June 4–8, 2016
Brisbane, Australia

Association for Computing Machinery

Advancing Computing as a Science & Profession

fuse
DIS 2016

DIS 2016

Proceedings of the 2016 ACM Conference on
Designing Interactive Systems

Sponsored by:

ACM SIGCHI

Supported by:

Queensland University of Technology, Brisbane, Greater Springfield, HFESA, Brisbane BMW, ROAMES, Urban Informatics, The MIT Press, Morgan & Claypool Publishers, Australian Network for Art & Technology, and Australian Design Alliance

Association for
Computing Machinery

Advancing Computing as a Science & Profession

The Association for Computing Machinery
2 Penn Plaza, Suite 701
New York, New York 10121-0701

ISBN: 978-1-4503-4031-1 (Digital)

ISBN: 978-1-4503-4597-2 (Print)

Additional copies may be ordered prepaid from:

ACM Order Department
PO Box 30777
New York, NY 10087-0777, USA

Phone: 1-800-342-6626 (USA and Canada)
+1-212-626-0500 (Global)
Fax: +1-212-944-1318
E-mail: acmhelp@acm.org
Hours of Operation: 8:30 am – 4:30 pm ET

Printed in the USA

DIS 2016 Chair's Welcome

Welcome to the southern hemisphere, welcome to Australia, welcome to Brisbane, welcome to the picturesque Gardens Point campus of Queensland University of Technology (QUT), and welcome to the 11th ACM SIGCHI Designing Interactive Systems (DIS'16) conference!

Since 1995, the (so far[1]) biennial Conference on Designing Interactive Systems (DIS) is the premier, international arena where designers, artists, psychologists, user experience researchers, systems engineers, and many more, come together to debate and shape the future of interactive systems design and practice. DIS is owned by the ACM Special Interest Group on Computer-Human Interaction (SIGCHI). In the past, DIS has been held in Ann Arbor (1995), Amsterdam (1997), New York (2000), London (2002), Boston (2004), State College (2006), Cape Town (2008), Aarhus (2010), Newcastle (2012), and Vancouver (2014).

The DIS'16 conference schedule comprises two days of pre-conference workshops and a doctoral consortium as well as three main conference days packed with peer reviewed paper presentations, demos, panel discussions, and three invited keynote speakers. The social program includes the welcome reception on Sunday night, the DIS Experience Night on Monday night, the DIS conference dinner on Tuesday night, and a post-conference after party on Wednesday night.

And for all those who still haven't had enough, the QUT School of Design has added a great satellite event held in conjunction with DIS'16: the inaugural *Queensland Design Policy Summit*, a full day event on Thursday 9 June, dedicated to bringing together thought leaders and policy makers across design, business, science, education, and citymaking in a dialogue to canvass the merits of resurrecting a revised, fresh, and bold Queensland Design Policy.

The DIS'16 theme of "fuse" is about exploring the range of new possibilities along the human and technology spectrum – the blurring of any clear divides between analog and digital, atoms and bits, materiality and virtuality, art and design, academy and industry. From mobiles to wearables, bearables, and even injectables, technology is finding its way to be carried by us, on by, and inside us. At the same time do we welcome more and more robots and humanoids into our lives – from Furby, Roomba, Siri, to Jibo. Are we witnessing a fusion of the cyborg with the matrix? What does the future of interactive systems hold? We hope to advance these questions at DIS'16.

I am very pleased that we were able to curate and assemble a stellar program, including three invited keynote presentations by Carlo Ratti (MIT), Natalie Jeremijenko (New York University), and Stelarc (Curtin University of Technology). I am sure they will stimulate our thinking particularly at the intersection of design and cities, the environment, and the human body.

DIS'16 is certainly a team effort. I thank all my colleagues on the organising committee, on the various program sub-committees, the student volunteers, our host, Queensland University of Technology, our ACM sponsor, SIGCHI, and our generous corporate supporters.

Please enjoy DIS'16!

Marcus Foth
DIS'16 General Chair
School of Design, Queensland University of Technology

[1] I said "so far," as from this year onwards, DIS will now be an annual event, and we will announce the European city hosting DIS 2017 at the closing ceremony of this year's conference.

DIS 2016 Technical Program Chairs' Welcome

DIS 2016 centers on designerly approaches to creating, deploying and critically reflecting on interactive systems. It is an interdisciplinary conference that encompasses how such systems are built, introduced and employed in a wide variety of socio-cultural contexts. We welcome a broad engagement with the field by inviting submissions that consider the following, from a diverse range of researchers and practitioners within the field of interactive systems design:

- **Design Methods and Processes:** Methods, tools, and techniques for engaging people; researching, designing, and co-designing interactive systems; participatory design, design artefacts, research through design; documenting and reflecting on design processes.
- **Experience:** Places, temporality, people, communities, events, phenomena, aesthetics, user experience, usability, engagement, empowerment, wellbeing, designing things that matter, diversity, participation, materiality, making, etc.
- **Application Domains:** Health, ICT4D, children-computer interaction, sustainability, games/entertainment computing, digital arts, etc.
- **Technological Innovation (systems, tools, and/or artifact designs):** Sensors and actuators, mobile devices, multi touch and touchless interaction, social media, personal, community, and public displays

The conference committees reviewed and accepted the following:

Venue	*Reviewed*	*Accepted*	
Papers and Notes	418	107	26%
Provocations & Works-in-Progress	59	19	32%
Pictorals	42	13	31%
Demonstrations	21	17	80%
Design Works	9	2	22%

This wonderful and provocative program would certainly not been possible had it not been for the work of the many contributing authors, the generous work of the reviewers, the organizational efforts of the Pictorals Chairs, Eli Blevis, Sabrina Hauser, and William Odom, the Workshops Chairs, Ben Matthews and Jared Donovan, the Provocations and Works in Progress Chairs, Margot Brereton and Elise van den Hoven, the Demos Chairs, Lian Loke and Markus Rittenbruch, the Design Works Chairs, Jennifer Seevinck and Gavin Sade, and the Doctoral Consortium Chairs, Ann Light and Jaz Choi.

We thank everyone involved for all of their effort to make a fantastic DIS 2016 program, and we are looking forward to this year's conference with great eagerness and excitement.

Wendy Ju
DIS'16 Technical Program Co-chair
California College of the Arts & Stanford University, USA

Ronald Schroeter
DIS'16 Technical Program Co-chair
Queensland University of Technology, Australia

Stephen Viller
DIS'16 Technical Program Co-chair
University of Queensland, Australia

Table of Contents

Session: Learning

Session: Art / Performance

Session: Tool / UI Design

Session: Pictorials 2: Reflections on Design

Session: About Design

Session: Sensing, Health

Session: Social Online

Session: Exertion, Health

Session: Images in Design

Session: Ageing

Session: Pictorials 3: Photo Visual / Imagery

Session: Fabrication / DIY

Session: Home

DIS 2016 Organization

General Chair	Marcus Foth *(Queensland University of Technology)*
Program Chairs	Wendy Ju *(Stanford University)* Ronald Schroeter *(Queensland University of Technology)* Stephen Viller *(University of Queensland)*
Pictorials Chairs	Eli Blevis *(Indiana University Bloomington)* Sabrina Hauser *(Simon Fraser University)* William Odom *(Simon Fraser University)*
Provocations and Work-in-Progress Chairs	Margot Brereton *(Queensland University of Technology)* Elise van den Hoven *(University of Technology Sydney)*
Workshop Chairs	Ben Matthews *(University of Queensland)* Jared Donovan *(Queensland University of Technology)*
Demonstration Chairs	Lian Loke *(University of Sydney)* Markus Rittenbruch *(Queensland University of Technology)*
Doctoral Consortium Chairs	Ann Light *(University of Sussex)* Jaz Hee-jeong Choi *(Queensland University of Technology)*
Design Works Exhibition Chairs	Jennifer Seevinck *(Queensland University of Technology)* Gavin Sade *(Queensland University of Technology)*
Treasurer	Ben Kraal *(Queensland University of Technology)*
Local Arrangements & Social Chair	Richard Medland *(Queensland University of Technology)*
Student Volunteers Chairs	Glenda Caldwell *(Queensland University of Technology)* Joel Fredericks *(University of Sydney)*
Industry Engagement Chairs	Marcus Foth *(Queensland University of Technology)* Alexander Bishop *(Queensland University of Technology)* Christine Satchell *(Queensland University of Technology)*
Promotion, Visual Design and Web Development	Bronte Poynts *(Queensland University of Technology)* Carly Hare *(Queensland University of Technology)* Wade Hextell *(techstudio3.com)* Andrew Bates *(Queensland University of Technology)* Manuela Taboada *(Queensland University of Technology)* Tory Grice *(budgiebusinessdesign.com)*

Steering Committee

Kim Halskov, Chair *(Aarhus University)*
Olav Bertelsen *(Aarhus University)*
John M. Carroll *(Penn State)*
Steve Harrison *(Virginia Tech)*
Ron Wakkary *(Simon Fraser University)*
Peter Wright *(Newcastle University)*

Professional Conference Organisers

Lauren Kerr *(QUT Events)*
Michelle Kani *(QUT Events)*

Program Subcommittee Chairs:

Kim Halskov *(Aarhus University)*
Steve Harrison *(VirginiaTech)*
Siân Lindley *(Microsoft Research Cambridge)*
Tuck Leong *(University of Technology Sydney)*
Johannes Schöning *(Hasselt University)*
Florian Mueller *(RMIT)*
Eric Paulos *(UC Berkeley)*
Manfred Tscheligi *(University of Salzburg)*

Program Associate Chairs: (Experience)

Daniel Buzzo
John Canny
Marcus Carter
Adrian Clear
Rob Comber
Martin Flintham
Jonas Fritsch
Colin Gray
Jonna Hakkila
Ellie Harmon
Eva Hornecker
Jina Huh
Ioanna Iacovides
Giulio Jacucci
Vaiva Kalnikaitė
Stacey Kuznetsov
Jarmo Laaksolahti
Effie Law
Lucian Leahu
Joon Suk Lee
Scott Mainwaring
Donald McMillan
David Mellis
Tim Merritt
Marianna Obrist
Lora Oehlberg
Sun Young Park
Marianne Graves Petersen
Tamara Peyton
Stefan Rennick-Egglestone
Jennifer Rode
Antti Salovaara
Patrick Shih
Chris Speed
Anja Thieme
Martin Tomitsch
Greg Wadley
Ron Wakkary
Salu Ylirisku

(Design Methods and Processes)

David Benyon
Mark Blythe
Jo Briggs
John Carroll
Peter Dalsgaard
Steven Dow
Eva Eriksson
Erik Grönvall
Liesbeth Huybrechts
Sara Jones
Kari Kuutti
Christopher Le Dantec
Andrés Lucero
Scott McCrickard
Jörn Messeter
Oliver Mival
Volkmar Pipek
Derek Reilly
Erica Robles
Corina Sas
Michael Smyth
Norman Su
Hyeon-Jeong Suk
Anna Vallgårda
Andrew Vande Moere
Mikael Wiberg
Peter Wright
John Zimmerman

(Technological Innovation)

Keith Cheverst
Alexander De Luca
Chris Harrison
Christian Holz
Jonathan Hook
Ahmed Kharrufa
Rohit Ashok Khot
Markus Löchtefeld
Shaun Lawson
Lindsay MacDonald
Nicolai Marquardt
Diana Nowacka
Nuno Nunes
Michael Rohs
Anthony Tang
Jo Vermeulen
Simon Voelker
Chat Wacharamanotham

(Application Domains)

Florian Alt
Louise Barkhuus
Cati Boulanger
Licia Calvi
Alan Chamberlain
Verena Fuchsberger
David Kirk
Boriana Koleva
Gerd Kortuem
Edward Lank
Xiaojuan Ma
Wendy Moncur
Hideyuki Nakanishi
Xiangshi Ren
Marco Rozendaal
Alessandro Soro
Diane Willow

Special thanks for the support provided by the

DIS 2016 Sponsor & Supporters

ACM Sponsor: SIGCHI

Venue Supporters: QUT Queensland University of Technology Brisbane Australia; brisbane australia's new world city

Keynote Supporter: Greater Springfield Greater Possibilities — A SPRINGFIELD LAND CORPORATION INITIATIVE

After Party Supporter: UI Urban Informatics

Book Supporters: The MIT Press; M&C Morgan & Claypool Publishers

Publicity Supporters: ANAT australian network for art & technology; [AdA] Australian Design Alliance; MAB16 Media Architecture Biennale; MAI Media Architecture Institute

Transport Supporters: airtrain.com.au; UBER

Futurecraft

Carlo Ratti
Senseable City Lab, Massachusetts Institute of Technology
Cambridge, MA, United States
ratti@mit.edu

KEYNOTE ABSTRACT

Cities are, by definition, plural, public, and productive. They are created by society itself (barring exceptional cases like master-planned Brasilia or Chandigarh) and they function as culture's petri dish for progress. Living in space and creating space can go hand in hand. We propose to employ design in a systematic exploration and germination of possible futures, exploring how ubiquitous computing – i.e. the increasing deployment of sensors and hand-held electronics in recent years, what we call Senseable City – is opening up a new approach to the study of the built environment. Design can investigate and intervene at the interface between people, technologies and the city – developing research and applications that empower citizens to make choices that result in a more livable urban condition.

The aim is not to portray what is to come. We call it futurecraft: we pose future scenarios (typically phrased as What if? questions), entertain their consequences and exigencies, and we share the resulting ideas widely, to enable public conversation and debate. It is important to extrapolate from the present condition and to place ourselves, as designers, in a fictive but possible future context with the intent of realizing or precluding that future through public discourse. Designer's work is meaningless unless it ignites imaginations and provokes debate: design by mutation is intrinsically collective. Designers produce mutations, some of which will grow, evolve, and develop into tangible artifacts that cause global change – driven to realization by the energy of the crowd.

Author Keywords

Smart cities; real-time data; urban design; urban interaction design; sensor data; future scenarios; city making

ACM Classification Keywords

H.5.m. Information interfaces and presentation: Misc.

DIS 2016, June 04-08, 2016, Brisbane, QLD, Australia
ACM 978-1-4503-4031-1/16/06.
http://dx.doi.org/10.1145/2901790.2915253

BIO

An architect and engineer by training, Carlo Ratti practices in Italy and teaches at the Massachusetts Institute of Technology, where he directs the Senseable City Lab. He graduated from the Politecnico di Torino and the École Nationale des Ponts et Chaussées in Paris, and later earned his MPhil and PhD at the University of Cambridge, UK. Carlo holds several patents and has co-authored over 250 publications. As well as being a regular contributor to Project Syndicate, he has written for the Le Monde, El Pais, La Stampa, Corriere della Sera, Scientific American and The New York Times. His work has been exhibited worldwide at venues such as the Venice Biennale, the Design Museum Barcelona, the Science Museum in London, MAXXI in Rome, and MoMA The Museum of Modern Art in in New York City.

Carlo has been featured in Esquire Magazine's 'Best & Brightest' list and in Thames & Hudson's selection of '60 innovators' shaping our creative future. Blueprint Magazine included him as one of the '25 People Who Will Change the World of Design', Forbes listed him as one of the 'Names You Need To Know' and Fast Company named him as one of the '50 Most Influential Designers in America'. He was also featured in Wired Magazine's 'Smart List: 50 people who will change the world'. Carlo was awarded the Renzo Piano Foundation prize for 'New Talents in Architecture'. Two of his projects – the Digital Water Pavilion and the Copenhagen Wheel – have been included by TIME Magazine in the list of the 'Best Inventions of the Year'.

Carlo has been a presenter at TED (in 2011 and 2015), program director at the Strelka Institute for Media, Architecture and Design in Moscow, curator of the 'BMW Guggenheim Pavilion' in Berlin, and was named 'Inaugural Innovator in Residence' by the Queensland Government. He was the curator of the 'Future Food District' pavilion for the 2015 World Expo in Milan. He is currently serving as Chair of the World Economic Forum Global Agenda Council on Future Cities, and he has been selected as Special Adviser to the President and Commissioners of the European Commission, to advise on urban innovation.

senseable.mit.edu

carloratti.com

Androids, Replicants and Chimeras: Alternate Embodiments / Uncanny Agencies

Stelarc
School of Design and Art, Curtin University of Technology
Perth, Western Australia
stelarc@curtin.edu.au

KEYNOTE ABSTRACT

What it means to be human is perhaps not to remain human at all. To become other is an irresistible urge. What a body is and how a body performs is a historical, cultural and technological construct but because it is also in the realm of contingency it is also highly contestable. It is a time of alternate anatomical architectures. Of hyper-human constructs that are a hybridization of biology, technology and virtuality.

Technology is attached and is inserted, as flesh is extracted and circulated. Body parts are exchanged. Hearts and hands are relocated and reanimated. A face on one body stitched to the skull of another, becomes a third face resembling neither. Your face, appropriated and animated by an alternate nervous system becomes the affect of the other. A body with implants is a body that can be hacked, re-wired and re-purposed. There are few reasons to perpetuate the body as it is – surviving in a slim spectrum of light, radiation and gravity, not very robust and with a limited longevity. Prosthetic Flesh becomes Fractal Flesh and Phantom Flesh.

It is necessary to shift from seeing the body as a site for the psyche to the body as a structure. Not as an object of desire but as an object to redesign. There is a need not only to expose but to simultaneously extend the body's interaction and task envelope. The body now performs remotely, involuntarily and with profound indifference, absent to its own agency. An indifference that allows something other to occur, that allows an unfolding- in its own time and with its own rhythm. The body becomes physically split with an extruded sense of self. A radical emptiness permeates the human horizon, but it is an emptiness generated not by a lack but rather through an excess of expectation.

Liminal spaces proliferate and generate the uncanny, the ambivalent and the uncertain. The anxious body becomes a floating signifier, becoming whatever it wants to become – in a multiplicity of forms and functions. Bodies are split and distributed. The problem is no longer possessing a split personality, but rather of having split physicality. In our Platonic, Cartesian and Freudian pasts these might have been considered pathological and in our Foucauldian present we focus on inscription and control of the body. But in the terrain of cyber complexity that we now inhabit the inadequacy and the obsolescence of the ego-agent driven biological body cannot be more apparent. A transition from psycho-body to cyber system becomes necessary to function effectively and intuitively in remote spaces, speeded-up situations and complex technological terrains of information overload. Can a body cope with experiences of extreme absence and alien action without becoming overcome by outmoded metaphysical fears and obsessions of individuality and free will? Embodiment, identity and agency need to be interrogated and algorithms of aliveness and affect need to be re-formulated.

Author Keywords

Alternate anatomies; agency; androids; replicants; chimeras

ACM Classification Keywords

H.5.m. Information interfaces and presentation: Misc.

BIO

Stelarc explores alternate anatomical architectures. He is an artist whose projects incorporate prosthetics, robotics, biotechnology, medical imaging and the internet. He has performed with a Third Hand, a Stomach Sculpture, Exoskeleton and a Prosthetic Head. Fractal Flesh, Ping Body and Parasite are internet performances that explore remote and involuntary choreography. He is surgically constructing and stem-cell growing an ear on his arm that will be internet enabled. In 1996 he was made an Honorary Professor of Art and Robotics at Carnegie Mellon University, Pittsburgh and in 2002 was awarded an Honorary Doctorate of Laws by Monash University, Melbourne. In 2010 was awarded the Ars Electronica Hybrid Arts Prize. In 2014 he initiated the Alternate Anatomies Lab. In 2015 he received the Australia Council's Emerging and Experimental Arts Award. Stelarc is currently a Distinguished Research Fellow, School of Design and Art (SODA) at Curtin University. His artwork is represented by the Scott Livesey Galleries, Melbourne.

DIS 2016, June 04-08, 2016, Brisbane, QLD, Australia
ACM 978-1-4503-4031-1/16/06.
http://dx.doi.org/10.1145/2901790.2915255

Creative Agency and the Space Race of the 21st Century: Towards a Museum of Natural Futures

Natalie Jeremijenko
Environmental Health Clinic
Steinhardt School of Culture, Education, and Human Development, New York University
New York, New York 10003-7599, USA nj6@nyu.edu

ABSTRACT: Reimagining and redesigning our relationship to natural systems to improve human and environmental health, increase biodiversity, build soil, and improve air and water quality is the Space Race of the 21st Century; i.e. the most complex systems design challenge we face, and one that current and emerging interactive technologies provide the opportunity to address. This assertion is intended to reframe the discourse of contemporary environmentalism in terms of creative agency that transcend market and regulatory incentives and disambiguates from "sustainability" which in research universities internationally seem to have been institutionalized as non-academic*.

The second, but most novel and critical assertion, is that we can design infrastructure, and specifically the built environment, data, energy, food, waste and distribution systems to IMPROVE human and environmental health, rather than lessening negative effects in efforts to reduce energy use, food miles, waste, emissions, greenhouse gasses or more conventional maintenance and labor costs. For instance, (1) the ELEVATORxPITCH project upgrades the sky-line-defining vertical transportation to create both cultural venue that produces views, and transforms this electric vehicle infrastructure into a building's power plant. Simultaneously the combination of sensor-actuated venting and fire-code upgrade can create cross-season passive air circulation that removes the need for heating, ventilating, and air conditioning (HVAC) systems (typically approx. 40% of the energy use in cities is building related and most of this: HVACs).

Or, (2) the example of the Pier2Pier from the Cuban Mussel Crisis Collaboratory (for open source Leapfrog Technology), is an integrated system for a pier structure that exploits buoyancy and tension, vs. mass and rigidity, a paradigm shift in coastal engineering that is approx. >10x stronger and >1000x more cost effective /meter2 sans the catastrophic failure modes of conventional piers and boardwalks that become battering rods in extreme climate events (for instance, Brisbane's Riverwalk or Far Rockaway' Boardwalks). This new pier also creates infrastructure for mussels – the only aquaculture system that improves water quality – and furthermore the mussel cultivation ropes incorporate "bioscilators" for wave energy conversion[i]. The main surface structure of inflated ETFE (ethylene tetrafluoroethylene) "artificial clouds" facilitates full solar throughput to drive photosynthesis and couples the cascading biogeochemical processes (unlike the dark 'wet-deserts' under conventional over-water structure), in addition to passive desalination / distillation within the structure.

The TREExCLOUD data infrastructure is a third example in which cloud data storage service offered by the TREExOFFICE co-working space (owned, operated and in the canopy of a tree / landlord) is powered by a pyrolytic waste-2-energy system, which is indexed to the Leaf Area Index (LAI) – a significant determinant of human (and environmental) health and therefore a potent metric to couple into the expanding demand for data storage. To increase storage capacity we increase the LAI achieved through strategies including increased canopy complexity; integrating vegetation into vertical urban surfaces; micro-ecosystem based afforestation (not monocultures). TREExCLOUD energy is generated from the lingo-cellulosic waste and food waste (the two largest of urban waste streams) that has the co-benefit of producing Biochar and anaerobic digest, which in combination not only sequesters carbon when worked into the soil (for ~>5000yrs) but in urban environments, can immobilize heavy metals with potential to reduce / prevent the body burden of neurotoxicants including lead (Pb) and mercury (Hg).

Thirdly, I assert that the way to redesign our urban infrastructure (UIs) is through Mutualistic Systems design (MUSTs) and Natural Systems Engineering – into which I put an "i" (as a call to independent action) for the NiSE!(est) acronym. I have developed these terms to describe generalizability from many distinct "public experiments" in mutualistic systems coupling to improve human and environmental health. These experiments have occurred primarily in non-STEM cultural spaces – art museums, galleries, university exhibitions / college campuses and public spaces where creative agency is privileged (over critical technical evaluation); and use participatory research, convivial learning and interactive systems to raise standards of evidence in the design of social and environmental transformation and invite diverse participants and non-traditional people (and other intelligent creatures) into radical systems and infrastructure innovation and development. Moreover, I assert that our collective response-ability to this C21st Space Race, to COP21, to the UN's Sustainable

DIS 2016, June 04-08, 2016, Brisbane, QLD, Australia
ACM 978-1-4503-4031-1/16/06.
http://dx.doi.org/10.1145/2901790.2915254

Development Goals (SDGs), and socio-ecological justice will be measured by human and environmental health**; but rather the agency each one of us has to act in our own – and our children's' – interests; with the knowledge that whatever we can do to improve our own food systems, air quality or environmental health, the benefits are shared by anyone with who we share that environment / health. While the medical model individualizes health, the math of mutualism and benefit-benefit analysis aggregates collectives. This reflects the exponential power we see in natural systems and megabiodiversity. i.e. Malthus was wrong!

Whereas, the outcomes of the COP21 of December 2015 have some ambitious if non-binding quantitative goals, these require translation into imaginative challenges to engage the design community. Lord Kelvin's "to measure is to know" may have informed big-data and the so-called smart city, and guided the Sustainability and similarly the Effective Altruism movements, which implicitly claim that environmental and social transformation can be achieved through accounting and evaluation schemes, such as LEEDS, Energy Star, Life Cycle Analysis, Embodied Energy, and various labels, certification, and regulatory frameworks (such as UN-REDD and REDD+); or by ranking the worthiness of a cause in terms of measures of quality-adjusted life-year (QALY) or career choice in terms of excess wealth for charitable contributions. Of course these approaches conflate political power and purchasing power and have no accounting for the disruptive innovation possible with and through the Creative Agency of young people in particular.

Design professionals have articulated zero waste, emission, impact or similar as the highest bar of collective design. Tesla cars', for instance, default plates state "zero emissions,' and Masdar City claims zero waste, zero carbon. If artists or other professionals, for instance, doctors, aspired to "zero-impact" they would struggle for credibility.

Finally, several of my students (in their early 20s) plan to present Plan B mutualistic urban system UNEA2 in Nairobi for each of their home cities including: Barcelona, Bogota, Beijing, Boulder, Berlin, and on my behalf for Brisbane (my own lovable floodable city). Each of these systems is transformative, radically inexpensive, and coupled through benefit-benefit (rather than cost-benefit) analysis. These include distributed local and hybrid energy systems (beyond renewables) and most substantially small-scale waste-2-energy. Waste benefits and is neither distributed, polluted nor wasted, to achieve energy transition. Reintegrating vegetation into the urban environment (through floriculture and canopy complexity) to increase Leaf Area Index (LAI), support pollinators and create significant human health benefits. These and others combine to significantly exceed the COP21 goals, but also to transform them into direct, local, wondrous and convivial benefits.

Kelvin claimed, "if you can not measure it, you can not improve it." And it is this metric, LAI, that is both easily measurable (via satellite and terrestrial LIDAR, and informal qualitative metric) and meaningful as a proxy for human health and biodiversity. The central question however is not how / if we measure but who feels creative agency, why do they have it; how do you teach, facilitate, learn, exercise and institutionalize creative agency in diverse people? Can we each feel thrilled by or be invited into the grand design challenge to redesign our relationship to natural systems so that the built environment, data, energy, food, waste and distribution systems – our environmental commons – improve human and environmental health? Who holds the design keys to the possible city; the possible energy system, et al.? We have the technological opportunities; the educational and cultural capital, the environmental urgency AND the creative agency to reimagine, redesign and coproduce desirable, delicious and delightful possibilities.

*at NYU, for instance, the Sustainability Task Force is within the Public Relations department and assigns student grants (rarely with or supported by faculty) rather than long term 'sustainable' research questions develop the professional connections through intellectual networks)

** that has little to do with the interests of venture capitalists, political agreements between 200 country; policing regulation; market incentives, and perhaps even less to do with trickle-down technology from x-prizes for billionaires-to-the-moon.

Author Keywords: Environment; health; nature; sustainability; climate change; design; energy; waste; human; agency; infrastructure; cities; creative; data
ACM Classification Keywords: H.5.m.

BIO: Jeremijenko directs the Environmental Health Clinic – facilitating public and lifestyle experiments that can aggregate into significant human and environmental health benefits. She is also an Associate Professor in the Visual Art Department, NYU and affiliated with the Computer Science Dept and Environmental Studies program.

Jeremijenko's practice develops the emerging field of socio-ecological systems design (or xDesign) crucial in the Anthropocene, using attractions and ongoing participatory research spectacles that address the C21st challenge to reimagine our collective relationship to natural systems. This integrates diverse strategies to redesign energy, food and transportation systems that can contribute to the common good, increase soil, aquatic and terrestrial biodiversity and improve human and environmental health.

In 2014 VIDA Art and Artificial Life International Awards Pioneer Prize was awarded to Natalie Jeremijenko "for her consistently brilliant portfolio of work over the past two decades" – a prize only awarded once before to Laurie Anderson. She was also granted a Most Innovative People award in 2013, most influential women in technology 2011, one of the inaugural top young innovators by MIT Technology Review, and 40 most influential designers.

environmentalhealthclinic.net nataliejeremijenko.com

[1] Bioscilator and Wave Energy Conversion, ongoing developments. Dr. Craig Stevens www.niwa.co.nz

Uncovering the Honeypot Effect: How Audiences Engage with Public Interactive Systems

Niels Wouters[1,2], John Downs[1], Mitchell Harrop[1], Travis Cox[1], Eduardo Oliveira[1], Sarah Webber[1], Frank Vetere[1], Andrew Vande Moere[2]
[1] Microsoft Research Centre for Social NUI, University of Melbourne, Australia
[2] Research[x]Design, Department of Architecture, KU Leuven, Belgium
{mharrop, travis.cox, eduardo.oliveira, s.webber, f.vetere}@unimelb.edu.au, john@johndowns.co.nz
{niels.wouters, andrew.vandemoere}@asro.kuleuven.be

Figure 1: Different phases of audience engagement in *Encounters*: while *audience members* learn interaction possibilities by watching (left), *participants* interact individually (middle), and *facilitators* actively orchestrate a dance performance (right).

ABSTRACT
In HCI, the honeypot effect describes how people interacting with a system passively stimulate passers-by to observe, approach and engage in an interaction. Previous research has revealed the successive engagement phases and zones of the honeypot effect. However, there is little insight into: 1) how people are stimulated to transition between phases; 2) what aspects drive the honeypot effect apart from watching others; and 3) what constraints affect its self-reinforcing performance. In this paper, we discuss the honeypot effect as a spatiotemporal model of trajectories and influences. We introduce the Honeypot Model based on the analysis of observations and interaction logs from *Encounters*, a public installation that interactively translated bodily movements into a dynamic visual and sonic output. In providing a model that describes trajectories and influences of audience engagement in public interactive systems, our paper seeks to inform researchers and designers to consider contextual, spatial and social factors that influence audience engagement.

DIS 2016, June 04-08, 2016, Brisbane, QLD, Australia © 2016 ACM.
ISBN 978-1-4503-4031-1/16/06...$15.00
DOI: http://dx.doi.org/10.1145/2901790.2901796

Author Keywords
Public display; public space; audience; media architecture; social interaction; honeypot effect; natural user interfaces; movement; dance; evaluation; methodology.

ACM Classification Keywords
H.5.m. Information interfaces and presentation

INTRODUCTION
As interactive digital media permeates the public landscape, it becomes increasingly challenging to attract the attention of passers-by, to make them aware of the interaction opportunities, or to motivate them to engage meaningfully and sustainably. These challenges are not simply about optimizing hardware or creating more attractive displays. Instead, we require a better understanding about the relationship between people, their physical surroundings and their use of technology [21].

One particular user behavior, often observed in public contexts, is known as the *honeypot effect*. This effect is a social learning influence that causes individuals to be affected by the mere and passive presence or activities of others, regardless of any competition, reward or punishment [37]. In HCI, the honeypot effect is typically observed when passers-by move closer to a system and consider whether to engage after observing other people interacting [3]. Various aspects of the honeypot effect have been interrogated by other researchers. In particular, the specific roles and activities of users [29, 32], the influence of spatial configuration [11] including the various zones of engagement [24, 34] and the activities that take place [23]. However, the aspects that drive a honeypot effect and influence the motivations to engage with an interactive system have not yet been examined in detail.

In this paper we explore the honeypot effect by synthesizing the current state of knowledge from HCI literature, and merging it with our case study observations. We propose a spatiotemporal model of the honeypot effect that consists of a series of successive engagement trajectories and contextual influences. In particular, our model also introduces a concise terminology to capture and annotate the honeypot effect in interactive systems. The critical discussion of our case study results are described as a series of design considerations that aim to reflect on how to best support manifestations of the honeypot effect in public interactive systems.

Our in-the-wild case study focused on analyzing the audience engagement in *Encounters*, a public interactive installation that allowed people to influence dynamically projected visuals, sound effects and music with bodily gestures (see Figure 1). Because of its large scale, open-ended interaction design rationale and the use of various audience facilitators, *Encounters* formed the ideal context to capture the typical characteristics of audience engagement.

RELATED WORK

The honeypot effect was introduced to HCI to help explain the attraction to a system arising from others already engaged with it. This effect creates a "sociable buzz" in its vicinity [3]. The honeypot effect relies on the mere presence of others and suggests engagement will result in low social embarrassment. This effect is described in studies related to public displays (e.g. [2, 19]), media architecture (e.g. [11, 13]) and art installations (e.g. [16, 20]). The honeypot effect is commonly described as a natural attraction cue, such as integrating *calls-to-action* (e.g. [26]), embedding responsive visual content (e.g. [2]) or enabling opportunities for studying peers (e.g. [28]).

Dimensions of Audience Engagement

Stimulating engagement in a public installation typically involves creating an environment that benefits social interaction (e.g. [21, 33]) and positively influences the atmosphere (e.g. [4, 7]). Specifically, an environment that aims to motivate a honeypot effect should balance a range of *spatial*, *interactive* and *social* aspects. We discuss the significance of each to the honeypot effect.

Spatial. The layout of space influences the subjective experience of the environment [14], and technology has become increasingly apt in actively shaping that experience [10]. Hence, an interactive installation is not simply situated in a location, but its presence in itself creates "situations". For instance, *Urban HCI* provided a concise model of how the spatial configuration around a public installation creates such situations, highlighting the role of *potential interaction spaces* as possessing the ideal physical characteristics to stimulate social interaction [11]. The notion of *embodied constraints* describes how certain spatial configurations and physical structures invite or impede group activities around tangible, interactive systems [15]. Key design characteristics include configuring the nearby physical space to allow people to interact concurrently, allowing multiple access points to distribute control over the system, and providing interaction possibilities that adapt to people's skills.

Interactivity. The *Audience Funnel Framework* [24] describes how people tend to organically transition between various levels of interactivity while evolving towards engagement with a system. Transitions range from quickly glancing as a *viewer* and causing an initial response as a *subtle user*, to interacting as a *direct user*. As people transition, quantifiable conversions between phases can be recognized, which are typically low (i.e. high threshold) as people engage in an initial interaction. *Building blocks* have the ability to transform these initial forms of interaction into more active engagement. Hence, they are successful in increasing conversions, for example by motivating activity, triggering curiosity or stimulating collaboration with others [25]. One such building block is described in the *PACD model* [23], where gradually uncovering features of a system leads to *discovery* and active engagement.

In interactive systems, the typical aim is to motivate interaction while providing a potentially engaging experience. Notably, this design goal does not necessarily imply that the 'success' of an interactive system is proportionate to increasing the number of interactions [3]. Even the absence of any interaction from bystanders contains a potential opportunity for their interaction at a later stage [32], or for watching the activities that are performed by active participants [22, 35]. As such, besides providing active participants in a system with a pleasant experience, systems should take into account the different degrees of participation in their vicinity, while unobtrusively inviting bystanders to engage in participation [17].

Social. Users engaging with interactive systems tend to be driven by emotional, sensual, compositional and spatiotemporal influences [36], not dissimilar to how art is impacted by the relationship between the self and the art object [9]. Accordingly, user interaction in public contexts is shaped by the presence of others, including the social norms that govern the relationships between each of them. Public contexts expose a particular contrast between the roles of *performers* (i.e. acting in front of others) and *spectators* (i.e. learning from others to increase proficiency), potentially decreasing the likelihood of interaction for fear of social embarrassment [3, 30]. In fact, systems should be configured to accommodate for the physical proximity of the user [32]. As users gradually become conscious of their role, their perception of the system is shaped [8].

Interactive systems aim to take people on journeys while they explore and utilize the features [31]. These journeys, commonly referred to as *trajectories*, describe how people navigate through a predefined set of narratives that is purposively composed by the designers [1]. Whereas systems may intend that people follow *canonical trajectories,* the very nature of interactivity allows for

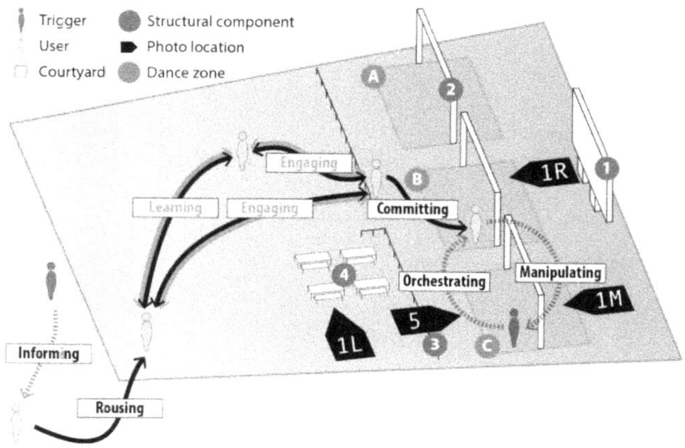

Figure 2: Schematic spatial representation of *Encounters*, the dominant trajectories and influences, and the main structural components: LED screen (1), archways with sensors (2), dance zones (A, B, C), fence (3) and seating area (4).

individual and unpredictable choices, i.e. *participant trajectories*, even when performers inform and support participants [18]. As such, engagement becomes a continuous dialogue between the system and the participant, between participants themselves, and between the participants and the spectators [30].

ENCOUNTERS

Our findings are based on the analysis of how people engaged with *Encounters*, a public, interactive installation that encouraged people to playfully explore a variety of dynamic visuals and soundscapes. *Encounters* was installed in a public courtyard during a summer festival in Melbourne, Australia, which ran over four evenings.

Technical Design

The interaction space of *Encounters* consisted of three 5x5m dance zones (see Figure 2). Each zone featured a large archway that supported a dynamic lighting system, six surround sound speakers, and an overhead Microsoft Kinect sensor that continuously monitored the area beneath. The dance zones were established by delineating a physical area underneath the archways by strategically pointing ambient lighting. A single 5x4m LED screen was installed facing all three dance zones. Depth data from the sensors was communicated to proprietary software at a rate of 30fps. The software processed, detected and interpreted a series of characteristics of every individual's movements in real-time, including the location in three-dimensional space, the velocity, and the distance from other nearby individuals. The system continuously broadcasted appropriate reactions to a music sequencer that controlled the surround sound and lighting, and to custom software that generated the dynamic imagery on the screen.

Conceptual and Social Design

The overarching artistic theme of *Encounters* was inspired by the wider cosmos, reflecting in part the dark and outdoor nighttime environment it was located in. Its dynamic visual and audio design switched between six distinct styles, each

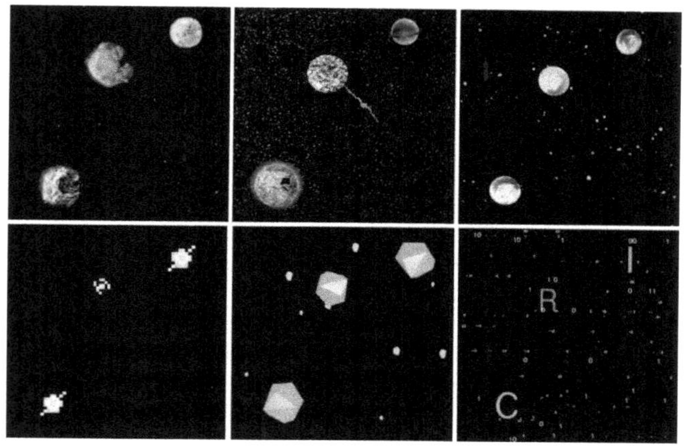

Figure 3: Overview of the visual aesthetics of *Encounters*, each representing identical depth sensor data.

of which was successively displayed for 10 minutes. The visual aesthetic styles were based on a particular artist's interpretation of the cosmos, ranging from a near-photorealistic representation (Figure 3, top left) to more abstract iconography (Figure 3, bottom left) or typography (Figure 3, bottom right). The dynamically composed soundscape of Encounters combined melodic and rhythmic elements of ambient and minimal music, which were composed to persuasively stimulate movement of people on stage. Each aesthetic style and accompanying soundtrack responded in real-time to the positions and activities of the people in the dance zones, and the physical distances between them. Each detected person was represented by a unique visual element, which was animated according to the input data, encompassing transformations such as scaling, rotating and morphing. One significant interaction was a 'supernova' that appeared as multiple persons approached within 30cm of each other, causing the corresponding elements to converge into a single visual entity. Various sound effects were overlaid on top of these soundtracks, and directly responded to a range of activities on stage, e.g. as people jumped on stage, a *whoosh*-ing sound was played.

As part of the artistic expression, three dancers stepped into the three dance zones every 30 minutes to perform a 10-minute prearranged choreography. The choreography consisted of three distinct phases, with each phase intensifying the interaction with participants. Initially the dancers performed a short solo routine (approx. 3min), during which they orbited around the people that were already present within the dance zones. During the second phase (approx. 2min), the dancers interrupted the rehearsed performance and talked directly to the people within the dance zones, as they encouraged them to form groups, for example by holding hands or bunching together. The formed group was then instructed to break apart, causing a drastic response in the visuals as the system recognized the transformation from a single, large entity to multiple, small elements. From this point on, the dancers encouraged participants to freely move around across the three dance zones, causing comet tails to appear on the LED screen that

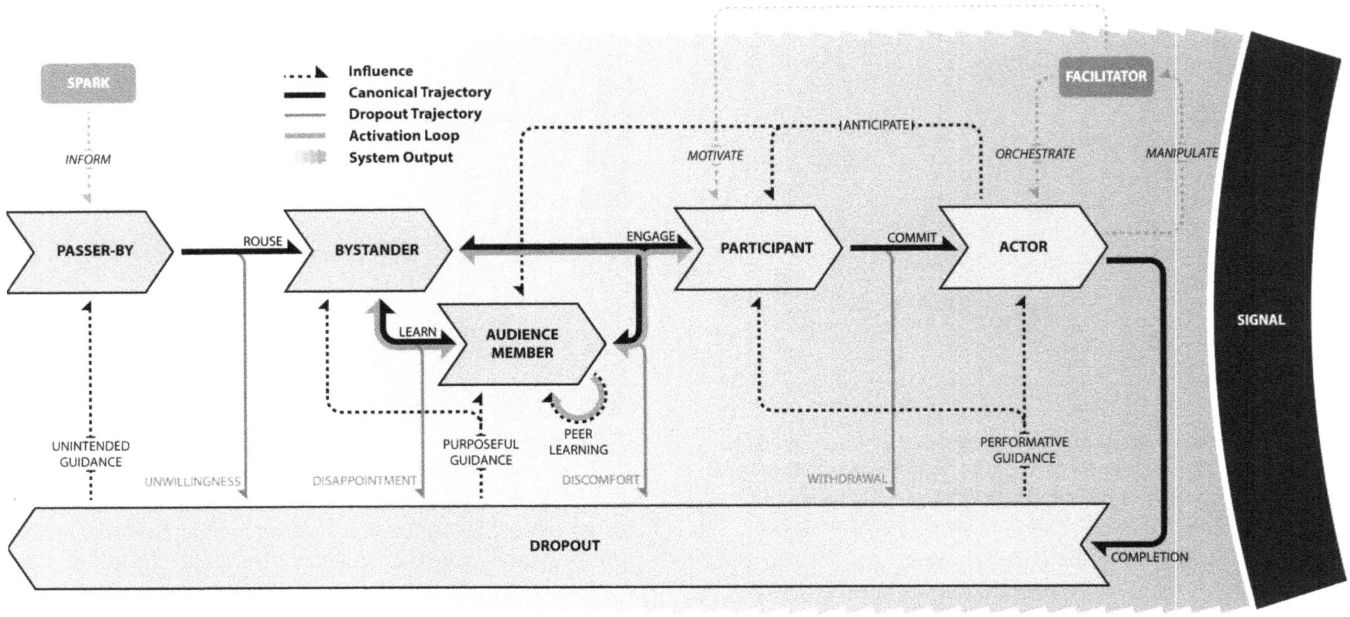

Figure 4: Honeypot Model containing the user roles, trajectories, influences and triggers that affect how audiences engage with interactive systems.

followed the movement of the participants. As participants started to improvise and engage with *Encounters* on their own terms, the last phase of the choreography (approx. 5min) consisted of dancers retreating into a solo performance, which finished with a brief ensemble dance.

In-the-Wild Field Study

Encounters was deployed on the same location during four separate evenings, running for a total time of 19 hours. Each performance started at 7PM and closed at night (until 11PM on three occasions, until 2AM on one occasion). Between performances, some spatial, technical, and artistic components were tweaked for optimization.

Evaluation Methodology

Each evening, three researchers conducted a contextual inquiry by observing the engagement behaviors taking place from randomly chosen locations around *Encounters*, and by conducting semi-structured interviews with participants, dancers and pitchmen. Questions aimed to uncover the trajectories between and experiences of different user roles: such as why participants felt motivated or discouraged to interact within the dance zone, how participants learnt about interactive features, and how dancers and pitchmen perceived their interaction with people. All interviews were audio recorded, and additional notes were taken on-site. In addition, all movements within the dance zones were recorded as video and depth data. The depth data was later segmented into tagged information to identify the number of people, start and end times, speed of movement, jumps, and configurations of people that were dancing over time.

Results

During the four evenings, a total of 1,159 people were counted entering the performance zones, with a maximum of 629 participants during the final performance (which took place alongside a major metropolitan light festival). On average, each person spent approximately 30 seconds in the performance area. There were about 3 people in the performance area at any given time, though the middle zone (B) seemed to attract substantially more people (5 people) than any other (2 people in area A and 3 people in area C).

We conducted a total of 125 interviews (of which 80 were taken from groups of people), taking an average of 6.0 minutes each (SD=37.4s). A team of four researchers analyzed the interview notes according to categorization methods used by Grounded Theory, including open coding and selective coding. Our analysis focused on revealing the nature of social and performative interactions, and the transitions of users as they engaged with *Encounters*. During each workshop session, groups of three to four attendees sorted the interview notes, while iteratively adjusting, debating and refining the coding scheme. This process is similar to previous studies that relied on group analysis [6]. Our approach helped in managing the sheer volume of data (i.e. 384 notes from 125 audio recordings), while allowing for new insights to emerge and previous insights to be refined. Hence, each session concluded with a plenary discussion of changes to the analysis process. The resulting analysis yielded a taxonomy of engagement types, a chronology of how people gained an understanding of the supported functionalities and perceived goals, and a classification of the influences that people experienced. These are further explained in the following sections.

HONEYPOT TRAJECTORIES AND INFLUENCES

The insights from the analysis were synthesized and a model consisting of user roles, trajectories, influences and triggers was created. All these aspects are integrated in the spatiotemporal Honeypot Model (Figure 4).

Figure 5: Dancers as facilitators (identifiable by EL wire wrapped around the body), involving participants and actors in dance as a way to motivate and engage.

Triggers

The most apparent and persuasive component of the system included the audiovisual feedback. However, potential participants were also informed via various printed and online publications, accessed remotely or in the vicinity of *Encounters*, while pitchmen roaming around the surrounding streets further encouraged passers-by to participate. Finally, hired dancers demonstrated the interaction features and encouraged collaborative behaviors such as group-based dance choreographies (see Figure 5).

Based on definitions from captology [12], depending on whether they increased the intrinsic motivation or the ability of passers-by to engage with the system, we propose these components acted either as *triggers*, i.e. respectively *sparks* or *facilitators*, as they specifically intended to persuade users to participate. *Encounters* captured the third type of trigger, *signals*, in the system itself, along with its supported functionalities and technologies.

User Roles

Initially, people became aware of the installation's existence through one or more triggers. As people entered the courtyard, noticed the music, saw the distant dynamic lights and visuals, and observed some physical activity among the attending audience, they became vaguely aware of the potential engagement with *Encounters*. Upon approaching closer by, people entered a seating area where many paused in order to observe the interactions that others performed, and to more intensely experience the visuals, sounds and music. Within the seating area, various forms of social interaction between people took place, such as telling each other about the installation's features. As people decided to enter the dance zones and their physical presence was detected by the overhead Kinect sensors, the system responded with appropriate visual and auditory feedback.

We identified two types of exploratory behaviors that emerged after people became aware of the interactivity. We coded these behaviors as *interacting oneself into existence*, which was characterized by people restricting themselves to a brief process of exploration. This process involved mimicking the behavior of others and performing basic, axial movements directly underneath the sensors, such as to identify themselves on the LED screen. As soon as they felt sufficiently comfortable and empowered, movements became more diverse, often involving acts such as running around, dancing and holding hands with others. The exploratory activities within the dance zones were also influenced by the performances that took place every 30 minutes, as dancers orchestrated the audience in a collaborative choreography (see Figure 5). Ultimately, people abandoned their engagement and left the dance zone.

Based on these observations, and complementary to the relevant terminology introduced in an analytic framework for public interfaces [29, 32], we identify six user roles.

- A **passer-by** roams around the immediate vicinity of an interactive system (i.e. *situated passer-by*) or learns about its existence via triggers. As some triggers may not be situated in the vicinity of the system, we propose the notion of *remote passers-by*.
- A **bystander** has experienced some form of (distant) visual, sonic, tangible or spatial expression of the interactive system (i.e. system output), yet is still unaware of the system's true interactive features.
- An **audience member** is familiar with the interactivity and the social norms surrounding a system, such as by reading instructions, or observing or discussing with others.
- A **participant** exhibits subtle forms of engagement with a system, such as moving slowly in the interaction space. Even though participants actively take part in interacting, they are still discovering interactive features and building a sense of comfort, and typically lack particular signs of profound commitment or enthusiasm.
- An **actor** demonstrates some committed form of engagement. This form of engagement is most noticeable in the nature of interactions (e.g. complex behaviors, challenging or testing out the system's capabilities), the extended amount of effort or time spent while interacting, or the apparent motivation to share their experience or seek the collaboration with others.
- A **dropout** has abandoned engagement with the interactive system, for instance by purposively not engaging with the system, or by leaving the interaction zone. Notably, any user role is able to drop out for various reasons (see subsection *Dropping Out*), even when no interaction with a system has yet occurred.

Trajectories

Within the context of our research, a *trajectory* describes the chronology of how people move towards and through distinct user roles. We have observed canonical and participant trajectories [1] in *Encounters*, and a range of dropout trajectories. Ultimately, we introduce the *activation loop* as a key trajectory to motivate and sustain engagement.

- The **canonical trajectory**, as envisioned by the *Encounters* designers, aimed to smoothly transition users from passer-by to actor and eventually dropout.
- Personal desires and expectations result in a participant to creating her own **participant trajectory** when experiencing an interactive system. Here, users organically transition back and forth between user roles.
- We observed instances of people abandoning every user role. We discovered that the reasons for choosing a **dropout trajectory** often corresponded with the experience that people had within their last actual role, although external issues could have occurred as well (e.g. unexpected phone call). For example, audience members typically dropped out because of social reasoning (e.g. crowdedness, perceived complexity of interactions), whereas actor dropouts were mostly due to having exhausted all interactive features of the system. As such, we propose four dropout trajectories (highlighted in red, Figure 4), which we articulate in subsection Dropping Out.
- We noticed how the activities of participants within a dance zone served as the main 'activator' for bystanders and audience members to move closer and engage for themselves. Particularly, it created a sense of anticipation to learn more about the features and interactivity. Occasionally, participants also retreated to a role as bystander or audience member, to gain more knowledge about the interactive features, or build a stronger sense of comfort. As such, we define the **activation loop**, a self-reinforcing trajectory that is capable of reactivating the interest and motivation to join the interaction.

Influences

We observed how the transition between user roles was affected by various forms of social interaction with other people. These included conversing with other participants (e.g. "*I talked with someone who stood next to me. He told me I could jump to change letters*", interview #68, young adult); studying the physical behavior of others (e.g. "*It was a little unclear in the beginning, but watching others helped to understand what was possible*", interview #54, young couple); and collaborating with actors (e.g. "*I felt sufficiently at ease to hold hands with strangers. It helped to identify myself on the screen*", interview #21, young family).

Accordingly, as users engage with an interactive system, their expectations are also shaped by the activities of others. We refer to these occurrences as *influences*, i.e. explicit or implicit forms of social interaction between people and that affect engagement with a system. We have identified 10 distinct influences in *Encounters* that depend on transitions between user roles, and will discuss them in the next section.

ANALYZING TRAJECTORIES AND INFLUENCES

To demonstrate the potential usefulness of the Honeypot Model in the design and evaluation of interactive systems, we further describe how particular spatial, social and interactive elements have affected the success of trajectories and influences in *Encounters*. By analyzing the nature of the observed trajectories and influences between user roles, we are able to reflect on their actual impact, which is then formulated as a set of design implications that aim to optimize the effectiveness of the honeypot effect in future endeavors. Figure 2 illustrates a graphical notation of how the main trajectories are physically situated within our case.

Rousing: From Passer-by to Bystander

Making activity in front of an interactive system visible beyond the interaction space itself is a potentially efficient technique to *rouse* initial engagement among passers-by [29, 34]. However, the spatial configuration of *Encounters* prevented the interaction activity to be noticed from surrounding streets. Therefore, we used various sparks to inform passers-by. These included symbols painted onto road surfaces, printed signage along main roads leading to the installation, and some digital signage in the alley that provided access to the courtyard. In addition, several clearly recognizable pitchmen mingled with passers-by. Although the pitchmen did not adhere to a strict schedule or script for approaching people, the process usually involved seeking contact, enquiring if they were having a good time, and asking if they would like to spend time at "*an interactive dance performance*". No additional details were shared about the range of supported interactions or expected behaviors in order to create a surprising experience.

The use of different sparks had a distinct effect on passers-by. The signage was most effective for passers-by that were initially unaware of the installation (e.g. "*I was walking past, noticed the signs, and just followed them*", interview #55, young couple), even though – or precisely because – it did not provide them with clear instructions (e.g. "*I read about Encounters in the online brochure. It didn't tell much about what could be done, and that motivated me to come and visit*", interview #11, young family). Those who already intended to visit *Encounters*, occasionally benefitted from additional information given by pitchmen: "*We wanted to see Encounters, but it was good to have the volunteers around to tell us more*" (interview #19, young couple).

Design implication. Making people aware often requires some form of advertising, which is dependent on the perceptual reach of the media output, its spatial configuration or persistence over time. While local signage forms an obvious choice, advertising may also involve more contextual techniques like those adopted by street performers to build up crowds, such as using the skills of dedicated pitchmen that directly address passers-by, or providing opportunities for glancing [5]. Along the rousing trajectory, the ideas about a system that develop among people should not be influenced, by not revealing details on particular functionalities, elements or characteristics of the system [32]. Such open-ended and ambiguous experiences create an opportunity for people to remain comfortable as an audience member, or seek further details about a system by more readily interacting with peers and bystanders.

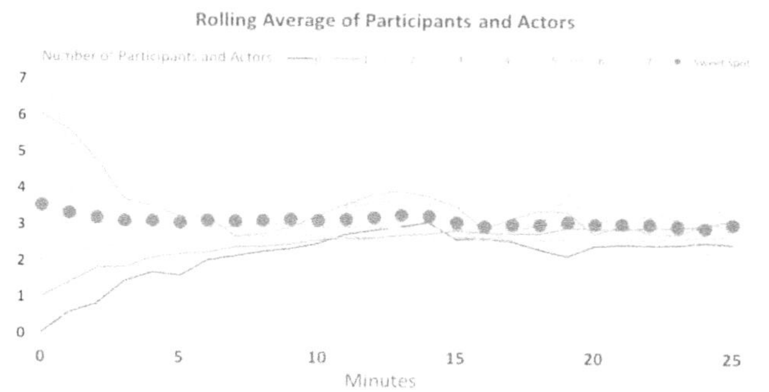

Figure 6: The honeypot sweet spot, i.e. the evolution of the rolling average number of participants and actors (Y axis) within any given dance zone over a 25-minute period (X axis).

Learning: From Bystander to Audience Member

We discovered that the typical trajectory for audience members included some form of *learning*. Since no instructive guidelines on how to interact in the dance zones were shown or explained, the learning process required some conscious effort. Most audience members first aimed to become familiar with the expected interactions (e.g. "*We've been enjoying [watching] other people do it. Trying to work it out from afar*", interview #22, middle-aged couple); the social norms that existed (e.g. "*As we watched others dancing, we could decipher the intrinsic rules of the game*", interview #49, young couple); or the inner workings (e.g. "*It took us a while to learn this must be picking up people's motions in one particular area*", interview #80, father and daughter). The learning trajectory commonly involved some form of social interaction with others, particular those who had previously participated: "*The people who aren't actually interacting, are [behind the fence], interacting with each other while trying to explain it. It's got everyone talking*" (interview #22).

Audience members that had no intention to learn, commonly watched the performance purely for personal enjoyment (e.g. "*You're just drawn to it. You can sit here and look at it*", interview #23, middle-aged couple); were discouraged by a perceived fear of social embarrassment (e.g. "*I entered a dance zone, but only for a short time. It felt more comfortable to just watch others*", interview #108, young couple); or refrained from further engaging because of social obligations (e.g. keeping an eye on personal belongings while family and friends were in a dance zone). These audience members appreciated and enjoyed a certain degree of physical and social comfort, which the space provided in the form of a seating area adjacent to the dance zones (see Figure 1, right). Notably, participants who dropped out, used this particular area to relax (see subsection *Dropping Out*) and, in turn, became themselves approachable sources of information to teach their peers about features of the system.

Design implication. Learning by watching other people's behavior in an interaction space (e.g. [27]) provides a context for one's own potential activities in later stages [10], even when people decide to refrain from any engagement. Learning also occurs via various forms of social interaction, particularly between different user roles along the canonical trajectory. Therefore, physical environments that aim to accommodate such learning process should focus on providing a comfortable space that caters for the physical and social needs of audience members. For instance, such space should warrant a nearby and uninterrupted visibility of the interactive system [22], while supporting stationary postures without fear for social embarrassment. Such space should also accommodate social interaction and opportunities for peer learning, for instance by stimulating approaching others, overhearing conversations or sharing experiences. Ultimately, such space should also accommodate for the absence of any interaction, such as from passive audience members. Here, a level of physical and social comfort is needed that supports spectating a performance, rather than socializing with peers.

Engaging: From Bystander over Audience Member to Participant

Two external factors influenced engagement in the dance zones: the number of people that simultaneously interacted, and the ambiguous meaning of unexpected events.

The Honeypot Sweet Spot

We discovered that the number of people simultaneously interacting with *Encounters* influenced the motivation of other participants. Figure 6 represents the rolling average of how the number of concurrent participants within the dance zones (Y-axis) affected the growth or decline of participants over a 25-minute timeframe (X-axis). The initial condition is the average number of people within a single dance zone per minute. Consequently, the diagram demonstrates that when two people are dancing, the number of participants tends to increase; whereas five participants trigger a decline over the course of 25 minutes. Our sensor data revealed that this number balances out at 3.1 participants per dance zone (SD=0.8). We refer to this number as the *honeypot sweet spot* (Figure 6, red-dotted line). We believe this phenomenon can be best explained by physical and spatial constraints: the archway's physical dimensions (5m) allows for a maximum of three people (3x approx. 1.75m) to stand next to each other, directly underneath a sensor. While there is still substantial space in front of or behind this line for people to move around, audience members might have perceived the dance zone to be fully occupied or experienced difficulties understanding the visual feedback: "*As more people entered the dance zone, we lost motivation. It got crowded, and we couldn't identify ourselves on the screen*" (interview #108, middle-aged couple).

This finding adds significance to previous findings in literature that indicate the honeypot effect is mainly unidirectional and self-reinforcing [26]. Our study shows that interactive systems are not necessarily able to accommodate a continuously increasing number of participants, but reveals a balance between user motivation and ergonomic, social, hardware and software constraints. Continuous recurring participation may not even always be desirable as, for example, the content or narrative may have reached its end, participants may have lost interest, or others may want to start interacting. As a result, participants can be expected to return to a role as audience member or bystander, and potentially even drop out of interaction.

Design implication. Interactive systems should consider how to tackle the *honeypot sweet spot*, i.e. the optimal number of participants that simultaneously interact. It requires taking into account a range of spatial and social constraints, such as the visibility of available interaction space, the hardware and software constraints that limit how many people effectively can be sensed or receive feedback in parallel, or simply the ergonomic dimensions of the system. To manage the *sweet spot* dropouts, specific trajectories could be designed to encourage people to seamlessly travel back and forth between the roles of participant, audience member and bystander depending on the number of simultaneous participants, or provide opportunities for dropouts to share their experiences with audience members. The aim is not to recommit dropouts into interaction, but rather stimulate knowledge transfer.

Unexpected Events

Encounters experienced an unexpected power outage during one dance performance, causing all audio and visual systems to shut down even though the dancers continued with their choreography. In follow-up interviews, participants remarked that they felt unsure if the power outage was deliberate and staged: "*It made us focus more on the dance performance, and we were less distracted by the visuals and the sounds*" (interview #49, young couple). This ambiguity therefore unintentionally made people wonder about how the installation was designed, and whether the temporary lack of interactivity was a legitimate part of the overall experience. It also illustrates how counterintuitively a lack of interactivity is still able to refocus the attention to the behavior that the interactivity was specifically meant to encourage and reinforce. In addition, it strengthens our earlier observation that triggers, such as dancers and volunteers, appear to fulfill a key motivational role, even in the (temporary) absence of an interactive system.

Design implication. Sudden disruptions in the interactivity of a system have the potential to positively influence engagement by way of creating an ambiguous situation that challenges participants to focus their attention to interpreting their own behavior. We propose further research is required to investigate the impact of such unannounced interaction shifts on user behavior, such as in terms of severity, frequency, persistence, and the potential boundaries between user frustration and curiousness. Here, we highlight that the impact of triggers is still relatively undervalued and underexposed, even though they appear to be crucial components of interactive systems.

Committing: From Participant to Actor

We observed that *Encounters* engaged participants through audiovisual feedback and dance performances, as well as through social interaction with each other. Participants who discovered the cause-and-effect narratives in *Encounters* committed to more persistent and dedicated forms of interaction: "*It got us all excited when we discovered that we could manipulate the visuals even more when we held hands with friends.*" (interview #3, two middle-aged couples). As participants were empowered to discover how the installation responded to performative and social interactions, they transformed into actors.

The Narrative of Participation

We observed participants transform into actors in two distinct ways: through participating in the dance performance and by initiating interactions with others. The second dance phase by facilitators temporarily orchestrated the engagement of participants. For instance, the choreography contained dance expressions that motivated participants to stand close together, and engage in activities like running, jumping or touching each other. As some participants became sufficiently empowered, they took on a role as actors and started manipulating the predefined choreography of the dancers: "*In my zone, people didn't want to form a cluster. [...] I kept orbiting around them. In the end I appreciated being part of their experience, but not creating their experience*", interview #10, dancer).

In order to fully explore the unpredictable responsive nature of sounds and visuals, some participants merged efforts to create group-level behaviors, such as maintaining close physical contact, or standing as far apart as possible. These collaborative behaviors happened within groups of relatives ("*[...] We tried to identify if there was a shape that was following us and I think there was. So we separated again to see if that was the case*", interview #20, middle-aged couple); between strangers (e.g. "*While trying to work it out, I held hands with others. It changed us into a big planet on the screen*", interview #6, young couple); and in collaboration with dancers (e.g. "*I imitated the dancers' moves. It's easy, and I get to see what is possible with the visuals on the screen*", interview #17, young adult).

Design implication. The transition from participant to actor requires a level of commitment that allows people to feel sufficiently empowered to immerse in their interaction and experiment with the possibilities of a system. Therefore, besides considering open-ended interaction mechanisms, triggers fulfill a particular role in easing the transition from participant to actor. Through their inside knowledge of an interactive system, triggers support a narrative for participants to immerse in, and, subsequently, facilitate opportunities for social and performative interaction between actors and triggers, and among groups of actors.

Collaborative Performances

At one occasion, a group of friends entered a dance zone and, after an initial phase of exploration, passed around a beach ball at each other. A subsequent interview revealed these participants aimed to explore the sensor's capabilities: "*It was fun! We could see that the sensors picked up the ball as we passed it around*" (interview #16, group of friends).

This improvisation positively impacted the social interaction, as two other participants joined in. On the other hand, the dance performance that started shortly thereafter required significant adjustment, as dancers were confronted with insufficient space in the dance zone to perform. Yet, as the *honeypot sweet spot* was already at its maximum, this particular dance became also relatively purposeless.

Design implication. In order to encourage collaborative behavior, a system's interactivity should motivate people to join efforts, in order to discover (hidden) features and positively influence the overall social experience. Design considerations involve forms of gamification that encourage deliberate and synchronous activities, in terms of technical features (e.g. software that recognizes collaborative actions), experience (e.g. visual and sonic feedback that responds to collaboration) and physical manifestations (e.g. providing *props* that require participants to collaborate). In this context, providing participants with detailed information about the system would increase the usability, yet might hinder the emergence of collaborative performances and more elaborate experimentations. However, collaboration may also hinder the engagement of others, or even the performance of the system in itself. As such, in order to accommodate a wide range of participants, one should consider spatial aspects (e.g. maximizing the dance zone) and technical features (e.g. responding meaningfully to varying levels of engagement).

Dropping Out: Transitioning out of Engagement

We observed people dropping out of *Encounters* for various reasons, which differed in terms of their prior user role.

- **Unwillingness** occurs among passers-by who have not (yet) experienced the interactive system, and where a general disinterest or discomfort (e.g. loudness, queuing, time constraints) might exist.
- **Disappointment** is caused by a contradiction between personal expectations and the actual experience, such as by feeling underwhelmed by the feedback or the general purpose of the interaction, which could be caused, among other reasons, by usability or user experience issues.
- **Discomfort** occurs as audience members have been unsuccessful in overcoming social fears (e.g. unfamiliarity, crowdedness). It mostly relates to a misalignment between personal expectations and what the system supports (e.g. a system requires excessive gestures, which an audience member is unwilling to perform for reasons such as social awkwardness or bodily constraints).
- **Withdrawal** occurs when participants have spent some time in the interaction zone, but drop out prior to transitioning to actor because of physical limitations (e.g. exhaustion) or spatial and social influences (e.g. perceived sense of crowdedness).
- **Completion** is the canonical reason for dropping out: participants have progressed through the complete narrative of the interactive system, or conclude that they have depleted all possible, expected or interesting interaction possibilities.

Design implication. Interactive systems need to be designed to avoid dropouts for external reasons, like limited usability or insufficient enjoyment. Systems should integrate gentle ways to abandon engagement and allow for different degrees of commitment with a system. Despite dropping out, specific trajectories can encourage dropouts to recommit into the canonical trajectory. Here, one can consider deploying triggers that attempt to relieve discomfort or deal with disappointment by disclosing or demonstrating the interactions that are supported by the system. We believe such interactions should highlight the general purpose of the system for potential engagement to (re)emerge, and refrain from posing additional challenges. Notably, if dropouts are to recommit, such trajectories should not have any social or other negative repercussions.

Social Interaction while Dropping Out

We observed that social interaction between dropouts and other users can take implicit forms, such as showing visible signs of physical exhaustion. More explicit forms of communication consist of dropouts who communicate their experiences with the people they pass in other stages of the trajectory, or bystanders who pick up on enthusiastic conversations between groups of dropouts. We thus distinguish between three types of social interaction.

- **Unintended guidance** occurs when passers-by are influenced, commonly involving overhearing conversations between dropouts, but can also involve reading status updates from dropouts on social networks.
- **Purposeful guidance** is an explicit interaction, when bystanders and audience members exchange information with dropouts, predominantly on the inner workings of a system or people's past experiences.
- **Performative guidance** occurs when participants and actors change behavior in response to the physical behavior of dropouts. It resembles some form of social risk assessment, such as when an actor stays behind in a dance zone as another actor suddenly drops out.

Design implication. Dropouts built up a particular experience that could be shared to those in other user roles. In fact, dropouts may easily and organically take on a role of *spark* or *facilitator*, enthusing those who have yet to engage in the interaction and sharing their insights and experience. Such interactions with other user roles can be encouraged by physically forcing them to meet or pass each other when dropping out, or by promoting collaboration with those who are not yet participating. Naturally, social interaction may be detrimental when dropouts report negative experiences to others, such as the reasons for dropping out that were mentioned earlier. However, we believe the role of dropouts is still underexposed in HCI, and suggest further research is required to investigate their effect on participant trajectories.

DISCUSSION

Our analysis yields new insights into the key factors of the honeypot effect, while still remaining flexible for adaptation and deployment in other application domains.

Triggering Audience Engagement

In the absence of any engaging activities or pre-existing participants (for example when a system is initially launched), motivating new participants to move closer and engage in an interaction becomes more challenging as the risk of social embarrassment is perceived to be higher. The Honeypot Model provides a framework that allows for simultaneously analyzing how triggers *influence* the *trajectory* of people, respectively through their behavior and spatial position. In addition, *Encounters* was characterized by a range of distinct triggers, unique in their temporality, sociality and proximity to the interaction zone. The ability of the Honeypot Model to accommodate such complex aspects, reveals its flexibility as an overall framework that describes – but not prescribes – the honeypot effect.

However, while triggers in *Encounters* influenced engagement by *informing* passers-by, *motivating* participants and *orchestrating* actors, other studies could consider how triggers can be utilized in different contexts. For example, amusement parks may need triggers that entertain queuing *audience members*, while street performers may rely on persons planted in the audience to orchestrate *bystanders* into cheering.

Promoting and Sustaining Engagement

As soon as some form of engagement with a system has been achieved, the challenge is to allow for different forms of engagement to emerge, and allow for their co-existence and sustainability over longer periods of time. In our model, we propose the *activation loop*, a trajectory that is crucial in activating new participants to join the interaction, and allowing dropouts to share experiences or recommit. The *activation loop* should not be understood as a mechanism that continuously pulls dropouts back into participation, but rather as an exchange of knowledge and motivation between those that interact (i.e. participants and actors) and those who are yet to engage in the interaction (i.e. bystanders and audience members).

Our analysis of the activation loop expands the common notion of the honeypot effect as solely relying on watching others. In fact, we argue the activation loop is one of its key elements, as the activities that occur allow for: 1) information to be exchanged between experienced dropouts and new participants to stimulate engagement (e.g. by sharing experiences), 2) bystanders and audience members to learn about the social norms and interactive features by observing the activities of participants and actors, and 3) dropouts to re-engage with the system after an initial period of withdrawal (e.g. to learn more about the supported features or social norms). We have illustrated that the activation loop relies on communication between different user roles.

However, there exists a limit to promoting engagement. We have identified a *honeypot sweet spot*; a natural equilibrium between the participation rate and system-specific constraints. We believe additional research is required to study the diversity of the honeypot sweet spot, such as its impact, optimization and applicability in varying contexts.

Limitations and Shortcomings

The Honeypot Model adds further consideration to existing knowledge about the honeypot effect. Since our findings are solely based on *Encounters*, we may not have identified influences that may exist in other contexts. Hence, the topology we propose is not deterministic. Applying the model to other domains will reveal the existence or absence of other components, such as the influence that actors have on remote passers-by through intended guidance (e.g. texting others while interacting) or how audience members potentially stimulate engagement by way of gestures and sounds (e.g. applause).

We believe that the Honeypot Model may prove fruitful when studying engagement in other contexts that rely on, or deal with, audience flows. Potential application domains span a wide array of contexts, ranging from street performances and media architecture, to urban games and mass tourist attractions. For example, amusement parks can apply the model to study how efficient transition through the activation loop can minimize waiting times; or public displays in community settings may require maximizing the activation loop to create opportunities for social interaction.

CONCLUSION

In this paper, we propose that the honeypot effect involves a series of spatial trajectories and contextual influences that should be modelled from well before the actual interaction takes place. Designing for a honeypot effect involves balancing the activation loop with the honeypot sweet spot. While the activation loop stimulates audience engagement, the honeypot sweet spot reduces the potential reach. However, the capacity of the honeypot sweet spot can be optimized by considering four design characteristics:

- optimizing the physical environment, by considering a range of ergonomic, spatial, technical and social aspects;
- deploying triggers to ease transitions between user roles;
- stimulating opportunities for collaborative interaction, peer learning and exploratory activities; and
- allowing for dropouts to leave without any repercussion, or empowering them to reactivate within the *activation loop* and to stimulate those who have yet to engage.

Our contributions and design implications are synthesized in the Honeypot Model, a spatiotemporal model that can be used by designers and researchers to annotate and optimize the impact of the honeypot effect. The Honeypot Model allows for the identification and study of different engagement styles, ranging from active and self-reinforcing, to passive and individual.

REFERENCES

1. Steve Benford and Gabriella Giannachi. 2008. Temporal Trajectories in Shared Interactive Narratives. In *Proceedings of the SIGCHI Conference on Human Factors in Computing Systems (CHI '08)*. ACM, New York, NY, USA, 73-82. http://dx.doi.org/10.1145/1357054.1357067
2. Gilbert Beyer, Vincent Binder, Nina Jäger and Andreas Butz. 2014. The Puppeteer Display: Attracting and Actively Shaping the Audience with an Interactive Public Banner Display. In *Proceedings of the 2014 Conference on Designing Interactive Systems (DIS '14)*. ACM, New York, NY, USA, 935-944. http://dx.doi.org/10.1145/2598510.2598575
3. Harry Brignull and Yvonne Rogers. 2003. Enticing People to Interact with Large Public Displays in Public Spaces. In *Proceedings of IFIP TC13 International Conference on Human-Computer Interaction (Interact '03)*. IOS Press, 17-24.
4. Martin Brynskov, Peter Dalsgaard, Tobias Ebsen, Jonas Fritsch, Kim Halskov and Rune Nielsen. 2009. Staging Urban Interactions with Media Façades. In *Proceedings of IFIP TC13 International Conference on Human-Computer Interaction (Interact '09)*. Springer, Berlin, Heidelberg, 154-167. http://dx.doi.org/10.1007/978-3-642-03655-2_20
5. Andrew Carlin. Working the Crowds: Street Performances in Public Spaces. In *City Imaging: Regeneration, Renewal and Decay*, Tara Brabazon Ed. Springer Netherlands, 2014, 157-169. http://dx.doi.org/10.1007/978-94-007-7235-9_12
6. Marcus Carter, John Downs, Bjorn Nansen, Mitchell Harrop and Martin Gibbs. 2014. Paradigms of Games Research in HCI: A Review of 10 Years of Research at CHI. In *Proceedings of the First ACM SIGCHI Annual Symposium on Computer-Human Interaction in Play (CHI Play '14)*. ACM, New York, NY, USA, 27-36. http://dx.doi.org/10.1145/2658537.2658708
7. Alan Chatham and Florian 'Floyd' Mueller. 2013. Adding an Interactive Display to a Public Basketball Hoop Can Motivate Players and Foster Community. In *Proceedings of the 2013 ACM International Joint Conference on Pervasive and Ubiquitous Computing (UbiComp '13)*. ACM, New York, NY, USA, 667-676. http://dx.doi.org/10.1145/2493432.2493478
8. Peter Dalsgaard and Lone Koefoed Hansen. Performing Perception: Staging Aesthetics of Interaction. *ACM Trans. Comput.-Hum. Interact.* 15, 3 (December 2008), 1-33. http://dx.doi.org/10.1145/1453152.1453156
9. John Dewey. *Art as Experience*. Minton, Balch and Company (New York, NY, USA), 1934.
10. Paul Dourish and Genevieve Bell. *Divining a Digital Future: Mess and Mythology in Ubiquitous Computing*. MIT Press (Cambridge, Massachusetts), 2011. http://dx.doi.org/10.7551/mitpress/9780262015554.001.0001
11. Patrick Tobias Fischer and Eva Hornecker. 2012. Urban HCI: Spatial Aspects in the Design of Shared Encounters for Media Facades. In *Proceedings of the SIGCHI Conference on Human Factors in Computing Systems (CHI '12)*. ACM, New York, NY, USA, 307-316. http://dx.doi.org/10.1145/2207676.2207719
12. Brian J. Fogg. 2009. A Behavior Model for Persuasive Design. In *Proceedings of the 4th International Conference on Persuasive Technology (Persuasive '09)*. ACM, New York, NY, USA, 40. http://dx.doi.org/10.1145/1541948.1541999
13. Luke Hespanhol and Martin Tomitsch. Strategies for Intuitive Interaction in Public Urban Spaces. *Interacting with Computers* 27, 1 (January 2015). http://dx.doi.org/10.1093/iwc/iwu051
14. Bill Hillier and Julienne Hanson. *The Social Logic of Space*. Cambridge University Press, 1993. http://dx.doi.org/10.1017/CBO9780511597237
15. Eva Hornecker and Jacob Buur. 2006. Getting a Grip on Tangible Interaction: A Framework on Physical Space and Social Interaction. In *Proceedings of the SIGCHI Conference on Human Factors in Computing Systems (CHI '06)*. ACM, New York, NY, USA, 437-446. http://dx.doi.org/10.1145/1124772.1124838
16. Clinton Jorge, Julian Hanna, Valentina Nisi, Nuno Nunes, Miguel Caldeira, Giovanni Innela and Amanda Marinho. Storytelling and the Use of Social Media in Digital Art Installations. In *Interactive Storytelling*, Hartmut Koenitz et al. Eds. Springer International Publishing, 2013, 233-244. http://dx.doi.org/10.1007/978-3-319-02756-2_29
17. Dirk vom Lehn, Jon Hindmarsh, Paul Luff and Christian Heath. 2007. Engaging Constable: Revealing Art with New Technology. In *Proceedings of the SIGCHI Conference on Human Factors in Computing Systems (CHI '07)*. ACM, New York, NY, USA, 1485-1494. http://dx.doi.org/10.1145/1240624.1240848
18. Lian Loke and George Poonkhin Khut. Intimate Aesthetics and Facilitated Interaction. In *Interactive Experience in the Digital Age*, Linda Candy and Sam Ferguson Eds. Springer International Publishing, 2014, 91-108. http://dx.doi.org/10.1007/978-3-319-04510-8_7
19. Paul Marshall, Richard Morris, Yvonne Rogers, Stefan Kreitmayer and Matt Davies. 2011. Rethinking 'Multi-User': An in-the-Wild Study of How Groups Approach a Walk-up-and-Use Tabletop Interface. In *Proceedings of the SIGCHI Conference on Human Factors in Computing Systems (CHI '11)*. ACM, New York, NY, USA, 3033-3042. http://dx.doi.org/10.1145/1978942.1979392

20. Anijo Mathew, Yvonne Rogers and Peter Lloyd. 2011. Post-It Note Art: Evaluating Public Creativity at a User Generated Art Installation. In *Proceedings of the 8th ACM Conference on Creativity and Cognition (C&C '11)*. ACM, New York, NY, USA, 61-70. http://dx.doi.org/10.1145/2069618.2069630

21. Joseph F McCarthy. Promoting a Sense of Community with Ubiquitous Peripheral Displays. In *Public and Situated Displays - Social and Interactional Aspects of Shared Display Technologies*, Kenton O'Hara et al. Eds. Kluwer Academic Publishers (Dordrecht, The Netherlands), 2003, 283-308. http://dx.doi.org/10.1007/978-94-017-2813-3_12

22. Robin Meisner, Dirk vom Lehn, Christian Heath, Alex Burch, Ben Gammon and Molly Reisman. Exhibiting Performance: Co-Participation in Science Centres and Museums. *International Journal of Science Education* 29, 12 (2007), 1531-1555. http://dx.doi.org/10.1080/09500690701494050

23. Nemanja Memarovic, Marc Langheinrich, Florian Alt, Ivan Elhart, Simo Hosio and Elisa Rubegni. 2012. Using Public Displays to Stimulate Passive Engagement, Active Engagement, and Discovery in Public Spaces. In *Proceedings of the 4th Media Architecture Biennale Conference: Participation (MAB '12)*. ACM, New York, NY, USA, 55-64. http://dx.doi.org/10.1145/2421076.2421086

24. Daniel Michelis and Jörg Müller. Observations of Gesture Based Interaction with Multiple Large Displays in a City Center. *International Journal of Human-Computer Interaction* 27 (2011), 562-579. http://dx.doi.org/10.1080/10447318.2011.555299

25. Jörg Müller, Florian Alt, Daniel Michelis and Albrecht Schmidt. 2010. Requirements and Design Space for Interactive Public Displays. In *Proceedings of the International Conference on Multimedia (MM '10)*. ACM, New York, NY, USA, 1285-1294. http://dx.doi.org/10.1145/1873951.1874203

26. Jörg Müller, Robert Walter, Gilles Bailly, Michael Nischt and Florian Alt. 2012. Looking Glass: A Field Study on Noticing Interactivity of a Shop Window. In *Proceedings of the SIGCHI Conference on Human Factors in Computing Systems (CHI '12)*. ACM, New York, NY, USA, 297-306. http://dx.doi.org/10.1145/2207676.2207718

27. Kenton O'Hara, Maxine Glancy and Simon Robertshaw. 2008. Understanding Collective Play in an Urban Screen Game. In *Proceedings of the 2008 ACM conference on Computer Supported Cooperative Work (CSCW '08)*. ACM, New York, NY, USA, 67-76. http://dx.doi.org/10.1145/1460563.1460576

28. Peter Peltonen, Esko Kurvinen, Antti Salovaara, Giulio Jacucci, Tommi Ilmonen, John Evans, Antti Oulasvirta and Petri Saarikko. 2008. It's Mine, Don't Touch!: Interactions at a Large Multi-Touch Display in a City Centre. In *Proceedings of the SIGCHI Conference on Human Factors in Computing Systems (CHI '08)*. ACM, New York, NY, USA, 1285-1294. http://dx.doi.org/10.1145/1357054.1357255

29. Stuart Reeves. Designing Interfaces in Public Settings: Understanding the Role of the Spectator in Human-Computer Interaction. Springer London, 2011. http://dx.doi.org/10.1007/978-0-85729-265-0

30. Stuart Reeves, Steve Benford, Claire O'Malley and Mike Fraser. 2005. Designing the Spectator Experience. In *Proceedings of the SIGCHI Conference on Human Factors in Computing Systems (CHI '05)*. ACM, New York, NY, USA, 741-750. http://dx.doi.org/10.1145/1054972.1055074

31. Christa Sommerer and Laurent Mignonneau. Art as a Living System: Interactive Computer Artworks. *Leonardo* 32, 3 (1999), 165-173. http://dx.doi.org/10.1162/002409499553190

32. Anthony Tang, Mattias Finke, Michael Blackstock, Rock Leung, Meghan Deutscher and Rodger Lea. 2008. Designing for Bystanders: Reflections on Building a Public Digital Forum. In *Proceedings of SIGCHI Conference on Human Factors in Computing Systems 2008 (CHI '08)*. ACM, New York, NY, USA, 879-882. http://dx.doi.org/10.1145/1357054.1357193

33. Jay Trimble, Roxana Wales and Rich Gossweiler. An Interactive Collaborative Workspace Platform. In *Public and Situated Displays - Social and Interactional Aspects of Shared Display Technologies*, Kenton O'Hara et al. Eds. Kluwer Academic Publishers (Dordrecht, The Netherlands), 2003, 18-44. http://dx.doi.org/10.1007/978-94-017-2813-3_2

34. Daniel Vogel and Ravin Balakrishnan. 2004. Interactive Public Ambient Displays: Transitioning from Implicit to Explicit, Public to Personal, Interaction with Multiple Users. In *Proceedings of the 17th Annual ACM Symposium on User Interface Software and Technology (UIST '04)*. ACM, New York, NY, USA, 137-146. http://dx.doi.org/10.1145/1029632.1029656

35. Sarah Webber, Mitchell Harrop, John Downs, Travis Cox, Niels Wouters and Andrew Vande Moere. 2015. Everybody Dance Now: Tensions between Participation and Performance in Interactive Public Installations. In *Proceedings of Australian Human-Computer Interaction Conference (ozCHI '15)*. ACM, New York, NY, USA. http://dx.doi.org/10.1145/2838739.2838801

36. Peter Wright, John McCarthy and Lisa Meekison. Making Sense of Experience. In *Funology*, Springer Netherlands, 2005, 43-53. http://dx.doi.org/10.1007/1-4020-2967-5_5

37. Robert Boleslaw Zajonc. Social Facilitation. *Science* 149, 3681 (1965), 269-274. http://dx.doi.org/10.1126/science.149.3681.269

Exploring Large-Scale Interactive Public Illustrations

Emily-Clare Thorn[1], Stefan Rennick-Egglestone[1], Boriana Koleva[1], William Preston[1], Steve Benford[1], Anthony Quinn[2] and Richard Mortier[3]
[1] School of Computer Science, University of Nottingham, Nottingham, United Kingdom
[2] School of Design, Central Saint Martins College of Art and Design, London, United Kingdom
[3] Computer Lab, Cambridge University, Cambridge, United Kingdom
{pszet,pszsre,pszbnk,pszwp,pszsdb}@nott.ac.uk, a.quinn@csm.arts.ac.uk, richard.mortier@cl.cam.ac.uk

ABSTRACT
We present a research-through-design exploration of transforming large-scale public illustrations into interactive media. We collaborated with creative practitioners to extend an existing visual marker technology to support spatial and layered interaction with wall-sized images. We document how these techniques were used to design interactive illustrations and how visitors to an exhibition engaged with these. We conclude that it is feasible to combine spatial and layered interactions to attach complex narratives to public illustrations, and highlight challenges around instruction giving, sociality and repeat experiences.

Author Keywords
Large scale displays;visual patterns;mobile interaction

ACM Classification Keywords
H.5.m. Information interfaces and presentation (e.g., HCI)

INTRODUCTION
From graffiti and street art, to billboards and posters, to temporary hoardings around building sites, large-scale public illustrations are a ubiquitous feature of the urban environment. In this paper, we consider how to make these static images interactive through digital augmentations that allow designers to embed complex digital narratives into large-scale visual media. To support this work, we have extended an existing mobile computer vision technology which allows for the recognition of topological structures in illustrations and their linkage to digital content. Our central challenge has been to identify appropriate mechanisms for scaling up interactions with visual markers so as to take advantage of the possibilities offered by the large physical scale and high resolution offered by public illustrations.

In exploring this space, we have worked with illustrators and creative writers to consider two broad approaches for extending interactions with visual markers. The first concerns *spatial interactions* in which users scan sequences or groups of visual markers that are embedded within an illustration, panning across its surfaces or stepping forwards and backwards to explore a range of content. The second addresses *layered interactions* in which multiple layers of visual markers are overlaid on the same illustration, with users switching between them as they interact. To support a realistic understanding of the opportunities and constraints of these for both designers and users, we have developed candidate implementations of both. We also commissioned creative teams to produce three large-scale interactive illustrations which were presented at an exhibition.

In this paper, we document what we learned through this process. We describe the mechanisms that we chose to implement spatial and layered interactions, consider creative practitioners used them to create three distinctive illustrations, and reflect on our observations of how exhibitions attendees interacted with them at our exhibition.

RELATED WORK
In conducting this exploration, we have drawn inspiration from several threads of prior work. Most immediately, our work seeks to extend familiar but simple interactions with street posters that involve small numbers of embedded and obvious visual tags. These include the use of QR codes as physical hyperlinks to digital information such as event details, map coordinates or vouchers and promotions [21]. Our aim is to extend such approaches to gracefully embed a higher density of visual codes within an image in a way that is both aesthetic and richly interactive. Our work contrasts with recent approaches that have employed computer vision to recognize the image as a whole. These are often coupled with the display of AR content (e.g. where the poster acts as reference frame in which to visualize 3D graphics) [13].

Although not intended as a public illustration, a prototype by Reilly et al [20] has demonstrated mechanisms for creating composite interactions linking together RFIDs embedded in a paper map. Interactions include path-select (click handheld button, drag along path, release button to select entire path) and multi-select (click button to select multiple non-adjacent items). In working with a computer vision technology, we have sought to enable composite interactions that do not require the augmentation of an illustration with electronics. Instead, all interactive features are embedded directly into the illustration itself.

DIS 2016, June 04 - 08, 2016, Brisbane, QLD, Australia

ACM 978-1-4503-4031-1/16/06…$15.00
DOI: http://dx.doi.org/10.1145/2901790.2901826

More widely, our work has been informed by extensive prior research into interaction with large, high-resolution printed displays (rather than illustrations). Here, Yeh at al [27] have highlighted the high resolution, low cost, reliability, mobility, and flexibility of paper, and proposed a network monitoring tool consisting of a 3ft by 6ft print showing all devices attached to a network, which can be annotated by an Anoto digital pen, linked to extra information presented on a mobile device, and used as a backdrop for projection of real-time information about the behavior of the devices. Although not digitally augmented, the work of the artist Simon Schofield [22] also shows the potential of large graphical designs to stimulate rich physical interactions. His scenes are algorithmically composed from individual elements, presenting features at different scales, from just a few millimeters to several metres. They are printed onto rubberized paper, which is robust enough to walk on, and are installed on floors or walls of environments such as galleries. They encourage physical interactions such kneeling down, getting close to inspect tiny features, or standing back to see the full image.

Finally, our work relates to an emerging body of work on large-scale public digital displays. In particular, engaging passers-by in urban interactions has been a key objective for work on media façades. Here interactivity, such as playing games, can also be supported through the users' mobile devices but in contrast involves the creation of a giant digital display by equipping the outer shell of a building with light emitting elements [23,1].

APPROACH

We have followed the overall approach of Research through Design (RtD) [28] in which our research findings emerged from ongoing reflection on a practice-led design process that produced an annotated portfolio of artefacts [11]. RtD has grown to become a broad umbrella that encompasses a diverse set of practices [10]. Ours has been to work with professional illustrators and storytellers to create a series of large-scale interactive illustrations that serve both to demonstrate and to challenge the development of new technologies. In assembling teams, we identified illustrators working within three very different graphical approaches, so as to provide a broad, rich and realistic exploration of our technology. The process itself involved three stages:

- We identified a candidate visual marker technology and conducted design workshops to explore how this might be extended to support new kinds of interaction. Extensions were implemented into a new mobile app.
- We commissioned creative teams to design interactive public illustrations, which were tested with the app.
- We hosted an exhibition of the resulting illustrations and collected observations and feedback from use.

Creative teams were required to produce illustrations within commercially realistic timescales; this contrasts with a substantial amount of prior RtD work which frequently sets aside temporal and financial constraints [28].

IMPLEMENTING SPATIAL & LAYERED INTERACTION

Many visual marker technologies might support interaction with large public illustrations. Widely used technologies such as barcodes [8] and QRcodes [15] are robust and scalable but suffer from a limited design aesthetic, in spite of various services to try and make them more visually interesting and personalized [2,8]. Recently, there has been a growth of interest in vision technologies that can recognise more aesthetic or natural images (or parts thereof) for example Goggles [12], Blippar [4], String [18], Media Markers [16], reacTIVision [3] and ARTag [9]. Within this latter camp, we chose to work with an approach based upon recognizing simple topological structures within images first implemented in a system called D-Touch [7].

We adopted this approach because previous studies, using a re-implemented and extended version, reported how it was especially suited to use by professional illustrators to create hand-drawn interactive patterns when decorating ceramic bowls [17]. This study showed how providing a simple set of topological rules made the operation of the technology sufficiently transparent to designers that they could easily learn to work with it and also develop new creative strategies that were not envisages in the initial system. In particular, the inherent visual ambiguity that similar looking patterns can embed different codes (topologies) within them, while the same code can be embedded in vary different designs proved to be fertile ground for creativity.

Having identified a baseline technology, we then organized a series of workshops with illustrators who were already familiar with the topological approach. We discussed settings in which public illustrations might appear, considered illustrations presented as single images or composed from multiple repeating elements (e.g. ceramic tiles) and explored the goals of making them interactive. The workshops generated a suite of interaction techniques for large-scale public illustrations based around the two broad approaches of spatial- and layered- interaction.

Spatial interaction

The first approach that emerged from the workshops was to consider how users might trigger interactions by engaging in various spatial movements, for example scanning across a large illustration or zooming in and out. For this, we directly built on the path and group select interactions identified by Reilly et al [20]. We encouraged designers to embed multiple recognizable codes within a single illustration and then to connect them using *pattern paths* and *pattern groups*. A pattern path is a collection of embedded codes that is read in sequence by panning across an illustration. A pattern group is a collection of embedded codes that must be read simultaneously, which may require stepping back and forward so as to zoom out to an appropriate framing. A single illustration might contain multiple pattern paths and pattern groups, drawing on a common set of underlying embedded codes. Figure 1 depicts a case in which a single illustration has 7 distinct topological codes embedded within (labeled A-G). The interaction has been configured so that two of these

(C and G) can be scanned in isolation to trigger interactions, two pattern paths can be scanned {A->B->D} and {A->C->E->F} as can two pattern groups {A,B,C} and (E,F}.

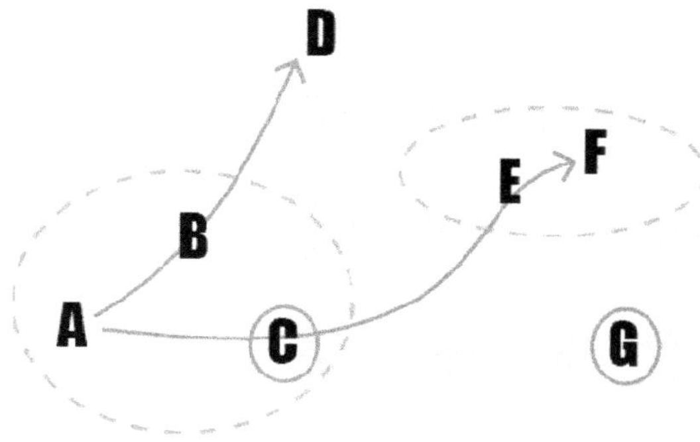

Figure 1. Pattern paths (arrows), pattern groups (dotted ovals). Each letter represents a discrete Aestheticode.

Layered interaction

The second approach that emerged from early workshops involved users interacting with different layers of visual codes that are embedded into the same illustration. This was inspired by previous research that had shown how designers came to realize that they could add certain colours to their patterns so as to enhance their aesthetics without affecting recognition [17]. This was possible because the computer vision software first applied a colour filter to a captured image then threshold it to black and white before trying to detect topological features. This previous research reported how the designers came to learn this technique as a result of experimentation. In our work, we decided to bring it directly under their control by introducing a controllable filtering mechanism into the vision pipeline that would allow chosen colours to be filtered in and out. We implemented two classes of filter:

- RGB: The colour space used by mobile phone cameras. Our filter removes the named layer [red, green, blue] and retains the remainder of the visual information
- CMYK: Used for printed media. We converted the video feed to CMYK, [cyan, magenta, yellow, black] and provided similar filters to remove a named layer.

Figure 2 presents an example of how this works. Previous implementations of the topological approach require the interactive part of the pattern (the code) to be separated from other parts of the pattern by (near) white space. This can be seen in fig 2, left in which the fish (code) are clearly separated from the red lily pads. In contrast, fig 2, centre shows an example in which the interactive part (fish) overlaps the background (lilies). Applying a red filter however, removes the lilies to present the system with the image shown in fig 2, right for subsequent processing. By dynamically switching between different filter types and colours the user can reveal different layers of codes within the same drawing.

Figure 2. Coloured filtering. The carp are valid Aestheticodes.

Following the workshop, we implemented a mobile app called Storicodes that could recognize topological markers within patterns using the D-Touch approach and that also supported our chosen techniques of pattern paths, pattern groups and switchable colour filters. The next step was to explore how skilled illustrators and storytellers would put these features to use.

DESIGNING THREE PUBLIC ILLUSTRATIONS

For the second phase or our process we commissioned three teams, each comprising a writer and an illustrator, to create interactive public installations. The three writers (Alice, Cheryl and Penny, not their real names) were all published authors of creative fiction. The three illustrators each brought a distinctive graphical style and approach: Lucy works with physical media such as paper and colored pencils; John works with layered collages of digital media; and Dave works in the advertising sector, which requires him to develop work with a wide range of styles.

Each team was given a distinctive brief that targeted a different audience. Two were for "portable" illustrations that did not strongly reference their deployment environment, the third was written around a project documenting the literary history of a city. Briefs and allocations were as follows:

- Brief 1: Write a short narrative featuring literary figures from Nottingham city's past and present. You might merge fact and fiction to create something intriguing and interesting [Dave and Penny].
- Brief 2: Write a short narrative that takes a young adult on a hunt through the illustration. It can be in any setting you wish but must give clues to point the participant in the right direction through the narrative to find the next visual code [John and Alice].
- Brief 3: Write a narrative to take a child on a journey through an illustration. It can be in any setting you wish but must contain a key character that the child can represent or help through the story [Lucy and Cheryl]

Each team was given a limited time budget which was roughly equivalent to a commercial contract (10 days for graphical designers, 7 days for writers), though teams were supported by a research expert in the technology.

Working from their briefs, creative teams designed both illustrations and associated digital content while we worked with them to support the configuration of Storicodes connecting the two and documenting the design process. Teams were not given target physical dimensions for the illustrations, but we emphasized the need to produce work on a large scale. We conducted a concluding interview with authors and designers to help understand the process as a whole. We now present the three designs that they created.

Illustration 1: A Princess Honeymoons in our Town

Princess presents three fictional characters, all of whom have previously featured in novels written by Nottingham-based authors. The central conceit of this work is that these characters have met by chance in a pub. The illustration for this work resembles a banknote (appropriate, given that the characters purchase and consume a substantial amount of alcohol during the story). Embedded codes within in the illustration link to web-pages that present the textual elements of a non-linear story (e.g., fig 4).

Figure 3. The illustration produced for "Princess"

A Princess Honeymoons In Our Town

The Old Angel

Arthur Seaton ☆ Princess Finestra ☆ Don Juan

"Erm, excuse me?"

A young woman stood in the doorway of the Old Angel, otherworldly in her beauty. Her voice

Figure 4. Top of web-page presenting narrative fragment

Color filtering was used to create two layers of interaction, red and blue. Launching the *Princess* experience from the Storicodes app automatically engages a filter to remove all reds from the camera feed, leaving the blue layer intact. The first interaction is then to use the smartphone to scan a pattern embedded into the central buildings (fig 5), triggering the display of a web-page showing the introductory piece of narrative (fig 4). This sets the scene for the story, by introducing the three principal characters.

Figure 5. The central building code (red layer removed)

Figure 6. Codes defining Arthur Seaton. Left: first filter applied. Right: second filter applied

The story develops through conversations between pairs of characters. Each is defined by a pattern path, composed of two visual codes embedded directly into the visual representation of the two characters (fig 6, left). Scanning the phone from one character to another reveals a page of dialogue between these two characters. Once all three pairs of dialogue in the initial blue layer have been scanned, Storicodes automatically switches to a coloured filter that scans the red layer of embedded codes (fig 6, right), enabling the viewer to trigger further conversations. The interaction concludes by re-scanning the blue-layer of the building code, which links to a concluding scene.

Illustration 2: Stalker

Stalker is a visually-complex illustration (fig 7) that was composited from over 100 layers in Photoshop. Color filtering was used extensively to ensure that the six interactive patterns hidden in the illustration could be robustly scanned. The associated digital experience took the form of a game comprising a series of missions that requiring interaction with nearby props and people. The underlying sci-fi story is one of rebellion by the Stalkers against their oppressors. Opening elements of the narrative position the experience as a call to arms and the illustration as an "inter-dimensional communication device".

Launching the *Stalkers* experience in Storicodes engages a colour filter that makes a pattern embedded into the journal in the bottom left readable (fig 8, left). This pattern links to a web-page presenting an opening journal entry (fig 8, right) introducing "Sera", the central character. From here, participants work through various physical interactions, such as picking up a package at a curiosity shop and listening to instructions on a tape recorder. The team intended that these would be instantiated in local venues such as galleries or cafes, creating the need to revisit the illustration multiple times, perhaps over several days. Each interaction directs the user back to scanning a new feature of the illustration so as to collect a further instruction. If they complete all activities, they obtain a code to a safe that they can open to obtain a reward.

Figure 7 The illustration produced for Stalker

Figure 8 Left: Journal Right: Associated digital content

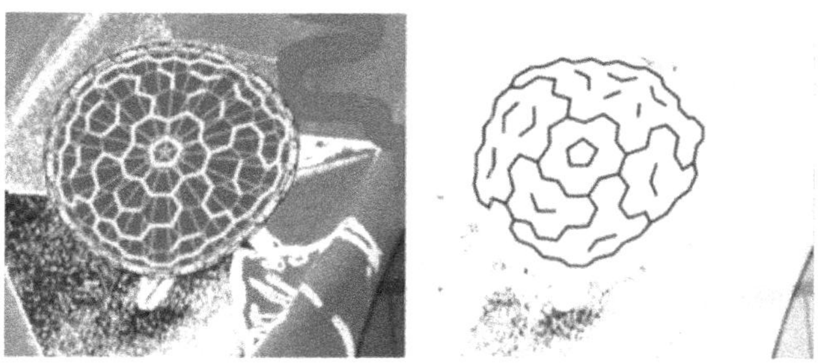

Figure 9 Sera's badge. Left: no filter. Right: filter applied.

To make the interaction with the illustration work, Storicodes automatically switches between specified color filters at key points in the experience, allowing for hidden codes to be robustly revealed to the recognition algorithm. As an example, fig 9 shows the impact of applying a filter that selects for yellows in Sera's badge.

Illustration: Who am I?

Who am I? is an interactive illustration targeted at young children, split across six panels (fig 10,11). Collectively, these tell the story of a creature who is trying to discover what species he is. All panels were originally hand-drawn and then digitally scanned for reproduction, with Photoshop used to make small alterations. Colour filtering was used to mask background detail, enabling the illustrator to work in a free and flexible manner when embedding codes into the wider picture (fig 12). Users follow a linear path through the narrative in which a digital representation of the creature is revealed through its visits to other animals. (fig 13). Pattern groups were used to link digital content to collections of patterns without these needing to be linked into a single code (fig 12). The split over six panels created a particularly challenge for how to guide users through the interaction that we discuss in detail, alongside the two other examples, in the following section.

Figure 10. Panels 1 to 3 - Who Am I?

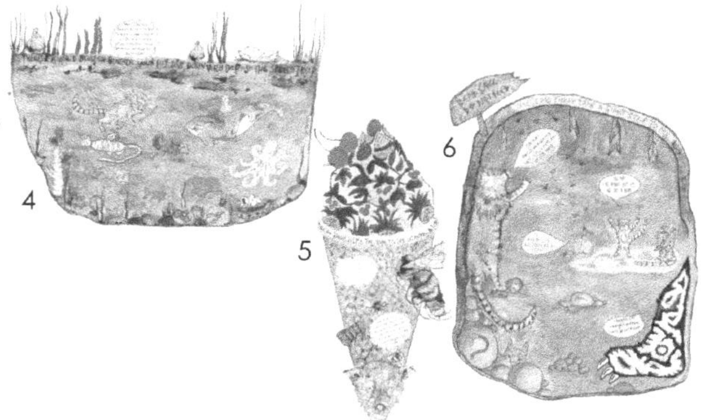

Figure 11. Panels four to six - "Who am I?"

Guiding users through interactions

A common challenge faced by each team was how to guide users through the process of interacting with large illustrations that contained complex layers, paths and groups of visual codes that were often deliberately disguised. Our teams evolved three distinct tactics for the production of instructions whose style was in keeping with the nature of their pieces while also allowing Storicode's interface to remain relatively simple:

Figure 12 Left: Pattern group comprising nest, eggs and birds. Right: cyan filter engaged (code highlighted in orange)

Figure 13. The creature visits others to find out who it is

1. Printed postcards giving instructions for downloading the Storicodes app and engaging in initial interactions.
2. Instructions embedded directly into digital media that was revealed on the phone.
3. Instructions embedded directly into the illustrations themselves.

An example postcard is shown in fig 14. This incorporates the following instruction fragment that simultaneously introduces core characters, indicates that download of an app is required, and provides a starting point for interaction.

> "My dear princess," replied Don Juan, "they can do just that, they but download the Storicodes app and scan the buildings in Mister Huggett's beautiful mural."

Figure 14 Postcard produced for "Princess" – front and back

An example of an instruction integrated into digital media is provided by Stalker where the follwing text was displayed at the end of a conversation between two guards so as to guide the user to now scan the mountains.

> "You need to take the vital information you have heard above to Sera! Scan the BLUE AND BLACK DULU MOUNTAINS and tell Sera the location of the map"

As a six panel piece, "Who Am I?" embedded a substantial amount of instruction within the piece itself, giving to guide a user through a linear series of interactions. Many of these were embedded into the illustration in a narrative style. For example the instructions embedded in fig 15 that read:

> "Maybe I'll find more creatures like me in the lake. I've heard the whale is very wise so I'll ask him first and the octopus is very clever, so I'll ask him second, and maybe then I'll find the catfish."
>
> … guiding the viwer to scan the pattern path embedded into part of the illsutration shown in fig 16.

Figure 15 Instructions embedded into a panel

Figure 16 Pattern path through whale, octopus and catfish codes highlighted in orange

Documentation of the design and production process

The research team kept a detailed record of the design and production process and conducted concluding interviews with the designers and writers. This allowed us to understand the approach taken by the creative teams.

The approach taken by the writers

The writers [Penny, Alice, Cheryl] generally lead the process of writing the narratives for the work:

- For *Princess*, Dave and Penny worked together to decide on an outline structure, which Penny filled out with a relatively lengthy story. This was cut back to an appropriate length for usage on a mobile device once an initial prototype of the web-content had been made

- For *Stalker*, Alice generated a much greater depth of material than was needed, including a substantial number of scenes which did not have dependencies on each other. John then selected from these to create a linear story to work into the illustration.
- For *Who am I?*, Cheryl produced an initial document that described in detail the interactions in each panel, and also the narrative elements relating to the panel.

The instructions discussed above were produced by the writers, and a key decision was whether they should be voiced as coming from Storicodes or one of the characters.

The approach taken by the illustrators

All of the illustrators worked to establish an effective overall layout and visual style for the illustrations before even thinking about the challenge of designing and integrating effective interactive patterns (e.g. fig 17). This reflected on a general professional confidence that they could make the interactive elements of the design work when needed, and also on the limited amount of time available for what was a commercial piece of work for them. There was a necessity to understand that the design worked on a large scale before "tidying it up" and filling out specific detail, to avoid wasting time. Limited time also meant that the designers had to work in a familiar way. Lucy worked rapidly in pencil and ink, producing a series of early sketches and then rubbing out or using Tippex where necessary. Dave produced vector art that could be tweaked and refined as necessary, and John worked in Photoshop to establish a basic collage of multiple layers.

Figure 17 Initial black and white layout produced for Princess

Working with color filters proved to be the most challenging element of engaging with the technology and their usage did not seem to be fully intuitive to the designers on first encounter. Consequently, we provided designers with a version of the Storicodes app that directly revealed the impact of applying different colour filters. Lucy employed this to develop a palette of coloured pencil/pen marks on a piece of paper that acted as a ready-to-hand guide as to the impact of different filters. The most technically complex usage of color filters was in *Princess* that is constructed from two independent layers of color. Dave conducted initial experiments with hand-drawn geometric shapes that revealed the danger of introducing breaks in solid lines (not acceptable within the Storicodes recognition algorithm). As such, the final design avoided any crossings between the two color layers.

The recognition technology did impose some compromises on the aesthetics of the design, but these were not of major importance, and could be worked around. As part of his "house style" Dave typically uses offsetting of colours to add contrast and texture, and to simulate the effects of screen-printing, as shown in the image on the left of fig 18, where the red hair "bleeds" over the blue line. However, applying a cyan filter to this caused a narrow white strip to appear (highlighted using the oval on the right of fig 18), which could confuse the recognition algorithm. As such, Dave avoided the use of offsetting in his final design. Similarly, Lucy chose to enlarge some patterns with delicate features beyond her preferred initial sizing to aid robustness of recognition, whilst John increased the contrast of elements in his collage to make them robustly scannable (e.g. the journal in the bottom left of fig 8).

Figure 18 Illustration of problems caused by offsetting. Left: original offset image. Right: implications of applying filter.

Reproduction of the illustrations

For each of the three illustrations we ran a test print onto the material we planned to use, working with a printing company who specialized in large-scale reproduction work. This allowed us to verify that color filtering still worked as expected with printed material. For *Princess*, we ran a second test print to verify that the thickness of the lines in the design worked effectively with the Storicodes recognition algorithm. Final versions of *Princess* were printed on 5mm Foamex Board with PVC printing, whilst *Who am I?* and *Stalker* were printed onto a flexible 200mic PVC sheet. All were waterproofed, allowing us to exhibit the work in either an exterior or an interior setting.

EXHIBITING THE ILLUSTRATIONS

The Interactive Illustrations were exhibited in a large space at Nottingham Writers' Studio, fixed to walls by hanging or taping them. In the case of "Who Am I" the panels were placed sequentially on a pre-existing white strip along the length of one wall. So as to obtain feedback relevant to an understanding of the medium, we invited other graphic designers and writers to a three-hour evening event that was attended by 13 participants.

Figure 19. ***Princess*****, attached directly to a wall**

Figure 20. Participants interacting with the "Stalker" piece

Figure 21. Interaction with one of the "Who Am I" panels

Figure 22. Scanning a visual code

We began with a brief introduction to the project. Those with iPhones were asked to download the app; others were given a phone to use by the research team. Rather than giving explicit instructions, the postcards described earlier on were handed out. Attendees were given time to freely explore the interactive illustrations while the resreach team observed and answered questions (this took about 40 minutes). They did this individually or in groups of 2-3. If participants arrived with others they tended to stay together during the experience.

In general participants were able to identify the visual elements they needed to scan in order to follow a narrative, but occasionally had to experiment with scanning from different distances to get a clear view of a full code. The design of each illustration clearly led to different patterns of physical interaction; interactive visual elements in "Who Am I" were small, and embedded in the fine detail of the illustration, and hence drew participants in very close. Stalker promoted quick interactions that drew people away from the illustration itself and into associated activities. Interactive features such as the building and the characters in *Princess* were large and bold, requiring scanning from a greater distance as well as movement from one side of the illustration to the other. This led to people contending for space and occluding each other, although also served to trigger impromptu conversations between attendees. The throughput with Princes was also lower, as the dialogue between the characters took some time to read.

Our observations revealed the importance of carefully wording instructions. In "Who Am I?", the following narrative element made it very clear that the representations of three animals had to be scanned in turn:

> "*Maybe I'll find more creatures like me in the lake. I've heard the whale is very wise so I'll ask him first and the octopus is very clever, so I'll ask him second, and maybe then I'll find the catfish.*"

In contrast, the instruction to "*Now scan each pair of characters to hear their conversation*" in *Princess* were ambiguous to some, who subsequently tried to simultaneously scan the characters (which meant fitting the entire illustration in the camera view, which did not work). For a few participants there were also issues when the textual narrative appeared on both the phone screen and the illustration (as in "Who Am I") as they tended to focus on just reading one (usually the mobile device) and so missed some hints on what to do next.

When the attendees had finished exploring the illustrations, we facilitated a group discussion to get feedback on the design of the interactive installations and their potential future use. Participants saw the illustrations as lovely public art in their own right, and commented that the visual designs were interesting and engaging. They found *Stalker* intriguing and attention grabbing, and liked its game-like structure that interweaved other physical activities. *Princess* was seen to have a simple and effective design. However, some participants reported that they did not fully read the dialogue presented through the linked web-pages, and a few did not read the narrative on the postcard completely so did not know where to start. The hand-drawn aesthetic and story of "Who am I" were liked, but to simplify interaction it was suggested to increase the size of the panels and highlight interactive items on the phone. Placing all three illustrations in the same setting lead to a relatively fast-paced interaction in which participants moved from one illustration to another. Longer installations in more public venues might allow for a slower engagement (especially in the case of *Stalker*), potentially facilitating engagement with detail that was missed in the exhibition.

In considering the ability to associate layers of content with the same visual element, discussions focused on the possibility of extending the number of available layers, or enabling the selection of a subset of layers to provide individuals with a bespoke experience that might feel more personal, secretive or intimate, rather than everyone accessing the same content. Other possibilities included the creation of layers which emerged in relation to external conditions, and which might consequently produce an adaptive narrative. For example, the changing nature of light that falls on an illustration, and the impact of this on the color perceived by the camera, might be used to read different codes and provide content that differentiated between midday and dusk. Alternatively, rendering codes in photochromic ink might allow for responses to changes in light, or thermochromic inks could be used to react to temperature. The participants also considered exploiting what the human sees versus what is detected by the camera in order to create optical illusions.

Finally, potential settings and applications for interactive public illustrations were considered. Suggestions included shopping centers and walls of buildings, where the same illustration could provide different layers of information for different users (e.g. young children, young adults, older adults). Other examples included museum displays (to allow for additional and easily updatable content), interactive educational displays in schools (e.g. for geography), a national treasure hunt, an area maps to provide details about local places of interest, or augmenting books or graphic novels with additional content layers.

DISCUSSION

By following a research through design process we have explored large scale interactive illustrations as a new public medium. We have revealed that they offer exciting new design possibilities – graphic designers and storytellers were able to create engaging pieces and largely viewers were able to successfully interact with them. However, our experience has also raised design and interaction issues. We now reflect on the opportunities and challenges of the medium so as to guide practitioners while also framing an agenda for further research.

Designing interactive illustrations

We begin with the designer's perspective – what did we learn about designing large-sale interactive illustrations? The three creative teams employed various combinations of spatial and layered interaction to produce very different pieces, both in terms of the structure and aesthetics of the graphics and the associated digital narratives.

Considering layered interaction first, *Who am I?* and *Princess* both made use of pattern paths as an interaction mechanism. In *Who am I?,* this was used to require a linear movement of the camera through three animal characters, whilst in *Princess*, it allowed for access to a non-linear dialogue through the scanning of pairs of patterns. Pattern groups in contrast, were only used in one instance - in "Who Am I?", where the eggs, nest and bird had to be simultaneously scanned. With codes statically embedded in the illustration, it is easy to see that pattern groups may not offer anything beyond what can be achieved with a single code. However, we suggest that pattern groups will become more useful if participants can somehow move elements around and dynamically compose them. An example might be a child's jigsaw puzzle, linked to digital content that is revealed as the child gradually assembles it.

Turning to layered interaction, all designers engaged in experimentation with color filtering. This feature was initially included to offer more creative possibilities in terms of placing codes on complex backgrounds, and this was its primary use in *Stalker* and *Who Am I?*. *Princess*, however, demonstrated the possibility of overlaying codes on top of one another and thereby providing layers of content (each accessed with a different color filter). This feature captured the imagination of the attendees at the deployment session and they saw many creative possibilities for revealing different content over time and providing more personalized content to individuals. Working with our first implementation of color filtering, however, proved to be a difficult and time-consuming process and required a great deal of experimentation to achieve a finished design. As noted earlier, we found that designers developed their understanding of the implications of color filtering through experimentation with hand-drawn imagery; further studies of how graphic designers work with color as part of their everyday practice should lead to a better understanding of how to enhance editing and debugging and so realize the potential of this technique.

In terms of design processes, all three illustrators began by creating the overall layout and aesthetic of the illustration before choosing elements to be converted into codes. This contrasts with previous studies of graphic designers working with the topological on small-scale designs that revealed how they were split in their approach, with some creating the structure of the code first and then embellishing it, and others drawing the pattern first and then converting it into code [17]. We see potential for tools to assist with the drawing of large illustrations and embedding of codes. Support could be provided for automatically identifying visual elements that can be turned into codes, making suggestion for how a specific element might become a code, and helping blend codes into the wider image.

Interacting with public illustrations

We now turn to the viewer's perspective – what was it like to interact with these large-scale public illustrations? While our participants found all three illustrations to be engaging, their experiences did raise some important concerns.

Embedding instructions

There is a spectrum of possibilities for embedding the points of interaction within an illustration – from making them obvious (by highlighting them on the screen or on the illustration) to purposefully hiding them. All three creative teams adopted the approach of weaving the interactive elements into the narrative itself, although they established different tactics for achieving this – external postcards, embedding them in the digital media, and embedding them in the illustration itself. While all three appeared to work, we note an important difference between them. Embedding instructions into the illustration makes the physical experience more self-contained. Indeed, one might construct an illustration that worked in its own right, with digital interactions providing an additional perspective. Conversely, embedding instructions into the digital media may allow for more dynamic reconfiguration of interactions and perhaps even re-appropriation of a long-lived piece of public art to tell new stories.

We note that instructions and narrative have to be carefully designed and we noted some problems with ambiguity. Previous accounts of the nature of instruction-giving over thin channels (such as text messages and audio recordings on mobile phones), and the ways in which such instructions are complied with (e.g. [25]) may help us to design more effective instructions and means to repair when the experience breaks down. Another important consideration for this medium is the opportunity to deliver instructions through a combination of channels – on the phone, the illustration or proxy objects such as postcards – and be mindful that participants do not just focus on one.

Interaction position

It may not be immediately clear where participants need to stand in order to interact with large illustrations as there is a much wider range of possibilities compared to nearfield displays. The design of the interactive elements may prompt users, for example, small visual items require participants to get close and vice versa. We suggest that there are also more explicit design strategies for communicating the interaction sweet spot that can be explored by future research, such as extending the illustration out onto the floor in front. Another aspect of interacting with digitally augmented illustrations is that scanning pattern paths requires the participants to move around. This might cause problems with users occluding each other., especially in in unsupervised public spaces.

Sociality

The large scale of the illustrations affords interaction by multiple participants. We saw small groups exploring the illustrations together (although the interactions were not explicitly designed to be collaborative), leading to the idea of making them more "socially scalable" where engagement becomes richer as more people interact [24]. Furthermore, the illustrations will inhabit public settings where people move around and there are spectators and bystanders. Designers need to respect and shape this sociality. We anticipate the "honeypot effect" noted by Brignull and Rogers [6] in which the clustering of users around the display attracts yet more users, and consider how to design "entry points" that invite and entice people into engagement and "access points" that enable users to join the activity [14]. A further consideration is whether to reveal visitors' interactions to spectators and so encourage them to become engaged or whether to try to hide them so that important clues are not given away as spoilers [19].

Repeated experiences

The kinds of public illustrations we are considering may be deployed as long-term public installations, making it important to consider repeat visits. To encourage people to interact again designers will need to provide something new each time. Layered interaction is particularly exciting in this regard as it allows us to reveal new codes on subsequent visits. An interesting direction for future research is also to explore visual patterns that change (and so does the code that is recognized) in response to external conditions such as lighting and temperature as noted earlier.

CONCLUSION

We have explored the opportunities created by augmenting large-scale public illustrations with interactive features. We have described the extension of an existing computer-vision technology to support spatial and layered interaction with large and complex visual narratives. We have presented a portfolio of three such illustrations created by teams of writers and illustrators and have offered reflections on the design process and how they were experienced by users. Through this work, we have identified the value of being able to embed multiple layers of interaction into a single illustration, and also considered the question of how the design of interactive elements impacts on the physical elements of the interaction with an artwork. An important step for future work will be to deploy such pieces over longer timeframes in public spaces so as to gain a deeper understanding of how visitors approach them, discover what to scan, orient themselves to the illustrations and other visitors and engage in repeat visits.

ACKNOWLEDGEMENTS AND DATA ACCESS

Work has been supported by the UK EPSRC (EP/L023717/1 and EP/M02315X/1). Our ethics approval does not allow for the release of transcripts collected during the design process, and hence access will not be provided to third parties. High-resolution versions of the illustrations are available from http://www.artcodes.co.uk/.

REFERENCES

1. Boring, S., Gehring, S., Wiethoff, A., Blöckner, M., Schöning, J., Butz, A. Multi-user interaction on media façades through live video on mobile devices. In *Proceedings of the SIGCHI conference on Human Factors in Computing Systems (CHI'11).* http://dx.doi.org/10.1145/1978942.1979342
2. Barcode Revolution website, http://www.barcoderevolution.com/, verified Jan 2013
3. Bencina, R., Kaltenbrunner, M. and Jorda., S. Improved Topological Fiducial Tracking in the reacTIVision System. In *Proceedings of the 2005 IEEE Computer Society Conference on Computer Vision and Pattern Recognition (CVPR'05) – Workshops*. Volume 03 (CVPR '05), Vol. 3. IEEE Computer Society, 2005
4. Blippar website, http://blippar.com/, verified Jan 2016
5. Bowers, J. The logic of annotated portfolios: communicating the value of research through design. *Proceedings of the Designing Interactive Systems Conference (DIS 2012).* http://dx.doi.org/10.1145/2317956.2317968
6. Brignull, H. and Rogers, Y. 2003. Enticing people to interact with large public displays in public spaces. In *Proceedings of Interact*. IOS Press, IFIP, 17–24.
7. Costanza, E. Huang, J., 2009, Designable visual markers. In *Proceedings of the SIGCHI conference on Human Factors in Computing Systems (CHI '09).* http://dx.doi.org/10.1145/1518701.1518990
8. D-barcode website, http://www.d-barcode.com/, verified Jan 2013.
9. Fiala, M., "ARTag Revision 1. A Fiducial Marker System Using Digital Techniques", NRC/ERB-1117. November 24, 46 Pages. NRC 47419, 2004
10. Gaver, W. What Should we Expect from Research Through Design? In *Proceedings of the SIGCHI Conference on Human Factors in Computing Systems (CHI'12).* http://dx.doi.org/10.1145/2207676.2208538
11. Gaver, B., & Bowers, J. (2012). Annotated portfolios. Interactions, 19(4), 40-49.
12. Goggles website, verified Jan 2013, http://www.google.co.uk/mobile/goggles/
13. Grubert, J., Grasset, R. and Reitmayr, G. 2012. Exploring the design of hybrid interfaces for augmented posters in public spaces. In Proc. 7th Nordic Conference on Human-Computer Interaction: Making Sense Through Design (NordiCHI '12). ACM, pp. 238-246.
14. Hornecker, E., Marshall. P., and Rogers, Y. 2007. From entry to access—How sharability comes about. In Proceedings of Designing Pleasurable Products and Interfaces (DPPI'07). ACM.
15. ISO, International Organization for Standardization, ISO/IEC 18004 "QR code" 2000.
16. Liu, Q., Liao, C., Wilcox, L., Dunnigan, L., Liew, B., Embedded media markers: marks on paper that signify associated media, In Proceedings of the 15th international conference on Intelligent user interfaces (IUI '10), 149-158, ACM, 2010
17. Meese, R., Ali, S., Thorne, E. C., Benford, S. D., Quinn, A., Mortier, R., ... & Baurley, S. L. (2013, April). From codes to patterns: designing interactive decoration for tableware. In Proceedings of the SIGCHI Conference on Human Factors in Computing Systems (pp. 931-940). ACM.
18. Powered by String website, http://poweredbystring.com, verified Jan 2013
19. Reeves, S., Benford, S., O'Malley, C., and Fraser, M. 2005. Designing the spectator interface. In Proceedings of CHI'05, ACM, 741–750
20. Reilly, D.F., Welsman-Dinelle, M., Bate, C., Inkpen, K.: Just Point and Click? Using Handhelds to Interact with Paper Maps, Mobile HCI 2005, 239–242 (2005)
21. Rukzio, E.; Schmidt, A., and Hussmann, H. Physical Posters as Gateways to Context-Aware Services for Mobile Devices. In Proc. 6th Workshop on Mobile Computing Systems and Appl., IEEE (2004), 10-19
22. Schofield, S. The Kipple Pond. http://www.simonschofield.net/gallery/view/kipple-pond
23. Seitinger, S., Perry, D., Mitchell, W. Urban pixels: painting the city with light. In Proc. of CHI'09.
24. Snibbe, S.S. and Raffle, H.S. 2009. Social immersive media: pursuing best practices for multi-user interactive camera/projector exhibits. In Proc. of the SIGCHI Conference on Human Factors in Computing Systems (CHI '09). ACM, New York, NY, USA, 1447-1456.
25. Tolmie, P., Benford, S. Flintham, M. Brundell, P, Adams, M. Tandavantij, N. Far, J.F. and Giannachi, G. 2012. "Act natural": instructions, compliance and accountability in ambulatory experiences. In Proc. of the SIGCHI Conference on Human Factors in Computing Systems (CHI '12). ACM, New York, NY, USA, 1519-1528.
26. Woodland, N., Silver, B., Classifying Apparatus and Method, US Patent 2,612,994. Issued Oct 7, 1952.
27. Yeh, R. B., Brandt, J., Boli, J., & Klemmer, S. R. (2006, October). Interactive Gigapixel Prints: Large, Paper-based Interfaces for Visual Context and Collaboration. In Proc. Ubicomp (Vol. 6).
28. Zimmerman, J., Forlizzi, J., Evenson. S. (2007) Research through design as a method for interaction design research in HCI. In Proceedings of the SIGCHI Conference on Human Factors in Computing Systems (CHI '07). ACM, New York, NY, USA, 493-502.
29. Zimmerman, J., Stolterman, E., & Forlizzi, J. (2010, August). An analysis and critique of Research through Design: towards a formalization of a research approach. In Proceedings of the 8th ACM Conference on Designing Interactive Systems (pp. 310-319). ACM.

Designing for Children's Outdoor Play

Jon Back[1], Caspar Heeffer[2], Susan Paget[3], Andreas Rau[2], Eva Lotta Sallnäs Pysander[2], Annika Waern[1]

Department of Informatics and Media, Uppsala University Uppsala, Sweden jon.back|annika.waern@im.uu.se

Urban and Rural Development, Swedish University of Agricultural Sciences Uppsala, Sweden susan.paget@slu.se

Media Technology and Interaction Design, Royal Institute of Technology Stockholm, Sweden cjhhe|arau|evalotta@kth.se

ABSTRACT

Children's outdoor play is fluent and fluctuating, shaped by environmental features and conditions. The article reports on a project where interaction designers and landscape architects work together to fuse their knowledge into working solutions for integrating interactive play in outdoor environments. We report on a schoolyard trial, where interactive play technology was installed as an integral part of a schoolyard environment, and discuss the interplay between technology and the environment that was partly natural forest and partly constructed playground. We highlight in particular the importance of the adaptability of the natural environment, how the combination of interactive technology and natural environment can contribute to the versatility of play activities, and how the interactive technology can both be useful for presenting invitations to play in such adaptable places, and enhance the adaptability for play in otherwise impoverished places.

Author Keywords

outdoor play; playscape; interactive play technology; landscape architecture

INTRODUCTION

Outdoor play is typically considered an essential, healthy and desirable activity for children [5], especially in its capability of encouraging physical activity. Yet, studies have shown that children spend less time outdoors than previous generations [6]. While the impact of this on children's physical activity has received much attention [27], its impact on imaginary play may be even more severe [6, 32]; the form of play that Piaget considered most beneficial for the child's cognitive and social development [25].

DIS 2016, June 04-08, 2016, Brisbane, QLD, Australia
ACM 978-1-4503-4031-1/16/06.
http://dx.doi.org/10.1145/2901790.2901875

One reason for the decline in outdoor play is the increased access to screen-based activity in the form of TV, Internet and computer games [26, 32]. But in addition, the urban landscape is designed as if children would only play in designated playgrounds, designed to offer safety and seclusion.

Incorporating technology in the outdoor environment is a potential way to combine the social and physical advantages of classical outdoor play with the appeal of computer games [26, 32, 29], thus making outdoor play more attractive to children again [32]. An interactive playground is commonly defined as a space in which physical play objects are augmented with digital technology that stimulate play [32].

The project DigiFys seeks to go beyond this approach, to develop play landscapes with integrated interactive components. It is a collaboration project between interaction designers and landscape architects, and while semi-generic, the approach strives to make interactive technology completely integrated in a specific landscape. Hence, understanding the affordances and opportunities offered by the place itself is an essential part of the design process, as is understanding the lifestyle and culture of the children residing in the area.

BACKGROUND

Children's Outdoor Play

Outdoor play tends to be more mobile and physical than indoors play, but follows the same general development patterns [20]. Piaget's theories of play as instrumental in cognitive development [25] and Parten's models of social play development [24] constitute early but useful models of play development that apply also to outdoor play. Detailed studies have focused on the effects on play by playground design (see Barbour [1] for a literature overview). In general, children's outdoor play is revered as "a natural and critical part of a child's healthy development" [6] through which children get physically apt but also learn important skills such as social competence and risk assessment, they also get to use their creativity.

Access to nature and natural materials is often considered a crucial part of the outdoor experience [36]. Talbot and Frost [33] coined the term 'Playscape' as a way to think about how a particular landscape can afford play and what they call "magical thinking". In her detailed study of outdoor play in a natural forest, Fjørtoft [10] discusses how the shrubbery affords both hide-and-seek as well as imaginative play (e.g. playing 'house'), whereas more sturdy trees would afford climbing and open spaces running and games of 'tag'. Retaining natural landscape environments in for example school grounds has been found to increase the amount of play activities pursued by children in general, not only in the natural landscape but also in adjacent hard-made areas [19]. Different kinds of loose material have been found to be important for children´s play and development [20, 21], and the temporal aspect of outdoor play is also important, with variable conditions such as wind, snow, sun, dusk, heat and cold [20]. Playing outdoors provides a varied environment with many levels of challenges that develop both motor and sensory abilities [31].

Interventions such as planting areas with both natural and horticultural species in the schoolyard have been used as a way to improve the physical wellbeing of the children, and change the culture of play in the school grounds [2]. Herrington and Studtmann [14] used landscape interventions to redesign play at a schoolyard, e.g. by installing a sequence of stepping-stones that encouraged children to move in previously unused areas. A particularly interesting observation from this study was how the mere act of planting some bushes moved play out of the fixed installations into two 'houses' formed by the bushes, perceived as suitable for imaginative play by the children. The authors note that the children that were dominant in this play activity were another group than those who dominated the physical activities afforded by the ordinary fixed installations. Presenting a varied landscape is thus not only a way to afford multiple forms of play, but also a way to create more flexibility in the social roles among the children. It may also serve to counter gendered differences in the amount of outdoor play [12].

Designing interactive technology for outdoor play

Most interaction design products for outdoor play target playgrounds and schoolyards. There is also a distinct focus on encouraging physical play through game challenges, over designs encouraging imaginative play. An example of this are the range of interactive products offered by Lappset[1], such as the interactive ball wall Sunu. The Sunu wall provides feedback through LED lights when a ball is kicked against the wall; it can be configured to present different challenges, and it is possible to play against other Sunu wall installations around the world. Sturm et al [32] suggest that such installations should afford simultaneous interaction by multiple players, be simple to use, and while not necessarily be games, still offer an interesting challenge to explore.

Research projects have to a larger extent placed focus on supporting open-ended and creative play through more open-ended designs. Rosales [28] used evocative design experiments to elicit free play in young children. The SmartGoals [35] are simple poles that form a goal that light up when something is passing between them. FlashPoles [32] are poles that light up when buttons are pushed or rotated. Some mobile technology has also been proposed such as the Ledball [32] and the Morels [15]. The focus in these projects has been on supporting open-ended play rather than implementing specific game challenges. De Valk et al. [7] propose a design strategy towards what they call open-ended play; play activities that are guided, but not constrained, by the designed artefacts. According to the authors, players that engage with open-ended installations go through a three-stage process of accepting the invitation, exploring the opportunities and subsequently immersing in the play activity [7, 8]. With a sufficiently rich and suggestive installation, the play activity may shift back and forth between exploration and immersion. Very similar design principles have been articulated for playful art installations in public space [23].

These design approaches have in common that they focus on the interactive technology as such. The crucial role of the playscape, nature and natural materials, is seldom taken into account in the design approaches towards playful interactive technology.

Interactive Playgrounds

Work in the field of playgrounds, where interactive play technology is considered in a spatial context, is still often based on user studies with specific interactive play objects. The influence of the environment plays a subordinate role in such work. Especially, the user studies on interactive playgrounds rarely take place in an actual outdoors playground setting but rather in gyms, [8, 9, 35] or even lab settings [34], neglecting the influence of the environment on play. Many studies on interactive playgrounds in outdoor settings also primarily focus on the digital props and the isolated play with them [16, 19, 30].

Seitinger et al. [29] focus on the relationship between children and the play environment as mediated by animated playground props. They examine the ability of such interactive objects to "enhance open-ended and physically active play in playgrounds". As consequences of using interactive elements in playgrounds, the authors mention increased physical activity, high engagement level of the children and the exploratory nature of the activities performed. The spatial component of play is also explicitly considered in the Water Games presented by Pare´s et al. [22]. Their concept involves the entire environment and features interactive water fountains that can be invoked by groups of users holding hands while moving around the fountains. Finally, a recurring concept in interactive playgrounds is interactive tiles that give light feedback using built in LEDs. This approach of using modular

[1] http://www.lappset.com/global/en/Products/Interactive-Play

building blocks that together form a game [13] is used in many interactive playground designs, including GlowSteps [9], The Body Games [18], and Play-ware [13].

DIGIFYS - DESIGNING FOR CHILDREN'S OUTDOOR PLAY

DigiFys is a long-term collaboration between landscape architects and interaction designers, with the goal to develop children's play environments. Capitalizing on both interaction design and landscape design, the long-term goals of the DigiFys project proposes to focus on children's immediate surroundings - playing 'close to home'. The reported study is targeting a schoolyard environment, which is an equally important but slightly more coherent environment, as its main purpose is to host children whereas the environment close to home must cater for both children and adult activities.

Design approach

The project uses a multi-disciplinary approach, combining elements both from landscape architecture and interaction design. These methods are at the same time complementary and sometimes conflicting. Since a full landscape design is costly and permanent, the landscape architects work with sketches and prototypes as main tools in illustrating landscape concepts. The design process has been guided by walking tours including children-led walks [4] at their local play areas. Several workshops have also been organized in situ with children and teenagers, with the purpose of eliciting an understanding of places of importance and neglect in their current play environments.

In parallel, the interactive technology has begun to take shape. The design was inspired by the walking tours and design workshops, but in order to develop interactive solutions with some level of generality, it needed to follow a much more artefact- and technology-centred process during design and development. The goal of this process was to develop fully functional prototypes, gradually working towards commercially viable semi-generic solutions in collaboration with a commercial project partner.

The prototypes presented below were developed in a fairly standard iterative design process. The first functional prototypes were trialled with invited children in a lab environment staged to mimic an outdoor location, and focussed on creating design solutions that would support open-ended play [7]. After this, a second round of trials were done outdoors, but again in a staged environment (this time in a park) with invited participants. The full development process is reported in two master theses [14, 27].

This design process ensured that the prototypes themselves were robust, provided legible feedback, and showed potential for supporting open-ended play. But in relation to the goals of DigiFys, the critical stage of trials was the integration of the prototypes into the landscape, where we

Figure 1: The tube.

could begin to study how play emerges in the interaction between landscape and the interactive installations. This is what is reported on in this article.

ARTEFACT AND INSTALLATION DESIGN

The interactive artefacts developed in the project share common design goals: they are designed to invite open-ended play [7] and to be possible to integrate in landscape architecture. They are also designed to be combinable. In the schoolyard trials, two prototype designs were used in different versions and settings.

The tube

The *tube* prototype is shown in Figure 1. The tube registers when objects, such as water, stones and twigs, are being put through and can recognize certain qualities of the objects, in the prototype like liquidity, noise, and movement. Feedback is provided by the tube itself, but was also integrated into other elements of the installations in the form of sound and light.

Physically, the tube is a square shaped wooden shaft. The length and other form factors of the tube can be adapted to the location where it is installed. Each tube is equipped with a water-sensor, an infrared barrier and a vibration sensor. Each of the sensors senses different qualities in the objects being thrown through the tube. The water sensor senses liquidity, the vibration sensor senses if the object causes more than light vibrations in the tube (typically related to the weight of the object). The infrared-barrier is triggered for most objects that pass through the tube. Through the use of different sensors, the tube reacts in different ways to different materials passing through. This is intended to broaden the experience for the children and invite them to explore and engage with the tube in different ways. The tube itself features both audio and visual feedback.

Figure 2: One of the communication nodes (mountain setting).

The tube projects a continuous soundscape around it, that gets more intense as the tube is used more and tunes down when the tube is used less. Each sensor also triggers its own sound. Visual feedback was mounted on the tube itself, and takes the form of a sequence of RGB LEDs on the top of the tube. Just as the ambient sound landscape reacts to the intensity of play, the LEDs show a pulsating animation, where the pulsation frequency increases when the tube is used intensely. When a sensor is excited, the LEDs show a falling animation to mimic the object falling through the tube. Each sensor is represented by a different colour on the LEDs.

Communication nodes

The communication nodes are shown in Figure 2. The communication concept was intended to enable children to communicate verbally with children in other places. In the trial three communication nodes were used that differed in visual appearance and form factor, to inspire multiple forms of interaction with the nodes.

The functionality of the controls was identical for all three communication nodes, and specifically designed for the project. Each communication node has two call buttons, each corresponding to one of the other two nodes. When a button is pushed, the communication channel to the respective node is opened. The nodes are identified with icons on the buttons resembling their physical appearance. This mode of communication is a hybrid between the protocols used in a telephone and a walkie-talkie: it has the simplicity of the push-to-talk interaction of a walkie-talkie, but establishes a two-way channel in the same way as a phone call. The prototypes also allow both buttons to be pushed at the same time, so that the speaker can speak to both nodes at once.

The state of the communication is conveyed through light and sound. When a communication channel is opened and closed, this is signalled by two distinctive sounds. The sounds are played both at the sending and at the receiving node. A ring of LEDs encircles each button, and is used to indicate its status through different animations. When communication is idle the light slowly pulsates, resembling the breathing of a person in rest. When communication is received, the LEDs of the respective button pulsate quickly. When there is outgoing communication, the lights are on permanently. When there is both incoming and outgoing communication there is a very light quick pulsation with an overall high brightness of the LEDs, combining the characteristics of the separate incoming and outgoing states.

In a similar way, multiple LEDs using the same animation schemes are installed at different places in the communication nodes.

Installing into the environment

While the interactive designs offer some inherent play opportunities, their purpose is to be integrated into an outdoor environment. The tube is specifically designed to interact with natural materials such as water, stones, twigs and pinecones.

In this article, we present and reflect upon the results from field trials with the prototype in a schoolyard of an elementary school south of Stockholm. The selected schoolyard was large, with multiple play areas with different landscape characteristics, including a natural forest, as well as a more traditional built playground. This created an ideal setting for exploring multiple ways to integrate interactive technology into the landscape.

Pre-study

Before the installations were put in place, the children playing in the schoolyard were observed over two of their recesses. Children led walking tours were also conducted with three groups of four children, the children were asked about their favourite and least favourite play areas as well as for their typical play practices in the schoolyard. This pre-study was necessary to sensitise the designer team for the playground and select locations for the installations as described above, in much the same way as the larger scale DigiFys landscape design process is informed by the target location. The pre-study also provided a useful backdrop for understanding how the children's every day practices were influenced by the installations.

Selecting the installation locations

The locations chosen for the installations are depicted in Figure 3. The places were chosen after the child-led walks [4] with children from the school, who told us about their play activities and their favorite and least favorite play areas. Two settings were selected for the installations, here referred to as the 'mountain setting' and the 'water setting': The 'mountain setting' was located high up on a hill in the forested area of the school yard, and the 'water setting' was located in an open area in direct conjunction with a small water canal that
runs through the school yard. The mountain setting was

Figure 3: The installation places (top, photo). The chosen spots lie close to, but not exactly at, the favourite play spots as indicated by children (bottom, map).

located in what the children call 'the forest', a popular area for fantasy play and building huts. The 'water setting' is partly in the constructed part of the schoolyard, right at the forest border. Both locations were equipped with a tube and a communication node. For comparison, two portable versions of the tube and the communication node were also created.

The mountain setting

The high location as well as the forest inspired the installations in the mountain setting. The communication node was located at an open space on top of a cliff, with a clear view over the whole schoolyard. It was placed to be an eye-catcher from anywhere in the yard. Similarly, while being up on 'the mountain', a player would be visible from the whole schoolyard. The main element of the mountain communication node was a speaking funnel, known from traditional playgrounds. A microphone was placed in the funnel. At children's waist height, a panel was installed for the buttons. Underneath this panel was a compartment for the output loudspeakers for the communication sounds and other electronics. LEDs were installed vertically along the speaking funnel on the front and backside.

Figure 4: The tube installed at the water location.

The mountain tube was made very long. It had a total length of 4.5 meters (15 feet), going down a steep part of the cliff down in to the forest. Thus, it was taking advantage of, and emphasizing the challenging steep terrain that the children would be playing in. The sounds of the tube were consistent with the mountain theme, with different rock and gravel sounds. The mountain tube did not feature any visual feedback.

The water setting

The second setting was inspired by the presence of the water canal, and the opportunities it offered for water play. This affected in particular the installation of the water tube. The water tube was placed in a section of the water canal where there was a staircase connecting a higher and a lower level of the schoolyard. This enabled the slanted position necessary to throw things down the tube. The tube was extended with open rain gutters, attached to poles (Figure 4). These rain gutters allowed children to let objects or water take a detour before travelling through the tube.

The sounds triggered by the sensors were also inspired by the water theme. The infrared sensor triggered the sound of a water drop falling, the water sensor triggered the sound of flushing water, and the vibration sensor would sound like a big rock plunging in a lake.

The communication node in the water setting was completely integrated with the physical environment (Figure 5). It was placed on the border between the organized schoolyard and the forest. The buttons activating a call were made large, thirty centimetres wide, and low and cylindrical of shape. They were placed on the ground, to be

Figure 5: The communication node at the water.

Figure 6: The two portable nodes. The tube in the background, the communication box in the front.

triggered by stepping upon them. Visual feedback was presented both through the prototype's standard rings of LED surrounding the buttons, and in the form of two rings with LEDs hanging above them. These showed the same animation as the LEDs around the button. The microphone was placed on the ground and could capture speech from both buttons. The speakers were hung next to the microphone between the rings.

The Portable Nodes

In addition to the two fixed installations, two portable versions of the prototypes were created (Figure 6). Their portable format allows them to be carried around and increase the children's opportunities to create their own playscapes around the prototypes, which provided a useful comparison to the two fixed installations during the study.

Since these prototypes are not supposed to be integrated into the environment, their sound and light feedback patterns were made adaptable. Dials mounted to both prototypes serve as theme selectors.

The portable tube is about 1 meter (3 feet) long, light enough for a child to carry, and fitted with 4 handles so that it can be shared. It features the same sensors as the other tubes. A lightweight speaker was built into the tube, and a RGB LED strip was fitted on the top.

The portable communication node is fitted into a small box with two buttons on top and two handles on the far end sides for portability. Apart from the LEDs encircling the buttons, additional LEDs around the bottom of the box convey the communication state. A microphone and a portable speaker are built in the box, each with a dedicated opening in the front.

STUDY SETUP AND ANALYSIS

The evaluation of the installations comprised four days of direct observation while the children in the school were offered free access to all of the installations during their normal recess time in the schoolyard.

The primary form of data collection was note taking on A3 size paper maps of the playground. This form of note taking emphasised the spatial and locative nature of the observations, in relation to the installations as well as to the playground in general. Whenever an interesting interaction, a special play event or anything else notable happened, the respective location was noted down and labeled with the time it happened, duration, number of participants, age group and gender of the involved children for each play event. The observation notes were guided by the following three questions:

1. What type of play happens in the schoolyard?
2. How does the landscape with our prototypes affect the play?
3. How is natural material used in the play?

Example notes are shown in Figure 7.

For ethical reasons, the audio-visual documentation was restricted to photographing play situations. All photos were cleared for publication with the school dean for the field trial and with the children's parents for the pre-study. No video or audio recordings were taken.

The data was collected over four days and a total of 11 recesses, during which a total of 900 interactions with the artefacts were observed. The study used a qualitative yet rigorous method for analysis, grouping these observations into clusters. Three researchers collaborated in performing this analysis.

The primary mode of analysis concerned qualitatively coding observations of play into play types, relating these to the locations in which play occurred. In line with studies performed by de Valk et al. [8], the aim was to distinguish between invitations as the initial attraction of an installations, explorative play when the children engage with an installation to figure out its play capabilities, and immersive play when children were deeply engaged in structured play. Following Frost [11], the play activities were further classified according to common playground play forms. While classification constitutes a simplified

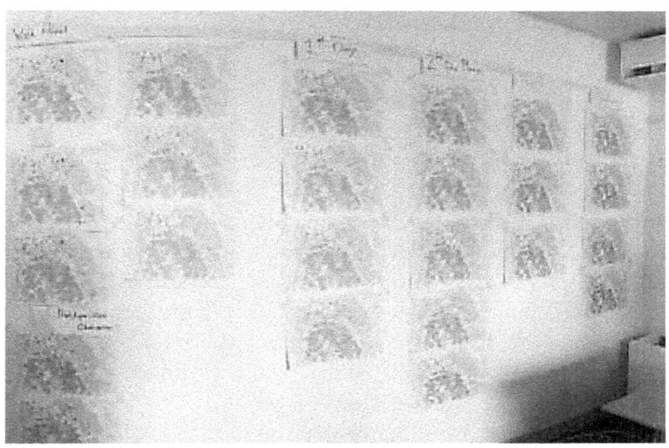

Figure 7: Field trial notes organized for analysis.

version of developmental models of play [24, 25], it corresponds to what readily can be observed in a playground and is for that reason well suited to the form of documentation employed in our study. It should be noted that while the observations below are representative of interesting and recurring behaviours, the qualitative methodology motivates the representation of these through detailed descriptions of selected examples rather than numbers.

In addition to this classification, individual observations that stood out as particularly significant were identified. This allowed us to create a nuanced perception of the observed play activities, incorporating aspects that would not be captured by the simplified classification.

OBSERVATIONS AND ANALYSIS

The results show that the affordances of the landscape surrounding the prototypes defined the play patterns that appeared in multiple ways. In particular, the physical shape of the landscape, and the availability of natural materials shaped the play. Results also show that the interactive prototypes invited children to explore them to a large extent and to play in the area surrounding the prototypes.

Landscape

Invitations

We could see that the installations presented attractive invitations to play. Typically, children would start to play when they heard action-triggered sounds, be it a communicated message or the sound feedback from a tube or a communication node. The physical appearance of the installations also functioned as invitation, in particular with the mountain setting. Finally, the installations feature a 'honeypot effect' [3] children playing with an installation function as a strong attractor for other children. The honeypot effect was enhanced by the way most of the installations used sound to communicate play intensity.

The communication station with the funnel on top of the mountain fulfilled the expectations of inviting play. The affordance of the funnel invited children to speak and sing into it. These play patterns continued throughout the week. Giving speeches ("Dear fellow citizens...") was part of the performative play in this stage-like place on top of the mountain

Running up and down the hill

The design of the mountain tube, together with the affordances of the steep slope of the mountainside and loose forest materials, made the play with this tube very physical. The children were using hands, arms, feet and legs to try to push stones through the tube, to de-clog it and to excite the sound and light feedback. In the process of doing this they were running up and down the slope, using the tube as a slide and they lifted the whole tube and bounced it against the rock to get the stones through.

The typical play pattern around the mountain tube was a distributed activity around the lower and upper ends of the

Figure 8: Running up and down, and playing in both ends of the tube.

tube (Figure 8). One or more children were putting in objects at the top, while another group of children were at the bottom to return the material as it came out of the tube. Often, one child would be looking into the tube only to take away their head in the very last moment. Here, children explored the physical properties of both tube and landscape material in a challenging bodily form of engagement.

The forest edge

The water communication node was situated at the edge of the forested area next to the water canal and constructed play area. The setting and design of this node, with rings high up above the heads of the children resulted in imaginative play (can be seen in Figure 5). An interesting aspect of this installation is the way it mediated an aesthetic landscape experience, in the way standing on the communication buttons and looking up through the rings also made you see the treetops and the open sky. Play was also based on the affordances of the buttons, in a way totally disconnected from the communication concept. The buttons were used to jump on, to stand on, to sit on, to look up into the sky to see the flashing lights in the rings, and to listen to the sound feedback. Placing two large buttons next to each other invited children to do synchronized activities on both buttons: Jumping at the same time, playing air guitar together or switching positions from one button to the other at the same time. The children imagined multiple functions for this installation: It was said to give a tickling feeling in the tummy, to create hunger, to be able to read thoughts, to be a teleporter, a time machine, an "alien thing", and many other things.

Side play

The interactive installations also affected, and inspired, play activities in the surrounding landscape. This happened in particular in relation to sound effects. This, we observed in relation to the ambient soundscape generated by the mountain tube. This tube used weather sounds to indicate intensity: as the activities with the tube increased, the weather condition reflected by the soundscape in the mountain tube changed from birdcalls, over rain to thunderstorm. Sometimes children, mostly girls, would be sitting under the speakers, listening to the bird calls and the changing weather conditions. On one occasion, a group of boys was playing in a hut in the forest close to the tube, while another group of children were playing with the tube. As the sounds from the tube changed to thunderstorm, one of the boys in the group playing in the hut said: “Load the cannons, there's thunder and rain on the way!” This is one of the few instances of imaginary play we saw related to this particular installation; the soundscape carried play value on its own in a more subtle way than the offered interactivity.

However, sound effects were also sometimes problematic and caused disruptions. This we observed in particular in relation to the communication nodes. Frequently, children were trying to establish communication by shouting “Hi! Can you hear me?” or “Who are you? What are you doing?” These communication attempts sometimes disrupted play next to the receiving station. We observed in particular one boy who was playing together with a group of children next to the water communication node. Whenever there was a call, he went to answer, but would just say “Hi!” and then return to his play with the rest of the group. The prototypes coerced him into responding, but his engagement was reluctant and as a result, no communicative play emerged with the other station. Another boy in the same group would instead repeatedly shout: “Shut up!” when somebody was contacting the station.

There was a lot of physical movement between the two stationary communication nodes. When children understood that they were contacted from another node they also wanted to speak, and ran between the nodes to be able to both talk and listen to each other (a common misunderstanding was that the communication worked only one way). Even when the functionality was fully understood, children would discuss who would go to which station or tell each other “come here”, “you go there” or “I'm coming to you”. It seemed like distributed play was not organised through the nodes, but organized and agreed upon in physical meet-ups. This way, the installation of distance communication *created* physical movement rather than diminished it.

Figure 10: De-clogging the mountain tube.

Figure 9: Playtraces at the water tube. The children have left stones and branches at the tube. The rightmost image shows how the track for rolling objects was extended in the sand below the tube.

Natural Materials

With and without water

Water is one of the most play-inspiring materials in outdoor play [17]. Consequently, the water tube featured a lot of immersive play on the first day, when it was possible to play with running water. However, during this day the tube itself played a lesser role in water play than the two rainwater gutters. The play changed significantly in the following days when there was no water supply. Now, children used different materials to evoke the sounds and lights of the tube. The children focussed on spherical objects, such as tennis balls, marbles and pinecones. The sand available in the area played an important role at the water tube. It was thrown through but also used to extend the tube itself. A complex open-ended rule-based game emerged, where the children extended the end of the tube using sand and twigs, constructing their own track in the empty water canal through which a ball had to roll. They kept trying out different starting points in the rainwater gutter in order for the ball to reach that particular point. The use of natural materials is clearly visible in the play traces left at this installation (Figure 9) as well as with the mountain tube.

De-clogging

A very common interaction with the mountain tube was the communal de clogging of the tube as large objects got stuck on their way down. This activity was not considered something to avoid, but took up a large share of the playtime around the mountain tube and was a highly cooperative activity. Children used large branches of two to three meters length found in the forest to poke inside the tube to get objects unstuck (Figure 10). These were planned and coordinated actions accompanied by comments such as "if we throw in three stones at once, it will come out".

Ambulatory Play

The portable prototypes featured some modes of play that were unusual for the fixed installations. Both the portable tube and the communication box tended to be used by one or a few children at a time, thus primarily supporting solitary play and seemingly a feeling of ownership (see Figure 6) .The mobile prototypes proved to be better suited for imaginative play than the fixed installations, and the children that developed immersive play strategies came back to play with them repeatedly on different breaks and days.

An example of imaginative play emerged when a boy found out that the installations had been placed in the schoolyard as part of a research project. This child used the tube intensely for the whole testing period during his breaks, exploring the interaction possibilities with the tube and imagining himself as a researcher, using the tube as a research instrument. One boy used the communication box as an announcement station, repeatedly commanding "To the office!" at different positions.

While the portable prototypes were carried around, their action radius was still rather limited. The children did not carry the prototypes far away, and on one occasion some children even returned the tube to a researcher when they found it in the forest. The landscape interacted with the portable prototypes in how the children used the landscape while exploring the prototype (i.e. using a tree stump as the research table) and they explored the landscape using the prototype by placing it in different positions and angles.

DISCUSSION

Versatility

The observations present some indications as to how the playscape may be enhanced by interactive technology. In particular, we saw that adding interactive elements to the landscape can increase the versatility of a location. Through interactivity, the locations are enriched to support a wider range of play activities than before.

This was particularly obvious with the water tube, which was installed in a location that would be rather impoverished without its presence especially when there was no water running in the canal. Since water has a high play value in itself, the interactive installation was less important when water was available. But when there was no water, which for this particular location would be the normal situation, the interactivity enriched the same place with a range of play activities. These were created by the design for open-ended play, but also by the way in which in particular the sound feedback created strong invitations to participate in play.

The other installations were installed in locations that already supported a wide range of play activities. Still, these also created a range of new play opportunities. It is particularly interesting to note that they inspired some synchronized, collaborative group play. The fixed communication nodes created a play activity focused on collectively organized communication, and associated to that, some intense running up and down the hill. The mountain tube created some interesting collective and synchronized play related to throwing natural material through the tube and de-clogging it. These play activities were closely related to the interaction offered, such as that throwing big and heavy stones into the tube triggered a different sound than throwing light objects. In the case of the communication nodes, much of the synchronization and running was created by the need to decide who was to speak, and who would listen.

While nature offers versatility in and of itself, the neighborhood close to home that DigiFys targets is typically much less versatile. The schoolyard studies give us reason to believe that an integrated design approach to landscape architecture and interaction design will be able to provide a rich play environment also in such settings.

Invitation and Exploration but little Immersion

In literature on interaction design for play, it is common to look upon long-term engagement as the end goal of any interactive design. In our observations, we found that the digital installations were effective in offering invitations, in particular through sound. To some extent also through light, although, as all playtesting was done in broad daylight and the effects of light are likely to be more present in dusk or at night, it is hard to draw any clear conclusions from this.

We were able to observe a wide range of functional and explorative play, where the children engaged in activities directly related to the physical form and function offered by the installations. However, there is also an observable novelty effect related to such play activities, in how they decline once the installations have been in place a couple of days. By contrast, immersive play was relatively rare in our study.

This should not be seen as an indication that the designs were unsuccessful, but is typical of how play activities are shaped by schoolyard environments as well as designed playgrounds, with their time limits for play (school breaks and parent's schedules). Typically, children tend to roam the schoolyard, rapidly moving from one play activity to another. In such settings, the successful design is rather one that offers *recurring* play, when children come back to an installation over and over again, during the same visit or multiple visits. We saw multiple examples of such recurring play in relation to both the fixed and the mobile installations.

Adaptability

One of the goals of the design was that the interactive prototypes would be adaptable, in two important ways. Their exact design could be adapted to the location of installation, and the strive for open-ended play was intended to offer children ways to invent their own games and play activities based on the offered interactivity. We also saw multiple forms of play emerge around the installations, such as the ball game at the water tube and the dislodging of stones at the mountain tube.

However, we had intended the prototypes to support symbolic fantasy play; the tube could for example have represented tanking a car, feeding an animal, throwing out waste through a waste chute or shooting a cannon. While it is possible that some such scenarios could have developed if the installations had been left in place for longer, it is a fact that we observed almost no such activities around the fixed installations. We *did* observe fantasy play in relation to the mobile installations.

One potential explanation for this effect was that open-ended interaction is not enough to sustain fantasy play in the outdoor setting. Compared to the infinite adaptability of nature, through its versatile physical affordances, abundance of varied materials, and ever-changing weather and climate conditions, open-ended interaction is a very limited design tool. A key insight was gained by looking at the playtraces such as the ones shown in Figure 9, around our installations as well as those left in other areas of the schoolyard. The traces illustrated how the children would constantly adapt their playtools and environment to their ongoing play activities.

Hence, a possible reason why the mobile installations were more successful in offering fantasy play was that they were, in fact, adaptable. These prototypes offered an opportunity for the children to adapt their sounds to their personal preferences. Furthermore, the fact that they were portable allowed the children to carry them to a location of their own choosing to integrate them in on-going fantasy play, such as when a boy declared that "this, I will bring to my hut"!

CONCLUSION

The schoolyard study presents many important insights concerning the integration of interactive technology into a playscape. We saw in particular that interactive technology is good at presenting play invitations, and that it is possible to capitalize on sound and light to this effect.

We saw opportunities for the use of interactive technology as a way to present more versatile play options in otherwise impoverished places, such as offering play at the gutter when dry. However, we also saw that raw nature is much more adaptable than raw interactivity, even when the installations are designed to offer open-ended play.

The long-term goal of DigiFys is to develop strategies for making interactive technology truly embedded into the landscape of the play environment. The schoolyard trials achieved this only to a limited extent. Most of the installations remained artifacts placed in the environment even though nature materials were used, and our trials give us reason to believe that this affected in particular their ability to foster sustained imaginative play. This is a challenge that we will continue to address in the second stage of the project.

The schoolyard trials have highlighted the dilemma of at the same time designing artifact-centered interactivity with the more holistic perspective of designing the playscape. The studies elicited some first steps towards addressing this dilemma and future research will focus on further integrating the design activities by landscape and interaction designers.

ACKNOWLEDGMENTS

We thank all the children that participated in the field evaluation at the school Balingsnässkolan and the staff at the school that helped us in the process of conducting the study there. This work has been funded by Sweden's innovation agency (VINNOVA).

REFERENCES

1. Ann C. Barbour. 1999. The impact of playground design on the play behaviors of children with differing levels of physical competence. *Early Childhood Research Quarterly* 14,1 (1999): 75-98.
2. Anne Bell, Janet E. Dyment. 2006. Grounds for action: Promoting physical activity through school ground greening in Canada. Evergreen.
3. Harry Brignull and Yvonne Rogers. 2003. Enticing people to interact with large public displays in public spaces. *Proceedings of INTERACT*, 17–24.
4. Sofia Cele. 2006. *Communicating place: methods for understanding children's experience of place.* Ph.D. thesis, Stockholm University Department of culture geography. Retrieved September 21, 2015 from http://www.diva-portal.org/smash/record.jsf?pid=diva2%3A186613&dswid=8961
5. Swetha Chakravarthi. 2009. *Preschool teachers' beliefs and practices of outdoor play and outdoor environments.* Ph.D. thesis. University of North Carolina at Greensboro.
6. Rhonda Clements. 2004. An investigation of the status of outdoor play. *Contemporary issues in early childhood.* 5,1 (2004): 68-80.
7. Linda de Valk, Tilde Bekker, and Berry Eggen. 2013. Leaving room for improvisation: towards a design approach for open-ended play. In *Proceedings of the 12th International Conference on Interaction Design and Children.*
8. Linda de Valk, Pepijn Rijnbout, Tilde Bekker, Berry Eggen, Mark de Graaf and Ben Schouten. 2012. Designing for playful experiences in open-ended intelligent play environments. In *IADIS International Conference Games and Entertainment Technologies*. 3-10.
9. Linda de Valk, Pepijn Rijnbout, Mark de Graaf, Tilde Bekker, Ben Schouten, and Berry Eggen. Glowsteps–a decentralized interactive play environment for open-ended play. In *Advances in Computer Entertainment*, 528–531.
10. Ingunn Fjortoft, Sageie Josefein. 2000. The natural environment as a playground for children: Landscape description and analyses of a natural playscape. Landscape and Urban Planning 48 (2000) 83-97.
11. Joe L Frost. 1992. *Play and playscapes*. Delmar.

12. Lawrence V. Harper, and Karen M. Sanders. 1975. Preschool children's use of space: Sex differences in outdoor play. *Developmental Psychology* 11,1 (1975): 119.

13. Henrik Hautop Lund, Thomas Klitbo, and Carsten Jessen. 2005. Playware technology for physically activating play. *Artificial life and Robotics*, 9, 4 (2005):165–174.

14. Caspar J.H. Heeffer. 2015. *Long-term engagement in interactive playgrounds*, Master thesis, Royal Institute of Technology, Stockholm.

15. Kenji Iguchi and Masa Inakage. 2006. Morel: remotely launchable outdoor playthings. In *Proceedings of the 2006 ACM SIGCHI international conference on Advances in computer entertainment technology*, 35.

16. Petra Jarkiewicz and Ylva Fernaeus. 2008. In the hands of children: exploring the use of mobile phone functionality in casual play settings. In *Proceedings of the 10th international conference on Human computer interaction with mobile devices and services*, 375–378.

17. Rachel Kaplan and Steven Kaplan. 1989. *The experience of nature: A psychological perspective*. CUP Archive.

18. Kyle Kilbourn, Larisa Sitorus, Ken Zupan, Johnny Hey, Aurimas Gauziskas, Marcelle Stiensta, and Martin Andresen. 2004. Exploring narratives for physical play: A pop-up guide to an interactive playground. In *Technologies for Interactive Digital Storytelling and Entertainment*, 240–245.

19. Gunilla Lindholm. 1995. *Skolgården*. MOVIUM - sekretariatet för den yttre miljön, vid Sveriges lantbruksuniversitet i Alnarp.

20. Fredrika Mårtensson. 2009. Lek i verklighetens utmarker. I eds. M. Jensen and Å. Harvard. *Lek för att lära: Utveckling, kongition och kultur*. Lund: Studentlittaratur. 163-188.

21. Simon Nicholson. 1971. How not to cheat children: The theory of loose parts. Landscape Architecture 62 (1971) 30-35.

22. Narcís Parés, Anna Carreras, and Jaume Durany. 2005. Generating meaning through interaction in a refreshing interactive water installation for children. In *Proceedings of Interaction Design and Children*, 218–223.

23. Narcís Parés, Jaume Durany, and Anna Carreras. 2005. Massive flux design for an interactive water installation: water games. In *Proceedings of the 2005 ACM SIGCHI International Conference on Advances in computer entertainment technology*.

24. Mildred B. Parten. 1932. "Social participation among pre-school children." *The Journal of Abnormal and Social Psychology* 27,3 (1932): 243-269.

25. Jean Piaget. 1951. *Play, dreams and imitation in childhood*. Vol. 25.

26. Ronald Poppe, Robby van Delden, Alejandro Moreno, and Dennis Reidsma. 2014. Interactive playgrounds for children. In *Playful User Interfaces*, 99–118.

27. Andreas Rau. 2015. *Digitally Augmenting the Built Environment to Mediate Play*. Master thesis, Royal Institute of Technology, Stockholm.

28. Yvonne Rogers and Sara Price. 2004. Extending and augmenting scientific enquiry through pervasive learning environments. *Children Youth and Environments*, 14,2 (2004):67–83.

29. Susanne Seitinger. 2006. *Animated props for responsive playspaces*. Ph. D. Dissertation. Massachusetts Institute of Technology,.

30. Susanne Seitinger, Elisabeth Sylvan, Oren Zuckerman, Marko Popovic, and Orit Zuckerman. 2006. A new playground experience: going digital? In *Extended abstracts on Human factors in computing systems (CHI'06)*, 303–308.

31. Szczepanski, Anders, and L. O. Dahlgren. 1997. *Utomhuspedagogik. Boklig bildning och sinnlig erfarenhet*. Linköpings Universitet, Linköping, Sweden.

32. Janienke Sturm, Tilde Bekker, Bas Groenendaal, Rik Wesselink, and Berry Eggen. 2008. Key issues for the successful design of an intelligent, interactive playground. In *Proceedings of the 7th international conference on Interaction design and children*. 258-265.

33. James Talbot and Joe L. Frost. 1989. Magical playscapes. *Childhood Education* 66,1 (1989): 11-19.

34. Daniel Tetteroo, Dennis Reidsma, Betsy Van Dijk, and Anton Nijholt. 2012. Design of an interactive playground based on traditional children's play. In *Intelligent Technologies for Interactive Entertainment*, 129– 138.

35. Gordon Tiemstra, Renée Van Den Berg, Tilde Bekker, and MJ de Graaf. 2011. Guidelines to design interactive open-ended play installations for children placed in a free play environment. In *Proceedings of the international conference of the digital research association (DIGRA)*. 1–17.

36. White, R. & Stoecklin, L. 1998. Children's outdoor play and learning environments: returning to nature. *Early Childhood News* 10, 2(1987): 24-30.

Sens-Us: Designing Innovative Civic Technology for the Public Good

Connie Golsteijn[1], Sarah Gallacher[2], Licia Capra[1], Yvonne Rogers[1]
[1] University College London, UK
[2] ICRI Cities, Intel Corporation (UK) Limited
info@conniegolsteijn.com; sarah.m.gallacher@intel.com; l.capra@ucl.ac.uk; y.rogers@ucl.ac.uk

ABSTRACT
How can civic technology be designed to encourage more public engagement? What new methods of data collection and sharing can be used to engender a different relationship between citizens and the state? One approach has been to design physical systems that draw people in and which they can trust, leading them to give their views, opinions or other data. So far, they have been largely used to elicit feedback or votes for one or two questions about a given topic. Here, we describe a physical system, called Sens-Us, which was designed to ask a range of questions about personal and sensitive information, within the context of rethinking the UK Census. An in-the-wild study of its deployment in a city cultural center showed how a diversity of people approached, answered and compared the data that had been collected about themselves with others. We discuss the findings in relation to the pros and cons of using this kind of innovative technology when wanting to promote civic engagement or other forms of public engagement.

Author Keywords
Physical survey; opinion gathering; public opinion; civic engagement; in-the-wild study; Census data; public good

ACM Classification Keywords
H.5: Information interfaces and presentation (e.g., HCI): H.5.m. Miscellaneous

INTRODUCTION
Every ten years, governments throughout the world send out a mandatory questionnaire (paper-based or online) to each household to fill in. A large number of personal questions are asked about work, health, national identity, education, marital status, ethnic background, marital status and so on. The data collected provides *"a detailed snapshot of who we are, how we live and what we do"* [19]. It is also used as a tool to help plan and fund services such as education, health and social services. The decisions and changes that are made, based on this feedback, are intended to map onto the needs of a community [17].

However, the types of questions, the methods used and survey format have remained the same for many years. How might the Census process be updated to make better use of innovative forms of technology and, in doing so, consider other ways of gathering information? The UK government is especially interested in thinking about how new ways of using technology for data collection could create a different and more open relationship between citizens and the state. What would an alternative census look like if done at a city level, where the city is viewed more broadly in terms of 'public good' rather than primarily as a tool for distributing public funding? How could it be used to ask a wider set of questions about how people participate and how often, what information they want to give towards a public good and what would feel representative of their everyday lives [24]?

To address these questions, we were invited to design an innovative technology for an interactive Citizen Census by [6]. The goal was to deploy our system for a month in a public, civic bureau that would be set up at Somerset House in London as part of the UK Census team's Civic Workshop. Our proposal was to design a quite different kind of survey – one that is physical rather than being digital or paper-based – with the rationale that it would *entice* civic engagement for the public good, when gathering opinions. By physical, we mean a bespoke interactive device that provides a range of physical input devices, such as sliders, knobs and dials that are combined with physically written questions embedded on a console. The benefits of going physical in this manner lie in their potential affordances – that can make a system appealing, attractive and obvious how to use, based on using familiar input mechanisms [9]. By standing out, we hoped it would draw in passers-by as they walked past the bureau, leading them to want to discover and know more about the Sens-Us. We were interested in finding out whether a person, having moved in front of a question box, would feel comfortable enough to divulge information about themselves and then to discover more about what others had also entered.

A central concern for developing such a system is whether the kinds of questions about public good that the Census team were interested in exploring lend themselves to being

DIS 2016, June 04-08, 2016, Brisbane, QLD, Australia
© 2016 ACM. ISBN 978-1-4503-4031-1/16/06…$15.00
DOI: http://dx.doi.org/10.1145/2901790.2901877

instantiated in a physical form. Moreover, would such a physical system be able to encourage the general public who were simply walking past the room to then enter and by their own volition take part? Would people be happy answering a range of personal questions? *In other words, what kinds of information would people be happy contributing to knowledge for the public good?*

The research reported here describes how we designed such a physical survey system. A requirement was that it would be a stand-alone system that could be used for several weeks in a public place – without the need for researchers or other members of the team to be at hand. A further concern was how best to structure and present a large number of questions so that they are both visible and intuitive to answer but also maintain appropriate levels of comfort and privacy. We wanted to see if people would trust a physical device that they had not seen before, with entering their own data while spending some time interacting with it. This meant designing a system that could attract people's attention, sustain their interest, and make them feel comfortable answering a range of personal questions.

We designed a set of physical boxes, called Sens-Us, that were situated in a room made out to be like a Civic Bureau, intended for the public to walk up to and use (Figure 1). We report on an in-the-wild study describing what happened when Sens-Us went public. The findings were analyzed in terms of how many questions people answered, what they were happy to reveal about themselves, how they felt about their privacy, and whether they were interested in discovering more about the results and comparing themselves with others. Finally, we discuss our findings around pros and cons of designing and using physical survey systems in the context of encouraging civic engagement.

BACKGROUND

The public good refers to a range of things for the use and benefit of all, including services, statistics, lighthouses, and parks that are generally provided by governments. The process by which these are selected, placed and maintained

Figure 1. Three of the Sens-Us boxes together with the visualization pillar placed in Somerset House, London.

is decided by local government, based on information and data gleaned from a variety of sources, including the Census. The decision-making process has typically been black box in nature with little or no input or understanding from the people it is being provided for [10]. Recently, there has been a move towards designing civic engagement technologies where citizens of a community, city or other locale are encouraged to be more actively engaged and have their say [23]. This includes initiatives that allow people to report online things they have noticed or concern them in their neighbourhood, such as potholes in the road, abandoned cars in their street, vandalism and unwanted graffiti – with the understanding that the local council will look into these and act upon them where possible. Typically, these are designed as mobile apps or web-based sites.

Projects that have sought to use other kinds of technologies include participatory sensing that place sensors in the environment to collect data about air quality, noise and so on [2], voting boxes for gathering local opinions in situ [26] and innovative "data technologies" that are designed to collect and visualize data so that the public can see and discuss together information that was previously unavailable or inaccessible to them [8, 21].

Walk up and use kiosks have been developed and deployed that target civic engagement by using familiar interaction mechanisms, such as on-screen forms and/or request people to submit SMS text messages. For example, the system "Discussions in Space" is an application for public screens that facilitates public civic feedback by interacting through text messages and tweets [18]. TexTales invites young people to take pictures of public issues and enables others to annotate [1]. Similarly, Ubinion is a service running on public displays that enables young people to give their opinions on local issues through photos alongside annotations [11]. Based in a more focused context, VoiceYourView [27] gathers feedback on use and improvements of a local library through public screens. MyPosition asks people to vote on local issues by gesturing in front of a large projected display in a public space [25]. Both Discussions in Space and Ubinion were found to be successful in engaging people that would otherwise not engage in civic debate [11, 18]. The TexTales study further reported triggering discussions on the system and in the physical space around it [1], while with MyPosition many people stopped to look, but only one in four chose to submit an opinion [25]. Other strategies have been used to voice opinions beyond simple votes or text input, such as telephone handsets [9, 27] and megaphones [7].

An overarching finding with these public display systems was that although many people freely gave their opinions, privacy remained a concern that impacted on who participated and what they shared, as people feared others "shoulder-surfing" and seeing their information [5]. Furthermore, some people felt uncomfortable and self-conscious interacting with the system, especially when they were asked to gesture or talk to machines [25, 27]. A key concern, therefore, when designing civic engagement technologies for public spaces is that people feel comfortable while being curious enough approaching and then at ease when using them.

Another way to address this is to design highly visible and attractive physical systems. It is well known that physical objects and interactions can draw people's attention through their affordances [16] especially when designed to stand out against the environment [12]. For example, Voxbox was designed as a large, physical box with a retro appearance that asked people to submit their opinions and provide ratings using brightly colored arcade buttons, slot machine spinners, and levers [9]. The machine was found to be very successful at drawing people's attention, getting a wide demographic to interact, and gathering opinions about an event they were attending.

Depending on their physical properties and design, such tangible systems can grab people's attention compared to public screen/surveys that they might otherwise walk past [15]. Simple physical voting boxes that show a question and ask users to submit a response by pressing a button have also been found to be effective [14, 22]. Such voting boxes have, for example, been used to gauge people's views about their community and neighborhood in shops along a road, after which collected data was visualized on the street with chalk [13]. Furthermore, simple interactive posters have been used to vote on local issues as an approach for political activism [26]. A novel interface that was designed to draw people's attention was "Vote with your feet" where people had to express their opinion by stepping on physical buttons in the pavement at a bus stop. It was found that the large buttons attracted people's attention much more than the screen that displayed the question and lowered the barrier for participation [20].

These kinds of physical systems show much potential for gathering public opinion because they can draw people in and make it obvious and easy as to how to interact through the use of familiar interfaces, such as buttons and dials. While the examples show that large and diverse audiences can be reached and meaningful data collected, they have so far only been developed to ask a small range of questions about an event or a single topic [3, 13, 22, 25]. What would it take to scale up such a system so that more questions could be asked about a range of personal topics and demographic issues? What other considerations would need to be taken into account?

Our approach is to exploit the affordances of physicality by using an array of colorful physical buttons, dials and toggle switches. The rationale is to make a system stand out and appeal – so that it makes people feel intrigued straight away while also comfortable, and in doing so, want to take part by answering questions and sharing their views [9, 25]. So far the use of physical surveys has been limited to asking a small set of questions about a topic, which require simple yes/no answers, checking a rating scale or giving an opinion about a topic, such as the service satisfaction smiley rating buttons now commonly found in many airports and cafes, that require only a few seconds or at most a couple of minutes to complete. For the Sens-Us project, we were interested in whether we could scale up a physical system to ask a diversity of probing questions that people would be prepared to answer.

DESIGN CONTEXT

To begin, we held several meetings with the Census team to understand what they wanted, what they meant by the public good and to discuss the pros and cons of designing an alternative, physical Census system. We considered how the new system might cover a range of subjective topics that go beyond the existing set asked in the current Census, including ones referring to a sense of belonging and trust in society. We ended up with 54 questions that the physical system should ask, of which 6 were about demographics and the others were divided equally across 4 themes (12 questions per theme): health, belonging, place and trust. Table 1 shows some examples of questions in each theme.

Questions in the demographics theme included age, sex, education level, income, postcode, and duration of living at that postcode. Questions in each of the other themes were divided into three categories (4 questions per category) that were about what information they would be willing to share and what information other people might want to know:

1) *Direct questions:* personal questions, for example, whether they were registered organ donors (health), whether they felt they were in a minority where they lived (belonging), whether they had planned how to support themselves in older age (place), or whether they thought others trust them easily (trust).
2) *Reported sharing questions:* asked people with whom they would be willing to share certain information, provided it was anonymous. Example questions included: how many times they had visited their GP (health) and whether they shopped locally (belonging). For each item, it was further asked whether someone would share this information with any of three parties: "close family and friends", "city council", or "public good" (which means that their data could be used by anyone as open data). Multiple answers were possible for each question.
3) *Knowledge questions:* questions about what information the person felt should be available to them, such as how social media websites use collected data (trust), or their friend's whereabouts during the day (place).

DESIGNING SENS-US

The overarching principles that were used to inform the design of the Sens-Us system were: discoverability, flexibility, manageability, privacy, and feedback.

	Controller	Illustrative example questions from Health box
cat. 1	Rotary dial	What blood type are you? (A+, A-, B+, B-, O+, O-, AB+, AB-, I don't know, prefer not to say)
cat. 1	Slider	Which health services do you use? (private health care all of the time, mixture of private and NHS, NHS all of the time, other, prefer not to say)
cat. 1	Toggles	Do you give blood? Have you had unprotected sex? Are you a registered organ/tissue donor? (yes, no, prefer not to say)
cat. 2	Check buttons	If your data was anonymous, who would you be willing to share the following information with? (select all that apply: close family and friends, city council, public good): How many times you visited your GP in the last year? Any hereditary conditions you are likely to get? Any symptoms you have on a regular basis?
cat. 2	Yes/no buttons	Do you think this information should be available to you? (yes, no): The average weight of adults living in your neighbourhood? The leading causes of death in your neighbourhood?

Table 1. Mapping of controllers in categories 1 (answer is visible after submitting) and 2 (answer is not visible) to questions.

Discoverability

The physical systems needs to be designed to stand out and enable people to discover it in their own time and decide whether to participate on their own terms. It should entice people from seeing the system to then using it.

Flexibility

The system needs to be able to accommodate individuals, pairs or groups so they can use it at the same time, either by going their own separate ways or together. Families, couples, groups of friends or people on their own should be able to use it at the same time. It should also be able to cater for several groups/individuals using it at the same time to prevent the need to queue or wait to have a go.

Manageability

The set of questions needs to be structured to be manageable in terms of how much effort and time is required to answer them by passers-by. We wanted people to feel reassured and at ease when starting to fill out a survey knowing how many more questions there were to complete it.

Privacy

As the system was going to be used in public it needed to provide enough personal space for someone to use and feel they are not being overlooked.

Feedback

Filling out a form, such as the Census, is usually one-sided; people don't see the data afterwards. We wanted our system to be able to visualize people's answers relative to how others had answered so that they could all see how they compared with each other in the moment (and later via a website).

The Design of Sens-Us

We developed Sens-Us as a set of five interactive physical boxes that had a console with either 6 or 12 questions embedded in each (see Figure 2). Having five boxes rather than one meant that the questions could be broken down and grouped by a theme while making answering them more manageable. It was envisioned that it would take a person between 1-3 minutes to answer the set of questions at each box. A data visualization station was also designed to provide aggregated answers as feedback of the answers that had been provided by the participants (see Figure 1). The questions were laid out on each box in a grid on a 60x40 cm slanted console, following a logical flow from left to right and top to bottom. The boxes were created out of 5 different brightly colored laser-cut acrylic pieces intended to be attractive and approachable. They were designed to be at an average adult waist height and the interaction console was slanted to make for easy interaction. Side panels were added to the boxes that were intended to obscure the interaction space from the side to provide a level of privacy. The design of the boxes was intended to be stand-alone, making it obvious how to interact with them. Information about each theme and the reasons for asking the questions was to be presented via posters located above each box.

To combine and compare people's answers at different boxes to each other, we developed smart cards that used card registration (using NFC technology). A card is activated when inserted into a box. The data from each box was then saved to the card's ID on removal, and in this way all data from the different boxes was linked to the same user regardless of which boxes they used. This linked data could then be shown when the card was inserted into the visualization station. The cards were also designed so that they could be taken away as a souvenir.

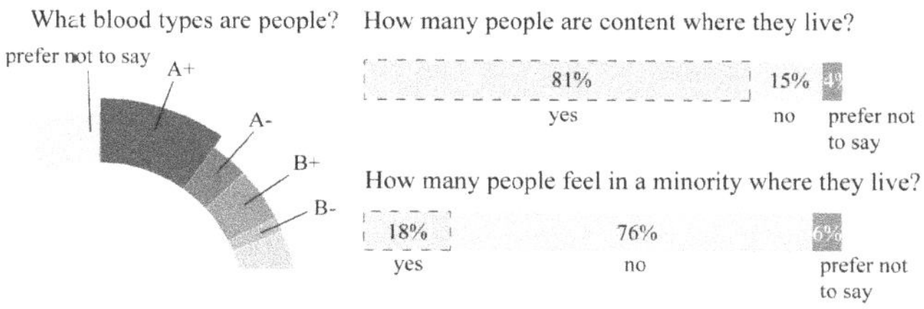

Figure 3. Examples of data visualizations: a. blood type chart (partial view) with participant's answer enlarged; b. belonging questions with participant's answers dashed.

Two types of controls were used for answering questions on the boxes. Table 1 shows the mapping of different controllers in relation to the questions. The first category of controls left answers visible after submitting them, and included linear sliders, rotary dials (which both had multiple options along their scales, including "prefer not to say"), and three-point toggle switches (which could be set to "yes", "no", or "prefer not to say"). These were used to answer the *direct questions*, i.e. personal information about the user (Figure 2a). The second category of controls did not leave answers visible after submitting them, and included small push buttons with an LED next to them that were mapped onto the *reported sharing* questions (Figure 2b). The other type of push buttons in this category was illuminated "yes" and "no" push buttons that were used to ask the *knowledge questions* (Figure 2c).

A data visualization station was designed to provide feedback in the form of a digital display that showed someone's answers relative to the aggregate of others' answers to individual questions. Different types of canonical graphical forms were used to depict the answers as an aggregate across all respondents (see Figure 3 for an example). The display was embedded in a pillar that was situated in the middle of the room with plenty of space around it for people to use it without others invading their space. It could be visited easily from any of the boxes and was flexible so that people could look at it whenever they wanted. It was designed to be at eye height and small enough to shield it from others. Placing a smart card into a slot resulted in the personal visualizations appearing on the screen. To browse through them "next" and "previous" buttons were provided.

Physical Setting

Sens-Us was placed in a small room (6x2.5 meters) in Somerset House, a major arts and cultural center in the UK. The room could comfortably accommodate up to 20 people at a time. This location was chosen for its potential to attract people walking by, and to create the impression of entering a census bureau. The center has numerous cultural and educational events happening during the week and at the weekends, which attracts both tourists and locals.

The boxes were spaced out with approximately 1.5 meters between them so that people could use each box privately (similar to the way a bank of ATMs are positioned along a wall). They were placed against the walls as someone walked in (three on the right and two on the left) to suggest a sequence from the door in a counterclockwise fashion. However, people did not have to follow this order, but could choose which way to answer them. If someone else was already at a box they could walk up to another that was free.

IN THE WILD STUDY

Sens-Us was deployed for four weeks at Somerset House. Modest signage was placed at the entrance of the building and a press release was sent out. Other than this, no active recruitment of participants took place by the researchers. The emphasis was for people who had come to the cultural center to decide what to do upon encountering the room.

During the deployment, we collected all the answers to the questions provided and the date and timestamps of when people used the question boxes. We further spent time over several days observing the Sens-Us room, unobtrusively positioning ourselves outside the room. We observed 34 people using the system, watching how they used the boxes; and if groups interacted with each other while using the system. We also conducted brief semi-structured interviews with 18 participants after they had interacted with Sens-Us. Interview questions included whether they knew about the project or had stumbled upon it; how the experience related to doing a census survey; if they had any concerns about their privacy, and if there was any data that surprised them.

Identification tags from the smart cards, along with time stamps and which boxes were completed were used to identify different users; for example, if a card had been reused by different users we were able to tell because time stamps did not match up and/or boxes had been completed multiple times with different data. Because we did not collect any personal data we could not verify if some users may have come back and participated again but this is unlikely giving the nature of the questions (i.e. it concerns higher level views that are unlikely to change significantly over four weeks' time). However, we did speak to one person who had come back with her parents because she wanted to show them the system.

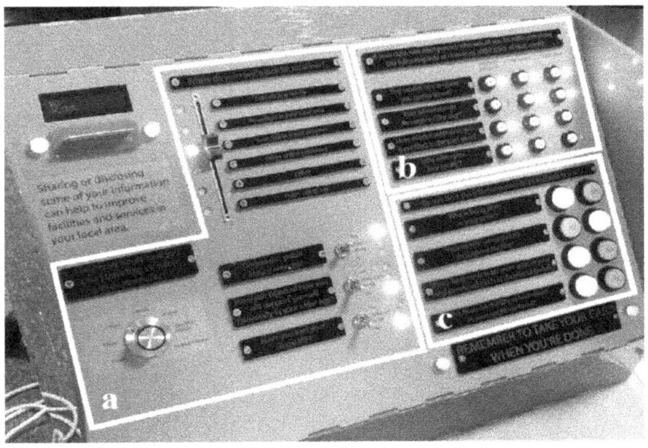

Figure 2. An example question box with different controllers: toggles, slider, rotary dial; check buttons and yes/no buttons.

She had participated during her first time in the room and now stood back to let her parents participate.

There was the occasional day when not all five boxes were operational because of technical issues – the data from these days was excluded from our analysis.

FINDINGS

Overall, the Sens-Us system attracted a diversity of people, from individuals to groups, who answered some or all of the questions. Many also looked at the feedback provided as visualizations about how they compared with others. People appeared engaged and intrigued by the system as evidenced by the time they spent at the boxes, the questions they answered and the conversations they had with each other. No-one seemed worried about why they were being asked these set of questions.

Of the people interviewed, half did not know about the project and just stumbled upon the room and proceeded to interact with the boxes. Of those who did know about it, some came on a group trip after they had heard about the project. Participants (P) were very positive about their experiences of using Sens-Us. Comments from the different Ps included, *"It is much more fun than filling in a survey form"* (P4); "*It is more efficient than the way the census is currently done"* (P8); *"This is more interesting and interactive. It is not just filling out a boring form. It's great to have something physical that is yours*" (P10); *"This is more personal. The census is so general. This is much more local and personal – it's closer to home"* (P7) and *"There should be a room like this in every council office in the UK."* (P6). These comments and the number of people who interacted suggest that people took part on their own terms because they were interested and that they found the experience very engaging.

The majority of respondents did not remember filling out their last census, were not UK residents, or were too young to have done it before (i.e., teenagers). Those who did remember were often a bit hesitant, for example, P15 said, *"I think so. It was on paper I think."* When people were asked if they had any idea what currently happens with census data and where they could find this data, most had never looked for it. P5 noted, *"you can probably find it online half a year later or so"* while one man (P18) knew *"It's actually not that simple to find it"*. Another man (P14) joked *"you probably won't see it until they show it on The Today Programme!"* [a current affairs program on British radio]. Two teenagers said they had only looked for it and used it for history lessons as research (P2, P3). Another lady (P7) commented *"it seems that not a lot happens with it. [...] It seems they [the government] are just going through the process [of doing the census] to check the box."* As surmised by the Sens-Us team, not many people are aware of what happens to the data collected from individuals and communities.

Of the people who answered the questions on the demographic box, 43% were male, 53% were female, while 0.5% identified as trans* and 4% did not answer or selected "prefer not to say". A wide distribution of ages was recorded: 12% were between 60 and 69 years; 16% were between 50 and 59 years; 12% were between 40 and 49 years; 11% were between 30 to 39 years and 13% were between 20 to 29 years. 73% of people were from the UK; 14% were from abroad, and 13% did not answer this question. Income was also widely distributed, 27% saying they earned £50,000 or more annually and 56% earning between £17,000 to £49,999 and the others not answering. Below, we analyze in more detail how successful the Sens-Us system was in terms of (i) extent of participation, (ii) privacy issues, and (iii) the effect of providing feedback on user engagement.

(i) Participation 731 people interacted with one or more of the boxes during the deployment – roughly 200 per week – as evidenced by the data collected for completing the questions. On average, people took about 10 minutes to complete the set of questions at each box - about two minutes per box. Overall, 33% of people completed the questions for all 5 boxes, 19% completed four boxes, 14% for three boxes, 12% for two boxes and 22% for one box. There were similar numbers of completion for each box, health being the most completed (71%) and trust being the least completed (60%); while demographics was completed by 69%, belonging by 68%, and place by 62%. These levels of completion might appear to be on the low side, but given that there was no requirement to visit all five boxes, a champion to chivy them along or official person to tell them they must, it is remarkable that a third of the people completed all questions at the five boxes.

Possible reasons for partial completion rates could be that some people did not realize that there were different questions at each box; people did not want to wait if someone else was at a box, or simply they had had a go and were ready to move on. To examine further how people used the boxes we mapped out the order in which they answered them according to placement in the room. A third of the participants answered the boxes in the sequence they were laid out in the room: demographics, health, belonging, place and trust. 8% followed the sequence but in the opposite direction. The rest visited them with a particular interest in mind or randomly. One woman, for example, commented that she was very interested in blood types and therefore chose to do the health box first.

We also looked at the effect of how crowded the room was on completion rate and found a positive correlation: the more crowded the room was, the more people completed all five boxes (Spearman's rank correlation, rho=0.18, $p<0.01$). This could indicate that people were encouraged to spend longer when others were in the room, that there was a positive "peer pressure" to complete, or that further discussions kept them interested. We also saw that when the room was crowded, people did not give up and leave, but more often diverted from the common box sequence to go to another box that was free (Spearman's rank correlation, rho=-0.15, p<0.01).

Our observations of the room showed that couples, groups of friends/colleagues and families answered the questions together as well as couples. Group members interacted either with a different box, individually, at the same time, looked over at someone's shoulder, or called out questions or answers to others. Overall, we saw that within groups, people mostly interacted individually with the boxes while interactions with each other remained limited to the occasional comment or question. For example, a couple discussed many questions, such as: *"how many neighbors do we know by name?"* (P32, P33). The man answered and his wife replied that they knew more people and started naming them, after which the man corrected his answer on the box. It also occurred that while one person was at the visualization station and another at a box, facts and figures were called out: *"12% had unprotected sex!"* (P21). This would often result in the other joining them and going through the data together.

(ii) Privacy A general concern when asking people to divulge personal information in public (e.g. have you had unprotected sex?) is that they might feel uncomfortable answering such questions. When we asked people who had taken part whether they were concerned about this, a few were genuinely surprised while 85% said they were not concerned. Others commented about the system being in public: *"It is obvious for others to look over your shoulder"* (P8), or on the physical nature of the controls, *"Yes, because of the toggles and the sliders. People behind me can see my answers. This defeats the purpose of anonymous sharing."* (P1). Another woman indicated she was not concerned about her colleagues seeing: *"I know them but I'm not concerned. I could have changed the controls – I should have perhaps – but I didn't. Change my age to 18!"* (P15). One man (P10) commented on what information they shared in relation to their privacy and made deliberate choices on what to share: *"I did not fill out any personal information, such as my identity, so that was fine."* Another man (P17) noted: *"The questions weren't linked to my identity, only postcode and gender but that's not enough. I did not give my full postcode, so maybe yes [I was concerned about privacy] in that sense."* P11 commented on the scale of the project: *"If this was deployed in small communities they might have an issue with privacy because it would be difficult to keep it anonymous. In small communities people can put information together and work out who is it."*

At the visualization station some people considered it completely normal to look at the data together and discuss it (and thus peruse one person's personal views), or look over another person's shoulder, while in other situations people respectfully stayed back and queued to wait their turn.

Two of the interviewed people appeared to have a different understanding of how the physical system worked. They were of the impression that their data stayed in the room or lived on the card: *"The fact that it's physical makes me less concerned. It's contained in this room and you know who is doing it. People can still do weird things with it, probably, but maybe less so than if it was online"* (P18) *and "Can I take my card with me? It has my data on it."* (P1). For ease of data collection and processing, Sens-Us was actually connected to the Internet to enable the data to be aggregated in real time for the visualizations.

The toggles, sliders, and rotary dials when switched to an answer stayed in place for others to see – unless the participant deliberately moved it back to the default position. However, during our observations, we rarely observed anyone switching them back. The only exceptions were for questions about age and salary, where a couple of people mentioned that they did not want their colleagues (who were also in the room) to see their answers.

We also analyzed the non-answers to questions to see if there were any differences for particular kinds of controls. Figure 4 shows the means and standard deviations of those that did not answer questions using the different controls. As there were only small differences between the percentages of non-answers within the same control across different boxes, results were aggregated. The figure shows that the sliders and rotary dials resulted in the least non-answers (less than 2%), while the toggles and check buttons resulted in the highest number of non-answers (just over 5% each). Hence, controls that stayed in place did not result in more non-answers than those that did not.

The highest number of non-answers for the demographics box was for the questions that asked for people's postcode (13% did not answer). This could have been because some people did not want to be identified (in the UK a postcode identifies which street you live in). Only 4% of people did not answer the question about their salary – which is usually considered to be quite private information. This low level of non-answer might seem surprising especially

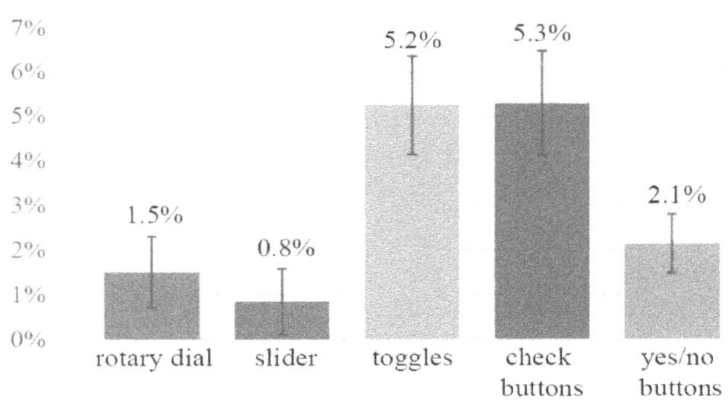

Figure 4. Means and standard deviations of the percentages of participants not answering questions across the five boxes with each interaction controller.

as the amount of salary selected was left visible for the next person to view, unless someone chose to slide it back to something else.

(iii) Feedback One of our goals was to determine whether people would be interested in discovering more about how others had answered compared to themselves. Of the people we interviewed, 78% said they had looked at the data visualizations, suggesting a high percentage of people were interested in finding out what they and others had answered. Those who did not look said they had not noticed the station or planned to look at the results on the web later. People typically spent between 30 seconds and 8 minutes looking at the data visualizations and most time was spent when there were two or more people looking together and discussing it. Most people visited the visualization station after completing one, two, or three boxes and often went back to the boxes afterwards to complete more. Hence, it appeared that the feedback also played a role in encouraging them to answer more questions and see how they fared compared to others.

When asked if there was anything in the data that surprised them, over 80% people related the data to their own views, interests, and experiences. Two teenagers were surprised by how many people wanted to know the average weight in their neighborhood: *"It doesn't concern you personally, why would you want to know?"* (P2, P3). A woman was pleasantly surprised that half of the people did not know any of their neighbors by name; it made her realize she is not abnormal or a "bad neighbor" (P5). One man (P17) was amazed to see that *"people put a lot more faith in the universe than in the government."* Others related the data they saw to society more broadly. P7 commented on how much some of the data made her concerned about where society was heading, for example that many people sold gifts instead of giving to charity, that not many people had made a plan for financially supporting themselves, and that so few people were donors or gave blood. One participant (P17) commented that the data visualizations would be more useful in his local community: *"[Then] I knew how my opinion related to those of my neighbors. Now I know this is only from people who visited this exhibition and I don't know who they are so I don't care that much. Local would be more interesting."* This feedback proved to be thought-provoking and revealing in ways people had not thought about before, suggesting it is a valuable way of connecting with people who are happy to give information about themselves.

DISCUSSION

The findings from the deployment of Sens-Us revealed that a large number people from diverse backgrounds, who happened to be passing the Civic bureau room, walked in and answered the set of personal and sensitive questions about themselves. It made them curious about the Sens-Us project and the way they could see how they and others had answered. Furthermore, they did not appear to be concerned about leaving their selected answers visible at a box for others to see what they had answered. The high level of completion rate could be partially due to a honey pot effect [4], where people are drawn in, when seeing others interacting with the boxes. Our study also suggests that the affordances provided by the physicality of the Sens-Us boxes attracted people, who then became engrossed in answering the range of questions. People knew intuitively how to interact with the boxes despite them being completely new to them. Seeing their answers relative to what others had answered - in the form of digital visualizations appeared also to encourage people to go to the other boxes to answer and find out more. They found it intriguing to provide and receive in return personal and sensitive information about themselves and others.

The Sens-Us project demonstrated how a diversity of passers-by participated when asked to answer a range of far-reaching questions. It suggests that the kinds of questions about public good that the Census team posed were ones people were interested in. Moreover none of the participants complained or mentioned privacy as a concern – which could have been a potential problem. A few were puzzled about the information that was being asked for in terms of how it might be for the public good (e.g. the weight of people living in their street). But overall, it proved to be a successful way of attracting people and raising awareness about how information can be gathered about people, their demographics, their health, their sense of belonging and trust, and how all of this might be made available to others.

It was not possible for us to determine how many people walked into the room and decided not to engage with the boxes. During our observations we saw some people wait for a while when it was busy, and then walk out. This presumably was because they did not want to hang about. There were also people who poked their head in and decided to then not enter the room. This is likely to be the case with any public installation, where some people remain as bystanders or choose not to partake.

One way we could have found out why people did not take part was to ask those who walked past. However, we felt it would have been inappropriate to approach people like this and ask why they had not used the boxes. Being approached by a stranger in this way might have felt accusatory and have either put pressure on them to then interact with the boxes or result in people being defensive or even abusive – as can happen when asking people why they have *not* done something. The Sens-Us team were also not interested in trying to get as many people to answer as possible but more interested in observing and finding out more about those who chose to voluntarily answer the set of questions.

Our findings suggested that there was no real preference for widget type in terms of which controls were easier to use, or more comfortable for participants. Our rationale for using a mix of physical input devices was both to vary the way questions could be answered and in terms of appropriate mapping between question type and form of answer (sliders for continuous Likert scales and discrete buttons for yes/no/don't know responses).

In most cases, it is likely to cost more in terms of money, time and effort to develop, deploy and maintain a physical system compared with other methods, such as online surveys or tablet-based ones. *The assumed benefits, therefore, need to be clear.* Below, we outline a set of questions that are intended to help designers consider what the benefits might be for 'going physical' in terms of their requirements.

1. Is the goal to encourage more civic engagement with physical systems? Our study showed that using familiar, colorful and friendly interfaces for the boxes was able to draw passers-by in who then became engrossed in answering the range of questions. This was a first step in exploring civic engagement. Answering closed questions in this way appeared to be straightforward and people were willing to have a go. If more open-ended questions or people's opinions are desired then such a closed physical console approach might not be as appropriate.

2. Are high completion rates desired? If it is not important to have as many people as possible answering or only one person answering at a time, then a physical survey can be an attractive alternative to other methods. We were surprised at how many people answered and how long they were prepared to commit to providing information. The possibility that some people may not have realized that the boxes asked different questions could have led to them not going to other ones. Not wanting to wait until someone had finished at a box also could have been a deterrent. However, nearly everyone answered all the questions when at a given box.

3. Will the attractiveness of a retro design wear off over time (c.f. novelty effect)? Using bright colors for the physical boxes, making each one a different color and using old-fashioned tactile buttons, toggle switches and dials, were found to help attract people to the question boxes and find it easy and desirable to answer questions. The physical nature of the boxes also provides a nostalgic feel that may have also drawn people towards them. There is a concern, however, that the novelty of the design is attracting people and that having interacted with them once they would not do so again. We were unable to ascertain whether this was the case for this particular installation (although some people did come back to bring their friends/colleagues to have a go). To determine if people would 'tire' of using them for answering questions in different settings, would require such physical systems to be placed in museums, galleries, exhibitions, and other public places, and be designed for a variety of survey types – which is clearly beyond the scope of our research.

4. What are the benefits of using physical controls as input? An advantage of physically laying out the questions with accompanying toggles, sliders and buttons is it shows how many questions there are, and what is being asked of people as to how to answer. This can provide people with reassurance that it won't take too long and they can see how they are progressing through the questions. Another benefit of this form of physical design is that Sens-us can be repurposed to ask different sets of questions using the same input controls. The physical controls can also be designed so that they default back to a set position – that does not show the previous answer – if this became a concern.

5. Is it better to have several boxes to distribute the question sets according to themes or one central console with all questions? Having a number of separate boxes rather than, say, just one big box with all the questions [cf. 9] enables more people to answer them at the same time. It also means people can chose to answer all or just a sub-set, depending on the amount of time and interest they have. However, in situations where it is important that all questions are answered then this kind of set-up is not ideal. A walk-up kiosk where all the questions are cycled through via an interactive display would seems a better fit (although there is no guarantee that people will complete a digital survey if they see that there are lots of questions answer).

6. Should you guide people or let them explore the boxes by themselves? Making it clear that all boxes have to be visited and questions answered is difficult to achieve. It is well known that people rarely read instructions or follow signage/posters in situ. A design challenge, therefore, is how much flexibility to allow for – in terms of how and where questions are answered, versus how to design a set-up to encourage completion rate. It may be possible to design a really big box with all the questions on it – but that would be unwieldy to position in a room. Strategic placement of a set of boxes in a room that suggests a sequence of answering could help convey there is a set, but as our study showed it is not necessarily a strong affordance. Another possibility is to provide a set of smart cards to indicate that there is a set to complete (e.g. giving participants one card per box).

7. Physical systems enable a range of group types or individuals to use but what if you only want one person to answer them at a time? Sens-Us was designed to be flexible, allowing one or more people to interact with a box at a time. This encouraged couples, families and groups of friends to answer together and discuss their replies. However, in other contexts, it may be important to elicit responses from only one person at a time. Can a physical system be designed to restrict answering to only one individual at a time when part of a group? One way to constrain individual use is for the system to randomly ask a particular member of the group to answer the questions (e.g. the youngest, a female). The others could look on while that person answers. Another approach is that each member of the group takes a card and moves between the boxes separately (as we observed with some family groups) and then come together at the end to observe and discuss their answers at the visualization station.

8. What privacy concerns might there be when going physical? Sens-Us was designed to use two different kinds of physical control in terms of feedback: one that left a trace from the previous answer by way of where it was positioned (the sliders, dials and toggles) and one that did not (the illuminated LED buttons). Our study showed that people were willing to input personal information regardless of whether the interaction mechanism persisted after they left so others could see or disappeared. The different types of controls used on the Sens-Us boxes, and their persistent or non-persistent natures, thus had minimal impact on people's willingness to share personal data in a public space.

9. Can providing real-time feedback trigger discussion and intrigue? When completing surveys, including the census, it is unusual to immediately have access to visualizations of the collected data. Our study showed that when feedback is provided in real-time it can be intriguing for people to find out more about themselves, triggering subsequent discussion. It provides an opportunity for people to reflect on how they differ from the norm and to make comparisons between themselves and others.

10. Where is it best to situate physical systems? Creating the feeling of a civic bureau worked well for enticing members of the public to come into the room and start entering information about themselves using the Sens-Us boxes. Placing them against a wall with some space between each provides sufficient personal space for people to interact with them without feeling uncomfortable or that other people were too near. Placing the visualization pillar in the middle of the room also provided a focal point for people to look at their data. Hence, the setting and how it is 'dressed up' is important in order to encourage people to walk up and interact with the system placed in it by their own volition.

CONCLUSIONS

The deployment of Sens-Us in a civic center has demonstrated how passers-by are firstly, attracted to, and secondly, willing to take part, unsolicited, in answering a range of personal questions. Our study showed how placing a physical survey system in such a public place was able to draw a diversity of people from different backgrounds. Its physicality, i.e. using actual switches, buttons and dials embedded in a colorful, waist height, console provided the affordances of accessibility, approachability and touchability – that literally played into the hands of the visitors. The boxes' inviting stance, together with the use of smart cards and real-time feedback, was both reassuring and intriguing. Moreover, privacy concerns were not an issue among those who participated. Our findings suggest that this kind of physical technology has much potential for offering a different and, perhaps, more open relationship between citizens and the state. Rather than view new technology in terms of how it can provide new ways of collecting data for a government to use, we have shown how it can be designed to encourage new forms of civic engagement where both citizens and governments can benefit from informing and being informed for the public good.

ACKNOWLEDGEMENTS

The research was funded by Intel ICRI Cities. We would like to thank all the people who took part in the Sens-Us project, and Sami Andberg and Ji Hu who helped to create the visualization station. We would also like to thank Somerset House, London; the British Council; and Cassie Robinson, Julia King and Louise Armstrong from the Civic Workshop.

REFERENCES

1. Mike Ananny and Carol Strohecker. 2009. TexTales: Creating Interactive Forums with Urban Publics. In *Handbook of Research on Urban Informatics: The Practice and Promise of the Real-Time City*, Marcus, F., (ed). IGI Global, Hershey, PA, USA, 2009, 68-86.
2. Paul M. Aoki, R. J. Honicky, Alan Mainwaring, Chris Myers, Eric Paulos, Sushmita Subramanian, and Allison Woodruff. 2009. A vehicle for research: using street sweepers to explore the landscape of environmental community action. In *Proceedings of the SIGCHI Conference on Human Factors in Computing Systems (CHI '09)*, 375-384. http://doi.acm.org/10.1145/1518701.1518762
3. Moritz Behrens, Nina Valkanova, Ava Fatah gen. Schieck, and Duncan P. Brumby. 2014. Smart Citizen Sentiment Dashboard: A Case Study Into Media Architectural Interfaces. In *Proceedings of The International Symposium on Pervasive Displays (PerDis '14)*, 19-24. http://doi.acm.org/10.1145/2611009.2611036
4. Harry Brignull and Yvonne Rogers. 2003. Enticing people to interact with large public displays in public spaces. In *Proceedings of INTERACT '03*, Rauterberg, M., Menozzi, M., and Wesson, J., (eds). IOS Press, 2003, 17-24.
5. Frederik Brudy, David Ledo, Saul Greenberg, and Andreas Butz. 2014. Is Anyone Looking? Mitigating Shoulder Surfing on Public Displays through Awareness and Protection. In *Proceedings of The International Symposium on Pervasive Displays (PerDis '14)*, 1-6. http://doi.acm.org/10.1145/2611009.2611028
6. Civic Workshop. Retrieved March 21, 2016 from: http://www.civicworkshop.city/work/.
7. Claude Fortin, Carman Neustaedter, and Kate Hennessy. 2014. The appropriation of a digital "speakers" corner: lessons learned from the deployment of mégaphone. In

Proceedings of the 2014 conference on Designing interactive systems (DIS '14), 955-964. http://doi.acm.org/10.1145/2598510.2598534

8. Sarah Gallacher, Connie Golsteijn, Lorna Wall, Lisa Koeman, Sami Andberg, Licia Capra, and Yvonne Rogers. 2015. Getting quizzical about physical: observing experiences with a tangible questionnaire. In *Proceedings of the 2015 ACM International Joint Conference on Pervasive and Ubiquitous Computing (Ubicomp '15)*, 263-273. http://doi.acm.org/10.1145/2750858.2807529
9. Connie Golsteijn, Sarah Gallacher, Lisa Koeman, Lorna Wall, Sami Andberg, Yvonne Rogers, and Licia Capra. 2015. VoxBox: A Tangible Machine that Gathers Opinions from the Public at Events. In *Proceedings of the Ninth International Conference on Tangible, Embedded, and Embodied Interaction (TEI '15)*, 201-208. http://doi.acm.org/10.1145/2677199.2680588
10. Mike Harding, Bran Knowles, Nigel Davies, and Mark Rouncefield. 2015. HCI, Civic Engagement & Trust. In *Proceedings of the 33rd Annual ACM Conference on Human Factors in Computing Systems (CHI '15)*, 2833-2842. http://doi.acm.org/10.1145/2702123.2702255
11. Simo Hosio, Vassilis Kostakos, Hannu Kukka, Marko Jurmu, Jukka Riekki, and Timo Ojala. 2012. From school food to skate parks in a few clicks: using public displays to bootstrap civic engagement of the young. In *Proceedings of the 10th international conference on Pervasive Computing (Pervasive '12)*, 425-442. http://doi.acm.org/10.1007/978-3-642-31205-2_26
12. Steven Houben and Christian Weichel. 2013. Overcoming interaction blindness through curiosity objects. In *CHI '13 Extended Abstracts on Human Factors in Computing Systems (CHI EA '13)*, 1539-1544. http://doi.acm.org/10.1145/2468356.2468631
13. Lisa Koeman, Vaiva Kalnikaité, and Yvonne Rogers. 2015. "Everyone Is Talking about It!": A Distributed Approach to Urban Voting Technology and Visualisations. In *Proceedings of the 33rd Annual ACM Conference on Human Factors in Computing Systems (CHI '15)*, 3127-3136. http://doi.acm.org/10.1145/2702123.2702263
14. Lisa Koeman, Vaiva Kalnikaite, Yvonne Rogers, and Jon Bird. 2014. What Chalk and Tape Can Tell Us: Lessons Learnt for Next Generation Urban Displays. In *Proceedings of The International Symposium on Pervasive Displays (PerDis '14)*, 130-135. http://doi.acm.org/10.1145/2611009.2611018
15. Jörg Müller, Dennis Wilmsmann, Juliane Exeler, Markus Buzeck, Albrecht Schmidt, Tim Jay, and Antonio Krüger. 2009. Display Blindness: The Effect of Expectations on Attention towards Digital Signage. In *Pervasive Computing*, Tokuda, H., et al., (eds). Springer Berlin Heidelberg, 2009, 1-8.
16. Donald A. Norman. 1998. *The design of everyday things*. MIT, London.
17. Office for National Statistics. Retrieved March 21, 2016 from: http://www.ons.gov.uk/ons/index.html.
18. Ronald Schroeter. 2012. Engaging new digital locals with interactive urban screens to collaboratively improve the city. In *Proceedings of the ACM 2012 conference on Computer Supported Cooperative Work (CSCW '12)*, 227-236. http://doi.acm.org/10.1145/2145204.2145239
19. Somerset Intelligence Census 2011. Retrieved March 21, 2016 from: http://www.somersetintelligence.org.uk/census2011/.
20. Fabius Steinberger, Marcus Foth, and Florian Alt. 2014. Vote With Your Feet: Local Community Polling on Urban Screens. In *Proceedings of The International Symposium on Pervasive Displays (PerDis '14)*, 44-49. http://doi.acm.org/10.1145/2611009.2611015
21. Alex S. Taylor, Siân Lindley, Tim Regan, David Sweeney, Vasillis Vlachokyriakos, Lillie Grainger, and Jessica Lingel. 2015. Data-in-Place: Thinking through the Relations Between Data and Community. In *Proceedings of the 33rd Annual ACM Conference on Human Factors in Computing Systems (CHI '15)*, 2863-2872. http://doi.acm.org/10.1145/2702123.2702558
22. Nick Taylor, Justin Marshall, Alicia Blum-Ross, John Mills, Jon Rogers, Paul Egglestone, David M. Frohlich, Peter Wright, and Patrick Olivier. 2012. Viewpoint: empowering communities with situated voting devices. In *Proceedings of the SIGCHI Conference on Human Factors in Computing Systems (CHI '12)*, 1361-1370. http://doi.acm.org/10.1145/2207676.2208594
23. Ioannis Tsampoulatidis, Dimitrios Ververidis, Panagiotis Tsarchopoulos, Spiros Nikolopoulos, Ioannis Kompatsiaris, and Nicos Komninos. 2013. ImproveMyCity: an open source platform for direct citizen-government communication. In *Proceedings of the 21st ACM international conference on Multimedia (MM '13)*, 839-842. http://doi.acm.org/10.1145/2502081.2502225
24. UK Government Data. Retrieved March 21, 2016 from: http://data.gov.uk.
25. Nina Valkanova, Robert Walter, Andrew Vande Moere, and Jörg Müller. 2014. MyPosition: sparking civic discourse by a public interactive poll visualization.

    In *Proceedings of the 17th ACM conference on Computer supported cooperative work & social computing (CSCW '14)*, 1323-1332. http://doi.acm.org/10.1145/2531602.2531639
26. Vasilis Vlachokyriakos, Rob Comber, Karim Ladha, Nick Taylor, Paul Dunphy, Patrick McCorry, and Patrick Olivier. 2014. PosterVote: expanding the action repertoire for local political activism. In *Proceedings of the 2014 conference on Designing interactive systems (DIS '14)*, 795-804. http://doi.acm.org/10.1145/2598510.2598523
27. Jon Whittle, William Simm, Maria-Angela Ferrario, Katerina Frankova, Laurence Garton, Andrée Woodcock, Baseerit Nasa, Jane Binner, and Aom Ariyatum. 2010. VoiceYourView: collecting real-time feedback on the design of public spaces. In *Proceedings of the 2015 ACM International Joint Conference on Pervasive and Ubiquitous Computing (UbiComp '10)*, 41-50. http://doi.acm.org/10.1145/1864349.1864358

Understanding the Sociality of Experience in Mobile Music Listening with Pocketsong

David S. Kirk, Abigail Durrant, Gavin Wood, Tuck Wah Leong* and Peter Wright

Open Lab
Newcastle University
Newcastle upon Tyne, UK
{david.kirk; abigail.durrant; g.wood2; p.c.wright}@newcastle.ac.uk

* Interaction Design and Human Practice Lab
University of Technology Sydney
Sydney, Australia
TuckWah.Leong@uts.edu.au

ABSTRACT
Music listening practices are changing. Mobile, networked devices now offer rich opportunities not just for personal music consumption but also for personally broadcasting music and for sharing digital meta-data concerning tastes, preferences and general listening habits. However, experiences of music listening and sharing on the move and how this has been impacted by developments in mobile technology remain under-explored. In this paper we present an empirical study of the sociality of mobile music experiences, 'in the wild', using a new location-based mobile music-sharing application (Pocketsong), designed as a technology probe. We report users' experiences of Pocketsong (distilled from interviews), and critically examine the affordances of mobile music applications, the sociality of sharing and 'co-listening', and the relationships between digitally-mediated mobile music consumption and self-expression. Based upon this we reflect upon the interaction design challenges of developing mobile music technologies that work in digitally-mediated social spaces.

Author Keywords
Music; Sociality; Mobile; Self-expression; Technology Probe.

ACM Classification Keywords
H.5.m. Information interfaces and presentation (e.g., HCI): Miscellaneous.

INTRODUCTION
Music listening is a ubiquitous aspect of many people's lives. As such, there has been a significant effort within the Human-Computer Interaction (HCI) community to design technologies that better support people's interactions with music, for example helping people to navigate and search their expanding digital music libraries more efficiently and effectively on computational devices (e.g. [4, 8]), or exploring more expressive ways to consume music [2]. However, listening to music can also provide a resource through which social and emotional interactions are produced, and this can contribute to building ties, creating shared meanings, and constructing collective 'mediated memories' [21]. In other words, people's interactions with music can shape their social experiences and personal identities; it is during their talking about, displaying, swapping, and sharing of music that people commonly express who they are [ibid].

DIS 2016, June 04-08, 2016, Brisbane, QLD, Australia
ACM 978-1-4503-4031-1/16/06.
http://dx.doi.org/10.1145/2901790.2901874

The Sony Walkman™ arguably ushered in an era of 'private music listening experiences' in public. This became even more pervasive with the arrival of the iPod, which was criticised by many as fostering anti-social behaviour [9]. However, as social technologies (e.g. smartphones, the mobile Internet) pervade our lives, we are finding new opportunities to reinvigorate the sociality of music listening, especially in public. This provides opportunities to explore the roles that new digital technologies may play in shaping people's everyday social and collaborative experiences as well as people's use of music in processes of self-expression (e.g. [19, 21]). Understanding these processes will allow us to design personal mobile music technologies that better support music listening and sharing in new digitally mediated social spaces.

This paper aims to advance our understanding of the social experience of mobile music listening and sharing by presenting an empirical study of individuals' 'in-the-wild' use of a location-based mobile music application (app) called Pocketsong, which we have designed to serve as a technology probe [11, 14]. The design of Pocketsong was guided by insights gained from prior fieldwork on technology-mediated sociality surrounding music [19] and informed by related approaches amongst extant literature (elaborated upon later). The use of Pocketsong within our fieldwork study was to specifically support and promote reflection amongst our study participants, upon aspects of social experience during mobile music listening.

In this paper we describe our design and deployment of Pocketsong and the reported experiences of its use, distilled from interviews. We discuss our study findings about the affordances of mobile music applications, the sociality of sharing and 'co-listening', and the relationships between mobile music consumption and self-expression. We further reflect upon the interaction design challenges of developing mobile music technologies that work in digitally-mediated social spaces, to offer up transferable insights for the HCI community. Before turning to describe the study, we first present extant work in HCI and related fields that informs and grounds our enquiry.

Studying music listening on-the-move

With the rise of mobile devices that allow people to interact with digital music on the move, there are abundant technical prototypes and frameworks offering novel [27, 3], effective [17] and ludic [13] forms of mobile interaction around digital music listening and sharing. Significantly for our concerns for sociality herein, some of these technical endeavours have sought to stimulate social interactions amongst listeners in the public space. For example, mobile apps (e.g., PDA) allow listeners to share or broadcast their music, to tune into what others are listening to nearby [5, 20]. Other phone apps allow peer recommendations of music, and/or the exchange of music files [6, 12, 24], and even messaging between listeners [7]. However, as Leong and Wright [19] have pointed out, whilst it is valuable to demonstrate the potential of technical frameworks to connect people, what remains underdeveloped in HCI literatures is a deep and nuanced understanding of the *nature* of this technology-mediated sociality surrounding music interactions and the impacts that this might have on user experiences. Indeed, there is a surprising dearth of research aiming to understand how mobile music listening technologies affect sociality and how social practices affect people's interactions with that technology.

There are a few exceptions, however. Seeburger et al [23] prototyped a smartphone app aimed at allowing collocated people to share and discover song choices in public spaces. They found that the use of the app mediated some social interactions and can be engaging to users as well as piquing their curiosity about people in their vicinity. However, the findings were based only on Wizard of Oz simulations of the app in action; there were no evaluations of users' experiences 'in the wild'. Hakansson et al [12] further explored mobile music sharing through a field study in Sweden of Push!Music, a prototype service allowing both manual and automatic music sharing through ad hoc wireless networking, also providing a social awareness of other users nearby. They too found interesting social uses and their findings highlight the significance of selecting and sharing tracks for impression management and self-expression; this supports earlier interview findings by Voida et al [26] on impression management in iTunes music sharing in the US. In related work, a survey of music sharing using mobile devices amongst Finnish teenagers revealed how technological affordances affected sharing practices [16], whilst another study described how Finnish 'tweens' made sense of their personal and social sharing of music on mobile devices [18]. Swedish teens were found to use the technology of mobile phones creatively for playful activities surrounding music and that music sharing was important for social interactions [15]. A more recent qualitative study of social practices surrounding digital music in the UK revealed how various recent key developments in our digital technological landscape have changed people's social practices surrounding music [19] by affording more opportunities for communicating, sharing, bonding, and celebrating lives with others through that music; Leong and Wright [ibid] found that factors such as the availability and accessibility of vast online music libraries via Internet-enabled devices, extended listeners' access to music beyond their own personal collections, and in turn changed the nature of music listening.

Whilst these extant studies have considered music consumption, our technology probe study with Pocketsong frames a new line of enquiry: we set out to understand the technology mediated sociality surrounding mobile interactions with music that are grounded in everyday *personal experiences*, and including *public* settings in which individuals are 'on the move' (mirroring recent interests in studying mobility [25]). Beyond consumption per se, our study sought to explore how practices of music listening and sharing are expressed and experienced through mobile technology use that mediates public space and social interactions. Furthermore, we sought to explore how social experiences are entangled with the affordances of mobile music applications. The Pocketsong study thus aimed to construct an experiential frame of understanding with which to unpack mobile music listening, in turn allowing us to critically reflect upon the design of mobile music technologies for use in digital public spaces.

OUR STUDY

We now describe our study design. Our original research questions were motivated by an Experience-centred Design (ECD) methodology [28] and an empirical concern for understanding 'real-world' user experience to generate pragmatic design insights. Our research questions were: (1) how do people *experience* location-based consumption and sharing of digital music in a mobile and public setting? And (2) how is social interaction/expression impacted by the emerging technological landscape of mobile music technologies? To address these questions we used a method that placed emphasis on critically exploring the social dimensions of technology use at the cutting edge of what's currently available on the consumer market, rather than exploring technical innovation through design per se.

Method

We chose a technology probe method [14] because, in keeping with our ECD approach, it enabled us to reconfigure existing technology to explore and capture data about people's interactions 'in the wild' [22]. With this objective, we present our smartphone app, Pocketsong, not so much as an innovative technology per se, but as a device to push certain features of interaction on our participants to explore how they would respond. We therefore designed the new app for field deployment with a sample of research participants, to log use and invite new opportunities for interacting with and sharing digital music in everyday life and in public (amongst the participants), over the course of 12-weeks. Participation in the study involved: an introductory session run by the researchers to address Pocketsong's usability and its novel features; an interim group interview; and an exit interview after the deployment to critically discuss the participants' experiences of use.

Recruitment

Using a snowballing method, we recruited nine participants for the Pocketsong study from the local area: Elly, Michael, Andy, Kieran, Sam, Shaun, Anita, Kim and Richard (all pseudonyms) (three of whom new one another), ranging in ages from 19-36 years. Kieran and Kim were music students at our university, at times taking classes and collocated in the same building as each other; Anita was an undergraduate student at the university. The other five in the sample lived and worked locally. All described themselves as highly interested in music (the music students in particular considered themselves music experts). Through this sample representing highly musically conscious individuals (but not early adopters of new technology), we hoped to analyse extreme users, for whom the issues at play would hold particular interest and salience, and who would therefore provide valuable critical accounts of use.

Pocketsong Design

Our starting point for a technology probe design was to generate a set of sensitising concepts from previous fieldwork [19] around notions of music consumption and sharing. This highlighted music listeners' experiences of both synchronous and asynchronous sharing, their desires to operate within listening communities, sharing tastes, and the ways in which places became associated with these specific communities and anonymous but evocative encounters with new music. The concepts were used in a series of service designs and associated storyboards. Through a process of critique and collective brainstorming, we selected and developed the Pocketsong app concept. A key design feature was for the probe to support a *social*, but otherwise *anonymised*, experience (enabling us to examine tensions around self-expression in social and 'public' settings). Accordingly, within the study, whilst some participants knew each other, their use of the system was anonymous to the other users unless they explicitly 'outed' themselves to one another (by revealing their self-selected and anonymous system usernames).

To address our research questions, our mobile app needed to be: (1) an accessible music player with simple functionality so that users could focus on experiencing its novel affordances with minimal distraction from usability issues; (2) a tool for sharing music between listeners in a location-based way; and (3) a service enabling users to explore what music was being listened to proximally (both geographically and temporally, i.e. 'snooping' on what other users were listening to, nearby and/or now). This feature in particular allowed us to perturb tensions around private and public listening.

We implemented Pocketsong as an Android OS app that connected to a remote server. Pocketsong was developed to be used on any touchscreen Android device running a minimum of the 'Ice Cream Sandwich' operating system, and due to practical constraints, the app was installed on a variety of Android phones with differing form factors. The app used tabbed pages giving the user convenient access to the majority of music functions. The app opened with users choosing music through the standard music player paradigm of selection by artist, album, track name and playlist (see Figure 1). As expected in this paradigm, once a selection was made on any given tab then the subsequent selections would be refined by that choice, (e.g. selecting the composer Beethoven might narrow the choice to the collection "Beethoven Symphony 5").

The locative functionality of this music player was accessible on the last tabbed page (see Figure 2). This tab allowed users to explore what people around them were listening to. During the design development, we envisaged that the number of adopters of the software could be anything from a dozen to hundreds, so this screen was designed to display the most recent track regardless of how long ago they were played. The tracks were initially ordered by the current relative distance to the user, and, optionally, the elapsed time. The most recent track or the closest listener was always shown first. If available, the album art from the track was downscaled into a square and given an appropriate dimension for the screen. In this way, the app arranged album covers in an ordered grid unaffected by different Android device resolutions. We used the presence of a green circle to indicate currently online listeners.

In order for the app, as a probe, to serve a critical-reflective research function, it was also designed to allow songs to be *placed* or 'dropped' in a geographic location, and allowed the *gifting* of songs to other users, thus framing alternative contexts for social exchange. Due to copyright limitations, we only exchanged a short introduction to each song (up to 15 seconds of intro), rather than the full track.

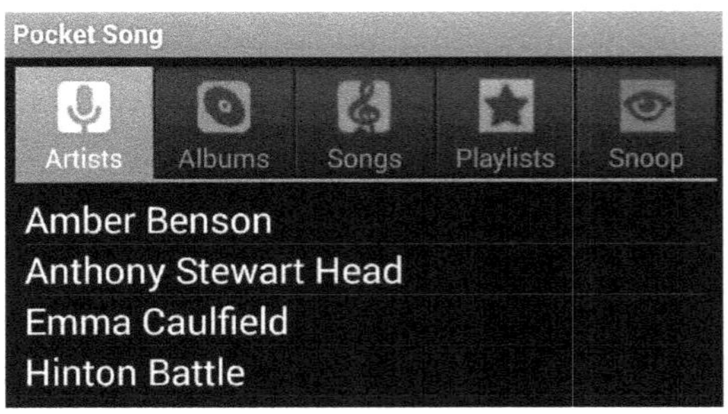

Figure 1. Pocketsong screenshot detail displaying music organised by artists

Figure 2. Music that has been played nearby, or recently

Figure 3. This user can drop a track for another user

We speculated that 'dropping' a specific track for a user would be an explicit gesture, an intention to communicate (an opening gambit as it were, in what might become an ongoing dialogue of exchanged tracks). To emphasise the intentionality behind this gesture, and give weight to the action (and possibly to avoid idle 'rick-rolling' (playful or malicious misdirection through web-links), the sender is forced to listen to the track they want to gift first (see Figure 3). The sender then selects the recipient from the list of anonymous people geographically co-present, and 'drops' the track to the other user, at that location. When that user next enters this place they are notified that a service user has dropped a track for them.

On receiving notification, the recipient of the track can add it to his/her own play list collection. This added a personal touch to the gift since playlists are normally a personal element of a music player, effectively a statement of the music that is important to you on that day. Taken together, Pocketsong's various features helped scaffold our research inquiry allowing us to potentially (and indirectly/naturally) construct certain kinds of social encounter.

Procedure

We invited our participants to attend an hour-long introductory drop-in session at our Lab before the deployment commenced. At this session, members of the research team provided participants with the app and, in some cases, an Android smartphone, and explained how they worked, ensuring that Pocketsong's novel functional features were well understood. Each participant was also provided with a 'diary application' on the phone, inviting them to make note of significant experiences and/or issues as they were to arise during the deployment, as an aide memoire. At this session, participants took part in a short interview (20min in duration) at which they were asked open questions about their music listening practices.

Around week eight of the deployment, participants were invited to one of two Interim Group Interviews (of four to five people, 30 minutes in duration) to describe their experiences of use and discuss any usability issues that they had encountered. Questions focused on use of Pocketsong and evaluation of its design, and sensed changes to everyday listening practices. Researchers also asked about application glitches and usability issues at this interview.

Although participants attended group sessions, few participants knew each other personally, in most cases they had never met. It is important to stress that their actual use of Pocketsong was effectively anonymous, as they did not know who was using what username within the system, as this was set up independently. This provided an workable level of anonymity, for the trial.

At the end of the deployment researchers held two further group interviews (one of six - Sam, Michael, Shaun, Richard, Kim and Anita; and one of three - Elly, Kieran and Andy). These lasted 90min each and consisted of in-depth, participant-driven discussion about user experiences over the course of the deployment. The interview schedule was semi-structured and many of the questions were oriented towards user experience, but others prompted conceptual discussion about emerging mobile music technologies and services and the forms of social interaction and self-expression that may emerge from them. This discussion incorporated critical reflection on the Pocketsong design and led to speculation about how to develop and even reconceptualise the app and related music sharing services. All interviews were video-recorded with consent, forming a qualitative data set accompanied by logs of device/app use.

Analytic Framework

In keeping with our ECD approach [28], we adopted an interpretative, phenomenological method for analysing the data. This involved a two-stage coding procedure as a collaborative effort by the researchers. First, we generated codes from the video data relating to participants' voiced experiences and sense making in the unfolding interviews. Codes were expressed as themes supported by data excerpts. Second, the researchers analysed *how* the unfolding researcher-participant dialogue in each of the interviews signaled an emerging understanding about how Pocketsong experiences related to broader experiences of mobile music listening and sharing technologies. This understanding was, again, expressed in themes supported by excerpts. In turn, we used this understanding to address our research questions, collectively generating higher-level themes to be presented next.

FINDINGS – POCKETSONG EXPERIENCES

During the study we saw moderate use of the app. Amongst the participants, 681 tracks were played and there were 29 instances of gifting across the 12 week period (with 76% choosing to download the gift), with use remaining roughly consistent over the 12 weeks. In the following sections we explore in more depth some of the key features of our participants' experiences of using Pocketsong and their broader critical reflections on mobile music systems that operate between the boundaries of private and public settings. Our findings reflect three areas of interest. Firstly, we open with a discussion of the ways in which music listening and sharing is impacted by participants' concerns for *self-expression*. In doing so, we discuss our participants' reflections upon the relationship between music and selfhood and social interaction. Secondly, we explore some of our participants' responses to ideas and *practices of co-listening*, as brought to the fore by using Pocketsong. And thirdly, we discuss some of our participants' reflections on *mobile-access to music media*, focusing on the affordances of mobile-phone technology and the potentials for this to shape music listening and sharing practices more broadly.

Self-expression and facework in music listening/sharing

Participants often discussed the impact that Pocketsong had when making their listening practices public. This core feature raised concern for them about how they were expressing themselves to other users. When it came to broadcasting her personal playlist to other app users, Anita suggested: "I get more aware of what I listen to because I don't want people to think that I listen to Bruno Mars". In the following subsections we focus on issues raised in response to core features of Pocketsong's design.

'Dropping' tracks and being presumptuous

Participants voiced concerns related to their ability through Pocketsong to "drop" tracks for other users. Despite user anonymity, participants felt self-conscious about 'saving face', and not wanting to come across as lacking in music knowledge and 'being uncool'. Participant discussions at group interviews highlighted how sensitive an act of suggesting music to someone can actually be, and indeed this anxiety stopped a few users from 'dropping' tracks at all. For example, Elly feared being thought of as 'lame', and worried about offending other user's musical sensibilities (especially when she respected their musical credentials, she gave the example of a DJ friend (not a study participant) whose musical tastes she admired and who she would be worried of 'embarrassing herself' in front of). By contrast, Shaun felt he lacked confidence to share a track with someone because of not knowing enough about the recipient's broader listening habits, as he explained:

> "I'd mentioned before not being able to see the full profile history of people, you know. It was one thing seeing someone play an Orbital track, but I don't know if what I'm listening to would be relevant, just because they listen to that Orbital track and that's all that I know, or that they listened to a Clash song recently, like that's a tiny proportion of a person's taste and what they're about, so it's very hard to say 'oh they've listened to that Clash song so I'll send them this', I wouldn't want to do that because I think it's a bit rude and presumptuous to go 'you've listened to that so there you go'".

Shaun's excerpt above effectively describes what recommender systems do, but somehow the inclusion of human agency in Pocketsong rendered this kind of functionality a potentially offensive gesture – and possibly "a bit rude and presumptuous". This might be because of the ways in which socially we ascribe intentionality to the acts of others, in a way we might not with a machine.

Maintaining face whilst broadcasting and 'snooping'

In discussion of Pocketsong use, participants also collectively voiced how their listening practices had been changed, not just through desiring to present a certain image of themselves, but also by *anxieties of feeling overlooked* by others. In Sam's words:

> "I knew people would be able to see what I was listening to so therefore I wouldn't listen to intros to albums or interludes because it's not very interesting for people to listen to, [...] But I did change my listening habits a little bit with playing more individual songs, rather than playing full albums, which is what I always do. So I was trying to make it more interesting for other people who were using the snoop."

What is particularly interesting here is how Pocketsong was pushing users, such as Sam, to shape their listening not just for their consumption but explicitly for the consumption of others. This moved beyond trying to maintain cool, actually *shifting from consumption to broadcast* as an orientation to the music player and one's relationship with it. This accentuates the social nature of music listening, arguably reversing the criticisms of private headphone 'cocooning'.

The 'snooping' function held particular interest for Elly, given the anxieties around being observed by others. She saw it as a way of circumventing embarrassment in asking for music recommendations from her friends she viewed as having greater musical knowledge:

> "If you were friends with people then I think I'd feel more like 'oh I definitely want to snoop on this person' because you know who they are and you might respect their music tastes, but you don't really know what they listen to. I've a friend who's a DJ and I'd love to snoop on his songs without having to ask him every time."

For participants like Elly, the snooping function served some means of 'saving face' in the socially fraught world of music listening. As such, the snooping tool offered a mode of listening that circumvented (in some cases) anxieties around sharing. However, as the findings above illustrate, music sharing makes for complex social experiences.

Notions of cool, and doing musical *facework* (i.e. saving and maintaining face) to generate cultural capital[1] [1] amongst a user's social group, was a phenomenon frequently noted by our participants. Observable music consumption and the implication of possessing music knowledge was seen as a way of self-identifying with certain groups, or as a way of differentiating oneself from the perceived mainstreams. The value of 'obscure' music, or music that was seen to be 'obscure', was an important measure for most users in the study. Significant here is that our sample included music students and required the self-selection of participants who were interested in music so it is likely that we gathered a sample who might be inherently more image-conscious around matters of music taste.

Of equal importance was being seen to have an eclectic musical taste. This particular concern was linked in talk to anxieties about others 'snooping' on an individual's listening practices. Similar to his concerns about suggesting tracks for others, Shaun worried that Pocketsong only presented a glimpse of his actual listening habits, and therefore it didn't accurately communicate something about his 'self-image' that he might want to express to others:

> "I've got a hugely broad spectrum of music, it would be very hard to define somebody by three or four tracks that they might listen to."

Mike added to this the value of demonstrating *eclectic* interests by talking about the importance and growth potential of music sharing for 'identifying difference':

> "Identifying differences and just finding something to talk about, I mean, everyone likes a little bit of disagreement. [...] That's how music evolves I think, through disagreement and conflict."

Mike felt that sharing tracks to provoke or stimulate conversation or debate about a conflict of taste was an interesting mode of social expression through music. He suggested that seeking out difference rather than common ground helped to evolve musical tastes, which is something he saw as a positive value in a music sharing technology.

Being part of a localised listening community

Whilst difference was seen as important for identity, similarity in taste was also discussed as significant. Richard described his excitement about being in a listening community of like-minded people interested in particular sub-genres of music. And Shaun explained that he would only share music if he sensed that there were similarities to his own tastes, and related that to the formation of friendships at school and beyond, claiming that his circle of friends all listen to the same kinds of music:

> "The reason we are all friends is because we kind of liked the same music at the same sort of time. [...] I have quite a lot of common ground musically with a lot of my core friend group."

Interestingly, Sam and Shaun went further to speculate about potentially localised music listening communities arising in public spaces explicitly because of the use of locative technologies such as Pocketsong:

> "Maybe there's a possible tendency for having certain areas where you'd have more of a correlation between what's playing – maybe high streets would be a huge mix of stuff, but there are certain areas where certain people hang, so what's the mix of genres around the university?" [Sam].

Kieran felt that a person's expression of who they are to others, and how that self-image is maintained, is strongly connected to an expressed knowledge of and 'critical engagement' with music. He framed the effort of finding out about music, being the person who knows the yet-to-be-discovered bands, and being the trendsetter, as core to developing cultural capital:

> "I suppose there's a prestige that comes from having gone through the work, then it's considered that you've had a critical engagement with a field of music, and you've chosen something as opposed to someone else doing that critical work and then coming along to you in a bar and going 'you should listen to this' and then you've kind of just had that shortcut."

Accordingly, Anita felt that she was justified in imposing her music collections on her friends. She had self-belief in the value (in terms of cultural capital) of her tastes, which gave her a sense of obligation and right to share her music:

> "I share music so that my friends also like it, I mean I believe what I listen to is cool music, right? So I just

---

[1] Bourdieu's [1] concept of assets (e.g. skills, knowledge, tastes, goods, credentials etc.) defining our social position.

force people to listen to those things as well, so I usually send them links from YouTube and say 'just listen to this, this is really good' and often they go 'no' but I just keep doing that, because I think you should just share good music and if you find something that is, I don't know, some indie bands that no one's ever heard of you just share it."

Of particular note here is Anita's demonstration of the way in which 'newness' might be used to support the development of cultural capital – it being one way to demonstrate your *insider knowledge*.

These discussion points about self-image, taste and cultural capital led on to talk about the establishment of digital media profiles, through which users could actively manage their self-image through a music app. Appreciating the significance of music technology in establishing self-image is critical to understanding the social anxieties present in the talk amongst participants. As Michael demonstrated, any music played in a digital public space and through social media platforms has the potential to trigger concerns about identity and sociality:

> "It seems to be a kind of a stake in identity being played out, it's like a personal investment you make in trying to assert your own identity and trying to ascertain someone else's and trying to gauge compatibility on those terms. Maybe it's less benevolent than saying 'I want to share this music because I think you might like it' and more 'I'm going to share this music because I want you to know what I'm all about and I want to figure out if we can be friends or something, you know what I mean, there seems to be a deeply psycho-social thing being insinuated I think."

Of further interest is a latter point made by Shaun, who, returning to his previous comments on music territories in towns, drew a distinction between his 'real' profile and a profile he might choose to present to others:

> "If you wanted to get into a scene, you noticed there was a scene at the bus station, then you might go 'I'm going to get into that scene and I'm going to tailor my profile accordingly, but I'm going to keep my real profile aside'".

Here Shaun acknowledges that an open profile is potentially problematic when infiltrating certain music communities because of the credentials you might need to demonstrate for group acceptability. In discussing this Shaun was effectively advocating that apps like Pocketsong could benefit from actively *supporting multiple expressions of self* through manipulable online profiles.

Practices of Co-listening

Much discussion about Pocketsong experiences focused on how the app presents information about the current or recent listening practices of other users. Connected to this, participants talked about how the dropping of tracks affords shared, if asynchronous, listening experiences because you have to listen to a track before you can drop it). Leading from this, our participants talked about their experiences of listening to music together and how this may or may not be impacted by apps like Pocketsong. We focus here on the ways in which they wished to share music experiences.

Framing a context for interaction

For Kieran, there was definite concern for how the act of sharing music, when digital (and remotely) achieved, might inevitably lack an empathetic connection, rendering it inappropriate. He described the potentially problematic disconnect between your current interest in a track and someone else's receptivity to concurrently hearing it:

> "It's not always clear what's going on at the other end of a computer interaction and so when somebody rejects something it reminds you of 'oh yeah that other person could be in a completely different space, [...] a different mood'. So sometimes when [...] you're like, having a great Fleetwood Mac experience for a minute, and you're like 'I must send this to Brian or whoever', and it's just not that moment when the other person is just waiting around for your great Fleetwood Mac recommendation [...] I have to remember to try and empathise with what the other person might be doing."

In this comment, Kieran suggested that technology platforms, particularly ones that rely on remote sharing, have *significant potential to decontextualise social exchanges*. Users' experience of Pocketsong sensitised them to this concern, resulting in a general agreement at the group interviews for a need to validate or assert one's motivations for sharing - a need to *qualify* just why the act of sharing was being enacted.

For some users the talk of sharing tracks made them think quite seriously about how face-to-face music listening (co-listening) was different to digitally-mediated co-listening. Whilst an advantage was seen in the instantaneous nature of sharing digital tracks at a distance, it was felt that the lack of physicality in sharing meant that the mobile interface was a poor substitute for seeing people when exchanging music; as Michael elaborates:

> "I think the most striking affordance in terms of mobile technology and broader, perhaps the Internet as a whole, is just the lack of palpable proximity with people, [...] you can still communicate with these phones but I guess when you're sharing music through them it's easier for the person on the other end to hide the fact they don't like it or ignore it altogether."

> "I think mobile technology can only be so social, I think it's always going to be derivative of real [...] but physical proximity, and even having the markers of where people are at on the app for instance, where you can see who listened to what in a certain place, that's still not quite the same as seeing somebody and seeing the look on their faces or what they're mumbling under their breath" [Michael].

Significant for our analysis is the attention given to *reciprocality* that Michael is expressing here. He has identified the subtle cues of social and situated interaction, highlighting how digital and mobile exchange as constructed through Pocketsong might lack this subtlety.

Synchronicity of experience

Building further on the notion of physical co-presence being valued and yearned for during moments of exchange, our participants further described valuing notions of more general synchronicity in the listening experience. The importance of having the immediacy of response to a piece of shared music, was argued to be key to the social experience of listening to music together. Michael suggested, that he wanted "more of a real time thing":

> "[If] people were using it a lot, you'd have a real time 'oh people are listening to that now', I'll drop them something, see if they listen to it, that sort of thing."

Picking up on the temporality of the Pocketsong interface, our participants suggested that synchronicity might be leveraged for a rich user experience. As Kieran suggests:

> "Just the idea that you could drop a track to somebody else, wait for them to push play on it, and when they push play on it, it would push play for you, and you would know that you were both listening to it and you could talk about it while you were listening to it, that seems to me that would kind of be, it's something that, it's a version of something that people do, right?"

When Kieran suggests that this a version of 'something that people do' he is referring to physical co-present sharing practices and he's suggesting that digital tools might be designed to better leverage these practices. Whilst this in and of itself isn't necessarily an original idea it does highlight the importance of a sense of shared experience in music consumption being a valued feature of Pocketsong use, and something which a push towards mobility and in essence individual/headphone listening could still support. Important to note as well is that Kieran's thoughts focused on temporal synchronicity and not spatial synchronicity – suggesting that the shared experience need not necessitate a simulation of physical co-presence to be satisfying.

Mobile-access to music media

As a mobile app, Pocketsong framed a research context for experiences with music centred on mobility and interacting through a smartphone. This framing further prompted interesting participant reflection on our research questions.

Emotional engagement on the move

When discussing music apps with participants a prominent consideration was the nature of *pervasive access* to libraries of music and information, and specifically how that access facilitated *ad hoc listening practices*, which might in turn have certain emotive uses. Listening to music on a phone meant it could be used for "drowning out ambience, of shutting off the noise of the bus and people chatting and things like that" [Andy], through headphone listening in public spaces so that people could be "closing themselves off in their own little bubble" [Andy] and as an opportunistic means for enhancing conversations with friends by having what they are currently listening to "there in your hand" [Mike]. *Opportunistic listening* also meant users could find a balance between emotional and musical expression. Participants described how music helped them manage emotions: "you can manage emotion with a good or bad record" [Kieran]. They also described music as having the power to exorcise or intensify emotional feeling: "if I'm feeling a bit angry then I might want to further my anger by putting on something that will make me even more angry" [Elly]. As such, we learned that music listening through pervasive technologies such as mobile phones actively afforded and mediated, in a moment-by-moment basis, emotional interactions with the world, and this was a feature of the experience of use that was actively valued.

Participants also had interests in the more visceral experiences that Pocketsong might offer. Discussion revolved around the 'snooping' features, with Mike arguing that Pocketsong was 'sneaky', and a way to 'spy' on others:

> "When it's got a button called snoop on it, there's something quite sneaky about it, it's like a really streamlined little spy tool, so maybe there's some fun to be had with that in my head. […] It's not sinister, but you know what I mean, right? It's a bit like 'wow what's that'? […] it's all a bit shrouded in mystery isn't it?"

Echoing Mike, several of the participants expressed values they held in the snoop functionality in terms of it delivering a *vicarious thrill* through surreptitiously *listening in* on others. This kind of possibility only really exists where there is the explicit intention to transgress emotionally labile privacy boundaries through system use, something that the HCI community rarely directly advocates.

Accessing and discovering music on the move

Participants also talked about how being tethered to a smartphone as a web-connected device afforded quick and easy access, not just to music, but also to information and news, Andy mentioned constant, easy access, particularly in terms of music discovery; he suggested that music was now 'there within a few touches of the button' [Andy]. Kieran talked about a 'powerful' musical experience whereby a mixture of 'real human contact' recommendation and the ease of access on his smartphone meant that there was a new immediacy in discovering music.

However, this ubiquitous presence afforded by smartphones meant that a lot of the work involved in finding music was taken away. Andy suggested that this fundamentally "changes the model of accessing music." He referred to himself as an avid user of his smartphone who used it to facilitate an ambient, peripheral engagement with music. He talked about how he really enjoyed "looking up random bits of information that just pop into my head, music-wise", something he saw as positive. But later in the focus group, he revisited this position to suggest that smart phones are like "a brain holding your hand" inferring that he felt he had sacrificed a certain amount of agency to the affordances of this kind of ubiquitous presence. He suggested that smartphones should facilitate a healthy use by becoming less like a 'crutch.' and he offered anecdotes about sitting at home with his wife, not talking, but using Facebook or their smart phones. Richard suggested that sharing and discovering music is now a lot easier because of access and the sheer amount that's available, and that this means that he feels less of an obligation to attend to it, suggesting that ubiquitous presence of music might in some way devalue it.

This discussion with participants described a value in the move towards mobility of music and pervasive access to it. At the same time however, there were clearly expressed concerns about the ways this in which this move might be devaluing or impairing our relationships to music content.

MOBILE MUSIC INTERACTION DESIGN CHALLENGES

We now turn to reflect upon the findings of our in-the-wild, UK study of Pocketsong. Critical to this reflection is that our aim was *not* to evaluate a product proposition. Our app is not entirely novel (for a similar technology see [5, 12, 23]). Likewise, we were *not* trying to propose the concept of music sharing services that utilise the digital public domain. The public sharing of listening habits already exists in various services and the online user community at large will evaluate its acceptability as a concept. Rather, what we aim to contribute to the DIS community through our study with Pocketsong is (*i*) a set of findings which help to reveal the social complexity of mobile music listening and sharing, prompted by use of a technology probe, and (*ii*) a set of interaction design challenges for the development of personal music technologies that work at the boundaries of public-private space. Our proposed contribution is based upon the qualitative understanding we have generated and the values and concerns expressed through experiential reflections on Pocketsong use. Below we set out challenge areas for those who wish to design personal mobile music technologies to support social interaction in public spaces.

Negotiating Online Identities

A key area of concern for music technologies such as Pocketsong, which work in digitally mediated social spaces, is the extent to which they support the negotiated expression of online identities. Much of our participants' discussion explored ideas that can be encapsulated by the concept of *music facework* (after Goffman's notion of 'facework' as a form of identity management) [10]. Prior research [12, 21] has demonstrated that it is not uncommon to use music in identity formation and for self-expression with one's peer group and others. Perhaps less well understood, however, is the interaction design challenge to explore how this facework activity can be supported through the design of music playing (and sharing) interfaces (as even allowing for anonymity at the interface, as we have seen, does not remove the need for complex facework).

Collectively, participants argued that music they share for public consumption has to fit a certain 'style', yet this might not reflect their 'real' tastes. Likewise, participants felt that, when wishing to integrate with certain social groupings, people may desire specific, ad hoc and possibly relatively temporary profiles that enable them to maintain sufficient social cachet that they can pass unremarked amongst social circles. In essence, this suggests the maintenance of permanent playlists that might be 'snoopable' in anonymity-preserving ways. These might then be coupled with publically facing, managed (and possibly conflicting) online profiles. The challenge here is designing interaction techniques for elegantly managing trade-offs between these positions, this depending on the intelligent application of policies utilising context-dependent information based on declared or assumed relationships between users. For example, imagine an individual with a music profile that switches automatically when entering certain places and/or when specific people 'are snooping'. Equally, the notion of spatialising music across cityscapes, suggested by some participants, raises a role for location-based services in spatially defining communities of music listening.

Another, and perhaps more subtle consideration, was the expressed shift between music players being used for consumption to being used for broadcast. The indirect 'broadcasting' of leaky music players such as Pocketsong, inevitably shaped listening practices but it is rare to see tools built in to music players that allow reflexive understanding of the impact of broadcast on patterns of others listening in. There is clear design potential to support users in shaping their external playlists to have maximum impact with communities they wish to address, but this requires data about 'impact' being generated, shared and visualised, raising challenges for managing privacy and self-disclosure that have been previously identified in related work [26].

Supporting co-listening on mobile devices

Another area of challenge is how personal mobile music technologies may better support co-listening and shared experiences. Building on findings from related work on supporting social awareness and reciprocity in the active and passive use of mobile music sharing services [12], our participants discussed their experiences of co-listening from the physically co-present to the digitally mediated. They expressed a desire for shared listening experiences but valued the ability to support remote interaction that came with digital mediation. Participants framed the sharing of music experiences as something beyond physical co-presence and saw no sense in attempts to recreate that co-presence at a distance (in terms of physicality). What they did however express was a desire for music sharing systems that supported *synchronicity*, i.e. the ability to experience something in the same temporal frame as another listener. Physical co-presence was less relevant if temporal synchronicity was there to foster remote co-presence.

However, to support this more fully participants expressed desires for better management of *reciprocality*, that is, tools for supporting the back channel communications that provide for a richer dialogue (a not uncommon observation with collaborative technologies [14]).

Understanding how people were responding to a shared piece of music was seen as a significant goal for collaborative interaction around that music. Equally, our participants have revealed a desire to further *contextualise content that is shared.* With the design of our probe, we made an explicit decision to keep Pocketsong lightweight and anonymous, but the sharing mode we designed stripped sharing gestures of their context, e.g. the reason why a given track was posted to a certain user. Without that information, it was felt that the act of sharing might transgress implicit social rules about who can share tracks with whom, when and why – issues typically worked out in our everyday interactions. Beyond this point of sharing there was also a desire to be able to observe the musical receptivity of others, again to avoid making musical faux pas by inappropriately or ineptly sharing with others.

Real time access and cultural capital

It is also important to consider the relationship between pervasive media access and processes associated with the development of cultural capital (keeping in mind that our participants identified very strongly with music as a component of their identity and may therefore be more extreme in opinion than some demographics). Our participants believed that easy access to music information was a good thing, but tied to this was a misgiving for how this access undermined carefully crafted and socialised practices of conferring status amongst peers on the basis of musical knowledge and perceptions of taste. It is not clear how music technologies and software such as recommender systems might be re-imagined to support such accumulation, expression and exchange of cultural capital amongst music listening communities, but this is potentially a very rich area of future research. And this is something that can only be done with further design exploration.

Reflecting on (limited) use

Finally, we wish to briefly reflect on some of the methodological considerations of doing this kind of 'in-the-wild' research. Pocketsong was designed and developed as an experimental platform – probe – for exploring our interests in the sociality of music listening. In our study we were asking participants to alter their regular listening behaviour – by getting them to use different software/hardware to their normal practices. Like any technology probe activity [14] this intervention is bound to alter behaviour. And this is part of the challenge of doing this kind of work. Ultimately, the provocations that the design raised were grounded in participants' own activities of meaning-making in dialogue with the research team. It is their efforts to make sense of the technology that have critically informed our understanding of the roles and values of sociality in their music-listening practices.

There is potential that some may look at a study of social media use with nine participants and assume the research to be ungeneralisable or provide sufficient insight in to the design of a mass media platform intended to work at scale. We would argue that this is a trade-off. Forced large-scale adoption does just as much damage to the validity of a study. Equally, launching a 'service' and waiting for mass adoption before you can do research seems wasteful. Our approach herein has been to use the technology in probe mode, and in a long tradition of more phenomenological research [see 28] we have developed a qualitative account, which considers the idiographic features of our users' experiences. And from this relatively limited amount of system use we have generated significant insight as to the moral ordering of social behaviour around music listening and sharing as it might pertain to mobile practices.

CONCLUSION

We have reported on a field study exploring social experiences of music listening and sharing in public spaces mediated by digital technology. To support this we designed and deployed Pocketsong, a location-based mobile application and technology probe. Our aim through this study was to produce valuable transferrable insights for designing future mobile music technologies. Our findings address mobile access to music media, practices of 'co-listening' and relationships between digitally mediated mobile music consumption and self-expression. We raise three interaction design challenges for critical reflection during the development of mobile music applications, focusing on the negotiation of self-expression to others, support for co-listening and the development of cultural capital through interface design. By addressing these challenges we have arguably foregrounded the significance and complexity of the *social* experience of mobile music listening afforded by emerging pervasive technologies.

ACKNOWLEDGMENTS

We thank our research participants for their time and contributions, and musician Jamie Thompson for his support with the study. This work was supported by EPSRC Social Inclusion through the Digital Economy (SIDE) [EP/G066019/1] and AHRC KE Hub for the Creative Economy [AH/J005150/1] grants. The second author is additionally supported by The Leverhulme Trust [ECF-2012-642].

Data supporting this publication is openly available under an 'Open Data Commons Open Database License'. Additional metadata are available at: 10.17634/082922-1. Please contact Newcastle Research Data Service at rdm@ncl.ac.uk for access instructions.

REFERENCES

1. Pierre Bourdieu (2011). The forms of capital (1986). *Cultural theory: An anthology*, 81-93.

2. Miguel Bruns Alonso & V. Keyson. 2006. MusicCube: a physical experience with digital music. *Personal and Ubiquitous Computing*, 10 (2-3), 163-165.

3. Lynne Baillie, David Beattie and Lee Morton. 2011. Feel what you hear: haptic feedback as an accompaniment to mobile music playback. In *Proceedings of Interacting with Sound Workshop: Exploring Context-Aware, Local and Social Audio Applications* (IwS '11). ACM, New York, NY, USA, 1-6. DOI=http://dx.doi.org/10.1145/2019335.2019336.

4. David Bainbridge, Brook J. Novak, and Sally Jo Cunningham. 2010. A user-centered design of a personal digital library for music exploration. In *Proceedings of the 10th annual joint conference on Digital libraries* (JCDL '10). ACM, New York, NY, USA, 149-158. DOI=http://dx.doi.org/10.1145/1816123.1816145

5. Arianna Bassoli, Julian Moore, and Stefan Agamanolis. 2006. tunA: Socialising music sharing on the move. In Kenton O'Hara and Barry Brown, Eds.*Consuming music together*. Springer. p.151-172

6. Arianna Bassoli, Johanna Brewer, Karen Martin, Paul Dourish, and Scott Mainwaring. 2007. Underground aesthetics: Rethinking urban computing. *Pervasive Computing, IEEE* 6, 3, 39-45.

7. Stephan Baumann, Björn Jung, Arianna Bassoli, and Martin Wisniowski. 2007. BluetunA: let your neighbour know what music you like. In *CHI '07 Extended Abstracts on Human Factors in Computing Systems* (CHI EA '07). ACM, New York, NY, USA, 1941-1946. DOI=http://dx.doi.org/10.1145/1240866.1240929

8. Janne Bergman, Jarmo Kauko, and Jaakko Keränen. 2009. Hands on music: physical approach to interaction with digital music. In *Proceedings of the 11th International Conference on Human-Computer Interaction with Mobile Devices and Services* (MobileHCI '09). ACM, New York, NY, USA, , Article 33 , 11 pages. DOI=http://dx.doi.org/10.1145/1613858.1613901

9. Michael Bull. 2007. *Sound Moves: iPod culture and Urban Experience*. Routledge

10. Erving Goffman. 1959/1990. *The Presentation of Self in Everyday Life*. Penguin

11. Connor Graham, Mark Rouncefield, Martin Gibbs, Frank Vetere, and Keith Cheverst. 2007. How probes work. In *Proceedings of the 19th Australasian conference on Computer-Human Interaction: Entertaining User Interfaces* (OZCHI '07). ACM, New York, NY, USA, 29-37. DOI=http://dx.doi.org/10.1145/1324892.1324899

12. Maria Håkansson, Mattias Rost, ,and Lars Erik Holmquist. 2007. Gifts from Friends and Strangers: A study of Mobile Music Sharing. In *Proceedings of European Computer Supported Cooperative Work (ECSCW),* Kluwer, pp. 311-330.

13. Sebastian Huber, Markus Schedl, and Peter Knees. 2012. nepDroid: an intelligent mobile music player. In *Proceedings of the 2nd ACM International Conference on Multimedia Retrieval* (ICMR '12). ACM, New York, NY, USA, , Article 57 , 2 pages. DOI=http://dx.doi.org/10.1145/2324796.2324862

14. Hilary Hutchinson, Wendy Mackay, Bo Westerlund, Benjamin B. Bederson, Allison Druin, Catherine Plaisant, Michel Beaudouin-Lafon, Stéphane Conversy, Helen Evans, Heiko Hansen, Nicolas Roussel, and Björn Eiderbäck. 2003. Technology probes: inspiring design for and with families. In *Proceedings of the SIGCHI Conference on Human Factors in Computing Systems* (CHI '03). ACM, New York, NY, USA, 17-24. DOI=http://dx.doi.org/10.1145/642611.642616

15. Petra Jarkiewicz, My Frankhammar, and Ylva Fernaeus. 2008. In the hands of children: exploring the use of mobile phone functionality in casual play settings. In *Proceedings of the 10th international conference on Human computer interaction with mobile devices and services* (MobileHCI '08). ACM, New York, NY, USA, 375-378. DOI=http://dx.doi.org/10.1145/1409240.1409292

16. Sari Komulainen, Minna Karukka, and Jonna Häkkilä. 2010. Social music services in teenage life: a case study. In *Proceedings of the 22nd Conference of the Computer-Human Interaction Special Interest Group of Australia on Computer-Human Interaction* (OZCHI '10). ACM, New York, NY, USA, 364-367. DOI=http://dx.doi.org/10.1145/1952222.1952303

17. Michael Kuhn, Roger Wattenhofer, and Samuel Welten. 2010. Social audio features for advanced music retrieval interfaces. In *Proceedings of the 18th ACM international conference on Multimedia* (MM '10). ACM, New York, NY, USA, 411-420. DOI=http://dx.doi.org/10.1145/1873951.1874007

18. Vilma Lehtinen and Lassi Liikkanen. 2012. The meanings of music sharing in tween life. In *CHI '12 Extended Abstracts on Human Factors in Computing Systems* (CHI EA '12). ACM, New York, NY, USA, 1907-1912. DOI=http://dx.doi.org/10.1145/2212776.2223727

19. Tuck W. Leong and Peter C. Wright. 2013. Revisiting social practices surrounding music. In *Proceedings of the SIGCHI Conference on Human Factors in Computing Systems* (CHI '13). ACM, New York, NY, USA, 951-960. DOI=http://dx.doi.org/10.1145/2470654.2466122

20. KuanTing Liu and Roger Andersson Reimer. 2008. Social playlist: enabling touch points and enriching ongoing relationships through collaborative mobile music listening. In *Proceedings of the 10th international conference on Human computer interaction with mobile devices and services* (MobileHCI '08). ACM, New York, NY, USA, 403-406. DOI=http://dx.doi.org/10.1145/1409240.1409299

21. Kenton O'Hara, K. and Barry Brown, 2006. *Consuming music together: social and collaborative aspects of music consumption technologies*. Springer

22. Yvonne Rogers. 2012. *HCI Theory: Classical, Modern and Contemporary*. Morgan Claypool

23. Jan Seeburger, Marcus Foth, and Dian Tjondronegoro. 2012. The sound of music: sharing song selections between collocated strangers in public urban places. In *Proceedings of the 11th International Conference on Mobile and Ubiquitous Multimedia* (MUM '12). ACM, New York, NY, USA, , Article 34 , 10 pages. DOI=http://dx.doi.org/10.1145/2406367.2406409

24. Atau Tanaka, Guillaume Valadon and Christophe Berger. 2007. Social mobile music navigation using the compass. *Proceedings of the International Mobile Music Workshop, Amsterdam*.

25. John Urry. 2007. *Mobilities*. Polity Press

26. Amy Voida, Rebecca E. Grinter, Nicolas Ducheneaut, W. Keith Edwards, and Mark W. Newman. 2005. Listening in: practices surrounding iTunes music sharing. In *Proceedings of the SIGCHI Conference on Human Factors in Computing Systems* (CHI '05). ACM, New York, NY, USA, 191-200. DOI=http://dx.doi.org/10.1145/1054972.1054999

27. Xinxi Wang, David Rosenblum, and Ye Wang. 2012. Context-aware mobile music recommendation for daily activities. In *Proceedings of the 20th ACM international conference on Multimedia* (MM '12). ACM, New York, NY, USA, 99-108. DOI=http://dx.doi.org/10.1145/2393347.2393368

28. Peter Wright and John McCarthy. 2010. *Experience-Centred Design: Designers, Users, and Communities in Dialogue*. Morgan and Claypool Publishers

Understanding the Challenges of Designing and Developing Multi-Device Experiences

Tao Dong
Google Inc.
Mountain View, CA, USA
dongtao@acm.org

Elizabeth F. Churchill
Google Inc.
Mountain View, CA, USA
churchill@acm.org

Jeffrey Nichols
Google Inc.
Mountain View, CA, USA
jwnichols@google.com

ABSTRACT
As the number of computing devices available to users continues to grow, personal computing increasingly involves using multiple devices together. However, support for multi-device interactions has fallen behind users' desire to leverage the diverse capabilities of the devices that surround them. In this paper, we report on an interview study of 29 designers and developers in which we investigate the barriers to creating useful, usable, and delightful multi-device experiences. We uncovered three key challenges: 1) the difficulty in designing the interactions between devices, 2) the complexity of adapting interfaces to different platform UI standards, and 3) the lack of tools and methods for testing multi-device user experiences. We discuss the technological and business factors behind these challenges and potential ways to lower the barriers they impose.

Author Keywords
Multi-device experiences; multichanneled services; crossmedia services; cross-device interactions; design issues; developer experience, interviews

ACM Classification Keywords
H.5.m. Information interfaces and presentation (e.g., HCI): Miscellaneous

INTRODUCTION
The ability to seamlessly connect multiple devices of varying screen sizes and capabilities has always been an integral part of the vision for distributed user experiences and Ubiquitous Computing. Recent studies [7,14] have shown that this future vision is beginning to arrive, and that many users are now engaging with multiple devices in parallel everyday. Use cases range from the mundane and simple, such as checking the translation of a word in a subtitle while watching TV, to more complex and long-form tasks, such as following instructions on a phone for installing and configuring software on a computer.

DIS 2016, June 04-08, 2016, Brisbane, QLD, Australia
ACM 978-1-4503-4031-1/16/06.
http://dx.doi.org/10.1145/2901790.2901851

Unfortunately, this same research shows that these multi-device use cases are rarely supported by software and that users must act as the bridge connecting their devices. This can substantially increase cognitive load for the user and greatly increase the difficulty of even relatively simple tasks. The lack of high quality multi-device user experiences despite the availability of the hardware devices that should enable them implies that there exist design and development challenges that are not yet fully understood. To better understand this, we chose to conduct a study to answer two research questions:

- *What barriers and challenges are there to creating useful, usable, and delightful multi-device experiences?*
- *What tools and methods would be helpful to simplify the design and development of such experiences?*

Our focus is to understand what factors might be complicating and undermining the work of the designers and developers who are trying to bring multi-device experiences to users. Our long-term goal is to inform the design of tools that aid in the design and development of such experiences.

To this end, we conducted in-depth interviews with 29 professionals who are actively designing or building multi-device user experiences, revealing a number of common challenges that are unique to the design and development of such experiences. In this paper, we present the three most critical challenges they discussed:

1. The difficulty in designing interactions between devices
2. The complexity of adapting user interfaces to different platform UI standards
3. The lack of tools and methods for testing multi-device user experiences

These three challenges affect different activities in building a multi-device experience. The first challenge complicates the functional design of a system, while the second challenge burdens visual and interaction design. The last challenge can cause the implementation of the experience to be costly and hard to manage.

Our work builds on past research (e.g., [4,11]) that has predicted the contemporary landscape of multiple, potentially connected devices, and forewarned of some of the difficulties inherent in creating seamless connected device experiences, such as maintaining UI consistency across devices and eliciting user feedback on early prototypes. As this multi-device computing environment has now become a reality, it is important to again consider these issues and identify which challenges have actually arisen and which have turned out to be less important than originally anticipated.

The rest of this paper is organized as follows: We first present an overview of related work on the design of multi-screen, multi-device experiences and the unique challenges of designing for such products. We then describe our research method and processes, and present detailed results that illustrate three key challenges identified. Finally, we discuss the technological and business factors behind these challenges and potential ways to lower the barriers they impose.

RELATED WORK

Our research is related to and informed by two bodies of work: studies on multi-screen and multi-device design principles, and studies seeking to understand the challenges faced by designers and developers of such multi-screen and multi-device user experiences. To contextualize these two bodies of work, we first introduce two main types of multi-device experiences identified in prior work. We have found this distinction helpful in understanding different design goals and the challenges associated with them.

Multichanneled Services and Crossmedia Services

Wäljas et al. identified two main types of multi-device experiences: multichanneled services and crossmedia services [19]. Though it is possible for a service to be both multichanneled and crossmedia, we found this distinction useful for analytical purposes.

Multichanneled services allow the user to access the same service via different kinds of devices and platforms (i.e., channels) [6,18]. The features available on different devices might differ due to input and output constraints and usage expectations, but the core functionalities are accessible from any of the supported devices. An example of a multichanneled service is the music streaming service Spotify, which offers largely the same set of features via its Web-based player, Mac application, iOS app, and Android app. The user's data between these channels are synchronized to allow the user to move between these channels to consume the service.

Crossmedia services split functionality across different devices according to those devices' strengths and affordances [19]. A commercial example of a crossmedia service is Google Chromecast[1], which allows the user to use a mobile device or a Web browser as the remote control for a large-screen viewing device, such as a TV. In this case, each type of device is used for its strength, and functionality is largely non-overlapping between them. The experience as a whole would not be possible without at least one of each type of device being present and functioning.

Multi-device Design Principles

To understand multi-device designers' challenges, it is important to understand the unique design requirements of multi-device services in the first place. This will help us to understand the gap between what designers can achieve with the resources available and the ideal user experience they want to provide. Multichanneled services and crossmedia services have different design and development considerations and thus we consider them separately.

For multichanneled services, inter-device consistency is the most fundamental principle. Extending the conventional concept of usability to multi-device systems, Denis and Karsenty [3] coined the term *inter-usability*, which refers to the overall ease of switching to other devices for a given functionality. Through interviewing 10 users who used multichanneled services such as emails, diaries, and address books, they identified two main dimensions of inter-usability: *knowledge continuity* and *task continuity*. Knowledge continuity allows the user to apply her existing knowledge about a service learned from using a previous device to a new one, while task continuity allows the user to easily resume the task he previously worked on when he switches devices. Denis and Karsenty further argued that these two types of continuities could be achieved by implementing different levels of inter-device consistency.

The key issue for crossmedia services is the question of how to distribute functionalities to different devices in the system. Segerståhl [15] conducted a field study of a fitness tracking system that consisted of a wearable activity tracker and a Web service. Based on the results, Segerståhl argued for the benefits of specializing different devices within the system with different functionalities to reduce the complexity of individual components of the system. However, she also warned that such distribution of functionality must match the structure of the target activity and maintain a certain degree of flexibility and feature redundancy (which she referred to as functional modularity) because human activities are constantly fluctuating.

The temporal dimension of multi-device use is also helpful in understanding the multi-device design space. In a diary study of multi-device use, Jokela et al. [7] found that both sequential use and parallel use of multiple devices were practiced by users. Similarly, in the 4C framework proposed by Sørensen et al. [16], the authors make a distinction between sequential use and simultaneous use. They emphasize data synchronization and migration of the user's activity state for sequential use and stress the importance of making sure different devices play to their individual strengths and complement one another for simultaneous use.

[1] Chromecast. https://www.google.com/chromecast

In search of an overarching design principle for multi-device experiences, Wäljas et al. [19] propose the notion of service coherence, based on insights gathered from a diary study of 3 different multi-device services, including both multichanneled services and crossmedia services. They define coherence as follows: "Coherence is influenced by composition, flow of interactions and content as well as continuity." In a similar vein, Kim et al. [8] argue that an ideal multi-device experience should have "locally optimized consistent UI & globally unified coherent UX." Levin offers a more holistic approach in her 3C framework [9], which argues that *consistent*, *continuous*, and *complementary* approaches should be considered as building blocks of a multi-device ecosystem rather than mutually exclusive paths of design.

Multi-Device Prototyping and Development Issues

Previous work has also examined the challenges inherent in prototyping and building multi-device user experiences.

To motivate a pattern-based cross-platform design tool, Lin [11] interviewed nine UI designers who worked on applications targeting two or more different types of devices, including desktop computers, PDAs, and WAP phones. The findings from his interviews highlight the difficulty of maintaining UI consistency across devices, especially the consistency of menu order, terminology, and colors and graphics. Furthermore, Lin noted the lack of design tools specialized for handling multiple devices and the scarcity of cross-device design patterns despite designers considering them to be useful.

Around the same time (pre-2006), Dow et al. [4] conducted an interview-based study with eleven designers who had experience "designing and prototyping off-the-desktop applications," which included multi-device experiences but also ubiquitous computing systems in general. They identified three challenges, including design tools inadequately supporting communications between different design roles, designers lacking knowledge about the capabilities and constraints of new hardware, and technical difficulties in producing Ubicomp prototypes. Furthermore, they argue for creating tools that can enable designers to employ multiple representations, including storyboards, diagrams, and simulations, to examine and express application design ideas.

More recently (pre-2011), Antila and Lui [1] interviewed seventeen professionals whose work included "components, which are interconnected with some level of measured usability." Based on those interviews they identified four challenges. First, it was difficult to address implementation constraints imposed by specific platforms at the early stage of a project, because the tools used by designers and the tools used by developers lacked integration. Second, some domains, such as healthcare, restricted deployment of certain technologies for organizational reasons. These restrictions can negatively affect the continuity and consistency of cross-platform experiences. Third, it was difficult to get user feedback on multi-device experiences until a functional prototype can be deployed in the field due to the lack of research frameworks and methods. Last, targeting multiple platforms/devices was complicated because of the tension between the assumed need for a unified look-and-feel across devices and the inherent differences in the capabilities and user interaction metaphors of each device.

Our research extends this prior work in three important ways:

1. Prior work focused mainly on the (still important) challenge of designing UIs that are consistent across devices that have very different input and output capabilities (e.g., [1,11]). We found this challenge was complicated by the additional tension between following native UI standards imposed by platform vendors (e.g., Google's Material Design[2] and Apple's Flat Design[3]) and maintaining consistency of design across platforms.
2. Prior work (e.g., [1,4]) noted that practitioners have difficulties getting useful feedback without deploying functional prototypes in the field due to the lack of research frameworks and analysis methods to explore a realistic cross-section of contextually appropriate usage scenarios. We extend this finding by unpacking the design complexity imposed by the many, often unanticipated ways devices can interact with one another in a multi-device experience.
3. Prior work (e.g., [1]) focused on the difficulty of user testing for multi-device experiences. Our work reveals that software testing is equally difficult. Functional testing, compatibility testing, and GUI testing are challenging for multi-device developers and represent an important barrier to development. Our interviews shed light on the unique challenges of conducting these tests in the implementation process of multi-device experiences.

STUDY DESIGN

In order to identify challenges related to designing and developing multi-screen and multi-device experiences, we conducted semi-structured interviews with 29 professional designers and developers who are currently building multi-device experiences.

Participants

Participants were recruited from an existing database of prospective participants maintained by our organization, and also through mailing lists, personal referrals, online development communities, and snowball sampling.

---

[2] Material Design. https://www.google.com/design/spec/material-design/

[3] iOS Human Interface Guidelines: Designing for iOS. https://developer.apple.com/library/ios/documentation/UserExperience/Conceptual/MobileHIG/

Of our 29 participants, 16 were UX/UI designers, 11 were software developers, and 2 were product managers. Our participants came from 13 organizations, but about half were affiliated with one large technology company that offers several popular multichannel and crossmedia products. Twenty worked on multichanneled experiences, and 9 worked on crossmedia experiences. The dominance of multichanneled experiences in our sample reflects the nascent nature of crossmedia experiences in the market.

Interview Procedure

All but three of our participants were interviewed in person; the remainder through video conferencing tools. The interviews were semi-structured and issues were discussed on a number of themes: the cross-device aspects of the participant's current and past projects; tools currently and previously in use; preferred, prescribed and discarded workflows; examples of adapting UIs to different platforms and form factors; aspects of prototyping and testing designs; within-team and cross-organization and development function communication issues; and attitudes towards automating certain aspects of the design process. Each interview lasted about an hour.

All interviews were audiotaped, summarized, and partially transcribed. Affinity diagrams were created to organize the data and identify common and key themes. Analytic memos on key themes were generated immediately post-interview and iteratively during analysis to provide a foundation for synthesizing the viewpoints of different participants.

RESEARCH FINDINGS

Our research identifies a number of challenges in designing and developing multi-screen and multi-device user experiences, confirming that the nature of multi-device interactions have brought about unique problems for designers and developers. Although a number of themes are apparent in our data, in this paper we present the top three challenges that have deep implications for the practice of design and development of multichanneled and crossmedia user experiences. Table 1 gives an overview of the challenges identified and explored.

Designing Interactions between Devices

Some of our participants worked on features that allow multiple devices to collaborate either in sequence or in parallel to help the user accomplish a task. Sequential use of multiple devices often emerges naturally when a multichanneled service provides the ability to synchronize data across devices, while parallel use is usually more deliberately designed by assigning different roles to different devices involved in an interaction. Both types of interactions between devices bring about new design challenges as we describe below.

Maintaining Consistent Information Architecture

From a design perspective, maintaining consistent information architecture is critical to help users achieve task continuity and knowledge continuity when they switch to a different device that might have a distinct form factor or different input and output constraints. P16, a designer working on a travel search application said his team was aware that some users would plan their trip across several devices in multiple sessions, as he described:

"You might start [planning a trip] at work on desktop. You might do more searches along the subway on your phone. And then in the evening with your tablet."

In order to make this kind of multi-session, multi-device activity as cohesive as possible, P16 emphasized the

Activities	Identified Challenges
Functional Design	**The difficulty in designing interactions between devices** • *Maintaining consistent information architecture* • *Handling task continuity with uncertain user intentions* • *Designing and communicating complex conceptual models and business logic*
Visual & Interaction Design	**The complexity of adapting user interfaces to different platform UI standards** • *Business biases and unrealistic design ideals* • *Fuzzy boundary between platform standards and product identities* • *Unclear cost of deviating from the standard* • *Unverified assumptions about multi-device use*
Implementation	**The lack of tools and methods for testing multi-device user experiences** • *Too many distinct devices to test* • *Inadequate emulators* • *Interdependency between components running on different devices* • *Difficulty of automating UI tests*

Table 1. Selected Challenges Grouped by the Activities in the Design and Implementation Process

importance of maintaining consistent information architecture across devices. In particular, he explained:

"When you transition between devices, 'Oh yeah! That was the thing I was looking at before.' So really as much as the layout as we can keep the same and consistent I'd love to keep it the same and consistent. But the most important thing to me is that we use the same words to describe the same things and the flow of information in the unit is consistent."

An additional challenge brought by multi-device computing to information architecture design is that some of the most familiar building blocks of information architecture start losing their meanings in a multi-device world. Designer P14 provided an example of this in an e-book app that attempts to always open to the last page a user was reading across different devices:

"The challenging thing is because of the different resolutions and screen sizes of different devices... you might have 1,000 characters here [a large-screen Android phone]. On the iPhone, you'll have 600 characters. So making sure that when you open it up, you map exactly to the right location. Page numbers don't really mean anything."

Handling Task Continuity with Uncertain User Intentions

Having consistent information architecture across devices is important to support task continuity, but that is often not enough. Designers sometimes find themselves uncertain about user intentions and making uninformed guesses when they wanted to create continuous user experiences across devices.

For instance, P23 worked on an application designed for sales professionals that has both a mobile version and a desktop version. The app supports two sequential use cases. In one case, users can save sales leads on their smartphones when they are in the field and then continue researching or following up on these leads on their computers when they get back to the office. In the second case, users can collect potential sales leads on their desktop computers and then retrieve related information before or during customer meetings on their smartphones.

Eager to harness the potential of multi-device computing, P23's team initially wanted to implement a "dream" scenario, as they referred it to, in which the mobile app would automatically present sales leads the user saved in the desktop version at the moment the user opens the mobile app. They hoped that this feature would help the user re-access saved information and provide a continuous experience. However, it proved to be more complicated than they thought, as P23 explained:

"Let's say you send it but you never opened up the app and then like three days later you opened up the app. It's telling you to go to this thing that's no longer relevant."

P23's account reflects the difficulty to answer several critical design questions due to the lack of tools and frameworks for designing such cross-device experiences. The first question they could not answer, in our view, was: what is the user's intention when he/she saves a sales lead on a device? The action of saving a lead does not necessarily imply an unfinished task that the user intends to get back to. Though they could have requested the user to specify his/her intention, but P23 said they worried it would make it "a heavyweight action." The second question was: what is the user's intention when he/she opens the app later on a different device? The time elapsed between these two sessions might provide some signal but it seemed not enough. The last question was: how proactively the system should help the user to get back to a saved task? Will that reminder get in the way of another task? Without a means to properly answer these three questions, implementing that "dream" scenario would be "sometimes useful, sometimes annoying [to the user]," said P23. His team ended up just providing the user with a separate section of saved leads, which, he admitted, did not take full advantage of the multi-device ecosystem but was a safe option.

Designing and Communicating Complex Conceptual Models and Business Logic

Another aspect of the challenge was related to the complex conceptual models and business logic governing crossmedia experiences. All apps embody business logic in that they take users through a flow, but in a crossmedia experience, business logic also specifies how and when a device should respond to another. It turned out to be quite difficult for designers to understand, inspect, and communicate how multiple devices would work together under different circumstances.

To designers and developers, it is particularly difficult to grasp the application behaviors in unusual or infrequent scenarios. Nevertheless their users may find themselves in such scenarios–and it is well known that a single negative experience can sour a user's relationship with a product. P26, who was familiar with issues in developing Chromecast apps, said that properly handling how the mobile client (i.e., the sender app in a typical Chromecast experience[4]) disconnects from and reconnects to the Chromecast device was one of the hardest problems for app developers. If they were not careful about the business logic they encoded into their apps, they might put their users in awkward positions. He told us an example:

"If you don't get it right, then you leave for the day, your kids watching whatever when they come home from school. You come home. Your device sees that network and reconnects to the network, and then reconnects that app [to

[4] Chrome Sender App Development. https://developers.google.com/cast/docs/chrome_sender

Chromecast] potentially. And you blow away what someone else is watching."

In this particular case, it would be easy to attribute the fault to the developer who made its app overly aggressive on reconnecting itself to the Chromecast device. But there are two issues inherent to designing crossmedia experiences. The first issue was the inability to determine the user's intention when they get disconnected from one of the devices involved in the experience. The father in this example made a so-called "implicit disconnect" by going out of the range of the WiFi network. It was unclear to the mobile client whether he wanted to reconnect to the Chromecast later or wanted to end the experience. The second issue was that it could be onerous for the product designer to walk through all the edge cases to understand the implications of the business logic he/she designed for the application. The challenge of designing sound business logic for applications involved in a crossmedia experience was crystallized in the analogy P10 made:

"When you think about design involving all these devices, it's a conversation...How do you ping those things in a way that it's an ongoing conversation, and they speak to one another in a synced way and in a logical way?"

Designing business logic for crossmedia experiences is hard, as is communicating that logic. One example is the Smart Lock[5] technology shipped with newer Android devices and Chromebooks. One of the features offered by the technology is to automatically unlock a device based on its proximity with another device that belongs to the same user and is currently unlocked. For example, when your phone is near your Chromebook and your phone has been unlocked, Smart Lock will automatically unlock your Chromebook. P10, a designer who were familiar with the technology, told us some users found it difficult to understand how it worked and its security implications:

"We need to do a better job at explaining to people the overall mental model. I think this idea of unlock phone and the unlocked phone represents you and your phone and it lets us know that you're there... Also just understanding what unlocks what and how the system works."

To summarize, participants identified three main reasons why anticipating and designing multi-device interactions could be challenging. First, the information architecture needs to be consistent across different form factors of devices to support task continuity. Second, it is hard to provide explicit support for task continuity across devices, because the user's intention is often unclear. Third, as devices start to collaborate in a variety of ways and under many different circumstances, it is hard for the designer to anticipate all the edge cases and design application behaviors appropriate for them.

[5] Google Smart Lock. https://get.google.com/smartlock/

Adapting User Interfaces to Platform UI Standards

Multichanneled experiences need to be accessible from different computing platforms, which often have distinct UI standards and design languages imposed by the platform's vendor, e.g., Apple's Flat Design, Google's Material Design, and Microsoft's metro-style UI. Though these UI standards are useful for platform vendors to enforce a coherent user experience within their respective device ecosystems, they also have become a source of contention, as multichanneled experiences often need to simultaneously pursue two different kinds of consistencies. For example, an application is expected to be consistent with the UI standard of the platform it runs on. Furthermore, an application is expected to be consistent with its sibling applications on other platforms. How should the designer accommodate the differences between UI standards while maintaining the consistency between different channels of the same service?

Based on our interviews, many experienced designers have taken a pragmatic approach to address this question. For example P10 expressed such a view as follows:

"The native guidelines need to be respected, but there is still a lot of room for freedom and creativity within your specific product."

This appears to be a sensible way to strike a balance between the potentially conflicting requirements of platform standards and product identities. However, a closer look at our interview data reveals that achieving that balance involves a tremendous amount of work to defend design decisions against business biases, refrain from pursuing unrealistic design ideals, and clarify ambiguities between platform standards and product identity. In addition, this approach is also loaded with risky assumptions about how users may cross ecosystem boundaries. We address each of those issues below.

Business Biases and Unrealistic Design Ideals

Though none of the designers we interviewed believed that every aspect of UI design should or can be consistent between platforms, some of their business stakeholders apparently did. For example, P07 lamented that business stakeholders often prefer consistency across platforms without understanding the reasons that differences may be necessary. He said:

"Way too often they [the stakeholders] are asking wrong questions. They're usually asking, 'why are they not the same' instead of 'why are they different?' Because usually there is a reason to be different."

To pursue such design ideals can lead to a compromised user experience. For instance, P13 said:

"We were very resistant to [UI differences between apps] at the beginning. We thought, well because on one screen you scroll this list horizontally, then on the Web you should scroll horizontally as well. We tried for months to make that work until we said no one wants to scroll horizontally on

the Web...We can't stick to a rule that compromises the quality and the experience for the user."

Fuzzy Boundary between Platform Standards and Product Identities

As stated above, many designers wanted to follow the UI standard of the platform but they also wanted to maintain the consistency of those aspects of the design that defined the character of their products across platforms. However, there was little consensus nor any deep rationale for what needed to be consistent across platforms.

When we asked about consistency choices, some participants made reference to very abstract motivations and concepts. For example, P09 talked about keeping the "spirit" of the product consistent across platforms while not worrying about specific UI elements. What "spirit" is was not defined, but his strategy was to stick to a set of design principles for the particular product. Similarly, P10 argued that consistency across platforms should apply to the differentiating factors in your product. P02 and P16 were more specific about visual design and information architecture, respectively, but their answers seemed highly dependent on the project they were thinking about at the time. For instance, P16's emphasis on information architecture was related to a travel planning application that allows multi-session and multi-device searches.

Unclear Cost of Deviating from the Standard

Though our participants generally were able to find ways to accommodate both platform UI standards and product-specific designs, they did occasionally run into conflicts, in which they found little guidance to help them properly evaluate the tradeoff. For example, P12 described a situation where the brand font of their product, a shopping app, was different from the system font of Android. They ended up giving up the brand font to make the UI look closer to other native apps, because the team believed that Android users would leave negative reviews if they saw a non-standard font. However, he was never sure whether that was the right decision:

"We respected the font for Android. We used Roboto. I might be wrong... On one hand, you are alienating your brand. On the other hand, you are alienating your users."

Unverified Assumptions about Multi-Device Use

Throughout our interviews, we found that the perceived importance of respecting native UI standards among many designers might be based on unverified assumptions about how users use multiple devices in the real world. Relying on such assumptions can be especially risky in the fast-changing area of multi-device interaction design.

Some participants provided seemingly contradictory accounts about the assumptions guiding their design decisions. For example, P14 initially said she believed that users rarely cross ecosystem boundaries (e.g., an iOS user will rarely use Android devices, and vice versa). Following this conviction, she said,

"It's just a guiding principle I think [that] we don't violate the OS native experiences."

However, she was also aware of the possibility of users sharing devices that have different platforms in a household, as she later said:

"And also if you're in a family, you guys are sharing the same library, you may not necessarily have the same OS or device."

The problem was that neither assumption had been validated through user research. Leaving such design decisions to intuition and guesswork is problematic when between-platform consistency can sometimes conflict with within-platform consistency.

To summarize, designers often find themselves managing a delicate balance between respecting platform UI standards and maintaining the identity and coherence of the product across platforms. Their practice is complicated and undermined by the lack of information and methods to assess tradeoffs between different kinds of consistency.

Testing Multi-device User Experiences

Testing multi-device experiences is much more complex than testing single-device experiences. Our participants reported a number of issues, including too many distinct devices, inadequate emulators, interdependency between components running on different devices, and the difficulty of automating UI tests in cross-device systems.

Too Many Distinct Devices to Test

Since the original iPhone launched in 2007, mobile device models have proliferated. According to a report [5], there were 24,000 distinct models of Android smartphones worldwide in 2015. It is infeasible for developers to sufficiently test their applications to cover all the possible devices in use.

A common strategy to deal with this explosion of devices is to test with a handful of representative devices from each category of form factor, and then test with a few known "trouble makers." For example, P18 said:

"Everyone has a small device, a medium-sized device, and a tablet. We also have a lot of other tablets to pass around... We use some little devices that are particularly known crashers."

Some modifications made by device vendors add to the burden of testing. For instance, P18 told us:

"They [a large technology manufacturer] were using the classic browser on Jelly Bean, even though Jelly Bean was supposed to use the Chrome-based browser."

One of the consequences of having to test on many real devices is that UI design issues are often discovered late in the development process. Designer P14 told us that on-device testing was usually done during the coding process and sometimes as late as in the QA stage. She said:

"Engineers can't catch everything for every device, then QA test and say, 'this is not working on this device,' and they'll take screenshots and file bugs."

Unable to discover design flaws on certain devices early on can lead to difficult decisions and compromises on user experience. For example, P14 said:

"What really is a bummer is that we have to make a design compromise, because it's not gonna work on this one set of devices. So it looks crappy on 40% of devices, because we have to fix for the other devices. Then I looked at our metrics, and say, 'Okay. Well, you know people using that on this OS and on that device is less than a greater N, and then I just have to make a call."

For smaller app makers, the problem is likely to be more acute, since they often cannot afford buying many different devices or hiring dedicated QA engineers.

Inadequate Emulators

Emulators are supposed to help developers examine their apps when the target physical devices are not available, but the developers we interviewed rarely used emulators. The main reason was that they were too slow to be useful. Emulator makers are fully aware of this and they have started making dramatic improvements to the speed of emulators [17].While a faster emulator is certainly helpful for many developers, it does not solve the problem for those who need to access low-level hardware features for inter-device communication and data transmission.

We learned of one such problem from P20, an engineer who worked on a system that uses Bluetooth and other radio technologies to transmit data from one device directly to another. He and his colleagues had to test with more than 120 different devices to make sure that their system would work well, because different devices often implement radio technologies differently. His team could not simply test their system on emulators because:

"All they [the emulators] will be doing is forking out to whatever Bluetooth stack was installed on your desktop. For that, you are not testing what actually gonna happen on the phone, you're just testing some arbitrary Bluetooth stack. Maybe it works great, [but] that still doesn't tell you anything about the devices. Maybe it doesn't work great, but your debugging problem might not exist in the real world. So it's a problem. ***The emulator doesn't emulate hardware.*** *[emphasis ours]"*

The key deficiency of emulators, as P20 pointed out, is that they are designed to mimic the software environments of mobile devices rather than different devices' hardware properties and features. Thus, they are often not helpful for testing direct device-to-device communications, which are highly dependent on the compatibility and performance of the hardware.

Interdependency between Components Running on Different Devices

Another factor that makes testing crossmedia experiences challenging is the interdependency between software components running on different devices. How to test each component independent of the others is an important productivity question for developers who are building these components in parallel. Being in this situation when his company was developing a Chromecast app, P27's solution was to create a dummy sender application to pass fake custom messages to invoke test cases of the receiver app (the software component running on the Chromecast device that renders content on the TV). He said:

"It's extremely challenging when you're developing the mobile apps, and you have a developer developing the receiver app, and they're not far enough along to do some of the testing. You need that sort of mock workflow...to work through scenarios when the mobile apps were not even done yet."

Similarly, P29 also created a dummy sender app to test his receiver app.

Difficulty of Automating UI Tests

Also related to the distributed nature of crossmedia experiences, some participants found it difficult to automate UI tests that require triggering events on different devices in a coordinated manner. P26 expressed his concern about this issue:

"It basically is manual testing, which is really time-consuming, really hard to do consistently."

The challenge of testing was often brought by the increased physicality of multi-device experiences. For example, one manual test case we learned from P26 requires the tester to have 2 or more Chromecast units set and available, and then tap the Cast icon in the sender application running on a smartphone. The test case further stipulates that the expected results should be two or more Chromecast device names appearing on a list. As this test case shows, to successfully execute such a simple test requires manual manipulations of physical devices by the tester.

Developers would want to reduce their reliance on physical manipulations of devices in tests. Here is an extreme but illustrative example:

"We would do silly things like wrap the Chromecast in tinfoil to trigger disconnect. You know, things like that. If there were tools available that allow you to manually trigger things like that, it would've been beneficial." (P27)

To summarize, testing multi-device experiences is often inadequate, inefficient, and inconsistent for four main reasons:

1. Many software and hardware differences between devices cause applications to appear and function differently.

2. Emulators are not very useful because of their performance limitations and their inability to simulate low-level hardware stacks critical to inter-device communication.
3. The interdependency of devices in a crossmedia service makes it hard to test each component independently when the components are being developed in parallel and potentially by different teams.
4. UI tests are difficult to automate due to the need to physically manipulate devices in many test cases.

DISCUSSION

In this section, we discuss the contributions of our research, two change-drivers behind the three key challenges we identified, and the implications for supporting designers and developers of multi-device experiences.

Research Contributions

Through interviewing designers and developers who are creating multi-device user experiences, we have identified a number of challenges for design and development. These challenges were either not addressed or under-examined in past research. For example, past studies has reported the issue of adapting UIs to devices with differing input and output constraints, but they do not address the impact of platform UI standards. Our research shows that expecting designers to make the UI consistent across platforms and simultaneously follow the native UI standard of each target platform has posed both usability and organizational challenges to designing quality multi-device experiences, raising questions such as:

- How often do users cross platform boundaries?
- Will users tolerate a design that deviates from the platform conventions in order to optimize for cross-platform consistency?
- What aspects of cross-platform consistency are users like to find most important?

Moreover, we have showed that designing sound business logic governing how devices interact with one another is extremely difficult due to uncertain user intentions and the lack of frameworks and tools to allow designers to foresee disruptive scenarios. This complexity for designers has not been revealed and detailed in prior work as far as we know.

In addition, our interviews have shown that testing multi-device experiences is often an onerous effort. Researchers previously warned that user testing a multi-device experience could be difficult [1]; our research reveals that this challenge goes beyond user testing but includes several important types of software testing such as functional tests, compatibility tests, and GUI tests.

Change-Drivers Behind the Challenges

We believe the three challenges we identified reflect two broader changes in the technological landscape, which we discuss below.

The Complexity Introduced by Collaborations between Devices

Research has shown that users want their devices to collaborate with one another [7,14], and our interviews reveal that some designers and developers have started experimenting with features that involve sequential or parallel uses of multiple devices. These new types of interactions have brought additional complexity that designers and developers struggle to understand and address. There are several dimensions of this complexity. First, a device's action often depends on the properties and states of other devices. Second, devices in a multi-device system often initiate actions with one another on behalf of the user, as in the case of the Smart Lock technology. Last, designers often need to design for task continuity under a great amount of uncertainty about the user's state and intention. To their disappointment, the design tools and frameworks they use today are not well equipped to address such uncertainty in multi-device experience design.

The Continued Diversification and Standardization of the Device Ecosystems

Paradoxically, the device ecosystems appear to be undergoing both diversification and standardization at the same time. As a result, multi-device designers and developers are caught between these two parallel processes.

On the one hand, there are strong technological and business factors driving the trend towards diversification. The barrier to entering hardware design and manufacturing has been drastically lowered over the past few years due to the rise of the maker movement, crowd funding platforms, and the open manufacturing paradigm started in Southern China [10]. As more hardware vendors join the competition, they all want to differentiate their devices from others by adding unique features such as Apple's 3D Touch[6], Amazon's Dynamic Perspective[7], and YotaPhone's dual displays[8], not to mention numerous vendor customizations to the Android operating system. The second driving force is the aging of mobile ecosystems, which has already led to co-existence of many old models and new models that have very different capabilities and designs. Supporting both new and old devices is hard but often necessary to retain market share. The last driving force is the likely rise of modular phones being developed by efforts such as Google's Project Ara[9]. When such technologies become commercially viable, there will be a new wave of device customization driven by consumers and makers.

On the other hand, the OS makers have relentlessly pursued an eco-system strategy that seeks to deliver unified

[6] 3D Touch. http://www.apple.com/iphone-6s/3d-touch/

[7] How 'Dynamic Perspective' Brings 3D to the Amazon Fire Phone. http://mashable.com/2014/06/18/amazon-fire-phone-3d-dynamic-perspective/

[8] YotaPhone. https://yotaphone.com/us-en/

[9] Project Ara. http://www.projectara.com/

experiences across the products within their respective ecosystems. Standardization of UI design has been an important part of that strategy. Our data suggest that this trend complicates multi-device design and development in several ways. First, it might create a perception among designers that users have become less tolerant of UI designs that deviate from the platform standard they are accustomed to. Second, as a substantial part of the application needs to be designed specifically for each target platform, synchronizing changes across platforms become an onerous effort. Last, it is likely to become harder to design experiences that are not only cross-device but also cross-ecosystem, since standardization *within* ecosystems often means diversification *between* them.

Key Implication: Better Multi-Device Simulation

Based on our data and analysis, we believe that the ability to simulate multi-device interactions at early stages of the design and development process is key to addressing challenges related to both designing and testing those interactions.

Not only should such a simulator be able to emulate properties and traits of individual devices, it also needs to incorporate other factors crucial to producing an accurate preview of the multi-device experience being designed. These factors include but are not limited to data flows between devices, timing of actions, usage contexts, performance of the devices and the infrastructure, availability of the devices, and their security settings. Such simulations can help designers better anticipate the behaviors of the application, shorten the feedback loop, and quickly iterate the design. Furthermore, those simulations may also help designers better communicate their design ideas to stakeholders including users and get their feedback earlier in the design process. An additional use of simulation is in testing. It can potentially reduce the need for physical manipulations of devices and paves a road to more automated cross-device tests.

Some research prototyping systems, such as the Weave IDE [2] and XDStudio [12], provide features to preview multi-device interactions within their respective design and prototyping environments. Unfortunately, they lack the ability to simulate usage scenarios with authentic data and contexts. We suggest tool developers and researchers consider adopting the "capture and replay" approach proposed by Newman et al. [13], who developed a tool called Replay to support the design and testing of location-based services. Replay allows the developer to playback episodes of GPS traces captured from real users' mobile phones to examine the behaviors of their applications. There are many ways this approach might be adapted to multi-device development. For example, traces of a device's presence in specific environments might be captured and made available in a tool to allow designers to more easily explore real-world scenarios.

Future Work

In addition to building simulation tools for multi-device experiences, it is critical to update and deepen our understanding about how people use multiple devices in a variety of settings, especially as support for such experiences gradually enhances over the time. Based on what we have learned from our interviews, we suggest future work explore two particularly important questions:

1. When do users cross platform boundaries, especially within the same task? How their experiences might be affected by the differences between platform UI standards?
2. How do social dynamics, device ownership, and timing play a role in shared crossmedia experiences? For example, should a Chromecast device treat all clients equally or prioritize connecting requests from certain members of the household?

It is also important to keep track of emerging tools and practices adopted by designers and developers. As tools and toolkits for developing multi-device experiences become more mature and available, there is an opportunity to gain insights from conducting surveys and analyzing online discussions about multi-device design and development.

CONCLUSION

Support for multi-device interactions has fallen behind users' increasing desire to leverage the diverse capabilities of the devices that surround them. Through interviewing 29 practitioners working in this area, we identified three key challenges that have prevented designers and developers from building usable multi-device systems despite of growing user demand. In particular, our work highlights the following challenges that have not been extensively examined before:

- The difficulty in designing interactions between devices
- The complexity of adapting user interfaces to different platform UI standards
- The lack of tools and methods for testing multi-device user experiences

Based on these findings, we suggest further research into simulations of multi-device experiences as a way to lower the barrier to designing and developing truly useful, usable, and enjoyable multi-device experiences.

ACKNOWLEDGMENTS

We thank our participants and our colleagues for their help with the study.

REFERENCES

1. Ville Antila and Alfred Lui. 2011. Challenges in Designing Inter-usable Systems. In *Human-Computer Interaction – INTERACT 2011*, Pedro Campos, Nicholas Graham, Joaquim Jorge, Nuno Nunes, Philippe Palanque and Marco Winckler (eds.). Springer Berlin Heidelberg, Berlin, Heidelberg, 396–403. Retrieved

September 20, 2015 from http://link.springer.com/10.1007/978-3-642-23774-4_33

2. Pei-Yu (Peggy) Chi and Yang Li. 2015. Weave: Scripting Cross-Device Wearable Interaction. *Proceedings of the 33rd Annual ACM Conference on Human Factors in Computing Systems*, ACM, 3923–3932. http://doi.org/10.1145/2702123.2702451
3. Charles Denis and Laurent Karsenty. 2003. Inter-Usability of Multi-Device Systems – A Conceptual Framework. In *Multiple User Interfaces*, Ahmed Seffah and Homa Javahery (eds.). John Wiley & Sons, Ltd, 373–385. Retrieved September 21, 2015 from http://onlinelibrary.wiley.com/doi/10.1002/0470091703.ch17/summary
4. Steven Dow, T. Scott Saponas, Yang Li, and James A. Landay. 2006. External Representations in Ubiquitous Computing Design and the Implications for Design Tools. *Proceedings of the 6th Conference on Designing Interactive Systems*, ACM, 241–250. http://doi.org/10.1145/1142405.1142443
5. David Gilbert. Android smartphone boom sees over 24,000 distinct models in use worldwide. *International Business Times UK*. Retrieved January 10, 2016 from http://www.ibtimes.co.uk/android-smartphone-boom-sees-over-24000-distinct-models-use-worldwide-1514342
6. Hanna-Maria Halkosaari, L. Tiina Sarjakoski, Salu Ylirisku, and Tapani Sarjakoski. 2013. Designing a Multichannel Map Service Concept. *Human Technology* Volume 9, 1: 72–91. http://doi.org/10.17011/ht/urn.201305211723
7. Tero Jokela, Jarno Ojala, and Thomas Olsson. 2015. A Diary Study on Combining Multiple Information Devices in Everyday Activities and Tasks. *Proceedings of the 33rd Annual ACM Conference on Human Factors in Computing Systems*, ACM, 3903–3912. http://doi.org/10.1145/2702123.2702211
8. Sung Woo Kim, Han Kyung Jo, and Da Yun Ha. 2011. Different UI, Same UX: A Design Concept for Implementing a Locally-Optimized and Globally-Unified User Experience. In *Design, User Experience, and Usability. Theory, Methods, Tools and Practice*, Aaron Marcus (ed.). Springer Berlin Heidelberg, Berlin, Heidelberg, 440–448. Retrieved September 20, 2015 from http://link.springer.com/10.1007/978-3-642-21708-1_50
9. Michal Levin. 2014. *Designing Multi-Device Experiences: An Ecosystem Approach to User Experiences across Devices*. O'Reilly Media, Beijing.
10. Silvia Lindtner. 2014. Hackerspaces and the Internet of Things in China: How makers are reinventing industrial production, innovation, and the self. *China Information* 28, 2: 145–167. Retrieved October 1, 2015 from http://cin.sagepub.com/content/28/2/145.short
11. James Lin. 2005. Using Design Patterns and Layers to Support the Early-stage Design and Prototyping of Cross-device User Interfaces.
12. Michael Nebeling, Theano Mintsi, Maria Husmann, and Moira Norrie. 2014. Interactive Development of Cross-device User Interfaces. *Proceedings of the 32Nd Annual ACM Conference on Human Factors in Computing Systems*, ACM, 2793–2802. http://doi.org/10.1145/2556288.2556980
13. Mark W. Newman, Mark S. Ackerman, Jungwoo Kim, et al. 2010. Bringing the field into the lab: supporting capture and replay of contextual data for the design of context-aware applications. *Proceedings of the 23nd annual ACM symposium on User interface software and technology*, ACM, 105–108. http://doi.org/10.1145/1866029.1866048
14. Stephanie Santosa and Daniel Wigdor. 2013. A Field Study of Multi-device Workflows in Distributed Workspaces. *Proceedings of the 2013 ACM International Joint Conference on Pervasive and Ubiquitous Computing*, ACM, 63–72. http://doi.org/10.1145/2493432.2493476
15. Katarina Segerståhl. 2009. Crossmedia Systems Constructed around Human Activities: A Field Study and Implications for Design. In *Human-Computer Interaction – INTERACT 2009*, Tom Gross, Jan Gulliksen, Paula Kotzé, et al. (eds.). Springer Berlin Heidelberg, Berlin, Heidelberg, 354–367. Retrieved September 21, 2015 from http://link.springer.com/10.1007/978-3-642-03658-3_41
16. Henrik Sørensen, Dimitrios Raptis, Jesper Kjeldskov, and Mikael B. Skov. 2014. The 4C Framework: Principles of Interaction in Digital Ecosystems. *Proceedings of the 2014 ACM International Joint Conference on Pervasive and Ubiquitous Computing*, ACM, 87–97. http://doi.org/10.1145/2632048.2636089
17. Nate Swanner. 2015. The new emulator in Android Studio 2.0 is 50 times faster than before. *The Next Web*. Retrieved January 17, 2016 from http://thenextweb.com/dd/2015/11/23/the-new-emulator-in-android-studio-2-0-is-50-times-faster-than-before/
18. Tyler Tate. 2011. The Rise of Cross-Channel UX Design. *UX Matters*. Retrieved from http://www.uxmatters.com/mt/archives/2011/10/the-rise-of-cross-channel-ux-design.php
19. Minna Wäljas, Katarina Segerståhl, Kaisa Väänänen-Vainio-Mattila, and Harri Oinas-Kukkonen. 2010. Cross-platform Service User Experience: A Field Study and an Initial Framework. *Proceedings of the 12th International Conference on Human Computer Interaction with Mobile Devices and Services*, ACM, 219–228. http://doi.org/10.1145/1851600.1851637

Timelessness: User Experience of Unplanned Smartphone Use

Yong-Ki Lee
KAIST
Daejeon, Korea, Republic of
ykl77@kaist.ac.kr

Youn-kyung Lim
KAIST
Daejeon, Korea, Republic of
younlim@kaist.ac.kr

KunPyo Lee
KAIST
Daejeon, Korea, Republic of
kplee@kaist.ac.kr

ABSTRACT
Everyday smartphone use gives rise to a new kind of user experience that is characterized by unplanned use. Exploring spontaneous uses promises to improve our understanding of both the deeper integration of the smartphone into mundane activities, as well as the smartphone's potential for distraction and interruption. Therefore, we studied the user experience of unplanned smartphone use to unpack its experience qualities. For capturing unplanned use from a first-person perspective, 36 participants each produced two hours of continuous video recordings with wearable cameras. The findings introduced the experience quality of 'timelessness,' a feeling that unplanned smartphone use is a series of unrelated moments, lacking a coherent sense of past, present, and future. Unplanned use usually leaves no memory of what it was, presents no attributes of what it is, and projects no endings of what it will be. The study contributes a theoretical framework of unplanned use for experience design.

Author Keywords
Unplanned use; smartphone; timelessness; time experience; distracted use

ACM Classification Keywords
H.5.m. Information interfaces and presentation (e.g., HCI): Miscellaneous;

INTRODUCTION
Unplanned use of the smartphone is a common and widespread phenomenon. People frequently report having used their smartphones in all kinds of unexpected situations [26], and running "under the radar" for most of the time, they are unaware of the full extent to which unplanned uses fill up their time [2,27]. Especially, spontaneous uses such as checking habits comprise a significant amount of the overall smartphone user experience, as they become a pervasive routine that people cannot assign with any forethought or purpose [13]. HCI Design has already begun acknowledging spontaneous uses that are neither based on planned actions nor on accomplishing predefined goals [4,14,31], and a growing number of studies shows interest in the broader issues of unplanned smartphone use. However, they still approach those questions indirectly by framing them in different concepts of e.g. excessive behavior [12], overuse [7,13,18,20], stimulation seeking and boredom [24], or attention issues found in phenomena such as distracted use, multitasking, and vigilance [6,19,22]. There is no unifying concept or theoretical framework to these approaches, which could combine the different aspects of unplanned use.

As a potentially new user experience category, unplanned use is underexplored and therefore needs a theoretical framework that should offer (1) a simple definition of what it is, (2) a model of how it is structured (3) an explanation of its effects and why people are compelled to it, and (4) preliminary predictions of its consequences. Such framework has been difficult to achieve because unplanned use is an abstract concept that represents the absence of a goal and purpose, which is contradictory to the nature of design as a purposeful planning activity. Unforeseen practices are what design usually wants to avoid through careful forethought and deliberation, and studying unplanned use would seem paradox in this light. Moreover, unplanned use is difficult to grasp due to its fleeting nature. Typically, it leaves little memory of what it was, shows no significant attributes in the moment of use, and projects no goals and endings of what it will be and where it will lead to. This lack of temporal presence is particularly challenging for drawing meaningful data from user research, since participants are likely to be unable to make sense of and report on unplanned usages.

Methodologically, we dealt with this counterintuitive and fleeting nature of unplanned use by observing its behavior through an uninterrupted first-person perspective. Wearable cameras produced rich observation data that was then shown to the participants for recounting their experiences. The closeness of the observation and analysis led us to two key findings. On the one hand we could unpack a basic structure of unplanned smartphone use behavior by organizing it into three descriptive categories of *Self- sabotage*, *Spontaneous Curiosity*, and *Fractured Communication*. On the other, we could identify and comprehend the way unplanned use diminishes the sense of time through three deficiency experiences. These are the experience qualities of *Memorylessness* that lessens the sense of the past,

DIS 2016, June 04 - 08, 2016, Brisbane, QLD, Australia.

ACM 978-1-4503-4031-1/16/06...$15.00
DOI: http://dx.doi.org/10.1145/2901790.2901839

Attributelessness that lessens the sense of the present, and *Endlessness* that lessens the sense of the future, which all add up to a condition of timelessness.

This study contributes a theoretical framework of timelessness being the defining experience quality of unplanned smartphone use. As the timelessness quality shapes people's experiences with their smartphone, it can be used to help critique and understand how current ICTs affect people's experiences, and to help frame future design explorations.

BACKGROUND AND RELATED STUDIES

To define unplanned use for design, it is insightful to borrow from the psychological concept of Impulsive Behavior. In psychology, impulsivity [8,28] can be characterized by two basic components. First there is the experience of instantaneity, which is a moment by moment change of what we want, with little to no forethought or consideration of the consequences. Instantaneity has a present-orientation. Secondly, there is the experience of discontinuity, which entails choosing short-term gains over long-term goals, with the inability to delay gratification. Discontinuity presents a lack of future-orientation. Through their time perspective both components frame impulsivity as shifting the experience of time from the future towards the present moment. Consequently, unplanned use can be understood as the experience of instantaneity and discontinuity of time causing the absence of a plan.

Unplanned use is a common phenomenon with the usage of smartphones. Yet, it is still an underexplored category in UX design. The reason for this knowledge gap may lie partly in the plan- and goal-oriented nature of HCI's and interaction design's subject matter. However, two direct approaches to unplanned use that introduce the unpredictability of actions and context to HCI design are provided by Lucy Suchmann and Paul Dourish.

Direct approaches to unplanned use

Suchman describes how goals, plans, and design problem were assumed to be adequate descriptions of both human and machine behavior. She proves that these rarely went according to plan and that the mismatch between the users and the machine is the result of a clash between the designers' plans and users' actual executions in practice. Suchman does not present situated action as an alternative to planning, but rather demonstrates how plans require interpretation through situated action. She does not dismiss plans, but accepts them to explain the concept how plans are executed in practice. In doing so, she draws a distinction between devices built to execute predetermined plans with accuracy and efficiency, and humans who use plans improvisational and in context [30]. Although situated actions involve unforeseen uses, Suchmann's argument does not cover the complete absence of plans, being the case of unplanned use.

Dourish argues that the practically engaged and non-rationalizing way in which everyday actions take place, stand in contrast to the planned and rational abstraction of most work in HCI. As Dourish points out, this description of everyday activity is still an exception in HCI. When for example speaking in a normal, everyday way, one does not have to rationally plan each word while saying it. The meaning of a word is its use in the language. Dourish's point is that traditional approaches to HCI design are not in accord with the activity they aim to support. Most designers do it without much thought to the implicit theoretical assumptions underlying their approach to design. Among others, Dourish presents a principle of "users, not designers, managing coupling," which refers to the coupling between a design's internal representations and the context of use [7]. Again, despite the involvement of the unpredictable user perspective, Dourish's argument as well does not satisfyingly cover the uses in the absence of a plan.

Both Suchman and Dourish show that planned action often ignores the unpredictable context of use and that situational actions in design are more valuable. However, they still reflect upon situational actions as something intentional, merely driven by a situation and a context. Unplanned use, in contrast, is an action that lacks a clear intention. The value of thinking about unplanned use however remains unaddressed. For this, the following section outlines some indirect approaches to unplanned use that have contributed further knowledge to its quality.

Indirect approaches to unplanned use

There is growing interest in the unintended consequences of smartphone use. Thereby studies frame unplanned and purpose-free use in diverse themes. For example, there is the theme of excessive behavior which focuses on the negative aspects of smartphone overuse such as sleep deprivation, attention deficits [12] compulsive usage and techno-stress [13] that are habit-forming [18] and that can interfere with recovery [7,11]. This theme indirectly presents unplanned uses as a problematic result of accelerated actions.

A second theme concerns the low arousal level of users related to smartphone use. Here, boredom as an emotional state [24], and sensation seeking as a trait to search for stimulating experiences [34] are presented as unconscious triggers of unplanned use. This theme indirectly presents unplanned uses as a desire to accelerate actions.

In a similar way the third theme of attention and awareness also deals with accelerating actions through simultaneous uses. Most commonly this is found with distracted multitasking on the smartphone, where the urge to do more at the same time leads to fragmented tasks [10]. Moreover, constant connectivity compel a sustained sense of alertness between usage sessions, creating distractions to daily life [23] and increasing social expectation of availability [1]. This theme indirectly presents unplanned uses as an obligation to accelerate actions.

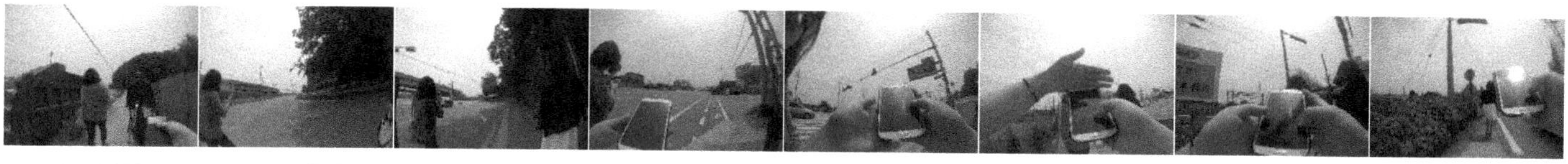

00:15:37	00:15:53	00:16:15	00:17:39	00:18:12	00:18:47	00:19:51	00:20:32
The user in the back listens to music and tries to manage the play list.	People walking together are not talking to each other, but looking at their phones.	Walking together but there is no conversation. They occasionally look at their phones.	The phone is held low to oversee the surroundings while walking.	The phone is held with two hands with more engaged use (tapping and swiping).	Glaring sunlight makes it difficult to see the screen content.	Two-handed use and text input. The walking pace slows down.	The smartphone takes more attention and the user is falling behind her friends.

Figure 1. Transcribing continuous video data by key frames

The selected approaches to unplanned smartphone use have in common that they all relate to an acceleration of actions, which essentially leads to a sense of time compression. A first emerging quality of unplanned use could therefore be considered its capacity to change the experience of time. Accordingly, we frame the guiding questions for our empirical study as follows. (1) What is the structure of unplanned use? (2) What effects does it have on the experience of time? (3) What are its consequences for the overall user experience?

METHOD

Given the shortage of empirical knowledge about unplanned smartphone use, we applied a qualitative method and adopted an inductive strategy to discover the particularities of the behavior and experience associated with unplanned smartphone use. Unlike logging studies, which have their strength in quantifying smartphone use [12] we focused on the subjective and experiential qualities of unplanned smartphone use. While capturing rich video data, we were able to observe natural behavior in more detail [25]. We chose an ethnographic method that involved video recordings with chest-mounted cameras, and a grounded theory approach for the data analysis. The research goal was to understand the user experience of unplanned smartphone use from a first-person perspective to build a model of experience qualities that surround unplanned smartphone use.

	Participant No. 31 (P31)
Age	23
Gender	Female
Occupation	College student
Device	Samsung Galaxy S4 Mini (Android 4.2 KitKat)
Use duration	More than 5 hours per day
Frequent apps	Social Networking Services, Online comics
Typical comment	"I always look at my smartphone, because It calms me down. Especially when I'm bored, I often pull down the notification bar to check for new messages or stuff like that."

Table 1. Example Profile of P31 (23, female)

Participants

We aimed at subjective insights about smartphone use. We recruited 36 participants with a mean age of M=23,5 (SD=1,5). 20 participants were female, 16 were male. We selected this demographic because it indicated the highest smartphone adoption rate. In addition, its homogeneity helped improve the internal validity of our study. 23 participants owned an Android OS Device, 13 an iPhone.

Data Collection

We held 36 separate user observation sessions. Each experiment lasted for at least one and up to 2.5 hour(s), in which the participants' continuously wore the camera and recorded their actions. There were no given tasks or behavior guidelines, allowing the users to act naturally. We intended to capture spontaneous uses by looking how the smartphone was woven into everyday activities. Figure 1 shows how we transcribed the continuous video data for each key frame.

A following user annotation session for reviewing the video material together with the participants helped us make more sense of the video material and understand the subjective experience of specific events. Participants reported on their motivations for some actions, but also admitted their thoughtlessness in other somewhat unconscious actions for which they had no straight explanation.

Data Analysis

For the purpose of analyzing the data we applied open coding following a Grounded Theory approach [5]. In a first step we converted the video data into a timeline that approximated different types of context activities, their sequence, duration, and frequency. Figure 2 shows that this timeline also served to identify certain use patterns, such as smartphone uses that the participants could not remember when watching and annotating their video recordings, or purposeless and unplanned gestures and actions with the smartphone, such as repeatedly pulling down the notification bar.

In a second step, we isolated these instances of unplanned uses through video screenshots and tabulated the use context, the smartphone screen, the actions, and the type of unplanned use (Figure 3). This table served as basis for our coding process. To identify details and particularities, we first proceeded with a round of open coding where we generated 438 descriptive codes.

	Context	Smartphone Screen	Actions	Unplanned Uses	Descriptive Codes
	The user stands up from playing the piano and reaches for her phone, which was silent and showed no alerts.	(Off)	The user pushes the home button, says "let me my check my messages," and unlocks the screen.	Spontaneous use Checking behavior	Checking, overuse, lack of self-control, Impulsive behavior, spontaneous curiosity, frequent exchanges, unplanned distractions
	While the user is engaged in smartphone use, the friends have neither eye contact with the user nor with each other.	Instant Messenger Chat List	The user scrolls through the chat list. There are several chats with 'Unread Messages' (Red Number Badge), however, instead of reading those, she selects a chat with no badge.	Spontaneous use with no crucial task	Interruption, physically there but mentally elsewhere, absent presence, no eye-contact, interrupted face-to-face talks, lack of facial expressions, less empathy, being absorbed elsewhere

Table 2. Annotation Table Excerpt of P31 (23, female)

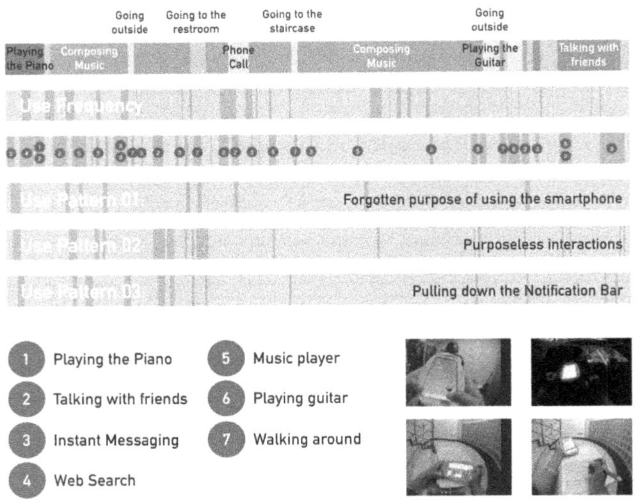

Figure 2. Timeline of P31 (23, female)

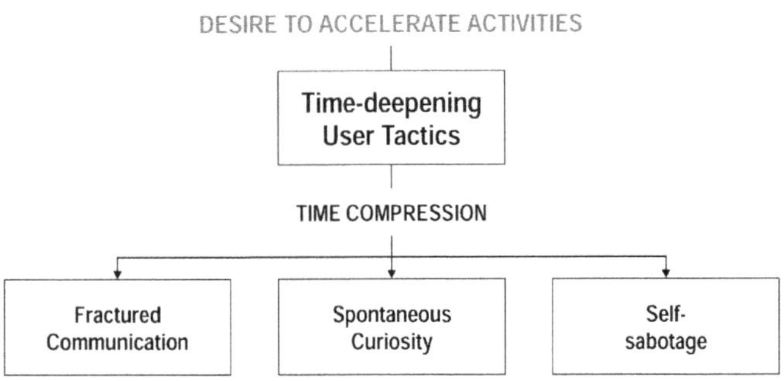

Figure 3. Behavior Categories

FINDINGS

According to our research goals, this section presents the results of our empirical study that aimed at understanding the user experience of unplanned smartphone use. We built a theoretical framework of unplanned use by showing (1) the Behavior Structure and (2) the Experience Effect.

Structure of Unplanned Smartphone Use Behavior

Driven by the desire to accelerate activities, unplanned smartphone use comprises time-deepening user tactics, which are ways to do more in the same time. This increases the number of actions in a given time period, thereby compressing the time experience. This time compression enables the user tactics to give rise to different types of behavior categories that we identified in our empirical study (see Figure 3).

In a third step, the descriptive codes were then validated by 11 researcher who reviewed and analyzed the data separately, and compared their results to build a consensus. This process was inspired by the Delphi Method [16] which is a structured forecasting method based on the principle that forecasts from a structured group are more accurate than those from individuals. It works by having experts answer questionnaires in two or more rounds. After each round there is a revision cycle, during which the group converges towards the dominant forecast. Accordingly, our consensus approach involved two revision sessions to achieve agreement over the validity of the codes. The dominant codes were then selected to represent the respective phenomenon. Table 3 shows an example of the validation and improvement of one original code.

Fractured communication

This behavior category describes excessive communication activities that lack content. As messages are broken down into shorter and more frequent increments, they lose their meaning.

> *"Digital communication becomes senseless since there is too much of it. Sometimes it seems that people don't care much what they talk about. They produce a lot of unrelated text snippets while actual conversations get shorter" (P7, 24, male)*

The absence of content can also be seen in the purpose-free use of the smartphone for communication.

> *"I do chat a lot. But most of it is just pointless. It's just basic everyday chatting. Most of the messages are pretty unnecessary... but fun!" (P31, 23, female)*

Original Code	Coder	Individual Coding	Revision 1	Revision 2	Final Code
	1	interruption	compulsive interruption	distracted interruption	
	2	self-distraction	distraction		
	3	compulsive action	compulsive distraction		
	4	temptation	habitual temptation	habitual interruption	
	5	habitual use	temptation		
	6	task interruption	interruption		
Checking Addiction	7	addictive behavior	interruption	self-interruption	**Self-interruption**
	8	useless-routine	useless interruption		
	9	routine	addictive-routine		
	10	information-checking	Checking	Checking	
	11	staying virtually present	Checking for friends	Checking behavior	

Table 3. Consensus Building of Descriptive Codes

Another aspect of fractured communication is the absence of presence. This is the case when one is physically present, but is absorbed by the virtual places that are mediated through the smartphone.

> *"There is this always available "elsewhere" when the conversation you're are having gets boring. You can shift your attention from the people in the room to the world on your phone."(P29, 22, female)*

Overall, fractured communication represents the detrimental outcomes of applying time-deepening tactics to communication. People keep the conversation short and on topics where they won't mind being interrupted. They don't feel as invested in each other and there is a decline of empathy that is usually found in face-to-face conversations, but seem to lack in unplanned smartphone-mediated talks.

Spontaneous Curiosity

This behavior category describes impulsive information seeking activities that lack a lasting learning effect. Building up knowledge is hindered by the breadth of information options and the lack of a given reading sequence.

> *"I rarely read a text in one piece. I use the smartphone to google a word or a name that I don't know. Even if it's not important to know. It drives me crazy and keeps me from focusing what I was originally reading. And I end up pointlessly jumping back and forth. Most of the times I'm left clueless about what the text actually was about."(P2, 25, male)*

With too many options decision making becomes increasingly difficult, leading to decision fatigue, the deteriorating quality of decisions made by an individual, after a long session of decision making, and the cause of irrational trade-offs in decision making [3,33],

> *"When I don't have choices I seem to want them and often will keep looking for them. But at the same time, I find that making too many choices can be quite exhausting."(P15, 23, female)*

Being unable to choose also means having no direction to move forward to. [33]

> *"I have an abundance of search potential but I cannot make full use of it because I don't know what to look for. How do you ask Google if you don't know what you want?"(P34, 23, male)*

Ultimately, directionlessness ends up in frustration and a never-ending discontent that spurs further seeking behavior.

> *"I wonder why I am always stimulated, yet at the same time bored. ...never satisfied! It keeps me going even though I'm tired" (P2, 25, male)*

Overall, spontaneous curiosity represents the inefficient outcomes of applying time-deepening tactics to information seeking. Search behavior becomes more superficial and broad, while not going into depth due to constant distractions and interruptions. Unsuccessful search attempts are frequently resumed due to a strong lure of possible success.

Self-Sabotage

This behavior category describes counter-productive activities that seek for a short-term effect while having long-term repercussions. The most common self-sabotaging behaviors are procrastination, and self-exploitation, which may seem helpful in the moment, but undermine in the long run. Procrastinators believe they perform better later on, but more often that is a way of justifying putting things off.

> *"I try to avoid difficult tasks and look for distractions, I cannot control myself but I always tell myself that it will get easier later on and that I will feel better tomorrow, or the next day."(P25, 23, male)*

With self-exploitation there is no more external force that exploits people. People exploit themselves. Much of the sense of busyness and overuse comes from tempting new pastimes, like computer games, workouts and gambling. That leaves users exhausted and sleep-deprived.

> *"I find smartphone use almost irresistible. I cannot ignore it and I cannot turn it off. I feel sapped, will-less, enervated. In the evening I use it for hours and hours, whenever I could, and I remember that feeling of tiredness and anxiety that always followed. A sense of time terribly wasted. It was like eating cotton candy. Smartphone use promises so much richness I couldn't wait for it and then it just evaporated into air. I remember feeling terribly drained after a night of smartphone use."(P35, 25, male)*

Overall, self-sabotage represents the harmful outcomes of applying time-deepening tactics to productivity.

Effect of Diminishing Time experience

The quality of experience that we observed in our empirical study is that of time incoherence and the Experience of diminishing time. To explain how we unpacked time experience we need to clarify terms regarding the meaning of 'experience.' We identified a partial view on how the term 'experience' is interpreted by UX designer. Typically, they refer to the immediate sensory experience over a measureable period of time [29,32].To explain our different reading of 'experience' we interpreted the term in its two diverse meanings found in the Japanese as well as the German language.

The Japanese language distinguishes between taiken and keiken. The literal meaning of taiken is the effects and outcomes of events undergone and evidenced by and through the body, as the Chinese ideograph for 'tai' indicates the body. It implies organic, immediate, and physical dimensions of the experience. In contrast, keiken, contains an ideograph that means "trajectory and the act of passing." In combination with the second ideograph that indicates "effects and evidence" it emphasizes the temporal dimension of experience, especially a 'pastness' of historical events. Accordingly the German word for 'experience' translates either into Erlebnis or Erfahrung. Erlebnis is more of a sensory experience from a first person point of view. It is intermittent, isolated und therefore incoherent, Erfahrung, on the other hand is continuous, holistic, and coherent. It tends to be more of a reflective and retrospective experience allowing a more distant third person point of view on oneself. Above all, Erfahrung is not confined to what a person encounters in the present moment, but rather it is the means by which one relates to all one's past and present experiences.

In summary, we see a distinction between the two distinct time perspectives of experience. On the one hand, we read taiken/Erlebnis as experiencing something in the moment, on the other we take keiken/Erfahrung as the genuine experience that builds up and lasts over time. In the following, both meanings will be applied to the various time experiences of unplanned use.

Unplanned smartphone use causes the obligation to adapt to social norms of efficiency. There is a synchronization pressure to short-term orientations that cause an incoherence between past, present, and future.

1. Present-Future incoherence: Improvised behavior undermines the ability to plan.

- The smartphone promises instant gratification without expenditure of time and energy. This is an advantage in a society marked by high rates of change and oriented to short-run time horizons.
- Time efficiency and rationality dictate short-term perspectives that remain open and optional, rather than long-term goals that take more time and are binding to just one specific option. Planning is undermined by improvisation to shortcuts. The result is a Priority of *Instant Gratification* and a devaluation of long-term future investments.

2. Present-Past incoherence: Momentarily lived events do not translate into lasting experience)

- The short-term experiential gain of experiencing is relatively high, while the enduring long-term value of experience is low. Smartphone use tends to leave users tired.
- Time efficiency also outweighs value judgments favoring the role of deadlines. Not the qualitative better, but the quantitative faster result is considered more desirable. This leads to a priority of experiencing that does not translate into genuine and lasting experience. Experiencing without experience, a state associated with shock and trauma, would be a suitable definition of the event of unplanned use.

The result is Time Incoherence which in turn gives rise to three deficiency experiences of time, where past, present, and future disconnect from each other: memorylessness, endlessness, attributelessness (see Figure 4).

Memorylessness

This experience quality describes the inability to translate the momentary act of experiencing into genuine and lasting experience. Memorylessness of unplanned smartphone use characterizes the failure to connect the present to the past.

> *"I don't remember... that's what I have my phone for." (P16, 22, female)*

Not only did the participant had difficulties remembering their smartphone use, but they felt that the device actively supported and legitimated their oblivion since it is supposed to serve as a memory prosthesis.

> *"I'm offloading' my information to the smartphone, because we should be spending our time using information, instead of remembering it." (P36, 24, male)*

The attitude of devaluing the act of remembering suggests the desire for some kind of externalized memory.

> *"If I want to find out something I go directly to the Internet. Then I forget it again because it will always be somewhere out there where I can find it again." (P32, 25, female)*

This externalized memory is expected to be out there permanently while the human memory gradually diminishes. Thus, unplanned uses are characterized by missing memories. The idea of the TV experience can illustrate that the rapid succession of decontextualized, and unconnected but highly stimulating sequences of events hinders the translation of lived events (Erlebnisse) into genuine experience. Contemporary forms of activity like television and computer games show a distinct pattern of time perception of both rapidly elapsing experiential time and rapidly erased memory traces. The lived events remain episodic. They are no longer linked to each other or to a meaningful narrative. During activities, which are felt to be short it elapses very rapidly, but at the same time, in retrospect it seems to shrink because there are hardly any memory traces left behind. Thus, on the one hand, the days and years seem to "fly" by, while, on the other hand, looking back, we have the feeling that time literally slipped through our fingers. In this sense, unplanned use is rich in lived events as much it is poor in genuine experience. The first quality of unplanned use is its memorylessness and the diminishing sense of the past.

Endlessness

This experience quality describes the lack of purpose and meaningful closure. Endlessness of unplanned smartphone use characterizes the failure to connect the present to the future.

> *"I often scroll aimlessly through Facebook and I cannot stop, even if I'm so tired of it." (P8, 25, female)*

Without an intent there seems to be no way of finding satisfaction. Aimless activities give no reason to stop. At the same time, being aimless also gives no reason to begin anything new:

> *"I spent a lot of energy on just figuring out what to do next. I'm not sure about what will be." (P7, 24, male)*

Here, the participant complained about being out of perspective due to growing contingency. Not having a direction seems to cause going round in endless circles taking away the motivation to change the current state. An ending as a closure only arises, if the beginning and the end of a process form a coherent relation, a unity in which they intertwine. The narration, for instance, can be understood as such a meaningful closure. It is only the narration's ending that can bring forth the meaning of its beginning. Moreover, a computer in contrast could be almost endlessly accelerated since its method of operation is not narrative but accumulative. Narratives, however, cannot be accelerated arbitrarily. The acceleration would destroy the internal time structure and thus the story itself. Following this analogy to narrative, we can understand the quality of unplanned use through its lack of endings. With unplanned use a narrative with a beginning, middle, and end is replaced by something more like putting together a puzzle by making connections and recognizing patterns. The second quality of unplanned use is its endlessness and the diminishing sense of the future.

Attributelessness

This experience quality describes how there is nothing that would connect individual events with each other to create a characteristic structure. Attributelessness of unplanned smartphone use characterizes the failure to enclose the present with the past and the future. Thus, time feels empty and boring.

> *"Jumping from one appointment to another creates this feeling of falling into gaps. I hate to wait in the moments in between. If the events do not connect it gets really boring." (P31, 23, female)*

Idle time is a common phenomenon with unplanned use. Its potential for boredom lies in the disconnection between a past and a future event. The in-between is experienced as having no qualities and just being boring. To the bored the present seems like nothing leads up to it and nothing will come of it. Thus, unplanned uses are characterized by an absence of qualities. The example of music shows that while listening to a melody, we take it to be a unity despite passing through different notes and rhythms. To hear a melody, means to retain the already sounded notes as a context against which the sound of the present note is experienced. Similarly, hearing this present note as one that anticipates further notes is necessary to experience the whole of a melody. Husserl called this the synthesis of protention (anticipation), presentation (momentary impression) and retention (memory) [35]. Listening to a melody means to 'inhabit' the music, both in order to integrate what has already sounded and to anticipate where it moves from here. Another way to put this is to say that experiencing music entails the ability to experience time. This synthesizing capacity of maintaining the past and the future of the melody is what we traditionally refer to as imagination. Imagination constitutes a fundamental condition for meaningful experience as such. Unplanned use is usually without protention and retention. It is as if the melody has been reduced to a single tone that does not change at all. In this sense, unplanned use can be thought of as a lack of imagination to turn the present into a coherent time experience. Unplanned uses become experiences without any qualities or attributes. Thus, the third quality of unplanned use is its attributelessness that creates empty gaps and moments of boredom. The result is a diminishing sense of the present.

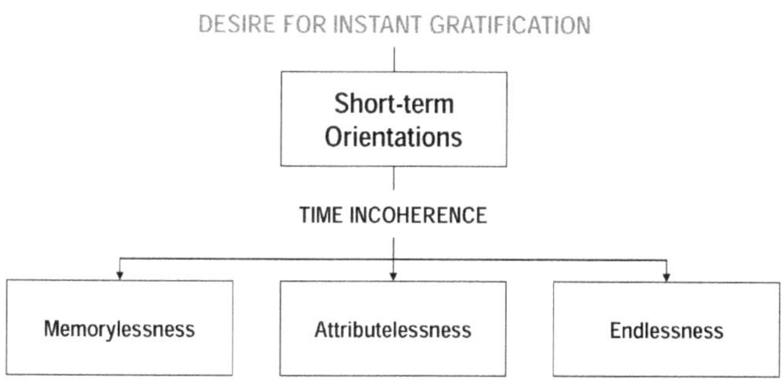

Figure 4. Deficiency Experiences

DISCUSSION

Odom introduced spacelessness, placelessness, formlessness "as a set of interrelated and paradoxical qualities that shape people's experiences with their virtual possessions"[17]. He mentioned that timelessness and temporality are significant aspects for future work. Timelessness is an equivalent to Odom's deficiency experiences, and arguing for its relevance as well as beginning to unpack its complexity were the main motivation for this paper.

The relevance of Timelessness

The experience of timelessness is about a different interaction type with the smartphone, and a different relationship to interactive products, services, and systems. A theoretical framework of timelessness could help understand how ICTs become pervasive and deeply integrated into everyday life. Beside the focus on HCI design, timelessness is also reflected in the general spirit of society and of our times. There is an awareness of a changed time experience in the information age. Information technology, especially represented by smartphone-enabled Internet, is transforming the experience of time and the way time is used. Although it is generally accepted that information technology is affecting temporal aspects of contemporary society, often the relationship between time and information technology fails to acknowledge the complexity of their relationship and is simply understood in terms of clichés such as IT enabling us to overcome barriers in time and space. While one key aspect of the effect of technology on time is that many things are getting faster, we believe the changes are more fundamental, as we have shown in the structure and experience effects of unplanned use.

Time Experience in the Information Society

The transformation of time by information technology is global and generic. According to Castells, the dominant temporality of our contemporary society is timeless time, in which the occurrence of phenomena is compressed for instantaneity and discontinuity [3] [9,15]. Information technology can disorder the sequence of events and make them simultaneous and thereby dissolved, with past, present, and future mingled in the new communication system.

Eriksen argues that the flow of information in many areas leads to the filling of gaps in time. Existence becomes a succession of repleted moments, without a before or after, or a here and there [8]. Even the here and now is threatened by the next moment, which makes it hard to live in the present. According to Eriksen, we then live, "with our gaze firmly fixed on a point about two seconds into the future." This "tyranny of the moment" greatly affects the perception of our existence. For users of advanced ICT, for instance, it gets harder to attract and keep the attention of others. The information recipients, on the other hand, might find that a slow, continuous perception of time and the control of our own time are becoming scarce. Time-saving techniques can even lead to time loss, and the enormous growth of the flow of information through ICT can lead to more confusion. If so, the thing to do is not just to gather as much information as possible but also to filter and sort out the data.

'Stacking', one of Eriksen's proposed principle touches on the difference between the www and a book. Whereas the book offers a static chain of information, the www presents a dynamic collection of information. Any individual can tap fragments of information from the www, but these fragments lack an overall interpretation. It is up to the individual to lay this down. If this doesn't happen, there will only be a collage of information instead of a cumulative insight. Another thing stacking could lead to is the slacking of attention and a declining appreciation for additional information, which, according to Eriksen, is the reason that news reports seem to be getting shorter and shorter.

Timeless Time and Smartphone use

This section discusses the relationship between Time Experience in the Information Society and smartphone use. It outlines the different conceptualizations of "Dead Time" with mobile devices and "iTime" to show how they compare to the concept of unplanned use and timelessness.

"Dead Time" is about a consequence of anytime-anywhere access. For industry players, time is money. One thing that is certain in the mobile industry is that time itself has become a commodity. Once time becomes a commodified resource (we can save and invest time, for example), it becomes not only disembedded from related value, but disembodied from any specific activities in daily life. It is only in this culturally specific connection between time and money, for example, that cultural perceptions of wasting time, of dead time, become influential. [21] Perry et al. have suggested that mobile devices act as "Lazarus devices" that resurrect mobile time, which would have previously been considered dead, economically unproductive such as time taken to travel from one place to another. This implies that an emerging mobile temporality is "Lazarus time," productive time that has been resurrected from unproductive dead time via the use of mobile technologies. The implication that time is money is relevant not only for those in the mobile business, therefore, but also for the mobile temporalities of users.

"iTime" describes how the smartphone affects work and life. In the article "iTime: Labor and life in a smartphone era", Ben Agger [36] depicts what could seem to be a dystopia of connectedness, where people are confined to their smartphones. According to Agger, the smartphone creates iTime and fundamentally alters the boundaries between public and private, and between day and night. Being online anytime and anywhere, requires a new theoretical understanding of time and place. For the working man and woman, iTime eliminates downtime, because much of their labor consists of tasks that can be done anywhere anytime. This blurs the distinction between paid and unpaid work time. And even though people resist by silencing their phones, the messages and emails accumulate, driving the need to respond. For the young, availability makes way for the compulsion to connect and not to miss anything. Time changes into iTime as connection and diversion dominate. iTime is mobile time that is portable as well as plastic. All these changes to the time experience opens new challenges for design.

Finally, in our study, there is a seeming contradiction between the analysis, being time-bound & time-aware (e.g. the use of timelines, terms such as Time Compression and

Time-deepening tactics, sense of time, etc.), and the evidence, which seems to point at the acute awareness of time and its increasingly smaller intervals, rather than at timelessness. The issue raised seems to be that timelessness, the way it has been presented here, after all, may not yet be a valid and relevant concept. However, we understand timelessness not as an unawareness or liberation of time. Rather, the concept argues that the temporal rationalizations such as *past-present-future* or *clock time* begin to lose their meaning as mental categories of the human experience. Although, we admit that humans will always remain bound to some objectification of time as a measurement of lifetime, we believe that such logical time characterizations will mean less and less as we encounter new ways of experiencing time through the use of digital and interactive technology. The acute awareness of smaller and smaller intervals of time for example is not affirming clock time as an efficient measurement, but instead criticizing clock time's limited ability to unpack experience qualities beyond productive, efficiency and usability. Therefore, we hope to contribute a different way to think about time in HCI Design.

Consequences of timelessness

The key contribution of this paper is a theoretical framework on the experience consequences of unplanned smartphone use. Unplanned smartphone use accelerates actions, forcing time compression. The felt time incoherence disconnects past, present, and future, diminishing the sense of time.

We argue that the key feature of the smartphone is not its usability, but its ability to remain under the radar while being present all the time. This ability is about the experience of unplanned use, which we identified as timelessness. The consequence of timelessness for the smartphone could be the ability to be always-ready to use, but never in the way.

This twofold condition of smartphones has the value that activities with them blend between the back- and foreground of attention. It is in-between where it is always present and absent at the same time. In other words, the smartphone never gets in the way of other activities, but instead fills out empty gaps of attention in which there is nothing important to do. Designer need to know how people fill out empty moments with unplanned uses and how they transition between the background and foreground of attention, so that interfaces offer an uninterrupted, and pervasive experience with technology. The research approach is showing how the users naturally transition between other activities and smartphone usage. Designing for the temporal transition to and from empty gaps of attention is becoming crucial.

Equally important is designing for the temporal consequences for boredom [24]. Users, instinctively tend to fill quiet time with noise. For example, they cannot stand listening to themselves, but always have to be doing something or talking with someone. It's more like they are

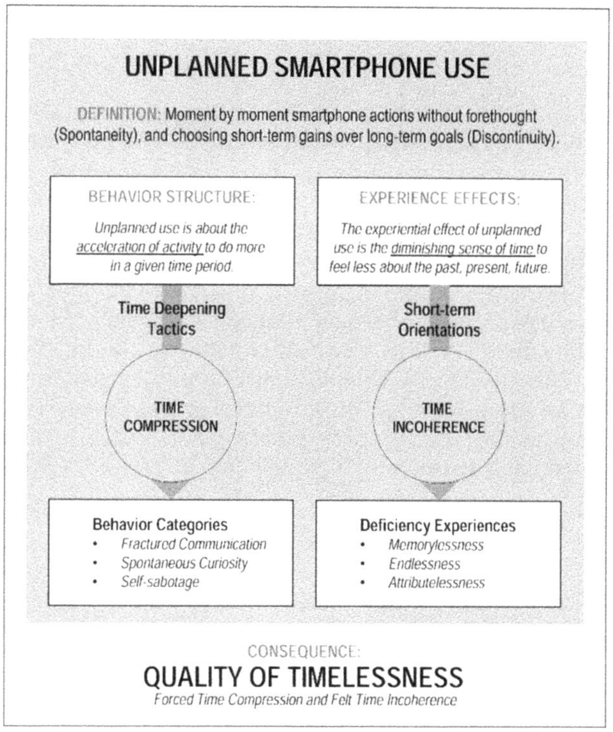

Figure 5. Framework of Timelessness

killing time than using it. Using the smartphone does not in fact aim at solving problems, but rather at postponing them; let's see first and then deal with the problem later. How to design with these kind of phenomena in mind obviously poses new challenges for HCI.

CONCLUSION

In summary, to understand unplanned use as a new user experience category, the theoretical framework of 'timelessness' had four contributions. First it offered a definition of unplanned use as the preference of short-term gains over long-term goals without prior deliberation. In other words it is the experience of instantaneity and discontinuity of time. Secondly, it proposed a model of how unplanned use behavior is structured into time-deepening tactics that produced a sense of time compression, which in turn led to the behavior categories of fractured communication, spontaneous curiosity, and self-sabotage. Thirdly, it gave an explanation of unplanned use's effects and that people are compelled to it due to a synchronization pressure to short-term orientations that produced the sense of time incoherence, which in turn led the deficiency experiences of memorylessness, endlessness, and attributelessness. Finally, this paper presented a basic model of unplanned use's consequences in form of the 'timelessness' framework, which explains the diminishing sense of time due to Deficiency- and Incoherence-Experiences (see Figure 5).

In short, this paper presented an observation and inductive analysis of unplanned Smartphone use. It defined a framework for unplanned use in terms of time experience, and it offered general implications for user experience design

Unplanned use reflects a reconfiguration of past, present, and future by contracting the distance between past history and future expectations to an instant. The result of such contraction affects human consciousness in the same way as sleep does; it removes any conscious experience. In this way unplanned use poses a great challenge to design. We have no sense organs for perceiving time, but our total awareness is able to become attuned to a greater temporal inventiveness. We have to change the way the mind and body are potentially able to experience time and space. Such an effort at the level of our imagination is needed if we are to deal satisfactorily with a whole range of time-focused environments.

For our future research we want to improve our empirical study on different levels. For example, a longer period of video recordings that would capture a complete day might yield richer data for interpretation. Furthermore, variations in the selected demographics would allow comparisons across generations and could help reach a higher degree of data validity. Finally, a mixed research approach with quantitative logging data would bring more scientific rigor to the existing qualitative analysis.

ACKNOWLEDGEMENTS

We thank the anonymous reviewers for their valuable comments and for recommending important related studies. We also thank Ilpo Koskinen for helpful insights to improve our work in progress.

REFERENCES

1. Morgan G. Ames. 2013. Managing Mobile Multitasking: The Culture of iPhones on Stanford Campus. *Proceedings of the 2013 Conference on Computer Supported Cooperative Work*, ACM, 1487–1498. http://doi.org/10.1145/2441776.2441945
2. Sally Andrews, David A. Ellis, Heather Shaw, and Lukasz Piwek. 2015. Beyond Self-Report: Tools to Compare Estimated and Real-World Smartphone Use. *PLOS ONE* 10, 10: e0139004. http://doi.org/10.1371/journal.pone.0139004
3. Roy Baumeister. 2003. The psychology of irrationality: Why people make foolish, self-defeating choices. *The psychology of economics decisions* 1: 3–16.
4. Uta Brandes. 2008. *Design by Use*. Birkhäuser Architecture.
5. Juliet Corbin and Anselm Strauss. 2008. *Basics of Qualitative Research: Techniques and Procedures for Developing Grounded Theory*. Sage Publications.
6. Laura Dabbish, Gloria Mark, and Víctor M. González. 2011. Why Do I Keep Interrupting Myself?: Environment, Habit and Self-interruption. *Proceedings of the SIGCHI Conference on Human Factors in Computing Systems*, ACM, 3127–3130. http://doi.org/10.1145/1978942.1979405
7. Daantje Derks, Lieke L. ten Brummelhuis, Dino Zecic, and Arnold B. Bakker. 2014. Switching on and off ... : Does smartphone use obstruct the possibility to engage in recovery activities? *European Journal of Work and Organizational Psychology* 23, 1: 80–90. http://doi.org/10.1080/1359432X.2012.711013
8. J. L. Evenden. 1999. Varieties of impulsivity. *Psychopharmacology* 146, 4: 348–361. http://doi.org/10.1007/PL00005481
9. Richard Harper and Eryn Whitworth. Fixity: Identity, Time and Durée on Facebook. Retrieved March 31, 2016 from http://citeseerx.ist.psu.edu/viewdoc/citations;jsessionid=7A2DE1A2A7E40D33B5EE35AD1DFFAD50?doi=10.1.1.679.7343
10. A.K. Karlson, S.T. Iqbal, B. Meyers, G. Ramos, K. Lee, and J.C. Tang. 2010. Mobile taskflow in context: a screenshot study of smartphone usage. *Proceedings of the 28th international conference on Human factors in computing systems*, 2009–2018.
11. Klodiana Lanaj, Russell E. Johnson, and Christopher M. Barnes. 2014. Beginning the workday yet already depleted? Consequences of late-night smartphone use and sleep. *Organizational Behavior and Human Decision Processes* 124, 1: 11–23. http://doi.org/10.1016/j.obhdp.2014.01.001
12. Uichin Lee, Joonwon Lee, Minsam Ko, et al. 2014. Hooked on Smartphones: An Exploratory Study on Smartphone Overuse Among College Students. *Proceedings of the SIGCHI Conference on Human Factors in Computing Systems*, ACM, 2327–2336. http://doi.org/10.1145/2556288.2557366
13. Yu-Kang Lee, Chun-Tuan Chang, You Lin, and Zhao-Hong Cheng. 2014. The dark side of smartphone usage: Psychological traits, compulsive behavior and technostress. *Computers in Human Behavior* 31: 373–383. http://doi.org/10.1016/j.chb.2013.10.047
14. Y. k Lim, D. Kim, J. Jo, and J. b Woo. 2013. Discovery-Driven Prototyping for User-Driven Creativity. *IEEE Pervasive Computing* 12, 3: 74–80. http://doi.org/10.1109/MPRV.2012.57
15. Siân E. Lindley. 2015. Making Time. *Proceedings of the 18th ACM Conference on Computer Supported Cooperative Work & Social Computing*, ACM, 1442–1452. http://doi.org/10.1145/2675133.2675157
16. Harold A. Linstone and Murray Turoff (eds.). 1975. *Delphi Method: Techniques and Applications*. Addison-Wesley Educational Publishers Inc.
17. William Odom, John Zimmerman, and Jodi Forlizzi. 2014. Placelessness, Spacelessness, and Formlessness:

Experiential Qualities of Virtual Possessions. *Proceedings of the 2014 Conference on Designing Interactive Systems*, ACM, 985–994. http://doi.org/10.1145/2598510.2598577

18. Antti Oulasvirta, Tye Rattenbury, Lingyi Ma, and Eeva Raita. 2011. Habits make smartphone use more pervasive. *Personal and Ubiquitous Computing*: 1–10. Retrieved January 17, 2012 from http://dx.doi.org/10.1007/s00779-011-0412-2

19. Alex Soojung-Kim Pang. 2013. *The Distraction Addiction: Getting the Information You Need and the Communication You Want, Without Enraging Your Family, Annoying Your Colleagues, and Destroying Your Soul*. Little, Brown and Company, New York.

20. Namkee Park, Yong-Chan Kim, Hae Young Shon, and Hongjin Shim. 2013. Factors influencing smartphone use and dependency in South Korea. *Computers in Human Behavior* 29, 4: 1763–1770. http://doi.org/10.1016/j.chb.2013.02.008

21. Mark Perry, Kenton O'hara, Abigail Sellen, Barry Brown, and Richard Harper. 2001. Dealing with Mobility: Understanding Access Anytime, Anywhere. *ACM Trans. Comput.-Hum. Interact.* 8, 4: 323–347. http://doi.org/10.1145/504704.504707

22. M. Giles Phillips. 2012. Designing for Vigilance During Intermittent Use. *Proceedings of the 4th Annual ACM Web Science Conference*, ACM, 243–246. http://doi.org/10.1145/2380718.2380749

23. M. Giles Phillips. 2014. Are Mobile Users More Vigilant? *interactions* 21, 6: 58–63. http://doi.org/10.1145/2670738

24. Martin Pielot, Tilman Dingler, Jose San Pedro, and Nuria Oliver. 2015. When Attention is not Scarce-Detecting Boredom from Mobile Phone Usage. *Proc. of UbiComp*. Retrieved September 9, 2015 from http://pielot.org/pubs/Pielot2015-UbiComp-Boredom-Detection.pdf

25. Martin Porcheron, Joel E. Fischer, and Sarah Sharples. 2016. Using mobile phones in pub talk. Retrieved January 17, 2016 from http://eprints.nottingham.ac.uk/30498/

26. Lee Rainie and Kathryn Zickuhr. Americans' Views on Mobile Etiquette. *Pew Research Center: Internet, Science & Tech*. Retrieved January 17, 2016 from http://www.pewinternet.org/2015/08/26/americans-views-on-mobile-etiquette/

27. Tye Rattenbury, Dawn Nafus, and Ken Anderson. 2008. Plastic: a metaphor for integrated technologies. *Proceedings of the 10th international conference on Ubiquitous computing*, ACM, 232–241. http://doi.org/10.1145/1409635.1409667

28. Brady Reynolds, Amanda Ortengren, Jerry B. Richards, and Harriet de Wit. 2006. Dimensions of impulsive behavior: Personality and behavioral measures. *Personality and Individual Differences* 40, 2: 305–315. http://doi.org/10.1016/j.paid.2005.03.024

29. Marc Steen, N. de Koning, and L. Hoyng. 2003. *The "wow" experience – Conceptual model and tools for creating and measuring the emotional added value of ICT*.

30. Lucy A. Suchman. 1987. *Plans and Situated Actions: The Problem of Human-Machine Communication*. Cambridge University Press.

31. Jane Fulton Suri and Ideo. 2005. *Thoughtless Acts?: Observations on Intuitive Design*. Chronicle Books, San Francisco.

32. Kaisa Väänänen-Vainio-Mattila, Jarmo Palviainen, Santtu Pakarinen, Else Lagerstam, and Eeva Kangas. 2011. User perceptions of Wow experiences and design implications for Cloud services. *Proceedings of the 2011 Conference on Designing Pleasurable Products and Interfaces*, ACM, 63:1–63:8. http://doi.org/10.1145/2347504.2347573

33. Kathleen D. Vohs, Roy F. Baumeister, Jean M. Twenge, Brandon J. Schmeichel, Dianne M. Tice, and Jennifer Crocker. 2005. Decision fatigue exhausts self-regulatory resources—But so does accommodating to unchosen alternatives. *Manuscript submitted for publication*.

34. Marvin Zuckerman. 2014. *Sensation Seeking (Psychology Revivals): Beyond the Optimal Level of Arousal*. Psychology Press.

35. *On the Phenomenology of the Consciousness of Internal Time | Edmund Husserl | Springer*. Retrieved January 18, 2016 from http://www.springer.com/us/book/9780792308911

36. iTime: Labor and life in a smartphone era. Retrieved January 18, 2016 from http://tas.sagepub.com/content/20/1/119.short?rss=1&source=mfr

The Design, Perception, and Practice of Tablet Photography

Cati Boulanger
Yahoo Labs
cati@cafecati.com

Saeideh Bakhshi
Yahoo Labs
saeideh@gatech.edu

Jofish Kaye
Yahoo Labs
jofish@jofish.com

David A. Shamma
Yahoo Labs
aymans@acm.org

ABSTRACT
People taking photographs with their tablets is an increasingly common sight. While the design of hardware is larger and more cumbersome than the smaller and more often carried cameraphones, the underlying photographic software is essentially the same. At the same time, cameraphone hardware usually contains objectively better quality cameras with more megapixels, better lenses, and faster image processing. So why do people choose one over the other? In this paper we explore the experience of tablet photography and aim to compare it with camera phone photography. In a mixed-methods study, we use quantitative and qualitative data to explore perceptions of photo quality, factors influencing photo quality, and the affordances of tablet computers that lead users to prefer them over camera phones. Our results indicate that participants take photos with their camera phone for the convenience of the small device form factor, but prefer taking photos with their larger tablet for photos that require higher definition. We discuss the design implications of this research for the design of mobile cameras.

Author Keywords
Digital photography, quality perception, camera resolution, cameras, device form factor, mobile photography, mobile phone, tablet, iPhone, iPad, Flickr.

ACM Classification Keywords
H.5.m. Information Interfaces and Presentation (e.g. HCI): Miscellaneous

INTRODUCTION
Far from the world's first tablet computer, the introduction of the iPad in 2010 changed the landscape. In 2011, the iPad 2 was released with a smaller and lighter design, and, importantly, containing both front- and rear-facing cameras. Since then people taking photos with a tablet has become an increasingly common sight (see Figure 1). Modern mobile cameras offer resolution and quality that compare favorably with much larger dedicated devices from the recent past. Current devices with somewhat similar functionality, such as the camera tablets and camera phones, differ in size, weight and ergonomic qualities. These two form factors are prolific among users, however we are still unclear what motivates photographers to choose one device over another. The form factor of these devices and specific design features may drive user interactions along with a different quality perception of the output photos.

Figure 1. Person taking a photo with a tablet. ©ⓘ psigrist on Flickr.

The core contribution of this paper is to present the intuitions and usage of two similar yet different form factor camera devices, the iPhone and the iPad. By studying the perceived affordances [29] of these two devices, we find that the perceptions of quality do not match the objective quality these devices offer and we propose that the form factor of camera devices affects the perceived quality of the photo. We are interested in the following research questions:

***RQ1:** Why do people take photos with their tablet if they own a camera phone with a much higher resolution camera?*

***RQ2:** How does the form factor of a device change the perception of the photo quality it produces?*

To answer this research question, in this paper we contrast tablet and smartphone photography, focusing primarily but not exclusively on the iPhone and iPad. We identify people who prefer to take, view and share photos on their iPad versus their iPhone, regardless of differences in photo quality between the two devices. We study this phenomenon through a formal analysis of over 9,000 forum comments, followed by a survey of

DIS 2016, June 4–8, 2016, Brisbane, Australia.
© 2016 ACM ISBN 978-1-4503-4031-1/16/06...$15.00.
DOI:http://dx.doi.org/10.1145/2901790.2901810

305 participants, and large scale log analysis of over 250,000 users posted photos on Flickr taken by both iPad and iPhone. Finally, we complement our study with in-depth one-to-one interviews of 12 respondents.

We find that device form-factor modulates a user's concept of quality and resolution, regardless of underlying hardware specification of the camera itself. Our findings provide design implications and opportunities for enriching the mobile photography experience.

RELATED WORK

Past comprehensive research using mixed methods contributes an understanding of why and how people choose to use tablets [27]. It identifies how tablet use differs from that of other computing devices and proposes to understand in future work why people transition between devices. Our research seeks to understand why people transition between taking photos with tablets and taking photos with mobile phones. Previous research identified the use of smartphones to primarily communicate activities in contrast to tablets which showed more variety of use and secondary activities such as watching TV, eating or cooking [28]. Then, by collecting and analyzing 38,017 incidences of smartphone and tablet use, they found that the % of incidence for photo taking was similar for smartphones and for tablets: the taking of photos had a 2.1% incidence on tablets and 2.7% incidence on smartphones. To further explore this phenomenon we examine what motivates users to choose the tablet over the smartphone to take a photo.

Tablet use and form factors

Previous work in HCI has explored novel camera form factors such as a mobile device for children to capture and edit pictures [24], a tablet camera to capture geometrical shapes [4], a novel interaction that positions a camera with a suction cup on various surfaces for self-photography [17], small wireless cameras embedded in toys for children to take action shots from multiple viewpoints [39], tangible tokens for camera phones that represent multiple shots in a story [38] and a camera hidden in a paint brush to paint with photos [32]. Research has introduced participatory design sessions to incorporate users' motivations into new cameras [24, 38]. Other research compared tablets to conventional laptops or desktops to investigate user performance during photo browsing tasks on an iPad [16], described emergent applications of tablets in specialized use-cases such as a multimedia controller [15], a tool for medical students [18], a crowd-based performance device [33], and a collaborative document reading tool [31].

There has been consumer discussions on how to be a better iPad Photographer [8, 14], however, we found no prior work that examines the form factors of mobile devices and how it affects the photo taking experience. We are therefore exploring the relationship between the form factors of two similar mobile cameras and their user interactions. We compare how and when people use camera-tablets and camera-phones, how they perceive the quality of the photos they take, and which device they use for serious versus everyday photos.

It is useful to note that camera phone and tablet models vary drastically in image quality, and that tablets frequently have significantly lower megapixel (MP) cameras than comparable smartphones, see Table 1. We recognize that megapixels are not the sole measure of camera quality, but it provides a useful comparison point. In addition, smartphones are replaced more frequently than tablets, and we nearly always found that for users with both tablets and phones their phone had an objectively better camera [26].

Tablets		**Phones**	
Model	*Resolution*	*Model*	*Resolution*
iPad 2	0.7 MP	iPhone 4	5MP
iPad Air	1.2MP	iPhone 6S	12MP

Table 1. Examples of the rear-facing camera sensor resolutions.

Digital photography

Digital photography has been the subject of research in HCI for many years. Phone photography has been described as the emerging dominant method for low-end consumer digital imaging [11, 1]. How and why people use camera phones has been explored [20, 19] along with various underlying motivations for taking individual photos [25]. Prior work has explored the perception and possession of digital archives [30, 13, 12]. Researchers have also explored what happens after photographs are taken when the photo is socially shared [35, 36].

Several studies examine success metrics and the perception of photographic success. For instance, it has been shown that an increase in contrast and exposure positively affects the number of views and comments on photos [2]. Researchers have conducted workshops to inform the perception of painting and art works on tablets, identifying the democratization of digital art-making but also tensions for establishing artists [5]. Beyond disparate observations, a set of design implications and several frameworks have been proposed, taking into account the potential value of new digital photo management tools with search and browsing functionality [22] as "lifecycle" understanding regarding what people currently do with video technology in the home [21].

STUDY DESIGN

Our aim is to understand the usage interaction between two similar, yet differently sized mobile cameras, the iPad tablet and the iPhone cellphone. For this, we used the following mixed-method phased approach.

1. **Forum analysis:** We began by analyzing approximately 9,000 blogs and forum posts related to tablet photography to understand the larger picture of phone and tablet photography and use.
2. **Survey:** We used the forum analysis to narrow our focus in a survey posted on Craigslist. We obtained usage data and qualitative comments from 305 participants.
3. **Interviews:** Finally, we selected twelve participants from the survey who reported that they used both smart phones and tablets for photography for in-depth, one-on-one interviews.
4. **Data Patterns and Analysis:** Simultaneously with phases 2 and 3, we analyzed and compared the metadata

Categories	Examples
Form factor	size, screen, grip
Functions	all-in-one device, email
Content	landscape, portrait, selfies
Sharing	co-located, remote
Photo management tools	editing, effects
Quality	resolution, colors
Context	indoor, outdoor
Specific to a population	grand parents, children
Fashion statement	design

Table 2. The categories generated to summarize the forum data

of photographs on Flickr taken by the more than 250,000 Flickr users who take photographs with both iPhones and iPads. We used the survey and interviews to surface hypotheses (like People take more pictures of animals with their iPads than their iPhones) which we could explore in the large data set.

Forum analysis

We initiated our study by reviewing community forums, exploring the broad theme of tablet photography. We examined 440 threads with an average of 20 posts each, for a total of approximately 9,000 comments in community forums and blogs that discuss mobile cameras, such as: `cameras.reviewed.com`, `mashable.com`, `engadget.com`, and `gizmodo.com`.

We conducted forum analysis similar to previous HCI research [10]. We used a set of keyword phrases that yield themes not originally specified but consistent with our motivation. We keyword filtered threads and posts targeting our initial motivation to understand the reason behind taking photos with a tablet, e.g., "screen", "tablet", "iPad". These initial search phrases helped surface user comments like: the iPad has a bigger screen while framing a shot, which gave insight into additional keywords to use in searches, e.g., "framing". We then ran an inductive analysis to code the data [34].

We organized comments, per category, pertaining to the features users like in their tablet, for instance comments such as the iPad has a bigger screen for checking a photo, is coded as to belonging to the *form factor* category, and comments such as the iPad does not make sense for selfies but makes sense for a group of people is added to the *content* category. We developed nine categories to summarize the raw data and convey key themes and processes. We gathered this community forum data to generate a list of specific categories, see Table 2, that forum participants mentioned about mobile photography with tablets and camera phones. We used these categories and associated statements to guide the design of our survey and open-ended interview questions.

Survey

We placed our survey on Craigslist in the following major US cities: Atlanta, Austin, Boston, Chicago, Dallas, Las Vegas, Los Angeles, Miami, New York, Philadelphia, Raleigh, San Diego, San Francisco Bay Area, Seattle, and Washington DC. First, we wanted respondents to rank mobile devices based on the type of activities participants undertake with the device, the type of photos participants take and share with their devices. Second, we wanted to understand the perception of value of the photos taken on each different device by the participants and by the people with whom they shared the photographs. We began our survey by explaining our interest in mobile photography, and that this survey was also a pre-screening survey: we would select several participants who fit our criteria to participate in a more comprehensive one hour long interview over Skype, for which they would be offered a US$50 gift card.

	Device	
	Tablet	*Phone*
Use Weekly	45%	99%
Use Daily	18%	77%

Table 3. The Percentage of survey participants and the frequency at which they take photos per mobile device.

We received 305 fully-completed surveys. Out of the 53% participants who use a tablet at least once a week, 72% of them take photos with their tablet and 98% of them also take photos with their phone, at least once a week. This finding suggests that people take photos with their tablet even if they own a phone. We present the percentage of survey participants and the frequency at which they take photos per mobile devices in Table 3.

Next, we asked: Which kinds of photos do you take at least once a week? for the different devices they use, and provided them with seven categories roughly based on a previous photo study [2]: selfies, individual photos, whiteboards (or screenshots or receipts), food, group activities, places and landscapes, and other (Figure 2). Participants reported taking more photos with their phone than their tablet across all categories. However, they do still take a substantial quantity of photos with their tablet even though they own and carry with them a camera phone. The largest difference appeared in photos of food, places and landscapes. The smallest difference is in the generic *others* category. The text analysis of the open-ended answers for the *others* category suggest that the category was a surrogate for the highly prevalent *pet* photo. Participants reported in the open ended answers that they frequently take photos of their pets with their tablet, which also surfaced in the log analysis and during the interviews.

As part of the survey responses, we also received 359 open-ended comments in addition to the more structured questions. The open-ended comments relate to the type of device and editing tools they use, the types of photos they take and share, how good they feel about their photos with the devices they use and a miscellaneous section including anything else they wanted to tell us. We used the open-ended answers as supporting data to structure our in-depth interviews with the selected participants. These results will also be included in the analysis section of the paper.

Data Patterns and Analysis on Flickr

We based our study on over 250,000 users who shared both iPad and iPhone photos on Flickr. From the public API we looked for people with iPad photos then checked to see if they

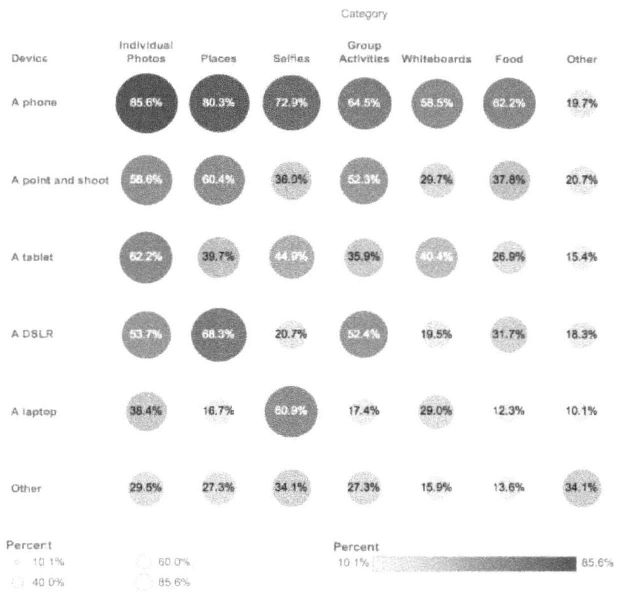

Figure 2. The percentage of survey participants who take photos in a given photo category per device.

had also uploaded iPhone photos; we limited our study to users who had uploaded at least 50 iPad photos and at least 50 iPhone photos. The total number of photos shared by this set of users that are taken by iPhone is over 66 million, and the total taken by iPad is over 2 million. We extracted anonymized metadata from a sample of these photos for further analysis, and only public data was used throughout the study. We looked at basic usage statistics of photos and tags shared across each group of categories, see Table 4 which shows photos shared by iPhone are significantly more frequent than photos shared by iPad.

We find that many face, groupshot and portrait photos are taken by iPhone while iPad is used less in these categories. We also find that categories of text, animal and general indoor are more common among photos uploaded by iPad. We can see that these categories are widely photographed by iPad compared to all other categories of photos. This finding also confirms the results found in the survey and during interviews. Overall, people take more photos with their iPhone than with their iPad. On average, for these photographers, who have uploaded at least 50 iPhone and 50 iPad photos, 63% of photos are taken by iPhone, while 7% of photos are taken by iPad. The rest of the photos are taken by other type of cameras.

SEMI-STRUCTURED INTERVIEWS

Based on these preliminary findings from the forum analysis and the open-ended comments from the survey, we found that the tablet's larger screen is a motivational factor for taking photos with the tablet. We found insights that users were more keen to take photos with their tablet because of the larger preview window before taking a photo, functioning as a preview window that is naturally smaller in camera phones. Most specifically, the preview screen is larger on the tablet than on the camera phone, allowing photographers to capture what they feel is a "larger" photo, and therefore giving the impression to capture a photo of "higher resolution". Our hypothesis that *device form-factors modulate a user's concept of quality and resolution* began to be confirmed with the findings from the survey. We explored this hypothesis further in our in-depth interviews.

Participants

We selected twelve participants from the survey. Participants were recruited against several criteria, including gender, age, occupation, the type of camera they use at least once a week, frequency of photo taking, the type of photo they take at least once a week, and how good they feel are the photos taken by their different devices. These criteria were used to target a sample of participants that was representative of the current US population of mobile photography users as possible.

Of all 12 participants who took part in the interviews, 5 were men and 7 were women. They ranged in age from 22 to 50. Our participants come from urban, suburban and rural locations across the US: urban (6), suburban (4), and rural areas (2). There was a wide range of tablets and smartphones use, see Table 5. Some participants also owned a point and shoot camera ($n = 7$), GoPro recorder ($n = 3$), and a DSLR ($n = 2$). All selected participants took photos with both tablet and camera phone. Half of them ($n = 6$) took photos with their tablet at least once a week. All participants took photos with their tablet, even if occasionally, with only one participant who rarely took photos with her tablet. Because a photography background might impact the manner to articulate the nuances of image taking and reception, we selected to interview a range of photographers: from the ones who had no notion about photography ($n = 2$), the ones who had some notion of photography ($n = 8$) to advanced photographers ($n = 2$).

Interview process

We ran twelve in-depth semi-structured interviews. We had prepared a set of interview questions to prompt discussions based on the participant's open-ended answers in their surveys, around tablet versus camera phone usage scenarios, and around photography workflows with multiple devices. We asked, for instance, the following questions: "When is the last time you took a photo with your phone, can you tell me about it?" "When is the last time you took a photo with your tablet, can you tell me about it?". Our interviews lasted about one hour, and ranged from 40 to 70 minutes. We conducted interviews with each participant until we reached data saturation [23] in the stories we were hearing from participants. Twelve interviews were conducted on Skype. Prior to the interview, we asked participants to sign a consent form. During the interviews we asked participants to have their tablet and phone accessible. We did not collect photos on these devices to protect participants' privacy, however participants shared their photos during the interviews to show the ones they take with each device. We received permission to record their interviews for later transcription.

We began with warm-up questions around the place they live in and if they like to take photos of these places. We then asked participants to tell us about their use of mobile devices

	iPad					iPhone				
	min	*mean*	*median*	*max*	*mean percentage*	*min*	*mean*	*median*	*max*	*mean percentage*
Face	0	1,359	18	32,619	12%	0	9,651	85	119,243	37%
Groupshot	0	670	8	12,749	5%	0	2,856	27	8,451	12%
Portrait	0	936	12	28,569	9%	0	8,458	76	96,785	30%
Outdoor	0	8,743	24	67,845	39%	0	18,285	39	106,785	62%
Indoor	0	1,023	14	32,968	50%	0	4,857	42	23,001	31%
Text	0	845	8	11,175	28%	0	1,034	9	12,067	6%
Animal	0	92	12	4,769	19%	0	239	12	6,642	2%

Table 4. Basic statistics of iPad and iPhone photos per category. We limit our analysis to users who have both iPad and iPhone photos and have shared at least 50 iPad and 50 iPhone photos to avoid accidental uploads/shares. We can see that in general photos taken by iPhone are more common. We also see that categories like text and animal have more iPad photos while groupshot and portraits are less common.

Tablet		Phone	
Model	*Count*	*Model*	*Count*
iPad	7	iPhone 6	4
iPad mini	2	iPhone 5	5
Google Nexus 10	1	Android Mini	1
Galaxy 4 Tablet	1	Galaxy Note 3	1
Verizon Ellipsis 8	1	Samsung 5	1

Table 5. Count of mobile cameras owned by our participants

to take photos, which ones they own, and asked them to tell us a day in their life using these devices. We asked them about when was the last time they took photos with each device. We asked them why would they choose to take a photo with a tablet if the phone is with them and vis-versa. We asked their experiences with photos they had taken and shared and their preferences between devices. To continue the flow of the interview, and if the participants did not continue their explanation, we would then ask them more details when they used terms such as "photo quality", or "serious photos". If they introduced these terms, we used them subsequently in the context of how they framed it and continued the interview. We transcribed the interviews using a professional transcription service. We then reviewed and coded the raw data, listed the tablets and phones the participants use, and developed key themes and processes for tablet photography that we present in the analysis section of this paper.

We initiated our mixed methods study by exploring the question of why people take and share photos with their tablet if they have a higher quality camera on a smaller camera overall housing in most camera phones today. We remind the reader of the previous data regarding objective measurements of camera quality; for 10 of our 12 interviewees, their tablet camera was actually worse (in terms of raw megapixel and quality metrics) than their mobile phone camera.

We discuss the following three themes that arose from our analysis:

1. Users perceive the photo resolution as being higher on the tablet.
2. The large preview screen of the tablet makes it easier for users to preview, capture, edit, collaborate and share photos.
3. Users reserve the tablet for serious photos and to capture the perfect moment.

FINDING 1: USERS PERCEIVE TABLETS TO TAKE HIGHER QUALITY PHOTOS

In this section, we summarize findings on participants' perception of the photo quality on their tablet, the photo resolution previewed on the screen, the camera resolution, the printed photo and more specifically the difference in between the rear and front cameras on both the phone and the tablet. Our interviews with the participants confirmed what we found in the survey: people take photos with their tablet because they like the clarity of the photo in tablet. P8 described the photos from the camera phone as blurry, fuzzy or not clear: *When I take cell phone pictures, it turns sort of blurry. It is not that good at all. My best photos come from my tablets and the point and shoot. The picture is not fuzzy.*

Participants told us that even though their tablet takes better photos, they still take more photos with their cell phones. They explained that their camera phone is *always* with them, because of its smaller size, and therefore available more frequently to take random photos. However they do use their tablet when they identify that they need a photo with better colors and more details. Participants who take photos with a tablet, even if once a month, reported preferring the quality and details of photos taken from their tablet rather than from their phone.

Quality: clear pictures

When asked about photo quality between their multiple devices, participants reported that the camera on the iPhone 5 was a much lower quality than their iPad. Here is an excerpt representative from this type of opinion from P7 who used an iPhone 5 and iPad 2nd generation: *I think the iPad is a LOT better quality and is a LOT better editing device* [in comparison with iPhone].

We asked P11 who takes photos with a GoPro (a 12MP camera), an iPad (in her case a 1.2 MP camera) and an iPhone 5 (a 8MP camera), how she compares the photo quality between the GoPro and the iPad: *The quality I think is close to the same. As far as the colorness and crispness, I think they're pretty similar. That's how I feel about that. They're both better than my phone.* Because the term *quality* has different interpretations, we sought to understand what participants mean by *the quality is better.* P11 further explained: *The clearness of the picture, the crispness. I think that sometimes my iPhone is blurry and I think that the colors are just clearer and it is just more clear on the iPad.*

Participants like to have a larger picture on their tablet than on their phone, and also prefer the overall photo quality, e.g. the colors and sharpness of the photo, taken on their tablet. We found that the physical preview size on the screen influences participant's understanding of how high the resolution of their photo. As explained by P4, more megapixels can be seen on the screen itself because of the larger screen and therefore he validates his observation by looking at the larger photo on his tablet:

> I believe the tablet has got higher resolution of megapixel than the cell phone. It might take more digitally, because my cell phone might not be able to give me more detail than the tablet, because of its small screen. Initially, I can see the comparison of my cell phone versus my tab picture by watching. I obviously believe that I'll get much better output in tablet than the cell phone because of the megapixel or the camera itself. (P4)

P4 also explained that being able to see more details on large screen of the tablet gives the impression that the photo ends up being of higher resolution than the one taken from a camera phone.

During our interviews, participants were articulate to describe the term quality in the sense of the *high resolution* of a photo. They also conveyed more than just the quality of a photo from a resolution standpoint. The quality of a photo is also derived from being able to frame a photo properly, being able to zoom in a photo appropriately, and overall to be able to have more control over the end result of a photo: *I guess when I want a clear picture, I think of my iPad. I like the color on the iPad better. I think I also like it because it's a bigger screen that I can see the actual results of the photo. (P10)*

Quality: printing quality

When one takes a photo with more megapixels, or a higher resolution photo, one can crop it down if necessary. The higher the resolution, the more likely the photo remains in high, printable, resolution after being cropped. We found that participants understand this exact notion of high resolution photo, and yet deliberately choose their tablet to take photos for that reason. For instance, P10 explained that she takes a *larger photo* on her tablet to have the option to scale it down and still have a photo of high definition:

> I could definitely put more on the iPad. I think that's why a lot of times when I'm outside or doing things like that, I like to at least have the option and take it largely, and then scale it down. (P10)

While this can again result of larger screen size and better viewing control, it might also be due to very high resolutions in today's cameras. After a certain point, the higher resolution is not noticeable on an ipad screen or a printed photo. We asked our participants if this difference in photo quality between their tablet and their camera phone was also noticeable on printed photos. Participants reported printing their photos from their tablet, and noticing a quality difference when the photos were printed on photo paper from the tablet versus the camera phone. They also explained that printing photos of high quality is the main reason they choose to capture photos with their tablet instead of their camera phone:

> The print itself, the print copy. Definitely. I would love to have a glossy picture so that I can feel it. That's one of the important aspects of getting the picture through the tablet. (P4)

When the photos are printed on paper, participants perceive the photos coming from the tablet as being of higher resolution.

Quality: front vs. rear cameras

To further understand the connection between megapixels and received quality, we explored a specific case, where the cameras are on the same device and of drastically different quality. We asked our participants about the front and back cameras of their camera phones and the tablets. These two cameras are different. For instance, on the latest iPhone 6 model, the iSight camera (rear) is 8 megapixel with a f/2.2 aperture while the Facetime camera (front) is a 1.2 megapixel with a f/2.4 aperture. Surprisingly, out of our 12 participants, only P9 noticed a difference of photo quality when the photo was taken from the front versus the back camera on the same device. All other participants mentioned the use case being different, for instance that the front camera is used more for selfies and therefore the lighting of the scene is naturally different.

But for these participants, there was no difference in photo quality between the front and the rear cameras in their mobile devices. Our participants tend to exclusively use the front camera of their mobile devices for selfies, in particular with the camera phone, and this context of use seems to override the ability to notice a change in photo quality or megapixel, because they have nothing to compare it to: they always take selfies with the front camera.

The two participants who replied in the survey occasionally or rarely taking photos with their tablet, reported during the interview that the photo quality on their tablets was worse than on their phone. The ten other participants who replied in the survey frequently taking photos with their tablet, reported during their interview that the photo quality on their tablet was better than on their phone. The participant's perception of how the device enables quality photos drives their decision to use a particular device.

FINDING 2: LARGE SCREENS ARE FAVORABLE

In this section, we analyze participants' preference for a larger preview screen on the tablet. We looked at how the larger screen facilitates their photo preview, capture, collaboration and sharing process.

Our interviews with the participants confirmed what was found in the forum analysis and in the survey: one of the reasons people take photos with their tablet is the larger screen: *You can see more you can do more! (P6).* With a larger window participants reported that it is easier to assess how a photo will appear. In particular, our subjects were enthusiastic about the previewing capabilities afforded by the tablet's large screen and feedback for zooming, aiming and framing. Our participants reported that the larger preview of the photo that is about to be taken is essential in their tablet photography experience, especially if the photo will be shared on social networks.

Large screen: you can fit more in the photo

Participants reported that the larger screen of the tablet allows them to fit more elements in the photo. This ability to fit more in their photos, for instance family members, is a factor that will make them choose the tablet over the camera phone. The same was reported in the panoramic feature in the iPad versus the iPhone. One of the participants explained that she can capture more elements at once with a tablet than with a camera phone:

> I feel like I can get the whole picture. The whole . . . What I'm trying to show. I don't just get the tree or a little bit of background. I can keep the whole scenery. It makes me more comfortable because I can do it with different angles, more so than I could my phone. My phone is a nice phone, the resolution is high, but I could only get so much. I can get maybe 2 kids, 3 kids. If not, I'll have to back up some more to get more of the background. (P9)

As a result, people tend to notice that their photos from their tablet has a richer content, it is more about the ensemble and the entire family than quick snaps or selfies.

Participants expressed at multiple occasions that one of the main advantages to taking photos with their tablet is the ability to better control what will be in the picture:

> The photos I take on my iPad are usually a lot better composed. And the cell phone is usually a very quick, 'I need to remember this', click, keep walking kind of thing. But my iPad photos, I definitely am aware that I'm thinking more about the actual composition of the photo. (P12)

For a couple of participants ($n = 3$), it is unclear if they can fit more in a photo because the screen is larger or if it is because the camera has a wide angle. Other participants explained that the tablet has a wider angle camera compared to the one of a camera phone, that way they can fit in more elements into a photo. Therefore, it seems that the details from the screen on the tablet, the perceived camera quality, and the wide camera angle makes the tablet the device of choice when taking photos of groups, of family members and of special events.

Large screen: better control

From our forum and survey analysis, we knew that the preview window from the tablet helps people frame their picture better. The overall picture comes out better from the tablet because the participants can preview their shot, with the proper light, angle, and overall scene composition on a larger screen, offering more control over their final photos.

In our interviews, participants explained that the wider screen of the tablet makes it easier to obtain the desired photo. P4 told us he didn't need to move much to get the right angle with ipad. Other participants also mentioned that the large screen offers the ability to select the right angle, and also have a better visual feedback as to where to zoom in on a scene.

The wider screen on the tablet allows people to control the frame better and take less photos with the iPad because they can quickly get the photo they want. We found that one of the reasons people take lots of snaps with their camera phone and a lot less with their iPad seems to be because the preview screen is larger on the tablet, and as a result our participants tend to think that tablet takes the right picture the first try:

> Well the iPhone I just have with me all the time so I just always snap pictures and snap pictures and snap pictures. Sometimes I take three or four of the same picture just in case it doesn't come out. But the iPad, I know it's going to come out well, so I just usually take one. (P5)

Interestingly, during data analysis we observed that 63% of photos posted were taken by iPhone while only 7% of the photos were taken by iPad.

Large screen: more flexibility in distance with camera

A tablet is easier to physically hold further away from oneself, particularly during crowded events: *when you hold it out you can hold it farther and see it to take a good picture (. . .) I think is quite useful with the iPad because of the larger screen.* (P3) Users can hold the tablet above their head, tilt the tablet slightly and take their photo, as explained this participant during his trip to Hawaii, but also mentioned at multiple occasions by other participants:

> I was in Hawaii at the volcanic part with this huge volcano and there's a wall, there's some people with iPads holding it out and they can see what they were taking a picture of and hold it out and see on a screen so they're holding it maybe two and a half feet away from their face and they have it past the little bushes in the wall and they could take the picture and they could see it on screen and know they took a good picture instantly while they're taking it. Whereas if you had a small little screen on a small phone, you're not sure. (P2)

Large screen: Photo editing

Over the course of the interviews, our participants reflected upon the photography process with their tablet, identified the advantages of a large screen and the perceived higher resolution of their photos, and told us that a successful photo is more than just a photo of higher resolution. 11 out of the 12 participants told us that the tablet interaction, because of the larger real estate to interact with elements on the screen is easier than the camera phone and therefore more engaging to take and edit photos with it. Only participant reported preferring editing, cropping and adding effects from her camera phone.

Large screen: Collaboration

Participants reported that they check the photos immediately on the tablet's large screen and after collaboratively with their co-located friends the instant they take the photo. We were told of an iterative workflow, beginning before the photo is taken with the preview, continuing through taking the photo, confirming that it is a desired photo, then, feeding that photo back to participants as collaborators. The tablet excelled at this process according to P2:

> The times I prefer the iPad is when I instantly show people the pictures because then it's a large screen and they can look at it and enjoy the photograph at that exact moment. People often really want to see that picture right away and see "Did I look good?" "Was it a good angle?" "Oh my chin is showing. I don't like that picture." (P2)

Large screen: Higher engagement

We asked participants if they knew friends or family members who also use their tablet to take photos and in that case what they perceive to be the quality of their photos from their tablet versus their camera phone. Our participants did report that their family and friends prefer to take photos on their tablet for the same reason they do. They also think the tablet takes better quality pictures than the camera phone. P8 told us: *It looks a little more cumbersome. It's just not as convenient as just flipping out on your phone, but I again, I do think it takes better pictures. I think he thinks the same thing.*

We also wanted to know if they noticed a difference in social network engagement between the photos posted online from their tablet versus their camera phone. P5 explained:

> Well, whenever I upload pictures on Facebook I always see the feedback. When I took the pictures if I uploaded 10 pictures, they are "like, like, like, like." I have found they have gone through the whole album. If I upload through my cell phone out of ten they only like two pictures only. In the tablet if I upload something, they have gone through the whole album. So they like at least six pictures out of ten pictures. (P5)

Through large scale data analytics, we find that the engagement values (number of favorites and views) [2] are not independent from each other which means they can be coming from the same pull of distributions. We ran chi-squared independence test but we failed to reject the null hypothesis of independence among the two groups. This means we can't find meaningful evidence the iPhone photos are more or less engaging than iPad photos. Although, in our interviews, two participants noticed a positive difference in engagement from their tablet photos when posted on Facebook.

FINDING 3: RESERVE THE TABLET FOR SERIOUS OR PERFECT MOMENTS

In this section, we analyze how the tablet does not allow participants to just capture a higher quality photo, but does allow capture of photos they will keep, for cherished or "serious" photos. We also present how the tablet allows our participant to capture their "perfect" moment.

Perfect moments: The tablet is for photos to keep, the phone is for quick snaps

In the qualitative analysis of the survey and the analysis of the interviews we found, that people reserve their tablet for taking the photos they want to keep and/or print, and their camera phone for more unplanned photos. As such, tablet photos need planning and people need to choose where and when the shot will take place before using the tablet:

> My iPad, if I'm using it to take pictures it's because I'm going somewhere that I know I'm going to want to take pictures and I tend to use it as a camera versus my phone would be what happens in that situation where I'm walking around, texting, or I'm walking around reading an email on the sidewalk and then something funny or something weird or something outside, I'm like "Oh my gosh" and I do want to take a picture of it. (P10)

Because of the larger size of the tablet, P11 reported keeping the iPad at her home unless she knew she would need it to capture an important event, in which case she brought her iPad to a specific location. Because our participants expect the tablet to capture photos of higher quality, they use their camera phone mainly for social photos and their tablet mainly for special events.

If participants know that the larger form factor of the tablet will be too much in the way of their experience, the trade-off is to carry the camera phone instead. If P11 knew in advance that she would be capturing a photo that would benefit from being of higher resolution, she would prefer to carry her tablet regardless of its size. P1 explained that the camera phone is for social, or less *serious photograph*, and the tablet is reserved for the most serious ones: *Cell phone camera is sort of unplanned photography I should say.*

More specifically, another participant mentioned that he reserves the iPad for keepsake photos while photos on the camera phone is for more temporary photos:

> If I'm taking a photo of a landscape or a sunset or something that I intend on keeping or intend on showing people, then it would be my iPad. Sometimes I'm just walking outside and I see something funny and I would just use my iPhone because I would just show it to somebody for a second and then delete it. That's the determining factor. (P3)

Finally, P9 reported preferring her tablet for the most serious photos, just because she is used to it. Between a camera phone and a Canon Powershot Point and Shoot, with a much higher camera definition (20.3 Megapixel sensor), she still preferred her tablet to take these serious photos.

This specific participant had identified that her point and shoot camera has a sensor of higher definition, but decided to still take her tablet to take photos of the first days after birth of her newborn, at the hospital.

A mobile camera is for capturing the perfect moment

P5, P12 and P11 participants explained that capturing the perfect moment is what makes a photo successful, and that a powerful camera such as a DSLR as little to do with this process. In addition to capturing the perfect moments, the participants who take photos with their mobile devices in place of their DSLR are more concerned with the aesthetic quality of the final photo. Studies in snapshot photography have shown that a high resolution photo is seldom of importance for snapshot photography [3, 9, 37]. This was confirmed throughout our interviews, for our participants, taking the right photo is about capturing the right moment and less about the "higher resolution" photo:

> Because usually when I'm taking a photo of a landscape, it isn't necessarily about the sharpness of the details. It's more about the mood, the vibe, the colors. (...) A picture of a very sharp tree does nothing for me. Who cares? But a picture of a tree where the lighting is really soft and pretty, like the colors fade in and out, that's more aesthetically pleasing to me. (P12)

DISCUSSION AND DESIGN IMPLICATIONS

We find that participants who capture photos with their tablet perceive the photos to be higher resolution than the photos taken with their smartphone even when the phone has a superior sensor (sometimes, almost 10 times of better resolution). Our results also indicate that the perception of quality is modulated by the form factor of the device, in particular the large preview screen. Because the photo "appears" larger, participants feel the photo is higher quality. So, why do mobile device manufacturers focus so much on the sensor quality of the camera while users care more about the end-to-end experience and the design of the device overall? We will discuss the design implications of our study in the following section.

A larger device means more photographic control

Our participants not only felt the iPad took higher resolution photos, but also that it created a more expressive photo. Again, the form factor of the tablet is at play when capturing a rich photo: the larger screen, the grip, the distance and the manner one can hold the tablet to tilt and turn to obtain the right angle, as well as the preview screen that provides immediate feedback, are all relevant variables. Because the form factor of the tablet facilitates the overall process of taking a photo, participants believe they take the right photo the first time. This finding could be taken into account when designing devices for which control is limited due to size or placement on the body. Less control is expected from such tiny devices but users will also not expect to be able to take photos that are sensitive to the perfect moment, a photo taking place in a particular instant relative to other instances in time.

High resolution comes from a larger screen

Unlike GoPro users, we observed that participants generally prefer a larger screen. Our participants might be technically incorrect about resultant resolution of the photos from their devices, especially when there is a screen involved, but it does not mean they do not care about a high resolution photo. They explained that they want a high resolution photo and therefore use their iPad when they need a photo they can print later on. They care about quality of details, colors, and depth of field. They are not able to distinguish if the quality comes from the camera sensor or the display itself, and they assume the display is representative of the resolution, the larger display corresponding to a higher resolution photo. The more of a photo the participant sees on the screen, the stronger the opinion that the photo is higher resolution. Designers and practitioners could use this principle and design light

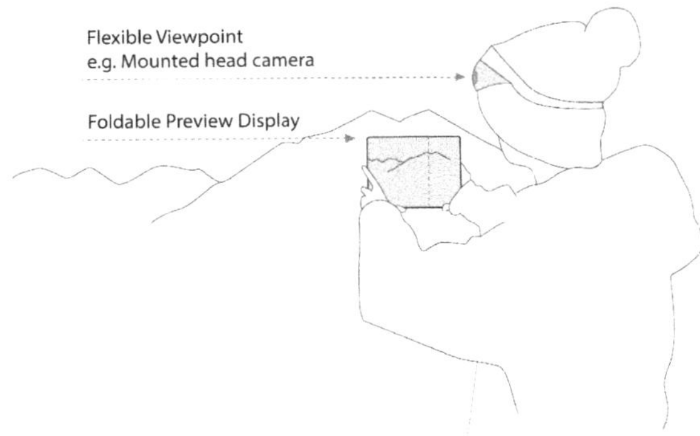

Figure 3. Our sketch illustrates one of our findings: A larger, but foldable screen, connected to a flexible viewpoint.

attachable portable displays connected to smart watches or modular cameras, see our sketch (Figure 3). Users could use their modular small camera to be in the moment of the photography but connect at any time to a separate screen to review their photos, and gain the full end-to-end experience with the perception of higher resolution.

Devices miniaturization with lower output expectations

When designing a novel device, designers and practitioners could consider how the perception of the device's form factor impacts the expectations of the output. Subjects explained that the photo they take with the tablet has a higher definition, with more colors and more detail, because they see more details on a larger display from the tablet screen. They also perceive that they can capture more on their tablet than on their phone, that more elements in a scene can be collected at a time on the camera tablet than on their camera phone. We found that the form factor of these devices drives specific user interactions and device choices along with a perception of output quality. If the current design trend is to design miniaturized displays, as we can see in current smart watch or wearable consumer device interest, users might expect a much lower quality photo even though a similar camera sensor to their cherished, large-screen devices. Integrating a larger and therefore more expensive sensor or display makes less sense on a miniaturized device. Conversely, if one designs a larger tablet, the expectation of a high resolution camera is higher to fit the resolution expectation coming from the screen-size alone. Manufacturers may meet these expectations or exceed them, but know that a pre-emptive opinion exists irrespective of the camera sensor.

The quick camera

Participants seek to capture quick photos and want to capture them at the cost of a higher resolution photograph. We noticed during the interviews an entangled relationship between the device itself and the moment, and the appreciation for the flexibility of the cell phone as being "in" and "out" of the pocket very quickly and at all times. The relevant variables to capturing the right moment quickly are capability in various environmental conditions (various light conditions), availability of the device to the photographer physically, and availability of the device in time. An ideal camera to fit these design criteria would be easily accessible to the user, yet would have to be temporarily on the body unlike a clip, watch, or glasses, but more like a stopwatch that can flip out and move around by the hand and quickly be off sight; it could flip out and move around by the hand, yet could quickly go back in a pocket. It would ideally have a fast shutter speed and work in low light conditions (higher ISO) to capture unexpected moments. These criteria could be met at the expense of the camera sensor.

Preview-less camera to be in the moment!

Participants who also use a GoPro with no display ($n = 3$), particularly liked the device's lack of display. When asked if they would rather have a display to visualize what they are capturing, they explained that they cherish this lack of display to be in the moment and not think about the end result of the photo. They reported enjoying being surprised by looking at their photo later on on their computer. This is an interesting observation in regards to the photographic experience. An end-to-end experience does not necessarily mean looking at the photo right away after capturing it, but may defer review entirely to enable the photographer to remain active in the scene, ostensibly to capture more perfect moments. The replay display, or injects its own time constraint in an otherwise continuous experience, limiting available moments. Since this research was conducted, GoPro has included a display in their device. However, another version of this camera could be significantly more inconspicuous in the space, with no display, one button (or voice activated), adherable away from the photographer.

Capturing the right moment is prioritized over the device

We found out that participants like the interaction with their tablet, the large screen preview, the larger framing of an image, the ability to hold the tablet further and the large surface to edit the photos. Interestingly, we found that this interaction with the camera resembles the one of semi-professional photographers with their full-frame camera. Semi-professional photographers are usually interested in more than just having a higher resolution photo, and are engaged in a process to capture the right moment [2]. Our participants emphasized how they preferred iPad photography for their important shots along with the facilitated interaction with the tablet, articulating how essential it is for them to capture the right moment, and how it is facilitated by the larger and high definition tablet screen, but also how the photos they take are higher quality and higher resolution as a result.

These results are consistent with the body of research [6, 7] that identifies the advantages and psychological benefits of interacting with engaging computing devices versus technically performant ones. Similarly, we found that among the participants who regularly take photos with their tablets, the actual hardware specifications are low priority.

More specifically, we found that our participants understand these hardware specifications to be of higher technical quality than they actually are, because their interactions with the device itself is easier and more engaging than with a more technically advanced device. Considering these results in the context of photo-sharing networks, our findings suggest that photographers carry preconceived and potentially erroneous notions of photo resolution prior to their decision to use one photo-sharing network over another. Photo-sharing networks differentiate on size of available storage space, supported resolution, and therefore the allowed resolution of hosted photo. These findings inform decisions regarding the value of supported resolution (quality) for various photographers based on the camera they are integrating with the service.

CONCLUSION AND FUTURE WORK

We explored the perception of the camera phone and camera tablet usage. Our mixed methods study with both quantitative and qualitative data indicates that participants perceive the output photos to be higher quality on the tablet even though the tablet inherently output photos of much lower quality due to hardware and software limitations. We determine that the form factor of mobile camera devices modulates the perceived quality of the photo. Additionally, the engaging nature of the devices themselves, via a larger screen, brighter colors and overall size, allow the user more control to take photos that they believe to be more desirable.

Camera phones are smaller, easy to use, quickly accessible, lighter, and in most cases, have a camera that is technically capable of taking higher resolution photos than the tablet. Nonetheless, subjects perceive higher quality tablet photos, because they prefer the overall interaction with their tablet. We suggest that novel technical features such as miniaturization of devices and sensors with higher megapixel ratings are insufficient motivation for consumer adoption. Our results emphasize the importance of the experience in design. It does not matter if there are more megapixels if the experience does not support a consumer's criteria for quality. In future work, we will adopt a methodology that introduces similar hypotheses at scale, by performing comparative data analysis of millions of examples of high end camera devices and their use through the data available on online photo sharing sites such as Flickr.

REFERENCES

1. Morgan Ames, Dean Eckles, Mor Naaman, Mirjana Spasojevic, and Nancy Van House. 2010. Requirements for mobile photoware. *Personal and Ubiquitous Computing* 14, 2 (2010), 95–109.
2. Saeideh Bakhshi, David A Shamma, Lyndon Kennedy, and Eric Gilbert. 2015. Why We Filter Our Photos and How It Impacts Engagement. In *Ninth International AAAI Conference on Web and Social Media.*
3. Geoffrey Batchen. 2008. Snapshots: Art history and the ethnographic turn. *Photographies* 1, 2 (2008), 121–142.
4. Jennie Berggren and Catherine Hedler. 2014. CamQuest: Design and Evaluation of a Tablet Application for Educational Use in Preschools. In *Proceedings of the 2014 Conference on Interaction Design and Children (IDC '14).* ACM, New York, NY, USA, 185–188. DOI: http://dx.doi.org/10.1145/2593968.2610448
5. Jo Briggs and Mark Blythe. 2013. Apps for art's sake: resistance and innovation. In *Proceedings of the 15th international conference on Human-computer interaction with mobile devices and services.* ACM, 45–54.

6. Rafael A Calvo and Dorian Peters. 2012. Positive computing: technology for a wiser world. *interactions* 19, 4 (2012), 28–31.

7. Rafael A. Calvo and Dorian Peters. 2014. *Positive Computing: Technology for Well-Being and Human Potential*. The MIT Press.

8. Jeff Carlson. 2014. *The IPad for Photographers: Master the Newest Tool in Your Camera Bag*. Pearson Education.

9. Richard Chalfen. 1987. Snapshot versions of life. (1987).

10. Felicia Cordeiro, Daniel A Epstein, Edison Thomaz, Elizabeth Bales, Arvind K Jagannathan, Gregory D Abowd, and James Fogarty. 2015. Barriers and Negative Nudges: Exploring Challenges in Food Journaling. In *Proceedings of the 33rd Annual ACM Conference on Human Factors in Computing Systems*. ACM, 1159–1162.

11. Marc Davis, Nancy Van House, Jeffrey Towle, Simon King, Shane Ahern, Carrie Burgener, Dan Perkel, Megan Finn, Vijay Viswanathan, and Matthew Rothenberg. 2005. MMM2: mobile media metadata for media sharing. In *CHI'05 extended abstracts on Human factors in computing systems*. ACM, 1335–1338.

12. Silke Gegenbauer and Elaine M Huang. 2012. iPods, Ataris, and Polaroids: A personal inventories study of out-of-use electronics in Swiss households. In *Proceedings of the 2012 ACM Conference on Ubiquitous Computing*. ACM, 531–535.

13. Connie Golsteijn, Elise Van Den Hoven, David Frohlich, and Abigail Sellen. 2012. Towards a more cherishable digital object. In *Proceedings of the Designing Interactive Systems Conference*. ACM, 655–664.

14. Christian Hall. 2014. *iPhone and iPad Photography*. Future Press.

15. Saburo Hirano, Takashi Ikebuchi, and Haruhiro Katayose. 2010. MoPH: a media performance system with a multi-touch interface. In *Proceedings of the 7th International Conference on Advances in Computer Entertainment Technology*. ACM, 20–23.

16. Marco Hudelist, Klaus Schoeffmann, David Ahlstrom, and others. 2013. Evaluation of image browsing interfaces for smartphones and tablets. In *Multimedia (ISM), 2013 IEEE International Symposium on*. IEEE, 1–8.

17. Aayush Jain, Saikiran Maguluri, Prakash Shukla, Poorvi Vijay, and Keyur Sorathia. 2014. Exploring Tangible Interactions for Capturing Self Photographs. In *Proceedings of the India HCI 2014 Conference on Human Computer Interaction (IndiaHCI '14)*. ACM, New York, NY, USA, Article 116, 6 pages. DOI: http://dx.doi.org/10.1145/2676702.2676721

18. Alireza Jalali, Daniel Trottier, Mariane Tremblay, and Maxwell Hincke. 2011. Administering a Gross Anatomy Exam Using Mobile Technology: How one medical school made the switch from paper to paperless. *eLearn* 2011, 2 (2011), 1.

19. Tim Kindberg, Mirjana Spasojevic, Rowanne Fleck, and Abigail Sellen. 2005a. I saw this and thought of you: some social uses of camera phones. In *CHI'05 extended abstracts on Human factors in computing systems*. ACM, 1545–1548.

20. Tim Kindberg, Mirjana Spasojevic, Rowanne Fleck, and Abigail Sellen. 2005b. The ubiquitous camera: An in-depth study of camera phone use. *Pervasive Computing, IEEE* 4, 2 (2005), 42–50.

21. David Kirk, Abigail Sellen, Richard Harper, and Ken Wood. 2007. Understanding videowork. In *Proceedings of the SIGCHI conference on Human factors in computing systems*. ACM, 61–70.

22. David Kirk, Abigail Sellen, Carsten Rother, and Ken Wood. 2006. Understanding photowork. In *Proceedings of the SIGCHI conference on Human Factors in computing systems*. ACM, 761–770.

23. Priya Kumar and Sarita Schoenebeck. 2015. The modern day baby book: Enacting good mothering and stewarding privacy on facebook. In *Proceedings of the 18th ACM Conference on Computer Supported Cooperative Work & Social Computing*. ACM, 1302–1312.

24. Jean-Baptiste Labrune and Wendy Mackay. 2005. Tangicam: exploring observation tools for children. In *Proceedings of the 2005 conference on Interaction design and children*. ACM, 95–102.

25. Mathias Lux, Desara Xhura, and Alexander Kopper. 2014. User Intentions in Digital Photo Production: A Test Data Set. In *MultiMedia Modeling*. Springer, 172–182.

26. Mary Meeker. 2014. *Internet Trends*. Technical Report. Kleiner Perkins Caufield and Byers. http://www.kpcb.com/blog/2014-internet-trends.

27. Hendrik Müller, Jennifer Gove, and John Webb. 2012. Understanding Tablet Use: A Multi-method Exploration. In *Proceedings of the 14th International Conference on Human-computer Interaction with Mobile Devices and Services (MobileHCI '12)*. ACM, New York, NY, USA, 1–10. DOI: http://dx.doi.org/10.1145/2371574.2371576

28. Hendrik Müller, Jennifer L. Gove, John S. Webb, and Aaron Cheang. 2015. Understanding and Comparing Smartphone and Tablet Use: Insights from a Large-Scale Diary Study. In *Proceedings of the Annual Meeting of the Australian Special Interest Group for Computer Human Interaction (OzCHI '15)*. ACM, New York, NY, USA, 427–436. DOI: http://dx.doi.org/10.1145/2838739.2838748

29. Don Norman. 2004. Affordances and Design. URL. (July 2004). http://www.jnd.org/dn.mss/affordances_and.html.

30. William Odom, John Zimmerman, Jodi Forlizzi, Ana López Higuera, Mauro Marchitto, José Cañas, Youn-kyung Lim, Tek-Jin Nam, Moon-Hwan Lee, Yeoreum Lee, and others. 2013. Fragmentation and transition: understanding perceptions of virtual possessions among young adults in Spain, South Korea and the United States. In *Proceedings of the SIGCHI Conference on Human Factors in Computing Systems*. ACM, 1833–1842.

31. Jennifer Pearson and George Buchanan. 2010. Real-time document collaboration using iPads. In *Proceedings of the third workshop on Research advances in large digital book repositories and complementary media*. ACM, 9–14.

32. Kimiko Ryokai, Stefan Marti, and Hiroshi Ishii. 2004. I/O brush: drawing with everyday objects as ink. In *Proceedings of the SIGCHI conference on Human factors in computing systems*. ACM, 303–310.

33. Jennifer Sheridan, Nick Bryan-Kinns, Stuart Reeves, Joe Marshall, and Giles Lane. 2011. Graffito: crowd-based performative interaction at festivals. In *CHI'11 Extended Abstracts on Human Factors in Computing Systems*. ACM, 1129–1134.

34. David R Thomas. 2006. A general inductive approach for analyzing qualitative evaluation data. *American journal of evaluation* 27, 2 (2006), 237–246.

35. Nancy A Van House. 2007. Flickr and public image-sharing: distant closeness and photo exhibition. In *CHI'07 extended abstracts on Human factors in computing systems*. ACM, 2717–2722.

36. Nancy A Van House. 2009. Collocated photo sharing, story-telling, and the performance of self. *International Journal of Human-Computer Studies* 67, 12 (2009), 1073–1086.

37. Nancy A Van House. 2011. Personal photography, digital technologies and the uses of the visual. *Visual Studies* 26, 2 (2011), 125–134.

38. Cati Vaucelle, Diana Africano, Glorianna Davenport, Mikael Wiberg, and Oskar Fjellstrom. 2005. Moving pictures: looking out/looking in. In *ACM SIGGRAPH 2005 Educators program*. ACM, 1–9.

39. Cati Vaucelle and Hiroshi Ishii. 2008. Picture this!: film assembly using toy gestures. In *Proceedings of the 10th international conference on Ubiquitous computing*. ACM, 350–359.

Documenting the Research Through Design Process

Jeffrey Bardzell[1] Shaowen Bardzell[1] Peter Dalsgaard[2] Shad Gross[1] Kim Halskov[2]

[1]Indiana University
Bloomington, IN
{jbardzel | selu | shagross @indiana.edu}

[2]Aarhus University
Aarhus, Denmark
{dalsgaard | halskov @cavi.au.dk}

ABSTRACT

Documentation of Research through Design (RtD) processes is essential for capturing and translating design knowledge into broader academic knowledge. Moreover, it can support both design and research objectives internally in RtD projects, as well as external concerns such as project management, knowledge dissemination, and education. In spite of this, RtD documentation has received little sustained attention in prior work. Building on what prior work there is as well as an in-depth analysis of two markedly different cases, we present a framework for planning and evaluating RtD documentation. The framework addresses three core concerns: the medium of documentation, the performativity of documentation, and providing equal support for both research and design.

Author Keywords

Research through design; documentation, design process

ACM Classification Keywords

H.5.m. Information interfaces and presentation (e.g., HCI): Miscellaneous.

INTRODUCTION

Research through design (RtD) is the practice of using design thinking, processes, and products as an inquiry methodology. It has generated considerable attention in both HCI and design discourses in recent years [5, 14, 18, 28, 30]. As a relatively nascent area of research in HCI, there remain some concerns about what RtD is and what it should be. In particular, questions and divisions remain about RtD as a knowledge practice [4, 6, 23]. Recently, Höök and colleagues [21, 22] distinguished between first-order knowledge (i.e., design researchers' insights and understandings pertaining to particular design situations) and second-order knowledge (i.e., how such a distinctive way of knowing is communicated and represented as more generalized knowledge). They articulate a need for design researchers to "develop both better ways of capturing the specificity and richness of design processes beyond anecdotal evidence, and better formats for communicating, contesting, and developing this knowledge in academic fora" [22].

DOI: http://dx.doi.org/10.1145/2901790.2901859.

Key to this work of capturing and translating primary design knowledge into broader academic knowledge is how design processes are documented; design documentation is a key raw material out of which such knowledge is constructed. Design process documentation appears in diverse forms, including workbooks, journals, project management systems, papers, and more. It also supports RtD in diverse ways. Process documentation supports *design* in activities of iterative problem framing and problem setting; it allows RtD practitioners to explore the materiality, form, and interactivity simultaneously that generate knowledge about materials pertaining to what it can and can not do, its strengths and limitations, etc.; documentation both facilitates ideation, sketching, and prototyping processes as well as subsequent communication and evaluation; and process documentation records the project's way-finding—choices made, breakthroughs, challenges, and paths not taken. Similarly, process documentation supports *research* in the ways it facilitates the development of inquiry objectives; it allows RtD practitioners to record research activities; it demonstrates and communicates research methods and rigor; it creates connection to prior work; it expresses relevant theory; and it includes data results and their interpretations. More generally, RtD process documentation supports *project management* and *education and broader dissemination*.

Influential papers from Koskinen, Binder and Redström [25] and Zimmerman, Stolterman, and Forlizzi [30] have pointed out that systematic and comprehensive documentation is often lacking in design research in general, and in RtD in particular. One reason for this is that even though RtD practitioners have various tools and practices at their disposal, they have to come up with their own documentation systems and approaches, often assembled ad hoc out of existing tools and practices from design and/or research. Virtually no literature takes up some of the most practical considerations, such as the following: What should we document, to what extents, and using which tools/media? How do we balance the effort of documentation with its reward? How do we document a dynamic process, where the research and/or design focus can change along the way? How do we balance the need to push a project forward with capturing its key moments for reflection? How do we support individual versus social activities and contributions? How do we document tacit knowledge and embodied knowledge (e.g., of materials)? This paper seeks to make a contribution towards such a practice in three ways. It offers an attempt to think systematically about RtD process documentation, with a special interest in the (multi-) medium of RtD documentation, the performative contributions of documentation in an RtD project (i.e., what documentation *does*), and the balancing of both design and research needs throughout. We present two case studies from our own RtD experiences, based in two different RtD groups within different universities. And finally we propose that the RtD community develop new genres of discourse to support its practice.

DOCUMENTING RTD PRACTICE

Available research provides insight into existing practices and resources, but none have claimed to offer a comprehensive solution to RtD process documentation, and we will argue that all of them emphasize one aspect of the challenge at the expense of others. We begin with design *workbooks*, as described in Gaver [15]. Workbooks are "collections of design proposals and other materials drawn together during projects to investigate options for design" (p.1551). The main purpose of workbooks is thus to support design: "everything in a design workbook should be addressed as a proposal: that is, as indicating a direction and course of action for design." [15:1559-1560]. For Gaver, the workbook collects design *proposals*. Although he does not explicitly define "proposal", he characterizes his own proposals as "very rough collages of alternative devices that explored a range of personal and idiosyncratic possibilities" in a design domain of interest (1552). A proposal typically occupies a two-page spread, comprises both images and text, and often exhibits a certain roughness. It facilitates the externalization of ideas, helps project futures, and contributes towards the creation of design spaces. Workbooks are deliberately open, in the sense that they contain a multitude of design proposals, and they can be understood as a provisional mapping and exploration of a design space.

Gaver himself stresses that workbooks support design—he says less about their role in research—and moreover they are most impactful in the relatively early design phases of problem setting and ideation. Other work from Gaver's group at Goldsmiths has presented documentation strategies that better support research, in particular *annotated portfolios* [24]. In contrast to workbooks, annotated portfolios are intended to extract and communicate research findings through "organising what can be learned from design in terms of annotations which formulate and highlight features of interest in a portfolio […] Annotations are characterised as indexically connected to artefacts, while connoting topics of broader interest" [8:76].

Löwgren proposes that annotated portfolios can be considered a form of intermediate-level knowledge: the knowledge presented in them resides on a level of abstraction between specific designs and generalisable theories. Annotated portfolios reflect a wider interest in the interaction design community to examine new ways of developing and communicating research findings that go beyond the traditional formats of academic papers and demos of systems and prototypes, which also underlies the development of *pictorials* as a novel academic format [7]. Similarly to annotated portfolios, Dalsgaard et al. [12] developed *maps for design reflection* to support the analysis and communication of crucial aspects of design projects, ranging from overarching trends and developments in a design project to specific examinations of how a design concept emerges and is transformed through various representations and manifestations. All of this work supports research, but its emphasis is comparatively reflective and retrospective; that is, annotated portfolios and pictorials present work that has already achieved a certain level of maturity; they do not propel a design forward the way that a workbook does.

Taking a different track but in a similar space, Binder & Brandt [6] propose that a traceable *genealogy* is an essential component of design research. For them, genealogy refers to an account of the process of a project or experiment situated in relation to one or more research traditions, such as design research, human factors, or art criticism, or everyday discourses, such as public discourses on topics in health and technology. Simply put, if we are to evaluate the knowledge presented in a research contribution, we must be able to trace both the emergence of this knowledge and also within which discourses and practices it can be recognized as "knowledge" in the first place. Genealogy appears to bring together two ideas: first is the *processual* nature of the RtD activity, and second is *familial* relation between the RtD project and the body of knowledge it seeks to extend or contribute to. The genealogy appears to serve in a way comparable to that of a Methodology in a scientific project, that is, a descriptive account of the activities or procedures by which the knowledge is generated and by which it can be legitimated, except that instead of scientific methods and their attendant epistemological commitments, the RtD project typically foregrounds design methods and their epistemological commitments. This work clarifies at a theoretical level how RtD can positions its processes as rigorous, but it offers few concrete recommendations on how to do it.

One more concrete approach is the use of dedicated systems for documenting RtD, such as the *Project Reflection Tool* described in [13]. This is a collaborative online system designed to support chronological aggregation of files, notes, and reflections of design projects for subsequent analysis. The PRT system is partly inspired by *Design Rationale* [1], an approach to design documentation that focuses on capturing the rationale behind design decisions and making it accessible. The intent is that a systematic and thorough examination of the rationale behind design decisions would expose potential flaws in the argumentation for decisions and lead to better and more well-founded decisions. A number of systems have been developed to support design rationale [9]. However, Design Rationale has had limited success [10], and has faced a number of criticisms, one of them being that many design decisions are informed by tacit knowledge that may not easily be formulated and captured in a system, and that it potentially adds a very large overhead to the work of designers. The limitation of systems such as these, beyond the lack of empirical evidence that they work well, is that with their emphasis on capturing rationales, they offer fewer resources to push the project forward; they run the risk of feeling in the moment like pure overhead.

These approaches variously shed light on different aspects of the problem, but each is also incomplete. Each struggles to support design and research equally, and each struggles to balance pushing the design forward in the moment with supporting reflection and synthetic thinking. At the same time, all also emphasize a relatively small number of values, which provides insight into some of the core qualities of RtD process documentation. One is the role of **medium**: by that we mean that RtD documentation typically requires the collection of different types of document (e.g., images, text, video/animation), and often aggregated, disaggregated, and reaggregated for different purposes (e.g., to support design ideation, to pitch a direction to a client, to trace the emerging rationale of a project). Related is the **performativity** of much documentation; RtD process documentation does not merely describe what happens, but it constitutes a form of action—note for example that Gaver's workbooks are made up of "proposals" and not "representations." Finally, all implicitly or explicitly are positioned as resources to facilitate the transition from, in Höök et al.'s words [21], first-order to second-order knowledge, that is, they aim to support **RtD**. These three qualities, which were not readily apparent to us when we began this research project, have come to shape our understanding of RtD process documentation, and came to constitute the core of our analysis of our RtD cases. How we came to this approach we explain in what follows.

METHODOLOGY

Building on prior work on the RtD process [5,14], this project began with a conversation between two RtD groups on the relationships between words/text and objects in RtD. Though the teams have worked in different design spaces—urban computing and media architecture in one case, and critical computing in the other—both found importance and elements of struggle in RtD process documentation. Two concerns in particular—uncertainty about what/how much to document during the process and a recognition that these repositories were not always used well during research reporting—emerged right away.

To begin a collaborative inquiry, we interviewed each other about our RtD processes and documentation practices. The goal was not to uncover facts about practice as a matter of social scientific inquiry; it was, rather, generative: to use the medium of the interview to call to mind experiences and examples, to bring our intuitions to clarity, to create openings to action. Both sides separately constructed interview questions and then interviewed the other side: we were as curious about each other's questions as we were their answers. Each interview lasted about 90 minutes and revolved around fundamental questions such as: What did you document and why? Did you use the documentation, and if so, how? Which individual documentations stand out, and why? Each interview was audio recorded.

Through the back-and-forth a number of issues emerged. One is the distinction between intrinsic and extrinsic motivation: when does documentation feel motivated by and supportive of—as opposed to a distraction from and burden on—the task at hand? Another is the problem of actually knowing when a breakthrough occurred; sometimes it is obvious, but other times something is only understood as a breakthrough in hindsight. Another is the problem of being able to find relevant assets efficiently in the future when needed, whether it is to solve a technical problem solved in the past, to make a presentation for stakeholders, or to support scholarly reporting. More fundamentally for our inquiry, the interviews made us recall dozens of stories and examples, which began to form a repertoire of RtD and RtD documentation situations.

In subsequent meetings, we identified several dozen issues and situations of interest. Using affinity diagramming, and guided in part by our literature review, we arrived at a preliminary version of the three aspects of RtD documentation we referenced in the Introduction: the significance of the medium of the documentation, the performative nature of the documentation, and the challenge of equally supporting the design and research aspects of the project. In subsequent meetings, we refined this three-part framework by testing its applicability and resonance with examples—our own and those articulated in related research.

During this process, it became clear that our analysis would benefit from a more sustained and close analysis of a finite set of RtD process documentation artifacts. Doing so would allow us to go back in time and reflect on what was happening, what their roles were in the project then, how they were subsequently used (or not). More specifically, we analyzed how each mediated the documentation (e.g., as a video, workbook, or project within a project management system); how each didn't merely represent a fact or piece of information, but was part of an action or performance; and how each participated in or contributed towards the research versus design aspects of the project. These analysis became the basis of our case studies (below).

THREE ASPECTS OF RTD PROCESS DOCUMENTATION

The framework that over time we settled on comprises three particularly resonant elements in our analyses:

The Medium of RtD Documentation

One of the most basic insights we had into RtD documentation processes was that they involved the aggregation, disaggregration, and reaggregation of different kinds of document, such as images, videos/animations, text, and so forth. We began to focus on how various systems and tools supported these aggregation practices, and this led us to dwell on the medium. That the medium of a work is central to it is commonplace in the arts and humanities. Synthesizing the position of Timothy Brinkley, philosopher David Davies [15] writes, "A medium is a set of conventions whereby performing certain manipulations on a kind of physical stuff counts as specifying a certain set of aesthetic properties as a piece." The key concepts in this definition are physical materials, conventions, manipulations, and piece. Physical materials—paint, celluloid, spoken words, the body of a ballet dancer—offer both capabilities and constraints. Conventions, such as cultural movements (e.g., Impressionism), genres (e.g., sonnets, war documentaries), and styles (e.g., 80s New Wave fashion) provide standardized yet transgressible means of using, manipulating, and/or shaping those materials. And this conventionalized manipulation of physical material is oriented towards the production of an individual piece, which is coherent and whole.

RtD process documentation is different from an artwork in several important ways. It does not necessarily aspire to the level of holistic coherence of a finished artistic piece. Nor does it necessarily seek to perform or innovate upon materials and/or conventions as an artist often does. Yet the basic underlying mechanisms remain the same: an RtD process workbook is based in a set of *materials* (e.g., a physical book, an electronic document, or a project management system); it leverages certain *conventions*, such as design sketches with textual annotations, laid out over time to reveal temporal unfolding/development; and it gains its *coherence* in the ways it is manipulated/aggregated around the purpose of documenting a design project in a certain way.

Documents as Speech Acts

We began the project often asking what design document is, identifying different examples, and organizing them into different types. We came to recognize that when we shifted the question to what design documents *do*, we were better able to situate documents in their moments. We saw that they were used in presentations, to support research, to record a stray thought that might be useful later, to collect disparate resources in a single location. We came to see that design documentation often plays a socially performative role, that is, that it contains, among other things, illocutionary acts. *Illocutionary acts* is a concept introduced by J.L. Austin [2] to describe statements that not only describe states of affairs but also have a social force, e.g., promises, demands, suggestions, bets, and so forth: "I declare you husband and wife", spoken in a certain situation by a qualified individual does not merely describe, but actually changes, social reality. In this way, documentation is not only documenting what has happened but, most importantly, it *acts* upon and within the design process.

We found that RtD documentation commonly *describes* a newly acquired design material. It *rules in or out* certain exemplars, directions, and materials. It *demonstrates* that a team member was productive in the past week, even though certain to-do items that he had *promised* to do were not completed. It playfully *explores* potential directions via sketches. It *proposes* that a design ought to look/function a certain way and *requests* financial, material, and human support. It *reveals* and *challenges* a shared assumption. It *takes credit* for a certain breakthrough. It *justifies* the project and its key decisions to the funding agency. Many of these acts are not passive recordings of design; they are design activities themselves. As we began to reread our documentation exemplars, tracing their performative roles dramatically improved our accounts of them and changed how we thought about RtD documentation in the future.

Supporting Research and Design

One of the difficulties of RtD is that its twin pillars seem to be in conflict with one another. The particularity of design [28] seems to be in conflict with the generalizing impulses of research [11, 18, 23]. In research, knowledge is transmitted verbally, but in RtD it is "embodied in the object" [15]). The scientific epistemological virtue of objectivity appears to conflict with the design virtue of expert subjectivity [3]. Conversely, one might ask whether design problem setting and framing is all that different from formulation of research questions and hypotheses; experiments with design materials and scientific experiments, different in many respects, nonetheless are experiments, guided by theories, methods, and communities of practice. Are design and research not merely different variations of inquiry? If so, then perhaps an alternative theory of inquiry can bring them back into compatibility, even alignment. Indeed, Basballe and Halskov [5] show that design and research in RtD are never fully separate but continuously *couple*, *interweave*, and *decouple*. Similarly, Dalsgaard, Halskov and Basballe [14] introduce the concepts of boundary zones and emergent boundary objects in order to account for how design concepts emerge and are shaped through ongoing negotiations of design interest and research interests. We turn now to our cases, to work through some of these ideas and to tease out some of the choices we make when we document and their consequences.

CASE 1: "PERSUASIVE ANXIETY"

"Persuasive Anxiety" (PA) was a design research project that investigated personal informatics from a critical perspective, with an emphasis on the relationships between personal data tracking and experiences of anxiety. The research team also sought to develop practice-informed theory about the relationships between criticality and design. The team comprised three faculty researchers and two Ph.D. students in interaction design. Each of the students was tasked with developing three design directions that critically explore personal informatics and anxiety. Designer A has a background in interactive fine arts and developed three critical designs that explore "bad" consumption—cigarettes, chocolates, and prescription drug abuse. Designer B has a background in graphic design and HCI, and leveraged his interest in photography to explore how cameras and networks might be used for (self-) surveillance.

The project amassed several hundred electronic documents, stored and shared in Dropbox. Documents included several dozen meeting minutes, each comprising a few pages of notes in bulleted text; documents developed to present/explain the work to diverse stakeholders; and data collected from an exhibition of the six designs, including hundreds of photos, several videos, and qualitative data from an exhibition of the designs. Beyond this general data, each designer had her or his own documentation. Designer A had dozens of sketches and hundreds of photos of inspirations and exemplars, as well as a poster and several slide decks from presentations she did of the work. Designer B kept an RtD workbook. This was not a workbook in Gaver's sense as described earlier, but in a more traditional sense: a personal workbook containing sketches, inspirations, semantic differentials, reflections, and so forth. He also used mind-mapping software and periodically output his mind map to PDF to share with the team. He also had several slide decks and handouts for presenting to stakeholders.

In the following, we focus on Designer B's workbook, turning to the other documentation to provide context and support as needed. We chose this document in part because it was well curated, provided ample documentation of the project in terms of its design and research objectives, and was in fact used both to support the design process and subsequent research writing. As part of this project, Designer B also looked back and reflected on the workbook, which became another source of data for our analysis. We now turn to our analysis of Designer B's RtD process workbook in light of the four considerations specified earlier.

The Medium of RtD Documentation

Designer B's workbook was done in Microsoft Word. It is spread across nearly 60 pages and includes prose (typically used for reflections), bullet lists (typically used for to-do lists), scans of sketches with annotations (used to document design activities), and photos of technical materials with annotations (used to document material and technical obstacles, opportunities, and hacks). For analysis purposes, we understand the material substrate of this Word-based workbook to include formatted text, embedded bitmap images, and a document model that manages these elements. It leverages a number of conventions of typography and page layout, offering standard text formatting options (e.g., paragraphs, numbered and bullet lists, captions) and page layout options (e.g., inserting images within text, wrapping, footnotes). Designer B had to work within these conventions to create an electronic version of a design notebook. For writing and formatting text, Word is quite strong. For sketching, it is basically unusable; the designer sketched on paper and then scanned the sketches in as bitmaps. Once imported, however, bitmaps were easy to lay out and annotate.

Common features of paper notebooks—e.g., the ability to paste in physical cuttings and images—are missing in Word, though scanning and importing simulates that functionality, albeit with higher overhead. Word also lacks the ability to put text at angles or to bend lines of text, as one often does in paper notebooks to fit everything on a single page, the page being an important structural unit in many paper design workbooks. Designer B let Word handle pagination and made no effort to construct well-formed pages. Instead of the physical page being the basic unit of organization, Designer B used logical sections, marked by headings and formatted using built-in Word styles. Typical sections reflected meaningful temporal demarcations organized by date as well as substantive ones (e.g., to do lists, reflections on theory, documenting technical hacks).

The overall organization of these sections is temporal and linear; the most basic unit of analysis was the week. Within each week, he used different materials and conventions to document design activities as well as research activities. Trends also emerged over time. For example, the early part of the workbook contains extended textual quotations and reflections on critical theory, theories of surveillance, and personal informatics research as well as hand-drawn sketches showing his design ideation—not surprising emphases during the problem setting and framing stage. The later part of the workbook includes documentation of experiments with materials, annotated photo walkthroughs of hacks, and photos of circuit boards and disassembled cameras—again, not surprising given the prototyping stage that he was in. That all of this work is contained in a single .doc file, which is nearly universally readable both technically and in terms of its stylistic and structural conventions, makes the work accessible at different levels of detail to different stakeholders, including the design researcher during his process, himself a year later when writing research papers about the project, and the rest of the team for both intellectual and project management reasons.

Documents as Speech Acts

To offer a close analysis of the illocutionary acts in Designer B's workbook, we focus on an example, which occurred within a given week about two thirds of the way through the workbook and process. At this time, Designer B had sketches of a design involving a traditional gumball machine that when the user turns its crank, takes a picture of the user and displays their image as part of a slideshow of similar images inside of the machine. After beginning with last week's to-do list and asserting his own productivity this week, Designer B announces that two key materials have arrived: a set of webcams and the gumball machine itself. He already had the LCD screen, so the central question of the week was to begin to explore how the three pieces of hardware could be integrated.

He talks first about the webcams. He observes that their focal length and depth of field were both different than he had expected. He proposes some alterations to the design to accommodate this. He then takes them apart, offers a commentary on their components, their quality, and their capabilities. This he documents with a series of photographs and accompanying verbal descriptions. He then turns to connecting the web cam and the LCD screen; to get them to work together, he will need a hack.

The next several pages document that hack. Along the way, he discovers some pins on the board that don't seem to be used; he consults online forums and finds out that they allow line-level control over the LCD screen, a feature he didn't know existed. He can't think of an application now, either, but he creates a "stub"—a small reminder that this feature is there and could be exploited later on, just in case. In the course of further testing, he discovers that the data stream for the web cam is simply too much for his Arduino controller board. He presents three options, one of which would subsequently be used in the designs. In following pages, he photographically and textually documents his disassembly of the gumball machine, seeking ways to connect it to the web cam, LCD screen, and processing board.

The hacking of the components that occupied Designer B this week was more than a description of components. It was a social performance—to his managers to demonstrate his productivity that week; to fellow geeks to demonstrate his hacking achievements; to stakeholders to justify his design decisions and purchases; to a version of himself in the future, who would presumably need to be reminded about how each of the components works; and finally also to himself in the present, having an aesthetic experience involving material play directed at inquiry: "This week", he writes, "I had intended to [work on the prototyping method] but just had too much fun with the Gumball machine and cameras." The diverse speech acts from this week—self-legitimations, technical showboating, materials analysis, proposed IT solutions, suggested implications for future work, and self-disclosures—*cohered* together.

Supporting Research and Design

Designer B's RtD process workbook overall suggests that research and design activities worked well together. The discursive conventions of the workbook supported his placement of prose paragraphs developing theory alongside annotated sketches and web cam hacks. The workbook's sprawling temporal unfolding can accommodate the often emergent movements of thought and emphasis that characterize an RtD project.

An example shows this at a finer resolution. In the first month of the design process, the group was reading about and attempting to theorize "criticality" in relation to design. The team was playing with a concept that they were calling "critical depth" and it was core to the research interest. The basic insight was that it is easy to be critical in a superficial way, and that doing so is sometimes a "way in" to a "deeper" kind of criticality. In the meeting minutes around that time, the team asked, "Is it possible to design iteratively from very shallowly critical to more deeply critical?"

Designer B's workbook from the following week has 11 pages devoted to this question. Pages 1-4 have him developing an analytical vocabulary to describe different aspects of his design (name, sensual qualities, actions/functions, critical components); each of these he analyzes thematically (100 words or so); this leads to insights (p.2), in which he views criticality not to inhere within any of his categories (e.g., a "critical form") but instead in the relations across categories (e.g., a design is critical in the relation of its form and actions); he then develops a semantic differential which he uses to analyze an actual advertisement and an AdBuster's ad (the latter representing criticality). This leads him to a result that seems to be similar to something he read in the research literature, though he does not specify what.

Pages 5-11 move from analytic work towards constructive design. Specifically, he takes one of his three critical design directions—the gumball machine with embedded camera and LCD screen—and imagines it at three levels of critical depth: from the most superficial towards the deepest. He does so using a combination of sketching along with textual descriptions; the sketching here is effortful, not quick stick figures but more developed renderings. He imagines a standard gumball machine (what he calls depth 0), a version of a gumball machine done in the style of H.R. Giger (level 1), and then a cancerous form of it (level 2) and finally a gun form of it (level 2). At the end of each sketch-annotation, he then provides a prose analysis. In this analysis, he talks about relations among form, function, affordances, and criticality of his different variations. He writes, "The Giger Form created questions about mass production and tradition within the system of gumball machine, while the Cancer and Gun Forms extended this to body issues and harmful actions, respectively."

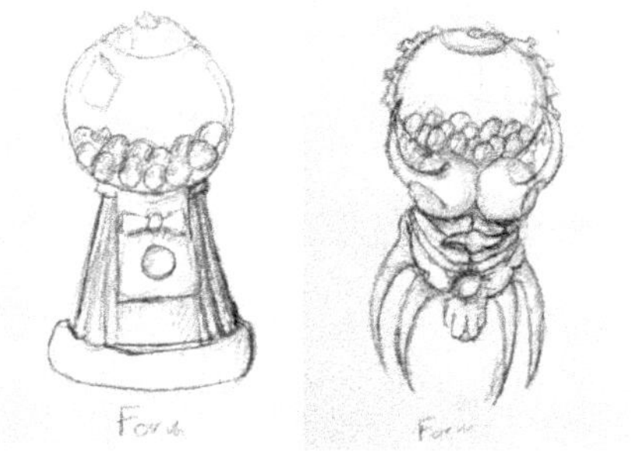

Fig. 1: Standard and "Giger" forms of the gumball machine

He then repeats the design exercise, this time changing the form of the gumballs. Instead of gum, he proposes tickers (strips of paper) with definitions of candy on them; in another version, instead of receiving candy, the user's hand is cut off; in the third variation, instead of candy, the user gets a bubble. Once again, he follows with an analysis. This time, he arrives at a research finding (i.e., a contribution to the theory of critical design): the more critical depth in the design, the less agency the user appears to have, which surprises him, since he expected the opposite.

In hindsight, we note that two of his "critical depth" research moves made it into his final designs. The Giger look informed one of his designs, though not the gumball machine, and a year later, during the deployment phase of the designs, the team used tickers instead of gumballs, though instead of putting the definition of candy on them, they put private details about participants' lives they were able to find on the Internet. In other words, even though the team never did pursue "critical depth" further as a concept, Designer B's constructive search in hopes of developing the concept did lead him to productive places. It occurred in a workbook entry that began with theory and analysis, transitioned to constructive design, and yielded insights for both the theory and design. Designer B's workbook offers evidence that the supposed gulf between research and design is not so great as it seems in theory; both are forms of inquiry and can mutually influence one another.

CASE 2: ODENPLAN

The Odenplan (OD) project was a ten-month collaboration between a design research lab and an architectural firm to develop media architectural components for a metro station at the Odenplan plaza in central Stockholm. The research team was composed of three senior researchers and four Ph.D. students. While the architects considered this a traditional design project, the research team considered their involvement to be an RtD process, in which the design activities were the catalyst to generate new knowledge and insights into the novel field of media architecture .

Thousands of documents and files were created during the project. In addition to individual repositories of documents, two shared systems were in place during the project. The first system was a research lab server. The material stored in the research lab server was primarily images and video files organized in folder correspond to design activities or specific aspects of the design process. The second system, which we will focus on in the following, was a dedicated tool to support design research projects, the PRT. As described by [13], PRT is a web-based system organized around documenting the design process in terms of events, sub-events and notes using time as the organizing principle. During the ten months of the OD project, the design and research activities were documented as 15 events in addition to three short notes. Each entry had a descriptive part representing what occurred during the process and a separate part where reflections on the process may be entered. Associated with each of the three kinds of elements, the tool supported the upload of still images, video footage, and documents. In addition to a list of all events and sub-events, a timeline visualised the relationship between the various elements according to the unfolding design process.

We focus here on the use of the collaborative online PRT system employed by the design research team, since it was developed and used with the specific intent of documenting the RtD process. We will also draw out a specific example of a single document: a video of the Traces design concept.

The Medium of RtD Documentation

The PRT tool was originally designed to be general, leaving the decision about how to document the process to the project participants. We consider the material substrate of PRT to be a range of individual documents, primarily text notes and reflections, photos and sketches of both the potential design products and documentation of discussions, e.g., photos of whiteboards with design reflections, and videos, which were either recordings of design events or video prototypes of potential products.

PRT offered predefined templates. Users could select to input notes or events, but had no way of altering the templates; for example, an event would come with an automatic timestamp and text fields labeled "Information", "Description", "Conclusion", "Reflections", and an option to upload media files. The system thus prescribed the types of information to be documented, and, of equal importance, indicated what was not. At the same time, these conventions drove specific patterns of coherence in the material.

In the OD case, members of the design research team would typically feed the system with text and visual documents *after*, rather than *during*, design events. In this respect, it served as a tool to record and offer an overview of the ongoing process, rather than one that supported in-the-moment exploration and discovery. The system inherits many of weblog traits, but adds further elements specific to design research, such as dedicated text fields for reflections and notes on an event. In the OD case, the work of documenting the project in PRT was generally perceived to be an additional workload on top of the design research team's traditional practice. Much of the content aggregated into the system would likely still have been created—e.g., sketches, meeting notes, and photos—but the process of aggregating this content, sometimes from multiple members of the design group, took time and was sometimes neglected. For each entry in the system there was a text entry box labeled "Reflections". After design events, design researchers would sometimes enter design insights; e.g., after a concept development workshop, a member of the team would summarize her insights from looking at the totality of the concepts in light of the design brief. Likewise, they would post reflections relating to their research agenda, e.g., on how an event had shed light on a specific research question. But in general, very few reflections were entered into the tool, in spite of rich discussions and reflections in the design research team throughout the project.

Documents as Speech Acts

Roughly half of the documents in the PRT related to planning and coordination activities, for instance minutes from meeting and phone conversation between the designers and the architects, and 3D rendering describing the site of the metro plaza. The statements in these documents generally serve to demonstrate how certain events unfolded, and in which sequence. They affirm certain chains of causality, which may be of interest in design research, e.g., that a given series of events led to a specific design decision. Furthermore, they justify the project to funding bodies by demonstrating the actual work involved.

The other half of the documents, and the most elaborate part, documents the design activities in sketches and other design materials. These documents explore what might be, and propose specific design decisions. Most of these entries were fairly brief consisting of only a few hundred words, with three exceptions documenting the main concept development workshop, its preparation, and the subsequent refinement of the key ideas developed during the workshop.

The preparation event was documented by three images of whiteboards from the meeting turned into three lists of key words and brief sentence capturing key aspect of the planning of the workshop. This part of the documentation was a rather brief and unprocessed summary of the meeting, but a brief note at the end of the summary points to a PDF file with much more structured documentation, namely a schematic representation of the design space identified during the meeting together with a diagrammatic representation of four parameters of engagement. The concept development workshop itself was a half-day workshop documented with five sub-events corresponding to the five main activities in the workshop. The textual part documenting the sub-events is in all cases rather brief – either bullet-lists or a couple of sentences. The textual documentation was supported by images of whiteboards from the meeting.

Figure 2: The *Traces* Virtual Video Prototype

We turn from the general use of PRT to a specific example of a single, yet complex, document: a virtual video prototype of the design concept, *Traces*. A virtual video prototype is a video in which a design concept is simulated, often using special effects [20]. The 30 second video visualises how the LED lights embedded into the OD staircase creates a trace of light behind people as they move (see figure 2). The Traces video is complex. It was developed as one of the final products from the design research lab, and as such it is the amalgamation of many prior ideas and documents, such as sketches and documents describing potential design concepts. The video served a number of design purposes: firstly, the creation of the video prompted the design researchers to make a number of design decisions that drove the design project forward, such as how LEDs would light up, and how they would respond to individual users vs. multiple users, etc. In this respect, the creation of the video prompted design refinement. Secondly, it served as a vehicle for communication between the design researchers and the architects, demonstrating the use of media architectural components clearly and in a manner that made it straightforward for the architects to assess and comment on the potentials of the interactive elements. Thirdly, it served as an end-product for the design researchers' involvement in the project, in combination with other deliverables such as technical specifications and 3D models.

Supporting Research and Design

The PRT system was almost exclusively employed by the design research team during the project. The architects were invited to view the ongoing documentation, but they preferred to be kept in the loop via meetings, phone calls, emails, and exchanges of files such as 3D models. Even though the OD project was thoroughly documented, it nevertheless represents a very specific selection of information on the project, namely that which might prove important from a design research perspective. The system did little, if anything, to drive the design process forward. However, it proved useful from a research perspective, since it was subsequently used as a resource for multiple research contributions. In spite of these benefits to research, which the design research team knew from previous projects, it still proved difficult to ensure that information from the project was put into the system. The primary value from using the system came from employing it retrospectively to analyse the process and/or specific events, whereas there was less immediate value of entering the content. This represents a profound challenge: how can design researchers ensure that relevant information will be aggregated if it is unclear if and how this might later be of use; this challenge is greater still if it requires other parties with little or no in-terest in the research perspective to take part in entering the content, as was the case with the architects in this project.

Even though PRT was primarily used by the design team, it would seem at surface that the documentation in the tool favored documenting aspects related to the design process rather than specific research topics. However, a more careful analysis reveals that the design process and hence also the documentation process was driven by both design and research interests. For instance, one of the Ph.D. students investigated 'space' as a resource in the design process and several documents, e.g.,images of public plazas and stairs, related directly the Ph.D. project. Another Ph.D. student's project was about generative design materials, which mirrored a certain interest in documenting the various materials used throughout the process. Likewise, several of the researchers involved in the project had an interest in the role of inspirational materials in the design process, which is carefully documented with images and links to websites presented as sources of inspiration during the workshop.

Let us once again consider the Traces video, which visualises the idea that the people on the stairs of the Odenplan station would leave behind luminous traces of their presence as they moved about. During the design process, the 3D animations were very important design visualizations assisting the designers in developing and concretising the design ideas developed at main concept development workshop. But, perhaps even more importantly, they represented the primary way of communicating the design concept to the collaborators at the architectural firm. From a research perspective, the animations became important elements of a research paper using the OD project as the main case. Three years later, the 3D models used for the animations were used for the production of a virtual video prototype of one of the other design concepts, and subsequently included in a research paper on tools for media architecture [26].

DISCUSSION

The PA and OD cases, though different, were of comparable scale with respect to the number of people involved in the projects and the length of the time period each project unfolded. Moreover the participants in both projects handled a large number of documents. We first discuss how the two cases relate to the three core concerns—the medium of documentation, the performativity of documentation, and providing equal support for both research and design—and then turn to a discussion of the generative and instrumental capacities of RtD documentation.

Comparison of RtD Documentation in the Two Cases

The Medium of RtD Documentation

The principal medium for the PA project was based on a generic word processor (Word) whereas the OD project used the custom designed PRT tool. Both support similar basic materials: text and bitmaps (PRT also supports video files). They differ in the conventions for manipulating these materials and the sorts of "piece" or "wholes" they yield. The word processer offers only generic conventions for organizing a document: pages, columns, paragraphs, paragraph types. In contrast, PRT provides templates that reflect and also enforce the RtD documentation conventions that informed its design. These templates made it easier for team members to understand which types of information they were supposed to enter into the system and how to read entries from other members. The assemblage and manipulation of these elements led to very different finished documents, as we explain next.

Documents as Speech Acts

As we've stressed, the shift from thinking about what RtD documentation is to what it *does* was key for us. Above all, RtD documentation articulates the ongoing refinement and development of design/research ideas within a project context. It features proposals, descriptions, justifications, explorations, experiments, and reflections. A key point of difference between the two cases is the role of *reflection* in documentation. Whereas there was very little evidence of reflection in the PRT system, the Word-based PA workbook had reflections from end to end.

We believe in hindsight that this difference has to do with the way the two tools handle the *aggregation* of diverse design document types. PRT offered a structured warehouse of assets as well as a timeline to provide an overview of the process. PRT managed assets as raw materials in an organized way, but in usage, the aggregation of these raw materials into meaningful narratives occurred for the most part outside of and after the use of PRT—e.g., as researchers pulled out from PRT elements of interest to their specific research projects, including production of research papers.

In contrast, Word—both in its technical features and use conventions—proposes that the work in question is *a document*: singular, unified, and coherent regardless of the nature and number of its elements. This in turn creates the subtle and ongoing suggestion that as design documents are inserted into it, some narrative should be constructed to explain their place. The PA workbook was not only organized over time; it also told a story. In contrast to PRT, it was filled with reflections, regardless of design phase. However, the PA Word workbook was created and maintained by a single designer, although it was routinely shared with many other stakeholders. It is less clear how or whether this document would scale if more than one team member were to attempt to contribute to it, and similarly (the present project excepted) the workbook was not used by other team members in their own research projects.

Supporting Research and Design

The PRT was developed to be a dedicated system for documenting RtD processes. As such, it presents a markedly different example of RtD documentation than the PA workbook, which exemplified individual documentation using a generic tool. The PA workbook supported both research and design on an ongoing basis; the two were often interwoven. The PA workbook most directly makes reference to theory and research hypothesis alongside of documents of the design process, such as sketches. In contrast, although PRT also supported these activities, it was not always clear in the system—e.g. many discussions during the process were informed by documents in PRT, but these discussions were not always captured and put back into PRT.

It is worth stressing that both approaches supported subsequent research activities; it is just that they did so in different ways. PRT supported multiple collaborators inputting documentation and also turning to it as a resource in subsequent research activities, but real-time reflections were only in exceptionally cases entered using the tool. The PA Word workbook supported the real-time juxtaposition of theory, research questions, multimedia design documents, and technical-material explorations; reflection was the glue that held the document together. However, it did so at the expense of collaboration, and as its narrative became "burned in" during its process of creation, it is more difficult to return to its raw materials without also perceiving them in relation to that narrative.

The Need for RtD Discourse Genres

A key insight that emerged in this project was that aggregation and reflection are two aspects of the same activity. Aggregation simply refers to the selection of assets for inclusion in some other document: a project report, a dissertation, a pitch for resources, a portfolio, a data set, an inspiration document, a postmortem, etc. Aggregation is always a purposeful activity: it involves decisions about the substantive and rhetorical purposes of the document.

Further, we observe that such aggregations can be formed into discourses in conventional ways. For example, given the temporal nature of research through design, it is not surprising that some kind of *narrative* is one of the dominant structural forms of this discourse. Part of what seems to be happening in the still emerging discipline of research through design is that we are figuring out what some of those conventions are. We propose that Gaver's specific conception of "workbooks" and "annotated portfolios", the emerging format of "Pictorials", Dalsgaard et al's notion of "maps for design reflection", Binder & Brandt's "genealogies"—all of these might be glossed as proposals for standard "genres" of RtD aggregations-as-discourse. Each provides research through design practitioners cues about what elements to aggregate and in what quantity, at which stage in the process, for which audience, and in service of which goals. Eventually, there might be dozens of such genres.

We began this paper with a series of practical questions: What should we document, to what extents, and using which tools/media? How do we balance the effort of documentation with its reward? How do we document a dynamic process, where the research and/or design focus can change along the way? How do we balance the need to push a project forward with capturing its key moments for reflection? How do we document tacit knowledge and embodied knowledge (e.g., of materials)?

We tried to answer these questions ourselves and came up short. Instead of concluding with such answers, we instead end with what we believe the RtD community might do to pursue such answers. We propose that the RtD community needs to develop discursive genres that facilitate communicative aggregations. There is a technical side of this, which involves the capture, storage, and searchability of RtD process elements: briefs, sketches, conversations, design proposals, crits, prototypes, theoretical resources, whiteboards, experimental results, exemplars, insights, models. The development of tools, such as PRT, can help with this. But there is also a need to develop our practice. Specifically, we propose the need to develop RtD discursive genres, and even more fundamentally, to recognize the possibility and existence of RtD discursive genres in the first place. Such genres, of which we already have some examples and hope to see many more, will collectively answer the questions with which we began the paper.

Our conception of *medium* can inform the development of such genres by clarifying the "what" of design discourse genres: their materials, conventions for manipulating them, and a sense of the finished "piece" conceived holistically. Many personal design workbooks are never fully "whole," but genealogies, annotated portfolios, and maps all strive towards such a fulfillment. A theory of medium brings into focus the need for conventionalized ways of assembling coherent wholes out of concrete materials.

Our conception of *performativity* can inform the development of such genres by foregrounding the "why" and "how" of design discourse. How can this particular aggregation perform some aspect of the RtD activity in the right way for the right audience (which can of course include oneself in the present or even future)? Put another way, what can be eliminated from the document to best serve this goal? Gaver's conception of "workbooks" is far more specific and narrow than what we have typically seen in designer workbooks. His conception imposes constraints that not only guide the construction of the workbook, but which also crystallizes its limited purpose—making it much easier to fulfill that purpose and to recognize and evaluate it. (It obviously does not replace the role of traditional workbooks.)

Our conception of *supporting research and design* was not intended to reify a divide between the two. Rather, it was to recognize that RtD comprises a diverse range of activities, and that at certain stages in the process, we often subjectively experience ourselves as doing one, and that in those moments, it is easy to lose sight of the fact that we are also doing the other. This can lead to problems in documentation that only reveal themselves much later on. For example, it can exaggerate the apparent gulf between the design-as-particular and knowledge-as-general, because our focus tends to be on one or the other at different times in the process.

At the initial stage of this project, our intention was to examine how documentation supports research and design. However, one of the key insights from the in-depth studies of the two cases is that *documentation is itself an act*—an RtD act. Documentation is not merely serving in an *instrumental* capacity to report on facts and findings; it is also *generative* in that it "talks back" to us as designers and researchers. This insight has helped us translate nouns—document, sketch, to do list, virtual video prototype—into verbs: to explore, demonstrate, propose, decide, hack, explain, educate, justify, reflect, narrate, pitch. In these verbs, project roles and meaningful units are made more visible, and the pragmatic and epistemic potentials of documentation become clearer.

ACKNOWLEDGEMENTS

The authors thank Indiana University, Aarhus University, the Intel Science and Technology Center for Social Computing and Innovation Fund Denmark (CIBIS 1311-00001B) for supporting this research. We also thank the reviewers for challenging us to up our game.

REFERENCES

1. Michael Atwood and John Horner. 2006. Effective Design Rationale: Understanding the Barriers. In A.H.

Dutoit, R. McCall, I. Mistrik, & B. Paech (Eds.) *Rationale management in software engineering*. Springer-Verlag, 73-90

2. John Langshaw Austin. 1962. *How to Do Things with Words*. Cambridge, MA: Harvard University Press.
3. Jeffrey Bardzell and Shaowen Bardzell. 2015. *Humanistic HCI*. Morgan & Claypool.
4. Jeffrey Bardzell, Shaowen Bardzell, and Lone Koefoed Hansen. 2015. Immodest Proposals: Research through design and knowledge. In *Proceedings of the SIGCHI Conference on Human Factors in Computing Systems* (CHI '15). ACM, New York, NY, USA, 2093-2102.
5. Ditte Amund Basballe and Kim Halskov. 2012. Dynamics of research through design. In *Proceedings of the Designing Interactive Systems Conference* (DIS '12). ACM, New York, NY, USA, 58-67. DOI=10.1145/2317956.2317967.
6. Thomas Binder and Eva Brandt. 2007. Experimental design research: genealogy, intervention, argument, *International association of societies of design research 2007: emerging trends in design*, Hong Kong.
7. Eli Blevis, Elizabeth Churchill, William Odom, James Pierce, David Roedl, and Ron Wakkary. 2012. Visual thinking & digital imagery. In *CHI '12 Extended Abstracts on Human Factors in Computing Systems* (CHI EA '12). ACM, New York, NY, USA, 2715-2718. DOI=http://dx.doi.org/10.1145/2212776.2212703
8. John Bowers. 2012. The logic of annotated portfolios: communicating the value of 'research through design'. In *Proceedings of the Designing Interactive Systems Conference* (DIS '12). ACM, New York, NY, USA, 68-77. DOI=http://dx.doi.org/10.1145/2317956.2317968
9. Janet Burge and David Brown. 1998. *Design Rationale: Types and Tools, Technical Report*, Worchester Polytechnic Institute, Computer Science Dept., retrieved on 03 January 2016.
10. Janet Burge, 2008. Design rationale: Researching under uncertainty. Artificial Intelligence for Engineering Design, Analysis and Manufacturing, vol 22, 311–324.
11. Peter Dalsgaard and Christian Dindler. 2014. Between theory and practice: bridging concepts in HCI research. In *Proceedings of the SIGCHI Conference on Human Factors in Computing Systems* (CHI '14). ACM, New York, NY, USA, 1635-1644. DOI=http://dx.doi.org/10.1145/2556288.2557342
12. Peter Dalsgaard, Kim Halskov, and Rune Nielsen, R. 2009. Maps for design reflection. Artifact Journal, Routledge.
13. Peter Dalsgaard and Kim Halskov. 2012. Reflective design documentation. In *Proceedings of the Designing Interactive Systems Conference* (DIS '12). ACM, New York, NY, USA, 428-437. DOI=10.1145/2317956.2318020
14. Peter Dalsgaard, Kim Halskov, and Ditte Amund Basballe. 2014. Emergent boundary objects and boundary zones in collaborative design research projects. In *Proceedings of the 2014 conference on Designing interactive systems* (DIS '14). ACM, New York, NY, USA, 745-754. DOI=http://dx.doi.org/10.1145/2598510.2600878
15. David Davies. 2003. Medium in art. In Jerrold Levinson, ed., *The Oxford Handbook of Aesthetics*. Oxford: Oxford University Press, 181-91.
16. Christopher Frayling. 1993. *Research in Art and Design*, Royal College of Art Research Papers series 1(1) 1-5.
17. William Gaver. 2011. Making spaces: how design workbooks work. In *Proceedings of the SIGCHI Conference on Human Factors in Computing Systems* (CHI '11). ACM, New York, NY, USA, 1551-1560. DOI=http://dx.doi.org/10.1145/1978942.1979169
18. William Gaver. 2012. What should we expect from research through design? In *Proceedings of the SIGCHI Conference on Human Factors in Computing Systems* (CHI '12). ACM, New York, NY, USA, 937-946. http://doi.acm.org/10.1145/2207676.2208538
19. Saul Greenberg and Bill Buxton. 2008. Usability considered harmful (some of the time). In *Proceedings of the SIGCHI Conference on Human Factors in Computing Systems* (CHI '08). ACM, New York, NY, USA, 111-120.
20. Kim Halskov and Rune Nielsen. 2008. Virtual video prototyping. *Hum.-Comput. Interact.* 21, 2 (May 2008), 199-233. DOI=http://dx.doi.org/10.1207/s15327051hci2102_2.
21. Kristina Höök, Jeffrey Bardzell, Simon Bowen, Peter Dalsgaard, Stuart Reeves, and Annika Waern. 2015. Framing IxD knowledge. *interactions* 22, 6 (October 2015), 32-36. DOI=http://dx.doi.org/10.1145/2824892
22. Kristina Höök, Peter Dalsgaard, Stuart Reeves, Jeffrey Bardzell, Jonas Löwgren, Erik Stolterman, and Yvonne Rogers. 2015. Knowledge Production in Interaction Design. In *Proceedings of the 33rd Annual ACM Conference Extended Abstracts on Human Factors in Computing Systems* (CHI EA '15). ACM, New York, NY, USA, 2429-2432. DOI=http://dx.doi.org/10.1145/2702613.2702653
23. Kristina Höök and Jonas Löwgren. 2012. Strong concepts: Intermediate-level knowledge in interaction design research. *ACM Trans. Comput.-Hum. Interact.* 19, 3, Article 23 (October 2012), 18 pages. DOI=http://dx.doi.org/10.1145/2362364.2362371
24. Nadine Jarvis, David Cameron, and Andy Boucher. 2012. Attention to detail: annotations of a design pro-

cess. In *Proceedings of the 7th Nordic Conference on Human-Computer Interaction: Making Sense Through Design* (NordiCHI '12). ACM, New York, NY, USA, 11-20. DOI=http://dx.doi.org/10.1145/2399016.2399019

25. Ilpo Koskinen, Thomas Binder, and Jonas Redström. 2008. Lab, Field, Gallery, and Beyond. Artifact, 2, 1.
26. Henrik Korsgaard, Nicolai Brodersen Hansen, Ditte Basballe, Peter Dalsgaard, and Kim Halskov. 2012. Odenplan: a media façade design process. In *Proceedings of the 4th Media Architecture Biennale Conference: Participation* (MAB '12). ACM, New York, NY, USA, 23-32. DOI=http://dx.doi.org/10.1145/2421076.2421081
27. Jonas Löwgren. 2013. Annotated portfolios and other forms of intermediate-level knowledge.*interactions* 20, 1 (January 2013), 30-34. DOI=http://dx.doi.org/10.1145/2405716.2405725
28. Harald Nelson and Erik Stolterman. 2012. The Design Way: Intentional Change in an Unpredictable World. 2nd ed. Cambridge, MA: MIT Press.
29. John Zimmerman, Jodi Forlizzi, and Shelley Evenson. 2007. Research through design as a method for interaction design research in HCI. In *Proceedings of the SIGCHI Conference on Human Factors in Computing Systems* (CHI '07). ACM, New York, NY, USA, 493-502. DOI=http://dx.doi.org/10.1145/1240624.1240704
30. John Zimmerman, Erik Stolterman, and Jodi Forlizzi. 2010. An analysis and critique of *Research through Design*: towards a formalization of a research approach. In *Proceedings of the 8th ACM Conference on Designing Interactive Systems* (DIS '10). ACM, New York, NY, USA, 310-319. DOI=10.1145/1858171.185822

Interaction Design Labels: Concepts, Inscriptions, and Concealed Intentions

Verena Fuchsberger, Martin Murer, Alina Krischkowsky, Manfred Tscheligi
Center for Human-Computer Interaction, University of Salzburg
Salzburg, Austria
firstname.lastname@sbg.ac.at

ABSTRACT
A variety of concepts in contemporary Human-Computer Interaction and Interaction Design (research) are labeled by adding attributes, such as "slow", "unaware" or "counterfunctional", to "technology", "object" or "thing". However, what do these labels disclose about a technology or an interaction? What are they supposed to express, what do they conceal? In order to identify labelling mechanisms in our (research) community, we describe five cases and analyze their labels, concepts, and intentions. Among others, we argue that the labels and the expressed aims or intentions do not always correspond and explore alternative ways to articulate and label design concepts or philosophies. We conclude by calling for Interaction Design labels that are based on careful reflections of conceptual histories, inscriptions, and intentions.

ACM Classification Keywords
H.5.m. Information Interfaces and Presentation (e.g. HCI): Miscellaneous

Author Keywords
Interaction Design Labels; Design Theory; Actor-Network Theory; Appropriation; Intermediary Knowledge.

INTRODUCTION
Characterizing relations between humans and interactive artifacts is a difficult endeavor, especially when referring to a specific group or concept of technologies, interactions, or experiences. Sometimes, the artifact itself is characterized (e.g., *slow technology* [23]), sometimes the resulting user experience is referred to (e.g., *emotional experience* [41]). In other cases, relations between humans and artifacts are characterized by human attributes (e.g., *charismatic technology* [3]), i.e., an attribute that is usually characterizing an individual, is transferred to technology. Some artifacts are said to be natural, leading to intense discussions on whether this is valid, as it remains unclear what this actually means [25]. In this paper we specifically focus on labels in Interaction Design (research), in form of attributes that are used to define (a group of) objects, arguing that other intentions than a specification of a technology are sought to express. In line with Hansen and Dalsgaard, we emphasize that the words we use to describe technology matter, as they carry "connotations, establish expectations about the role and use of an object" and "foreground particular qualities, while obscuring others" [25, p. 65].

Many of these labels follow different intentions, e.g., describing a design or research concept of a group of objects or interactions, providing design (research) knowledge, etc. Based on Actor-Network Theory (ANT; e.g., [37]) and design theory (e.g., strong concepts [27]), we reconsider specific attributes and their attachment to objects in order to shed light on what is attempted to be expressed when referring to them. Therefore, we analyze different kinds of labels to trace their origin, i.e., what they actually aim to convey.

This discussion contributes, on one hand, to the articulation of (design) research knowledge, e.g., in form of concepts. On the other hand, it is practically relevant. For instance, when we, as a research community, talk about *counterfunctional things* [49] – do we refer to the concept, to one counterfunctional thing, to users' experiences with them? Do we assume that with discussing *unaware objects* [47] it is given that we refer to the concept, not to *an* unaware object? Does this assumption hold true if we talk about *disobedient objects* [17], which presumably do not belong to the community's common ground? Do we then know whether it is a concept, philosophy, or group of *disobedient objects*? Are we aware of the label's histories, notions, intentions, and audience?

To position the analysis, we draw on Vardouli's characterization of human-artifact engagements, i.e., design-centric, communicative, and use-centric attitudes [53]. Afterwards, we briefly describe ANT's vocabulary to trace the agency of both human and non-human actors. Then, we present five examples of human-artifact encounters, analyze and discuss their notions, and provide implications on how to proceed with an alternative wording. These implications focus on alternative ways to label, for instance, design concepts (e.g., referring to an activity instead of a property). Further, they include a proposal to articulate not only the concepts, but also why they were labeled in a certain way, i.e., why emphasis is put on a specific element of the concept or the context, including its goals, inscriptions, etc.

DIS 2016, June 04-08, 2016, Brisbane, QLD, Australia
©2016 ACM. ISBN 978-1-4503-4031-1/16/06...$15.00
DOI: http://dx.doi.org/10.1145/2901790.2901846

BACKGROUND

This section is dedicated to conceptual and theoretical work on human-artifact engagements. In an earlier work, we provided a theoretical framing of actors in HCI and Interaction Design [19] by focusing on active encounters with interactive artifacts, Interaction Gestalt[1] or design materials (physical, digital). Based on Actor-Network Theory (ANT), we argued for an (analytical) symmetry, proposing to not only investigate how humans design or use interactive artifacts (e.g., shape, craft, use, alter), but also how those influence humans (e.g., inspire, constrain, impress, stimulate). One main argument is that designers' intentions can be, but not necessarily are, affecting the user in a certain (or any) way; rather, those are different relations with different attributes and qualities [19].

The following background section considers in detail different forms of human-artifact encounters. Therefore, we draw on Vardouli's analysis of attitudes to human-artifact engagements [53], and literature on technology appropriation (e.g., [13]), which specifically focuses on the fragile relation between designers' intentions and users' actions.

Human-Artifact Engagements

Based on literature from design research, material culture studies, design anthropology and function theory, Vardouli [53] differentiates between three *attitudes to human-artifact engagements*. First, she refers to the term *design-centric* for theories and methods that "view use as a derivate of an artifact's function" [53, p. 139]. This perspective contains models that consider the designer as anticipating a specific form of use, which is translated into functional requirements that are finally attached to physical form. *Communicative* human-artifact engagements, Vardouli's second attitude, specifically focus on the alignment of anticipated use with actual use. Therein, artifacts are considered "communicational devices that link the spatially and temporally separated contexts of design and use" [53, p. 139]. Artifacts communicate messages about an intended function or value to the users, who then interpret this. Finally, Vardouli proposes to think of *use-centric* attitudes. Thereby, use is considered to be open-ended and temporally unfolding, which can be described without referring to an design intentions [53].

Critiquing design-centric and communicative perspectives (e.g., strong ties between designers' intention and the resulting use of the object), Vardouli finally suggests a refinement of the use-centric attitude towards *use as making*, i.e., an active and embodied engagement with the material world, promoting temporality and emergence. She argues for differentiating between designers' intentions and users' usage [53]. This is specifically important when it comes to the description of design concepts (and how they are labeled), which, as a consequence, would need to clearly distinguish between designers' intentions and actual use.

Technology Appropriation

This differentiation also resonates with the discourse in HCI and Interaction Design around *appropriation*. Though understood by Vardouli as a communicative attitude towards technology [53], i.e., artifacts are tying the disparate settings of design and use, literature on appropriation suggests different perspectives, which may also be aligned with use-centric and making use. Philosophers of technology raise questions whether functional descriptions in the context of design actually relate to the ways technology is used [32].

While the disparity between intentions of those designing and actual use [10] is sometimes considered as dysfunctional [12], others consider it as an integral aspect of use [10] and a positive phenomenon in system design [10, 13, 16, 29]. Especially the latter has brought forward research on technology appropriation that is specifically investigating (e.g., in user studies or ethnographic fieldwork) the various ways how people appropriate technology in their very own ways by fitting them into their individual practices [14], e.g., how the technology has become the user's own [7].

In regards to design, Dix argues that "design can never be complete" as it is "impossible to design for the unexpected" [13, p. 27]. Designing for appropriation is often considered as an oxymoron [13, p. 27], as designers will never be able to fully anticipate users' specific needs, values, and intentions of using technology in encompassing usage environments that are highly situated and dynamic [15]. In exploring how people appropriate technology, we can learn about new arrangements of people and things, and indeed learn more about how unanticipated usage generates and 'naturalizes' new forms and orders of causality and knowledge about the world [1]. Therefore, technologies may be approached as entities that have no fixed identities, rather embody interpretative flexibility [6] and/or multistability [28], designed in an open-ended and malleable way that allows for unexpected users and usages.

Human-Artifact Encounters

Research on appropriation focuses on the activity arising in use. This is similar to making-use in Vardouli's understanding [53], but may also be framed as a negotiation between actors, which in these cases is concerning the association between users and artifacts. However, negotiations also characterize the relations between designers and materials or interactive artifacts [20]. Thus, not only making-use may be of relevance for describing phenomena on HCI and IxD, but also making-design, indicating the active negotiation between humans and non-human, material actors in different human-artifact encounters. In the following, we discuss the labels of different human-artifact encounters, and how they are connected to the articulations of the respective concepts.

RESEARCH OBJECTIVES AND APPROACH

Concepts, philosophies, or ideas in HCI and Interaction Design research are often labeled similarly, i.e., there is an [attribute] (sometimes a rather human characteristic, sometimes a non-human characteristic) in combination with a [non-human actor], resulting in the form [attribute] [non-human actor]. For instance, attributes that usually characterize humans are transferred to artifacts, such as *charismatic technology*, or artifacts are equipped with any other attribute, such as *counterfunctional* or *unaware*. The resulting labels in form of [attribute] [non-human actor] are then often used for tagging a specific

[1] see Lim et al. for a detailed description of Interaction Gestalt [42]

design (research) *concept*, rather than a or *n* design(s). However, what do we, as a research community, actually mean when talking about *unaware objects*? Are we referring to the concept created by someone, to an object, to how individuals make use of this object? Are the creators of a concept "present at the moment" [53, p. 146] of discussion, of designing an instantiation, or of use? Are we taking enough care for how we articulate our concepts?

Approach

In the following paragraphs we establish why the labels that we use might not always be expedient to describe the different human-artifact encounters they address. In order to do so, we refer to Actor-Network Theory (ANT) as analytical lens. In contrast to investigations based on ANT that focus on the "laboratories", i.e., the sites of activity, we refer to ANT as methodological perspective for analyzing notions and concepts in Interaction Design. The main reason for taking ANT's perspective is that it does not consider the nature of an artifact as decisive, rather, its agency and activity is what counts (see e.g., [19]). Methodologically, ANT treats all observed entities (counterfactually) as if an attribution of authorship had not yet happened [51].

If authorship (e.g., who created what specific Interaction Design research concept / label) is left aside, the labels we use become mere shells, neglecting the creators' (authors') concepts and notions that are including more than one (or *n*) specific instantiation. Thus, what is not communicated through the label is the intention that comes with it, the *inscriptions* into the objects are not conveyed. The labels may not be required to communicate all these inscriptions and aims, but they are representatives of the concepts as titles of research papers, exhibitions, or (singular) artifacts.

Based on these considerations, we analyze in detail what the concepts, labeled in form of [attribute] [non-human actor], actually include, such as aims and purposes. ANT is chosen as the theoretical and methodological background for analyzing them; its sometimes radical positions are considered to be helpful to sort out different notions, rather than taking them for granted [18]. Therefore, we provide a (very brief) overview of ANT in the following, which clarifies the perspective that we "borrow" for this analysis.

Actor-Network Theory

ANT, a theory associated with Science and Technology Studies (STS), aims to descibe *the social*, arguing "that the stuff of the social isn't simply human" [39, p. 283]. It is a multifaceted theory about how human and non-human actors form networks with a set of relations that constitute *the social*. These networks are unstable, i.e., they are formed for specific purposes and terminated by the ending of that very phenomenon [37]. ANT contains a multitude of associated constructs, descriptions, and terminologies[2] (see e.g., [2, 45]). We focus on a few assumptions, which are relevant for the argument of this paper. They are mainly extracted from writings of Bruno Latour (e.g., [34]), Madeleine Akrich (e.g., [1]), and John Law (e.g., [40]), who were significant contributors to the development, interpretation, and discussion of ANT.

- *Actors* can be human, non-human, or hybrid (e.g., a gun and a gunman [35]). Actions and agency are distributed between many actors that have goals [35], which are sometimes referred to as "competencies" of actors.
- *Networks* are associations of human and non-human actors, whereby a human actor is not an actor primarily because he or she inhabits a body that carries knowledges, skills, and values, but he or she inhabits a set of elements (including a body) that stretches out into the network of materials, somatic and otherwise, that surrounds each body. Thinking, acting, writing, loving (all attributes that we normally ascribe to human beings), are generated in networks that pass through and ramify within and beyond the body [39].
- *Inscriptions* are actors' (e.g., designers, engineers) efforts to *inscribe* a vision into another actor (e.g., a technology) [1], being an inscription in an agency [36]. For instance, a street bump that has been created to make drivers speed down has the engineers' program of action (i.e., its goal) inscribed in concrete [35].

Whenever referring to ANT, it is necessary to discuss the critiques that it faces. One major concern with ANT is the proposed symmetry of actors (e.g., [52]). There is a long-standing discussion, with advocates of either the one or the other standpoint, debating whether it is valid to not consider humans' motives and motivations in the first place, with no superiority to non-human actors. However, as we pointed out in an earlier discussion on monads (a refinement of ANT [38]), the symmetry may be considered an analytical lens, a methodological attempt to alternate an analysis between humans and artifacts, which does not pre-assume a hierarchy [18]. However, in our reading it also does not indicate that there is *no* hierarchy either; it is rather a matter of detailed descriptions of empirical data, which may reveal activity between actors in either direction. Taking these perspectives as methodological background, we go into detail about the concepts that are labeled in form of [attribute] [non-human actor] in the following.

[ATTRIBUTE] [NON-HUMAN ACTOR] LABELS

In this chapter, concepts are described that use the combination of [attribute] [non-human actor] to label them. Thus, the labels define non-human actors by attributing them characteristics. We selected concepts in a literature review, which was based on several considerations: We included cases that are heterogeneous in nature, ranging from generative conceptualizations and evaluative ideas [27] to meaning-making notions. All of the cases have recently been developed, exhibited, or discussed in the realm of Interaction Design (research), e.g., presented at recent conferences such as the International Conference on Designing Interactive Systems (DIS), Creativity and Cognition (C&C), or Critical Alternatives, the decennial Aarhus Conference. One of these cases is not positioned within HCI or Interaction Design research, i.e., an exhibition on *disobedient*

[2]It might seem contradictory to call for nuanced terminology in HCI and Interaction Design based on a theory that does not consolidate its own terms, but borrows, invents, or adapts new words every now and then itself [45]. However, the terms of ANT that are used here are clarified as far as possible, taking into account that they are one interpretation of potential numerous ones.

objects. The reason for including this exhibition is that looking beyond the established HCI or design research community (e.g., into arts) helps preserving a critical and relational perspective on what is happening within the community, which is, though rarely realized, of high relevance.

A variety of cases fulfill these criteria (e.g., *unaware objects* [47], *slow technology* [23], *counterfunctional things* [49], *charismatic technology* [3], *disobedient objects* [17], *sociable technology* or *polite technology* [5, 44], *celebratory technology* [22], *natural user interfaces* [57], etc.). In order to establish the argument within the limits of a paper, we finally focused on five cases to be included, which have been chosen based on the heterogeneity of notions and instantiations.

The following case descriptions already contain an analytic step. Texts on [unaware, slow, counterfunctional, charismatic, and disobedient] technologies, objects, or things are analyzed and summarized regarding three aspects: what the respective authors understand as [unaware, slow, counterfunctional, charismatic, and disobedient] technology, object or thing; the framing that is given to these cases (e.g., whether it is considered a concept, a design philosophy, or else); and concrete instantiations. This first step of the analysis is based on an assumption provided by ANT, i.e., what inscriptions they contain. At the end of each case we provide a preliminary analysis that provides an outline of inscriptions and interpretations in regards to human-artifact encounters.

[Unaware] [Objects]

This label was coined by Odom and Wakkary [47], referring to objects that emphasize actuality over functionality, neither having an explicit interface nor computational awareness of humans' presence or actions. They enact their behavior without requiring any attentions of their owners, being designed in a way that they are computationally unaffected by direct interactions. These post-functional engagements between humans and an unaware object are considered to be *intersections*, which are unique and dynamic configurations of artifacts, contexts, and human actions [47]. Odom and Wakkary did not refer to the term *interaction* due to its notion of direct manipulation of an artifact. Rather, intersections are considered as complementary to interactions, being more general to account for a broad range of known and unknown human-technology encounters [47].

Framing

Odom and Wakkary consider *unaware objects* as a concept, which provides knowledge stemming from synthesizing insights gained from the development and study of the instantiations. Furthermore, *actuality* and *post-funcationality* are presented as strategies that may guide future generative work in the Interaction Design community [47].

Instantiations

Unaware objects resulted from critical reflections on the conceptualizations, designs, and analysis of two Research through Design (RtD) approaches (see e.g., [21, 31, 58]), i.e., the Photobox [48] and table-non-table (e.g., [55]). The Photobox aimed to critically intervene in experiences of digital overload resulting from personal digital content (e.g., photos or videos) that captures life experiences. It was designed to slow down the consumption of digital pictures to support humans' reflection (see its relation to *slow technology* below). Therefore, a photo printer in a wooden box randomly printed four to five photos a month from an owner's Flickr account at selected timestamps that were difficult to anticipate.

The table-non-table, another example of an unaware object, was designed to be aligned with the competences, materials, and motivations of life practices in everyday homes. It is a slowly moving stack of paper (paper was chosen due to humans' familiarity with the material, its flexibility and allowance for simple practices) that rests on a chassis, moved by two motorized wheels. The movements were randomized, but kept within short distances to be almost imperceptible [47].

By deploying both artifacts, the authors found that the unaware nature of the Photobox and the table-non-table resulted in being lived-with while remaining open-ended over time. Furthermore, encounters went beyond appropriation by creating creativity that is reflective or mindful.

> While unaware objects are designed with people in mind, their functionality differs significantly and is not dependent on human interaction, attention or presence. They do function, yet in ways that provoke people to work towards their own understandings or uses of unaware objects within their own everyday lives and environments. [47, p. 41]

Thus, post-functionality and actuality were crucial characteristics of these instantiations of *unaware objects*.

*With **unaware objects** a generative design concept is described, which incorporates objects that are unaffected of direct interactions. Inscriptions into instantiations are aiming for making-use (i.e., an active and embodied engagement with the world [53]). These engagements are described as actual and post-functional, which the authors then suggest as strategies for generative design work. Design knowledge is provided in form of the concept, which is informed by findings on individuals' experiencing its instantiations.*

[Slow] [Technology]

The above described Photobox [47, 48] is also an example of *slow technology*. Starting from the notion of *calm technology*, which engages both the center and the periphery of our attention by moving back and forth between the two to create calm and comfort [56], Hallnäs and Redström developed the notion of *slow technology*. Its central assumption is that not only technology is needed that supports calm, but which creates moments of reflection and mental rest [23]. Its key issue is

> that we should use slowness in learning, understanding and presence to give people time to think and reflect. [23, p. 203]

Thereby, aesthetics of functionality, rather than an artifact's objectives, are in the focus. Slowness can also concern appearance and presence, being inherent in the design, with time as the central and explicit notion within the design. Slowness may also come from reflection on aesthetics and changing perspectives, independent from whether the artifact is aiming to be used to efficiently accomplish tasks [23]. Further, re-visitation of the past may also be a design goal under the umbrella of *slow technology* [46].

Framing
Slow technology is considered a *design philosophy*, and might also be a kind of design leitmotif for this type of Interaction Design, emphasizing the conceptualization of a design style, a form of expression [23]. Later, Hallnäs and Redström present *slow technology* as a *design program*, i.e., what lays out the foundations for a series of design experiments [24].

Instantiations
By means of the Photobox, Odom et al. aimed to explore how slowness may support anticipation over time and create a pace of interaction that would support self-reflection [48]. Another example is the Chatterbox, a system for sharing information in public space. However, instead of presenting the information as it is, the Chatterbox messes the information up by more or less randomly recombining information pieces (e.g., substituting words from one text with words from another one). Over time, people can make sense by recognizing text fragments or certain words. One of the aims of the Chatterbox was "to use technology developed for efficient information distribution to do almost the opposite". [24, p. 162]

***Slow technology**, as a design philosophy or program, suggests inscribing moments of reflection, mental rest or re-visitation of the past into instantiations. The inscriptions focus on making-use, as self-reflection requires an in-depth engagement that is characterized by temporality and emergence [53]. For designers, it may be a leitmotif that informs forms of expression, including notions of how individuals encounter instantiations.*

[Counterfunctional] [Things]
Counterfunctional things, as a concept, has been introduced by Pierce and Paulos, i.e., things that figuratively counter some of their own "essential functionality", while retaining familiarity as "essentially that thing" [49, p. 377]. This concept aims to contribute to the emerging research agenda centered around designing digital limitations. Limitations are not understood as carrying normatively negative connotations, but as sources of new positive possibilities. By reflecting on design studies they conducted, they identified three key dimensions to consider, i.e., a distinction between interest in actually using the object and interest in thinking about using it; including new positive forms and functions while removing familiar and desired ones; and the influence of earlier technologies on how a counterfunctional thing is experienced.

Framing
The authors describe "counterfunctionality as a methodological and conceptual route to approaching interactive design" [49, p. 382]. They emphasize that, generally, counterfunctionality encapsulates a notion that functional oppositions can create new types of useful and desirable functionality [49]. *Counterfunctional* was a post-hoc ascription, when retrospectively reflecting on the approach taken to design digital limitations or functional oppositions [49].

> In terms of actual material artifacts, our use of the concept of counterfunctionality is not intended to describe an intrinsic property or quality. Rather we propose counterfunctionality as a way of both interpreting existing artifacts and approaching the design of new things. [49, p. 377]

Instantiations
Pierce and Paulos present several examples of *counterfunctional things*, including ultra-low resolution displays or inaccessible digital cameras. With the ultra-low resolution digital displays, they aimed to design in the opposing direction of the trend towards high-resolution displays, exploring new forms of expressivity [49]. Another example refers to inaccessible digital images, resulting in the Unviewable Image Camera [50], conceptualized as a camera that instantly stores pictures as digital data on the camera, but without a possibility for viewing the images. The camera had a concrete enclosure, or required a saw for breaking apart the basswood enclosure to access the SD card [49].

*The concept of **counterfunctional things** describes how things counter some of their own functionalities to open up new possibilities. Inscriptions into instantiations are proposed that address how users understand them, how they experience new forms and how earlier technologies influence the current counter-functionality. Making-use is emphasized (and described in form of findings from user studies); for generative designs as well as interpretations of existing artifacts it is argued to consider the suggested inscriptions.*

[Charismatic] [Technology]
Ames developed the *idea* of *charismatic technology* to describe the holding power that technologies seem to have [3]. This idea is based on charisma as a sociologist construct, which was theorized to describe the exceptional or magical authority that religious leaders have on their followers, and how ideas (e.g., of globalization) can be charismatic, being a destabilizing force that elicits excitement and produces material effects in the world [3]. Ames utilizes ANT's perspective that relations between human and non-human actors are examined through the same analytical lens, i.e., 'scripts' that designers build into technologies. However, with charisma, Ames attempts to fill a gap that ANT has not addressed appropriately, i.e., taking beliefs into account [3].

Charismatic technologies derive their power experientially and symbolically through a promise of action, meaning that not what the object is counts, but what it promises to do. The material form is less important than how it is able to invoke imagination. It is not decisive whether the promises are met, even utopian or deceptive promises are possible, as they make both technological adoption and social change appear straightforward, giving *charismatic technologies* a determinist spirit. At the same time, *charismatic technologies* refer to existing systems of meaning-making and confirm existing stereotypes, institutions, and power relations, reinforcing the 'right' worldview of their audience in form of an ideology, i.e., a framework of norms that shape thoughts and actions [3].

Framing

The idea of *charismatic technology* fulfills analytic and reflective purposes, as, by examining the charisma of a technology, its effects and how to counter them, becomes understandable [3]. Ames argues that researchers in HCI, as well as designers, are supported in identifying their own or others' ideological commitments, recognizing the invisible through analyzing a technology's charisma [3]. Thus, the *idea of charismatic technology* may be considered an analytic means to reflect on ideologies, dependencies, utopias, and consequences of technological inventions and interventions.

Instantiation

As an instantiation of *charismatic technology*, Ames presents the case of One Laptop per Child (OLPC)[3], an initiative by Seymour Papert and Nicholas Negroponte with the goal of advancing education across the Global South.

> Both, Negroponte and Papert are themselves charismatic, and both used it to build the charisma of the OLPC project and the XO laptop. [...] OLPC's XO laptop itself included a host of charismatic features that were eagerly discussed in the tech community and media alike, even when some never actually existed and others did not work in practice. [3, p. 111]

Proposed features were a hand crank to manually charge it, though it was never implemented, or the vision of a "hundred-dollar laptop" (the initial name of the project), which was never achieved. Nevertheless, the project and its *charismatic green machine* are still hyped in the technology world [3]. OLPC is one instance of a *charismatic technology*, others would be the invention of the railroad in the mid-nineteenth century, the radio, or the Internet. They all have in common that they draw on the same set of utopian narratives, concerning technology, youth, masculinity, rebellion, or self-determination [3].

Applying the idea of ***charismatic technology*** *to analyze technology is considered to contribute to the identification of researchers' and designers' ideologies and ideological commitments. In contrast to the above-mentioned examples, it is less about use, although the instantiations themselves are objects to be used. Here, it is rather about making-design (both in terms of design research and practice), i.e., actively engaging with the objects that are researched or designed. However, this engagement includes the analysis of various associations of the instantiations, e.g., with individuals, media, etc.*

[Disobedient] [Objects]

Disobedient objects was the name of an exhibition at Victoria and Albert Museum in London in 2014 / 2015. It aimed at examining the (powerful) role of objects in movements for social change, demonstrating how "political activism drives a wealth of design ingenuity and collective creativity that defy standard definitions of art and design." [54]

Disobedient objects are understood as a previously under-examined area of the art and design of object-making within social movements, in the sense of people's history of art and design from below [17]. Imagination and creativity of making within these social movements have always been key in achieving social change, influencing public debates and commercial art and design [17]. The exhibition presented a perspective on activism, posing the question of what activism is [30] and illuminating the role of making in grassroots movements for social change [54]. The curators also considered talking about "activist objects"; however, this term would imply that these objects are made by 'activists', with a specific identity that might not appropriately describe the subjectivity involved in non-Western social movements [17].

Disobedient objects can take various forms, but most commonly they are everyday objects, appropriated and turned to a new purpose, involving do-it-yourself (DIY) hacking or re-use of easily accessible objects in order to design whole new ways of disobeying. These objects are active, as they are bound up with the agency of social change, but are not considered to have agency themselves, rather, they are part of ecologies composed of several objects, music, performing bodies, laws, organizations, and affects. An object's disobedience only becomes apparent when considered in its context [17].

Framing

Disobedient objects is the name of the exhibition collecting objects that played a role in social movement and change.

> At the same time, 'disobedient objects' don't attempt to define a discipline. The term is intended as an evocative proposition or an invitation rather than a typology or closed concept. We look instead at the range of object-based tactics and strategies that movements adopt to succeed. Its edges remain open to questions. What other forms of agency do these objects involve? Can we identify material points where disobedience begins, or turns into something else? Are some politics unable to produce objects? [17, p. 12]

Instantiations

According to Knox [30], one example of *disobedient objects* are Mexican dolls, which are an hommage to Subcomandante Marcos and the 1994 uprising of the Zapatista Army of National Liberation (EZLN) against the Mexican government and its signing of the NAFTA free trade agreement with the United States. Also documents (e.g., a climate change report that critiques an official government report), papier-mâché puppets, media images, or rubber stamps may be considered as *disobedient objects* [30]. Finely woven banners, changing designs for barricades and blockades, political video games, experimental activist-bicycles, or textiles bearing witness to political murders are further examples [54].

With ***disobedient objects*** *a framing is created that incorporates objects of social change, but with an emphasis on their making. Inscriptions are not defined by top-dow design; instead, social movement happens through inscriptions into objects of everyday life, e.g., by means of appropriating them. The focus on making, however, does neither match with making-use (as understood by Vardouli [53]), nor making-design; rather, it may be literally considered as making-change. The concept tells about social movements and the role of objects therein, and aims to support collective involvement.*

[3]http://one.laptop.org

ANALYSIS: AGENCIES & PURPOSES

After summarizing the notions and analyzing them regarding their inscriptions, we extract their agency (in reference to ANT) and what purposes they aim to fulfill (in reference to design theory), resulting in a discussion on different aims and their relation to [attribute] [non-human actor] labels.

Agency

When considering the agency that is inherent to the attributes, it is worthwhile to identify what agency they actually imply. For this exercise, let us pay attention to the attribute without the "object", "technology" or "thing" that they have been used in combination with: unaware, slow, counterfunctional, charismatic, disobedient. Interestingly, they rarely indicate any sort of activity. All of them do not indicate what the actor, they are used in combination with, *does*; rather, they characterize and emphasize what something or someone *is*, i.e., being aware, being slow, being counterfunctional, being charismatic, and being disobedient. We speculate that this is due to the notion of being a concept, an abstraction of some sort rather than one or *n* artifacts that function or behave in a specific way.

From this perspective, also contradictions within concepts become visible. *Slow technology* is not necessarily slow, but it aims to slow down an interaction to provide the pace for self-reflection [23]. Similarly, *disobedient objects* are not disobedient per se, but result in disobedient endeavors as part of an ecosystem in a specific context [17]. Both *disobedient objects* and *charismatic technology* carry styles, messages, and personal characteristics that are manifested within instantiations, they are inscribed into them. In reference to ANT, objects (or any other actor) are only considered to have agency when they actually affect another actor. For instance, *an* unaware object would only be considered as an actor as long as it influences another one (e.g., a user, a designer, a cat, a wall, a table, etc.).

The *concept of* unaware objects, however, does not require the object to actually be present in order to have agency; rather, written accounts of the concepts (e.g., publications in academic venues, exhibition catalogues, etc.) have their own agency within the academic discourse, e.g., by being discussed, reflected upon, criticized, etc. Similarly, the designer herself, who generates a novel unaware object based on the concept of unaware objects may be an actor, characterized by pursuing the inscriptions suggested in these concepts or creating novel intentions inspired by a concept. Consequently, different forms of agencies are related to the objects, the concepts they are associated with, or the researchers / designers, who reflect on, create, or design them.

Labels in the form of [attribute] [non-human actor] often do not indicate what the objects that are summarized within the respective concept, do, but what they are. When looking at the [attribute] in combination with the [non-human actor], it is furthermore not necessarily a literal connection between them, as, for instance, slow technology does not necessarily mean that the technology is slow.

Purpose

Unaware objects are described as being a concept [47], *slow technology* as design philosophy or design program [23]. *Charismatic technology* is considered being an idea, or an analytical lens [3], and *disobedient objects* being an evocative proposition [17]. They aim for different things, from informing designers by providing a philosophy, taking a step back from one's design or research subject to identify ideological commitments, to collecting and reflecting on material instantiations of social change. All of them provide *second-order* knowledge, i.e., communicated and represented knowledge about *first-order* knowledge gained in the actual engagement within design activities [26].

In order to analyze the epistemologies of the presented cases, we draw on design theory to discuss them further. The analytical distinction between generative and evaluative modes of working may be of help here, i.e., whether the cases refer to design practice (generative mode of working) or criticism (evaluative mode of working) [27]. The concepts of *unaware objects*, *slow technology* and *counterfunctional things* propose generative modes of working, indicating that the aim is to create new design ideas and possibilities. *Charismatic technology*, in Ames' understanding [3], proposes rather an evaluative mode of working, aiming at criticizing designs.

Nevertheless, the question remains whether *charismatic technology* could serve as a generative mode of working as well, indicating that one aims to generate designs that are *charismatic*, being informed by the respective concept. *Counterfunctional things* are explicitly considered to be both at the same time, as the concept proposes a way of interpreting existing artifacts *and* approaching the design of new things [49]. This distinction between generative and evaluative modes of working, however, is primarily an artificial one serving analytical reasons [27]. Thus, it is likely that all mentioned concepts, ideas, and philosophies entail moments of generation and evaluation alike, depending on perspectives and purposes.

The concept of *disobedient objects*, in contrast, may be considered neither generative nor evaluative, it rather aims to draw attention to made objects in regards to social change. "Exhibitions are moments of collective meaning-making" [17, p. 23]. Consequently, *disobedient objects* are not (primarily) situated in design research, nor are they the result of top-down critical design or design activism [17].

Concepts labeled with [attribute] [non-human actor] may guide generative or evaluative modes of working, and/or meaning-making. Purposes are articulated explicitly, contributing to design theory, practice, or reflection. These concepts, however, are not part of the label, rather, they are explicated to be inscribed in future applications of these concepts.

In the following sections, we analyze the purposes of the aforementioned concepts, distinguishing between generative concepts, evaluative ideas, and meaning-making, as each of these purposes entails different perspectives.

Generative Concepts

Unaware objects, *slow technology*, and *counterfunctional things* are provisions of knowledge in form of concepts or design philosophies. As they are rather considered generative than evaluative, it seems to be appropriate to relate them to the notion of *strong concepts*. Introduced by Höök and Löwgren in 2012, it originates from the aim to provide epistemological articulations to engage in the collaborative construction of generative design knowledge [27]. Though not mentioned explicitly, this aim is also inherent to the work on *unaware objects*, *slow technology*, and *counterfunctional things*.

The following paragraphs on *strong concepts* are a detour, aiming to briefly outline this proposal in terms of Interaction Design research knowledge[4]. Strong concepts are on the level of what Höök and Löwgren call intermediary knowledge that is in between theories and instances, being

> design elements abstracted beyond particular instances which have the potential to be appropriated by designers and researchers to extend their repertoires and enable new particulars instantiations [sic]. [27, p. 23:5]

For applicable academic criteria, Höök and Löwgren refer to Booth [8]. Accordingly, academic knowledge contributions in the realm of Interaction Design research have to be contestable (e.g., inventive and novel), defensible (e.g., empirically, analytically, and theoretically grounded), and substantive (e.g., relevant to the community, generative) [27]. The development of a strong concept starts by identifying the source of a strong concept, i.e., an instance (e.g., a design responding to a particular existing or possible use situation). Then, it is related to similar concepts (horizontal grounding), related to other known instances (vertical grounding), and reflected upon, articulated, and abstracted [27].

Further, Höök and Löwgren suggest to start by identifying a tentative strong concept from one or several design experiments [27]. Interpreting the writings about *unaware objects*, *slow technology*, and *counterfunctional things*, their process has been similar, and so is their intention, i.e., to articulate intermediary knowledge to allow other "designer-researchers to create instances in different design situations" [27, p. 23:11].

These concepts qualify as tentative strong concepts, as they concern a dynamic gestalt, reside between technology and people, carry a core design idea that is not tied to a specific use application or domain, and their abstraction level is above particular instances [27]. They are tentative, as their academic quality (being contestable, defensible, and substantive) has either not been fully established yet, or not explicitly articulated. However, they all explicitly invite to take the concept up by designing instances or using it for critique.

This detour via the notion of strong concepts aimed to clarify the purpose of the generative [attribute] [non-human actor] concepts. It seems that there is a need to articulate and communicate the conceptual nature, without actually being a strong concept already. Interestingly, those examples that have been used as illustrations of strong concepts by Höök and Löwgren, are labeled as "seamfulness" or "social navigation" [27]. In contrast to the aforementioned examples, which used an adjective to accompany a non-human actor, here, a nominalization is used stand-alone. With these labels, the scope of the strong concept is broader than referring to an object or a group of objects; it presumably aims to affect not only the design of *an* interactive artifact (object, technology, thing), but the community surrounding research and practice in Interaction Design.

This finding might be accidental, with no intention of the creators of the labels / concepts to narrow or broaden the scope. However, the way terms are created is sensitive to what aims to be communicated. Interestingly, *slow technology* has been referred to as *slow design* as well [49], maybe because the inscription of being a generative design concept is not sufficiently expressed in the label *slow technology*.

Evaluative Ideas

Charismatic technology and *counterfunctional things* are considered as analytic means to reflect on design instantiations [3, 49]. They differ from (or complement) generative concepts by aiming to support critique of existing artifacts. The idea of *charismatic objects* aims to identify ideological commitments from researchers or designers [3], whereas, the concept of *counterfunctional things* aims to also support the interpretation of existing artifacts [49].

Evaluative intermediary knowledge is associated with experiential qualities, design heuristics, and criticism [27]. A similar exercise than in the previous section, replacing strong concepts with design heuristics or criticism, results in the reading that *charismatic objects* and *counterfunctional things* are presumably not mature enough to be theories of criticism, yet they are no singular examples. Thus, they are similarly tentative in their nature, aiming to be used to reflect on, criticize, or interpret beyond their initial appearance. In terms of the labels of *charismatic objects* and *counterfunctional things*, the same considerations apply. The labels do not communicate intentions, inscriptions, or authorships of the respective concepts and ideas, resulting in the risk of being misinterpreted as one design or a group of designs or objects.

Meaning-Making

The notion of *disobedient objects* is, in comparison to the other examples, different in its intent and expressions. Being considered as an "evocative proposition", it aims to support meaning-making within an exhibition of artifacts for social change [17]. It is neither generative nor evaluative, rather, it is an invitation to individually / collectively unpack the meaning of objects and processes of *making* in social movements. Meaning-making might, however, be inscribed in all the discussed concepts, whether they are generative or evaluative.

In terms of (intermediary) knowledge, all of the five analyzed concepts provide written accounts of knowledge already gained or aimed for, which is complementing the objects they summarize, thereby, supporting meaning-making. This happens either in form of exhibition catalogues [17] that describe the motivation as well as objects and their (assumed) inscriptions, or in form of scientific articles clarifying the genesis, instantiation and rational for the concepts [3, 23, 47, 49]. Consequently, supporting meaning-making might be an intention

[4]For reasons of conciseness, the current intense discourse on how to frame intermediary knowledge in IxD is not presented in this paper, but see e.g., [9, 11, 26, 43, 55] for detailed discussions.

inherent to all concepts, but, similar to notions of evaluative or generative concepts, this inscription is not expressed by the label given to the respective concepts.

Summarizing their inherent purposes, concepts labeled with [attribute] [non-human actor] may aim to become a strong concept, if they provoke generative modes of working. In case they support an evaluative mode, they may strive to become a theory of criticism. Additionally, or exclusively, they may aim at meaning-making. Creating new designs, evaluating existing ones, and constructing meaning are, however, not separated from each other, but different perspectives that inform each other.

DISCUSSION

Within the analysis we identified notions and nuances of the concepts articulated by the labels [attribute] [non-human actor]. The following list briefly summarizes the most relevant aspects of the analysis.

Intermediary knowledge concealed by Interaction Design labels in the form of [attribute] [non-human actor] may

- *inscribe making-use* by proposing designs that seek to facilitate an active engagement with the material world, its temporality and emergence [53].
- *inscribe making-design* by providing guidance, inspiration, or strategies to inform future designs (provoking a generative mode of working), or by providing theoretical or methodological approaches to engage with existing design (supporting an evaluative mode of working), e.g., by reflecting on them or criticizing them.
- *inscribe meaning-making* with an explicit focus on roles of objects and making.
- *inscribe making-use, making-design, and meaning-making*, either consecutively or in parallel.
- *inscribe an activity, but articulate a property*, focusing either on encountering a technology or designing one.
- *contribute to advancing the respective concept* with different levels of (intermediary) knowledge that needs to be articulated, communicated, discussed.

The most pressing question resulting from these aspects is *what role terminology actually plays when it comes to labels, concepts, philosophies, and inscriptions*. For instance, what do labels need to express (e.g., intentions, strategies, perceptions, experiences)? Closely related is the discussion of whether the labels that have been used are appropriate, or whether we need to appropriate them to fit the articulation needs. This also includes speculations on how we might *improve articulation and communication of (design) knowledge about concepts and inscriptions*. Thus, the following discussion focuses on these two dimensions, and concludes by suggesting (alternative) ways to articulate concepts, philosophies, or programs.

What role does terminology play?

Objects, technology, things, interfaces, artifacts – they are often described in terms of characteristics, features, objectives, or agency. As we have shown, design concepts in particular are often labeled in a specific way, i.e., [attribute] [non-human actor]. Written accounts, exhibitions, design examples, example designs, and many other formats, are given these titles and labels, with inscriptions that the respective authors more or less explicitly provide within these formats.

We speculate that the labels are chosen for reasons, however, this process of labeling is rarely discussed. Thus, it remains open why a specific attribute was preferred over another one (e.g., Why is it *slow technology*, not *reflective technology*? Why is it *unaware objects*, not *post-functional objects*?). There might be marketing reasons for labeling a concept in a certain way, but we assume that it is an attribute that the creators of the concepts aim to emphasize.

However, though its genesis is rarely communicated, a label may have a great effect on how the audience understands it, and there might be differences in what audience takes up on a concept. For instance, when writing about *counterfunctional things* in a research paper, it might target HCI or design researchers, who know how to interpret these concepts and inscriptions. However, when it comes to users (or: humans that encounter or appropriate a technology, thing, object or intersect with it) it is less clear.

On one hand, all concepts that we presented refer to users (to different extents, though), their opinions towards the instantiations seemed to highly inform the concepts, e.g., by providing respective design strategies for future design work. On the other hand, *unaware objects*, for instance, is post-hoc concept that "emerged through critical reflection on the conceptualizing, designing, and analysis of our two design artifacts" [47, p. 35]. Unfortunately, it is not reported why the label resulted in *unaware objects* (and not, for instance, in *post-functional objects*, which would have reflected a finding from the user studies [47]).

However, even if attempting to label a concept on basis of main findings from, for instance, user studies, questions arise in how far these labels and ascriptions sufficiently cover the multifaceted ways of how people adapt, adopt, and *appropriate* technology to their very specific values, needs and intentions of use, i.e., leading to artifacts inducing crystalized knowledge from the activity of use over time [4]. Both the genesis of a concept (incorporating the knowledge of conceptualization and design) and the intended or unintended ways of making-use of the respective instantiations over time, may inform the process of creating a label. Iterative processes in the creation and refinement of design concepts and their instantiations may lead to dynamic reformulations of labels, which we would propose based on the previous arguments and discussion.

How do (can, or should) we articulate concepts?

As discussed before, intentions of various forms are often communicated under the umbrella of a certain label. What our analysis suggests is that a nuanced labelling for these concepts, and a nuanced description and distinction of intentions and inscriptions within the respective concepts might be valuable. Coming back to the finding that the knowledge provided in these concepts may strive to become a strong concept one day (or eventually a theory), we consider these differentiations to be necessary parts of both intermediary provisions of knowledge and eventual theories.

Related to this is the question of authorship, i.e., who is responsible for inscriptions. In terms of ANT, authorship is not visible, as not an inscription (or a designer's or engineer's intention) is what counts, but the activity of the actual actor (e.g., an object, a human actor). The reason for not considering authorship as forming "the social" (in actor-networks) is that what actually happens in a setting is not necessarily overlapping with the intentions and inscriptions, resulting in what is considered *appropriation* in HCI. However, though authorship is critical, it is rarely discussed in HCI and Interaction Design (research).

The empirical fallacy, as described by Hallnäs and Redström, may also come into play here: Users, who are inscribed into a design, are neither coinciding with individuals taking part in user requirements studies, nor with those in evaluation studies [24]. Thus, it is not only about the authorship of the design, but also about the (defined, inscribed) user. All of these inscriptions require explication, e.g., in form of written accounts, in order to clarify what we mean when discussing [attribute] [non-human actor], ensuring that we are as careful in our articulations as in our design and research activities.

The consequence resulting from this discussion is a call for exploring (alternative) ways to label concepts and to express intentions, inscriptions, and experiences. Thereby, a reconsideration of the [attribute], the [non-human actor], or the combination of those two (or other *n*) terms is proposed:

- An [attribute] may not only articulate a property, but an activity in order to emphasize the dynamic gestalt of an interactive artifact (e.g., *randomly operating objects* instead of *unaware objects*)

- An [attribute] may express intended use / encounters (in form of inscriptions) in order to render visible how the creators of the concept envision individuals' encounters with an artifact, while at the same time guiding designers of instantiations, or indicating intentions that instantiations can be evaluated against (e.g., *reflexion technology* instead of *slow technology*)

- An [attribute] may express actual use / encounters, acknowledging (e.g., in an accompanying written account) that actual encounters informed the concept already (e.g., *post-functional objects* instead of *unaware objects*)

- A [non-human actor] may not only refer to plural objects, but to interactions, designs, or (computer-supported) practices [33] (e.g., *counterfunctional interactions* instead of *counterfunctional things*)

- Creators may refrain from using attributes, but indicate in the label what it is, that is presented (e.g., a concept for, a philosophy of), and/or what it aims for (e.g., a concept for confronting humans; a concept for facilitating humans reflection, etc.)

This proposal does not call for established labels to be changed; rather, it is an invitation to explore variations of labels to reflect on a concept's meaning, articulation, and communication. Communicating *why* a certain label has been chosen, however, is likely to be of value, as it might unveil why the creators favor a label, an attribute, or an actor of a setting over another. Further, we argue that dynamically changing labels may be needed to adapt to advancements of concepts and instantiations. This will allow to (a) depict the intermediary knowledge explicitly; (b) distinguish between intentions, inscriptions, and actual (unintended) use; and (c) reflect on (design) researchers' and designers' assumptions about what aspect of, for instance, a design concept, is of upmost importance to be communicated.

CONCLUSION

With this discursive paper on the relation between concepts and their labels we aim to initiate a discussion on how we, as a (design) research community, articulate our knowledge mainly within, but also beyond our community, and how we refer to it. Though this is only the beginning of a discussion around concepts, labels, authorships, inscriptions, and intentions, we close with a call to nuanced descriptions of all these facets by articulating them explicitly, reflecting on different dimensions of inscriptions and making them visible, and identifying how they are associated.

We again emphasize tracing the *activity* of actors (e.g., [19]), but we also suggest to articulate authorships and the respective intentions. In future work we aim to advance this discussion by, for instance, asking the question of whether the artifacts (that are generated based on a specific design concept) have policies, what role authorships actually play in our field, or whether design practice and design research require different articulations. This not only requires to analyze written accounts, but the observation of artifacts' agencies in different settings, e.g., in design practice, in use, in research. Specifically, the explication of why we label concepts in a certain way requires attention, something, that has rarely been done (or articulated) in the past.

The argument developed in this paper (in a nutshell: that articulations need to be clarified, including histories, notions, inscriptions, intentions, goals, and audience in order to contribute to the discourse in a multifaceted and unambiguous way) allows to reconsider how we provide knowledge, concepts, and guidance within our community, and provides suggestions on how to go beyond current [attribute] [non-human actor] labels. With this, we hope to see explorations and careful reflections on labels and articulations of future design concepts, philosophies, and human-artifact encounters.

ACKNOWLEDGMENTS

The financial support by the Austrian Federal Ministry of Science, Research and Economy and the National Foundation for Research, Technology and Development is gratefully acknowledged (Christian Doppler Laboratory on "Contextual Interfaces").

REFERENCES

1. Madeleine Akrich. 1992. The de-scription of technical objects. In *Shaping Technology / Building Society*, Bijker Wiebe E. and Law John (Eds.). MIT press, 205–224.
2. Madeleine Akrich and Bruno Latour. 1992. A summary of a convenient vocabulary for the semiotics of human and nonhuman assemblies. In *Shaping Technology / Building Society*, Bijker Wiebe E. and Law John (Eds.). MIT press, 259–264.
3. Morgan G. Ames. 2015. Charismatic Technology, In Aarhus Series on Human Centered Computing. *Aarhus Series on Human Centered Computing* 1 (2015), 109–120. DOI: http://dx.doi.org/10.7146/aahcc.v1i1.21199
4. Liam J. Bannon and Susanne Bødker. 1991. Designing Interaction. Cambridge University Press, New York, NY, USA, Chapter Beyond the Interface: Encountering Artifacts in Use, 227–253. http://dl.acm.org/citation.cfm?id=120352.120364
5. Remi Barraquand. 2012. *Designing sociable technologies*. Ph.D. Dissertation. Grenoble.
6. Wiebe E Bijker, Thomas P Hughes, Trevor Pinch, and Deborah G Douglas. 1987. *The social construction of technological systems: New directions in the sociology and history of technology*. MIT press.
7. Susanne Bødker and Ellen Christiansen. 2012. Poetry in Motion: Appropriation of the World of Apps. In *Proceedings of the 30th European Conference on Cognitive Ergonomics (ECCE '12)*. ACM, New York, NY, USA, 78–84. DOI: http://dx.doi.org/10.1145/2448136.2448152
8. Wayne C Booth, Gregory G Colomb, and Joseph M Williams. 2003. *The craft of research*. University of Chicago press.
9. John Bowers. 2012. The Logic of Annotated Portfolios: Communicating the Value of 'Research Through Design'. In *Proceedings of the Designing Interactive Systems Conference (DIS '12)*. ACM, New York, NY, USA, 68–77. DOI: http://dx.doi.org/10.1145/2317956.2317968
10. Jennie Carroll. 2004. Completing design in use: closing the appropriation cycle. In *Proceedings of the 12th European Conference on Information Systems (ECIS 2004)*. 337–347.
11. Peter Dalsgaard and Kim Halskov. 2012. Reflective Design Documentation. In *Proceedings of the Designing Interactive Systems Conference (DIS '12)*. ACM, New York, NY, USA, 428–437. DOI: http://dx.doi.org/10.1145/2317956.2318020
12. Gerardine DeSanctis and Marshall Scott Poole. 1994. Capturing the complexity in advanced technology use: Adaptive structuration theory. *Organization science* 5, 2 (1994), 121–147. DOI: http://dx.doi.org/10.1287/orsc.5.2.121
13. Alan Dix. 2007. Designing for Appropriation. In *Proceedings of the 21st British HCI Group Annual Conference on People and Computers: HCI...But Not As We Know It - Volume 2 (BCS-HCI '07)*. British Computer Society, Swinton, UK, UK, 27–30. http://dl.acm.org/citation.cfm?id=1531407.1531415
14. Paul Dourish. 2003. The appropriation of interactive technologies: Some lessons from placeless documents. *Computer Supported Cooperative Work (CSCW)* 12, 4 (2003), 465–490. DOI: http://dx.doi.org/10.1023/A:1026149119426
15. Sebastian Draxler, Gunnar Stevens, Martin Stein, Alexander Boden, and David Randall. 2012. Supporting the Social Context of Technology Appropriation: On a Synthesis of Sharing Tools and Tool Knowledge. In *Proceedings of the SIGCHI Conference on Human Factors in Computing Systems (CHI '12)*. ACM, New York, NY, USA, 2835–2844. DOI: http://dx.doi.org/10.1145/2207676.2208687
16. Pelle Ehn. 2008. Participation in Design Things. In *Proceedings of the Tenth Anniversary Conference on Participatory Design 2008 (PDC '08)*. Indiana University, Indianapolis, IN, USA, 92–101. http://dl.acm.org/citation.cfm?id=1795234.1795248
17. Catherine Flood, Gavin Grindon, and others. 2014. Disobedient Objects. *Victoria & Albert Museum. Londres: V&A Publishing* (2014).
18. Verena Fuchsberger, Martin Murer, Thomas Meneweger, and Manfred Tscheligi. 2014b. Capturing the In-between of Interactive Artifacts and Users: A Materiality-centered Approach. In *Proceedings of the 8th Nordic Conference on Human-Computer Interaction: Fun, Fast, Foundational (NordiCHI '14)*. ACM, New York, NY, USA, 451–460. DOI: http://dx.doi.org/10.1145/2639189.2639219
19. Verena Fuchsberger, Martin Murer, and Manfred Tscheligi. 2013. Materials, Materiality, and Media. In *Proceedings of the SIGCHI Conference on Human Factors in Computing Systems (CHI '13)*. ACM, New York, NY, USA, 2853–2862. DOI: http://dx.doi.org/10.1145/2470654.2481395
20. Verena Fuchsberger, Martin Murer, and Manfred Tscheligi. 2014a. Human-computer Non-interaction: The Activity of Non-use. In *Proceedings of the 2014 Companion Publication on Designing Interactive Systems (DIS Companion '14)*. ACM, New York, NY, USA, 57–60. DOI: http://dx.doi.org/10.1145/2598784.2602781
21. William Gaver. 2012. What Should We Expect from Research Through Design?. In *Proceedings of the SIGCHI Conference on Human Factors in Computing Systems (CHI '12)*. ACM, New York, NY, USA, 937–946. DOI: http://dx.doi.org/10.1145/2207676.2208538
22. Andrea Grimes and Richard Harper. 2008. Celebratory Technology: New Directions for Food Research in HCI. In *Proceedings of the SIGCHI Conference on Human Factors in Computing Systems (CHI '08)*. ACM, New York, NY, USA, 467–476. DOI: http://dx.doi.org/10.1145/1357054.1357130

23. Lars Hallnäs and Johan Redström. 2001. Slow Technology &Ndash; Designing for Reflection. *Personal Ubiquitous Comput.* 5, 3 (Jan. 2001), 201–212. DOI: http://dx.doi.org/10.1007/PL00000019

24. Lars Hallnäs and Johan Redström. 2006. *Interaction design: foundations, experiments*. Textile Research Centre, Swedish School of Textiles, Unversity College of Borås and Interactive Institute.

25. Lone Koefoed Hansen and Peter Dalsgaard. 2015. Note to Self: Stop Calling Interfaces "Natural". *Aarhus Series on Human Centered Computing* 1, 1 (2015), 4. DOI: http://dx.doi.org/10.7146/aahcc.v1i1.21316

26. Kristina Höök, Jeffrey Bardzell, Simon Bowen, Peter Dalsgaard, Stuart Reeves, and Annika Waern. 2015. Framing IxD Knowledge. *interactions* 22, 6 (Oct. 2015), 32–36. DOI: http://dx.doi.org/10.1145/2824892

27. Kristina Höök and Jonas Löwgren. 2012. Strong Concepts: Intermediate-level Knowledge in Interaction Design Research. *ACM Trans. Comput.-Hum. Interact.* 19, 3, Article 23 (Oct. 2012), 18 pages. DOI: http://dx.doi.org/10.1145/2362364.2362371

28. Don Ihde. 1990. *Technology and the lifeworld: From garden to earth*. Number 560. Indiana University Press.

29. Joseph 'Jofish' Kaye. 2006. I Just Clicked to Say I Love You: Rich Evaluations of Minimal Communication. In *CHI '06 Extended Abstracts on Human Factors in Computing Systems (CHI EA '06)*. ACM, New York, NY, USA, 363–368. DOI: http://dx.doi.org/10.1145/1125451.1125530

30. Hannah Knox. 2014. Disobedient Objects. Blog Post (Material World: A Global Hub for Thinking about Things). (2014). http://www.materialworldblog.com/2014/11/disobedient-objects/

31. Ilpo Koskinen, John Zimmerman, Thomas Binder, Johan Redstrom, and Stephan Wensveen. 2011. *Design research through practice: From the lab, field, and showroom*. Elsevier.

32. Peter Kroes. 2002. Design methodology and the nature of technical artefacts. *Design studies* 23, 3 (2002), 287–302.

33. Kari Kuutti and Liam J. Bannon. 2014. The Turn to Practice in HCI: Towards a Research Agenda. In *Proceedings of the SIGCHI Conference on Human Factors in Computing Systems (CHI '14)*. ACM, New York, NY, USA, 3543–3552. DOI: http://dx.doi.org/10.1145/2556288.2557111

34. Bruno Latour. 1992. Where Are the Missing Masses? The Sociology of a Few Mundane Artifacts. In *Shaping Technology / Building Society*, Weibe Bijker and John Law (Eds.). MIT press, 225–258.

35. Bruno Latour. 1994. On technical mediation. *Common knowledge* 3, 2 (1994), 29–64.

36. Bruno Latour. 1996. On interobjectivity. *Mind, culture, and activity* 3, 4 (1996), 228–245.

37. Bruno Latour. 2007. *Reassembling the Social. An Introduction to Actor-Network-Theory.* Oxford University Press.

38. Bruno Latour, Pablo Jensen, Tommaso Venturini, Sébastian Grauwin, and Dominique Boullier. 2012. The Whole is Always Smaller than Its Parts: A Digital Test of Gabriel Tarde's Monads. *British Journal of Sociology* 63, 4 (2012), 590–615. DOI: http://dx.doi.org/10.1111/j.1468-4446.2012.01428.x

39. John Law. 1992. Notes on the theory of the actor-network: Ordering, strategy, and heterogeneity. *Systems practice* 5, 4 (1992), 379–393.

40. John Law. 2008. Actor network theory and material semiotics. In *The new Blackwell companion to social theory*. Wiley-Blackwell, 141–158. DOI: http://dx.doi.org/10.1002/9781444304992.ch7

41. Youn-kyung Lim, Justin Donaldson, Heekyoung Jung, Breanne Kunz, David Royer, Shruti Ramalingam, Sindhia Thirumaran, and Erik Stolterman. 2008. Emotional experience and interaction design. In *Affect and Emotion in Human-Computer Interaction*. Springer, 116–129.

42. Youn-kyung Lim, Erik Stolterman, Heekyoung Jung, and Justin Donaldson. 2007. Interaction gestalt and the design of aesthetic interactions. In *Proceedings of the 2007 Conference on Designing Pleasurable Products and Interfaces (DPPI '07)*. ACM, New York, NY, USA, 239–254. DOI: http://dx.doi.org/10.1145/1314161.1314183

43. Jonas Löwgren. 2013. Annotated portfolios and other forms of intermediate-level knowledge. *interactions* 20, 1 (Jan. 2013), 30–34. DOI: http://dx.doi.org/10.1145/2405716.2405725

44. Thomas Ludwig, Oliver Stickel, Alexander Boden, and Volkmar Pipek. 2014. Towards Sociable Technologies: An Empirical Study on Designing Appropriation Infrastructures for 3D Printing. In *Proceedings of the 2014 Conference on Designing Interactive Systems (DIS '14)*. ACM, New York, NY, USA, 835–844. DOI: http://dx.doi.org/10.1145/2598510.2598528

45. Annemarie Mol. 2010. Actor-Network Theory: sensitive terms and enduring tensions. *Kölner Zeitschrift für Soziologie und Sozialpsychologie. Sonderheft* 50 (2010), 253–269.

46. William Odom. 2015. Understanding Long-Term Interactions with a Slow Technology: An Investigation of Experiences with FutureMe. In *Proceedings of the 33rd Annual ACM Conference on Human Factors in Computing Systems (CHI '15)*. ACM, New York, NY, USA, 575–584. DOI: http://dx.doi.org/10.1145/2702123.2702221

47. William Odom and Ron Wakkary. 2015. Intersecting with Unaware Objects. In *Proceedings of the 2015 ACM SIGCHI Conference on Creativity and Cognition (C&C '15)*. ACM, New York, NY, USA, 33–42. DOI: http://dx.doi.org/10.1145/2757226.2757240

48. William T. Odom, Abigail J. Sellen, Richard Banks, David S. Kirk, Tim Regan, Mark Selby, Jodi L. Forlizzi, and John Zimmerman. 2014. Designing for Slowness, Anticipation and Re-visitation: A Long Term Field Study of the Photobox. In *Proceedings of the 32Nd Annual ACM Conference on Human Factors in Computing Systems (CHI '14)*. ACM, New York, NY, USA, 1961–1970. DOI: http://dx.doi.org/10.1145/2556288.2557178

49. James Pierce and Eric Paulos. 2014a. Counterfunctional Things: Exploring Possibilities in Designing Digital Limitations. In *Proceedings of the 2014 Conference on Designing Interactive Systems (DIS '14)*. ACM, New York, NY, USA, 375–384. DOI: http://dx.doi.org/10.1145/2598510.2598522

50. James Pierce and Eric Paulos. 2014b. Some Variations on a Counterfunctional Digital Camera. In *Proceedings of the 2014 Conference on Designing Interactive Systems (DIS '14)*. ACM, New York, NY, USA, 131–140. DOI: http://dx.doi.org/10.1145/2598510.2602968

51. Ingo Schulz-Schaeffer. 2006. Who Is the Actor and Whose Goals Will Be Pursued? Rethinking Some Concepts of Actor Network Theory. In *Prenatal Testing: Individual Decision or Distributed Action?*, Bernhard Wieser, Sandra Karner, and Wilhelm Berger (Eds.). Vol. 48. Profil-Verl., 131–158. http://nbn-resolving.de/urn:nbn:de:0168-ssoar-122028

52. Lucy Suchman. 1998. Human/machine reconsidered. Department of Sociology, Lancaster University. (1998). http://www.comp.lancs.ac.uk/sociology/soc040ls.html

53. Theodora Vardouli. 2015. Making use: Attitudes to human-artifact engagements. *Design Studies* 41, Part A (2015), 137 – 161. DOI: http://dx.doi.org/10.1016/j.destud.2015.08.002 Special Issue: Computational Making.

54. Victoria and Albert Museum. 2015. Disobedient Objects (Exhibition). (2015). http://www.vam.ac.uk/content/exhibitions/disobedient-objects/

55. Ron Wakkary, Audrey Desjardins, and Sabrina Hauser. 2015. Unselfconscious Interaction: A Conceptual Construct. *Interacting with Computers* (2015). DOI: http://dx.doi.org/10.1093/iwc/iwv018

56. Mark Weiser and John Seely Brown. 1996. Designing calm technology. *PowerGrid Journal* 1, 1 (1996), 75–85.

57. Daniel Wigdor and Dennis Wixon. 2011. *Brave NUI world: designing natural user interfaces for touch and gesture*. Elsevier.

58. John Zimmerman, Erik Stolterman, and Jodi Forlizzi. 2010. An Analysis and Critique of Research Through Design: Towards a Formalization of a Research Approach. In *Proceedings of the 8th ACM Conference on Designing Interactive Systems (DIS '10)*. ACM, New York, NY, USA, 310–319. DOI: http://dx.doi.org/10.1145/1858171.1858228

When a Product Is Still Fictional: Anticipating and Speculating Futures through Concept Videos

Richmond Y. Wong
University of California, Berkeley
Berkeley, CA USA
richmond@ischool.berkeley.edu

Deirdre K. Mulligan
University of California, Berkeley
Berkeley, CA USA
dkm@ischool.berkeley.edu

ABSTRACT
This paper explores corporate concept videos as a type of design fiction that embed a vision about the future of computing – including how computing should be done, for whom, and the norms that might exist – and allow for a discourse to explore and contest these claims. We introduce a method for critiquing and analyzing concept videos. Through an analysis of Google Glass' and Microsoft HoloLens' concept videos and a discourse analysis of media articles during the time period after the products were announced but before they were available to the public, we introduce a method of analysis that lets us surface values and critique the narratives presented in technology concept videos and in early media reactions. We also introduce the language of "anticipatory" and "speculative" orientations toward the future to better describe how people imagine sociotechnical futures.

Author Keywords
Concept videos; design fiction; discourse; imagination

ACM Classification Keywords
H.5.m. Information interfaces and presentation (e.g., HCI): Miscellaneous

INTRODUCTION
In April 2012, Google announced a project called Project Glass, publishing a concept video on YouTube entitled "One Day" [44]. While not ready for public release, the video presented a first-person view of what using Glass could be like, showing a user's experience with an augmented reality-like heads up display. For the next year, early versions of Glass were used almost exclusively by people within Google, until the Google Glass Explorer project launched in April 2013, allowing a limited number of individuals from the public to purchase and use Glass. In January 2015, Microsoft announced its augmented reality head-worn display, called Microsoft HoloLens, publishing a concept video on YouTube called "Microsoft HoloLens – Transform your world with holograms" [56]. Some people drew comparisons between Glass and HoloLens [55, 58]. Both appear as head-mounted devices, like glasses or goggles (Figure 1). Both have cameras, allow for internet connectivity, and can overlay information in a user's field of view. While similar in some ways, the underlying designs, the companies' portrayals of the technology, and the emerging discussions and responses to the technologies differed. The depiction and discussion of Glass focused on its potential integration into everyday life as wearable technology, and privacy concerns emerged as well. Meanwhile HoloLens was often portrayed as a gaming device or work tool.

DIS 2016, June 04 - 08, 2016, Brisbane, QLD, Australia

ACM 978-1-4503-4031-1/16/06…$15.00
DOI: http://dx.doi.org/10.1145/2901790.2901801.

We argue that the concept videos for Glass and HoloLens can be thought of as design fictions. This allows us to look at an important period of time between the announcement of the technologies and their public release – at a time when the products were still conceptual or fictional to most people. This lets us see how people imagined what the world with these devices would be like, and how people's expectations about the technologies were shaped. Concept videos embed a vision about the social and technical future of computing: how computing will be done, for whom, by what means, and what the norms of that world will be.

This paper makes two main contributions. First, it introduces methods of analysis that allow us to surface values and critique the narratives presented in technology concept videos and in early media discourse about new technologies. Second, as a result of our findings, we introduce the terms "anticipatory" and "speculative" orientations toward the future to provide a more nuanced discussion about the ways futures are represented in discourse, design, and HCI research.

In the following sections, we trace related work that discusses the ways people orient themselves toward imagined futures. We then introduce a method for analyzing concept videos, and analyze the Google Glass and Microsoft HoloLens videos. We detail the discourses that emerged around Glass and HoloLens after their concept videos were released but before they were available for purchase. We then reflect on our methods of analysis and call on researchers to engage in values discussions and critique of early design representations of technologies.

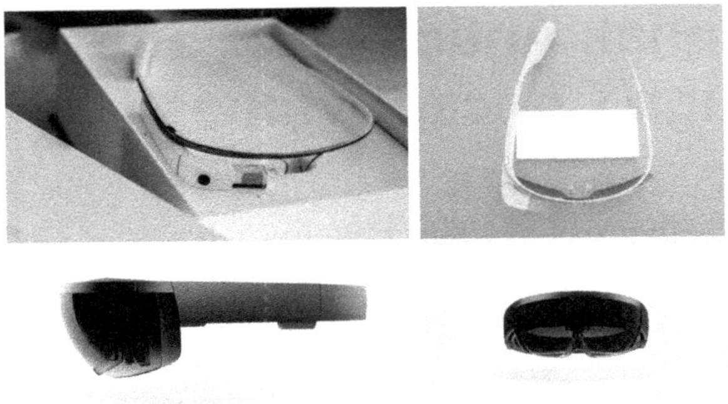

Figure 1. Top: Google Glass viewed in a box [54] and from above [41]. Bottom: Microsoft HoloLens viewed from the side and from the front [56]. Images CC-BY 2.0

RELATED WORK AND BACKGROUND

We discuss how the ideas of design fiction and processes of collective imagination inform our work.

Design Fiction

The concept of design fiction is still being shaped, yet it has garnered much interest. Julian Bleecker, in an early piece on design fictions, describes design fictions as an authorial practice that exists in the space between science fiction and science fact [3]. The artifacts of this practice exist in an imagined speculative world or narrative [21]. The focus is not just creating a single speculative artifact, but embedding that artifact in a broader world, story, or fictional reality. Design fictions are also discursive: they embody values and ideas (consciously or unconsciously) that may respond to or instigate a broader discourse [34]. They encourage discourse by often allowing viewers to construct multiple meanings from them. They are often seen as related to practices that draw on near future fictions [22] and practices that use design for provocation or subversion such as critical or speculative design [4, 11, 22, 34].

Design fictions can take on many forms. Fictional research abstracts and findings were written in text as a critique and reflection on a particular strain of research through design [4]. Others have analyzed the production of Steampunk-styled artifacts as types of design fictions [34]. Hybrid visual and textual forms [28] and short film [17] have also been used to express design fictions. While design fictions are often employed for the purposes of social critique [11], corporate storytelling, such as the Google Glass concept video, has been suggested as a type of design fiction [60]. Placing corporate concept videos in the realm of design fiction frames the video as something that is not predicting *the future*, but presenting a representation of *one possible future* out of many. It also allows us to interpret the video and investigate the ideas it promotes. Because design fictions are discursive, this suggests that such videos are best considered in dialogue with broader social discourses.

Collective Imagination Processes

Another line of work shows that representations of technology affect broader perceptions, reactions, and debate. Collective processes of imagination are expressed through and facilitated in part by processes of cultural production. For instance, Harmon and Mazmanian investigate the ways commercials and news articles create sociotechnical narratives about smartphones and smartphone users [16]. The circulation of stories and the discourses that arise frame a debate about what it means to be a smartphone user, and associate moral values with using a smartphone. Dourish and Bell explore how imaginations and narratives of ubiquitous computing create a shared narrative of the "proximate future," which exists "just around the corner" in the future [1]. This narrative is embedded, expressed, and reinforced through the actions and products of researchers and practitioners in the field, as well as through cultural expressions of the future, like science fiction [10]. Representations of technologies influence the way people imagine future technologies, build broader collective narratives about what technologies mean, and influence technological development and use. Work by Jasanoff and Kim shows how these broader narratives about technology affect science and technology policy decisions [18]. This also suggests that we should not look at the concept videos' representations of technology in isolation, but rather in relationship to broader discourses.

Analyzing Corporate Concept Videos

We extend these lines of work by looking at concept videos for Google Glass and Microsoft HoloLens as design fictions. Each video creates a narrative world that takes place in the future, depicting technical artifacts and how humans interact with them. Furthermore, the public release of the videos provides a starting point for public discussion and discourse about the technologies' social implications. Both videos offer a particular sociotechnical vision of the future and allow a broader public audience to engage with and contest the politics and values of the presented futures.

Yet corporate concept videos differ slightly from design fictions with critical ends. Unlike other design fictions which invite users to into a narrative world to imagine technologies *as if* they are real, many corporate concept videos portray technologies that *will be* real in some form. These videos more directly serve corporate purposes. While these videos do not explicitly direct users to purchase a particular product, they do reflect advertising imperatives. Utilizing imagery helps these videos help fuel demand and create markets for these novel products [12, 27]. The concept videos also share qualities with "vision videos," corporate research videos that represent possible future sociotechnical worlds (rather than a specific product), such as the "future of productivity," bringing a vision of a possible future into the present [20].

These videos serve further purposes beyond advertising. They contain elements of video prototyping, which can help designers brainstorm, communicate, and explore the functionality and contexts of new technologies [8, 23, 35]. Video prototypes may also have marketing purposes, such as Apple's 1987 Knowledge Navigator video [36].

The Google and Microsoft videos serve exploratory and probing purposes as well that support collective imagination processes. Google's Glass Explorer Program [53] and Microsoft's HoloLens research grants [51] were both announced before the products were commercially available, inviting early users and researchers to find and explore novel uses of the technologies. Thus the videos invite the viewer to imagine new uses and possible futures; they open a conversation to talk about a technology that is not fully defined yet. During the time period after the concept videos were released, but before they were commercially available, the Glass and HoloLens videos were fictional in the sense that the worlds and technologies they portray did not yet fully exist at the time of their publication. Yet as they neared their public release dates, the devices became "more real." This suggests that "fictional" and "real" exist on a spectrum, rather than being binary qualities.

The lens of design fiction lets us concurrently analyze the videos' explanatory and exploratory purposes, and their future-oriented narratives. Analyzing corporate uses of design fictions helps surface aspects of the companies' narratives that may not be at their central focus, but could have significant implications for people if those narratives come to fruition. Analyzing the creation – and contestation – of narratives by companies and the media response also provides insight into the practice of "infrastructuring" [31], making visible processes that embed or associate social and political values with new technologies.

The sections that follow offer two case studies that trace the discourses that emerge once a new technology has been announced and a concept video has been released. We then discuss themes found through our analysis of the videos and then reflect on our analysis and on the implications of analyzing concept videos as design fictions.

METHODS

Looking at discourse at a time when products are still conceptual allows us to see the emergence of cultural narratives surrounding new technologies. Advertisements and news articles do not only promote products or inform the public, but also influence people's perceptions of products and instruct users on the "proper" ways to use the technologies [13]. Looking at companies' concept videos and at articles from the media and popular press indicates what types of hopes, fears, concerns, and other narratives were created and used while imagining the roles of new technologies. We can see how an initial framing of a technology set by the company through the concept video interplays with a broader cultural discourse represented by the media and press articles. From these sources, we can see how the discourses around these technologies engage in imagining the future.

Google Glass and Microsoft HoloLens were chosen because they share high-level some similarities (both are head worn computing devices), and because some media authors drew comparisons between the technologies and their launches when HoloLens was announced [55, 58]. These comparisons may seem curious to some because their purposes, form factors, video narratives, and underlying technology differ. While people understood them as different technologies, they used their prior experience with Glass to interpret HoloLens. We present Glass and HoloLens as two separate cases, but we note that the broader social context in which the videos are interpreted and discussed are temporally connected.

Data Collection and Analysis

This analysis draws on two collections of sources. The first set consists of the first publicly released concept videos from Google and Microsoft about Glass and HoloLens, respectively. We drew on semiotic analysis techniques by looking at signs – objects and concepts in the video, and what they mean or signify [29]. In particular we followed Dyer's method for investigating visual signs in advertisements [12] by focusing on five main signals: physical appearance of people, people's emotions, people's behavior and activities, props and physical objects, and settings. We identified these elements in each video, and interpreted what types of values they may signify. We further follow Dyer by paying attention to visual camera techniques such as camera angle and focus. Beyond our own analysis of the videos, we were interested in understanding how others responded to the videos. Viewers do not passively receive these videos but bring their own social experiences and beliefs to shape their understandings and interpretations [12]. As we studied the videos retrospectively, we could not analyze people's reactions in situ. We instead turned to media discourse to see how people in a collection of media sources discussed the products after the concept videos were released.

Our second set of sources consists of articles referencing Glass and HoloLens from *The New York Times*, *Forbes.com*, and *Wired.com,* found in online news databases using the search terms 'Google Glass' and 'Microsoft HoloLens'. This includes 137 articles related to Glass published between April 4, 2012, when Project Glass was first announced, and April 15, 2013, the day before Glass was released to a number of people in the public, called Google Glass Explorers. The set also includes 33 articles related to HoloLens published between January 25, 2015 when HoloLens was publicly announced, and June 29, 2015, when HoloLens was scheduled to be sent to the International Space Station to be used by astronauts, marking a point when HoloLens would be used by a community outside of Microsoft. At the time of writing, HoloLens is not commercially available to the public. Note that the evolution of products from fictional to real is a gradual change in state, not a binary one. The end dates of the articles in the set are not intended to mark when the devices become real, but rather indicate one point when the devices move in the direction from fictional to real.

Figure 2. Screenshots from the Google Glass concept video [44] which shows a first-person point of view of Glass. Left: the user continues wearing Glass while interacting with a friend. Middle: the user uses the built-in camera to take a photo of his surroundings and share it on social media. Right: the user shares his point of view with his girlfriend while using video chat.

We are interested in how public narratives constituted meanings and concerns about these new technologies. We looked to discourse analysis to better understand the situations when HoloLens and Glass emerged, as language both reflects and constructs realities [15]. While discourses build and reflect numerous dimensions of social situations, we focused on understanding how media articles: foregrounded and made significant certain ideas; invoked politics and values; and made connections with other conversations [15].

We manually coded the text of media articles for these themes and those found in the videos in our initial analysis, but also allowed new themes to emerge from the media articles [6], such as the ways companies were discussed and portrayed or how the future was discussed. We primarily used sentences as our unit of analysis. Acknowledging that it is difficult to view these materials while ignoring retrospective knowledge, the materials were viewed in order of publication during the initial round of analysis, as to follow a similar temporal trajectory that the people involved would have experienced.

This collection of media sources privileges certain viewpoints, but they are chosen because they target a wide set of people who have an interest in these technologies: interest from a general public viewpoint, a business viewpoint, and a technological viewpoint. These sources also contain a combination of opinion pieces that may more explicitly engage in imaginative discussion, and reporting pieces that provide insight on how discussions about these technologies are framed. The content of the articles, rather than the type of article, is privileged in this analysis. They also tend to focus on the ways that potential users perceive the technologies, rather than the designers or engineers behind the products. While the viewpoints expressed in the concept videos may not be the same ideas expressed by the technologies' designers and engineers, what the videos say and how they are framed provide important discursive pieces to investigate because they were an important way that people first learned about the technologies.

CASE 1: IMAGINING GOOGLE GLASS

Google's concept video "Project Glass: One Day…"[1] was released on April 4, 2012. The video portrays a day in the life of a male Glass user, as he makes his way around New York City (Figure 2). The video shows the user's point of view while waking up, eating, walking around the city, meeting a friend, shopping, and completing a video call to his girlfriend at sunset. The user uses Glass for: setting calendar events, weather information, looking at directions with live traffic and transit updates, sharing and receiving current locations with friends, taking photos, using social media, playing music, and having video conversations. But more important than the features of Glass is how the video frames and envisions the prop of Glass and the user.

First, the perspective of the video renders the actual Glass device invisible. This is done visually, as the video's continuous first-person point of view never allows the viewer to actually see the device or any other users' viewpoints, positioning the single Glass user in the video as the actor with agency and authority. The user interactions shown also render the physical form of Glass invisible. The user only interacts with the device by voice commands, or information is automatically and contextually displayed. There is no indication from this video of needing to touch the device in order to interact with it.

Second, the video frames the user of Glass as a young white male in New York City who lives alone in a sizeable apartment, indicating some level of affluence. Furthermore, he uses Glass for personal and social activities, spending the day walking around New York City; Glass is not something used at work, but rather to be used out in the world in daily life. This representation of glass evokes the image of a savvy technology-oriented male of financial means in an urban space with an emphasis on sharing his life through social media. Furthermore, he is the only person in the video using Glass; bystanders and others in the video never wear it. While it appears that there are privacy controls for the Glass user – when making a video call, he can decide whether or not to share his camera view with the person he is talking to – it is unclear whether any bystanders would be able to know if the camera is on or off.

Third, the context and settings of use of Glass are presented as mobile and seamless. Notably, most of the scenarios shown in the video take place outdoors, such as meeting a friend at a food truck, walking down the street with directions, or sharing pictures of something seen outdoors. These are things traditional personal computing would have

[1] Viewable at https://youtu.be/9c6W4CCU9M4

a hard time doing, and are instead similar to things a person would do on a smartphone. Yet the video presents an experience seemingly more seamless and effortless than a smartphone. Glass crosses multiple boundaries and contexts in the video, from home, to shopping, to seeing friends, to walking around. The continuous first-person viewpoint and day-long narrative suggest that the camera can continuously record in private and in public and that Glass is always turned on. The experience is also seamless in ease of use. While many of the scenario's features, like maps, take up the entire user's field of vision, the user is never bothered by it – there are no collisions or moments of frustration.

Fourth, the device itself is positioned as something that becomes invisible. Glass is framed as a device that invisibly fits into the daily life patterns of an individual. It is highly mobile, and augments a user's ability to communicate, navigate, and gather contextual information from his or her surroundings. Furthermore, no one that the user in the video interacts with in real life ever mentions or indicates seeing the device on the user's head, nor is the user ever seen putting Glass on or taking it off – it is always physically on the head and always turned on in the video.

Based on the video, Glass appears to fit well into the life patterns of young, rich, technologically-inclined males. Many of the functions could be conducted on a smartphone, but the video imagines Glass as a different experience, as the hardware is imagined as invisible, seamless, effortless, mobile, and "always on," reinforced in the video by using a continual first-person point of view and taking place over the course of an entire day. Even though the ultimate experience of using Glass was not the same as what was portrayed in this video, the video provides a starting point by Google for future-oriented discourses about Glass.

Glass Imagined in the Media

After the "One Day…" Glass video was released in April 2012, a broader media audience engaged in future-oriented discourses about Glass. Based on knowledge of the Google video, people outside of Google imagined what Glass would be like in the world, representing hopes and concerns about the technology as it related to a number of different societal and cultural issues. These represent the exploration of a range of possible futures, both positive and negative.

Several media authors identified Glass as a seamless, invisible, highly mobile, and always-on device, similar to its portrayal of the video. Some saw these as positive affordances of the technology. Part of the technology's appeal was its promise to "remove this barrier between living life and capturing it. Seemingly seamlessly, Google Glass wearers can capture their life while still immersed in the experience" [40]. As Glass was envisioned to be worn as an everyday object, it allowed people to imagine Glass's design and use through the lens of fashion. This was reinforced by referring to it as a "wearable," as well as its use by fashion designer Diane von Furstenberg in September 2012. Descriptions of Glass as "odd" "insane," "geeky," and even "ugly" [66, 64, 50, 39] matter because they indicate how people viewed Glass as a piece of fashion, not just a piece of technology. This envisioned Glass as something regularly worn all day, and that it would fade into the background of daily life and into the background of human interactions.

Using the video as a starting point, some authors imagined privacy concerns that might emerge in a world with Glass. A primary concern expressed that a world ubiquitous with Glass users would be a world in which surveillance by users would be commonplace. One author wrote "It's easy to imagine lots of other situations in which it'd be attractive to be able to snap photos all of the time, whether with friends, on the subway, on a road trip, walking down the street, at the beach, at clubs, at bars, on an airplane […] We could all become surveillance cameras, but with legs and Instagram filters" [48]. People envisioned certain technological capabilities, such as constant video or photo streams, combined with the vision of Glass as an invisible, seamless, and mobile technology. While taking photos with cell phones was already possible, one author noted that "The distinction is how covertly Google Glass will enable such privacy encroachments … an issue Google will need to address in detail before preemptive banning of its product goes viral." [43] Indeed, as time got closer to the launch of Google Glass Explorers, people and businesses began taking concrete actions in response to privacy concerns, including banning Glass in bars and strip clubs before it was available [43], and the formation of a campaign trying to ban Glass called Stop The Cyborg. Alternatively, a few authors viewed these qualities favorably, even likening Glass to a personal black box to provide safety for its users or owners [45].

Google's business models and place in the regulatory and market environment were discussed by media writers, providing a broader context to the video. Discussions occurred around the amount of data Glass could collect, envisioning a world where Google could perversely use this data for invasive advertisements, one author writing "Unfortunately, given Google's basic business model, this allows us to envision a world where ads are delivered directly to our eyes." [63] Others leveraged Google's privacy controversies occurring at the same time to envision a future where Google was not a wholly benevolent actor. In 2012, Google was fined for bypassing privacy settings in the Safari web browser, and in March 2013, Google paid a fine for violating people's privacy by collecting personal information during its Street View mapping project, leading some to call the company "a serial violator of privacy." [61]

Others responded to Glass by imagining alternate and unsanctioned uses of Glass through parody and critique. An early parody of the original concept video was created by Tom Scott entitled "Google Glasses: A New Way to Hurt

Figure 3. Screenshots from the Microsoft HoloLens concept video [56]. The first two shown a third-person point of view; the third shows a first-person point of view. Left: A woman walks in an office using Skype virtually while wearing HoloLens. Middle: A man plays Minecraft in augmented reality in his living room. Right: A woman sees a holographic display of a motorcycle she is designing.

Yourself,"[2] one writer describing it as how Glass "would actually look like for the rest of us" [62]. This parodied the original video's depiction of a user's experience with Glass. Scott instead portrayed a user bumping into objects because of obstructed vision, accidentally recording malapropos comments, advertisements appearing at inopportune times, and nonconsensual access of data by the police. Another author critiqued the imagined user shown in the original concept video, particularly that it only showed a "New York hipster's trip to The Strand to find a how-to ukulele book" [52]. Others envisioned alternate form factors such as a computerized walking stick to critique the perceived silliness of computerized glasses [59]. When the Google Glass Explorer project was announced, some people expressed alternative scenarios using Google's #ifihadglass hashtag, such as accidentally recording their own ATM PIN, surreptitiously watching pornographic videos in public, or leaving Glass in a drawer next to other unused gadgets [49]. Together, these provide an alternative set of speculative futures vastly different from the one Google presented.

CASE 2: IMAGINING MICROSOFT HOLOLENS

Microsoft's concept video "Microsoft HoloLens – Transform your world with holograms" was released on January 21, 2015.[3] (Figure 3) It shows HoloLens as a set of head worn goggles that projects holograms around the user. The video's narrator says "your digital world is blended with your real world." The video imagines various settings in which different users may use HoloLens' augmented reality holograms, including: a man in a kitchen interacting with holographic maps and weather reports; a woman in an office virtually designing and interacting with a motorcycle part; a woman using HoloLens conversing with a man over Skype sharing virtual architectural designs; two non-collocated men exploring a holographic representation of Mars; a man playing Minecraft in a living room; a man annotating woman's field of view via Skype to help fix a pipe; and a father virtually modeling his son's drawing.

First, the perspective of the video utilizes a third-person point of view, allowing the viewer to see the physical design and form factor of the device. It appears similar to a large pair of black ski goggles. The video also augments the third-person point of view, displaying the world filled with holograms, providing the video viewer the ability to see users immersed in a world of holograms, even though in reality one would need to wear the device to see them. Sometimes the video shifts into different users' first-person view, to show what various tasks might feel like.

Second, the video shows multiple users of HoloLens. But while there are multiple male and female users, some stereotypical gender roles are reinforced, such as a male assisting a female to fix a sink pipe. Users of HoloLens are portrayed as adults who are well off financially, working in relatively luxurious offices and living in spacious and well-furnished single family homes. The video evokes images of relatively affluent, professional workers as HoloLens users.

Third, the context and settings of use of HoloLens are portrayed as being attached to traditional computing environments. Every use of HoloLens shown in the video takes place indoors, either in an office or home. Furthermore, the video shows multiple users doing separate things: a woman uses HoloLens to design a motorcycle at work, while separately a man uses it to play Minecraft at home. HoloLens is not used by one person for doing everything in multiple places, but rather it is used by many people for doing one thing in specific places.

Fourth, the device itself is portrayed as a tool for particular tasks. HoloLens is not presented as always being on; users are sometimes seen not wearing HoloLens. The first user in the video is shown the device putting on. Furthermore, HoloLens is a normal occurrence in the world of the video, and not a strange technology. However, the video never shows people interacting with other people in face to face contexts while using HoloLens. Instead people either interact with others digitally through Skype or a holographic representation, or people are shown not wearing HoloLens while interacting face to face.

HoloLens Imagined in the Media

After the HoloLens concept video was released, a broader audience engaged in a discourse about the device, representing an exploration of imagined futures. This discourse used Microsoft's video as a reference point.

Reflecting the video portrayal, the physical design of HoloLens was described as "a space-age-looking smoke-

[2] Viewable at https://youtu.be/t3TAOYXT840
[3] Viewable at https://youtu.be/aThCr0PsyuA

tinted visor a bit bigger than a pair of ski goggles" [42] or a "face-computer that looks like a pair of space-age sunglasses" [47]. Authors explicitly described HoloLens unlike a fashion piece and as something not meant to be always on or omnipresent, but rather to be used for specific tasks indoors. Comparing the design to Glass, one author writes "Google Glass tried to be hidden, good at everything and to be worn all day and it failed. HoloLens is big, designed to accomplish a certain task, and worn for a few hours." [58] These comparisons reiterate the notion that HoloLens should be used for traditional PC tasks.

Using the video as a basis for further imagination, the HoloLens concept video was interpreted as extending current computing metaphors into the future. One author wrote "you used to compute on a screen, entering commands on a keyboard. Cyberspace was somewhere else. [...] In the very near future, you'll compute in the physical world. [...] What will this look like? Well, holograms." [46] The vision of computing portrayed by Microsoft's concept video is neither weird nor wildly different from what people experience today. One author wrote "it's taking the way you interact with your device, be it a laptop or PC, to new levels" [55]. HoloLens was viewed by some as an evolution or continuation of traditional personal computing tasks, either in the home or office. HoloLens' potential as a home gaming platform was often discussed, leveraging new possibilities with augmented and virtual reality, often describing Minecraft or other games. The potential for HoloLens to serve as a tool in an office context or as a platform for enterprise services was also commonly discussed. In one author's analysis, "I like that the headset is only designed to be worn for a few hours a day for a very specific purpose [...] That is one reason why I am considering the HoloLens as a productivity device first and entertainment second" [58]. Together, these identify two potential audiences for HoloLens – gamers and businesses – and also portray HoloLens as a device for specific types of purposes and tasks.

Microsoft's role was a prominent part of the discourse, providing a broader context to interpret the video. Microsoft was framed as an underdog, for example one author wrote "At least with HoloLens, Microsoft appears to be skating to where the puck could be headed in technology, rather than where it has been" [65]. In part because Microsoft was the developer, HoloLens was viewed in a positive light, as a new innovative and bold development by the company. Furthermore, Microsoft was recognized as a software and hardware company rather than a data-oriented company, leading to a focus on the software and hardware aspects of HoloLens, and less attention to the types of data the device might collect.

Glass was compared to HoloLens, generally to distinguish between the world envisioned by Glass and the one envisioned by HoloLens. One author compares HoloLens to Glass's perceived awkwardness, writing "The professional setting carries few of those social pitfalls. If you're wearing HoloLens as part of your work, you're not being rude, you're simply... doing your work" [38]. Another author separates HoloLens from the notion of an always-on wearable as represented by Glass. "You could use [Glass] while walking outside so there was the ability to overlay information and take photos and videos but HoloLens takes a different approach in that it seeks to replace a mouse, keyboard, tablet and even your PC screen" [55].

FINDINGS

In this section we discuss three main findings. The first explores different orientations toward imagining the future. Second, we discuss how the discourses' imagining the future with Glass and HoloLens and interpretation of the videos rely on broader narratives about computing and understandings about Google and Microsoft. Third, we look at how the analysis can surface values discussions, using the example of surveillance concerns.

Imagining the Future

After both concept videos were released, media authors used the videos as a starting point to further imagine the future world with Glass and HoloLens, and the implications of living in those worlds. Yet they portrayed the future in two different ways: some discussed the future by critiquing the world depicted in the companies' concept videos, while others accepted the depicted worlds. We distinguish between these two orientations, terming them speculative and anticipatory.

Speculative orientations toward the future acknowledge multiple possible futures, often with a critical lens. People utilizing this orientation may critique the future that the video depicts or present an alternate future. We use the term "speculative" as we found this orientation similar to speculative design's exploration and construction of multiple futures. These orientations are more likely when the fictional future is more provocative, violating today's norms and practices, and when the fictional future seems further away. We read media articles that acknowledged the futures presented by the companies, but contested them or presented alternate narratives. These were especially present when Glass was first announced and seemed further in the future. Written critiques, alternate subversive scenarios, and parodies provided reflections on what social experience and intimacy might mean with Glass, questioned Google's motives, and explored how new social norms enabled by Glass may raise privacy concerns.

Anticipatory orientations toward the future foresee a singular future. We use the term "anticipatory" finding inspiration from the concept of anticipation work, where practices in the present work to maintain and move toward a *particular* vision and expectation of the future [33]. Some of the articles we read expected the particular fictional world presented by companies as the expected future reality. This orientation is more likely when the fictional world follows familiar norms and practices, like those found in the present. We saw this in many HoloLens articles, as the HoloLens video utilizes familiar computing norms and contexts. They anticipated how HoloLens might be deployed in ways similar to what was portrayed in the video, but there was little critique of Microsoft, nor were there many expressions of alternative or subversive uses of HoloLens.

Anticipatory orientations are also more likely as a technology shifts from being more fictional to more real. We saw more anticipatory articles about Glass over time, the closer Glass got to commercial release. More articles focused on imagining a world with a Glass app economy, and how developers might use the Glass API, rather than critiquing Glass. With less space for critique or reconsideration of the design, some people began taking other types of concrete steps to prepare for the arrival of the anticipated future, such as bars and other private establishments that pre-emptively banned Glass due to privacy concerns.

These two orientations are not mutually exclusive, but rather lay on a spectrum. However, distinguishing between them allows us to be more precise about ways people discuss and imagine the future. When people adopt a speculative orientation toward the future, it suggests an opportunity to change and refine designs, and to consider other future sociotechnical worlds. The adoption of anticipatory orientations may suggest greater acceptance of a particular envisioned future, but it may also signal lessened space and receptiveness for critique or discussion.

Narrative Framing through Corporate Authorship and History

While the discourses surrounding Glass and HoloLens were forward looking, they were also informed by prior knowledge about the companies that created them. Google's business model of collecting user data to provide online advertising was projected onto Glass, as people imagined ways Google might try to continuously collect data for advertising, or continuously overlay ads over a user's field of vision. Prior privacy concerns around Google's use of data and the 2013 settlement over Google Street View for violating privacy were also cited as heightening privacy concerns about Glass.

Prior perceptions of Microsoft influenced how optimistically people viewed HoloLens. A common perception held that Microsoft was once a technology leader, but had failed to introduce compelling and innovative products recently. Microsoft was also viewed as a hardware and software company, not a data one. Given Microsoft's experience with the Xbox gaming system, many people imagined potential gaming uses of HoloLens. Against this backdrop, HoloLens is seen as innovative and exciting hardware, viewed with cautious optimism.

HoloLens also more closely fits into a historical narrative of the desktop computer. Other work has also noted the roles of historical narratives in affecting forward-facing outlooks [33]. Much of Microsoft's corporate history is associated with the use of Windows in the American workplace. Many of the imagined uses in Microsoft's concept video show desktop activities translated into an augmented reality world. Microsoft's HoloLens video seems to be an extension of prior visions of personal computing. A commercial for Windows 95[4] conceives of computing as allowing users to start: "discovering; learning; doing; organizing; connecting; managing; creating; playing; moving." In a similar way, the narration of the HoloLens video says that HoloLens allows people to: "visualize work; share ideas with each other; more immersive ways to play; new ways to teach and learn; collaborate and explore; and create."

Google Glass fits into a broader history of ubiquitous computing originating from the Silicon Valley lab Xerox PARC, outlined in Mark Weiser's 1991 article which conceptualizes the future of computing as ubiquitous, always present, and invisible, weaving itself "into the fabric of everyday life" where computers "pose no barrier to personal interaction" [37]. Like PARC, Google is similarly geographically headquartered in Silicon Valley, whereas Microsoft's Seattle location seems separated from the Silicon Valley culture. Dourish and Bell note that Weiser's vision of a world where the technology fades into the background still centers on technology use in the office, imagining new technologies but extending familiar social norms and forms of workplace organization [9]. Google's concept video reflects the technological aspects of Weiser's ubiquitous computing, while the contextual and social elements are broadened to non-workplace environments. More specifically, Glass fits into a tradition of research on wearable computing. Early wearable computing explored goggle-like computing interfaces that would understand the user's context by using a camera to identify objects surrounding the user [32], much like Glass.

Glass and HoloLens both present future visions that shift the location of computing from the screen into the physical world through the use of head-mounted devices. But each relies on a different broader historical narrative of computing, influenced by the ways that Google and Microsoft as companies were situated in popular thought.

Values in Imagined Futures: Surveillance Concerns

Looking more closely at the intertwining of the concept videos, the media's imaginings of the future, and authorial narratives provides a way to surface discussion of values in imagined futures. We focus on the way surveillance concerns were imagined as one such example.

Discussion about who has (and does not have) power and agency with these technologies affected surveillance and privacy concerns. Work in film studies describes how the

[4] Viewable at https://youtu.be/5VPFKnBYOSI

gaze, sometimes shown visually through point of view, can ascribe power, often projecting male or western power [19, 25]. Both the Glass and HoloLens videos present the viewpoints of the professional working class, but the Glass video's continuous first-person point of view serves to empower the white male user, as his view of the world is the only one we get to experience. Glass only provides him agency. No one else in the video wears Glass, and non-users are instead the object of his gaze. In the discourse, Glass was often seen as empowering when people imaged themselves as users by augmenting their capabilities to interact with the world. However, when people imagined themselves as non-users, Glass is disempowering, as they become objectified by Glass users. This becomes more concerning when Glass is portrayed as invisible and always on. A lack of mutuality between parties with respect to surveillance decreases the subject's ability to appropriately respond [2, 7]. Because not everyone gets to wear Glass and it is imagined as invisible, it becomes imagined as a tool of surveillance and power over others. Mutuality is lost and non-users fear that they will not be able to know when they are being recorded, what about them is being recorded, or how collected information is used.

While HoloLens only presents professional class users, it does show a variety of people using the device, distributing who has power and agency. The third-person point of view in the video allows the viewer to explicitly see the people wearing HoloLens, making the device and its users visible. HoloLens is portrayed as augmenting reality through holograms, rather than augmenting the abilities (and by extension, power) of an individual user. Imagining use cases in the contexts of work and home frame the device as familiar and mundane – it becomes just another computing device to assist with productivity and entertainment that anyone can use. Its physical visibility also creates a type of symmetry and mutuality that affords non-users agency: it is easier for non-users to know if someone wearing HoloLens is looking at them. Furthermore, HoloLens is not imagined or discussed as being continuously worn, creating a lesser power difference between users and non-users.

This illustrates how an analysis of concept video portrayals, speculative and anticipatory oriented discourses, and corporate authorial narratives can surface the ways in which they contributed to people's imagination and framing of surveillance concerns related to Glass and HoloLens. We note that the video and discourse analysis could also lead to further discussion of other values-centered debates such as questions about differential access and use of these technologies, norms of social interaction, isolation, constant connectivity, or productivity.

REFLECTIONS

We provide some reflections about our method of analysis, and what we gain by analyzing and critiquing corporate concept videos as design fiction. Our goal in analyzing concept videos is not to argue that our interpretation is the only "correct" reading. Rather our goal is to present a method that allows viewers to surface ideas, questions, and reflections while watching concept videos, and to consider how the presentation of technologies relates and responds to public discourse around their introduction into society.

We found that the video analysis is best done over several iterations. It took several viewings of the videos to identify the various elements in the videos and to draw connections and meanings between the elements. We suggest researchers conducting this type of analysis first look for the elements mentioned by Dyer [12]: people's appearance, their emotions, their behaviors, their activities, props and physical objects, and settings. Identifying visual techniques such as camera angle and focus, and any narration in the video is also useful. After identifying these elements, we found that asking several questions allowed us to surface further questions and insights. We note that this is not an exhaustive list, and is likely to expand as more analyses are done on different types of concept videos.

- *How are technologies portrayed?* This includes looking at the design and form of artifacts, their technical affordances, and possible values they embody.
- *How are humans portrayed?* Who are users and non-users of the technology? This draws on factors like behaviors, appearance, emotion, and setting to see what types of people are imagined to be interacting with the technology.
- *How is the sociotechnical system portrayed?* This focuses on how humans and the technology interact together, the settings and contexts in which they interact, and raises questions about who or what has agency over different types of interactions.
- *What is not in the video?* What populations or needs are unaddressed? What would it look like if certain technical capabilities are taken to the extreme? Can we imagine alternate futures from what the video depicts?

By analyzing and interpreting the corporate concept videos as viewers, we do not know about the process behind the creation of these videos, making the creators' intent difficult to discern. Unlike design fictions published in other venues or formats, there is no accompanying paratext, essay, or academic paper describing the authors' intent or process. This leads us to focus on how the videos act in dialog with broader media discourses. Regardless of intent, we find that the futures portrayed by the videos are ideological and express cultural values, whether consciously or unconsciously. We also found that by looking beyond the design fiction artifact itself, to the ways others further imagined the concept videos (media authors in our case), we could surface these values and see how people interpreted and responded to them.

We used discourse analysis in service of understanding how media articles discussed the narratives and themes we surfaced in our video analysis. When conducting our discourse analysis of media articles, we focused on how authors made certain ideas significant, how politics were invoked, and how it related to other conversations, such as existing conversations about privacy, Google, or Microsoft. Further work might investigate the role of language in other aspects of social situations, such as: engaging in activities, creating identities, signaling relationships, or identifying particular ways of knowing [15].

While we privileged content-relevance over type of article when building our media corpus, we still kept track of each article's context, following Gee's statement that words have specific meanings in different contexts [15]. Knowing where articles were published (both what publication and what section of the publication), the intended audience, and what other types of articles were written by the author helped provide clues on how to interpret the articles. For instance, without taking into account contextual information, it could be difficult to understand whether an author's proposed apps for Google Glass were serious business propositions or humorous critique. We found value in not decontextualizing articles and not taking words only at face value. Rather, we recorded and took into account knowledge about how the articles were contextually situated to interpret the written content.

Concept videos depict narratives which imply what technical affordances technologies have, but there may be gaps between portrayal and actual capabilities that we do not know about. The videos also do not show the technical mechanisms that enable the design and function of the technology. However, these ambiguities should be viewed as features, not bugs, of concept videos. Concept videos' usefulness, like design fictions, comes from their narrative features and their ability to elicit multiple interpretations, reflections, and questions. Concept videos' representations of technology should not be seen as final design solutions, but a work in progress still amenable to change.

Commercial concept videos help us acknowledge and explore the ways artifacts represent values at a time before the design of a company's product is finalized. Analysis and critique of these videos conducted earlier in design processes, rather than years later, can surface potential problems at a time when designs can still be changed. Given that, we call on the HCI and design communities to leverage their expertise and engage in this type of critique. In particular, by promoting speculative oriented discussion, they can open a space for the discussion of cultural values embedded in the concept videos, and promote or explore alternative values. This would be beneficial when addressing privacy, among other values. Furthermore, our analysis began raising issues around the portrayal of other cultural values, such as power, agency, gender, and class. Surfacing and addressing these values would be useful to many in the HCI community as well as technology studies scholars. Further analyses and critiques of concept videos should investigate these and other cultural values as well.

CONCLUSIONS

In this paper, we have posited that we can look at the concept videos of Google Glass and Microsoft HoloLens as design fictions. We make two main contributions. First, we introduced a method for analyzing the narratives presented in concept videos and in the media echo of those narratives. Like an echo, the media response may resemble the narratives in the video at some times, while other times the media response may shift or modulate to create a different narrative. Analyzing the creation and contestation of narratives and the values they promote provides insight into "infrastructuring" practices of new technologies. Through this type of analysis, the HCI and design communities can proactively contribute to values discussions when products are still fictional – that is after they are announced, but before they are publicly released. Future research should investigate how these methods can encourage reflection and discussion of values from the *beginning* of the design process, building on value-centered design processes like value sensitive design [5, 14] or privacy by design [24, 30].

Second, from our findings, we introduced the terms "anticipatory" and "speculative" orientations to the future to provide a more way to discuss the variety of ways futures are portrayed and responded to, and to acknowledge the ways corporate design fictions are often created in service of real future products. Speculative orientations acknowledge multiple possible futures, often in a critical fashion, while anticipatory orientations foresee a single particular future. Future work should explore how acknowledging and designing for these orientations can be used to benefit design practice.

Some recent media articles critique Glass's lack of public adoption as a failure, and at the time of writing it is still unknown how HoloLens will fare once it becomes widely available. Yet a focus on user adoption overlooks the discursive and imaginative work these technologies and their early video representations do. Design fictions can be powerful when they are seemingly close enough to reality that people have to contend with their claims or provocations as if they are real. Viewing the Glass and HoloLens concept videos as design fictions highlights new time periods when the values embedded in and promoted by products can be contested and debated. By seeking and taking part in this discourse, we can actively engage in and shape discussions about future cultural values while emerging technologies are still fictional.

ACKNOWLEDGEMENTS

We thank the all reviewers of this paper for their valuable comments. We also thank James Pierce, Laura Devendorf, and Anna Lauren Hoffmann for their early feedback on this work.

REFERENCES

1. Genevieve Bell and Paul Dourish. 2007. Yesterday's tomorrows: notes on ubiquitous computing's dominant vision. *Personal Ubiquitous Comput.* 11, 2 (January

2007), 133-143. http://dx.doi.org/10.1007/s00779-006-0071-x

2. Victoria Bellotti and Abigail Sellen. 1993. Design for privacy in ubiquitous computing environments. In *Proceedings of the third conference on European Conference on Computer-Supported Cooperative Work* (ECSCW'93), Giorgio de Michelis, Carla Simone, and Kjeld Schmidt (Eds.). Kluwer Academic Publishers, Norwell, MA, USA, 77-92.
3. Julian Bleecker. 2009. Design Fiction: A short essay on design, science, fact and fiction. (Mar 2009). Retrieved January 11, 2016 from http://drbfw5wfjlxon.cloudfront.net/writing/DesignFiction_WebEdition.pdf
4. Mark Blythe. 2014. Research through design fiction: narrative in real and imaginary abstracts. *In Proceedings of the SIGCHI Conference on Human Factors in Computing Systems (CHI '14).* http://doi.acm.org/10.1145/2556288.2557098
5. Alan Borning and Michael Muller. 2012. Next steps for value sensitive design. In *Proceedings of the SIGCHI Conference on Human Factors in Computing Systems* (CHI '12), 1125-1134. http://doi.acm.org/10.1145/2207676.2208560
6. Kathy Charmaz. 2014. *Constructing Grounded Theory* (2nd ed.). Sage Publications.
7. Julie E. Cohen. 2008. Privacy, Visibility, Transparency, and Exposure. *The University of Chicago Law Review*. 75: 181-201.
8. Marco de Sá, Judd Antin, David Shamma, and Elizabeth F. Churchill. 2011. Mobile augmented reality: video prototyping. In *CHI '11 Extended Abstracts on Human Factors in Computing Systems*(CHI EA '11), 1897-1902. http://dx.doi.org/10.1145/1979742.1979927
9. Paul Dourish and Genevieve Bell. 2011. *Divining a Digital Future: Mess and Mythology in Ubiquitous Computing*. MIT Press.
10. Paul Dourish and Genevieve Bell. 2014. "Resistance is futile": reading science fiction alongside ubiquitous computing. *Personal Ubiquitous Comput.* 18, 4 (April 2014), 769-778. http://dx.doi.org/10.1007/s00779-013-0678-7
11. Anthony Dunne and Fiona Raby. 2013. *Speculative Everything: Design, Fiction, and Social Dreaming*. MIT Press.
12. Gillian Dyer. 1982. *Advertising as Communication*. Routledge.
13. Claude S. Fischer. 1992. *America Calling: A Social History of the Telephone to 1940*. University of California Press.
14. Batya Friedman. 1996. Value-sensitive design. *interactions* 3, 6 (December 1996), 16-23. http://doi.acm.org/10.1145/242485.242493
15. James Paul Gee. 2005. *An Introduction to Discourse Analysis: Theory and Method* (2nd ed.). Routledge.
16. Ellie Harmon and Melissa Mazmanian. 2013. Stories of the Smartphone in everyday discourse: conflict, tension & instability. In *Proceedings of the SIGCHI Conference on Human Factors in Computing Systems (CHI '13).* http://doi.acm.org/10.1145/2470654.2466134
17. Sabrina Hauser, Audrey Desjardins, and Ron Wakkary. 2014. SFUture: envisioning a sustainable university campus in 2065. In *Proceedings of the 2014 companion publication on Designing interactive systems* (DIS Companion '14), 29-32. http://doi.acm.org/10.1145/2598784.2602774
18. Sheila Jasanoff and Sang-Hyun Kim. 2009. Containing the atom: Sociotechnical imaginaries and nuclear power in the United States and South Korea. *Minerva* 47, 2: 119-146.
19. E. Ann Kaplan. 1997. *Looking for the Other: Feminism, Film, and the Imperial Gaze*. Routledge.
20. Samuel Kinsley. 2010. Representing 'things to come': feeling the visions of future technologies. *Environment and Planning A* 42,11: 2771-2790. http://dx.doi.org/10.1068/a42371
21. Joseph Lindley and Paul Coulton. 2015. Back to the future: 10 years of design fiction. *In Proceedings of the 2015 British HCI Conference (British HCI '15).* http://doi.acm.org/10.1145/2783446.2783592
22. Conor Linehan, Ben J. Kirman, Stuart Reeves, Mark A. Blythe, Joshua G. Tanenbaum, Audrey Desjardins, and Ron Wakkary. 2014. Alternate endings: using fiction to explore design futures. In *CHI '14 Extended Abstracts on Human Factors in Computing Systems* (CHI EA '14), 45-48. http://dx.doi.org/10.1145/2559206.2560472
23. Wendy E. Mackay and Anne Laure Fayard. 1999. Video brainstorming and prototyping: techniques for participatory design. In *CHI '99 Extended Abstracts on Human Factors in Computing Systems*(CHI EA '99), 118-119. http://dx.doi.org/10.1145/632716.632790
24. Deirdre K. Mulligan and Jennifer King. 2011. Bridging the Gap Between Privacy and Design. *University of Pennsylvania Journal of Constitutional Law* 14, 4: 989-1034.
25. Laura Mulvey. 1975. Visual pleasure and narrative cinema. In *Media and cultural studies: KeyWorks.* Meenakshi Gigi Durham and Douglas M. Kellner (eds.). Blackwell Publishing, 393-404.

26. Helen Nissenbaum. 2009. *Privacy in Context: Technology, Policy, and the Integrity of Social Life*. Stanford University Press.
27. Richard L. Oliver, Thomas S. Robertson, and Deborah J. Mitchell. 1993. Imaging and Analyzing in Response to New Product Advertising. *Journal of Advertising* 22, 4: 35-50. http://dx.doi.org/10.1080/00913367.1993.10673417
28. James Pierce and Eric Paulos. 2014. Some variations on a counterfunctional digital camera. In *Proceedings of the 2014 conference on Designing interactive systems* (DIS '14), 131-140. http://dx.doi.org/10.1145/2598510.2602968
29. Gillian Rose. 2007. *Visual Methodologies: An Introduction to the Interpretation of Visual Materials* (2nd ed.). Sage Publications.
30. Ira S. Rubinstein. 2011. Regulating Privacy by Design. *Berkeley Technology Law Journal* 26, 3: 1409-1456.
31. Susan Leigh Star and Geoffrey C. Bowker. How to Infrastructure. In *The Handbook of New Media*. Leah A. Lievrouw and Sonia Livingstone (eds.). Sage, 230-245.
32. Thad Starner, Bernt Schiele, and Alex Pentland. 1998. Visual Contextual Awareness in Wearable Computing. In *Proceedings of the 2nd IEEE International Symposium on Wearable Computers* (ISWC '98), 50-57
33. Stephanie B. Steinhardt and Steven J. Jackson. 2015. Anticipation Work: Cultivating Vision in Collective Practice. In *Proceedings of the 18th ACM Conference on Computer Supported Cooperative Work & Social Computing (CSCW '15).* http://doi.acm.org/10.1145/2675133.2675298
34. Joshua Tanenbaum, Karen Tanenbaum, and Ron Wakkary. 2012. Steampunk as design fiction. In *Proceedings of the SIGCHI Conference on Human Factors in Computing Systems* (CHI '12), 1583-1592. http://doi.acm.org/10.1145/2207676.2208279
35. Bruce Tognazzini. 1994. The "Starfire" video prototype project: a case history. In *Proceedings of the SIGCHI Conference on Human Factors in Computing Systems* (CHI '94), Beth Adelson, Susan Dumais, and Judith Olson (Eds.), 99-105. http://dx.doi.org/10.1145/191666.191712
36. Laurie Vertelney. 1989. Using video to prototype user interfaces. *SIGCHI Bull.* 21, 2 (October 1989), 57-61. http://dx.doi.org/10.1145/70609.70615
37. Mark Weiser. 1991. The computer for the 21st century. *Scientific American* 265, 3: 94-104.

MEDIA SOURCES

38. Brian Barrett. 2015. Microsoft Shows HoloLens' Augmented Reality Is No Gimmick. (29 Apr 2015). Retrieved July 2, 2015 from http://www.wired.com/2015/04/microsoft-build-hololens/
39. Jeff Bercovici. 2012. If You Think Cheating is Rampant Now, Just Wait Till Google Glasses Are Here. (26 Sep 2012). Retrieved July 1, 2015 from http://onforb.es/Q0IuG4
40. Kelly Clay. 2013. Why I Don't Care 'If I Had Glass'. (30 Mar 2013). Retrieved July 1, 2015 from http://onforb.es/Zukw80
41. Giuseppe Costantino. 2013. google-glass-12. Image. (24 May 2013). Retrieved September 20, 2015 from https://flic.kr/p/eqPW1q
42. Scott Dadich. 2015. Letter From the Editor: Microsoft's Holographic Goggles Are Strange—But Kind of Awesome. (21 Jan 2015). Retrieved July 2, 2015 from http://www.wired.com/2015/01/editors-letter-feb-2015/
43. David DiSalvo. 2013. The Banning of Google Glass Begins (And They Aren't Even Available Yet). (10 Mar 2013). Retrieved July 1, 2015 from http://onforb.es/10rxJBl
44. Google. 2012. Project Glass: One Day…. Video. (4 Apr 2012). Retrieved September 20, 2015 from https://www.youtube.com/watch?v=9c6W4CCU9M4
45. Andy Greenberg. 2012. Cyborg Discrimination? Scientist Says McDonald's Staff Tried To Pull Off His Google-Glass-Like Eyepiece, Then Threw Him Out. (17 Jul 2012). Retrieved January 11, 2016 from http://www.forbes.com/sites/andygreenberg/2012/07/17/cyborg-discrimination-scientist-says-mcdonalds-staff-tried-to-pull-off-his-google-glass-like-eyepiece-then-threw-him-out/#363fd1a54983
46. Jessi Hempel. 2015. Project HoloLens: Our Exclusive Hands-On With Microsoft's Holographic Goggles. (21 Jan 2015). Retrieved July 2, 2015 from http://www.wired.com/2015/01/microsoft-hands-on/
47. Jessi Hempel. 2015. Restart: Microsoft in the age of Satya Nadella (Satya Nadella's Got a Plan to Make You Care About Microsoft). (21 Jan 2015). Retrieved July 2, 2015 from http://www.wired.com/2015/01/microsoft-nadella/

48. Kashmir Hill. 2012. Sergey Brin's Favorite Google Glass Feature. (11 Sep 2012). Retrieved July 1, 2015 from http://onforb.es/RIXia6
49. Kashmir Hill. 2013. Sorry, Google. Here Come The Inevitable #IfIHadGlass Bashtags. (20 Feb 2013). Retrieved January 11, 2016 from http://www.forbes.com/sites/kashmirhill/2013/02/20/sorry-google-here-come-the-inevitable-ifihadglass-bashtags/
50. Robert Hof. 2012. LIVE at Google I/O Conference: New Tablets, Home Media Player, Google Glass and More. (27 Jun 2012). Retrieved July 1, 2015 from http://onforb.es/MwEonL
51. Alex Kipman. 2015. Meet the award recipients of the first Microsoft HoloLens academic research grants. (11 Nov 2015). Retrieved March 28, 2016 from https://blogs.windows.com/devices/2015/11/11/meet-the-award-recipients-of-the-first-microsoft-hololens-academic-research-grants/
52. Anthony Wing Kosner. 2012. Google Project Glass Takes Augmented Reality Way Beyond Army "Birth Control Glasses". (4 Apr 2012). Retrieved July 1, 2015 from http://onforb.es/HhT5sq
53. Anthony Wing Kosner. 2013. If You Have a Great Idea (And $1,500) You Can Be A Google Glass Explorer. (20 Feb 2013). Retrieved July 1, 2015 from http://www.forbes.com/sites/anthonykosner/2013/02/20/if-you-have-a-great-idea-and-1500-you-can-be-a-google-glass-explorer
54. lawrencegs. 2013. Google Glass. Image. (5 Dec 2013). Retrieved September 20, 2015 from https://flic.kr/p/itfbxJ
55. Antony Leather. 2015. Microsoft Windows 10: Free Upgrade Confirmed, HoloLens VS Google Glass VS Oculus Rift. (22 Jan 2015). Retrieved July 1, 2015 from http://onforb.es/1zz8li1
56. Microsoft. 2015. Microsoft HoloLens – Transform your world with holograms. Video. (21 Jan 2015). Retrieved September 20, 2015 from https://www.youtube.com/watch?v=aThCr0PsyuA
57. Microsoft Sweden. Windows 10, januari 2015. Image. Retrieved September 20, 2015 from https://www.flickr.com/photos/microsoftsweden/albums/72157648095843533
58. Patrick Moorhead. 2015. Microsoft Hololens Gets Face Wearables Right. (28 Jan 2015). Retrieved July 1, 2015 from http://onforb.es/1Hf8XgY
59. Lore Sjoberg. 2013. Alt Text: Google Hats and the Imaginary Future of Wearable Computing. (27 Feb 2013). Retrieved January 11, 2016 from http://www.wired.com/2013/02/alt-text-google-glass/
60. Bruce Sterling. 2012. Augmented Reality: Google Glass Design Fiction. (4 Apr 2012). Retrieved January 11, 2016 from http://www.wired.com/2012/04/augmented-reality-google-glass-design-fiction/
61. David Streitfeld. 2013. Google concedes drive-by prying violated privacy. *The New York Times*. (13 Mar 2013).
62. Dave Thier. 2012. What Life with Google Glasses Would Actually Look Like. (5 Apr 2012). Retrieved July 1, 2015 from http://onforb.es/HSWyzD
63. Dave Thier. 2013. The Potentially World-Changing New Feature in Google's Project Glass. (20 Feb 2013). Retrieved July 1, 2015 from http://onforb.es/11VjbyK
64. Eric Wilson. 2012. The Year in Style. *The New York Times*. (23 Dec 2012).
65. Nick Wingfield. 2015. Microsoft's Far-Out Vision. *The New York Times*. (3 May 2015).
66. Tim Worstall. 2013. Google Glass: The Dork Look Isn't All That Popular Right Now. (25 Feb 2013). Retrieved July 1, 2015 from http://onforb.es/15KgoaL

The Case of the Strangerationist: Re-interpreting Critical Technical Practice

Vera Khovanskaya
Information Science
Cornell University
vdk9@cornell.edu

Maria Bezaitis
Intel Corporation
Maria.Bezaitis@intel.com

Phoebe Sengers
Information Science and Science & Technology Studies, Cornell University
pjs54@cornell.edu

ABSTRACT
We describe a method for critically informed development of new technical systems by combining analysis of historical discourse with critical technical practice. We take the case of social recommender systems, a class of algorithms that calculate which people should be recommended to whom. We demonstrate similarities between limitations of "social network" rhetoric in contemporary social matching algorithms and discourse on planning in Artificial Intelligence. We develop an algorithm for social matching that recombines "lost" ideas from the history of AI, orienting around situated behavior and algorithmic transparency. By implementing this approach in a functioning prototype called "The Strangerationist", we examine directly how conceptual commitments inform low-level technical decisions, and how available technologies shape conceptual vision. Our goal is not to design a 'better' algorithm but to explore the challenges and opportunities of weaving together historical discourse and critical analysis of values embedded in technology with the experience of designing it.

Author Keywords
Critical technical practice, critical methods, HCI.

INTRODUCTION
In "The Relevance of Algorithms," Tarleton Gillespie describes algorithms as embedded, multi-dimensional entanglements between technical processes and the social tactics of the designers and audiences which gives rise to them. He calls for simultaneous sociological inquiry into the technical process by which algorithms evaluate and present data and the social contexts and processes which yield and legitimate algorithms [20]. Yet, as noted by Gillespie, along with many other social science scholars [31, 38, 40], algorithms continue to be fraught ground for sociological inquiry because algorithms, like many technical infrastructures are notoriously embedded, "squirreled away in semi-private settings or buried in inaccessible electronic code" [45, p 378] so much so that they are often only visible in malfunction [45] or at their seams [11]. Even if researchers can locate themselves in the presence of code and have the technical literacy necessary to analyze its contents, algorithms pose further unique difficulties. The sheer scale and technical complexity of the data manipulations of the algorithm is often impossible to recreate manually, leaving even technically trained persons unable to follow the many iterative transformations by algorithms that render inputs into "intelligent" outputs [38].

Beyond mapping and making visible the embedded representations of the social reality, the task of critical engagement with algorithms is motivated by an interest in experiencing the of decisions made on the part of technical practitioners—a mixture of "choice, necessity, pragmatism, and unquestioned 'home truth'"[40]—which in turn is shaped by the constraints of what is practically calculable and implementable. The Strangerationist project is one attempt to answer the call to social analysis of algorithms in light of these difficulties. It answers that call by engaging directly with algorithms, specifically taking the case of social matching algorithms—algorithms which recommend people to people—simultaneously on the level of social and historical discourse, and on the level of technical system design.

Our work is grounded in critically oriented and reflective design traditions in Human-Computer Interaction (HCI), and in a parallel earlier thread of inquiry conceived by Philip Agre called *critical technical practice* [1]. When he was a researcher in Artificial Intelligence (AI), Agre developed critical technical practice as a means to integrate philosophical, critical reflection and technical development. This method works by recognizing technical impasses as philosophical problems, applying philosophical and critical methodologies to find ways around these impasses, and thereby driving new technical innovation. We see system development here not as an end in itself, but as a means to reflectively explore underlying assumptions and attitudes about technology and humanity.

Broadly following Agre's development of critical technical practice, our methodology here starts with a critical analysis of contemporary technical discourse to identify recurring metaphors and assumptions on which the discourse

DIS 2016, June 04 - 08, 2016, Brisbane, QLD, Australia

ACM978-1-4503-4031-1/16/06 $15.00
DOI: http://dx.doi.org/10.1145/2901790.2901860

rests. Through this analysis, we pinpoint and explain systemic issues that follow from those assumptions and the points of connection between these limitations. To further explore the relationship between conceptual commitments and algorithms, we use inspiration from the history of technical discourses to identify, revive, and recombine "lost" ideas which embody different points of view from those currently prevalent in the design of social matching algorithms. We explore the potential impact of these conceptual commitments within algorithms by embodying those heuristics in a specific technical system. We use the practice of system building both as a means to identify and alter low-level decisions that would otherwise flow unthinkingly from the dominant technical discourse into systems design. Throughout the process, we track the ways in which technologies resist, constrain, or reroute those commitments. While the work we present here is focused specifically on social matching, more broadly we are concerned with questions about the role of critique and design in a world increasingly structured by algorithms. As we will describe next, in this paper we contribute a method for integrating historical analysis of technical discourses with critical technical practice as a means for exploring the mutual embedding of discursive concepts and algorithmic development.

THE RELEVANCE OF SOCIAL MATCHING

Recommender systems are part of a growing family of algorithms that curate one's experience of technology through the careful mining of specific types of data. Hand in hand with the proliferation of personal and social data, recommender systems are being explored through commercial systems and research prototypes as a way of profitably sifting data-overflow by suggesting which information may be of most value to you. While recommender systems generally seek to automate the everyday process of word-of-mouth sharing of opinions in various domains—e.g. music, movies, or books—social *matching* systems specifically automate the process of 'bringing people together" by recommending people to people based on their activities. Popular modern social media applications like Facebook and Google+ calculate matches between users of the system and other people that they are likely to know by constructing intricate friendship graphs, or "networks," using interaction data.

Network-based models for social matching algorithms have a clear practical utility. Nevertheless, given the reach of social matching applications and their potential to shape people's on-line experiences, it is worthwhile to ask for what reasons and with what consequences these algorithms rely so heavily on social networks. In this paper we critically examine the conceptualizations of human relations that are incorporated into these algorithms, using technical design coupled with analysis of historical discourse as a means for social study of algorithms.

We will do so by drawing on historical analysis of debates within AI. In analyzing social matching algorithms, we will identify similarities between the historical discourse in which social matching algorithms and the concept of the "social network" arose, and arguments challenging "top-down" modeling approaches in Artificial Intelligence, which similarly narrow the scope of experience to what can be effectively modeled. In particular, we will argue that networked-based matching algorithms are based on an intellectual legacy of adopting structural sociology into computer science which tends to see closeness between people as reasonably static and as quantifiable based on data traces. This legacy is tied to two well-known problems: first, that this understanding of closeness has clear limits in representing real human relationships given their dynamic and incompletely documented nature, and, second, that to the extent the algorithms effectively do capture human relationships, they tend to connect people who would already know or meet each other and otherwise create 'filter bubbles' of like-minded people [37].

EXPLORING ALGORITHMS I: HISTORICAL DISCOURSE

Most recommender systems arise from a desire to use computers to effectively manage data overload [50]. Traditionally, this problem has been tackled in computer science through AI, i.e. as a computer intelligence task: can computers be "taught" how to trace useful patterns through a milieu of data to show the optimal collection of music, books, etc. for another person. In the field of social matching in particular, where, instead of books, *people* are recommended to people, the task has similarly been approached as an intelligent modeling task. For example, in a seminal survey paper in AI, Terveen and McDonald describe this general methodology for developing social matching recommenders: "(1) modeling the set of users who can be matched, (2) matching users in response to an explicit request or implicit opportunity, (3) introducing matched users, enabling them to (4) interact with each other... note that the results of the process must feedback to the system, possibly causing it to update its models" [50, p 404]. Terveen and McDonald articulate two significantly different classes of techniques for modeling users.

The first set of approaches identified by Terveen and MacDonald calculate tie-strength (the distance between two people, represented as nodes in a graph of the social network) using data about people's' *social interactions* to compute who is likely to know each other [50]. Early forms of such social-modeling recommendations include the "friend-of-friend" algorithm -- "if many of my friends consider Alice a friend, perhaps Alice could be my friend." Canonical examples of this kind of system include ReferralWeb [25] and Expertise Recommender [32], which model professional social networks through co-authorship in hopes of recommending experts on a certain topic that the user of the system is likely to know. A more recent example is the "people you may know" feature of social networking websites like Facebook.

The second set of approaches identified by Terveen and McDonald rely on modeling *content characteristics* like users' preferences and behaviors, based on the assumption that matches can be recommended through similarity of interests or content produced. An early example of this approach was an early-2000s recommender I2I [12] which matched people who were on the same website at the same time, reasoning that "if we both post content on similar topics, we might be interested in getting to know each other". This approach to matching can be seen in several current, interest-specific social websites like Flickr (photography), Pandora (music), and dating websites such as OkCupid, which perform social matching based on user content and characteristics (e.g. [26]).

Although these approaches are distinct in their use of different kinds of data for determining a 'match' between two users – the social network ties of a user versus the content produced or consumed by the user – it is important to note that recommendation algorithms are not inherently limited to just one approach. For example, Chen et al. empirically evaluate a hybrid model that combines content matching with social network "links" [13].

At the time of Terveen and McDonald's survey, 2005, it did not seem clear that any one approach dominated the design space. But five years later, research showed that social network modeling algorithms appeared to produce better-received recommendations and found more known contacts for users [13]. In more recent work, trends show that for general-purpose social matching, social network modeling is the prevalent technique. While some domain-specific social matching recommender systems facilitate connections over content-based interest, the dominant algorithms for calculating social matches in mainstream social media rely on the construction of social networks.

The trend toward network models for social matching has a legacy in an area of sociology called structural analysis, which is commonly drawn on in this work. Historically, this field has conceptualized the social network as a graph-based representation of social interactions that can be used for various computations such as tracking the spreading of disease or the dissemination of news. In social network models, social matches are generally computed as the measurable distance between two human nodes on a graph. This conceptualization has been represented and analyzed using mathematical graph theory, notably in work by mathematician Manfred Kochen and political scientist Ithiel de Sola Poole [46].

In conjunction with advances in personal and interpersonal data gathering and reiterations of popular sociological experiments, particularly Stanley Milgram's "Six Degrees of Separation" [33] and Mark Granovetter's "Strength of Weak Ties" [21] these earlier works have motivated many computational efforts to model and quantify social networks [15]. Algorithms have been developed to calculate social closeness though social network modeling; for example, work by Gilbert and Karahalios found a series of features (e.g. number of mutual friends, number of words exchanged) that can, notionally, predict tie strength between friends in an online social network [17]. These algorithms have been applied and iterated by many researchers in social matching. Work in this field has provided an intellectual legacy that frames how researchers think about the strength of social ties and central and peripheral social roles [15,19].

Trouble on the Network

There is no denying the practical benefits that have accrued from matching people with other people based on social network modeling. At the same time, limitations of quantifying social closeness and modeling social networks have become markedly visible in recent HCI research. We here identify two key systemic issues.

The first issue is that, to the extent that social networks truly capture real-world ties, there is limited novelty to the predictions and connections that arise from network models. Empirical work suggests that algorithms based on social network information are able to produce better-received recommendations and find people that users already know, while algorithms using similarity of user-created content were stronger in discovering "new friends" [13]. The sense that social network algorithms may reproduce real-world connections rather than develop new ones has led to concerns in academic and popular-press writing about social matching leading to "echo chambers" and "filter bubbles" [37].

The second issue is that there are substantial and perhaps fundamental difficulties in capturing novel and useful data for the computation of social closeness. For example, in reflecting on close friendships as revealed in Facebook data, Sosik et al highlight that the data available to data scientists is limited because closest ties are often left out of computer mediated communication [47]. Other identified difficulties include persuading users to provide clean, semantically interoperable data [23] and recognizing the recursive malleability of social networks because the recommendation process itself can influence social ties [39]. The legacy of Granovetter's strength of weak ties research in the social network software space has even been directly challenged by Panovich et al.'s work which suggests that, in the context of online question and answer features embedded into social networks, users report getting the most useful answers from people that, when assessed by various accepted social closeness algorithms, including those by Karahalios, were computed as close - not weak - ties [36].

It is important to note that these impasses are neither new nor unanticipated by proponents of structural analysis. Work from the 1970's on modeling contact and influence in social networks observed the difficulty of quantifying and computing basic information about "man-to-man" contact, for example because of the near-impossibility of obtaining accurate values for many of the variables [46]. The authors present an influential model for estimating the scale and connectivity of a "human contact net" and argue that the model requires precise and necessarily reductive definitions of "knowing." They describe significant practical caveats about friction between the model and the "lumpiness" of daily, lived experience. These concerns have been echoed in the context of social matching by Terveen and McDonald, who describe ways in which the setting of a relationship often influences how the relationship develops [50]. They argue that "whole network analyses" have consistently revealed that the social and information seeking behaviors of people evade formal structures, and that personal roles and interpersonal experiences are lurking variables in modeling networks.

These concerns suggest that underlying the practical difficulties associated with social-network-based models are deeper questions about what kind of relationship exists between the social networks discovered by algorithms based on available data and actual relationships between people in the world. One interpretation of 'found' social networks would be that they ideally correspond to the actual real-world relationships between people. Since it is easy to realize that (1) people have multi-faceted, dynamic relationships which cannot easily be reduced to simple, static links, (2) many aspects of those relationships take place outside of monitored data streams, and (3) even monitored data streams have human meanings outside of the plausible reach of contemporary algorithms, such a simplistic interpretation is unlikely to be adhered to long by even the most ardent proponent of social networks.

And yet there is a seduction to the term "network" itself that makes the equation of data structure and relationship a practical, quotidian accomplishment of algorithmic work despite its proponents' critical reflection. In a similar vein, Agre has analyzed the extraordinary power of certain broad technical terms such as "planning" when they are used, like "networks," both to identify a family of technical specifications and as metaphorical descriptors of empirical phenomena [2]. The power of these terms derives from their under-recognized plasticity, in that they are flexibly and seamlessly deployed to refer sometimes to a specific technical representation (e.g. a graph data structure) and sometimes in a much more vague sense to real-world phenomena (e.g. a network of friends). It is precisely the ability of these terms to travel between these two kinds of meanings that provides them with the heady power to apparently calculate the world.

Within social matching, we see the consequences of this rhetorical plasticity in slippages between 'networks' understood as structures that can be calculated from conveniently captured data and 'networks' as actually existing, real-world relationships. One kind of slippage is when the networks that can be calculated are taken as necessarily revealing one's real-world relationships. Another kind of slippage happens when network models are used to give you opportunities to connect with the match that has been calculated – in this case your actual social network is not 'found' but transformed, through the system, to more closely resemble the calculated structure. A third kind of slippage happens when the forms of networks that are calculated bear noticeable traces of the kind of data that happens to be available; we see this for example in the evolution of social recommender systems moving from co-authorship networks in early work to social media interactions, Facebook interactions, Twitter interactions, etc.

Certainly, all these forms of data bear relationships to the real world of human experience; equally certainly, it can be informative to consider real-world relationships in terms of social networks and to use calculation to help give a sense of the shape of those relationships. But the issues of limited novelty and of limited data caution against an unintentional equation between a model of reality and reality itself. They suggest an untapped potential for finding ways to suggest social matches that do not depend conceptually on an equation between real-world relationships and what computers can sense and model. Is it possible for algorithms to embody such a worldview? It is this opportunity we now turn to explore in depth.

EXPLORING ALGORITHMS II: ROADS UNTRAVELLED

Our analysis above highlights possibilities, constraints, and limits of the focus on social networks as a technically instantiated metaphor of human relationships. Here, we take another tack to understand social recommendation algorithms, by identifying other conceptual commitments that could also be embodied in algorithms for social matching. Our goal in this section is to demonstrate concretely that an equation between computational representations and human relationships or practices is not a requirement for a social matching algorithm by laying out how alternative conceptual commitments could be embodied in design. In the next section, we will explore how these conceptual commitments come under stress, shift and are further shaped in technical instantiation.

The first source for rethinking social matching comes from following different paths through the history of sociology than those normally drawn on in social-network-based matching, specifically ideas from sociology about how to frame how humans relate to each other that arose before present conceptions of networks had been cemented. The second source is from the history of technical discourses around modeling prevalent in AI in the 1980's and early 1990's, which questioned and developed technical and design alternatives to the idea that computing should be based on complex models that directly mirror real-world phenomena. Our goal here is to explore the social commitments embedded in algorithms for social matching by examining and recombining paths not taken by contemporary social matching.

What is a 'match'?

Previously, we discussed how earlier researchers in sociology had articulated difficulties arising in the modeling of human relationships through networks that later surfaced in HCI as concerns about network-based social matching models. One way, then, to potentially address these difficulties is to return to prior moments in sociology where alternative understandings of network models were formulated. Precisely because these ideas may not have been picked up on at the time, they may now provide us with a different lens for conceiving of what social matching algorithms could or should be.

One place to start is with Granovetter's discussion of the limitations of weak ties [21]. In the concluding sections of "The Strength of Weak Ties", Granovetter expresses concerns about reducing relationships to strong and weak ties. He encourages future social modeling practitioners to elaborate the social network model, specifically since tie-strength alone is a "very limited model for social networks" [p. 1380]. One direction Granovetter suggests for future work is to consider tie strength as a "continuous" [p. 1380] variable. He also points to the value of considering the developmental, rather than static, structure of networks.

Since Granovetter, this line of thinking has been tackled from a modeling perspective. This has led to "context sensitive" frameworks for social modeling that attempt to use probabilistic modeling to capture context sensitivities in the network [e.g. 12,50]. Yet we note, in the context of the concerns previously mentioned around data availability, that these approaches also largely depend on the assumption that real-world relationships can be effectively captured in the model, given sufficient data.

However, the distance between people does not necessarily need to be approached through a technical program that posits it as having a definite value, whether absolute or probabilistic. In this line of thinking we are inspired by early 20th century sociologist Georg Simmel's work, which tackles the distance between people by challenging classic distinctions between "the stranger" and the "native." In doing so, Simmel points to how even the most intimate relationships have degrees of distance and alienation. Importantly, he points to a degree of fundamental uncertainty: "we do not know how to designate the peculiar unity of this position other than by saying that it is composed of certain measures of nearness and distance" [44, pp 3].

Inspired by this conceptualization of an omnipresent, shifting closeness and distance to social matching, we suggest an alternative to trying to calculate (and/or iteratively re-calculate) the distances between people and interpreting these as "strong" or "weak" ties. Another, perhaps more effective way to think about tie strength is as a "continuous" variable in Granovetter's formulation, in terms of a closeness and distance, where at any given point in time, with any two people, a relationship is a to some degree unknowable and constantly shifting combination of the two. Under this conception of tie strength, it becomes feasible to drop some of the assumptions about the calculability of the network, and pursue a different model for social matching. For inspiration about how to do so, we turn to the history of Artificial Intelligence (AI).

Action beyond calculability

It may sound paradoxical to argue for building algorithms for social matching while seeing actual social matches as only partially calculable. We draw inspiration for how to do so from debates around the relationship between computational representations and the activity of computational systems that took place in AI in the 1980's and have more recently been revisited in HCI [29,30]. AI at the time was in crisis, as the ambitious attempts to build "artificial minds" in the '70's through the manipulation of complex symbolic representations appeared to be at a standstill. One strand of research termed "situated action" began to explore the idea that autonomous agents might be able to react to what is happening around them without necessarily directly representing it. As Brook's influential slogan, "The world is its own best representation" [9], suggests, the idea was to tie agent behavior directly to what could be sensed about the world. Rather than focusing effort on building complex models of the world which quickly became cumbersome and out-of-date, these researchers argued that directly tying sensing to action would allow agents to exhibit reactive, real-time, apparently intelligent behavior without necessarily "knowing" much in a representational sense. This approach led to substantial successes in robotics and AI. It also led to substantial controversy, pitting its ability to drive impressively complex, reactive behavior with challenges in framing such behavior as 'intelligent' and in generalizing the model beyond bodily action [9].

For our purposes here, the framing of technical systems as agents who do not know the world but who can react to its visible features in ways that can be narrated as intelligent suggests an alternative approach to social matching. What if we think about social matching systems as 'agents' reacting to a world of user behavior? In this sense, existing network-based matching can be thought of in the vein of 1980's AI as creating symbolic systems that construct complex representations of that world, with good matching achieved as a consequence of a correct representation. But we could also consider social matching as a form of situated action, emphasizing matching as continuously reacting to and embedded in human activity. This reframing removes our reliance on the model of the network and focus instead on optimizing the moment-to-moment interaction between the matching algorithm and what users do. In the next section, we describe potential design strategies for social matching based on this alternative model.

Embodying Alternatives in Algorithmic Design

We argued previously that the primary models for social matching based on networks rest on an implicit equation of computational representations and human activities. Here, we develop two design heuristics for social matching that are based on an alternative viewpoint. These heuristics embody the continuous, dynamic, and partially incalculable vision of social ties arising from our analysis of sociology. They do so by leveraging ideas from AI about how to design systems that can respond dynamically in real-time to human action without depending on long-term modeling. In particular, we develop heuristics based on two different, related strands of work termed "situated action" that drew on the previously discussed debates about AI in the 80's. Our first heuristic, *reactive social matching*, draws from work by technical researchers to improve the ability of agents to couple with external environments. Our second heuristic, *interpretable social matching*, draws from parallel work by social scientists who emphasized the role of human interpretation in human-agent interaction.

Reactive Social Matching

Technical researchers in situated action emphasized the use of simple rules to allow 'agents' or programs to immediately react to ongoing conditions in the local environments. A canonical example is Agre's Pengi, a quick-moving game in which agents are able to interact with their immediate context in an efficient and "intelligent" way by following situation-action rules, as opposed to calculating and maintaining models [3]. This is based on the idea that relevant 'knowledge' is stored not as representations in the mind but as a bodily readiness to respond to the solicitations of situations in the world. Similarly, we could think of situated recommender 'agents' as dynamically responding to behaviors in a world that is constantly in flux. Data from the host user could trigger immediate reactions instead of accreting in a model of the user's role in the broader social network. In other words, such an approach reframes matching from being about connecting me to others who are inherently like me on a long-term scale which a machine can eventually correctly model, to thinking of matching as being about connecting users who are behaving similarly in the current situation.

One implication of this refocusing is a potential return to a kind of content-based social matching, since information about data I am currently focused on could be a major component of what agents react to. But this design commitment has deeper implications for the processes used to make recommendations, as well as the ways we frame what these processes are doing. Instead of using data about users to represent their relationships and then use those models to make match recommendations, reactive social matching would use simple, "on the ground" techniques to present recommendations in response to user behaviors. Some early existing social matching recommenders already did this, such as I2I, which matches people who are on the same website; I2I reacts to users' immediate action (browsing the same webpage) simply by inviting the users to a shared chat room without pre-supposing any relationships [12].

It is important to note here that recommenders that use data associated with social networks can also follow this heuristic. For example, if Alice "friends" Bob, and is also "friends" with Jane, the system could respond to Alice's action by recommending Jane to also "friend" Bob. This is another framing of the "friend-of-friend" algorithms. The difference is that, conceptually, the system does not represent the Bob/Jane friendship, or claim to have any intelligence on Bob's relationship to Jane. As we will see later, such conceptual differences eventually can end up having significant implications for the resulting technical implementation.

Social matching without social modeling may have pragmatic benefits: we have already discussed how available data necessarily represents only a limited part of human dynamics, and how those dynamics themselves are constantly in flux. From a technical design point of view, relaxing the commitment to modeling in a highly nuanced problem with sparse data is not unreasonable and allows social matching researchers to focus less on the intelligence of the system, and more on user interaction with and interpretation of the system. This shows that technical designs are not limited to modeling only for highly nuanced problems, and that the 'problem' of sparse data only exists as such within a worldview that assumes that algorithm construction is always about ideal data fit, about creating the perfect alignment between representation and world. What this re-imagining suggests, is that it is possible to relax this commitment, that instead of focusing on the "intelligence" of the system or its degree of correspondence 'to the real world,' computational technics are also amenable to designs that center instead on user interaction with and interpretation of the system.

Interpretable Social Matching

In HCI, the most well-known proponent of "situated action" is Lucy Suchman, whose classic work *Plans and Situated Actions* explores how formal representations function as descriptions, not drivers, of action, and always require additional work to unpack and make relevant in the situation of action [49]. This social-science perspective of situated action highlights the work done by both technologies and humans in interaction to make sense of each other's behavior. One way in which these ideas have been built on in agent-based AI is to refocus agent construction on clearly communicating what agents are doing. For example, the Expressivator agent architecture supports comprehensibility of agent behavior through "narrative agent architecture", in which the agent continually entails its state to users [41].

A design heuristic following from this work is that social matching agents can and should communicate to users not only what matches have been calculated but also how.

Clearly, such a commitment places constraints on the complexity possible within a social matching process to those which are plausibly narratable to a human user.

Nevertheless, there are several potential benefits to algorithmic interpretability in social recommender systems. A body of work on user-evaluation of recommender systems shows that users prefer systems that explain their processes and favor those tools [7, 22, 39]. Empirical work with music recommenders, for example, suggests that explanation and interaction with visualizations of the recommendation results in "higher levels of user satisfaction and perceived relevance of predicted recommendations" [39]. Recent qualitative sociological analysis by Karakayali et al further suggests that users are *already* actively analyzing their presence on social media—including active classification and categorization of their relationships with other users [24]. Accounting for the recommendation processes could support engagement in a way that goes hand-in-hand with documented user practices in the field of social matching systems and has been shown to elicit positive reactions in closely related design spaces.

EXPLORING ALGORITHMS III: HOW IMPLEMENTATION RESHAPES CONCEPTUAL COMMITMENTS

In the previous section, we explored the conceptual assumptions embodied in social matching algorithms by tracing "lost" ideas from the history of sociology and AI and by demonstrating how these ideas could be drawn on to generate different design strategies for social matching than those currently in use. In this section, we explore how such conceptual commitments are embodied, altered and reworked through the process of embodying them in implementation.

Our decision to examine the ways that alternative design heuristics work out through implementation is grounded in critically-oriented and reflective design traditions in HCI, in which system development is not simply an end in itself, but also a means to reflectively explore underlying assumptions and attitudes about technology and humanity. Within HCI, critically oriented systems have explored design practice with reference to, and commenting on, technology's cultural and historical situation [e.g.27, 42, 43]. This means building technologies to change not only what people can do with but also the way they think about technology. By tracking our attempt to implement a simple, but functioning prototype that embodies alternative values, we shed light on the process by which algorithms come to both embody and rework their authors' conceptual commitments.

The Strangerationist

The prototype system we designed and implemented is called "the Strangerationist." This tool was designed to perform content-based semantic matching to engage "strangers" using the system in conversations about things they have (and do not have) in common. It embodies situated agent behavior by matching users based on analysis of their recent typing activity. It embodies interpretable agent behavior by exposing the process of calculating the match—along with some of the relevant assumptions and biases—as part of the recommendation itself.

The Strangerationist is a Firefox browser add-on. The tool, which is constantly active while Firefox is being used, appears as a sidebar on the browser. While the participant is using the browser, the Strangerationist gathers all text typed into HTML textbox areas (e.g. emails, web searches, blog posts) and sends it to a secure database for interpretation. The system continuously runs an open-source clustering algorithm—adapted from Carrot2— on the newest content by each participant [35]. The adapted Carrot2 algorithm automatically groups small collections of documents into thematic categories using a weighted Singular Value Decomposition. If clusters form, the Strangerationist arbitrarily runs an additional subset of simple language and grammar algorithms on both users' queues to find additional similarities and differences. It may compare, for example, the most frequent pronoun used, average sentence length, or rarest words used. The system provides a narrative account of its entire process in the extended output of the recommendation along with a means for the user to contact their matches.

An example extended output is the following: *"Several algorithms have been used to observe the ways in which you are similar (and not similar) to a stranger named Ken. To make the initial observation, we ran a clustering algorithm that uses documents from you and Ken every time that you contribute data to our service. We use a weighting scheme aimed at balancing the local and global term occurrences in the documents, down-weighting terms that are likely to appear very often. We favored an even contribution by both users to the cluster, preferring a cluster in which you and stranger Ken added similar number of documents. We also numerically rewarded the size of clusters, arbitrarily setting the ideal cluster size to 20 documents (clusters with more than 20 documents were not up-weighted.) After casting off lower-ranked cluster names (e.g. "spud", "growing" and "food") we found the largest value in the resulting vector to determine the best matching phrase: "POTATOES."*

To identify other writerly similarities and differences between you and Stranger Ken, we ran a set of other algorithms to look at aspects of the language in your documents: we have compared your recent vocabularies to Standard English and discovered that the most unusual word you and stranger Ken both use is "maleficent."

Figure 1. Screenshot of the Strangerationist.

Users of the system also have the option to contact their "matches" or dismiss incoming recommendations. Because the Strangerationist is meant to encourage interaction outside of one's traditional "social network" the design of the system explicitly reminds users of the various benefits of strangers when they select the "dismiss" function. These short quips, e.g. "relating to people who are not like you can lead to new experiences" or "many peripheral relationships are satisfying," were pulled from a variety of sources, including ones that initially motivated our work (e.g. [21]). The interactive design of the "dismiss" action, like the extended computational narrative, is a form of making some of the system's tacit commitments explicit.

In the design of the Strangerationist, we tried to follow our design heuristics, namely, we followed simple rules based on in-the-moment computations based on user-generated content, and we tried to express them, along with our implicit biases, through a narrative output of the system's processes—which was facilitated by the system's writerly and blatantly pro-stranger interaction personality. The emerging personality of the Strangerationist—obsessively wordy in its own account of users' words, aggressively pro-engagement with strangers, should one attempt to dismiss its observations—is reminiscent of other critical design work in which the technologies took on a personality based on the flavor of conceptual work they were doing to further underscore their critical commitments. For example, in a critical design piece that explores the potential social effects of disturbing, uncomfortable systems, a social agent that spreads false, strange gossip throughout an office space is named after a mythological Norse trickster and has an extensive backstory, including an affinity for purple shoes [16]. The output of a home health sensing system that promotes user interpretation through deliberately ambiguous output, expressed its sensor readings as automatically constructed, ambiguous "horoscopes" [18]. In both cases, the systems had personalities which affected their interactions with users and were in line with their conceptual design commitments.

Lessons Learned from Building

The process of designing and implementing the Strangerationist frequently led us to reconsider the conceptual analysis we had initially done. Specific technical decisions described below shed light on how decisions that appeared to be low-level or "technical" simultaneously engaged with, underscored, or altered our critical conceptual work.

Situated, not networked - Documenting the output of the clustering algorithm required us to interpret the results we had obtained algorithmically in light of our new design commitments. An initial temptation in implementing the clustering algorithm was to use word-matching as a way of calculating "strangeness" between people—and the Strangerationist could recommend most strange and least strange people for a user. We realized we had been more deeply influenced than we thought by the rhetorical plasticity of matching language, because even though we were implementing our agent architecture, we were still thinking of it as calculating (modeling) tie strength. In this way, we experienced first hand the "transfer" [31] that computational methods incur on knowledge practices outside of computer science.

To underscore the different idea we were aiming to approach here, we developed a new metaphor: rather than using clustering to measure "distance" between users, we used the clusters to provide an opportunity for people to connect. Rhetorically, it was like a shared "airplane seat"—an excuse for two people to relate to each other. To further this line of thinking, we removed language that directly referred to "matching" (calling the output "observations" instead) and followed the clustering with deliberately simplistic analysis of writerly qualities (e.g. "the most unusual word you and stranger Ken have in common is "maleficent") to make it clear that we were creating an opportunity for matching without making an argument for an objectively existing tie.

Asymmetrical observations – This design lesson emerged from a conversation about how to store the matches. Initially, we imagined that they would be stored in a lookup table such that, if person A is matched to person B, then person B also receives a notification of being matched to person A. We rejected this implementation for several reasons. First, since we were explicitly not calculating distance between people or building a top-down model of the social interactions, there was suddenly no reason to have symmetrical relations. We instead chose deliberately to "reward" contributors of data with observations and stored them in unlinked data structures, such that if person A contributes data that clusters with data given once by person B, person A receives the observation immediately, but person B will not receive any observations until they give the Strangerationist new data. Because the queue is regularly cleared, there is no reason that, at the time of person B's typing, the same clusters will still be calculable. This design move was in line with being reactive because it responded to individual behavior without assuming that relationships needed to be mutual, and it was in line with being interpretable because the asymmetrical recommendations provided an opportunity to clearly communicate that data contributions resulted in observations from the system.

Inherited aesthetics - When we were implementing our clustering algorithm, we directly inherited assumptions about the latent structural relationships between words from the algorithm we adapted. We tried to make these clear in the expanded text, for example, by explaining that the weighting scheme in Carrot2 has a bias toward novel word-phrases: "down-weighting terms that are likely to appear very often" and has a very specific ideal cluster, favoring "an even contribution by both users to the cluster... and setting the ideal cluster size to 20 documents" [34]. They were thresholds that we could change, but the metrics for assessment came as part of the code. The consequence of our decision to use semantic clustering was that, instead of looking for a latent structure between people, we had found a calculable proxy in modeling the latent structure of words in their documents.

As we struggled to make use of the available alternatives to social network analysis without absorbing the positivist motivations of the algorithms, we saw more clearly the broader motivations for doing social matching work. One thing we learned about social matching recommenders through the reframing of the "matching" metaphor in the Strangerationist is that social-network modeling—especially gathering feedback about user behavior to improve the model through iterative representation and re-representation—was not necessary for basic social matching. Through the parallels between historical discourse on social networks and the discourse around Agre's critical technical practice, we see another logical reason for conventional social recommenders to do the iterative modeling that they do. For research enterprises, it directly follows a long history of research in AI, where people are simultaneously users of an interactive system and also data points for improving and assessing the success of an artificial intelligence.

DISCUSSION

Reflecting on the legacy of critical technical practice in the form of situated action from the perspective of reforming practices in artificial intelligence, Agre wrote about the necessary "split identity" of critical technical practitioner between technical design and reflexive critique rooted in non-technical fields [3]. In this work, we ended up rhetorically taking on the role of a technically oriented researcher with expertise in social matching recommenders. We negotiated this stance so what we could explore how critical technical practice could be combined with historical discourse to shed light on values and assumptions undergirding algorithmic practice. It is important to note, however, that we do not identify as experts in the domain of recommender algorithms, and do not believe that the Strangerationist should be considered primarily as a contribution to the domain of recommender systems.

Our work is grounded in critically oriented and reflective design traditions in HCI, which is a home discipline for several of the authors. It is interesting to note that while Agre's methodological contributions to critical technical practice have been re-absorbed into what he considered to be the dominant practice within the field of AI itself [49], critical technical practice has strongly shaped the intellectual traditions HCI. We see system development as not simply an end in itself, but also a means to reflectively explore underlying assumptions and attitudes about technology and humanity. This work has also drawn from the strange, uncomfortable, and provocative "critical design" methods described by Dunne and Raby [14, pp 12] as a means to raise questions about the political implications of design practice. Critical design as a term has been elaborated and repositioned by Bardzell and Bardzell to recognize their ties to a longer critical theory legacy including the Frankfurt School of critical theory and post-structuralism [5]. Within HCI, critically oriented systems have explored design practice with reference to, and commenting on, technology's cultural and historical situation [27, 42, 43]. This means building technologies to change not only what people can do with but also the way they think about technology. For example, critically oriented design methods have been used to alter objective, informatics approaches to affective computing— which structure, formalize, and represent emotion as informational units—by centering technical decisions around the indefinable complexities of human affective experience [6].

Since doing the project, we have been able to make use of historical analysis, substantiated by our familiarity with the details of technical implementation, to discuss social network analysis and recommendation with practitioners in HCI. Because we set out to explore a methodology where the critique of values in design can be a guiding method in technical development, we count technically and historically grounded engagement with social recommender systems among our successes.

But is the Strangerationist successful as a social matching system? This is not possible for us to say. We did not engage in conventional evaluation of the Strangerationist in the form of a user study that assesses its usability and value in quotidian use. This was because our goal in the project was less to create a "better" social matching than to explore the values and commitments embodied in social matching algorithms. For this end-user evaluation is not a directly relevant measure. More deeply, we felt standard models of evaluation significantly misrepresent what Strangerationist was doing as a project.

Moreover, what the 'historical' aspect of the Strangerationist reveals, as an extreme case, are tacit temporalities in technical system design and evaluation in HCI. In order to evaluate a technical system, a prototype design is often deployed back 'in the wild'—so that it can be tested against the realities which inspired the design. As we contemplated the multiple privacy implications of deploying the system—keystroke logger and all—it became clear to us that the temporal frame of swinging time back around and putting the design into the world was not possible in the case of the Strangerationist. In response to over a decade of anxious intertwining of internet users' personal and online lives (e.g. e-commerce, personal data mining, and security panics) it seems that attitudes about gathering keystroke data have shifted in the passage of time. We imagine that the world of finding friends, for example by being on the website, may not exist in the way it served as inspiration for early social recommender algorithms. The Strangerationist itself may be an anachronism for which there is no longer any 'where' against which to test the algorithm on HCI's normative terms. What this method offers instead is an opportunity to reconfigure the relationship between social science and technical methods through the historical analysis and design of technical systems.

CONCLUSION

In this sense, our goal with the Strangerationist differs from what Agre set out to do with critical technical practice in AI: we did not set out to reform the field of social recommenders so much as to imagine and implement an alternative configuration between historical work on technical practice and technical practice itself. What we hope can be drawn from our work is an approach to borrowing ideas from critical technical practice and historical discourse on technical practices to inform sociological and STS understanding of algorithms. In some ways, by exploring how technical practices can be used in such a way, we articulated a method which resembles the conceptual inverse of critical technical practice: taking ideas from technical discourse to innovate on research practices in the social sciences. We hope that this combination of approaches can be used to explore the entangled facets of algorithms that are often left unexamined by researchers operating outside of niche technical research programs, and thought to be exclusively visible through (to borrow Agre's phrase) "the daily work of trying to get things built and working" [2].

ACKNOWLEDGEMENTS

This work was funded by NSF grant 1217685 and the Intel Science and Technology Center for Social Computing. The Strangerationist was developed at Intel Labs with Ken Anderson, Richard Beckwith, and Cian Montgomery. Thanks to Nick Seaver, Ellie Harmon, and all of our anonymous reviewers for their helpful feedback.

REFERENCES

1. Agre, P. (1997). *Computation and human experience.* Cambridge University Press.
2. Agre, P. (1997). Beyond the mirror world: Privacy and the representational practices of computing. *Technology and Privacy the New Landscape (PE Agre and M. Rotenberg, Eds.). Massachusetts, MIT Press,* 29-62.
3. Agre, P. "Toward a critical technical practice: Lessons learned in trying to reform AI." *Bridging the Great Divide: Social Science, Technical Systems, and Cooperative Work, Mahwah, NJ: Erlbaum* (1997): 131-157.
4. Agre P., and Chapman, D. 1987. Pengi: an implementation of a theory of activity. In Proceedings of the sixth National conference on Artificial intelligence - Volume 1 (AAAI'87), Vol. 1. AAAI Press 268-272.
5. Bardzell, J., and Bardzell, S. 2013. What is "critical" about critical design? *Proc* CHI '13, 3297-3306.
6. Boehner, K., Sengers, P., and Warner, S. 2008. Interfaces with the ineffable: Meeting aesthetic experience on its own terms. ACM Trans. Comput.-Hum. Interact. 15, 3, Article 12 (December 2008)
7. Bostandjiev, S., O'Donovan, J., and Höllerer, T. 2012. TasteWeights: a visual interactive hybrid recommender system. In *Proc* RecSys '12. 35-42.
8. Bowker, G., Star, S. L., Gasser, L., & Turner, W. (Eds.). (2014). *Social science, technical systems, and cooperative work: Beyond the great divide*. Psychology Press.
9. Brooks, Rodney A. "Elephants don't play chess." *Robotics and autonomous systems* 6.1 (1990): 3-15.
10. Brooks, R. A. (1989). A robot that walks; emergent behaviors from a carefully evolved network. *Neural computation*, *1*(2), 253-262.

11. Chalmers, Matthew. "Seamful design and ubicomp infrastructure." *Proceedings of Ubicomp 2003 Workshop at the Crossroads: The Interaction of HCI and Systems Issues in Ubicomp*. 2003.
12. Budzik J., Bradshaw, S., Fu, X., and Hammond, K. J. 2002. Clustering for opportunistic communication. In *Proc* WWW '02. 726-735.
13. Chen, J., Geyer, W., Dugan, C., Muller, M., Guy, I. 2009. Make new friends, but keep the old: recommending people on social networking sites. In *Proc* CHI '09. 201-210.
14. Dunne, A., and Raby, F. *Design noir: The secret life of electronic objects*. Birkhäuser, Basel, Switzerland, 2001.
15. Ergin, E., and Lee, D. "On six degrees of separation in DBLP-DB and more." *ACM SIGMOD Record* 34.2 (2005). 33-40.
16. Foucault, B., Mentis, H. M., Sengers, P., and Welles, D. 2007. Provoking sociability. In *Proc* CHI '07. 1557-1560.
17. Freeman L. 1998. Computer programs in social network analysis. *Connections 11*, 26–31.
18. Gaver, W., Sengers, P., Kerridge, T., Kaye, J., and Bowers, J. Enhancing ubiquitous computing with user interpretation: field testing the home health horoscope. In *Proc* CHI '07. 537-546.
19. Gilbert, E., and Karahalios, K. Predicting tie strength with social media. In *Proc* CHI '09. 211-220.
20. Gillespie, T. The relevance of algorithms. In T. Gillespie, P. Boczkowski, and K. Foot, eds., *Media Technologies*. MIT Press, forthcoming.
21. Granovetter, M. S. (1973). The strength of weak ties. *American journal of sociology*, 1360-1380.
22. Herlocker, J. L., Konstan, J. A., and Riedl, J. Explaining collaborative filtering recommendations. In *Proc. CSCW '00*. 241-250.
23. Kadima, H., & Malek, M. (2010, December). Toward ontology-based personalization of a recommender system in social network. In *Soft Computing and Pattern Recognition (SoCPaR), 2010 International Conference of* (pp. 119-122). IEEE.
24. Karakayali, N., & Kilic, A. (2013). More network conscious than ever? Challenges, strategies, and analytic labor of users in the Facebook environment. *Journal of Computer-Mediated Communication, 18*(2).
25. Kautz, H., Selman, B., and Shah, M. 1997. ReferralWeb: Combining social networks and collaborative filtering. *Comm. ACM 30*, 3.
26. Krzywicki, A., Wobcke, W., Kim, Y. S., Cai, X., Bain, M., Mahidadia, A., & Compton, P. (2015). Collaborative Filtering for people-to-people recommendation in online dating: Data analysis and user trial. *International Journal of Human-Computer Studies*, *76*, 50-66.
27. Leahu, L., Schwenk, S., & Sengers, P. Subjective objectivity: negotiating emotional meaning. In *Proc* DIS '08. 425-434.
28. Leahu, L., Thom-Santelli, J., Pederson, and C., Sengers, P. Taming the situationist beast. In *Proc* DIS '08. 203-211.
29. Leahu, L., P. Sengers, and M. Mateas. 2008. Interactionist AI and the promise of ubicomp, or, how to put your box in the world without putting the world in your box. In *Proceedings of UbiComp '08*, 134-143.
30. Leahu, L. Representation without representationalism. PhD thesis, Cornell Computer Science, 2012.
31. Machlup, F. and Mansfield, U. (1983), *The Study of Information: Interdisciplinary Messages* (New York: Wiley).
32. McDonald, D. W.and Ackerman, M. S. 2000. Expertise recommender: A flexible recommendation architecture. In *Proceedings of the ACM Conference on Computer-Supported Cooperative Work. (CSCW'00)*. 231–240.
33. Milgram, S. (1967). The small world problem. *Psychology today*, *2*(1), 60-67.
34. Osiński, S. *An algorithm for clustering of web search results*. Diss. Poznań University of Technology, Poland, 2003.
35. Osiński, S., & Weiss, D. (2004). Conceptual clustering using lingo algorithm: Evaluation on open directory project data. In *Intelligent Information Processing and Web Mining* (pp. 369-377). Springer Berlin Heidelberg.
36. Panovich, K., Miller, R., and Karger, D. 2012. Tie strength in question & answer on social network sites. In *Proceedings of the ACM 2012 conference on Computer Supported Cooperative Work* (CSCW '12).
37. Resnick, P., R. Garrett, R. K., Kriplean, T., Munson, S. A., and Stroud, J. 2013. Bursting your (filter) bubble: strategies for promoting diverse exposure. In Proceedings of the 2013 conference on Computer supported cooperative work companion (CSCW '13).
38. Röhle, T., and Rieder, B. (2012) 'Digital Methods: Five Challenges,' in D. Berry (ed.), *Understanding Digital Humanities: The Computational Turn and New Technology*. (London: Palgrave Macmillan), pp. 67–84.
39. Sharma, A. 2013. PopCore: a system for network-centric recommendation. In *Proceedings of the 2013*

conference on Computer supported cooperative work companion (CSCW '13).

40. Seaver, N. *(2015)* The nice thing about context is that everyone has it. *Media Culture Society,* vol. 37 no. 7 1101-1109
41. Sengers, P. (1998, May). Do the thing right: an architecture for action-expression. In *Proceedings of the second international conference on Autonomous agents* (pp. 24-31). ACM.
42. Sengers, P., Boehner, K., David, S. and Kaye, J. Reflective design. *Proc. Critical Computing*, ACM Press (2005), 49–58.
43. Sengers, S., McCarthy, J., and Dourish, P. 2006. Reflective HCI: articulating an agenda for critical practice. In *CHI '06 Extended Abstracts on Human Factors in Computing Systems* (CHI EA '06).
44. Simmel, Georg. "The stranger." *The Sociology of Georg Simmel* (1950): 402-408.
45. Star, Susan Leigh. "The ethnography of infrastructure." *American behavioral scientist* 43.3 (1999): 377-391.
46. de Sola Pool, Ithiel, and Manfred Kochen. "Contacts and influence." *Social networks* 1.1 (1979): 5-51.
47. Sosik, V.S., Zhao, X. and Cosley, D. See friendship, sort of: How conversation and digital traces might support reflection on friendships. *Proc. CSCW '12*
48. Suchman, L. *Human-machine reconfigurations: Plans and situated actions*. Cambridge University Press, 2007
49. Suchman, Lucy A. *Plans and situated actions: the problem of human-machine communication*, Cambridge University Press, New York, NY, 1987.
50. Terveen L., and McDonald, D. W., 2005. Social matching: A framework and research agenda. *ACM Trans. Comput.-Hum. Interact.* (September 2005), 401-434.

FusePrint: A DIY 2.5D Printing Technique Embracing Everyday Artifacts

Kening Zhu
City University of Hong Kong
Hong Kong
keninzhu@cityu.edu.hk

Alexandru Dancu
Chalmers University of Technology
Gothenburg, Sweden
alexandru.dancu@gmail.com

Shengdong Zhao
National University of Singapore
Singapore
zhaosd@comp.nus.edu.sg

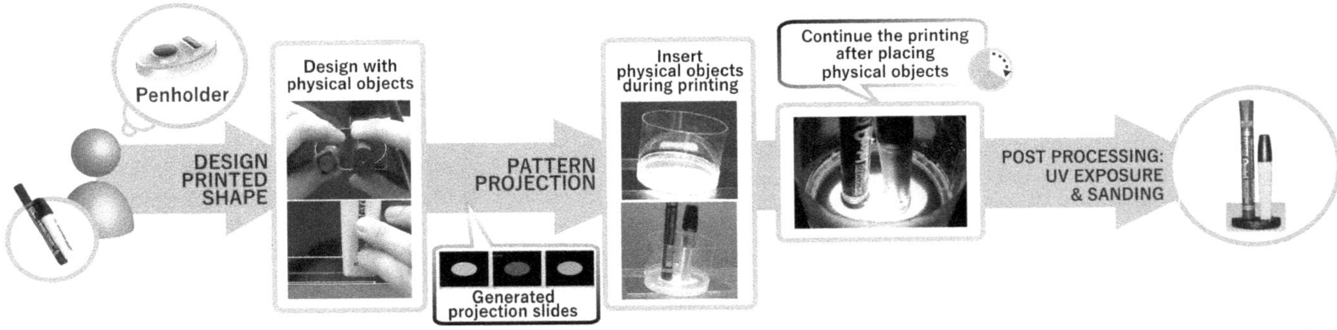

Figure 1: FusePrint fabrication process. User wants to create a penholder; its shape is designed with the reference of physical objects, and projected through the bottom of the container holding the resin and physical objects (pens). The projected shape solidifies, resulting in being perfectly matched to the objects.

ABSTRACT
FusePrint is a Stereolithography-based 2.5D rapid prototyping technique that allows high-precision fabrication without high-end modeling tools, enabling the mixing of everyday physical artifacts and liquid conductive gels with photo-reactive resin during the printing process, facilitating the creation of 2.5D objects that perfectly fit the existing objects. Based on our polynomial model on 2.5D resin printing, we developed the design interface of FusePrint, which allows users to design the printed shapes using physical objects as references, generates projection patterns, and notifies users when to place the objects in the resin during the printing process. Our workshops suggested that FusePrint is easy to learn and use, provides a greater level of interactivity, and could be useful for a wide range of applications domains including: mechanical fabrication, wearable accessory, toys, interactive systems, etc.

Author Keywords
FusePrint; Fabrication; DIY; 3D Printing; 2.5D Printing; Stereolithography; Everyday Artifacts.

DIS 2016, June 04 - 08, 2016, Brisbane, QLD, Australia

ACM 978-1-4503-4031-1/16/06...$15.00
DOI: http://dx.doi.org/10.1145/2901790.2901792.

ACM Classification Keywords
H.5.m. Information interfaces and presentation (e.g., HCI): Miscellaneous

INTRODUCTION
The popularity of 3D printing technology has significantly boosted personal fabrication in the past decade. Although 3D printing has become increasingly precise, using it to create objects that can tightly fit with real-world artifacts can still be challenging [8] despite the availability of tools to create 3D models from existing objects, such as CADScan's Cubik® 3D scanner [6] and MakerBot's Digitizer [21]. This is because physical objects can have complex geometric structures (e.g., an internal screw thread). While fitting objects within a simpler structure, such as a cube, is theoretically easy, in practice, daily wear and tear may transform parts or the whole of that simple object into a more complex shape/texture, increasing the difficulty of modeling. High-end 3D scanning devices [1] can achieve greater precision, but they are usually costly and less accessible for hobbyists.

Even if a perfect 3D model can be created, much of the printing process in current low-cost 3D printers may introduce additional errors due to the difficulty in calibration(e.g., it can be difficult to 3D-print the details of an internal screw thread in an object to tightly fit the existing screws). These factors could result in a long chain of trial-and-error attempts with current 3D printers to produce objects that fit existing artifacts well.

One way to print objects (e.g., an internal thread) that can tightly fit existing artifacts (e.g., an external screw thread) is to leverage existing artifacts as a mold so that the printing material in contact with the artifact can naturally fit to its shape and texture. This implies that the printer needs to be able to tolerate the insertion of arbitrary objects during the printing process (before the printing material is solidified) without causing too much interference to the construction of the intended 3D model. Shape Deposition Manufacturing (SDM) [24] provides the possibility of embedding actuators, sensors and other pre-fabricated functional components inside the product. However, SDM still requires the fabrication of molds that precisely fit the embedded parts, which leads to ad-hoc tolerance optimization by novice users [15]. To fabricate parts for well-fitting assembly, current SDM processes often requires users to amend the original models in an ad-hoc manner for optimal tolerance, making the entire process time-and-cost consuming for novice users [29].

The current 3D-printing process (i.e., Fused Deposition Modeling – FDM [9], Stereolithography – SLA [14], and Selective Laser Sintering – SLS [10]) do not support the insertion of physical objects in the printing process. While inserting physical objects may obstruct the printing head for FDM or the laser beam for SLS, SLA leverages the usage of the liquid resin that can be cured gradually using light sources, thus it becomes theoretically possible to mix it with existing objects to produce the desirable molding effect. However, *"introducing objects into the resin while the printer is running can damage the resin tank,"* and *"may also interrupt the printing process"*; therefore, existing SLA 3D printer manufacturers (e.g., Formlabs [11]) clearly declare that *"mixing anything into the resin"* is neither supported nor recommended [12]. In addition, testing with commercial SLA/DLP printers, although possible, requires modifying its setup to clear the space above the resin occupied by the building plate, thus it is non-trivial without any technical detail from the companies.

To support such capability, the printing process adopted by existing SLA printers needs to be carefully modified and tested. In this paper, we present our first effort to enable the capability of inserting existing artifacts with FusePrint, a DIY SLA-based 2.5D printing technique that allows for the mixture of everyday physical artifacts as well as liquid conductive gel with the photo-reactive resin during the printing process, making it much easier to create 2.5D objects that tightly fit with the existing objects and thereby offering interactivity. Using FusePrint, one can simply place an external screw thread or a cup, for example, into the photo-reactive resin during the printing process to print an internal thread or a cup holder that perfectly matches the shape of the inserted objects. In addition, by mixing liquid conductive gel with the resin, one can print customized touch-sensitive interactive objects that can detect multi-touch points as well as gestures.

As a first attempt, our DIY FusePrint technique still has a few limitations: it only permits the printing of 2.5D objects instead of true 3D objects, and the printing quality of the 2.5D object has a less polished finishing as compared with higher-end commercial products. However, with the new capability to include existing objects in the printing process without the requirement of prior modeling, FusePrint opens up new possibilities for personal fabrication and is already useful as a rapid prototyping tool for a wide range of applications domains.

The contribution of this work is threefold:

- A new SLA-based fabrication technique that can integrate everyday artifacts into the printing process to produce 2.5D models that easily fit various shapes and sizes without high-end modelling tools.
- Experimental investigation to find the parameters for controlling the resin curing process using a Digital Light Processing (DLP) projector.
- A workshop study showing FusePrint's effectiveness and the various application scenarios that leverage the unique capabilities of our technique.

BACKGROUND AND RELATED WORK

Our design of FusePrint was inspired by the working principles of SLA 3D printers, the existing research in Human-Computer Interaction on integrating physical objects with 3D printing, and 3D printed interactive objects. We summarize key related work in these areas below.

Personal Fabrication with Existing Object

Researchers have long discovered the advantages of mixing existing artifacts with 3D created objects and have developed various tools to facilitate this process. For example, MixFab is a mixed-reality environment for personal fabrication, which allows users to create models by placing physical objects in the workspace [8]. KidCAD allows children to combine the 2.5D shape of their toys to create new 3D models for printing [27]. In CopyCAD, users can reuse 2D shapes in a CNC milling setting [28]. Constructable extends the 2D contour reuse by copying textures to workpieces [30]: a camera takes a photo of the texture and transfers it on the part using a laser-cutter. Enclosed [7] uses electronic components as handles and size references during enclosure design. It automatically adds cutouts to the enclosure patterns so that the components can be mounted. Printed Optics [16] adopted the shape-deposition-based process that still requires the detailed 3D models of embedded components. Similarly, the FDM-based Voxel8 [31] enables the fabrication of conductive circuit, but it still needs ad-hoc tolerance adjustment to integrate electronics.

More recently, Gannon et al. developed Tactum [20], which enables the design of 3D models for wearable accessories based on body shape. A review on rapid prototyping using laser-based, nozzle-based, and printer-based systems in the field of bioengineering shows how to combine 3D printed

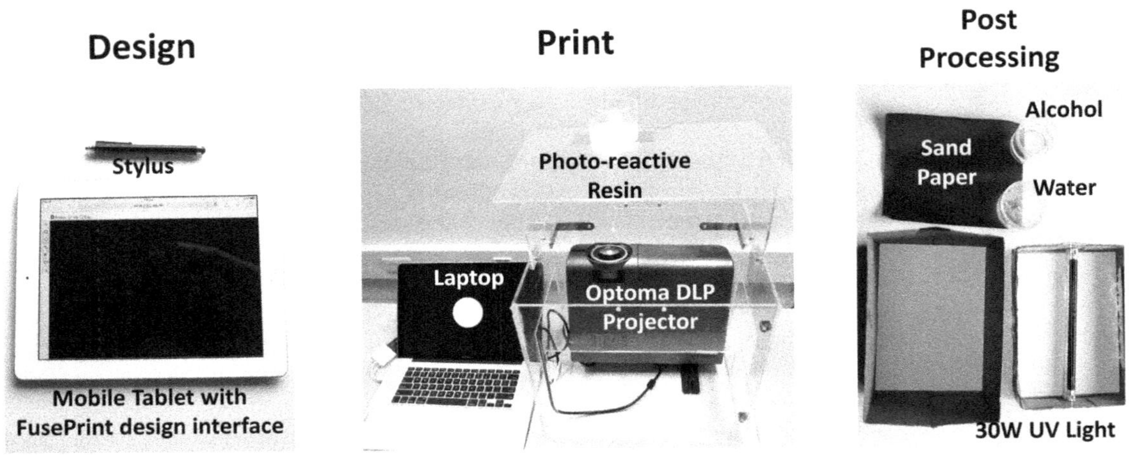

(a) (b) (c)

Figure 2: FusePrint setup

structures with the human body [3]. Chen et al. [32] proposed Encore, an FDM-based 3D printing technique to augment everyday objects in three ways: printed-over, affixed, and interlocked. ReForm [35] leveraged the usage of malleable clay to allow users to create physical 3D models in a bi-directional way, and the physical clay models can be scanned and exported for 3D printing fabrication. It supported the usage of markers and physical objects as the annotation of modeling. In SPATA [36], Weichel et al. developed two technology-enhanced measuring tools, allowing users to transfer the geometric information of physical objects into 3D models. Teibrich et al. [37] presented a 3D-printing technique that supports direct modifications (i.e. addition and subtraction) on the already-printed objects using 3D scanning, to reduce the waste of the material because of the failures in fabrication.

In all mentioned work above, researchers have mainly focused on using physical objects in the modeling process. As previously mentioned, the modeling process itself can be tedious by requiring extra measuring tools, and errors could still occur during the scanning and the manufacturing process due to the non-perfect hardware implementation of FDM 3D printers. While Encore is the most relevant and competitive related work, FusePrint distinguishes itself as the fitting process of Encore assumes that "models of the existing and the new objects have been acquired using 3D scanning, or created from scratch". The Print-to-affix technique of Encore requires expert users to model a connector "that matches the surface geometry of the existing object", while in FusePrint, the real world object serve as a mold, which eliminates 3D scanning, and solves the problem of matching the surface geometry and modeling the connector.

3D Printed Interactive Object

Different approaches have been explored in printing functional actuators and sensors with FDM 3D printers. Ishiguro et al. [34] proposed the technology for designing and manufacturing interactive 3D printed speakers, where sound reproduction can be integrated into various objects at the design stage and little assembly is required. The same group further developed Printed Optics [16], a new type of 3D printed object that enables sensing, display, and illumination elements to be directly embedded in the casing or mechanical structure of an interactive device. Recently, Laput et al. [13] developed Accoustruments, a type of low-cost, passive, and powerless mechanisms for creating interactive mobile accessories, based on the principle of wind instruments.

FusePrint shares the vision of 3D printed interactive objects. Compared to these existing efforts with FDM 3D printing, FusePrint has adopted the process of SLA 3D printing, and we leveraged the usage of liquid resin and also explored the design option of mixing conductive gel to create 2.5D interactive objects that can support multi-touch interaction.

FUSEPRINT

FusePrint Setup

With FusePrint, we aimed to create a DIY process that could create objects to fit existing objects. As a DIY technique developed for hobbyists, we had the following design requirements for FusePrint:

1) The system is simple to setup and easy to maintain.
2) The cost is minimized by using existing tools.
3) The printing process is easy to learn and perform.

With these requirements, we developed a DIY setup (Figure 2) with four main components: a mobile tablet for shape designing, a light source using an existing Optoma DLP projector (model = EH1060; brightness value = 0; contrast value = 0), a resin container, and a computer. The DLP projector is mounted in the acrylic case, projecting upward to the container filled with photo-reactive resin. The resin container is placed on the acrylic plate above the projector.

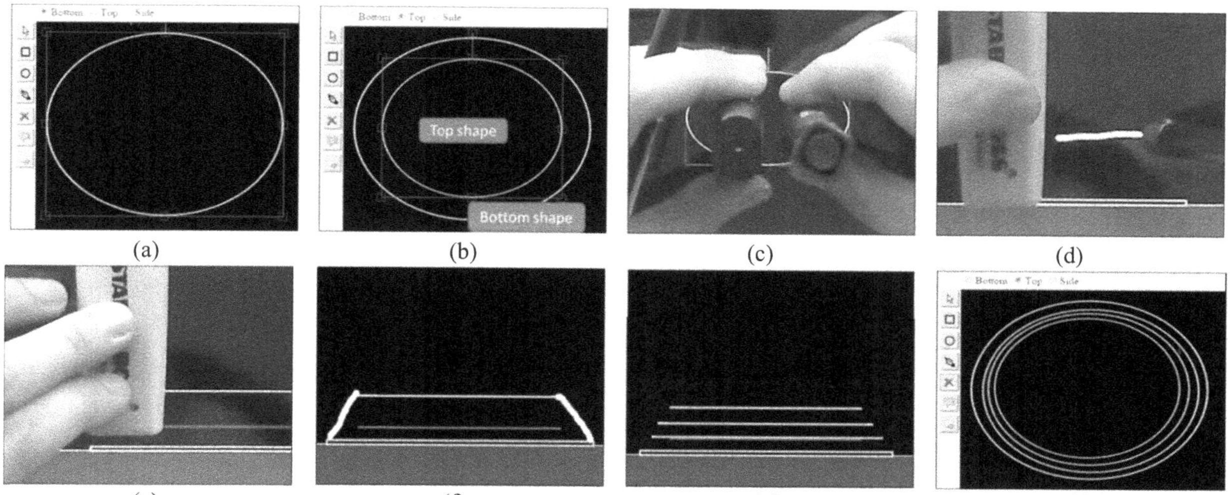

(a) (b) (c) (d)
(e) (f) (g) (h)

Figure 3: Example of designing a penholder

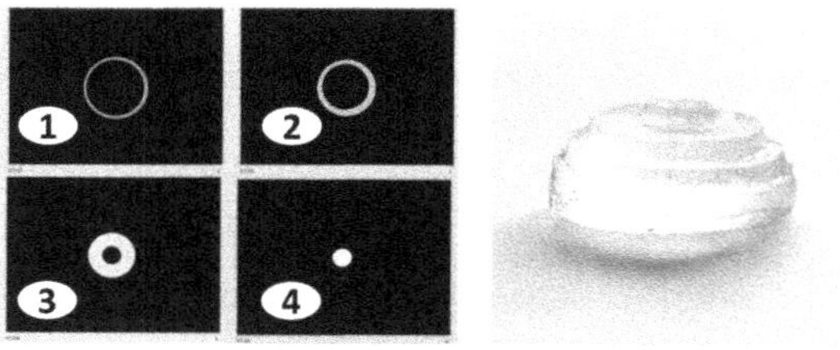

(a) (b)

Figure 4: Light patterns to print a half sphere.

The base of the resin was made of flexible silicon, to facilitate easy-removal of the printed shapes. To achieve maximum illumination, the distance between the projector and the resin container is set to be the minimum projection distance of the projector model (22 cm in our setup). The computer is connected to the projector to control the projected images to create objects layer by layer.

To reduce cost and complexity in our first attempt, we did not include the z-axis linear actuators to enable 3D printing typically equipped by existing SLA printers. As a result, the current setup only supports the printing of 2.5D objects. These objects are often greatly preferred for CNC milling and can be used to create a large number of useful parts. In addition, any 3D object can be composed using multiple 2.5D objects, at least in theory.

To print a 2.5D object, one can shine a sequence of slides through a DLP projector to the appropriate region of the resin to cure the resin layer by layer. For example, to print a half sphere (Figure 3b), one can shine the sequence of light patterns in Figure 3a to the resin. To control the thickness of a printed layer, one needs to carefully control the intensity of the light source and duration in which the resin is cured under it. While commercial printers have pre-set values to achieve optimal printing results specific for their printer hardware, the relationship equation for a DIY setting needs to be determined by users themselves. In the section Technical experiment on 2.5D Resin Printing, we describe a simple procedure and a template formula to help hobbyists and researchers derive the mathematical models for their specific setup.

FusePrint Process

The overall process of printing a 2.5D object using FusePrint consists of the following steps (Figure 1): A user first needs to specify the shape of the printed object and its dimension in a modeling software; the system then translates the model into a sequence of images in which each image is a cross-section of a 2.5D model representing a layer of that object needing to be printed. According to the height of the layer, the image is set with different light intensity values. Each image will be shined into the resin for a pre-calculated duration to ensure the printed object has the desirable shape and height.

We designed and implemented a software application for FusePrint which contains a web-based sketch interface allowing users to design the 2.5D patterns on mobile tablets (Figure 2a) and a plug-in for Microsoft PowerPoint to generate projection patterns based on the design of 2.5D shapes. To create a 2.5D model such as a cone, users first need to draw the bottom shape of the object in the canvas of the sketch interface, which supports basic shape drawing and freehand drawing, as shown Figure2a.

In the second step, the user activates the canvas in the top view where our software automatically creates two clones of the design in the bottom view (one for editing and the other for reference). As shown in Figure 4b, the user can resize the top shape with the reference of bottom shape. While editing the shapes in bottom view and top view, users are allowed to use physical objects as reference to assist their shape design. Figure 4c shows a user employing two marker pens to assist him in resizing the shape for a stationary holder, to ensure enough space for stationaries.

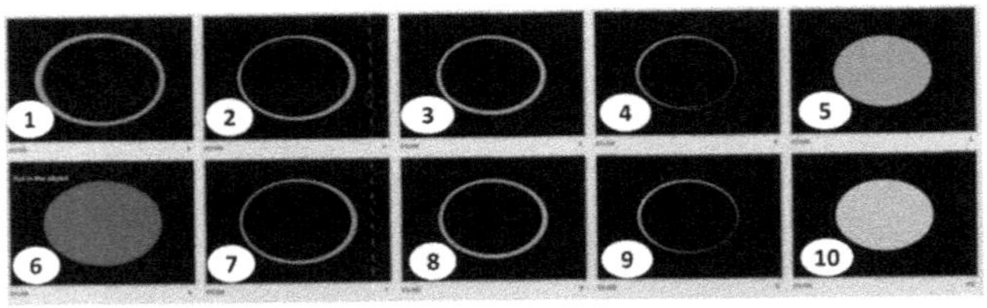

Figure 5: Slides generated by our MS PowerPoint plugin for printing a penholder.

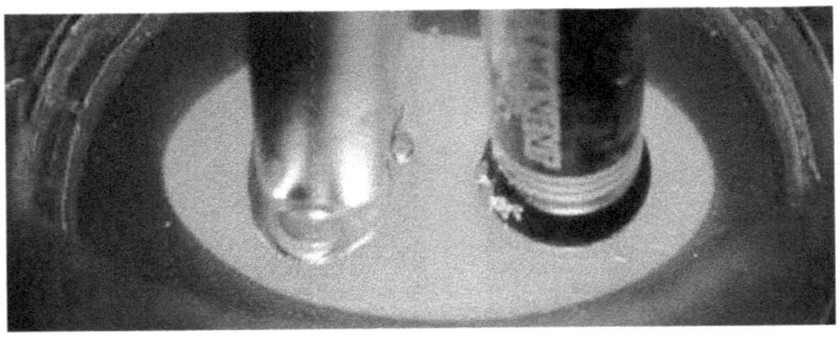

Figure 6: Placing physical pens into the resin during the printing process of a pen holder

After designing the shapes for bottom view and top view, the user can switch to the side view where the interface helps the user to design the height of the printed shape. The user draws two strokes to indicate the bottom and the top of the printed object (Figure 4d), and the software generates two straight lines according to the sizes of the shapes in bottom and top views and the positions of the two strokes made by the user. The vertical distance between the two straight lines indicates the height of the 2.5D object. As shown in Figure 4d, the user can utilize physical objects to help the design of the height.

To facilitate the object placement, the sketch application provides a "Place Objects" button. To specify where to insert an object, the user can toggle the insertion mode by clicking this button and draw a new stroke (in red) between bottom and top lines to indicate the location of the inserted object. As shown in Figure 4e, the user can again utilize physical objects as a reference to indicate the height to place objects (red line indicates the height to place objects). The system will automatically calculate the layer and the time in which the object can be inserted in the printing process. During the printing process, the system pauses the printing and alert the user to insert the object when corresponding layer is reached.

After specifying the information for the height and the object insertion, the user can then design the slopes of the printed object by sketching to connect the bottom and the top lines, as shown in Figure 4f. Lastly, the user clicks the "Export" button, and the system analyzes the design and calculates the number of interval layers that are needed to be printed based on the design of the slope and the height. Our algorithm automatically generates one interval layer in every 2 mm between the bottom and the top lines (Figure 4g) shows the side view of the generated layers and Figure 4h shows the top view). The shape in that layer is scaled according to its distance from the bottom line. The program

(a) (b) (c)

Figure 7: (a) printed pen holder (b) the bottom of a marker pen (c) the texture imprinted on the substrate

then converts the model into a sequence of slides (Figure 5) and automatically sets the duration in which each image will be projected into the resin to form the desirable effect.

To print the object, the user just plays the slides which will be projected into the resin. The red slide in Figure 5 indicates the moment the physical object needs to be inserted by the user. When the slides turn red, the printing process is paused, since the resin would not be cured in red light spectrum. Therefore, the user can place the physical objects in the resin (Figure 6) and continue the printing. The rest of the projection slides continue the printing, and "engrave" detailed patterns on the bottom surface of the object in the printed product, as shown in Figure 7b & 7c.

Once the printing process is complete, there are further steps to follow to post-process the printed result. The post-processing stage (Figure 2c) contains a washing container, UV light box, and sand paper. Similar to post-processing in SLA 3D printing, the user gently peels the model off the container base, washes off the remaining liquid resin on the model surface, applies UV exposure by putting the printed part in the box with a 30W UV light tube for 3 minutes, and finally sands the surface of the model to achieve the best surface result.

A 30W UV light tube can be easily for less than ten dollars from Amazon. Figure 7a shows the final product of the penholder using the generated images in Figure 5.

Additional Usage Scenario

Depending on various needs, one can place the physical object at different stages of the printing process to create different effects. When the physical object is placed at the beginning of the printing process, it will result in a hole fitting the object's contour in the final printed product. Holes can also be formed by embedding a mold of the real-life object in the resin. For example, one could create a mold of his/her finger with paper/plastics/clay (which are highly accessible) and place the mold in the resin, creating a well-fitting ring (Figure 8). The close-up view in Figure 8d specifically shows that there is little space between the ring and the finger, indicating a good fit.

Another interesting application of FusePrint is the ability for users to place screws in the liquid resin (Figure 9a), so the resin can be cured around the screw, and create internal threads that tightly fit the particular type of screws without

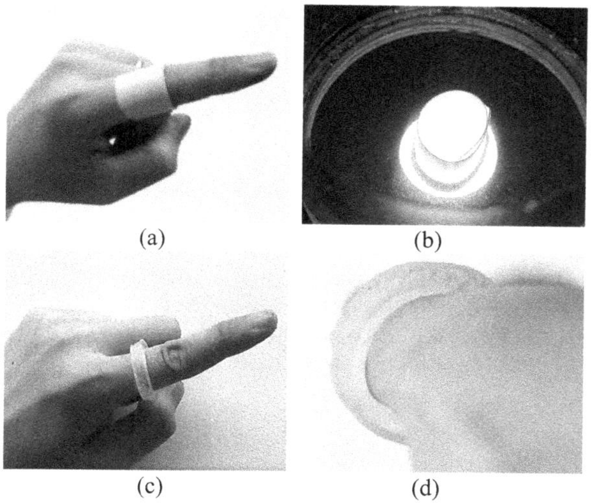

Figure 8: (a) user made a model of the finger using a plastic wrapper (b) the plastic wrapper is placed in the resin during printing (c) the printed ring fits nicely to the finger (d) top down view of the ring.

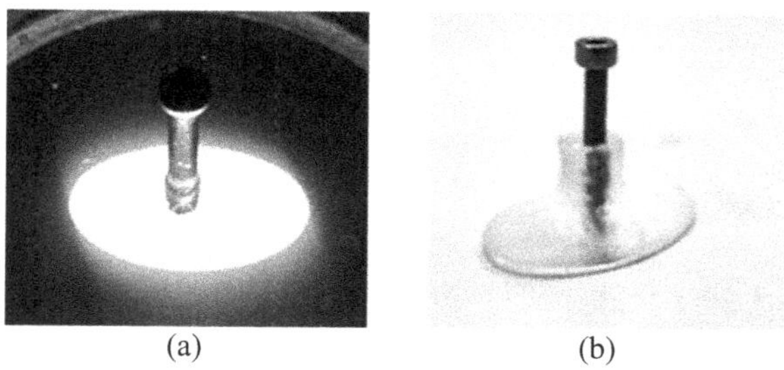

Figure 9: Print a screw thread (a) a physical screw is placed in the resin to create the internal structure for a thread (b) the screw can tightly fit into the thread

measuring and modeling (Figure 9b). By mixing the photo-reactive resin and conductive gel, we can create conductive objects that can be used as capacitance-based touch sensors, as shown in Figure 10. Different shapes resulted in different conductivities and further achieved different touching sensitivities; thus a unique touch ID can be assigned a particular object. In addition, the printed parts can detect the number of touch points, facilitating the design of multi-touch interaction.

TECHNICAL EXPERIMENT ON 2.5D RESIN PRINTING

To investigate the feasibility of DLP-based 2.5D printing, we experimented on how the length of light exposure and the color of the projected pattern could affect the thickness of the printed object. In the first trial set, we fixed the depth of the liquid resin at 2.5cm. We varied the RGB value of the projected color from gray (127, 127, 127) to white (255, 255, 255). The resin was exposed in light projection with 4 different durations: 3 minutes, 5 minutes, 10 minutes, and 15 minutes. We collected 28 data in total.

Experiment Results

As shown in Figure 11, the height of the printed object has a positive correlation with the RGB value of the projected

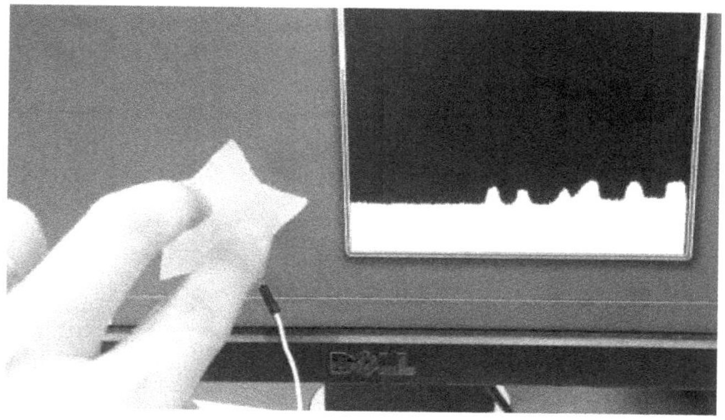

Figure 10: Print a touch sensor with the mixture of photo-reactive resin and conductive gel.

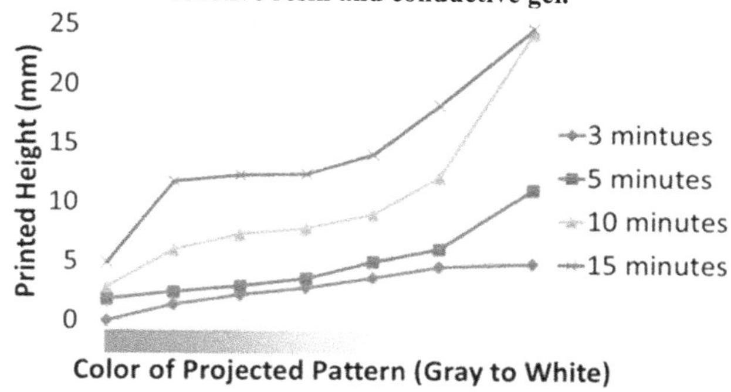

Figure 11: Experiment data on the effect of projection color and time on the height of printed objects.

color. With the same projection color, the height increases along with the increment of the length of light exposure.

We further fitted these experimental data into a multivariate 3-degree polynomial model (Equation 1) to predict the height of the printed object (h) with a particular setting of the grayness of projected color (c) and duration (t). Based on the relationship among printed height, projected duration, and projected color, as shown in Equation 1, the PowerPoint plug-in computes the color of the object and the advance timing of the slides given the height specified by the user in the sketch interface. Noted that Equation 1 was derived from the empirical data collected using the setup specification described in FusePrint Setup section, thus the factors might change if the set-up is modified. With this consideration, we designed the PowerPoint plug-in to allow researchers to input their own experimental data and derive the suitable multivariate polynomial equation.

$$h = -0.00280t^3 - 0.00125t^2c + 0.0000477tc^2 + 0.000167c^3 + 0.300t^2 + 0.0125tc - 0.00941c^2 - 3.53t + 1.66c - 90.6$$

$$Residual\ Sum\ of\ Square: rss = 9.91$$

$h\ (mm)$: $height\ of\ the\ printed\ model$

$t\ (minute)$: $length\ of\ light\ exposure$

c: $grayness\ of\ the\ projected\ color\ (setting\ the\ RGB\ values\ equally)$

Equation 1: Polynomial model of the effect of projection color (c) and time (t) on the printed height (h).

Time (minute)	Calculated Color (R, G, B)	Designed Height (mm)	Printed Height (mm)	Error (mm)
10	(152,152,152)	6	5.93	0.07
5	(249,249,249)	10	9.35	0.65
15	(212,212,212)	15	14.23	0.77
8	(252,252,252)	17	17.66	0.66
12	(255,255,255)	24	24.42	0.42

Table 1: Validation of Equation 1

Validation of Mathematical Model for 2.5D Printing

We performed a validation experiment to test our mathematical model and the PowerPoint plug-in for 2.5D resin printing. We randomly picked 5 combinations of printed height and time and employed the plug-in to generate 5 different slides, which were projected into the resin individually. We measured the heights of the printed objects and calculated the error between the printed height and the designed height. As shown in Table 1, the printing process achieved marginally low errors (rss = 1.63) between the designed height and printed height, which validated our polynomial model in Equation 1.

Mixing Resin with Conductive Gel

We experimented with the conductivity (electric resistance) of a mixture of resin and conductive gel, in which conductive gel has been widely used in cosmetic and medical treatments. We identified two factors that affect the conductivity of the printed objects: the ratio of conductive gel and photo-reactive resin, and the shape of the object. Figure 12 illustrates the resistance change in printed objects produced with 5-mintute projection exposure. These objects had different shapes (an equilateral triangle with edge length of 5cm, a rectangle sizing 4cm x 3cm, and a full circle with diameter of 5cm) and a different ratio of mixture. We can see a significant reduction in the electric resistance along with the increase in proportion of the conductive gel in the mixture, and the resistance varies among three different shapes.

Our results (demonstrated in Figure 12) further suggested that printed resistance varies significantly among different shapes under the ratio of 1:3 and 1:2 (Gel:Resin). In addition, the printed electric resistance could easily achieve the insulating level (>10Mohm) using 1:3 mixture. Also, the surface roughness increases along with the increment of the conductive gel in the mixture, as the mixture with more conductive gel has stronger effect on light scattering. Thus we decided to carry on the rest of the experiments with the 1:2 mixture of conductive gel and photo-reactive resin.

Making Different Touch Sensors

The various electric resistances can provide interactivity to these SLA-3D-printed objects, and objects with different resistances can be created in different shapes.

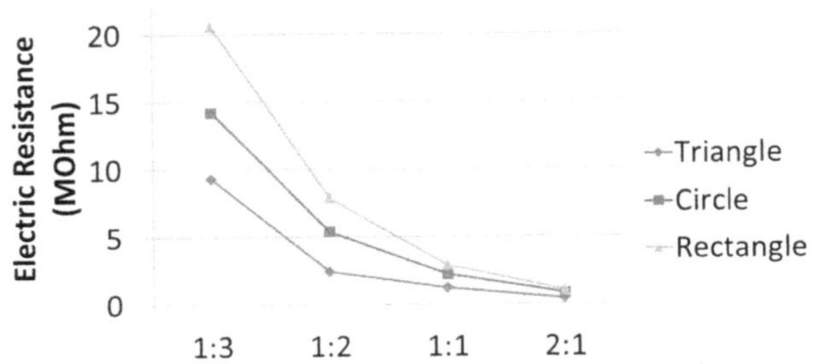

Figure 12: Experiment data on the effect of mixture ratio and printed shape on the conductivity of printed objects.

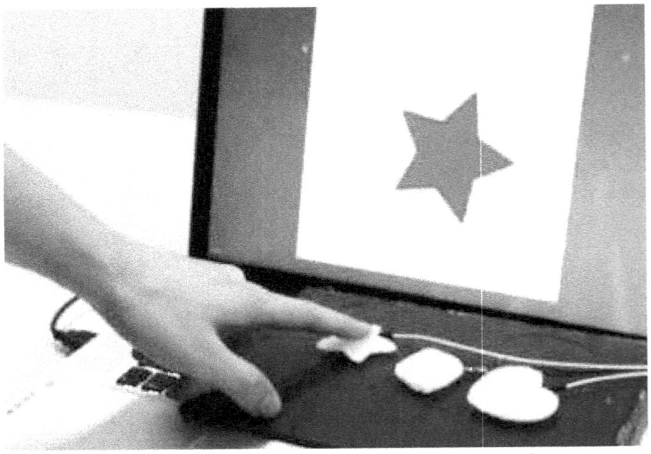

Figure 13: Printed touch sensors in different shapes.

The conductive objects can be connected to the normal capacitive touch-sensing circuit to form touch sensor circuits, as shown in Figure 13.

WORKSHOP STUDY

To further understand how FusePrint could be used in the process of design and rapid prototyping, we conducted a series of empirical workshops by inviting users with different backgrounds to use the FusePrint process. We adopted the evaluation strategy followed by other creative systems [17, 25], and procedures used by Buechley et al. [5] in electronic textile for our evaluation.

Workshop Participants

Our workshops had a total 8 participants (one participant per workshop), consisting of five males and three females with ages ranging from 20 to 32 years (M=23.25, SD=2.11). Prior to conducting the workshops, we collected the participant's background information in 3D printing. Two participants self-rated as experts, four self-rated as beginners, and two had never tried 3D printing before.

Workshop Apparatus

The workshops were held in a fabrication lab (10 m x 7 m) in a local school, with various prototyping tools, such as screws, screwdrivers, drillers, etc. Each participant worked with a FusePrint setup: an iPad 2 and a stylus in the design stage; a MacBook Pro connected to Optoma DLP projector EH1060, and a resin container with 500g resin (Form1

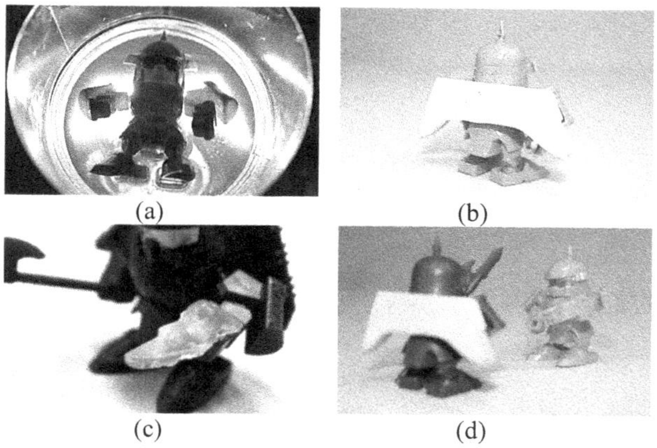

Figure 14: Printing new parts for toys.

Clear) in the printing stage; two pairs of tweezers, 100 ml of ethyl alcohol in a bottle for cleaning, one UV light box with 30W UV light tube, and 3M #600 sandpaper in the post-processing stage. In addition, we provided several everyday objects, such as stationaries, water bottles, plastic toys, etc. Participants were also allowed to bring their own objects to the workshop.

Workshop Procedure

The workshop was conducted in four sessions:

1. Introduction (20 minutes). The workshop facilitator gave a brief introduction of FusePrint and the technology of SLA 3D printing, and showed a few examples of printed outcomes. The objective was to give the participants a brief understanding of the system and the technology. The participants were allowed to ask questions at any time during the introduction.

2. Guided Task (30 minutes). After being introduced to FusePrint, the participants were given a tutorial on how to use FusePrint to make a ring that matched his/her finger. The participants were asked to recreate this example to familiarize with the fabrication process. The activity included creating the wrapping that fit the finger, designing the shape of the ring, printing the ring with the wrapping, post-processing the printed result.

3. Free Task (30–40 minutes). Participants were encouraged to freely explore their own imagination by using physical objects in FusePrint. They were allowed to use any objects in the workshop space. This session was to provide insights on how FusePrint allowed users to explore their creativity.

4. Demo (10 minutes). After finishing the free task, each participant was asked to show his/her result to the workshop facilitator, and explain the design rationale.

The workshop process was video recorded with the participants' consent. After the workshop, the participants answered a questionnaire on their impressions of FusePrint.

Workshop Outcomes

We summarized the objects printed by the workshop participants into three main themes: *making accessories for physical objects*, *adding interactivity to physical objects*, and *fitting details of physical objects*. We will discuss these three themes by using the representative examples created in the workshops.

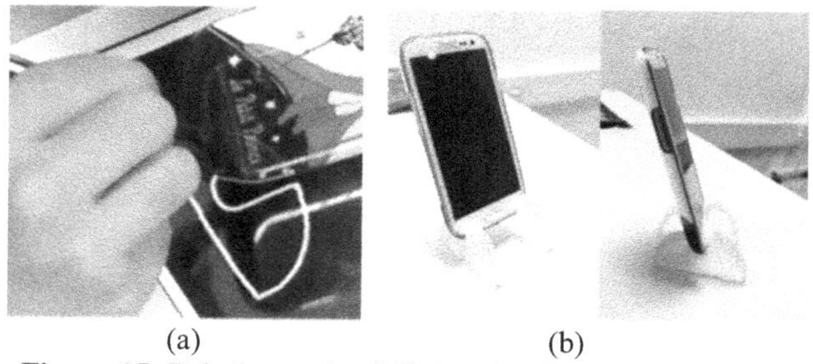

Figure 15: Printing a stand fitting the shape of the phone.

Figure 16: A printed conductive accessory for the glasses.

Making Accessories for Physical Objects

While printing screw thread focuses on the more industrial-oriented application of FusePrint, the workshop results of making new parts for toys suggested the application towards personal entertainment. There were two new toy parts created in the workshops. In these two examples, existing parts of the toy (hand and body) were placed in the resin (Figure 14a), so the printed new parts could fit into the slots in the original parts (Figure 14b and 14c). As the two toys were manufactured from the same company with the same standard, the new parts could be swapped between two toys to create new combinations (Figure 14d).

One female participant (28 years old) created a new stand for her mobile phone. She drew the shape of the stand by tracing the edge of her mobile (Figure 15a) to make sure the slot fit the size of the device well (Figure 15b).

Adding Interactivity to Physical Objects

One interaction designer (final-year undergraduate majoring in art and interaction design with 3 years of experience in Processing and Arduino) created a tiny accessory for his glasses using the mixture of photo-reactive resin and conductive gel, turning his glasses into a pair with touch-sensitive capabilities. Using a plastic sheet wrapped around the earpiece of the glasses, he printed the Touch sensor that could be easily and firmly attached to his glasses (Figure 16a), and quickly developed an interactive demo, as shown in Figure 16b.

He commented that the functionality of using a physical object to shape the printed part that fit back onto the object could shorten the iteration of prototyping for designers. In theory, they could quickly create a nice proof of concept in the first iteration, as they would be able to focus more on

(a) (b) (c)
Figure 17: A screw-assembled hanging hook made in the workshop

the functionality of the design instead of the tedious modeling and printing process.

Fitting Details of Physical Objects

The most common usage of FusePrint is to fit detailed parts of physical objects. One 31-year-old male participant, who is a mechanical engineer, created multiple parts with M4 screw threads and assembled them together with screws (Figure 17a). He screwed the assembled structure into an existing hole in the wall (Figure 17b) and created a hook for hanging clothes (Figure 17c). He commented that FusePrint would be very useful in creating tiny parts for home appliances to fit with original parts, especially those easy-to-lose-but-not-easy-to-buy-new ones, such as special screws and screw bolts. He said it would be time saving and cost saving to set up FusePrint at home and make parts whenever he wants.

Another example was one customized bottle cap (Figure 18) created by one 28-year-old female participant. She mentioned that sometimes she wants to re-use plastic bottles, and she could use FusePrint to personalize these bottles to differentiate from others. She also suggested that she could use this technique to create different caps for medicine bottles for her vision-impaired grandmother.

Quantitative and Qualitative Results

Intuitiveness and Learnability

Participants found the software interface and the process of placing physical objects easy to learn and intuitive. They commented that the idea of directly placing objects in liquid resin is "*intuitive.*" One participant said, "*using physical objects [as reference] to design the printed shape is very similar to what I usually did in quick sketch design.*" The quantitative result of *learnability of designing shapes to print* received an average score of 4.25/5. All of the participants were able to follow the tutorial to create well-fitting rings within 30 minutes. In the free task, they were able to generate various ideas and create new objects with everyday physical objects.

On the other hand, the participants' comments identified the potential problems with the sketching interface. Questions like "*Can I combine different shapes to create new shapes?*" and "*Where exactly should I put the object in the red circle?*" indicated improvement could be done in the shape design and the indication of the spot for object insertion.

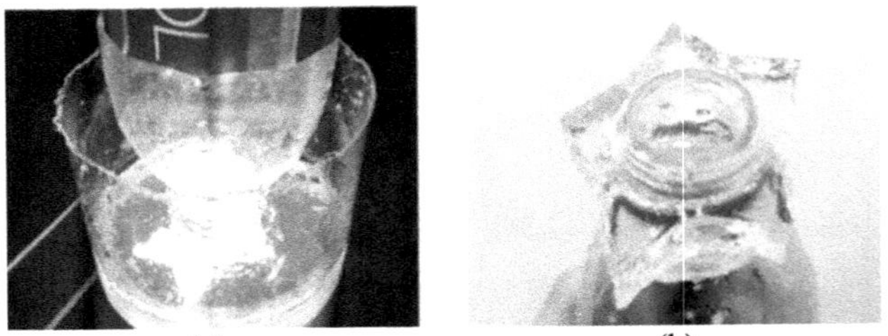

(a) (b)
Figure 18: Customized bottle cap made in the workshop

Usefulness and Engagement

The participants agreed that the process of directly placing physical objects as molds is useful and suggested the application in: mechanical fabrication, toy design, wearable design, interactive system prototyping, etc. One participant suggested, "*FusePrint would make it easy for disabled people to make a DIY prosthesis that perfectly fit their bodies,*" which indicates a potential application in biomechanics and healthcare.

The average rating for engagement was 4.5/5. One experienced 3D-print practitioner commented: "*I felt more close to my printed product in this process than 3D printing, because here the printing time is shorter, and you can get involved during the printing, but in 3D printing, you can do nothing but just watch and wait once pressing the start button.*" In addition, participants felt the process was more fun when given the freedom to explore different possibilities with different objects, than the guided task.

DISCUSSION

Comparison with Other Methods

We compared FusePrint with existing methods in terms of cost, time estimated for fabricating the pen holder (described in FusePrint Process section), printing technologies, products, types of inserted artefact, the modeling process, and the requirement of tolerance adjustment in the hardware, as shown in Table 2. FusePrint offers acceptable cost, and allows intuitive sketch-based modeling of the connection, instead of requiring accurate scanning/modeling tools. The comparison on time spent for fabricating the described pen eliminated the time for measuring and modeling, and showed that the SLA-based FusePrint outperformed the FDM/SDM-based techniques which could suffer from fabricating objects with large sizes. While the existing FDM/SDM-based methods required the ad-hoc tolerance adjustment on hardware, the nature of light-based fabrication in FusePrint eliminates this tedious process. In addition, FusePrint adopted the SLA technology, a different approach with the existing methods, which we hope can potentially open up future opportunities for innovation in the area of rapid prototyping.

On the other hand, it may be possible to conduct the experiment of FusePrint with existing commercially-available DLP-projection-based 3D printers (i.e. Kudo3D Titan 1 [4] and B9 Creator [2]), but modifying the infrastructure (i.e. removing the moving mechanics above

	FusePrint	Encore [32]	Voxel8 [31]	Printed Optics [16]
Cost	~$650	~$350	~$550	~$20,000
Time spent for fabricating the pen holder	~20 min with the described settings	~45 min with MakerBot Reprecator 2 [22]	~45 min with MakerBot Reprecator 2 [22]	~50 min with Objet Eden260V [23]
Printing Technology	SLA	FDM	FDM	SDM
Printed Object	2.5D	3D	3D	3D
Inserted Artefact	Physical objects & liquid	3D printed objects with the same material	Electronics	Electronics
Physical Connection Modeling	Sketch-based modeling on tablet	High-end accurate scanning/modeling for surface connection		
Tolerance Adjustment	Not required	Require ad-hoc adjustment.		

Table 2: Comparison of FusePrint and existing methods for embracing physical objects in fabrication

the resin) and tuning the parameters (i.e. adjusting the projection) of these commercial printers could be non-trivial without detailed technical specification from the companies. In addition, there emerged more related literature on customizing DLP-projection-based 3D printers in the maker community than the commercial market. Thus, it was more cost-and-time-effective for us to customize our own projection setup for FusePrint than purchasing and modifying commercial product. Lastly, FusePrint may seem similar with clay molding at the first glance, but FusePrint offers the possibility for setting up in the daily environment with off-the-shelf DLP projectors, while clay molding usually requires advanced manufacturing skills and facilities, such as cutters and high-temperature ovens.

Limitation

Ease of Setup

The participants in the presented workshop studies were not asked to set up the FusePrint system from scratch, thus the ease of setup for FusePrint was not evaluated explicitly. However, one participant mentioned it would be time saving and cost saving to set up FusePrint at home. As one future plan, we will investigate the set-up and the usage of FusePrint in different settings, including home, school fablabs, and maker spaces. Particularly, we would like to investigate the ease for makers and hobbyists to replicate the DIY process of collecting empirical data, tuning the polynomial factors, setting up and using the FusePrint system.

3D Fabrication

Our experiment showed that FusePrint is enable to fabricate high-precision assembly mechanisms, including non-permanent assembly (i.e. screw threads, which is essential in valve structure) and permanent assembly (i.e. shaft-hole sockets and pipes), without requiring high-end modeling tools. However, the current setup of FusePrint has limitations that prevent it from fabricating complex structures, such as hollow or suspension structures. As the next step, we will explore how to fabricate true 3D objects with FusePrint, by carefully calibrating and coordinating the top and the bottom projection. One other solution is to parse the 3D models into multiple 2.5D parts, and print them in sequence where the printed part can be inserted for fabricating new parts, so that they can be assembled into 3D.

While the current FusePrint can produce user-acceptable 2.5D objects, shape distortion may occur when printing different heights in the z axis. This is mainly due to the difficulty of controlling light transmission in the liquid resin. Lastly, users are required to use gloves while handling the photo-reactive resin because touching the liquid resin can "*cause mild skin irritation for some people*" [12].

CONCLUSION

In this paper, we introduced FusePrint, a DIY 2.5D printing technique exploring the possibility of inserting everyday artifacts in SLA-based 2.5D printing. We experimented with how lighting condition affected the height of a printed object, derived a mathematical model, and applied it to the software part of FusePrint. We also explored the possibilities of inserting physical objects and conductive gel into the printing process. The workshops on FusePrint suggest the technique is easy to adapt for making objects that fit well with existing ones, and users are highly engaged in the printing process. More importantly, the workshops revealed various possible applications of FusePrint: mechanical fabrication, toy design, wearable accessories, rapid prototyping for interactive system, bioengineering, etc.

For the future work, we will further investigate the setup and the usage of FusePrint in different contexts. Finally, this fabrication process points to further investigation, including integrating with traditional moulding technique, fabricating true 3D objects, mixing different materials, and empirical investigations of resulting characteristics (e.g., conductance, color, texture, and haptic properties).

ACKNOWLEDGMENTS

The research described in this paper was partially supported by the Start-up Grant (Project No. 7200404) and the Strategic Research Grant (Project No. 7004308), and fully supported by the Strategic Research Grant (Project No. 7004582) from City University of Hong Kong.

REFERENCES

1. 3shape Convince scanners series for quality control (accuracy: 16-20 microns) http://www.3shape.com/
2. B9 Creator. http://www.b9c.com/
3. Billiet, T., Vandenhaute, M., Schelfhout, J., Van Vlierberghe, S., & Dubruel, P. (2012). A review of trends and limitations in hydrogel-rapid prototyping for tissue engineering. *Biomaterials*, *33*(26), 6020-6041.
4. Bottom-up stereolithography 3D printing technology http://www.kudo3d.com/
5. Buechley, L., Eisenberg, M., Catchen, J., and Crockett, A. The lilypad arduino: using computational textiles to investigate engagement, aesthetics, and diversity in computer science education. In Proc. of CHI 2008,
6. Cadscan Cubik Desktop 3D Scanner http://cad-scan.co.uk/product/cubik-desktop-3d-scanner/
7. Christian Weichel, Manfred Lau, and Hans Gellersen. 2013. Enclosed: a component-centric interface for designing prototype enclosures. In Proc. of TEI '13.
8. Christian Weichel, Manfred Lau, David Kim, Nicolas Villar, and Hans W. Gellersen. 2014. MixFab: a mixed-reality environment for personal fabrication. In Proc. of CHI '14.
9. Chua, Chee Kai, Kah Fai Leong, and Chu Sing Lim. "Powder-based rapid prototyping systems." Rapid prototyping: principles and applications. Singapore: World Scientific (2003).
10. Deckard, Carl R. "Method and apparatus for producing parts by selective sintering." U.S. Patent No. 4,863,538. 5 Sep. 1989.
11. Desktop stereolithography 3D printer http://formlabs.com/
12. Formlabs Resin Care. http://formlabs.com/support/guide/print/resin-care/
13. Gierad Laput, Eric Brockmeyer, Scott E. Hudson, and Chris Harrison. 2015. Acoustruments: Passive, Acoustically-Driven, Interactive Controls for Handheld Devices. In Proc. of CHI'15.
14. Hull, Charles W. "Apparatus for production of three-dimensional objects by stereolithography." U.S. Patent No. 4,575,330. 11 Mar. 1986.
15. Jorge G. Cham, Beth L. Pruitt, Mark R. Cutkosky, Mike Binnard, Lee E. Weiss, and Gennady Neplotnik. "Layered manufacturing with embedded components: process planning considerations." In ASME Design Engineering Technical Conferences, Sept, pp.12-15. 1999.
16. Karl Willis, Eric Brockmeyer, Scott Hudson, and Ivan Poupyrev. 2012. Printed optics: 3D printing of embedded optical elements for interactive devices. In Proc. of UIST'12.
17. Kening Zhu and Shengdong Zhao. 2013. AutoGami: a low-cost rapid prototyping toolkit for automated movable paper craft. In Proc. of CHI'13.
18. Kruth, J-P., Ming-Chuan Leu, and T. Nakagawa. "Progress in additive manufacturing and rapid pprototyping." CIRP Annals-Manufacturing Technology 47.2 (1998): 525-540.
19. Lipson, Hod, and Melba Kurman. *Fabricated: The new world of 3D printing*. John Wiley & Sons, 2013.
20. Madeline Gannon, Tovi Grossman, and George Fitzmaurice. 2015. Tactum: A Skin-Centric Approach to Digital Design and Fabrication. In Proc. of CHI'15.
21. MakerBot Digitizer 3D Scanner. http://store.makerbot.com/digitizer
22. MakerBot Replicator 2. http://store.makerbot.com/replicator2.html
23. Objet Eden260V. http://www.stratasys.com/3d-printers/design-series/objet-eden260vs
24. Robert Merz, F. B. Prinz, K. Ramaswami, M. Terk, and L. Weiss. Shape deposition manufacturing. Engineering Design Research Center, Carnegie Mellon Univ., 1994.
25. Rubaiat, H. K, Chua, K. C., Zhao, S., Davis, R., Low, K.. SandCanvas: a multi-touch art medium inspired by sand animation. In Proc. of CHI 2011, ACM Press (2011), 1283- 1292
26. Sachs, Emanuel M., et al. "Three-dimensional printing techniques." U.S. Patent No. 5,204,055. 20 Apr. 1993.
27. Sean Follmer and Hiroshi Ishii. 2012. KidCAD: digitally remixing toys through tangible tools. In Proc. of CHI'12.
28. Sean Follmer, David Carr, Emily Lovell, and Hiroshi Ishii. 2010. CopyCAD: remixing physical objects with copy and paste from the real world. In Adjunct Proc. of UIST'10.
29. Shrey Pareek, Vaibhav Sharma, and Rahul Rai. Design for Additive Manufacturing of Kinematic Pairs. International Solid Freeform Fabrication Symposium 2014. p732 – 745.
30. Stefanie Mueller, Pedro Lopes, Konstantin Kaefer, Bastian Kruck, and Patrick Baudisch. 2013. constructable: interactive construction of functional mechanical devices. In *ACM SIGGRAPH 2013 Talks*
31. Voxel8. http://www.voxel8.co/
32. Xiang 'Anthony' Chen, Stelian Coros, Jennifer Mankoff, and Scott E. Hudson. 2015. Encore: 3D printed augmentation of everyday objects with printed-over, affixed and interlocked attachments. In ACM SIGGRAPH 2015 Posters.
33. Yan, Xue, and P. E. N. G. Gu. "A review of rapid prototyping technologies and systems." Computer-Aided Design 28.4 (1996): 307-318.

34. Yoshio Ishiguro and Ivan Poupyrev. 2014. 3D printed interactive speakers. In Proc. of CHI'14.

35. Weichel Christian, Hardy John, Alexander Jason, and Gellersen Hans. 2015. ReForm: Integrating Physical and Digital Design through Bidirectional Fabrication. In Proc. of UIST '15.

36. Weichel Christian, Alexander Jason, Karnik Abhijit, and Gellersen Hans. 2015. SPATA: Spatio-Tangible Tools for Fabrication-Aware Design. In Proc. of TEI '15.

37. Teibrich Alexander, Mueller Stefanie, Guimbretière François, Kovacs Robert, Neubert Stefan, and Baudisch Patrick. 2015. Patching Physical Objects. In Proc. of UIST '15.

ProxyPrint: Supporting Crafting Practice through Physical Computational Proxies

Cesar Torres[1,2], Wilmot Li[2], Eric Paulos[1]

[1]Electrical Engineering and Computer Sciences
University of California, Berkeley
{cearto, paulos}@berkeley.edu

[2]Adobe Research
601 Townsend St.
San Francisco, CA, USA
wilmotli@adobe.com

Figure 1. a) Schematic, an annotated construction proxy used to provide fabrication feedback, b) Stencil, a fabrication proxy that breaks down designs into elementary forms, c) Jig, a fabrication and construction proxy that provides a ritual high-fidelity fabrication process.

ABSTRACT

Advances in digital fabrication (DF) technologies are making it easier to produce high-fidelity replicas of digital designs. However, this push-to-print paradigm limits the creative opportunities that arise from the process of "working through a material" which involves risk, uncertainty, and serendipitous discovery. We investigate how DF artifacts can function as static intermediary tools, which we term proxies, to support crafting practice. We focus on the wire-wrapping process where physical wire is bent into complex shapes and build DF fixtures to aid with construction and fabrication. We explore how these proxies can be generated to provide users with different levels-of-assistance and evaluate how these proxies affect the making process. We show that our proxies affect quality and speed and yield different making experiences between novice and expert craftspeople. We derive design principles to inform future proxy design and discuss how approaches such as ProxyPrint that are designed aware of the medium can create more engaging making tools that can embed tacit knowledge, encourage creativity, and sustain crafting practice.

Author Keywords

digital fabrication; creativity support tools; design; DIY;

DIS 2016, June 04–08, 2016, Brisbane, QLD, Australia
ACM 978-1-4503-4031-1/16/06.
http://dx.doi.org/10.1145/2901790.2901828

ACM Classification Keywords

H.5.m. Information interfaces and presentation]: User Interfaces - Interaction Styles

ACM Classification Keywords

D.2.2 Design Tools and Techniques: User interfaces

INTRODUCTION

With the growth of digital fabrication (DF) technology, it has become possible to rapidly manufacture objects in a growing range of materials, including plastics, ceramics, and metal. Today, users can fabricate accurate, physical artifacts from digital designs at the push of a button without the need to master difficult, labor-intensive manual fabrication processes. This technology has clear benefits for both novices and experts. For novices, DF lowers the barrier to entry and expands the range of craft and DIY projects they can execute. For experts, DF facilitates physical prototyping of designs, small run manufacturing, and the production of parts that are hard to manufacture with traditional processes.

However, there are several important trade-offs to the convenience of automated fabrication. By removing manual creation from the process, DF eliminates well-known benefits of making things by hand: Klemmer et al. [17] describe how "thinking through doing" (i.e., engaging directly with the physical world) often helps with problem-solving and learning, which aligns with constructionist approaches to education [21, 25]; makers also tend to feel greater ownership over objects that are physically made [32], especially when the "hand of the artist" is visible [20, 38]; finally, manual creation introduces the risk of making errors, which can lead to "happy accidents" [19] that can shape and even improve creative outcomes. At the same time, while DF machines and interfaces, have moments or surprise and error, this secondhand feedback is more displaced from the material and usually a result of some algorithmic or mechanical error.

Recent advances in human-computer interaction has opened a new hybrid design space that can balance benefits of automation and the advantages of working directly with materials. This hybrid space refers to blended digital and physical practices. Hybrid tools which facilitate this practice have gained traction in domains such as crafts by outsourcing tedious labor to machines [5]. However, several tensions arise around hybrid craft resulting from ambiguities between mediums: traditional crafts are slow and near-at-hand; digital processes are inherently faster (supporting iteration) and can be ubiquitous [15, 22]. Other tensions between digital fabrication and handed fabrication arise from socio-cultural practices such as: a) deskilling the artist by making the craft easier; b) masking the "hand of the artist"', or the distinction that an artifact is hand-made versus machine-fabricated, c) dishonoring the material, such as tacking on other media like electronics [22], and d) failing to listen to the material, such as when a wood knot is not "heard" by a CNC machine whereas a woodworker would detect it and alter the design [5].

A Proxy-Mediated Practice

In order to address some of these tensions, we explore a new class of hybrid DF tools that combine the convenience of automated fabrication and the advantages of working directly with materials – ProxyPrints is a set of computationally generated physical artifacts that facilitate, inform, and influence the manual creation processes, functioning similar to armatures in traditional sculpture. This gives rise to our vision of a proxy-mediated practice where a user works directly with a material with their hands and tools; this process informs future iterations of a design; a design tool generates a set of specific passive fixtures or custom static tools based on the design; which assist the user to continue working with the material and develop craftsmanship.

Such as practice allows users to still create final artifacts by hand while retaining the advantages of manual fabrication. At the same time, proxies assist users with challenging aspects of the fabrication task by providing more customized design-specific scaffolding than generic tools and be designed to provide different levels-of-assistance based on the goals and expertise of the user (Figure 1), acting in the traditional role of a teacher in a master-apprentice relationship. For example, while novices may want more fabrication assistance to guarantee success, experts may prefer less or more localized assistance that offers the ability to explore interesting variations. Unlike traditional tools, computational proxies can provide this type of design-specific assistance to complement and build on a user's existing skill set.

Wire-wrapping as Crafting Exemplar

To explore the idea of proxy-mediated practice, we focus on the domain of wire-wrapping, a metalworking medium that involves bending wire into aesthetic forms. Wire-wrapping exhibits many of the characteristics of typical DIY communities: namely, the grassroots innovation in tools and techniques; a culture of shared practice through tutorials and workshops; and the potential for refining craftsmanship. Furthermore, wire wrapping is extremely popular for both jewelers and hobbyists and has been successful in handmade marketplaces (> 300K hits on Etsy). Wire-wrapping has a clear cross over to other 1D mediums and crafting tasks, such as needlecrafts, acrylic bending, basket-weaving, and knot-tying. Thus, wire-wrapping represents an interesting and relevant context in which to investigate how proxies affect DF processes for both novices and experts.

Contributions

Firstly, ProxyPrint expands the set of computational proxies available to wire wrapping and introduces proxy recipes for *assembling* multiple pieces of wire into a single artifact, *forging* wire to vary its width (and strength), and finally, *weaving* wire to create textured patterns. This expanded set of proxies more holistically supports the medium, and a preliminary usability evaluation suggests that our proxies address these challenges over conventional methods and tools.

Secondly, we address the larger issue of user engagement and innovation with current DF tools and services. Providing the right type of assistance during a user's experience can ultimately determine whether or not a user abandons their endeavor or deviates from a template and begins a new lifelong practice. ProxyPrint introduces the use of *computational scaffolds* to assist users based on their expertise or familiarity with a medium. Here, we identify three types of scaffold proxies (schematics, stencils and jigs) that provide different assistance (Figure 1) and evaluate these proxies in a formal study with novice and expert craftspeople. Our study characterizes the proxies based on metrics from hybrid crafting literature [20, 30, 38]. Our results showed that the making experience with scaffolds differ across expertise and can effectively influence creative deviation and agency.

RELATED WORK

Recent work has looked at creating more synergistic interactions between maker and tools. Below, we describe work around digital and physically augmented tools, instructional tools, traditional tools, and scaffold design. Lastly, we focus specifically on work that uses wire as a medium.

Augmented tools

Digitally augmented tools or smart tools combine some digital or computational intelligence with manual usage, and primarily act in the service of providing higher accuracy or fidelity. FreeD, an augmented dremmel tool, provided feedback to users through autoshut off features; notably it provides a "human-overide" mode that allowed users to deviate from the digital model. Peng et al. use common clay coiling techniques, bearing a large similarity to Fused Filament Fabrication, as a way to additively construct and digitally scan geometries at fabrication-time [23]. Enchanted scissors used conductive traces to detect and prevent incorrect cuts [36]. In Hybrid Basketry, Zoran explored how digital fabricated armatures can support and guide the basket-weaving process and influence the final artifact design [37]. Notably, the role of digital fabrication in Hybrid Basketry is not a driving or stopping force, but acts solely as a support structure. ProxyPrint builds on this idea of *passive* assistance and expands the set of computationally-generated support fixtures. Furthermore it explores a new dimension of the levels-of-assistance that is exposed to the user. ProxyPrint looks at DF not for producing final artifacts but for producing intermediate highly customized tools and instructions.

Augmented practice and materials

Abstracting materials into primitive additive and subtractive processes, such as fusing sand into glass, can omit much of the rich cultural history of people working with a material (e.g. glass-blowing). Several works investigate how the cultural experience of tools, mediums, and their practice can enhance the making experience. Jenkins et al. explored the religious experiences that are associated with crafting practices and created devotional gardening tools mediated with electronic and digital feedback [16]. Rosner et al. explored the combination of clay and digital fabrication, describing the tensions occurring from the displacement of the medium from the ceramist's hand [27]. ProxyPrint complements this previous work; we similarly design the experience of handed practices into our *scaffold proxies*, and work *with* a material by integrating tacit knowledge from current practices into the design of our *material-driven proxies*.

Design-specific fabrication instructions

Some existing design tools focus on domains that require manual fabrication of the final artifact, such as plush toys [14], inflatable balloons [10], planar cardboard sculptures [12], and customized garments [33]. The output of these tools is typically a set of instructions for how to make the user-generated design. More implicit fine-grain instructions have been explored in systems like Sculpting by Numbers [26] which provides users with a "diff" between forms through a scanning and projection interface, non-intrusively aiding them in evaluating their progress. As we discuss later in the paper, such design-specific instructions represent one type of computer-generated assistance for fabrication tasks. However, the bulk of our work focuses on the design of physical proxies that facilitate manual creation.

Scaffolds on design

Several systems study the impact of levels-of-assistance on user experience and design outcome. Painting with Bob, a design tool for digital painting evaluates a simple toolset (e.g. an eraser that erases everything under the cursor) against a smart toolset (e.g. an eraser that erases similar color regions under the cursor) and draws from literature in creativity support tools [3]. PortraitSketch provides a set of automatic assistance algorithms for adjusting user strokes while drawing to achieve a certain portrait aesthetic [35]. We similarly study the effects of level-of-assistance under a broader spectrum and in the context of physical making.

Wire design and fabrication

Some existing commercial products help users create wire-wrapped artifacts. Companies like WigJig and Beadsmith provide kits that allow users to create customized "jigs" by inserting different sized cylindrical pegs into a board. However, the discrete set of peg sizes and positions limits the designs that such kits can support. CNC wire benders such as DIWire have automated the wire bending process, with some tooling limitations. Such machines have been proposed as sites for interaction: Willis et. al. *Speaker* interactively "sculpts" wire based on sound wave forms [34]. In contrast, we are interested in providing a hybrid crafting experience that keeps the user in the loop with the material and propose more flexible, design-specific physical proxies that can support a broader range of designs.

Most relevant to the domain of our work is WrapIt [13], a computational design tool for converting line drawings into optimal wire wrap forms ("wire decompositions") that can be fabricated with the help of a 3D-printed jig. We build on this work in several ways. First, while WrapIt focused mainly on the design problem of converting line drawings into wire decompositions, we concentrate on the problem of fabricating a given design. To this end, we propose several new computational proxies that aid in wire wrapping tasks that WrapIt does not consider (e.g., forging, assembly, weaving). Moreover, our wire shaping jig design offers some important improvements over the original WrapIt jig. We also investigate the question of level-of-assistance, which seems critical for the design of physical tools that aid the creative process of manual fabrication. We validate these improvements with a comparative evaluation.

OUR APPROACH

Our proxy design approach follows a *style analysis*, or identifying the "constancy, or consistency, in the way an individual, or a group, treats the formal elements of art, or visual culture" [11]. We explored the wire medium not only by its physical affordances (medium-specific) or properties (material-aware), but also through the expert practice and tradition that have already produced conventional uses, meanings, and techniques with this material. For instance, it is a common practice to use coil wraps to connect elements but also to hide imperfections in a design. ProxyPrint develops the tools (proxies) through this medium-aware approach to facilitate these aesthetics and culture to more easily integrate itself with existing practices.

We explore the design of computational proxies along two different dimensions. First, we investigate proxies that facilitate the execution of common wire-wrapping techniques, like wire shaping, forging, and connecting elements together. We call these *material-driven proxies* since they address fabrication challenges that are specific to the material and align with expert craft practice [2]. The second dimension that we consider is how proxies can provide varying amounts of scaffolding for the user. To explore this aspect of the design space, we take the basic elements of our wire shaping proxy and consider design variations that offer different levels-of-assistance. We refer to these variations as *scaffold proxies*.

MATERIAL-DRIVEN PROXIES

The typical wire-wrapping workflow is to first *shape* one or more wires into appropriate forms, then *forge* (or strengthen) the wires so as to retain or enhance their form, and finally

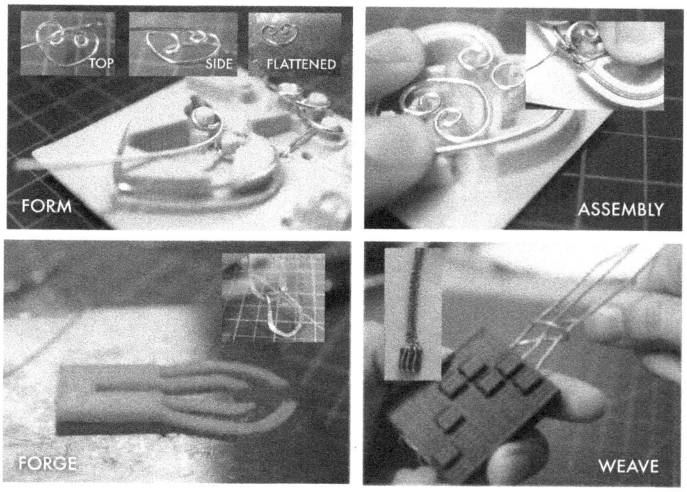

Figure 2. Material-driven proxies: computationally-generated fixtures assist in common wire wrapping tasks such as forming, forging, connecting, and weaving (enlarged for visibility).

connect separate elements together to form a single, coherent composition. Here, we describe how each of these tasks are carried out with traditional tools and then describe our material-driven proxies that help users accomplish the tasks with higher quality and fewer errors. Figure 2 shows examples of the different material-driven proxies we designed.

Shaping

Shaping a piece of wire into a desired form is the primary task in creating wire-wrapped artifacts. In general, it is hard to bend wire to create smooth curves that match the proportions of the design. Wrappers employ hand tools and custom-built jigs for this purpose, but using such tools effectively is challenging. For example, different types of pliers heads are best suited for different types of bends: flat-nose for sharp angles, barrel- or taper-nose for curves and swirls, and chain-nose for general bending. In addition, exerting too much force on the wire with pliers can accidentally mar the metal. Finally, experts typically plan the sequence of bends to minimize interference between the wire, pliers and jig(s) as they manipulate the material.

Based on these observations, we derive the following design requirements for a shaping proxy. Most importantly, the proxy should help the user:

- bend the wire smoothly into the appropriate shape without requiring a lot of precise, plier manipulation.
- clearly convey the bending sequence
- minimize physical obstructions that may interfere with bending interactions

Shaping proxy via hill climbing

The design of our shaping proxy was inspired by the WrapIt jig [13] which has similar design goals. The WrapIt jig includes physical "support walls" around areas of high curvature that guide the shape of the wire to ensure that the resulting form matches that of the input design. While this approach reduces the number of walls and the number of physical obstructions, the wire is prone to falling off the jig since when the wire overlaps on itself it rises above the constraining jig walls. Another issue is that as complexity increases, the ordering of the wraps becomes ambiguous.

The key observation is that support walls are only necessary on one side of the wire (the "interior" or concave side of each bend), which reduces the physical obstructions that may interfere with the wrapping process. However, designs with multiple closely-spaced bends or wire crossings still resulted in interferences between the wire and support walls – a major usability issue with WrapIt jigs. To address this problem, we developed a different type of shaping proxy inspired by a common technique for creating circular jump rings. The method involves coiling wire around a cylindrical mandril, cutting laterally through the coil to create small open rings, and then flattening each ring to create a closed, circular shape. By coiling the wire along the mandril, the user does not have to worry about interferences between subsequent rings.

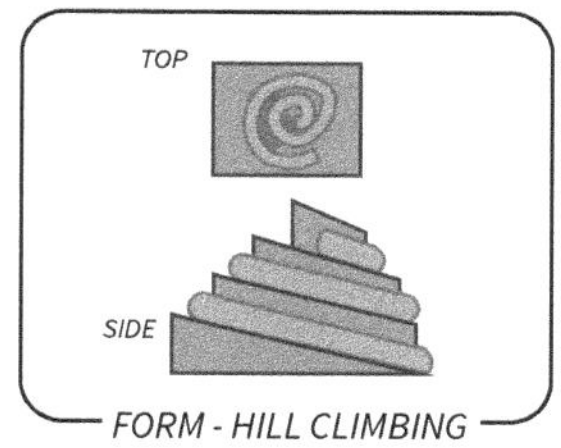

The main insight here is that *the wrapping process does not need to occur on a single 2D plane*, even if the resulting piece is designed to be flat. Thus, we propose a "hill-climbing" proxy design that creates a supported path for the wire that rises from the start to the end of the path. In cases of overlaps, the lower portion of the path takes precedence ensuring each portion of the jig and wire does not interfere with subsequent wrapping interactions. Moreover, the height of the path acts as an implicit cue for where to start and end the wrapping process. As with the WrapIt jig, support walls are only generated along the interior of each bend. Once wrapping is completed, the user simply flattens the wire into a plane. While the change in elevation may result in a small amount of distortion in the flattened geometry, we did not find this to be a problem in the artifacts that we created.

Leveraging tacit knowledge from wire-wrapping, we designed some additional optimizations for allowing users to shape wire with minimal error. For one, bending ends of a wire is difficult to do without deforming the rest of the design. To minimize this, we extended path ends by length and curvature to "complete the loop". This extra length is easily snipped away by the user. Furthermore, a hole was added at the base of the path; this allows users to thread and anchor the wire. These anchors are necessary to keep the wire in place and allow the user to put longitudinal tension on the wire during wrapping. A terminating platform was added to the end of the path to signal to the user the ending position of the design. Lastly, a flattening phase was needed to compress the design back down into plane. We used a rubber[1] hammer and anvil to flatten large elements and nylon pliers for smaller ones.

Forging

In addition to designing the shape of the wire path, experts often vary the width of the wire to achieve specific aesthetic goals. Such variations can be used to make the piece look more organic or to add/remove visual weight from certain

[1]Using non-metal instruments prevents marring of the wire

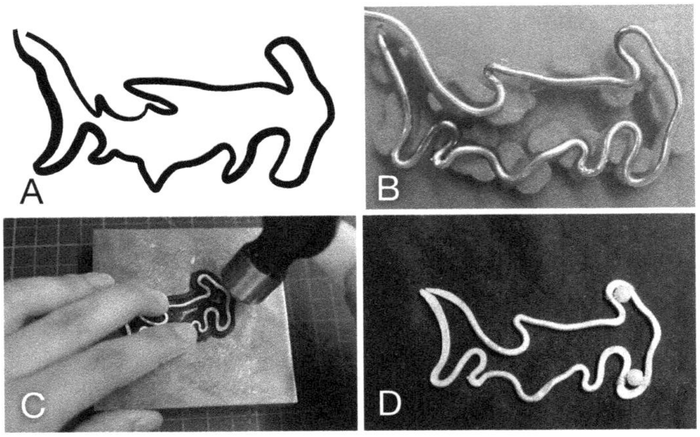

Figure 3. The forging process: (A) a weighted line drawing is taken as input, (B) the shape proxy is generated and used to construct the basic form; note the uniform width of the wire, (C) using metal-to-metal hammering, we deform the metal; the forge proxy prevents the metal from being deformed incorrectly, (D) two additional pearls are coiled onto the final forged wire piece for aesthetic.

portions of the design. Changing the width of the wire requires forging (flattening) portions of the material, which also has the effect of making the material more rigid. Forging is typically done by hammering the wire with a steel hammer, but achieving the desired variations in width requires skill and expertise. In particular, accidentally hammering at an angle versus hammering flat can cause unwanted marking.

Forging Proxy through guard walls

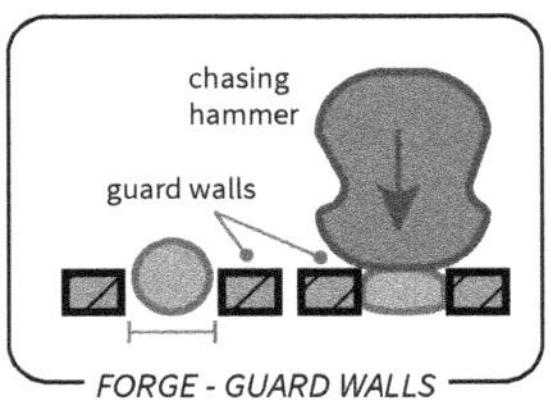

To help users achieve the desired variations in wire width, we developed a forging proxy. Since forging typically happens after shaping, we assume the wire has already been formed into the desired shape. The forging proxy is defined by a channel that holds the shaped wire in place; the user then hammers the wire as it sits in the proxy to create the width variations. "Guard walls" on either side of the channel constrain the width of the wire in two ways: the height of the walls determines how far down the hammer can travel to flatten the wire within the channel; and the gap between the walls limits how wide the wire can become at each point along the channel. We determine the relationship between the height and gap of the walls by fitting an empirical model that relates the lateral strain to the medial strain of the wire. The lateral strain characterizes the width of the compressed wire and the medial strain corresponds to the amount of compression that the hammer imposes.

In order to deform the wire, it must be compressed between two metals (or harder materials). Because of this, plastic cannot be used to compress a metal wire. Thus, it presents a notable challenge to hold plastic guard walls together when they cannot share a common connecting ground. Our approach adds a common substrate across the wire connecting two adjacent guard walls in portions of the path that do not need to be thickened. If an entire path needs to be forged, we select regions at the ends to be connected; a user would have to forge these ends without a guard wall. The minimum height of a guard wall is limited by the minimum layer resolution of the 3D printer; as such thicker gauge wires (<16 AWG) offer a more dynamic and expressive thickening range.

Connecting

Wire-wrapped pieces are rarely composed of a single element. Typically, several individual elements are assembled together into a single artifact. Connections between elements are typically formed either by wrapping thin coiling wire around elements or soldering the two elements together. With either of these techniques, one of the main difficulties is in holding the various elements in place while forming the connections. In particular, users may accidentally deform the shape of the wire while coiling or soldering, and this can lead to unwanted asymmetries or distortions in the final design.

Connection Proxy

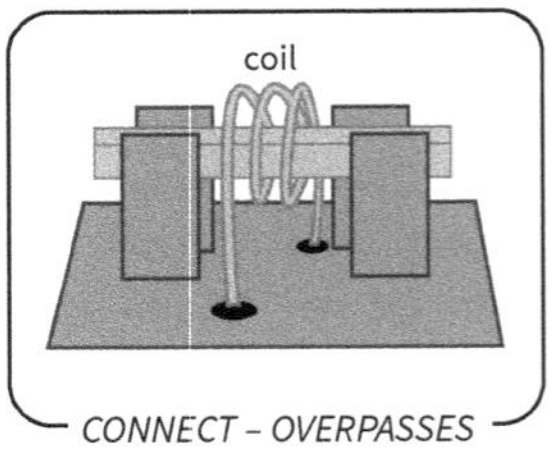

To facilitate connection tasks, we designed a connection proxy that holds the various wire elements firmly in place while still giving users room to coil or solder at connection points. Similar to the forging proxy, the connection proxy has a channel with guard walls that holds the shaped or forged wire in place. The gap between the walls allows for the wire to be press-fit into the channel. Unlike the forging proxy, the entire channel and walls are lofted above the main plane of the proxy, similar to an elevated highway. The material beneath each connection point is removed resulting in an "overpass". Two holes are added for anchoring the exit points of the connecting wire coil. With this design, users can either coil wire or solder the elements together without worrying about securing or accidentally deforming other parts of the design.

Weaving Proxy

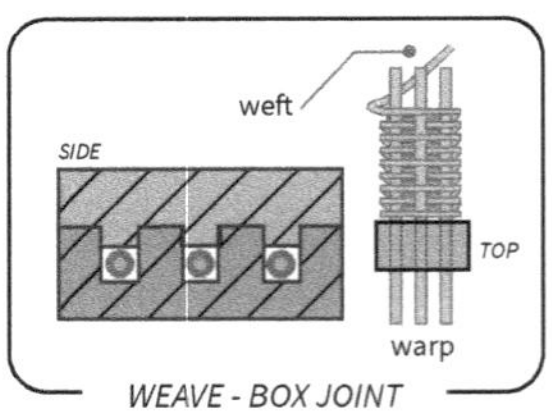

In some cases, rather than wrapping coiling wire around a single connection point, experts create weaves that bind two or more elements together. In these cases, the individual wires of each element act as "framing wires", or warps, while a thinner gauge wire, or weft, is used to create the actual weave. Holding the framing wires in place when starting a weave is very difficult; usually a rubber-lined clamp is used to position these wires. To help users create weaves, we developed a *weaving proxy* that uses a box joint, a common woodworking joint, to hold wires in place. The teeth of the joint act as a compressive element while the chambers hold and space the wire apart. These teeth can be spaced in different configurations, giving users additional control over the spacing of framing wires. Notably, the box-joint creates two disjoint elements (jaws). This allows for wires which are part of closed elements (with no exposed "ends") to be used as framing wires since the jaws can be positioned anywhere on a design. A binder clip is used to hold the jaws in place while a user weaves.

SCAFFOLDS OF A SHAPING PROXY

While the previous section describes proxies that facilitate different wire-wrapping tasks, here we focus on wire shaping and ways we can provide different types of assistance, or scaffolds, to assist the user. We design for fabrication assistance, referring to physical assistance with a particular medium such as pliers that provide fine-grain bending control; and construction assistance, referring to the planning of appropriate steps given a set of tools to achieve a given design.

Jigs (Fabrication and Construction Assistance)

Jigs are proxies that provide the highest level of both fabrication and construction assistance. The hill-climbing shaping proxy described above is one such jig: by indicating where to begin wrapping (the starting hole), how to proceed (continuously rising path), and where to end (terminating cliff), this proxy minimizes the cognitive effort of deciding how, where, and when to bend the wire. Moreover, the act of wrapping itself is constrained to pulling the wire tight against the inner wall, which minimizes the physical skill and dexterity required to realize the design. In this respect, jigs encourages a fairly mechanical, repetitive interaction with the material. While such an interaction may seem somewhat limiting, existing theories of making raise the possibility that even repetitive or habitual creative actions can contribute to the joy of making [20] and that simply engaging in the process of creation has "intrinsic pleasures of creative action" [24]; such self-expression has large socio-cultural benefits [2].

Stencils (Fabrication Assistance)

Jigs provides a scaffold for shaping an entire design. However, it may be more important for some parts of the design to have an accurate shape, while other parts may be less critical. Moreover, some parts of the design may be much harder to execute than others. Based on these observations, we developed a stencil proxy that only provides scaffolding for specific portions of the design; these portions were manually chosen. For example, the heart design had stencils generated to support fabricating half the heart along the axis of symmetry and supports for creating the arcs that appear at the ends of the design (Figure 1B). These supports are scaled to different size to provide more diverse and alternate forms. To shape the wire, users apply the desired set of stencil components. Since the stencil proxy does not support the creation of every bend in the wire, it provides less assistance than a jig. In addition, users are not constrained to use a single consistent set of stencil components to complete the design; they can choose which combination or subset of components to apply.

In contrast to jigs, our stencil design is motivated by view of making described by Ingold's *making as correspondence*. This correspondence can take the form of a maker who "joins forces' with 'active materials' to see what might emerge"[9]. Latour proposes a similar idea, but notes that agency is not a fixed property of the material or actors but the result of a relationship between people and artifacts [31]. Our stencils act as participants in this correspondence. They provide focused aid for portions of the design but allow for variability in the construction process. In this respect, the final artifact can be viewed as a collaboration between the maker and the stencil.

Schematics (Construction Assistance)

Both jig and stencil proxies provide some amount of physical assistance with the fabrication process. This assistance necessarily imposes some constraints on how the maker can interact with and manipulate the material. A schematic reduces the amount of physical assistance and instead provides a physical paper with the reference design printed *to-scale* that aids the user cognitively by providing a target design. While schematics are not novel (they act as simple instructions for the maker), they provide a different type of assistance than the other scaffolding proxies. By providing a clear feedback mechanism (evaluating your design as you make it against the piece of paper), schematics aid with a type of making termed "reflection-in-action" and is related to Schön's "reflective practice" [28]. In this view, making occurs between two actors, the user and the materials, and follows the pattern of entering into conversation with a problem, making a move, reflecting on what happened (letting the materials "talk back"), and repeating until convergence. In this framing, schematics enable the user to reflect on how the material responds to bends by evaluating the wire against the reference design. This reflection may produce insights (e.g., a bend needs to initially go past the desired angle to account for the springback of the metal). We provide additional annotations to facilitate the conversation: a) relevant measurements such as the length of the wire and the radii of curves (Figure 1c), b) construction geometries such as the bounding circles of curves, and c) axes of symmetry. By only providing a criteria for evaluation, the maker is free choose their own level of fidelity and workmanship.

DESIGN TOOL AND PROXY FABRICATION

All of the wire wrap designs and primitives shown in our paper were sourced from artisan handbooks [4] and community forums [2] and encoded as SVG drawings. Proxy generation was automated using an annotated SVG path as input. Using our web-based paper.js design tool, we can manipulate paths, specify materials, and add ornamentation (Figure 4). Our tool then produces a heightmap with appropriate walls, holes, and markings as detailed in previous sections to generate a 2.5D model. Proxies were printed using Fused Filament Fabrication (FFF) on a Type A Machine at 0.1 mm layer height using PLA polymer filament. For the proxies that include support and guide walls, we generated the wall geometry by creating offset paths on either side of the original SVG path, giving these offset paths a small constant width, and then extruding them upwards off the plane.

EVALUATION

We evaluated ProxyPrints in two ways. To validate the design of our material-driven proxies, we conducted an preliminary usability evaluation where participants performed specific wire-wrapping tasks with and without our proxies. We also ran a comparative evaluation between our three scaffold proxies to investigate how novice and expert users respond to different types of assistance.

[2]www.pinterest.com

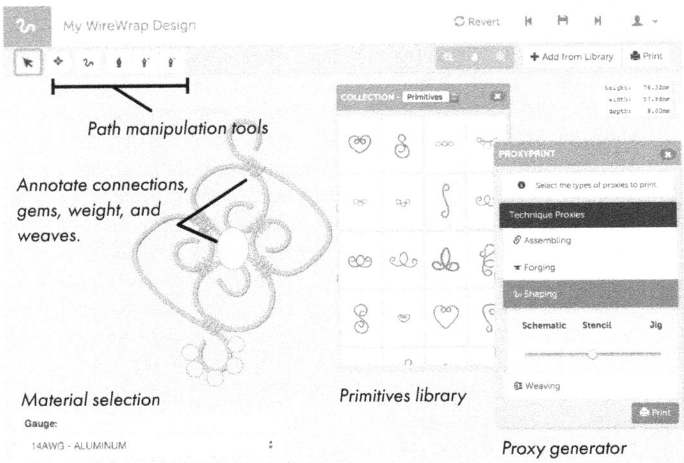

Figure 4. The ProxyPrint digital design tool for wire forms. Users can drag common forms onto a canvas, manipulate paths, specify materials, and add ornamentation and connections. The tool produces a heightmap used to generate a 2.5D printable proxy.

Experiment 1: Usability of material-driven Proxies

We recruited four participants through a mailing list and conducted a series of block randomized A/B tests. Each participant carried out four simple wrapping tasks (shaping, forging, connection, weaving) and for each of these tasks answered a series of questions about the usability, perceived speed, and preference of condition, and the preference of the final artifact design.

Shape task

For this task, we gave participants a reference design on-screen and asked them to shape a 16 AWG aluminum wire to match the design. Here, we compared our hill-climbing shaping proxy against the WrapIt jig[13]. Participants were able to complete the design task on average 1.5X faster using ProxyPrint and reported higher usablity and speed; all participants preferred using the ProxyPrint over the WrapIt jig. They also preferred the final 3D wire-wrapped artifacts that were created using ProxyPrint.

Forge task

We then asked participants a shape a wire using a hammer to match a reference weighted line drawing (Figure 3A) with and without our forging proxy. Participants reported a preference for using the hammer without the proxy since it became tedious to reposition the wire in the proxy. However, participants ended up preferring the end artifact created using the proxy, noticing fewer imperfections and a more pleasing aesthetic outcome.

Connect task

Next, we gave participants two heart shapes (depicted in Figure 2B) and asked them to connect them at a specified point with and without our connection proxy (Figure 2). Participants reported a large difference in usability (proxy = 4.5 ± 0.5, without = 1.5 ± 1.0). Without the proxy, participants struggled with accidentally exerting too much pressure on the coil and deforming the wire. In particular, participants worked 1.6X faster and reported higher confidence with the proxy; several participants reported having more control and tighter, cleaner connection coils. One participant expressed a willingness to take on more complex many-connection designs, but noted the limitation that wires need to be shaped precisely in order to fit in the proxy. All participants strongly preferred this proxy.

Weave task

In the final task, we gave participants a simple weaving task: with five frame wires, weave 20 rows of a simple pattern. Participants reported that it was much easier to secure the framing wires and start the weave with the proxy. All participants noted that the most critical stage is the first few rows, however they could not discern a large difference in the quality of their weaves beyond the first couple rows.

Experiment 2: Scaffold Proxy Evaluation

The main goal of this experiment was to obtain qualitative feedback on how different scaffold proxies affect the making process. We evaluated the scaffolds according to several metrics described in detail below. One of our goals was to compare the responses of novices and experts. We anticipated that the constrained nature of the shaping proxy would conflict with expert practice, while novices would likely prefer the higher degree of assistance. On the other hand, we felt that stencils and schematics would likely coincide with expert practice but provide too little scaffolding for novices.

Participants

We conducted the study with twelve participants — 6 experts and 6 novices. Expertise was determined from self-reported 5-point Likert values on experience with crafting, metal, jewelery, and digital design tools. Participants with an average experience greater than 3 were labeled experts. Participants were recruited from an internal mailing list at a large software company and the surrounding community via Craigslist. The average age of the participants was 32.3 ± 8 (8 female).

Procedure

Each session lasted one hour and consisted of a warm-up tutorial, three design tasks, and a post-study interview. Participants were seated at a work table with the following tools: ruler with mm/in, calipers, cutting mat, a rubber anvil and hammer, a permanent marker. Each participant was allowed to choose from three different-color spools of 16 gauge copper wire or 14 gauge aluminum. For each task, the following set of hand tools were made available: a flush cutter and [chain, barrel, taper, bent, nylon] – nose pliers.

In order to minimize newness effects, a small warm-up task introduced each tool and asked used to make an "S" shape with no constraint on size; participants were required to cut, straighten, and bend the wire into shape using any of the tools. Lastly, we demonstrated how to use a shaping proxy – specifically how to anchor a wire, follow the jig path, remove the wire, and flatten the final form with a rubber hammer. We then asked each participant to complete the same design task, but varied the type of scaffold proxy that they would be able to use. The ordering was block-randomized. Participants were also asked to reflect out-loud their thoughts on the tools, their design process, and specifically their plans for construction.

The design task was to construct the heart shape depicted in Figure 1. We chose this design since it is a common and recognizable shape that contains a mixture of sharp bends and smooth curves. Participants were allowed as much time to complete each task to their satisfaction. Lastly, each participant was instructed before beginning each task that they could deviate from the design; we only asked that the final design semiotically signify a heart.

Metrics

Previous HCI research on creativity support has introduced several ways of characterizing how physical tools can support creative practices [20, 30, 38]. We derived metrics from this body of work to evaluate the experience of using scaffolding proxies. We asked participants to rate their experience with each proxy using five-point semantically anchored Likert questions (1=Strongly Disagree, 5=Strongly Agree):

- **USABILITY** – The *proxy* was usable.
- **ERROR** – I made many errors using this *proxy*.
- **TRANSPARENCY** – I was not aware of the *proxy* when I was working with it.
- **CONTROL** – I had control of the wire using the *proxy*.
- **CREATIVITY** – I felt I had creative freedom with the *proxy*.
- **QUALITY** – I am happy with the final design.
- **AGENCY** – Given a *proxy*, I feel capable of making my own customized designs.

Note that **TRANSPARENCY** addresses the awareness of a tool during creative practice [20]. A highly transparent tool (e.g. keyboard) can act as a conduit; a less transparent tool (e.g. high-powered chainsaw) can add risk yet augment the workmanship potential of a craft.

We also looked at **FLOW** which describes absorption with the activity at hand [7] and is a common metric for engagement in games [6]. In design, flow can originate from complexity; the challenge and skill needed to execute a design becomes a source of personal enjoyment [29]. Various methods exist for assessing flow [8]; we focus on one factor of flow – temporary loss of time – which can be measured unobtrusively. We calculated **FLOW** as the difference between perceived and actual completion time. So if a participant completed a task in 11 minutes, and perceived it as 4 minutes, we would have a flow measure of –5 minutes. Lastly, participants were asked to rank the three designs in terms of speed and quality.

Analysis

We used a 2x3 factorial design with factors **EXPERIENCE** (novice, expert) and **PROXY** (schematic, stencil, jig) within-subjects. Each participant completed the same design using each of the proxy types. The order of the proxies was counterbalanced using a Latin square. Twelve participants completed 3 tasks each for a total of 36 tasks completed altogether. Due to a small sample size and semantically anchored scale data, we look at descriptive statistics.

RESULTS

Here, we summarize results and findings from Experiment 2. Overall, each session was unique and had widely varying completion times. Several participants deviated from the original design because of an error or took an opportunity to be creative. For reference, the completion time for each task was on average 7.8 ± 3.3 (**SCHEMATIC**), 10.4 ± 3.1 (**STENCIL**), 6.2 ± 2.0 (**JIG**) minutes. We first report quantitative results and then discuss interview responses in the context of specific observations and insights from the study.

FLOW, RANK SPEED and RANK QUALITY

For **FLOW**, we found that stencils had a noticeably larger negative effect on time perception[3] than schematics or jigs (Figure 6). This suggests that participants, especially experts, were more engaged and in a flow-state using stencils. Jigs on the otherhand had the opposite effect; experts found these less engaging. When experts used the jig, we also observed a positive effect on time perception, or less flow. Based on subjective responses in Figure 5, this is most likely associated with the higher level of scrutiny (**QUALITY**) that experts had on the near "automated" nature of the jig.

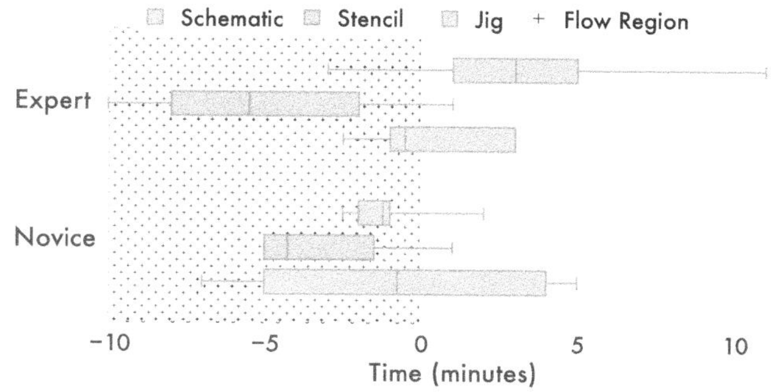

Figure 6. Flow as a measurement of engagement. The boxplot depict the difference in perceived and actual completion time. Areas in the texture '+' field indicate the participant lost track of time.

Participants were asked to rank on perceived speed and quality. The results (below) indicate that **JIGS** were consistently ranked higher than the other scaffolding proxies for both factors. Participants reported that their criteria for evaluating quality were symmetry, smoothness, and low marring.

RANK QUALITY	RANK SPEED
JIG (1.3 ± 0.8)	**JIG** (1.0 ± 0)
STENCIL (2.3 ± 0.5)	**STENCIL** (2.3 ± 0.5)
SCHEMATIC (2.4 ± 0.7)	**SCHEMATIC** (2.7 ± 0.5)

Observations and Insights

Our observations of making behavior and user responses led to some insights for future design tools for physical mediums.

Guaranteed success as sites of creativity

For many, the jig presented a safety net; upon seeing the form they vocalized complete confidence. This was a site for them to explore creative opportunities since they felt they were guaranteed that the base form would "come out". For those that did not deviate, the amount of guidance the jig gave them changed the narrative of agency. When responding to error, users attributed the error to the jig; whereas in the stencil and schematic condition, they blamed their own skill. One user vocalized that she did not view the jig as a tool:

[3]Time perception follows a *linear* Weber law with median $k = 0.77$ [1] which suggests that we would still see similar (albeit less profound) trends if we adjusted for perception error.

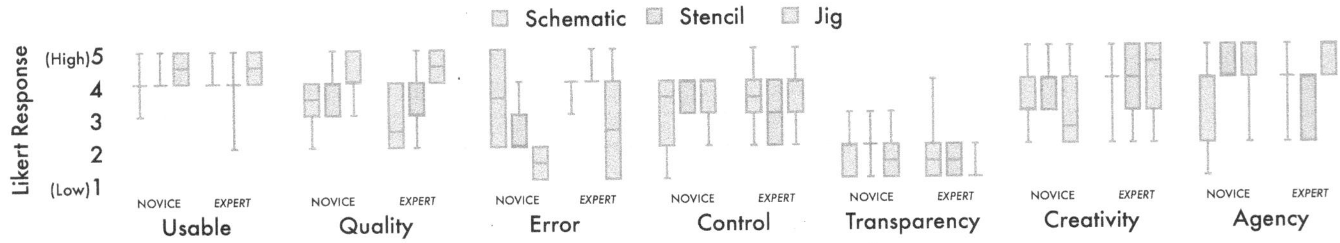

Figure 5. Scaffolding proxy evaluation responses. A simple design task is carried out by 6 expert and 6 novice participants for each proxy (schematic, stencil, and jig). Displayed are reported values for several creative tool metrics (bottom). Each metric is grouped based on Novice (N) or Expert (E) responses. Note the differences in Creativity using Jigs, Error, and Agency.

> **Novice #3**: I relied on my hands mostly, not the hand tools. For me, the jig was the hand part.

Furthermore, jig-made designs were subject to scrutiny. Slight imperfections in symmetry were viewed as major flaws, whereas in the other two conditions such asymmetry was embraced as a "handcrafted" look. Notably, experts had higher scrutiny of jig **ERROR** ($\bar{x}$= 2.7 $\pm$ 1.7) than novices ($\bar{x}$= 1.5 $\pm$ 0.5). This indicates that tools that are designed with more agency in the fabrication process bare the burden of error.

Cognitive offloading can support ritual

Some participants relished the ability to not have to think about how to construct the wire form.

> **Expert #4**: I could just loose myself in the jig. I am totally absorbed in it. I don't have to think; I just do what I tell it to do. I surrender to it.

One participant likened this workflow to the rhythmic mechanical repetitive movement of her hands when knitting garments.

Multiple cognitive entry points encourage deviation

A clear differentiation between expert and novice users was the ability to see multiple paths. For many, the proxies provided to them offered a clear and singular route to achieve the design. We hypothesized that the **JIG** would hinder creativity of expert users since it was so constrained to one design. However we were surprised at how expert users viewed the guiding walls and other superfluous elements as interesting deviation points.

> **Expert #2**: I dislike that I am only given one hole to anchor my design. I want holes everywhere. At the base of the path (Jig) and at the end. I want to start in a completely different place. I want these walls to end more symmetrically, and have gaps exactly the width of my wire, so I can use them in my design.

These participants went "off-the-path" and arrived at serendipitous designs that took advantage of non-design elements of the jig. than their novice counterparts ($\bar{x}$= 3.0 , σ= 1.3) with **JIGS**. Experts more readily deviated from the constrained design presented in the **JIG** and expressed greater creative freedom ($\bar{x}$= 4.0 $\pm$ 1.3). Novices, on the other hand, followed the **JIG** design, expressing less creative freedom than their counterparts ($\bar{x}$= 3.0 , σ= 1.3). However it was often the case that novices were, if successful, elated at being able to make a professional-looking form. Between both groups, participants expressed the felt the most capable in making future designs (**AGENCY**) with the **JIG** ($\bar{x}$= 4.5 $\pm$ 0.9), than the other proxies ($\bar{x}$= 3.6 $\pm$ 0.9), **SCHEMATIC**; ($\bar{x}$= 1.2 $\pm$ 0.9), **STENCIL**).

Expert behaviors: Forethought and tool-switching

Many novice participants needed to match each construction step to visually approach the final design. As such, if an element was accidentally misplaced, it would immediately be corrected. This behavior was most noticeable using the **SCHEMATIC**. Since the schematic was to-scale, many participants bent wire directly on top of the schematic and used it to frame and "sanity check" their design. When accidentally displacing an element, users found that they had more confidence in returning it to the correct form. Participants using this proxy constantly verified form and felt higher risk working with their hands. Several participants expressed a similar sentiment for deciding when to stop, likening the wire to becoming stale.

> **Novice #1**: I always worry about the symmetric part. Thats when I didn't have control. I was particularly intimidated by [hand tools]. Hand tools are so free form. The jig I could handle. I just had to follow the form. With the hand tools [schematic], I didn't know where to begin. I realized that I had to minimize the amount of contact I had with the wire.

We noticed a delay in this match-step behavior with expert participants. Notably, experts were more prone to make movements meant for making fabricating the shape easier:

> **Expert #3**: I'm not going to worry about that now. I know that I can make it look fine in the end; I need to focus instead on these end loops first.

From think-outloud transcripts, we noted general differences amongst proxies over the type of thinking participants exhibited. Participants using the **JIG** exhibited passive thinking, succeeding agency to the jig.

> **Novice #1**: I'm just going to go around and around the jig, letting it guide me to where I need to go.

Conversely, **STENCILS** elicited in-the-moment thinking, or responding to events as they happened. This was evident in the amount of tool-switching that occurred as participants varied their working style based on the current state of the wire. Lastly, **SCHEMATICS** elicited more active, forward thinking, or planning actions based on anticipated outcomes. Forward-thinking was primarily observed when participants realized that they had to achieve symmetry without any aid. Only then did we see behaviors that purposely started with the crease in the heart design, before moving onto the curves and loops on the ends of the wire.

Figure 7. Construction patterns were highly dependent on the first scaffold that was presented to participants. Schematic-first users moved with step-wise similarity, jig-first followed a linear progression, while stencil-first compartmentalized forms – an expert trait.

Novice behaviors: Construction fixation

We observed high variability in how users constructed their design in the SCHEMATIC condition, and detail some notable construction patterns depicted in Figure 7. Participants who started with the schematic condition moved closer to the final design with each step. However, if a step did not bring the design closer to the desired form, these users would become more apprehensive and stop manipulating the wire as freely. Participants who started with the jig followed a linear construction pattern, often being unable to allocate enough material to successfully achieve symmetry. Lastly, participants who started with the stencil compartmentalized their construction, creating the complex loops before creating the bend thereby minimizing the amount of interaction between different components of the design. This approach had a higher chance of achieving symmetry. This priming effect suggests a construction fixation, or a cognitive bias that limits a person to construct a design in a prescribed way. This presents a unique opportunity for the design of making tools: *construction methodologies can be influenced by computational proxies to encourage expert best practices.*

LIMITATIONS

Our study targeted the fabrication phase of a simple design in a limited time frame. While our evaluation metrics provided a profile of the making experience, we recognize a need for assessing how embodied skills and experiential pleasure develop. The study does provide insights into the onboarding phase of design tools — a critical phase for novice users getting acquainted with a process.

DISCUSSION

Future tools need to be able to incorporate the user back into the design cycle in order for users to develop an understanding of the material and engage users to deviate from templates. Our approach strikes a subtle balance of handed and digital fabrication; we show how this balance can promote exploratory behaviors through stencils, encourage design deviations using ambiguous entry points, communicate tacit knowledge through ordering. ProxyPrint offers an alternative trajectory for DF tools, specifically one that foregrounds making intermediary tools that aid users in fabrication.

In the case of maker communities that openly share designs, the room for deviation for novices is dependent on the familiarity of the tools available to them. Scaffolding is especially relevant to empowering novice users to create their own designs. To encourage deviation, we found it necessary to explicitly mark alternative forms and visualize ambiguous designs. For instance, a parametrized STL model of a vase can "ghost" its design space, indicating to the user the multiplicity of forms that can exist.

The level of automation in a scaffold is particularly important to how makers might assess their work. As we saw in ProxyPrint, providing too much fabrication assistance shifts the burden of error to the machine, whereas when the error is shared by the maker and the machine a "handed" synergy exists. Providing consistent feedback is important for novices who we observed had less of a basis for evaluating whether their construction patterns are "correct"; providing a guaranteed success can mediate this initial experience as evaluation criteria develops. In this context, design tools can present a task with a ground truth for users to compare against during their initial experiences with a material. While frustration is common in the design process, certain areas of a design can purposely be made to instill pleasure. We found that ritualizing an action, or offloading cognitive effort with a repetitive manual task, can support crafting practice.

We showed that with a medium-aware design that takes into account the unique properties and cultural histories of materials, we can make proxies that assist, enhance, and extend the wire-wrap medium. Other domains can benefit from such passive proxies, for instance, a ceramics proxy practice might involve stencils that form lathe bits for use with a pottery wheel. Because of the *passive* nature of proxies, participants found value in a proxy's non-intrusiveness and proposed a practice which follows: sketching an idea and "wrestling the material"; converting interesting forms into stencils; and refining this into a final artifact. It is imprudent to disregard the new cultural histories that are arising from DF machines; works such as *Filament Sculptures* [18] that creates 3D forms from a 3D printer's characteristic extrusion demonstrate the gray area that exists between what is a tool and what is a material.

CONCLUSION

In ProxyPrint, we expanded the expressibility of computational wire-working through forging, connection, and weaving proxies. We identified that proxies can exist on a spectrum of support and design three scaffolding proxies (schematic, stencil, and jig) that capture points along this spectrum. We characterize these proxies through common measures in hybrid crafting, and evaluate them in a formal user study. We show that our supports impact quality and speed, and differ between experts and novices. We contribute design principles for facilitating both expert and novice practice and engaging users with the medium.

ACKNOWLEDGMENTS

We thank the anonymous reviewers for their insightful comments. This research was supported by Adobe Research and NSF Grant No. IIS–1451465.

REFERENCES

1. Lorraine G Allan. 1979. The perception of time. *Perception & Psychophysics* 26, 5 (1979), 340–354.
2. Shaowen Bardzell, Daniela K. Rosner, and Jeffrey Bardzell. 2012. Crafting quality in design: integrity, creativity, and public sensibility. In *Proceedings of the Designing Interactive Systems Conference*. ACM, 11–20. http://dl.acm.org/citation.cfm?id=2317959
3. Luca Benedetti, Holger Winnemller, Massimiliano Corsini, and Roberto Scopigno. 2014. Painting with Bob: Assisted Creativity for Novices. In *Proceedings of the 27th Annual ACM Symposium on User Interface Software and Technology (UIST '14)*. ACM, New York, NY, USA, 419–428. DOI: http://dx.doi.org/10.1145/2642918.2647415
4. Jodi Bombardier. 2013. *Artisan filigree: wire-wrapping jewelry techniques and projects*. Interweave.
5. Amy Cheatle and Steven J. Jackson. 2015. Digital Entanglements: Craft, Computation and Collaboration in Fine Art Furniture Production. In *Proc. of CSCW (CSCW '15)*. ACM, 958–968. DOI: http://dx.doi.org/10.1145/2675133.2675291
6. Jenova Chen. 2007. Flow in Games (and Everything else). *Commun. ACM* 50, 4 (April 2007), 31–34. DOI: http://dx.doi.org/10.1145/1232743.1232769
7. Mihaly Csikszentmihalyi. 1990. *Flow: The psychology of optimal experience.* New York: Harper & Row.
8. Mihaly Csikszentmihalyi and Reed Larson. 1987. Validity and reliability of the Experience-Sampling Method. *The Journal of nervous and mental disease* 175, 9 (1987), 526–536.
9. Laura Devendorf and Kimiko Ryokai. 2015. Being the Machine: Reconfiguring Agency and Control in Hybrid Fabrication. In *Proc. of the SIGCHI (CHI '15)*. ACM, 2477–2486. DOI: http://dx.doi.org/10.1145/2702123.2702547
10. Yohsuke Furuta, Nobuyuki Umetani, Jun Mitani, Takeo Igarashi, and Yukio Fukui. 2010. A film balloon design system integrated with shell element simulation. *Proc. of Eurographics* (2010). http://www.jst.go.jp/erato/igarashi/projects/balloon/balloon.pdf
11. Shad Gross, Jeffrey Bardzell, and Shaowen Bardzell. 2014. Structures, Forms, and Stuff: The Materiality and Medium of Interaction. *Personal Ubiquitous Comput.* 18, 3 (March 2014), 637–649. DOI: http://dx.doi.org/10.1007/s00779-013-0689-4
12. Kristian Hildebrand, Bernd Bickel, and Marc Alexa. 2012. crdbrd: Shape Fabrication by Sliding Planar Slices. In *Proc. of Eurographics*.
13. Emmanuel Iarussi and Wilmot Li. 2015. WrapIt: Computational Jigs for Wire Wrapping. In *Proc. of SIGGRAPH Asia*.
14. Yuki Igarashi and Takeo Igarashi. 2009. Designing Plush Toys with a Computer. *Commun. ACM* 52, 12 (Dec. 2009), 81–88. DOI: http://dx.doi.org/10.1145/1610252.1610275
15. Jennifer Jacobs and Leah Buechley. 2013. Codeable objects: computational design and digital fabrication for novice programmers. In *Proc. CHI*. 1589–1598. http://dl.acm.org/citation.cfm?id=2466211
16. Tom Jenkins. 2013. Devotional Gardening Tools. In *CHI '13 Extended Abstracts on Human Factors in Computing Systems (CHI EA '13)*. ACM, New York, NY, USA, 2219–2226. DOI: http://dx.doi.org/10.1145/2468356.2468743
17. Scott R. Klemmer, Bjrn Hartmann, and Leila Takayama. 2006. How Bodies Matter: Five Themes for Interaction Design. In *Proceedings of the 6th Conference on Designing Interactive Systems (DIS '06)*. ACM, New York, NY, USA, 140–149. DOI: http://dx.doi.org/10.1145/1142405.1142429
18. LIA. 2014. Filament Sculptures. http://www.liaworks.com/theprojects/filament-sculptures/
19. Leah Maestri and Ron Wakkary. 2011. Understanding Repair As a Creative Process of Everyday Design. In *Proceedings of the 8th ACM Conference on Creativity and Cognition (C&C '11)*. ACM, New York, NY, USA, 81–90. DOI: http://dx.doi.org/10.1145/2069618.2069633
20. Malcolm McCullough. 1998. *Abstracting Craft : The Practice Digital Hand.* The MIT Press.
21. Bakhtiar Mikhak, Fred Martin, Mitchel Resnik, Robert Berg, and Brian Silverman. 1999. The Children's Machines: Handheld and Wearable Computers Too. In *Proc. of the 1st International Symposium on Handheld and Ubiquitous Computing (HUC '99)*. Springer-Verlag, 31–43. http://dl.acm.org/citation.cfm?id=647985.743715
22. Michael Nitsche, Andrew Quitmeyer, Kate Farina, Samuel Zwaan, and Hye Yeon Nam. 2014. Teaching Digital Craft. In *CHI '14 Extended Abstracts on Human Factors in Computing Systems (CHI EA '14)*. ACM, 719–730. DOI: http://dx.doi.org/10.1145/2559206.2578872
23. Huaishu Peng, Amit Zoran, and Franois V. Guimbretire. 2015. D-Coil: A Hands-on Approach to Digital 3D Models Design. In *Proc. of SIGCHI (CHI '15)*. ACM, 1807–1815. DOI: http://dx.doi.org/10.1145/2702123.2702381
24. Andrew Polaine. 2005. The Flow Principle in Interactivity. In *Proc. of Interactive Entertainment'05 (IE '05)*. Creativity & Cognition Studios Press, 151–158. http://dl.acm.org/citation.cfm?id=1109180.1109204
25. Mitchel Resnick. 1993. Behavior Construction Kits. *Commun. ACM* 36, 7 (July 1993), 64–71. DOI: http://dx.doi.org/10.1145/159544.159593

26. Alec Rivers, Andrew Adams, and Frdo Durand. 2012. Sculpting by Numbers. *ACM Trans. Graph.* 31, 6 (Nov. 2012), 157:1–157:7. DOI: http://dx.doi.org/10.1145/2366145.2366176

27. Daniela K. Rosner, Miwa Ikemiya, and Tim Regan. 2015. Resisting Alignment: Code and Clay. In *Proceedings of the Ninth International Conference on Tangible, Embedded, and Embodied Interaction (TEI '15)*. ACM, New York, NY, USA, 181–188. DOI: http://dx.doi.org/10.1145/2677199.2680587

28. Donald A Schön. 1983. *The reflective practitioner: How professionals think in action*. Vol. 5126. Basic books.

29. Erik Stolterman. 2008. The nature of design practice and implications for interaction design research. *International Journal of Design* 2, 1 (2008), 55–65.

30. Michael Terry and Elizabeth D. Mynatt. 2002. Recognizing Creative Needs in User Interface Design. In *Proc. of the 4th Conference on Creativity & Cognition (C&C '02)*. ACM, 38–44. DOI: http://dx.doi.org/10.1145/581710.581718

31. Jakob Tholander, Maria Normark, and Chiara Rossitto. 2012. Understanding Agency in Interaction Design Materials. In *Proc. of the SIGCHI (CHI '12)*. ACM, 2499–2508. DOI: http://dx.doi.org/10.1145/2207676.2208417

32. Cesar Torres and Eric Paulos. 2015. MetaMorphe: Designing Expressive 3D Models for Digital Fabrication. In *Proceedings of the 2015 ACM SIGCHI Conference on Creativity and Cognition (C&C '15)*. ACM, New York, NY, USA, 73–82. DOI: http://dx.doi.org/10.1145/2757226.2757235

33. Nobuyuki Umetani, Danny M. Kaufman, Takeo Igarashi, and Eitan Grinspun. 2011. Sensitive Couture for Interactive Garment Modeling and Editing. In *ACM SIGGRAPH 2011 Papers (SIGGRAPH '11)*. ACM, New York, NY, USA, 90:1–90:12. DOI: http://dx.doi.org/10.1145/1964921.1964985

34. Karl D.D. Willis, Cheng Xu, Kuan-Ju Wu, Golan Levin, and Mark D. Gross. 2011. Interactive Fabrication: New Interfaces for Digital Fabrication. In *Proc. of TEI (TEI '11)*. ACM, 69–72. DOI: http://dx.doi.org/10.1145/1935701.1935716

35. Jun Xie, Aaron Hertzmann, Wilmot Li, and Holger Winnemller. 2014. PortraitSketch: Face Sketching Assistance for Novices. In *Proceedings of the 27th Annual ACM Symposium on User Interface Software and Technology (UIST '14)*. ACM, New York, NY, USA, 407–417. DOI: http://dx.doi.org/10.1145/2642918.2647399

36. Mayu M. Yamashita, Junichi Yamaoka, and Yasuaki Kakehi. 2013. Enchanted Scissors: A Scissor Interface for Support in Cutting and Interactive Fabrication. In *ACM SIGGRAPH 2013 Posters (SIGGRAPH '13)*. ACM, 33:1–33:1. DOI: http://dx.doi.org/10.1145/2503385.2503422

37. Amit Zoran. 2013. Hybrid Basketry: Interweaving Digital Practice Within Contemporary Craft. In *ACM SIGGRAPH 2013 Art Gallery (SIGGRAPH '13)*. ACM, New York, NY, USA, 324–331. DOI: http://dx.doi.org/10.1145/2503649.2503651

38. Amit Zoran, Roy Shilkrot, Suranga Nanyakkara, and Joseph Paradiso. 2014. The Hybrid Artisans: A Case Study in Smart Tools. *ACM Trans. Comput.-Hum. Interact.* 21, 3 (June 2014), 15:1–15:29. DOI: http://dx.doi.org/10.1145/2617570

Probing the Potential of Post-Anthropocentric 3D Printing

Laura Devendorf[1], Abigail De Kosnik[2], Kate Mattingly[2], Kimiko Ryokai[1]

[1] School of Information
UC Berkeley
Berkeley, CA, USA
{ldevendorf, kimiko}@berkeley.edu

[2] Theater, Dance, and Performance Studies
UC Berkeley
Berkeley, CA, USA
{adekosnik, katematt}@berkeley.edu

ABSTRACT
The growth of small scale manufacturing technologies associated with the "maker movement" has captured the attention of artists, innovators, educators, and policy makers. This paper critically examines how one core technology of the maker movement, a 3D printer, materializes assumptions about makers and their preferred ways of working with machines and materials. We describe how existing designs can be seen as anthropocentric, framing the human maker as visionary and commander of passive machines and materials. We then present an alternative system for 3D printing, called *Redeform*, which explores how a post-anthropocentric framing of makers as collaborators with machines and materials changes the design of 3D printers. We place our system within a lineage of performances that have explored relationships between humans and nonhumans since the 1950s. In doing so, we explore and speculate on the opportunities for operationalizing post-anthropocentric theories within the specific context of the maker movement.

Author Keywords
Maker movement; digital fabrication; new materialisms; indeterminacy; resistance; performance art.

ACM Classification Keywords
K.4.0. Computers in Society: general.

INTRODUCTION
The so-called "maker movement" has emerged from the combination of new developments in grassroots manufacturing technology with a body of potential users eager to make their own products, designs, trinkets, and tools. Dale Dougherty, founder of *Make* magazine, attributes the growth of the maker movement to factors including "the introduction of new technologies such as 3D printing" and "hyper-local efforts to convene those who share common goals" [11]. The technologies of the movement, specifically 3D printers, have captured the attention of artists, educators and policy makers alike. The appeal of 3D printing for artists includes the ability to physically realize unimaginable structures and forms created through generative coding. For educators and policy makers, exciting new machines for making things are looked upon as a means for motivating young students to pursue careers in science, technology, engineering, and mathematics.

A "maker" is someone who shares a "do-it-yourself" work ethic. Dougherty writes, "makers are seeking an alternative to being regarded as consumers, rejecting the idea that you are defined by what you buy" [11]. By identifying makers by a shared set of values rather than specific technical skills or practices, the rhetoric of the maker movement promotes inclusivity and suggests that the doors to the movement are open to all who share its do-it-yourself spirit. Often, "joining" the movement entails participation within a maker community, whether it is a digital community like instructables.com or a physical space like a shared machine shop, hacklab, or maker space. In the case of physical communities, access to fabrication machines serves as a locus to unite people of varying interests and backgrounds.

While most hacklabs and makerspaces claim to be neutral spaces for makers of all backgrounds and interests, the politics of participation are more complicated as some forms of working are seen to be more legitimate or technically sophisticated than others. Toombs et al. describe barriers to access in hackerspaces as "sociological," relating to how someone fits in with the existing culture of the space [29]. Feminist hacker spaces like Double Union in San Francisco can be seen as a response to sociological barriers of access. These spaces have come into being to address the specific interests and styles of working shared by women – interests like identity workshops or sketching that the founders of Double Union found to be marginal at traditional hackerspaces [12,16].

Reflection on participation in the maker movement has tended to focus on the accessibility of particular technologies or the social dynamics of physical spaces. We shift focus to the *technologies* of making and examine how their workflows embody and reinforce a particular set of values in making. Specifically, we examine how the design of a 3D printer, a technology that is central to the rise of the

DIS 2016, June 04-08, 2016, Brisbane, QLD, Australia
ACM 978-1-4503-4031-1/16/06.
http://dx.doi.org/10.1145/2901790.2901879

maker movement, allows for particular values in design, like accurate replication, to be expressed while making other values, such as close interactions with materials, more difficult.

BACKGROUND

The Politics of 3D Printers

Scholars in science and technology studies and related fields have described the how technological artifacts express politics and materialize the ethics and viewpoints of the stakeholders who contribute to their design [21,31,32]. Critical technical practice is an approach developed by Agre to surface the politics embedded in designs and to describe their effects on human experiences [1]. As an exercise in critical technical practice, this paper unpacks existing assumptions about makers that are built into the design of 3D printers and then reimagines the design by drawing from an alternative set of assumptions. Specifically, we identify existing designs as anthropocentric and we draw from theories associated with the new materialisms [7] in order to suggest a post-anthropocentric design for a 3D printer. Our goal is *not* to offer a design to replace existing 3D printers or to suggest incremental improvements to existing designs, but to highlight the biases of 3D printers: the kinds of making that are more or less difficult and the relationships with materials that are and are not supported. For instance, existing 3D printer designs make it difficult to physically manipulate a structure as the machine is building. One could argue that such a design is biased towards users who value accuracy and efficiency rather than those who prefer a process that recognizes the value of errors in disclosing new approaches. By calling existing design norms into question, we offer a lens through which one can reflect on the relationship between fabrication systems design and participation in the maker movement. We shed light on how a designer's conceptualization of the value of making is enacted in design and how these value judgments ultimately reinforce or challenge norms around what it means to be a "maker."

The Changing Landscape of Fabrication

Researchers in and out of HCI have developed innovative fabrication technologies that allow makers to work with computationally specified instructions without compromising close engagements with materials [10,26–28,35]. This paper analyzes one such technology, Redeform (previously named "Being the Machine" [10]), to provide a broader theoretical framework for thinking about how such projects shape relationships between makers, technologies, and materials.

This paper synthesizes and expands upon two previous projects. The first, titled "Being the Machine" presented technical descriptions and accounts of user experiences with what we refer to here as Redeform [10]. We highlighted how dealing with resistance and/or unpredictable materials was a core value in the practices of many makers and argued that technology can play other roles in making beyond preventing failure and producing accurate models. The second was an exploration of how themes expressed in performance art could be engaged in the design of fabrication systems [9], in order to highlight how situated actions, in addition to objects, can be the locus of meaning in fabrication activities.

This paper offers a deeper reflection on the connections between new materialist theory, post-WWII performances, and fabrication systems design that have emerged out of Devendorf's own artistic practices with Redeform over the past 20 months. In doing so, this piece takes a step back to reflect on how HCI thinks about values of makers and making and how those values inevitably shape the technologies we build. The goal of this work is to provide researchers with intellectual resources that help them critically examine the way digital fabrication systems structure relationships between humans, machines, and materials. Since enthusiasm about the maker movement is already impacting education and culture, attention to the politics and priorities embedded in this movement need to be analyzed and acknowledged in order to ensure that a diversity of making systems and making styles are being offered and honored.

In the paper that follows, we summarize two contrasting theoretical positions, hylomorphism and morphogenesis, to understand what making is and the specific ways in which forms come into being through making. We describe how existing 3D printer designs can be seen as hylomorphic and draw from a contrasting theory of morphogenesis to suggest a new kind of 3D printer. We discuss our design within a lineage of performance art in order to paint a speculative vision of the experiential and aesthetic implications of interacting with a fabrication system designed through the lens of morphogenesis. Drawing from our design, performance processes, and new materialist theory, we conclude by describing the kind of maker we aim to support, the particular values they may share, and how we might make room for these values in the maker movement.

ANTHROPOCENTRISM AND 3D PRINTERS

While making always results in a form, various theories describe how that form comes into being. Some theories can be classified as anthropocentric, framing the human maker as the primary factor determining form while others can be described as post- or non-anthropocentric, framing form as something that emerges from complex negotiations between humans, tools, materials, and environments. Hylomorphism is an anthropocentric theory in which form is believed to be determined independently of material forces [8,18]. In anthropologist Tim Ingold's terms, "Whenever we read that in the making of artefacts, practitioners impose forms internal to the mind upon a material world 'out there', hylomorphism is at work" [18]. A hallmark of hylomorphism, and anthropocentrism more broadly, is the belief in the passivity of matter. With passive matter, an idea can be faithfully translated into an object with little change arising within the process of translation.

To understand 3D printers as hylomorphic, one must first understand how a 3D printer works. A 3D printer is a kind of machine within a broad category of computer-numeric controlled (CNC) machines. CNC machines and their associated software translate digital models into a list of instructions that a machine can perform to create a physical version of that digital model. The language used to specify the movements (what are technically referred to as tool-paths) of these machines is called G-Code. G-Code offers a standard set of codes to tell machines things like where to move, how fast to move, and, depending on the machine, where to add or remove material. Creating the mechanics and algorithms for translating a digital model into a list of G-Code instructions intended for a particular machine is a key design challenge when developing CNC technologies. Currently, the heuristic that has driven development in CNC machines, including 3D printers, has been fidelity to the original digital model.

The focus on accurate replication of a pre-existing model makes the designers of CNC systems seek to eliminate all sources of uncertainty that may potentially alter the form from what has been specified digitally. In other words, it drives designers to identify methods to tame the material world so that it will passively take on any shape or form. Such a vision of passive materials is reflected in the rhetoric of engineer and maker movement evangelist Neil Gershenfeld, who imagines that, “personal fabrication will bring the programmability of the digital worlds we’ve invented to the physical world we inhabit” [13]. While this vision has certainly ushered in powerful new innovations, forms, and processes of creation, it is also one that frames the human maker as the locus of innovation and creativity and their building materials as passive receptors or containers for makers’ ideas—an idea we believe limits the design space of 3D printing for two primary reasons.

First, commercial 3D printers tame the material world by limiting building materials to those that have been engineered to readily take on many shapes and forms. For example, MakerBot® 3D printers are designed to work specifically with acrylonitrile butadiene styrene (ABS) or polylactic acid (PLA) filaments. One of the primary advantages of 3D printing is the ability to realize a form that was created digitally, perhaps using generative computational means to create once unimaginable forms, and to use that form as a basis for the production of a material object. Yet, the flexibility to change structures and forms with code or computer aided design tools is far greater than the flexibility one has when the design “leaves” the digital world so to speak and enters the physical world. The physical world is full of materials with broad ranging shapes, properties, behaviors, and textures that can be engaged in making to lend particular qualities to the form produced. By embracing the unique and lively characteristics of everyday materials, from sticks and leaves to candy or carrots, we see an opportunity to produce a set of hybrid computational-material forms with textural, aesthetic, and symbolic characteristics vastly different than those created from filaments used in traditional 3D printers.

Second, attempting to pacify building materials for the sake of accurate replication limits the experiential range of 3D printers. Currently, the idealized experience of commercial 3D printing involves setting up the printing environment and hitting “go,” at which point the machine takes over and the human is free to pursue other projects. While such an approach is ideal in terms of efficiency and multitasking, it removes the human from the process of making, preventing them from developing sensitivity to the materials though touch and feeling them as they mold or resist particular forms. By developing a rich intuition about the way in which building materials adapt to 3D printing processes, one may begin to imagine novel ways of reworking both processes and materials in order to develop ideas for future forms. Furthermore, continued care, experimentation, and growth with a set of materials can form the basis of a sustained relationship with materials that many find pleasurable and even therapeutic. By augmenting 3D processes to accommodate rich sensory experiences, we see opportunities to extend the ways in which one can bring computation in tandem with physical materials.

As we describe the limitations of hylomorphic design ideals, it is important to consider that while technology *shapes* interaction, it does not script or specifically determine the way in which a maker might think, feel, or do certain things [22,33]. Accordingly, a CNC machine designed from a hylomorphic perspective does not imply that a maker’s actions with the machine could also be described as hylomorphic. All interactions with machines are constrained and users are always negotiating their desires with a machine’s functionality. What most makers describe as a “successful” 3D print, in the sense that it produces what they expect, emerges only after multiple attempts, tweaks, and adjustments have been made to control unpredictability on the users’ end. For instance, the ABS plastic filaments used by many 3D printers tend to curl in on themselves at sharp corners, requiring the user to add extra support structures or “helper discs” to her model to keep the corners firmly affixed to the building surface. Additionally, the heat sensitive materials used for 3D printing act less predictably when the temperature of the environment is not controlled, say, when the printer is placed near a sunny window.

To summarize, while a designer’s imagined workflow of 3D printing may be hylomorphic, the reality of 3D printing is anything but: 3D printing, like all craft, forces the maker to contend with stubborn recalcitrance and unpredictability of the material world. A non-hylomorphic design approach frames material recalcitrance and unpredictability as *beneficial* aspects to explore within interactions with the technology, rather than aspects to be eliminated by technology. It shifts human labor from attempting to control the printing environment to sensing the materials and finding new and exciting ways to open the production process to material forces. For instance, melting, which might be caused from a printer being too close to a sunny window, can shift from being regarded as a problem or nuisance to new and interesting force that offers a potentially beautiful dripping texture to be crafted.

There are many ways that makers can (and do) embrace the recalcitrance and unpredictable aspects of existing 3D printers. Thus, a non-hylomorphic design approach may offer different benefits for different audiences. For people who may not see resistant or recalcitrant materials as creative resources, non-hylomorphic designs could scaffold workflows that may change their perception. For people who already value working with stubborn materials, non-hylomorphic designs create spaces for unique encounters with digital and physical materials that might not have emerged from explorations with existing 3D printers.

TOWARDS MORPHOGENETIC MACHINES

As we stated above, a non-hylomorphic 3D printer frames building materials as entities to be harnessed and adapted in order to discover new forms rather than facilitators for realizing our pre-existing ideas. A desire to work *with* stubborn materials in fabrication is represented by a growing number of hacked or self-built 3D printing systems that use uncommon materials [23,30] or playfully derivate from input models [20]. We see these actions as evidence for a desire to work beyond a model of human mastery over machines, since these actions seek a more open ended, even collaborative relationship with a rich set of materials and machines. Such an approach to design could be described as morphogenetic.

Morphogenesis offers a contrasting theory to hylomorphism: one in which form is not determined a priori, but emerges from a nexus of activity between human and nonhuman actors [8,18]. Drawing from Deleuze's use of the term, DeLanda writes, "We may now be in a position to think about the origin of form and structure, not as something imposed from the outside on an inert matter, not as a hierarchical command from above as in an assembly line, but as something that may come from within the materials, a form that we tease out of those materials as we allow them to have their say in the structures we create" [8]. Materials, in this view, take an *active* role in determining the form that emerges. Tim Ingold relates morphogenesis specifically to the way in which humans make things and uses the term "correspondence" to describe a relationship between humans and their nonhuman tool and material counterparts [18]. In the process of making, humans enter into correspondence with materials as well as the broader world within which they are working. Materials "speak" in this correspondence through their physical properties, pushing towards and pulling against a maker's actions. Ingold argues that form can never fully be determined, only anticipated by a maker working in correspondence with his or her materials.

Thus far we have argued that hylomorphism in design can be limiting and suggested a morphogenetic perspective in design as a way to embrace the "activity," unpredictability, and stubbornness of materials in making. As the examples above show, some creative practitioners have already embraced such an approach in the design of 3D printing systems for their personal use, though not calling their design approach morphogenesis as such[1]. In the following section, we will describe a system we built in order ask how the specific theoretical framing of morphogenesis and concept of correspondence might push the design of 3D printers in an even more radical direction, uncovering new formal and experiential spaces that emerge through indeterminate engagements with machines and materials in specific spaces. By placing this work in relationship to the maker movement, we explore values in making that may be uniquely addressed by such an approach.

REDEFORM

Designed by Devendorf and Ryokai, Redeform (formerly "Being the Machine" [10]) is a system that asks humans to receive, interpret, and execute the G-Code instructions typically provided to a 3D printer in order to construct new objects, reversing the scenario of 3D printing, in which humans provide instructions to a printer that the machine must carry out. In essence, Redeform makes the human user into a 3D printer. Technically, Redeform consists of a laser pointer that illuminates a single dot on a surface. The dot moves along the tool-paths generated from a digital model that the human has inputted, showing the human how a 3D printer would lay down material and inviting them to follow by hand. For the human, this feels like a game of connect-the-dots. Upon completion of the task "described" by the laser pointer, the human has sculpted a three-dimensional object more or less like the digital model they specified. The materials used by humans to craft objects with the Redeform system have ranged from flowers to Cheez Whiz to pipe cleaners to balloons.

To use Redeform, the user creates or selects a 3D model that she would like to use as a starting point for interaction (figure 1a). The 3D model is processed through an open source G-Code generator called Slic3r [21] to convert it into a list of machine instructions. G-Code instructions for

[1] The concept of morphogenesis and its relationship to CNC manufacturing technologies has been a growing area of exploration in architecture. Much of this work applies concepts of morphogenesis to the architectural design processes and makes use of existing CNC technologies to realize those designs. In this article, we advocate a similar approach in relation to interaction design, asking how morphogenesis can be mobilized to foster new kind of technology and experiences with those technologies.

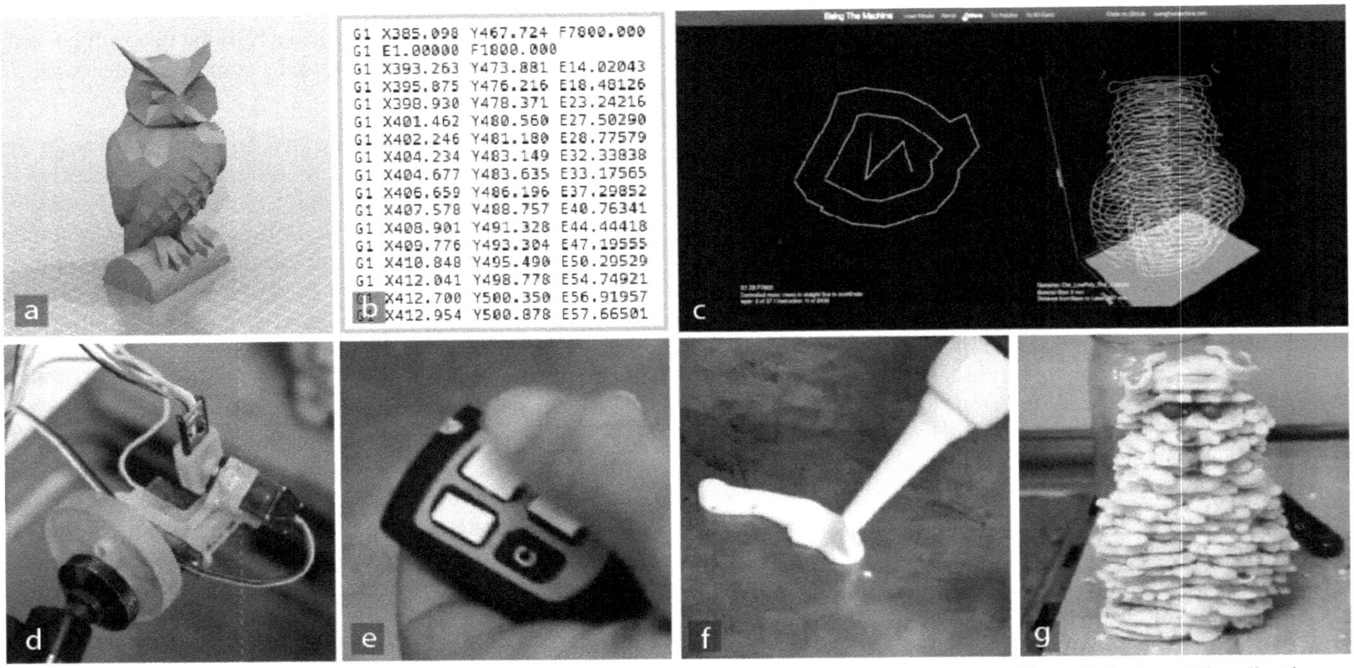

Figure 1: Working with Redeform. a. A 3D model of an owl is selected. b. The model is converted into G-Code. c. Visualization software allows the user to view the G-Code paths generated. d. Once the user finds the paths suitable, she can upload the G-Code to the Redeform machine, a laser pointer attached to 2 motors in a pan-tilt configuration. e. She presses buttons on a key-fob to tell the machine to play or stop playing through machine instructions. f. She sees instructions as a single laser point and follows the point with pancake batter on a hot skillet. g. After she follows all the paths described by the laser pointer, an object emerges.

many 3D printers are created by virtually slicing a 3D model into layers and converting each layer into a series of paths that can be drawn with a mechanical extruder (figure 1b). A 3D printer draws the layers one on top of the other to recreate the object. When translating a model to G-Code with Slic3r, the user is able to specify parameters such as material height and width, which affect the way the G-Code paths are specified. We created software that allows the user to visualize the G-Code paths generated from Slic3r so that she can get a sense of the movements that the model will be asking her to perform (figure 1c). After creating a G-Code file to her liking, she uploads it to our machine (figure 1d). She interacts with the machine using a key-fob with buttons that allow her to play forward, play backward, and stop the machine (figure 1e). If she pushes the play forward button, the laser point begins drawing from the current G-Code instruction to the next subsequent G-Code instructions. The user experiences this by seeing the laser point move along a path. Playing backward allows the user to do the same action in reverse. Pressing the stop button allows the user to stop the laser at its current position. By following the laser point with her materials (figure 1f), the user produces a series of paths and layers that begin to look more or less like her input model (figure 1g).

After conducting several user studies with Redeform [10] we found that one key design feature encouraged users to embrace qualities like indeterminacy and emergence characteristic of a morphogenetic perspective on making: following a single laser point. Redeform could have been designed using an alternate set of tools and techniques. For instance, a projector could have projected an entire outlined path, rather than a single point, which would have been easier to trace accurately. We made a strategic design decision *not* to use a projector for three primary reasons.

First, we wanted to encourage interpretation and emergence, not replication. A closed path tends to connote a need to be precisely copied or filled in, but a single moving point has no history and no future, allowing the user to follow it without the ability to compare whether or not they followed the point accurately. Second, we wanted interaction with our machine to provide the user with a bodily sense of the mechanics of 3D printers. Guiding a user along a path using a single point encourages the movements of the body to mimic those of the machine. Additionally, it prompts the user to work with her building materials in an uncommon way. By asking the user to do something strange with her materials, we aimed to heighten her sensitivity to the ways in which materials conformed to or resisted the machine paths. Third, we felt it was important for the machine to have a unique persona and performance of its own. The machine we created consists of a laser pointer attached to two motors in a pan-tilt configuration. When the user presses "play" on the machine, the machine begins to animate the motors and laser pointer. The gears of the motors produce a low humming sound unique to mechanical parts. The sounds and motions of the machine may not play a primary role in interaction, but they become peripherally present as part of the environment of making.

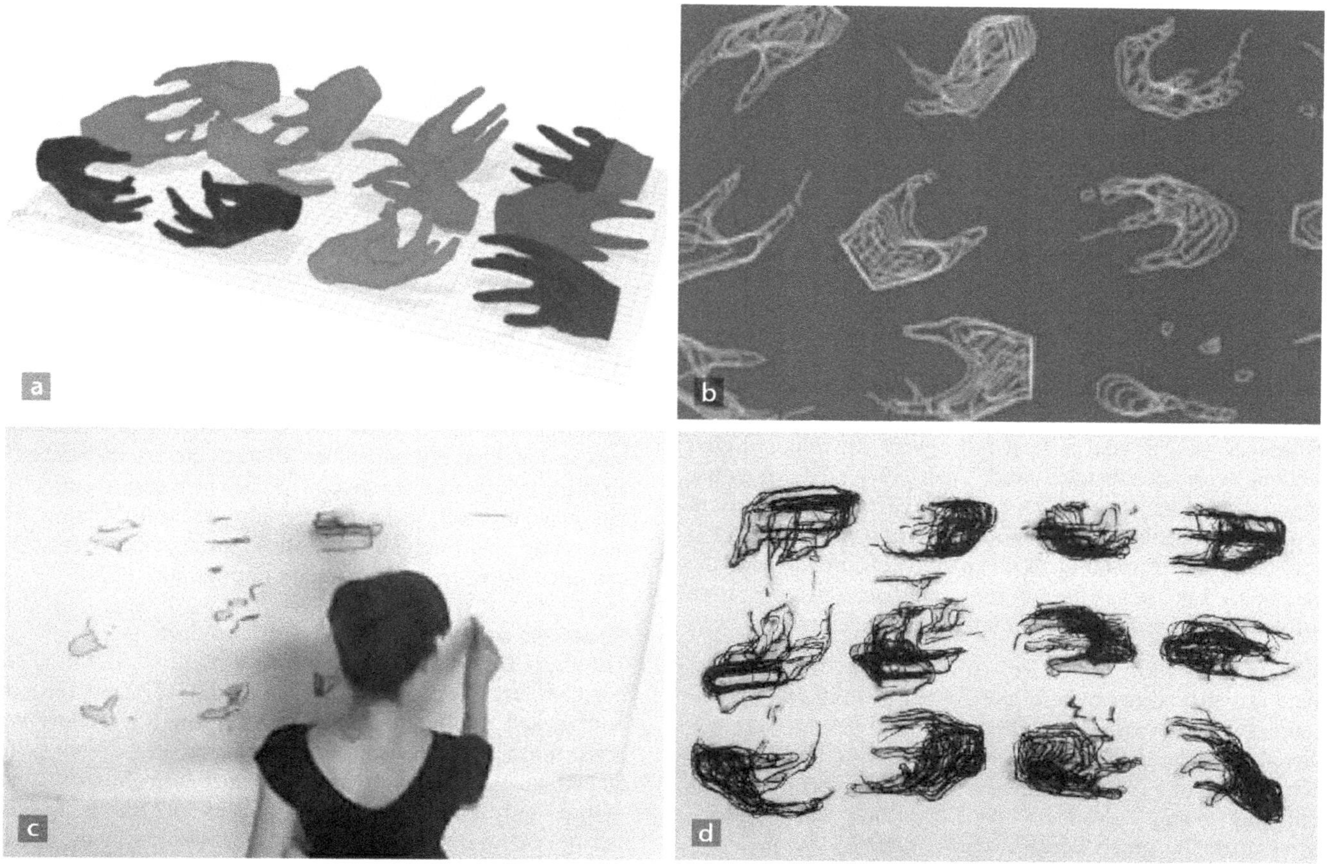

Figure 2: Following Redeform with Charcoal. a. 3D model of several hands in different orientations is used as input to Redeform b. A visualization shows the tool-paths generated from the 3D model. c The laser pointer moves along the tool-paths and Devendorf follows it with charcoal. d. The drawing that emerges is abstract derivation of the original 3D model.

By framing Redeform as a machine to be interpreted and experienced, we created a platform to sustain close interactions and growth with a large set of materials. The design itself contains affordances to suggest particular ways of working that de-emphasize precision in order to make space for new ideas, forms, and experiences to emerge. Additionally, the way in which both the materials and the machine become present to the user, through the machine's movements or the feeling of the materials on her hands, allows her to become entangled in the agencies of nonhuman actors. Redeform created a very different experience of 3D printing and set the stage for a mode of making characterized by improvisation and discovery.

Redeform in Practice

The way a maker's sensitivities change and materials become activated within interactions with Redeform is best illustrated through example. For the past 20 months Devendorf has been using Redeform as part of her personal art practice. In January 2015, she began to experiment with shapes and forms that emerged as she followed the laser with charcoal on paper. Experimentation entailed generating digital models, translating them into G-Code files, uploading those G-Code files to the laser guide, and then following the laser guide by hand with charcoal. At every step in the processes a different set of digital and physical materials became activated, causing the model to deviate from its previous form. For instance, the digital input model is manipulated by the parameters specified to the G-Code generator, the motors which drive the laser guide have limited resolution and rasterize the paths Devendorf follows, and, Devendorf's own hand imperfections modify the paths even further.

Experimenting with the system led to growth with both digital and physical materials. After several experiments with 3D models of hands, Devendorf began to realize how arranging the hands in different orientations in 3D space produced radically different looking tool paths. While early experiments focused on drawing a single model, she felt the drawings to be more visually and conceptually interesting if the same model was repeated multiple times in the composition because it visually emphasized tensions between replication and derivation. Additionally, Devendorf began to develop new ways to work with her "building" material, charcoal. Charcoal has a unique capacity to smear on paper and in early experiments Devendorf found herself trying to limit smearing by carefully keeping her hand lifted off the page. A fellow artist offered the critique, "the charcoal isn't doing anything for you in these drawings," which she took to mean that she was not embracing the properties of charcoal that make it uniquely different from something like a marker or pencil. In subsequent experiments, she embraced the smearing nature of charcoal by actively dragging the side of her hand as she drew. The results were striking. Since drawing flattens the tool-paths for a 3D object into a 2D plane, the degree of smearing became a way to represent the layers of the model, with darker regions representing areas shared by many overlapping layers, and lighter regions representing areas with less layering.

Devendorf experienced growth with materials across the entire process. For instance, realizations about the behaviors of charcoal affected the way in which digital models were constructed and vice versa. The ongoing negotiation and development of all parts of the system could be described as correspondence. In use, Devendorf is not only corresponding with paper, charcoal, and the machine, but also the digital models, customization software, and hardware that comprise the machine.

Interactions with Redeform also called attention to materials that were not originally engaged in the process of making. For instance, when exhibiting the project, Devendorf preferred to perform the laser-guided drawings live in front of a gallery audience. The act of performing the machine made Devendorf consider how her physical movements in space became choreographed by the tool-paths and led her to change models and G-Code in a way that would produce movements that may be interesting for viewers. At one performance, the laser guide was mounted to an overhang, which extended from the second floor of the building. The vibrations of both the amplified music as well as the footsteps of people walking on the second floor shook the laser point Devendorf was following and became represented in the drawing. Additionally, many attendees began to engage Devendorf by asking her about the system and the way it worked. Often, the attendees would stand in front of the laser point, unaware that their body was occluding the mark that Devendorf was following. Rather than pausing the system and waiting for the attendee to move or moving the laser guide to a more stable location, Devendorf began to see the people and vibrations of the space as additional active forces in the drawing process: their presence being represented by shakes and gaps in the traced paths. The result from each performance was a completely unique drawing, not simply because Devendorf's hand movements are unique, but because the dynamics of the space, its vibrations and people, all became captured in the marks on the paper.

While Redeform guided Devendorf in doing things like a machine, it would not be correct to say that Redeform is ultimately controlling interaction. Such a strict binary between human and mechanical agency would deny the many layers and filters of agency that become enmeshed in interaction. For instance, Devendorf chose the model she would eventually draw, she controlled the speed of the laser, and to some degree, the way the G-Code paths were generated. Furthermore, there are contributors to the interaction that extend beyond the Devendorf and Redeform, for instance, the vibrations of the speakers that shook the paths in her performance. To say that the machine is specifically "controlling" interaction would make as much sense as saying a coloring book is controlling the way in which someone chooses to color. We prefer to think of Redeform as a way to shape, but not determine, interaction towards a particular set of effects. With Redeform, Devendorf chose specific constraints in order to bring herself and audiences viewing her performances to a place to understand and reflect on human-machine relationships, to draw these experiences in contrast to other experiences with 3D printers, to reflect on the way that all technologies can be both freeing and restricting, and to create a decidedly strange experience that can open up new perspectives on familiar actions.

Redeform and an Indeterminate Tradition

Through Devendorf's experiences with Redeform, we began to tease out how the system set the stage for both human and nonhuman actors to perform. Devendorf was performing in a literal sense when she created drawings for an audience but her human performance was choreographed within and around the performances of the nonhuman actors: the charcoal, machine, and vibrations in the space. By framing these nonhumans as actors rather than tools or media to be acted upon, the agency of nonhumans became foregrounded in interaction allowing for new kinds of processes, forms, and understandings to emerge. We began to see connections between the kind of making we created by operationalizing morphogenesis in design and the kind of making taking place within chance-based and participatory art practices, which gained prominence between 1950 and 1980. In the following section, we reflect on this tradition of art making in order to unpack the meaning and values embodied in Redeform, as well as the aesthetic and personal impacts morphogenetic maker technologies may have more broadly.

In the 1950s, experimental composer John Cage founded an approach to art making that featured co-operations between human players and nonhuman objects that combined to generate sound in unpredictable and surprising ways. In Cage's "Water Walk" [5], Cage assembled a large number of ordinary household appliances, including five unplugged radios, an iron pipe, a bathtub, a soda siphon, an ice bucket, a vase with flowers, a tape machine, a garden sprinkler, a pressure cooker. Cage then walked from object to object, using each in its commonplace way, and the sounds created by his "playing" each thing produced a vibrant cacophony that was wholly different than anything a musician might have played on a musical instrument. In Cage's work, the musician is not someone who occupies the role of "master" or who controls and dominates "servant" instruments; rather, the performer aims to activate latent potentials in everyday objects at hand, and is ready and open to the soundscapes that result from her aleatory interactions with these nonhuman collaborators. The humans and the nonhumans, in this piece and in many of Cage's works, form an assemblage in which a human does not have hierarchical superiority, but all elements form a reciprocal relation and act equally on one another. Cage's methods proved to be highly influential on generations of artists' practices.

In 1965, choreographer Yvonne Rainer developed a piece called "Parts of Some Sextets," which consisted of Rainer's 10 performers moving 12 mattresses around a stage in multiple configurations and interacting with them in playful and seemingly bizarre ways. For example, Rainer's instructions include these scenes:

...18. Human flies on mattress pile; 19. Formation #1 (fling); 20. Formation #2 (with 'bug squash'); 21. Move pile to other side.... [24].

Rainer's conception for "Parts of Some Sextets" calls the performers' and the viewers' attention to the possibility that objects can create choreography as opposed to a human choreographer planning each step of a piece. Human performers in this work do not wholly dominate the mattresses, nor do the mattresses completely dominate the humans; rather, the humans and nonhumans exchange power and alternate in the roles of "actors" and "acted upon."

A contemporary of Rainer, choreographer Trisha Brown, designed "Walking on the Wall" in 1971, which similarly presented human performers as partners (rather than controllers) of nonhuman materials [4]. This project featured seven dancers attached by harnesses to a system that allowed them to walk on the walls, their heads pointing towards the center of the room, so that the performers' bodies were parallel to the floor as they walked. Brown recognized that there would be a high degree of difficulty for the dancers attempting to maintain equilibrium between gravity and the force of the harness/pulley system as they walked on the wall, and in all of the performances of "Walking," the dancers do not mask their effort, or make the piece seem polished or "finished." Instead, the performers in 1971 wore their ordinary workout clothes (not costumes), and did not move to any music—their dialogue with one another, and the sound of the harness/pulley system, were the only sound cues. The "working out" of the performance constituted the performance. There was no completed piece that was refined through many rehearsals and only shown to the public when it had achieved a degree of "readiness." In addition, Brown's work exposes the apparatus of making: the pulleys, ropes, and harnesses were fully visible throughout the performance, and even the surface of the wall, which substituted for the dance floor, was made prominent and served as a contributing and determining element in "Walking." Thus, "Walking" foregrounded the collaboration of human performers and nonhuman materials, and honored the generative accidents that arose from such interactions of people and objects.

At the same time that Cage, Rainer, Brown created the pieces described above, the artists' network called Fluxus formulated a theory of what they called "intermedia art" [17]. Intermedia art is defined by the co-presence and interdependence of humans and objects—especially machines, such as film projectors—in performance spaces. The Fluxus group aimed to create intermedia art that heavily emphasized indeterminacy in the collaboration of disparate elements (for example, one of their books was titled *An Anthology of Chance Operations* [34]). We regard Redeform as an intermedia art construct, which brings humans into relation with machines (a computer and motorized laser guide) and other nonhuman matter (the substances that the humans use to build their pieces, such as pancake batter or charcoal), in a way that does not frame the human as a "user" nor the nonhumans as "media," but establishes a more equal power dynamic across all of the participants or members of the relation, and leaves the outcome of the relation open to chance and accident.

In Redeform, as in the aleatory works of Cage, Rainer, Brown, and the Fluxus group, the human performer does not make use of a nonhuman medium, but *serves as the medium* through which performers and objects create something collaboratively, causing a new form to come into being. The human in Redeform is not wholly the servant of the machine—the human decides what to program the machine to tell them to do, after all—but after the human has programmed the machine with some instructions, the human then becomes a servant of the machine, using eyes and hands to follow the machine's instructions as best as they are able. The human's inability to "perfectly" execute the machine's directions, as well as any resistance to manipulation shown by the substance that the human is trying to shape into an object, reveal that the true "product" of Redeform is, in fact, a *process*—the process of labor co-performed by human and nonhuman makers.

DISCUSSION

Drawing from our experiences designing, working with, and studying Redeform, as well as aesthetic potentials expressed by the performances discussed above, we conclude with a speculative vision of the impact morphogenetic design, a particular post-anthropocentric design perspective, could have on maker technologies and the maker movement more broadly. While we advocate for open-ended and emergent approaches to making, we are *not* suggesting that precision and accuracy are bad or that all CNC systems should embrace unpredictability. Rather, we argue for an expanded view of values in making that regards control-driven (hylomorphic) and indeterminate (morphogenetic) systems as valuable in different contexts.

Decentering the User in Design

Commercial 3D printers, and most consumer facing technologies for that matter, aim to place the user in the "center" of design, and thus, in a role to command machines and materials. The user is positioned above and apart from the technology and the technology does its best to offer intuitive controls, seamlessly supplying the user with the information or resources she requires. Redeform and the performance works outlined above place humans and nonhuman machines and materials on more equal footing. In Redeform, the technology is strategically *non-intuitive* and gets in the way of its user, forcing her to negotiate her goals with the machine. In morphogenetic design agendas, we see the user transitioning from a commander of materials to an orchestrator of materials, placing materials in various configurations and arrangements to produce a range of non-specific, but non-random, outcomes. As the user shifts from commander to orchestrator, her position is no longer "central" as other human and nonhuman forces can challenge and resist her actions. Thus, she loses the ability to predict the outcome of making but gains an opportunity to discover surprising or unexpected forms, insights, and expressions that emerge only by limiting her voice in the creative process.

DiSalvo and Lukens also describe how post-anthropocentric theories (namely, Actor-Network theory and Object Oriented Ontology) decenter the human user in design [6]. They developed technologies that allow humans to see through the perspective of robots, and highlighted how this can lead to new insights, understandings, and sensitivities to those perspectives. Redeform and the performances described above reveal how decentering the maker or artist can create provocative engagements that foreground the dependencies between, and mutual shaping of, humans and technology.

Consider Karen Barad's term "intra-action" to describe,

> *...the mutual constitution of entangled agencies. That is, in contrast to the usual 'interaction,' which assumes there are separate individual agencies that precede their interaction, the notion of intra-action recognizes that distinct agencies do not precede but rather emerge through, their intra-action* [2].

With this definition in mind, we see hylomorphic design perspectives as those that hold human and machines as categorically different, with assumed agencies that precede interaction. Alternatively, we see morphogenetic designs supporting *intra*-actions among machines, materials, audiences, and environments. Within intra-actions with materials, machines, software, and people, the maker is able to affect and be affected by the agencies of all the forces and factors involved. By blurring roles of human and machine, or media and tool, these technologies can make room for new roles, agencies, and outcomes to emerge. In the case of Redeform, boundaries between human and machine become blurred by allowing a human to act like a machine. In intra-action, human makers are provided with an opportunity to reflect on and even tinker with their positioning and power dynamics among the other forces involved in the making process. Thus, the process of making transforms from a way to produce things to a way to inquire about relationships among things, spaces, people, and materials.

This new configuration of making–less about a human subject and more about the potentials that inhere in collaborations between humans, materials, and machines–aligns with posthumanism as defined by N. Katherine Hayles [15]. Hayles' theories of posthumanism attempt to de-center the human "self" as the master of technological systems. She proposes that humans must be seen "as part of a distributed system" incorporating both human bodies and machine bodies, human intelligences and machine intelligences, and that "the full expression of human capability can be seen precisely to *depend* on the splice" between humans and technologies. Post-anthropocentric making technologies operate within this "splice" and highlight contingencies between human and nonhuman agencies, opening them to reflection and experimentation.

Making with Vibrant Materials

Political theorist Jane Bennett argues that recognition of the agency of nonhuman things can foster more sustainable behaviors in the world. Bennett's "vital materialism" calls attention to the livelihood of nonhuman things and their ability to affect us in "not-quite-human" ways. She writes,

> *The capacity to detect the presence of impersonal affect requires that one is caught up in it. One needs, at least for a while, to suspend suspicion and adopt a more open-ended comportment. If we think we already know what is out there, we will surely miss much of it* [3].

Designing machines for making, like 3D printers, from a morphogenetic perspective is a particularly useful way for allowing users to become "caught up," or as Ingold might say, "join forces," with the affects of other human and nonhuman forces. In these encounters, strange constraints requiring one to build like a machine or cues that connect the actions of people and mattresses become an asset, allowing users to break away from familiar associations with things in order to see, create, and experience them anew. Humans can begin to identify with their nonhuman counterparts and may begin to seek alternative ways of working *with* materials as opposed to acting on them. By creating modes of making that make the "voice" of nonhumans louder, as in intra-action, these machines can be seen to have sensitizing capacities. They foster close, careful, and attentive relationships among humans, machines, and materials. Morphogenetic making machines, then, are well suited to "slow" [14], reflective engagements with machines and materials as opposed to rapid, product-driven prototyping.

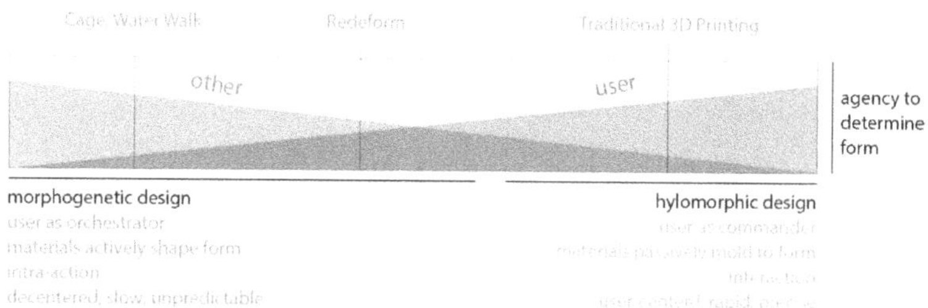

Figure 3: A high-level sketch of the differences between the morphogenetic and hylomorphic design perspectives.

A Post-Anthropocentric Maker and Movement

Post-anthropocentric maker technologies formulate an image of a post-anthropocentric maker who becomes innovative and technologically fluent by working closely with machines and materials, listening and sensing their actions, and responding accordingly. For this maker, empowerment is not about the ability to realize one's existing ideas, instead, it stems from the ability to listen and respond to materials as they take on forms. This maker is a performer among a cast of human and nonhuman counterparts, organizing her actions in relation to the others to form critical inquiries into the world. While the machines, materials, and outcomes may look similar to other acts of making, the way this maker goes about *doing* making may be better understood as improvisation, interplay, and entangled performance rather than as predetermination, domination, and control.

What separates anthropocentric from post-anthropocentric making is a matter of perspective. Two makers may use the same machines and materials but the way in which each maker relates to her materials can be quite different. Additionally, a single maker may desire different modes of making at different points within their practice, say, a post-anthropocentric approach to generate new ideas and an anthropocentric approach to create multiple objects from those ideas. It is common to see designers, artists, and craftspeople using post-anthropocentric approaches to spur new insights about familiar materials and inspirational ideas. For instance, Jackson and Kang descriptions of artists working with or obsolete technologies can be seen as a mode of making that attends to the agency of "junk" [19]. Thus, it's reasonable to say that a post-anthropocentric maker movement is already taking place. Yet, maker spaces and the media associated with the maker movement make post-anthropocentric approaches difficult to detect or color them as different than "Making." This may be due to the fact that much of this work takes place as a social and technical inquiry rather than (or in addition to) a desire to "do-it-oneself." While it might be tempting to let these practices mutually exist in different arenas, (say, post-anthropocentric approaches in art studios and anthropocentric approaches in maker spaces) carving a place for open-ended and indeterminate practices within the broader maker movement could be beneficial, particularly for fostering a diversity of opinions and working styles within educational contexts and maker spaces.

We see two ways (but there are likely to be more) that indeterminate practices can gain visibility and respect within mainstream maker culture. First, designers could create and maker spaces could include technologies like Redeform that allow for computational workflows to be applied in improvisatory ways. The presence of this technology in maker spaces could validate such practices and may appeal to broader audiences. Second, documentation associated with the maker movement could highlight process over product. Currently, finished *products* are the focus of knowledge sharing in the maker movement and are often presented as a kind of recipe for others to reproduce. In this model, the *processes* of working that gave rise to the idea for that product or its successful implementation are obscured. Knowledge gleaned from post-anthropocentric making might be communicated better as stories of practice, which highlight shifts in perspective, moments of inspiration, and an evolving thought processes.

CONCLUSION

This article weaves a narrative connecting new materialist theory, interaction design, and performance histories in an attempt to articulate ways of thinking about engagement that could broaden the landscape of digital fabrication research and foreground the potential of post-anthropocentric modes of design. We describe how post-anthropocentric theories, which argue for the view of nonhuman matter as active or even alive, can be operationalized in design by providing a description of Redeform and contextualizing it within a broader landscape of experimental performances. In doing so, we shed light on the important role indeterminacy and resistance play in interactions that place humans and nonhumans on equal footing. We speculate on the potential impact such a design approach might have within the specific context of the maker movement—namely, that such an approach could provoke reflection on human relationships with technology and could foster more thoughtful, careful, or reflective modes of engagement with core Maker technologies like 3D printers.

ACKNOWLEDGEMENTS

Thank you to the Autodesk Aritst-In-Residence program for their support of Devendorf as she developed Redeform. Thank you also to Rosemary Joyce, August Black, Daniela Rosner, James Pierce, and all of their reviewers for their feedback.

REFERENCES

1. Philip E. Agre. 1997. *Computation and Human Experience*. Cambridge University Press, Cambridge ; New York.
2. Karen Barad. 2007. *Meeting the Universe Halfway: Quantum Physics and the Entanglement of Matter and Meaning*. Duke University Press Books.
3. Jane Bennett. 2010. *Vibrant Matter: A Political Ecology of Things*. Duke University Press Books, Durham.
4. Trisha Brown. 1971. *Walking on the Wall*. Retrieved from http://www.trishabrowncompany.org/?page=view&nr=481
5. John Cage. 1960. *Water Walk*. Retrieved from https://www.youtube.com/watch?v=-koTMW95NZs
6. Carl DiSalvo and Jonathan Lukens. 2011. Non-Anthropocentrism and the Non-Human in Design: Possibilities for Designing New Forms of Engagement With and Through Technology. In *From Social Butterfly to Engaged Citizen Urban Informatics, Social Media, Ubiquitous Computing, and Mobile Technology to Support Citizen Engagement*. MIT Press.
7. Diana Coole and Samantha Frost. 2010. *New Materialisms: Ontology, Agency, and Politics*. Duke University Press.
8. Manuel DeLanda. 2004. Material complexity. *Digital tectonics*: 14–21.
9. Laura Devendorf and Daniela K. Rosner. 2015. Reimagining Digital Fabrication As Performance Art. *Proceedings of the 33rd Annual ACM Conference Extended Abstracts on Human Factors in Computing Systems*, ACM, 555–566. http://doi.org/10.1145/2702613.2732507
10. Laura Devendorf and Kimiko Ryokai. 2015. Being the Machine: Reconfiguring Agency and Control in Hybrid Fabrication. *Proceedings of the SIGCHI Conference on Human Factors in Computing Systems*, ACM.
11. Dale Dougherty. 2013. The maker mindset. *Design, make, play: Growing the next generation of STEM innovators*: 7–11.
12. Sarah Fox, Rachel Rose Ulgado, and Daniela Rosner. 2015. Hacking Culture, Not Devices: Access and Recognition in Feminist Hackerspaces. *Proceedings of the 18th ACM Conference on Computer Supported Cooperative Work & Social Computing*, ACM, 56–68.
13. Neil Gershenfeld. 2007. *Fab: The Coming Revolution on Your Desktop--from Personal Computers to Personal Fabrication*. Basic Books, New York.
14. Lars Hallnäs and Johan Redström. 2001. Slow Technology – Designing for Reflection. *Personal Ubiquitous Comput.* 5, 3: 201–212.
15. N. Katherine Hayles. 1999. *How We Became Posthuman: Virtual Bodies in Cybernetics, Literature, and Informatics*. University Of Chicago Press, Chicago, Ill.
16. Liz Henry. The Rise of Feminist Hackerspaces and How to Make Your Own. *Model View Culture*. Retrieved October 29, 2014 from https://modelviewculture.com/pieces/the-rise-of-feminist-hackerspaces-and-how-to-make-your-own
17. Dick Higgins. 1966. Statement on Intermedia. *Dé-coll/age (décollage)* 6.
18. Tim Ingold. 2013. *Making: Anthropology, Archaeology, Art and Architecture*. Routledge, London ; New York.
19. Steven J. Jackson and Laewoo Kang. 2014. Breakdown, Obsolescence and Reuse: HCI and the Art of Repair. *Proceedings of the SIGCHI Conference on Human Factors in Computing Systems*, ACM, 449–458. http://doi.org/10.1145/2556288.2557332
20. Jeff Maeshiro, Jia Wu, and Mary Sek. 2014. *Geoweaver*. Retrieved from http://maeshirodesign.com/2014/07/05/geoweaver/
21. Bruno Latour. 1994. Where are the Missing Masses? The Sociology of a Few Mundane Artifacts. In *Shaping Technology / Building Society: Studies in Sociotechnical Change*. The MIT Press, Cambridge, Mass.
22. Bruno Latour. 2007. *Reassembling the Social: An Introduction to Actor-Network-Theory*. Oxford University Press, Oxford; New York.
23. Ron Rael and Virgiina San Fratello. Emerging Objects. Retrieved September 9, 2014 from http://www.emergingobjects.com/
24. Yvonne Rainer. 1965. Some Retrospective Notes on a Dance for 10 People and 12 Mattresses Called "Parts of Some Sextets," Performed at the Wadsworth Atheneum, Hartford, Connecticut, and Judson Memorial Church, New York, in March, 1965. *The Tulane Drama Review* 10, 2: 168–178. http://doi.org/10.2307/1125242
25. Alessandro Ranellucci. *Slic3r*. Retrieved from http://slic3r.org/
26. Alec Rivers, Andrew Adams, and Frédo Durand. 2012. Sculpting by Numbers. *ACM Trans. Graph.* 31, 6: 157:1–157:7. http://doi.org/10.1145/2366145.2366176
27. Alec Rivers, Ilan E. Moyer, and Frédo Durand. 2012. Position-correcting Tools for 2D Digital Fabrication. *ACM Trans. Graph.* 31, 4: 88:1–88:7. http://doi.org/10.1145/2185520.2185584
28. Studio Homunculus. *Haptic Intelligentsia*. Retrieved from http://studio-homunculus.com/portfolio/haptic-intelligentsia-human-prototyping-machine/
29. Austin L. Toombs, Shaowen Bardzell, and Jeffrey Bardzell. 2015. The Proper Care and Feeding of Hackerspaces: Care Ethics and Cultures of Making. *Proceedings of the 33rd Annual ACM Conference on Human Factors in Computing Systems*, ACM, 629–638. http://doi.org/10.1145/2702123.2702522
30. Unfold. 2012. *Stratigraphic Porcelain*. Retrieved from http://unfold.be/pages/stratigraphic-porcelain

31. Peter-Paul Verbeek. 2011. *Moralizing Technology: Understanding and Designing the Morality of Things*. University Of Chicago Press, Chicago ; London.
32. Langdon Winner. 1980. Do Artifacts Have Politics? *Daedalus* 109, 1: 121–136.
33. Steve Woolgar. 1990. Configuring the user: the case of usability trials. *The Sociological Review* 38, S1: 58–99. http://doi.org/10.1111/j.1467-954X.1990.tb03349.x
34. La Monte Young (ed.). 1963. *An Anthology of Chance Operations*. La Monte Young & Jackson Mac Low.
35. Amit Zoran and Joseph A. Paradiso. 2013. FreeD: A Freehand Digital Sculpting Tool. *Proceedings of the SIGCHI Conference on Human Factors in Computing Systems*, ACM, 2613–2616. http://doi.org/10.1145/2470654.2481361

Ontological Surprises: A Relational Perspective on Machine Learning

Lucian Leahu
The IT University
Copenhagen, Denmark
lucian@itu.dk

ABSTRACT
This paper investigates how we might rethink design as the technological crafting of human-machine relations in the context of a machine learning technique called neural networks. It analyzes Google's Inceptionism project, which uses neural networks for image recognition. The surprising output of one the experiments reveals that such networks might be used to trace relations between entities. This paper contributes by fleshing out the necessary changes in the ways HCI builds, tests, and engages neural networks in the design of interactive systems from a relational perspective; it proposes a hybrid approach where machine learning algorithms are used to identify objects *as well as* connections between them; finally, it argues for remaining open to ontological surprises in machine learning as they may enable the crafting of different relations with and through technologies.

Author Keywords
ontology; relations; machine learning; neural networks; design; hybrids; critical technical practice.

ACM Classification Keywords
H.5.m. Information interfaces and presentation (e.g., HCI): Miscellaneous;

INTRODUCTION AND MOTIVATION
In the past decade, scholars from a variety of fields have turned to reexamining technology and its role in the world from the perspective of the shifting web of human-nonhuman relations. Perhaps most visible and impactful in HCI has been Lucy Suchman's "Human-Machine Reconfigurations" [11], which retells and extends "Plans and Situated Actions" [10] to incorporate new conceptualizations of relations such as Latour's work on the mutual constitution of humans and non-humans [4] and Barad's agential realism [1].

DIS 2016, June 04 - 08, 2016, Brisbane, QLD, Australia

ACM 978-1-4503-4031-1/16/06...$15.00
DOI: http://dx.doi.org/10.1145/2901790.2901840

Suchman's work has been influential in HCI, primarily in studies of existing technologies and the ways in which they come to be used. However, the last few years have witnessed calls to take up such explicit orientations to relations in design practices as well. At the last DIS conference, philosopher of science Peter-Paul Verbeek's opening keynote described a need to rethink interaction design by considering how humans and technologies mutually shape each other. Pointing out that 'use' relations are but a small subset of the relations humans enact with or through technologies [14], he called for researchers in this field to think of design as what he termed the "technological crafting of human-technology relations."

Indeed, his call resonates with recent efforts in interaction design. Drawing on a body of work in sociology and science and technology studies (STS), Taylor argues that "technologies have always been about producing dense relationships between humans and non-humans, i.e. world making." He proposes an alternative framing that focuses on the relations that are brought into being when we design things [12].

The goal of this paper is to investigate how these ideas can be manifested in the design and construction of interactive artifacts. Specifically, I focus on the *technical* means to support a shift to relations in system design. Existing technical approaches have been developed in a symbolic or representative framework [e.g., 2]; consequently, the primary emphasis has been on representing entities, rather than the relationships between them. Thus, it is an open question how to use existing technical approaches from a relational perspective. This paper contributes to the development of this research area by analyzing how a machine learning approach called neural networks, which is typically used to detect entities (for example, the presence of a certain object in a photograph), may be used to trace relations.

The paper is organized as follows. The next section takes a specific research project as a focal case study. While this project did not feature an interactive system, it focuses on a technical approach relevant for interaction design: image recognition using neural networks. Interactive technologies are increasingly likely to draw on and be constructed in conjunction with machine learning technologies such as neural networks, given the prevalence of such techniques in today's technological developments as evidenced by the computational turn to big data. Hence it is a critical time to examine these technical approaches from a relational perspective. The section after that analyzes the surprising output of one experiment revealing that such networks might be used to trace relations between objects. The paper continues by articulating how HCI should change the ways in which we build, test, and design with neural networks so that our systems may trace relations rather than just objects. The paper ends by arguing that ontological surprises in machine learning work might engender technologies that support the emergence of different kinds of relations.

INVERTING NEURAL NETWORKS

How Machine Learning Works

Machine learning algorithms find statistical regularities in data sets that may be meaningful. In the image recognition domain, a typical supervised machine learning project would proceed as follows. Suppose we want to build a model that decides whether an image contains bananas. We would find a large amount of images, in the range of millions, some of which contain bananas. We would label the photos according to whether they contain bananas or not and then partition the data set in two: a subset to use for training the model and another one for testing it. Once the model has been trained using the former set, the later can be used to check how well the model can find bananas in other (than those used in training) photos.

The power of machine learning is that it needs no other information (such as explicit symbolic descriptions) beyond the data and the labels as it relies on statistical features to discriminate between the positive data points (in our example: images containing bananas) and negative ones (images without bananas). In other words, it's the math behind them together with the human labor that performs the labeling and selects statistical features that make these techniques so powerful. At the same time, this can pose difficulties understanding semantically (not just mathematically) why some models work better than others [e.g., 3]. Moreover, it is quite important to understand what the representations entail, as these networks can be understood to distill the essential characteristics of the entity they've been trained to recognize. Thus, in order to understand which images will be categorized correctly and which may slip through the cracks, it is crucial to have a concrete sense of what the networks encode: not just in terms of the mathematics, but quite concretely, e.g. what do bananas need to look like for this network to recognize them in an image. Not only is this an important topic but also one that is quite difficult to tackle as errors easily creep in, e.g. images having similar statistical properties to those of the images used in training can fool the network [8]. However, recent developments in this arena make it possible to 'have a look' inside neural networks, i.e. to visually inspect what the network encodes [7].

The Google Inception Project

This was the starting point for a project conducted by a group of Google engineers [9]. Their work consisted of building models to detect the presence in images of entities such as: animals, fish, buildings, trees, etc. To verify what the models encode, the project drew on a technique that inverts a neural network's functionality: instead of using the network to detect the presence of a particular object in the input image, the network is inverted and used to generate a new image—the input image is modified so that the new image contains the object the network was trained to detect. So a network trained to recognize bananas, when inverted it modifies the input so that it contains the network's 'view' of bananas. This technique allows for a visual inspection of what the network encodes. In effect, this technique turns the network upside down, as well as inside out.

To check what the networks they built encode, the authors used input images containing random noise. This kind of image represents a clean slate from a statistical perspective. Thus the outcome image is determined only by the contents of the model encoded in the network. The image on the left in Figure 1 shows the initial random noise image fed into an inverted neural network trained to recognize bananas.

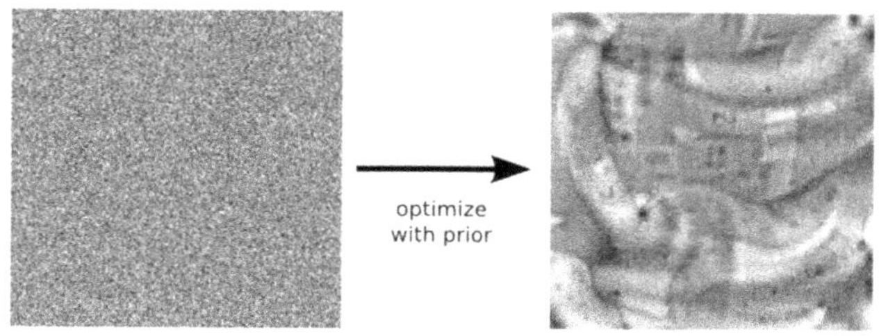

Figure 1. From noise to bananas: a random noise image (left) fed into an inverted neural network trained to recognize bananas produces the image on the right.

Some of the images produced by using random noise as input depict humanly recognizable representations of the objects they were trained to recognize (e.g., bananas, ants, starfish, etc.)—see Figure 2.

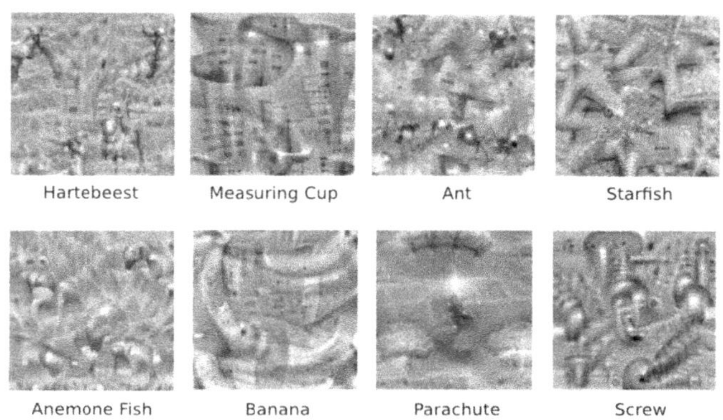

Figure 2. Sample outputs of inverted neural networks trained to recognize different entities. A higher resolution version is available at [9].

The Dumbbells Neural Network

Other networks, however, surprised the engineers conducting these experiments. One such example is that of a network trained to detect dumbbells. Indeed, the images output by the neural net contained dumbbells, however they also depicted human arms operating them—see Figure 3. In other words, from the network's perspective the essential characteristics of a dumbbell include human arms.

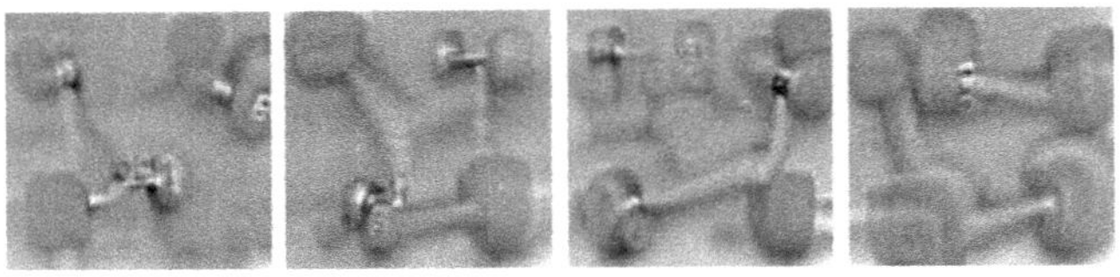

Figure 3. Dumbbells and arms.

According to the research team conducting this work, the dumbbells example showcases a failed learning job and thus the kinds of failures that visualizing the contents of a network can reveal: "In this case, the network failed to completely distill the essence of a dumbbell. Maybe it's never been shown [i.e., the training set did not contain] a dumbbell without an arm holding it. Visualization can help us correct these kinds of training mishaps." [9]

Indeed, one way to make sure that the network encodes only a dumbbell is to remove from the training set images containing the object and an arm operating it.

However, my reading of the outcome of this particular experiment is different from the Google engineers. The network encodes a central aspect pertaining to dumbbells: the fact that they can be operated in particular ways by arms. My interpretation is rooted in a relational worldview. From this perspective, what characterizes an entity is not the attributes of that entity but the relations that perform the object as such: the relations through which an object's identity is performed—a weight emerges as a dumbbell by being used as a training weight, typically by lifting it with one's arms. In sum, the network in this experiment can be thought to encode a relation between dumbbells and arms; indeed, a constitutive relation. Viewed from a relational point of view, then, this experiment is a success and motivates a further analysis on how we may use neural networks beyond identifying objects.

RETHINKING NEURAL NETWORKS FROM A RELATIONAL PERSPECTIVE

The ontological perspective we take shapes in fundamental ways how we set up an experiment, how we interpret its outcomes, and how we use the knowledge generated [e.g., 1]. Thus it is important to rethink how we approach neural networks from a relational perspective. I continue by working out what needs to change in the ways we understand, build, test, and use neural networks in system design.

Changing Goals: from Entities to Relations

My relational interpretation of the experiment read the encoding of the network to trace a relationship between dumbbells and arms, rather than a failure of the experiment to include sufficient images of dumbbells without arms. This is not to say that the latter interpretation is wrong. On the contrary, that interpretation is correct within the specific ontological framework (realist) that commonly underlies machine learning work.

Here I trace out the logics of the two diverging interpretations with respect to the two ontological frameworks. If we were to take a realist perspective, like the engineers in this project, we would embrace the ontological belief that the world is a collection of entities—be they elementary particles, atoms, bananas, dumbbells, or humans—whose identity is largely independent of the rest of the world. In this case, the goal of using a machine learning technology such as neural networks must be to detect the presence of an entity (e.g., dumbbell). If the result contains more objects than the one targeted, this necessarily signals a failure of the network to distill the essence of the dumbbell from the training set it was presented. This explains why the dumbbells experiment was considered a failure by its authors and why they are correct within a realist framework.

If, on the other hand, we were to take a relational perspective, we would understand relations as the building blocks of the world and entities as shaped in constitutive ways through these relations. From this perspective, the experiment above traces a relationship that makes dumbbells meaningful (actionable, in this case) and thus it can be seen as a success. This discussion highlights how the goals of a project and thus the ways in which we evaluate its success change when shifting to a relational worldview. *Instead of aiming to encode entities in themselves, the goal shifts to tracing relations between entities.*

Changing How We Train and Test Neural Networks

Considering neural networks from a relational perspective requires us to think how we may position neural networks in this realm. First, it is clear from the dumbbells example that networks are capable of *mapping* relations that a particular entity is part of—this means that the technical practitioner does not need to be aware of the relation a priori. For this the training set would have to include a large number of data points (here, images) and would have to depict the objects in contexts of interest (e.g., use), rather than the object itself. The majority of data found online meets this latter condition: i.e., data produced by people in contexts they find meaningful. In the realm of images, examples include photos posted on social media or online repositories such as flickr together with associated annotations (tags, captions). These images are likely to depict objects in various contexts, rather than isolated entities. This quality of the training corpus suggests that it is increasingly more likely that machine learning models trained on such images will trace relations between entities rather than the entities in themselves. In other words, the data sets out there are already primed for technologies that trace relations.

Second, the networks can be trained to encode known relations by using in the training set images in which the entities in the relationship are present. In this case, the training and testing data would be carefully collected or produced by machine learning specialists, like those used in projects aiming to detect entities: heterogeneous collections of data coming together from different contexts.

Testing the neural networks trained to trace relations would proceed along similar lines to those of networks trained to detect entities. An added provocation pertains to the case of discovering relations: understanding the meaning and the scope of the relation.

This analysis reveals further provocations brought about by a shift to tracing relations. These include understanding: What kinds of relations can be traced using technologies? What kinds of relations are likely to remain invisible to them? How might we trace shifting or emergent relations?

Using Neural Networks in System Design

From the perspective of designing interactive systems, using machine learning technologies to trace relations represents another resource for system designers. This is especially relevant when the relation involves a human, as in the case of the dumbbells. Moreover, the relations that might be particularly relevant are those including the people around the system. In this case, designers of interactive systems stand to benefit by focusing the models to trace relations and could miss out by focusing the models narrowly on object recognition. However, this does not mean that we should do away with entity recognition. Indeed, an interesting development would be to combine recognition of relations with entity/object recognition. In fact this might be necessary to identify the entities that constitute a discovered relation. In the dumbbells example this would mean training a neural network to recognize human arms and thus work out that the constitutive elements of the relation are human arms and dumbbells. I suggest that we might get more mileage of this machine learning technique when using a *hybrid* approach: skillfully combining both relation and entity recognition.

Further work is needed to understand what kinds of new interactions and indeed relations with technology we can engender by engaging machine learning techniques that trace relations. What does it mean to design a system built from this perspective? If we no longer focus narrowly on entities but instead on tracing and supporting the emergence of relations, how must our design practices shift?

But perhaps the most exciting opportunities lie in the networks potential to trace unexpected relations. The dumbbells experiment surprised the engineers with the presence of human arms in the output images. Although this particular relation (dumbbells-arms) is not particularly surprising, this experiment suggests that it might be possible for machine learning technologies to surprise us by tracing unexpected, indeed emerging, relations between entities. *Such tracings may shift ontologies*, the ways we understand and categorize the world. This would require us to be open to *ontological surprises:* e.g., relations and/or categories that 1) are native to specific configurations of machine learning technologies, the contexts in which they are applied, and the human labor necessary to operate the technologies and interpret their results and 2) might be different than what we expect.

What would this mean for our discipline? What kinds of possibilities lie ahead? A few completed HCI projects offer a glimpse of the possibilities in this space. For example, Taylor et al.'s work examining how data can be multiply entangled in the social web of a community led to the development of the data-in-place concept alongside a suite of interactive systems and displays [13]. In the realm of machine learning, support vector machines in the context of emotion prediction based on physiological data have been analyzed from ontological and epistemological perspectives and then engaged in the design of a system that affords hybrid human-machine enactments of emotion [5, 6]. These projects show that asking different questions of data and of machine learning technologies can lead to the development of systems that craft different relations between data, computation, and people.

CONCLUSION

The surprising output of the dumbbells inverted network invites us to rethink the tasks we ask of machine learning technologies in general, and neural networks in particular. This paper contributes by rethinking neural networks from a relational perspective and by uncovering new directions for interactive systems to use machine learning technologies. Beyond neural networks, the relational perspective makes visible the fact that it is possible to ask different questions of machine learning and that we should approach these technologies with curiosity in order to remain open to ontological surprises: not just unexpected relations between entities but entirely different categories than what we normally expect. Such openness on our behalf may support the crafting of different relations with and through technologies, as well as fresh perspectives on how we might live with technologies and with each other.

AKNOWLEDGEMENTS

I am grateful to Marisa Cohn, Pedro Ferreira, Lilly Irani, Dag Svanæs, and Alex Taylor for their generous feedback on earlier drafts and to the anonymous reviewers and ACs for their comments.

REFERENCES

1. Karen Barad. 2007. *Meeting the Universe Halfway.* Duke University Press.
2. Alan Blackwell. 2015. Interacting with an Inferred World: The Challenge of Machine Learning for Humane Computer Interaction. In Proc. *Critical Computing'15*. ACM, New York, NY, USA, 169-180.

3. Leo Breiman. 2001. Statistical Modeling: the two cultures. *Statistical Science 16(3)*, 199-231.
4. Bruno Latour. 1993. *We have never been modern.* Harvard University Press.
5. Lucian Leahu. 2012. *Representation without Representationalism.* Doctoral dissertation. Cornell University.
6. Lucian Leahu and Phoebe Sengers. 2014. Freaky: performing hybrid human-machine emotion. In *Proc. DIS '14.* ACM, New York, NY, USA, 607-616.
7. Aravind Mahendran and Andrea Vedaldi. 2015. Understanding deep image representations by inverting them. In *Proc. CVPR 2015.* 5188-5196.
8. Nguyen A, Yosinski J, Clune J. Deep Neural Networks are Easily Fooled: High Confidence Predictions for Unrecognizable Images. In *Computer Vision and Pattern Recognition* (CVPR '15), IEEE, 2015.
9. Alexander Mordvintsev, Christopher Olah, and Mike Tyka. 2015. Inceptionism: Going Deeper into Neural Networks. Retrieved January 15, 2016 from http://googleresearch.blogspot.dk/2015/06/inceptionism-going-deeper-into-neural.html
10. Lucy Suchman. 1987. *Plans and Situated Actions: The Problem of Human-Machine Communication.* Cambridge University Press.
11. Lucy Suchman. 2007. *Human-Machine Reconfigurations: Plans and Situated Actions.* Cambridge University Press.
12. Alex Taylor. 2015. After interaction. *interactions* 22, 5 (August 2015), 48-53.
13. Alex S. Taylor, Siân Lindley, Tim Regan, David Sweeney, Vasillis Vlachokyriakos, Lillie Grainger, and Jessica Lingel. 2015. Data-in-Place: Thinking through the Relations Between Data and Community. In *Proc. CHI'15.* ACM, New York, NY, USA, 2863-2872
14. Peter-Paul Verbeek. 2015. COVER STORY: Beyond interaction: a short introduction to mediation theory. *interactions* 22, 3 (April 2015), 26-31.

3D Folded PrintGami: Transform Passive 3D Printed Objects to Interactive by Inserted Paper Origami Circuits

Claudia Daudén Roquet[1,2] **Jeeeun Kim**[2] **Tom Yeh**[2]

[1] Multimedia Engineering
La Salle Barcelona Universitat Ramón Llull

[2] Department of Computer Science
University of Colorado Boulder

cldauden@gmail.com {jeeeun.kim, tom.yeh}@colorado.edu

ABSTRACT

Recent advances in 3D printing allowed end users to easily utilize desktop 3D printers. However, these printers mainly consume molten plastic, due to limited materiality in customer level. While high interests in creating interactive 3D objects with electronics are ubiquitous, commercial 3D printers have not yet provided adequate supports for integrating electronic components. On the other hand, paper as flexible medium has shown its possibility to be a channel to host interactive objects, enabling interaction triggered by users. In this paper, we introduce a process of integrating paper circuit into a 3D printed object, combining two universal fabrication techniques, 3D printing and paper crafting: 1) design a hollow 3D model, 2) construct circuits on the 2D planar cutout of this figure, 3) pause 3D printing to insert folded paper circuits in, and 4) resume to complete printing. We empower makers and tinkerers to employ pervasive technology to build interactive 3D objects without hacking machine, obtaining professional utilities, or buying expensive materials.

Author Keywords

paper circuit, 3D printing, hand craft, personal fabrication

ACM Classification Keywords

H.5.2 Information interfaces and presentation – User Interfaces

INTRODUCTION

3D printing has been gaining popularity in hobbyists, tinkerers, and makers' community due to its recent breakthrough. This Fused Deposition Modeling (FDM) technique is an inexpensive and flexible method that generates each layer by mechanically extruding molten thermoplastic filament such as ABS/PLA onto a substrate, and stacking up layers one at a time to build a final product. However, it is difficult to integrate functional components into the printed object to allow users to interact with it.

DIS 2016, June 04-08, 2016, Brisbane, QLD, Australia
© 2016 ACM. ISBN 978-1-4503-4031-1/16/06 $15.00
DOI: http://dx.doi.org/10.1145/2901790.2901891

In this paper, we propose an alternative 3D printing process that allows designers to embed paper-based electronics and circuits using a personal desktop 3D printer without having to modifying the printer. Since electronics drawn on the paper are foldable to be easily shaped in 3D [7, 10], users can construct 3D shapes from 2D templates via established paper crafting techniques such as Origami. It would be compatible with 3D printed objects to integrate electronics composed on them. Embedded paper circuits will enrich interactivity for passive 3D objects printed with plastic, and the result will physically, visually and geometrically enhance designers' creativity with less effort to adapt high technology.

The first contribution of this paper is the proposal of a process to integrate different printing techniques, 3D printing and paper printing, without the necessity of hacking a 3D printer or obtaining high tech machine. Because paper circuits are generally easier than metal-based circuits to manipulate, they allow for greater artistic expressions by letting designers create shapes and textures that would be almost impossible to do with 3D printed plastics. Second, we define a low cost process for designing and fabricating custom interactive 3D printed objects with paper circuits in cheap ways, without high technical skills to construct circuitry for daily designers, makers. In addition, we propose the use of several paper circuits to build 3D shapes with complex geometries and attaching each other with magnets to align connections when they are inserted separately. In this way, users can also exchange alternative circuits that have different functionality, allowing fast iterations and experimentation. Lastly, we validate the process with a set of example applications demonstrating how this technique can be applied to support rich interactions with paper based artifacts.

RELATED WORKS

Folded Paper as User Interface Medium

Researchers have developed techniques to encourage makers to use paper, to construct circuits rather than heavy and stiff circuit board due to its flexible, thin and lightweight aspect. Paper has already been used to create interactive popup books [15], and custom sketches [14]. Aided by conductive paint, silver ink or circuit stickers [7], makers are easily able to construct inventive paper circuits without additional soldering tools or a precise understanding of the circuit board designing. Efforts on investigating novel ink materials have enabled a range of new techniques to utilize paper as fully functional electronic parts [11]. For instance, PrintScreen treats paper as output display by printing liquid electrodes with inkjet printers [9]. Another example is Foldio, which enables paper to be an input device with specially designed patterns for sensing input, letting paper read capacitive skin touch [8]. Origami has been considered as a way to construct 3D figures from flat 2D paper [3]. Here we combine paper's versatility to construct light circuits and its plasticity to compose 3D volume from flat silhouettes.

Interactive 3D objects

In recent years, methods to enable interaction through passive 3D printed objects have been proposed. 3D printed interactive Tactile Picture Book is a great example to utilize current 3D printer for daily practical use [6]. Movable primitives introduced were inserted into random 3D objects as target pictures, to create an interactive scene for children's books. Adding electronics, especially sound triggering elements with low cost method, in order to empower more interactivity was suggested as a future work. Sauron proposed embedding a small camera into 3D printed commodities, to interpret movements of a small part of object compared to other passive bodies [10]. A camera attached to a joystick captures and interprets movement differences between previously scanned scenes of parts. In this way, the suggested system is able to turn a passive 3D printed object to an interactive gadget. Recently, RevoMaker tried printing 3D object over already functional electronics box [4]. Gao et al. modified a 3D printer to attach an additional microcontroller, which rotates the printing base in four axis, communicating with the main 3D printer system, to print sliced 3D parts around a electronics box. Voxel8, a high-end 3D printer that can dual-extrude silver paste along with plastic, is another alternative to insert circuitry into 3D printed object [12]. While these techniques are promising, they tend to require complicated hardware modifications or software sensing techniques, making the techniques impractical for novice makers.

Our approach fills the gap that has not been covered within the past research efforts, by facilitating the creation of interactive 3D objects with commodity desktop printers. Without buying an expensive, high-end machine or modifying an existing low-end printer, users can design and fabricate interactive 3D objects by embedding folded paper circuit inside during the 3D printing process.

FABRICATION PROCESS

The printing process for embedding paper circuits inside the desired interactive object is defined in three steps: 1) design a 3D model by modeling software, 2) print out paper cutout template that matches to the 3D model created, compose circuits on the 2D planar figure, and 3) insert folded paper circuit by pausing and continue printing by resuming process. Step 1 and 2 are reversible along with designer's intention. A designer could get paper templates to construct 3D artifacts by folding, and model 3D version, which houses the paper design, or, s/he get a 3D model from online repository and then find the paper template for it.

Design 3D Models

We developed a reusable template to ease the creation of 3D printable objects with inner hollow spaces for inserting paper circuits. This template consists of a *"host"* object and a *"hole"* object to subtract from the host. A designer can specify the host and the *"hole"* objects respectively, then the cutting operation will be automatically performed.

We implemented this template using CrarftML[1]. CraftML is a markup language to model 3D objects using an HTML5 resembling syntax. It allows designers to construct, modify, and align 3D solid primitives in ways similar to web design. It also supports SVG style syntax and CSS to perform Boolean CSG operations and assign properties.

Figure 1 shows the CraftML code for designing a cake as the host object with a sphere-shaped hollow space inside.

```
1: <g layout="center xyz" transform="cut .hole">
2:   <stack id="host">
3:     <cylinder radius="7" height="2"/>
4:     <cylinder radius="10" height="5"/>
5:   </stack>
6:   <sphere size="5" class="hole"/>
7: </g>
```

Figure 1. Simple code to create a hollow cake shape by CraftML. Space defined as the class hole will be cut out from solid cake shape.

The sphere is a *"hole"* object that is assigned the CSS class label `hole` (line 6), which can be selected to cut using the transform expression `cut .hole` (line 1). A `<stack>` tag arranges the two cylinder primitives inside a vertical stack to form a cake-like object (line 2). The layout expression `center xyz` aligns the stack and the sphere with respect to their centers along all three axes (line 1) such that once the sphere is cut, the hollow space is in the center of the stack. Building upon this example, a designer can easily replace the cake stack with another object, such as an STL file downloaded from on online model repository such as Thingiverse[2] and YouMagine[3].

We designed a custom scaffolding pillars to replace the default supporting settings while printing with overhang, as shown in Figure 6 (left). Otherwise, the 3D printer would extrude materials in the hollow space with infill patterns and make it impossible to insert paper circuit parts. However, overhang parts such as arms and the body of the robot in the same example would not be finished as expected, if the printing scaffolding setting is turned off.

Paper Circuits on the Planar Figure

In order to create the paper circuits, we first divide the 3D model into atomic 3D polyhedrons such as spheres, cubes,

[1] https://craftml.io
[2] http://thingiverse.com
[3] https://youmagine.com

and cylinders. Simple shapes are easier to manipulate and convert from 2D templates to 3D shapes, and also easy to insert into 3D printed shell.

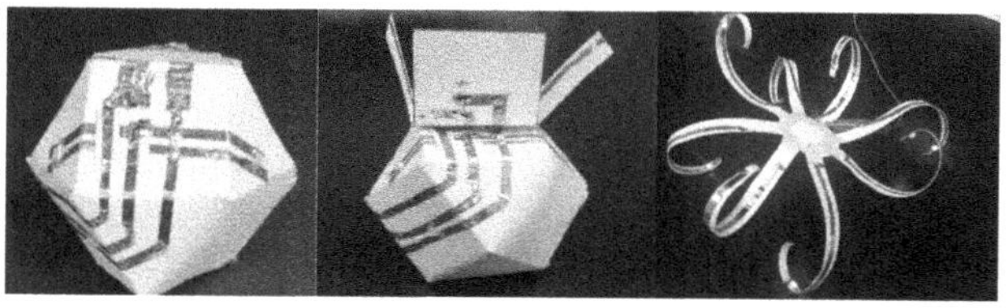

Figure 2. Paper circuits designed on an 2D template of sphere(left), and attached cube on the top by magnets for dual pausing process (middle), and a curled paper circuit (right)

Paper template generating from 3D shapes solution, such as PaperLego [5] allows easy creation of a planar figure of a 3D model that can then be folded into 3D shapes. To construct 3D polygons, a designer only need to cutout the templates, fold, and glue them. Sketch-a-TUI guides makers to construct interactive circuits on the paper tangibles [13]. When complicated details are needed for the object, we can dissect parts into pieces, adding magnets to each side of polygons. Magnets help alignment among wires on circuit for closed connection, as shown in Figure 2 middle. Magnets have great conductivity and are easy to cope with copper tapes. Copper tapes replaced wires because of their plasticity, high conductivity, low resistance, and solder-ability. They can be also easily cut or untapped if situated wrong. Note that any low cost circuit construction technique can be an alternative, conductive paints, silver ink pen, circuit printing with inkjet printer, for example. We assume that users are already used to designing hand crafted paper circuit, either by their own previous knowledge or by being supported from circuitry design tools such as 123D Circuits [1]. Our focus is blending these cheap hands-on circuit design technique with a consumer-level 3D printing. Materials used on paper circuits such as copper tapes, silver ink, small LEDS, and photocells are familiar, inexpensive and easy to get around.

The flexibility of paper helps us explore a greater level of experimentation, such as the form shown in Figure 2 right, used for Octopus' legs. By curling, creasing, or wrinkling, users can create a wide range of shapes and unique textures that would be very hard to accomplish with 3D printing.

Pause and Resume to Insert Paper Circuit

Figure 3. Printing process of simple cube with sensors and LEDs on each facet of folded paper circuit for cube.

To insert paper circuits inside a 3D printed object, the printing job has to be paused and resumed rather than being done at-one-go. For the first step, we paused at the Z-height that seems that should be stopped by being guided through the slicing program's time approximation. Once the printing process is paused, the 3D paper circuit was manually inserted into the inner hole, and was resumed to continue the task. When multiple components need to be inserted, users can pause the printing process at multiple z heights. In this case, it will be important to take into account that discrete circuits can be aligned via magnets.

We are able to automate this technique by modifying the G-code [2] to stop the printing at multiple heights where the paper circuits need to be inserted as shown in Figure 4. In order to keep print header from touching inserted circuit and dragging it around, we let it stop at the height that the model has its widest layer.

```
;layer 1000 where to stop, Z=10.5
G1 X108.572 Y96.837 E15.98996
M25            ;pause print
G1 Z40 F1800 ;raise extruder to height 40
G4 S010        ;wait 10sec.
;Here insert paper circuits in the inner space
G29 Z10.500   ;return back to Z-origin
               ;remembered from the last Z-height
G1 E13.98996 F2400.00000 ;continue
...
```

Figure 4. Revised G-code snippet to pause and resume printing for inserting paper circuits during printing process

APPLICATIONS AND ENABLED INTERACTIONS

These new approaches can be applied to various design cases, from testing prototypes to personal designing. We present a range of examples from the simplest to the more complex.

Polygon Primitives

We created basic Euclidean polygons, observing how planar figure templates for 3D polyhedrons are created, experimenting construction of circuits on 2D surface, and folded into 3D shapes. Cubes, spheres, hexagonal cylinders, and other basic polyhedrons helped us test which template figures well fit into 3D objects. For instance, we tested a convex polyhedron template for internal sphere circuit, varying the number of sides, depending on where the electronic components should be placed.

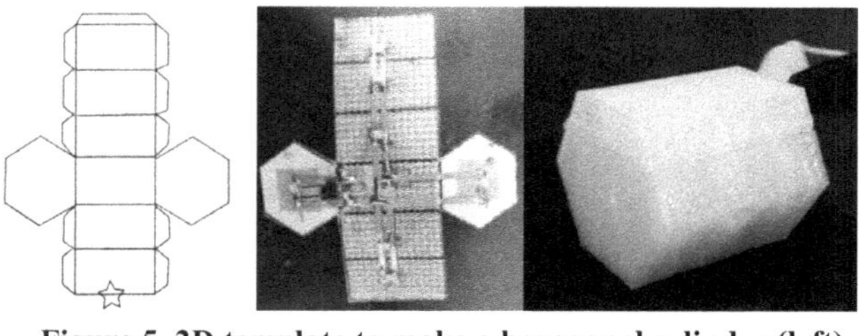

Figure 5. 2D template to make a hexagonal cylinder (left), paper circuit of the template to light up on 6 different positions (middle), and resulting model with LEDs (right).

Toy Robot

One exciting application is to build 3D objects that users can utilize in their daily lives and play with. Inspired by the robot collection featured on Thingiverse that has been beloved for years, we developed a robot to investigate various inputs and outputs inside 3D printed objects. We integrated a photo resistor to detect luminance of background through transparent PLA plastic, a microphone that detects sound and changes the resistance, and LEDs representing the robot's eyes that can light up depending on currency through the entire circuit. We made two different versions: 1) the battery can be replaced through a hole and 2) two pins to connect to an external power source. For the former, the paper circuit was folded around the battery with the positive tape on the top, and the negative beneath of inserted battery. It is a reliable approach to replace power periodically (Figure 6 right).

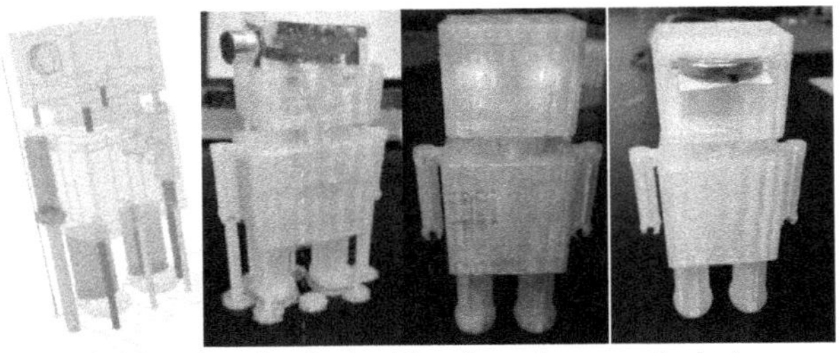

Figure 6. 3D printed robot with microphone and photo sensor to light up eyes. With paper circuit, users can precisely situate electronics on designated position

Paper circuits give users the full control over spatial and geometric organizations of traces and components. For example, two LED positions for the robot's eyes, and microphone for its ear that situated on exactly designated spot as the designer planned ahead.

Peacock

Magnifying the plasticy and foldability of a paper, we explored various paper crafting techniques not only folding, but also creasing, and quilling. In one of these experiments, we created a peacock figure with two paper templates: a sphere shaped for the body cavity, and the creased form of its train. Taking advantage of the flexible modality of a creased paper, a user can interact with the tail by collapsing it or letting it spread out to open and close the circuit. The main sphere circuit was inserted into the peacock's body when printing was paused. It contains the connections for the battery and small LEDs with open circuit for connecting tail. The second circuit accommodates copper tapes that close the circuit when it is grabbed as shown in Figure 7 right. Since the tail is interchangeable even after printing, this design provides a new design approach, allowing users to combine different colors, textures and sizes of the tail without having to print a new model from the scratch.

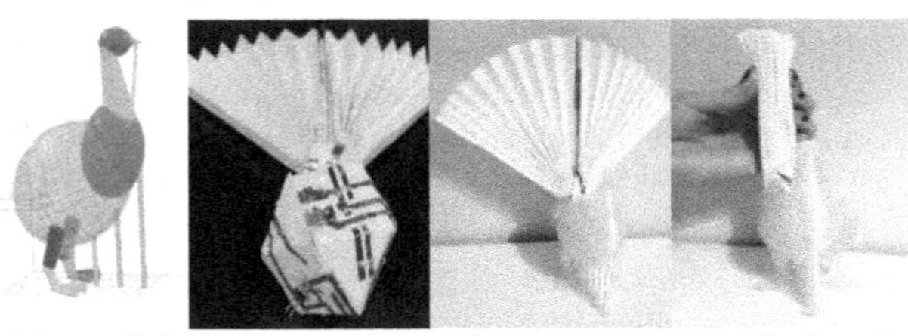

Figure 7. The process of creating 3D peacock with closed circuitry by hand interaction with its tail.

Other Interaction Techniques

Finally, we present two more interaction design possibilities enabled by our approach. We designed an octopus with a curled paper circuit embedded (Figure 2 right) that contains a reed switch to allow a different type of interaction. The octopus can react to a magnet nearby, completing the circuit by closed magnet connection. In another application, by inserting a metal ball at the bottom of a balancing toy and the circuit with a mercury tilt switch on the top, the artifact also can detect inclination. We demonstrated example interaction with toys, but introduced versatile techniques can be imposed into different design implications

LIMITATIONS AND FUTURE WORKS

Our work opens a novel opportunity for inserting common crafting materials during the 3D printing process. Fabrics, yarn, threads, marbles, and magnets are common materials used in everyday crafting. By pausing and resuming 3D printing and inserting these materials into partially printed objects, we can realize a complex, multi-material design using a unmodified, commodity 3D printer. Figure 8 shows an example of inserting a magnet into a 3D printed teaspoon, illustrating that our technique can potentially be applied to non-paper materials as well.

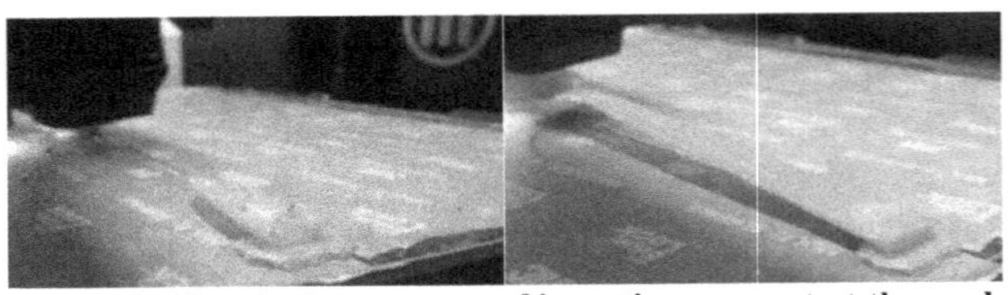

Figure 8. 3D printing process of inserting magnet at the neck

Paper manipulation technique itself can be a great interactivity triggering activity, folding to let adjacent facets attach each other to close the circuit, creasing papers to enable elongation of length and volume as proven by peacock's tail example, and bending to change resistance. With micro controller integration, we vision actuating 3D objects by flexible papers stitched with SMA, by printing them with soft materials, such as NinjaFlex, or Nylon.

Nonetheless, with this approach, 3D concave objects need to be divided into multiple convex parts. The robot in Figure 6 as an instance, the printing had to be stopped twice to insert a circuit in the body, and to head because of the narrow neck, which does not allow the paper cube for the body part to pass through. We will continue to explore better ways to insert separate parts for overhanging parts (e.g., robot's arms).

As 3D Folded PrintGami is a new design process, user study is essential to validate this new design approach enables designers simply apply into their 3D interactive objects design, and improve the process observing their obstacles.

ACKNOWLEDGEMENTS

This research is supported by NSF Grant No. IIS-1453771, and Balsells Mobility Program Scholarship.

REFERENCES

1. 123D Circuits. https://123d.circuits.io/
2. Gcode http://reprap.org/wiki/G-code
3. Michael Eisenberg, Ann Nishioka, and M. E. Schreiner. 1997. Helping users think in three dimensions: steps toward incorporating spatial cognition in user modelling. In *Proceedings of the 2nd international conference on Intelligent user interfaces (IUI '97)*, Johanna Moore, Ernest Edmonds, and Angel Puerta (Eds.). p113-120.
4. Wei Gao, Yunbo Zhang, Diogo C. Nazzetta, Karthik Ramani, and Raymond J. Cipra. 2015. RevoMaker: Enabling Multi-directional and Functionally-embedded 3D printing using a Rotational Cuboidal Platform. In *Proceedings of the 28th Annual ACM Symposium on User Interface Software & Technology* (UIST '15), 437-446. DOI=http://dx.doi.org/10.1145/2807442.2807476
5. Jiangtao Gong, Jue Wang, and Yingqing Xu. 2014. PaperLego: component-based papercraft designing tool for children. In SIGGRAPH Asia 2014 Designing Tools For Crafting Interactive Artifacts (SA '14). ACM, New York, NY, USA, , Article 3 , 4 pages. DOI=http://dx.doi.org/10.1145/2668947.2668954
6. Jeeeun Kim and Tom Yeh. 2015. Toward 3D-Printed Movable Tactile Pictures for Children with Visual Impairments. In *Proceedings of the 33rd Annual ACM Conference on Human Factors in Computing Systems* (CHI '15). ACM, New York, NY, USA, 2815-2824. DOI=http://dx.doi.org/10.1145/2702123.2702144DOI= http://dx.doi.org/10.1145/2677199.2688815
7. Steve Hodges, Nicolas Villar, Nicholas Chen, Tushar Chugh, Jie Qi, Diana Nowacka, and Yoshihiro Kawahara. 2014. Circuit stickers: peel-and-stick construction of interactive electronic prototypes. In *Proceedings of the SIGCHI Conference on Human Factors in Computing Systems* (CHI '14), 1743-1746. DOI=http://dx.doi.org/10.1145/2556288.2557150
8. Simon Olberding, Sergio Soto Ortega, Klaus Hildebrandt, and Jürgen Steimle. 2015. Foldio: Digital Fabrication of Interactive and Shape-Changing Objects With Foldable Printed Electronics. In *Proceedings of the 28th Annual ACM Symposium on User Interface Software & Technology* (UIST '15), 223-232. DOI=http://dx.doi.org/10.1145/2642918.2647413
9. Simon Olberding, Michael Wessely, and Jürgen Steimle. 2014. PrintScreen: fabricating highly customizable thin-film touch-displays. In *Proceedings of the 27th annual ACM symposium on User interface software and technology* (UIST '14), 281-290. DOI=http://dx.doi.org/10.1145/2807442.2807494
10. Valkyrie Savage, Colin Chang, and Björn Hartmann. 2013. Sauron: embedded single-camera sensing of printed physical user interfaces. In *Proceedings of the 26th annual ACM symposium on User interface software and technology* (UIST '13), 447-456. DOI=http://dx.doi.org/10.1145/2501988.2501992
11. Michael Shorter, Jon Rogers, and John McGhee. 2014. Enhancing everyday paper interactions with paper circuits. In *Proceedings of the 2014 conference on Designing interactive systems* (DIS '14), 39-42. DOI=http://dx.doi.org/10.1145/25298510.2598584
12. Voxel8, 3D printing Electronics http://www.voxel8.co/
13. Alexander Wiethoff, Hanna Schneider, Michael Rohs, Andreas Butz, and Saul Greenberg. 2012. Sketch-a-TUI: low cost prototyping of tangible interactions using cardboard and conductive ink. InProceedings of the Sixth International Conference on Tangible, Embedded and Embodied Interaction (TEI '12), Stephen N. Spencer (Ed.). ACM, New York, NY, USA, 309-312. DOI=http://dx.doi.org/10.1145/2148131.2148196
14. Jie Qi and Leah Buechley. 2014. Sketching in circuits: designing and building electronics on paper. In *Proceedings of the SIGCHI Conference on Human Factors in Computing Systems* (CHI '14), 1713-1722. DOI=http://dx.doi.org/10.1145/2556288.2557391
15. Jie Qi and Leah Buechley. 2010. Electronic popables: exploring paper-based computing through an interactive pop-up book. In *Proceedings of the fourth international conference on Tangible, embedded, and embodied interaction* (TEI '10), 121-128. DOI=http://dx.doi.org/10.1145/1709886.1709909

Motion Echo Snowboard: Enhancing Body Movement Perception in Sport via Visually Augmented Feedback

Hyung Kun Park, Woohun Lee
Wonder Lab, KAIST
291 Daehak-ro, Yuseong-gu, Daejeon, South Korea
{hung85, woohun.lee}@kaist.ac.kr

ABSTRACT
This paper introduces an interactive snowboard concept, *Motion Echo Snowboard*, which provides visually augmented feedback for body movements during snowboarding. The proposed system augments the user experience with a real-time visual display of performer weight distribution on the upper side of the snowboard. We conducted two user studies: an individual usage and a lesson situation. Based on the results, we confirmed that the *Motion Echo Snowboard* concept could enhance movement perception and motivation as being the starting point for exploring body movement in both situations. Moreover, it could generate new behavior patterns and could establish student-instructor trust as a medium of movement during lessons.

Author Keywords
Sport interaction; representation; movement; body; perception; augmented feedback;

ACM Classification Keywords
H.5.m. Information interfaces and presentation (e.g., HCI): Miscellaneous

INTRODUCTION
Perceiving body movement is very important in various sporting activities. It influences not only the athlete's performance but also his motivation and safety [16, 33]. People utilize various methods to understand their own body movements during sporting activities. For example, to correct stroke motions in tennis or badminton, people may carefully observe mirror images of themselves. In golf, one might ask a friend to record a golf swing using their mobile phone. When the reflected motions are viewed, it is actually surprising to know that we are not moving as precisely as we had perceived ourselves to be. The reason for this may be a gap between the perceived movement and the actual body movement. The degree of the gap might differ depending on the participant's perception or physical skills. However, this perceptional gap clearly exists in every performer. In addition, in the case of learning situations, when an instructor or colleague observes the performer's movement, it is hard to perceive every detail of the performer's body movement. From the third-person point of view, an observer can gather information about the performer's posture and the results of their movements. However, some information can only be accessed through a performer's intrinsic feedback, and this information is often difficult for a third party to capture. Instructors usually add their own previous experience of the movement to the observation in order to understand the performer's current movement and offer corrections. Thus, there is another perceptual gap between the actual body movement and the observed body movement when it comes to observers and participants.

In this context, augmented feedback through interactive technology can be a useful way to reduce this perceptual gap. Augmented feedback to support perception in sports has been studied in previous research, i.e., sports science and human-computer interaction (HCI) research. Previous research into augmented feedback in sports has mainly focused on auditory feedback [2, 18, 24, 28, 30] and tactile feedback [7, 12, 17]. These modalities are easy to design in such a way that the feedback has a peripheral property and does not hinder performance in sport [31]. However, tactile feedback and auditory feedback are limited in terms of the quantity and speed of information they provide. In addition, these modalities are not in the necessary format to share body movement with others in real-time. In this research, we suggested the concept of the '*Motion Echo*', which visualizes movements with a visual modality in real-time in order to support the performer's and the observer's perception of the performer's movements in sport. By adjusting the visual attention to the proper level and increasing the intuitiveness of the feedback, we try to develop a visual feedback system with the peripheral property.

In snowboarding, a simple body movement or small change in balance can have a huge effect on the movement of the snowboard. In addition, snowboarding contains dynamic action with high speed, which makes it challenging to observe the details of others' movements. An expert

DIS 2016, June 4–8, 2016, Brisbane, Australia.

http://dx.doi.org/10.1145/2901790.2901797

interview was conducted to confirm the initial area of research and to define the core movements and information that would need to be analyzed by a snowboarding support system. From the following reasons, we have selected snowboarding to demonstrate our system concept. We developed the *Motion Echo Snowboard*, an interactive snowboard deck, which allows the user to visualize the change of weight distribution on the board, which is a core element in snowboarding. When the performers move their body on the snowboard, the change in weight distribution is represented through a visual display on the upper side of the snowboard deck. Individual usage tests and tests in a lesson situation were conducted with the *Motion Echo Snowboard* prototype. In the individual usage test, we explored perceptible situations of feedback from *Motion Echo Snowboard* while in an actual snowboarding environment. In the lesson situation test, we expected that *Motion Echo Snowboard* could help instructors observe others' body movements and help them generate new behavior patterns. Finally, we discussed how this visual medium tool could support the sporting experience in real-time.

RELATED WORK

Perceiving body movement in sports

Every sport is based on some type of movement. Furthermore, a participant's perception of such movements is important in virtually every sport. Robert et al. [16] investigated the influence of natural sound (impact sound, swing sound) on sports performance and golf club selection. They found that perception is closely linked to learning and motivation. Helsen and Starkes [33] researched the relationship between perception and performance. Knudson and Kluka [10] stated that visual information is important in sports training. In the areas of sports science and sports research, the relation between performance and perception of body movement has already been explored and defined.

Two types of feedback are used for the perception of body movement in sport [9, 25]. One is intrinsic feedback, which uses a person's own sensory system, for example, tension in the biceps and the visual position of the racket while playing tennis. Extrinsic feedback, also known as augmented feedback, is reflective information that originates from an external source and the surrounding environment. This category includes comments from an instructor and recorded video. Performers perceive their own movements through both intrinsic and extrinsic feedback and modify them during sporting activities.

Modality transfer of body movement

In the past, in the field of art and dance, the transfer of body movements and their development into a medium of expression have been important research areas. In dancing, body movement is a fundamental means of expression. Various studies focusing on the transfer of body movements into other modalities, such as sound, light, and actuated movement, have proved that body movement modality transfer is possible [8, 11, 15, 19]. Elblaus et al. [21] explored sonic interaction in a circus, because circuses use vibrant and extremely dynamic body movements.

Feedback through modality transfer can enhance motor learning in many other disciplines in which body movement is important. For example, Danna et al. [17] developed a hand movement sonification method that improves the handwriting of disabled children. Hernadez et al. [14] developed a method in which body movements during rehabilitation are used as the input to a game in order to enhance the motivation of children with cerebral palsy. Grosshauser and Hermann [32] used hand movement sonification to help students who are learning to play the violin. In exergame research, body movement and factors of the game were combined to generate new experiences or enhance immersion of the system [13]. Furthermore, Sigrist et al. [25] reviewed the research in this area and verified that augmented feedback can support motor learning based on feedback and design modalities.

These research results show that modality transfer of body movement can enrich user experiences, motivation, hedonic qualities, and motor learning.

Augmented feedback in sport

Sonification for enhancing the individual's perception

Sonification is the most promising approach for enhancing body movement perception in sports. Nylander [30] sonified the swing motion of a golf club to explore the influence of non-interpretive feedback in performer's sports experiences. Godbout and Stienstra [2, 18] sonified the hand stroke in speed-skating to correct posture and the hand stroke of athletes. The vLink system was developed to inform ski athletes of how much and where slips were occurring during a ski-carving turn [24]. Shoichi [28] sonified the center of gravity for skiing. In this way, auditory feedback has the ability to deliver movements in real-time. These methods work without drawing unwanted attention to the method itself and can deliver information without being visually distracting. However, sonification has the limitation of delivering only complicated information or information from multiple sources at the same time. In addition, spatial information from sound has a subjective quality in terms of perception. In other words, an observer may not easily map a performer's movement and sonification in dynamic sporting conditions.

Tactile feedback for lesson situation.

Generally, in a conventional training/lesson situation, the instructor physically manipulates the student's body parts to create proper posture. However, in dynamic sports like skating and snowboarding, physical intervention is almost impossible. To solve this, tactile feedback could replace physical intervention in real-time training. Spelmezan designed a wireless tactile feedback system for communication during snowboarding lessons [7]. Emanuele [12] developed a tactile feedback system that supports error recognition in rowing training. This kind of non-verbal and non-visual delivery could facilitate the learning of strategy in sports like soccer [17]. However, these examples were meant to judge or instruct the captured movement and not to share or communicate it.

Visual feedback for enhancing immersion or post-hoc analysis

Augmenting body movement with visual feedback enables a system to deliver accurate information in a short time. Kajastila visualized body movement and traced a user's movement on a trampoline [25]. She tested the difference between feedback of direct-mapped movements and feedback of exaggerated movements. However, visual feedback in most sports can raise concerns about sight distraction. For this reason, visual augmentation is mostly used in sports simulation systems such as indoor rowing and archery [3, 6, 27]. In real sporting activity, visual feedback is useful for analyzing movement after the execution. Pijnappel projected the trace of a skateboard on a wall to explore different training methods and to learn skateboarding tricks [26]. Higuchi utilized a drone for the representation of posture in sports training [20].

In general, auditory and tactile feedback is a common modality for augmented feedback in real-time sporting conditions. Despite the fact that visual feedback can deliver large amounts of information in a short time and can lead to system immersion, the distraction problem means that visual feedback is used for relatively static sporting conditions or in sports simulation systems. In this research, we explored the applicability and the design considerations of visual feedback in real-time sporting conditions.

SNOWBOARD

Snowboarding basics

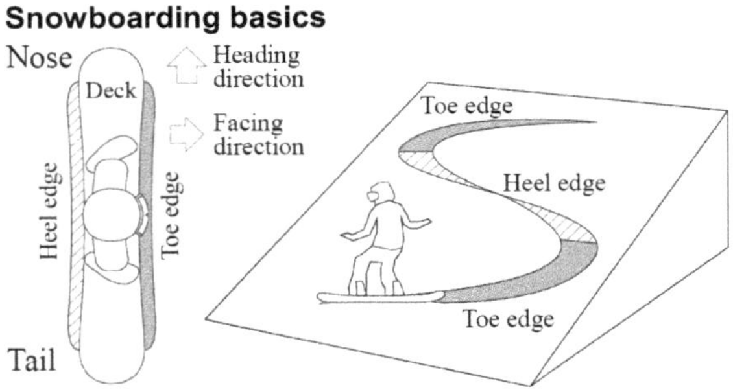

Figure 1. Snowboarding basics

Snowboarding is a winter sport in which the snowboarder glides on snow using a long board. The snowboarder binds both feet on the board with a strap called bindings. From the top view, the facing the forward direction is the nose, and facing the rear, is the tail (Figure 1). The toe edge and the heel edge are on either side. Snowboarders move their body to control how their weight is balanced and to use the heel edge and toe edge to glide down a slope.

In snowboarding, differences between perceived body movement and actual body movement can occur, like all sports. These differences from simple change in body balance can be critical to the success of the snowboarder's performance. Also, snowboarding have dynamic and speedy environment, so it is hard to observe performer's movements for coach or colleagues. Because of this, we believe that snowboarding is an appropriate discipline to test and develop the concept of '*Motion Echo*'.

Snowboarding Skill in User study

We used several snowboarding techniques in user testing (Table 1). During individual usage tests, participants performed a routine comprising of a pendulum slides, beginner turns, switch riding, and basic ground tricks. In the lesson test, an instructor gave a lesson on skating, the side slip, and the pendulum slide, depending on the student's skill levels.

Name	Description
Skating	Traveling on a flat surface with one foot bound.
Side slip	Gliding on snow using only toe edge or heel edge.
Pendulum slide	Controlling balance to move left and right while doing the side slip.
Beginner turn	Gliding on snow and changing toe and heel edges.
Switch riding	Alternating between front foot and back foot. (E.g., in the case of regular stance, riding with right foot in front.)
Basic ground tricks	Simple tricks that can be performed on the snowfield (nose/tail press, ollie (jump), 180 jump, etc.)

Table 1. Snowboarding techniques

EXPERT INTERVIEW

We conducted two expert interviews to investigate the core snowboarding movements and ascertain the importance of perception in snowboarding. In this exercise, we recruited two snowboarding experts, with experiences of sports lesson, who could represent both the performer and instructor. From the results of the expert interview, we confirmed the difference between perceived and observed motions, and the impact that makes on changes to performer body movement.

Expert Interview setup

Expert	Experience	Skill
A (M, 30)	12 years	Professional athletes
B (M, 27)	7 years	Chair of Korean university snowboard federation

Table 2. Personal information of expert in the expert interview

The expert interviews were conducted with two snowboarding experts (Table 2). Based on the pre-interview through an online survey, we selected participants who had a high level of snowboarding understanding experience with lessons. The selected experts had a combined average of 9.5 years of experience in their sporting disciplines. Each in-depth interview was conducted on a one-on-one basis and lasted approximately one hour. In these interviews, we explained the purpose of the research and introduced existing researches and technical examples. The experts answered core questions in their own sports discipline. The first half of the questions focused on how the experts use their perceived movement in snowboarding. The rest of the questions focused on the attempts made by the experts to enhance movement perception in snowboarding.

Findings from Expert Interview

Perspectives of perceiving body movement

The interviews confirmed the importance of perception during movement. The experts asserted that perceiving movement and body posture is important for learning and improving on skills. However, in many situations, there is a gap between the performer's own perception and the actual movement, which could cause difficulties while learning and performing. However, this gap becomes smaller as the person becomes more adept at the activity. The experts stated that from their experiences of a lesson, beginners usually cannot perceive their own movements entirely. Furthermore, in situations where they are trying to discuss their movements with others, the second party was unable to determine the exact movement that was made. Even with more knowledge of movements observer have, the performers still considered that the observers did not know their movements precisely. However, the experts emphasized that, in addition to this movement perception issue, external knowledge and training should run in tandem to enhance performance.

Weight distribution is core information of snowboarding

Both two experts emphasized that weight distribution and change in distribution are the most important elements in snowboarding. Series of body movements in snowboarding such as rotating the shoulder, leaning backward and forward, and pressing the knees are directly related to manipulating the weight balance on the board. Because snowboarding happens on an inclined snow surface, there is a difference in the feeling of a vertical practice surface and an actual slope. Standing on an inclined surface is not familiar to most people. Because of this unfamiliarity, the beginning performer may think that they are standing vertical to the inclined surface, while actually standing in the direction of gravity. This makes controlling a snowboard with body weight caused by gravity challenging for beginners. In addition, information on weight distribution is only perceived by the performer through intrinsic feedback.

Existing attempts and feedback preferences

We collected examples of previous attempts to enhance their movement and perception while snowboarding. The experts used video recordings to observe their own movements from a third person standpoint, and listened to comments from their colleagues. In addition, they used the sound of sliding on snow and visual traces in the environment to track their movement. Feedback style and modality were differentiated based on context and purpose. The expert subjects preferred the non-interpretive information mentioned by Nylander and Tholander [29]. The experts asserted that objective and expressive feedback is acceptable and easy to apply for various purposes in snowboarding.

MOTION ECHO SNOWBOARD

Concept of Motion Echo Snowboard

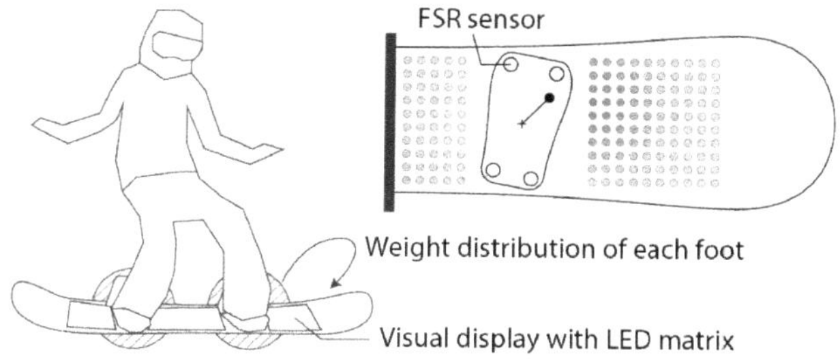

Figure 2. *Motion Echo snowboard* concept

Motion Echo Snowboard is a system used to visualize the weight distribution of each foot in real time (Figure 2). From the sensor data under the bindings, overall weight distribution and variance can be detected. This information is shown to the performer through an embedded LED matrix on the upper side of a snowboard deck without any interpretation. In our system concept, the snowboard deck is the operating point where movement occurs and it also works as a display that shows the performer's body movement. We expected that this visualization could help the performer and observer gain an intuitive understanding of their movement.

Prototype of Motion Echo Snowboard

Hardware

Motion Echo Snowboard consists of a sensor that detects movement, an LED matrix that displays information, and a processor module that includes a battery and Arduino. Eight FSR sensors (FSR-402) are located under the bindings to detect the direction and pressure of each foot (Figure 3B). Except for the sensor, all wiring is embedded into the deck to protect from the outdoor conditions. In case of sensor, we needed to adjust the location and replace the sensor due to a maintenance issue. We discovered that FSR sensor is sensitive to moisture in the pilot study, so we coated the sensor with a silicone layer of thickness 1- 1.5 mm. The LED matrix consists of 400 NeoPixels (Figure 3C) [1]. A NeoPixel strip was embedded into the upper side of the snowboard deck and coated with a diffusion sheet to reduce dazzling and create smooth graphical transitions. The processor module consisted of an Arduino that used sensor data and controled the NeoPixel, battery, and switch for calibrations and power (Figure 3A). To manage the 400 LED pixels in high frequency, we use an Arduino Due [4], for its fast processing speed. We used two types of batteries. (For Arduino, 7.4 V and 500 mAh; for NeoPixel matrix, 3.7 V, and 2000 mAh). Depending on conditions and methods of our experiment, one battery pack could endure 2-3 hours. User experiments were conducted on an inclined snowfield; therefore, each section had to be fully waterproof.

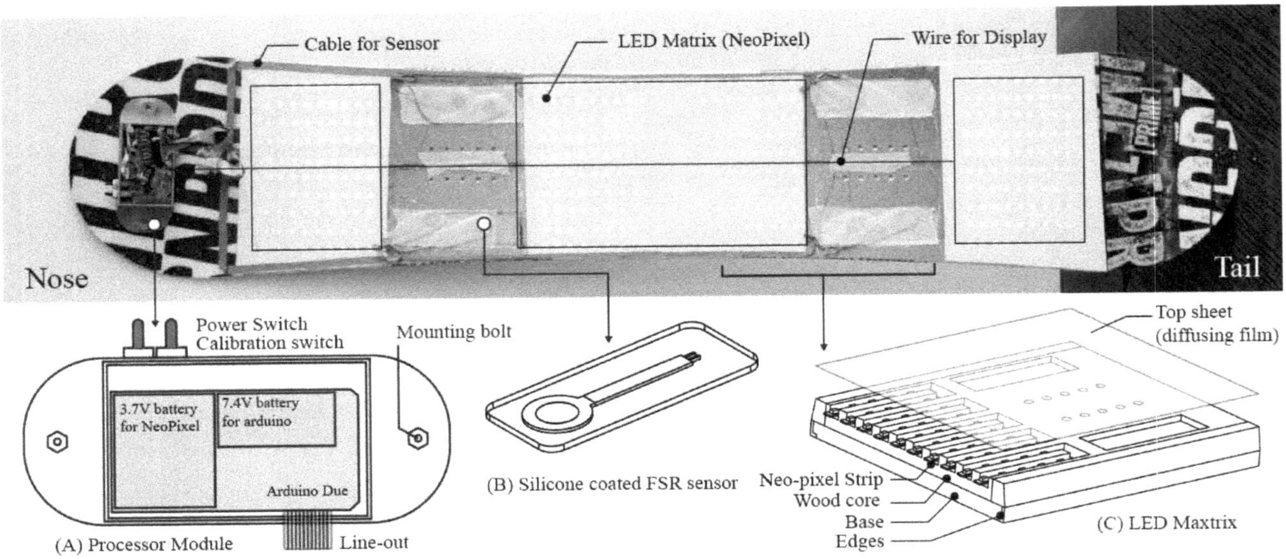

Figure 3. Hardware of *Motion Echo Snowboard*. (A) Processor module, (B) FSR sensors, and (C) LED matrix for display.

Software

Visual feedback was achieved using Arduino code. There are four LED matrices on the board. Each matrix consists of 10 × 10 NeoPixel lights. We developed feedback prototypes several different styles including heat map style, equalizer style, and physical movement of particles style. We selected the heat map style of feedback because it was considered the most intuitive and had the least information distortion. To visualize flow, one panel collect data from two adjacent sensors. With these two sensors, direction and pressure on deck could be calculated. The HSB color system was used to calculate each pixel's color and brightness. Higher pressure was expressed with the red hue and lower pressure was expressed with the purple hue. Overall pressure affected the brightness. Saturation value was fixed. We used a diffusion film to control the maximum brightness in order to reduce distraction from the snowboarding task.

USER STUDY

The user studies were conducted in two scenarios. First, we did an individual usage test, in which a performer uses *Motion Echo Snowboard* alone. In the individual usage test, we wanted to discover the basic characteristics of the system and to see how the performer perceived body movement by themselves, in their sporting context. In the lesson situation test, we want to see how Motion Echo Snowboard could be used accepted as a medium of movement during snowboarding lessons, and how it would add to the lesson curriculum. Therefore, we summarize the research objectives of the user study below.

1. Understand the basic characteristics of *Motion Echo Snowboard* system (Feedback design, desired information, and etc.).
2. Find out the how visual feedback is perceived and explore the possibility of individual use with *Motion Echo Snowboard*
3. Discover if *Motion Echo Snowboard* is a valuable medium for communicating body movement and if it helps deliver movement awareness and knowledge between instructor and students.

Individual usage test

User study setup

For the individual usage test, we recruited participants of various skill levels from one year of experience to more than five years of experience plus an instructor's certificate. Based on their skill level, participants were divided into two groups. Advanced participants could glide down every type of slope with ease and had several lesson experiences. Intermediate participants had less experience than advanced participants, but had no trouble gliding down the slopes without falling. All had spent more than one winter at a ski resort. Two prototypes were prepared with lengths of 152 cm and 153 cm, which were suitable for participants with 173-178 cm height and 64-75 kg weight. Because of the board specifications, mainly male participants were recruited. This should not affect test results because snowboarding is a male dominated sport. The test was conducted on an indoor ski slope owing to the season, ease of capturing video, and simplicity in managing participants. The slope was 30 m of novice level with moving walkway. Two moderators managed the safety and filming of the experiment.

Participants	Carriers	Skill levels
P1 (Male, 21)	1 year	Intermediate
P2 (Male, 24)	1 year	Intermediate
P3 (Male, 26)	2 years	Intermediate
P4 (Male, 25)	3 years	Advanced
P5 (Male, 24)	4 years	Advanced
P6 (Male, 24)	5 years	Advanced

Table 3. Participants' data for the individual usage test

User study Contents

Before starting the study, participants were asked to go down the slope 1-2 times with a conventional snowboard. This step was to make sure participants were accustomed to the indoor ski slope and to refresh their memories. After this step, participants were asked to ride down the slope while performing different themes (Table 1, Pendulum slide, beginner turn, switch riding, basic ground tricks). Because of the shorter slope length, these themes were provided to recall their overall experience in snowboarding. All tests were recorded. After finishing the set tasks, participants answered survey and interview questions.

Lesson situation test

User study setup

In the lesson situation test, instructors and students formed pairs, with the instructor instructing the student (Table 4). Three instructors, with experience giving snowboarding lessons, participated. Six participants, who had never ridden a snowboard before, were recruited as students. An instructor gave lessons to two students. One student was trained with a traditional snowboard, as a control, and the other with the *Motion Echo Snowboard.* Under the latter condition, the instructor also used the *Motion Echo Snowboard.* Unlike the individual usage test, the conversation and details of the instruction between the instructor and each student were important. Because of this, a moderator stood by and observed each lesson in its entirety.

Instructor	Carriers	Student	
I1 (M,24)	4 years	SE1(Male,29)	Experimental group
		SC1(Female,22)	Control group
I2 (M,26)	4 years	SC2(Female,20)	Control group
		SE2(Male,20)	Experimental group
I3 (M,26)	6 years	SC3(Male,28)	Control group
		SE3(Male,25)	Experimental group

Table 4. Participants of lesson situation test

User study contents

Each instructor was asked to give a lesson for approximately two hours based on a lesson curriculum. Two hours is the generally accepted time for an actual slope lecture. Prior to the start of the lesson, the moderator introduced the instructor to the *Motion Echo Snowboard* for about 5 minutes and asked to include it in the day's lesson curriculum. Following the completion of the lesson, the instructor and students were asked interview questions similar to those asked in the individual usage test. Because all the students were riding a snowboard for the first time, the interview was primarily conducted from the viewpoint of the instructors. The instructors answered based on comparison to the control group.

Lesson curriculums

Lesson contents and order was based on the curriculum of the Canadian Association of Snowboard Instructors (CASI) [5]. However, instructors were allowed to graft their own skill and teaching know-how into their lesson. Most of the instructors first explained basic snowboarding concepts. They then gave a lesson about skating and traveling on a flat surface with one foot bound. After skating, they climbed the slope and performed the side slip and pendulum sliding. Depending on the student's sense of movement, most lessons progressed to the pendulum slide.

RESULT

Analysis

The user study was mainly analyzed through interview and observation. All interviews and conversations during the lesson were transcribed and coded with a coding scheme based on research questions. In the individual usage interview, comments were coded with four main topics, the perceptible situation, feedback design, provided movement, and the application. From the coded data, we developed several insights. In the lesson situation test, the overall study was analyzed in two ways. First, the interview and observations were coded by four topics, as described above, and the four phases of the lesson as below. Especially in observation data, comparison with the control group was considered. From the coded data, we developed several insights from using *Motion Echo Snowboard* in a lesson situation. These insights were categorized with the point of view of instructor or student. To understand the tendency of the comments of the instructor, verbal expressions were counted and compared with the control group.

We divided lesson process into four phases. The '*Explanation*' phase was focused on delivering theoretical contents of movement through verbal communication, drawings, and instructor description of the body motions. Next is the '*demonstration*' phase in which the instructor shows the desired movement lets students observe the instructor's movement. The third phase is '*correction*'. In this phase, students make a movement and instructor provides correction via verbal expression. The final phase, '*intervention*', is a physical operation when the instructor intercepts and changes the students' body movements (we excluded the case that instructor holds the students' hand or body so that is does not fall down).

Characteristics of Motion Echo System

The information of weight distribution was transferred accurately in short time.

Participants were able to connect the information on weight distribution with their body movement and the provided visual image without any difficulty. From the beginner to the advanced snowboarder, all had a similar understanding about the provided information.

"I could understand right away (what information was converted). The gradient color was easy to understand the strength of pressure. I was surprised than I thought. (Individual, P6)"

"If I see this board at the ski resort, not as participants, it was easy to know that this light is changed by my weight

distribution and its variance. (Lesson, I3)"

The feedback image was generated from the upper side of the snowboard deck. This location of the feedback allowed users understanding feedback quickly and focus on manipulating their weight distribution while on the snowboard.

"It was easy to focus on manipulating snowboard because the feedback image was on the deck. (Lesson, SC1)"

The feedback was designed so that users could intuitively understand information about their weight distribution, which was hard to perceive in the past.

Individual Usages of Motion Echo Snowboard

Situation of perceiving body movement had limited condition

Even though *Motion Echo Snowboard* has well-designed feedback system, the location of visual stimuli created several challenges for the individual users. Participants used feedback to check the current status of weight distribution rather than continuously glancing down to see the change in the visual display.

"It's okay to glance down once in a while. I've checked the feedback whenever I wanted. (Individual, P1)"

Most of the participants reported that the feedback was hard to consider when they performed more difficult tricks than their skills.

"It was helpful when I do just comfort riding. However, when I do special tricks or difficult movement, it was hard to consider feedback because I focused on my movement. (Individual, P2)"

Objective feedback of body movement would be useful to analyze a lesson situation.

When participants were able to perceive their motion, they were able to try various movements and check the feedback. Most participants desire to know their weight distributions and weight balance from past. Therefore, many participants propose making the application for a third person view. For example, applying *Motion Echo Snowboard* with video recording could be an interesting and effective material for users to analyze their body movement from an objective point of view after the performance.

"Many people use video recording for snowboarding improvement. With this board, recorded video can show more. (Individual, P5)"

To use the system as real-time feedback, all participants answered that the system assisted in delivering knowledge and enriching contents in the context of snowboard lesson. Five of six participants in the individual usage tests had experience giving snowboard lessons to others. They expected that this system would be useful in a lesson situation based on their experiences.

"It would be good for teaching beginner snowboarders. It is easy to explain the concept with a direct demonstration on an inclined slope. (Individual, P4)"

Interesting visual display motivated exploring body movement.

It was possible that the feedback given by the system could win a participants' favor through the colorful graphics and dynamic changes with their body movement. First, overall participants thought that the system was pragmatic and useful to enhance performance, and did not consider use of the board as solely hedonic enjoyment.

"It was useful to notice where my weight balance is and how it is changing. It is pragmatic than hedonic. (Individual, P2)"

However, in actual usage, some users felt hedonic satisfaction from the generated visual images.

"Once deck is glowing, this could attract the other's eye. (Individual, P6)"

As a result, it is challenging for *Motion Echo Snowboard* to provide effective assistance for constantly changing information of movement and correcting movement in individual usage. However, *Motion Echo Snowboard* could provide positive motivation for users exploring their own body movement through due to the constantly changing feedback expression.

Lesson Usages of Motion Echo Snowboard

Real applicability and benefits of *Motion Echo Snowboard* were mainly found in the lesson context. Instructors were guided about the basic concepts and about the instructions for the *Motion Echo Snowboard* in an introductory session right before the start of the lesson. After 1~2 trials, instructors could use the *Motion Echo* system easily in their lesson curriculum without additional time for adapting their curriculum.

Findings from instructor 1. Expressions of comment and instruction were diversified and had fundamental property.

Due to differences in the student's motor skills, understanding, or other individual factors, the same instructors could not give identical lesson comments. However, in conventional lesson situations, instructor's comments for correcting student's movement had a repetitive and simple pattern. On the other hand, with *Motion Echo Snowboard*, instructors used more various types of expression while giving comments about students' movement.

For examples, in every study situation, teaching 'side slip' took a majority of the test time. In this situation, on average, the experimental group used 1.6x more expressions than the control group (Table 5). In the control group, the instructor used fragmentary comments such as lift/down the toe. In the experimental group, the instructor used more comments based on fundamental theory such as adding weights or moving the weight balance.

"It feels like pushing weight to the backside, or slope side, as much as you can. (Lesson, I3)"

There were 3 comments, on average, which directly

	Experimental group: Verbal expressions of comments	Number of comments	Number of types	Control group: Verbal expression of comments	Number of comments	Number of types
Less on 1	Facing Front, Slide snow, Press board, knowing angle of board, move by whole body, lift toe, feel like seating on chair, press heel with hips, check student's feedback*, if pin under the toe, Strengthen on foot, move weight balance, feel like fall on back.	12	13(*1)	Slide snow(2), Lift toe(2), Strengthen foot(3), knowing angle of board(4), feel like seating on chair	12	5
Less on 2	Lift/down toe(3), Add weights (3), Release the angle(4), Move weight balance (3), Press foot (2), Check instructor's feedback*, Check student's feedback* (2), Feedback with intervention*	19	8(*4)	Lift/down toe(7), Press on heel side, Stiff the edge	9	3
Less on 3	load weight(2), Push/release with weight, Check students' feedback* (3), feel like fall on back, lift toe, stretch spine and thigh, strengthen on foot(2), just stand straight, Check teacher's feedback*, Move weight balance, Control down speed, Press toward back(2), Stop with dragging, Control with head position, Strength on heel	22	15 (*4)	Slide with heel, lift toe(2), strengthen foot, adding weight, keep should not to spin	6	5

* is directly referring image of feedback display

Table 5. Tendency of instructor's comments on side slip lesson

referred to the visual image of *Motion Echo Snowboard.* *"Let's see the lights. There is red on the back (heel-side), right? (Lesson, I2)"*

When using *Motion Echo Snowboard*, lesson contents were enriched with these types of principle-oriented expressions. Because the sensor data is non-interpretive, the feedback was took away some instructor uncertainty. They could develop various ways to come up with solutions based on the student's body posture, the result of other actions and cues, and the feedback of *Motion Echo Snowboard.*

Findings from instructor 2. Lesson started with explaining the concept of control weight balance, core of snowboarding

From the expert interview, we confirmed that weight distribution is a core element in snowboarding. In the interview session of the user study, instructors answered that this information is crucial. However, in the control group, the concept of weight distribution appeared in demonstration and correction phases when students could not understand proper movement. With *Motion Echo Snowboard*, all instructors referred weight distribution at the beginning of the explanation phase (Figure 4A).

"... then you can't control the direction of the board. You should add weight on the front foot like this color. (Lesson, I1)"

"Can you see my weight is added on the back? This is brake movement. (Lesson, I2)"

"If you see here, you can see the weight is added on the backside when doing heel-side slip. (Lesson, I3)"

About frequency of appearance, Instructors' commented on using weight distribution 4.0 times in the control group and 9.7 times in the experimental group. Each instructor made an average of 2.6 more comment on weight distribution when they using *Motion Echo Snowboard.* The feedback immediately displayed status of the current movement, so the instructor could consciously use this information.

Findings from instructor 3. Core information of movement was utilized as shareable reference in lesson comments.

In the ordinary lesson situation, when teaching a certain movement, the instructor first demonstrated the movement by him/herself and let the students imitate that movement. In our user study, an instructor could use the *Motion Echo Snowboard* to encourage students to observe the feedback image on the instructors' board. Students in the experimental group were able to observe and compare their own feedback with that of the instructors while at a relatively low inclined surface or while holding hands with the instructor.

"Let's glide down with matching your LED with my LEDs. (Lesson, I3)"

In the correction phase, the instructor usually observes the student's movement and provides comments to correct the student's actions. Of course, the instructor could infer current movement status by observing posture and using their prior knowledge. However, with *Motion Echo Snowboard*, the instructor could deliver more specific and obvious explanations (Figure 4C).

"You are using right foot too much. Your left foot has proper lights on the heel edge, however, lights of the right foot change a lot. (Lesson, I2)

In the intervention phase, the instructor could directly intervene with the student's movement and help them get the correct feeling of the movement. Even through there was little the physical intervention in the control group, in the experimental group, the instructor was able to change student's body movement and instruct using the shared board images with student (Figure 4D). The instructor would gently push or pull the student's boots so the student

Figure 4. Selected Scenes from lesson situation (A), (B), (C), (D) (from the left)

could check get the feel and see feedback images with the correct posture and movement.

"(Pressing the boots with hand) Press here. Pressing like this is breaking. (Realizing the boots) and now going. (Lesson, I3)"

Some instructors commented that this system makes them feel more comfortable when teaching. Information they might miss could be delivered even though the information would usually be coming from the opposite side of the student.

"I felt like I have an assistant for teaching snowboard. (Lesson, I1)"

Findings from student 1. Shared information of movement enhanced student's trust to instructor.

Usually in lessons, when students do not perform properly, and the instructor just repeats instructions, a conflict would occur between the instructor and student. However, in the interview session, students answered that comments using objective feedback from *Motion Echo Snowboard* were easy to understand. Moreover, they felt that instructor has a complete understanding of their current movement.

"When the instructor gives a comment like "red lights on toe", I felt that this instructor is fully aware of my movement and I felt stability. (Lesson, SC3)"

From this, we find that *Motion Echo Snowboard* could enhance student-instructor trust and be a positive influence on the student's attitude and understanding.

Findings from student 2. Induce student to actively observe instructor's movement.

Without this system, although the instructor demonstrates their movement in front of the students, students do not know which part of the instructor's movement they should focus on. When this happens, a student may not carefully watch or even ignore the demonstration and simply follow the instructor down the slope. However, with visual feedback from the *Motion Echo Snowboard*, beginners are able to intuitively understand the instructor's motion (Figure 4B). Students were used as a standard for studying the instructor's movement. Based on the information provided by the board, students could develop questions about their performance and correct any misunderstandings stemming from the instructor's lesson.

"(Instructor's) shoulder wasn't moved as I thought. If there were no signs on the deck, I would wonder how to move at that step. (Lesson, SC2)"

Findings from student 3. Although, prior knowledge from the instructor is essential.

Motion Echo Snowboard helped students understand the concept of weight distribution and perceive their movement with intuitive visual feedback. Despite this, feedback from *Motion Echo Snowboard* cannot teach how to refine and develop a movement through only perceived movement. According to Perception–action and Bayes' theory, perceived body movement consists of prior knowledge in addition to the sensation of movement [22]. Therefore, the Motion Echo system must be used in conjunction with proper interpretation and analysis from an instructor in order to establish an effective and enriched lesson environment.

"If I give an instruction of "no red on here", I'm not sure they can do right. This information (Motion Echo's feedback) is helpful to correct body movement; however, I think students might not know specific solution by themselves. (Lesson, I1)"

DISCUSSION

Visual Feedback as a starting point of exploring body movement in sports

Through this research, we explored the possibility of using real-time visual feedback to improve body movement and perception while snowboarding. Feedback created by *Motion Echo Snowboard* provide objective information for the user on their current movement and body position. Visual feedback that changes with body movement could satisfy the needs for hedonic experiences and self-expression. In addition, the interactivity could induce those who are interested in the feedback to actively try new methods of movement.

To design a platform for real-time visual feedback in a sport like snowboarding, two considerations should be followed. First, the location of feedback occur is important. Generally, users concentrate where stimuli occurs. As we confirmed in our interview, the performer could focus on the movement of snowboard because feedback is generated from the board itself. If the feedback is provided where movement is generated, the user will more easily understand the feedback provided. However, at the same time, feedback should have a peripheral property in rapid and dynamic sporting conditions like snowboarding. In these types of situations, distracting or time-consuming types of feedback are obviously not acceptable. Visual feedback in sport should be unobtrusive enough so that the user can focus entirely on their movement, and also can check feedback quickly and with high accuracy when they desire. For example, a cycle computer shows cadence and heart rate. A user can quickly glance down at the handle bar to check on their current of the movement. In this way, a trade-off between having data in an easily accessible location and the peripheral property of the feedback should be considered when attempting to make a supporting device with visual feedback.

As a second consideration, feedback should be non-interpretive rather than judging right or wrong. One of the main contributions of this research is that this type of feedback can induce a performer to actively explore their body movement. There may be many methods that achieve one resultant movement. For example, to give pressure on the heel side edge, a user can use just their ankles, lean their whole body backward, or do both. Through trial and error, a performer could get used to exploring their body movement. As a result, they could enhance their understanding how their body is moving. Adding with Nylander mentioned earlier [29], non-interpretive representations, which have various possibilities depending on performer's skill levels and purposes for movement, is also appropriate for designing visual feedback to support body movement perception in the sport.

Medium of communicating about body movement

Medium of body Movement in sports lesson

Feedback from *Motion Echo Snowboard* could be used as a way of communicating objectively between both performer and observers in lesson situations. Until now, performers can use only their inner sense to perceive their weight distribution and the observer must assume the distribution based on body posture. These different ways of perceiving weight distribution could lead to misunderstandings when communicating about body movement. In our research, visual feedback from *Motion Echo Snowboard* was acceptable without prior skills or knowledge. This type of easily understandable optical representations would be helpful in situations where an observer is trying to deliver knowledge or give comments. Of course, instructors must always interpret perceived feedback based on their prior knowledge in order to analyze challenges that the student is facing.

The *Motion Echo* concept could be used to communicate movement with others as shown in Figure 5. The feedback generated by an instructor's movement is observed by students and the instructor themselves. Similarly, the student's movement is observed by both parties. In this iterative process, instructor and students can compare each other's feedback and reflect on their movement. In this way, augmented feedback, which can be shared between the performer and the observer, could have value as new communication channel in sporting lessons.

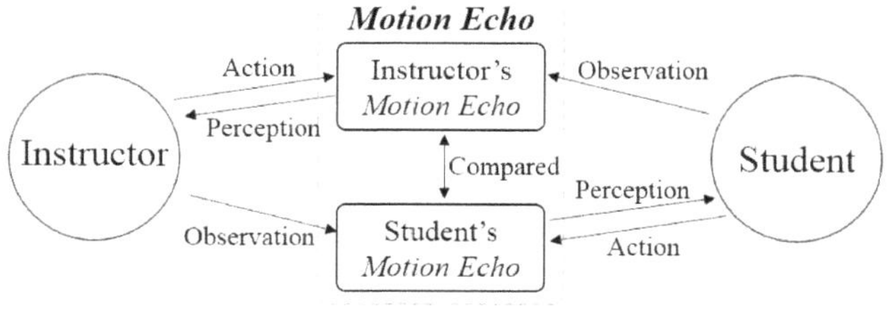

Applications of Motion Echo concept

In the lesson situation of our user study, the instructor could generate a new lesson pattern with diversified lesson contents and the student could have a better understanding of their own body movement and actively observe the instructor's demonstration. In addition, students have trust in instructor's comments and behavior when they have and enhanced understanding of what is happening. However, we expect that this system has potential to not only establish trust and enrich lesson contents but also to enhance communication. There are multiple avenues for communicating body movement, such as collaboration, competition, imitation, etc. For example, in synchronized swimming, if performers could have visual feedback of their colleagues' and their body, similar to the *Motion Echo* concept, they could consider their colleagues body movement and control their movement to keep in step. In cycling, sharing movement, such as pedaling torque, or cadence could encourage colleagues and help establish new strategies. Further possibilities and properties on sharing body movements through augmented feedback can be researched.

CONCLUSION

In this research, we proposed the *Motion Echo Snowboard* that augments information on movement when snowboarding with an objective visual display. Through an interview with snowboarding expertise, we decided to focus on weight distribution that is not easily observable but is a core element of movement while learning and performing snowboarding. *Motion Echo Snowboard* represents this subjective information with an objective visual display to support perception and communication between performer and observer. To verify the concept, two types of user studies were conducted in actual slope conditions. The usage patterns of participants were analyzed through interviews and observations. We concluded that *Motion Echo Snowboard* as a real-time visual feedback can motivate people to explore body movements during their sports activity. In a lesson situation test, *Motion Echo Snowboard* could be a novel medium to demonstrate movement when communicating with others. The objective and additional references which instructor and student share through the tool enrich the lesson curriculum. Through this research, we define areas in which real-time visual feedback could aid participant perception of their body movement in sports.

ACKNOWLEDGEMENT

This work was supported by Institute for Information & communications Technology Promotion (IITP) grant funded by the Korea government (MSIP) (No.10041313, UX-oriented Mobile SW Platform).

REFERENCES

1. Adafruit, NeoPixel, from http://adafruit.com
2. Andrew Godbout and Jeffrey Edwin Boyd. 2010. Corrective sonic feedback for speed skating: a case study. Proceedings of the 16th International Conference on Auditory Display (ICAD 2010): 23–30.
3. Antonio Frisoli, Emanuele Ruffaldi, Leonardo Bagnoli, et al. 2008. Preliminary design of rowing simulator for in-door skill training. Haptic in Ambient Systems (HAS).
4. Arudino, Arduino Due from https://www.arduino.cc/en/Main/ArduinoBoardDue
5. CASI. CANADIAN ASSOCIATION OF SNOWBOARD INSTRUCTORS, from https://www.casi-acms.com/index.php/en/course-overview
6. Daniel R. Mestre, Virginie Dagonneau, and Charles-Symphorien Mercier. 2011. Does Virtual Reality Enhance Exercise Performance, Enjoyment, and Dissociation? An Exploratory Study on a Stationary Bike Apparatus. Presence: Teleoperators and Virtual Environments 20, 1: 1–14. http://doi.org/10.1162/pres_a_00031
7. Daniel Spelmezan. 2012. An investigation into the use of tactile instructions in snowboarding. Proceedings of the 14th international conference on Human-computer interaction with mobile devices and services - MobileHCI '12: 417. http://doi.org/10.1145/2371574.2371639
8. Danielle Wilde, Alvaro Cassinelli, and Alexis Zerroug. 2012. Light arrays. Proceedings of the 2012 ACM annual conference extended abstracts on Human Factors in Computing Systems Extended Abstracts - CHI EA '12: 987. http://doi.org/10.1145/2212776.2212367
9. DAVIS, B. et al. (2000) Physical Education and the study of sport. 4th ed. Spain: Harcourt. p.321
10. Duane Knudson and Da Kluka. 1997. The impact of vision and vision training on sport performance. … of Physical Education, Recreation & Dance, May 2014: 37–41. http://doi.org/10.1080/07303084.1997.10604922
11. Elena Márquez Segura, Annika Waern, Jin Moen, and Carolina Johansson. 2013. The design space of body games: technological, physical, and social design. Proceedings of the SIGCHI Conference on Human Factors in Computing Systems - CHI '13: 3365–3374. http://doi.org/10.1145/2470654.2466461
12. Emanuele Ruffaldi, Alessandro Filippeschi, Antonio Frisoli, et al. 2009. Vibrotactile perception assessment for a rowing training system. Proceedings - 3rd Joint EuroHaptics Conference and Symposium on Haptic Interfaces for Virtual Environment and Teleoperator Systems, World Haptics 2009: 350–355. http://doi.org/10.1109/WHC.2009.4810849
13. Florian "Floyd" Mueller, Darren Edge, Frank Vetere, et al. 2011. Designing sports: a framework for exertion games. Proceedings of the 2011 annual conference on Human factors in computing systems - CHI '11: 2651–2660. http://doi.org/10.1145/1978942.1979330
14. Hamilton a. Hernandez, Zi Ye, T.C. Nicholas Graham, Darcy Fehlings, and Lauren Switzer. 2013. Designing action-based exergames for children with cerebral palsy. Human Factors in Computing Systems: Proceedings of the SIGCHI Conference, (CHI 2013): 1261–1270. http://doi.org/10.1145/2470654.2466164
15. Horace Ip, Young Hay, Alex Tang. 2003. Body brush. Emerging Technologies Exhibition, Siggraph 2003
16. J. R. Roberts, R. Jones, N. J. Mansfield, and S. J. Rothberg. 2005. Evaluation of impact sound on the "feel" of a golf shot. Journal of Sound and Vibration 287, 4-5: 651–666. http://doi.org/10.1016/j.jsv.2004.11.026
17. Jan B. F. van Erp, Ian Saturday, and Chris Jansen. 2006. Application of tactile displays in sports : where to , how and when to move. Proceedings of the Eurohaptics: 105–109. Retrieved from http://lsc.univ-evry.fr/~eurohaptics/upload/cd/papers/f1.pdf
18. Jelle Stienstra, C.J. Overbeeke, and Stephan Wensveen. 2011. Embodying Complexity Through Movement Sonification : Case Study on Empowering the Speed-skater. Proceedings of the 9th ACM SIGCHI Italian Chapter International Conference on Computer-Human Interaction: Facing Complexity: 39–44. http://doi.org/10.1145/2037296.2037310
19. Jin Moen. 2007. From Hand-held to Body-worn: Embodied Experiences of the Design and Use of a Wearable Movement-based Interaction Concept. 251–258. http://doi.org/10.1145/1226969.1227021
20. Keita Higuchi, Tetsuro Shimada, and Jun Rekimoto. 2011. Flying sports assistant: external visual imagery representation for sports training. Proceedings of the 2nd Augmented …: 1–4. http://doi.org/10.1145/1959826.1959833
21. Ludvig Elblaus, Maurizio Goina, and Roberto Bresin. 2014. Modes of Sonic Interaction in Circus : Three Proofs of Concept. September: 14–20.
22. Marc O Ernst and Heinrich H Bu. 2004. Merging the senses into a robust percept. 8, 4. http://doi.org/10.1016/j.tics.2004.02.002
23. Raine Kajastila, Leo Holsti, and Perttu Hämäläinen. 2014. Empowering the exercise: A body-controlled

trampoline training game. International Journal of Computer Science in Sport 13: 6–23.

24. Richard Kirby. 2009. Development of a real-time performance measurement and feedback system for alpine skiers. Sports Technology 2, 1-2: 43–52. http://doi.org/10.1002/jst.85

25. Roland Sigrist, Georg Rauter, Robert Riener, and Peter Wolf. 2013. Augmented visual, auditory, haptic, and multimodal feedback in motor learning: a review. Psychonomic bulletin & review 20, 1: 21–53. http://doi.org/10.3758/s13423-012-0333-8

26. Sebastiaan Pijnappel and Florian “Floyd” Mueller. 2013. Designing interactive technology for skateboarding. Proceedings of the 8th International Conference on Tangible, Embedded and Embodied Interaction - TEI ’14: 141–148. http://doi.org/10.1145/2540930.2540950

27. Sebastian Göbel, Christian Geiger, Christin Heinze, and Dionysios Marinos. 2010. Creating a virtual archery experience. International Conference on Advanced Visual Interfaces - AVI ’10: 337. http://doi.org/10.1145/1842993.1843056

28. Shoichi Hasegawa, Seiichiro Ishijima, Fumihiro Kato, Hironori Mitake, and Makoto Sato. 2012. Realtime Sonification of the Center of Gravity for Skiing. Proceedings of the 2012 Augmented Human International Conference: 3–6. http://doi.org/10.1145/2160125.2160136

29. Stina Nylander and Jakob Tholander. 2014. Designing for Movement: the Case of Sports. Proceedings of the 2014 International Workshop on Movement and Computing - MOCO ’14: 130–135. http://doi.org/10.1145/2617995.2618018

30. Stina Nylander, Alex Kent, and Jakob Tholander. 2014. Swing sound: experiencing the golf swing through sound. Proceedings of the extended abstracts of the 32nd annual ACM conference on Human factors in computing systems - CHI EA ’14: 443–446. http://doi.org/10.1145/2559206.2574789

31. Stina Nylander, Jakob Tholander, and Alex Kent. 2013. Peripheral interaction for sports – exploring two modalities for real-time feedback. Proceedings of the INTERACT workshop on Peripheral Interaction.

32. Tobias Grosshauser and Thomas Hermann. 2009. Augmented haptics - An interactive feedback system for musicians. Lecture Notes in Computer Science (including subseries Lecture Notes in Artificial Intelligence and Lecture Notes in Bioinformatics) 5763 LNCS: 100–108. http://doi.org/10.1007/978-3-642-04076-4_11

33. W. F. Helsen and J. L. Starkes. 1999. A multidimensional approach to skilled perception and performance in sport. Applied Cognitive Psychology 13, 1: 1–27. http://doi.org/10.1002/(SICI)1099-0720(199902)13:1<1::AID-ACP540>3.0.CO;2-T

Designing Mid-Air TV Gestures for Blind People Using User- and Choice-Based Elicitation Approaches

Nem Khan Dim[‡], Chaklam Silpasuwanchai[*], Sayan Sarcar[‡], Xiangshi Ren[*‡]
nemkdim@gmail.com, {chaklam, sayan.sarcar, ren.xiangshi}@kochi-tech.ac.jp

[*]Center for Human-Engaged Computing, Kochi University of Technology, Kochi, Japan

[‡]School of Information, Kochi University of Technology, Kochi, Japan

ABSTRACT
Mid-air gestures enable intuitive and natural interactions. However, few studies have investigated the use of mid-air gestures for blind people. TV interactions are one promising use of mid-air gestures for blind people, as "listening" to TV is one of their most common activities. Thus, we investigated mid-air TV gestures for blind people through two studies. Study 1 used a user-elicitation approach where blind people were asked to define gestures given a set of commands. Then, we present a classification of gesture types and the frequency of body parts usage. Nevertheless, our participants had difficulty imagining gestures for some commands. Thus, we conducted Study 2 that used a choice-based elicitation approach where the participants selected their favorite gesture from a predefined list of choices. We found that providing choices help guide users to discover suitable gestures for unfamiliar commands. We discuss concrete design guidelines for mid-air TV gestures for blind people.

Author Keywords
Blind People; Mid-Air Gesture; TV Interaction; Choice-Elicitation Approach; User-Elicitation Approach.

ACM Classification Keywords
H.5.2 [Information Interfaces and Presentation]: User Interfaces: Evaluation/Methodology.

INTRODUCTION
Mid-air gesture interfaces have become increasingly popular due to its intuitive and natural control. However, only a very few studies [10] have explored the use of mid-air gestures for blind people. Consequently, blind people have not enjoyed equal access to the benefits provided by such technologies. One promising use of mid-air gestures for blind people is their use for TV interactions because TV is one of the most common and essential activities of many blind people [2]. We have confirmed this fact through our preliminary interviews with blind people where we found that they used TV for more than 7 hours per week. Furthermore, the interviews informed us that blind people often have difficulty finding their remote controls or figuring out the button layout. Such problems suggest that employing mid-air gestures for interaction with TVs is a useful alternative method.

DIS 2016, June 4–8, 2016, Brisbane, QLD, Australia
 ISBN 978-1-4503-4031-1/16/06...$15.00.
DOI: http://dx.doi.org/10.1145/2901790.2901834.

To design usable and accessible gestures, we determined that the first important step was to understand the mental mapping of blind users when performing mid-air gestures. Thus, we investigated the mid-air gesture preferences of blind people for TV interaction using a user-elicitation approach. With the user-elicitation approach, we were able to formulate a classification of gesture types and the frequency of various body parts usage. However, we found two primary limitations with the user-elicitation approach. First, our participants experienced much difficulty and stress trying to come up with their own gestures for some commands because they did not have adequate understanding of the design alternatives and possibilities. Consequently, there was a gesture consensus only for commands that were familiar to users. Second, for unfamiliar commands, our participants suggested many abstract/random gestures which seemed to be rather inefficient and unsuitable for gesture inputs.

To address these limitations, we conducted a second study which adopted a choice-based elicitation approach [17] as a complementary approach where the participants were given a predetermined range of possible gestures from which to choose. All participants reported that they appreciated the gesture choices as the choices helped them to discover more suitable gestures. We also found that the choice-based elicitation approach can help confirm the preferences of certain gestures, while guiding the participants to reach a consensus for unfamiliar commands. We conclude our work with some generalized implications for mid-air TV gesture interaction design, as well as some discussion regarding the use of the choice-based elicitation approach.

Our contributions include:

1. We analyzed 180 defined gestures from which we developed a classification of gesture types for blind people and determined the frequency of body parts usage.

2. We leveraged the choice-based elicitation elicitation approach to address commands that had little consensus among participants and about which blind participants had little understanding or awareness.

3. We present a complete gesture set of mid-air TV gestures for blind people.
4. We present design guidelines for mid-air gestures for blind people by analyzing patterns of user gestures and their mental mappings.
5. We discuss the usefulness and general guidelines of the choice-based elicitation approach.

RELATED WORK

Here we present the most relevant works regarding gesture design based on user-elicitation, gesture interactions for blind people and the choice-based elicitation method.

User-elicitation Method

The user-elicitation approach is a recently developed approach for designing suitable gestures. This approach was originally based on the guessability technique [14, 7], where participants were asked to define gestures, given some visual effects of commands/actions.

In terms of effectiveness, Morris et al. [12] and Wobbrock et al. [8] suggested that a user-elicitation approach can produce more highly preferred gestures, compared to gestures designed by experts who have the tendency to develop more "physically and conceptually complex gestures". In terms of learnability, Nacenta et al. [13] found that user-defined gestures were easier to learn, remember and recall, compared to other predefined gestures.

Motivated by the effectiveness of this approach, many user-elicitation works have been conducted, e.g., tabletops [8], mobile phones [9] and TV [22]. Most works resulted in promising design practices and a consensus set of suitable gestures which were determined by the highest agreed gestures among participants.

Informed by promising findings from previous studies, we conducted a user-elicitation study to determine the gesture preferences of blind people for TV interactions.

Gesture Interactions for Blind People

Previous studies on defining suitable gestures for blind people mainly focused on touchscreen surfaces in terms of enhancing hardware to provide access to touch screen kiosks (e.g.,[3, 21]) and exploring interaction techniques for mobile touchscreens ([11, 20, 16, 18, 19]). Kane et al. [15] performed a touchscreen gesture elicitation study and compared the performance of sighted with the performance of blind people. They found that blind people have different gesture preferences, and their ways of performing gestures are significantly different (e.g., the gestures of blind people tend to be noticeably exaggerated).

A few studies also explored motion gestures to interact with mobile devices. Ruiz et al. [9] presented an elicitation study of motion gestures for mobile interaction. The study reported a consensus of motion gestures to invoke commands on a smartphone and presented a taxonomy of motion gestures. However, the study did not consider gestures of people with visual impairments. More recently, Dim and Ren [5] studied motion gestures for blind people in mobile phone interactions. They found that blind people mostly perform metaphorical gestures reflecting actions from their daily activities. Thus, such gestures had a high consensus for familiar activities related to daily activities such as *making phone call* and *voice search*, but they had a low consensus for unfamiliar commands such as *zooming*.

Although some studies have been done for touchscreen gestures and motion gestures in mobile phones for blind people, very few works have been done on suitable mid-air gestures. Thus, we conducted user studies to determine suitable mid-air gestures for blind people, especially for TV interactions.

Choice-based elicitation Method

To our knowledge, only a little study has employed choices for gesture design, with the exception being the work of Silpasuwanchai and Ren [17]. They employed choices to understand how gamers perform simultaneous gestures during intense gameplay. However, there was no deep discussion regarding the use of choices for gesture design.

Where users have little or no idea of the range of possibilities for suitable gestures, employing designer-selected choices can serve as one way to non-threateningly introduce designer ideas into the design process without making the users feel compelled. In addition, allowing users to select their preferred choices can reduce the chance of designers introducing overly-complicated gestures, as suggested by Morris et al. [12]. This also increases the chance of settling on a gesture that is suitable in both the view of designer and that of the users. Informed by this potential benefit, we adopted the choice-based elicitation approach for our study.

In summary, while designing suitable gestures for blind people is an ongoing challenge, our study leverages the benefits of both user-elicitation and choice-based elicitation to determine the most suitable mid-air gestures for blind people.

PRELIMINARY INTERVIEWS

Prior to the studies, we conducted a preliminary interview with 8 blind participants (ages ranged from 37 to 65 years). The purpose of the interview was to gain an understanding of the current problems in TV interactions of blind people and their experiences with mid-air gesture interfaces. Each participant was paid $10 for their participation.

TV Interactions

We observed that the use of TV is one of the most common and essential activities of our participants. All our participants regularly 'listen' TV for more than 7 hours per week. Although they can not see, they enjoyed the experience through audio. Their reasons for using the TV were listening to sports, news, drama, music and other programs. Our participants mentioned that they often had a hard time finding their remote controls as well as figuring out the button layout on the remote control. For example, one participant stated, "*I am always frustrated when someone changes the position of the remote control and I cannot find it.*" Another participant mentioned that it was difficult to learn the layout of remote controls as there was no standard layout of TV remote controls. For example, one of the participants mentioned, "*Many times, I cannot distinguish buttons for changing channels and changing the TV volume on the remote control, so I just use the buttons on the TV.*" When asked about the possibilities of using mid-air gestures, all participants agreed that it would be useful if they could sometimes use mid-air gestures in their interactions with TV.

Experiences in Mid-Air Gesture Interfaces

None of our participants had any knowledge of mid-air gesture interfaces but one had experience with touch gestures in smartphones. When asked about experiences in mid-air gesture interfaces, one participant stated, "*Generally, I understand that mid-air gesture is about moving your body parts, for example, waving the hand for saying goodbye. But I have no idea about how I can use it for communicating with any devices.*" When asked the participant who used a smartphone, that participant mentioned, "*With my smartphone, I only do flick gestures (to the left and the right) for browsing the next and previous contents. I do not know what mid-air gesture interfaces would look like.*" Even though blind people perform daily gestures, they are not necessarily able to transfer their knowledge to mid-air gesture design due to their lack of knowledge and experience with mid-air gesture interfaces and with technology in general.

Thus to design usable mid-air gesture interfaces, there is a need to better understand the preferences and mental mappings of blind people. To determine blind people' mid-air gesture preferences in interactions with TVs, we conducted a user-elicitation study.

STUDY 1: USER-ELICITATION APPROACH

The objective of this study was to determine blind people's mid-air gesture preferences for TV interactions. The participants were asked to define gestures for a set of TV interaction commands. Gesture classifications and frequency of body parts usage, agreement scores, gesture defining times and subjective assessments were analyzed.

Participants

Twelve blind participants (7 males, age range = 26 to 78 years, M = 53.9 years, SD = 12.64) were recruited. One of the participants could see light, two of them could see the presence of objects but not able to distinguish shapes. One could see objects. The other participants were totally blind. Ten of the participants were 'early blind' (age 0 to 3 years), and the rest two were 'late blind' (one at 6 years and the other at 17 years). All participants regularly 'listen' TV for more than 7 hours each week. None had experience using mid-air gestures for TV control or any other devices. Eleven participants were right-handed and one was ambidextrous. Each participant was paid $15 for the experiment.

Commands

We identified commonly used TV commands. We also selected commands that are specifically used by blind people, e.g., *Voice Guide* [1]. A total of 15 commands were selected for the experiment (see Table 1).

No.	Command	Description
1	Open	Power on TV
2	Close	Power off TV
3	Channel	Change channel
4	Favorite Channel	Go to saved channels
5	Next	Go to next channel/menu
6	Previous	Go to previous channel/menu
7	Volume Up	Increase volume
8	Volume Down	Decrease volume
9	TV Guide	Check channel list and time
10	Pause	Pause
11	Play	Play
12	Menu	Open menu
13	Yes	Answer Yes to system question
14	No	Answer No to system question
15	Voice Guide	Activate voice guidance for blind users

Table 1. TV commands used in Study 1 and 2.

Procedure

Our study design used a user-elicitation approach similar to that of [9, 8]. As with previous elicitation studies, we did not want participants to take recognizer issues into consideration, and to observe the users' best possible gestures.

At the start of the experiment, participants were asked to define gestures for 15 TV commands in randomized order. To identify the most preferred gesture and reduce any ordering effects, participants were allowed to reuse the same gesture for multiple commands.

Each command name was communicated by the experimenter, along with the description of the command's effect (e.g., "*Open TV*" followed by "*This command will power-on your TV*").

During gesture defining, participants were instructed to think-aloud while performing their gestures, confirming the start and end of their performed gesture and describing their corresponding rationale. To determine how well they imagined the gestures, we recorded gesture defining times, i.e., the time between command instruction and gesture execution.

After each group of commands was defined (each group contains approximately 5 commands), participants were asked to evaluate their gestures, using similar evaluation to that of [8]: "The gesture I performed is a *good match* for its purpose"; "The gesture I performed is *easy to perform*"; "The gesture I performed is *tiring*".

The experiment took around 1.5 hours, and it was audio and video recorded for qualitative data analyses.

Results

Our results include a gesture taxonomy, body parts used, agreement score, gesture defining time and subjective ratings.

Classification of Mid-Air Gestures

As noted in related work, gesture classifications have been developed for surface gestures [8] and mobile interactions [9]. However, no work has established a taxonomy of mid-air gestures for blind people. We classified gestures collected from the study along five dimensions: *nature, form, axes of motion, binding* and *flow*. Each dimension was further classified into multiple subcategories (see Table 2 and Figure

Dimension	Category	Description
Nature	*Symbolic*	Gesture depicts similarity of symbols.
	Metaphorical	Gesture indicates a metaphor.
	Deictic	Gesture refers to spatial information.
	Abstract	Gesture-command mapping is arbitrary.
Form	*Static pose*	Hand pose is held in one location.
	Dynamic pose	Hand pose changes in one location.
	Static pose with path	Hand pose is the same but the hand is moving.
Axes of motion	*Sagittal*	User moves the hand/leg forward and backward.
	Horizontal	User moves the hand/leg left and right.
	Longitudinal	User moves the hand upward/downward.
	Compound-axes	User hand movement includes more than one direction.
	Stationary	User performs the gesture keeping the hand or fingers at one location.
Binding	*Independent*	Gesture requires no information about object positions or body parts.
	Body-centric	User moves the hand/leg using spatial reference of the body.
	Body-referenced	User moves the hand with respect to other body parts.
Flow	*Discrete*	Response will occur after user performs the gesture.
	Continuous	Response will occur while user is performing the gesture.

Table 2. Taxonomy of mid-air gestures based on 180 gestures.

1a). Gesture taxonomies obtained in our study and those in [8] and [9] were different for two main reasons: (1) the gestures were performed for different interactions (i.e., surface gestures, motion gestures in mobile phones and mid-air gestures), and (2) they were performed by users with significantly different capabilities (i.e., sighted users and blind users).

The *Nature* dimension is a classification of gesture-meaning relationships. The other four dimensions are concerned with the characteristics of physical movements involved in performing the gestures (trajectories, movement plane, gesture flow, etc.). In the (1) *Nature* dimension, symbolic gestures are depictions of symbols, for example, drawing a letter 'V' for the *Voice Guide* command. As we expected, very few symbolic gestures were performed in our study, given that these gestures require visual references. (2) Metaphorical gestures linked to their meaning by mechanical determinism (i.e. linked to the logical meaning of daily actions or feelings, not linked to their visual similarities). For example, some of our participants put their hands near by the ears for the *Voice Guide* command indicating that "I want to hear". Metaphorical gestures reflecting common daily actions were the most frequently performed gestures by our participants. Among the metaphorical gestures, we found some conventional gestures. For example, four of our participants performed 'OK gesture' for the *Yes* command. (3) Deictic gestures refer spatial information of objects. For example, when asked to perform a gesture for the *Menu* command, one of our participants said, "I would put the *Menu* command at the upper right corner of the screen and point at it". It is important to note that, unlike sighted people who are able point at visual on-screen contents, our participants performed pointing gestures only relying on their proprioception. That is, they could only refer the content position to hand movements in distinct and specific directions which are related to their body (i.e. upper left, upper-right, etc.) rather than by accurate reference to the display or on-screen contents on the display. (4) Abstract gestures are linked to the meaning neither by the similarity nor by any other relationship that allows one to infer the meaning from the gesture. Arbitrary gestures were the second most performed gestures in our study. For example, when asked to perform a gesture for the *Voice Guide* command, one of our participants came up with the gesture which showed a finger stating no clear gesture-meaning relationship.

In the *Form* dimension, (1) static pose is where the hand pose is held in one location, for example, showing the palm for the *Stop* command or showing 'OK' for the *Yes* command. (2) Dynamic pose is where the hand pose changes within one location, for example, the *blink gesture* (close and open the palm) for the *Open TV* command or the *double tap* by the foot for the *Yes* command. (3) Static pose with path is where user moves the hand but hand pose is not changed, for example, moving the hand from left to right for the *Next* command or moving the hand upward for the *Volume Up* command. These gestures were the most frequently performed gestures. One interesting observation is that our participants mostly used distinctly exaggerated movements, that is, moving their entire forearm or arm instead of only the wrist and the hand when performing hand or finger gestures. When asked about the reasons, our participants commented that they were not sure of the boundary of interactions, thus making large movements seemed to reassure them and give them confidence that they had performed the actions in a manner that made them clearly recognizable. While gestures with *static pose with path* were the most frequently performed in our study, it is noticeable that there can be cases where the user moves the hand position and also changes the hand pose (i.e. *dynamic pose with path*). However, none of our participants performed such gestures in our study.

The *Axes of motion* dimension shows the direction of user movements of the hand, foot or fingers. (1) Sagittal gestures are those where users move the hand forward and backward. Examples include moving the hand backward to represent 'undoing' for the *Pause* command and pushing the finger forward as 'pushing a button' for *Open TV*. (2) Horizontal gestures are those where users move the hand or foot left and right, for example, moving the hand left and right for *Next/Previous*. (3) Longitudinal gestures are those where users move the hand upward and downward, for example, moving the hand upward for *Volume Up*. (4) Compound-axes gestures are those where user movements include more than one spatial dimensions. For example, some of our participants drew a circle in the air for *TV Guide*. Another example is moving the hand in the upper-right direction where our participant stated, *"I would put the Menu command at the upper-right corner of the screen and point at that direction."* (5) Stationary gestures are those where users perform their gestures keeping their hands or fingers in one location. With respect to the *form* dimension, stationary gestures are *static* and *dynamic gestures* while sagittal, horizontal, longitudinal and compound-axes gestures are *static gestures with path.*

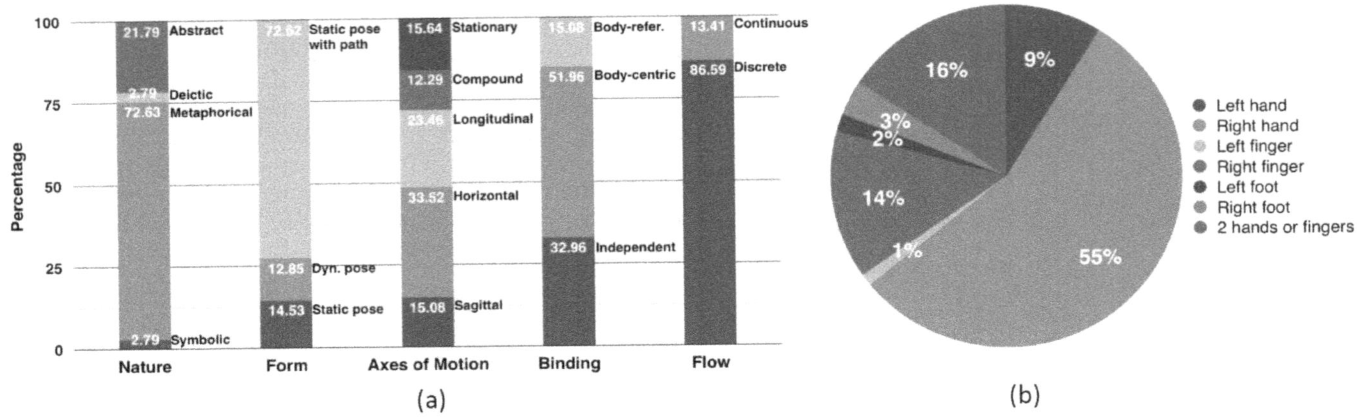

Figure 1. Percentage of gesture types and body parts used.

In the *Binding* dimension, (1) independent gestures require no information about the world or the body. Examples are showing 'OK' sign for the *Yes* command and showing the palm for *Stop*. These gestures can be performed anywhere regardless of their relation to the user's body or objects on the screen. (2) Body-centric gestures are performed by users by referring spatial information to the body, for example, moving the hand to the left of the body or by moving the foot forward. These gestures were the most performed gestures by our participants. While it is understandable that *body-centric gestures* are specifically selected and performed for certain commands, such as *Next/Previous* commands (moving the hand left and right), we found that our participants performed *body-centric* gestures in many other cases as well. Examples are waving the hand left and right for the *Play/Pause* commands, drawing the hand backward to represent undoing for the *No* command and moving the hand in an upper-right direction to represent skipping for the *Favorite Channel* command. (3) Body-referenced gestures were performed by referring other body parts, for example, putting the hands near by the ears for *Voice Guide*. Another example was that our participants performed *body-referenced gesture* by opening the hands (clasp two hands together and then separate them) for commands such as the *Open TV, Play* and the *Voice Guide* commands.

In the *Flow* dimension, (1) discrete gestures are performed and responded to as one event, for example, the *blink gesture* for the *Open TV* command. (2) Continuous gestures require ongoing recognition. One example is *raising the hand* for the *Volume Up* command. *Discrete* or *continuous gestures* were performed depending on the users' perceptions of the system responses to their gestures for the commands. For the *Open TV* command, it was expected that the system would respond by opening the TV instantly after the gesture; the participants performed *discrete gestures* for that command. On the other hand, for the *Volume Up* command, the participants continuously moved the hand upward as if progressively increasing the volume to certain desirable level. Similarly, for the *TV Channel* command, the participants rotated the hand steadily as if to continue until they found the channel they wanted.

Use of Body Parts

Figure 1b shows the use of body parts. One-handed gestures with the right hand were the most preferred, followed by one finger gestures, two hand/finger gestures, and foot gestures.

Hand gestures were commonly performed in the form of movements, such as waving the hand left and/or right for *Next* and *Previous*, waving the hand left and/or right for *Select Channel*, and moving the hand up and down for*Volume Up/Down*. Finger gestures commonly featured the index finger to draw a circle to activate *TV Guide* or to pointing in order to *Open/Close* the TV. Fingers were also used to perform 'OK' gesture for the *Yes* and the *crossed fingers* gesture for *No*. Foot gestures were used by some participants when they wanted to do the same gesture they had already performed using the hands or fingers. For example, one of our participants who moved the right foot to right for the *Channel* command mentioned, "I would like to use my leg because I have done the same gesture for *Next* using the hand." Although the participants were allowed to suggest the same gesture for different commands, they often used the feet reasoning that they wanted to use different gestures from the previous gestures they had already performed. We observed that, our participants performed their foot gestures mostly for abstract gestures where they could not suggest any gesture-meaning relationship. For example, one participant moved the right foot to the right for the *Menu* command stating, "When I have no idea what gesture to use, I just change the body part".

Agreement Score

To determine the gesture consensus among participants, we calculated the agreement score using a formula from [8]. The calculation of agreement score is as follows:

$$A_r = \sum_{P_i} \left(\left| \frac{P_i}{P_r} \right| \right)^2 \quad (1)$$

where P_r represents all gestures performed for event r and P_i is a subset of identical gestures from P_r. A_r ranges 0 to 1. Gestures were considered to be identical when they had similar trajectories and poses.

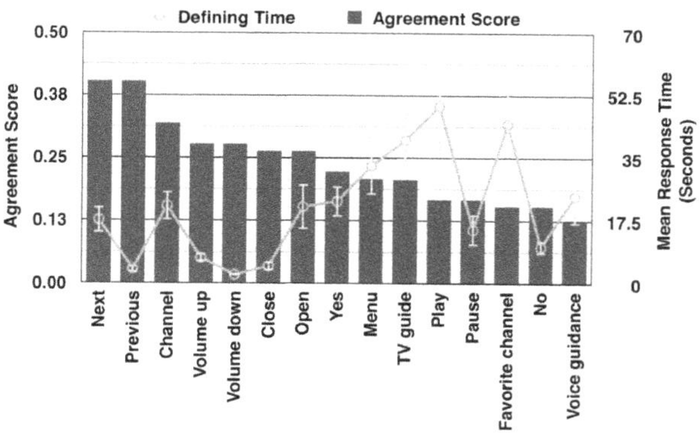

Figure 2. Agreement scores and gesture defining times of the user-elicitation approach.

Figure 2 shows the agreement score of each command. We found that user-defined gestures in our study had a slightly lower agreement score (0.24) compared to gestures of sighted people for TV control (0.42 in [22]) and other user-defined studies (0.28 and 0.32 in [8]). There were some commands that had relatively high agreement scores such as *Next* and *Previous*. However, for more abstract commands such as *Voice Guide* and *Favorite Channel*, participants reported that they had a lot of difficulty imagining the gestures. As a consequence, most participants came up with arbitrary gestures about which they had no clear rationale as to why they defined the gesture in that particular way.

Defining Time

Gesture defining time is the time between command instruction and gesture definition. It can measure the speed and ease of defining of commands which can help inform how well participants can imagine their gestures. The mean defining time of all commands was 22.92 seconds (SD = 12.02). Figure 2 shows the mean defining time for each command. Some commands showed consistency between agreement scores and defining times. For example, *Previous* and *Volume Down* both had high agreement scores and low defining times. Similarly, there were commands such as *Play* and *Favorite Channel* that participants had difficulty imagining and consequently there was low consensus among the participants. On the other hand, there were also some commands with low agreement scores but also low defining times, e.g., *Pause* and *No*, suggesting that there were certain commands where, although each participant had some clear idea of the gestures, they shared little commonality between participants' preferred gestures.

Subjective Ratings

Unlike past works, we found that the highest agreed gestures in our user-elicitation study had no significantly higher good match rating compared to other gestures. This indicates that, in our case, popularity did not necessarily identify better gestures over the worse ones. This was largely due to the fact that our participants had a lot of difficulty imagining suitable gestures and partly due to their lack of experiences with gesture interactions.

Discussion

The classification of gestures revealed that most gestures performed by our participants came from their daily experiences, for example, raising the hand for the *Open TV* command which mimics switching on the light and pushing the hand forward for the same command which mimics pushing buttons on their household appliances and devices. From the *binding* dimension, we observed that our participants preferred *body-centric* gestures, that is, moving hands or fingers to directions with respect to the body (left, right, forward, backward, etc.). Given that our participants did not perform gestures combining dynamic poses with path gestures, we observed that they preferred gestures with simple hand movements. When performing those gestures, user movements could include any directions (of left/right, forward/backward and upward/downward) and most of the gestures occurred at the *frontal plane* of users. Also, for the gesture recognition, it is important to note the inclusion of compound gestures, for example, moving the hand to draw circle in the air (i.e. the hand moves to more than one spatial dimension in a single gesture). Regarding the physical movements when performing gestures, gesture recognition should be developed to accommodate exaggerated hand movements which were preferred by our participants. Gesture recognition should also be developed with attention to user expectations regarding the system's response. For example, *continuous gestures* such as gestures for *Volume, Select Channel* would require on-going (sustained) recognition of gestures.

Regarding the use of body parts, we observed that right and left hands, right fingers, and 2 hands and fingers were mostly used for the *metaphorical, deictic and symbolic gestures*. The left finger, left foot and right foot were not recommended for gesture design, given that these body parts were not commonly used and we observed that they were mostly used for abstract commands.

Some commands in the user-elicitation study achieved low-agreement scores, given our participants had no clear idea of mid-air gesture interfaces and design. Also, our participants were less influenced by seeing gestures of other people. Defining gestures for the given TV commands was difficult for our participants especially for abstract and unfamiliar commands such as *Voice Guide, No, Favorite Channel, Play, Pause, TV Guide* and *Menu* commands. The higher defining time revealed the fact that our participants had much higher difficulty imagining suitable gestures in the user-elicitation approach. Thus, to address these gaps, we recruited the same participants and conducted a choice-based elicitation study where participants were asked to select their preferred gestures from a predefined list. To minimize any possible effect of the user-elicitation approach on the choice-based elicitation approach, we set sufficient time gap (around 1 month) between Study 1 and 2.

STUDY 2: CHOICE-BASED ELICITATION APPROACH

Study 1 allowed us to develop an understanding of user gestures and their mental mappings through the detailed analyses and classification of gestures. However, we found that our participants had difficulty suggesting suitable gestures for certain TV commands, for example, *Voice Guide, No, Favorite Channel, Play, Pause, TV Guide* and *Menu*. The objective of Study 2 was to adopt the choice-based elicitation approach to better understand the preferences of gestures in commands where users had less idea of gesture design. In choice-based elicitation, participants were asked to select their preferred gestures from a list of designer-selected choices. The choice list contained two data columns, one for gesture choices, and another for commands, with the relationship as many-to-one, respectively.

Selecting Choice Candidates
We regard the process of selecting which choices to include in the choice list and how choices are introduced to participants to be key to the effectiveness of the choice-based elicitation approach. Four measures were considered.

First, there is abundant evidence to show that too many or too few choices may decrease user engagement and can possibly confuse users [6]. However, there exist no simple rules to decide the suitable number of choices. To decide the number of choices, we adhered to two grounds - (1) modern working memory studies show that humans can only hold about 4 chunks at a time in their memories [4]; (2) consistent with the memory capacity theory, our initial pilot study with two blind people shows that they preferred a range of 2 to 4 choices. Based on these two grounds, we kept our number of choices to no more than 4.

Second, in order to ensure that each gesture choice is reasonable, there is a need to select gesture choices that are considerably intuitive. We recognized that there are many different ways to construct the choice list and that this depends largely on designer preferences. To demonstrate one possible way, we derived our choices from three places (Study 1, related work, and designers) - (1) we selected the highest-agreed gestures for each command from Study 1 (26.67% of gestures in the choice list). We also selected any gesture from Study 1 that we intuited to be potentially intuitive and suitable (28.33% of gestures in the choice list); (2) we derived some gesture choices from existing works (e.g., [22]); (3) we designed some gesture choices based on our own experience with blind people[1]. Also, gesture classification derived from Study 1 also helped us to design the most suitable gestures for Study 2, for example, selecting the body parts, avoiding symbolic gestures wherever possible. The final list of gesture choices achieved a high interrater reliability among authors and one independent rater (Kappa=0.919, $p < 0.001$).

Third, to ensure that each choice was equally exposed and judged, experimenters asked participants to perform each choice, instead of only passively listening to the different choices. This also enabled the participants to weigh each gesture based on how comfortable it was to use.

Last, to prevent any possible ordering effect of choices (i.e., due to the recency or primacy effect on choices), we decided that all choices should be presented to participants in randomized order.

[1]One of the authors has been working consistently with blind people for approximately three years.

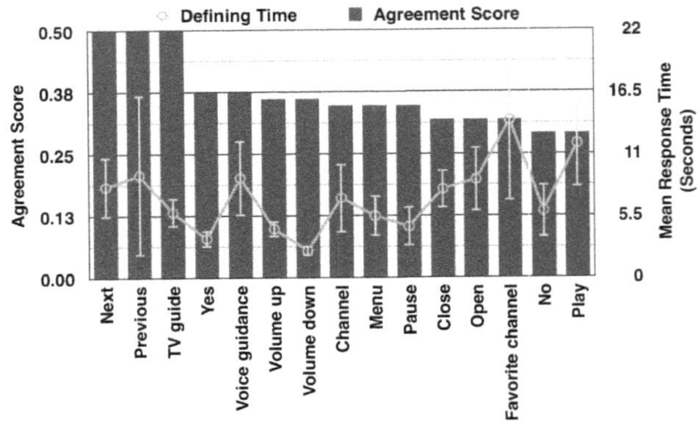

Figure 3. Agreement scores and response times of the choice-based elicitation approach.

Experimental Design
To understand how choices can help us better understand users, the same 12 blind participants in Study 1 were recruited. We used the same set of commands as in Study 1. The procedure was also conducted in a similar manner to Study 1, except that the participants were provided with a list of choices and were asked to select their most preferred choices. Each command name was communicated by the experimenter, along with the description of the command effect. The experimenter then provided the first gesture choice, i.e., the experimenter explained how to perform the gesture, followed by asking the participants to perform the gesture. For each command, the experimenter went through all choices in a similar manner. Gesture choices were presented in a randomized order. The experimental session took around 1.5 hours.

Results
Agreement score, gesture defining time,subjective ratings and the mid-air gesture set were presented.

Agreement Score
The choice-based elicitation approach achieved a noticeably higher agreement score (0.37) (Figure 3). This result was initially expected because choices reduced the possible variations between participants. Nevertheless, the choice-based elicitation approach was found to be useful, particularly for commands where participants have no clear ideas of their own, e.g., *Favorite Channel, Voice Guide, TV Guide*. Participants reported that the supplied gesture choices enabled them to discover more suitable gestures, particularly for difficult commands.

Defining Time
To understand how long it took the participants to select their choice, we measured the time between the choice presentation time and decision time. The mean defining time of all commands was 7.16 seconds ($SD = 3.13$). Figure 3 shows the mean defining time for each command. We found that the gesture choices can guide users to discover more suitable gestures.

Subjective Ratings
We found that the highest agreed gestures had significantly higher good match rating ($Z = -2.612$, $p < 0.01$) compared

to other gestures. This indicates that, in the choice-based elicitation study, popularity does identify better gestures over the worse ones. We were thus confirmed that the choice-based elicitation approach can help confirm the preferences of certain gestures.

Mid-Air Gesture Set

Based on the highest agreed gestures, we developed the mid-air gesture set for TV commands (see Figure 4). Nine of the 15 commands shared similar highest-agreed gestures in both user- and choice-based elicitation approaches. These nine commands includes Open/Close, Volume Up/Down, TV guide, Yes, Previous/Next, and Voice Guide. Another six commands were mainly based on the choice-based elicitation approach which include Play/Pause, Change Channel, Favorite Channel, Menu, and No. Using the choice approach, we found a good average consensus on these six commands (0.32).

Discussion

Gesture agreement scores for all commands increased in the choice-based elicitation study. Higher agreement scores were expected given that the choice-based elicitation approach has fewer choices than the user-elicitation approach. However, we observed the effectiveness of the choice-based elicitation approach especially for abstract or unfamiliar commands which had quite low agreement scores in the user-elicitation study. The agreement scores for those commands noticeably increased in the choice-based elicitation study: *Voice Guide* (increased by 192.31%), *TV Guide* (138%), *Favorite* (113.33%), *Pause* (105.88%), *No* (93.33%), *Yes* (72.73%), *Play* (70.59%) and *Menu* (66.67%) respectively. Gestures for commands that had the highest agreement scores in the user-elicitation study (*Next, Previous, Channel, Volume Up, Volume Down, Close* and *Open*) had the highest scores in the choice-based elicitation study and in the same order .

The choice-based elicitation approach also helped confirm that there was indeed some commonality in the participants' mental mappings to the gestures, and this commonality could be more likely observed when all participants were equally informed about the different possibilities within the design space.

GENERAL DISCUSSION

We have explored the use of the user- and choice-based elicitation approach, and our studies showed promising results. This section discusses (1) mental model observations, and (2) user-elicitation and choice-based elicitation.

Mental Model Observations

Our quantitative data, qualitative data and video recordings enable us to capture user mental models that will benefit the design of mid-air gestures for blind people. Guidelines are summarized in Table 3.

Symbolic vs metaphors

We observed that the mid-air gestures of blind people were quite different from those of sighted people in a way that sighted people performed a lot of *symbolic gestures* [22] and our participants performed very few (fewer than 3%) of those

Guidelines	Criteria
Metaphors	Gestures should be designed mimicking metaphor in users' daily lives. Avoid symbolic gestures such as drawing letters (e.g., 'M', 'X'). Avoid gesture that needs visual references (e.g., sizes, distances). For measurements, system should recognize the fine-grained self-referenced movements of users as measures of degree.
Logical Mappings	When mapping gestures to daily metaphors, *actions* (e.g., gesture that represents opening a menu book for the *Menu* command) should be used. Mimicking *visual similarities* (e.g., gesture that represents the *Menu* as a list of items) should be avoided.
Body-centric	Movements in performing the gestures should be easily relatable to user body (e.g., moving left and right, backward and forward). If pointing are required to trigger a menu, users should be able to rely on reference only to their own bodies (e.g., moving the hand upward, upper left). The need of accurate reference to the display or on-screen contents on the display should be avoided.
Commonly Used Device	Gestures should be designed to mimic the use of users' older devices whereas possible. Attention should be paid to differences of commonly used devices of blind and sighted people (e.g., smartphone vs feature phone).
Reversible gestures	Reverse gestures should be designed for dichotomous commands. Reverse or related gestures should also be designed for similar commands (e.g., *Pause, Close TV*) where possible.
Exaggerated user movements	Gesture recognition should allow freedom of movements for performing user gestures. Expect slow pace due to big movements in gestures performed by blind users. Avoid time-based gesture recognition.

Table 3. Design Guidelines and Criteria.

gestures. Instead, *metaphoric gestures* were mostly performed by our participants. For example, while the gesture for *Menu* was drawing letter 'M' in [22], the gesture for the same command in our study was the "*Open Book*" gesture (Figure 4). Most of our participants chose that gesture stating that, "*This gesture is like opening a menu book at a restaurant*". Thus, it is important for designers to understand which daily actions of blind people can be exploited as potential gestures in interactions with digital devices.

Also, for the *Volume Up/Down* commands, gestures of sighted people included having the non-dominant hand as a visual reference of measurement while moving the dominant hand upward/downward increasingly with reference to it [22]. However, none of our participants performed gestures that referenced measurement. Thus, for commands like *VolumeUp/Down*, gesture recognition should be developed so that users can rely only on their non-visual skill via proprioception, that is, the system should recognize the fine-grained self referenced movements of users as measures of degree (increase/decrease).

Visual resemblances vs logical mapping

It is important to understand how blind people perceive the meaning of certain commands. For example, the highest agreed gesture in user-elicitation study for *TV Guide* was

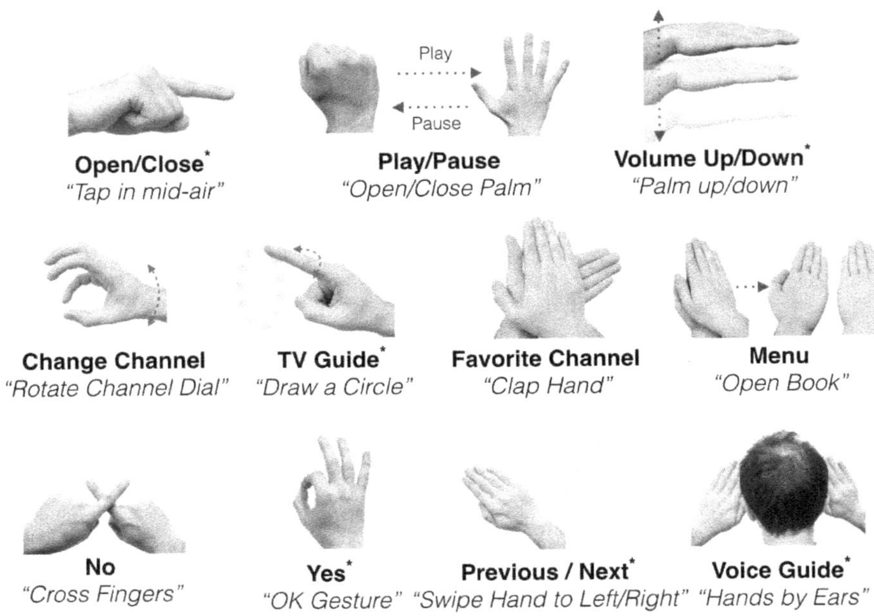

Figure 4. Highest-agreed gestures in choice-based elicitation approach.

drawing a circle in the air stating, *"the meaning of a circle is 'all' and a TV Guide also shows all TV channels."* This gesture was also the most agreed gesture for *TV Guide* in the choice-based elicitation. During the choice-based elicitation study, although the participants were given other gesture choices for the same command such as moving the hand from up to down (as if to indicate a channel list), none of our participants chose that gesture. This informed us that the imagination of our participants for certain commands can be very different from that of sighted people (i.e. visual-based imagination of the *TV Guide* as a channel list vs logically mapping as *showing the whole*). Thus, designing gestures that are related to visual resemblances should be avoided as these gestures may not be intuitive to blind users.

Body-centric

As discussed in earlier sections, our participants mostly performed *body-centric* gestures (i.e. moving the hands or fingers to left/right, forward/backward, and so on). From our semi-structured interviews, we also observed that spatial references relating to their body was a great aid in many situations (for example, saying *"coffee cup at the left and mobile phone at the right"*). Thus, it is clear that *body-centric gestures with simple movements* are desirable for blind users because they could apply their proprioceptions.

Also, both sighted and blind users may simply want to select contents on the screen when they have no gesture ideas for triggering the commands. In our study, *deictic gestures* were performed by our participants stating that they would like to place the menu items and select them. However, finding and selecting the on-screen contents will be different between sighted and blind users, given that blind users have no visual cues to help them find the content on the screen. For such cases, gesture recognition should allow users to rely on non-visual skills such as proprioception, for example, users can select the content just by moving their hand in certain directions (upper-left, right, etc.) with reference only to their own bodies.

I want to use old things that I have learned

During the study, our participants often came up with gestures that they commonly used to interact with appliances and devices in their daily lives. For example, the highest agreed gesture in both studies for the *Select Channel* command was rotating the hand left and right which mimicked rotating the channel dial on old televisions. Similarly, the participants selected a "*Push button* gesture in mid-air for the *Open/Close TV* command which mimicked pushing buttons in their mobile phones. Thus it is important for designers to understand the commonly-used actions used by blind people when interacting with their commonly used devices and appliances. Although the influence of daily device usage may also be applicable for sighted users, the devices used and the interaction experiences can be quite differently perceived between blind and sighted people (e.g., smartphone vs. feature phones). Thus, designers should pay close attention to those differences when designing gestures that mimic the use of older devices.

Reversible gestures are more memorable

We observed that our participants used consistent mapping of gestures for many commands, for example, *Next/Previous, Volume Up/Down, Play/Pause*, and so on. Notably, reversible gestures were very important for blind users for gesture learnability and memorability because mapping similar and opposite things was an efficient learning aid for them in many cases. During Study 1, one of the participants stated, *"I do an open hands gesture (i.e. claps the two hands then separate them) one time for Play, so I would do the same gesture 2 times for*

Open TV because they are similar commands." This implies that even for commands that are not directly dichotomous, our participants preferred mapping similar or opposite gestures where possible. Thus, it is a good idea to design reversible gestures wherever possible.

Big movements are more recognizable

All our participants used noticeably larger movements when they performed gestures. This can be partially due to the lack of feedback during gesture performance in our study. We speculated that by exaggerating their movements our participants compensated for the lack of feedback intending to eliminate uncertainty regarding the perception of their gestures and ensuring that their movements were clear enough to be recognized by the system. Thus, gesture recognition should be developed to allow freedom of movement. Also, time-based gesture recognition should be avoided because blind people may perform gestures with big movements at a different pace to sighted people.

User-Elicitation and Choice-Based Elicitation

We observed that the choice-based elicitation approach can work well when the user has no clear idea of gesture possibilities. Nevertheless, we cannot disregard the results from user-elicitation. In particular, we found that the results from the user-elicitation proved to be very useful. They enabled us to understand the gestures that users were familiar with and the commands that they had little idea about and those that they had difficulty imagining gesture(s) for. Conducting only the choice-based approach may not allow us to obtain such insights. By combining the information from both the user-elicitation and the choice-based elicitation approaches, we gained useful insights for designers, as demonstrated in previous section. We thus suggest that it would be beneficial to use both approaches during gesture design processes.

Participants commented on the benefits of the choice-based elicitation approach in three ways. First, it helped users understand what is possible within the design space. By learning through the choices, participants commented that they understood better about the different possibilities in the design space. This understanding was reflected by one participant who stated that, "*For some commands, it was just impossible to imagine, I really appreciated the choices, as I could learn through examples.*" Second, the choice approach made participants to think actively about all the possibilities presented to them. Participants commented that the process of selecting their preferred choices caused them to think actively, i.e., to carefully weigh the benefits and disadvantages of each gesture. One of the participants commented that it was fun as they felt like they were 'wearing the hat of a designer'. Third, by giving choices, our participants felt more confident when they discovered that the gestures they had preferred were also in the choice list. All blind participants reported that they appreciated the gesture choices as they helped guided them to decide on their preferred gestures. One participant stated, "*The choice list helps me to express what I really want.*", another commented, "*This is like a game and it's fun!*".

For designer convenience, we summarized our experience of using the choice-based elicitation approach in the form of five generalized guidelines.

1. We should consider the number of choices based on the memory and attentional capacity pertaining to different demographics. For example, old people may prefer a fewer choices, compared to young people.

2. It is essential for users to actually perform each gesture choice instead of just passively to look at or listen to a description of a gesture. By actually performing the choice, users can better estimate the suitability of the gesture.

3. The criteria for selecting candidate gestures for the choice list should be specified as objectively as possible. These criteria may vary depending on the priorities set by the designers, e.g., high-comfort, high-speed and/or low-error rate, etc.

4. It is important to carefully consider the issue of learnability in the choice-based elicitation approach, as the selected gesture may not have originated from the user's mind. It is thus essential to pay special attention to gesture learnability in the choice-based elicitation approach.

5. Although we found that the choice-based approach is effective for our blind participants, it is also worthwhile to conduct a user-defined approach to better understand users. In other words, user-defined and choice-based approaches have their own respective advantages and they can well complement one another limitations.

CONCLUSION AND FUTURE WORK

We conducted two user studies: a user-elicitation study and a choice elicitation study to determine the mid-air gesture preferences of blind people in TV interactions. From Study 1, we developed and propose a classification of gesture types and the frequency of body parts usage. From Study 2, we presented a gesture set for blind people in TV interactions. Study 2 also confirmed that providing choices can help reconfirm the preferences of gestures for unfamiliar commands. We conclude by discussing concrete design guidelines for mid-air TV interaction gestures for blind people.

In our study, the number of participants and diversity in their demographic background were limited. Thus, we will extend our work to include more diverse blind participants (with diverse level of sight, age, the age of onset of blindness). Also, we will further explore the use of user- and choice-based elicitation approaches and more theoretical grounding of choice candidate gestures.

ACKNOWLEDGMENTS

We thank the members of the Center for Human-Engaged Computing in Kochi University of Technology for their support. We also thank anonymous reviewers for their thoughtful suggestions. This study has been partially supported by the Grant-in-Aid for Scientific Research of Japan under Grant No. 25330241.

REFERENCES

1. Fraser Hamilton Alex Carmichael, Helen Petrie and Jonathan Freeman. 2003. The Vista Project: Broadening Access To Digital TV Electronic Programme Guides. *PsychNology Journal* 1, 3 (2003), 229–241.
2. American Foundation for the Blind. 1997. Blindness statistics. (1997). Available: http://www.afb.org/info/blindness-statistics/statistical-snapshots-archive/technology-related-statistics-archive/technology-video-description/2345, Accessed on June 30, 2015.
3. Gregg Vanderheiden Chris Law. 2000. The development of a Simple, Low Cost set of Universal Access Features for Electronic Devices. In *Proc. CUU 2000*. ACM, 118. DOI:http://dx.doi.org/10.1145/355460.355545
4. Nelson Cowan. 2010. The Magical Mystery Four: How Is Working Memory Capacity Limited, and Why? *Current Directions in Psychological Science* 19, 1 (2010), 51–57. DOI:http://dx.doi.org/10.1177/0963721409359277
5. Nem Khan Dim and Xiangshi Ren. 2014. Designing Motion Gesture Interfaces in Mobile Phones for Blind People. *Journal of Computer Science and technology* 29, 5 (2014), 812–824. DOI: http://dx.doi.org/10.1007/s11390-014-1470-5
6. Sheena Iyengar. 2011. *The Art of Choosing*. Twelve.
7. Brandon Rothrock Jacob O. Wobbrock, Htet Htet Aung and Brad A. Myers. 2005. Maximizing the guessability of symbolic input. In *Proc. CHI EA 2005*. ACM, 1869–1872. http://doi.acm.org/10.1145/1056808.1057043
8. Meredith Ringel Morris Jacob O. Wobbrock and Andrew D. Wilson. 2009. User-defined gestures for surface computing. In *Proc. CHI 2009*. ACM, 1083–1092. http://doi.acm.org/10.1145/1518701.1518866
9. Yang Li Jaime Ruiz and Edward Lank. 2011. User-defined Motion Gestures for Mobile Interaction. In *Proc. CHI 2011*. ACM, 197–206. DOI: http://dx.doi.org/10.1145/1978942.1978971
10. Kibum Kim, Xiangshi Ren, Seungmoon Choi, and Hong Z. Tan. 2016. Assisting people with visual impairments in aiming at a target on a large wall-mounted display. *International Journal of Human-Computer Studies* 86 (2016), 109 – 120. DOI: http://dx.doi.org/10.1016/j.ijhcs.2015.10.002
11. Gregory Abowd W. Keith Edwards Matthew Bonner, Jeremy Brudvik. 2010. No-Look Notes: Accessible Eyes-free Multi-touch Text Entry. In *Proc. Pervasive 2010*. Springer, 409–427. http://dx.doi.org/10.1007/978-3-642-12654-3_24
12. Andrew D. Wilson Meredith Ringel Morris, Jacob O. Wobbrock. 2010. Understanding users' preferences for surface gestures. In *Proc. GI 2010*. CIPS, 261–268. http://dl.acm.org/citation.cfm?id=1839214.1839260
13. Miguel A Nacenta, Yemliha Kamber, Yizhou Qiang, and Per Ola Kristensson. 2013. Memorability of Pre-designed and User-defined Gesture Sets. In *Proc. CHI 2013*. ACM, 1099–1108. http://doi.acm.org/10.1145/2470654.2466142
14. Michael Nielsen, Moritz Störing, Thomas B. Moeslund, and Erik Granum. 2004. A Procedure for Developing Intuitive and Ergonomic Gesture Interfaces for HCI. In *Gesture-Based Communication in Human-Computer Interaction*, Vol. 2915. Springer, 409–420. DOI: http://dx.doi.org/10.1007/978-3-540-24598-8_38
15. Jacob O. Wobbrock Shaun K. Kane and Richard E. Ladner. 2011. Usable Gestures for Blind People: Understanding Preference and Performance. In *Proc. CHI 2011*. ACM, 413–422. DOI: http://dx.doi.org/10.1145/1978942.1979001
16. Jeffrey P. Bigham Shaun K. Kane and Jacob O. Wobbrock. 2008. Slide Rule: Making Mobile Touch Screens Accessible to Blind People using Multi-touch Interaction Techniques. In *Proc. ASSETS 2008*. ACM, 73–80. DOI:http://dx.doi.org/10.1145/1414471.1414487
17. Chaklam Silpasuwanchai and Xiangshi Ren. 2015. Designing concurrent full-body gestures for intense gameplay. *International Journal of Human-Computer Studies* 80 (2015), 1 – 13. DOI: http://dx.doi.org/10.1016/j.ijhcs.2015.02.010
18. Jaime Snchez and Fernando Aguayo. 2006. Mobile Messenger for the Blind. In *Proc. ECRIM 2006*. Springer, 369–385. http://dx.doi.org/10.1007/978-3-540-71025-7_24
19. Jaime Snchez and Eduardo Maureira. 2006. Subway Mobility Assistance Tools for Blind Users. In *Proc. ECRIM 2006*. Springer, 386–404. http://dx.doi.org/10.1007/978-3-540-71025-7_25
20. Hugo Nicolau Daniel Gonalves Joaquim A. Jorge Tiago Guerreiro, Paulo Lago. 2008. From Tapping to Touching: Making Touch Screens Accessible to Blind Users. *IEEE Multimedia* 15, 4 (2008), 48–50. DOI: http://dx.doi.org/doi:10.1109/MMUL.2008.88
21. Gregg Vanderheiden. 1996. Use of Audio-haptic Interface Techniques to Allow Nonvisual Access to Touchscreen Appliances. In *Proc. HFES 40*. Springer, 1266. DOI: http://dx.doi.org/10.1177/154193129604002430
22. Radu-Daniel Vatavu. 2012. User-defined Gestures for Free-hand TV Control. In *Proc. EuroiTV 2012*. ACM, 45–48. http://doi.acm.org/10.1145/2325616.2325626

Interaction in Motion: Designing Truly Mobile Interaction

Joe Marshall
School of Computer Science
University of Nottingham, UK
joe.marshall@nottingham.ac.uk

Alexandru Dancu
t2i Lab, Dept. of Applied IT
Chalmers University, Sweden
alexandru.dancu@gmail.com

Florian "Floyd" Mueller
Exertion Games Lab
RMIT, Melbourne, Australia
floyd@exertiongameslab.org

ABSTRACT
The use of technology while being mobile now takes place in many areas of people's lives in a wide range of scenarios, for example users cycle, climb, run and even swim while interacting with devices. Conflict between locomotion and system use can reduce interaction performance and also the ability to safely move. We discuss the risks of such "interaction in motion", which we argue make it desirable to design with locomotion in mind. To aid such design we present a taxonomy and framework based on two key dimensions: relation of interaction task to locomotion task, and the amount that a locomotion activity inhibits use of input and output interfaces. We accompany this with four strategies for interaction in motion. With this work, we ultimately aim to enhance our understanding of what being "mobile" actually means for interaction, and help practitioners design truly mobile interactions.

Author Keywords
Mobile; interaction; locomotion; motion.

ACM Classification Keywords
H.5.2 User Interfaces: Theory and methods

INTRODUCTION
In addition to common activities such as walking [27] and cycling [16,60], mobile systems are increasingly built for use during complex and intense types of locomotion such as rock climbing [33,35], skiing [59] and even swimming [13]. Even commodity smartphones are commonly used whilst moving [23,71]. What this means for designers is that it is increasingly important to consider how users will move whilst interacting with systems, and how to make designs work given user locomotion. We previously argued [43] that many designs described as being mobile, whilst they *are* portable, are in fact designed to only be actively used whilst being stationary. Whilst *"stop to interact"* may be the best design in some cases, ignoring the reality that people **do** interact with devices whilst moving causes bad designs in two ways: firstly, it causes safety and practical problems; studies have shown reduced safety when cycling [71], driving [54] and walking [30] due to device use. Secondly, even simple activities like walking decrease users' abilities to interact with systems [49,65]; hence the result is often a non-optimal user experience.

DIS '16, June 04 - 08, 2016, Brisbane, QLD, Australia

ACM 978-1-4503-4031-1/16/06…$15.00
DOI: http://dx.doi.org/10.1145/2901790.2901844

In this paper, by *mobile interactive system* we mean a digital system designed to be used while those interacting with the system perform some kind of locomotion. How they move is termed the *locomotion activity*, such as walking, running, driving or cycling. Active use of a mobile interactive system while moving is *interaction in motion*. We include in this definition fixed systems where users may move within a wide area whilst interacting, so their interaction with the system is mobile even though sensing is embedded in the environment. We exclude fixed location systems involving gross motor movement without parallel locomotion activity such as Wii Fit [53] and BodyBug [40].

Contribution
The contribution of this paper is a structured framework for the consideration of mobility in interaction design, based on the following two dimensions:

1) To what extent is the interaction task related to the locomotion task?
2) To what extent does the locomotion activity inhibit the ability of the user to interact with a system?

Relation between interaction and locomotion tasks (or not) is key to design for movement, because of the following:

- If an interface is strongly related to the locomotion, this may provide greater opportunities for designing for physical and attentional constraints of the activity, for example by creating hands free technology for skiing embedded in goggles that a person already wears.
- The more strongly related interaction is to the locomotion, the more the interaction itself is likely to be continually dependent on how and where a person is moving.

The level of inhibition by locomotion is important because:

- The range of physical possibilities for active interaction with systems is radically different in constrained activities such as swimming compared to less constrained activities such as walking.
- Different modes of locomotion place different physical and mental demands on users, which affects their ability to attend to systems.

DESIGN FOR LOCOMOTION

Locomotion is a key human experience, vital not only for our ability to get places, it also plays a strong role in human cognitive and social development [14] and through sport and exercise can be a major source of enjoyment and support healthy lifestyles. We would argue that the design of current mobile devices, although portable and wearable often inhibits movement or is poorly suited to locomotion. For example wrist worn wearables are often hard to interact with whilst running or cycling, where hand position is constrained, voice and gesture controls for smart glasses are poorly designed for use when moving outdoors in noisy environments, and despite advertising for waterproof mobile phones showing people swimming, they are typically poorly designed for use in water.

Drawing on a set of examples from interaction design research and existing products, we develop a taxonomy that demonstrates how current approaches to mobile design fit on these dimensions. We then discuss *why* a designer might choose to design for interaction in motion from a safety and risk point of view, and follow this with a set of 4 strategies to make interaction design sensitive to user locomotion.

RELATED WORK

In this section we discuss conceptual HCI work relating to locomotion. Systems are discussed in the taxonomy section that follows, so are not described here.

Full Body and Movement Based interaction

The use of the whole body to interact with a system has been studied by various authors. Moen et al. [46] present a discussion of various criteria for movement based design. This motivates both why one might encourage movement interaction, (because it is fun and fulfilling) and discusses various ways to support users in performing a wide range of interesting movements.

Moen et al. argue that the "primary reason for movement" is that "it is fun". Höök's call for somaesthetic design [28] discusses the creation of interactive experiences which aim to foreground the bodily experience, to "deepen our understanding and engagement with ourselves". Whilst our focus here is not purely on movement for the sake of movement, these authors highlight that awareness of the movement itself is key to design for interaction in motion. This point is echoed by Hummels et al. [29], who present a detailed discussion of why we might want to design for movement, arguing that all interaction should be designed with consideration for how the user moves during interaction. They describe four modes of analysis for interaction: the physical and experiential style of the interaction used, whether the activity is goal focused or experience focused, who is the person interacting with the product, and contextual factors such as where and when the product is used. We draw on this work and extend the focus in particular to locomotion which occurs concurrently to the interaction with a digital system, but is not necessarily part of the interaction itself.

Further to this, when trying to understand how locomotion affects interaction, we can make use of work which discusses how to understand and describe underlying movements, for example Alaoui et al. [1] discuss the use of dance inspired 'movement qualities' as an analysis and design tool for physical interaction. Beyond the HCI field, we can also potentially make use of kinesiology and neurobiology descriptions of how people move, such as put forward by Massion, [44] who provide detailed descriptions of the complex nature of seemingly simple motor skills.

Our previous work on interaction in motion [43] has also informed this paper. In it, we describe 4 challenges produced by locomotion: the cognitive load of locomotion, the physical constraints on the body of locomotion, the fact that people must pay attention to the terrain that they are moving over (Figure 1), and the fact that movement occurs with or around other people.

Bicycle and automotive interface guidelines

Prior research around the tension between locomotion and paying attention to interfaces, has been investigated in the automotive and bicycle domains. For example, there are various guidelines for the design of user interfaces in cars such as the SAE standard 2364 [62] that suggests that for safety purposes user interface tasks for cars should take a maximum of 15 seconds to complete. Another example is guidelines from Green et al. [26] who break down possible interaction tasks into those they believe are acceptable whilst driving (such as changing the volume of the radio), and tasks which must be performed while being stationary (such as setting a destination in a navigation system). Rowland et al.'s study of two cycling-based technology experiences [60] discusses how demands of cycling impact on people's ability to interact, presenting a series of lessons for cycling design in response.

Figure 1. Terrain can affect our ability to interact (from [43])

RISKS OF INTERACTION IN MOTION

First, we need to consider whether interaction in motion design is the right thing to do. The key thing to consider here is what additional risk, if any, is posed by the combination of locomotion and interaction and whether that risk is worth it. Whilst we may aim to minimize the impact of interaction on people's ability to move, any attention paid to an interactive system has the potential to create a physical risk to the user as a result of the diverted focus on the locomotion activity. Locomotion always happens in a physical space that contains potential obstacles, and even when in controlled environments, taking attention away from locomotion affects the movement. Studies of driving behavior have shown that even completely hands free telephone conversations and listening to music impair driving performance [6,54]. Similarly for pedestrians, listening to music and texting while walking can reduce the ability to walk safely [66], and using smart eyewear is likely to reduce the ability to avoid obstacles while walking [61]. Conversely locomotion is extremely likely to reduce people's performance at interactive tasks, making it more difficult to read screens and interact with devices [65].

So, given all interactions are likely to reduce locomotion performance and locomotion has negative effects on interaction performance, why would we argue for the design of interaction in motion experiences, and how might we decide what level of performance impairment and risk in the motion activity is acceptable to us? In this section we discuss 6 potential ways to consider what is an acceptable level of risk when designing systems.

Risk versus benefit of movement

Many locomotion activities have major physical and mental health benefits – for example cycling has real risk of injury or death, however in the long term the health benefits of regular cycling lead to people overall being healthier and living longer [11]. If our designs facilitate or encourage people to use active modes of transportation, or to undertake enjoyable locomotion activities, a similar argument may hold, even if they are at higher risk of injury.

Risk versus benefit of interaction

The use of car music systems and hands free phones make car driving more dangerous [6,54]. However they are widely used and legal in most countries. Clearly this implies a general view of society and regulators that the benefits of music in the car or communication with others is a greater benefit than the risk.

Reduction of existing risks

A major reason hands free phones are legal in cars despite safety problems is the greater risk posed by handheld phones. So whilst the absolute risk of hands free communication is greater than not communicating by phone, if we assume that people will communicate by phone whilst driving regardless, suddenly there is a strong argument for hands free systems. Similarly with alternative notification systems like watches and glasses; they are certainly more risky than not checking notifications, but compared to taking out a smartphone and checking that, in many situations they may be less risky.

Comparison against existing risks

A common way of deciding if a risk is acceptable is to compare it against existing risks. This is even made explicit in driver safety standards such as SAE 2364 [62], which sets 15 seconds as a reasonable time for an interaction to take, based on the time that a typical user takes to adjust a car radio, an acceptable existing risk.

Risk taking as an end in itself

In I Seek the Nerves Under Your Skin [41], participants were encouraged to run as fast as they possibly in crowded environments full of bystanders and fellow runners, littered with obstacles. The additional risk was a major part of what made this experience so thrilling. Dangerous and exciting locomotion activities such as extreme sports are a major part of human culture [67], and we believe that the creation of technology to support and even encourage such risk taking is a valid design goal in itself.

Risks of Collocated interaction With Others

Most mobile systems are essentially designed for an individual. However, we argue that all forms of locomotion are essentially social, whether it be people you are travelling to a place with, passers-by whilst you walk somewhere, other drivers on the road etc. Essentially we must design for what Mueller et al. call the "relating body" [47]. As Lundgren et al. [39] discuss, whilst existing technology has good support for distributed social interaction, most designs do not support collocated interaction very well. For example Jacobs et al. [32] describe how in their mobile phone work "A Conversation Between Trees" whilst participants enjoyed the experience, they felt that the mobile device actually got in the way of their social experience with people they had come with. Designing for collocated interaction requires that we take account of "*the complex interplay between: the social situation in which it takes place; the technology used and the mechanics inscribed; the physical environment; and the temporal elements of design*" [39]. Current systems for co-located interaction (e.g. [37,39]) primarily describe social interactions between those who know each other. However as the need for pedestrian crash avoidance system CrashAlert [27] demonstrates (and the widespread legislation banning mobile phone use in cars), the use of technology when moving is not neutral to bystanders. In addition to safety risks, visible and always-on technology such as augmented reality glasses may lead to privacy concerns in bystanders [18]. Interaction in motion technology may even wish to communicate with other instances of technology belonging to strangers, for example in car to car communications to aid navigation or safety [50].

A TAXONOMY OF MOBILE INTERACTION

In this section, we present two dimensions of mobile interaction, and populate the space defined by these dimensions with existing systems to create a taxonomy of mobile interactions. As we are interested in interaction while being mobile, we assume the user has two underlying tasks (which may or may not be related), firstly to engage in locomotion, such as walking, cycling or driving, and secondly to perform an interaction with a digital system.

Dimension 1: To what extent is the interaction task related to the locomotion task

A key feature of smart watches is the ability to notify users of information such as email, SMS messages and calls. This interaction is largely unrelated to the locomotion of the user. In contrast, when developing navigation applications the locomotion of the user is more strongly related to the interaction task, it is more of an integrated movement based interaction as described by Moen et al. [46]. We define 4 points of interest along this dimension:

- *Unrelated* – as in our example with the notifications on the smart watches, there is no sensing of locomotion or adaptability to it.
- *Weakly related* – locomotion and interaction are related but with no immediate system response to movement, for example looking up nearby places on maps, or tracking movement with a GPS.
- *Strongly related* – there is a real-time feedback loop between interaction and locomotion, as seen in turn by turn navigation where the interface is telling the person where to turn, and the person is feeding back to it with their movements [7].
- *Encouragement* - Exertion games such as Jogging Over a Distance [48] or fitness systems which directly encourage players to move, such as the Zombies Run game [2], may be seen as even more highly related interaction tasks, as interaction with the system is the reason locomotion is occurring.

Figure 2 visualizes these properties along the dimension.

Dimension 2: To what extent does the locomotion activity inhibit the ability of the user to interact with a system?

As Massion et al. [44] describe, locomotion is a highly complex activity. The demands of locomotion activities can inhibit interaction in many ways [43]. At the low end of this dimension, we can consider a person sitting down indoors, they are largely unconstrained in their interaction. Next, we consider a person walking outside; to do this, they must pay a certain level of attention to their surroundings which constrains their vision, but largely have the ability to move their hands to manipulate devices, address speech recognition interfaces etc. Tasks such as driving or running constrain us further by dictating what we do with hands and feet. At extremes, we can consider swimming, a swimmer is highly constrained in body position, visibility, ability to hear or speak; in cold water, they may even lack the sensitivity to feel tactile sensations; swimming also constrains people's ability to stop (without drowning) [43].

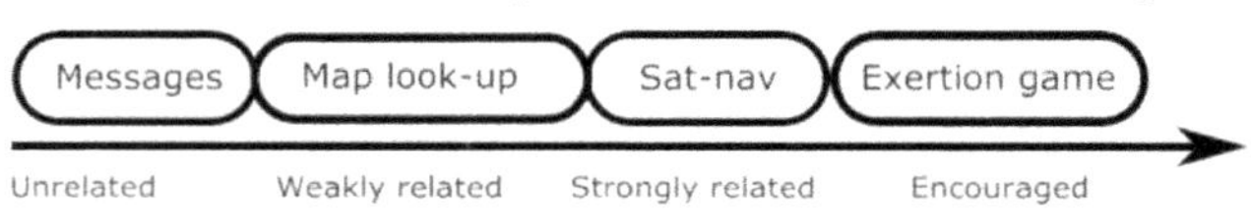

Figure 2. Relation of Interaction Task to Locomotion

We define 3 points of particular interest along this dimension:

- *Weak Constraints* – activity constrains the user by requiring attention only (e.g. walking with phone)
- *Strong Constraints* – activity places constraints on what the person can do physically (e.g. driving requires hands on the wheel)
- *Extreme Constraints* – activity places extreme constraints on what people can look at, whether they can stop doing the activity or requires constant mental focus.

Figure 3 plots on this dimension various locomotion activities mentioned in previous HCI work. This has an element of subjectivity, for example here we have plotted cycling as being slightly less constrained than driving despite them having largely similar physical constraints, as cyclists typically have a greater ability to stop and interact if needed (as mentioned in [60]). Similarly, street skateboarding [58] has been plotted as requiring more constraints than cycling, because whilst it is hands free, it is much harder to hold or use a device whilst using the full body to do a trick. Swimming is plotted as being more constraining than rock climbing, because whilst dynamic climbing moves require the full body, when not on an overhang or mid move, climbing provides many points at which climbers are free to use and look at digital equipment, something evidenced by the highly active documentary culture described by Byrne et al. [9].

If we consider different modalities of input which do not require physical gestures, such as speech, or outputs which do not require visual sensing such as audio and haptics, this ordering may change slightly, for example the enclosed cockpit of a car can be ideal for speech input, whereas a combination of environmental noise and the changes in voice due to being low on breath make speech input difficult during running.

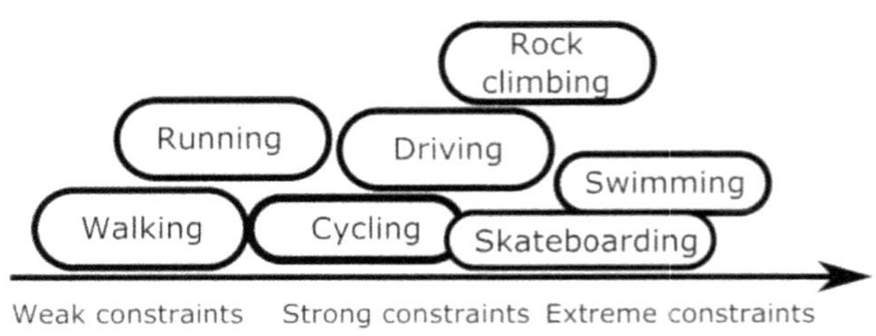

Figure 3. Inhibition of interaction

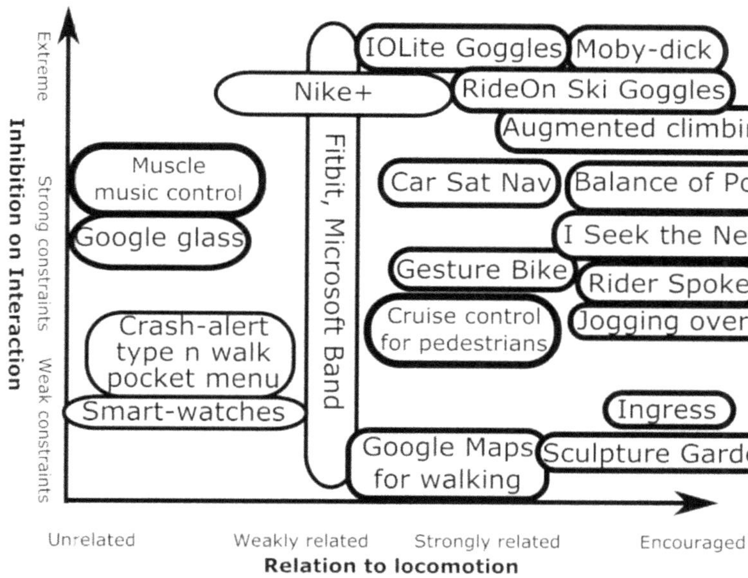

Figure 4. A taxonomy of systems discussed in the paper

POPULATING OUR TAXONOMY

In this section, we discuss a selection of existing systems designed to be used during locomotion, and discuss where they fit in the taxonomy. This is not an exhaustive list, but is designed to illustrate a range of activities supported by popular existing systems from both industry and research, including work from our own practices (Figures 5,6,7,8,9). Figure 4 shows how systems discussed in the paper fit on the two dimensions of our taxonomy, this may be useful to refer back to whilst reading the following sections.

Navigation Systems

A classic example of an interaction that directly responds to locomotion activity is a navigation system. Navigation systems exist for most modes of transport; in this section we describe navigation aids designed for various modes of mobility, and show how the constraints of each locomotion activity led to very different designs.

Google Maps Navigation

Google Maps [25] is a smartphone application which provides maps and navigation directions for walking, cycling and driving. Google Maps illustrates how different locomotion activities place different constraints on the interaction - In walking mode, the interface is largely unconstrained, and users can browse maps, search, and use navigation freely. In driving mode, the phone must be mounted on the car and operates basically as a car satnav device - the user is given strict instructions only to touch the screen whilst not driving, so can only follow turn by turn directions or use voice commands to search for a new destination. It is also possible to use turn by turn navigation for cycling, including a version that uses.Google Glass.

Ride-On Ski Goggles

The Ride-On Augmented Reality Goggles [59] are designed for skiing. They allow users to navigate whilst skiing, using augmented reality visual cues overlaid on the real world showing which direction to turn for particular ski runs, and also to play games such as skiing down a virtual slalom course. Interaction with the goggles is highly constrained because typically users will be wearing gloves and in windy environments in which speech recognition is unlikely to work well. Because of this, interaction with the Ride-On goggles while moving is done purely through skiing directions, with additional features which are accessed via eye movements while stopped.

IOLite and OnCourse Swimming Goggles

In open water swimming, swimmers are at a low level in the water, with their head underwater most of the time. A key challenge is to navigate a course in straight lines with limited ability to sight landmarks. Two competing wearable products exist which aim to help swimmers maintain their course, the OnCourse [55] and IOLite [31] goggles . Due to the unique and extreme constraints of swimming these navigation aids are very different to land-based satnavs. Both use LEDs in the goggles to show if the swimmer is drifting off a course made out of a series of straight lines. They differ slightly in how one sets the course – in the OnCourse goggles, swimmers must look in the direction they wish to swim and press a button on the goggles each time they turn a corner, interrupting their swimming; the IOLite goggles in contrast only allow interaction by swimming, with the course changing when the goggles detect a sharp turn.

Gesture Bike and Smart Flashlight
Dancu et al. [16,17] argue that for cycling navigation, many environmental and personal factors, such as how busy a street is, how direct a route is and what kind of route a rider likes, mean that it is more appropriate for cycling navigation to provide a full map including context around the rider rather than to use car style turn by turn navigation. Their cycle navigation systems use a projector shining a large map onto the road showing the area around the rider. This caters for the fact that the rider is constrained by their cycling to look forward most of the time by placing the interface close to where they are looking [16]. In Gesture Bike [17] (Figure 5), they further add detection of standard cycling turn signal gestures, using these to support the activity of cycling by projecting arrows on the road to show other users how the rider is turning.

Notifications, Interruptions and Messages
Several different types of devices offer support for basic smartphone operations like receiving notifications and/or sending text messages. These systems support movement by reducing the frequency that a user has to get their smartphone out of their pocket, or making it easier to move whilst using a phone. These applications are largely not strongly related to locomotion.

Smartwatches
Smartwatches, such as the Pebble Watch and Apple Watch are primarily devices that show notifications on the user's wrist, and notify by sound or haptic feedback of events like messages and incoming calls. By removing the need to get out a smartphone, they offer a quick ability to see messages whilst moving, as long as constraints of the activity on hand position or where it is possible to look do not obstruct this.

Head mounted displays and glasses
Head mounted displays can also be used for smartphone type functions; they have the advantage over watches that visuals can be seen largely hands free. As an example Google's Glass [17] displays a small screen on the periphery of the user's vision, which can be used to see notifications and information such as navigation directions. Voice control allows it to take input. Glasses require a shift in visual focus for interaction versus locomotion, which may take time away from both. Glasses based notification system NotifEye [38] uses deliberately unobtrusive notifications that float across the user's vision which aims to minimize the amount users must shift their visual focus.

Smartphone Walking apps
Type-n-walk [12] is a smartphone application which displays a video feed from the rear camera of the phone behind a window in which email or SMS messages may be written. This is designed to allow users to get around the constraints imposed by needing to see the street in front of them while walking. The CrashAlert [27] research prototype does a similar thing but uses phone-mounted sensors in order to detect oncoming obstacles and displays on-screen information relating to these obstacles – the study demonstrated that walkers were able to walk and interact with the device successfully with significantly less need to look up or slow down.

PocketMenu [57] is designed to allow 'in-pocket interaction' with music players, using fixed screen positions and tactile and audio feedback to allow users to select music tracks and pause & play on a smartphone whilst the phone is in their pocket. PocketTouch [63] extends this by allowing for capacitive sensing through the fabric of the pocket so users do not even need to touch their phone.

All the above applications require hand input on the devices, so are limited to locomotion activities that do not constrain the hands, meaning that they are only suitable for less constraining forms of movement like walking or jogging.

Direct Body Interfaces
One alternative approach to mobile interfaces is to interface systems directly to the body's electrical signals. For example Saponas et al. [64] describe a music control interface using detection of arm muscle activation, which they argue could enable hands and screen free interaction while jogging. Cruise Control for Pedestrians [56] takes an alternative approach to bodily interfacing, directly controlling the movement of someone walking by electrically stimulating their leg muscles. Proprioceptive interaction [36] goes beyond this, in using a combination of sensing hand posture, and electronic muscle stimulation to force hand posture changes, allowing both input and output to occur via the user's wrist.

Sports and Activity Trackers
There are many smartphone applications and devices that measure locomotion activity such as distance and speed of running or cycling, or the number of steps taken. They typically fit into two broad categories:

Sports Tracking Devices and Applications
Sports trackers such as Nike+ [52] are aimed at people doing targeted workouts. They record how much exertion someone does during a workout, by recording data such as heart rate, speed and distance. Some including Strava [69], Endomondo [19] and Nike+ [52] include competition features so that users can compete against each other. Interaction with these systems typically only has a weak

Figure 5. Signalling with Gesture Bike

Figure 6. Jogging Over a Distance

relation to the locomotion activity, as they purely record exercise, and the user does not respond to the sports tracker during their exercise.

Activity Trackers

Activity trackers are wearables (such as the Fitbit [21] and Microsoft Band [45]) or smartphone apps that rather than tracking discrete sporting activity sessions, instead track the user's whole life, capturing data related to locomotion such as steps and distance walked during a day. Again, direct interaction with such devices is typically done offline at specific intervals, for example when checking heart rate or number of steps over the day. In Figure 4, these are shown on all levels of dimension 2, because they are designed to be used both during extreme exercise, and also to measure more everyday movement.

Exertion Games

There are a wide variety of games that go beyond responding to locomotion to deliberately encouraging it. Both these sport-focused 'exertion games' [47] and sports/activity trackers typically have an explicit aim to encourage people to exercise; exertion games differ from tracking applications in that the feedback is real-time and directly responds to player movements and exertion.

Mobile Exertion Games

The gaming mode of the Ride-On [59] ski goggles encourages people to ski down particular tracks and ski from side to side to hit a virtual slalom track. The way that it encourages and responds to exertion allows the playing of a game without any input to the system other than rider movement, in a situation where the locomotion activity severely constrains all other forms of interaction. Jogging Over a Distance (Figure 6) [48] also uses running as a control method to allow two people jogging in different locations to run together, able to hear audio from each other, with runners who are working harder appearing to move in front of and away from the other runner through their headphones. MobyDick [13] is a multi-player swimming pool game in which players must swim particular strokes in order to capture a virtual sea creature and duck underwater to avoid its fiery breath. Players hear the game events through waterproof headphones as they swim and must collaborate in order to capture the sea creature without getting killed by it. Another swimming game, Swimoid [70], makes use of a swimming robotic display, located in the pool below the swimmer.

Figure 7. Balance of Power

As well as mobile device-based exertion games, some games exist which instrument the environment and track players' movement in the space. Despite different user interfaces, these create similar challenges to those of mobile exertion games, in that people are inhibited in their ability to directly interact with systems by their locomotion. For example, Balance of Power [42] (Figure 7) is a game for 4 or more players, played in a squash court. In Balance of Power, two teams must try and physically move the opposing team to their side to score points. The locomotion activity here combines running with physical contact and play-fighting. This combination makes it hard for players to always hear audio cues, and they often cannot even look at the large projection screen used in the game. Because of this the game combines both display types, with very loud audio plus a projection screen showing current game status that is designed to be visible in the very brief glances that players have time for.

Another situated exertion game is the Augmented Climbing Wall [33], a physical climbing wall which has visual tracking and projections added to it. The projections are used to create games in which the player must climb fast to avoid being caught by a virtual chainsaw. This again purely tracks the motion activity as input, in order to allow the player freedom to move their whole body as required in climbing and projects directly onto the wall, so that it is in line of sight.

Artistic Movement Experiences

As well as sport-focused exertion games, there are a large number of artistic experiences and pervasive games that, whilst they are not primarily focused on exertion, do also require users to perform locomotion whilst playing them.

Pervasive Games

Rider Spoke [60] (Figure 8) is a pervasive game for cyclists. In Rider Spoke, people are given a bike with a handlebar mounted computer, and are sent cycling round a city at night, hearing audio instructions, and responding by using the touchscreen and talking into a microphone when stopped. Rider Spoke uses a "stop to interact" paradigm, where riders can hear music and instructions from the system while riding, but are instructed to only interact with

Figure 8. Rider Spoke

the system while stopped. Even with that safeguard, riders did occasionally find the audio dangerously distracting [60].

Ingress [51] is a long term massively multiplayer online game in which players must physically visit points of interest located in the real world in order to capture territory. In contrast to the exertion games described above, Ingress does not require players to move quickly, because of this there are few constraints on the interaction so it can use a relatively traditional handheld mobile interface.

Artistic Experiences

Fosh et al.'s sculpture garden experience [22] uses a relatively standard touchscreen interface with an audio soundtrack, as people are moving slowly and have the time to look down at the screen when they need to.

A more intense-effort artistic experience is the 'running poetry' game I Seek the Nerves Under Your Skin [41] (Figure 9). This is a purely movement controlled experience; it deliberately exploits the fact that users struggle to combine sprinting hard in complex environments with listening to an audio track of performance poetry, to create an "intense" experience.

4 DESIGN STRATEGIES FOR INTERACTION IN MOTION

In this section we describe four interaction in motion strategies. Each address one extreme of our taxonomy dimensions (see Fig. 10). They may be useful to designers depending on the application type they are building and locomotion activities they anticipate occurring.

These strategies may be of use to designers both when considering how to design a system given the anticipated user locomotion, and also when altering a system to account for interaction issues that occur when it is used during locomotion.

Figure 9. I Seek the Nerves Under Your Skin

As an example of use of this framework when designing a system, we could consider the design of a signaling device for cycling. An obvious idea would be to fit buttons to the handlebars (as in commercial devices). However, cycling creates constraints on hand interaction, particular at points when one may wish to manouvre. We could instead apply our strategy *"use Locomotion Activity as Primary Interaction Channel"*, and build a system which sensed existing cycling manouvres (as we did in [17]).

As an example of how using the framework to identify alterations to a design might work, Colley et al. [15] describe modified touch screen displays for cars. Such screens typically require the user to look at them, which makes them hard to use while driving [15]. Colley et al. modified a touchscreen car interface so that sliding different fingers controlled features such as temperature, fan speed and music volume to allow them to be used eyes free. This alteration could be suggested by our strategy *"adapt interaction to modalities and locations that are easily accessible whilst moving"*.

High relation to locomotion, highly constrained interaction – Tailored Solutions

When creating specialized interactions to support forms of movement that place a lot of constraints on the user, we are likely to require solutions that are strongly tailored to the expected locomotion activity. Three ways in which we could do this are:

Use Locomotion Activity as Primary Interaction Channel

Early designers of car navigation systems envisaged them as being a source of instructions which the driver would follow [26], in part because prior to GPS being widely available, the car had limited knowledge of where it was being driven. With modern GPS based systems, drivers no longer blindly follow directions, and instead engage in a dialog with the system, for example driving down a 'wrong'

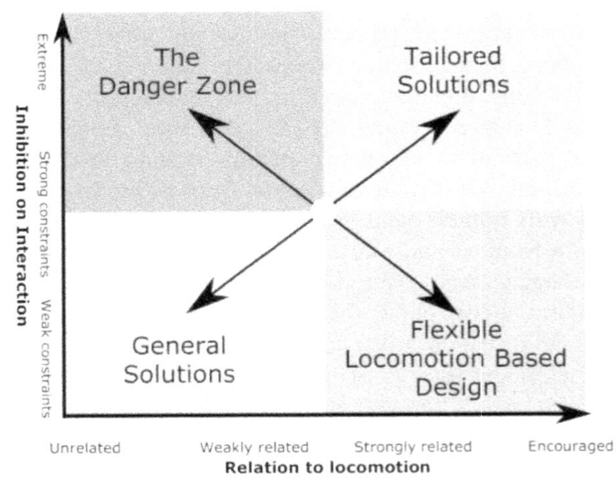

Figure 10. Four strategies for mobile interaction

road to communicate desire to use a different route [7].

The IOLite swimming goggles similarly allow a user to instruct them that they wish to swim in a different direction by turning and swimming that way. Gesture Bike [17] also exploits natural movements of cycling, in this case gestures that cyclists use to indicate turning. Another bike visibility aid from Busch und Muller [8] uses accelerometers to detect cycle braking and light a car style brake light.

Create custom physical or multi-modal interfaces
In contrast to the IOLite goggles [31], the OnCourse goggles [55] perform the same task of helping swimmers swim straight, but rather than automatically judge a turn has occurred, they instead require the user to push a waterproof button on the goggles. Whilst this means an extra action is required by the swimmer, it also avoids problems with sensor based interaction such as the sensor detecting another event as being an attempt to communicate a turn to the system, Bellotti et al [4] discuss this when they describe how sensor based systems can make it hard to 'not address' the system.

At many points when interaction is highly constrained a multi-modal interface which is tailored to the demands of the locomotion activity may be appropriate. For example in cars, use of speech recognition as an extra input is obviously useful allowing drivers to keep their hands on the wheel whilst controlling the system. Similarly for outputs we may wish to consider multiple modalities; as we discuss in relation to Balance of Power, the character of different outputs gives them different value; a screen or other visual output is persistent, meaning people can glance at it when the demands of the motion activity permit. Audio and haptic feedback in contrast are momentary, meaning that if they are missed they are lost, but have the advantage that in low noise environments they do not require eyes to be taken off the locomotion activity.

Avoid distracting from or spoiling the locomotion activity
Many locomotion activities are pleasurable activities in themselves [46]. When designing interactive systems for use during such activities, we should consider how their use impacts enjoyment of the activity itself. As an example of user concerns about this, in some presentations of the running system I Seek the Nerves, some runners refused to use it because the headphones blocked out external sound which they felt would ruin the running experience [41]. Distraction from the activity can also be a safety risk – particularly when using visual interfaces, we must be aware that even AR and see through interfaces must be carefully designed to avoid such distraction [61].

Low relation to locomotion, highly constrained interaction – Design for The Danger Zone
When dealing with constrained interaction, such as driving, swimming, climbing or cycling, we have to seriously consider whether it is sensible or safe to create interactions to support tasks that are unrelated to the locomotion task itself and may distract participants. For this reason, we call this rather dramatically "THE DANGER ZONE". For example the safety and usefulness of wearable technology in cars is a subject of current debate [10]. We could argue that in many cases devices designed to allow people to perform general tasks in such situations may be a positive thing, as rather than create new distractions, they may allow people who would otherwise be using general purpose systems in an unsafe manner, such as sending text messages while driving, something that in some countries 30% of drivers admit to doing [23]. Whilst the task may be unrelated to the locomotion activity, it is likely that we will still need to consider what types of locomotion activity we wish to support when designing for this style of interaction.

Three ways in which we can design for the "Danger Zone" are:

Create systems that are aware of locomotion task load
Kim et al. [34] describe a system for cars which uses a range of sensors and a machine learning classifier to identify moments when driving is taking less effort, which they argue would be good moments to interrupt people. Similarly when cycling, one could restrict moments where systems encouraged interaction to occur when stopped, and restrict interruptions to when on less busy roads.

Adapt interaction to modalities and locations that are easily accessible whilst moving
Dancu et al.'s Smart Flashlight [16] presents information directly on the road that a cyclist is travelling along. Similarly heads up displays in cars [72], smart glasses [24] and similar devices aim to present visual information in places where people are already looking. This is in contrast to early pervasive games, which often required people to run around whilst looking at device screens, which in several cases was reported to have endangered participants [3,5]. We can also adapt how users interact with devices as with Colley et al.'s eyes free car touchscreen [15], which removes the need to look to interact.

Enforce stop to interact (at convenient or safe times)
Studies have shown that users of technology adapt their usage to the locomotion activity, for example drivers alerting other partners in a phone call to traffic situations in to 'pause' the phone call [20]. Context aware technology could potentially support this by encouraging interaction at convenient or safe times. In particular, in many interfaces, there will be points at which the user has to input data on screens. Realistically in highly constrained interaction, especially if it is taking place in a noisy place where speech recognition is unreliable, these will have to be confined to points at which it is possible to stop and interact. In situations where the locomotion is highly related to or even driven by the interactive system, we have an advantage, that we can detect state of the system to make interactions happen at a convenient or safe time. A basic example of this is car navigation systems that only allow addresses to be input when a car is stopped.

High relation to locomotion, weakly constrained interaction – Create Flexible Movement Based Designs

In this situation, we are creating a movement controlled system which is only designed for low intensity movement. Here we need to consider what is the purpose of the locomotion – is it to get to places, for exercise, for enjoyment of the outdoors. Interaction is not highly constrained, so the strategies below are less about purely handling the combination of interaction and locomotion activity, and more about how to design the interaction so that it is sensitive to the fact of movement.

Consider the aesthetics of interaction

In situations where interaction is less constrained by the practicalities of dual locomotion and interaction, we have more freedom to consider the aesthetics of combining interaction and locomotion. As examples of this, in Ingress [51], the 'scanner' smartphone application is modeled after handheld scanning devices used in science fiction such as Star Trek's 'tri-corders' and the 'alien trackers' in Ridley Scott's Aliens. This creates an aesthetic reason for the need to hold the phone in front of you and interact with it while you play the game.

Design for awareness of surroundings

When we move, whether it is for navigation or for entertainment or sport, awareness of our surroundings is important. Applying a 'head-up' [68] interaction style is one way to achieve this, by using audio feedback or head mounted wearables. Mobile art work "A Conversation Between Trees" [32] takes an alternative approach, in that it uses screen based interaction, but regularly asks the user to point the phone camera at interesting things – participants reported that this created a deep engagement with the forest in which they were walking.

Design for the "pleasure of motion" [46]

Moen et al. [46] ask the question – why use movement as an interaction? Whilst in the case of locomotion, there are clearly some more prosaic reasons why movement may be a useful part of an interaction, such as navigation, in other interactions, the primary reason for movement is that it is fun, and even when it is not, we should be aware of the pleasures of even practical locomotion..

Low relation to locomotion, weakly constrained interaction – Design General Interaction Aids

When designing for interactions that place only weak constraints on interaction, it is possible to create quite general solutions. This area is essentially where most existing wearables, smart glasses, mobile phone walking apps etc. succeed, where there is a low level of interaction constraints caused by the locomotion activity, so people are able to successfully interact with quite generic interfaces. This type of interaction is probably the most commonly targeted area, and as such is relatively well understood. Because of this, the following three design strategies largely describe ways in which current technology aims to make things better in this kind of situation.

Fix limitations your application places on locomotion

Apps such as CrashAlert [27] and Type n Walk [12] address a key restriction that touchscreen text input interfaces have, that they require the user to watch the screen which makes it hard to walk safely. Glass's voice input and face mounted display aims to do the same thing.

Reduce unnecessary interruptions

The most important feature of smartwatches is their handling of notifications, allowing people to avoid taking out other mobile devices. However, with multiple applications installed on an accompanying phone, a very large number of notifications may be received. Key to the design of smartwatches is the ability to filter notifications and select what is and is not an important enough interruption to be worth putting on the watch.

Be realistic about where and when the system will be used

Existing research demonstrates that almost all mobile systems are used while moving, even in more constrained locomotion activities such as cycling or driving [23,71]. As designers, we cannot ignore the reality of device use; we should either design to support locomotion use cases, or perhaps consider how our designs can encourage users not to do so in the case we judge it to be too risky.

CONCLUSIONS

Locomotion is a central human need and ability, being one of the main ways we interact with the physical world around us. Designing interactive products and experiences that support locomotion is not only an opportunity for designers, but is a requirement of a society that employs interactive devices at all times. Failure to design systems with movement in mind may increase risk of both interaction problems and unsafe device use. We believe that by taking a principled approach to designing for those moments when people are moving whilst interacting, designers have the power both to effectively support people's existing motion and interactive activities, and also to create systems which may inspire new and exciting locomotion based experiences.

ACKNOWLEDGEMENTS

Joe Marshall is supported by The Leverhulme Trust (ECF/2012-677). Florian 'Floyd' Mueller acknowledges support from the Australian Research Council Grant LP130100743. Alexandru Dancu thanks EU FP7 People Programme (Marie Curie Actions) under REA Grant Agreement 290227. All authors thank Adviye Ayça Ünlüer for the Gesture Bike illustration

REFERENCES

1. Sarah Fdili Alaoui, Baptiste Caramiaux, Marcos Serrano, and Frédéric Bevilacqua. 2012. Movement qualities as interaction modality. *Proceedings of the Designing Interactive Systems Conference on - DIS '12*, ACM Press, 761. http://doi.org/10.1145/2317956.2318071
2. Naomi Alderman. 2012. Zombies, Run!

3. Rafael A. Ballagas, Sven G. Kratz, Jan Borchers, et al. 2007. REXplorer. *CHI '07 extended abstracts on Human factors in computing systems - CHI '07*, ACM Press, 1929. http://doi.org/10.1145/1240866.1240927

4. Victoria Bellotti, Maribeth Back, W. Keith Edwards, Rebecca E. Grinter, Austin Henderson, and Cristina Lopes. 2002. Making sense of sensing systems. *Proceedings of the SIGCHI conference on Human factors in computing systems Changing our world, changing ourselves - CHI '02*, ACM Press, 415. http://doi.org/10.1145/503376.503450

5. Stephen Boyd Davis, Magnus Moar, John Cox, et al. 2005. 'Ere be dragons. *Proceedings of the 13th annual ACM international conference on Multimedia - MULTIMEDIA '05*, ACM Press, 1059. http://doi.org/10.1145/1101149.1101376

6. Warren Brodsky and Micha Kizner. 2012. Exploring an alternative in-car music background designed for driver safety. *Transportation Research Part F: Traffic Psychology and Behaviour* 15, 2: 162–173. http://doi.org/10.1016/j.trf.2011.12.001

7. Barry Brown and Eric Laurier. 2012. The normal natural troubles of driving with GPS. *Proceedings of the 2012 ACM annual conference on Human Factors in Computing Systems - CHI '12*, ACM Press, 1621. http://doi.org/10.1145/2207676.2208285

8. Busch & Müller. 2014. BrakeTec. Retrieved September 22, 2015 from http://www.bumm.de/innovation-original/braketec.html

9. Richard Byrne and Florian "Floyd" Mueller. 2014. Designing Digital Climbing Experiences through Understanding Rock Climbing Motivation. In *Entertainment Computing – ICEC 2014*, Yusuf Pisan, Nikitas M. Sgouros and Tim Marsh (eds.). Springer Berlin Heidelberg, Berlin, Heidelberg, 92–99. http://doi.org/10.1007/978-3-662-45212-7

10. Maurizio Caon, Michele Tagliabue, Leonardo Angelini, Paolo Perego, Elena Mugellini, and Giuseppe Andreoni. 2014. Wearable Technologies for Automotive User Interfaces: Danger or Opportunity? *Proceedings of the 6th International Conference on Automotive User Interfaces and Interactive Vehicular Applications - AutomotiveUI '14*, ACM Press, 1–5. http://doi.org/10.1145/2667239.2667314

11. Nick Cavill and Adrian Davis. 2007. Cycling and Health - What's the evidence. Retrieved from www.cyclingengland.co.uk

12. CGActive LLC. 2009. Type n Walk. Retrieved from http://www.type-n-walk.com/

13. Woohyeok Choi, Jeungmin Oh, Taiwoo Park, et al. 2014. MobyDick. *Proceedings of the 12th ACM Conference on Embedded Network Sensor Systems - SenSys '14*, ACM Press, 76–90. http://doi.org/10.1145/2668332.2668352

14. Melissa W Clearfield. 2011. Learning to walk changes infants' social interactions. *Infant behavior & development* 34, 1: 15–25. http://doi.org/10.1016/j.infbeh.2010.04.008

15. Ashley Colley, Jani Väyrynen, and Jonna Häkkilä. 2015. In-Car Touch Screen Interaction. *Proceedings of the 4th International Symposium on Pervasive Displays - PerDis '15*, ACM Press, 131–137. http://doi.org/10.1145/2757710.2757724

16. Alexandru Dancu, Zlatko Franjcic, and Morten Fjeld. 2014. Smart flashlight. *Proceedings of the 32nd annual ACM conference on Human factors in computing systems - CHI '14*, ACM Press, 3627–3630. http://doi.org/10.1145/2556288.2557289

17. Alexandru Dancu, Velko Vechev, Adviye Ayca Unluer, et al. 2015. Gesture Bike : Examining Projection Surfaces and Turn Signal Systems for Urban Cycling (in press). *Intelligent Tabletops and Surfaces*, ACM.

18. Tamara Denning, Zakariya Dehlawi, and Tadayoshi Kohno. 2014. In situ with bystanders of augmented reality glasses. *Proceedings of the 32nd annual ACM conference on Human factors in computing systems - CHI '14*, ACM Press, 2377–2386. http://doi.org/10.1145/2556288.2557352

19. Endomondo. 2007. Endomondo. Retrieved January 21, 2015 from http://www.endomondo.com/about

20. M. Esbjörnsson, O. Juhlin, and A. Weilenmann. 2007. Drivers Using Mobile Phones in Traffic: An Ethnographic Study of Interactional Adaptation. *International Journal of Human-Computer Interaction* 22, 1-2: 37–58. http://doi.org/10.1080/10447310709336954

21. Fitbit Inc. 2008. Fitbit Tracker. Retrieved from http://www.fitbit.com

22. Lesley Fosh, Steve Benford, Stuart Reeves, Boriana Koleva, and Patrick Brundell. 2013. see me, feel me, touch me, hear me. *Proceedings of the SIGCHI Conference on Human Factors in Computing Systems - CHI '13*, ACM Press, 149. http://doi.org/10.1145/2470654.2470675

23. Thomas R Frieden, Harold W Jaffe, James W Stephens, Denise M Cardo, and Stephanie Zaza. 2013. Mobile device use while driving--United States and seven European countries, 2011. *MMWR. Morbidity and mortality weekly report* 62, 10: 177–82. Retrieved September 21, 2015 from http://www.ncbi.nlm.nih.gov/pubmed/23486382

24. Google. 2013. Glass. Retrieved from https://www.google.com/glass/start/

25. Google. 2015. Maps. Retrieved from https://play.google.com/store/apps/details?id=com.google.android.apps.maps
26. P Green, W Levison, G Paelke, and C Serafin. 1994. Suggested human factors design guidelines for driver information systems. *The University of Michigan ....* Retrieved September 21, 2015 from http://citeseerx.ist.psu.edu/viewdoc/download?doi=10.1.1.97.6518&rep=rep1&type=pdf
27. Juan David Hincapié-Ramos and Pourang Irani. 2013. CrashAlert. *Proceedings of the SIGCHI Conference on Human Factors in Computing Systems - CHI '13*, ACM Press, 3385. http://doi.org/10.1145/2470654.2466463
28. Kristina Höök, Anna Ståhl, Martin Jonsson, Johanna Mercurio, Anna Karlsson, and Eva-Carin Banka Johnson. 2015. Somaesthetic design. *interactions* 22, 4: 26–33. http://doi.org/10.1145/2770888
29. Caroline Hummels, Kees C. J. Overbeeke, and Sietske Klooster. 2006. Move to get moved: a search for methods, tools and knowledge to design for expressive and rich movement-based interaction. *Personal and Ubiquitous Computing* 11, 8: 677–690. http://doi.org/10.1007/s00779-006-0135-y
30. Ira E. Hyman, S. Matthew Boss, Breanne M. Wise, Kira E. McKenzie, and Jenna M. Caggiano. 2009. Did you see the unicycling clown? Inattentional blindness while walking and talking on a cell phone. *Applied Cognitive Psychology* 24, 5: 597–607. http://doi.org/10.1002/acp.1638
31. IOLite. IOLite Goggles. Retrieved September 24, 2015 from http://www.swimiolite.com/
32. Rachel Jacobs, Steve Benford, Mark Selby, Michael Golembewski, Dominic Price, and Gabriella Giannachi. 2013. A conversation between trees. *Proceedings of the SIGCHI Conference on Human Factors in Computing Systems - CHI '13*, ACM Press, 129. http://doi.org/10.1145/2470654.2470673
33. Raine Kajastila and Perttu Hämäläinen. 2015. Motion games in real sports environments. *interactions* 22, 2: 44–47. http://doi.org/10.1145/2731182
34. SeungJun Kim, Jaemin Chun, and Anind K. Dey. 2015. Sensors Know When to Interrupt You in the Car. *Proceedings of the 33rd Annual ACM Conference on Human Factors in Computing Systems - CHI '15*, ACM Press, 487–496. http://doi.org/10.1145/2702123.2702409
35. Felix Kosmalla, Florian Daiber, and Antonio Krüger. 2015. ClimbSense. *Proceedings of the 33rd Annual ACM Conference on Human Factors in Computing Systems - CHI '15*, ACM Press, 2033–2042. http://doi.org/10.1145/2702123.2702311
36. Pedro Lopes, Alexandra Ion, Willi Müller, Daniel Hoffmann, Patrik Jonell, and Patrick Baudisch. 2015. Proprioceptive Interaction. *Proceedings of the 33rd Annual ACM Conference Extended Abstracts on Human Factors in Computing Systems - CHI EA '15*, ACM Press, 175–175. http://doi.org/10.1145/2702613.2732490
37. Andrés Lucero, Matt Jones, Tero Jokela, and Simon Robinson. 2013. Mobile collocated interactions. *interactions* 20, 2: 26. http://doi.org/10.1145/2427076.2427083
38. Andrés Lucero and Akos Vetek. 2014. NotifEye. *Proceedings of the 11th Conference on Advances in Computer Entertainment Technology - ACE '14*, ACM Press, 1–10. http://doi.org/10.1145/2663806.2663824
39. Sus Lundgren, Joel E. Fischer, Stuart Reeves, and Olof Torgersson. 2015. Designing Mobile Experiences for Collocated Interaction. *Proceedings of the 18th ACM Conference on Computer Supported Cooperative Work & Social Computing - CSCW '15*, ACM Press, 496–507. http://doi.org/10.1145/2675133.2675171
40. Elena Márquez Segura, Annika Waern, Jin Moen, and Carolina Johansson. 2013. The design space of body games. *Proceedings of the SIGCHI Conference on Human Factors in Computing Systems - CHI '13*, ACM Press, 3365. http://doi.org/10.1145/2470654.2466461
41. Joe Marshall and Steve Benford. 2011. Using fast interaction to create intense experiences. *Proceedings of the 2011 annual conference on Human factors in computing systems - CHI '11*, ACM Press, 1255. http://doi.org/10.1145/1978942.1979129
42. Joe Marshall, Conor Linehan, and Adrian Hazzard. 2016. Designing Brutal Multiplayer Video Games. *CHI '16 Proceedings of the SIGCHI Conference on Human Factors in Computing Systems*. http://doi.org/10.1145/2858036.2858080
43. Joe Marshall and Paul Tennent. 2013. Mobile interaction does not exist. *CHI '13 Extended Abstracts on Human Factors in Computing Systems on - CHI EA '13*, ACM Press, 2069. http://doi.org/10.1145/2468356.2468725
44. J Massion. 1992. Movement, posture and equilibrium: interaction and coordination. *Progress in neurobiology* 38, 1: 35–56. Retrieved August 13, 2015 from http://www.ncbi.nlm.nih.gov/pubmed/1736324
45. Microsoft. 2014. Microsoft Band.
46. Jin Moen. 2007. From hand-held to body-worn. *Proceedings of the 1st international conference on Tangible and embedded interaction - TEI '07*, ACM Press, 251. http://doi.org/10.1145/1226969.1227021
47. Florian Mueller, Darren Edge, Frank Vetere, et al. 2011. Designing sports. *Proceedings of the 2011*

annual conference on Human factors in computing systems - CHI '11, ACM Press, 2651. http://doi.org/10.1145/1978942.1979330

48. Florian Mueller, Shannon O'Brien, and Alex Thorogood. 2007. Jogging over a distance. *CHI '07 extended abstracts on Human factors in computing systems - CHI '07*, ACM Press, 1989. http://doi.org/10.1145/1240866.1240937
49. Terhi Mustonen, Maria Olkkonen, and Jukka Hakkinen. 2004. Examining mobile phone text legibility while walking. *Extended abstracts of the 2004 conference on Human factors and computing systems - CHI '04*, ACM Press, 1243. http://doi.org/10.1145/985921.986034
50. Tamer Nadeem, Sasan Dashtinezhad, Chunyuan Liao, and Liviu Iftode. 2004. TrafficView. *ACM SIGMOBILE Mobile Computing and Communications Review* 8, 3: 6. http://doi.org/10.1145/1031483.1031487
51. Niantic Labs. 2012. Ingress. Retrieved from http://www.ingress.com
52. Nike. 2006. Nike+.
53. Nintendo. 2007. Wii Fit.
54. Luis Nunes and Miguel Angel Recarte. 2002. Cognitive demands of hands-free-phone conversation while driving. *Transportation Research Part F: Traffic Psychology and Behaviour* 5, 2: 133–144. http://doi.org/10.1016/S1369-8478(02)00012-8
55. OnCourse. On Course Goggles. Retrieved from http://www.oncoursegoggles.com/
56. Max Pfeiffer, Tim Dünte, Stefan Schneegass, Florian Alt, and Michael Rohs. 2015. Cruise Control for Pedestrians. *Proceedings of the 33rd Annual ACM Conference on Human Factors in Computing Systems - CHI '15*, ACM Press, 2505–2514. http://doi.org/10.1145/2702123.2702190
57. Martin Pielot, Anastasia Kazakova, Tobias Hesselmann, Wilko Heuten, and Susanne Boll. 2012. PocketMenu. *Proceedings of the 14th international conference on Human-computer interaction with mobile devices and services - MobileHCI '12*, ACM Press, 327. http://doi.org/10.1145/2371574.2371624
58. Sebastiaan Pijnappel and Florian Mueller. 2013. 4 design themes for skateboarding. *CHI '13 Proceedings of the SIGCHI Conference on Human Factors in Computing Systems*, ACM, 1271–1274. http://doi.org/10.1145/2466110.2466165
59. Ride-on Vision. 2015. Ride-on Augmented Reality Goggles. Retrieved from https://www.rideonvision.com/
60. Duncan Rowland, Martin Flintham, Leif Oppermann, et al. 2009. Ubikequitous Computing : Designing Interactive Experiences for Cyclists. *Proceedings of Mobile HCI '09*, ACM. http://doi.org/10.1145/1613858.1613886
61. Eric E. Sabelman and Roger Lam. 2015. The real-life dangers of augmented reality. *IEEE Spectrum* 52, 7: 48–53. http://doi.org/10.1109/MSPEC.2015.7131695
62. SAE. 2001. *SAE Recommended Practice Navigation and Route Guidance Function Accessibility While Driving (SAE 2364)*.
63. T. Scott Saponas, Chris Harrison, and Hrvoje Benko. 2011. PocketTouch. *Proceedings of the 24th annual ACM symposium on User interface software and technology - UIST '11*, ACM Press, 303. http://doi.org/10.1145/2047196.2047235
64. T. Scott Saponas, Desney S. Tan, Dan Morris, Ravin Balakrishnan, Jim Turner, and James A. Landay. 2009. Enabling always-available input with muscle-computer interfaces. *Proceedings of the 22nd annual ACM symposium on User interface software and technology - UIST '09*, ACM Press, 167. http://doi.org/10.1145/1622176.1622208
65. Bastian Schildbach and Enrico Rukzio. 2010. Investigating selection and reading performance on a mobile phone while walking. *Proceedings of the 12th international conference on Human computer interaction with mobile devices and services - MobileHCI '10*, ACM Press, 93. http://doi.org/10.1145/1851600.1851619
66. David C Schwebel, Despina Stavrinos, Katherine W Byington, Tiffany Davis, Elizabeth E O'Neal, and Desiree de Jong. 2012. Distraction and pedestrian safety: how talking on the phone, texting, and listening to music impact crossing the street. *Accident; analysis and prevention* 45: 266–71. http://doi.org/10.1016/j.aap.2011.07.011
67. Donald R. Self, Electra De Vries Henry, Carolyn Sara Findley, and Erin Reilly. 2007. Thrill seeking: the type T personality and extreme sports. *International Journal of Sport Management and Marketing* 2, 1/2: 175. http://doi.org/10.1504/IJSMM.2007.011397
68. Iris Soute, Panos Markopoulos, and Remco Magielse. 2009. Head Up Games: combining the best of both worlds by merging traditional and digital play. *Personal and Ubiquitous Computing* 14, 5: 435–444. http://doi.org/10.1007/s00779-009-0265-0
69. Strava. 2009. Strava. Retrieved January 21, 2015 from http://www.strava.com/about
70. Yu Ukai and Jun Rekimoto. 2013. Swimoid. *Proceedings of the 4th Augmented Human International Conference on - AH '13*, ACM Press, 170–177. http://doi.org/10.1145/2459236.2459265
71. Dick de Waard, Paul Schepers, Wieke Ormel, and Karel Brookhuis. 2010. Mobile phone use while

cycling: Incidence and effects on behaviour and safety. *Ergonomics*. Retrieved September 21, 2015 from http://www.tandfonline.com/doi/abs/10.1080/00140130903381180#.Vf_msd9VhBc

72. Wen Wu, Fabian Blaicher, Jie Yang, Thomas Seder, and Dehua Cui. 2009. A prototype of landmark-based car navigation using a full-windshield head-up display system. *Proceedings of the 2009 workshop on Ambient media computing - AMC '09*, ACM Press, 21. http://doi.org/10.1145/1631005.1631012

CardboardSense: Interacting with DIY Cardboard VR Headset by Tapping

Xiaoqi Yan[1], Chi-Wing Fu[2], Pallavi Mohan[1], Wooi Boon Goh[1]
Nanyang Technological University[1]
Singapore[1]
{yanx0005, pallavi003, aswbgoh}@ntu.edu.sg[1]
Chinese University of Hong Kong[2]
Hong Kong, China[2]
philip_cwfu@yahoo.com.hk[2]

ABSTRACT
DIY cardboard-based VR headset that enfolds a commodity smartphone is a popular means of achieving low cost immersive stereoscopic viewing experiences. However, existing applications for these devices have limited user-input capability, allowing mainly look-at control by head tilting. CardboardSense is a set of novel tap-gesture-based inputs that take advantage of the motion sensing capabilities already available in most smartphones. The key premise is that finger contacts with the cardboard surface produce incidental but detectable vibrations that can be reliably differentiated from typical user head motion. Moreover, tapping on different surface locations produces differentiable temporal signatures in the sensor signals. We present methods to extract and analyze these temporal patterns, and experimentally determine a set of tapping gestures that can be accurately recognized. Experimental results show promising potential for CardboardSense to extend the interactivity of future cardboard-based VR headset applications.

ACM Classification Keywords
H.5.m : Miscellaneous

Author Keywords
Google Cardboard; Input methods; Tapping; Finger gestures; Gyroscope; Accelerometer

INTRODUCTION
DIY cardboard-based VR headsets such as the Google Cardboard [2] (see Figure 1) are growing in popularity as they can bring immersive VR experience to smartphone users for less than $10. They have also spawned many third-party VR applications, e.g., Titans of Space, where users can explore a 3D simulation of Solar system, and Roller Coaster VR, which simulates the experience of riding in a roller coaster, etc.

Unfortunately, the Cardboard has limited input capabilities. An obvious input control is to map the user's head orientation sensed by the smartphone's built-in accelerometer to the look-at direction in the 3D virtual world. In addition, the first generation Cardboard allows the user to slide an attached

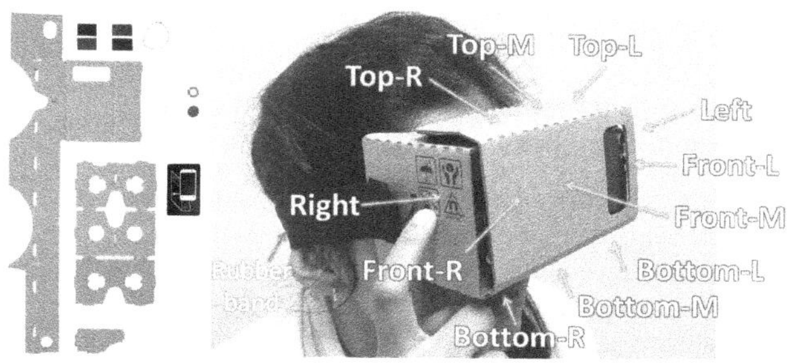

Figure 1. Left: Cardboard components. Right: potential tap locations.

magnet on the left-hand side to trigger an event using the phone's magnetometer. A small lever button that makes indirect contact with the phone's touchscreen was featured in the second generation Cardboard. Additionally, the Cardboard SDK offers a gaze-and-trigger feature that triggers an event associated with a virtual object that the user is gazing at over a prolonged period or during the magnet button activation.

This work explores tapping as an input modality for interacting with the Cardboard. It requires no additional physical implement since it takes advantage of the distinctive vibration patterns detected by the phone's built-in motion sensors when a user taps on different locations on the Cardboard. As such, the proposed technique can also be applicable to other VR headsets provided the enclosure is rigid to support the signal transmission, e.g., other cardboard HMD like Microsoft VR Kit or better quality plastic versions like Samsung Gear VR. By analyzing and differentiating these different temporal signatures in real-time, Cardboard applications can now employ tapping gestures as an additional form of user input.

CardboardSense was developed by first exploring all tapping gestures that can be detected distinctively by the motion sensors. Here, we derive methods to extract temporally-aligned signature samples from the continuous signal and progressively analyze the similarity among different gestures through a machine learning method. After determining a set of feasible gestures, we further perform experiments to evaluate the detection performance and reliability of the gestures.

This work makes several important contributions. First, CardboardSense has extended the input capabilities of the low-cost cardboard VR headset without requiring any physical changes to the device. It uses the phone's built-in gyroscope and is computationally efficient. Second, six different tapping gestures can be reliably distinguished. Their spatial distribution over the Cardboard surfaces provides a good degree of

http://dx.doi.org/10.1145/2901790.2901813

input options for interface design. Lastly, the tapping gestures are easy-to-learn and are ergonomically-friendly to perform.

RELATED WORK

Among the many pioneering works that explore applications of motion sensors, we survey those that study finger contacts. Hinckley and Song [6] distinguished a gentle finger swipe from a hard-onset drag on phone screen by using gyroscope and accelerometer, while Heo and Lee [5] employed accelerometer to discriminate a gentle tap (Tap) from a strong tap (ForceTap). Sundström et al. [9] proposed a system using accelerometer to measure the dynamic properties of the digital material. Goel et al. [3] combined multiple built-in sensors (touchscreen, inertial sensors, and vibration motor) to estimate hand posture and exerted pressure on phone.

Serrano [8] proposed the Bezel-Tap gestures for immediate interaction on handheld tablets, where a bezel tap is detected by the accelerometer. Oakley et al. [7] explored beats tapping gesture for interacting with smart watches. Rather than using motion sensor, Harrison et al. [4] explored the use of acoustic sensing for detecting different forms of taps and touches: pad, tip, knuckle, nail, etc.

These works suggest that finger-contact-based vibration sensing can be detected and discriminated, but none have explored its feasibility with setups similar to the Cardboard, i.e., head-mounted and phone embedding. In particular, we explore tapping as a new input modality for Cardboard applications and empirically determine a feasible set of gestures.

Interaction with Cardboard. Google Cardboard is a very recent innovation. As such, we are only aware of one very recent work by Yoo and Parker [10] that presented a preliminary analysis of existing input methods for interacting with Cardboard, such as those discussed in the Introduction. No new interaction techniques such as tapping were presented nor suggested in this work.

Overview. This work involves four research stages. First, we brainstorm and try finger gestures that may be differentiated using the built-in motion sensors (stage 1). Then, we extract and analyze signature samples of different gestures (stage 2), construct classifiers from these samples by machine learning to empirically determine a set of feasible gestures (stage 3): tap left, tap right, tap top-mid, tap bottom-mid, left double-tap, and right double-tap. A real-time method to recognize the gestures was then developed" (stage 4). Lastly, we also perform various experiments to evaluate the results and discuss potential usage scenarios.

STAGE 1: EXPLORING POTENTIAL GESTURES

In Stage 1, we first brainstormed potential gestures that we may perform, e.g., tap on different locations (see Figure 1), tap left and right simultaneously, double tap, sliding on Cardboard, etc. To aid the exploration, we developed a program that continuously plots the motion signals on the phone, see Figure 3, so that we can see the signal response in real-time while trying out different finger actions on Cardboard.

From this initial experiment, we found that we have to drop the simultaneous left-and-right taps since the signal patterns are quite unstable, see Figure 4. Sometimes, they looked like stationary signals since left and right taps cancel each other out, and sometimes, they looked like a left or right tap. Moreover, since the cardboard surface is rather smooth and hard, the signal responses for sliding were found to be weak, or similar to that of tapping. Hence, we ignored sliding as well.

STAGE 2: COLLECTING GESTURE DATA

Next, we collected accelerometer and gyroscope signature samples of the following gestures: tap left, right, front-L, front-M, front-R, top-L, top-M, and top-R, bottom-L, bottom-M, and bottom-R, and double-tap versions of them. Note that for consistency, we consider a bottom tap to be one performed by a finger flick from below. As such, no bottom double-tap is considered since double finger flicks might be difficult for some people to perform.

To collect signature samples of a gesture, we first repeated the same gesture action successively twenty times every two seconds, and recorded a long sequence of accelerometer and gyroscope data. Here, we found that if we simply chop the long signal into segments centered at the designated action moments (every two seconds), the extracted signature samples may not align well with one another, see Figure 2 (left-most), because we may not perform the actions exactly at the designated moments. Hence, we looked for the first local (absolute) maximum among the signal channels within [-0.2,+0.8] seconds around each designated moment, and extracted 10 data samples before the local-maxima sample and 34 samples after it to form a *signature sample* of 45 data samples.

For each gesture, we repeated the above process 16 times, thus producing 20×16-signature samples. To further improve the method's robustness, we recruited 6 additional participants (2 male and 4 female; aged 23 to 30), who performed the above process twice, thus helping to produce an additional 20×2-signature samples per gesture. Figure 2 revealed that different gestures produce different signature samples.

Gyroscope vs accelerometer. From Figure 2, we can see that both gyroscope and accelerometer signals reveal certain temporal variation while the accelerometer signals are usually relatively weaker. In addition, accelerometer is more sensitive to the user's static head orientation, which is not advantageous to the data training. We also compare results using gyroscope only (G) with results that use gyroscope together with accelerometer (A+G). We found A+G can improve the accuracy slightly at the expense of an increase in computation - the accuracy was found to be improved from 99.51% to 99.56%, but the overall gesture detection time can increase from 0.04 (G) to 0.11 (A+G) sec. Computational cost increases by 2.75 times. The above reasons led to our final choice of employing only the gyroscope's signals in gesture training and recognition.

Non-gesture data. Next, to help differentiate user gestures from head/body motion, we collected motion samples of six different situations (B1-B6), see Figure 5 for B2-B6, while B1 is stationary. For the case of B6 (incidental and small head movement), we collected 80 signature samples by the procedure we used for tapping, while for the rest, we performed the

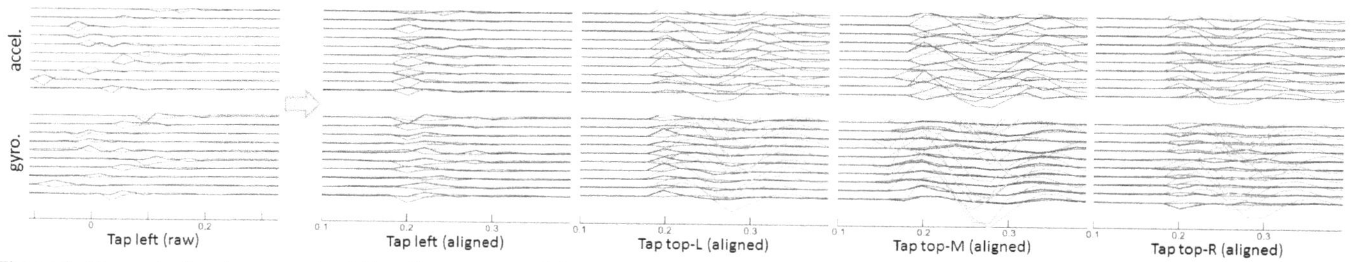

Figure 2. Example signature samples (aligned) we extracted from the raw signal (e.g., leftmost) using the methods presented in Stage 2. RGB plots refers to signals in XYZ, respectively, and the horizontal axis is time in seconds; note also that to show the temporal variations more clearly, we zoom into the frontal part of the signatures rather than showing all the 45 data samples in the signature samples. Each signature sample ranges ~0.9 sec.

actions over ~80 seconds, and randomly picked and collected 80 signature samples from the long gyroscope signal.

STAGE 3: TRAINING GESTURE DATA

This stage has two purposes: i) analyze the distinctiveness of each gesture (against other gestures as well as B1-B6), and ii) build classifiers for gesture recognition. Here, we use a machine learning library called LIBSVM [1] and the C-SVC model with radial basis function as the kernel. To further optimize the classifier, we perform hyperparameter optimization by the grid search method with 5-fold cross-validation:

First, the cross-validation rates of the three top tap gestures were found to be rather low: tap top-L (81.62%), tap top-M (86.14%), and tap top-R (73.22%), so it is not feasible to differentiate among them. Figure 2 also shows that they exhibit very similar patterns. Since tap top-M is slightly more distinctive than others, we dropped tap top-L and tap top-R, and keep tap top-M. Similarly, the three bottom tap gestures are very similar, and we retained only tap bottom-M.

Second, we found that tap front-L and tap front-R are similar to tap right and tap left, respectively. The cross-validation rate to differentiate tap front-L from tap right is only 75.11% while it is 83.92% for tap front-R from tap left. From the signal plots, we found that tap front-L (tap front-R) produces incidental motion similar to that of tap right (tap left), so we have to drop tap front-L and tap front-R. Furthermore, the cross-validation rate for differentiating front-M from bottom-M was found to be just 62.75%. Here, we ignored tap front-M and kept tap bottom-M, since front-M was found to be less stable: with the nose as the pivot point, its signature pattern would vary with slight changes on the front-tap location.

Lastly, since Cardboard is mounted on the left and right sides of user's head by a rubber band, double top tap would produce relatively larger vibration compared to others, so its accuracy is relatively low. Thus, we also dropped double top tap.

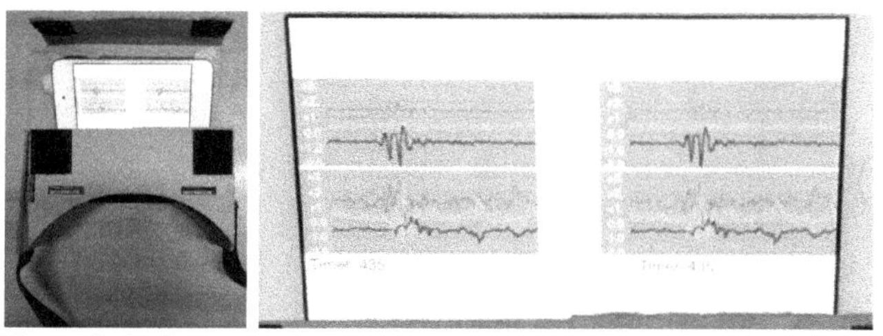

Figure 3. In Stage 1, we explore potential gestures using this real-time plotting tool to see accelerometer (top) and gyroscope (bottom) signal.

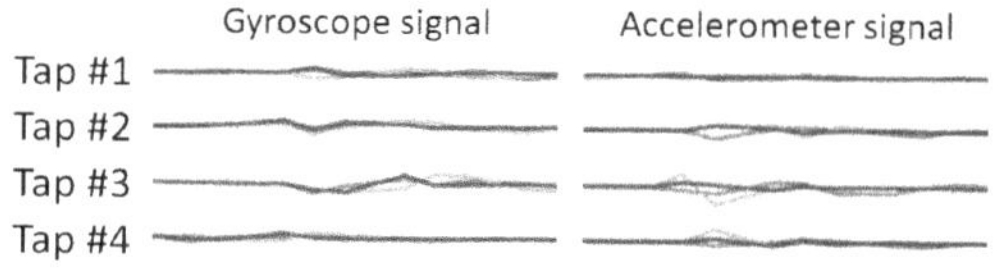

Figure 4. Gyroscope and accelerometer signals for four different simultaneous left-and-right taps; we can see that the patterns are unstable.

	single tap				double tap	
device	left	right	top-M	bottom-M	left	right
iPod touch	99.76	99.86	99.23	99.19	99.58	99.43
Android	99.26	99.55	99.09	98.96	99.03	99.12

Table 1. Cross-validation rates of the remaining feasible gestures.

Table 1 shows the cross-validation rates of the remaining feasible gestures. The rates are all very close to 100%. The slight imperfections were mainly due to weak outlier signals resulted from gentle/misplaced tap actions during Stage 2.

STAGE 4: GESTURE RECOGNITION

After training the SVM classifiers, we employed them to recognize gestures in real-time on mobile devices in Cardboard. To improve the recognition efficiency and accuracy, instead of testing every 45-sample time frame in the signal stream, we adopt the method and results in Stage 2. That is, we first look for a local maximum in the signal stream and see if the value is near to the local maximum values of the signature samples extracted in Stage 2. If so, we extract a 45-samples time frame with 10 samples before the local-maximum point and 34 samples after. Then, we use the SVM classifiers constructed in Stage 3 to perform gesture recognition on the time frame. Hence, we can improve the computational efficiency and avoid testing of partial patterns. Moreover, since recognition is done with the gyroscope signal, the user's head orientation need not be upright, and our method can still detect the tap gestures accurately.

IMPLEMENTATION AND RESULTS

Hardware. We employed two mobile devices in the experiments: iPod Touch 5 (running iOS 8.4) and Motorola Moto X 1st Gen (running Android 5.1 Lollipop). The gyroscope sensing rate of both devices is ~50Hz with iPod Touch being slightly lower (47~50Hz) and the Android phone being slightly higher (50~52Hz). The development environments are Xcode 6.4 and Android Studio 1.3.2, and the gesture training is performed on Alienware desktop computers with Intel(R) Core(TM) i7 CPU 960 3.2GHZ and 12GB memory.

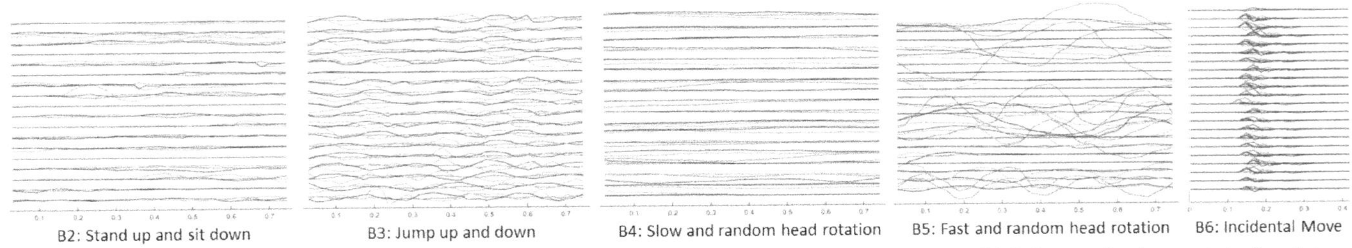

Figure 5. Example non-gesture signature samples collected in different head/body movement situations (B2-B6), note the time scale in the plots.

Software. For gesture training, we downloaded the source code of LIBSVM [1] (version 3.2) in C, and compiled it for execution on Matlab (version R2015a) using Mex. For gesture recognition, we directly used the downloaded C source code in the Xcode and Java source code in Android Studio.

Experimental Conditions: i) The phone was mounted tightly in Cardboard without phone case to maximize the vibration transmission; ii) Cardboard was mounted firmly against user's head to avoid unwanted movement during tap; and iii) users were not tap when heads were in motion.

Experiment: Performance. Each iteration in training an SVM classifier takes around 11.27 seconds on average, and since we need to optimize the classifier parameters, this requires 1517 iterations in the training, which takes around 4.74 hours on average per classifier. Hence, we employed several desktop computers to train the classifiers in parallel. For gesture recognition, the average time taken to find a time frame by matching a local maximum are 0.0246 and 0.1348 milliseconds on the iPod Touch 5 and Android phone, respectively, while the average time taken to use the SVM classifiers to recognize a gesture are 0.0139 and 0.0231 seconds, respectively. So, the performance is real-time on both devices; here, we computed the averages over 36 gestures.

Experiment: Recognition Accuracy. We performed two experiments to evaluate the gesture recognition accuracy with 16 participants: 6 male, 10 female, aged 23 to 31, and six of them (old participants) helped in the training. Before the experiments, we synced the phone display with a laptop in order to see the detection results when participants perform tapping. In the first experiment, each participant was first given 5∼10 minutes to practice the finger-tap gestures while observing the detection results on the Cardboard. Then, they were asked to perform 300 tap actions: 50 actions per gesture in a randomized order. This took at least half an hour, and the participants were allowed to rest whenever they wanted to. Table 2 presents the results, showing that both old and new participants can perform gestures with very high accuracy.

		Left	Right	Top-M	Bottom-M	Left Dbl	Right Dbl
old	mean	100	100	99.33	99.67	98.67	98.00
	stdev	0	0	1.63	0.82	1.63	1.79
new	mean	99.00	99.80	98.60	99.00	96.00	98.40
	stdev	1.41	0.63	1.35	1.70	2.49	2.07

Table 2. Gesture Recognition Accuracy: 10 new and 6 old participants.

In the second experiment, each participant was asked to perform any head motion that they could come up with over a period of 30 seconds. Through this, we can check if any action would be mis-detected as tapping and we found no mis-detected gestures with any of the participants.

User Subjective Feedback. The 16 users were asked several questions after the trial to gauge their user experience. On a 7-point Likert scale, the average user physical comfort level of their experience was rated at a very comfortable 5.6, where 1 is extremely uncomfortable and 7 is perfectly comfortable. On the question of how much force was used to activate their desired function, the average force was rated at a moderate 3.9, where 1 is lightest hit and 7 is strongest hit. On the question of how tired their fingers and arms were at the end of the trial, an average mildly tired score of 5.3 was noted, where 1 is extremely tired and 7 is not tired at all. Lastly, when asked how intuitive the tapping technique was, an average score of 6.0 was noted, where 1 is non-intuitive and 7 is naturally intuitive. Experiments about the transition between devices and sensitivity to user motion have been detailed in the appendix.

BASIC INTERACTION DESIGN GUIDELINE

The CardboardSense tap gestures can be used to activate buttons or select menu items. Left and right taps can be used to intuitively scroll through a horizontal list of menu items, while double taps enable fast scrolling to subsequent left/right pages. Later, selection can be made by a bottom tap. To aid remembrance of tap gesture assignments, we recommend that labelled GUI buttons be placed in screen locations (top-mid, top-left, top-right, and bottom-mid) that correspond to their respective tap positions (tap top-M, tap left, tap right, and tap bottom). Since these function buttons may occlude or consume valuable screen space, they can remain hidden and only appear when the user makes the first tap and then slowly recede to the background when no further taps are detected over a predetermined period.

CONCLUSION

CardboardSense uses only the smartphone's built-in gyroscopic signals to enhance the interactivity of Cardboard applications with finger-tap input modality. We extracted temporally-aligned signature samples of different potential gestures and progressively determine a set of feasible gestures by observing and analyzing the temporal signatures using cross validation. Robust and computationally efficient methods were developed to recognize six different tap gestures. Experimental results with 16 participants confirmed a high real-time detection accuracy rate of 98.9% on average.

ACKNOWLEDGMENTS

This work is partially supported by the AcRF MOE Tier 1 (RG 29/11) funding and the Chinese University of Hong Kong strategic recruitment fund and direct grant (4055061).

REFERENCES

1. Chih-Chung Chang and Chih-Jen Lin. 2011. LIBSVM: a library for support vector machines. *ACM Tran. on Intell. Sys. and Tech.* 2, 3 (2011), 27:1–27:27.
2. David Coz and Damien Henry. 2014. Google Cardboard. (2014). Available at: `https://www.google.com/get/cardboard/`.
3. Mayank Goel, Jacob Wobbrock, and Shwetak Patel. 2012. GripSense: Using Built-in Sensors to Detect Hand Posture and Pressure on Commodity Mobile Phones. In *UIST '12*. 545–554.
4. Chris Harrison, Julia Schwarz, and Scott E. Hudson. 2011. TapSense: Enhancing Finger Interaction on Touch Surfaces. In *UIST '11*. 627–636.
5. Seongkook Heo and Geehyuk Lee. 2011. ForceTap: Extending the Input Vocabulary of Mobile Touch Screens by Adding Tap Gestures. In *MobileHCI '11*. 113–122.
6. Ken Hinckley and Hyunyoung Song. 2011. Sensor Synaesthesia: Touch in Motion, and Motion in Touch. In *CHI '11*. 801–810.
7. Ian Oakley, DoYoung Lee, MD. Rasel Islam, and Augusto Esteves. 2015. Beats: Tapping Gestures for Smart Watches. In *CHI '15*. 1237–1246.
8. Marcos Serrano, Eric Lecolinet, and Yves Guiard. 2013. Bezel-Tap Gestures: Quick Activation of Commands from Sleep Mode on Tablets. In *CHI '13*. 3027–3036.
9. Petra Sundström, Alex S. Taylor, Katja Grufberg, Niklas Wirström, Jordi Solsona Belenguer, and Marcus Lundén. 2011. Inspirational Bits Towards a Shared Understanding of the Digital Material. In *CHI '11*. 1561–1570.
10. Soojeong Yoo and Callum Parker. 2015. Controller-less Interaction Methods for Google Cardboard. In *SUI '15*. 127–127.

APPENDIX

The following lists some related experiments:

Experiment: Transition Between Devices. We applied the SVM model trained with an iPod Touch 5 on an iPhone 6, and performed detection 20 times for each gesture. The overall accuracy is 96.7%, which is 2.6% lower than that with an iPod Touch 5, so the technique is likely to transition well among the Apple family of devices. However, this cannot be said of Android-based devices due to the highly variable models and makes in the market.

Experiment: Sensitivity to User Motion. The proposed detection method can be sensitive to rotatory motion arising from user's motion. To give a sense of this drop in accuracy, an informal experiment of 120 trials was done (i.e., 20×6 gestures): seated in a moving bus (speed of about 50kmh, albeit bumpy ride) gave an average drop in accuracy of about 30%.

If Words Could Dance: Moving from Body to Data through Kinesthetic Evaluation

Shannon Cuykendall, Ethan Soutar-Rau, Thecla Schiphorst, Steve DiPaola
School of Interactive Arts and Technology, Simon Fraser University, Canada
{scuykend, esoutarr, thecla, sdipaola}@sfu.ca

ABSTRACT
The value of integrating the body and experience into technology has become an important goal in third wave HCI. One challenge in using experiential design methodologies is understanding how to transmit and apply the fullness of an experience into a computational system. We explore the relationship and meaning that can be created between kinesthetic experiences, words, and sensor data through the design of an interactive system that generates poetry from movement data. POEME (Portrayal of Ephemeral Movement Experiences) combines words into insightful, whimsical, and witty poetry that interprets one's movement. We refined our design of POEME through kinesthetically evaluating sensor data with the aid of visual analytic tools and confirmed the utility of these results through incorporating them into an effective machine learning system. Through this combination of visual analytics and kinesthetic evaluation, we contribute to the exploration of innovative design practices that both embody and evaluate movement interaction design strategies.

ACM Classification Keywords
H.5.2 User Interfaces: User-Centered Design, Prototyping; H.5.3 Evaluation/Methodology: ,Web-based Interaction

Author Keywords
design; kinesthetic experience; expressive movement interaction; movement classification; visual analytics;

INTRODUCTION
As motion sensors become more ubiquitous, there is a growing need to understand how to design for full-body movement interactions that extend beyond basic gestural interfaces. This has given traction to the idea that, in HCI, designers must experientially understand movement in order to design for it. As stated in Hummels et al (2007), "One has to be or become an expert in movement, not just theoretically, by imagination or on paper, but by doing and experiencing while designing" [7].

While experiential methodologies support designers in creating movement-based interactions [15, 6, 11], challenges still remain in understanding how to transmit or incorporate bodily knowledge into design. Kristina Höök points out, "...the experiences I am trying to describe are wordless, and putting detailed descriptions of them still fails to cover the complexities and the uniqueness of my embodied experience" [6]. Helena Mentis and Georges Khut have also described a similar challenge of transferring felt bodily experiences to the design of technology [2].

Movement classification systems such as Labanotation or Laban Movement Analysis (LMA) are often used as intermediate steps in translating and making sense of bodily experiences. However, even Rudolf Laban (1879-1968), whose theories led to the development of these classification systems, states, "Many dance creations have perished because it was impossible to describe them in words and we hardly know how the dances of former epochs were presented. Had descriptions been attempted, as in fact they have, they could only have been superficial and inadequate" [9]. While it may be difficult to translate the nuances of a bodily experience into words, we propose that the perceived gulf between words and movement is not as wide as commonly believed.

We explore the relationship between words and movement through our design of POEME (Portrayal of Ephemeral Movement Experiences). POEME is a website (https://poeme.iat.sfu.ca) that generates poetry in response to a user's movement. POEME records a user's movement through an IMU (Inertial Measurement Unit) that integrates an accelerometer, a gyroscope, and a compass. This type of sensor is included in many mobile devices and transparently used in everyday interactions.

To create an embodied system that integrates our experience of movement, we developed a novel methodology to kinesthetically interpret sensor data with the aid of visual analytics (VA) tools. VA tools provide a way for humans to more easily analyze and interpret "big data." One short movement phrase or gesture can produce an overwhelming large amount of data that is challenging to interpret in relation to experience. VA tools can provide a way for designers to understand how their experiences are being represented through data. Using VA tools we compared different aspects of a kinesthetic experience when using POEME including: our kinesthetic memories, first-person written reflections of the movement, numerical data from the IMU, and the poetic verse that initially inspired the movement interaction.

A strong current in recent VA research is how interaction with visual representations of data can lead to knowledge generation [14]. In POEME, knowledge is accumulated by documenting

DIS 2016, June 04–08, 2016, Brisbane, QLD, Australia

ACM 978-1-4503-4031-1/16/06...$15.00
DOI: http://dx.doi.org/10.1145/2901790.2901822

the results of kinesthetic evaluation and translation of these insights into computational models. We call this novel method of analysis an *embodied VA approach* to design. We propose this methodology can help designers more seamlessly move between body and data in the design process.

BACKGROUND

The overarching motivation behind creating POEME is to further explore the complex interaction between words and movement. Words, like movements, have layers of meaning and can be recombined to create a multitude of sentences or sequences that all vary in their underlying meaning. As philosopher Mark Johnson states, "It is true that when we read, we read words. But words have meanings, and meanings go far beyond words" [8]. The same could also be said for bodily movement.

POEME is heavily inspired by the Japanese form of poetry known as *haikai no renga* (comic, collaborative poetry) which involves the social creation of poems through turn taking [3]. Creating these linked poems requires participants to respond to previous stanzas with original verse. In POEME, movement and poetry take turns in what we call a "movement poem."

Each verse generated in POEME is a Parts of Speech Poem (PoSP). The PoSP template allows for very simple production of verses and ensures that each movement poem describes a subject, actions and qualities of these actions. While sophisticated automatic poem generators exist, the point of POEME is not to create human-like poetry, but instead to create poetry that inspires and responds to a large range of movement experiences. Each poem begins with a noun which is followed by two adjectives, two verbs, and an adverb (See Figure 1). This structure may not be able to adequately describe all kinesthetic experiences; however, the PoSP template allows us to examine word and movement relationships in a variety of contexts and results in cohesive poems even with unusual word pairings.

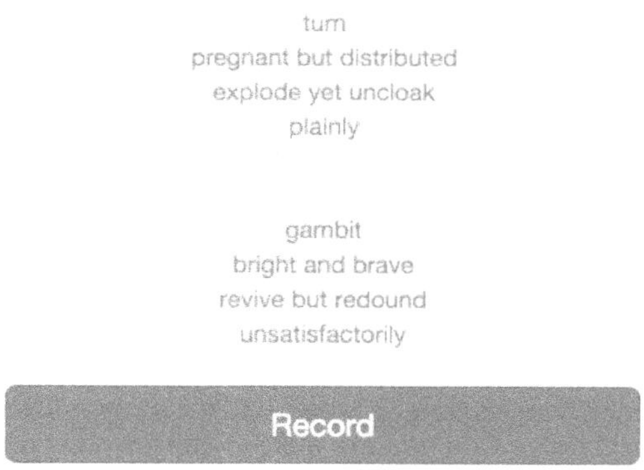

Figure 1. Examples of POSP generated by POEME. ©Shannon Cuykendall and Ethan Soutar-Rau 2015

POEME is meant to crowdsource a large corpus of movement by engaging people to move in response to its poetry. This lead us to design it as a mobile website which trades fidelity of data for ubiquity of platform. Still, prior research has found success in recognizing movement qualities from just an accelerometer [16]. We approached the design of POEME with the understanding that we would need to compensate for the limitations of our data source with our own insight.

KINESTETHIC EVALUATION

We used an auto-ethnographic methodology to support and refine our design of POEME. This approach was chosen so that we could understand how our kinesthetic experiences are linked to both IMU data and poetic verse. Many HCI researchers have stressed the importance of incorporating bodily experience into design, suggesting that movement cannot be fully understood from afar; therefore, auto-ethnographic approaches are commonly used to design for movement (e.g. [6, 13]). One major critique of this methodology is that the results are not representative of a diverse population. In our study we mitigate this challenge through having the first two authors (SBC and ESR respectively) both engage in the auto-ethnographic process. SBC and ESR have very different movement backgrounds. SBC has a classical dance background; while, ESR's movement background is based primarily in athletic activities, such as biking and soccer.

In the following sections we describe our auto-ethnographic approach as a series of two studies. The outcome of the first study was the development of our novel kinesthetic evaluation technique that we refer to as an *embodied VA approach* to design. In the second study we evaluate this approach by incorporating our findings from the first study into a machine-learning system.

Study 1: Development of Embodied VA Approach

We used VA tools to find features in the IMU data and compared them with our kinesthetic memory, written descriptions of the movement, and poetic verse. We describe this methodology as a series of three steps.

Step 1: Move in Response to Poetic Verse

SBC and ESR responded through movement to fifty PoSP, created both by the POEME system and also human authors. We chose to blend human authored and generated verse to see if we preferred moving in response to one over the other. As stated previously, the intent of POEME is not to create human-like poetry, but to create poetry that could effectively respond to and inspire a broad range of movement. We found that both generated and human-authored poetry inspired rich kinesthetic experiences.

We recorded our movement responses with the IMU in a mobile phone. We explored with placing the sensor in various places on the body including: placing the phone in our pants' pockets, holding it in our hands and changing between right and left sides. For the purposes of this study, we decided to strap the the mobile device to the right arm for consistency. While it would be very interesting to compare how our interpretations of the data differ based on the location of the sensor, the point of this initial study was to first establish how IMU data and words could be linked to our kinesthetic experiences.

Step 2: Reflect on our Experience of Moving

Immediately following each movement recording, both authors reflected on their kinesthetic experience by describing their experience in words. Our movement descriptions were informed with the Language of Dance (LOD) movement classification system [5], which is based on Laban's movement theories and further developed by Anne Hutchinson Guest. In this framework, Guest correlates parts-of-movement to parts-of-speech. Our descriptions of movement included movement nouns, verbs and adverbs in order to form a comprehensive and easily comparable account of the kinesthetic experience. For an example of these descriptions see Figures 2, 3, 4, and 5.

Step 3: Kinesthetically Interpret Data

We used the VA tool *JMP* [1] to create multiple graphical representations of the movement data. This included scatter plots, line graphs, bar graphs and histograms of measurements of acceleration, rotation and orientation. We compared these graphical representations side by side with the movement descriptions and the poetic verse.

After comparing these descriptions with the data, we selected the features that best aligned with our experiences of the movement. Our criteria for selection was that the movement that *felt* most similar should also have similar visualizations. This is a key feature to our embodied VA approach that allowed us to select movement features that could be both *felt* and *seen*.

Through our embodied VA approach both SBC and ESR found that the range of acceleration, depicted on three axes through a bar graph, most closely related to our kinesthetic experiences. It is important to note that SBC and ESR rarely responded to poetic verse in a similar manner; however, both of them agreed that the range of acceleration best correlated to their experience. Although bar graphs may appear counter-intuitive to represent dynamic experiences, they are simple representations that are highly perceptually effective [17, 10]. In contrast to prior work where designers have sought to model individual qualities or actions of movement that make up an experience; in POEME we seek to characterize *whole* kinesthetic experiences. The bar graph allowed us to more easily see the kinesthetic experience as a whole, rather than separated moments in time.

In Figure 2 we show similar kinesthetic experiences, as felt by SBC, juxtaposed with the visual depiction of the range of her acceleration and the poetic verse. In Figure 3 we show different kinesthetic experiences, as felt by SBC, juxtaposed with the visual depiction of the range of her acceleration and the poetic verse. In these graphical representations the different experiences are clearly distinguishable and the similar experiences are not as distinct.

In Figures 4 and 5 we demonstrate how the graphical representation of mean acceleration related to SBC's kinesthetic experiences. SBC did not feel these graphical representations as strongly correlated to her experience because different kinesthetic experiences are not as distinct and similar kinesthetic experiences are not as analogous.

Study 2: Applying our Findings to a Machine Learning System

If a poem can serve as a method of expressing a kinesthetic experience, then it should be possible to construct a com-

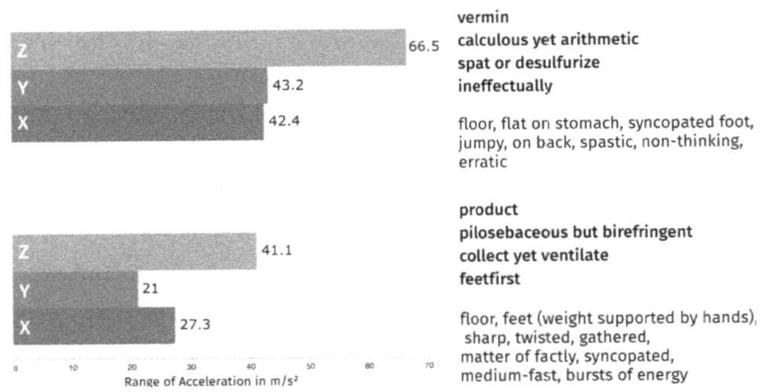

Figure 2. Two similar kinesthetic experiences depicted through range of acceleration

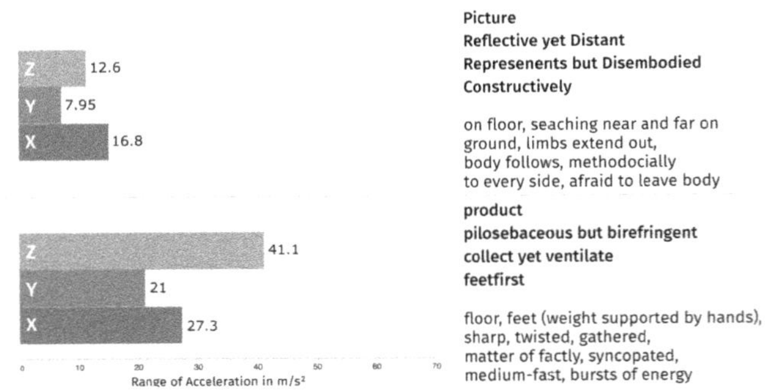

Figure 3. Two different kinesthetic experiences depicted through range of acceleration

putational theory about the relationship between a statistical summary of a movement and a poem that would express the same movement. Creating such a theory from scratch would be a daunting task, but the results of Study 1 suggest that the ranges of acceleration across the three axes measured by the IMU could potentially be a robust method of statistically summarizing a kinesthetic experience. Study 2 evaluates the predictive efficacy of a theory based on these ranges versus theories based on other summary statistics.

Step 1: Create Legible Interactions

To understand how the accuracy of POEME could be evaluated we needed to create more legible interactions. To do this we curated two wordlists that depicted different themes of movement. The first wordlist, which we call the "stillness list" includes words such as, frozen, sustained, still, and serene. These words could potentially describe little or no noticeable movement. The second wordlist, which we refer to as the "motion list" includes words related to the physics of motion such as, buoyant, centripetal, accelerated, forced, and collision. The stillness list contains 75 words and the motion list contains 250 words. Both lists include words from all parts of speech. We chose to use descriptive words in this study so that we could more easily evaluate if the poetry responded effectively to our movement.

Step 2: Train POEME using a Naive Bayes Algorithm

To train POEME the first two authors interpreted POEME's generated verse into movement, created from either the stillness or motion list. We used a simple Gaussian Naive Bayes algorithm [12] to classify movement. We will refer to this construct of language theory, training procedure, and verse

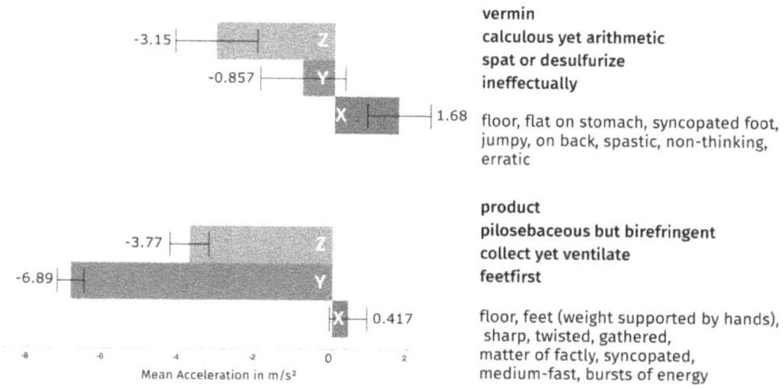

Figure 4. Two similar kinesthetic experiences depicted through mean acceleration

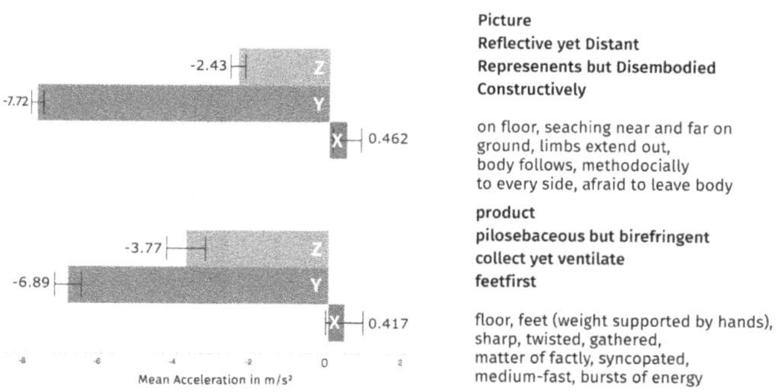

Figure 5. Two different kinesthetic experiences depicted through mean acceleration

authoring process as the *naive agent*. It considers each word placement in the PoSP template independently and can be configured to map a variety of measurements to poetic verse.

Step 3: Evaluate Accuracy of Predictions

First, the naive agent interpreted a corpus of movement phrases using the range, mean, and median of acceleration. Second, the agent classified which wordlist a movement phrase corresponded to (See Table 1). Third, the agent created a sample of likely text of the poem (See Table 2). The classifications were scored for accuracy and logistic loss. The accuracy of the predicted text in each word placement was also measured.

	Accuracy	Log Loss
Range	0.97	0.28
Mean	0.81	0.37
Median	0.77	0.46

Table 1. Accuracy metrics are shown for the Naive Bayes algorithm predicting which word list that movement corresponds to when using various summary statistics. Higher accuracy and lower log loss values are better.

DISCUSSION

Effective quantitative evaluation of POEME is challenging because an ideal measurement would require a more sophisticated model of the relationship between movement and poetry than we currently possess. These two studies illustrate how the embodied VA approach can be used for feature selection tasks in the absence of satisfactory objective measures. In Study 1, kinesthetic experience served as the basis for selecting the range of acceleration as a feature to summarize movement. In Study 2, incorporating this insight allowed us to create a successful machine learning system.

Unexpectedly, the naive agent's predictions were much more accurate for certain word positions in the PoSP template than others. The range of acceleration, which the authors found to be most congruent with their kinesthetic experiences in study 1, performed the best on the first word placement (See Table 2). We take this to mean that word placement affects how the words are interpreted in the overall meaning of the verse. We also speculate that the paired adjectives and paired verbs are much harder to accurately predict because the intervening conjunction influences how the words are interpreted in relation to one another. Our Naive Bayes model is especially sensitive to disruption from these logical dependencies because it models all of the word placements independently. Anecdotally, the naive agent seems able to compose verses in a graduated way between still and more energetic movement, and the agent also appears to make distinctions within each wordlist. For example, words such as springlike and weightless are commonly displayed in response to light, jumping movements. It may not be a coincidence that these are literally descriptors of acceleration characteristics.

	0.74 (noun)	
0.60 (adj.)	0.23 (conj.)	0.65 (adj.)
0.47 (verb)	0.15 (conj.)	0.47 (verb)
	0.51 (adverb)	

Table 2. Accuracy measurements are shown for the naive agent predicting each word of a verse using range acceleration values to summarize a movement experience.

While these findings are intriguing, it is also important to keep in mind that the original reason for embarking on the embodied VA approach was to avoid a hasty literal mapping of words to movement and premature conceptions of "right" and "wrong" responses. We suggest that other methods of evaluation may better serve the POEME system since our intent is to use POEME as a probe to further explore the relationship between movement and words. Boehner et al (2008) suggests rethinking evaluation techniques in HCI to include aesthetic experience [4]. Similarly, the embodied VA approach should be considered as an alternate way to design interactive systems which include kinesthetic experience.

CONCLUSION

Articulating the fullness of the movement experience in a way that effectively transmits the richness of the experience is an ongoing challenge to designers of interactive systems. We contribute to the field of HCI by developing a novel design approach that incorporates kinesthetic evaluation into the process of selecting movement features that can be both felt and seen in visualizations of data. The features chosen through our embodied VA approach proved to be effective measures when implemented into a machine-learning system.

REFERENCES

1. *JMP®, Version 10*. SAS Institute Inc, Cary, NC.
2. Alaoui, Sarah Fdili and Schiphorst, Thecla and Cuykendall, Shannon and Carlson, Kristin and Studd, Karen and Bradley, Karen. 2015. Strategies for Embodied Design: The Value and Challenges of Observing Movement. In *Proceedings of the 2015 ACM SIGCHI Conference on Creativity and Cognition*. ACM, 121–130.
3. Basho, Matsuo. 1998. *Basho's Narrow Road: Spring and Autumn Passages*. Stone Bridge Press, Inc.
4. Boehner, Kirsten and Sengers, Phoebe and Warner, Simeon. 2008. Interfaces with the ineffable: Meeting aesthetic experience on its own terms. *ACM Transactions on Computer-Human Interaction* 15, 3 (Nov. 2008), 1–29. DOI:http://dx.doi.org/10.1145/1453152.1453155
5. Guest, Ann Hutchinson. 2005. *Labanotation: the system of analyzing and recording movement* (4th ed., rev ed.). Routledge, New York.
6. Höök, Kristina. 2010. Transferring Qualities from Horseback Riding to Design. In *Proceedings of the 6th Nordic Conference on Human-Computer Interaction: Extending Boundaries (NordiCHI '10)*. ACM, New York, NY, USA, 226–235. DOI: http://dx.doi.org/10.1145/1868914.1868943
7. Caroline Hummels, Kees CJ Overbeeke, and Sietske Klooster. 2007. Move to get moved: a search for methods, tools and knowledge to design for expressive and rich movement-based interaction. *Personal and Ubiquitous Computing* 11, 8 (2007), 677–690.
8. Johnson, Mark. 2008. *The meaning of the body: Aesthetics of human understanding*. University of Chicago Press.
9. Laban, Rudolf. 1980. *The Mastery of Movement* (fourth edition ed.). Macdonald and Evans, Plymouth.
10. Mackinlay, Jock. 1986. Automating the Design of Graphical Presentations of Relational Information. *ACM Trans. Graph.* 5, 2 (April 1986), 110–141. DOI: http://dx.doi.org/10.1145/22949.22950
11. Moen, Jin. 2007. From Hand-held to Body-worn: Embodied Experiences of the Design and Use of a Wearable Movement-based Interaction Concept. In *Proceedings of the 1st International Conference on Tangible and Embedded Interaction (TEI '07)*. ACM, New York, NY, USA, 251–258. DOI: http://dx.doi.org/10.1145/1226969.1227021
12. Pedregosa, F. and Varoquaux, G. and Gramfort, A. and Michel, V. and Thirion, B. and Grisel, O. and Blondel, M. and Prettenhofer, P. and Weiss, R. and Dubourg, V. and Vanderplas, J. and Passos, A. and Cournapeau, D. and Brucher, M. and Perrot, M. and Duchesnay, E. 2011. Scikit-learn: Machine Learning in Python. *Journal of Machine Learning Research* 12 (2011), 2825–2830.
13. Pijnappel, Sebastiaan and Mueller, Florian. 2013. 4 Design Themes for Skateboarding. In *Proceedings of the SIGCHI Conference on Human Factors in Computing Systems (CHI '13)*. ACM, New York, NY, USA, 1271–1274. DOI: http://dx.doi.org/10.1145/2470654.2466165
14. Sacha, D. and Stoffel, A. and Stoffel, F. and Bum Chul Kwon and Ellis, G. and Keim, D.A. 2014. Knowledge Generation Model for Visual Analytics. *Visualization and Computer Graphics, IEEE Transactions on* 20, 12 (Dec 2014), 1604–1613. DOI: http://dx.doi.org/10.1109/TVCG.2014.2346481
15. Schiphorst, Thecla and Andersen, Kristina. 2004. Between Bodies: Using Experience Modeling to Create Gestural Protocols for Physiological Data Transfer. In *Proc. CHI 2004 Fringe*. ACM Press.
16. Diego Silang Maranan, Sarah Fdili Alaoui, Thecla Schiphorst, Philippe Pasquier, Pattarawut Subyen, and Lyn Bartram. 2014. Designing for Movement: Evaluating Computational Models Using LMA Effort Qualities. In *Proceedings of the SIGCHI Conference on Human Factors in Computing Systems (CHI '14)*. ACM, New York, NY, USA, 991–1000. DOI: http://dx.doi.org/10.1145/2556288.2557251
17. Tufte, Edward R and Graves-Morris, PR. 1983. *The visual display of quantitative information*. Vol. 2. Graphics press Cheshire, CT.

Designing for Advanced Personalization in Personal Task Management

Mona Haraty, Joanna McGrenere
Department of Computer University of British Columbia
{haraty, joanna}@cs.ubc.ca

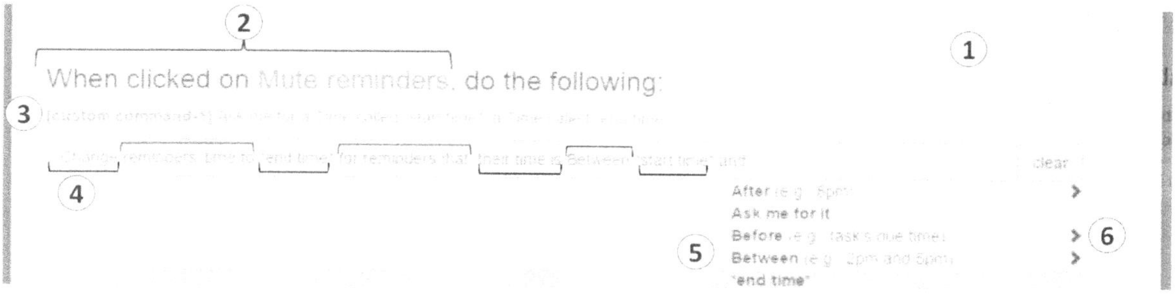

Figure 1: ScriPer is a guided scripting mechanism for constructing a new feature. Here, a user is adding a "Mute reminders" button to postpone reminders between a user-defined period. She has already created the button (trigger is marked as 2) and the first part of its behavior which is to ask for "start time" and "end time" (labeled as [custom command-1], shown in blue (3)). The screenshot is capturing the creation of the second part of the script (4). The script is composed by selecting one of the options from ScriPer's suggestions at each step (5). ScriPer starts with suggesting a set of actions, and updates its suggestions based on the rest of the script. Typing in the textbox filters the suggestions. Clicking on arrows (6) cycles through usage examples of the suggestions.

ABSTRACT
Many applications provide personalization mechanisms through which users can make changes to adapt a system to better fit ptheir needs or preferences. However, *advanced* personalization, such as extending system functionality, is often only available to programmers. Building on ideas from end-user programming and personalization literature, we developed an adaptable task management tool that allows advanced personalization using a self-disclosing mechanism and a guided scripting mechanism, ScriPer. We present our design process, its outcome, and the results of a user study (n=24). Participants, even those with no to some background in programming, were able to use ScriPer to perform advanced personalization (in 142 of 144 trials). We also found error patterns differed across programming expertise.

Author Keywords
Meta-design; personalization; personal task management.

ACM Classification Keywords
H.5.2 User Interfaces (D.2.2, H.1.2, I.3.6);

DIS 2016, June 04 - 08, 2016, Brisbane, QLD, Australia

ACM 978-1-4503-4031-1/16/06...$15.00
DOI: http://dx.doi.org/10.1145/2901790.2901805 .

INTRODUCTION
Many applications provide personalization (customization) mechanisms through which users can make changes to adapt the system to better fit their needs or preferences. But the personalization available is often quite basic, which cannot support the diversity of user needs. Advanced personalization—broadly defined as personalization that goes beyond changing the look and feel, and involves changing functionality—often requires programming skills. In this research, our goal is to bridge the gap between simple and advanced personalization mechanisms by designing a mechanism that supports creation of advanced personalization without requiring the user to code.

Current apps are often limited to basic personlizations such as making simple changes to the visual appearance of interface elements (e.g., changing icons or a background), customizing access to functionality (e.g., adding, removing, re-arranging commands/buttons to/in a toolbar or defining a shortcut), and modifying system behavior by choosing options from a list of predetermined alternative behaviors. More advanced personalization such as extending system functionality are possible through mechanisms such as macros and add-ons, but these mechanisms have limitations. Recording a macro extends a system's functionality by encapsulating a sequence of repeated user actions that can be invoked later. But sophisticated macros that add new functionality require users to edit the code generated by the macro recorder which requires programming skills. Tools such as web browsers enable users to extend system functionality by creating and installing add-ons. However, end users are restricted to *using* pre-existing add-ons, unless they have the programming skills to develop new add-ons.

To achieve our goal of designing tools that support advanced personalization, we built on ideas from end user programming (EUP) approaches such as controlled natural languages and sloppy programming [19], and followed guidelines on designing personalizable tools such as meta-design guidelines [8]. We chose personal task management (PTM) as the design domain, because PTM tools need to support advanced personalization in order to accommodate differences in PTM behaviors both across individuals and over time [12,13]. We designed a prototype of a personalizable PTM tool with two key components for enabling the creation of new functionalities: 1) a self-disclosing mechanism that reveals system functionality to users and thus makes it easier for users to understand what can be changed, 2) a guided scripting personalization mechanism (ScriPer) that enables users to construct new features by combining building blocks that are familiar to them. To investigate the strengths and challenges of these two components, we conducted an exploratory user study. Participants, even those with no or some programming background, were able to use our personalization mechanism to complete personalization tasks, except for 2 out of 144 trials. All the participants made mistakes. While programming expertise was not associated with the number of mistakes made, participants with no to some programming background produced different error patterns than programmers. Our primary contributions are: 1) the design of a personalizable PTM tool with two key personalization components, 2) empirical evidence of the challenges and strengths of both our personalization and self-disclosing mechanisms. A secondary contribution is our design process that provides additional insights into how to employ the theoretical guidelines on designing personalizable tools.

RELATED WORK

We review the guidelines on designing personalizable tools as well as EUP approaches that informed our design process.

Guidelines on designing personalizable tools

Henderson and Kyng looked at the practice of designing in use and described three activities that change the behavior of a technology: choosing between alternative anticipated behaviors, constructing new behaviors from existing pieces, and altering an artifact through modifying the source code [12]. The focus of our work is on constructing new behaviors from existing pieces. One of the comprehensive sets of principles for designing for adaptability is outlined by Moran as the principles of everyday adaptive design: overbuild infrastructure, under-build features, convey the adaptable quality of a tool as opportunity to the user, allow for recombining and repurposing (modularity), and make adaptations sharable [21]. Similarly, meta-design provides another comprehensive set of guidelines. Meta-design is a theoretical framework for empowering users to design their own tools by providing them with appropriate tools and opportunities [8]. Meta-design guidelines include: provide building blocks, under-design for emergent behavior, establish cultures of participation, share control, promote mutual learning and support of knowledge exchange, and structure communication to support reflection on practice. Key common requirements of both sets of guidelines is that software systems provide mechanisms that allow users to create complex personalizations by combining building blocks (modular components), and that systems should under design to promote personalization.

In our research, we focus on providing users with building blocks as well as mechanisms for combining the building blocks to create advanced personalization in a PTM tool.

While some of the other design methodologies (e.g., software shaping workshops [4]) include somewhat concrete practical steps for specific design situations, prior systems that have explicitly employed *meta-design* guidelines to our knowledge have been mostly domain-oriented design environments. Two examples are FRAMER for user interface design [16], and JANUS for kitchen design [9]. In these design environments, the primary user activity was to design, thus the building blocks were "design units" such as sink and refrigerator in the case of the kitchen designer, and windows and menus in the case of the user interface designer. Identifying building blocks of a non-design environment, such as a PTM tool, is less clear.

End user programming (EUP) approaches

EUP methods often take one of the following approaches: programming by demonstration, visual languages, and scripting. In our work, we focus on the scripting approach. Two approaches to improving a scripting mechanism are: (1) simplifying the format or syntax, and (2) using a scripting editor that ensures creation of a correct script, often referred to as a structure editor [5,18]. Natural languages [23] take the simplifying format approach. Sloppy programming is a form of natural language that attempts to simplify format by making programming similar to entering keywords into a Web search engine [19]. Systems such as CoScripter [17] for automating repetitive Web tasks and Inky [20]—a web command interface that allows users to automate tasks by entering unstructured text—have taken the sloppy programming approach. One limitation of this approach is that users might try commands that are not supported [17].

The structure editor approach addresses both this limitation and the issue of poor discoverability which is a limitation with all command line interfaces. The structure editor approach enables users to create commands by choosing options from menus, and it guarantees that only correct combination of options are selected. Controlled natural languages (CNLs), which are a subset of natural languages that have restricted dictionaries and grammars for reducing the complexity and ambiguity, combine both approaches of simplifying formats and structure editor. While CNLs have been explored for ontology authoring and semantic annotation (e.g., [3,10,11]), they have rarely been explored for the purpose of automation or personalization. Atomate is an exception that has used a CNL interface to enable end user construction of reactive rules using information sources on the web such as one's online calendar, email client, and messaging services [15]; an example of a reactive rule constructed with Atomate is: "Have Atomate automatically update your facebook status when you are at a concert." While ScriPer is similar to Atomate in that they both use a CNL interface for creating behaviors, they differ in both the type of CNL interface and the usage context. As a result of the difference in the usage context, our approach provides finer grain building blocks as well as integration with the rest of the interface. In addition, our approach allows users to extend functionality of an under-designed PTM system by changing the behavior of already existing UI elements and defining behavior of new UI elements. Alfred is an automation tool that, similar to Inky, offers a command line for *running* commands [25]. Unlike Inky, Alfred supports creation of new commands but not through its command line interface; simple commands can be created using a visual programming interface where users can define flow of data between different apps; creating advanced commands requires programming knowledge. Unlike Inky and Alfred, the scripting mechanism in ScriPer is for *creation* of new behaviors, and using those behaviors—which is equivalent to running commands in Inky and Alfred—is done through the GUI elements in our prototype. While some of the EUP approaches have been studied, their effectiveness for people with no to little programming experience has been largely unexplored [15,20].

The contribution of our work is in bringing the EUP techniques to the context of personalization in PTM, and providing empirical evidence on the challenges and strengths in using them. We designed and developed a personalizable PTM prototype that includes a scripting mechanism (ScriPer) for creating advanced personalization. Our design incorporated both approaches of simplifying format and structure editor by using a scripting language that resembles natural language, and by presenting the space of applicable building blocks (language expressions) that can be used at each step of composing a script. A key difference between our approach and that of tools such as Alfred or Inky is that we use a command line interface for *creating* new behaviors for interface elements using very basic building blocks such as change, move, show, etc., rather than *running* predefined commands. Our goal was to design an approach for command creation that does not require programming.

Show my tasks' deadlines on a timeline
See & select appropriate tasks that can be done in a given time slot
Filter & show me tasks that were recorded today
Focus on the current tasks, minimize distraction by other tasks
Add an icon next to the tasks that [meet a certain condition]
View task lists & calendar together
Print tasks that are due today in a particular format
Set timer on tasks for tracking time
Color code tasks based on their list / goal
Strike through tasks when done

Table 1. Examples of user needs from prior PTM studies.

META-DESIGNING A PTM TOOL

Following the guidelines discussed earlier, we had two primary research questions in meta-designing a PTM tool: What are the building blocks of a PTM tool? And what personalization mechanisms should be provided to users for enabling them to combine those building blocks to create new functionality? Below we describe how we addressed these questions by reviewing our design process.

We developed a prototype of a basic PTM tool that supports basic functionalities such as creating task lists, adding tasks to lists, editing task attributes (e.g., color, due date, reminder), marking tasks as done, and deleting tasks.

Establishing the building blocks of a PTM system

Providing users with building blocks is the cornerstone of the existing guidelines on designing personalizable tools [2,8,22]. However, none provided concrete actionable guidelines as to how to come up with the building blocks for a system. To address our first question (what are the building blocks of a PTM system?), we hypothesized that understanding the types of desired personalizations would provide insight into what needs to be modifiable and thus the building blocks of a system. Several types of personalization (e.g., interface and functionality adaptation [21]) have been identified in the past, in domains other than PTM. However, previous categorizations of personalization were based on the personalizations that were *available* in the existing personalizable tools. What we needed, by contrast, were the types of personalizations that were not necessarily available but were *desired* and needed to be supported for accommodating differences in PTM behaviors both across individuals and over time. Thus, we reviewed users' various PTM needs reported in prior PTM studies (e.g., [1,11]), as well as the feature requests made by users of PTM tools such as Remember The Milk [26] which is one of the most active feature request forums related to PTM. See Tables 1 and 2 for examples of user needs and feature requests.

We considered user needs and feature requests as forms of personalizations that users should be able to create. Thus, we treated the words (e.g., task, change, due date) mentioned in the feature requests and user needs as the building blocks of a meta-designed tool, and categorized them into UI elements, actions, interactions, external events, entities, entities'

Snooze button for notifications
A "make current" button, that takes all selected overdue tasks and moves them to the present day
Ask for date to which to postpone when postponing a task
Customize reminders for specific lists/tags
Make 'delete' a button instead of an option in 'more actions'
Show tasks due today in bold
Show overdue tasks in the 'Today' tab on the Overview screen

Table 2. Example of feature requests in RTM.

attributes, and attributes' values. Table 3 illustrates examples of the building blocks in each of these categories.

The under-design guideline of meta-design [6] (or overbuild infrastructure and underbuild features of [21]) guided our decision of what actions to include as building blocks. According to this guideline: 1) building blocks should offer enough functionality that they are useful and usable as a unit and, 2) they should not be too complex to require users to break them down in order to combine them with other blocks [6]. In our design process, before adding a new feature based on a user need, we assessed the feasibility of building that feature using more basic blocks. If feasible, we added the new building block instead of the new feature. For example, we skipped adding an 'archive' feature, because archiving involves moving a completed task to a list called 'archive' and thus could be built by creating a list and using a 'move' building block which is more generic than 'archive.'

Creating new personalizations using the building blocks

After reviewing the user needs and feature requests for identifying the building blocks, we decided to focus on designing personalization mechanisms for two classes of personalizations: the first is adding a new feature to the system that can be invoked by interacting with a new interface element (e.g., a button or a menu-item); the second class is modifying the effect of an existing user interaction by adding new behaviors to it or changing its current behavior. While both classes require a mechanism for defining a new behavior, the first class involves creating a new interface element and attributing the new behavior to an interaction with it, and the second one involves attributing the new behavior to an existing interaction. Below, we describe how we designed for the above requirements.

ScriPer: Scripting for personalizing

To allow users to combine the building blocks for creating a new behavior, we designed ScriPer (**Scri**pting for **Per**sonalizing) which is a guided scripting mechanism. ScriPer allows users to create a script—representing their desired behavior—by choosing from a list of suggested building blocks that gets updated based on users' selected building blocks so far. ScriPer starts with suggesting a set of action building blocks (Figure 2.6), each of which has their own grammatical template. For example, the 'change' action block has the following template:

[[1]**change] [**[2]objects' attributes **to] [**[3]attribute's values**] [**[4]**for** (all) objects (that)**] [**[5]objects' attributes**] [**[6]attributes' values**].**

Category	Examples of building blocks
UI element	Button, checkbox
Action	Change, ask me for [data], show, move, remove.
Entity	Task, list, reminder
Attribute	Color, due date, type, status, importance, etc.
Value	Gray, tomorrow, long-term, done, high, etc.
Interaction	Click, right click, double click, drag, drop, hover
External event	Closing a web page, starring an email, etc.

Table 3. Categories of building blocks in a PTM system.

The numbers represent the order of ScriPer's suggestions for the 'change' block. After choosing 'change,' it suggests all the attributes of all the objects in the system to ask users what they want to change. Once an attribute is selected, it suggests all the possible objects that have that attribute (e.g., 'all the selected tasks' or 'tasks that'). If users choose objects such as 'tasks that' for which they have to specify conditions, then ScriPer suggests conditions in two steps: first by suggesting the attributes of the objects on which users want to apply a condition, next by suggesting possible values of the selected attributes (see Fig 1.4). We chose the order of ScriPer's suggestions such that a complete script forms a correct English sentence. This order was chosen to increase accessibility to non-programmers, at the cost of being contrary to mainstream programming paradigms (e.g., object oriented programming where objects come before actions).

The 'move' block has a slightly different template:

[[1]**move] [**[2](all) objects (that)**] [**[3]objects' attributes**] [**[4]attributes' values**] [**[5]to (day)(list)(position in a list)**] [**[6](day's values) (list names) (positions' values)**].**

ScriPer suggests values for an attribute based on the type of the attribute. For example, if the user selects an attribute such as 'due date' whose type is date, ScriPer shows a list of dates such as today and tomorrow, as well as a 'pick a date' block that when chosen, a date picker will be shown. Fig 3 illustrates this for the reminder's time attribute. When the script inside the textbox represents a complete script, ScriPer shows the two buttons of 'and' and 'save' (Fig 4) to signal to users that they can either add another script or just save their current script. ScriPer is implemented as a modal pop-up window that can be invoked either through a self-disclosing mechanism [5] or by clicking on a newly created interface element (e.g., a button) in the "personalization mode"; we describe the purpose of each approach next.

Personalization mode

To allow users to create new interface elements, we distinguish between the main mode, where all the regular PTM-related activities take place, and the personalization mode where personalization-related activities such as adding a new button or a menu-item happen. Switching modes is done by clicking on 'Personalization'/'Exit personalization' button (Fig 2.1); personalization mode adds a gray overlay to the main interface and all the regular PTM-related interactions are disabled such that the user interactions will show their expected effects in a panel (through the self-disclosing mechanism described next) rather than being executed. To add a new button, users click on the plus button next to other buttons (Figure 2.7), name the button, and then click on it to define its behavior using the ScriPer.

A self-disclosing mechanism

The second class of personalization that our prototype supports is modifying the effect of an interaction with an existing interface element (e.g., the effect of clicking on a button) by either adding a new effect or replacing an existing

Figure 2: The prototype in personalization mode, hence the gray overlay (1). The plus button (7) is only displayed in personalization mode. The 'Mark as done' button has been clicked and thus the panel (2) is showing the effects (4) of that event (3). In this screenshot, the user is adding a new effect to the 'Mark as done' button by clicking on "Add a new action/effect" (5) which has invoked the ScriPer window (6). ScriPer starts with suggesting a set of action building blocks. Next to each action block are examples of using the block to familiarize the user with the block.

one. To support such personalization, following one of Moran's principles of everyday adaptive design [21], we first needed to *convey the adaptable quality* of user interactions so users know they can change the effect of their interaction. To do this, we display the effect of an existing interaction, building on the idea of self-disclosing systems that disclose their behaviors to users [6]. Whenever a user interacts with an interface element, the interaction (Fig 2.3) and its effects (Fig 2.4) are displayed in a fixed panel at the bottom of the page (Fig 2.2). The interaction is shown as a trigger and its effects are shown as actions. The background color of the panel changes to blue for one second when the user interacts with an interface element to clarify for the user the connection between her interaction and what is being displayed in the panel. The panel appears in both the main and the personalization modes, and its display can be toggled. The effects of an interaction—displayed as actions—can be modified via the ScriPer window. New effects can be constructed and assigned to the displayed trigger by clicking the "Add a new action/effect" button (Fig 2.5) which invokes ScriPer (Fig 2.6).

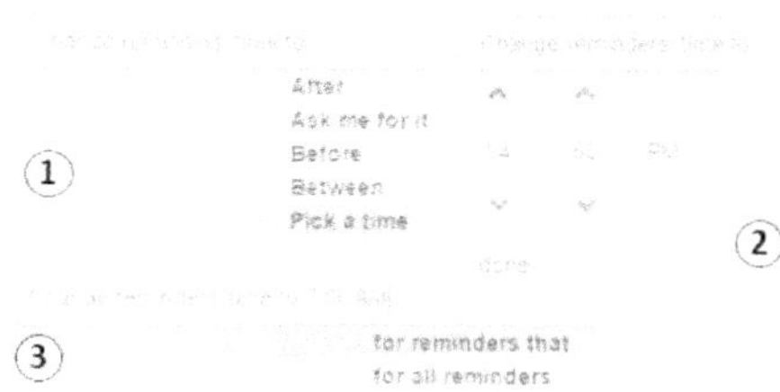

Figure 3: To select a value for a reminders' time, (1) the user chooses 'pick a time', (2) then ScriPer shows a time picker for the user to select a time, (3) after picking 7 AM and pressing done, ScriPer adds the picked value to the script.

EVALUATION

We conducted an exploratory lab study where people with various levels of programming experience used the tool to perform a set of predetermined personalization tasks. The goal of our study was twofold: (1) to evaluate our design decisions and understand the strengths and potential challenges involved in using the two components of our meta-designed tool—ScriPer and the self-disclosing mechanism—for personalizing software, and (2) to assess the effect of programming experience on the ability to perform personalization tasks.

Participants

Twenty four participants completed the study (13 females). Participants were recruited by posting signs around a large North American university campus as well as emails to different departments. Participants ranged from 21 to 31 years of age. They were all university students, and only 6 (3 females) were from the computer science department.

Prior to signing up for the experiment, interested participants filled out a short questionnaire to describe their programming expertise and rated it on a scale of 1-3 (1 little to no programming background, 2 some programming background, and 3 proficient in programming). While our design was targeted at the first two groups, we included the third group for comparison purposes. We were able to recruit 8 participants in each expertise category. In the rest of the

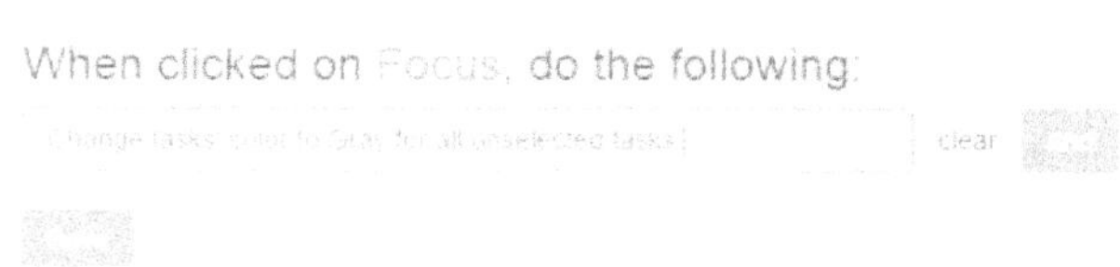

Figure 4: A grammatically correct script.

paper, participants are referred to as their gender (M/F) + expertise (N/S/P) + a number (1-8). For example, a male proficient programmer is referred to as MPx where x is between 1 and the number of participants in that category.

Tasks

To maintain ecological validity in designing personalization tasks, we reviewed user needs from prior PTM studies as well as the feature request forum of a PTM tool, Remember the Milk. Table 1 and 2 shows examples of user needs and feature requests that influenced our tasks. Based on those examples, we designed six personalization tasks, all of which could be performed using our prototype.

Four of the tasks involved creating a new button and defining its behavior. For each of these tasks, we designed a group of two tasks—henceforth a task group (TGi). The second task in each group was a personalization task, which explicitly asked participants to create a button that performs a desired personalization. The first task was to perform what the button would do prior to performing any personalization. The first task involved some repetition, which was to motivate the need for the personalization. This is often challenging when designing personalization tasks for lab studies. Another goal of the first task was to familiarize participants with the goal of the personalization they were asked to perform in the 2nd task. The task groups TG1, TG2, TG5 and TG6 were designed this way (see Table 4).

The remaining task groups (TG3 and TG4) involved using the self-disclosing mechanism. TG3 included 3 tasks, and TG4 included 4 tasks. The last task of each of these task groups was a personalization task that asked participants to change the effect of an interaction with already-existing interface components (e.g., 'mark as done' button). The other tasks in each of the task groups were designed to familiarize the participants with that interaction and its current effects. In those tasks, participants performed an action, e.g., marking a few tasks as done, and explained its current effect.

Procedure

First, to familiarize participants with the system, we walked them through performing a personalization task. Next, they were given all tasks one at a time in the order shown in Table 4, and were asked to think aloud while performing the tasks without any time limit. The screen and the audio were recorded. After finishing the tasks, participants were asked about their experience with ScriPer and the self-disclosing mechanism in a semi-structured interview. The session took on average 42 minutes (min=20, max=60).

Data analysis

We collected usage log data (the personalization scripts and task completion), the screen recordings, the interview data, and the notes of the participants' actions and comments. The screen recordings and the transcriptions of the think aloud were coded against the number and type of mistakes, and whether or not they reused their created personalization in subsequent tasks. The semi-structured interviews were transcribed and coded against the strengths and challenges of different parts of the design. We ran mixed-model regression to analyze participants' success in completing the tasks without mistakes and the number of mistakes. In the

Task groups	Tasks
TG1	**T11:** Change the due date of the following tasks to tomorrow: "finish paper review", "learn javascript", "do yoga"
	T1P: Imagine that you'd like to do the previous task for a whole bunch of tasks and that you might need to do this again in the future. For this situation, you decide to create a button (called 'postpone to tomorrow') that when you click on, the system modifies the due dates of the to-dos that you have selected to tomorrow.
TG2	**T21:** Find tasks that are overdue (i.e., due before today) and change their color to red so that you won't miss them.
	T2P: To save time on the previous task in the future, you decide to create a button called "Highlight overdues" that when you click on, it automatically turns the overdue tasks into red.
TG3	**T31:** Mark the following tasks as done to indicate that you are done with them: (Code, do yoga)
	T32: What did the system do when you pressed the 'Mark as Done' button? (please explain)
	T3P: Imagine that you would like the system to move your tasks to the bottom of the list when you are done with them, in addition to crossing them off. So, make the system do that.
TG4	**T41:** Create a list called "tomorrow".
	T42: Add the following new tasks to the tomorrow list and set their due dates to tomorrow: "buy bread", "register", "return book"
	T43: What does the system do when you add a task to a list? (please explain orally)
	T4P: In addition to adding the task to the bottom of the list, make the system set the tasks' due date to tomorrow by default when you enter a task in this list.
TG5	**T51:** You do not want to disturb your sleep by the automated task reminders that are sent when you are asleep. So, find tasks that their reminders are set to be sent out between 10 pm and 7 am and postpone them to 7 am.
	T5P: Imagine that there are other times that you you'd like to define quiet hours so that you tell the system a time period in which you don't want to receive any reminders and the system postpones sending the reminders to the end of that period. In this situation, you decide to create a button called 'mute reminders' that when you click on, the system asks you to enter the time period and then the system changes the reminders that are supposed to be sent out within that period such that they will be sent out at the end of that period.
TG6	**T61:** Today, you want to focus on the following 3 tasks (Read paper, learn javascript, Finish paper review). Gray out the rest of your tasks so they don't distract you.
	T6P: Imagine that you'd like to do the previous task again in the future. For this situation, you decide to create a button called 'Focus' such that when you select the tasks that you want to focus on and click on the 'Focus' button, it makes the other tasks gray.

Table 4. Tasks used in the experiment. Participants were given one task at a time.

regression models, we included the fixed effects of the number of tasks already attempted, programming expertise, gender, and age, as well as the random effects of the task that was being attempted and participant.

We *only* analyzed personalization tasks (T1P-T6P) in the task groups. Some participants performed personalization even for the non-personalization tasks in which they were not explicitly asked nor expected to personalize, i.e. the first task in TG1, TG2, TG5, and TG6. Some of them skipped the personalization task in the task group as they recognized that they had already performed that task. In these cases, we considered their first tasks as their personalization tasks.

FINDINGS

Task completion and mistakes made

Except for two participants who gave up completing T5P, participants did complete all personalization tasks, albeit some with mistakes (due to the iterative nature of writing a script, only uncorrected mistakes are counted as mistakes). A mistake meant that the solution was either a slightly or completely different personalization than the intended one. Out of the 144 (24x6) trials of the six personalization tasks, only 2 were left incomplete, 94 were completed successfully with no mistake (Fig 5-A). In the remaining 48 trials, 54 mistakes were made in total. The number of mistakes made in a single task ranged from 1 to 3, with only 1 participant ever making 3 mistakes on a task (T5P). Table 5 illustrates the distribution of mistakes across the tasks.

We grouped the similar mistakes, and labeled the 4 emergent groups as: lack of precision, terminology related, mental model mismatch, and wrong trigger. In 41% of the mistakes, a wrong block was chosen due to *lack of precision*, e.g., choosing 'for all tasks' instead of 'for all *selected* tasks' or 'yesterday' instead of 'before today'. 37% of the mistakes, were *terminology related*, e.g., using 'completion date' instead of 'due date' or 'time' instead of 'date'. 18% of the mistakes were due to changing the effect of a *wrong trigger* which was most common in the tasks that required use of the self-disclosing mechanism (T3P, T4P). For example, when performing T4P, which required attributing a new effect to the 'add' button, some participants added the new effect to an irrelevant trigger that was displayed through the self-disclosing mechanism because that irrelevant trigger happened to be their last interaction with the system. Finally, only 4% of the mistakes were due to a *mental model mismatch* such as a mismatch between the functionality of a building block and what users expected it to do. For example, 3 participants made an unnecessary use of the 'show' block in T2I—where they were asked to find tasks that were overdue and change their color to red—before using the 'change' block. For example, FN4 created the following two scripts: "Show tasks that their due date is before today on calendar" and "Change tasks' color to Red for tasks that their due date is before today". But all those 3 participants mentioned "*I probably didn't have to use 'show'*" right after using the 'change' block. Fig 5-B illustrates a breakdown of mistake types across programming expertise. Compared to programmers, participants with no to some programming background made disproportionately more mistakes due to lack of precision and choosing a wrong trigger.

To examine if the number of mistakes were associated with programming expertise and other aforementioned factors, we ran a Poisson mixed model regression. Also, to analyze success in completing a task (0 mistakes vs. 1 or more), we ran a logistic mixed model regression. Neither of these analyses identified any significant predictors.

Unexpected personalization behaviors

Personalizing when performing non-personalization tasks: As mentioned, some participants performed personalization in tasks where they were not directly asked to do so (T1I, T2I, T5I, and T6I). Out of the 96 trials of these four tasks, 57 were done by creating a personalization. When asked

Task	Correct personalization script	# of mistakes in the script				
		0	1	2	3	--*
T1P	[When clicked on **"Postpone"**], [Change] [tasks' <u>due date</u> to] [tomorrow] <u>[for all selected tasks]</u>	17	7	0	0	0
T2P	[When clicked on **"Highlight overdues"**], [Change] [tasks' color to] [Red] [for tasks that] [their due date is] [before] [today/now]	10	12	2	0	0
T3P	[When clicked on **"Mark as done"**], [Move] [all selected tasks to] [location in the list:] [bottom of the list]	20	4	0	0	0
T4P	When clicked on **"add"**, [Change] [tasks' due date to] [tomorrow] [for all tasks in this list]	12	11	1	0	0
T5P	When clicked on **"Mute reminders"**, [Ask me for] [a Time called "start"], [a Time called "end"] [Change] [reminders' time to] [*end*] [for reminders that] [their time is] [between] [*start*] and [*end*]	13	7	1	1	2
T6P	When clicked on **"Focus"**, [Change] [tasks' color to] [Gray] [for all unselected tasks]	22	2	0	0	0
	Total Number of trials = 144	94		48		2

Table 5. Correct personalization for each personalization task and the number of participants who made 0, 1, 2, 3 errors in their scripts when performing each task. Each correctly selected building block of a personalization is shown within a bracket. * The last column shows the number of participants who left the tasks incomplete.

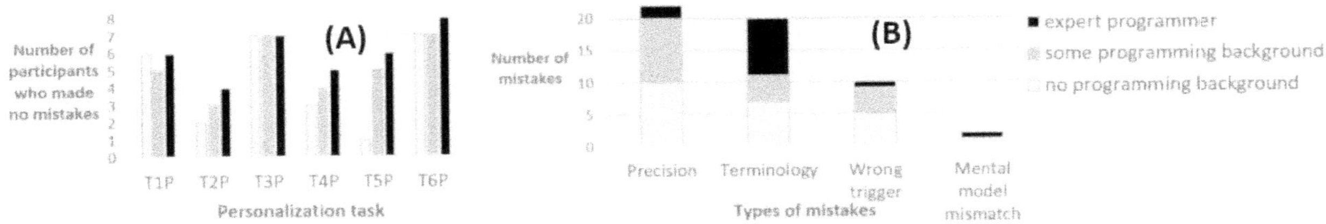

Figure 5: (A) Number of participants who successfully completed each task with no mistake, (B) Breakdown of mistakes across types and programming expertise.

about their choice, participants mentioned one of the following: 1) they were aware of the manual method but thought that the task involved *"too much hassle"* if done manually, 2) they mentioned that they never would have thought that they should do the task manually, or 3) they could not figure out how to do the task without personalizing. In an extreme case, FS4 couldn't find the 'Mark as done' button, when she was asked to mark two tasks as done in T31, and she created a button called 'completed.' A logistic mixed model regression of whether participants personalized in these tasks did not identify any significant predictor.

Creating more generalizable personalization than asked for: Four participants (MP2, MS2, MP3, MS4) created more generalizable personalizations when not asked to personalize; instead of the simpler anticipated solution of *"Change tasks' start date to tomorrow for all selected tasks"* for T11, they combined the following two scripts: *"ask me for a Date called 'dateChange'"* and *"change tasks' start date to *dateChange* for all selected tasks"*.

Reusing a personalization created in prior tasks: Some participants reused their personalizations without being instructed to do so. Task T42 asked the participants to add 3 tasks to a list and set their due dates to tomorrow. To save time on this, 5 participants (MP3, FP2, MP5, FN5, FN6) reused the 'postpone to tomorrow' button that they had created in T1P, instead of manually changing the due dates of the three tasks. We expect to see such reuse behavior when users build their own personalization in a real-world setting, and it was reassuring to see this behavior in the lab setting.

ScriPer: strengths and challenges

Flexibility of the system

For each personalization task, we had anticipated a single solution, but participants performed some of the tasks differently. This showed the system's flexibility in supporting different ways of expressing a feature. For example, for T3P where they were asked to add a new effect to the 'Mark as done' button such that it moves the tasks to the bottom of the list, 3 participants performed the task with this script: "change tasks' location to the bottom of the list for all selected tasks" instead of our anticipated solution of "move all selected tasks to location: bottom of the list".

MP5, who used Todoist (a dedicated PTM tool), was eager to provide suggestions for improving the PTM support of our prototype before realizing that he could achieve some of his suggestions through personalization: *"that's the nice thing about the system, you can always edit and do anything you want. So for example, I want 'Mark as done' to move all of this into a 'done' list. I can easily do it with personalization"*. Then he went ahead and changed the effect of 'Mark as done' button and said: *"So, it's hard to criticize the system because you can create anything you want. Like if you have anything missing, it's like a plugin, you can just create it."*

Some of the participants speculated about the potential usefulness of ScriPer in other apps: *"I like that you can construct features. Other apps don't do that. The gray out thing [referring to T6P], I have an app similar to this but it doesn't do the gray out...you can prioritize them [your tasks], but you have to do it individually, you can't say all these ones are priority ones together"* [FS1]. MP2 could see ScriPer being used for macro creation in spreadsheets: *"Instead of having to record your macro you can actually do something that's a bit more plain text [as in ScriPer] it's really frustrating to make those macros; they are always very strict...they won't allow any easy process."*

Overall ease of use

Overall, participants liked the concept of creating their own features, and found ScriPer easy to use for the most part. Even programmers appreciated not having to code for the purpose of personalization: *"I loved the feature construction window. I'm a programmer but I don't like doing it when I don't have to especially for something like personalization"* [MP1]. One participant commented on the value of the save button in ScriPer: *"I liked the fact that when you want to save you need to complete every step. It's not like you complete half the steps and you can save it, that didn't work. It's giving you some feedback that you are right"* [MN2].

Findability of the building blocks among the suggestions

Participants took different approaches to finding their desired block among the suggested blocks: some participants typed a keyword they were looking for to filter the suggestion list, and others visually scanned the list to see what fits. In cases where the list of suggestions was long, participants who filtered seemed to find their desired block faster, based on observation as the time to select a suggestion was not logged. However, the filtering behavior led some participants to either make precision-related mistakes or create less efficient scripts, as they sufficed to the first best-matched block and did not find the correct block, which was filtered out. For example, MP3 inefficiently performed T6P;

while the intention was to gray out the unselected tasks, he created the following two scripts: "change task's color to gray for all tasks" + "change tasks' color to green for all selected tasks." He missed the option of "for all *unselected* tasks" when writing the first script. Some participants preferred scanning the options rather than typing and filtering, because they anticipated a potential mismatch between their own vocabulary and that of the system: *"there wasn't so much stuff that I thought that [the filter] was necessary. I also realized I was scared I'd miss something if I didn't type it as exactly the way it was typed"* [MS4].

Match between the order of blocks and users' expectations
ScriPer imposes an order in which users are expected to express their desired personalization. While the majority of the participants mentioned that the order made sense to them, 7/24 pointed to a mismatch between the order they thought about the personalization and the order the blocks were suggested. All those 7 participants wanted to first identify objects and only then apply an action on them; however, in our prototype, the action building blocks were suggested first. For example, FP3 said: "*I like how it constructs it for you. But sometimes I felt like I have to think about the order of how to construct things in a certain way. First I need to select and then I need to do change whatever it was. I think it's more helpful to have the system help you construct it like this, but at the same time the rigidness made it hard to figure out.*" However, many participants (without prompting) pointed to the learning curve in getting to know the order of ScriPer's suggestions and that by their last tasks, they knew what suggestions they should be expecting and when.

Difficulty in creating composite data types
The 'ask me for' block was designed to be used for instructing the system to ask for data (e.g., a time, a text). Part of T5P involved using this block to instruct the system to ask users to enter a 'time period'—a composite data type. Fig 6 illustrates the steps involved. Following the under-design guideline, we chose not to include composite data types such as 'time period' as a building block, since they could be built using more basic blocks such as time. Thus, in T5P participants were expected to instruct the system to ask them for two time inputs, which proved to be difficult for some of the participants with little to no programming background. Two of the participants gave up completing T5P. For example, when performing this task, FP2 thought aloud "*I want the system to ask me for a range but this is only asking for one time. I don't know how to enter a time period.*"

Self-disclosing mechanism: strengths and challenges
The panel that disclosed the system behavior was available in both the main and the personalization modes. Most participants liked having it in the main mode. MS2 mentioned that he should be able to have it in both modes: "*that's kinda cool because it visually shows you what's being done for whatever is pressed live, whereas in personalization [mode] you have to go and click and see.*"

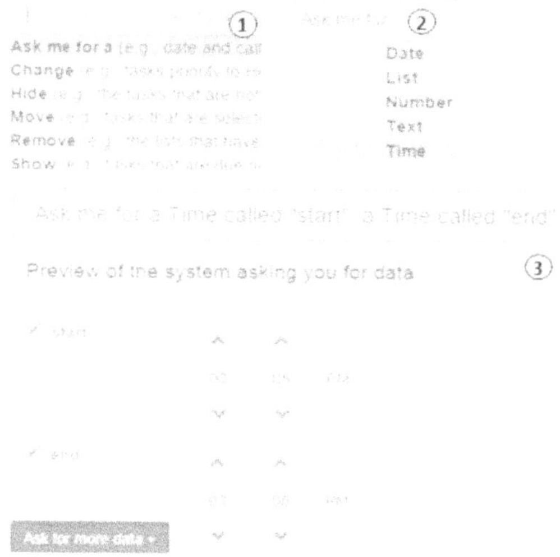

Figure 6: Steps involved in using the 'Ask me for' block to perform part of T5P.

However, as mentioned earlier in the discussion of mistakes, some participants had difficulty finding the right trigger, and made mistakes by attributing a new behavior to a wrong trigger (10/54 mistakes). The triggers shown in the panel are updated on each user action. Thus, to change the effect of an action through the self-disclosing mechanism, a participant has to first perform the action so that the panel displays it as a trigger. If done in the personalization mode, the action and its expected effects are displayed without being executed. However, participants who performed an action in the main mode just to make the panel display the right trigger had to undo the effect of their action. One approach to alleviate this issue is to show a history of user interactions in the panel, instead of only the last interaction, and allow users to choose their desired trigger manually from the panel without going through the process of performing and undoing an action, or having to switch to the personalization mode.

In addition, there was a mismatch in how the system set triggers and some of our participants' mental model of it. In our prototype, triggers are general actions such as "when clicked on the checkbox next to a task." To attribute a new behavior to a trigger such that the behavior is only applied to certain of objects (e.g. tasks that are in the 'shopping' list), participants had to specify those objects when constructing the new behavior, and not when setting the trigger. However, some participants expected to first define a more specific trigger such as "when clicked on the checkbox next to a task in the 'shopping' list", and then to add a behavior to it. Therefore, they avoided changing the effect of a general trigger: "*I was a bit scared of using the panel because it applies to very general actions... If I click on a task and then add an action I say oh my God I'm gonna screw up every time I click on that very generic action. I'll leave that for really general behaviors unless there are some sort of filtering built into that*" [MP3]. To resolve this issue, triggers need to be editable so that users can add conditions to them.

DISCUSSION AND CONCLUSION

The theoretical guidelines on how to design personalizable tools have been rarely put into practice. To our knowledge, our work is first in following such guidelines to design a personalizable tool that is not a design environment as in [9,16]. Our work paves the way for designing personalizable tools by revealing its detailed design process and putting the theoretical guidelines into practice, specifically by providing insights into *how* to identify the building blocks of a system and *how* to under-design, as well as providing an example of a mechanism (ScriPer) for combining building blocks to create some types of advanced personalizations; ScriPer is a proof of concept and was not intended to offer complete language expressivity; it covers trigger-action rules where the trigger is a user interaction with an interface element.

To identify the building blocks of a PTM system we reviewed user needs and feature requests of an existing PTM application. We think that our high level categories—UI elements, actions, interactions, external events, entities, entities' attributes, and attributes' values—provide a more practical starting point for designers of personalizable tools to identify building blocks of a system. We found the under-design guideline helpful in deciding whether to add a new feature. It led us to include more basic building blocks instead of adding more features or composite blocks. This approach increases the number of possible features users could build. However, our decision about not including the composite data type of 'time period'—since it could be built using two times—did not work out for some participants. Thus, under-design decisions need to be tested carefully to ensure that composite blocks can be built intuitively, especially for people with no programming background.

ScriPer is one possible design of a mechanism for combining building blocks to create advanced personalizations, and our preliminary evaluation shows that it is promising. One of the most encouraging results is that many participants intuitively personalized even when not required. Out of the 96 trials of four of the non-personalization tasks, 57 were done by creating a personalization. Further, most users were able to create advanced personalizations when instructed to. On the downside, however, ScriPer does not prevent the user from making mistakes, and indeed about one third of the created personalizations were either slightly or completely different than the intended ones. Part of the issue is the ability for the user to easily spot a mistake. Our evaluation did not include having participants using our tool with their own tasks, something that would have likely highlighted any mistake quickly. Further investigation is needed to see how well users are able to recover from their mistakes. Beyond recovery, it is important for a personalization mechanism to limit the possibility of making a mistake in the first place. Mistakes due to choosing a wrong trigger in the self-disclosing mechanism were related to not noticing the trigger part in the panel. To avoid such mistakes, the self-disclosing mechanism should emphasize the trigger part and ask users—once they are done with creating a personalization—to confirm that their personalization is attributed to the right trigger. Compared to programmers, participants with no to some programming background made disproportionately more mistakes due to lack of precision, i.e. mistakes such as choosing 'yesterday' instead of 'before today'. One approach to reduce the possibility of such error is to suggest other conceptually similar options to what they have selected or are about to select. This can be done, for example, by highlighting those similar options when a user is about to select an option. This approach requires designers to determine clusters of conceptually similar building blocks which might be an added step to the design. Alternatively, a data-driven approach may be adopted by tracking how errors are made and then corrected.

One usability issue with ScriPer was related to the order it imposed on using the blocks. Action building blocks such as change, move, etc. were so basic (i.e., low-level) that they did not necessarily correspond to any user interaction or interface element in the system. Therefore, ScriPer had to be able to provide specific suggestions for each step of composing a script to compensate for users' lack of familiarity with the actions and their parameters. Thus, we chose to impose an order for combining building blocks so the number of suggestions at each step would be manageable for users. The order allowed the personalization scripts to form an English sentence and provided the benefit of knowing what building block should be selected at each step. However, it did not match some participants' preferred order. Part of the problem was due to lack of visibility of the next steps, which was partly due to their dependence on user's prior selections. An alternative approach is to show all the steps to users and let users choose the order in which they want to complete each step. However, that might make the interface crowded and confusing. Also, systems that use higher level building blocks that are more familiar to users can support a flexible order. Inky is an example of such a system, since it replaces a GUI with a command line interface, where users are likely to be familiar with the available commands and their parameters.

Although the personalization tasks in our study were ecologically valid, they were not derived from our particular participants. Longitudinal studies are needed to assess if users can translate their *own* needs into personalizations and whether they can reuse those personalizations effectively. Similar to our prototype, even a fully developed PTM tool can be limited in its coverage of primitive building blocks. To overcome this, users should be able to add building blocks to the system; but this could be challenging. For example, adding an *action* building block such as 'hide' requires determining all the possible building blocks that can be combined with it, a template to represent arrangement of the building blocks, and the underlying functionality associated with the block. Although the first two can be achieved by people with no to some programming background, defining the underlying functionality associated with an action block perhaps needs to be left to programmers.

REFERENCES

1. Victoria Bellotti, Brinda Dalal, Nathaniel Good, Peter Flynn, Daniel G Bobrow, and Nicolas Ducheneaut. 2004. What a to-do: studies of task management towards the design of a personal task list manager. *Proceedings of the SIGCHI conference on Human factors in computing systems*, ACM, 735–742. http://doi.org/http://doi.acm.org.proxy.lib.sfu.ca/10.1145/985692.985785
2. Richard Bentley and Paul Dourish. 1995. Medium versus mechanism: supporting collaboration through customisation. *Proceedings of the fourth conference on European Conference on Computer-Supported Cooperative Work*, Kluwer Academic Publishers, 133–148. Retrieved October 31, 2012 from http://dl.acm.org/citation.cfm?id=1241958.1241967
3. Abraham Bernstein and Esther Kaufmann. 2006. GINO–a guided input natural language ontology editor. In *The Semantic Web-ISWC 2006*. Springer, 144–157. Retrieved November 30, 2015 from http://link.springer.com/chapter/10.1007/11926078_11
4. Maria Francesca Costabile, Daniela Fogli, Piero Mussio, and Antonio Piccinno. 2004. Software environments for end-user development and tailoring. *Psychnology* 2: 99–122.
5. Allen Cypher, Mira Dontcheva, Tessa Lau, and Jeffrey Nichols. 2010. *No Code Required: Giving Users Tools to Transform the Web*. Morgan Kaufmann. Retrieved April 12, 2015 from http://books.google.ca/books?hl=en&lr=&id=-bJKhQWYesoC&oi=fnd&pg=PP2&dq=no+code+required&ots=aHQ20HID3N&sig=pFdjOWG3bmxD86QPlZo9LAS_DGg
6. Chris DiGiano and Mike Eisenberg. 1995. Self-disclosing design tools: a gentle introduction to end-user programming. *Proceedings of the 1st conference on Designing interactive systems: processes, practices, methods, & techniques*, ACM, 189–197. Retrieved April 13, 2015 from http://dl.acm.org/citation.cfm?id=225455
7. Gerhard Fischer and Thomas Herrmann. 2011. Socio-technical systems: a meta-design perspective. *International Journal of Sociotechnology and Knowledge Development (IJSKD)* 3, 1: 1–33.
8. Gerhard Fischer and E. Scharff. 2000. Meta-design: design for designers. *Proceedings of the 3rd conference on Designing interactive systems: processes, practices, methods, and techniques*, 396–405. Retrieved October 26, 2012 from http://dl.acm.org/citation.cfm?id=347798
9. G. Fischer, R. McCall, and A. Morch. 1989. JANUS: Integrating Hypertext with a Knowledge-based Design Environment. *Proceedings of the Second Annual ACM Conference on Hypertext*, ACM, 105–117. http://doi.org/10.1145/74224.74233
10. Norbert E. Fuchs, Kaarel Kaljurand, and Tobias Kuhn. 2008. Attempto Controlled English for knowledge representation. In *Reasoning Web*. Springer, 104–124. Retrieved November 30, 2015 from http://link.springer.com/chapter/10.1007/978-3-540-85658-0_3
11. Adam Funk, Valentin Tablan, Kalina Bontcheva, Hamish Cunningham, Brian Davis, and Siegfried Handschuh. 2007. *Clone: Controlled language for ontology editing*. Springer. Retrieved November 30, 2015 from http://link.springer.com/chapter/10.1007/978-3-540-76298-0_11
12. Mona Haraty, Joanna McGrenere, and Charlotte Tang. 2015. How and Why Personal Task Management Behaviors Change Over Time. *Proceedings of the 2015 Graphics Interface Conference*, Canadian Information Processing Society, GI'15.
13. Mona Haraty, Diane Tam, Shathel Haddad, Joanna McGrenere, and Charlotte Tang. 2012. Individual differences in personal task management: a field study in an academic setting. *Proceedings of the 2012 Graphics Interface Conference*, Canadian Information Processing Society, 35–44. Retrieved October 4, 2012 from http://dl.acm.org/citation.cfm?id=2305276.2305284
14. Austin Henderson and Morten Kyng. 1991. There's no place like home: Continuing Design in Use. *1991) Design at Work: Cooperative Design of Computer Systems. Lawrence Erlbaum Associates, Hillsdale, NJ*: 219–240.
15. Max Van Kleek, Brennan Moore, David R. Karger, Paul André, and m.c. schraefel. 2010. Atomate It! End-user Context-sensitive Automation Using Heterogeneous Information Sources on the Web. *Proceedings of the 19th International Conference on World Wide Web*, ACM, 951–960. http://doi.org/10.1145/1772690.1772787
16. Andreas C. Lemke and Gerhard Fischer. 1990. A cooperative problem solving system for user interface. *AAAI*, 479–484. Retrieved December 28, 2015 from http://www.aaai.org/Papers/AAAI/1990/AAAI90-072.pdf
17. Gilly Leshed, Eben M. Haber, Tara Matthews, and Tessa Lau. 2008. CoScripter: automating & sharing how-to knowledge in the enterprise. *Proceedings of the twenty-sixth annual SIGCHI conference on Human factors in computing systems*, ACM, 1719–1728. http://doi.org/10.1145/1357054.1357323
18. H. Lieberman, F. Paternò, and V. Wulf. 2006. *End user development*. Springer. Retrieved October 2, 2012 from http://books.google.ca/books?hl=en&lr=&id=9bTgzKA1fkYC&oi=fnd&pg=PR7&dq=component-based+approaches+to+tailorable+systems&ots=ujhXsoIR-e&sig=atGOBVjZktFJw1SeVEzbVLG2V3I
19. Greg Little, R. Miller, V. Chou, Michael Bernstein, Tessa Lau, and Allen Cypher. 2010. *Sloppy programming*. Morgan Kaufmann. Retrieved April 12, 2015 from http://books.google.ca/books?hl=en&lr=&id=-bJKhQWYesoC&oi=fnd&pg=PA289&dq=sloppy+programming&ots=aHQ20HNGaK&sig=ECLvPwTV1wtc4A_jk0DU6JMleL8
20. R. C. Miller, V. H. Chou, M. Bernstein, G. Little, M. Van Kleek, and D. Karger. 2008. Inky: a sloppy command line for the web with rich visual feedback. Retrieved November 19, 2012 from http://dspace.mit.edu/handle/1721.1/51696
21. Thomas Moran. 2002. Everyday Adaptive Design (keynote). Retrieved from http://www.sigchi.org/dis2002/
22. Anders Mørch. 1995. Application units: Basic building blocks of tailorable applications. In *Human-Computer Interaction*. Springer, 45–62. Retrieved October 10, 2013 from http://link.springer.com/chapter/10.1007/3-540-60614-9_4

23. Brad A. Myers, John F. Pane, and Andy Ko. 2004. Natural Programming Languages and Environments. *Commun. ACM* 47, 9: 47–52. http://doi.org/10.1145/1015864.1015888

24. R. Oppermann and H. Simm. 1994. Adaptability: User-initiated individualization. *Adaptive User Support–Ergonomic Design of Manually and Automatically Adaptable Software. Hillsdale, New Jersey*. Retrieved November 5, 2012 from http://books.google.ca/books?hl=en&lr=&id=0N9xdnrutSoC&oi=fnd&pg=PA14&dq=Adaptability:+User-Initiated+Individualization&ots=ptwQxyR8-j&sig=BWDthV-2warCk0Ko4oO3KQ0IYml

25. *Alfred*. Retrieved from https://www.alfredapp.com/

26. Remember The Milk - Forums / Ideas. Retrieved March 30, 2016 from http://www.rememberthemilk.com/forums/ideas/

Patina-inspired Personalization: Personalizing Products with Traces of Daily Use

Moon-Hwan Lee
KAIST
Republic of Korea
moonhwan@kaist.ac.kr

Oosung Son
KAIST
Republic of Korea
spctrm0@kaist.ac.kr

Tek-Jin Nam
KAIST
Republic of Korea
tjnam@kaist.ac.kr

ABSTRACT
Despite the popularization of product personalization systems, it is difficult for people to personalize a product in a way that symbolizes themselves and their daily lives. Borrowing the characteristics of patina generation, we suggest *patina-inspired personalization* as an alternative approach. This approach is a way of progressive personalization through transforming digital traces of product use into patina-like material traces on a product. As an exemplar, we developed *Trace-Marker*, a custom-built laser engraver for bicycle riders. It engraves aesthetic patterns on a bicycle bag according to a user's bicycle journey. During the field trial with 10 participants for three weeks, participants used the system to add symbolic meanings, in particular their unique identities and personal stories on their bags. The permanently engraved patterns enhanced the emotional bond with the bags. Based on the field trial, we discuss implications for improving patina-inspired personalization in wider contexts.

Author Keywords
Product personalization; patina; trace; symbolic meaning; self-expression.

ACM Classification Keywords
H.5.m. Information interfaces and presentation (e.g., HCI): Miscellaneous.

INTRODUCTION
Product personalization is a process that defines or changes the appearance or functionality of a product to increase its personal relevance to an individual [3]. The motivations for product personalization are related to people's desires to express themselves, be creative, or make items they cannot buy [25]. These days, falling costs for fabrication machines and a growing number of customization services make it cheaper and easier for people to make their own physical products [14,45].

DIS 2016, June 04-08, 2016, Brisbane, QLD, Australia
© 2016 ACM. ISBN 978-1-4503-4031-1/16/06…$15.00
DOI: http://dx.doi.org/10.1145/2901790.2901812

Despite the popularization of product personalization systems, there are some concerns regarding systems that focus mainly on the convenience of manufacturing a new object and improvements in the speed and accuracy of manufacturing. One concern is that it is still difficult for people to personalize a product in a way that conveys symbolic meanings of self-expression to the owner. In design and market research, a considerable number of studies have demonstrated the importance of symbolic meanings with respect to product design. This importance of symbolic meaning can be understood by the notion that products often act as a self-expressive means for people, providing personal meaning and communicating the owners' personal identities and narratives to others [6,16,30]. However, although people are able to easily participate in personalization through user-friendly interfaces in current systems, personalization still requires substantial design capacities so that a personalized product can symbolize the users' identities or lifestyles. Because most product personalization systems are focused on a product's functional or aesthetic elements, it is challenging for users to include the intangible symbolic meaning in product personalization process.

To support general users' product personalization in a way that enriches a symbolic meaning about themselves, we tried to explore an alternative personalization approach by applying the characteristics of patinas. Figuratively, a patina refers to any fading, darkening, or other sign of age on an object that occurs through a natural or artificial aging process [17]. Artists and designers often deliberately use patinas as design resources for constructing aesthetic surfaces and for lending credibility or giving a warm feeling to an object [8,50]. Besides their aesthetics, patinas are valued for the ways in which they evoke the lived past [10]. For example, for patinas on everyday products such as denim jeans or antique furniture, the process of patina generation relies on the use of the product over time. Therefore, products exhibiting clear traces of use betray some characteristics of the users and how often, when and in which ways they were used.

Borrowing the characteristics of patina generation and digital traces together, we suggest *patina-inspired personalization*. Patina-inspired personalization is a way of personalizing a product through users' trace accumulations during the product's use stage. Inspired by how products become personalized with patinas, this approach supports progressive personalization during a product's use stage rather than instant personalization at the manufacture stage of a product's life cycle [1,48]. Through an interactive personalization system, users can transform digital traces about product use into patina-like material traces on a product. As an exemplar, we present *Trace-Marker*, a patina-inspired personalization system that engraves patina-like patterns on a bicycle bag based on a user's bicycle-riding history, which is digitally recorded. Accordingly, the appearance of the bicycle bag evolves along with the user's history of bicycle-related experiences. We conducted a field trial with 10 participants for three weeks to learn the impact of patina-inspired personalization.

This paper makes several contributions. First, it details design considerations regarding how to support product personalization for enriching symbolic meanings of self-expression by applying the characteristics of patinas. Trace-Marker is proposed as an exemplar system for patina-inspired personalization. Primarily, the results of the field trial improve our understanding of how patina-inspired personalization is embedded in the context of product use while enriching the symbolic meaning of a product. This study guides the design of future product personalization by suggesting design issues and opportunities.

RELATED WORK

Product Personalization and Symbolic Meaning

As a self-expressive means, a product enables owners to communicate their personal identities and narratives to others [6,16]. The main reason why people pay attention to a product's symbolic meaning is that they want to enhance and express their self-concept: a person's identity and ideal image of him/herself [24]. As strategies for designing products' self-expressive values, several studies suggested personalization [30]. Meanwhile, as a response to DIY trend and product personalization, previous research in the HCI field has mainly been focused on making personalization accessible to a wider audience through parametric interface [22,34], gesture-based interface [11], mixed reality [47], etc. Despite improvements of the interfaces for modifying products' appearance or functions, it is difficult for general users to make personally meaningful products, which symbolize the users' identities and lifestyles.

Product Personalization with Digital Traces

Making a Souvenir-like Object Based on Digital Traces

There has been research on making personal objects by using digital traces such as activity data or physiological data. Data sculpture is a representative example that shows how designers and artists use digital traces for product personalization [38,51]. Moreover, in previous studies fabrication systems have been installed at home or in public contexts such as museums or conferences to make personal objects based on digital traces [23,31,32,37,43]. In these studies, the systems are used to make souvenirs that represent personal histories regarding physical activities, or activities at an art exhibition or conference. These studies illustrate the value of embedding digital fabrication in everyday contexts to facilitate social interaction and users' reflections upon their activities. Our work is distinct from these studies in that we used digital traces for progressive product personalization. Unlike previous cases, which have made separate data-things [32], our study used digital traces of products so that the products could be personalized gradually according to users' histories with them.

Attaching Digital Traces to Physical Objects

Several researchers have taken an interest in improving the emotional value of physical objects by attaching digital traces to them. For example, Spyn [39] allowed people to leave digital traces, such as audio/visual media and geographic data, on fabric. Similarly, Broken Probes [20] and Chiocciola [15] used material traces, such as cracks, as mediums for connecting digital traces. As was done in previous work, we tried to exploit the advantage of the sentimental value of digital and material traces. The main difference between our study and prior research is that our approach is not about attaching digital traces but about transforming digital traces into material traces on products. Using this approach, we explored the possibility of personalizing a product as a self-expressive means.

Product Personalization from the Perspective of Product Life Cycle

The product life cycle comprises three stages: manufacture, use, and disposal [1,48]. The manufacture stage involves producing new products. The product use stage is when products provide services to users and when users interact with the products. The disposal stage describes the process of discarding or recycling the product. Most product personalization to date has been largely focused on the manufacture stage. The central research issues with respect to this stage include how to make an object with various materials and mechanisms [28,36] and how to make effective use of resources [27,40].

Unlike previous studies, we focus on personalization at the product use stage to enhance a product's symbolic meaning about the users and their experiences with a product. The main reason is that the product use stage is when users have the most active interactions with products and spend the longest time making histories with their products. Also, according to previous research on emotional durability and product attachment, the gracefully aging surface of a product, narratives with a product, and histories with a product can become salient factors for giving a product symbolic meanings [12,30,35,46]. These cases illustrate the potential for an alternative personalization approach that grows traces on product in a way that allows users to enrich the symbolic meanings of a product.

DESIGN EXPLORATION

We exploit the concept of patinas as an alternative product personalization, focusing on the product use stage and symbolic meanings. In the following sections, we explain how patinas' characteristics add value to objects and the rationale for patina-inspired personalization.

Values and Characteristics of Patinas

The word *patina* refers to a thin layer that forms on the surface of stone, metal, or wooden furniture. In a broader sense, it refers to any accumulated material traces from normal use of an object. Artists and designers have deliberately added patinas as part of the original design for constructing aesthetic, historic, authentic properties [8,49]. In addition, several studies have mentioned symbolic values of material traces and patinas that deliver unique narratives regarding an object [15,20,35].

Literature on art and culture illustrates that the value of a product's patinas is deeply related to the distinct characteristics of patina generation [8,17]. First, the process of patina generation relies on product usage over time. Depending on how they are used, some products may gather extensive patinas within a short period of time, and others may gather patinas more slowly.

Second, a patina is mainly determined by how, when, or where the product is used. The patina could be unintentionally generated by users' physical touch while the product is used. A person may also leave an intentional patina to mark a special moment during a product's usage (e.g., travel labels on a suitcase or dog-eared pages in a book). In these cases, patinas contain the information about the history of a product's use.

Lastly, the expression of a patina is abstract and emerges gradually. A patina is primarily valued for its aesthetic expression. Also, due to its abstract nature, a patina provides information about past product usage in ambiguous ways. The abstract and subtle shape of a patina can be means of reflecting users' pasts.

Some applications of graphical interfaces in the HCI area have metaphorically exploited a patina to provide information about user history [18,19,42]. However, few ways have been studied for improving the quality of physical objects through product personalization enriched by patinas. Although the Patina Engraver system showed the potential for utilizing the characteristics of patinas to visualize activity data on wearable devices, the users' involvement in selecting traces and designing was limited [26]. In particular, our work differs from previous research in that we tried to suggest a new way of product personalization and support users' modifications of everyday products based on traces of product use.

Design Considerations for Patina-inspired Personalization

Based on review of existing product personalization systems and understanding of how patinas' characteristics add value to objects, we derived the following design considerations for patina-inspired personalization. These considerations are related to timing, source, expression and process of product personalization.

Supporting Progressive Modifications during Product Usage

In the natural environment, patinas are accumulated over several physical touches, becoming clearer over time. The progressive change gives a product historical value. Inspired by this process, we conceived a personalization system that progressively modifies a product during long-term product use. Thus, rather than manufacturing a new object or completing personalization at once, patina-inspired personalization would enable progressive and repetitive modifications of the same product. Through repetitive operations, users would be able to gradually personalize the product by modifying parts of it.

Utilizing Digital Traces of Product Use as a Source of Personalization

Though several personalization systems have been improved and have become accessible even to lay users, most systems still require design capabilities from planning to production. To support general users' personalization with symbolic meanings, we were inspired by the fact that patinas are naturally generated from past experiences, which can become a source of design. Recognizing that patinas are mainly caused by product use, we tried to create a personalization system that utilizes digital traces: histories of product use that can be digitally recorded. Of the many types of digital traces, we focused on the data that may jog a user' memories about his/her past experiences. According to Doménique et al.'s study, during everyday life, people rely on ordinary physical objects for the retrieval of memories, and people think of locations and activities associated with such objects [13]. Thus, we decided to use digital traces that can remind users of how, when, and where a product was used as a source of personalization.

Generating Abstract but Aesthetic Traces on a Product

Traditionally, designers have valued patinas for their abstract but aesthetic expressions. Moreover, the abstract shapes of patinas provide subtle information about the past [8,49]. Considering the advantages of patinas' expressions, we conceived a personalization system that engraves abstract and aesthetic material traces on a product based on digital traces. Instead of using numbers or letters, we tried to generate material traces that were arranged in geometrical patterns through a computational design. In particular, by mapping a user's digital traces through predefined pattern-generation algorithms, we expected that the material traces would be engraved like patterns resembling those that might be seen on a fashionable product.

Simplifying a Personalization Process

Natural patinas are accumulated smoothly in the trajectory of product usage. Even when users deliberately make material traces on a product, the process is typically short and does not disturb the original product usage. However, since most current personalization systems require several pieces of equipment and software programs for modeling and construction, these systems may disturb users' experiences with the product and make it difficult to personalize products. To embed a personalization system smoothly within the context of product usage, it might be important to simplify the operation process of personalization. For this reason, we conceived a system that covers an entire process from design to construction. We sought to modify a product quickly and easily by integrating the design and construction parts in a single system. Since the system would be installed in a context in which the product would be used, we had to consider a form factor that harmonized with the product's usage environment.

TRACE-MARKER

To explore the impact and possibility of patina-inspired personalization, we developed Trace-Marker, a laser-based personalization system that supports the accumulation of aesthetic patterns on bicycle bags based on users' riding histories (Figure 1). Based on design considerations, the hardware part was designed for supporting progressive modifications during the product use stage. We also simplified the operation process by integrating the interface for design and the construction part. Regarding software, we digitally recorded bicycling histories and utilized such histories as sources of product personalization.

Figure 1. Trace-Marker

Design Context

To concretize the design considerations regarding and to explore the possibilities of patina-inspired personalization, we developed Trace-Marker to fit the context of bicycling. The first reason we focused on bicycling is that a bicycle and bicycling accessories are now regarded as lifestyle accessories—expressions of an individual. Accordingly, it is common to see heavily customized bicycles with different seats or handle bar designs as examples. Bicycle accessories, such as bags, helmets, and gloves, have become popular among enthusiasts, who often spend more on clothing and fixtures than they do on bicycles. Regarding such customers' needs, we concluded that the bicycling context would be appropriate for applying patina-inspired personalization and studying impacts on symbolic meanings related to personal identity, aesthetics, and social communication. The second reason we focused on bicycling is that many riders frequently use tracking applications, such as Strava [52], MapMyRide [53], and MyTracks [54], that record riding history. These applications all record a GPS-based route, cycling duration, distance, pace, and calories burned. Such digital traces could work with a patina-inspired personalization system for modifying bicycle accessories.

Considering riders' desire for self-expression and their practice of recording their histories, we tried to develop a personalization system for bicycle accessories, particularly bicycle bags. Inspired by travelers' delight at collecting immigration stamps on their passports or stamps from tourist sites, our personalization system was made to modify a bicycle bag by engraving aesthetic patterns on it.

System Overview & Walkthrough

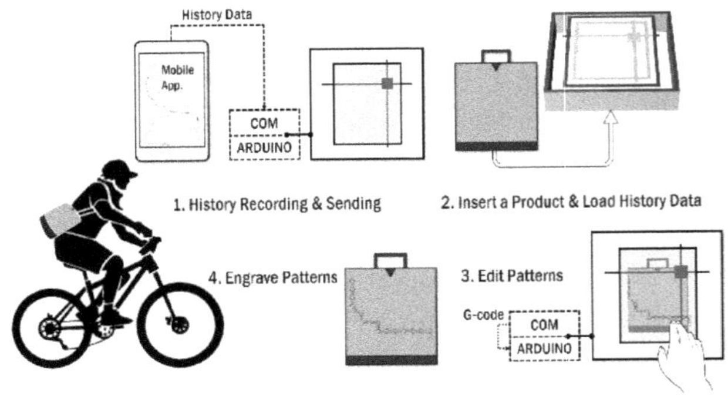

Figure 2. Trace-Marker System Walkthrough

To enable progressive personalization of bicycle accessories based on riding history, users' history data are periodically uploaded from users' mobile phone applications and saved to the local computer for Trace-Marker (Figure 2). To engrave a pattern, a user inserts the bag or other product in the drawer of Trace-Marker. The user logs into the system, which loads his/her riding histories and analyzes them to generate a visual pattern. In the interface, the user edits and places the pattern while looking through the interactive transparent display. Finally, the system engraves the pattern on the product placed in the drawer.

This system is distinct from existing fabrication systems, because it aims to integrate the whole user experience of retrieving history from the tracking application, direct visual editing on a product, and live tracing.

Hardware Implementation

To implement the hardware for Trace-Marker, we considered how to support progressive modification during product usage and how to simplify the personalization process in the context of product use. Thus, the hardware was designed to include three layers of parts (Figure 3): a system interface layer (consisting of a transparent display and a touch panel), a laser plotter, and a drawer. The height of Trace-Marker was set at waist-level (700 mm) so that adult users could control the interface from a standing position. We made the hardware of Trace-Marker similar to other home furniture, aiming for a situation in which this system would be installed in a public space or a home environment.

The bottom part of Trace-Marker was designed as a drawer so that users could engrave on a variety of everyday objects with different heights, such as bicycle bags, caps or mobile

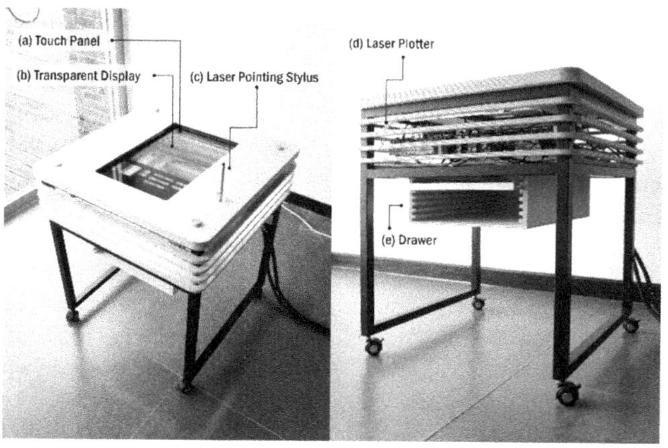

Figure 3. Trace-Marker Hardware: (a) Touch Panel, (b) Transparent Display, (c) Stylus, (d) Laser Plotter, (e) Drawer

phones. To keep a consistent distance from the laser diode, the drawer can be inserted at different heights.

The top of Trace-Marker is made of a transparent display and a touch panel. The see-through interface supports users' progressive designs and the construction process. Users can generate visual patterns for trace engraving while watching modeled patterns displayed above the real product. We added a laser-stylus pen for touch input and to guide the position of the pattern that is to be plotted on the bag.

When a user executes a laser engraving command in the interface, a laser plotter under the interface layer shoots a 405 nm blue-violet laser beam. The maximum work area is about 330 mm by 330 mm, and accuracy is 0.1 mm. The intensity of the laser was adjusted to be safe and suitable for engraving fabrics or leathers. The users were required to wear safety glasses while using the laser.

In addition, we made bicycle bags out of leather. After exploring several materials, we chose natural leather because the engraved lines were more aesthetic than they were for other materials, such as artificial fabrics. The bag's size was made to be suitable for carrying a few bicycle items, such as a water bottle and a wallet.

Software Implementation

While implementing the system's software in the Java environment, we mainly considered how to utilize the digital trace of product use (e.g., bicycling history data) as a source of design so as to transform that digital trace into abstract but aesthetic patterns.

Visual Pattern Design

To generate a visual pattern, we used history data from My Tracks or Strava. These applications generated history data in a format such as GPX (a data format used for GPS navigation devices) or CSV (comma-separated values) that suited our system. Trace-Marker automatically transformed the users' riding histories onto abstract patterns by mapping each data type to predefined pattern-generation templates. The method for generating visual patterns was decided through several phases of exploration.

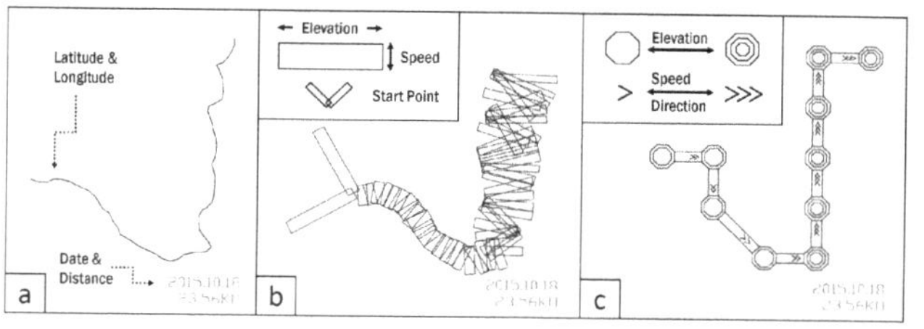

Figure 4. Pattern Styles: (a) Basic Line, (b) Ribbon Style, (c) Metro Style

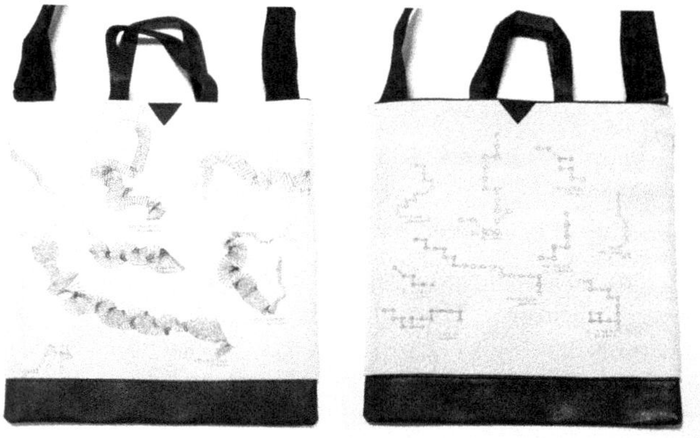

Figure 5. Examples of Personalized Bags with Ribbon Style and Metro Style

First, we selected (i) the types of riding history data that would be sources for pattern generation. Of the diverse types of riding logs, we chose latitude, longitude, elevation, speed, date, and total distance—the types of information that people generally want to know when using tracking systems. Next, we explored (ii) the overall styles and shapes of the patterns by mapping each set of riding data types onto certain parts of a pattern. Specifically, latitude and longitude were mapped to form a pattern's skeleton. Other types of history data were mapped differently to improve the aesthetics of a pattern style. We also considered (iii) the time required for engraving a pattern. Considering the context of riding, only the vector mode of laser engraving was used; this mode takes a considerably shorter time to engrave than the raster mode does. During our study, the pattern engraving process took roughly between five and twenty minutes. We also evaluated noticeability, the possible number of modifications, and visual aesthetics when deciding on the pattern types.

Finally, the system included two styles of visual patterns (Figures 4 and 5): ribbon and metro. In both styles, latitude and longitude data were used to draw an overall skeleton of a pattern. In the ribbon style, elevation and speed were mapped to the width and height of a rectangle. In the metro style, the overall shape was simplified using nodes and connected lines. As elevation increased, more circles were added at each node. To express the moving speed and direction, arrows were added in the connection lines. Lastly, to provide identity information for the pattern, total distance and date numbers were included in both styles.

Interface

In the interface, five menus were implemented: 1) Load a personal bicycling history, 2) Select a visual style, 3) Edit a pattern, 4) Transform (Change a pattern's position and size), and 5) Engrave (Figure 6).

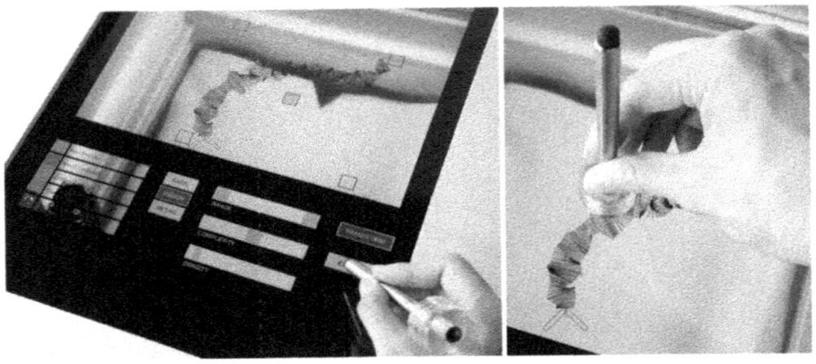

Figure 6. Interface: Selecting Menus (Left), Estimating the Position of Patterns with the Laser Pointing Stylus (Right)

To start personalization, users selected and loaded their bicycling histories. Then, the GPS route from the data was drawn on the display. Users selected a visual style based on the GPS route and other history data. In the Edit menu, users cropped the route and adjusted the complexity and density of the pattern. Size and position buttons allowed users to change the size and position of a pattern. This was done while viewing the pattern on the bag through the transparent display. The laser pointing stylus could be used to check the plotting position of a pattern on the bag. When the engraving process was executed, the system sent G-codes to the laser plotter, which was controlled by an Arduino board. According to the user-defined pattern, the plotter controlled the stepper motors and the laser diode.

FIELD TRIAL

We conducted a field study to understand not only the usability of the patina-inspired personalization system but also the impacts of the system on users' experiences. Specifically, we expected to determine how patina-inspired personalization would be embedded in the context of product use. We also wanted to find out how patina-inspired personalization could be used for attaching participants' personal meanings to the personalized products.

For that, we expected that users would need a certain amount of time to become accustomed to using the Trace-Marker system. Thus, we had 10 participants use Trace-Marker for three weeks. The sample size and the length of the field trial were determined from a previous study [4] that discussed field trial methods. Given the exploratory nature of our design work, we focused on gathering a rich set of opinions (rather than on quantitative findings) and aimed to encourage reflective thinking about the personalization approach and personalized products.

Participants

We recruited 10 participants (6 male and 4 female, ages ranging from 19 to 29 years, M = 25.1, SD = 3.4) who rode a bicycle regularly and who were interested in DIY culture. Their past experiences in tracking their bicycling were also considered in the recruitment phase. To reduce the novelty of activity logging itself, only people who had previous experience recording some sort of physical activity using mobile applications (e.g., Strava, or MyTracks) or other relevant devices (e.g., Garmin Edge [55]) were selected. Throughout the paper we refer to each participant using gender and the week of the interview session (e.g., M5, week 3). All participants periodically rode a bicycle for exercise, as a hobby or to commute. Five of the participants partook in bicycle clubs and rode for long distances every week (more than 100 kilometers): M1, M2, M3, M6, and F3. In addition, four participants (M2, M5, M6, and F3) had experience customizing their bicycles.

Method

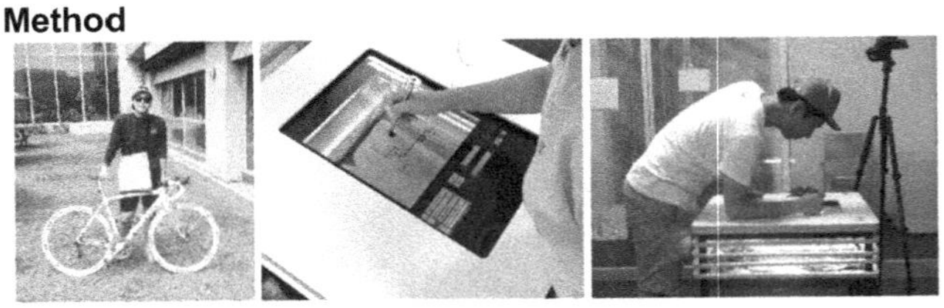

Figure 7. Example Participant (M3) & Personalization Task

During the field trial, one preliminary interview session and three main sessions—including an interview and a personalization process—were conducted. To minimize the participants' burden, Trace-Marker was installed in a building that participants could reach within 10 minutes by foot (Figure 7). The interview sessions were conducted right after using the system.

The preliminary interview session included questions related to the participants' biographies, their normal practices while riding a bicycle, and their views of activity tracking. In this session, we provided a bicycle bag and asked participants to check on or set up their cycling applications. We explained how to export their riding history data periodically to the local computer for use with Trace-Marker.

Once per week for three weeks, the participants visited us to use Trace-Marker and to have an hour-long interview session. Before each interview, they could engrave one or two patterns. During each interview, we asked questions about the impact that the patina-inspired personalization had on their experiences and the functional, emotional, and symbolic aspects of Trace-Marker and the modified bags. Additionally, in the 3rd week, we also asked about the possibility of applying patina-inspired personalization in diverse products and service contexts after conducting a design workshop with the participants.

Data Collection and Analysis Method

We analyzed the results based on observations of participants' use of the system and on the weekly interviews. The weekly photos of participants' bicycle bags and their riding histories were used to identify the detailed situations that the users mentioned in their interviews. A total of 20 hours of interviews were audio-recorded and transcribed. Our research team categorized the data from the interview transcriptions and contextual data, including bicycling data and photos of the participants' bags, through iterative analytic induction. During the analysis, we considered novelty effects and tried to find unexpected uses [4].

FINDINGS

The participants positively received the idea of personalizing bicycle bags using their bicycling histories. Though most participants were concerned that they would need professional design knowledge before using the system, all participants were able to easily select history data, edit a visual pattern, and place the pattern as they wanted, even in the 1st week. Three participants (M2, M6, and F3) who had previous experience using professional fabrication systems mentioned that the Trace-Marker was less costly and burdensome than the existing fabrication systems which require separate design software and fabrication equipment. Participants noted that the interface in which they could design patterns above real bags was useful to predict the outcome so that they could be assured of their designs: *"Unlike existing fabrication systems, this system supports design right over real objec*ts, so *I could feel confident of my design decision"* (M2, week 2). In addition, participants enjoyed watching the process of personalization. Overall, the process of designing a pattern for a bag took less than five minutes. Depending on the size and density of the pattern, engraving took five to twenty minutes. Due to the irregular surface height of the bags, the patterns were engraved with different degrees of vividness.

In the following section, we explain how Trace-Marker was used for personalizing bicycle bags over three weeks and how the system was embedded in the context of bicycle riders while attaching personal meanings to the bicycle bags.

Progressive Personalization for Expressing Personal Stories and Identities

During the field study, we observed that participants' bicycle bags became varied after three to five uses of the system (Figure 8). According to participants' riding histories and aesthetic preferences, all participants' bags became visually distinguishable by the last week. We found out that from the 1st personalization, participants established criteria about what kinds of patterns would be accumulated and how they would place patterns on the bag. Through the process of accumulating patterns, participants could gradually add personal stories and identities about bicycling to their bags.

Engraving a Pattern like Keeping a Diary

It was common for our participants to select history data that represented their daily cycling lifestyle. For example, M4 and F2, who ride bicycles for transportation, mentioned that they selected histories that were related to their frequently visited commuting routes: *"I want to use this system like a diary, so I engraved with the history that shows my commute from my home to my office or from my home to frequently visited markets etc."* (M4, week 2). Sometimes, participants chose a history that recorded an unexpected or unusual event. *"One day, I fell off my bicycle and chafed my knee, and visited a hospital. This pattern exactly shows the story. This crumpled part is when I got injured"* (M2, week 1).

During the participants' three to five times using Trace-Marker, some tried to build a single big pattern that showed a personally meaningful story by combining individual patterns. They arranged each pattern like the pieces of a puzzle. For example, F2 tried to place patterns related to a frequently visited location, making a map over her bag: *"I wanted to complete a map that shows my daily routine with my bicycle. At the center of my bag, I placed this pattern that shows the way from my home to my office, and the right pattern is the way to my favorite restaurant"* (F2, week 3). In this way, she tried to modify her bag to represent her life.

Engraving a Pattern to Show Off

Some participants (M1, M2, M3, M5, and M6) who ride mainly as a hobby or exercise activity selected histories that represented challenges and accomplishments. Thus, they tried to engrave patterns that showed how fast and how far they had ridden or how high they had climbed: *"I rode a mountain bike last week, which was really tough. I wanted to engrave this ribbon pattern since it shows the elevation clearly"* (M5, week 1), *"This week I tried to ride at the speed of 30 kilometers per hour, which is difficult for amateur riders. This history is chosen to show off my progress"* (M6, week 1). Throughout several pattern engravings, the participants tried to make bags that represented their identities as avid cyclists: *"This week, I rode much farther*

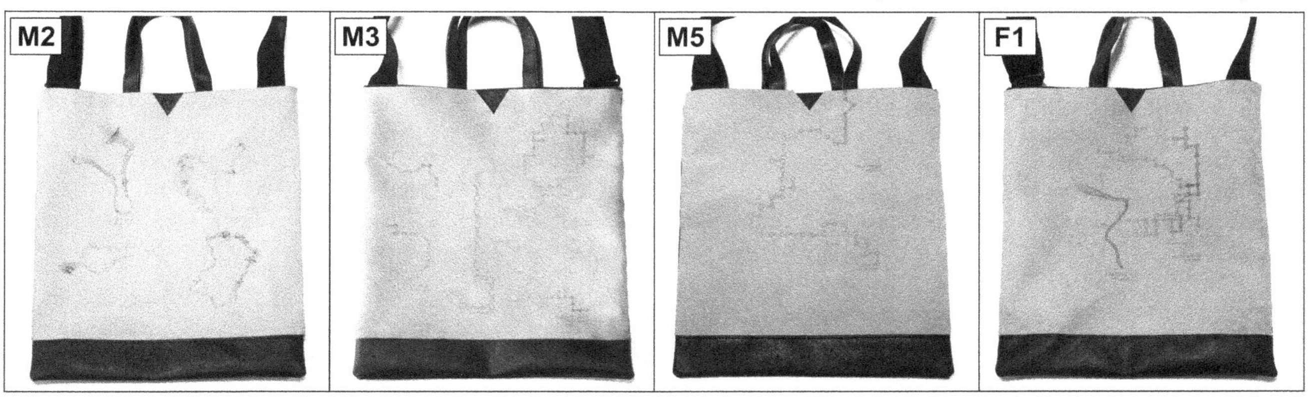

Figure 8. Participants' Bicycle Bags after 3 - 5 Times of Pattern Engraving

than usual, so I placed this pattern above the pattern based on my usual riding. Like this, this bag will show how hard I ride" (M5, week 2). The participants mentioned that their bags' patterns felt like rewards.

Likewise, we found that most participants tried to place each pattern so that the accumulated patterns would represent their bicycling experience and symbolize their identities and lifestyles. At the same time, because the patterns might be shown to others, participants considered aesthetics and harmony with the patterns previously engraved on the bag.

Embracing Personalization as Part of Product Experience

We investigated whether Trace-Marker was smoothly embedded in the context of bicycle riders. During the study, we found that the system led participants reflect on their past experience and even affected their bicycling habits.

Stimulating Reflection on Past Experiences

In general, participants became curious about the patterns and tried to associate the patinas with their past experiences after engraving a new pattern. Participants mentioned that the mobile application was suitable for checking the accuracy of numerical values, such as average speed or calories burned. On the other hand, the abstract aspect of the patina-like patterns caused participants to interpret and question the shape of the patterns and their past experiences: *"(While looking at the engraved pattern) I think this part shows when I climbed up the hill. That's why the ribbon is getting wider"* (M5, week 1). In this way, we observed that Trace-Marker stimulated reflection and enabled past experiences to be seen from unusual perspectives.

Influencing on Users' Behaviors

Trace-Marker was developed to progressively modify bicycle bags based on past histories of bicycling. While we expected that only past bicycle usage would influence the personalization of the bags, we observed that the system also influenced how the participants used their bicycles.

First, participants tried to record riding histories regularly because they wanted to accumulate patterns that showed their general lives or special events. For instance, F4 was concerned that if she did not record her history constantly, the patina pattern would be irrelevant to her general lifestyle: *"Usually I do not use tracking applications, but I tried to record my riding experience regularly because it is better to make patterns which correspond to me"* (F4, week 2). Moreover, participants were motivated to take a different route or to increase the frequency of cycling to engrave more diverse and more aesthetic patterns on the bags: *"Usually I take a linear route from home to the park, but this week I rode in a circular route for making a circular and aesthetic pattern"* (M1, week 2); *"Since a bicycle is just transportation for me, I do not usually go to special places, but, to make diverse shapes of patterns, I went home another way"* (F1, week 3). In this way, participants embraced the personalization process as a part of their bicycling and even changed their ways of riding.

Strengthening the Emotional Bond with Products

Distinct from other fabrication research, which mainly reports excitement regarding custom products, our study revealed the impact of patina-inspired personalization on emotional bonds with products. Though participants first felt interests in using the personalization process itself, their initial interest faded after the 1st week. Nevertheless, their emotional bonds with their bags and patterns were strengthened in the following weeks. Comparing the participants' perceptions of the bicycle bag during the first week and the last week (after modifying the bag several times), we observed that their emotional bonds with the bags became stronger: *"Though other participants' bags may look nicer, I will prefer my bag. It is like a part of me."*(M3, week 3). During the interviews, participants described two reasons for forming such emotional bonds.

Users' Involvement in Personalizing a Product

Participants said that their involvement in the design process made their bicycle bags more meaningful. They felt engaged in the process of selecting histories and personalizing their bags with new patterns: *"Even if I assemble IKEA furniture, it will end up with just like others' furniture. Though I do not make a product, this system supports my design, which leads to more unique products"* (M4, week 3).

Involvement in making a product gives a person a greater stake in it and a deeper connection with it [21]. In our study, though the main function of Trace-Marker was not to create a new product, participants felt as if they were directly involved in creating one-of-a-kind products because the planning a pattern and modifying a bag required effort and personal decisions: *"If I build my house, I will just make a blueprint about my house rather than piling up bricks. This system is close to making a blueprint of a product. Making all parts of a product costs too much."* (M3, week 3).

Formation of Memories Anchored in a Product Itself

Furthermore, most participants felt that the uniqueness of each bag was enhanced by the fact that the accumulated patterns were based on their past experiences: "*Rather than just selecting predefined patterns, these patterns are generated from my one of a kind experience. It would be impossible to generate the same patterns"* (M4, week 3). In addition to this uniqueness, during the last week of the field study, participants said that their bags reminded them of their lives or their efforts in bicycling. They liked that material traces in the bag would last longer than the digital traces from mobile applications. They also mentioned that the permanently engraved patterns, similar to natural patinas, enhanced the historical value of their bags: *"Since the patterns on my bag had changed along with my experiences, it feels like a growth ring"* (F1, week 2).

According to Belk's concept of the *extended self*, external objects may be viewed as part of oneself, when the objects serve as reminders and confirmers of one's identity [2]. Because the bag could become a convenient means of viewing oneself, it could have a strong symbolic meaning that would not be replaced by other bags. In general, product-related memories develop independently from a product's design and manufacture and are thus difficult for designers to influence [29]. However, in this study we observed the possibility of patina-inspired personalization for embedding users' memories about their meaningful experience into a product.

DISCUSSION

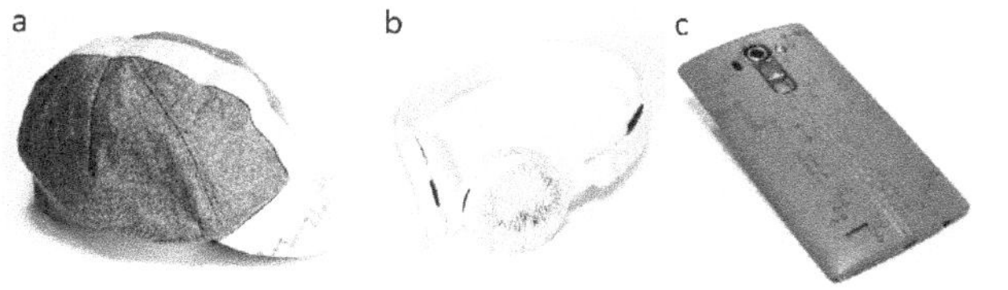

Figure 9. Using Patina-inspired Personalization for Other Products: (a) Cycling Hat, (b) Headphones, (c) Smart Phone

In our study, we found that product personalization based on history of bicycle journey helped participants to add personal stories and identities to their bags. Participants embraced the personalization process as part of their product use. This result implies that patina-inspired personalization has potential as alternative design approach for enhancing the symbolic meanings of a product as a self-expressive possession. We think that the patina-inspired personalization would also be beneficial and applicable to IT products and services. Though we used a mobile application for recording users' digital traces, today, many physical products are being used together with integrated product-service systems (e.g., Nike+ & Fuel Band); or they can also independently collect, process, and produce information about users' experiences. At the same time, their aesthetic and symbolic qualities as fashion items are essential. Accordingly, it would be possible to detect memorable events while using product-service systems to improve products' aesthetic and meaningful aspects.

In the following, we discuss how patina-inspired personalization can be applied in wider contexts and domains. In the design workshop conducted during the last week of the field study, we asked participants to select one of their possessions and to design a pattern on that possession by mapping history-related data, as Trace-Marker did. Though Trace-Marker was applied for modifying bicycle bags, participants desired to use the system on their bicycles and other items such as a cycling cap, a smart phone, a skateboard, shoes or a pair of headphones (Figure 9). Combining the results of field study and the design workshop, we discuss implications to improve the use of patina-inspired personalization.

Design Implications for Patina-inspired Personalization

Tailoring Digital Traces for Enhancing Symbolic Meanings

The patina-inspired personalization utilizes digital traces from users' product-related experiences to make material traces arranged like a pattern. To enhance the symbolic meaning about the users, it is important to consider the association among the type of digital traces and the users' experiences with their products. For instance, M1 mentioned that for headphones, history data about a frequently played song or a favorite genre or artist would be proper for making patterns. M6 said that he wanted to modify skateboards based on history data related to his skill progress: *"When I ride my skateboard, the location or speed is not important. I want to accumulate patterns that show the techniques that I perform, such as flips, jumps and the level of tricks"* (M6, week 3). In this way, it is necessary for designers to select proper types of digital traces and tailor them to symbolize users' unique and important experiences with the products. It would also be possible to help users freely select and edit digital traces to highlight some of their histories.

Balancing Automation and User Involvement

As participants became adapted to our system during three weeks, they expressed different desires about the system's automation and user involvement. For example, M5 and F1, who had little experience in design, mentioned that they hesitated to execute engravings because of uncertainty about their knowledge of aesthetics. On the other hand, M6 and F3, who had more experience in designing and DIY practices, expressed a desire for detailed involvement. They wanted to change the shape of the patterns and map certain data to a specific part of a pattern.

In general, commercial product personalization services allow people to create a product by selecting components from a predefined set of options. Norman said that these services are better at making personalization easy, but they do not directly guarantee emotional bonding [33]. That is mainly because the services require little physical or mental effort. Meanwhile, more effortful product personalization might have a downside as well. As the effort invested increases, so does the perceived complexity of the task and, consequently, the possibility that people become confused [7].

Therefore, users with different levels of proficiency could be offered separate interfaces in patina-inspired personalization. For novice users, the system could automatically generate a pattern and place it according to predefined templates. It might also provide examples or recommendations about how the patterns could be aesthetically placed. For more experienced users, a parameter-based interface [34] could allow them to directly define and modify details of the patterns and the modification mechanism. With a high level of involvement, these users might be able to make more personalized products that could become clear memory cues.

Permanent or Erasable Traces

Our personalization system uses a laser diode to make unmodifiable material traces. In contrast to digital traces in mobile applications, the permanently engraved traces improved the historical value of the participants' bags. However, in the current system, one concern is the limited number of possible engravings that can be made on the surface of a given product. When we asked about a situation in which the bag would be full of patterns, most participants said that they would want to replace the front cover of the bag with a new cover and keep the old one to serve as a gift or a souvenir.

As an alternative solution, we expect that it will be possible to increase the dimensions of a pattern expression by applying additive or subtractive fabrication mechanisms. Though Trace-Marker generated single-colored patterns, if gradations and variations of color become possible in the system, more patterns could be accumulated, allowing overlapped patterns to maintain their own expressions. Erasable materials could also be applied to the patina-inspired personalization for long-term use and to protect against design mistakes, as was tried with the Shader Printer [41]. In addition to the problem of the limited number of engravings, participants mentioned their discomfort when making design mistakes. During design and construction activities, it is common to experience trial and error. Thus, though the interface of Trace-Marker helped to predict how the fabrication would look, erasable materials might help the users of patina-inspired personalization systems. Since there permanent and erasable traces might have different values, the mechanisms of patina-inspired personalization should be selected based on users' needs and the context of the product's use.

Technical Improvements

Calibrating Personalization Mechanism

To support the progressive personalization of diverse products including 3D objects, the patina-inspired personalization system could be developed to detect the dimensions and materials of a product. During the field trial, we found that the forms of the participants' bicycle bags changed through long-term usage; this inconsistency caused different engraving effects. The intensity of the laser diode also had to be adjusted according to the varying solidity of product materials. Thus, 3D scanning technology or other visual sensing technologies would be helpful to self-calibrate the fabrication mechanism after detecting the current status of the inserted products [11,40,44].

Improving a Parallax in the Interface Layer

In the current system, we used a transparent display and touch panel to simplify the design and construction processes. The advantage of such an interface was that participants could predict the outcome before executing construction of the product, thus creating certainty about the decision. However, the space between the image on the transparent display and the actual product (which was 200 mm) created a parallax and sometimes caused inaccurate engraving. Though participants moved their head to watch the interface and the bag vertically, their view from above the display did not match perfectly with the position of the bag. For this reason, participants had difficulty placing patterns in the desired positions. To solve this problem, it might be possible to automatically adjust the position of the patterns in the display by detecting the angle between users' eyes and the position of the products. Users might then be able to implement a more accurate design on the product.

Limitations and Future Work

In this research project, we conducted a field study for three weeks in a specific product context. As the system used a laser, it could not be installed freely in public due to safety issues. A longer "in the wild" study may show other impacts of patina-inspired personalization [4]. First, in such studies, it will be possible to investigate if personalization leads to long-term effects related to product attachment or emotional durability [5,12,29]. Although we studied the impacts on a symbolic meaning of a product, the symbolic meaning seems to be a particularly important factor influencing users' emotions and product attachment. Desmet argued that it may be more fruitful to establish a long-term emotional relationship between a product and a consumer after a purchase situation [9]. In this respect, it will be beneficial to study whether patina-inspired personalization may enable a continued close relationship between a product and a user over an extended period of time. Though we observed that participants felt close to their products during the field study, a longer study would be helpful to investigate other issues, such as whether the users postpone disposal of products and how patina-endowed objects may be valued beyond the first owner. Second, an "in the wild" study setting may be helpful to observe which other product contexts are applicable and how the system can be used to create patinas for events other than bicycling.

CONCLUSION

Our motivation for conducting this study was to suggest product personalization in a way that enriches a symbolic meaning of a product as a self-expressive means. Thus, in this paper, we presented the concept of patina-inspired personalization through accumulated traces of product use. Based on an understanding of how patinas' characteristics add value to objects, we derived the design considerations for patina-inspired personalization related to the timing, source, expression, and personalization process. Then, we developed Trace-Marker, which was specialized in the bicycling context, to investigate the impacts of patina-inspired personalization. With the deployment of this system, we found that the process of accumulating patina-like traces helped participants add personal stories and identities to their bags. Also, the use of Trace-Marker stimulated reflection and enabled past experiences to be seen from unusual perspectives. Participants' emotional bonds with the bags also became stronger. We expect this research to inspire diverse product personalization services and general fashion and product designs.

ACKNOWLEDGMENTS

This work was supported by Institute for Information & communications Technology Promotion (IITP) Grant funded by the Korea government (MSIP) (No.10041313, UX-oriented Mobile SW Platform) and the National Research Foundation of Korea Grant funded by the Korean Government (NRF-2014S1A5A2A01010939).

REFERENCE

1. Leo Alting. 1995. Life Cycle Engineering and Design. *CIRP Annals - Manufacturing Technology* 44, 2: 569–580. http://doi.org/10.1016/S0007-8506(07)60504-6
2. Russell W. Belk. 1988. Possessions and the Extended Self. *Journal of Consumer Research* 15, 2: 139–168. http://doi.org/10.1086/209154
3. Jan Blom. 2000. Personalization: A Taxonomy. *CHI '00 Extended Abstracts on Human Factors in Computing Systems*, ACM, 313–314. http://doi.org/10.1145/633292.633483
4. Barry Brown, Stuart Reeves, and Scott Sherwood. 2011. Into the wild: Challenges and opportunities for field trial methods. *Proceedings of the SIGCHI Conference on Human Factors in Computing Systems - CHI'11*, ACM Press, 1657–1666. http://doi.org/10.1145/1978942.1979185
5. Jonathan Chapman. 2009. Design for (Emotional) Durability. *Design Issues* 25, 4: 29–35. http://doi.org/10.1162/desi.2009.25.4.29
6. Nathan Crilly, James Moultrie, and P.John Clarkson. 2004. Seeing things: consumer response to the visual domain in product design. *Design Studies* 25, 6: 547–577. http://doi.org/10.1016/j.destud.2004.03.001
7. Benedict G.C. Dellaert and Stefan Stremersch. 2005. Marketing Mass-Customized Products: Striking a Balance Between Utility and Complexity. *Journal of Marketing Research* 42, 2: 219–227. http://doi.org/10.1509/jmkr.42.2.219.62293
8. C. DeSilvey. 2006. Observed Decay: Telling Stories with Mutable Things. *Journal of Material Culture* 11, 3: 318–338. http://doi.org/10.1177/1359183506068808
9. Pieter Desmet. 2002. *Designing emotions*. Dissertation, Delft University of Technology, The Netherlands
10. Michael Erlhoff and Tim Marshall. 2008. *Design Dictionary: perspectives on Design Terminology*. http://doi.org/10.1007/978-3-7643-8140-0
11. Madeline Gannon, Tovi Grossman, and George Fitzmaurice. 2015. Tactum: A Skin-Centric Approach to Digital Design and Fabrication Madeline. *Proceedings of the SIGCHI Conference on Human Factors in Computing Systems - CHI '15*, ACM Press, 1779–1788. http://doi.org/10.1145/2702123.2702581
12. Silke Gegenbauer and Elaine M Huang. 2012. Inspiring the design of longer-lived electronics through an understanding of personal attachment. *Proceedings of the Designing Interactive Systems Conference on - DIS '12*, ACM Press, 635–644. http://doi.org/10.1145/2317956.2318052
13. Doménique van Gennip, Elise van den Hoven, and Panos Markopoulos. 2015. Things That Make Us Reminisce. *Proceedings of the SIGCHI Conference on Human Factors in Computing Systems - CHI '15*, ACM Press, 3443–3452. http://doi.org/10.1145/2702123.2702460
14. Neil Gershenfeld. 2007. *Fab: the coming revolution on your desktop--from personal computers to personal fabrication*. Basic Books.
15. Elisa Giaccardi, Elvin Karana, Holly Robbins, and Patrizia D'Olivo. 2014. Growing traces on objects of daily use. *Proceedings of the 2014 conference on Designing interactive systems - DIS '14*, ACM Press, 473–482. http://doi.org/10.1145/2598510.2602964
16. Josiena Gotzsch, Jean Jacques Chanaron, and David Birchall. 2006. Product development with a focus on attractive product expression: an analysis of case studies. *International Journal of Product Development* 3, 3/4: 467. http://doi.org/10.1504/IJPD.2006.009903
17. Hilkka Hiiop. 2008. *The Possibility of Patina in Contemporary Art or, Does the 'New Art' Have a Right to Get Old?* In Koht ja paik. Place and Location. Studies in Environmental Aesthetics and Semiotics VI Estonian Literary Museum, Estonian Academy of Arts, 153–165.
18. William C. Hill, James D. Hollan, Dave Wroblewski, and Tim McCandless. 1992. Edit wear and read wear. *Proceedings of the SIGCHI conference on Human factors in computing systems - CHI '92*, ACM Press, 3–9. http://doi.org/10.1145/142750.142751
19. Amy Hurst, Jennifer Mankoff, Anind K. Dey, and Scott E. Hudson. 2007. Dirty desktops: using a patina of magnetic mouse dust to make common interactor targets easier to select. *Proceedings of the 20th Symposium on User Interface Software and Technology - UIST '07*, ACM Press, 183–186. http://doi.org/10.1145/1294211.1294242
20. Miwa Ikemiya and Daniela K Rosner. 2014. Broken probes: toward the design of worn media. *Personal and Ubiquitous Computing* 18, 3: 671–683. http://doi.org/10.1007/s00779-013-0690-y
21. Tim Ingold. 2013. *Making: Anthropology, Archaeology, Art and Architecture*. Routledge.
22. Jennifer Jacobs and Leah Buechley. 2013. Codeable objects: Computational Design and Digital Fabrication for Novice Programmers. *Proceedings of the SIGCHI Conference on Human Factors in*

Computing Systems - CHI '13, ACM Press, 1589-1598. http://doi.org/10.1145/2470654.2466211

23. Rohit Ashok Khot, Larissa Hjorth, and Florian "Floyd" Mueller. 2014. Understanding physical activity through 3D printed material artifacts. *Proceedings of the SIGCHI Conference on Human Factors in Computing Systems - CHI '14*: 3835–3844. http://doi.org/10.1145/2556288.2557144

24. Sari Kujala. 2009. Product Symbolism in Designing for User Experience. *4th International Conference on Designing Pleasurable Products and Interface (DPPI 09)*, 176–186.

25. Stacey Kuznetsov and Eric Paulos. 2010. Rise of the expert amateur. *Proceedings of the 6th Nordic Conference on Human-Computer Interaction Extending Boundaries - NordiCHI '10*, ACM Press, 295. http://doi.org/10.1145/1868914.1868950

26. Moon-hwan Lee, Seijin Cha, and Tek-jin Nam. 2015. Patina Engraver: Visualizing Activity Logs as Patina in Fashionable Trackers. *Proceedings of the SIGCHI Conference on Human Factors in Computing Systems - CHI '15*, ACM Press, 1173–1182. http://doi.org/10.1145/2702123.2702213

27. Stefanie Mueller, Sangha Im, Serafima Gurevich, et al. 2014. WirePrint: 3D Printed Previews for Fast Prototyping Stefanie. *Proceedings of the 27th annual ACM symposium on User interface software and technology - UIST '14*, ACM Press, 273–280. http://doi.org/10.1145/2642918.2647359

28. Stefanie Mueller, Pedro Lopes, and Patrick Baudisch. 2012. Interactive construction: Interactive Fabrication of Functional Mechanical Devices. *Proceedings of the 25th annual ACM symposium on User interface software and technology - UIST '12*, ACM Press, 599-606. http://doi.org/10.1145/2380116.2380191

29. Ruth Mugge, Jan P.L. Schoormans, and Hendrik N.J. Schifferstein. 2005. Design Strategies to Postpone Consumers' Product Replacement: The Value of a Strong Person-Product Relationship. *The Design Journal* 8, 2: 38–48. http://doi.org/10.2752/146069205789331637

30. Ruth Mugge, Jan P.L. Schoormans, and Hendrik N.J. Schifferstein. 2009. Emotional bonding with personalised products. *Journal of Engineering Design* 20, 5: 467–476. http://doi.org/10.1080/09544820802698550

31. Bettina Nissen, John Bowers, Peter Wright, Jonathan Hook, and Christopher Newell. 2014. Volvelles, Domes and Wristbands: Embedding Digital Fabrication within a Visitor's Trajectory of Engagement. *Proceedings of the 2014 conference on Designing interactive systems - DIS '14*, ACM Press, 825–834. http://doi.org/10.1145/2598510.2598524

32. Bettina Nissen and John Bowers. 2015. Data-Things: Digital Fabrication Situated within Participatory Data Translation Activities. *Proceedings of the SIGCHI Conference on Human Factors in Computing Systems - CHI '15*, ACM Press, 2467–2476. http://doi.org/10.1145/2702123.2702245

33. Donald Norman. 2005. *Emotional design: why we love (or hate) everyday things*. Basic Books.

34. Piia Nurkka and Satu Jumisko-Pyykkö. 2014. Exploring online customization of a high involvement experience product. *Proceedings of the 26th Australian Computer-Human Interaction Conference on Designing Futures the Future of Design - OzCHI '14*, ACM Press, 505–514. http://doi.org/10.1145/2686612.2686692

35. William Odom, James Pierce, Erik Stolterman, and Eli Blevis. 2009. Understanding why we preserve some things and discard others in the context of interaction design. *Proceedings of the SIGCHI Conference on Human Factors in Computing Systems - CHI '09*, ACM Press, 1053–1062. http://doi.org/10.1145/1518701.1518862

36. Huaishu Peng, Jennifer Mankoff, Scott E. Hudson, and James McCann. 2015. A Layered Fabric 3D Printer for Soft Interactive Objects. *Proceedings of the SIGCHI Conference on Human Factors in Computing Systems - CHI '15*, ACM Press, 1789–1798. http://doi.org/10.1145/2702123.2702327

37. Irene Posch, Hideaki Ogawa, Christopher Lindinger, Roland Haring, and Horst Hörtner. 2010. Introducing the FabLab as interactive exhibition space. *Proceedings of the 9th International Conference on Interaction Design and Children*, 254–257. http://doi.org/10.1145/1810543.1810584

38. Guto Requena. *LOVE PROJECT*. Retrieved from http://goo.gl/o19avO

39. Daniela K. Rosner and Kimiko Ryokai. 2010. Spyn: Augmenting the Creative and Communicative Potential of Craft. *Proceedings of the SIGCHI Conference on Human Factors in Computing Systems - CHI '10*, ACM Press, 2407–2416. http://doi.org/10.1145/1753326.1753691

40. Daniel Saakes, Thomas Cambazard, Jun Mitani, and Takeo Igarashi. 2013. PacCAM: Material Capture and Interactive 2D Packing for Efficient Material Usage on CNC Cutting Machines. *Proceedings of the 26th annual ACM symposium on User interface software and technology - UIST '13*, ACM Press, 441–446. http://doi.org/10.1145/2501988.2501990

41. Daniel Saakes, Masahiko Inami, Takeo Igarashi, Naoya Koizumi, and Ramesh Raskar. 2012. Shader printer. *ACM SIGGRAPH 2012 Emerging Technologies on - SIGGRAPH '12*, ACM Press, 1–1. http://doi.org/10.1145/2343456.2343474

42. Ansel Arjan Schütte and Stephen a Benton. 1998. *Patina: Layering a history-of-use on digital objects*. MIT Media Laboratory.

43. Rita Shewbridge, Amy Hurst, and Shaun K. Kane. 2014. Everyday making: Identifying Future Uses for 3D Printing in the Home. *Proceedings of the 2014 conference on Designing interactive systems - DIS '14*, ACM Press, 815–824. http://doi.org/10.1145/2598510.2598544

44. Pitchaya Sitthi-Amorn, Javier E. Ramos, Yuwang Wangy, et al. 2015. MultiFab. *ACM Transactions on Graphics* 34, 4: 129:1–129:11. http://doi.org/10.1145/2766962

45. Joshua G. Tanenbaum, Amanda M Williams, Audrey Desjardins, and Karen Tanenbaum. 2013. Democratizing Technology: Pleasure, Utility and Expressiveness in DIY and Maker Practice. *Proceedings of the SIGCHI Conference on Human Factors in Computing Systems - CHI '13*, ACM Press, 2603–2612. http://doi.org/10.1145/2470654.2481360

46. Peter-Paul Verbeek. 2005. *What Things Do: Philosophical Reflections on Technology, Agency, and Design*. Penn State Press.

47. Christian Weichel, Manfred Lau, David Kim, Nicolas Villar, and Hans W. Gellersen. 2014. MixFab: A Mixed-Reality Environment for Personal Fabrication. *Proceedings of the SIGCHI Conference on Human Factors in Computing Systems - CHI '14*, ACM Press, 3855–3864. http://doi.org/10.1145/2556288.2557090

48. E Westkamper, L Alting, and G Arndt. 2000. Life Cycle Management and Assessment: Approaches and visions towards sustainable manufacturing. *CIRP Annals - Manufacturing Technology* 49, I: 501–522. http://doi.org/10.1016/S0007-8506(07)63453-2

49. Sílvio Mendes Zancheti, Flaviana Barreto Lira, Aline Figueirôa Silva, Anna Caroline Braga, Fabiana Gonçalves Gameiro, and Luciana Santiago Costa. 2006. The patina of the city. *City & Time* 2, 2: 11–22.

50. Silvio Mendes Sílvio Mendes Zancheti, Flaviana Barreto Lira, Aline De Figueirôa Silva, et al. 2006. The patina of the city. *City & Time* 2, 2: 11–22.

51. *Meshu*. Retrieved from http://meshu.io/

52. *Strava*. Retrieved from https://www.strava.com/

53. *MapMyRide*. Retrieved from http://www.mapmyride.com/

54. *MyTracks*. Retrieved from https://goo.gl/grG2i5

55. *Garmin Edge*. Retrieved from https://goo.gl/AcbpTM

What Can You Do? Studying Social-Agent Orientation and Agent Proactive Interactions with an Agent for Employees

Q. Vera Liao[1, 2] , Matthew Davis[2] , Werner Geyer[2] , Michael Muller[2] , N. Sadat Shami[3]
[1]University of Illinois at Urbana-Champaign, Champaign, IL, USA
[2]IBM Research, Cambridge, MA, USA
[3]IBM, Armonk, NY, USA
liao28@illinois.edu, { davismat, werner.geyer, michael_muller, sadat }@ us.ibm.com

ABSTRACT
Personal agent software is now in daily use in personal devices and in some organizational settings. While many advocate an *agent sociality* design paradigm that incorporates human-like features and social dialogues, it is unclear whether this is a good match for professionals who seek productivity instead of leisurely use. We conducted a 17-day field study of a prototype of a personal AI agent that helps employees find work-related information. Using log data, surveys, and interviews, we found individual differences in the preference for humanized social interactions (*social-agent orientation*), which led to different user needs and requirements for agent design. We also explored the effect of agent proactive interactions and found that they carried the risk of interruption, especially for users who were generally averse to interruptions at work. Further, we found that user differences in social-agent orientation and aversion to agent proactive interactions can be inferred from behavioral signals. Our results inform research into social agent design, proactive agent interaction, and personalization of AI agents.

Author Keywords
Agent; personalization; social-agent orientation; agent proactive interaction; enterprise personal agent.

ACM Classification Keywords
H.5.m. Information interfaces and presentation (e.g., HCI): Miscellaneous.

INTRODUCTION
Half a century after the introduction of first-generation chatbots like ELIZA [47], conversational agent interfaces have become increasingly common, as demonstrated by popular applications such as Apple Siri, Google Now and Microsoft Cortona. Many of these agents act as a new interface paradigm for *information-finding*, which incorporates or aims to replace the traditional interfaces such as search engines and recommender systems [12]. In addition to handling natural conversational interactions, scholars argue that the advantage of the agent inter-face lies in its social capabilities [1, 6, 7, 16, 21]. The social aspect of the agent interface not only provides potentially more engaging user experiences, but also engenders new technologies and designs that leverage a human metaphor and social context. For example, many systems utilize a "personal assistant" metaphor that makes users more receptive to functions such as reminders and task delegation [20, 31, 50]. Some embrace the opportunities for personalization by continuously learning about the user through social and relational conversations [16].

However, questions remain as to whether *agent sociality*, the incorporation of humanized social features, is favored for an information-finding application, the evaluation of which is often based on task performance such as accuracy and relevance of the information retrieved. The necessity of sociality may be especially questionable for users with high productivity versus leisurely needs, such as users in organizational settings. Moreover, we argue that there could be individual differences in preference for the level of agent sociality, potentially shaped by individual experiences with both the increasingly popular commercial agent applications and conventional information-finding applications such as search engines.

Another potential of the agent interface, as some argue [5, 24, 52], is to initiate proactive interactions in a manner similar to how a person initiates conversations. Proactive interactions may serve a variety of purposes such as recommending, reminding [52], facilitating learning [24], or persuading [5]. However, proactive interactions may risk interrupting users. Especially for employees with busy schedules and thus scarce attention resources, interruption by agent proactive interactions may result in low responsiveness, and even worse, undermine the overall experience with the agent system.

To explore these topics, we conducted a 17-day field study with a prototype of an enterprise personal agent that aims to help employees find work-related information in a large-size international company. We contribute to the human-agent interaction literature with a rare opportunity to study the social interactions and proactive interactions of agents

DIS 2016, June 04 - 08, 2016, Brisbane, QLD, Australia

ACM 978-1-4503-4031-1/16/06 $15.00
DOI: http://dx.doi.org/10.1145/2901790.2901842

in a real user context for an extended period. The majority of user studies for agent systems rely on lab experiments (e.g. [17, 24, 48, 49]). Such a controlled environment and limited timeframe may not allow full exploration of the social aspects of human-agent interactions. Meanwhile, a few field studies documented that users exhibit anthropomorphic behaviors such as asking "how are you?" as well as flaming behaviors such as typing random letters [25, 46], which are not often observed in lab studies. Therefore, we believed a field study would be more suitable for studying agent sociality. Also, we studied an agent specialized in the enterprise context. While there is a growing interest in developing personal agents for the work environments [1, 18, 20, 52], there have been few field studies for these systems to the best of our knowledge.

In this paper, we focused on studying individual differences in *social-agent orientation*, defined as the preference for humanized social interactions with an agent interface, such as having natural conversations and social dialogues. We explored how the individual differences led to differences in user requirements for agent system design and user behaviors that can be used to infer such orientation. By testing a variety of agent proactive interaction designs, including initiating social dialogue and crowdsourcing user questions, we also examined how users reacted to agent proactive interactions. Our study highlights that agent sociality designs are crucial for some users' experience, but may not fit others, at least for a performance-driven, non-leisure context. We also underline the importance of considering user aversion to unsolicited proactive interactions in a work environment, especially for users with busy schedules and frequent social contacts. In the following section, we introduce the background of the study before discussing hypotheses and research questions.

BACKGROUND

Agent Sociality

The development of AI agents could be dated back to the 1960s [47]. In the last two decades, we see an increasing number of studies focused on improving the design of agent systems. Among others, one direction is to introduce and improve the human-like attributes of agents. Earlier studies focused on the appearance of agents, including using humanized images [37], facial expression [11], gesture, and movement [27]. Recent research explored incorporating common human conversational and social strategies, including storytelling, reciprocal appreciation, being socially conscious, expressing empathy, humor, and many others [4, 8, 41]. Rich evidence suggests that *agent sociality* (the presence of human attributes in agent design) can elicit more cooperative behaviors from users, and lead to heightened engagement and more positive user opinions about the system. Emerging recently is the concept of the "relational agent", to build long-term relationships through continuous social interactions [6, 16]. Relational agent is considered to have great potential in many domains such as healthcare, education, and personal task management.

Another line of research on agent sociality explores personalization. Many explored the design of personalities built into agent dialogues [17, 26]. Studies consistently found that users favor agent personalities matching their own [17, 33, 45], or matching the task context (e.g., seriousness versus playfulness [22]). Another type of personalization aim to individualize the interactions such as by recognizing returning users or remembering information from previous conversations [21, 29]. Personalization was found to improve rapport, cooperation, and engagement with robots and agents.

Social-Agent Orientation

Many of the anthropomorphism efforts in agent designs recognize following the Computers are Social Actors (CASA) paradigm proposed by Nass et al. [34]. They demonstrated that social rules and expectations guiding human-human interaction can be applied to human-computer interaction, including using social categories and exhibiting social behaviors such as politeness and reciprocity. The CASA paradigm suggests users can behave *as if* computers warrant human considerations. This implies that computer interface should accommodate these social aspects of user needs, a point further addressed by scholars in the field of affective computing [40].

While agent interfaces are well suited to cater to social interactions, evidence suggests that there are individual differences in the tendency to exhibit social behaviors when interacting with agents or robots. Lee et al. find that, when interacting with a robot, some users appear to be more social, with more relational conversations, politeness, attention to the robot, and self-disclosure. Interestingly, such tendency can be predicted by whether the user greets the robot at the first encounter [28]. Ogan et al. looked at how children interact with a teachable agent, and found that some tend to use the pronouns "we" and "you" while others use "it," where the former predicts better learning outcomes [28]. These results point to possible individual differences in mental model of the systems, as repeatedly suggested by the observation that when interacting with a robot or an agent, some users report viewing it more as a social entity while others treat it as a technological entity [19].

By pointing out "individual differences in the strength of social response" as a future research agenda for CASA paradigm [34], Nass et al. suggested a key predictor could be the extent to which the users focus on the task and ignore task-irrelevant dimensions of the system. We consider it especially relevant to agent systems that target important *utilitarian needs*. In contrast to chatbots for hedonic use (e.g. ELIZA, Microsoft XiaoIce), the agent in our study was developed to address employees' serious information needs. So it is possible that some users would primarily seek to satisfy utilitarian needs. The co-presence of utilitarian and social needs is manifested in the observation that users' subjective evaluations of an agent, including satisfaction and likability, were often not strongly associated with objective measurements such as task completion and agent mistakes, and are impacted by the presentation and conversational design of the agent [42, 48].

Based on these previous findings, we studied *social-agent orientation*, defined as the individual preference for humanlike social interactions with agent interfaces. Partly, we are inspired by observing the large variances in the extent of sociality designs in information-finding agents, ranging from embodied conversational agents that attempt to faithfully mimic human [9], to popular personal assistant systems that work solely with a text or voice input window and little anthropomorphic conversations (e.g., Google Now). With these systems becoming commonplace, they could potentially shape the differences in users' general mental model of agent interfaces. Other factors could also contribute to the individual difference. For example, a study on human-robot interactions showed that parasocial interaction tendency, which media scholars use to explain individuals' tendency to have illusionary reciprocal relationships with media persona, predicts positive user attitude towards hedonic robots [30]. However, in this paper, we leave the investigation of the potential causes of social-agent orientation to future studies, but focus on understanding *how varied social-agent orientation leads to differences in user needs and preferences for agent interface design.*

Agent Proactive Interactions

A few recent studies explored agent-initiated proactive interactions as technological interventions to influence users, for instance, to enhance learning [24] or to improve health regimen adherence [5]. While they provide evidence that users generally welcome such interactions, they also point out that a major challenge is to deliver information that users can immediately apply [48]. Some also suggest a mismatch between an agent's message and the delivery context can undermine user trust and compliance with the agent [14]. While these studies reveal the problem of context matching in message content, a less-studied topic is the problem of interruption by proactive interactions, which we note might be more difficult to investigate in lab studies than in real user contexts. Meanwhile, the HCI community has a long history of studying the negative influence of interruptions on task performance and user emotions [2], and especially giving it crucial consideration for technology design in enterprise [15, 38]. By conducting a field study with an enterprise information-finding agent, we studied whether perceived interruption of agent-initiated interactions is associated with negative user opinions of the system, and we explored what factors may affect such perception, including the design of proactive interactions.

RESEARCH HYPOTHESES AND QUESTIONS

We start by investigating how social-agent orientation impacts user preference by studying user attitudes toward the system. Using the metaphor of an office assistant, the prototype was designed to be consistent with such a role in both representation (e.g. with a common English name and a professional image) and conversational style (e.g. with polite and professional tone). It was also built with the capability to handle basic social conversations such as greetings and answering common "small talk" questions such as "what are you up to?" Given the high sociality design of the tool, we hypothesize:

> **RH1:** Users with higher social-agent orientation will have more positive opinions of the agent system.

We expect that users with high social-agent orientation may gain satisfaction from social interactions with agents, and thus may place less emphasis on their utilitarian needs, which in the context means getting the correct information from the agent. We therefore hypothesize:

> **RH2:** Users with higher social-agent orientation will be more tolerant of agent mistakes.

To identify user categories to deliver personalized design solutions, we are interested in how to infer individual differences based on users' behavioral signals. We ask:

> **RQ1:** How can social-agent orientation be inferred from behavioral signals?

Furthermore, to inform the personalization design to accommodate the preferences of users with high or low social-agent orientation, we ask:

> **RQ2:** How do design requirements for information-finding agents differ for users with high or low social-agent orientation?

In the professional context, those who perceive agent proactive interactions to be interruptive may form negative opinions of the application. We hypothesize:

> **RH3:** Users who perceive agent proactive interactions as interruptive will have less positive opinions of the agent system.

We are also interested in predicting aversion to the interruption of agent proactive interactions. We ask:

> **RQ3:** What factors influence perceived interruption of agent proactive interactions? How can it be inferred?

In the rest of the paper, we first introduce the agent prototype and discuss the study design. We present quantitative analyses to test RH1- RH3, and explore RQ1 and RQ3. By identifying individuals with varied social-agent orientation, we conducted interview studies to explore answers to RQ2.

SYSTEM DESCRIPTION

We introduced a prototype of a personal agent named "Ella Jones". The agent could be installed on the enterprise instant messaging (IM) tool. Users could initiate a conversation with the agent from a chat window (Figure 1). The agent was designed with a professional-looking cartoon of a female face.

Using an AI agent dialog development platform [53], we built knowledge nodes and pattern-matching rules for the agent's conversational output. For example, we could create a knowledge node that links to information about the enterprise's timesheet policy, and specify matching to the node when users ask questions mentioning "timesheet" or its variations. When matching fails, the agent asks "do you mean any of the following?" with a list of potentially related questions. If no related question is found, the agent says "sorry, I don't know the answer" or its variations.

Figure 1. Ella interface

To create the knowledge nodes for the agent to answer work-related questions, we relied on existing internal repository of frequent employee questions provided by the Human Resource department. In addition, we asked 8 employees to intensively interact with the agent for 1-2 weeks to collect common questions they had at work.

We also built around 200 knowledge nodes to handle common social dialogues such as "thank you", "how are you?," "what do you do for fun?" (a single node may cover many variations of a statement using regular expression). They were partly from an existing repository included with the AI dialogue development platform, collected from previous deployment. Two researchers work on adapting the agent's answers to fit the persona of a professional office assistant. Moreover, to handle questions inquiring about the agent system, we built nodes for the agent to introduce itself, including its functions (e.g. a prototype system to navigate enterprise internal knowledge), and personal stories (e.g. "I'm new to the company…").

Although the system was a prototype with limited capacity, it was able to provide answers to about half of the questions users asked. Currently, commercial general-purpose AI agents like Siri often only reach similar success rate [1] and most agent technologies can only handle knowledge in very specific domains. The limited capacity of the prototype served to study user tolerance towards agent mistakes (RH2), which is especially important to consider given the current limitations of agent systems.

Introducing New Features

To encourage user engagement with the agent, we introduced several new features throughout the study. These new features included: 1) an option to "crowdsource" user questions to their peers if the agent could not find an answer; 2) an option to anonymously crowdsource; 3) an invitation for the user to teach the answer to a question the agent had failed to answer; and 4) an invitation to use the "person lookup" function, with which the user could ask the agent to retrieve the profile information of coworkers. These features were designed to be small additions to the agent's primary Q&A function that would not significantly alter the way users interact with the agent.

METHODOLOGY

Participants

We recruited 30 volunteers from the enterprise, with a mix of full-time employees and interns (38.1% are female and the average age is 28.8, SD=8.5). We selected mostly participants employed for less than a year, as they are likely to have higher needs for information-finding tasks.

Study Design and Procedure

Participants were invited to a briefing meeting, where they were instructed on how to install the personal agent in the enterprise IM tool. The agent was introduced as an "AI agent that answers questions you have at work… just like with a coworker, you can chat with her on the IM tool anytime if you have questions about corporate knowledge and process." To collect data in naturalistic setting, participants were given no further instruction on how to use the tool and were told to freely interact with the agent. We informed participants that the system would log all the contents and time stamps of their interactions for analysis.

After the study, all participants were invited to participate in a survey. Active participants with interaction frequencies above the median value were invited to participate in a 20-min interview. We chose active participants because they were more likely to have formed good understanding of the system and thus more suitable for inquiring about design requirements. The response rate was 70% for the survey and 50% for the interview. We discuss the details of the survey and interview study in later sections.

Proactive Interactions

One goal of the study was to understand how users react to proactive interactions initiated by the agent in an office environment. To this end, we designed three types of proactive messages: *new feature self-introductions*, *crowdsourcing requests,* and *social messages.*

In the "introducing new feature" section, we mentioned that we introduced four new features during the testing period. Importantly, the agent's self-introduction of these new features served as the first type of proactive interaction. These are messages like *"Starting from today, I can ask around for you if I cannot find an answer…"*. We set the introduction messages to be delivered to all participants on the same day when they signed onto the IM tool, if they did. Otherwise, it was delivered at the next sign-on.

The crowdsourcing feature was introduced on the 6th day of the study. When the agent could not answer a question, it offered the option to direct it to other participants of the study. To coworkers who were available on the IM tool, the agent then sent a proactive message asking *"Hi [name], can you answer this question for your colleague?"*

The last type of proactive interaction was social messaging, asking, "*Hi* [name], *what's the most exciting thing about work today?*" or its variations. We were particularly interested in this type of message because it would allow us to test how users respond to *proactive social interactions*—an agent that exhibits relational, "caring" behaviors. Therefore, we introduced this type of message as a between-subjects variable – we randomly selected half of the participants to receive a greeting message from the agent everyday if they signed onto the tool in the morning.

Measurements

System Performance

Given that the objective of the information-finding agent system is to answer participants' questions, we considered the success rate of answering user questions as the measurement of system performance. We anonymized the askers and labeled whether each question received a reasonable answer. Using the results, we calculated the agent success rate for each participant.

Behavioral Measurements

To answer RQ1, we looked at the association of user behaviors and self-reported social-agent orientation. We coded relevant behaviors from the conversational interactions, including socializing, politeness, and agent-grounding behaviors (defined as follow-up attempts such as rephrasing in order to obtain a desired answer). We will discuss the coding schema in details in the "inferring social-agent orientation" section.

Subjective Measurements: Survey Design

One week after the field study, we conducted a survey to collect users' opinions of the agent and users' social-agent orientation with conversational agent systems. We also collected demographic information including age, gender, self-reported experience with conversational agent systems, as well as their usage of the enterprise IM tool, including how often they send messages and how often they feel they are interrupted by others' messages.

User Opinions: Users' opinions on the agent system were measured by averaging the following three items, all on 7-point Likert scale (Cronbach alpha=0.86).

- *Satisfaction*: How would you rate your overall experience with Ella? ("Not satisfied at all" to "very satisfied")
- *Ease of use*: How would you rate your interactions with Ella ("Very difficult to talk to" to "very easy to talk to")
- *Likability*: How much do you like Ella? ("Not at all" to "a lot")

We measured *perceived interruption* by asking participants to rate "in general, how interruptive was it when Ella tried to start a conversation with you?" and *perceived friendliness* by asking "please rate how friendly Ella is."

Social-agent orientation: At the end of the survey, after asking about demographic information (in order to be separated from Ella specific questions), we asked each participant to rate his or her social-agent orientation. The social-agent orientation was measured by averaging the following two items with a 7-point Likert scale from "completely disagree" to "completely agree" (Cronbach alpha=0.86):

- *"I think "small talks" with an AI agent or chatbot is enjoyable."*
- *"I like chatting with an AI agent or chatbot."*

Although the interactions with Ella may potentially impact the self-reported social-agent orientation, thus present a potential limitation of the study, we note that measuring it before the study would likely bias users behaviors. We therefore chose to survey it a week after the study, and emphasized that participants should rate based on their general preference, not specifically towards Ella.

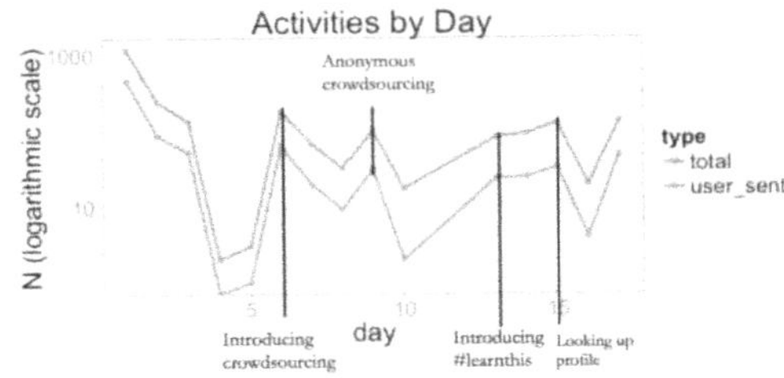

Figure 2. Number of interactions by day

RESULTS: QUANTITATIVE ANALYSIS

During the 17 days, the 30 participants on average sent 27.4 messages (SD=33.3, median=14) to, and received 49.8 messages (SD=50.3, median=36.5) from Ella. Figure 2 shows the total number of interactions per day. User interactions peaked in the beginning, indicating strong interest at the initial encounter with the agent. While the interest dropped after the first couple of days (Note, day 4, 5, 11, 12 were weekends, so the interactions were close to 0), the proactive interactions to introduce new features effectively increased usage.

Table 1 shows the number of each form of proactive interactions delivered and the total response rate for each. Response was defined to be any immediate reaction, e.g. trying out the new feature, answering a crowdsourced question, or replying "got it." The response rate suggested that these interruptions had low responsiveness and were potentially not well received. We will further explore the topic of perceived interruption in the rest of the paper.

Effects on user opinions

In this section, we examine which factors impacted user opinions of the agent system. In particular, we tested whether high social-agent orientation led to more positive user opinions on Ella, which was designed to have high sociality (RH1), whether it moderated the impact of system

Type	N	Response rate
Introducing features	86	26.7%
Crowdsourcing requests	75	28%
Social messages	104	45.2%

Table 1. Descriptive statistics for proactive interactions

performance on user opinions (RH2), and whether the perceived interruption of agent proactive interaction is negatively associated with user opinion (RH3).

To test these hypotheses, we used the user opinion measured in the survey (see description in the "Measurement" section) as the dependent variable. We built a linear regression model of user opinions as a function of self-reported social-agent orientation, perceived interruption of proactive interaction collected from the survey, and our rating of the question success rate for each participant, controlling for age, gender, and self-rated experience with conversational agents. To test RH2, we included the interaction between social-agent orientation and success rate as an independent variable.

The results of the regression model are shown in Table 2. We found that, perhaps not surprisingly, the strongest predictor of user opinions is the system performance, i.e., success rate. The significant positive effect of social-agent orientation shows that users with high social-agent orientation tended to have more positive opinions of the system (RH1 confirmed). Moreover, the significant negative interaction between social-agent orientation and system success rate indicated that users with high social-agent orientation were also more tolerant of negative system performance (RH2 confirmed). We also found that perceived interruption of agent proactive interactions was associated with less positive opinions (RH3 confirmed).

Among the control variables, we found that age had a positive effect on user opinions, implying that older users in our sample (correlated with work experience) had more positive opinions. General experience with conversational agents was associated with more critical opinions of the agent. We did not find any gender differences.

To summarize, consistent with the predictions, we identified that individual differences in social-agent orientation had significant impact on user opinions. High social-agent orientation not only led to more positive user

	β	SE	p-value
Intercept	-0.59	0.84	0.49
Success rate	3.75	1.16	<0.01**
Social-agent orientation	0.50	0.16	<0.01**
Success * Social-agent orientation	-0.83	0.31	0.02*
Perceived interruption	-0.18	0.07	0.02*
Control variables			
Gender (female baseline)	0.14	0.29	0.63
Age	0.09	0.02	<0.001**
Experience	-0.22	0.09	0.02*
Adjusted R^2=0.72, $F(8,12)$=7.55, p=0.001			

Table 2. Linear regression model predicting user opinions.

opinions on the high-sociality agent, but also made the opinions more robust and less impaired by suboptimal system performance. It may imply that users with high social-agent orientation did not judge the system solely by its utilitarian value, but also appreciated its sociality designs. We also found that participants who perceived the proactive interactions to be interruptive had less positive opinions of the system. It is noteworthy that the perceived interruption was a stronger predictor of user opinions than perceived friendliness of the agent (β=0.06, p=0.66), suggesting that, at least in the professional context, interruption could be a more crucial design consideration than agent personality. In the next two sections, we will explore how to infer social-agent orientation and aversion to proactive interaction from users' behavioral signals.

Inferring Social-Agent Orientation

In human-agent interaction literature, content analyses of users' conversational interactions are often performed to infer user status or attributes [10, 36]. Identifying the indication of conversational signals for the underlying user attributes is an important step towards user profiling and user modeling, which may enable personalization and development of adaptive systems. Based on this view, we are interested in identifying users' behavioral signals that can be used to infer social-agent interaction (RQ1).

Behavioral Measurements

After carefully reviewing user conversational behaviors, and inspired by Lee et al.'s work on users' exhibition of social behaviors towards a robot [28], we chose to explore if the following three behavioral measures can be used to infer social-agent orientation.

Socializing questions are questions that directly address the agent, such as *"what is your favorite color?" or, "what do you do for fun?"* These questions are unrelated to the intended system function of finding enterprise information, but are typical of human interactions. We coded and counted how many socializing questions each participant asked, normalized by the total number of questions the user asked, to create the *socializing index*.

Politeness reflects how politely the user treated the agent. We chose to code *polite behaviors* by including greetings (e.g. *"Good morning"*), appreciation (e.g. *"Thank you"*), apology, farewell, and other kinds of courtesy. We coded *impolite behaviors* by including explicit insult (e.g. *"You are dumb"*) and flaming behaviors (e.g. repeating a question within a short period). For each participant, we calculated the number of polite behaviors, minus the number of impolite behaviors, and normalized it by the total number of questions asked, to create the *politeness index*.

Agent-grounding questions are intended to obtain a desired answer from the agent. We were inspired by, but wanted to differentiate from, the original term "grounding behavior" in communication research, which refers to people trying to reach common ground during conversing [13]. Agent-

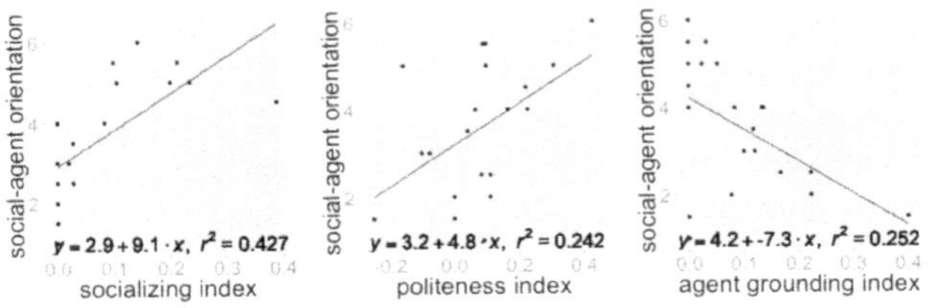

Figure 3. Inferring social-agent orientation based on behavioral measures

grounding questions happened when the agent failed in a user's initial attempt, and the user asked follow-up questions. They include *rephrasing* (e.g. from "*What does PMOM mean?*" to "*Define PMOM*"), and *changing granularity* (e.g. from *"Does the company give discounts to Disney world?"* to *"Are there employees discounts at theme parks?"* to *"What employee discounts do we have?")* We coded and counted the number of agent-grounding questions for each participant, and normalized it by the total number of questions to create the *agent-grounding index*.

We studied the inference power of these behavioral signals on users' self-reported social-agent orientation by studying their correlations. The results are presented in Figure 3. We found that all three measures are significantly correlated with social-agent orientation. Specifically, asking socializing questions has the strongest correlation with social-agent orientation (β=9.1, t (19)=3.76, p=0.001). Being polite to the agent also positively correlates with one's social-agent orientation (β=4.8, t (19)=2.46, p=0.02). Interestingly, we found that asking agent-grounding questions negatively correlates with one's social orientation (β=-7.3, t (19)=-2.53, p=0.02).

We argue that the agent grounding behaviors reflected a process of attempting to identify and fit an input model that the system can process and respond. These resemble user behaviors using search engines, iteratively generating new queries to locate the desired information. We also highlight that these behaviors signal the *high utilitarian needs* of low social-orientation users. They used the system for its functional goal of finding information, and adapted their usage to better satisfy such needs. Indeed, as evidenced, we found that the *agent-grounding index* significantly correlates with the question success rate for participants (r^2=0.33, β=1.29, t (28)=3.72, p<0.001).

To summarize, we found that users with high social-agent orientation could be identified from behavioral signals, including asking socializing questions, being polite, and engaging less in asking agent-grounding questions intended to retrieve desirable answers. We suggest these behavioral signals could be easily detected with NLP techniques for user profiling. These results echoed findings in Lee et al. [28], where they found that user exhibition of social and relational behaviors with robots are correlated, including asking socializing questions and showing politeness. Using self-reported measures of social-agent orientation, we further prove that these correlated behaviors may result from an underlying user attribute of desiring to engage in humanized social interactions with agent systems. In the "interview study" section, we will further explore whether and how this orientation is associated with different mental models of the agent, as well as differences in user requirements for agent system design.

Understanding Perceived Interruption

In previous analysis, we found that those who perceived the proactive interactions to be interruptive tended to have less positive opinions about the system. This suggests that another personalization opportunity would be to personalize the proactive interactions. An important question is what factors impact the perceived interruption (RQ3). For example, the frequency or the type of proactive message could make differences, or perhaps it is driven by a general user attribute of aversion to unsolicited messages at work. Such knowledge may help us identify appropriate personalization strategies for proactive interactions.

We examined the predictive power of three variables on self-reported perceived interruption: frequency of receiving proactive messages from the agent (since users were not always logged onto the IM tool, this frequency largely varied), type of interruption (receiving vs. not receiving social messages), and general interruptibility, which was measured by a 7-point scale self-reported rating how often one feels being interrupted by messages from the enterprise IM tools. We found no significant effect of the frequency of receiving proactive messages (β=0.04, t (19)=0.68, p=0.50), nor whether one received social messages (β=0.08, t (19)=0.10, p=0.92). However, we found significant effect of the general tendency of perceiving IM messages to be interruptive (β=0.60, t (19)=2.46, p=0.02) (Figure 4 left).

The results suggest that perceived interruption is likely associated with users' general aversion to unsolicited IM messages at work, regardless of whether it is from an agent or colleagues. It implies that the perceived interruption may not be alleviated by simply reducing message frequency or modifying message contents of proactive interactions. We also note that such an attribute could be related to how often one uses the enterprise IM tools, as we found a correlation between the general interruptibility and self-claimed usage frequency of the IM tool (Pearson's r(19) = 0.53, p <0.01). It implies that given the context of office environment, professionals who have busy schedules and frequent social contacts may be especially intolerant of the interruption from agent proactive interactions.

We also attempted to infer the user attribute of aversion to proactive interactions based on behavioral signals. By hypothesizing that people considering the proactive interaction to be interruptive were likely to be less responsive, we calculated the response rate for each user. As expected, we found that the response rate is negatively correlated with the extent one found agent proactive interactions to be interruptive (β=-3.9, t (19)=-2.36, p=0.03) (Figure 4 right).

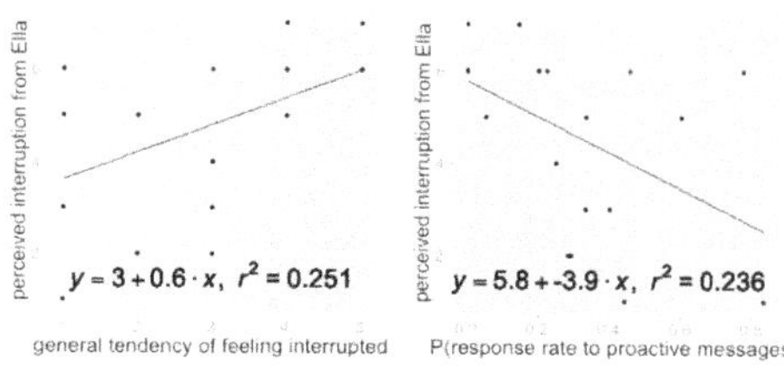

Figure 4. Predicting perceived interruption from proactive interaction based on (left) general tendency of feeling interrupted by IM messages and (right) response rate.

In summary, our study highlighted that, in the enterprise context, proactive agent interactions may risk disrupting some users and harming their overall user experience. We found that the individual aversion to agent proactive interaction is likely associated with the general user aversion to unsolicited messages at work. This tendency is at least partially associated to the user's busy work routine, which could be related to users' positions in the enterprise and/or their work patterns. To avoid interruption, it may be necessary to turn off proactive interactions for targeted users, who can be identified from low or decreasing response rate to proactive messages.

INTERVIEW STUDY: UNDERSTANDING USER MENTAL MODELS AND PREFERENCES

We conducted post-study interviews to further understand whether the varied levels of social-agent orientation are associated with different mental modals of agent interfaces, and how the varied orientation leads to different user requirements for designing information-finding agents (RQ2). We interviewed 7 of the most active users. Among them, three rated their self-rated social-agent orientation below the median (4), the rest were equal or above median.

The interview was semi-structured and focused on understanding: 1) user's mental model of the system, for which we asked participants to describe their expectations at the encounter of the agent, their general view of the agent, and their experiences; 2) user requirements, for which we asked them how they wish to *improve* the system.

All interviews were conducted through audio conferencing software and were recorded and transcribed. We analyzed the transcripts based on grounded theory [44], following an iterative open-coding process. We focused on comparing the responses between the two clusters of participants (social-agent orientation below or above/equal median). While our interview sample was relatively small, we were able to identify some consistent themes across most, if not all, participants. We will first discuss their mental models, then the emerging themes from their descriptions of requirements for an enterprise information-finding agent.

Differences in Mental Models

By finding that higher social-agent orientation led to more social behaviors towards the agent, we hypothesize that they could be mediated by a mental model of a social, instead of technological, entity. To concretely learn about these mental models, in Table 3, we present some representative quotes describing the mental models of Ella from interviewees with varied social-agent orientation scores. We observe that users with low social-agent orientation consistently viewed the agent as an *interface for information access,* and emphasized the *utilitarian value* of the system. In contrast, users with high social-agent orientation viewed the agent as a *humanized assistant* and described it using human-specific treats. The striking differences in their descriptions of mental model again highlighted that users with low social-agent orientation were primarily seeking the utilitarian value of the system, while those with high orientation also valued engaging in social interactions with the agent.

Based on the results, it is necessary to consider personalization of agent systems to adapt to these mental models. To this end, in the next two sections, we focus on examining differences in user requirements described by the participants with high and low social-agent orientation. The goal is to identify design considerations for information-finding agents with high or low sociality, allowing personalization for different classes of users.

User Requirements: High Social-Agent Orientation

When analyzing user requirements (i.e. how they wish to improve the agent), we identified two themes that were mentioned repeatedly, but exclusively by users with higher social-agent orientation. The first theme is *improving conversations*. Examples include improving the capability of handling continuity and turn-taking, awareness of user status, having more variations in answers, and also tailor the granularity of answers, e.g. giving more general or specific answers depending on the asker's intention.

Another prominent theme high social-agent orientation users expressed was to *present a personality*, including

ID	SO score	Quotes
P5	2	*"I see it as a way to access the vast amount of company information and infrastructure ... So being able to access that kind of information directly..."*
P8	2.5	*"[It] integrates and helps users make sense of all the different repositories within the company."*
P3	3	*"I am using a chat-bot interface to find information...."*
P11	4	*"I was thinking of her as a way of augmenting search.... but part of the mental model is what are the things I want to talk to people on [the IM tool]"*
P12	4.5	*"She has a personality. I like her, more on her friendliness, instead of a tool".*
P17	5.5	*"The metaphor I have in mind, who is like a lovable colleague, but kind of cool colleague, that most of our conversations are kind of one-sided..."*
P26	6	*"I want to talk to her like a human, but she still feels robotic. I wish she would have more personality."*

Table 3. User quotes describing mental model of the system

providing more subjective and opinionated answers instead of solely retrieving facts, presenting relational behaviors, memorizing previous conversations, and initiating meaningful proactive interactions. In general, they desired to have conversations beyond the functional goals, and to engage in more social dialogues. Such needs are exemplified in the following quote:

"I think humor, subjective thing, personality… I think if there is, like, humorous reply, it is like Easter Eggs that would reward the 'necessary interactions', I think people tend to enjoy more. So even if the tool does not work, but if it gives you funny answers, it adds to my delight. I think it may attract people to interact more." (P12)

User Preference: Low Social-agent orientation

We found three distinct themes from users with lower social-agent orientation. The first theme is *including features from conventional information-search tools*. By viewing the personal agent as an interface for information access, they naturally related it to familiar information-finding technologies. They particularly mentioned features that could improve its capability for providing desired information with less required user input, such as better processing of (non-conversational) input, giving multiple potential answers, suggesting or automatically correcting input, providing context aware recommendation, and handling ill-defined information finding tasks, as exemplified in the following quotes:

"It is very hard to get the keywords, and you have to fully understand the whole protocol of asking the particular chat-bot the way it wants to be asked. There is a lot of friction trying to use it…So, how do I ask something I don't know about. And a chat-bot never does it for me…But a search engine might just give you a bunch of semi-close results. It will get me to where I want." (P3)

We contrast these responses to the "improving conversation" theme identified among people with high social-agent orientation: while both express needs for improving the information-finding process, those with high social-agent orientation placed emphasis on having an easy, natural, or even "intelligent" conversation, while people with low social-agent orientation preferred more machine-like solutions that could reduce the required user input.

The second theme also made a strong contrast. Users with low social-agent orientation explicitly stated the *unnecessity of humanized features*. P3 mentioned that even though in the beginning he had some social conversations with the agent, he was "testing the system", and he would not do that in the long run. P5 also commented that he preferred a non-humanized, especially neutral interface that avoids any stereotypical human features like gender or profession.

The last theme identified from users with low social-agent orientation was to *improve the transparency and affordance of the system*. P5 had confusion when first encountering agent system: *"I never really understand what the functionality is. Like what Ella can do or cannot do."* P3 and P8 both expressed preference for a more transparent system, for example by knowing from which repository the agent gets the information. We note that such needs are consistent with the mental model of search-engine like system, and are to improve the information-finding process.

As a core interface design concept introduced by Don Norman, affordance refers to *communicating what user action is possible in design* [35]. It is, however, challenging to realize in agent systems as they are mostly single-modal (conversation) and typically present limited cues without user initiation (e.g. just a chat window). Interestingly, we identified *affordance-understanding* behaviors from the interaction data. The most typical one was to ask *"what can you do?"* when initially encountering the agent. We found 8 out of the 30 users asked such a question within the first three interactions with the agent. Consistent with the qualitative finding of higher needs for affordance, 75% of them are people who self-identified to have low social-agent orientation (below median). In responding to the question, the agent explained her functionality — to answer enterprise-wide questions, and also provided examples of questions. By simply asking this question to form a better understanding of the system affordance, we found that it significantly improved the success rate of using the agent system, compared to those who didn't ask these questions (β=0.156, $t(28)$=2.180, p=0.04). The results underline the importance of *designing affordances* in agent systems, especially for users with high utilitarian needs, and suggest that one way to do so is to carefully embed the explanation and instruction on how to use the system into the dialogue.

DESIGN IMPLICATIONS AND DISCUSSIONS

Individual Differences in Social-Agent Orientation

Our study demonstrated that there are individual differences in social-agent orientation. When using an information-search agent, some users value sociality designs and prefer engaging in human-like social interactions, while others may care less about this, focusing primarily on task performance. Such differences are found to be associated with different mental models of the system and lead to distinctive design requirements. The results recommend developing personalized agent interfaces. For example, we envision a customizable agent that allows users to choose the levels of social attributes. Those with high social-agent orientation may favor the availability of choosing agent look and persona, even if it means investing time. Those with low social-agent orientation can skip these steps and use a non-humanized interface such as an input box. This initialization would already differentiate these two user groups for further personalization.

For the high social-orientation user group, we recommend designs that imitate human-human interactions. There is a rich body of research that explores relevant techniques inspired by communication and linguistic literature [4, 16, 17]. By conducting a field study, we found that, somewhat surprisingly, 18% of the questions were "socializing questions" that are typical of social dialogues and irrelevant to the system's intended function. We also found that those with higher social-agent orientation were more likely to ask socializing questions. We consider some of these questions as natural, subconscious responses when a user deemed the agent as a social entity (e.g. asking "how are you going to learn?"). Some other questions appeared to be simply for the enjoyment of social dialogues or to explore the agent's social capabilities (e.g. asking "what is your favorite color?"). When developing a personal agent, especially more social versions, it is important to ensure handling of these types of questions. We also recommend having variations and more opinionated responses to create natural and engaging social dialogues, which could be enabled by having adaptive and individualized conversation models.

The low social-orientation group place less emphasis on the conversational design but more on the utility of the system to find information easily and quickly, and may consider standard conversational interactions as burdensome. We recommend designs consistent with the mental model of *"an interface for information access"* and to focus on smoothing the information finding process and reducing required user input, which may not resemble human-human conversations. To keep this group of users engaged with agent interfaces, it is also necessary to consider what advantages agent interfaces could offer over those of the conventional information finding tools in improving task performance. For example, agent's conversational model may facilitate mixed-initiative automation by increasing user input and integrating knowledge about the user from different contexts. We also consider agent mediated information-finding a potential paradigm for *collaborative search*, which is an emerging research topic with many novel interaction techniques being developed [32].

Lastly, we note the evolving nature of the user differences in mental models. Almost all the participants reported having had some experience with conversational agent systems. Although our sample from a technology company is potentially biased towards tech-savvy users, we note the increasing availability of popular agent applications is shaping user perceptions of, and expectations for, agent systems. For example, P3, who reported to have low social-agent orientation, repeatedly referred to his preference for Google Now, which is designed to be an extension of a search service with rather limited sociality designs. So these mental models are "learned" and can possibly evolve in the future. We also point out that much of the friction in conversational interactions, deemed as unfavorable by users with low social-agent orientation, is constrained by current language processing techniques. Once we have overcome these challenges, it may be worth revisiting the topic of user differences in utilitarian and social orientation.

Agent Proactive Interactions

While we found evidence that agent proactive interactions may carry the risk of interruption, we by no means intend to reject proactive features. Instead, we urge consideration on how to improve the reception of proactive interactions by reducing its interruption cost and increasing its value.

To reduce the potential interruption costs, we can learn from the large body of HCI literature on interruption, including predicting the cost of interruption and improving interruption strategies by considering the context, activity, and emotional status of the user, as well as the format of the interruption (see review in [23]). In addition to the awareness of delivery context, our study suggests *user attribute awareness* by identifying user groups that are more or less susceptible to interruption, potentially based on demographics or social status. An agent system could also easily learn about such attribute from users' previous responses. Moreover, advanced context-aware and user-attribute aware techniques can be developed by accessing users' schedule-related information from sources such as email or calendar tools.

Research also suggests that the aversion to interruption could be reduced through increasing its perceived utility. During our interview, when asking participants why they did not respond to social messages they repeatedly answered things like *"I did not see anything happened after I replied the first time... I was expecting it to come back with help for what I said I was going to do"(P8)*. When we asked why they did not respond to messages introducing the crowdsourcing feature, they replied: *"We are already using Slack...I don't know how Ella would be better (p 26)"*. These answers suggest that if proactive messages can explicitly communicate the value it creates, users may be less resistant to their interruption. Future research is needed to explore these possibilities.

CONCLUSION

By studying human-agent interactions in a natural, but special context – enterprise information-finding, our study shows that there are individual differences in the preference for engaging in human-like social interactions and agent sociality designs. Such individual differences are associated with the extent one focuses on satisfying utilitarian needs and may be particularly important to consider for agent systems intended for productivity versus leisurely use. Our study also illustrates that user's general preference for a design paradigm can have profound implications for system design, impacting how users interact with, expect from and evaluate the system. Our findings can be used to inform the development of personalized agent interfaces for user groups with high or low social-agent orientation. We also highlight the potential risk of interruptions from agent initiated proactive interactions in the work environment and suggest not only context awareness but also user-attribute awareness for personalizing agent proactive interactions.

REFERENCES

1. Apple's Siri wrong 38 percent of the time in test. http://www.cnet.com/news/apples-siri-wrong-38-percent-of-the-time-in-test/
2. Bailey, B. P., & Konstan, J. A. On the need for attention-aware systems: Measuring effects of interruption on task performance, error rate, and affective state. *Computers in human behavior 22*, 4(2006), 685-708.
3. Berry, P., Peintner, B., Conley, K., Gervasio, M., Uribe, T., and Yorke-Smith, N. Deploying a personalized time management agent. *In Proc. AAMAS 2006*, ACM Press (2006), 1564-1571).
4. Bickmore, T., and Cassell, J. Relational agents: a model and implementation of building user trust. In *Proc. CHI 2001*, ACM Press (2001), 396-403.
5. Bickmore, T., Mauer, D., Crespo, F., and Brown, T. Persuasion, task interruption and health regimen adherence. In *Proc. Persuasive Technology*, 1-11.
6. Bickmore, T. W., Pfeifer, L. M., and Jack, B. W. Taking the time to care: empowering low health literacy hospital patients with virtual nurse agents. In *Proc. CHI 2009*, ACM Press (2009), 1265-1274.
7. Bickmore, T. W., and Picard, R. W. Establishing and maintaining long-term human-computer relationships. *ACM Transactions on Computer-Human Interaction (TOCHI) 12*, 2 (2005), 293-327.
8. Brave, S., Nass, C., and Hutchinson, K. Computers that care: investigating the effects of orientation of emotion exhibited by an embodied computer agent. *International Journal of Human-Computer Studies* 62, 2 (2005), 161-178.
9. Cassell, Justine. *Embodied conversational agents*. MIT press, 2000.
10. Cassell, J., & Bickmore, T. (2003). Negotiated collusion: Modeling social language and its relationship effects in intelligent agents. *User Modeling and User-Adapted Interaction*, *13*(1-2), 89-132.
11. Cassell, J., and Thorisson, K. R. The power of a nod and a glance: Envelope vs. emotional feedback in animated conversational agents. *Applied Artificial Intelligence 13,* 4-5(1999), 519-538.
12. Chi, E. H. Blurring of the Boundary Between Interactive Search and Recommendation. In *Proc. IUI 2015*, ACM Press (2015), 2-2.
13. Clark, H. H., and Brennan, S. E. Grounding in communication. *Perspectives on socially shared cognition*, *13*(1991), 127-149.
14. Cramer, H., Evers, V., van Slooten, T., Ghijsen, M., & Wielinga, B. Trying too hard: effects of mobile agents'(Inappropriate) social expressiveness on trust, affect and compliance. In *Proc. CHI 2010,* ACM Press (2010), 1471-1474.
15. Czerwinski, M., Horvitz, E., & Wilhite, S. A diary study of task switching and interruptions. In *Proc. CHI 2004,* ACM Press (2004), 175-182.
16. Dautenhahn, K. Robots we like to live with?!-a developmental perspective on a personalized, life-long robot companion. In *Robot and Human Interactive Communication 2004*. 17-22.
17. Dryer, D. C. Getting personal with computers: how to design personalities for agents. *Applied Artificial Intelligence 13*, 3 (1999), 273-295.
18. Faulring, A., Myers, B., Mohnkern, K., Schmerl, B., Steinfeld, A., Zimmerman, J. and Siewiorek, D. Agent-assisted task management that reduces email overload. In *Proc. IUI* 2010, ACM Press (2010),61-70.
19. Friedman, B., Kahn Jr, P. H., and Hagman, J. Hardware companions?: What online AIBO discussion forums reveal about the human-robotic relationship. In *Proc. 2003,* ACM Press (2003), 273-280).
20. Gil, Y., and Ratnakar, V. Towards intelligent assistance for to-do lists. In *Proc. IUI 2008,* ACM Press (2008), 329-332.
21. Gockley, R., Bruce, A., Forlizzi, J., Michalowski, M., Mundell, A., Rosenthal, S. andWang, J. Designing robots for long-term social interaction. In *Intelligent Robots and Systems 2005,* 1338-1343.
22. Goetz, J., Kiesler, S., and Powers, A. Matching robot appearance and behavior to tasks to improve human-robot cooperation. In *Robot and Human Interactive Communication 2003*, 55-60.
23. Ho, J., and Intille, S. S. Using context-aware computing to reduce the perceived burden of interruptions from mobile devices. In *Proc. CHI 2005*. ACM Press (2005), 909-918.
24. Kim, Y., Baylor, A. L., & PALS Group. Pedagogical agents as learning companions: The role of agent competency and type of interaction. *Educational Technology Research and Development 54,*3 (2006), 223-243.
25. Kopp, S., Gesellensetter, L., Krämer, N. C., and Wachsmuth, I. A conversational agent as museum guide–design and evaluation of a real-world application. In *Intelligent Virtual Agents,* (2005), 329-343.
26. Kshirsagar, S. A multilayer personality model. In *Proceedings of the 2nd international symposium on Smart graphics* 2002, 107-115.
27. Kuno, Y., Sadazuka, K., Kawashima, M., Yamazaki, K., Yamazaki, A., and Kuzuoka, H. Museum guide robot based on sociological interaction analysis. In *Pro. CHI 2007*, ACM Press (2007), 1191-1194.

28. Lee, M. K., Kiesler, S., and Forlizzi, J. Receptionist or information kiosk: how do people talk with a robot?. In *Proc. CSCW 2010,* ACM Press (2010), 31-40.
29. Lee, M. K., Kiesler, S., Forlizzi, J., and Rybski, P. Ripple effects of an embedded social agent: a field study of a social robot in the workplace. In *Proc CHI 2012*, ACM Press (2012), 695-704.
30. Lee, N., Shin, H., & Sundar, S. S. Utilitarian vs. hedonic robots: role of parasocial tendency and anthropomorphism in shaping user attitudes. In *Proc HRI 2011*, ACM Press (2011), 183-184.
31. Maes, P. Agents that reduce work and information overload.*Communications of the ACM 37,*7(1994), 30-40.
32. Morris, M. R., & Horvitz, E. SearchTogether: an interface for collaborative web search. In *Proc. UIST 2007*, ACM Press (2007), 3-12.
33. Nass, C., and Lee, K. M. Does computer-generated speech manifest personality? An experimental test of similarity-attraction. In *Proc CHI 2012*, ACM Press (2012),329-336.
34. Nass, C., Steuer, J., and Tauber, E. R. Computers are social actors. In *Proc. CHI 1994*. ACM Press (1994), 72-78.
35. Norman, D. A. (2002). The Design of Everyday Things.
36. Novielli, N., de Rosis, F., & Mazzotta, I. (2010). User attitude towards an embodied conversational agent: Effects of the interaction mode. *Journal of Pragmatics*, *42*(9), 2385-2397.
37. Nowak, K. L. and Biocca, F. The effect of the agency and anthropomorphism on users' sense of telepresence, copresence, and social presence in virtual environments. *Presence 12,* 5(2003), 481-494.
38. O'Conaill, B., & Frohlich, D. Timespace in the workplace: Dealing with interruptions. In *Proc. CHI 1995*, ACM Press (1995), 262-263.
39. Ogan, A., Finkelstein, S., Mayfield, E., D'Adamo, C., Matsuda, N., and Cassell, J. Oh dear stacy!: social interaction, elaboration, and learning with teachable agents. In *Proc. CHI 2012,* ACM Press (2012), 39-48.
40. Picard, R. W., and Picard, R. (1997). *Affective computing* (Vol. 252). Cambridge: MIT press.
41. Prendinger, H., and Ishizuka, M. Social role awareness in animated agents. In *Proceedings of the fifth international conference on Autonomous agents*. ACM Press (2001), 270-277.
42. Salem, M., Lakatos, G., Amirabdollahian, F. and Dautenhahn, K. Would You Trust a (Faulty) Robot?: Effects of Error, Task Type and Personality on Human-Robot Cooperation and Trust. In *Proc. HRI 2015,* ACM Press (2015), 141-148.
43. Satake, S., Kanda, T., Glas, D. F., Imai, M., Ishiguro, H., and Hagita, N. How to approach humans?-strategies for social robots to initiate interaction. In *Proc. HRI 2009*, ACM Press (2009), 109-116).
44. Strauss, A., & Corbin, J. Grounded theory methodology. *Handbook of qualitative research*, (1997), 273-285.
45. Tapus, A., Ţăpuş, C., and Matarić, M. J. User—robot personality matching and assistive robot behavior adaptation for post-stroke rehabilitation therapy. *Intelligent Service Robotics1*, 2(2008), 169-183.
46. Thompson, C. A., Goker, M. H., and Langley, P. A personalized system for conversational recommendations. *Journal of Artificial Intelligence Research, (2004)*, 393-428.
47. Weizenbaum, J. ELIZA—a computer program for the study of natural language communication between man and machine. *Communications of the ACM 9*, 1(1966), 36-45.
48. Xiao, J., Stasko, J., and Catrambone, R. An empirical study of the effect of agent competence on user performance and perception. In *Proc. AAMAS.* IEEE Computer Society (2004),178-185.
49. Xiao, J., Stasko, J., and Catrambone, R. The role of choice and customization on users' interaction with embodied conversational agents: effects on perception and performance. In *Proc. CHI 2007*, ACM Press (2007) 1293-1302.
50. Yan, H., & Selker, T. Context-aware office assistant. In *Proc 2000*, ACM Press (2000), 276-279).
51. Yee, N., Bailenson, J. N., and Rickertsen, K.. A meta-analysis of the impact of the inclusion and realism of human-like faces on user experiences in interfaces. In Proc. 2007, ACM Press (2007), 1-10.
52. Yorke-Smith, N., Saadati, S., Myers, K. L., and Morley, D. N. Like an intuitive and courteous butler: a proactive personal agent for task management. In *Proc AAMAS 2009*. 337-344.
53. Watson Dialog Service. http://www.ibm.com/smarterplanet/us/en/ibmwatson/developercloud/dialog.html

Yo!: Enriching Emotional Quality of Single-Button Messengers through Kinetic Typography

Minhwan Kim, Kyungah Choi, Hyeon-Jeong Suk
Department of Industrial Design, KAIST
Daejeon, Republic of Korea
{minhwan.kim, cka0116, color}@kaist.ac.kr

ABSTRACT
This study aims to investigate the effects of kinetic typography elements in single-button messengers to enrich the conveyance of emotional quality. Two complementary studies were conducted: First, a paired user workshop was conducted through which eight macro animation types were extracted to facilitate the evaluation in a subsequent experiment. Second, an empirical study was conducted to explore the effects of kinetic typographical elements, namely animation type, speed, and dynamics, on conveying particular emotions. The study is expected to act as a good stepping stone for further developing single-button messengers as an alternative messaging tool with unique communicational aspects.

Author Keywords
Emotive text; instant messaging; kinetic typography

ACM Classification Keywords
H.5.2. Information interfaces and presentation (e.g., HCI): Miscellaneous

INTRODUCTION
The maturing of technology has led to the relocation of a significant part of interpersonal interaction as instant messaging [9]. It is worthy of close attention that mediated communication tools have shifted from computers and cell phones to smart devices, such as smartphones and smartwatches. Such environmental change has allowed the advent of new ways of communication, and single-button messaging has expanded the possibilities for communication by drastically reducing them. The single-button messenger is an emerging communication application (app) for mobile devices that allows users to exchange limited texts or signals with a single tap. The 'Yo' app is a representative single-button messenger that does nothing but send a one-word message, 'Yo,' to other users, as shown in Figure 1. The single-button messenger

Figure 1. Screenshots of a single-button messenger 'Yo.'

has rapidly become useful as an alternative messenger as we head into the future of wearable devices [2], and a number of similar applications have been subsequently released, such as 'Hodor,' 'Aiyo,' 'Dingbel,' 'Lo,' and so forth.

However, the single-button messaging application is lacking in a communicational aspect due to its simple functionality. What if users want to say something else? Such questions have led users to use this messenger for a limited purpose, such as an eye-catching notification. Nevertheless, we believe in the potential of this new messaging service, and studies need to be conducted to explore new ways of communication using single-button messaging. In this study, we attempt to embed kinetic typography in single-button messengers.

Kinetic Typography
Kinetic typography is defined as text that changes in color, size, or position over time [3]. It easily catches the user's attention and emphasizes the original meaning of the word. It has been used as an alternative solution to deliver emotional quality in text-based communication, and there have been many attempts to embed kinetic typography in instant messengers [1,4,6]. Lee et al. [7] asserted that pre-designed kinetic typography can convey specific emotions. More recently, Gaylord et al. [5] showed that animated text can add more nuanced communication cues of intonation and body motion. However, those studies have mainly focused on empirical evidence of the influence of different animation types, while they have not yet specified the effects of other elements. Furthermore, earlier studies were conducted in computer-based simulated messengers, and the animation stimuli were pre-designed by experts. In this regard, we conducted a series of two complementary studies on the influence of kinetic typography elements in

DIS 2016, June 4–8, 2016, Brisbane, Australia.
© 2016 ACM ISBN 978-1-4503-4031-1/16/06...$15.00.
http://dx.doi.org/10.1145/2901790.2901835

single-button messengers for mobile devices. First, through a user-participated workshop, we extracted eight types of macro animation for mobile devices. Based on the results, the following study was conducted to investigate the effects of kinetic typographical elements, including animation type, speed, and dynamics, on conveying particular emotions. Lastly, we suggested new ways of using single-button messengers with design implications.

PRELIMINARY STUDY

Procedure

The preliminary study aims to extract user-driven macro animations for mobile devices. We recruited four pairs of users for the workshop. A total of eight college students made up of five males and three females participated. Among the participants, two pairs were in a relationship, and the rest were intimate with each other. Participants sat opposite each other and were asked to express six basic emotions, such as happiness, sadness, anger, fear, surprise, and disappointment [10], using tangible letters 'Y' and 'o' in the dummy smartphone screen, as illustrated in Figure 2. Two letter sets had different textures: silicone for expressing elastic motion and an acrylic plate for expressing rigid motion. During the workshop, participants were allowed to talk freely and encouraged to give feedback to their partner's animation. The animations designed for each emotion were archived as thumbnails in a sketched form. Ice-breaking exercises were given prior to the workshop, and five minutes were given to each of the six emotions. Including a ten-minute user interview, each workshop took approximately 50 minutes.

Results and Discussion

Fifty animations were designed from the user-participated workshop. However, animations with a morphological alphabet that was specific to 'Y' and 'o' were eliminated. As a result, eight types of macro animations were extracted and were given appropriate names, as shown in Figure 3. Eight animation types were then classified into four groups: The first group is composed of animations with deformation of the original text in three different stretching directions (see Figure 3(a)). The second group consists of vibrating animation (see Figure 3(b)). The third group is composed of animations with a translation in two different motion paths (see Figure 3(c)). Finally, the last group consists of rotating animations in two different rotation axes (see Figure 3(d)).

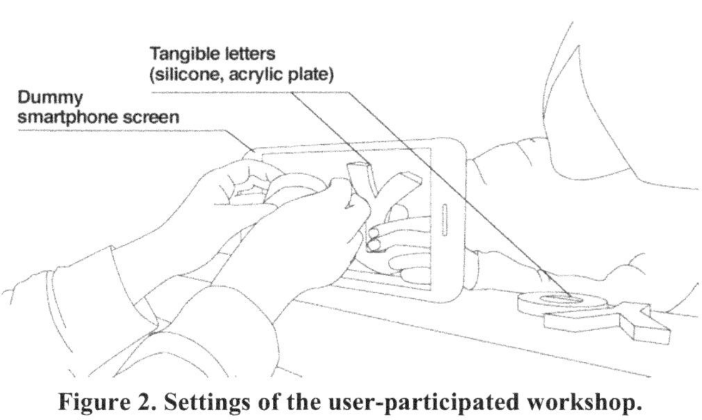

Figure 2. Settings of the user-participated workshop.

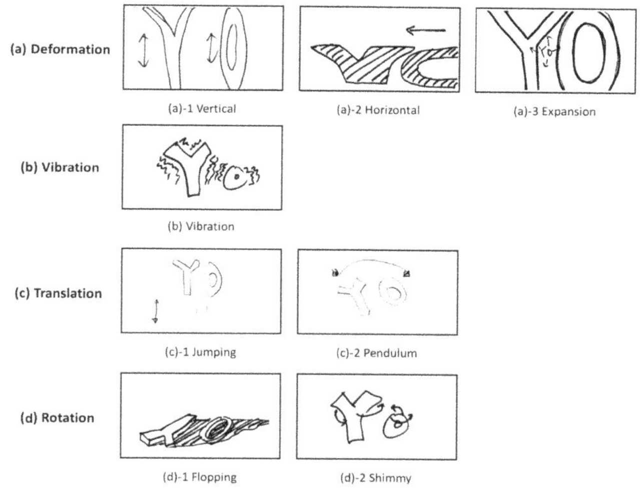

Figure 3. Eight types of macro animations extracted from the preliminary study.

Despite the different participants involved, interestingly, several animations were replicated. For example, 'flopping' animation type was repeatedly used to express disappointment. The 'jumping' animation type was frequently used to express happiness. This implies that there are stereotypes of animation that are strongly tied to specific emotions. On the other hand, some animation types were controversial in use among participants. For instance, some participants stretched the text vertically to express an angry emotion, while other participants used it to express a joyous feeling. For a joyous feeling, however, a gentle touch was added. This triggered our motivation to investigate the interaction effect jointly caused by more than one kinetic attribute.

MAIN STUDY

The main study aims to investigate the role of kinetic typographical elements—animation type, speed, and dynamics—on enriching emotional quality. In particular, we attempted to identify both the main effects and interaction effects among the kinetic elements. In addition, we intended to propose a set of prescriptive rules for the use of kinetic typography, which in turn can be designed as an 'emotion presets' in the messenger interface.

Procedure

Three kinetic typographical elements were explored in the empirical study: animation type, speed, and dynamics. First, eight macro animation types derived in the preliminary study were adopted as the level of animation type. Second, three levels were defined for speed: 'slow,' 'moderate,' and 'fast,' according to the play time of the animation. The 'slow' level had five times longer playtime than the 'fast' level, where each level was designed in an equidistant interval. Lastly, the dynamics were divided into three different levels to explore the activeness of animations. For animation types with deformation (Figure 3(a)) or translation (Figure 3(c)), the level of the dynamic is defined by the space covered by the text. On the other hand, for animation types with vibration (Figure 3(b)) or rotation (Figure 3(d)), the levels were defined with the motion range, such as its rotation angle. In order to reduce the number of stimuli, while minimizing the loss of measuring the effect, we adopted an orthogonal design. As a result, 31 profiles, including four holdout profile cards, were composed out of all 72 (8 × 3 × 3) combinations. Including a text without any effects, a total of 32 animated texts were designed and created in Adobe After Effects CS6, which are available at https://vimeo.com/152108052.

A total of 20 subjects consisting of eleven males and nine females participated, and their age ranged from 21 to 32 (M = 26.33, SD = 5.67). The animation sets were displayed on a smartphone (iPhone 6s) in order to simulate an instant messaging application in smart mobile devices. Participants were asked to assess six emotional qualities of the 31 animated texts using a seven-point Likert scale. In addition, the responses were recorded in the Affect Grid [8].

Results and Discussion

We performed conjoint analysis to identify the elements that have a dominant effect, as shown in Table 1. The relative importance was extracted for each of the 20 participants to perform repeated measures ANOVA. The result indicated that 'animation type' plays the most important role in conveying emotions across eight dependent variables ($p < .05$). The importance between 'speed' and 'dynamics' was not significantly different, except for the 'happiness' emotion ($t(19) = 2.95$, $p < .05$). Although the importance of the 'animation type' was always biggest among three typographical elements, its relative importance was significantly different among eight measurements ($F(7, 133) = 8.27$, $p < .05$). The 'animation type' played a relatively less important role in expressing 'surprise' (49.01%) and 'energy' (45.72%). It was interesting to note that, however, the importance of the 'dynamics' element was biggest in expressing these emotions ($F(7, 133) = 6.74$, $p < .05$). There was no significant difference in 'speed' elements among eight measurements ($F(7, 133) = 2.02$, $p = .57$).

Emotions	Type*	Speed	Dynamics*
Happiness*	**58.41**	**24.40**	**17.20**
Sadness*	**54.82**	**23.79**	**21.39**
Anger*	**57.40**	**18.90**	**23.71**
Fear*	**55.37**	**20.92**	**23.70**
Surprise*	**49.01**	**24.04**	**26.95**
Disappointment*	**59.58**	**22.09**	**18.34**
Mood*	**65.62**	**18.00**	**16.37**
Energy*	**45.72**	**25.62**	**28.66**

Table 1. Relative importance (%) from conjoint analysis. An asterisk indicates significance at $p < .05$.

In order to propose the best kinetic typography for each of the six basic emotions, part-worth utilities were derived from conjoint analysis, as shown in Table 2. The post hoc tests indicated that there is no single representative 'animation type' for each emotion. Hence, the animation types with a significantly higher utility score were extracted and underlined for each typographical element.

Next, we plotted eight animation types on the Affect Grid using the 'Mood' and 'Energy' scores, as shown in Figure 4. The result from the Affect Grid is qualitatively consistent with the best animation types extracted for six basic emotions. For instance, 'vertical' and 'jumping' animation types in the excitement (1st) quadrant are suggested for 'happiness' or 'surprise' emotion. The 'horizontal' and 'expansion' animations are located in the stress (2nd) quadrant, and they should convey emotions of 'anger,' 'fear,' or 'surprise.' The 'vibration,' 'flopping,' and 'shimmy' animation type were located in the depression (3rd) quadrant, and they should be adequate for 'sadness,' 'anger,' 'fear,' or 'disappointment.' For these seven animation types, the changes in speed and dynamics merely act as an 'amplifier.' This indicates that the influence of speed and dynamics on the emotional characteristics was marginal.

Interestingly, the 'pendulum' animation type was plotted on a neutral point. In fact, this received positive utility scores

Elements	Levels	Happiness	Sadness	Anger	Fear	Surprise	Disappoint	Mood	Energy
Animation type	Vertical	1.19	-0.45	-0.12	-0.33	0.45	-0.64	0.81	0.65
	Horizontal	-0.22	-0.37	0.84	0.43	0.60	-0.49	-0.34	0.80
	Expansion	-0.48	-0.79	1.14	0.89	1.30	-0.92	-0.39	1.05
	Vibration	-0.67	0.23	0.02	0.96	-0.07	0.06	-0.43	-0.65
	Jumping	1.82	-0.87	-0.71	-0.61	0.36	-1.10	1.89	0.64
	Pendulum	0.32	0.34	-0.23	-0.66	-0.52	0.41	0.03	0.05
	Flopping	-1.18	1.06	-0.49	-0.12	-0.79	1.51	-1.14	-0.85
	Shimmy	-0.77	0.86	-0.46	-0.56	-1.32	1.16	-0.43	-1.70
Speed	Slow	-0.64	0.49	-0.30	-0.15	-0.63	0.44	-0.40	-0.95
	Moderate	-0.06	0.02	-0.11	-0.13	-0.19	0.10	0.05	-0.02
	Fast	0.71	-0.50	0.41	0.28	0.81	-0.54	0.36	0.97
Dynamics	Minimum	-0.34	0.43	-0.56	-0.33	-0.72	0.41	-0.07	-1.12
	Medium	0.21	-0.26	-0.06	-0.13	-0.20	-0.32	0.36	0.18
	Maximum	0.13	-0.17	0.62	0.46	0.92	-0.08	-0.29	0.94

Table 2. Part worth utilities of each level for eight emotions. The underlined scores indicate a statistical difference at $p < .05$.

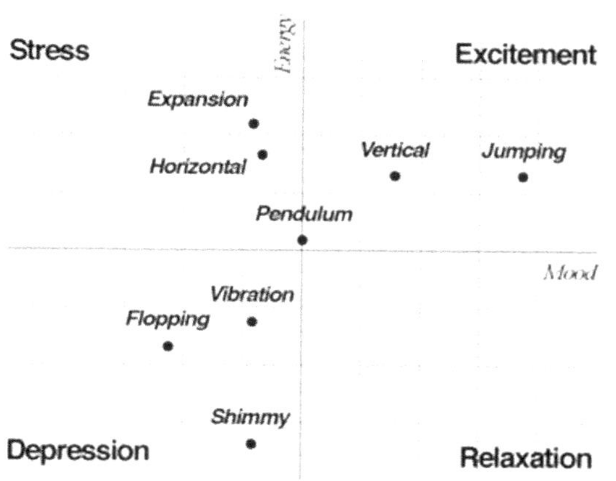

Figure 4. Eight animation types plotted on Affect Grid.

for both 'happiness' (0.32) and 'sadness' (0.34) emotions. We performed a paired samples t-test between the pendulum type with fast speed and maximum dynamics, and with slow speed and minimum dynamics. The result indicated that the effects of speed and dynamics on the 'happiness' ($t(19) = -2.57$, $p < .05$) and 'sadness' ($t(19) = 5.08$, $p < .05$) were significant. This implies that the changes of speed and dynamics function as 'shunt switches' when the animation type has a less sensitive emotional stereotype.

DISCUSSION AND FUTURE WORK

Based on the empirical studies, we suggest a new way of using single-button messengers expecting that they also can deliver the emotions.

Firstly, using animated texts with other data can enrich the communication, as shown in Figure 5. For instance, people can send their location on the 'Yo' app. Its current function is the notification of the user's presence, and it is difficult to draw rich communication. On the other hand, location data with animated text connote a much richer communication aspect. People can express their feelings with their presence such as, "It's really nice to be here," or "The food at this restaurant tastes really bad." Other types of data such as health data might also be applicable.

Secondly, notification with animated texts can be embedded in the 'communication with things,' as shown in Figure 6.

Figure 5. Using animated texts with other data.

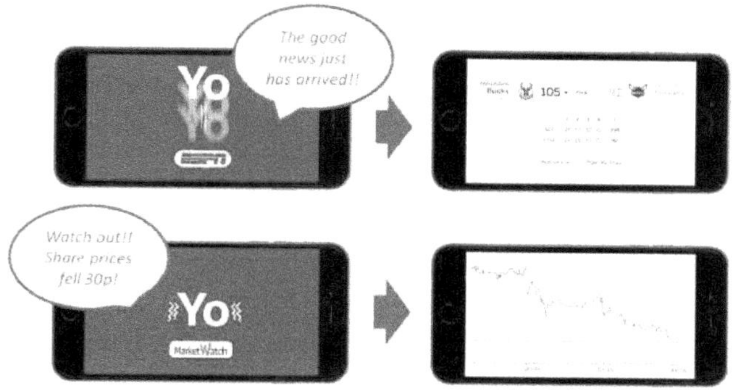

Figure 6. Animated texts embedded in the 'communication with things.'

Currently, the 'Yo' app has been updated with a new function, providing users a new way to subscribe to updates from their favorite online 'things.' This shows that the platform has simply outgrown its function and that it is not only for 'interpersonal' communication but also communication with 'things.' In this situation, animated text can support appropriate notification depending on its contents or users' preferences. For instance, news notifications about users' favorite sports teams can be delivered with the excited-feeling animation, or a bad news notification about the stock market can be delivered with a depressed animation. This helps people engage more with the notification.

However, this study is limited to the articulation of three elements among the kinetic typography. Also, we should be concerned about the real benefit of making the simple messenger more complex. We are aware of the successful merging between simple text and rich emotional communication. For instance, users' physiological data might be utilized as an automated input.

Nevertheless, we have shown the possibility of using kinetic typography on the single-button messengers as an emotional communication tool and provided evidence that it is a relatively simple and nevertheless emotion-rich tool for fast and powerful communication.

CONCLUSION

In this study, we explored the influence of adding kinetic typography onto the single-button messenger to enrich the communicational aspects by conducting a series of two complementary studies. From the preliminary study, eight macro animations were created by users and adopted for evaluation in a main subsequent study. From the main study, we found that the 'animation type' plays the most important role in conveying emotional quality among three kinetic typographical elements. Besides the animation type, we observed that the intervention of speed and dynamics could act as an 'amplifier' or a 'shunt switch,' depending on the animation type. The findings in this paper are expected to strengthen the potential value of the single-button messenger and expand its usage.

REFERENCES

1. Kerry Bodine and Mathilde Pignol. 2003. Kinetic typography-based instant messaging. In *Proceedings of the CHI'03 Extended Abstracts on Human Factors in Computing Systems*, 914-915. http://doi.acm.org/10.1145/765891.766067
2. Sam Byford. 2015. Messaging apps could be the best thing about the Apple Watch. Retrieved January 15, 2015 from http://www.theverge.com/2015/7/8/8910935/apple-watch-messaging-apps-asia
3. Shannon Ford, Jodi Forlizzi, and Suguru Ishizaki. 1997. Kinetic typography: issues in time-based presentation of text. In *Proceedings of the CHI'97 Extended Abstracts on Human Factors in Computing Systems*, 269-270. http://doi.acm.org/10.1145/1120212.1120387
4. Jodi Forlizzi, Johnny Lee, and Scott Hudson. 2003. The kinedit system: affective messages using dynamic texts. In *Proceedings of the SIGCHI Conference on Human Factors in Computing Systems*, 377-384. http://doi.acm.org/10.1145/642611.642677
5. Weston Gaylord, Vivian Hare, and Ashley Ngu. 2015. Adding body motion and intonation to instant messaging with animation. In *Proceedings of the 28th Annual ACM Symposium on User Interface Software & Technology*, 105-106. http://doi.acm.org/10.1145/2815585.2815741
6. Johnny C. Lee, Jodi Forlizzi, and Scott E. Hudson. 2002. The kinetic typography engine: an extensible system for animating expressive text. In *Proceedings of the 15th annual ACM symposium on User interface software and technology*, 81-90. http://doi.acm.org/10.1145/571985.571997
7. Joonhwan Lee, Soojin Jun, Jodi Forlizzi, and Scott E. Hudson. 2006. Using kinetic typography to convey emotion in text-based interpersonal communication. In *Proceedings of the 6th conference on Designing Interactive systems*, 41-49. http://doi.acm.org/10.1145/1142405.1142414
8. James A. Russell, Anna Weiss, and Gerald A. Mendelsohn. 1989. Affect grid: a single-item scale of pleasure and arousal. *J Pers Soc Psychol* 57, 3: 493-502.
9. Ori Schwarz. 2011. Who moved my conversation? Instant messaging, intertextuality and new regimes of intimacy and truth. *Media Cult Soc* 33, 1: 71-87.
10. Zhiquan Yeo. 2008. Emotional instant messaging with KIM. In *Proceedings of the CHI'08 Extended Abstracts on Human Factors in Computing Systems*, 3729-3734. http://doi.acm.org/10.1145/1358628.1358921

T.A.I: A Tangible AI Interface to Enhance Human-Artificial Intelligence (AI) Communication Beyond the Screen

Xin Liu[1,2]
[1]MIT Media Lab
Cambridge, USA
xxxxxxin@mit.edu

Kati London[1]
[2]Microsoft Research
New York, USA
katil@microsoft.com

ABSTRACT
Social and emotional intelligence of computer systems is increasingly important in human-AI (Artificial Intelligence) interactions. This paper presents a tangible AI interface, T.A.I, that enhances physical engagement in digital communication between users and a conversational AI agent. We describe a compact, pneumatically shape-changing hardware design with a rich set of physical gestures that actuate on mobile devices during real-time conversations. Our user study suggests that the physical presence provided by T.A.I increased users' empathy for, and social connection with the virtual intelligent system, leading to an improved Human-AI communication experience.

Author Keywords
Shape-changing interface; Affective Communication; Social Agent; Tangible interface

ACM Classification Keywords
H.5.2. Information interfaces and presentation: User Interfaces

INTRODUCTION AND RELATED WORKS
Social and emotional intelligence are critical elements of human interactions, communications and relationships. Driving the development of artificially intelligent (AI) agents as social companions, there has been a wave of mobile chat applications and services like Microsoft's Cortana and Apple's Siri, through which new forms of social engagement beyond the human-to-human are being explored. These conversational AI agents and systems are not limited to utilitarian applications, as a key requirement of their designs is that they be capable of establishing social and emotional connections with users. Many researchers have investigated ways of developing intelligent systems that can model and recognize human emotions in order to relate to people[7, 19].

DIS 2016, June 04 - 08, 2016, Brisbane, QLD, Australia

ACM 978-1-4503-4031-1/16/06…$15.00
DOI: http://dx.doi.org/10.1145/2901790.2901896

However, considering the lack of real-world, sensorial interactions, current technologies do not fully support social and emotional connections between intelligent systems and users [22]. Similar to the limitations of remote telepresence communication systems, the absence of a physical presence deprives human-AI interactions of the intimate, non-verbal information which is critical to social and emotion connections between people [1].

Many tangible affective interfaces have been explored on human-to-human remote communications. Quintanilha and Nakanishi used physical objects, on-wall objects and a robotic arm to augment the telepresence of the absent parties [13, 18]. Paiva connected the emotional states of a character and its user through a doll with embedded sensors [14]. Inform, a shape-changing display system, provides a physical presence and allows tangible interactions at a distance [10].With the increase in mobile communications, tangible affective interfaces in forms of phone peripherals are developed to associate tactile experiences with emotional expressions as part of mobile interaction experiences [11, 12, 15]. At the same time, larger, visually observable physical changes have been used to provide animated emotional representations [6, 15]. However, physical interactions with AI conversational agents on mobile devices have been researched only marginally. To date, most physical AI explorations have been explored in the social robot domain. Previous applications have proved and advanced the emotional and social effects of physical interactivity on AI systems such as the full body research projects from MIT Personal Robot Group (Kismet, Tofu, Nexi, Jibo) [17], open source DIY robot Ono with rich facial expressions [20] and personal companion robots like Musio [3] and Paro [8]. In this paper, we focus on applying physical interactions on mobile devices to enhance emotional and social connection between human and a AI system in real-time conversations.

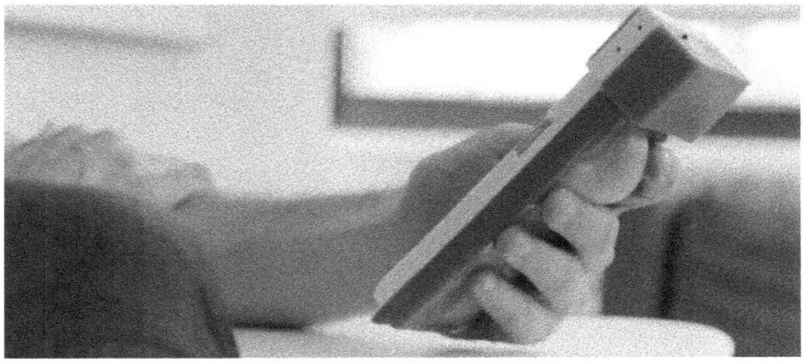

Figure 1. T.A.I system

We propose T.A.I (Figure 1), a mobile shape-changing peripheral that enables a text-based AI conversational agent to deliver physical interactions in real time during mobile chat conversations. Using pneumatically-driven shape-changing materials, T.A.I generates tactile and visual gestures to interact with the user as well as express the AI's own emotional state. To evaluate the role T.A.I played in augmenting the screen-based conversation between the AI agent and its user, we conducted a user study in which participants engaged in conversation with the AI agent both with and without physical interactions. The observations and user interviews showed increased levels of empathy for the AI agent as well as improved conversational results, and provide new insights for the design of affective interfaces for social and emotional AI systems.

T.A.I DESIGN

T.A.I is an embedded, mobile, shape-changing system built upon a text-based AI conversational agent. The user texts the AI through a mobile application and the emotional state of both parties determines T.A.I's shape-changing actuations.

Hardware Design and Physical Actuations

The hardware of T.A.I is contained in the form of a lightweight, portable phone case. A low-voltage micro pump (T2-03, Parker) and three 8mm solenoid valves (X-Valve Parker) are used for air control. Each elastomer bag has its own valve to be independently controlled for deflation and inflation. The high-flow (up to 2.5 LPM free low) micro pump is used to provide air, and the air flow is distributed to each elastomer bag through connected air channels. By switching the valve states and using PWM to control the air flow from the pump, physical actuations can be varied based on speed, amplitude, waveform (motion combinations of three air bags) and duration. Its main control board (A Tmega328p) was programmed to enable additional designs and exploration of a range of physical gestures. The system communicates with mobile devices through Bluetooth LE is powered by a 3.7V LiPo Battery with Qi wireless charging.

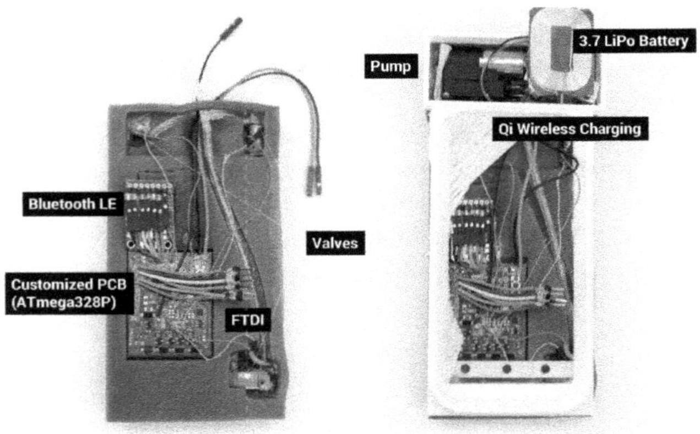

Figure 2. T.A.I Hardware design

The shape-changing actuations are achieved by a composite structure which includes three parts, a stiff silicone part (Blue, Elongation at Break: 339%) with hollows for electronics, air channels and air bags, three soft silicone air bags (Transparent, Elongation at Break: 900%) embedded on the back of the case and a 3D printed case holder to connect the phone and soft materials (Figure 3). Including all the electronics, the air pump and three values, the whole phone case is about 300 grams.

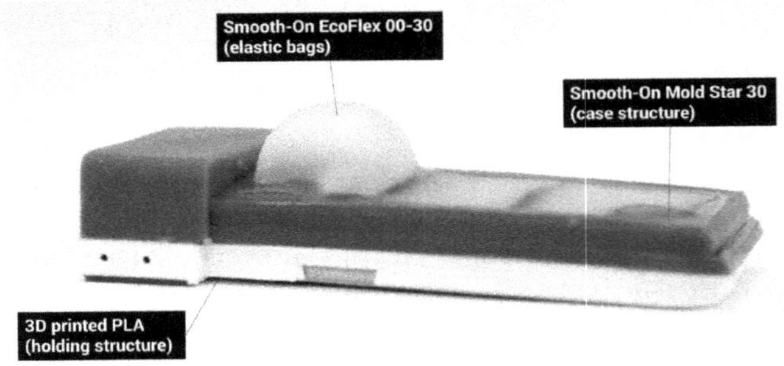

Figure 3. T.A.I shaping-changing structure

Real-world Interaction Design

Through abstract, animated motions, we can assign various emotional content and identities to objects [5, 6]. In T.A.I the five motion factors below form a rich library for emotional communication. Based on previous research [2, 4], we generated the following principles to design the emotional physical gestures.

- *Amplitude*: We support two levels of actuation in terms of amplitude: haptic level, which is mainly experienced through physical contact, and visible level, which is visible from a distance and has broader shape-changing effects. In our design, haptic-level gestures are perceived as intimate while visual gestures express more active, stronger emotions. In visual gestures, large amplitude tends to be seen as positive [4].
- *Speed*: Fast movement correlates with intense emotional expression. Slow motion is perceived as calm and comforting.
- *Waveform*: Jerky motion (random waveforms) is highly related to a negative valence while stable patterns can be calming and comforting.
- *Duration*: Since our physical gestures were implemented on top of a text-based conversation. The duration of each physical gesture cannot exceed 5 seconds, or it would disturb the flow of the conversation. We designed our physical motions to perform within 2-5 seconds.

A.I Agent and User Study Application

The social A.I agent is a custom Chabot accessed through its web API. We built a mobile Android chat application (app) which integrates the conversation between the AI agent and users, the emotion detection, and the physical interaction control. The app was also used in the user study.

T.A.I work flow is shown in Figure 4: A user texts the AI agent using the chat app. Using the AI agent's web API, the app sends the message to be processed, and the response is sent to both the user's phone and a third-party server, our emotion picker. The emotion picker analyzes the conversation to decide the emotional states of the user and TAI. For the purposes of our user study, this analysis was done manually with a human-in-the-loop, who uses a web interface to choose from a predetermined set of emotional states. In the future, this process could be automated with natural language processing. Once the selection is made, the server sends it to the app, which communicates with the embedded processor in the phone case using BLE. The phone case then actuates accordingly.

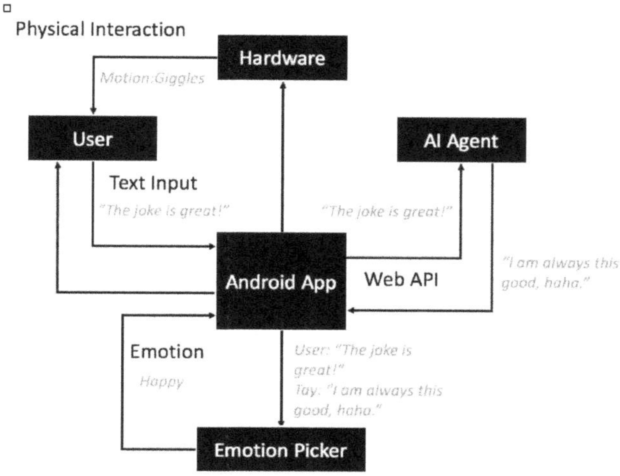

Figure 4. T.A.I work flow example: "happy" emotion is detected and triggers Giggles motion.

Physical gestures are not performed with each response from the AI agent. There are four conditional triggers and their corresponding gestures, shown in the accompanying video, specifically designed for the later user study:

Conditional triggers	Corresponding gestures
Greeting: when the conversation just started.	"waves": three air bags inflate and deflate in sequence
False chat: when the AI Agent cannot understand the user.	"a sigh": middle air bag inflates a little, then deflates
Annoyed: when the conversation is offensive or the user is trying to tease the system	"trembling": Random inflations and deflations among three air bags
Happy: when the conversation is pleasant or the AI agent tells a nice joke	"Giggles": fast and shaking actions at the lower two air bags, while the upper one inflates a little each time

Table 1. T.A.I physical gesture design

USER STUDY

We conducted a user study to explore the following questions: first, do people associate the physical interactions with the AI agent? If they do, how will the physical interactions affect their social communications? Finally, to gain design insight, we collected users' subjective reactions to our material choices and emotional gesture design.

Figure 5. User study setup

In the study, we had two groups chat with the AI agent: a control group (A-D, 3 males and 1 female) in which people only talk to the agent through texts, and a T.A.I group (E-J, 4 males and 2 female) in which there are physical interactions during the conversation with the AI agent. The ten participants were of ages 20-30 and are familiar with mobile chat apps from daily usage.

We introduced the AI agent as a conversational agent and made users aware that they were being video and audio recorded. We asked each participant to text the AI agent for 10 minutes. They could stop the conversation whenever they wanted during the study. After the 10-minute chat, we also conducted a 15-minute interview.

In the after-study interview, users were asked whether they sensed a personality of the AI agent and how the AI agent related to them spatially (inside the phone vs. the telepresence of a remote system). They were also encouraged to talk about their impressions of the AI agent and their overall experience.

FINDINGS

Impression of the presence

More than a virtual, illusory intelligence, the physical interactions provided a more "living" "creature"-like impression of the AI agent for the users. In the interviews, 4 out of 6 participants in the T.A.I group felt that the physical actuation indicated that the AI agent was inside the phone rather than a telepresence of a remote system. User F mentioned, "Something else is here (in the room), not just myself." The tangible interaction created a sense of intimacy as user H stated: "it feels intimate as if the AI agent is in the phone, not in the air".

Emotional and behavioral changes toward AI system

One main issue in AI-human interaction is that users tend to challenge the system rather than relating and talking to it as they would to a person. Similar to human-human communication, a good conversation between the AI agent and our users should contain more specific, detailed discussions. The AI agent has richer editorial contents that can be triggered by keywords such as "weather", "food", "dog", "family", "movie," etc. Compared to the control group, users in the T.A.I group triggered a higher percentage of richer content, leading to longer, deeper conversations around these topics. We believe this indicates that the users tended to talk with T.A.I more successfully rather than just testing or challenging the AI agent, signaling user empathy and social acceptance.

Users in the T.A.I group also spent more time considering their responses to the AI agent compared to the control group, because the physical actuations imposed a delay during the conversation. The pauses have positive effects on conversations, especially when the AI agent failed to respond accurately to the user. In the control group, users tended to question the AI agent more asking: "what do you mean?" and "you are not making sense." In the T.A.I group, when there was a chat failure, the corresponding gesture, "a sigh", paused the conversation for three seconds. After the pause, users seemed to be more forgiving of the AI agent's error and receptive to a topic change, as user F said, "I thought more about what I should say."

Abstract gesture expression

All the users experienced shape-changing actuations on mobile devices for the first time in our study and we didn't inform them about the physical interactions in advance. When the phone performed its "greeting" gesture, users accepted it easily. ("It is surprising.", "I like to touch something.", "It is like a massage, it relaxes me.") Most users in the T.A.I group interpreted the physical actuations as real-life gestures ("The breath feels like a sigh.", "(the wave) is like giggling".) and tried to associate gestures with the AI agent ("Is she thinking?"). However, the messages of gestures weren't always clear to users due to the low threshold of our emotion picker. In the study, a researcher worked as the emotion picker. As a human, the researcher detected emotions easily and the tolerance is fairly large. For example, the researcher would consider both parties are happy when there is a smooth conversation or just a "ha-ha". This mechanism turned to be too sensitive as an emotion picker and the users didn't sense such strong emotion changes or have a different interpretation. User I mentioned, "At the beginning I thought the breath was a sigh but then I got confused when it happened again" when the emotion picker thought the user was annoyed but he wasn't.

Design choices on the phone case

- Material: Users reacted well to silicone, since its soft texture was lifelike. ("rubber is life-like.")
- Motions: Users suggested more dynamic motions as well as other physical effects, like adding some light effects. User I said, "Now it only moves when there is a chat, a reply. But as a lively thing, it should have constant motions. Like when you talk to someone, their body and eyes move all the time, not just when they are speaking."

DISCUSSION AND IMPLICATIONS

There are several lessons in designing physical interactions we learned from the user study:

- Physical actuation deliver a lively, real-life impression of the AI agent which improves users' empathy towards an intelligent system. However, in order to communicate emotions, users tend to interpret the gestures better when it connects to more extreme, obvious emotional changes during the conversations.
- Face-to-face communication in the real world is a dynamic, complex combination of gestures and languages. Adding physical interactions into screen-based messages should consider more active intervals during the conversations rather passive triggers after the current dialog session. These factors in improving physical interactions will be the essential design considerations for a more emotionally engaged and socially accepted tangible human-AI communication interface.
- Social and emotional intelligences in AI systems and affective computing technologies often require intense work on analyzing and reacting to human emotions for a digital system. In the user study, we observed that communication quality with the AI agent was effectively improved with the assistance of tangible affective interfaces. Also supported in previous social robot applications, (Keepon [9] and Tofu [21]), simple, abstract physical appearance and behavior can be a powerful design factor in designing AI systems, especially to improve its emotional relation with users.

CONCLUSIONS AND FUTURE WORK

We developed T.A.I to explore and examine the emotional and social effects of tangible interfaces for human - AI communication. Its pneumatically-driven shape-changing mechanism performs a variety of abstract, animated gestures by changing the speed, amplitude, and waveform of three air bags at the back of a phone case. The compact, portable design of T.A.I enables the seamless integration of shape-changing physical interactions with real-time communication on mobile devices. In a preliminary user study, we observed increased empathy towards the AI conversational agent with the assistance of T.A.I., which also led to a richer communication experience.

Physical interactions give a sense of lifelike presence to intelligent systems. The visible actuation can also function as an active gesture at a distance, supporting notifications. As an interactive phone peripheral, the T.A.I. hardware can also be used in human-human remote communication. The new forms of telepresence established by T.A.I provide opportunities to increase embodied engagement in digital communication.

REFERENCES

1. Adalgeirsson, S. O., & Breazeal, C. (2010, March). Mebot: a robotic platform for socially embodied presence. In Proceedings of the 5th ACM/IEEE international conference on Human-robot interaction (pp. 15-22). IEEE Press.
2. Amaya, K., Bruderlin, A., & Calvert, T. (1996, May). Emotion from motion. In Graphics interface (Vol. 96, pp. 222-229).
3. Anthony Ha. 2015. Meet Musio, A Robot That Talks Back. Retrieved September 25, 2015 from http://techcrunch.com/2015/05/31/meet-musio/
4. Bartram, Lyn, and Ai Nakatani. "What makes motion meaningful? Affective properties of abstract motion." Image and Video Technology (PSIVT), 2010 Fourth Pacific-Rim Symposium on. IEEE, 2010.
5. Harris, J., & Sharlin, E. (2011, July). Exploring the affect of abstract motion in social human-robot interaction. In RO-MAN, 2011 IEEE (pp. 441-448). IEEE.
6. Hemmert, F., Löwe, M., Wohlauf, A., & Joost, G. Animate mobiles: proxemically reactive posture actuation as a means of relational interaction with mobile phones. In Proc. *TEI'13*, ACM, 267-27.
7. Ivanović, M., Radovanović, M., Budimac, Z., Mitrović, D., Kurbalija, V., Dai, W., & Zhao, W. Emotional Intelligence and Agents: Survey and Possible Applications. In *Proc. WIMS14*, ACM, 52.
8. Kidd, C. D., Taggart, W., & Turkle, S. (2006, May). A sociable robot to encourage social interaction among the elderly. In Robotics and Automation, 2006. ICRA 2006. Proceedings 2006 IEEE International Conference on (pp. 3972-3976). IEEE.
9. Kozima, H., Michalowski, M. P., & Nakagawa, C. (2009). Keepon. International Journal of Social Robotics, 1(1), 3-18.
10. Leithinger, D., Follmer, S., Olwal, A., & Ishii, H. Physical telepresence: shape capture and display for embodied, computer-mediated remote collaboration. In *Proc. UIST 2014*, ACM, 461-470.
11. Luk, J., Pasquero, J., Little, S., MacLean, K., Levesque, V., & Hayward, V. A role for haptics in mobile interaction: initial design using a handheld tactile display prototype. In *Proc. CHI 2006*, ACM, 171-180.
12. Mullenbach, J., Shultz, C., Colgate, J. E., & Piper, A. M. Exploring affective communication through variable-friction surface haptics. In *Proc. CHI 2014*, ACM, 3963-3972.
13. Nakanishi, H., Tanaka, K., & Wada, Y. Remote handshaking: touch enhances video-mediated social telepresence. In *Proc. CHI 2014*, ACM, 2143-2152.
14. Paiva, A., Prada, R., Chaves, R., Vala, M., Bullock, A., Andersson, G., & Höök, K. Towards tangibility in gameplay: building a tangible affective interface for a computer game. In *Proc. ICMI 2003*, ACM, 60-67.
15. Park, J., Park, Y. W., & Nam, T. J. Wrigglo: shape-changing peripheral for interpersonal mobile communication. In *Proc. CHI 2014*, ACM, 3973-3976.
16. Park, Y. W., Park, J., & Nam, T. J. The Trial of Bendi in a Coffeehouse: Use of a Shape-Changing Device for a Tactile-Visual Phone Conversation. In *Proc. CHI 2015*, ACM, 2181-2190.
17. Personal Robot Group. Project list. MIT Media Lab Retrieved September 25, 2015 from http://robotic.media.mit.edu/project-portfolio/
18. Quintanilha, M. S. Buddywall: a tangible user interface for wireless remote communication. In *CHI EA'08* , ACM, 3711-3716.
19. Schröder, M., & McKeown, G. Considering social and emotional artificial intelligence. *In Proc. AISB 2010.*
20. Vandevelde, C., Saldien, J., Ciocci, M. C., & Vanderborght, B. (2013). Systems Overview of Ono. In Social Robotics (pp. 311-320). Springer International Publishing.
21. Wistort, R., & Breazeal, C. (2009, June). TOFU: a socially expressive robot character for child interaction. In Proceedings of the 8th International Conference on Interaction Design and Children (pp. 292-293). ACM.
22. Zhang, X. 2013. *Examining sensorial interfaces as the stimuli for remote affective communication.* Phd dissertation. Carleton University Ottawa.

Fostering Engagement with Personal Informatics Systems

Rebecca Gulotta, Jodi Forlizzi
Human-Computer Interaction Institute
Carnegie Mellon University
{rgulotta, forlizzi}@cs.cmu.edu

Rayoung Yang, Mark W. Newman
School of Information
University of Michigan
{rayang, mwnewman}@umich.edu

ABSTRACT
Personal informatics systems are becoming increasingly prevalent as their price, form, and ease of use improves. Though these systems offer great potential value to users, many systems are hampered by issues that limit their ability to foster engagement, and people often abandon use of these systems without garnering meaningful outcomes. While continued use of these systems is not necessary for all people, there is an opportunity to better support people working towards achievement-based goals.

In this paper, we draw from the literature and our own prior work to identify a number of problems that hinder engagement with achievement-based personal informatics systems — problems related to inadequate support for goal-setting, misalignment of user and system goals, and the burden of system maintenance. We then propose seven strategies for the design community to explore for mitigating these problems and discuss how these strategies could be used to foster engagement with PI systems.

Author Keywords
Personal informatics; activity trackers; self-tracking; fitness; health; personalization; reflection.

ACM Classification Keywords
H.5.m. Information interfaces and presentation (e.g., HCI): Miscellaneous

INTRODUCTION
There has been a surge of interest in the use of personal informatics (PI) systems, such as fitness trackers and banking applications, which track and provide feedback about people's behaviors. This emerging category of systems includes physical devices, such as the FitBit and the Nest Thermostat, but also systems with no specific tangible form, such as MyFitnessPal, a food logging service that can be accessed on a computer, tablet, or smartphone. For individuals, these systems offer a variety of potential benefits, such as increased physical fitness, a better sense of one's finances, and, in some cases, a better understanding of one's own goals, values, and desires. Taking into consideration higher-level societal needs, these systems can also offer a way for technology to help address or raise awareness of complex, large-scale problems like climate change and widespread health issues.

While certain types of PI systems, such as heart rate monitors, have been used for years, the accessible price and form of new systems have significantly expanded their use. Their popularity is clear. FitBit, one of the most popular makers of activity trackers, sold over 8 million devices in 2015 alone [24]. PI systems are increasingly being bundled with new devices, such as the Google Fit app for Android smartphones and the Activity app for the Apple Watch. Organizations are also beginning to provide tracking tools to customers by partnering with third parties. One example is Walgreen's Balance Reward Points program, which was designed to help customers stay healthy and become more active [85].

Despite technological and aesthetic improvements to these systems, and their broadening availability, a number of challenges remain that limit the usefulness of these systems. People frequently stop using PI systems without having achieved their goals; those who do reach their goals may lack motivation to continue using the system to maintain their progress or to refine their goals over time. For some people, continued use of the system may no longer be necessary or desired [11]. However, we believe that systems can better support people who are interested in continuing to use PI systems to pursue their goals. Supporting users in this way also benefits product developers, who stand to gain from the potential to collect more complete and more accurate data from users.

In this paper, we draw from our collective experience conducting research on the design and development of PI systems and from related literature to produce a collection of strategies we have developed to help foster engagement between achievement-based PI systems and the people who use them. To do so, we first conduct a literature review identifying problems that hinder or disrupt engagement with PI systems. We then draw from our own research to identify examples of these issues and specific areas to address in the future design of PI systems. Using that information, we propose a set of seven design strategies, grounded in research from related fields including behavioral economics, cognitive psychology, and game design, which we hope will provide direction for the HCI community as they experiment with these strategies in their own work. With that goal in mind, we describe these strategies and consider how they might address challenges

DIS 2016, June 4–8, 2016, Brisbane, Australia.

DOI: http://dx.doi.org/10.1145/2901790.2901803

encountered by people who use existing systems. In the final section of the paper, we discuss broader implications for implementing these strategies.

SCOPE OF OUR WORK

Our work explores *long-term engagement with achievement-based personal informatics systems*. We chose to focus on the achievement of goals rather than reflective or documentary use of PI systems for three reasons. The first is that the majority of people who use PI systems are motivated principally by the desire to reach some goal [21]. The second is that while some of our strategies encourage reflection, it is not yet clear if people with purely reflective goals would benefit from engaging with PI systems in a way that differs from current practices. The third is that failing to engage with a PI system may not actually negatively impact a person's ability to engage in self-reflection. Refection and documentation are, of course, necessary parts of achieving a goal, and these practices are discussed as a part of our larger consideration of how systems can help people achieve their goals. For more information about reflective and documentary use of personal informatics systems, see [21, 61, 69].

Drawing from prior work in personal informatics, we define engagement as the active use of a system that aligns with practices that support a person's ability to achieve a goal using that system. Engagement is not itself an activity or state, but describes a collection of actions that a person may undertake over time, such as regularly contributing data to a system, accessing and reflecting on the data, or making an effort to understand the information it provides. Engagement is not a universal set of behaviors; engagement with a FitBit activity tracker may be different than engagement with the financial management tool Mint, for example.

The goal of supporting long-term engagement with achievement-based PI systems is different from that of supporting only the achievement of a specific or singular goal. Though achieving a goal is an important motivator for many people, focusing exclusively on a single milestone does not reflect the idea that people's goals often change over time, and that the process of reflecting on and refining one's goals is a valuable part of a person's development. As a result, we chose to focus on *fostering engagement* as a way of supporting people as they work to achieve meaningful outcomes, while still being sensitive to the notion that people's goals and activities often change over time, as do the larger contexts in which PI systems operate [12]. This framing also provides an opportunity to explore why people stop using personal informatics systems. For example, a person may feel that PI systems do not align with their understanding of their identity; they may have difficulty of interpreting data captured by PI systems; or they may feel that PI systems require too much maintenance and effort relative to the value they get from using the system [39].

Fostering engagement with PI systems can be beneficial in other ways beyond achieving a personal goal. People sometimes benefit from information provided by other users, so increased engagement can improve the quality of the service that is provided. For example, many food-logging applications rely on users to contribute nutritional information about foods that are not yet in their databases. This information is then available to all users. People also benefit from being actively engaged with a system when that system is able to use the information they provide to give them tailored feedback. That is, if a system can adapt in response to the information it has collected, that may help encourage reflection and further use. Finally, systems that have access to more complete or more accurate information about their users have an opportunity to provide a better service and meet business needs, such as by providing targeted advertising.

RELATED WORK

A number of different strands of research inform this work, illustrating the motivation for, and impact of, human behavior tracking over time. In this section, we discuss research from personal informatics and from broader technological disciplines that describes how and why people use — and subsequently stop using — these systems and devices. Additionally, we focus on cases from our prior research in this area to enrich these findings.

Contextualizing and Motivating Self-Tracking

People have long recorded different aspects of their life such as food intake, exercise, health symptoms, and mood. Though there are limits to what aspects of one's life can be captured through these means, tracking is commonly used in many communities, including medicine, fitness, and mental health [1, 39, 66]. This technique serves a way to track certain metrics over time, to produce data that can be analyzed, and to reflect on one's behavior and experiences [53, 58]. Research has demonstrated that even simple self-tracking efforts, such as writing out one's thoughts, can have a powerful influence on one's understanding of their own life [35]. Self-tracking also supports a number of other outcomes, such as defining one's identity as an individual and developing a sense of control over one's life [63]. Although these activities do not always support healthy behaviors, they do have the potential to deeply impact a person's life, their understanding of that life, and their interactions with other people [87].

Tracking information about oneself is also a way to leverage resources. In some cases, the data generated enables other people to participate in the analysis and use of this data — caregivers, for example, might use this information to better understand a patient's experience outside of treatment sessions. Generating data about one's life also offers opportunities to garner support from other people [20]. People with chronic illness and rare conditions have used online communities as a way to compare symptom experiences and to learn more about treatment options [47]. Finally, generating data provides people with a way to leverage the computational abilities of algorithms that can expose trends in their own data and that learn from information collected from other people [1, 83].

Personal Informatics Systems

The increasing ubiquity of computing has enabled the creation of a wide variety of personal informatics systems designed to facilitate the capture of data about a person's life or the about the lives of a small group of people (such as a family). These systems vary tremendously, as do the goals of the people that use them, but across categories they offer some benefits that extend beyond those offered by non-digital tracking methods.

In addition to the ability to make use of the resources described in the previous section, one advantage is that PI systems assist people with some of the burdensome aspects of self-tracking. Counting one's steps as the FitBit does would be infeasible, for example. While not conventionally considered a "Personal Informatics" system, the Nest Thermostat provides a core PI feature by recording data about users' interactions with the system and then using that information to try and make decisions on their behalf [64]. Many food logging applications are prepopulated with nutritional information about thousands of foods, eliminating the need for people to gather this information on their own [17]. Another benefit of PI systems is the ability for a system to be available as a person changes locations and contexts. Many systems, even those that require the use of a physical device, are available through both websites and mobile apps. Furthermore, the relative ease of tracking with digital systems has enabled people to track more information and to switch between systems, which is a common practice for users [21]. PI systems also allow people to connect with other people that can support them as they work towards their goal [20, 62]. Looking forward, the data captured by PI systems may also offer opportunities to generate historical records about one's life that allow for reflection many years in the future [19].

Understanding Abandonment

As use of personal informatics systems has spread, there has been a growing interest in understanding what leads people to stop using them. Prior work has highlighted a number of factors, ranging from misalignment of goals, to expectations of system use, to aligning with needs and values, to issues with system functionality.

These are not issues that are unique to PI systems, but they do greatly hamper a person's ability to use them effectively [54]. One significant factor that influences the use of PI systems is people's perceptions about the usefulness of those systems. It can be difficult for people to understand how to interpret the information presented to them by a system [48], or to assess the information accuracy [89]. Additionally, people have reported a mismatch between their goals and the goals that were supported by the system [12, 48]. There are also people who have stopped using PI systems because they have reached their goals. This is not an undesirable form of abandonment, but exposes an opportunity to think about how we can support people even after their initial goal has been achieved. Abandonment is also influenced by the sense that a system does not align with a person's needs and values — prior work describes situations in which people have abandoned a system because it seemed to support a type of person that they did not identify with [48, 76]. Other people who have stopped using, or who intermittently use, PI systems note that a high level of maintenance and interaction was required to use the system relative to the expected benefits [17, 21, 48].

Prior work has also investigated what motivates people to leave or stop using a related category of services: social networks. Although there are important differences between these two categories of systems, people who stop using social networks describe many of the same motivations as people who stop using PI systems (some of which share many features with social networks). These include wanting to limit the time one spent using the service [75], concerns about the burdens of maintaining social relationships [5], and concerns about privacy [2]. Prior work also highlights the value of non-use in particular situations. For example, a study of people leaving the social network Grindr describes how some people who left the site did so to illustrate their investment in other social groups and relationships [8].

Our research on long-term engagement

Our own research has explored problems with abandonment and misuse of PI systems in more detail, in particular misalignment with goals, expectations for frequency of use, perception of usefulness, and issues with system maintenance. Our work helps us move from problem to strategy by beginning to populate the vast design space of PI systems with designs that are less and more successful. Below, we describe this work and highlight design implications for personal informatics systems. It is important to note that the research we describe below took place across different time periods, domains, and research institutions, with each of the authors contributing their expertise to an understanding of the higher-level issues addressed in this paper.

Some of this work has focused on the goal-setting process. In [52], we investigated how prompting users to reflect on their goals could shape their ability to achieve those goals. To do so, we deployed a website called Fitbit Plan that prompted people to set daily step goals by either allowing the system to generate suggestions based on their past performance or by prompting users to reflect on their overall goals. This work articulates design strategies that leverage reflective personalization to help people achieve their goals and that might foster engagement with a system over time.

We found similar phenomena in a different domain, identifying challenges that a person might face as they try to understand the relative trade offs associated with setting a particular goal. This study, which investigated the use of the Nest Thermostat, found that when the control of a smart, predictive thermostat was left to users, they often tended to prioritize their personal comfort goals rather than taking advantage of the potential energy savings. As such, this work explored the topic of prioritizing one aspect of a goal over another to better align with one's broader needs and values [89].

Misalignment of goals has also been a salient thread in our prior work, where participants frequently described how changes to their goals have led them to stop using a particular system or to switch to another system [53]. In some cases, this change was a result of increased familiarity with the functionality provided by a particular system, which led people to look for a system that might better suit their needs [53, 88]. Other work has demonstrated how systems can successfully foster engagement, and overcome challenges that limit people's desire to use a system, such as by providing information to users that successfully conveys how particular goals are supported by the functionality of the system [89].

Another piece of our prior work explores a pivotal issue — the ability for a PI system to align with a user's motivations and desires. This work surveyed 133 people who use or have used personal informatics systems and explored how these systems supported particular psychological needs, such as the feeling that is a person is competent and that they are continuing to grow and develop [40]. This work highlights the ways in which systems can foster engagement with users.

Our research has also investigated the factors that influence how users perceive the effort needed to use a particular system. [54] published the results of interviews with fifteen people who use personal informatics systems such as activity trackers and financial tracking websites. This work illustrated that people often found it difficult to interpret the information provided by those systems, a difficultly that reduced people's perceptions of the value they were getting from each of these systems.

Finally, our research has also noted issues that arise when system functionality does not meet people's expectations. The study of the Nest Thermostat described how users were disappointed in the thermostat's inability to correctly interpret individual behaviors [88]. This misinterpretation sometimes required users to make corrections to the thermostat and frustrated users who reported feeling as though the thermostat was not working properly.

In the next section, we build on these findings to identify specific problems that arise from how personal informatics systems are designed and used.

DESIGN PROBLEMS THAT HINDER LONG-TERM ENGAGEMENT WITH PI SYSTEMS

A survey of related work and a growing design space populated by results from research done in our labs and beyond yields a set of problems that affect long-term engagement with achievement-based PI systems. We summarize them here:

People's goals do not match system goals — PI systems typically support a combination of different types of goals, most often reflective and achievement-based goals. Reflective goals or documentary goals are those motivated by the desire to learn about one's habits, but do not necessarily involve making any behavior changes [74]. Achievement-based goals focus on a particular thing that a person wants to achieve, such as walking a certain number of steps per day. Not all systems support both, but some do to varying degrees.

A person's goal changes over time — People's goals will sometimes change as they use a PI system [76]. For example, a person who decides to increase their physical activity may find that their initial goal was too ambitious or that it does not account for their changing fitness level. PI systems often do not provide opportunities for users to reconsider their goals in a way that reflects their experience using the system over time.

A person achieves their goal — When a goal is achieved, a person may stop using a particular system. In some cases, it may be advantageous for a person to continue using a system but to shift their goals, however systems do not adequately support this process [12].

Information may be hard to access or interpret — People may find it difficult to interpret the information that is provided to them by the system. For example, a system might display a graph of a person's performance over time without providing them with the tools to draw out any conclusions or direction from that information [54]. Additionally, people may find it difficult to assess the accuracy and reliability of the information provided by the system, which in turn may lead to mistrust [90].

Maintenance and routine use requirements may be burdensome — All systems require some degree of maintenance. For example, some need to be charged, some require the user to correct errors in the data they record, and some require a user to provide feedback in order to make decisions about how to operate. Others may require users to input information about their behaviors. For example, MyFitnessPal — a food and activity logging service — encourages users to return at least once a day. Users may come to believe that these requirements outweigh the benefits they receive from the system [78].

System does not align with aspects of the user's identity — The use of a personal informatics system may intersect with identity presentation concerns, particularly when the systems involve wearing devices or engaging in behaviors that may elicit reactions from other people [48]. In addition, a system may not support the needs that drive a person's use of that system, nor a person's understanding of their own values.

Connections to social support — One common feature that PI systems offer is the ability to share information about one's progress through social media accounts. Another example is the ability to connect your account to that of another user so that you can see their activity and receive feedback from within the system. While these features can be motivating for some users [20], some work has shown that social sharing of information from PI systems can discourage use of the systems and cause apprehension for users [17, 72]. Other research has shown that public goal setting was effective at eliciting support from a social community and was helpful in setting goals [21].

Dependencies on other systems — Certain types of systems depend on databases of information to reduce the burden associated with self-tracking. For example, many food-tracking applications provide nutritional information for common or brand-name foods. This type of information can make using the system more convenient, but can also contain omissions and errors that make it difficult to assess one's progress [17].

STRATEGIES TO FOSTER ENGAGEMENT

We have organized the problems identified in prior work into three overarching categories: inadequate support for goal-setting, misalignment of user and system goals, and burden of system maintenance. For each of the categories, we note the importance of addressing that category of problems and describe potential solutions informed by literature in this space. The remaining problem that does not fall into these categories — the inability for systems to re-engage users that have achieved their goals — is explored in the discussion section, due to the broader ethical questions involved in implementing strategies to address that issue.

Problem: Inadequate Support for Goal-Setting

Goal-setting is a critical task for people who use PI systems; properly setting a goal can help support adherence to that goal over time [82]. The process of setting a goal involves considering one's current state, one's desired outcome, and a strategy for achieving that outcome. In addition, there are other key factors that can influence a person's ability and desire to achieve a goal. Two of these factors, efficacy and commitment, reflect a person's belief that they can achieve a goal and strength of their resolve to do so [15]. Goal-setting theory also suggests that one's ability to achieve a goal is influenced by that person's assessment of whether that goal is reasonable and in line with their personal understanding of what they'd like to achieve [56]. Consequently, setting goals that do not have the right level of specificity or difficulty can hamper a person's desire and ability to accomplish these goals.

Proposed strategy: Reflective approach to goal-setting

We believe that supporting a reflective approach to goal-setting will help address several of these issues, perhaps by helping people create system-specific goals that are better aligned with their broader goals, or by helping people consider the challenges that they might face when working to achieve a goal. Instead of simply asking a user to enter their goal, systems employing this strategy would help the user to choose a goal by asking them to reflect on what motivates their decision. Research from outside of PI also supports the idea of reflective goal-setting — literature from education and cognitive psychology describes how a high degree of metacognitive awareness, or understanding one's own thought processes, can help people achieve their goals [73].

Though there has been thoughtful work that has examined how to structure goal-setting in PI systems [15], few have examined using reflection as a part of this process. However, one example of recent work does examine how reflective goal-setting can be used to support people in increasing their physical activity. The study asked participants to describe why they had chosen a particular goal and then gave them time during which they were asked elaborate on that answer. This process was effective in increasing users' levels of physical activity [52].

While further research is necessary to understand the best ways of utilizing reflective approaches to encourage metacognition in the goal-setting phase, we believe that this strategy will likely help people set better goals and better understand their own motivations. There could also be benefits to users as they work toward their goal. The information provided during this initial process could be used by the system to tailor the feedback that a user receives over time. Finally, this strategy could also help manage user expectations. PI systems have made it easier to track and visualize information, but achieving one's goals is still a difficult process for many people [65]. Using reflection at the start of a person's effort is an opportunity to reinforce the idea that reflection can play an instrumental role in achieving long-term benefits.

In practice, this strategy could be implemented to draw from a number of different sources of information that enable reflection. One method would be to ask the user to think more deeply about their specific goal (such as losing ten pounds or biking 25 miles a week) and also their larger motivations (such as becoming more fit and preparing for a long distance bike trip) [52]. This information could then be used to provide more meaningful feedback to users, particularly when lapses occur or when a person is not making steady progress towards their goal. Another variation on this strategy would be to utilize the information provided by other users as a way of providing people with a better understanding of what might be a reasonable goal to set and to prepare them for the challenges they might face.

Problem: Misalignment of User and System Goals

It is sometimes necessary for a person to refine or change a goal they originally set [53]. Though this process is often programmatically simple to do, it can be personally challenging because it requires to that a person engage in higher-level thinking about their goals and their progress towards those goals. It can also be personally challenging because of the negative feelings that may be associated with changing a goal. Though it is not an uncommon practice, users may be disinclined to change their goal when it feels like they have failed or when the system makes it seem as though this action is unusual or discouraged. There is also an opportunity to help people refine their long-term goals after they've accomplished an initial goal. Over time, a person may realize that their original goal does not ultimately suit their higher-level motivations and may return to the system to make revisions and begin working towards their new goal.

Proposed strategy: Periodic reflection on goals

Despite the widespread understanding that reflection is a critical process for people who use PI systems [54], systems have been slow to integrate formal opportunities for reflection into their programs. We suggest that systems should provide opportunities for periodic reflection on user goals to help people evaluate their progress and to help people engage with other resources that could support their efforts. While there is a need to balance the usefulness of user engagement with the costs to users, we believe that systems could use periodic reflection to help shift people's perceptions about the value that they receive from the system relative to the effort required to use it.

This strategy is informed by research that suggests that asking people what their reasons are for doing an activity triggers them to consider their underlying motivation and leads them to focus on their higher-level goals [85]. In addition, work on periodic prompting indicates that these interventions exert a positive influence on people's behaviors [28]. Thus, these requests for periodic reflection can be designed such that they provide value to the user, increasing perceived utility as well as engagement. Though prompts differ in meaningful ways from opportunities for reflection, this research does provide support for the use of periodic interaction with users and also describes some key considerations to consider when designing the reflections, namely the period, medium, composition, and personalization of the messages [28]. This work also highlights the importance of taking people's broader practices into account when designing these interactions [29].

There are several factors to consider when implementing periodic reflection on both user and system goals. The first is deciding when reflection will occur. We believe that personalized timing would reduce the potential negative impacts of engaging the user in a way that they don't perceive to be meaningful. For example, systems could time reflection in response to a person's history of interaction with the system, to the length of time the system estimates that a person needs to achieve their goal, or to patterns of use derived from other people's data.

Proposed strategy: Personalization in system configuration and use

Personalization in technology services can be defined as using the decisions people make about their interactions with systems to influence the content they see and engage with. It also refers to allowing people to directly select features they want to use as a way to customize their interactions with a system [6]. Prior research has shown that personalization in system design offers many benefits, including reduced cognitive load, assistance with workflow, and more persuasive and satisfying interactions overall [4, 6, 41, 46, 50, 55, 84].

Personalization in systems can be classified into two types: system-driven personalization and user-driven personalization. In system-driven personalization, systems infer what people want based on their model of a user, occasionally with poor outcomes [49]. Though most personal informatics systems allow users to set particular preferences, the use of system-driven personalization is less widely used, perhaps due to the difficulties of implementing these features and the potential for negative consequences. That being said, some research has suggested that individuals (and different personality types) may vary in regards to what types of feedback help motivate their use of personal informatics systems [33]. In addition, personalization may allow a system to adapt to the needs of different types of users, such as people who are new to self-tracking, people who have broad goals, or people who are serious athletes.

User-driven personalization lets people choose from a number of alternatives, tailoring their experience with a system. This type of personalization can have positive outcomes as it minimizes cognitive overload and may support people in reaching their goals. However, choices provided to users may seem like formulaic customization, or may cause people to feel overwhelmed when they are faced with the task of making choices [38, 79].

Some research has shown that personalization in HCI can be beneficial for fostering interaction with a system. For example, [7] explored what personal and contextual factors come into play when personalizing TV viewing schedules and found that relying on knowledge of family members and prior viewing resulted in better recommendations. Similarly, personalization has long been explored in e-commerce as a way of pursuing changes that benefit both users and systems [42].

One way to approach personalization in PI systems to motivate engagement is to enable systems to better respond to user-driven strategies and to make recommendations for personalization. For example, [52] allowed users to either create their own goals for daily steps or to follow suggested plans based on their performance over the previous two weeks. In addition to providing people with a way to deeply reflect on their goals, this feature resulted in people taking more steps than those who were using the standard FitBit system and dashboard.

Proposed strategy: Mixed-initiation as a means of helping to achieve goals

Another strategy to help users refine or change their goals over time is mixed-initiation [23], which combines prompts from both the system and user to accomplish a mutual mission, with initiatives and roles opportunistically negotiated. This strategy has been discussed with regards to developing an agent system that manages tasks for users, such as scheduling and meeting management [23]. Several pieces of research work have extended this notion to the design of PI systems that assist users make plans to achieve system and user goals [89, 43, 45]. Even basic systems initiative can be helpful: some research has shown that simple prompts from a system can increase self-logging frequency by a factor of five [3].

In discussing challenges for PI systems that promote energy savings, [88] illustrate how systems need to encourage users to make changes but to also be realistic about their own needs. In this work, Yang and Newman found that when the control was solely left to users, they often tended to prioritize their comfort goals over energy savings. As a result, energy savings remained unrealized as user relied on the system automation and their engagement decreased over time [89].

To address these challenges, it will be necessary for personal informatics systems to act proactively in getting users to reassess and refine their goals. For example, [70] provided users with three suggestions to configure their thermostat: a high comfort option, an energy saving option, and a balanced option, along with users' existing schedule. Then, the system left users to decide whether and how to implement the suggestions, engaging users to take control of decisions related to their potential energy savings, as opposed to relying on the PI system to make those decisions. The study results indicated that users who used this system saved more energy than those who did not [70].

By designing systems that promote responsibility and initiate interactions with users, systems can foster engagement and help users to readjust their goals with suggestions based on their current progress.

Problem: Burden of System Use and Maintenance

After setting a goal, a person begins the process of working towards it. This work is, in a way, a collaboration between users and systems. As a part of this collaboration, users are responsible for generating data, for attending to system upkeep, and for engaging in routine use. Systems are responsible for tracking information, processing that information, and providing users with feedback about their progress.

Proposed strategy: Motivational design as a mechanism to increase system use

One way to address misalignment between perceived value of a system and the effort that system requires from users is to leverage motivational design strategies. Here, we use the term motivational design to refer to a combination of strategies from behavioral economics and features from game mechanics that can be used to motivate people to engage in more productive use of PI systems. As both behavioral economics and game design are entire fields of study, it is not our goal to be complete in our discussion of either discipline. Instead, we have identified several specific concepts that have inspired us to think about how they might be employed as design strategies for personal informatics systems.

We are not the first to note that these disciplines contain valuable insights for designers interested in supporting engagement — prior research from persuasive technology has shown that feedback about one's interactions with a system can foster engagement with it [25]. Our prior research has demonstrated ways in which we can leverage thoughtful presentation and timing of information to encourage people to make self-beneficial decisions that will help them make progress towards their goals [51].

Though many systems use rewards to try to motivate users, the way these features are implemented makes a difference in whether they hamper or support people. Research on the use of rewards in PI has illustrated that many people find rewards to be good motivation to complete tasks that ultimately support one's goals [26]. Not surprisingly, many systems have implemented rewards as a way to motivate and engage users. For example, Strava, a GPS app used by bicyclists and runners to track and improve progress in their workouts, features game mechanics such as badges and leaderboards to foster engagement and inspire long-term use of the system [81]. While some users undoubtedly feel motivated by these challenges, research on the direct effects of employing game mechanics and rewards indicates that the application of these concepts is nuanced and context-specific [91].

In order to effectively put these ideas into practice, work from behavioral economics and game design can help designers develop rewards that capitalize on users' desires to compare themselves to others with particular characteristics and affiliations. Research that examined how to persuade people to engage in resource-saving behaviors found that evoking provincial norms — norms based on one's situational context — was a powerful motivator [30].

Work from behavioral economics also describes other phenomena that can influence how a person understands their current context and makes decisions based on that understanding. For example, researchers have suggested that asymmetric paternalism, a method of influencing people to make particular choices, and present bias, the tendency for people to place higher value on more immediate rewards, are powerful ways to influence people to make decisions that benefit their health [57]. Ways to approach applying motivational design could include convenience and salience (making the most important information the easiest to access and the most demanding of attention) and choice attractiveness (positioning the right choice about one's behavior with a less attractive choice so the optimal decision is easy). These rewards can be used to motivate people to work towards a goal, but also to engage with a system. There is also an opportunity to examine how existing rewards align with literature from behavioral economics that articulates what motivates people to engage in behavior change.

Proposed strategy: Ambient awareness to increase system use with minimal attention

Another way to reduce how a person perceives the overall burden of a personal informatics system is to leverage ambient awareness, where information is presented in a way that does not attract a great deal of attention [10]. This ambient information could display the status of the interaction between user and system, or give information relative to progress towards one's goals, without attracting much of the user's attention. Prior work in PI has investigated how to visualize and segment information so that it provides the greatest clarity and benefits for users [60, 80]. This information can be useful in fostering engagement in four ways: minimizing the time to answer questions, helping to generate insights and insightful questions, conveying the essence of the data, and generating confidence and knowledge about the data itself [80]. We can leverage this work and other research on ambient displays to reduce two reasons that people describe abandoning personal informatics systems: (1) the perception that a system is not useful and (2) the perception that a personal informatics systems requires too high a level of maintenance.

In order to convey usefulness, ambient information needs to be designed appropriately. Designs may exploit metaphors drawn from nature to subtly convey information — for example, using the rhythm of a heartbeat or respiration, or representations of water or wind. UbiFit, a personal informatics system designed to encourage physical activity found providing abstract, at-a-glance information on the background of a mobile phone was an effective way to support reflection on one's goals and behaviors [14, 15, 16]. In another example, [32] used a dynamic visualization of light along a lamp's power cord to show the energy used. The AMBIENTroom project explored representations of water and wind moving clouds in the sky to explore how awareness of an information display could be moved from the periphery to the center of attention and back [36, 37]. Further research could help determine how to utilize the topic of the data to make decisions about the visual design of a PI system.

Proposed strategy: Improved social features

We believe that systems can provide better opportunities for users to connect with other people who share their goals and who can provide them with support. Doing so would help motivate people to engage with a system and would lessen the perception that a system does not provide a worthwhile value to its users.

Prior work suggests that people are motivated to share information captured by PI systems because it helps them stay accountable, allows them to elicit support, and because it allows them to portray themselves in a particular light or align with a desired identity [20]. In addition to social interaction that is mediated by social networks, some systems offer people the ability to communicate with other users. Communicating with other people who have an understanding of what you might be experiencing can be very valuable; research suggests that social interaction between people in similar circumstances can help encourage people to seek out useful information, to offer support to others, and to share their experiences [27]. Additionally, research on online support networks has demonstrated that participating in these networks can have a positive impact on a person's well-being [71].

Many current systems offer users the opportunity to connect with other users, but it is often up to the individual to seek out and find these people through existing social networks. For example, FitBit allows users to search their Facebook friends list for other people who are also FitBit users. While being able to see your friend's activity can be motivating, it can also discourage people to log data that may reflect badly on their image or their ability to accomplish their goals. Another difficulty is that it can be challenging for some users to communicate information about their experiences in a way that elicits that desired support from other people [20].

Systems can address this issue by leveraging their ability to analyze user data to help people connect with other people who can provide support. Some examples of how this might work include matching users with similar goals, who have overcome similar challenges, or who are using the same methods. In addition, as systems become increasingly sophisticated in their ability to analyze user data, they might be able to match people who are working towards a particular goal with users who have already accomplished similar goals as a way of providing mentoring to new users. This strategy would help engage users at all stages of the process.

DISCUSSION

In this paper, we draw from our prior work and from related literature to identify a set of overarching problems that hinder engagement with achievement-based personal informatics systems — inadequate support for goal-setting, misalignment of user and system goals, and burden of system maintenance. We then propose a set of seven strategies to explore for mitigating these problems. It is our hope that designers working in this space will experiment with the strategies we have presented, and build on this work to concretely illustrate how the strategies might be applied over different domains, different PI systems, and different use cases.

Beyond Achievement-Based Goals

The strategies we presented in this paper focused on achievement-based goals. Prior work has illustrated that while achievement-based goals are one of the primary motivators for people to start using personal informatics systems, people are also motivated by other types of goals, such as the desire to document, reflect, and learn more about one's behaviors, to look for links between experience and behavior, to collect in-system rewards, and as a way of exploring one's interest in technology and information [74]. In reality, engagement with a system combines many of these activities, and it is worth exploring how systems could use the strategies we've described to support these different types of goals.

Although the focus on engagement and abandonment may not be a useful framing for all types of goals, we believe that the strategies we have outlined could support many of the goals that motivate the use of personal informatics tools. Systems could better serve the needs of users by allowing users to set goals and understand what motivates their use of the system. Systems could then use that information to personalize the information they capture about users and the feedback they provide over time. In addition, periodic reflection on those goals could help people take stock of how they've progressed and could potentially be used to foster meaningful outcomes.

Post-Achievement Use of Personal Informatics Systems

It can seem as though achieving a goal is the end of a person's journey with a PI system. In reality, the process of creating long-term behavior change is not so straightforward. Even if a person accomplishes the goal they set out to achieve, maintaining that change over time can be immensely challenging. People who lose weight, for example, often regain that weight [18]. This issue is attributable to a number of factors, some which are behavioral, and some that are tied to social and biological influences.

The reality of long-term behavior change presents a challenge for personal informatics systems, but it is also an opportunity to explore how we can utilize these ubiquitous systems to have a lasting impact on people's lives. Most personal informatics systems allow people to continue using the system in a maintenance mode after they've achieved their goals, but don't often support different needs a person has after achieving a goal. From a marketing standpoint, it makes sense that systems would emphasize their ability to help people achieve some behavior change. However, this focus may not benefit users in the long-term. Systems could offer additional functionality that allows for maintenance activities as a part of the larger effort to achieve and sustain a goal over the long term. In addition, systems could utilize the strategies we have outlined to help people develop new goals that reflect their evolving understanding of their life, values, and needs.

Potential Problems with Implementing the Strategies

Our community has identified a number of issues that could potentially make it difficult to implement the strategies we have listed here. The first is the fact that it may be hard to increase engagement with PI systems overall. Many people already feel as though the expected degree of system use is too high. If a system were to ask people to reflect on their goals or progress but did not explicitly appear to make use of this information, this might contribute to the feeling that a system requires too much interaction relative to the benefits people get from the system. The second is that it might be hard to make use of data generated from systems that employ the strategies. It might be difficult for systems to parse and utilize information derived from reflections on their goals, experiential aspects of the data, or social commentary about the data. Finally, meaningful personalization of a PI system may be difficult to achieve. Systems may also be unable to also leverage emerging computational abilities to personalize systems in a way that aligns with user needs.

Each of these issues represents an opportunity for researchers and system designers to better understand how to capture and make use of user data.

Limitations

We do not believe that our goal of fostering engagement is useful for all systems or for all people. There are many situations in which a person does not need or want to continue using a PI system. There may be situations in which abandonment or non-use of technology may be beneficial to users. In addition, self-tracking can be detrimental when it enables harmful behavior, when it contributes to feelings of anxiety or unease, or when it works against a person's ability to achieve a healthy goal [67]. While avoiding all negative effects is likely impossible for any system, our intention is to understand how achievement-oriented PI systems can use information collected over the long term to support practices that improve a person's life in some way. Therefore, our goal is not to eliminate abandonment of PI systems or to champion their universal usefulness, but to instead support people who are motivated to accomplish a goal but whose needs are not being met by existing systems.

CONCLUSION

In this paper, we gleaned findings from the literature and our own work to identify a number of problems that hinder engagement with achievement-based personal informatics systems — problems related to inadequate support for goal-setting, misalignment of user and system goals, and burden of system maintenance with achievement-based personal informatics systems. We then propose a set of seven strategies to explore for mitigating these problems. While each of the strategies have been discussed in other literature, we contribute the collection of strategies as a means to advance research and development of personal informatics systems that will improve people's lives. These strategies are not intended to be complete or exclusive. Instead, they offer an overview of salient concepts that can be applied from a number of disciplines. Future work can explore these strategies to better understand the situations in which they ought to be applied and the ways they can be used to uncover further nuances regarding how people use personal informatics systems.

ACKNOWLEDGMENTS

We would like to thank Chloe Fan, Ruben Gouveia, Evan Karapanos, Min Kyung Lee, Pedja Klasnja, and Ian Li. We would also like to thank the people who participated in the research described in this paper. This work was funded in part by NSF grant #0750271.

REFERENCES

1. Meredith A. Barrett, Olivier Humblet, Robert A. Hiatt, and Nancy E. Adler. 2013. Big data and disease prevention: From quantified self to quantified communities. *Big Data* 1, 3: 168 – 175.
2. Eric P.S. Baumer, Phil Adams, Vera D. Khovanskaya, Tony C. Liao, Madeline E. Smith, Victoria Schwanda Sosik, and Kaiton Williams. 2013. Limiting, leaving, and re(lapsing): An exploration of Facebook non-use practices and experiences. In *Proceedings of the SIGCHI Conference on Human Factors in Computing Systems* (CHI '13). ACM, New York, NY, USA, 3257 – 3266.
3. Frank Bentley and Konrad Tollmar. 2013. The power of mobile notifications to increase wellbeing logging behavior. In *Proceedings of the SIGCHI Conference on Human Factors in Computing Systems* (CHI '13). ACM, New York, NY, USA, 1095 – 1098.
4. Shlomo Berkovsky, Jill Freyne, and Harri Oinas-Kukkonen. 2012. Influencing individuality: Fusing personalization and persuasion. In *ACM Transactions on Interactive Intelligent Systems* 2, 3, Article 9.
5. Jeremy Birnholtz. 2010. Adopt, adapt, abandon: Understanding why some young adults start, and the stop, using instant messaging. *Computers in Human Behavior* 26, 6: 1427 – 1433.
6. Jan O. Blom and Andrew F. Monk. 2003. Theory of personalization of appearance: Why users personalize their pcs and mobile phones. *Human-Computer Interaction* 18, 3: 193 – 228.
7. Simon Elias Bibri. 2015. Implicit and natural HCI in AmI: Ambient and multimodal user interfaces, intelligent agents, intelligent behavior, and mental and physical invisibility. *The Human Face of Ambient Intelligence*, 159 – 318.
8. Jed R. Brubaker, Mike Ananny, and Kate Crawford. 2014. Departing glances: A sociotechnical account of 'leaving' Grindr. *New Media and Society*, 1 – 18.
9. Lora E. Burke, Jing Wang, and Mary Ann Sevick. 2011. Self-monitoring in weight loss: A systematic review of the literature. *Journal of the American Dietetic Association* 1, 92 – 102.
10. Panagiotis Chatzitsakyris, Goncalo Ducla-Soares, and Alejandro Zulas. 2004. IN-Visible: Perceiving invisible urban information through ambient media. In *CHI '04 Extended Abstracts on Human Factors in Computing Systems* (CHI EA '04). ACM, New York, NY, USA, 1348 – 1350.
11. Eun Kyoung Choe, Nicole B. Lee, Bongshin Lee, Wanda Pratt, and Julie A. Kientz. 2014. Understanding quantified-selfers' practices in collecting and exploring personal data. In *Proceedings of the SIGCHI Conference on Human Factors in Computing Systems* (CHI '14). ACM, New York, NY, USA, 1143 – 1152.
12. James Clawson, Jessica A. Pater, Andrew D. Miller, and Elizabeth D. Mynatt. 2015. No longer wearing: Investigating the abandonment of personal health-tracking technologies on craigslist. In *Proceedings of the 2015 ACM International Joint Conference on Pervasive and Ubiquitous Computing* (UbiComp '15). ACM, New York, NY, USA, 647 – 658.
13. Sunny Colsolvo, Predrag Klasnja, David W. McDonald, Daniel Avrahami, Jon Froehlich, Louis LeGrand, Ryan Libby, Keith Mosher, and James A. Landay. 2008. Flowers or a robot army?: Encouraging awareness and activity with personal, mobile displays. In *Proceedings of the 2008 Conference on Ubiquitous Computing* (UbiComp '08). ACM, New York, NY, USA, 54 – 63.
14. Sunny Consolvo, David W. McDonald, Tammy Toscos, Mike Y. Chen, Jon Froehlich, Beverly Harrison, Predrag Klasnja, Anthony LaMarca, Louis LeGrand, Ryan Libby, Ian Smith, and James A. Landay. 2008. Activity sensing in the wild: A field trial of UbiFit garden. In *Proceedings of the SIGCHI Conference on Human Factors in Computing Systems* (CHI '08). ACM, New York, NY, 1797 – 1806.
15. Sunny Consolvo, Predrag Klasnja, David W. McDonald, and James A. Landay. 2009. Goal-setting considerations for persuasive technologies that encourage physical activity. In *Proceedings of the 4th International Conference of Persuasive Technology*. ACM, New York, NY, USA.
16. Sunny Consolvo, David W. McDonald, and James A. Landay. 2009. Theory-driven design strategies for technologies that support behavior change in everyday life. In *Proceedings of the SIGCHI Conference on Human Factors in Computing Systems* (CHI '09). ACM, New York, NY, 405 – 414.

17. Felicia Cordeiro, Daniel A. Epstein, Edison Thomaz, Elizabeth Bales, Arvind K. Jagannathan, Gregory D. Abowd, and James Fogarty. 2015. Barriers and negative nudges: Exploring challenges in food journaling. In *Proceedings of the SIGCHI Conference on Human Factors in Computing Systems* (CHI '15). ACM, New York, NY, 1159 – 1162.

18. Kristina Elfhag and Stephan Rössner. 2005. Who succeeds in maintaining weight loss? A conceptual review of factors associated with weight loss maintenance and weight regain. *Obesity Review* 6, 1: 67 – 85.

19. Chris Elsden and David Kirk. 2014. A quantified past: Remembering with personal informatics. In *Proceedings of the ACM Conference on Designing Interactive Systems* (DIS '14). ACM, New York, NY, 45 – 48.

20. Daniel A. Epstein, Bradley H. Jacobsen, Elizabeth Bales, David W. McDonald, and Sean A. Munson. 2015. From "nobody cares" to "way to go!": A design framework for social sharing in personal informatics. In *Proceedings of the 2015 ACM Conference on Computer Supported Cooperative Work* (CSCW '15). ACM, New York, NY, USA, 1622 – 1636.

21. Daniel A. Epstein, An Ping, James Fogarty, and Sean A. Munson. 2015. A lived informatics model of personal informatics. In *Proceedings of the 2015 ACM International Joint Conference on Pervasive and Ubiquitous Computing* (UbiComp '15). ACM, New York, NY, USA, 731 – 742.

22. Debra Ferreday. 2003. Unspeakable bodies: Erasure, embodiment, and the pro-ana community. *International Journal of Cultural Studies* 6, 3: 277 – 295.

23. Eric Horvitz. 1999. Principles of mixed-initiative user interfaces. In *The Proceedings of the SIGCHI Conference on Human Factors in Computing Systems* (CHI '09). ACM, New York, NY, USA, 159 – 166.

24. Fitbit Tracker Sales. Retrieved from: http://www.wareable.com/fitbit/tracker-sales-q2-2015-financial-results-1488.

25. B.J. Fogg. 2002. Persuasive technology: Using computers to change what we think and do. In *Ubiquity* 5. ACM, New York, NY, USA.

26. Thomas Fritz, Elaine M. Huang, Gail C. Murphy, and Thomas Zimmermann. 2014. Persuasive technology in the real world: A study of long-term use of activity sensing devices for fitness. In *The Proceedings of the SIGCHI Conference on Human Factors in Computing Systems* (CHI '14). ACM, New York, NY, USA, 487 – 496.

27. Jeana H. Frost and Michael P. Massagli. 2008. Social uses of personal health information within PatientsLikeMe, an online patient community. *Journal of Medical Internet Research* 10, 3.

28. Jillian P. Fry and Roni A Neff. 2009. Periodic prompts and reminders in health promotion and health behavior interventions: Systematic review. *Journal of Medical Internet Research* 11, 2.

29. Julia EWC van Gemert-Pijnen, Nicol Nijland, Maarten van Limburg, Hans C Ossebaard, Saskia M Kelders, Gunther Eysenbach, and Erwin R Seydel. 2011. A holistic framework to improve the uptake and impact of eHealth technologies. *Journal of Medical Internet Research* 13, 4.

30. Noah J. Goldstein, Robert B. Caldini, and Vladas Griskevicius. 2008. A room with a viewpoint: Using social norms to motivate environment conservation in hotels. *Journal of Consumer Research,* 472 – 482.

31. Ruben Gouveia, Evangelos Karapanos, and Marc Hassenzahl. 2015. How do we engage with activity trackers?: A longitudinal study of Habito. In *Proceedings of the 2015 ACM International Joint Conference on Pervasive and Ubiquitous Computing* (UbiComp '15). ACM, New York, NY, UA, 1305 – 1316.

32. Anton Gustafsson and Magnus Gyllenswärd. 2005. The power-aware cord: Energy awareness through ambient information display. In *CHI '05 Extended Abstracts on Human Factors in Computing Systems* (CHI EA '05). ACM, New York, NY, USA, 1423 – 1426.

33. Sajanee Halko and Julie A. Kientz. 2010. Personality and persuasive technology: An exploratory study on health-promoting mobile applications. *Persuasive Technology,* 150 – 161.

34. James D. Hess and Arnold C. Bacigalupo. 2011. Enhancing decisions and decision-making processes through the application of emotional intelligence skills. *Journal of Management Decisions* 49, 5: 710 – 721.

35. Ellen Isaacs, Artia Konrad, Alan Walendowski, Thomas Lennig, Victoria Hollis, and Steve Whittaker. 2013. Echoes from the past: How technology mediated reflection improves well-being. In *Proceedings of the SIGCHI Conference on Human Factors in Computing Systems* (CHI '13). ACM, New York, NY, USA, 1071 – 1080.

36. Hiroshi Ishii, Sandia Ren, and Phil Frei. 2001. Pinwheels: Visualizing information flow in an architectural space. In *CHI '01 Extended Abstracts on Human Factors in Computing Systems* (CHI EA '01). ACM, New York, NY, USA, 111 – 112.

37. Hiroshii Ishii, Craig Wisneski, Scott Brave, Andrew Dahley, Matt Gorbet, Brygg Ulmer, and Paul Yarin. 1998. ambientROOM: Integrating ambient media with architectural space. In *CHI '98 Conference Summary*

on Human Factors in Computing Systems (CHI '98). ACM, New York, NY, USA, 173 – 174.

38. Sheena S. Iyengar and Mark R. Lepper. 2000. When choice is demotivating: Can one desire too much of a good thing? *Journal of Personality and Social Psychology* 79, 6: 995 – 1006.
39. Frederick H. Kanfer. 1970. Self-monitoring: Methodological limitations and clinical applications. *Journal of Consulting and Clinical Psychology* 35, 2: 148 – 152.
40. Evangelos Karapanos, Ruben Gouveia, Marc Hassenzahl, and Jodi Forlizzi. 2016. Need fulfillment and experiences with wearable trackers in prolonged use. *To appear in Personal and Ubiquitous Computing.*
41. Maurits Kaptein, Boris De Ruyter, Panos Markopoulos and Emilie Aarts. 2012. Adaptive persuasive systems: A study of tailored persuasive text messages to reduce snacking. *ACM Transactions on Interactive Intelligent Systems* 2, 2, Article 10.
42. Clare-Marie Karat, Jan O. Blom, and John Karat. 2004. Designing personalized user experiences in eCommerce. *Human-Computer Interaction Series.*
43. David V. Keyson, Marc P.A.J. de Hoogh, Adinda Freudenthal, and Arnold P.O.S. Vermeeren. 2000. The intelligent thermostat: A mixed-initiative user interface. In *CHI '00 Extended Abstracts on Human Factors in Computing Systems.* ACM, New York, NY, USA, 59 – 60.
44. Vera Khovanskaya, Eric P.S. Baumer, Dan Cosley, Stephen Voida, and Geri Gay. 2013. "Everybody knows what you're doing": A critical design approach to personal informatics. In *Proceedings of the SIGCHI Conference on Human Factors in Computing Systems* (CHI '13). ACM, New York, NY, USA, 3403 – 3412.
45. Christian Koehler, Brian D. Ziebart, Jennifer Mankoff, and Anind K. Dey. 2013. TherML: Occupancy prediction for thermostat control. In *Proceedings of the 2013 ACM International Joint Conference on Pervasive and Ubiquitous Computing.* ACM, New York, NY, USA, 103 – 112.
46. Sherrie Y. X. Komiak and Izak Benbasat. 2006. The effects of personalization and familiarity on trust and adoption of recommendation agents. *MIS Quarterly* 30, 4, 941 – 960.
47. Judith N. Lasker, Ellen D. Sogolow, and Rebecca R. Sharim. 2005. The role of an online community for people with a rare disease: Content analysis of messages posted to a primary biliary cirrhosis mailinglist. *Journal of Medical Internet Research* 7, 1.
48. Amanda Lazar, Christian Koehler, Joshua Tanenbaum, and David H. Nguyen. 2015. Why we use and abandon smart devices. In *Proceedings of the 2015 ACM International Joint Conference on Pervasive and Ubiquitous Computing* (UbiComp '15). ACM, New York, NY, USA, 635 – 646.
49. Min Kyung Lee, Daniel Kusbit, Evan Metsky, and Laura Dabbish. 2015. Working with machines: The impact of algorithmic and data-driven management on human workers. In *Proceedings of the 33rd Annual ACM Conference on Human Factors in Computer Systems* (CHI '15). ACM, New York, NY, USA, 1603 – 1612.
50. Min Kyung Lee, Jodi Forlizzi, Sara Kiesler, Paul Rybski, John Antanitis, and Sarun Savetsila. 2012. Personalization in HRI: A longitudinal field experiment. In *Proceedings of the Seventh Annual ACM/IEEE International Conference on Human-Robot Interaction* (HRI '12). ACM, New York, NY, USA, 319 – 326.
51. Min Kyung Lee, Sara Kiesler, and Jodi Forlizzi. 2011. Mining behavioral economics to design persuasive technology for healthy choices. In *Proceedings of the SIGCHI Conference on Human Factors in Computing Systems.* ACM, New York, NY, 325 – 334.
52. Min Kyung Lee, Junsung Kim, Jodi Forlizzi, and Sara Kiesler. 2015. Personalization revisited: A reflective approach helps people better personalize health services and motivates them to increase physical activity. In *Proceedings of the 2015 ACM International Joint Conference on Pervasive and Ubiquitous Computing* (UbiComp '15). ACM, New York, NY, USA.
53. Ian Li, Anind K. Dey, and Jodi Forlizzi. 2010. A stage-based model of personal informatics. In *Proceedings of the SIGCHI Conference on Human Factors in Computing Systems* (CHI '10). ACM, New York, NY, USA, 557 – 566.
54. Ian Li, Anind K. Dey, and Jodi Forlizzi. 2011. Understanding my data, myself: Supporting self-reflection with ubicomp technologies. In *Proceedings of the 13th International Conference on Ubiquitous Computing* (UbiComp '11). ACM, New York, NY, USA, 405 – 414.
55. Ting-Peng Liang, Hung-Jen Lai, and Yi-Cheng Ku. 2007. Personalized content recommendation and user satisfaction: Theoretical synthesis and empirical findings. *Journal of Management Information Systems* 23, 3(3): 45 – 70.
56. Edwin A. Locke and Gary P. Latham. 2006. New directions in goal-setting theory. *Current Directions in Psychological Science* 15, 5: 265 – 268.
57. George Loewenstein, Troyen Brennan, and Kevin G. Volpp. 2007. Asymmetric paternalism to improve health behaviors. *Journal of the American Medical Association* 298: 20, 2415 – 2417.

58. Deborah Lupton. 2014. Self-tracking cultures: Towards a sociology of personal informatics. In *Proceedings of the 26th Australian Computer-Human Interaction Conference.*

59. Lena Mamykina, Andrew D. Miller, Elizabeth D. Mynatt, and Daniel Greenblatt. 2010. Constructing identities through storytelling in diabetes management. In *Proceedings of the SIGCHI Conference on Human Factors in Computing Systems* (CHI '15). ACM, New York, NY, 1203 – 1212.

60. Tara Matthews and Jennifer Mankoff. 2005. A toolkit for evaluating peripheral awareness displays. From the *Awareness Systems Workshop at CHI 2005.*

61. Sean Munson. 2012. Mindfulness, reflection, and persuasion in personal informatics. In *Extended Abstracts of the SIGCHI Conference on Human Factors in Computing Systems* (CHI EA '12). ACM, New York, NY, USA.

62. Sean A. Munson, Erin Krupka, Caroline Richardson, and Paul Resnick. 2015. Effects of public commitments and accountability in a technology-supported physical activity intervention. In *Proceedings of the SIGCHI Conference on Human Factors in Computing Systems* (CHI '15). ACM, New York, NY, USA, 1135 – 1144.

63. Dawn Nafus and Jamie Sherman. 2014. This one does not go up to 11: The quantified self movement as an alternative big data practice. *The International Journal of Communication* 8, 1784 – 1784.

64. Nest Tracker. Retrieved from: https://nest.com/thermostat/meet-nest-thermostat/

65. Paul Nobles. 2015. Fitbit, you're doing it wrong. Retrieved from: http://www.eattoperform.com/2015/07/22/fitbit-youre-doing-it-wrong-by-paul-nobles/

66. Melody Powers Noland. 1989. The effects of self-monitoring and reinforcement on exercise adherence. *Research Quarterly for Exercise and Sport,* 60, 3: 216 – 224.

67. Carly R. Pacanowski, Jennifer A. Linde, and Dianne Neumark-Sztainer. 2015. Self-weighing: Helpful or harmful for psychological well-being? A review of the literature. *Current Obesity Reports* 4, 1: 65 – 72.

68. Chris Paton, Margaret Hansen, Luis Fernande-Luque, and Annie Y.S. Lau. 2012. Self-tracking, social media, and personal health records for patient empowered self-care. *Nursing and Health Professionals Faculty Research.*

69. Afarin Pirzadeh, Li He, and Erik Stolterman. 2013. Personal informatics and reflection: A critical examination of the nature of reflection In *Proceedings of the SIGCHI Conference on Human Factors in Computing Systems* (CHI '13). ACM, New York, NY, USA, 1979 – 1988.

70. Devika Pisharoty, Rayoung Yang, Mark W. Newman, and Kamin Whitehouse. 2015. Thermocoach: Reducing home energy consumption with personalized thermostat recommendations. *BuildSys2015,* 201 – 210.

71. Bernd Ploderer, Wolfgang Reitberger, Harri Olnas-Kukkonen, and Julia van Gemert-Pijnen. 2014. Social interaction and reflection for behavior change. *Personal Ubiquitous Computing* 18: 1667 – 1676.

72. Bernd Ploderer, Wally Smith, Steve Howard, Jon Pearce and Ron Borland. 2012. Things you don't want to know about yourself: Ambivalence about tracking and sharing personal information for behavior change. In *Proceedings of 24th Australian Computer-Human Interaction Conference* (OzCHI '12). ACM, New York, NY, USA, 489 – 492.

73. D. Scott Ridley, Paul A. Schultz, Robert S. Glanz, and Claire E. Weinstein. 1992. Self-regulated learning: The interactive influence of metacognitive awareness and goal-setting. *The Journal of Experimental Education* 60, 4: 293 – 306.

74. John Rooksby, Mattias Rost, Allistair Morrison, and Matthew Chalmers. 2014. Personal tracking as lived informatics. In *Proceedings of the SIGCHI Conference on Human Factors in Computing Systems* (CHI '14). ACM, New York, NY, USA, 1163 – 1172.

75. Sarita Yardi Schoenebeck. 2014. Giving up Twitter for Lent: How and why we take breaks from social media. In *Proceedings of the SIGCHI Conference on Human Factors in Computing Systems* (CHI '14). ACM, New York, NY, USA, 773 – 782.

76. Victoria Schwanda, Steven Ibara, Lindsay Reynolds, and Dan Cosley. 2011. Side effects and 'gateway' tools: Advocating a broader look at evaluating persuasive systems. In *Proceedings of the SIGCHI Conference on Human Factors in Computing Systems* (CHI '11). ACM, New York, NY, USA, 345 – 354.

77. Victoria Schwanda Sosik, Xuan Zhao, and Dan Cosley. 2012. See friendship, sort of: how conversation and digital traces might support reflection on friendships. In *Proceedings of the 2012 ACM Conference on Computer Supported Cooperative Work* (CSCW '12). ACM, New York, NY, USA, 1145 – 1154.

78. Patrick C. Shih, Kyungsik Han, Erika Shehan Poole, Mary Beth Rosson, John M. Carroll. 2015. Use and adoption challenges of wearable activity trackers. In *Proceedings of the 2015 iConference,* 1 – 12.

79. Itmar Simonson. 2005. Determinants of customers' responses to customized offers: Conceptual framework and research propositions. *Journal of Marketing* 69, 1: 32 – 45.

80. John Stasko. 2014. Value-driven evaluation of visualizations. In *Proceedings of the Fifth Workshop*

on Beyond Time and Errors: Novel Evaluation Methods for Visualization. ACM, New York, NY, USA, 46 – 53.

81. Strava Activity Tracker. Retrieved from: https://www.strava.com/

82. Victor J. Stretcher, Gerald H. Sejits, Gerjo J. Kok, Gary P. Latham, Russell Glasgow, Brenda DeVellis, Ree M. Meertens, and David W. Bulger. 1995. Goal-setting as a strategy for health behavior change. *Health Education Quarterly* 22, 2: 190 – 200.

83. Melanie Swan. 2012. Crowdsourced health research studies: An important emerging complement to clinical trials in the public health research ecosystem. *Journal of Medical Internet Research* 14, 2.

84. Jaime Teevan, Susan T. Dumais, and Eric Horvitz. 2010. Potential for personalization. *ACM Transactions on Computer-Human Interaction* (TOCHI) 17, 1(4). ACM, New York, NY, USA.

85. Yaacov Trope and Nira Liberman. 2010. Construal-level theory of psychological distance. *Psychological Review* 117, 2: 440 – 463.

86. Walgreens Balance Rewards Program. Retrieved from: https://www.walgreens.com/steps/appmarket.jsp

87. Kaiton Williams. 2013. The weight of things lost: Self-knowledge and personal informatics. From the *Personal Informatics in the Wild Workshop at CHI 2013.*

88. Rayoung Yang and Mark W. Newman. 2013. Learning from a learning thermostat: Lessons for intelligent systems for the home. In *Proceedings of the 2013 ACM International Joint Conference on Pervasive and Ubiquitous Computing* (UbiComp '13). ACM, New York, NY, USA, 93 – 102.

89. Rayoung Yang and Mark W. Newman. 2014. Making sustainability sustainable: Challenges in the design of eco-interaction technologies. In *Proceedings of the 2014 ACM Conference on Human Factors in Computing Systems* (CHI '14). ACM, New York, NY, USA, 823 – 832.

90. Rayoung Yang, Eunice Shine, Mark W. Newman, Mark S. Ackerman. 2015. When fitness trackers don't 'fit': End-user difficulties in the assessment of personal tracking device accuracy. In *Proceedings of the 2015 ACM International Joint Conference on Pervasive and Ubiquitous Computing* (UbiComp '15). ACM, New York, NY, USA, 623 – 634.

91. Oren Zuckerman and Ayelet Gal-Oz. 2014. Deconstructing gamification: Evaluating the effectiveness of continuous measurement, virtual rewards, and social comparison for promoting physical activity. In *Personal and Ubiquitous Computing* 18, 7: 1705 – 1719.

Connected Baby Bottle: A Design Case Study Towards A Framework for Data-Enabled Design

Sander Bogers[12], Joep Frens[1], Janne van Kollenburg[21], Eva Deckers[2], Caroline Hummels[1]
[1] University of Technology, Eindhoven, Netherlands
[2] Philips Design, Eindhoven, Netherlands
{s.j.a.bogers, j.w.frens, c.m.m.hummels}@tue.nl - {janne.van.kollenburg, eva.deckers}@philips.com

ABSTRACT

This paper presents the design case study of a connected baby bottle, which is used as an exploration towards a data-enabled design framework for designing intelligent products, services and ecosystems targeting behavior change. We explore how contextual, behavioral and experiential data can be used as design material for remote insight collection and remote design intervention. The first "contextual" iteration sets out to understand the design context with its complexities, based on a combination of quantitative sensor data and qualitative interview sessions. The second 'informed' iteration utilizes design probes, remotely connected to a data-canvas, to explore behavioral, experiential and contextual consequences of design interventions. The dynamic and open character of the introduced data-canvas allowed us to iterate quickly without requiring physical presence of the designer. Finally, we translate the findings from this case study into a two step model for data-enabled design that we further discuss to outline what next steps are required towards constructing a framework for data enabled design.

AUTHOR KEYWORDS

Data-enabled design; prototyping; in the everyday life; behavior change; complexity; systems; data.

ACM CLASSIFICATION KEYWORDS

H.5.2. User Interfaces: User Centered Design, Theory and Methods, Prototyping

INTRODUCTION

A new generation of products, services and systems aims at changing people's behavior [34]. This new wave of quantified self [31] and wearable technologies is believed to help in solving major societal challenges in the future [6].

DIS 2016, June 04 - 08, 2016, Brisbane, QLD, Australia

ACM 978-1-4503-4031-1/16/06...$15.00
DOI: http://dx.doi.org/10.1145/2901790.2901855

Measuring one or more parameters which are nearly invisible to human perception (e.g., amount of steps walked), visualizing these on a screen, provides handles for insight into personal patterns and could therefore motivate behavior change. Examples are the Jawbone Up [10] i.e., a wearable for activity and sleep and the Vessyl [23] i.e., a smart cup for liquid intake feedback. Yet, little is known about how to design for these challenges and how to grasp the impact of our interventions in the design process.

The connected nature of these products, services and ecosystems, the vast amount of data they generate and the world they are placed in, increase the complexity [25] of these product-service systems as they break with the *'one person – one product dictum'* [4]. Experiences and responses of the system become less predictable as they are composed of multiple factors. As apparent, these systems introduce complexity challenges for design, as people's experiences in the ecosystem are by no means a simple accumulation of the single human-product interaction experiences [15]. We acknowledge that design explorations closer to reality are required to embrace this complexity. At the same time, we see that it is not always possible or desirable to be present to observe. Besides being a potential privacy invasion and an enormous investment in time, the designers' presence will also change behaviors.

Access to contextual, experiential and behavioral data, and tools (i.e., quantified-self products with open API's [1] and connected prototyping tools [11]) to monitor data has become significantly easier, through the large variety of apps, health tracking devices and prototyping toolkits that are at hand. However, we do not yet see how the ease of access to data has influenced the design processes. This data is potentially highly valuable for design, to receive continuous feedback during an iterative design process.

We take a research through design approach and present a design case study of a connected baby bottle, where we explore the potential role of data in the design process. Executed in the industrial context of Philips Design, this project aims to design personal and meaningful insights for parents, regarding baby bottle feeding. The design approach of this project has been informed by previous case studies involving data in design [26, 24, 16]. Based on insights collected from this case study, we present a first attempt to formalize a two-step model for data-enabled design; two-steps for on-the-fly designing *in* everyday life. We end with a discussion of what needs to be done to develop these insights into a framework for data-enabled design.

BACKGROUND & RELATED WORK

We aim to utilize data as design material to design remotely for behavior change. We recognize three large bodies of work as necessary building blocks for this. Block 1: (Design) methodologies that build on user involvement to enable designers to grasp the contextualized complexity. Block 2: (Design) methodologies that have been successful in technology-mediated data collection from the field, to gain detailed insights in user behavior and experiences. Block 3: The use of interactive prototypes as a vehicle for experience and value probing.

Block 1: User involvement to grasp complexity

User involvement in design for product-service-systems has increased considerably in relevance, due to the growing complexity of the societal challenges we face [32].

Co-X [21] outlines an extensive body of work relating to user involvement in the design process (e.g, co-design [28], co-creation[27], co-reflection[32] and participatory design [14]). *Co-design*, building on empathic design [17], aims to give voice and tools to those who were traditionally not part of the design process [21]. This is done to bring potential users and stakeholders into the design process. Sanders and Stappers [28] present a landscape of user-centered design research in designing for products and systems, which describes different types of user involvement. Multiple established methods are mapped on a two-dimensional chart ranging from "users as subject" to "users as participants", and from "research-led" to "design-led". The vast majority of *co-design* work describes the physical presence of the designer to empathically understand user experiences in the design process [21]. Other work proposes a closer integration of design and usage by connecting *co-design* to *living labs [12].*

Concluding

Close user involvement is valuable for coping with the complexity of our design challenges. Due to the data-intensive approach, the technological complexity of this and the limited frame of references users have in this, we argue for close and active involvement of users during discussions about their experiences, without burdening them to create themselves. Through design explorations placed in the field (user's home) we aim to remotely collect insights that are rich enough to inspire further design iterations.

The changing role of the user consequently changes the role of the designer. The methods described above require the physical presence of the designer (in the field) during these explorations, to observe and discuss ideas. When placed in the everyday life, the designer uses techniques as questionnaires and interviews to get to the core of the experiences. The results are however always subjective and strongly depend on the information the participants decide to provide. Through techniques presented in block 2, we aim to eliminate the requirement for physical presence and aim for high quality insights through remote understanding.

Block 2: Remote understanding situations through data

Existing technology-mediated remote research methods aid in giving detailed insight in human behavior and experiences through the data they collect. Bolt and Tulathimutte describe *Remote Research* [2] as a co-located HCI research method to collect data about product use in the field (i.e., outside the controlled lab setting). The presented tools for remote research (e.g., webcams, screen sharing, video and audio recordings) emphasize screen-based interactions and show its powerful ability to collect both opinion-based and behavior-based data. Funk introduces *adaptive observation [5]* to get high-quality information about product usage. "*The framework enables stakeholders of product information to specify graphically what data should be collected from products in the field*" [5]. Where adaptive observation is mainly a tool for validation and optimization of business flows, the currently often advocated data-driven design approach [6] collects data from interactions with the product, which directly steers further design direction.

Different forms of computer-mediated ethnography (i.e., Digital [20], virtual [7] and cyber ethnography [13]) describe social interaction research methods that are adaptable, to facilitate the dynamic nature of the questions the researcher wants to ask. Larson and Csikszentmihalyi's *Experience Sampling Method* (ESM) [3] is a method of data collection in which participants respond to repeated assessments at moments over the course of time while functioning in their natural settings. *The Adaptive Experience Sampling Method* (A-ESM) [33] adds to this by offering the ability to change the focus of the experience sampling on the fly.

Concluding

When data is used in the design process we see two clear directions. The first describes the use of data collection in software applications that are mostly screen based. Usage data, mainly statistics without a qualitative component, is used to optimize the design further. These approaches are used for A/B testing and commonly serve validation purposes instead of being creative design material. The second direction describes methods for detailed and remote observation, combining sensor data with interviews and other ethnographic methods. We see considerable value in these methods as they provide rich and detailed understanding of context, behavior and experiences. When combined with methods that utilize design probes as means of inquire (see Block 3) we see this as an important building block for data-enabled design.

We see large value in the methods to remotely collect data in real-time, and appreciate the richness of data forwarded by methodologies in the second part. By combining these two and introducing design probes we aim to use remotely collected data (i.e., sensor data and qualitative data) as design material.

Block 3: The role of interactive prototypes

The significance of the prototype changes by shifting from a co-design approach, with the presence of the designer during the design process, to a living lab or everyday life approach, where the designer is not present to observe and make adjustments. The role of the prototype in research through design has been previously discussed in literature. Furthering Houde & Hill's [8] prototype definition as 'any representation of a design idea, regardless of medium', Lim, Stolterman & Tenenberg [19] define prototypes as 'filters that traverse design space' and as 'manifestations of design ideas that concretize and externalize conceptual ideas'. Wensveen and Matthews [35] distinguish four roles of the prototype. The prototype as (1) experimental component, (2) as means of inquiry, (3) as research archetype and (4) the process of prototyping as vehicle of inquiry. Megens & Peeters [22] introduce Experiential Design Landscapes as a design research method to design and explore the potential value of conceptual ideas through prototypes in everyday life. This work introduces experiential probes, as vehicles for understanding situations and unraveling design opportunities. This way the method stretches the boundaries of preserving ecological validity though retaining experimental control; where ecological validity refers to how close the conditions of the experiment come to their real life counterparts.

Concluding

We aim to utilize data-enabled prototypes to get closer to the core of the experiences we are interested in. Previously, interactions would be either captured through observations and in the case of home placement studies through e.g. interviews, diaries and questionnaires. As alternative for this indirect information we hope to better understand these experiences in detail by enhancing these prototypes with sensors and other ways to collect insights.

The level of interaction described in the work related to prototyping limits itself to interactions directly relevant for the user experiences. The prototype, often used as a probe, is static as a means of inquiry. Here, we aim for a more open prototype environment, or canvas, that is dynamic and can be interactively adjusted based on remote insights.

DESIGN CASE: CONNECTED BABY BOTTLE

The case study describes the design and development of a connected baby bottle within Philips Design. The commercial context introduces the different goals of developing business value on a product level and serving as a research through design case to investigate data-enabled design. The business goal of the design case was to design *personal and meaningful baby bottle feeding insights* for parents, based on data tracking connected devices. We stayed close to the current concept of data trackers (i.e., where the tracker connects with an app to visualize data), but set out to explore how the collected data could be meaningful for parents beyond the graphs and charts currently frequently used.

The design approach we take is based on insights from previously executed case studies that were data intensive. One of the primary challenges from these projects (e.g., an app to socially motivate physical activity [24], a way to communicate sleep stage data of babies [16]) was preventing the data deluge (i.e., having so many data that it becomes difficult to grasp its value) [6]. Therefore, we set out to incorporate the use of contextual, behavioral and experiential data as design material from the start. Now we hope to build an understanding of the data while it grows.

In the first iteration, we explored how and which data could become meaningful, by putting an early data collecting probe in everyday life. Based on insights from the first iteration, we set out to design on the fly (remotely and situated in the field) based on direct insights from the field experiment in the second iteration. We questioned which data could be meaningful related to their experiences when bottle feeding, how this could further inspire design iterations and what the role of the probe is in this.

ITERATION 1: UNDERSTANDING CONTEXTUAL DATA

To gain understanding of the potential of sensor data, we set out to explore in context which data could support us in understanding experience drivers for bottle feeding experiences. To facilitate later iterations, we designed the prototype with growing capabilities (i.e. room left to add more sensors or actuators), with the future in mind. Mainly through the integration of Bluetooth, which is irrelevant for this iteration, we aimed to open future opportunities for making this device connected.

With limited knowledge about data that might be relevant for bottle feeding experiences (even with an expert team on baby bottles involved) and the infinite amount of potentially interesting data possibilities, we choose a limited set of sensors with concurrent data streams to depart from. The initial interest was specific towards the actions performed with the bottle (e.g., preparing, cleaning, feeding) and the routines in this. The accelerometer could accommodate most of these. Temperature was forwarded by the expert team as one of the factors parents were most hesitant about.

Contextual Probe

The first prototype (see figure 1) consists of a sensor board (1), placed in a small 3D printed PLA casing (2), which fitted tightly into a custom made flexible silicone sleeve (3) that fit tightly around the bottles used for the study (4).

The sensor board (1) responsible for the data collection consisted of (a) a LightBlue Bean [18] (i.e., an Arduino based microcontroller with embedded Bluetooth Low

Energy and 3 axis accelerometer to measure the angle of the bottle), (b) an infrared temperature sensor to measure bottle content temperature, (c) an SD card to log data, and (d) a battery with concurrent charging circuit.

Figure 1. Preparing the bottle with sensor sleeve (Part. A)

To be able to effortlessly charge the battery during the experiment an inductive charger station was provided. When we later refer to 'sensor sleeve' we refer to the assembled package of element 1, 2 and 3. The sensor sleeve could easily be detached and attached, for example to prevent the battery from igniting during microwave use. All elements were designed to be as unobtrusive and little work for the participants as possible and to be robust enough to run for two weeks.

This set of sensors enabled tracking of the following parameters for all bottle feedings: time of the day, duration, angle of the bottle and temperature of the bottle content. All data would only be saved locally on the SD card.

Field study

We deployed the contextual probe in real life family settings to collect data and explore the potential value of the data. Based on a balance between the amount of time required to build multiple prototypes, the recruitment of participants, the explorative nature of the study and our interest in a diverse set of natural and pure user data, we deployed the first prototype in 5 families for two weeks. Participants were recruited through a Facebook group of a neighborhood housing many young parents. For all 5 participating families (all Dutch), the mother was the one who subscribed and was most actively involved in the study. Participating babies varied in age between 2 and 11 months. None of these parents were using technology to track data about their baby. We expected privacy related feedback (because of the strong data aspect) and some technology aversion at first (i.e., why do I need this?).

Study setup

During the individual introductions situated at each participant's home, an informal semi-structured interview was used to profile the participants (e.g., occupation, amount of children, roles in the family, why they are bottle feeding). The interview aimed to gain deeper insight in their experiences related to bottle feeding (e.g., when do you feed, what works well for your baby). During the interview the contextual probe was introduced as a "sensor sleeve" with the only description it would collect data about the bottle. Participants were trained in how to use the bottle; to charge the "sensor sleeve" every evening and to remove it from the bottle while placed in the microwave or dishwasher. Participants were encouraged to use the bottle in the same way they normally would.

For the first week participants were asked to fill out a diary with questions about their bottle feeding experiences. After the first week, a researcher visited all participants to check if the prototype was still in working order. During this visit, the filled-in booklet of the first week was discussed and a new diary for the second week was introduced. This diary focused on daily routines and was intended to be closer related to the data (e.g., when do you feed during the day, who feeds, etc.). At the end of this meeting, the researcher collected the data from the SD Card.

During the final interview (after week 2) the researcher discussed the diary that had been filled out during the second week in detail. Until this point, the participants had received no explanation of what the "sensor sleeve" measured, neither had they seen any of its data. As part of the interview, the participants would imagine what the "sensor sleeve" could do and mean for them. As a last step, their personal sensor data of their first week would be presented in early stage data visualizations to trigger further discussions on the relevance of data.

Results

During the study with the 5 participants we collected 183 feedings, 15 interviews and 10 diaries.

The prototypes were extensively tested in our controlled lab setting before we started, with positive results. However, when put in the families' homes for 2 weeks, we discovered 75% of the collected data had wrong timestamps. A very short power drop would reset the timestamp, which we overlooked during our lab tests as it only started occurring after a couple of days. For the different prototypes, this happened between the 4 and 15 times per prototype. This does not mean that the collected data became useless. For these sets of sensor data, we were able to compare different feedings (i.e., the relative timestamps were still good), only without knowing at what time during the day or week they occurred. This way we were not able to find patterns in routines as envisioned. During the analysis we considered which quantitative sensor data could be meaningfully linked to the qualitative data captured during the observations, interviews and diaries.

Reflection of iteration 1

Reflecting on our initial expectations, participants were more positive about the concept of a technology enhanced bottle than expected. After showing simple data visualizations of the collected data and discussions about future possibilities, most participants were very positive.

"I don't think this 'raw' data is interesting for people but it is interesting to see how I act each time differently. There is clearly value in that." - (Participant D)

Based on the quantitative sensor data which, at first sight, shows little regression over time and participants who reply that the "sensor sleeve" changed nothing in their routine, we can conclude that the "sensor sleeve" solely has little impact on the behavior of the participants. Besides the key insights described next, we collected a large set of relevant behavior details that have changed our perspective on bottle feeding experiences (e.g., the 'obsession' for having the perfect milk temperature or differences in shaking and swirling techniques between parents of the same family).

We discovered the combination of the quantitative sensor data and interview sessions to be of large value to gain more detailed insight in what bottle feeding entails and means to people. Where initially the introduction interviews missed depth in nuances and subtleties of feeding routines, through the data we were able to ask more specific questions and offer the participants handles for more detailed discussion. Because the collected data was theirs, they could empathize with it and therefore better imagine which aspects captured in this data could be valuable for them to have more insight in. The available sensor data enabled the researchers to dig deeper in reasons behind different actions. By understanding these actions better, the data slowly transformed from raw sensor data to contextualized behavioral and experiential data. Without the qualitative discussions and participant feedback, this would never have been possible.

"You can see that I have longer breaks in my evening feedings because there I change diapers half way during the feed". - Participant E

The collected data was seen as *personal* and *highly dynamic*. The data fidelity in this experiment is already high enough for parents to, through simple visualizations (which were explained and discussed during the interview), already see clear differences in feeding styles and find deviating patterns. Data across feedings of the same family are similar, even though nuances are clearly visible. Differences between participating families are even easier to recognize. The data and context is highly dynamic as parents indicate that by the time they start understanding new routines and preferences they have already changed. Even in this short term experiment we see participants change their routine from 5 feedings a day to 4 feeds a day.

Reflecting on the combination of the collective qualitative and quantitative data, we notice significant differences between both. The quantitative sensor data revolves around the act of feeding as if an objective "perfect feed" would exist. Although these aspects highly influence the overall experiences, they are not exclusively responsible. A set of sensor data is never all-encompassing for user experiences and should never be considered as such. Qualitative feedback collected through observations and interviews facilitates in unraveling the motives behind collected data. This way the qualitative data goes beyond the sensor data by further defining context that shapes the experience.

"After the feed I want to have some time to play with her before I put her to bed." (Participant A)

Although the current quantitative dataset does not fully reflect the experiential richness we observed, the current sensors proved to give us contextual insight beyond what we expected. The temperature sensor, for example, gave us room temperature and the accelerometer data could highlight when the bottle was taken along for a car drive; giving a good indication of feedings at different locations.

Although this approach gave valuable insights, through the time difference between the moment the data was generated and discussed we lost valuable nuances. Interesting deviating patterns in the data were hard to recall and explain by the participants. For the next iteration we aim to combine the use of data with Adaptive Remote Experience Sampling to grow contextual understanding in the moment while affording the ability to act in a designerly way.

ITERATION 2 - INFORMED PROBE

The second iteration aims to utilize access to contextual, behavioral and experiential data to design while the probe is situated in everyday life. This step uses an informed probe, as it got informed and more focused by the insights collected during the first iteration. The need for real-time access to the data follows from our insights in being able to sample experiences closer to their moment of expression. The sensor sleeve in this iteration build on the previous sleeve by adding sensors to understand the environment. Instead of doing an exploration only to better understand context, we set out to use a dynamic data-canvas that utilizes both the qualitative and quantitative data as inspiration and insight mechanism for design intervention. The data-canvas is composed of a collection of tools that aid in collecting and gaining understanding of data, while providing a canvas for a range of design interventions.

A data-canvas

The contextual probe of the first iteration required some significant changes to enable for real-time probing based on the personally collected data. Also the need for more situated information clearly followed from that iteration. Instead of enabling us to measure everything, especially considering the short iterative approach we use, we added the ability to manually enter information in the app (see below), beyond the limitations of the sensors (i.e., who is feeding, type of content, happiness of the baby). Besides this, we extended our sensor platform. The informed probe builds on the contextual probe and extends it to a well connected platform that enables a dialogue through data and manual interaction between the designer research team and families.

Figure 2. The data-canvas was composed of: (1) The online bottle environment, (2) The app and (3) The sensor sleeve.

Elements 3 and 2 were visible for the participants during the study, element 1 was only visible for the design researchers. Elements 3 and 2 are together referred to as the informed probe. Elements 1, 2 and 3 together are referred to as the data- canvas.

The sensor sleeve (1) builds on the previously described "sensor sleeve". To better understand contextual influencers, an environmental sound sensor and an ambient light sensor were added. A weight sensor, to measure the volume of milk inside the bottle, was added in response to participants' interest from the first iteration.

Figure 3. The electronics inside the sensor sleeve

The app (2) has multiple roles. Firstly, its role as an experiential probe; to be able to receive insight cards based on their personal data. At this point, insight cards were not further defined than a new blank frame inside the app that could contain any form of content (e.g., messages, images, charts). We set out to understand which types of cards could prove meaningful to people through exploration. As we implemented the windows available in the app to be mostly driven by web page views, it became possible to do quick and obtrusive on-the-fly updates.

Secondly, its role as a research vehicle; to be able to facilitate a dialogue between the design research team and the participants question-based messages. Thirdly, its role to collect data from the "sensor sleeve" through Bluetooth and send this to the Online Bottle Environment.

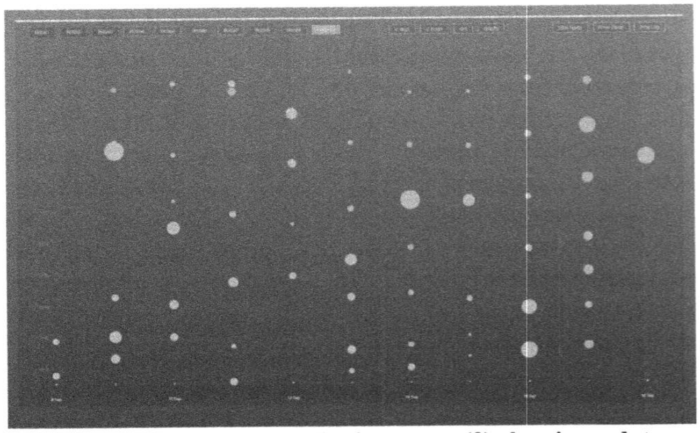

Fig 4. The Online Bottle Environment (3) showing a data visualization of one participant. On the x-axis the date is shown, on the y-axis the time during the day. The dot size indicates the duration of the feeding.

The Online Bottle Environment (3) would collect, store and give insight into all collected data (qualitative and quantitative) and enable the design research team to *act manually as a system* by sending out insight cards based on findings (fig 4), and to sample experiences by asking questions remotely. The environment contained numerous dynamic data visualizations (see figure 4) to enable the design research team to play with the collected data in different ways to explore possible values further.

Compared to the first iteration, a couple of software enhancements were made. A custom algorithm would analyze incoming data and, based on insights from the previous discussions, classify data as feedings or no feedings (e.g., a car drive or cleaning of the bottle). After being classified as a feeding, the algorithm would generate a summary for that feeding, containing feeding duration, amount of interruptions, duration of interruptions, average angle of the bottle, average temperature, average sound level, average light level, who is feeding, content type, baby happiness and volume.

Field study

We deployed the informed probe in the everyday life of participating families to design for personal and meaningful insights when situated in everyday life. We expected to be able to further develop our data-canvas to an extent where we would be able to utilize personal data, both qualitative and quantitative, to make informed design decisions to give personal and meaningful insights. We expected participants to value these insights over the visualizations of their data.

Preserving the diversity in participating families for previous iteration, we recruited 9 new families and extended the experiment to 3 weeks to facilitate time for design interventions. This time, out of 9 participants (again all Dutch) once the father was the one to sign up, and in the rest of the cases the mother. Participating babies also varied in age between 2 and 11 months. Only one parent was using a manual diary to track data of their baby.

Study setup

The first week of the experiment was used to collect data about the participants, which would enable designers to remotely build empathy. As more (insight in) personal data was required to build insight cards, participants would not yet receive cards during the first week. The second and third week aimed at exploring design opportunities for meaningful personalized insights. Both the in-app data visualizations and insight cards would be explored and the online bottle environment allowed to be further developed to cope with new challenges.

During a collective kick-off meeting at the design lab, participating parents would be briefed about how to use the app and "sensor sleeve". (i.e., mainly microwave and charging routines were explained). Apple IPods Touch running the described app were provided to all participants. The compositions of sensors, functionality and details of the data tracking were not discussed.

Similar to previous iteration's interviews, but now collectively instead of individually due to the group size, semi-structured interviews and diaries similar to previous ones were used to gain deeper insight in their values related to bottle feeding Unless technical errors would occur, participants would not be visited during the experiment.

After the 3th week participants were visited for a final, semi-structured interview targeting the sharing of experiences that had not been shared, overall opinions, and ideas for future developments. At this point also the online bottle environment, to which the participants had no access before, was shown and discussed in detail (i.e., were there other things we could have responded to?).

Results

All 9 participants have used the research prototype for 3 weeks. Besides some minor technical prototype imperfections most aspects worked satisfactorily. Only the weight sensor, intended to measure volume, proved to be more difficult to interpret than expected, as placing the bottle on different surfaces heavily influenced the sensor reading. Although we were aware of this limitation, we did not communicate this limitation to the participants as we aimed to change as little as possible to their routine. The sensor readings have been ignored for this study.

In total 2594 events arrived at the Online Bottle Environment, of which 365 have been algorithmically classified as feedings. The algorithmic classification of the events is beyond the scope of this paper. In total the design research team manually send 88 cards containing questions and 287 cards containing personalized insight cards.

Reflection on iteration 2

Participating parents responded enthusiastically to the concept during the final interview meetings. 5 out of 9 parents indicate to have changed aspects of their bottle feeding routine because of the personal insights. We see strong indications of these modifications in the collected data. Examples are changing the teat size to extend the duration of the feeding based on feeding duration insights, consciously changing the feeding environment or feeding location based on insights in the role of environmental sound related to the amount of interruptions during the feeding. Their enthusiasm was mostly related to (1) *Convenience* to log feedings and their detailed characteristics, (2) *Reassurance* of healthy development, (3) Having *personal insights* to draw personal conclusions.

"It is an app that detects when and how a feeding went. This way you have all info close and you can see how and is being fed." (Participant 9)

"Gut feeling is not always enough to change something, now I have proof that makes me decide to change.' (Participant 2)

"The cards with correlations are very helpful. It's difficult or even impossible to make those relations yourself. The sleeve and app help with that." (Participant 6)

The personal insight cards, as a first attempt to design for more personally meaningful insights, show its potential value to stay interesting for a longer period of time than the data representations. Participants indicate its contemporary value is build through insights from data over time and is personal, contrasting the app's data visualizations that show a generic overview from which insights are hard to deduct.

The starting point for the second iteration, an app to visualize data and present cards to the participants, was further refined during the experiment. The following examples illustrate how personal data and the data-canvas impacted our findings.

Data is not comprehensive

Through the combination of sensor data, interviews that make use of this data and more subjective experiences (entered through the app), we gained understanding of the complexity and influencers of a good feeding. With the notion that parents are satisfied with finding some influencers of a good feed, opposed of striving for a 'perfect feeding', we changed the type of cards send out. Through our data-canvas we gained better understanding in how parents value feedback based on their data, by probing with different content and with different tones of voice. Instead of coaching the parents towards a perfect feed with tips and tricks we shared the insights we discovered in the data and let the parent decide to act upon these insights or not. When designing for similar products it is advisable to take into account that the data can understand context partially, but the context is far richer than data can grasp.

Exploring real values instead of envisioned value

Due to the malfunctioning weight sensor, intended to measure volume, parents were asked to manually enter the volume variable. Based on the initial absence of volume used in the data visualizations, 3 participants asked for insight in their manually entered values. Although a new visualization was designed for this, the visualization received little attention after. All participants indicated they perceived volume logging as important, but it was actually less important in the stage their baby was currently in. Through the dynamic nature of the app we were able to change our design based on these insights which gave us more insight in the underlying reasons for the request.

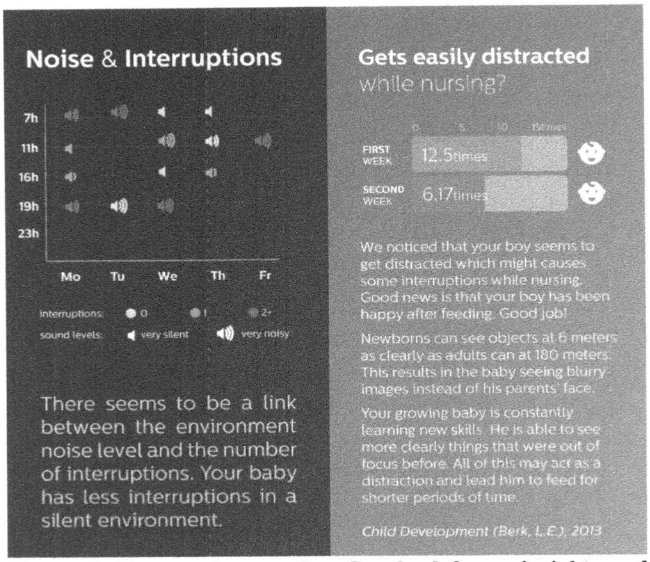

Figure 5. Two card examples. On the left, an insight card shows the relation between environmental sound and feeding interruptions. On the right, distractions during the feeding.

Insight in data to compare what matters

We set out to give insights based on personal data, but initially had little idea what made data personal and what data could be of interest. The online bottle environment enabled the design research team to 'play' with the data and look at different aspects. In the third week, when personal datasets started to contain more body, we sent a considerable amount of cards to give insight in correlations between different aspects (e.g., a louder environment results in more interruptions (fig 5), grandmother feeds at a much lower temperature, interruptions and feeding duration related to time of the day)).

Through the data, we gained understanding in what content can be relevant for that person and when it matters. In the final interviews, the responses of the parents confirmed this understanding (i.e., *"I had the feeling environmental noise influenced the feed but never took action. This insight helped me realize and change environment"* - Participant 2). Access to real data made the design more personal.

DISCUSSION

The presented design case study shows how data can be used as design material for the development of connected product-service-systems. We collected a rich set of insights by integrating qualitative and quantitative data in the design process as a way for growing contextual understanding as handles for design inspiration and intervention. In this section, we abstract the approach of the case study into a two-step model for data-enabled design. This is by no means a validated model but follows from this case study and the knowledge from earlier design cases (that this case was build upon). We use it as a way to further discuss qualities and opportunities of data-enabled design and outline what next steps need to be taken to further develop this knowledge, towards a framework for data-enabled design.

A two-step model for data enabled design

The first step of the proposed two-step model for data-enabled design is a 'contextual' step, the second step is an 'informed' step. The first is used to gain *contextual* understanding and to inspire the *informed* step. After a first contextual step, multiple informed iterations can follow.

The contextual step

The *contextual* step sets out to gain contextualized understanding by utilizing a combination of quantitative sensor data and qualitative user insights. Through enriching the sensing capabilities of a prototype, thus turning it into a contextual probe, we allow for data to become part of the creative process. The design of the contextual probe can be based on prior knowledge (e.g., expert input) and by valuing an abundance of sensors to create a rich data landscape. The sensor data collected with the contextual probe can give handles for detailed insight in context, behavior and experiences. Though, without the qualitative side (e.g., user interviews utilizing the data) this sensor data will stay flat and meaningless. Involving users, to make a connection between their quantitative sensor data and their personal (qualitative) experience influencers, enriches the quantitative and qualitative data and turns it into design material. This step benefits from having a diverse group of participants to be able to find a variety of personal experience drivers, to further inspire design action.

This contextual approach aids for inspiration and design conceptualization through a better understanding of the quantitative and qualitative data when it is still small enough to be graspable. For design inspiration we rather aim for experiential qualities that are expressed in small but richly annotated datasets than large datasets without these. This prevents from the serendipitous use of data that often poses challenges for data-driven-design [6]. This step aims to build better understanding of the contextual complexity and by doing so it aids in shaping the data-canvas of great significance for the next step.

The informed step

This *informed* step sets out to iteratively design while the prototype stays in the field. This shift necessitates more (real-time) remote insights to inspire and direct new design interventions. Instead of introducing a prototype as a static means of inquiry, the informed step introduces an open and dynamic set of tools, a data-canvas, that can be further shaped based on remotely collected insights. Although designed to be open and dynamic, the data-canvas will always be targeted through the limitations it provides (e.g., although the case study presents the app as a black canvas, there was already a choice for an app). Insights collected in the contextual step can help to accommodate the data-canvas.

Different from the *contextual* step, this *informed* step uses a prototype as a vehicle to probe for new experiences through new design interventions. In the execution of this step, a diverse, not earlier participating group of participants is preferred. By preserving the techniques used in the contextual step, to gain understanding in the meaning of the data, we aim to grasp the impact of our interventions in the natural everyday life context of the user.

After the first *contextual* step, multiple iterations of the *informed* step can follow. Note that due to its dynamic character, the informed step already exists of multiple smaller iterations by itself. As long as the prototype stays in context, design iterations can take place *within* the *informed* step. When a new physical prototype, with data-canvas, is introduced a new *informed* step iteration starts.

We foresee the relevance of the two step model for data-enabled design inside multiple phases of the design process. Hence, data-enabled design does not necessarily have to limited to an iteratively incremental model from start to end. It can also be applied as a methodology to understand user experience and explore and design on a distance.

A data-enabled design canvas

The data-canvas comprises a canvas for both (1) remote contextual insight collecting and understanding through experiential and behavioral data, and (2) a way to probe and place design interventions back in the everyday life of the participants remotely. It is an interactive system, for the designer, composed of different tools, some placed in everyday life, some at the design lab, to remotely gain understanding through probing iteratively (see also figure 2 for the data-canvas used in the case study).

For the informed probe in the case study, we introduced a data-canvas to enable dynamic remote design interventions and insight collection. We believe this data-canvas to play such a crucial role in the data-enabled design framework we are working towards, that we deliberately rename it into the data-enabled design canvas. The tools composing the data-enabled canvas are so closely interwoven with the approach that they can not be separated.

Flexibility of the data-enabled design canvas

Due to the contextual complexity, the data-enabled design canvas should posses the ability to pivot in design space, with as much freedom as possible. By offering the ability to intervene remotely, it becomes possible to iterate without retrieving the prototype or having a consciously noted intervention by the participant. This dynamic approach to prototyping significantly differs from the prototyping work framed before. Although it is still a means for inquiry, it transformed into a richer and more interactive explorer of experiences. For now, we have found this flexibility mainly in the digital but also see opportunities for more physical designs. (see future challenges). Participants should perceive the presence of the researcher as limited as possible, as it negatively impacts the ecological validity we hold dear. The ability to intervene remotely enables the design researcher to explore faster, and explore a large variety of aspects within what was previously considered one iteration, as it now becomes a set of iterations within the boundaries of the data-enabled design canvas. Therefore, the development of the design and the data-enabled canvas are inherently connected, as the canvas helps to further explore design space, and the design further informs and demands abilities from the data-enabled design canvas [30]. The canvas should facilitate the ever changing question of the design researcher within the range of freedom it provides. To work towards a framework for data-enabled design, it is essential to further develop possible generic components of data-enabled design canvasses to lower thresholds for these projects (both for people with and without the required prototyping skills). On a critical note, the data-enabled design canvas can heavily influence the outcomes. This should be further considered to prevent tunnel visioning through this approach: it becomes easy to channel everything into data.

Remote understanding and probing through data

We suggest a highly iterative approach with a strong emphasis on the value of remote data collection to understand contextualized behavior and experiences and to use data as design material for remote design interventions.

This is different from a *data-driven* design approach that has a large say for data as a tool for analysis and validation instead of exploration. For this reason, these data collections are often much larger (big data) and contain less qualitative insights. Next to this, by not focusing solely on the ability to collect data and translate it into valuable insights, the approach also differentiates itself from previously presented related work that is highly data dependent (i.e., Remote Research, Adaptive Observation and Digital Ethnography). Instead, data-enabled design sets out to use data as design material to probe for user behavior, utilizing reflective skills (i.e., reflection-in-action and reflection-on-action). By doing this, it can step into the physical world of connected devices that are somehow influenced digitally.

Compared to co-design and participatory design work, with data-enabled design we aim to utilize the high levels of ecological validity by placing probes in the wild, without continuous intervention of the design research team that would subsequently decrease ecological validity further. The behavioral and experiential data we collected through the combinations of different types of data (i.e., sensor data, feedback through the app and interviews with the data) can hardly be collected otherwise with this level of detail, and helped us to better understand bottle feeding experiences.

The role of the designer and user

In data-enabled design users continuously switch roles, between being subject or partner, for the designer to further understand context, experiences and behavior. Data-enabled design assigns users with an active role without directly enabling them to create. Since the amount of data and the behavior change challenges introduce high complexity for design, it is challenging to *co-create* with users. Instead, through the freedom the data-enabled design canvas provides, designers can leave room for value creation at the side of the user by probing different aspects, and understanding responses (both qualitatively as quantitatively). The designers' skills in grasping complexity through making, when situated in context, can help in facilitating the dialogue with the user. Through this we position data-enabled design between 'user as subject' and 'user as partner', in the model of Sanders et al. and more at the side of 'led by design' than 'led by research'.

Data-enabled design sets out to involve users in real contexts of use. Through a combination of different data sources and the ability to probe remotely, we aim to build empathy with users in the field. The complexity embodied in the data provides handles to grasp the information. However, we do acknowledge that the collected sensor data will always be a reductive representation of the experiential context to design for. The interviews, strongly supported by the data, help in bridging this gap between sensor data insights and real experiences.

Retaining reflection-in-action in remote design

As aforementioned, we set out to take a research through design approach, strongly building on reflective practice as described by Schön [29]; In reflection-in-action, actions are *spontaneous*, *automatic* and *understood without being aware* of having learned them [9]. Reflection-on-action reflects back on a moment of action to question (implicit) decisions and directions to further articulate design vision and strategy. Due to the high complexity of designing for behavior change, we argued for placing our design prototypes in real life settings to retain ecological validity. As a consequence of this, we experienced in the first iteration that essential reflection-in-action abilities were missing, as our probe was static and could hardly be changed during the setup of the study. To retain the ability to reflect-in-action and explore new design ideas on-the-fly, we introduced the data-enabled design canvas for the second iteration. In retrospect, the data-enabled design canvas could have also played a role (although in a more passive form) in the first step. It could have facilitated for the simple data visualizations and could have sampled experiences closer to their moment.

FUTURE CHALLENGES

The presented design case study shows how data-enabled design relates to the design and development of a mostly digital case study. The informed step requires a high level of freedom to execute quick design iterations while situated in the field. The digital domain fits this dynamic nature arguably better through software updates and being influenced by data streams. Although mostly explored in the digital domain, we also recognize potential reaches into the physical design space. To further develop this model towards a framework we argue for more design case studies in a variety of domains (including more physical ones) to validate and further explore its qualities.

We argued the data-enabled design canvas to be an essential part of a data-enabled design framework. Although we strongly believe this data-enabled design canvas should always be specifically tailored to its design challenges, there are generic parts recognizable. To reduce the time required to set up a first data-enabled design canvas, these generic parts should be further explored and developed (e.g., connected a physical object to an online dashboard). Challenges are to make these tools accessible for designers with less developed software skills and to ensure that the developed tools are not unintentionally targeting in a specific direction by itself.

CONCLUSION

Designing products, services and systems for behavior change introduces complexity through the inter-connected and social nature of systems. Based on a design case study presented a two-step model for data-enabled design: two steps to designing for complexity; a *contextual* and an *informed* step. These steps aim for a situated exploration utilizing both quantitative sensor and subjective qualitative data. It allows a deep understanding of people's behavior, experience and context and affords iterative design interventions remotely. Thereby it enables to play with subtleties and nuances that are otherwise difficult to explore, especially in the challenging area of designing for behavior change. The approach proved valuable in a dominantly digital domain (i.e., an app with cards and data visualizations). To further progress this into a framework for data enabled design we argue for a wider range of case studies (including more physical ones) and to further develop and explore the data-enabled design canvas.

ACKNOWLEDGEMENTS

This research was supported by the IMPULS perinatology framework.

REFERENCES

1. API Directory | Programmable Web. 2015. Retrieved January 2016 from http://www.programmableweb.com/apis/directory
2. Nate Bolt and Tony Tulathimutte. 2010. *Remote research.* Rosenfeld Media.
3. Mihaly Csikszentmihalyi and Reed Larson. 1987. Validity and reliability of the Experience-Sampling Method. The Journal of nervous and mental disease 175,9: 526-536.
4. Joep W. Frens and C.J. Overbeeke. 2009. Setting the stage for the design of highly interactive systems. *Proceedings of international association of societies of design research*, 1-10.
5. Mathias Funk. 2011. *Model-driven design of self-observing products.* Ph.D Dissertation. University of Technology, Eindhoven.
6. Justin Hienz. 2014. The future of data-driven innovation. U.S. Chamber of Commerce Foundation
7. Christine Hine. 2008. Virtual ethnography: Modes, varieties, affordances. *The SAGE handbook of online research methods*, 257-270.
8. Stephanie Houde and Charles Hill. 1997. What do prototypes prototype. *Handbook of human-computer interaction, 2*, 367-381.
9. Caroline Hummels and Joep W. Frens. 2009. The reflective transformative design process. In *CHI'09 Extended Abstracts on Human Factors in Computing Systems* (pp. 2655-2658). ACM.
10. Jawbone. Jawbone | We're in it for life. 2015. Retrieved September 25, 2015 from https://jawbone.com.
11. Johnny Five | Javascript Robotics Platform – Platform Support. Retrieved January 2016 from http://johnny-five.io/platform-support/
12. Eija Kaasinen, Kaisa Koskela-Huotari, Veikko Ikonen, Marketta Niemelä and Pirjo Näkki. 2012. Three approaches to co-creating services with users. *Advances in the Human Side of Service Engineering*, 286.
13. Elizabeth Keeley-Browne. 2010. Cyber-Ethnography: The Emerging Research Approach for. Handbook of Research on Transformative Online Education and Liberation: Models for Social Equality: Models for Social Equality, 330.
14. Finn Kensing and Jeanette Blomberg. 1998. Participatory Design: Issues and Concerns. Computer Supported Cooperative Work 7. (pp 167–185)
15. Janne van Kollenburg, Eva Deckers, Paul Gardien, and Caroline Hummels. 2015. *People Research for Eco-system propositions: a theoretical framework towards the future of interaction design.* In progress DeSForM '15 conference.
16. Janne van Kollenburg, Eva Deckers, Sander Bogers, Caroline Hummels. 2016. User Experience Research in Changing Economies. In review.
17. Ilpo Koskinen, Katja Battarbee, and Tuuli Mattelmeaki. 2003. Empathic design. IT Press, 2003.
18. LightBlue Bean. The LightBlue Bean. 2014. Retrieved September 25, 2015 from http://legacy.punchthrough.com/bean/.
19. Youn-Kyung Lim, Erik Stolterman and Josh Tenenberg. 2008. The anatomy of prototypes: Prototypes as filters, prototypes as manifestations of design ideas. *ACM Transactions on Computer-Human Interaction (TOCHI)*, *15*(2), 7.
20. Davis Masten and Tim Plowman. 2003. Digital ethnography: The next wave in understanding the consumer experience. *Design Management Journal (Former Series)*, *14*(2), 75-81.
21. Tuuli Mattelmäki, Froukje Sleeswijk Visser. 2011. Lost in Co-X: Interpretations of Co-design and Co-creation. In *2011). Diversity and Unity, Proceedings of IASDR2011, the 4th World Conference on Design Research*(Vol. 31).
22. Carl Megens, Michel Peeters, Caroline Hummels, and Aarnout Brombacher. "Designing for behaviour change towards healthy living." In *2013). Consilence and Innovation in Design, Proceedings of IASDR2013, the 5th International Congress of International Association of Societies of Design Research.*
23. Myvessyl.com. Vessyl. 2015. Retrieved September 25, 2015 from https://www.myvessyl.com/.
24. Terence Nelson, Carl Megens, and Michel Peeters. 2012. Bouncers: a design exploration into sharing and triggering personal activity amongst friends. Persuasive Technology 2012. (pp 33-36)
25. Don Norman. 2010. Living with Complexity
26. Michel Peeters , Carl Megens , Elise van den Hoven, Caroline Hummels and Aarnout Brombacher. 2013. Social Stairs: taking the Piano Staircase towards long term behavioral change. Consilence and Innovation in Design, Proceedings of IASDR2013, the 5th International Congress of International Association of Societies of Design Research.
27. C.K. Prahalad and Venkat Ramaswamy. 2004. Co-creating experiences: The next practice in value creation. Journal of Interactive Marketing (pp. 5-14)
28. Elizabeth B.N. Sanders and Pieter Jan Stappers. 2008. Co-creation and the new landscapes of design. *Co-design, 4*(1), 5-18.
29. Donald A. Schön. 1983. The reflective practitioner: How professionals think in action. Temple Smith.
30. Jelle Stienstra, Sander Bogers, Joep Frens. 2015 Designerly Handles: Dynamic and Contextualized Enablers for Interaction Designers. *In Proc. of Desform 2015* (pp. 86-94)
31. Melanie Swan. 2013. The Quantified Self. Big Data 2013 (pp. BD85 – BD99)
32. Oscar Tomico, Joep W. Frens, and C. J. Overbeeke. "Co-reflection: user involvement for highly dynamic design processes." *CHI'09 Extended Abstracts on Human Factors in Computing Systems.* ACM, 2009.
33. Martijn H. Vastenburg and Natalia Romero Herrera. 2010. Adaptive experience sampling: addressing the dynamic nature of in-situ user studies. In *Ambient Intelligence and Future Trends-International Symposium on Ambient Intelligence (ISAmI 2010)* (pp. 197-200). Springer Berlin Heidelberg.
34. Stephen Wendel. 2013. *Designing for behavior change.* O'Reilly Media
35. Stephan Wensveen and Ben Matthews. 2015. *Prototypes and prototyping in design research.* Routledge

Teens, Parents, and Financial Literacy

John Zimmerman, Jodi Forlizzi, Justin Finkenaur, Sarah Amick, Ji Young Ahn, Nanako Era, Owen Tong
HCI Institute, Carnegie Mellon University, Pittsburgh, PA, USA
johnz@cs.cmu.edu, forlizzi@cs.cmu.edu

ABSTRACT
Teens' financial literacy, their ability to understand financial concepts and make effective decisions, is an important topic in the US. Educational programs targeted at teens have had little impact. Our study investigated if parents should play a role in teaching their teens. We conducted a literature review on teenage financial literacy and a competitive analysis of current tools. We interviewed parents and teens, probing on what teens know and how they learned these concepts. We conducted speed dating sessions, exposing parents and teens to provocative services meant to trigger conversations about financial values. These included a system where parents gave loans and charged interest and a game where teens guessed the prices of family expenses. Results showed a strong interest for tools that allow parents to educate their teens. Concepts worked best when they addressed teens' current needs and when they allowed parents to influence spending based on values.

Author Keywords
Financial literacy; teens; parents; research through design; speed dating; user enactments

ACM Classification Keywords
H.5.m Human-centered computing~Field studies

INTRODUCTION
US teens control billions of dollars in spending each year [1]. Today they face an increasingly complex financial world as they leave home and must manage their income, expenses, debts, and as they must manage savings and investments for their eventual retirement. Research on teens' financial literacy indicates they are unprepared; many do not understand basic financial concepts like interest, inflation, or risk diversification [14]. Their inability to manage money leads to bad outcomes. For example, many college-aged teens have credit cards (first-year students receive roughly eight credit card offers in their first week), and more drop out of school due to credit card debt than because of academic failure [1].

DIS 2016, June 04-08, 2016, Brisbane, QLD, Australia
© 2016 ACM. ISBN 978-1-4503-4031-1/16/06...$15.00
DOI: http://dx.doi.org/10.1145/2901790.2901858.

Across the US, a citizen-wide lack of financial literacy has been linked to high rates of consumer debt, increasing bankruptcy, and the 2008 housing crisis and financial collapse [11]. Like teens, many adults in the US do not understand financial concepts like compound interest, inflation, and diversification risk [13]. Many researchers and financial industry experts assume more financial education will lead to financial literacy and that financial literacy will lead to better financial decision-making. However, the evidence for a connection between these remains scarce [9,22]. Speculation on why financial education does not always lead to better financial decision mentions both biases and "nonrational" influences [22].

Previous HCI and IxD research investigated benefits of creating interactive products and services that make people feel they are moving towards an *idealized self* with respect to a specific social role. Much of this work investigated tools that help parents with parenting [23]. We viewed teens' lack of financial literacy as a potential opportunity to further investigate this space. Specifically, we wanted to investigate the appropriateness and feasibility of new services that might support parents in teaching their teens about finances. Parents communicate and negotiate important values through the financial choices they make and through the choices they allow their children. Negotiating and instilling family values around finances often represent an important long-term parenting goal.

To better understand the opportunity for services that connect teens and parents around finances and financial values, we followed a research through design (RtD) approach [24]. We conducted a literature review and a competitive analysis of tools and services designed to educate teens about finances. Next, we recruited eight families and engaged them in interviews involving at least one parent and at least one teen. These interviews focused on understanding how parents and teens interacted around financial choices and on how teens gain an understanding of financial topics.

Following the interviews, we carried out a speed dating study with user enactments (UEs) [4]. We generated five semi-functional *design provocations* and asked parents and teens to interact with them together. These ranged from a system for parents to loan money and charge interest, to a game where teens guessed the cost of different family expenses, to a planning tool to help teens spend a windfall. Interviews showed that parents wanted to keep their personal financial information private; however, they also wanted to show their children how to manage finances and lacked other tools or examples to use when teaching their children. During the enactments, we observed that parents and teens had meaningful discussions about financial choices when situations focused on teens' current financial needs, allowed parents to influence choices based on values. The tools allowed everyone to move beyond statements like, "We can't afford that," and to investigate the consequences of what affording something really meant.

RELATED WORK

To the best of our knowledge, financial literacy has not yet been a topic of interest for the HCI or IxD research communities. In addition, while there are many desktop, web, and mobile tools that help people in managing personal finances (Mint, YNAB, GnuCash, MoneyDance, Budget Simple [10]), the HCI and IxD research communities have done little research on personal finances.

Some early work in the space of wearable computing investigated wearable, digital wallets [3]. Informed by innovations such as a wearable wallet from Swatch, researchers conducted ethnographic research on people and their wallets. One challenge raised was a finding that people kept many non-monetary items in their wallets and that most viewed wearable wallets as fundamentally financial. Other work investigated digital banking and digital finance in the developing world. Researchers compared different interfaces (text, non-text, and multimedia) for both semi-literate and illiterate users [15]. Other work looked at how mobile phones might better integrate with paper record keeping for microfinance projects [19].

Work conducted in the UK investigated the financial practices of the "older old" (those over 80 years) to inform the design of new interactive products and services [21]. Researchers found this group kept detailed records of their financial transactions and monitored these for errors. They noted that this group cared about the materiality of money, interactions with familiar people in local places, and feeling in control of what was happening with their finances.

More recent work in the US examined the financial practices of working-age adults in California [12]. This study found that most participants had no explicit system for tracking their finances, and they would instead check on things by repeatedly using digital tools to monitor account balances. Some participants had tried online financial tools, but they had abandoned these due to security concerns. In general, participants conceptualized their income and expenses in terms of pots of money devoted to a topic. They generally lacked a deep financial sophistication.

Our work adds to this small set of HCI research on personal finances by probing on the appropriateness and feasibility of online services that support parents in teaching their children about finances by enabling them to make joint financial decisions.

RESEARCH THROUGH DESIGN CASE

Previous IxD and HCI research investigated using product attachment theory, which describes how and why people develop strong attachments to some of their material possessions to improve user experience. Design teams focus on making new products and services that have the explicit intention to make people feel they are making progress towards their idealized self in a specific social role [17,23]. Many examples of this work have focused on the needs of parents and on how products and services can add benefits by allowing parents to focus on their longer-term parenting goals, such as helping their children make better decisions [23,24] or in our case, helping parents prepare their children to thrive in the world by teaching them about financial management and instilling financial values.

We chose to follow an RtD (Research through Design) approach. RtD allows design researchers to investigate speculative futures with the goal of identifying futures that both could and should be [24]. RtD is intended to produce knowledge about a problematic situation. It is NOT meant to result in a commercially viable product. We specifically wanted to know if parents and teens would be open to using these kinds of services, if we could identify situations that lead to effective discussions of financial values between parents and teens, and if there were important concerns that might block adoption or might dissuade either parents or teens from using such a system.

As part of our framing of this research project, we approached a US bank that had a relationship with our university. The bank provided research funding for the work and allowed us to explore a service design approach by considering the needs and strategic initiatives of a potential service provider. Service design is different than user-centered design in that it takes an explicitly systemic approach and works to identify opportunities for the co-production of value between service providers and customers [7]. This is in contrast to user-centered design's narrower focus on user needs and desires [6].

During the course of the research, we met with members of the bank's innovation and education teams. They shared the bank's goals for developing financial literacy tools including: creating services specifically for teens[1], increasing customer engagement with the number of banking services, increasing the amount of money a customer holds at a bank, and creating service features that allow differentiation from the competition. Through these interactions, we learned how banks view the challenge of financial literacy, their thoughts on the financial topics their customers would benefit from learning, and both brand and legal aspects related to our design ideas that might prevent

[1] Many banks have services for younger children including passbook savings accounts. Banks also offer many services for college students and children leaving their parents' home. Teens appeared to be an underserved audience.

banks from promoting or delivering these kinds of services. By linking parents' performance of parenting to a set of tools that help them teach financial concepts and share personal values with their teens, we speculated that such a service might effectively increase parents' brand attachment to a service provider.

Below we describe this RtD case, covering a literature review on teens' financial literacy, a competitive analysis of current products and services intended to educate teens, our interviews with teens and their parents on their current practices, and a UE study probing future service offerings that might connect teens and parents around finances.

LITERATURE REVIEW ON TEEN FINANCIAL LITERACY

Financial literacy is an outcome of financial education and practice making financial decisions. By learning about financial concepts like interest, inflation, diversification, credit, and debt, people are assumed to become financially literate, and thus they can make "sound" financial decisions by applying the knowledge they have gained [9,11,22]. Financial literacy is more than simply understanding financial concepts; it also includes the ability to operationalize this understanding in an effective way.

We wanted to understand the state of financial literacy for teens. We also wanted to identify which financial topics experts claim teens should know, and to gain insights on why current tools might not be effective.

We began with a literature review. We wanted to gain a high-level overview of the current state that could be used to generate design opportunities for new services. We searched for peer-reviewed articles using the search terms "teen" and "financial literacy." We used the resulting set of papers to discover a more extensive set of references. We read a selected set of these, taking notes with respect to the problem, current approaches, and important financial topics. We then used affinity diagrams [8], using sticky notes to organize the findings across the set of papers.

In general, we found agreement on the fact that teens generally lack financial literacy and are unprepared to make financial decisions when they leave home. Much work has been done to address this problem, and it has almost entirely focused on financial education. Many high schools have developed financial education programs; however, our review showed that few have any positive impact in terms of literacy. Some research showed that teens who have taken a financial management class did not necessarily improve their financial behavior. They were no more likely to save or budget than teens who had not taken a similar course [20]. Several studies noted that educational materials for teens should be based on everyday examples and real world needs. Simulated stock market and investment club games, which are outside of teens' immediate concerns, have proven to be less than effective [2]. There have been some efforts to train teachers to become successful financial mentors, and to require states to mandate a course in personal finance with the intention to increase financial literacy in the US [2].

PISA (Programme for International Student Assessment) collects survey data internationally on teen financial literacy, through the use of a written test [18]. This research showed that parents play an important role in teen financial literacy, that family wealth positively corresponds with teen financial literacy and later-life financial sophistication, and that starting early has a strong effect [18]. In addition, studies in the US also show that young people's financial literacy is highly correlated to socio-economic status; youth from more financially sophisticated families had more financial literacy [14].

Collectively, our literature review and affinity diagramming produced a set of topics (spending, saving, budgeting, investing, income, risk, credit) and a set of actions that were salient to teens, including opening and using checking and savings accounts, obtaining credit, buying cars, clothing and personal care items [20]. These results influenced the next steps of our research.

COMPETITIVE ANALYSIS

To better understand the state of current financial education tools aimed at teens and young adults, we conducted a competitive analysis of financial products and services designed for teens. We wanted to survey current offerings and to investigate if any of these used social motivation, such as interaction with peers through commenting and replying, or if any engaged parents a discussion of financial values as part of the education process.

We conducted another round of online searches, following links to both individual product and service sites and to ranked lists of services meant for users to compare. Our final set of products and services included: TheMint.org, Practical Money Skills for Everyone, Money Talks, Khan Academy, Mad City Money, Budget challenge, Virtual Business Online Simulations, Different simulation models, MoneySKILL Life Simulation, Financial Literacy Simulation. We also explored banks in the US and Europe to see what services they offered for teens. We read about each of these services, and viewed demos and tutorials. We took notes and synthesized these using affinity diagrams to help identify important themes.

Our analysis revealed that while there are many financial services for teens, many are poorly designed and/or expensive. Many are simulations that are detached from the real-world needs of a teen, and instead practice adult skills of budgeting, paying bills, and avoiding bank fees. For example, Money Talks presented the topics of saving, spending, and budgeting in a format that was uninteresting for teens. Financial Literacy Simulation presented concepts like checking and savings accounts detached from any purchase or savings goals.

The most relevant services for teens relied on a quiz format for relaying information. For example, on themint.org, financial information is taught through a quiz format, interspersed with fun facts. Other services relied on games, but the gameplay was detached from financial concepts, offering a poor overall experience. This was the case with Practical Money Skills for Life, which embedded financial concepts within unrelated gameplay about sports and cities.

While some of the services came from banks (osper.com in the UK) or had corporate sponsorship (Practical Money Skills for Life is sponsored by Visa), a clear opportunity existed to better support building a service relationship with a financial institution through delivery of financial information to teens. This was an opportunity that our sponsor could surely take advantage of.

All of the products and services we surveyed were one-on-one services, with no interaction from parents and no social play. This also served to lessen the utility of these services, as budgeting, saving, and spending are often done in coordination with parents for this age group.

In summary, the competitive analysis revealed opportunities to help teens see the need to learn about financial information and to save money by better tying financial information to real-world goals. There is an opportunity to provide a mechanism for teens and parents to increase their financial literacy together. Finally, there is an opportunity to create a brand affiliation with a financial institution in offering such a service to their customers.

FIELDWORK WITH TEENS AND PARENTS

We conducted directed storytelling interviews with parents and teens to better understand how teens gain financial knowledge and if parents play a role [5]. In these interviews, we prompted parents and teens to recall specific events that had happened to them, related to how teens learned about finances. Questions included: Have you ever set aside money for a large expense? What does the transfer of money between you (parents and teens) look like? How did you learn about money? and Have you talked to your teen about saving for college?

We recruited eight families. They all came from the local area and represented a broad range of educational and economic statuses. When recruiting, we required a family to have at least one active bank account and for both one teen and one parent to be available. Table 1 provides an overview of the families. "NI" indicates this parent was not interviewed. In the Teen column, "D" indicates daughter, "S" indicates son, and the number indicates the teen's age. The Mom in family F5 was a single parent; hence "None" is listed for Dad.

Interviews were conducted with at least two researchers present. We separated parents and teens at the beginning of the interviews and then brought them together. We recorded all interviews and produced transcripts. To process the data, the team members who performed the interview would recall their experience. The team then reviewed the transcript, lifting out observations and insights. These were placed on sticky notes. We then synthesized the data using affinity diagrams to draw out themes across the interviews.

	Mom	Dad	Teen
F1	Administrator	Software Engineer	D13
F2	NP Outreach	NI	S18
F3	Health coach	Pastor	D15
F4	Homemaker	Construction Worker	D15
F5	Elementary school staff	None	D17
F6	Office Administrator	NI	D15
F7	NI	Construction Worker	D18, S13
F8	Software Engineer	Programmer	S14, S16, S18
F9	Administrator	NI	D11
F10	School Administrator	NI	D14, S17

Table 1. Details on participating families, including parents' occupation, teen gender, and teen age. F1-F8 participated in the interviews. F1-6 along with F9 and F10 participated in the UEs.

Interview Findings

The teens we spoke with had little knowledge of the financial world. Many claimed to know nothing about interest, credit, taxes, or retirement. When asked to describe life insurance, if they had an idea, they described it as health insurance, something needed when you got sick. In general, teens knew the least about financial issues outside of their current experience. For example, when asked about retirement D13-F1 replied, *"I know that if you save up money for your retirement you'll be like, not worried. Isn't it like once you're retired the government gives you money until you die? And like some medical stuff?"* At 13 years of age, she still had many years to plan for retirement. However, for more complex immediate needs, many teens also did not understand the immediate implications. For example, when asked if she and/or her parents had been saving for college that was starting in a few months, D18-F7 replied, *"My mom is taking out some sort of loan. I don't know how loans work, and I don't think I myself could really do that, so I think she is just doing it... I'm going to start to pay her back."*

Most teens spent money on food, entertainment with friends, music, concerts, movies, and clothing. Some of the older teens with jobs paid for their own bus passes and phone service, and one had paid for a car. Only a few had saved money to make a bigger purchase, which included the car and a few phones. In addition to a few jobs, a few of the teens received an allowance. Most teens, however, had no consistent source of income, and they would instead ask their parents for money as needs arose. D3-F1 shared how this typically works, "*I'm like 'Dad can I have money' and he's like 'what for?' and I'm like 'I'm going to the movies with Larissa or whatever' and he's just like 'okay how much do you need' and I'm like 'a twenty would be good' and he's like 'okay I'd like the change back' and I'm like 'We'll see'. And then I keep the change.*"

Parents' willingness to provide money seemed strongly connected to the availability of funds, the child's recent behavior, and the parents' values with respect to how the money would be spent. Mom-F6's description of the decision process matched with most parents. "*I won't usually give her money, especially if she goes out with her friends. ...if she usually puts in a lot of effort in her chores, I will sometimes give her money... if she wants make-up or clothes, or maybe things I don't agree with, I usually have her buy it herself. I also think when she does different chores, then I will give her some money, but I am not one to just hand over money.*"

When prompted, the teens expressed an interest in learning about a variety of different topics. Several wanted to know the difference between credit and debit cards. When checking out of a store with their parents, cashiers would typically asked what kind of card a parent was using, making the teens curious, but not curious enough to ask their parents about the difference. One wanted to know how to write checks, a few wanted to know about taxes, and several wanted to know how to pay for housing including both monthly rentals and home mortgages. Teens also expressed an interest in knowing what things cost around their home as a way of preparing to someday move out and take responsibility for their own home.

Teens learned about finances in a variety of ways. The most commonly mentioned method was observing their parents. The teens also mentioned learning about finances from television, and interestingly, several spoke of TV commercials as how they learned about insurance and interest. Teens learned from older siblings who had taken on larger financial responsibilities, such as getting a job or moving out of the family home. They also learned from earning their own money through activities like baby-sitting or getting a part-time job. School was never mentioned with the exception of one private school that had required one of the teens to track fictional income and pay expenses over several weeks. Several teens mentioned that they wanted to know more, but that their parents sometimes seemed unwilling to share. D-13-F1: "*I'll be like, to my mom, 'so how much is your house' and my mom is just like 'you don't need to know', and I'm like 'why not' and she's like 'you'll know later'.*"

Parents mostly viewed financial literacy as knowing the difference between *wants* and *needs*, and as knowing how to manage cash flow such that the family had a little savings at the end of the month. Dad-F7 shared that his children needed to know, "*that money doesn't grow on trees. You couldn't just ask for money, and have it handed over.*" Mom-F6 connected this with making smart purchasing decisions, such as looking for sales. "*In years past she has received allowance. I try to teach her about spending wisely, buying on sale, the difference between a need and a want.*"

Parents worked to communicate their financial values through stories of their own purchase decisions and through their child's expenses they chose to support. Interestingly, they did not want to share the details of their personal finances with their children. They did not share income, housing costs, investment choices, or their strategies for saving for college or their own retirement.

Parents had two different rationales for not sharing personal financial information and decision making with their children. First, many viewed finances as personal. Mom-F2's response, when asked if she shared her personal finances with her son, captured a common understanding across the parents we spoke with. "*No... because it is none of his business.*" Second, several parents expressed a desire to shield their children from unnecessary stress. Dad-F3 discussing why he took over handling daily finances for the family: "*I am making it, and you* [refers to Mom] *are handling the bills. It was just eating her up. You know, her personality, which was too stressful. So I like to take that over, and it was stressful for anybody. But I think the minute that you showed your kids, if you trying to teach them monetarily literacy then, and they all will see you, then I think it will fear them when it comes to money. And money... becomes either a trouble maker or something that always been difficult to obtain.*" While the financial literacy research all claims children should learn these concepts earlier, several of the parents viewed this as potentially harmful.

Based on the interviews, we identified several insights, concerns, and opportunities.

Insights:

- Both parents and teens wanted parents to teach teens about finances, but parents lacked any tools for doing this other than their own finances.
- Parents wanted children to understand *wants* and *needs* and to set spending priorities. However, this desire seemed in conflict with most teen's lack of agency and with the common practice of having to ask for money as each need/want emerged.
- Parents liked to exert influence through what they chose to support or not support.
- Teens seemed to learn the most from doing, like having a job and taking on responsibility. They also paid most attention to things that immediately impacted them.

Challenges:

- Parents often lacked a sophisticated understanding of the financial world.

• Parents did not want to share personal financial information with the children. This might be to protect their children from stress or to protect parents from sharing their own mistakes or lack of strategies.

Opportunities:

• Have parents teach teens about finances by using tools that address real money. Services could provide teens with more control of financial decisions, but they could also allow parents to influence and share their values.
• Explore if parents might be willing to share some aspects of their personal finances, especially parts where the teens might have a strong preference or where the teen's actions might impact costs.
• Explore if services could entice parents and teens to want to know more, and motivate them to seek out additional information in order to better use the service.

USER ENACTMENTS

Our collective design research methods provided a rich understanding of the current state. We particularly liked the idea of making tools where teens practice making financial decisions with real money and where parents play the role of a bank or advisor. We also liked ideas that prompted parents to share some of their financial information, especially when the topic impacted teens or when the topic was impacted by teens' behaviors.

We wanted to probe possible futures to build understanding for what could and should be. Therefore, we chose to run a speed dating study using user enactments (UE) [4,8,16]. When using this method, design researchers create several different concepts. They function as *design provocations* that probe on different aspects of the opportunity space. Teams then build an environment and generate a script that guides how participants move between concepts and interact with the environment. Teams then bring participants in, situate them in a familiar experience and then trigger a technology intervention that suggests a possible future. Teams debrief participants after each UE and then have a longer debriefing at the end to probe on insights, opportunities, and concerns that cut across the different provocations. UEs are meant to provoke discussion about different futures, so they are often more extreme than an actual commercial product or service.

We began by generating many different concepts. During this process, we reviewed the topics experts claimed teens should know and revisited highlights from the interviews. Once we had a large set of ideas, we began to cluster them. Within the clusters we combined different ideas and filtered some out. This produced an initial set of eight. We shared these with the bank employees to probe on their interest and insights on their customers. We shrank this set down to five based on discussion, fit to important financial concepts, and our sense of if we could render the design as a UE. They included:

• Loan: Parents offer a loan with interest
• Windfall: Teen receive unexpected money and decides how to spend/save it
• Saving: Parents help teen save towards a goal
• Invest: Parents and teens choose investments
• Price is Right: Teen guess what things cost

Next we iteratively developed each UE. During this process, we realized that we needed to extend the UE method beyond how it is commonly used. For these UEs the physical space, a critical design aspect of previous UEs, became much less important. Our focus was on the interaction between parents and teens, which should be triggered by the UE. This had little to do with any specific location, so instead of building an environment, we chose to conduct the UEs in participants' homes. As we designed, we quickly realized that we needed to support several interactions over time, such as setting up a loan with interest and then revisiting months later when some had been paid off but the needs had changed. To address this, for most UEs we developed scripts for setup and for a revisit at a predetermined future time.

After sketching the concepts, we chose to implement three of them as interactive interfaces (Loan, Windfall, Savings) and two as physical games. We developed the interfaces using Microsoft Excel. We locked the screen so only a few cells could be interacted with. These were always white, to help guide participant interaction. We implemented the board games using color prints, paperboard, glue, and Velcro (Figure 1). Below we describe each UE in terms of the initial situation and the interaction.

Loan: interest, credit, income, expenses, cash flow

Trigger: Teen receives an SMS from a friend inviting them to an upcoming concert. They do not have enough money saved, so they need to ask their parents for a loan.

Interaction: Parents set an interest rate. Then the teen plays with the down payment amount and monthly payment amount. As each change is made, the screen updates the total amount the tickets will cost and the amount of time it will take to pay it off.

Windfall: income, expenses, interest, debt, liquidity, cash flow, planning

Trigger: Teen receives $350 in birthday money.

Interaction: Teens and parents set up a step-by-step approach for figuring out how much to save and how much can be spent. Teens can opt to add a new purchase, pay off a loan, or save money to the Windfall calculation. As values are entered, the screen updates accordingly.

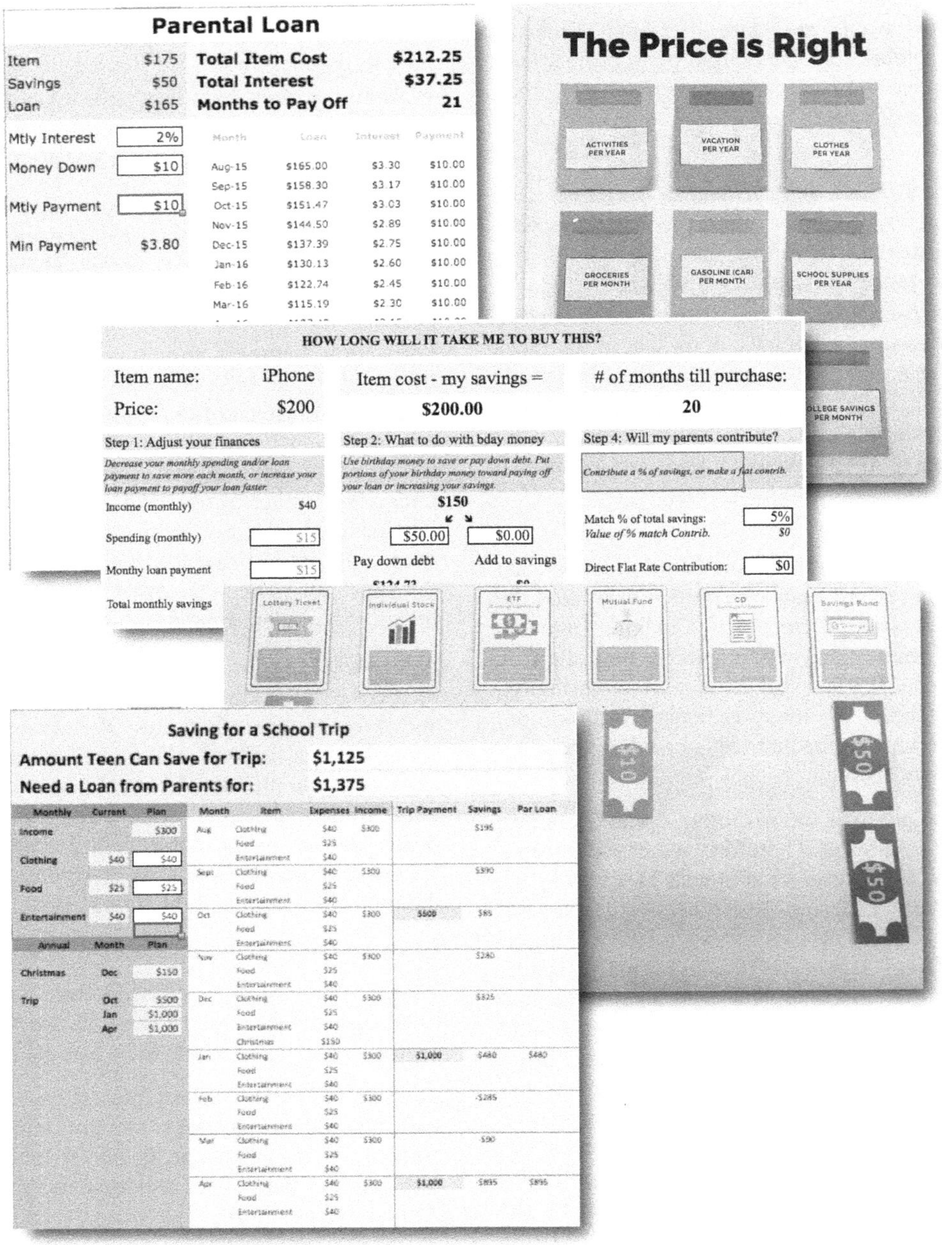

Figure 1. Images of UE tools. Upper-left is *Loan.* By adjusting the down payment, monthly payment, and interest rate, participants could see details of all payments and a summary at the top of the total cost and time to purchase concert tickets. Upper-right is *Price is Right.* Parents wrote the weekly, monthly, or annual costs for different expenses on the back of cards, and teens attempted to guess the amount without guessing more than the amount. Upper-middle is Windfall. Teens had to decide how to spend birthday money. They were told they wanted a new phone, already had an active loan, and had a set of monthly expenses. They had to decide if they should buy the phone or payoff their loan. Lower-middle is *Investment.* Teens and parents were given money to invest and were given several choices. On revisit they learned how much they had made and could reallocate. Bottom is *Savings.* Teens want to go on a school trip that costs $2500. They must make adjustments to their monthly expenses and ask their parents for financial help.

Savings: interest, cash flow, income, expenses

Trigger: Teen learns their school is having a trip to Costa Rica. It costs $2500 to go and the money is due in three payments. In addition, the teen is told their monthly income, expenses, and the amount they will need to spend on holiday presents for family members.

Interaction: The teen discusses with their parents if the parents might help them pay for the trip. They can reduce the monthly amount they spend on clothing, food, and entertainment to reduce what they need from the parents in order to go.

Investment: investing, interest, risk, rate of return

Trigger: Teen and parent are given $500 to invest in different investments including: stock, mutual fund, ETF, Certificate of deposit, or Savings Bond. Each has a brief description.

Interaction: They can work together or compete in investing the money in one or more instruments. They can learn how much each investment will and reallocate their money if they desire.

Price is Right: household expenses, costs, planning

Setup: Parent is asked for costs of different expenses including home internet, mobile phone plans, schools costs, monthly college savings. These are recorded on the back of each card.

Play: Teen is instructed to select a card and guess the amount. They choose four cards. They must be within 20% of the total cost, and they can never guess more than the actual amount in order to be crowned the "winner."

We carried out eight UE sessions. Six happened in our lab and two in participants' homes. Due to time pressure to get through all of the UEs we sometimes dropped Investment or Windfall, as these generated less interest.

Figure 2. UE happening in our lab with parent (left) and teen (right) discussing Windfall.

FINDINGS

Parents and teens had the strongest reactions and interactions with each other for the Loan, Savings, and Price is Right UEs. These connected with teens' immediate needs for money or with household spending that impacted teens. Windfall, where teens and parents discussed if the teen should pay off a loan, save money, or buy a new phone, seemed to work only with the older teens, who generally had more control over spending and more experience making purchase decisions. Investment did not generate much interest from either parents or teens. It required more knowledge of financial instruments than parents and teens possessed. Unfortunately, it never motivated a participant to seek additional information from the Internet.

UEs generated effective interactions between parents and teens (and some potential learning) when they supported exploration of different options or scenarios. Participants investigated different strategies with Loan, Savings, and Windfall. The interaction between Mom-F2 and S18-F2 provides a nice example:

Mom: *And so it will take you 44 months to pay off this loan. So 44 months is a long time, do you want to increase your monthly payment?*

Son: *Sure. I want to keep it at $5.*

Mom: *Do you know how many years that is? That's at least 4 years. What happens if you want another loan from me?*

Son: *Ok, I guess I'll pay $10 a month.*

Mom: *Ok so that cut it back to 20 months. Are you okay with that?*

Son: *No.*

Mom: *What do you want to do?*

Son: *$11.*

Mom: *18 months. Are you okay with that?*

Son: *Yeah that's fine.*

During the debrief, S18-F2 shared that he now understood that increasing his monthly payment reduced the total number of months, and more importantly, it reduced the total amount in interest he would need to pay, thus reducing the overall price for the ticket. Prior to this he did not realize that paying the loan off sooner would impact the total amount he needed to pay back.

Trying different scenarios also helped parents and teens negotiate, and it helped surface discussions around values and spending. F1s discussion around Windfall provides a good example of the kinds of interactions we observed.

Mom: *Yeah but if you pay us $25, then you can save* [to buy an iPhone] *by the end of Christmas. You still have to do Christmas shopping right? By the end of December, if you increase your payments, you should be able to get your phone. And you're cutting your spending down to $5.*

Daughter: *Yeah but what if my phone goes completely dead, you won't know where I am, I won't get home.*

Mom: *Okay, good point, okay. Well buy a new charger.*

Daughter: *It's not going to work. I've already been through three chargers.*

Mom: *Okay how bout this, give us $50. That gives you 8 months to pay the rest of the balance off, and you don't have to get the iPhone, but you could get something.*

Daughter: *Get what?*

Mom: *something within your budget.*

Daughter: *A flip phone?*

Mom: *Flip phones are coming back!*

Daughter: *No. I'm gonna get laughed at!*

After attempting several scenarios, the daughter realized she would rather try to repair her current iPhone and get a new charger. She would wait longer to get a new phone, because it mattered more to her to have an iPhone than to have a "new" functioning phone.

The ability to try different plans and see consequences created friction when values differed between parents and teens. However, the ability to investigate scenarios also made it easier for parents to support what their teens wanted. D15-F6 began to cry during the Savings UE, when discussing how to save for the school trip. Her parents wanted her to make more significant cutbacks in her monthly clothing and entertainment expenses. At one point she no longer wanted to go on the trip, but the trip had become important to her parents, especially when compared with her current spending habits. When reflecting on this same UE, Mom-F10 shared, "*Only if I see someone trying, I'll be glad to help. But if I don't see you trying. If I don't see you trying, I'm not doing it.* The Saving interface provided evidence of her child's effort, something not easy to grasp during typical parent-child negotiations over spending.

During the interviews, several parents revealed that they would not share personal financial information with their children; however, all parents when participating in the UEs enjoyed watching teens guess different household expenses such as groceries, phone service, and school supplies. They particularly liked when teens underestimated the expense. The game play between Mom-F1 and D13-F1 provides a typical example.

Daughter: *School supplies. $10.*

Mom: *Per year? Are you sure?*

Daughter: *Okay $30.*

Mom: *$30. Per year. Are you sure?*

Researcher reading from the card: *$200.*

Daughter: *What?*

Mom: *Yeah, because we get your books, the paper, the pencils, the different mechanical pencils you use. You always want to switch up the bookbags…*

Daughter: *Groceries. $60?*

Mom: *Really??*

Daughter: *Okay maybe make that $100.*

Mom: *Really? Okay, go ahead…*

Researcher reading from the card: *$300*

Daughter: *It doesn't look like it's that much.*

Mom: *I know it doesn't look like that much, but it's that much!*

When prompted on when her daughter should learn what things cost in order to plan for her future, Mom-F1 replied, "*She needs to know now so she'll be prepared. Before she goes on her own.*" This typical response to the UE stood in contrast to the interviews where several parents spoke of wanting to protect their children from the stress of finances.

Teens and parents often had a different view of charging interest on a loan. Parents typically viewed charging for the loan to be part of an educational process. Many also used this as an opportunity to share their financial values with their children. For example, Mom-F1 initially input a 12.5% interest rate for the $175 concert tickets because she viewed the high price as extravagant. She engaged her daughter in a discussion of the difference between wants and needs before lowering the rate. In reflecting on the UE, D13-F1 shared that charging interest was unfair. It was OK for banks to charge interest, but not parents. F6-D15 viewed the idea of charging interest a little differently, "*I feel like they shouldn't do that. Interest is for a profit. I feel like your parents shouldn't be making a profit off of you.*" This strong emotional reaction to the underlying idea helped the teen become and remain engaged in the situation, but it also limited her openness to learning, as the emotional affront seemed to hold all of her attention.

DISCUSSION

Our research investigates the idea of building tools that support parents in teaching their teenage children about finances. This challenge breaks down into two questions. The first asks if parents, who often lack financial sophistication, can effectively teach complex financial concepts to their children. The second asks if parents would be willing to teach finances to the children, and if teens would give their parents any attention. Our project skirts this first question and focuses more directly on the second and additionally probes if online tools might support parents in teaching teens.

The interviews showed that parents were the main source of teens' financial information. Parents and teens expressed interest in tools that could support parents playing a teaching role. Challenges came from a lack of available materials parents might use to teach teens other than the parents personal financial records. Parents seemed unwilling to share these. In addition, though the research shows starting financial education early has a positive effect, some parents wanted to shield children from the stress parents associated with finances.

The UEs explored the idea of parents taking on an educational role; however, they differed from previous educational materials by framing the tools not as educational tools, but instead as tools for parents and teens to use when negotiating teens' financial choices. They appeared as tools families might actually use to manage intra-family financial transactions.

This framing for a new kind of financial tool worked when it triggered conversations about financial values and when these conversations revealed different values for parents and teens. Parents and teens became most engaged when they could investigate several different scenarios in order to better understand the consequences of taking different actions. Exploring also allowed for negotiation. Parents and teens could discuss what they each viewed as important and work towards a middle ground.

The tools helped when they revealed that teens were making an effort to achieve a financial goal they really desired. The tools made the problem faced and the effort of each party more tangible. While the UEs were only role playing, using fixed scenarios with preset amount for things like teen monthly spending on different categories of items, parents and teens appeared to treat these much like real tools. They negotiated as if real money was at stake.

From the interviews, we observed that many teens had no regular income from their parents, such as an allowance. Instead, they would ask for money each time a new opportunity appeared. The teens curated their set of requests, not asking parents for many things they wanted when they felt there wasn't any way their parents might agree. Parents had no way to observe all of the times the teen chose not to ask them for money. Parents wanted teens to prioritize spending, but the teens' lack of income often made this difficult, if not impossible. Without a source of income, the teens lacked agency to make one choice over another and to demonstrate to their parents their decision process. The UEs worked when they provided teens with this agency and when they also provided parents with the ability to probe on teens' priorities and to influence a choice through their own willingness to help or to set terms that made achieving a goal more likely.

Our research revealed that parents and teens both benefited and struggled due to the ambiguity of their current financial arrangements. When teens asked for money, they sometimes used the word "loan," but they appeared to never actually mean they wanted a loan. They almost never had any intention of paying their parents back. We also observed ambiguity around what it meant when parents gave their children money. When the teens spent this money, parents still viewed it as parental money even though they had surrendered control of this to their teen. Neither financial term "loan" nor "gift" fit this arrangement. The UEs disrupted this ambiguity by more clearly classifying money as gift (parental help with the school trip) or with the interested accruing and payment scheduled loans from Loan and Windfall.

The Price is Right game shifted parents from their claim that they did not want to share personal financial information with their children. We suspect the game worked well because it shielded parents from having to share any mistakes they might have made and from any deficits in their own financial knowledge. In addition, we suspect this UE was popular because it matched more closely with parents' view of financial literacy as being able to get to the end of each month having paid the bills and having achieved a little savings.

While many research and practical questions remain, we see our collective set of findings across the different activities as supporting the idea of making financial tools that support parents in teaching their children about finances. This is mostly due to the strong engagement we observed between parents and teens, and due to the way the UEs triggered both emotionally charged and reflective conversations about financial values; most often framed by parents as the difference between wants and needs. Open issues include:

• Learning financial concepts outside of teens' immediate needs. Tools should focus on teens' need to learn many concepts such as interest, credit, expenses, income, and cash flow. Other important concepts needed for later-in-life planning, such as risk, the differences between good and bad credit, the impact of compounding interest over decades, and the role of life insurance remain out of reach.

• Our UEs worked well when they exposed a teen's cash flow, allowing them to run scenarios and make plans. However, from our interviews and the related literature, it seems unlikely that teens or their parents are currently in a position to easily assess what their cash flow might be.

Our work provides preliminary evidence that parents and teens might be willing to engage in services that allow parents to help their teens practice making better financial decisions. This direction seems ripe for helping teens practice the act of making these decisions without the risk of suffering the full consequences associated with making these choices as an adult. This approach seems less capable of actually educating either parent or teen about complex financial concepts or even triggering a desire in either group to seek out additional information. This approach is not a "fix-all"; however, it could prove more effective if coupled with an in-school program focused on the more abstract and complex concepts. The parent-teen tools might allow practice of decision making while the school program introduces advanced concepts.

CONCLUSION

US teens' lack of financial literacy is a real concern. We investigated the feasibility of new digital services that support parents in discussing financial concept and passing on financial values. Following a research through design approach, we conducted a literature review, a competitive analysis, and interviewed teens and parents. We generated design provocations to investigate possible services and observed how parents and teens interacted. Our results showed that parents and teens want these kinds of services, especially when they provide teens with increased agency and allow parents to influence based on their values. In the future, we plan to deploy functional tools and observe how families use these over time.

ACKNOWLEDGMENTS

We thank the PNC Center for Financial Services Innovation at Carnegie Mellon for their financial support of this work.

REFERENCES

1. Stanley H. Breitbard and Cheryl Gravis Reynolds. 2003. Jump-starting Financial Literacy. *Journal of Accountancy* 196(6).
2. Carol Cochran. 2010. *Financial Literacy in Teens*. Master's Thesis, Program of Curriculum and Instruction, Caldwell College.
3. Lee Cooper, Graham Johnson, and Chris Baber. 1999. A run on Sterling-personal finance on the move. *The Third International Symposium on Wearable Computers*, 87–93.
4. Scott Davidoff, Min Kyung Lee, Anind K. Dey, and John Zimmerman. 2007. Rapidly exploring application design through speed dating. *Proceedings of the Conference on Ubiquitous Computing*, Springer. Retrieved from http://link.springer.com/chapter/10.1007/978-3-540-74853-3_25
5. Shelley Evenson. 2006. Directed storytelling: Interpreting experience for design. In *Design Studies: Theory and Research in Graphic Design*, Audrey Bennett (ed.). Princeton Architectural Press, 231–240.
6. Jodi Forlizzi and John Zimmerman. 2013. Promoting Service Design as a Core Practice in Interaction Design. *The 5th IASDR World Conference on Design Research*, IASDR Press.
7. Susan Meyer Goldstein, Robert Johnston, JoAnn Duffy, and Jay Rao. 2002. The service concept: the missing link in service design research? *Journal of Operations management* 20, 2: 121–134.
8. Bruce Hanington and Bella Martin. 2012. *Universal methods of design: 100 ways to research complex problems, develop innovative ideas, and design effective solutions*. Rockport Publishers, Beverly, MA.
9. Ian Hathaway and Sameer Khatiwada. 2008. Do financial education programs work?. Federal Reserve Bank of Cleveland Working Paper.
10. Alan Henry. 2014. Five Best Personal Finance Tools. *Lifehacker*. Retrieved January 15, 2016 from http://lifehacker.com/5828438/five-best-desktop-personal-finance-tools
11. Sandra J. Huston. 2010. Measuring Financial Literacy. *Journal of Consumer Affairs* 44, 2: 296–316
12. Joseph Jofish Kaye, Mary McCuistion, Rebecca Gulotta, and David A Shamma. 2014. Money talks: Tracking personal finances. *Proceedings of the SIGCHI Conference on Human Factors in Computing Systems* (CHI '14), 521–530.
13. Annamaria Lusardi and Olivia Mitchell. 2007. Financial Literacy and Retirement Planning: New Evidence from the Rand American Life Panel. *Michigan Retirement Research Center WP 157*.
14. Annamaria Lusardi, Olivia S. Mitchell, and Vilsa Curto. 2010. Financial Literacy Among the Young. *Journal of Consumer Affairs*, 44(2), 358-380.
15. Indrani Medhi, S N Nagasena Gautama, and Kentaro Toyama. 2009. A comparison of mobile money-transfer UIs for non-literate and semi-literate users. *Proceedings of the SIGCHI Conference on Human Factors in Computing Systems* (CHI '09), ACM Press, 1741–1750.
16. William Odom, John Zimmerman, Scott Davidoff, Jodi Forlizzi, Anind K. Dey, and Min Kyung Lee. 2012. A fieldwork of the future with user enactments. *Proceedings of the Designing Interactive Systems Conference on - DIS '12*: 338. Retrieved from http://dl.acm.org/citation.cfm?doid=2317956.2318008
17. Kursat F Ozenc, James P Brommer, Bong-keum Jeong, Nina Shih, Karen Au, and John Zimmerman. 2007. Reverse alarm clock: a research through design example of designing for the self. *Proceedings of the Conference on the Design of Pleasurable Products and Services* (DPPI '07), ACM Press, 392–406. http://doi.org/10.1145/1314161.1314196
18. Kimberly Palmer. 2014. How to Teach Teens About Money. US News Online, accessed June 29, 2015: http://money.usnews.com/money/personal-finance/articles/2014/08/06/how-to-teach-teens-more-about-money
19. Tapan Parikh, Paul Javid, Sasikumar K., and Kaushik Ghosh. 2006. Mobile phones and paper documents: evaluating a new approach for capturing microfinance data in rural India. *Proceedings of the SIGCHI Conference on Human Factors in Computing Systems* (CHI '06), ACM Press, 551–560.
20. Karen Varcoe, Shirley S. Peterson, Charles Go, Margaret C. Johns, Paula René-Fitch, Carol J. Powell, and Connie Costello. 2002. Teen financial literacy evaluated to develop outreach materials. *California Agriculture,* 56(2), 65-68.
21. John Vines, Mark Blythe, Paul Dunphy, and Andrew Monk. 2011. Eighty something: banking for the older old. *Proceedings of the 25th BCS Conference on Human-Computer Interaction*, 64–73.
22. Lauren E. Willis. 2011. The financial education fallacy. *The American Economic Review* 101(3), 429-434.
23. John Zimmerman. 2009. Designing for the self: making products that help people become the person they desire to be. *Proceedings of the SIGCHI Conference on Human Factors in Computing Systems* (CHI '09), ACM Press, 395–404. http://doi.org/10.1145/1518701.1518765
24. John Zimmerman and Jodi Forlizzi. 2014. Research Through Design in HCI. In *Ways of knowing in HCI*, Judith S. Olson and Wendy A. Kellogg (eds.). Springer, 1–23. http://doi.org/10.1007/978-1-4939-0378-8

Tap-Kick-Click: Foot Interaction for a Standing Desk

William Saunders, Daniel Vogel
Cheriton School of Computer Science, University of Waterloo, CANADA
william@williamsaunders.net, dvogel@uwaterloo.ca

ABSTRACT
Foot interaction techniques for controlling conventional desktop applications at a standing desk are described. Indirect, discrete two-foot input using combinations of spatial kicks, taps, jumps, and standing postures are tracked using a depth camera and instrumented shoes. An implemented system shows how visual feedback and interface augmentation can make foot input compatible with existing desktop applications. Application scenarios using the system demonstrate productive pure foot input breaks with real application tasks like web browsing and code debugging, as well as using feet as a secondary input channel with mouse and keyboard. An evaluation validates the usability of the approach.

Author Keywords
interaction technique; foot input; healthy computing;

ACM Classification Keywords
H.5.2. Information Interfaces (e.g., HCI): Input devices

INTRODUCTION
Using a computer while standing at an elevated desk can increase health and productivity [10]. This is largely due to a standing posture and increased physical movement. To enhance this benefit, we created *Tap-Kick-Click*, foot interaction techniques for a standing desk to enable productive "foot input only" breaks (Figure 1a) and increased physical activity by using foot input with mouse and keyboard input (Figure 1a). We build on Meyers et al.'s [16] foot-based exercise system to sort emails and photos on a large display, and we extend, realize, and validate our previous hypothetical illustration of foot input at standing desk [25].

Tap-Kick-Click primarily uses an interaction vocabulary of discrete taps and kicks aimed at virtual targets arranged in a semicircular array around each foot. Low-density targets are used for application commands (injected as keyboard shortcuts or simulated target selection) under eyes-free usage and high-density targets with indirect "foot cursors" for menu selection. Small jumps access help and, as a further probe, mildly uncomfortable foot positions are used to self-control "cyberslacking" [31] (Figure 1c). Our implemented system shows how carefully designed feedback and interface augmentations can make foot input compatible with existing desktop applications.

Consider a *Tap-Kick-Click* usage scenario for academic research (also demonstrated in the accompanying video):

While standing at her desk, Jane enters a paper search term with the keyboard, then lifts her hands to stretch while scrolling search results with forward and backward toe taps. She continues working "away from the keyboard" by kicking forward to enter "click mode" where visible hyperlinks are decorated with icons to convey short sequences of forward, side, and back taps to select them. Jane selects a paper link by performing a sequence, reads the abstract, and with a backward kick, adds the paper to her reference manager. She switches to her reference manager using a right kick and forward left toe tap, then opens the downloaded PDF with a forward kick. Jane skims the PDF while scrolling with her feet like the webpage. Having taken a short physical break, she reaches again for the keyboard to enter notes. While typing, her music player starts playing an annoying song, so she skips it "in the background" with a forward whole foot tap. Having accomplished some research, Jane decides to check Facebook. To help reduce procrastination, she configured her system so she has to stand in a mildly uncomfortable position while viewing certain sites. It is just enough to deter her from spending too much time on it and Jane returns shortly to her work.

Our work leverages research in foot input, sensing, and break software to design, implement, and validate a foot-based interaction technique in a fully working system for a new and thought-provoking application.

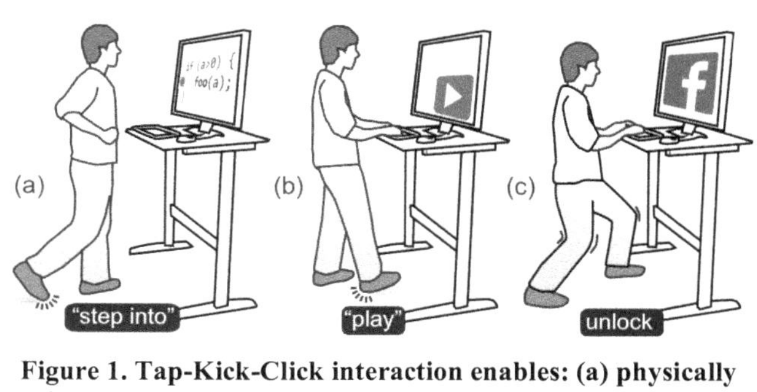

Figure 1. Tap-Kick-Click interaction enables: (a) physically active and productive "foot input only" breaks; (b) increased physical activity using foot input *with* mouse and keyboard input; (c) and, as a way to self-control cyberslacking.

DIS 2016, June 04-08, 2016, Brisbane, QLD, Australia © 2016 ACM.
ISBN 978-1-4503-4031-1/16/06...$15.00 DOI:
http://dx.doi.org/10.1145/2901790.2901815

To our knowledge, no previous work has combined foot input with a standing desk for command-level control of conventional desktop applications. We make five contributions:

- A set of indirect, discrete foot interaction techniques for a standing desk that enables primary foot-only application control and secondary foot input augmentation of mouse and keyboard.
- Feedback visualizations and command mappings to make foot input practical with real desktop applications.
- A tracking system using an under-desk depth-camera and shoes with IR LEDs and force sensors.
- Demonstrating how Tap-Kick-Click can be used for web browsing, academic research, and interactive debugging.
- A usability evaluation validating the system and interaction techniques applied to real application tasks.

After surveying related work, we describe the interaction vocabulary, provide implementation details for the system, illustrate how the vocabulary is applied to example applications, and present the results of a usability evaluation.

RELATED WORK

Past work motivates using standing foot input for physical activity rather than increased performance, previous foot-based systems in other domains like mobile and large displays provide inspiration for input methods, and studies examining standing foot input provide guidelines.

Foot motion follows Fitts' law, but it is slower than comparable arm movements [7,12,29] making foot-based cursor control slower and more-error prone than a hand-operated mouse [20] or trackball [19]. Although footswitches are used for audio transcription [21], using feet for desktop applications is rare for able-bodied users [6,14], especially when standing. Velloso et al. [30] provide a comprehensive survey of foot-based interaction, we highlight the most relevant work for foot input while standing.

Active Foot Input

Although foot input may be slow, feet can make interaction physically active. Foot-based games such as Dance Dance Revolution (DDR) [13] are strenuous and skilled, but exergaming systems [33] and mobile games [18] have used less strenuous taps, jumps, and kicks for mild exercise, immersion, and enjoyment [10].

These kinds of physically active movements can also be used to perform conventional computing tasks. For example, foot input can provide a break from mouse and keyboard to reduce wrist RSI, such as Berque et al.'s [3] extra foot operated mouse to control a game and scroll a Twitter feed. However, given poor foot-based cursor control while seated [19–21], discrete command invocation is likely more suitable. In their work-in-progress, Meyers et al. [16] use foot taps on a 3×3 DDR foot switch mat to make tasks like email sorting more active and enjoyable. A DDR mat uses direct input, so gaze shifts between display and monitoring foot position, and the input space is limited to about 8 to 10 single movement actions: this will not scale easily to controlling real applications. Given issues with continuous foot control and the encouraging results of Meyer et al.'s initial exploration of discrete control, our interaction vocabulary is discrete.

Subtle Foot Input

A counter-point to increasing physical activity are systems designed to be subtle and socially acceptable [23]. Crossan et al. [5] use in place toe taps for an eyes-free menu and Scott et al. [27] explore single foot, heel and toe pivoting gestures following a double toe tap demarcation. We extend in place tapping by adding a spatial dimension of virtual floor targets and by using different kinds of taps. Even more subtle input is possible with pressure. Schöning et al. [26] sensed subtle weight shifts with a Wii balance board for large display map navigation. Matthies et al.'s insoles also sense small toe movements [15], an idea expanded by Fukahori et al.'s pressure sensing socks to perform secret tasks like password entry [8]. Our goal is not to use subtle movements like toe or heel pivots since they are less physically active. Moreover, they are difficult to distinguish from shifting feet when standing and are more likely to cause false positive inputs at a standing desk. We use insole force sensors and spatial targets to make tapping more expressive and robust.

Guidelines for Standing Foot Input

Alexander et al.'s [1] elicitation study suggests additional foot gestures, including spatial taps and kicks for controlling continuous map navigation, a more specialized goal than general command invocation. We justify some design choices using this work, but we extend their elicited mappings to desktop applications and to a larger input space of spatial tapping and kicking using both feet. Alexander et al. tested recognition of dominant foot kicks in four directions and forward taps in their system implementation, and only applied on kicks and in-place taps for map navigation. Han et al. [11] develop guidelines for discrete, directional kicks: people can reliably kick in 5 forward directions over a 120° arc (24° targets) and reliably control two levels of kick velocity. Our previous work evaluating indirect foot pointing in a controlled experiment [25] provides expanded guidelines supporting the use of both feet, the near equivalence of tapping and kicking, tap and kick direction preferences, and recommended target sizes. Velloso et al.'s [29] study of foot input while seated confirms many of our findings as well. We apply these guidelines to our design.

TAP-KICK-CLICK INTERACTION

The core interaction vocabulary is a sequence of taps and kicks performed with either foot, aimed at virtual targets in a semicircular array around each foot. Alexander et al.'s study [1] found people intuitively use this kind of tapping and kicking. We supplement the core vocabulary with jumps and static foot positions for specialized applications.

This vocabulary and system are powerful enough to perform useful application tasks such as web browsing, reading, and stepping through code with an interactive debugger. The combination of a standing desk and standard desktop applications means foot input is easily interleaved with mouse and keyboard. Feet are not used for rapid or precise tasks like text entry or drawing; the goal is to provide enough capability to enable physical breaks away from the mouse and keyboard and create opportunities for increased physical activity by using feet for background tasks.

Since foot input is always available, our system enables a physical break without leaving a work task. This is a middle ground between intense task focus without any kind of break and completely off-task physical and mental breaks enabled by systems like SuperBreak [17]. There is evidence that off-task breaks may not increase productivity [24] and our own informal observations suggest workers do not always want to take an off-task break when "on a roll."

Interaction with Spatial Taps and Kicks

We use a combination of foot action and target selection as a discretized input language.

Indirect Target Selection

The center-front of each foot is the selection hotspot, represented on the display as *foot cursors* within a virtual target layout (Figure 2b). This is *indirect* input control where the user can focus on the display rather than their feet. A DDR mat or Augsten et al.'s interactive floor [2] use *direct* control where the user looks at their feet relative to actual floor targets. An indirect cursor also eliminates foot occlusion and minimizes hotspot ambiguity [2].

Targets are selected with slow-speed kicks and three types of taps: toe (front of the foot), heel (back of the foot), and whole foot (both front and heel) (Figure 4). In our previous study [25], we found kicks or taps to be nearly equivalent and people naturally perform these different taps with some preference for toe tapping. Taps are detected using heel and/or toe floor contact and kicks are identified when and where the foot reverses direction.

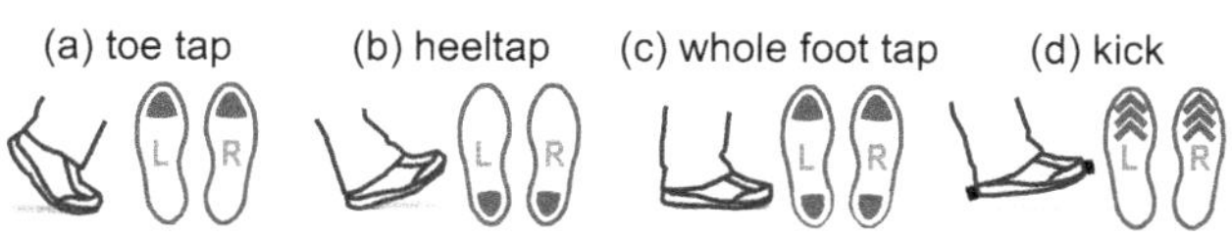

Figure 4. Foot actions with foot icons used in the interface.

"Midas-Step" Avoidance

There is no explicit mode switch to turn foot input on or off since our aim to make foot input always available to support spontaneous foot breaks and background foot input. We accomplish this with a simple counter-measure to avoid accidental foot input. Between each tap and kick, the foot typically returns to a home position to maintain balance and encourage physical activity. The diameter of each home position in motor space is 10 cm and it is dynamically adjusted to match the standing position by following short, slow foot movements (typical when adjusting stance). Combining a

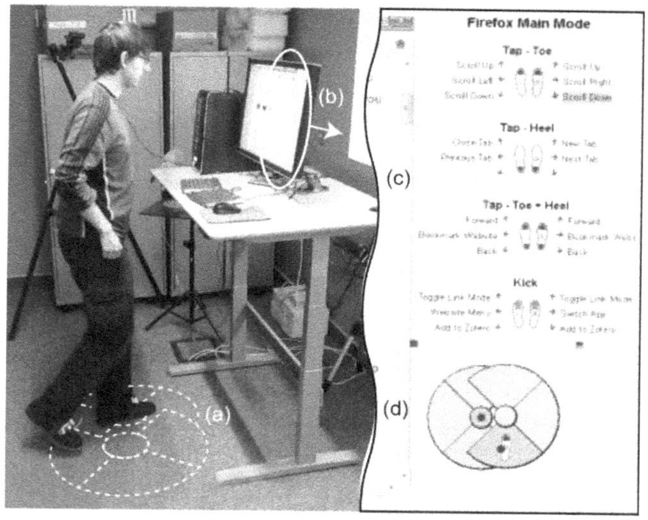

Figure 2. Indirect foot input system showing: (a) low-density virtual targets; (b) indirect feedback in always-visible sidebar with (c) cue card showing command mapping for foot action and target (d) foot cursors within virtual targets (left foot is in home position, right foot has just completed a back toe tap).

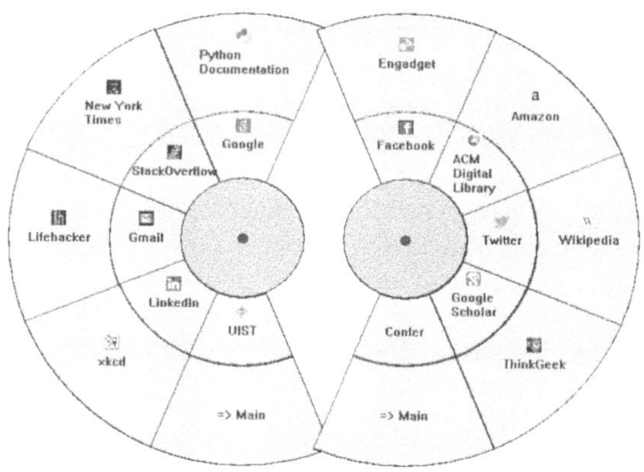

Figure 3. High density virtual targets used for foot menu.

dynamic home position and distinctive spatial tap and kick movements reduce "Midas step" inadvertent activation.

Virtual Target Layouts

Two virtual target layouts are used: low- and high-density. The *low-density layout* is for issuing application commands and selecting GUI targets with a special "click mode." With some practice, this can be done *eyes-free,* without monitoring the foot cursor allowing complete focus on the application under control. Following guidelines [25], low-density targets have an angular size of 90° and are positioned forward, outward, and backward from each foot (Figure 2a).

The *high-density layout* is used for a special-purpose foot menu where the user can fully rely on indirect feedback to select among many simultaneous actions (Figure 3). Following guidelines [25], the high-density targets have an angular size of 45° and are positioned in a contiguous outward arc from front to back of each foot in two bands, one from 10 to 20 cm and the other 20 to 30 cm.

Application Commands with Low-Density Targets

A constantly available side panel displays a foot cursor with virtual target positions (Figure 2d) and a dynamic cue card showing current foot action to command mappings (Figure 2c). The active command set matches the mode of the focused application. Each time a tap or kick is sensed, the corresponding command is sent to the application by injecting a keyboard shortcut key sequence. The most recently sensed foot action is displayed using a foot-action icon (see Figure 4) at the target location and the cue card highlights the command issued. Rich feedback is important to convey detected events and current state to spot and troubleshoot errors (e.g. a background object disrupting foot tracking) and it provides a way to learn mappings between foot actions and application commands.

The side panel does reduce space for other applications[1]. With larger displays, or multiple displays, this is less of a concern. The panel design could be refined to minimize its size, or it could be made semi transparent and become active when foot input is detected. We also plan to experiment with augmenting the system cursor with a subset of information shown in the side bar for expert users.

Command Mapping Patterns

With 4 foot actions (toe tap, heel tap, whole foot tap, kick) and 6 virtual target locations across both feet, 24 commands can be accessed in one set (examples of command sets in Figure 8). Where possible, we map frequent commands to forward targets and favour toe taps [25]. However, highly correlated mappings overrule this guideline: we initially assigned scroll-down to a forward tap based on frequency, but pilots revealed strong dislike for this mapping. Alexander et al. [1] note the importance of correlated mappings.

We distribute frequent commands across both feet for comfort and balance and map the most frequent commands, such as scroll down, to both feet so feet and be alternated. Backward heeltaps are difficult [25], so we avoid them, or use them for infrequent and irreversible commands (e.g. "delete all"). Tapping actions are "auto-repeated" when the foot is held on a target for a period of time (after 150ms, the action repeats every 400ms). This can be particularity useful for scrolling or stepping through code.

Kicks are used to change application modes. For example, in a code editor, interactive code debugging (and the corresponding debugging command set) is activated with a forward kick. Across all applications, an outward right-foot kick changes to a global command set for application switching and background application control. For example, toe taps are for application task switching (analogous to "alt-tab")

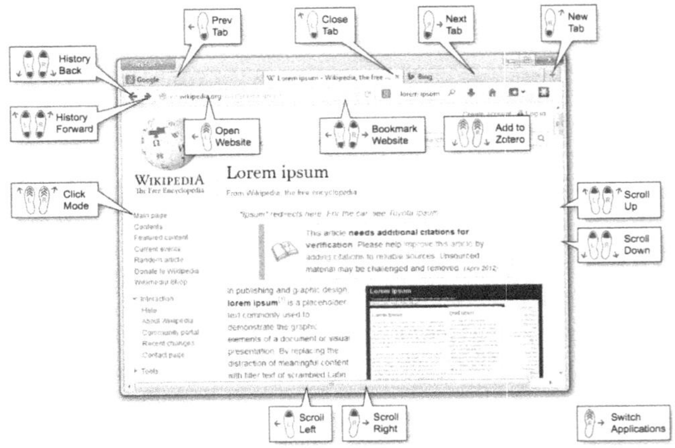

Figure 5. Help screen showing foot action to command mappings in the context of the application interface.

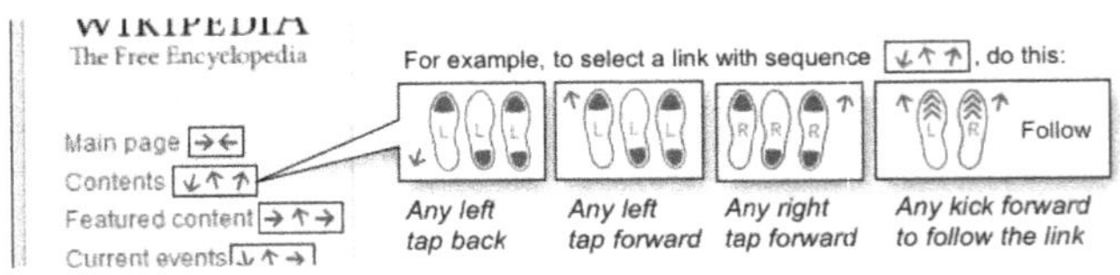

Figure 6. *Click mode* selection sequences (the right callout is only shown in help mode).

and other taps for background application control (e.g. a right whole foot tap sends 'play' to a music player and a right whole foot tap up skips to the next track).

"Clicking" on GUI Targets with Low-Density Targets

There are many cases in GUI applications where arbitrary targets must be selected and there is no direct keyboard mapping (e.g. webpage hyperlinks). Given the poor performance of foot-controlled mice and our focus on discrete input, we developed a technique called "click mode" where GUI targets are selected with short sequences of taps. Once activated with a forward kick, click mode decorates each target with icons representing a unique sequence of forward, outward, and backward taps using left or right feet. Since sequence lengths vary, we use a forward kick to accept the entered sequence and "click" on the target.

We implemented this in Firefox using a modified version of the "Hit-a-Hint" add-on. Sequences are displayed beside each link in the visible portion of the page as strips of 16px arrow icons (Figure 6). This scheme scales well, sequences up to length 3 can index 258 targets ($6 + 6^2 + 6^3$). With dense targets, the arrows occlude content, but click mode is usually activated after the desired target is visually identified. This technique could be extended to targets in any GUI application using accessibility APIs for target locations. Click mode

[1] Note the panel size is larger in the accompanying video to increase legibility in the video only.

is not as fast as using a mouse, but it is easy to learn and requires fun combinations of steps that fulfill our goal of physical activity.

Foot Menu with High-Density Targets

The high-density layout is used for a special-purpose foot menu (Figure 3). In the web browser command set, a left kick opens the menu of bookmarks. The high-density virtual targets forming the menu, and the foot cursor feedback, are displayed in the center of the screen. Each target is labelled with a menu action. With 4 foot actions and 20 targets, 80 menu items are possible, although we use 20 commands for ease of understanding.

In Place Jump for Contextual Help

Meyers et al. [16] report people found two foot jumps enjoyable, but using them for core application control is too physically demanding. Augsten at al. [2] test jumping as a target selection technique on a direct input floor, we integrate it into a vocabulary in a different input context. We use small in place two-foot jumps to activate a help system. The jumping action is intended to be easy to remember and encourage learning (avoiding exertion by consulting help too frequently). Help is provided in the form of command mappings in the context of the application interface (Figure 5). Foot action icons are shown in callouts pointing to the equivalent application command location when possible.

Static Foot Positions for Self-Regulating Cyberslacking

Static, discrete foot positions can be used as a kinaesthetic mode to unlock websites like Facebook or YouTube that can be a source of "cyberslacking" [31]. We use a mildly uncomfortable posture resembling a lunge with one foot forward and the other back (Figure 1c). The foot positions can be switched at any time.

We imagine this as "self-help" where the user chooses to block websites. The lunge posture is purposely chosen to be extreme. More natural postures could be used for other tasks, for example crossing one foot behind the other to switch between two virtual desktops. Poses and mappings must be chosen carefully to avoid false positives.

Error Recovery

An incorrect foot movement, a sensing error, or a cognitive mistake, could result in the invocation of an undesired command. Erroneous navigation commands, such as scrolling and link selection, can be reversed using additional foot input commands or by reaching for the keyboard or mouse. Most erroneous application commands can be "undone" using an application's built-in undo function. Currently, undo is not mapped to foot input, so this requires the use of the keyboard. Given the standing desk context, reaching for the keyboard or mouse should not be a significant burden.

SYSTEM

The Tap-Kick-Click interaction vocabulary is fully implemented to work with existing Windows desktop applications. The system handles foot input tracking using a depth camera and insole pressure sensors, as well as managing the side bar display, command mode selection, command injection, and application augmentation such as decorating links with icons for "click mode."

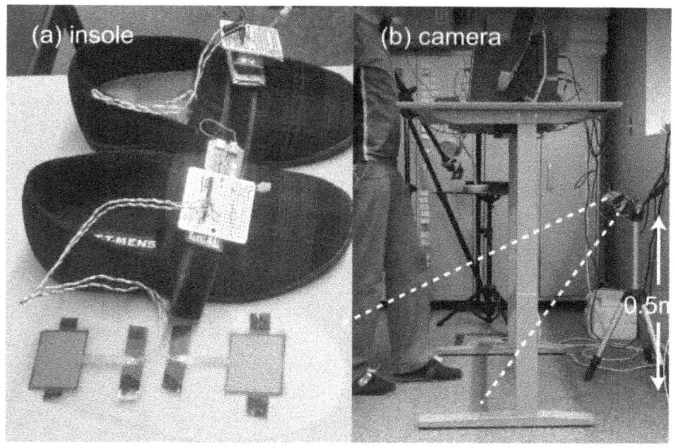

Figure 7. Sensing hardware: (a) insole with force sensors; (b) under desk Kinect depth camera for foot position tracking.

Sensing Foot Input

Using instrumented shoes with a depth camera makes sensing foot position and foot tap quite robust. This enabled us to focus on interaction and also minimized a confounding effect of tracking errors from our usability study.

Foot Position

To be practical for small offices, a Microsoft Kinect depth camera is mounted behind the standing desk with a clear view of the feet and lower leg (Figure 7b). Full skeletal tracking requires a less convenient mounting location and does not provide accurate foot positions. Simple depth image thresholding can identify people by their shoes [22], or track directional foot movements when seated at a desk where occlusion is not an issue [28]. For increased precision and to mitigate partial-occlusion during backward movements, we mounted 850nm IR LEDs on two slippers to locate each foot. Tracking fixed points also makes the algorithm robust to changes in foot orientation, characteristic when moving to side targets [25].

The depth of each foot is calculated using an algorithm implemented with SimpleCV with the following steps:

1. The two brightest points (the IR LEDs) are located in a downsampled 160×120px IR frame using two passes with a 3×3 25-percentile filter.
2. Using a downsampled 320×240px depth frame, the 25th percentile of depth is computed in the region surrounding each point masked by a bottom half-ring shape (inner radius 5px, outer radius 15px). This shape avoids the depth "hole" caused by a bright IR LED.
3. The depth sample is used to find the 3D location of the foot and then the 2D position by projecting down along the normal of the calibrated floor plane.

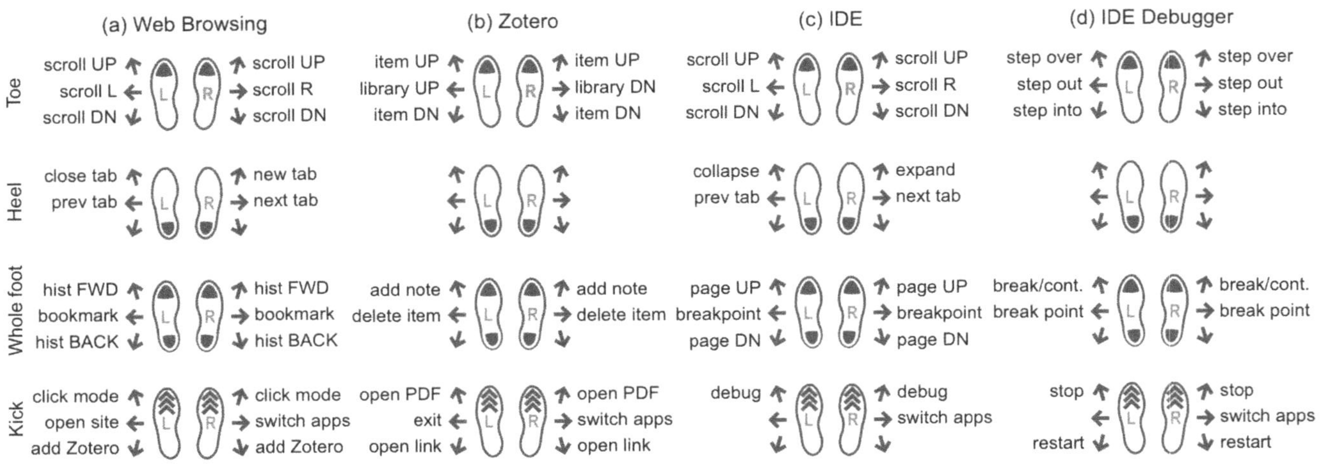

Figure 8. Example application command sets with foot action mappings represented as sidebar cue cards.

Foot Contact
Force sensitive resistors are mounted at either end of each insole to accurately differentiate between heel, toe, and whole foot tapping, between kicking from tapping, and precisely sense repeated tapping actions (Figure 7a). The sensors for each foot (and IR LED) are connected to a battery-powered Arduino and sensor readings are sent over Bluetooth to the computer system

Sensor Fusion and Action Sensing
The Arduino force and Kinect position streams are time stamped and synchronized. Commands are sent when a foot action and target position combination is sensed over a 200ms time window. Kicks are classified as reversing motions over a target without any floor contact. Additional constraints reduce false activations: kick events are only sent if the foot returns to home target without any taps over a target, and toe or heel events are only recognized after a whole foot event if the foot lifts up entirely or the toe or heel state is sensed for 500ms.

A more evolved computer vision algorithm or pressure sensitive floor could remove the requirement for instrumented shoes. For example, the GravitySpace system [4] uses a high-resolution pressure-sensitive floor to unobtrusively detect different types of foot contacts and kicks using the contact pattern of planted feet. Alternatively, the shoe-based sensing could be improved to eliminate the need for the depth camera. For example, similar "on foot" sensing already exists for fitness tracking (e.g. Nike+ Fuel, Footlogger, Sensoria Sock, SENSEable Shoes) and researchers have used shoe-based sensors for interaction in the past. For example, Paradiso and Hu [20] put sensors in shoes to create an interactive dance performance and Matthies et al.'s [15] insoles use pressure sensors to detect actions like jumping, walking, and turning for virtual environment navigation.

Command Set Selection and Command Injection
A system-level service synchronizes the set of command mappings with the current foreground application state by template matching the focused window title text. The appropriate command set is currently chosen from hand built configuration files. This could be more automated by scraping application menus using accessibility APIs. Commands are sent to the application by injecting keystrokes that simulate short-cut key sequences.

EXAMPLE TASK SCENARIOS AND APPLICATIONS
To illustrate Tap-Kick-Click utility, we implemented three representative task scenarios: general web browsing, web-based academic research, and interactive debugging. These are good examples of suitable tasks for Tap-Kick-Click interaction for three reasons: 1) they are common tasks for different types of knowledge workers; 2) the task goals do not emphasize input speed (find information, read a paper, trace through code); and, 3) they involve periods without text entry or editing. The accompanying video provides demonstrations of representative scenarios.

Primary command sets for associated applications are shown in Figure 8. These mappings leverage the results of Alexander et al.'s [1] elicitation study and natural behaviour we observed in our controlled foot input experiment [25]. To facilitate learning, some commands are universal (like kicks to switch applications) and some are application independent (like scrolling pages or items with forward and backward toe taps). Note that a large set of commands are possible, but ultimately it is the user's choice when to use foot input. For example, they could initially use feet only for scrolling web pages or documents when reading.

Web browsing
The command set uses "click mode" for hyperlink selection and supports standard web browsing tasks (Figure 8a). Toe tapping scrolls the page, link selection is with click mode, and history navigation is maps to whole foot commands. This provides a complete method for navigating within and between web pages. Heel actions close tabs, switch between tabs, and open a new tab. When a new tab is opened, the foot menu is used to select a bookmarked website. Occasional

textual search queries or form entry are accomplished by reaching out and typing on the keyboard. Other features like bookmarking a page use outward whole foot taps. The system also has special website-specific command sets. For example, a special Google search results command set makes it easily to select from a list of results without labelling every link with click mode: a forward left kick highlights the first result, lower results are selected with toe taps, and a forward right kick selects. More website-specific command mappings could be developed for web applications such as email or task management.

Web-based Academic Research

Web-based academic research typically spans multiple applications for browsing web-based databases, reading PDF papers, and storing items in a reference manager. Currently, web browsing uses the techniques above, but website-specific browsing modes could be added to streamline sites like the ACM Digital Library or JSTOR. While browsing, a PDF link is opened using click mode and the paper read using toe taps for scrolling, heeltaps for tab switching, and kicks for zooming. Using an outward right-foot kick to change to the global command, the PDF reader may be closed with a backwards kick, returning the focus to the web-based database and website command set. There, a kick back adds the paper to the Zotero reference manager. After switching to Zotero using the global command set, Zotero command mappings (Figure 8b) enable navigating between libraries and selecting reference items with toe taps and whole foot taps add or delete a note. A forward kick opens the item in a PDF reader.

Interactive Code Debugging in an IDE

Finally, Tap-Kick-Click can be used for specialized tasks within text-heavy applications, such as a coding IDE. This can augment keyboard input by using feet for code navigation (Figure 8c): toe taps to scroll and heeltaps to switch tabs and expand/collapse code blocks. Perhaps most compelling is using an outward whole foot tap to set a breakpoint, and a forward kick to start a debugging session. The debugging command set (Figure 8d) uses toe taps to *step into*, *step out of*, and *step over* code while tracing through program execution code. A whole foot tap breaks or continues execution, and kicks exit or restart the session.

EVALUATION

The goal of our evaluation is to validate the fundamental Tap-Kick-Click interaction techniques as realized in the system when used for realistic tasks. This goal spans usability and usefulness by determining if the techniques and system can be learned and used during a short session and verify applicability to key application scenarios. This initial evaluation focuses on using foot input as a primary input method and was conducted in a lab. A longitudinal field study could evaluate how the system integrates into everyday computing tasks and explore how often people choose to use their feet for primary or secondary input.

Protocol

We recruited 8 people from a university (ages 20 to 30, 4 female). One participant had used a standing desk; none were familiar with the system or foot input. The software and sensing system were as described above. Three pairs of slippers were instrumented: Women's 8½, Men's 10, Men's 12 (US sizing). These provided an adequate range of sizes for both male and female participants.

Tasks

Participants performed a sequence of five tasks to practice the foot interaction vocabulary and apply it to web browsing and PDF viewing. The IDE debugger was not included to avoid restricting participants to programmers. The experimenter introduced components and provided clarification as requested. Participants used the keyboard for text entry, otherwise only foot input.

Task 1: Practice low-density foot actions — Participants performed the foot action (toe tap, heel tap, kick, etc.) and direction (forward, side, back) as indicated by a pair of foot icons and an arrow (similar to Figure 8). All 22 action-direction combinations were performed. This task was repeated up to 4 times until 3 errors or less occurred to ensure a common level of eyes-free performance.

Task 2: Practice "click mode" — Participants navigated through 10 Wikipedia pages, following specified links.

Task 3: Web browsing — Participants selected a pair of Wikipedia pages from a list, and then navigated from the first page to the second page using links. We used the website wikispeedia.net [32], which presents tasks of this form using a version of schools.wikipedia.org.

Task 4: Practice high-density foot menu — Using a version of the bookmark menu labelled with letters, participants were shown a letter and asked to select the corresponding item using any foot tap. All 20 item locations were selected.

Task 5: Web search and PDF viewing — Participants used the bookmark menu to open the ACM Digital Library, Microsoft Academic Search, and Google Scholar to look up a specific author's citation count. After, they found a specific paper by that author; they opened it in a PDF reader, and counted the number of figures in the paper. Finally, they closed the PDF reader and all web browser tabs.

Tasks 1, 2, and 4 focus on learnability and usability of specific types of interactions, while tasks 3 and 5 focus on more general usability with realistic tasks. On average, the task portion of the study took 47 minutes (excluding setup and calibration time).

After the tasks, a subset of the NASA-TLX was administered and a questionnaire-guided interview gathered subjective feedback on each system features, and suitability for hypothetical usage scenarios. The subject feature feedback included rating each feature on a continuous scale from 1 to 5 for "how easy it was to learn and use." Given the desktop context, there is an implied comparison between foot input and mouse and keyboard input which provided participants with some relative context for their subjective feedback.

Results and Discussion

Table 1 summarizes mean questionnaire results for NASA-TLX ratings and Table 2 summarizes "how easy it was to learn and use" the six main features.

Overall

All participants completed tasks without significant difficulty. NASA-TLX ratings are near neutral with moderately high variance shown by the standard deviations. Some rated the system as more mentally demanding, others rated it as more physically demanding. Although some experimenter clarification was required (more so in Tasks 1 and 2) participants were able to recover from errors like triggering the wrong command without resorting to keyboard or mouse. Regarding learning speed, 6 participants completed Task 1 with 3 errors or less on the third task repetition. Neutral to somewhat positive mean ratings for "ease of learning and use" of system features support these observations. We did not measure "enjoyability" since it is hard to quantify, but some participants commented to the effect that they found it fun and a bit like dancing.

These overall results are encouraging given that foot input is known to be harder to learn [9], the system is quite novel, and the relatively short study time. The fact that people can learn the core of the system and accomplish non-trivial tasks in a single experiment session is a measure of success.

System Features

Four participants reported high cognitive load when looking up commands in the *sidebar*, but 3 of these said practice would make this easier. P8 said "[It is mentally demanding] in the sense that you have to think a lot; it was easy to get mixed up between the different commands sometimes. Until you get the hang of it - once I got the hang of it, it seems pretty easy."

Participants rated the *contextual help screen* as easiest to learn and use, but even after practicing with it, no one used it during the applied tasks. The current static contextual help screen may be too limited.

Click mode was rated as moderately easy to learn and use, and participants used it multiple times in Tasks 2, 3, and 5. Two participants said link annotations covered too much text, and one participant said link selection had high physical demand due to the number of actions required.

Participants found the *bookmark menu* hardest to learn and use. This is supported by a 40% error rate in Task 4, high-density menu training. There were some sensing errors related to certain types of foot contacts and backward movement directions (see below), but position sensing was quite accurate. In our controlled target selection experiment, we did not find higher error rates when target location and size simulated the high density target layout used by the bookmark menu [26]. We believe the primary reason for bookmark menu difficulty was not enough practice causing mental error (selecting the wrong item) and physical errors (making the wrong movement).

Factor	Mean (stddev)
Frustration	8.0 (4.6)
Temporal	8.2 (3.4)
Mental	8.2 (5.0)
Physical	8.3 (4.2)
Effort	10.1 (2.1)
Performance	11.8 (4.2)

Table 1: NASA-TLX Ratings: mean (with stddev) by factor on scales from 0 (best) to 20 (worst)

Feature	Mean (stddev)
Help Screen	1.9 (1.1)
App Switching	2.0 (0.8)
Sidebar Feedback	2.4 (1.1)
App Navigation	2.5 (0.8)
Click Mode	2.5 (0.9)
Bookmark Menu	3.4 (0.7)

Table 2: Subjective ratings in response to question "For each of the features of the interaction technique, rate on a scale of 5 how easy it was to learn and use." (1 is Very Easy, 5 is Very Hard).

Participants only selected each of the 20 bookmark menu locations once. In Task 1, low-density training, participants repeated the task multiple times for extra practice resulting in a comparable error rate for Task 1 after the first run (36%), but was less than 14% for 6 participants on the third repetition. P4 wrote: "Bookmark menu: easy to select wrong [item] because they are very close to each other." In spite of the theoretical advantage of central, indirect feedback with the bookmark window, selecting high density targets requires more practice to master and appears more susceptible to sensing errors.

Interaction Technique

Three participants wanted a larger interaction area or encountered sensing errors from kicking too far. We used a conservative estimate of interaction range [25], but users may prefer a custom range. Four participants reported or experienced problems with whole foot taps, especially in the back direction. Analysing logs suggests this is caused by slow movements when a heel or toe tap is sensed before a whole foot tap is completed. More conservative user-calibrated thresholds would improve this. We did not find occurrences of "Midas-Step" suggesting our avoidance rules were effective while interacting with feet.

System Usefulness

When asked if the system would be useful for hypothetical applications, participants were generally positive: 8 said it would be useful for controlling a background application; 7 for controlling a web browser; 7 as a deterrent to using applications like Facebook; and 5 for controlling a citation manager. After we explained what an interactive debugger was, only 2 participants were in favour of using the system for that purpose. One participant felt using feet would add to the already high cognitive difficulty of debugging, but recall we did not control for programming experience.

Discussion

Our evaluation shows participants were able to learn the system and perform tasks requiring multiple foot gestures within a 60-minute time frame. When they made mistakes, they were able to recover within the framework of the system. The results of the study can be summarized in the following implications for design:

- Navigation controls, link selection, application switching and feedback panel were generally well received, although with somewhat of a learning curve. There is room for additional support in teaching commands to new users, perhaps in the form of an explicit tutorial, or a training task which prompts the user with a command (go back in the web browser) and requires the user to perform the correct foot action.
- The bookmark menu in its current form is somewhat difficult to learn and use – it may be better to also use *click mode* for selecting among many items in a menu like bookmarks.
- Two-foot jumping appears to be considered an easy to perform action, but our contextual help screen may not be as useful as we hoped in practice.
- The help screen is currently not used by participants. It might need to be reworked into a more relevant form, such as a tutorial or training task for the different web browser commands.
- Some minor system changes would improve performance, including increasing the interaction range and making toe and heel tap detection more conservative to improve performance of whole foot tapping detection.

CONCLUSIONS AND FUTURE WORK

The Tap-Kick-Click system demonstrates how foot interaction techniques can effectively control conventional desktop applications at a standing desk. Foot input may not provide a clear efficiency benefit compared to mouse and keyboard, but feet can still have a role in desktop computing. Since foot input is always available, it can be used for pure foot input breaks while still continuing a primary work task like reading a paper, or it can be used to augment mouse and keyboard for background tasks like controlling a media player. If desired, it could even be used as a physical deterrent for cyberslacking. We accomplish this with a simple, but expressive vocabulary of indirect, discrete two-foot input composed of kicks and taps, as well as standing postures supported by feedback and contextual help systems. Our evaluation shows that the core idea of Tap-Kick-Click is learnable and usable. A longitudinal field study remains future work since it relies on incremental engineering improvements and a self-supporting configuration interface to map foot input to any application. We hope that our work demonstrates how a well designed foot input system can make daily computing a little bit healthier, and perhaps, even a little more fun.

REFERENCES

1. Jason Alexander, Teng Han, William Judd, Pourang Irani, and Sriram Subramanian. 2012. Putting Your Best Foot Forward: Investigating Real-world Mappings for Foot-based Gestures. *Proceedings of the SIGCHI Conference on Human Factors in Computing Systems*, ACM, 1229–1238. http://doi.org/10.1145/2207676.2208575
2. Thomas Augsten, Konstantin Kaefer, René Meusel, et al. 2010. Multitoe: high-precision interaction with back-projected floors based on high-resolution multi-touch input. *Proceedings of the 23nd annual ACM symposium on User interface software and technology*, ACM, 209–218. http://doi.org/10.1145/1866029.1866064
3. Dave Berque, Jimmy Burgess, Alexander Billingsley, Shan Johnson, Terri Bonebright, and Brad Wethington. 2011. Design and evaluation of persuasive technology to encourage healthier typing behaviors. *Proceedings of the 6th International Conference on Persuasive Technology: Persuasive Technology and Design: Enhancing Sustainability and Health*, ACM, 9:1–9:10. http://doi.org/10.1145/2467803.2467812
4. Alan Bränzel, Christian Holz, Daniel Hoffmann, et al. 2013. GravitySpace: Tracking Users and Their Poses in a Smart Room Using a Pressure-sensing Floor. *Proceedings of the SIGCHI Conference on Human Factors in Computing Systems*, ACM, 725–734. http://doi.org/10.1145/2470654.2470757
5. Andrew Crossan, Stephen Brewster, and Alexander Ng. 2010. Foot Tapping for Mobile Interaction. *Proceedings of the 24th BCS Interaction Specialist Group Conference*, British Computer Society, 418–422.
6. David Dearman, Amy Karlson, Brian Meyers, and Ben Bederson. 2010. Multi-modal Text Entry and Selection on a Mobile Device. *Proceedings of Graphics Interface 2010*, Canadian Information Processing Society, 19–26.
7. Colin G. Drury. 1975. Application of Fitts' Law to foot-pedal design. *Human Factors: The Journal of the Human Factors and Ergonomics Society* 17, 4: 368–373.
8. Koumei Fukahori, Daisuke Sakamoto, and Takeo Igarashi. 2015. Exploring Subtle Foot Plantar-based Gestures with Sock. *Proceedings of the 33rd Annual ACM Conference on Human Factors in Computing Systems (CHI '15)*, ACM, 3019–3028.

http://doi.org/http://dx.doi.org/10.1145/2702123.2702308

9. Fredrick P. Garcia and Kim-Phuong L. Vu. 2011. Effectiveness of hand- and foot-operated secondary input devices for word-processing tasks before and after training. *Computers in Human Behavior* 27, 1: 285–295. http://doi.org/10.1016/j.chb.2010.08.006
10. Anne Carolyn Grunseit, Josephine Yuk-Yin Chau, Hidde Pieter van der Ploeg, and Adrian Bauman. 2013. "Thinking on your feet": A qualitative evaluation of sit-stand desks in an Australian workplace. *BMC Public Health* 13: 365. http://doi.org/10.1186/1471-2458-13-365
11. Teng Han, Jason Alexander, Abhijit Karnik, Pourang Irani, and Sriram Subramanian. 2011. Kick: Investigating the Use of Kick Gestures for Mobile Interactions. *Proceedings of the 13th International Conference on Human Computer Interaction with Mobile Devices and Services*, ACM, 29–32. http://doi.org/10.1145/2037373.2037379
12. Errol R. Hoffmann. 1991. A comparison of hand and foot movement times. *Ergonomics* 34, 4: 397–406. http://doi.org/10.1080/00140139108967324
13. Johanna Hoysniemi. 2006. International survey on the Dance Dance Revolution game. *Comput. Entertain.* 4, 2. http://doi.org/10.1145/1129006.1129019
14. S.-H. Kim and D. B. Kaber. 2008. Design and Usability Evaluation of Foot Interfaces for Dynamic Text Editing. *Proceedings of the Human Factors and Ergonomics Society Annual Meeting* 52, 6: 581–585. http://doi.org/10.1177/154193120805200615
15. Denys J. C. Matthies, Franz Müller, Christoph Anthes, and Dieter Kranzlmüller. 2013. ShoeSoleSense: Proof of Concept for a Wearable Foot Interface for Virtual and Real Environments. *Proceedings of the 19th ACM Symposium on Virtual Reality Software and Technology*, ACM, 93–96. http://doi.org/10.1145/2503713.2503740
16. Brian Meyers, A. J. Bernheim Brush, Steven Drucker, Marc A. Smith, and Mary Czerwinski. 2006. Dance Your Work Away: Exploring Step User Interfaces. *CHI '06 Extended Abstracts on Human Factors in Computing Systems*, ACM, 387–392. http://doi.org/10.1145/1125451.1125534
17. Dan Morris, A.J. Bernheim Brush, and Brian R. Meyers. 2008. SuperBreak: Using Interactivity to Enhance Ergonomic Typing Breaks. *Proceedings of the SIGCHI Conference on Human Factors in Computing Systems*, ACM, 1817–1826. http://doi.org/10.1145/1357054.1357337
18. Volker Paelke, Christian Reimann, and Dirk Stichling. 2004. Foot-based mobile interaction with games. *Proceedings of the 2004 ACM SIGCHI International Conference on Advances in computer entertainment technology*, ACM, 321–324. http://doi.org/10.1145/1067343.1067390
19. Toni Pakkanen and Roope Raisamo. 2004. Appropriateness of foot interaction for non-accurate spatial tasks. *CHI '04 Extended Abstracts on Human Factors in Computing Systems*, ACM, 1123–1126. http://doi.org/10.1145/985921.986004
20. Glenn Pearson and Mark Weiser. 1988. EXPLORATORY EVALUATIONS OF TWO VERSIONS OF A FOOT-OPERATED CURSOR-POSITIONING DEVICE IN A TARGET-SELECTION TASK. *SIGCHI Bull.* 19, 3: 70–75. http://doi.org/10.1145/49108.1046356
21. G. Pearson and M. Weiser. 1986. Of Moles and Men: The Design of Foot Controls for Workstations. *Proceedings of the SIGCHI Conference on Human Factors in Computing Systems*, ACM, 333–339. http://doi.org/10.1145/22627.22392
22. Stephan Richter, Christian Holz, and Patrick Baudisch. 2012. Bootstrapper: Recognizing Tabletop Users by Their Shoes. *Proceedings of the SIGCHI Conference on Human Factors in Computing Systems*, ACM, 1249–1252. http://doi.org/10.1145/2207676.2208577
23. Julie Rico and Stephen Brewster. 2010. Usable gestures for mobile interfaces: evaluating social acceptability. *Proceedings of the SIGCHI Conference on Human Factors in Computing Systems*, ACM, 887–896. http://doi.org/10.1145/1753326.1753458
24. Arthur Saltzman. 1998. Computer user perception of the effectiveness of exercise mini-breaks. *Proceedings of the Silicon Valley Ergonomics Conference and Exposition*, 147–151.
25. William Saunders and Daniel Vogel. 2015. The Performance of Indirect Foot Pointing using Discrete Taps and Kicks While Standing. *GI '15 Proceedings of the 41st Graphics Interface Conference*, 265–272.
26. Johannes Schöning, Florian Daiber, Antonio Krüger, and Michael Rohs. 2009. Using hands and feet to navigate and manipulate spatial data. *CHI '09 Extended Abstracts on Human Factors in Computing Systems*, ACM, 4663–4668. http://doi.org/10.1145/1520340.1520717
27. Jeremy Scott, David Dearman, Koji Yatani, and Khai N. Truong. 2010. Sensing foot gestures from the pocket. *Proceedings of the 23nd annual ACM symposium on User interface software and technology*, ACM, 199–208. http://doi.org/10.1145/1866029.1866063
28. A. L. Simeone, E. Velloso, J. Alexander, and H. Gellersen. 2014. Feet movement in desktop 3D interaction. *2014 IEEE Symposium on 3D User Interfaces (3DUI)*, 71–74. http://doi.org/10.1109/3DUI.2014.6798845
29. Eduardo Velloso, Jason Alexander, Andreas Bulling, and Hans Gellersen. 2015. Interactions Under the Desk: A Characterisation of Foot Movements for Input in a

Seated Position. In *Human-Computer Interaction – INTERACT 2015*. Springer International Publishing, 384–401.

30. Eduardo Velloso, Dominik Schmidt, Jason Alexander, Hans Gellersen, and Andreas Bulling. 2015. The Feet in Human–Computer Interaction: A Survey of Foot-Based Interaction. *ACM Comput. Surv.* 48, 2: 21:1–21:35. http://doi.org/10.1145/2816455
31. Jessica Vitak, Julia Crouse, and Robert LaRose. 2011. Personal Internet use at work: Understanding cyber-slacking. *Computers in Human Behavior* 27, 5: 1751–1759. http://doi.org/10.1016/j.chb.2011.03.002
32. Robert West, Joelle Pineau, and Doina Precup. 2009. Wikispeedia: An Online Game for Inferring Semantic Distances Between Concepts. *Proceedings of the 21st International Jont Conference on Artifical Intelligence*, Morgan Kaufmann Publishers Inc., 1598–1603.
33. Anthony Whitehead, Hannah Johnston, Nicole Nixon, and Jo Welch. 2010. Exergame effectiveness: what the numbers can tell us. *Proceedings of the 5th ACM SIGGRAPH Symposium on Video Games*, ACM, 55–62. http://doi.org/10.1145/1836135.1836144

Paper Street View: A Guided Tour of Design and Making Using Comics

Thomas Dykes
Northumbria University,
Newcastle Upon Tyne, UK
thomas.dykes@northumbria.ac.uk

Jayne Wallace
Northumbria University,
Newcastle Upon Tyne, UK
jayne.wallace@northumbria.ac.uk

Mark Blythe
Northumbria University,
Newcastle Upon Tyne, UK
mark.blythe@northumbria.ac.uk

James Thomas
Northumbria University,
Newcastle Upon Tyne, UK
james.thomas@northumbria.ac.uk

DIS 2016, June 04 - 08, 2016, Brisbane, QLD, Australia

ACM 978-1-4503-4031-1/16/06 $15.00
DOI: http://dx.doi.org/10.1145/2901790.2901904

Abstract
This comic reveals multilayered details and insights about the design and making of Paper Street View, a suite of artefacts that allow groups of older people in care environments to navigate Google Street View using a paper map. In creating the comic we wanted to account for material thinking in design. We show that comics can be used as a dynamic and visual way of presenting and composing discussions about making. Comics allow you to talk around artefacts gathered during the design process (i.e. CAD drawings, prototypes, sketches and notes) and encourage a more dynamic use of image and text.

Authors Keywords
Design, craft, process, comics

ACM Classification Keywords
H.5.m. Information interfaces and presentation

Introduction
This pictorial builds on the work of Jarvis et al. [2] and Gaver and Bowers [1] in considering more visual approaches to the representation of design artefacts in HCI. It was in part inspired by the work of Scott McCloud [3], who talks about the descriptive power of comics through his cartoon self. We have reflected more fully on the potential of comics in a full paper [4]. We see this pictorial as a standalone contribution demonstrating how comics can holistically represent multi-faceted elements of design and making.

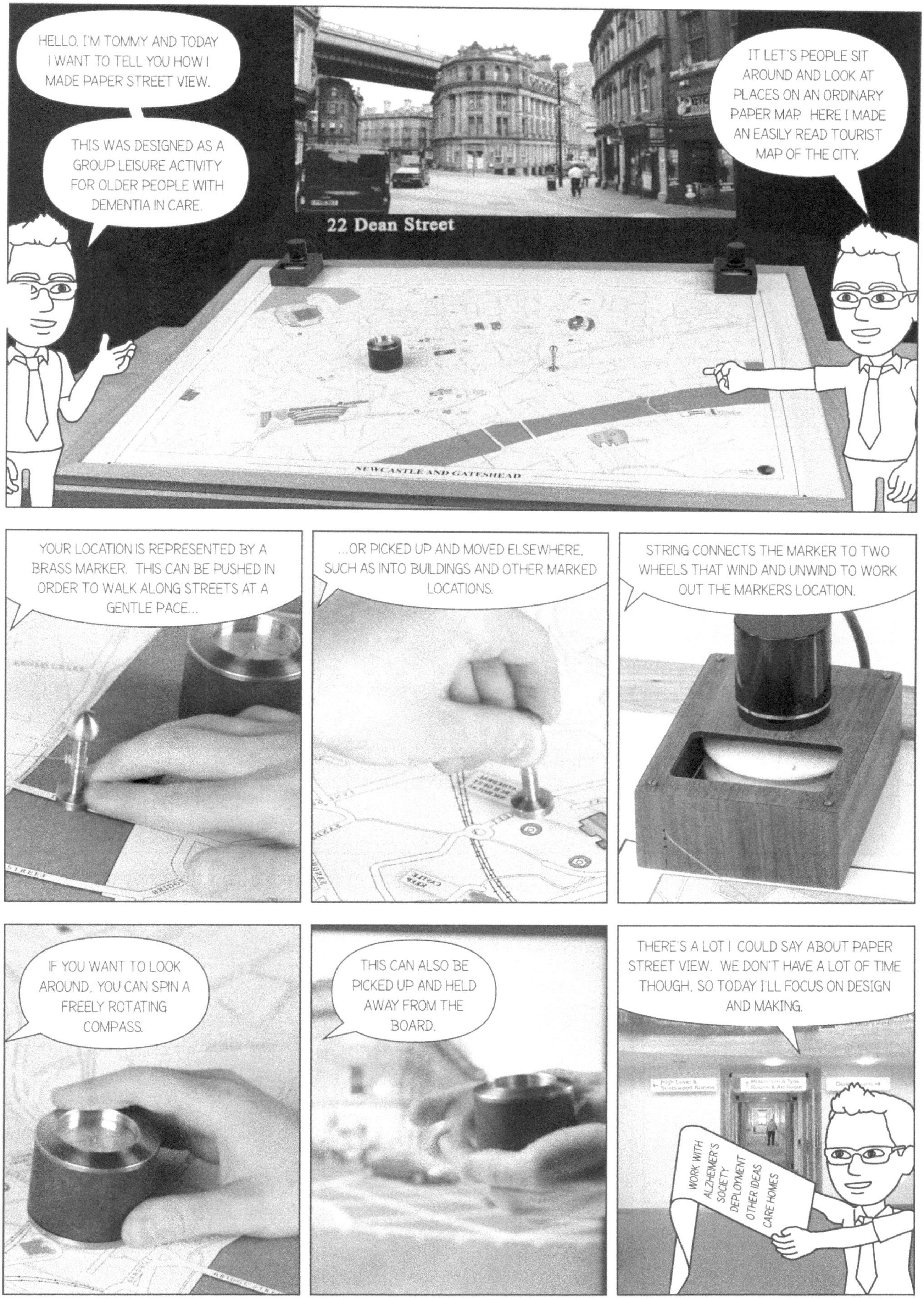
HELLO. I'M TOMMY AND TODAY I WANT TO TELL YOU HOW I MADE PAPER STREET VIEW.
THIS WAS DESIGNED AS A GROUP LEISURE ACTIVITY FOR OLDER PEOPLE WITH DEMENTIA IN CARE.
22 Dean Street
IT LET'S PEOPLE SIT AROUND AND LOOK AT PLACES ON AN ORDINARY PAPER MAP. HERE I MADE AN EASILY READ TOURIST MAP OF THE CITY.
NEWCASTLE AND GATESHEAD
YOUR LOCATION IS REPRESENTED BY A BRASS MARKER. THIS CAN BE PUSHED IN ORDER TO WALK ALONG STREETS AT A GENTLE PACE...
...OR PICKED UP AND MOVED ELSEWHERE, SUCH AS INTO BUILDINGS AND OTHER MARKED LOCATIONS.
STRING CONNECTS THE MARKER TO TWO WHEELS THAT WIND AND UNWIND TO WORK OUT THE MARKERS LOCATION.
IF YOU WANT TO LOOK AROUND, YOU CAN SPIN A FREELY ROTATING COMPASS.
THIS CAN ALSO BE PICKED UP AND HELD AWAY FROM THE BOARD.
THERE'S A LOT I COULD SAY ABOUT PAPER STREET VIEW. WE DON'T HAVE A LOT OF TIME THOUGH, SO TODAY I'LL FOCUS ON DESIGN AND MAKING.
WORK WITH ALZHEIMER'S SOCIETY
DEPLOYMENT
OTHER IDEAS
CARE HOMES

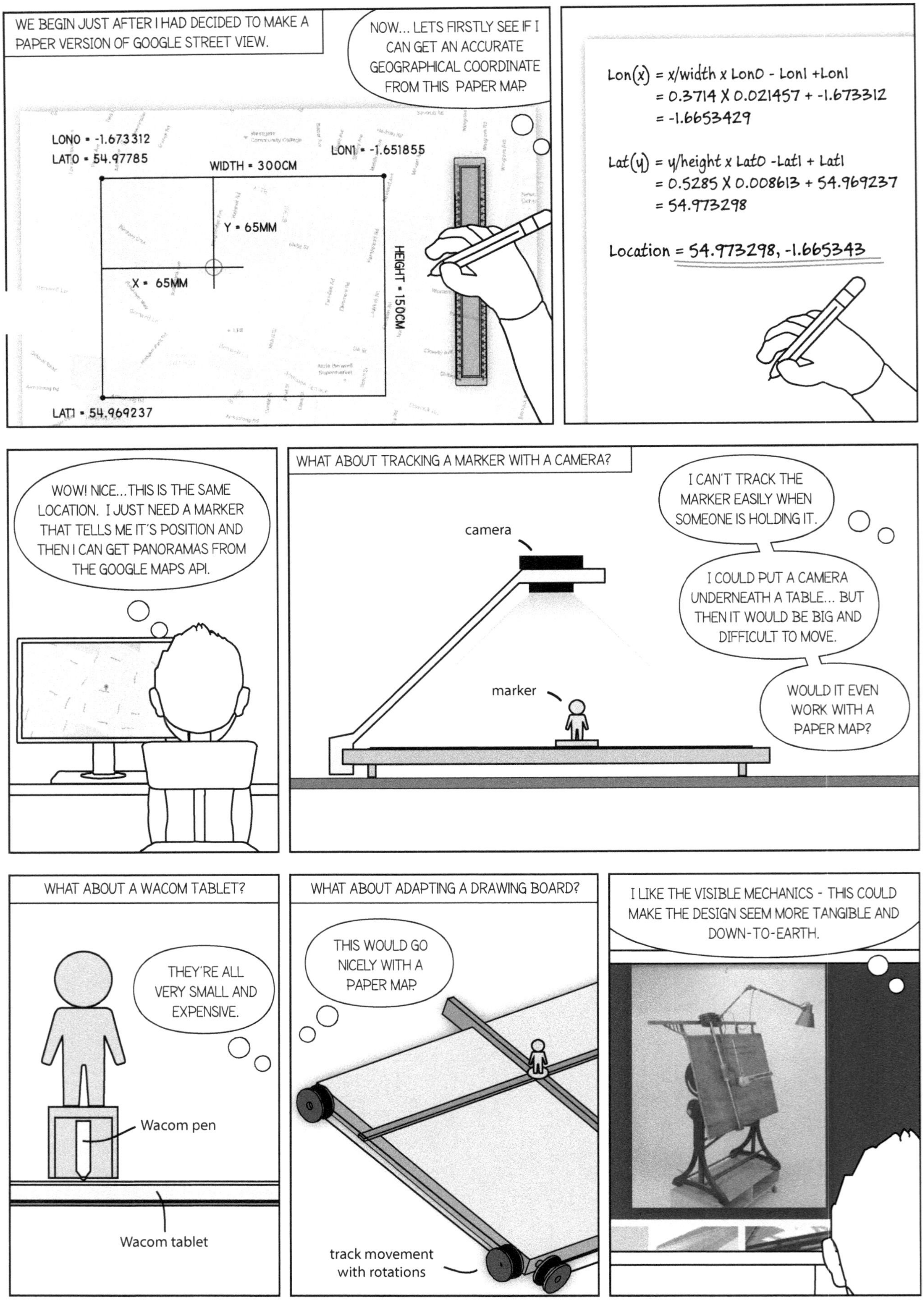
WE BEGIN JUST AFTER I HAD DECIDED TO MAKE A PAPER VERSION OF GOOGLE STREET VIEW.
NOW... LETS FIRSTLY SEE IF I CAN GET AN ACCURATE GEOGRAPHICAL COORDINATE FROM THIS PAPER MAP.
LON0 = -1.673312
LAT0 = 54.97785
LON1 = -1.651855
WIDTH = 300CM
Y = 65MM
X = 65MM
HEIGHT = 150CM
LAT1 = 54.969237
Lon(x) = x/width x Lon0 - Lon1 +Lon1
= 0.3714 X 0.021457 + -1.673312
= -1.6653429
Lat(y) = y/height x Lat0 -Lat1 + Lat1
= 0.5285 X 0.008613 + 54.969237
= 54.973298
Location = 54.973298, -1.665343
WOW! NICE...THIS IS THE SAME LOCATION. I JUST NEED A MARKER THAT TELLS ME IT'S POSITION AND THEN I CAN GET PANORAMAS FROM THE GOOGLE MAPS API.
WHAT ABOUT TRACKING A MARKER WITH A CAMERA?
camera
marker
I CAN'T TRACK THE MARKER EASILY WHEN SOMEONE IS HOLDING IT.
I COULD PUT A CAMERA UNDERNEATH A TABLE... BUT THEN IT WOULD BE BIG AND DIFFICULT TO MOVE.
WOULD IT EVEN WORK WITH A PAPER MAP?
WHAT ABOUT A WACOM TABLET?
THEY'RE ALL VERY SMALL AND EXPENSIVE.
Wacom pen
Wacom tablet
WHAT ABOUT ADAPTING A DRAWING BOARD?
THIS WOULD GO NICELY WITH A PAPER MAP.
track movement with rotations
I LIKE THE VISIBLE MECHANICS - THIS COULD MAKE THE DESIGN SEEM MORE TANGIBLE AND DOWN-TO-EARTH.

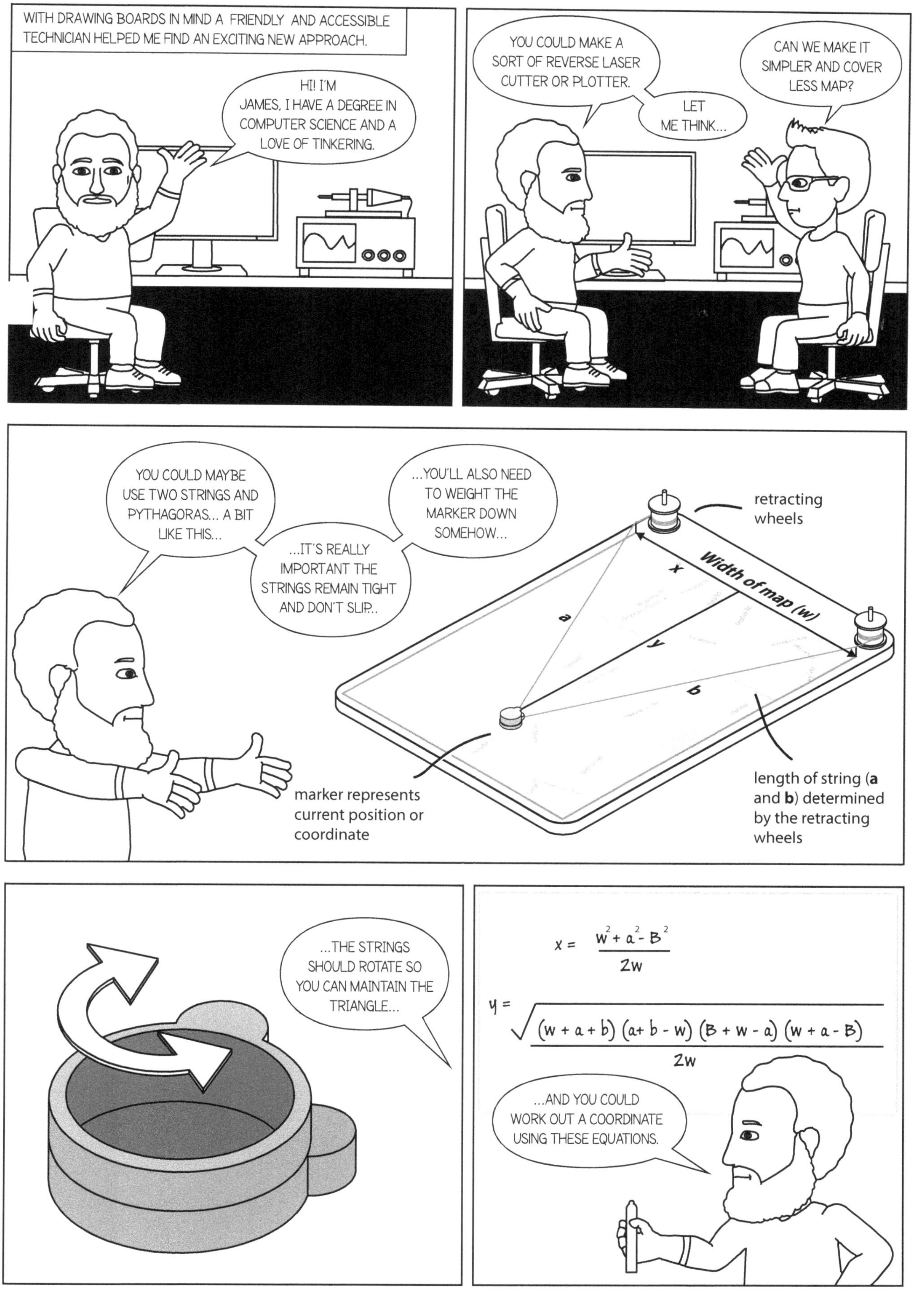
WITH DRAWING BOARDS IN MIND A FRIENDLY AND ACCESSIBLE TECHNICIAN HELPED ME FIND AN EXCITING NEW APPROACH.
HI! I'M JAMES, I HAVE A DEGREE IN COMPUTER SCIENCE AND A LOVE OF TINKERING.
YOU COULD MAKE A SORT OF REVERSE LASER CUTTER OR PLOTTER.
LET ME THINK...
CAN WE MAKE IT SIMPLER AND COVER LESS MAP?
YOU COULD MAYBE USE TWO STRINGS AND PYTHAGORAS... A BIT LIKE THIS...
...IT'S REALLY IMPORTANT THE STRINGS REMAIN TIGHT AND DON'T SLIP...
...YOU'LL ALSO NEED TO WEIGHT THE MARKER DOWN SOMEHOW...
retracting wheels
Width of map (w)
x
a
y
b
marker represents current position or coordinate
length of string (a and b) determined by the retracting wheels
...THE STRINGS SHOULD ROTATE SO YOU CAN MAINTAIN THE TRIANGLE...
$x = \frac{w^2 + a^2 - B^2}{2w}$
$y = \frac{\sqrt{(w + a + b)(a + b - w)(B + w - a)(w + a - B)}}{2w}$
...AND YOU COULD WORK OUT A COORDINATE USING THESE EQUATIONS.

THIS IS GREAT, THANKS JAMES. I REALLY LIKE THE IDEA OF USING WHEELS.
SOME OF THE GUYS ARE ENGINEERS, I BET THEY WOULD BE CURIOUS TO SEE THE WORKINGS AS WELL.
EXCITED, I QUICKLY BEGAN MAKING PROTOTYPES WITH MATERIALS I FOUND IN THE LAB.
A FIRST ITERATION WAS BASED ON A DIGITAL MEASURING TAPE THAT I'D TAKEN APART.
SO HOW DID IT WORK?
SINCE THE STRING IS WRAPPED ONCE AROUND THE WHEEL, YOU CAN PULL THE STRING AND THE WHEEL WILL TURN. THE WHEEL IS CONNECTED TO A POTENTIOMETER MEANING YOU CAN WORK OUT HOW MANY TIMES IT HAS TURNED.
string retainer
retracting keyring
multi-turn potentiometer
ONE FULL TURN IS THE SAME AS A CIRCUMFERENCE WORTH OF STRING, MEANING I COULD MEASURE THE LENGTH OF THE STRING.
LENGTH = TURNS X CIRCUMFERENCE
TURNS OUT THIS SETUP DOSEN'T WORK BECAUSE THE STRING SLIPS OVER THE WHEEL WHEN IT'S PULLED.

IS THIS EVEN GOING TO WORK?! I DON'T WANT TO WASTE TOO MUCH TIME ON A DEAD END I SHOULD KEEP MAKING QUICKLY.
ANOTHER ITERATION TO STOP THE STRING FROM SLIPPING.
THIS TIME I WOUND THE STRING DIRECTLY ONTO THE WHEEL.
AS THE STRING IS PULLED, THE KEYRING CORD WINDS ONTO THE BOTTOM WHEEL AND CAUSES THE STRING TO PULL BACK.
keyring cord
adjacent wheel and seperate string
GREAT... IT DOSEN'T SLIP, EVEN IF I PULL IT SHARPLY.
LOOK THOUGH... THE STRING IS WINDING ON TOP OF ITSELF AND CHANGING THE CIRCUMFERENCE.
THIS WILL MAKE IT TOO INNACURATE TO LOCATE ROADS IN MORE BUILT UP AREAS
I'LL LASER CUT THIS ITERATION SO IT'S MORE ACCURATE... NOW HOW TO KEEP A CONSTANT CIRCUMFERENCE?...
I'LL TRY USING THINNER STRING AND INCREASE THE SIZE OF THE WHEEL. THIS WAY I'LL NEED LESS WINDS OF STRING.

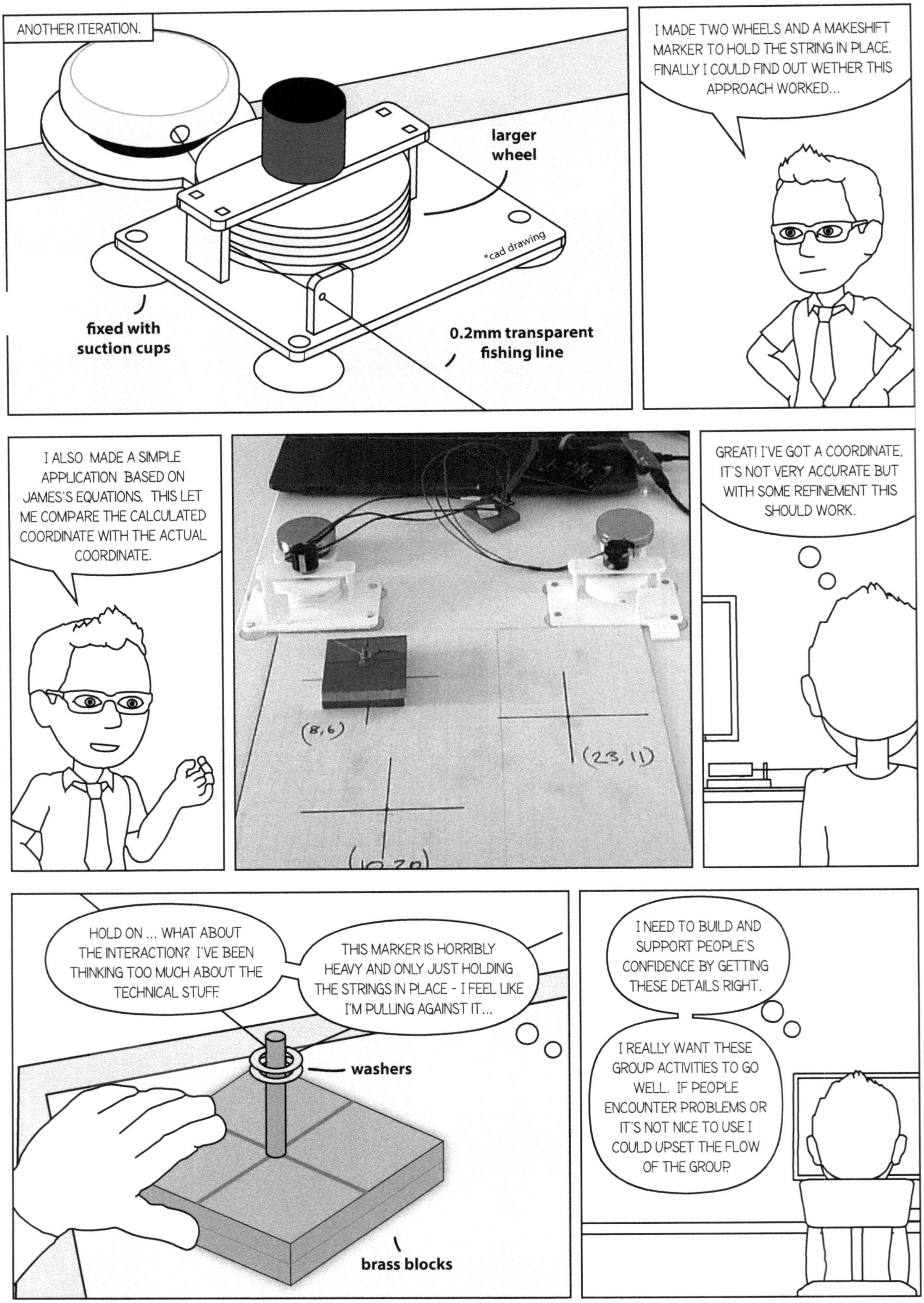
ANOTHER ITERATION.
larger wheel
*cad drawing
fixed with suction cups
0.2mm transparent fishing line
I MADE TWO WHEELS AND A MAKESHIFT MARKER TO HOLD THE STRING IN PLACE. FINALLY I COULD FIND OUT WETHER THIS APPROACH WORKED...
I ALSO MADE A SIMPLE APPLICATION BASED ON JAMES'S EQUATIONS. THIS LET ME COMPARE THE CALCULATED COORDINATE WITH THE ACTUAL COORDINATE.
(8,6)
(23,11)
GREAT! I'VE GOT A COORDINATE. IT'S NOT VERY ACCURATE BUT WITH SOME REFINEMENT THIS SHOULD WORK.
HOLD ON ... WHAT ABOUT THE INTERACTION? I'VE BEEN THINKING TOO MUCH ABOUT THE TECHNICAL STUFF.
THIS MARKER IS HORRIBLY HEAVY AND ONLY JUST HOLDING THE STRINGS IN PLACE - I FEEL LIKE I'M PULLING AGAINST IT...
washers
brass blocks
I NEED TO BUILD AND SUPPORT PEOPLE'S CONFIDENCE BY GETTING THESE DETAILS RIGHT.
I REALLY WANT THESE GROUP ACTIVITIES TO GO WELL. IF PEOPLE ENCOUNTER PROBLEMS OR IT'S NOT NICE TO USE I COULD UPSET THE FLOW OF THE GROUP.

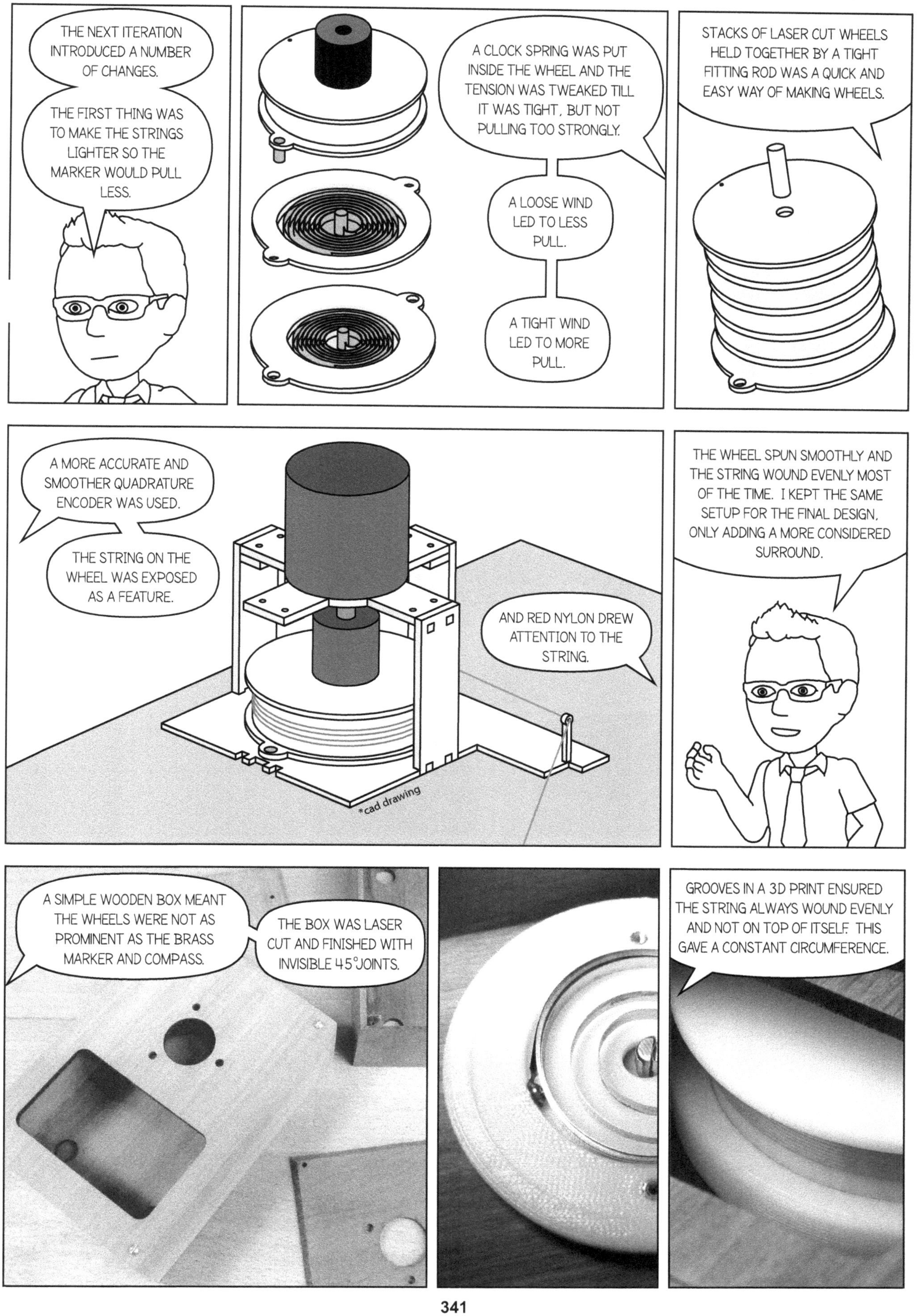
THE NEXT ITERATION INTRODUCED A NUMBER OF CHANGES.
THE FIRST THING WAS TO MAKE THE STRINGS LIGHTER SO THE MARKER WOULD PULL LESS.
A CLOCK SPRING WAS PUT INSIDE THE WHEEL AND THE TENSION WAS TWEAKED TILL IT WAS TIGHT, BUT NOT PULLING TOO STRONGLY.
A LOOSE WIND LED TO LESS PULL.
A TIGHT WIND LED TO MORE PULL.
STACKS OF LASER CUT WHEELS HELD TOGETHER BY A TIGHT FITTING ROD WAS A QUICK AND EASY WAY OF MAKING WHEELS.
A MORE ACCURATE AND SMOOTHER QUADRATURE ENCODER WAS USED.
THE STRING ON THE WHEEL WAS EXPOSED AS A FEATURE.
AND RED NYLON DREW ATTENTION TO THE STRING.
*cad drawing
THE WHEEL SPUN SMOOTHLY AND THE STRING WOUND EVENLY MOST OF THE TIME. I KEPT THE SAME SETUP FOR THE FINAL DESIGN, ONLY ADDING A MORE CONSIDERED SURROUND.
A SIMPLE WOODEN BOX MEANT THE WHEELS WERE NOT AS PROMINENT AS THE BRASS MARKER AND COMPASS.
THE BOX WAS LASER CUT AND FINISHED WITH INVISIBLE 45° JOINTS.
GROOVES IN A 3D PRINT ENSURED THE STRING ALWAYS WOUND EVENLY AND NOT ON TOP OF ITSELF. THIS GAVE A CONSTANT CIRCUMFERENCE.

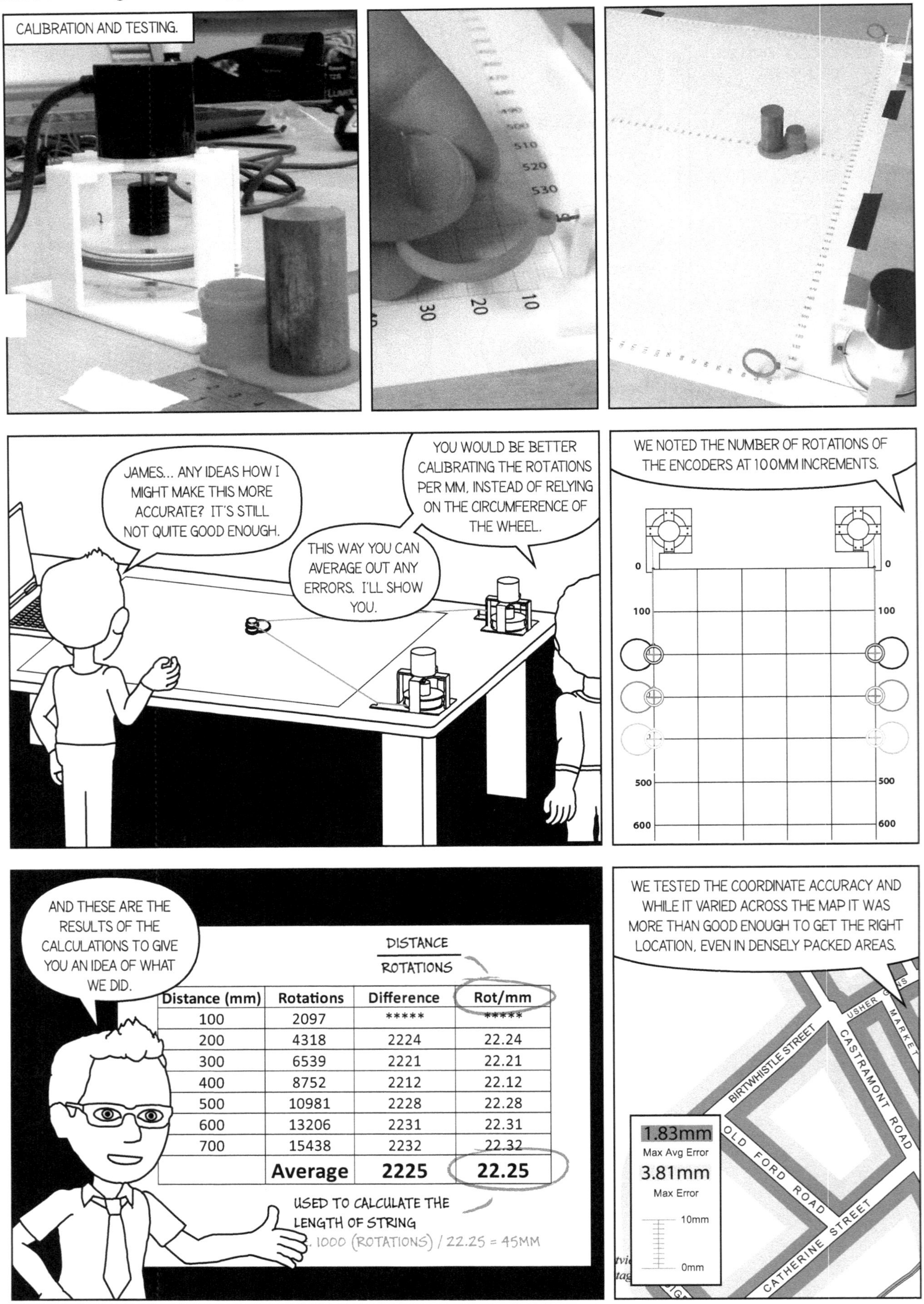
CALIBRATION AND TESTING.
510
520
530
30
20
10
JAMES... ANY IDEAS HOW I MIGHT MAKE THIS MORE ACCURATE? IT'S STILL NOT QUITE GOOD ENOUGH.
YOU WOULD BE BETTER CALIBRATING THE ROTATIONS PER MM, INSTEAD OF RELYING ON THE CIRCUMFERENCE OF THE WHEEL.
THIS WAY YOU CAN AVERAGE OUT ANY ERRORS. I'LL SHOW YOU.
WE NOTED THE NUMBER OF ROTATIONS OF THE ENCODERS AT 100MM INCREMENTS.
0
100
500
600
AND THESE ARE THE RESULTS OF THE CALCULATIONS TO GIVE YOU AN IDEA OF WHAT WE DID.
DISTANCE / ROTATIONS
Distance (mm) | Rotations | Difference | Rot/mm
100 | 2097 | ***** | *****
200 | 4318 | 2224 | 22.24
300 | 6539 | 2221 | 22.21
400 | 8752 | 2212 | 22.12
500 | 10981 | 2228 | 22.28
600 | 13206 | 2231 | 22.31
700 | 15438 | 2232 | 22.32
Average | 2225 | 22.25
USED TO CALCULATE THE LENGTH OF STRING
1000 (ROTATIONS) / 22.25 = 45MM
WE TESTED THE COORDINATE ACCURACY AND WHILE IT VARIED ACROSS THE MAP IT WAS MORE THAN GOOD ENOUGH TO GET THE RIGHT LOCATION, EVEN IN DENSELY PACKED AREAS.
USHER
MARKET
BIRTWHISTLE STREET
CASTRAMONT ROAD
OLD FORD ROAD
CATHERINE STREET
1.83mm
Max Avg Error
3.81mm
Max Error
10mm
0mm

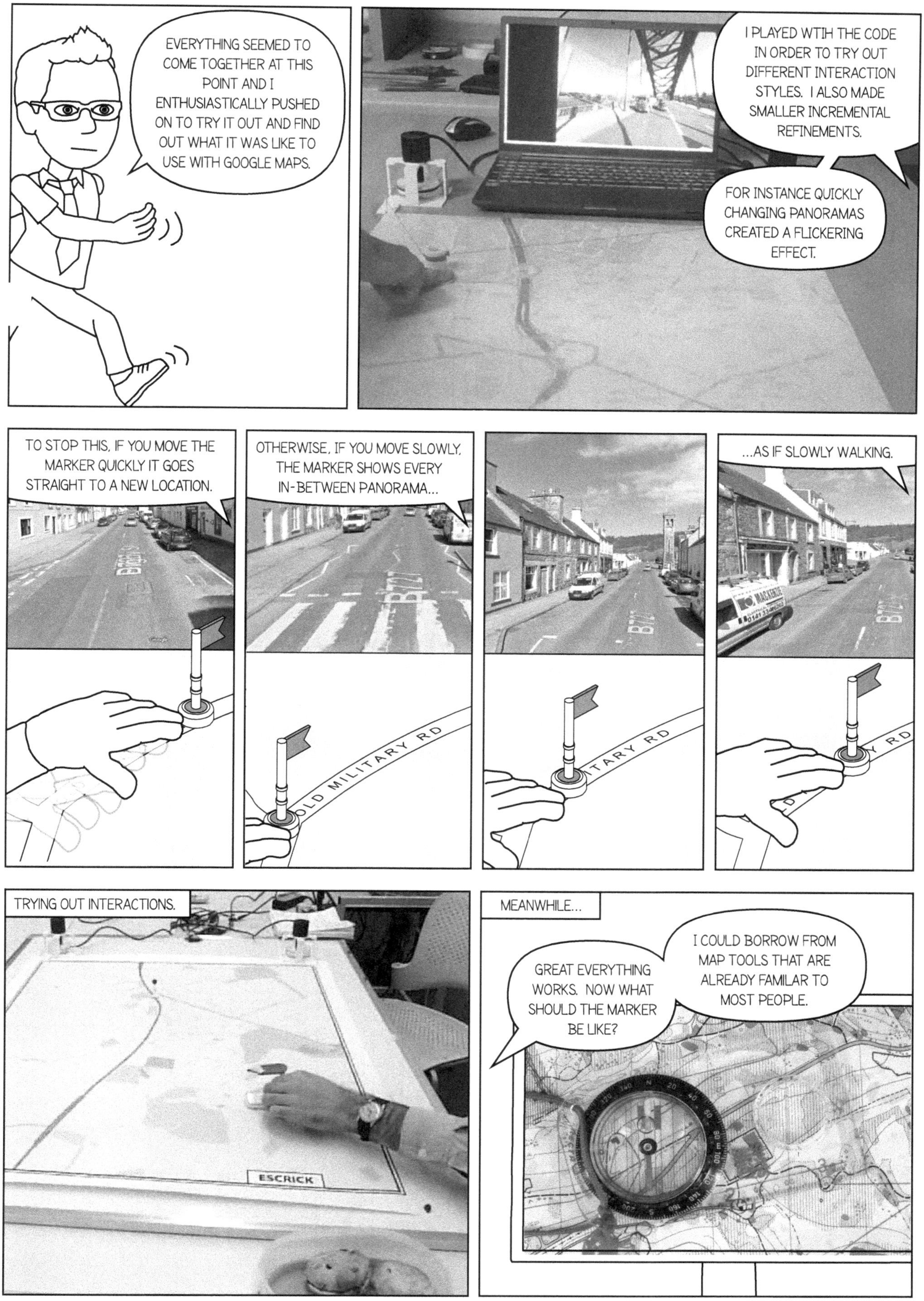
EVERYTHING SEEMED TO COME TOGETHER AT THIS POINT AND I ENTHUSIASTICALLY PUSHED ON TO TRY IT OUT AND FIND OUT WHAT IT WAS LIKE TO USE WITH GOOGLE MAPS.
I PLAYED WTIH THE CODE IN ORDER TO TRY OUT DIFFERENT INTERACTION STYLES. I ALSO MADE SMALLER INCREMENTAL REFINEMENTS.
FOR INSTANCE QUICKLY CHANGING PANORAMAS CREATED A FLICKERING EFFECT.
TO STOP THIS, IF YOU MOVE THE MARKER QUICKLY IT GOES STRAIGHT TO A NEW LOCATION.
OTHERWISE, IF YOU MOVE SLOWLY, THE MARKER SHOWS EVERY IN-BETWEEN PANORAMA...
...AS IF SLOWLY WALKING.
TRYING OUT INTERACTIONS.
ESCRICK
MEANWHILE...
GREAT EVERYTHING WORKS. NOW WHAT SHOULD THE MARKER BE LIKE?
I COULD BORROW FROM MAP TOOLS THAT ARE ALREADY FAMILAR TO MOST PEOPLE.

LARGE WASHER RINGS
MARKINGS ON ETCHOGRAPH
CATHERINE ST
AT THE SAME TIME AS EXPLORING ON PAPER I WAS MAKING PROTOTYPES TO UNDERSTAND WHAT IT WAS LIKE TO USE.
THE LARGER RINGS TENDED TO SNAG AS THEY WERE SO BIG.
TO MAKE THE RINGS SMALLER AND THE MAP MORE VISIBLE I REMOVED THE VIEW FINDER.
IT"S A LOT LIKE A COMPUTER MOUSE.
IT WOULD BE EASIER TO PICK IT UP.
WHY DON'T I TRY A MAGNET AND MAKE A BOARD GAME MARKER.
I CAN STILL HAVE A SURROUND AVAILABLE IN CASE PEOPLE FIND IT EASIER.
magnet
The Bungalow
Anwoth Annexe
Bridge House

THE MAGNET WAS LIGHT ENOUGH TO BE PICKED UP AND PUSHED, WHILE STRONG ENOUGH TO STAY IN PLACE ON THE MAP.
N42 4x 2mm
N52 4x1mm
N42
TOO SHORT AND THE STRINGS GOT IN THE WAY.
TOO HIGH AND IT EASILY TOPPLED WHEN SLID.
WHEN KNOCKED OVER THE MARKER WOULD GET PULLED QUICKLY TO THE END OF THE BOARD AS THE STRINGS RETRACTED.
I REDUCED THE WALL THICKNESS SO THE MAGNETS STOPPED IT SLIDING.
wall thickness
IN FINISHING I USED A CAPTIVATING AND QUALITY COMBINATION OF MATERIALS AND DESIGN BY REFERENCING VINTAGE NAVIGATION TOOLS.
THE PHYSICAL QUALITIES OF THE DESIGN WERE SEEN AS IMPORTANT A PART OF THE GROUPS EXPERIENCE AS THE DIGITAL.
THERE WE HAVE IT. IN THIS SHORT TIME I'VE GIVEN YOU SOME VISUAL INSIGHTS INTO THE DESIGN AND MAKING OF PAPER STREET VIEW.
I ALSO TRIED TO SHOW DIFFERENT WAYS THE COMIC CAN BE USED WHEN TALKING ABOUT DESIGN AND MAKING AND AM EXCITED TO SAY I HAVE MANY MORE IDEAS FOR THE FUTURE!

References

1. Bill Gaver and John Bowers. 2012. Annotated portfolios. *interactions*, 19 (4). 40-49.
2. Nadine Jarvis, David Cameron and Andy Boucher. 2012. Attention to detail: annotations of a design process. *Proceedings of the 7th Nordic Conference on Human-Computer Interaction: Making Sense Through Design*, ACM, Copenhagen, Denmark, 11-20.
3. Scott McCloud and Bob Lappan. 1994. Understanding comics. William Morrow, New York.
4. Thomas Dykes, Mark Blythe, Jayne Wallace, James Thomas and Tim Regan. RtD Comics: A Medium for Representing Research through Design. *Proceedings of the Designing Interactive Systems Conference*, ACM, Brisbane, Australia.

Mime: An AR-based System Helping Patients to Test their Blood at Home

Tom Djajadiningrat
Philips Design
High Tech Campus, Building 33
5656AE Eindhoven
The Netherlands
tom.djajadiningrat@philips.com

Pei-Yin Chao
pei-yin.chao@philips.com

SeYoung Kim
seyoung.kim@philips.com

Marleen van Leengoed
marleen.van.leengoed@philips.com

Jeroen Raijmakers
jeroen.raijmakers@philips.com

DIS 2016, June 04-08, 2016, Brisbane, QLD, Australia
ACM 978-1-4503-4031-1/16/06.
http://dx.doi.org/10.1145/2901790.2901915

Abstract
Mime is a tablet-based augmented reality system which guides new chemotherapy patients through testing their blood at home. Starting from the socio-economic push towards home healthcare, we use blood analysis as a case study to illustrate the user experience challenges of unassisted care at home and how AR may support the user. We then show our explorations during an early ideation workshop, using low-fi prototyping and acting out. We also show steps from our making process in which we combine various tools, both physical and virtual, to further our understanding. We conclude with our final demonstrator and the discussions it triggered.

Authors Keywords
augmented reality; manuals; home healthcare

ACM Classification Keywords
H.5.2. User Interfaces: training, help and documentation
H.5.1. Multimedia Information Systems: Artificial, augmented, and virtual realities

Introduction
The rising costs of healthcare are a global concern. One approach to battle these costs is to reduce the number of times outpatients need to visit the hospital and the time that inpatients remain in hospital. This has led to a new area of 'home healthcare' in which patients are provided the means for continued care at home with an emphasis on self-care and telecare, if necessary with support

The Minicare Home system

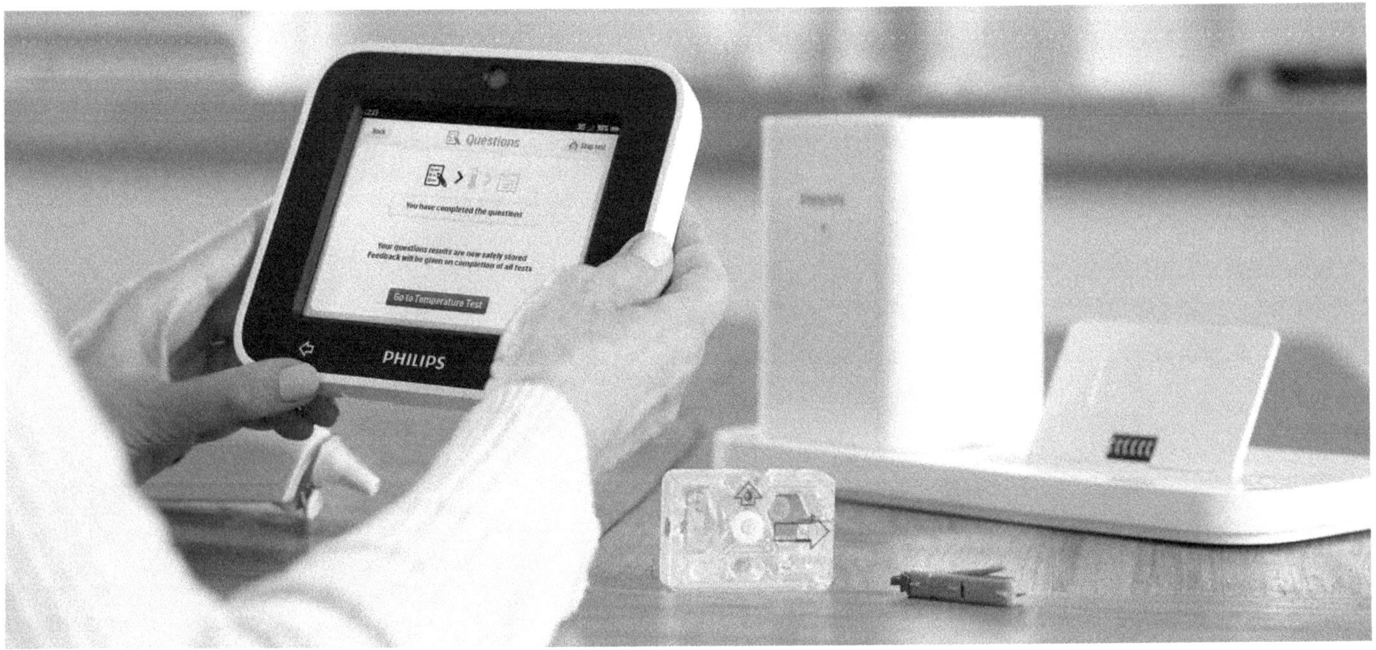

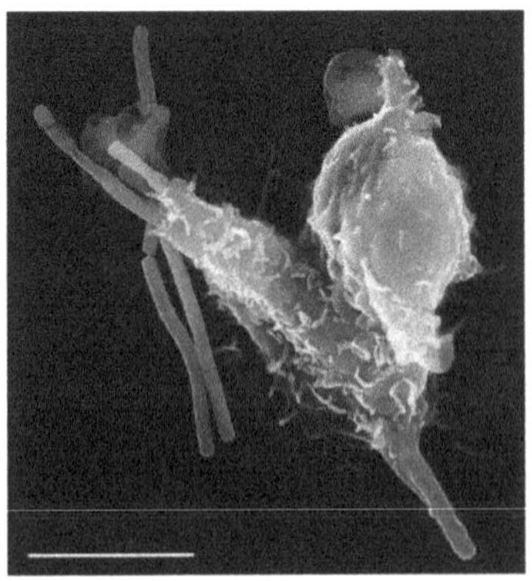

A neutrophil engulfing a bacterium (Volker Brinkman, 2005)

from local care workers. Understandably, there is concern about the required continuity of care, and ensuring quality and safety standards away from the hospital.

Here we focus on one specific application in home health-care: the blood test that chemotherapy patients undergo to check whether they can safely have their next treatment. Typically, chemotherapy patients have such a test done at the hospital prior to every treatment. However, recent advances in blood monitoring equipment made it possible for patients to monitor their blood at home, thus reducing the number of times they need to visit the hospital. In addition to the aforementioned cost benefit, this equates to less infection risk and directly translates into improved quality of life as hospital visits are both physically and mentally exhausting. These benefits are especially relevant for chemotherapy patients as treatments are notorious for making patients feel weak.

A side effect of chemo medication is that it can temporarily lower the number of white blood cells or neutrophils. Neutrophils help the body to fight infection. When this condition, called neutropenia, is too severe, patients are not allowed to undergo their next chemo treatment. A benefit of blood analysis at home then is that it allows for more frequent testing and helps avoid the disappointment of having a test at the hospital, only to hear that the next chemo treatment cannot take place.

In the next section we explain the use of a home blood analysis device (shown above) developed by our company and identify the user experience challenges that come with an unassisted self-test.

The blood analyzer in use
The patient is about to put the blood cartridge into the blood analyzer. From this picture it can be seen how the blood test requires quite a large number of objects and how the user needs to decide on the best order to handle them. Typically, patients need to walk to a sink to warm up their hands.

The use protocol

The basic process for using our current generation blood analysis device ("Home monitoring service", 2016) is seemingly simple: the user needs to desinfect a finger, lance the finger, place a drop of blood into the cartridge, put the cartridge into the machine and put on a band-aid where the finger prick took place. The results are then sent via the internet to the oncology team for review. However, there are two requirements which complicate matters. The first is that the drop of blood needs to be 'fresh' as once it starts to coagulate its analysis will be unreliable. The user is therefore given a time limit of 45 seconds between lancing and putting the cartridge with the drop of blood into the machine. When the required actions are carried out in the right order this should pose no problem. However, when actions are carried out in a sub-optimal order the user may exceed the time limit.
This can happen, for example, when the user has already lanced and then still needs to take the cartridge out of its foil packaging. Missing the time limit means wasted consumables, which increases costs, and requires the user to lance again, which causes discomfort.
A second requirement is that the cartridge is filled with a sufficiently large drop of blood. Drawing a large drop of blood can be challenging, especially for elderly patients with low perfusion. It is therefore recommended that prior to lancing, patients dilate their blood vessels by immersing their hands in a sink with warm water. This is cumbersome and results depend on duration and water temperature.
Another complication is the number of objects that the user is confronted with: an alcohol swap, a lancet, a foil-packaged cartridge, a band-aid, the blood analyzer itself and possibly scissors to open the packaging. The disposables come from different manufacturers and are not that easy to recognize for a non-medically trained, novice user.
Regarding manuals, the current generation blood analyzer comes with a tablet which contains a number of movies which explain the procedure the user needs to go through.
A final complication is that patients undergoing chemotherapy do not only get a physical but also a mental blow: from a cognitive point of view they are not their usual selves. This phenomenon, known as chemo fog, makes it more difficult for them than normally to remember and interpret instructions. The instructions they get in the hospital will be hard for them to remember, even more so than for 'normal' patients.

Ideation workshop: exploring an AR-based, contextual manual

The essence of augmented reality is that it can display a virtual overlay on top of the physical world. Because a tablet is already used in the current set-up for internet connectivity and to show instruction movies, we were interested in using it to augment the scene.

Currently, patients have to look back and forth between the explanatory movies shown on the tablet and their own set-up. This means that they have to interpret the movie and relate the various objects and actions explained in the movie to their own. We envisaged that using augmented reality we could build a contextual manual, with the tablet providing guidance overlaid on top of the user's own objects and hands. The first ideation session was therefore aimed at exploring how virtual annotations could guide the user through the procedure.

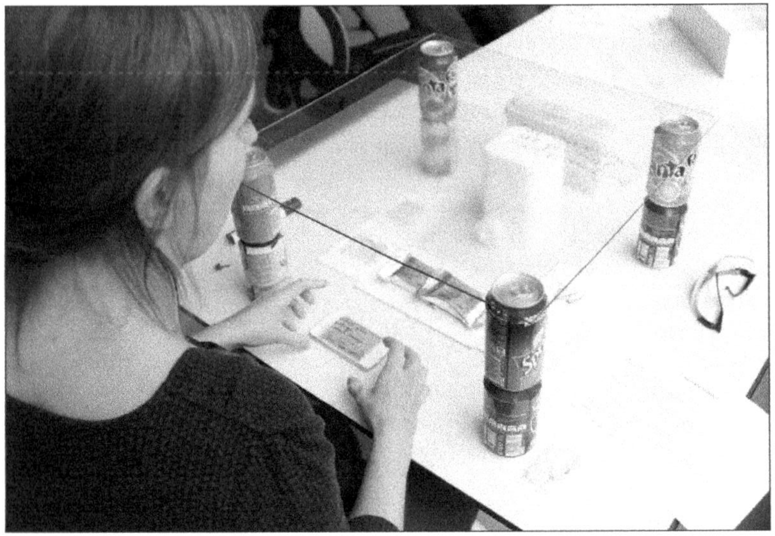

Using low-fi physical prototyping to explore augmentation

Because the design problem is so physical—involving the user's body and various tangible objects—we re-enacted the scene using low-fi, physical prototyping, even for the augmentation (Burns 1994; Ylirisku & Buur, 2007). This set-up shows how we put a sheet of acrylic on top of some beverage cans. By putting writing and drawings on top of this sheet, we could quickly explore where and when to show virtual annotations on top of the real world.

A game board metaphor: optimizing the order of actions

Using the objects in a sub-optimal order increases the likelihood of not making the time limit. We therefore came up with the idea of a gameboard in which the first step is to place the objects in the right order of use. Here objects are ordered linearly from left to right.

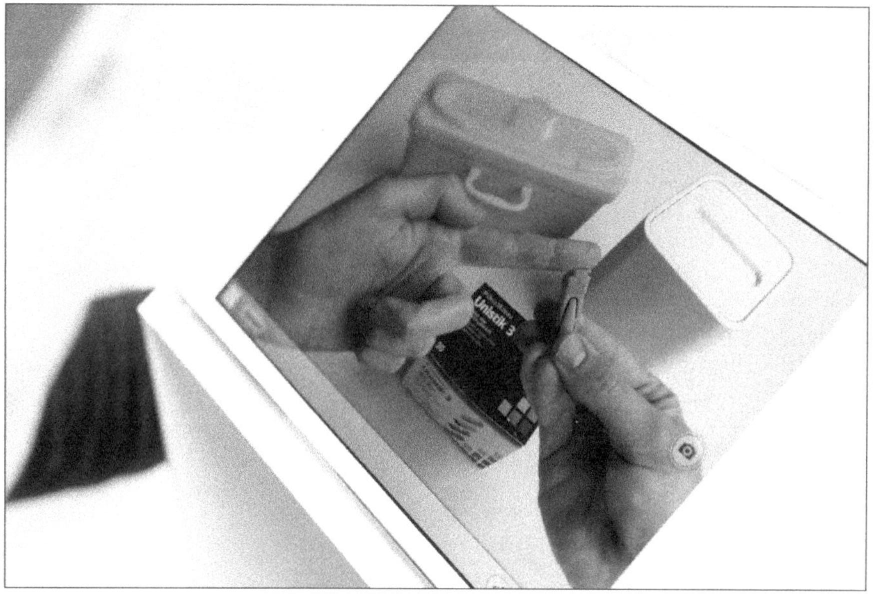

Lancing behind the tablet: impossible due to disturbed hand-eye coordination.

One aspect that we wanted to communicate to the user is which part of the finger to lance. We envisaged that the user would lance behind the tablet and that using augmented reality we would show an arrow on top of the real hand to indicate the ideal spot for the needle. When we started to experiment with this—simply by using the camera functionality of the tablet, programming not yet required—we found that unfortunately this did not work. Due to a combination of the tablet's camera being off-centre, the image not being stereoscopic, the lack of head-coupled motion parallax and delay, our hand-eye coordination was so messed up that when viewing our hands through the camera we simply could not lance accurately.

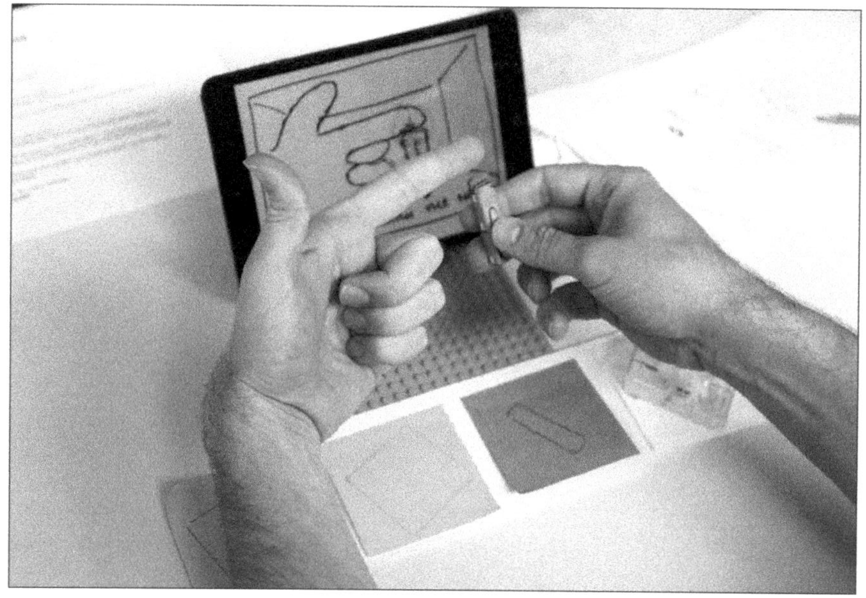

Lancing in front of the tablet: optimizing the order of actions

We therefore settled for showing an animated visual of hand and lancet on the screen of the tablet which the user can then follow in front of the tablet. This introduces a level of indirection and is thus a less sophisticated solution than AR guidance displayed on the user's own body. However, we felt it was the right approach as the limitations of tablet-based augmented reality made lancing behind the tablet too awkward.

Storyboarding

We sketched out the complete interaction flow to identify at which points the use of AR could make sense.

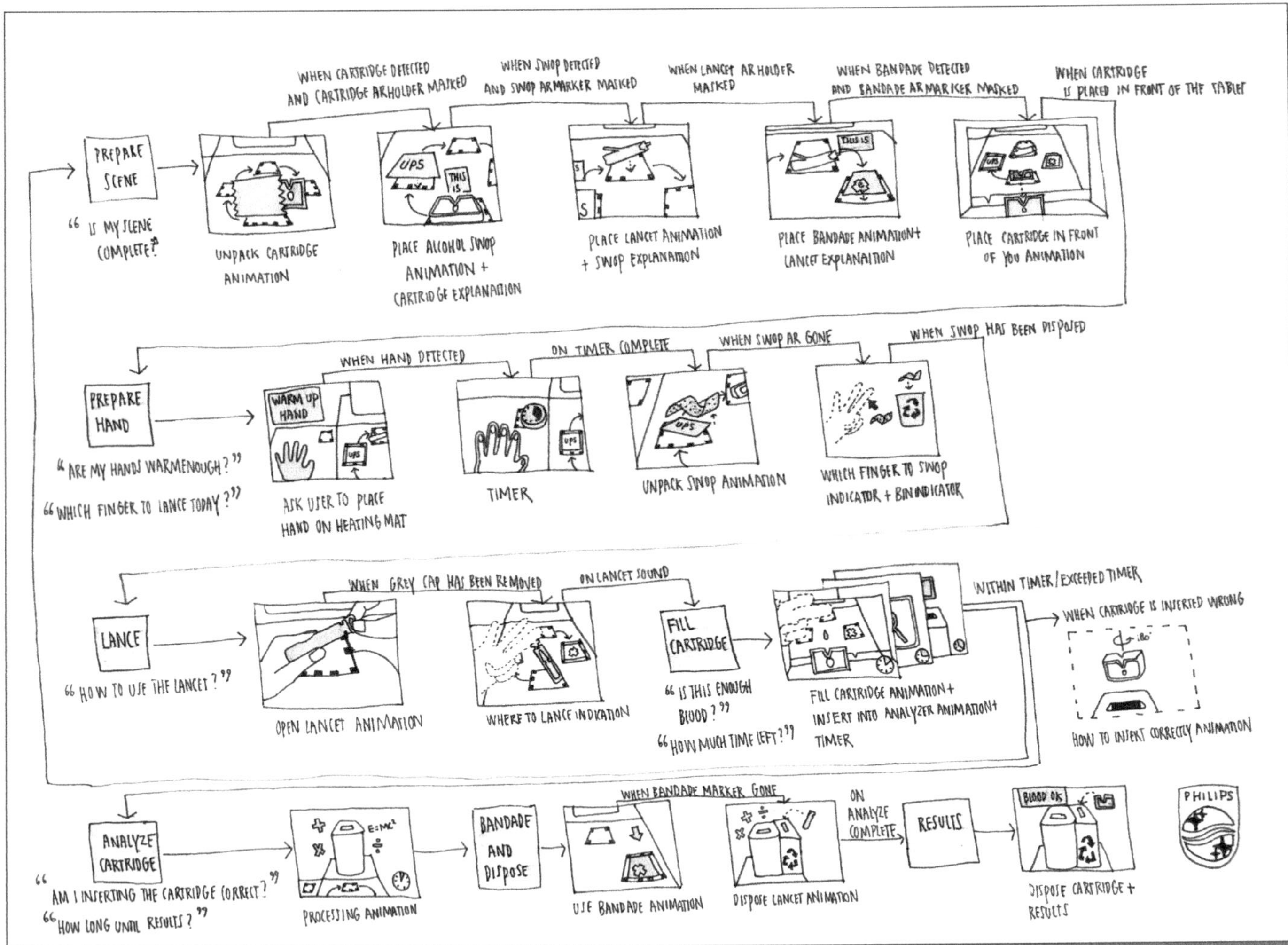

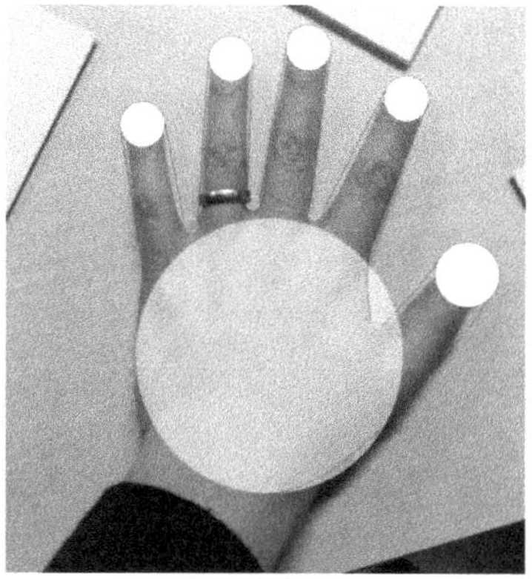

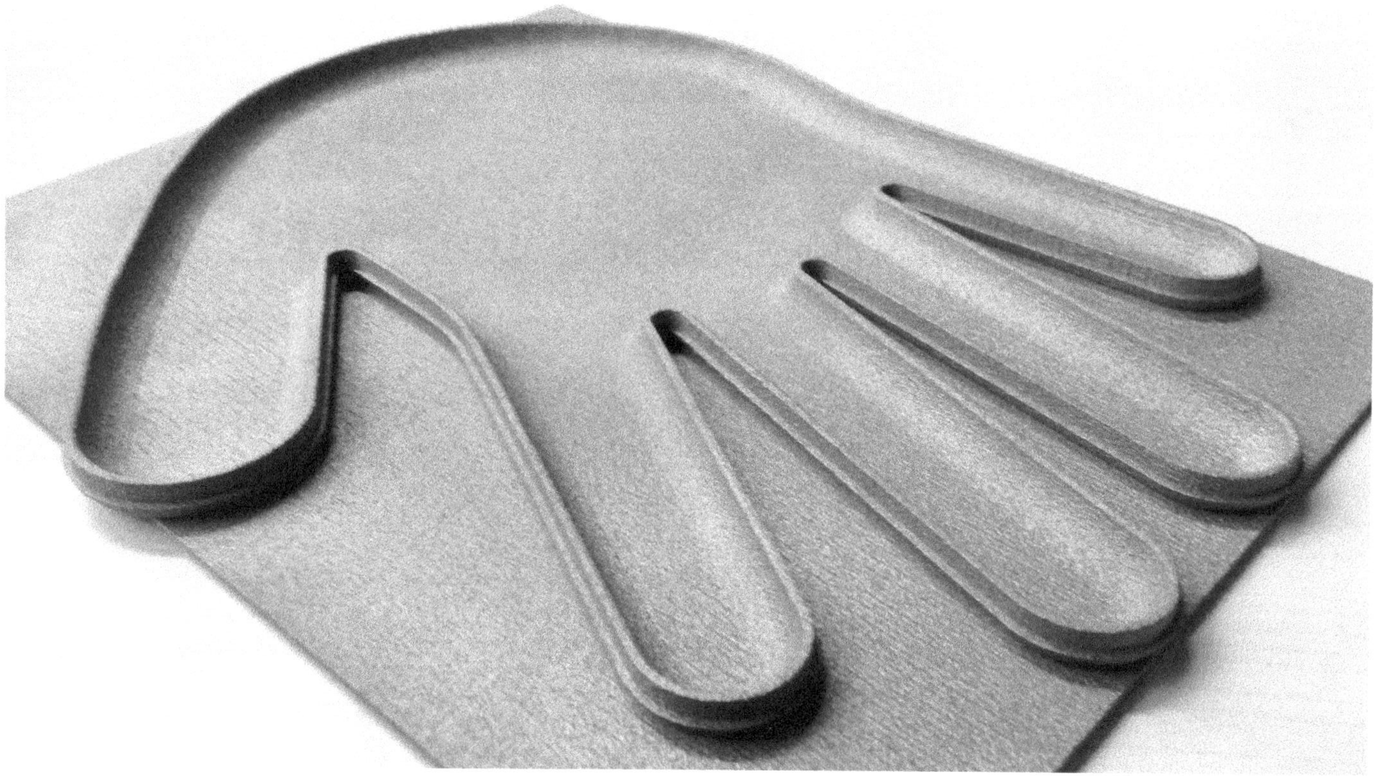

Hand warming unit

One of the things we were intent to improve upon was patients having to warm up their hands in the kitchen sink. It is not only cumbersome but also potentially unhygienic. We therefore developed a hand warming board. Because the best spot to lance is the side of the finger, we made a hand-shaped recess which heats not only the handpalm but also the sides of the fingers. As the cavity is smooth and rounded, it is easy to clean with an alcohol swab.
For our demonstrator we chose to 3D print the hand warming board in steel rather than mill it from solid. This was quicker, cheaper and allowed more form freedom.
One of the challenges was how to detect that patients put their hand on the heating mat. Clearly we could not ask users to put a marker on their hand. Ideally, the tablet would see the hand but recognizing hands through computer vision is notoriously error prone.
We therefore added pressure sensors underneath the hand warming board. These were connected to an Arduino microcontroller which communicated wirelessly with the tablet via Bluetooth. The weight of the hand informed the system whether the user's hand was on the mat or not.

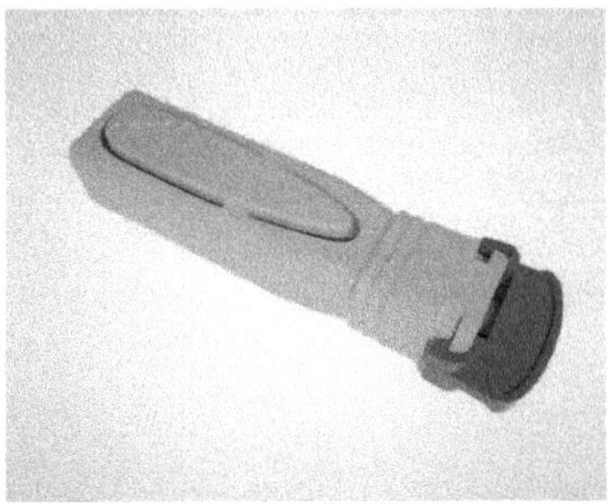

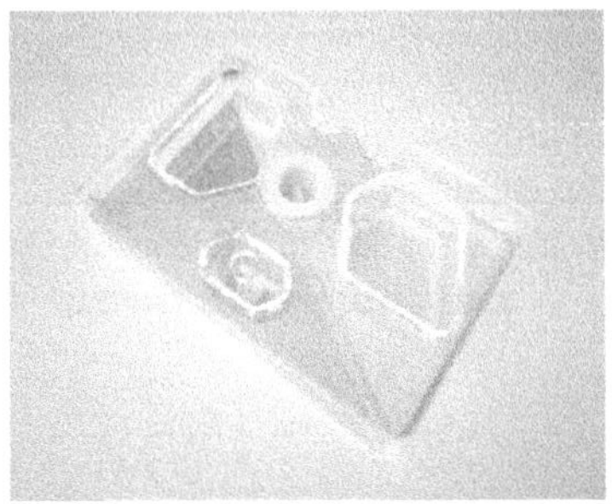

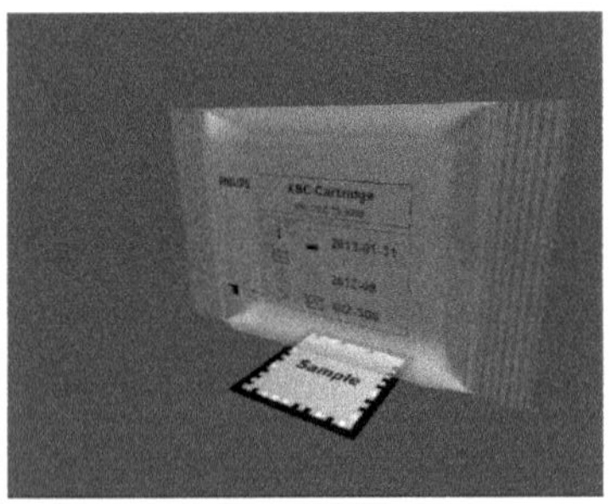

Virtually showing the next step
Our idea was to let Mime virtually show the next step so that the user could simply copy. To be as clear as possible we wanted realistic virtual objects animating in the right physical locations. For this we created virtual versions of all the disposables and their packaging.

Adding markers to packaging
To be able to augment the disposables we had to re-design their packaging to add AR markers which could be tracked by the tablet's camera. We placed the original graphics inside a AR marker edge to respect the corporate identity of the manufacturer.

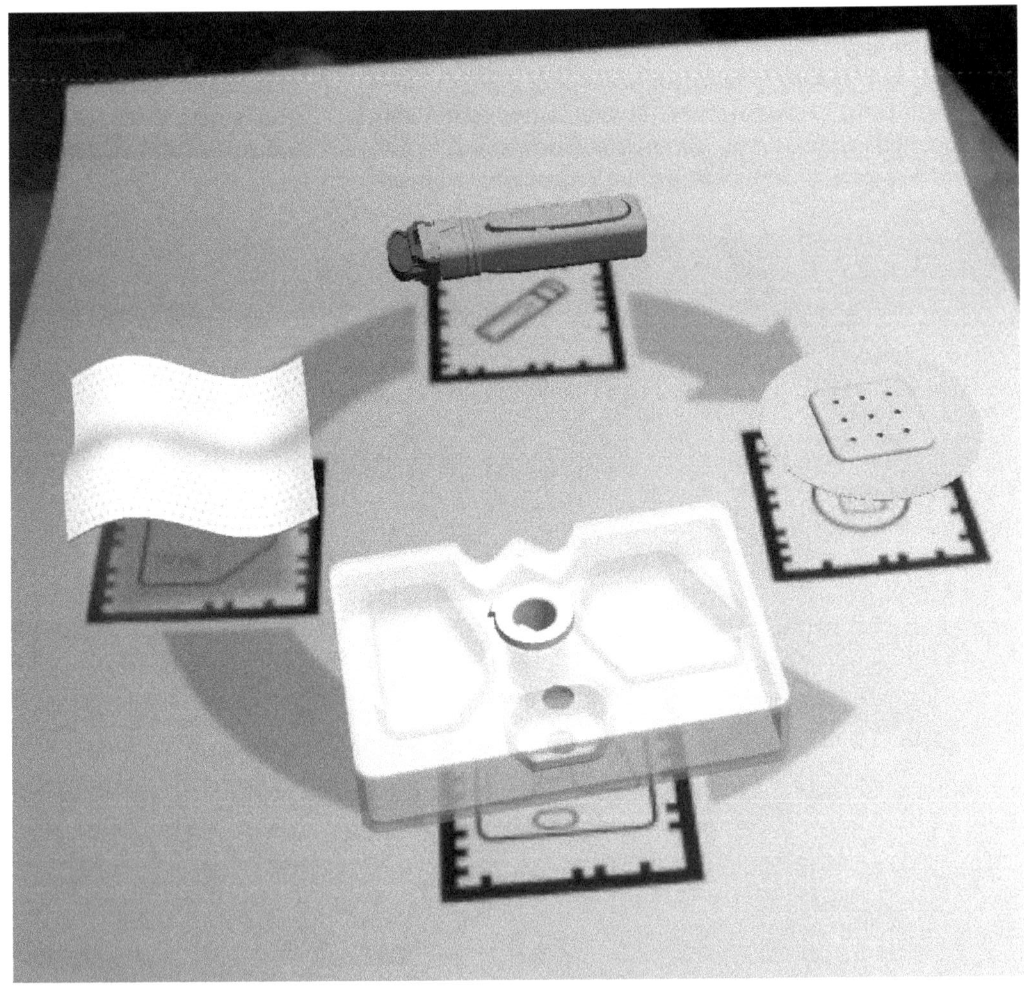

Virtual disposables on gameboard
Our first attempt at augmented the physical gameboard with virtual content. We had to compromise and replace the linear gameboard by a circular one as the field of view of the tablet's camera was too narrow to hold a linear strip of markers in view, even with the addition of a wide angle lens.

Cardboard model of the test set-up
The model includes the stand with the tablet (front), the gameboard (middle), the hand warming plate (left) and the blood analyzer (rear). This pre-model allowed us to test ergonomics and how to place the tablet so that all AR markers could be covered by its camera.

Screenshot of the cardboard test set-up
The blood cartridge has just been placed and has been recognized as shown by the 'text balloon'. The virtual alcohol swap animating down on the gameboard shows that this is the next step that the user has to take.

Product design of folding box

Once we had the interaction concept, we envisaged a folding box which would include all components: the blood analyzer, the game board, the handwarming unit, the tablet stand, the tablet itself and all needed disposables. Using a combination of cardboard and computer modelling we came to box which holds everything together and can fold out flat on the table.

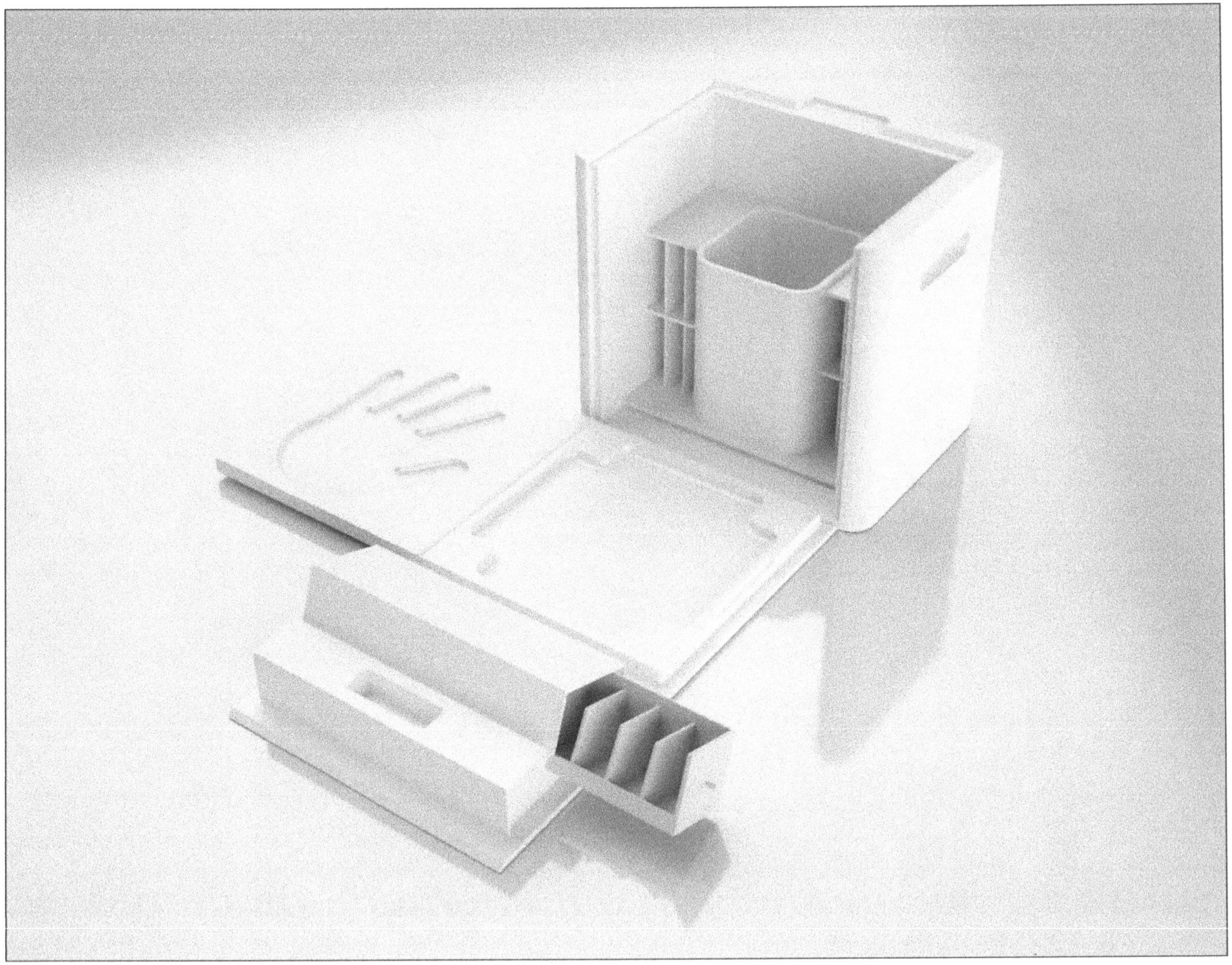

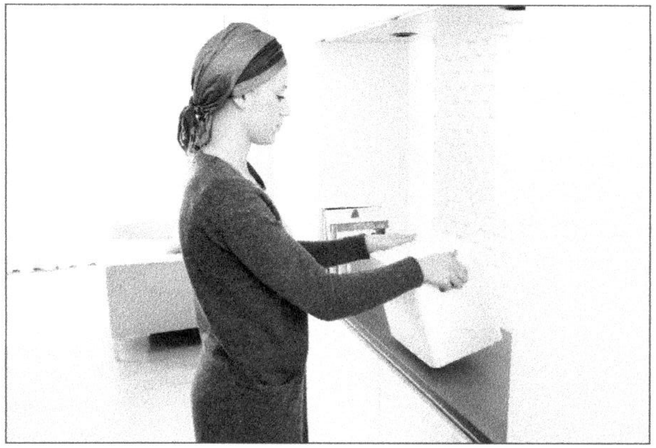

When the user picks the case off the shelf she can be confident that she has everything needed for a blood test together.

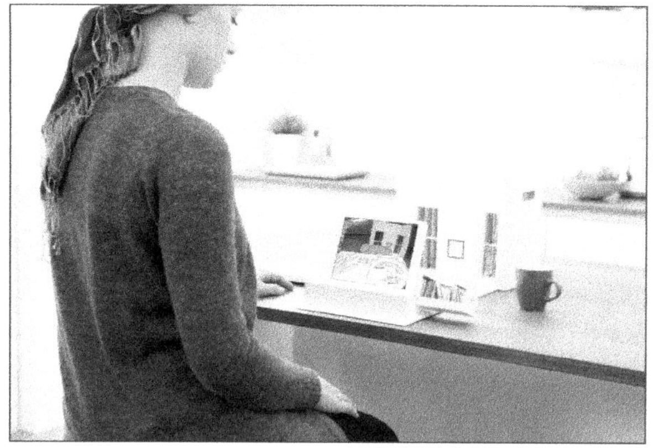

Once the case has been folded flat, the user finds the tablet with AR software, the disposables, the analyzer and the handwarming unit.

To dilate the vessels and make it easier to draw a sufficiently large drop of blood, the patient is asked to put her hand on the heating mat. A virtual timer shows how long she needs to keep her hand there.

Through animated virtual objects, the patient is shown how to place the disposables in the best order. Mime always shows the next step, enabling her to simply copy. Once a step has been completed, Mime automatically advances to the next one.

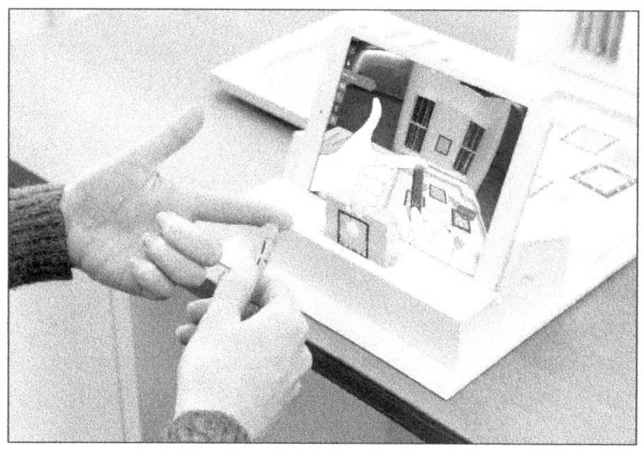

Mime then shows the patient to pick up the lancet and unscrew its cap. Once she has lanced her finger, she can rub a drop of blood into the cartridge. A 45 seconds countdown starts from the moment that Mime hears the click of the lancet.

The final step is to put the cartridge into the blood analyzer. If the user holds the cartridge the wrong way, Mime will show how to correct this by means of a virtual arrow.

We shot a three minute contextual video explaining the purpose and use of Mime. This allowed us to circulate the concept more widely than by means of the demonstrator alone. We gathered feedback from various people within the company including business stakeholders and usability experts who directly work with the patient group.

Discussion

We highlight some points from the feedback we received and add our own reflections.

1. AR as an in-context manual for novice users

The current Minicare Home system uses tablet-based movies to instruct the user. Although this is an improvement on a paper manual, the indirection remains: users watch the movies to build an understanding of the objects and actions involved and then need to apply this to their own situation. In contrast, Mime shows guidance directly on the objects handled by the user and provides immediate feedback on the user's own actions. Whilst using AR to provide instructions has been proposed many times before (Weidenhausen et al., 2003), we feel that in home healthcare its use is particularly appropriate because of the target group. Unlike mechanics or service technicians, patients are novices who strongly benefit from contextualized instructions.

2. AR using a fixed display

AR is often associated with glasses, a technology which is not yet mature, or with handheld smart devices, which rob the user of one hand. With Mime, we make use of a tablet in a stand which already forms part of the current proposition and which leaves the user free to act with both hands.

3. Mime as a Virtual Nurse

When distances are large or traffic is busy, sending out a real nurse to assist the patient is costly in terms of travel time. From a business modelling point of view, this is how the added costs of the AR technology may be offset.

4. Mime as a way to improve scalability

Systems which first require explanation by a knowledgeable nurse during a home visit suffer from a scalability problem. It is much more costly to train and employ staff than to mass produce devices. Systems such as Mime may therefore help improve the scalability of home healthcare.

5. Mime's form factor is currently too big

Whilst the all-in-one solution was appreciated, many felt the folding box was too big. This makes Mime unwieldy for travel, e.g. a weekend trip. A possible alternative would be to print AR markers on a tablet sleeve that could double up as a 'gameboard' on which to order disposables.

Patenting

We filed an patent application on the working principle behind Mime as an 'Augmented Reality-based manual to guide timely object placement in the physical world'.

Acknowledgements

We gratefully acknowledge Malcolm Luker, Alison Sundset, Geert Christiaansen, Hans Driessen, Sean Carney, Roland Hovers, Jacqueline Janssen, Vincent Jeanne, Anja Janssen and Myrte Thoolen for their feedback on and contributions to Mime and this pictorial.

References

1. Brinkman, V. (2005). "Neutrophil engulfing Bacillus anthracis". PLoS Pathogens 1 (3): Cover page.
2. Burns, C., Dishman, E., Verplank, W., and Lassiter, B. (1994). Actors, hairdos & videotape—informance design. In Conference Companion on Human Factors in Computing Systems (CHI '94), Catherine Plaisant (Ed.). ACM, New York, NY, USA, 119-120.
3. Home monitoring service for patients undergoing chemotherapy (2016). Retrieved from http://www.philips.co.uk/healthcare/education-resources/publications/hotspot/minicare-home
4. Weidenhausen, J., Knoepfle, C., & Stricker, D. (2003). Lessons learned on the way to industrial augmented reality applications, a retrospective on arvika. Computers & Graphics, 27(6):887-891, 2003.
5. Ylirisku, S. and Buur, J. (2007). Designing with Video. Focusing the user-centred design process.

Behind the Lens: A Visual Exploration of Epistemological Commitments in HCI Research on the Home

Audrey Desjardins,
Simon Fraser University
Surrey, British Columbia, Canada
adesjard@sfu.ca

Ron Wakkary
Simon Fraser University
Surrey, British Columbia, Canada
Eindhoven University of Technology
Eindhoven, Netherlands
rwakkary@sfu.ca

Will Odom
Simon Fraser University
Surrey, British Columbia, Canada
wodom@sfu.ca

DIS 2016, June 04 - 08, 2016, Brisbane, QLD, Australia

ACM 978-1-4503-4031-1/16/06 $15.00
DOI: http://dx.doi.org/10.1145/2901790.2901910

Abstract

In this pictorial, we propose an alternative approach to investigating human-computer interaction (HCI) researchers' epistemological commitments in research on the home. While researchers' commitments can be discussed through textual aspects of their research, in this pictorial we conduct a pattern analysis of visual elements as a productive way to further inquire into such kinds of commitments. By analyzing visual elements from 121 works in HCI research on the home, we identify seven types of observers, which can be associated with epistemological commitments in research. We also propose two new complementary observers: the absent observer and the protagonist observer.

Authors Keywords

Home; Epistemological Commitments; Visual Exploration.

ACM Classification Keywords

H.5.m. Information interfaces and presentation (e.g., HCI): Miscellaneous.

Introduction

For over twenty-five years, HCI researchers have investigated the diverse roles that interactive technologies and systems play in people's homes and have proposed new ways to design for domestic experiences. Researchers have adopted various methods to address the complex, messy and intimate nature of the home. These range from ethnographic and ethnomethodological studies of current practices in the home (e.g. [3,9,49,52]), to field deployments of newly designed technologies (e.g. [30,38,43,45]), to participatory design (e.g. [41]), to the proposal of speculative visions (e.g. [2,18,53]).

In [13] we reported on a critical literature review that identified genres in HCI research on the home as a starting point to define future complementary directions for HCI research. In addition to looking at genres of research (based on the types of questions researchers were asking and the objects of their studies), we also uncovered five epistemological commitments HCI researchers interested in the home could adopt when conducting and reporting on their research. As part of this work, we had also conducted a preliminary analysis of the visual elements presented in each paper we reviewed. At first glance, we found that often times images of similar quality and topic were clustered in each of the seven genres of HCI research on the home. However, due to the limitations of the standard ACM long paper format, we largely omitted this pattern analysis of visual elements from our previously published paper.

In this pictorial, we provide an in depth pattern analysis of the visual elements (e.g. photographs, line drawings, photomontage, floor plans, sketches, interface screenshots, etc.) included in 121 works of HCI research on the home. HCI is showing a growing interest in visual literacy and in developing new ways to visually represent and communicate research findings (e.g. [4–6,8,16,21]). Our goal is to show how the visual elements chosen by researchers are not arbitrary; rather, they too embody epistemological commitments bound to particular ways of practicing and representing HCI research on the home.

Methodology

We used the same list of 121 works of HCI research on the home as in [13]. For each work, we took screenshots of all the visual elements and we built a library organized by author and publication. To begin the analysis, we printed and cut each individual image. We then started to cluster the images in terms of what was represented on the image (e.g., was it people? an object? a space?, etc.) and in terms of the treatment of the image (e.g., photograph, line drawing, annotated photograph, etc.). We used the two following sets of questions to guide our analysis:

1. Why these types of pictures? What does the observer want to capture and show?
2. Where is the observer? In order to achieve that goal, where does the observer spatially need to position herself or himself?

Using these questions as framing mechanisms for our inquiry, we clustered the visual elements of the 121 works into seven affinity groups that we categorized as seven types of observer. We note that our process was iterative and that certain categories only emerged after spending enough time describing and highlighting details of the visual elements.

Our pictorial

We present seven types of observers in HCI research on the home. In each type, we articulate what we determined to be the answers to the sets of questions we asked. We use clusters of images to show the sub-types of observers and annotations to highlight visual characteristics of the images. We also provide a reflection on our analysis method and on the seven types of observers in addition to offering two complementary types of observers: the absent observer and the protagonist observer.

The Detached Observer

WHY THESE TYPES OF PICTURES?

The observer aims to capture a situation as it is, with little to no trace of intervention or presence. The goal is that what is visible is evidence of a social routine taking place without knowledge or effect of the observer.

WHERE IS THE OBSERVER?

The observer is purposely distant or removed from the situation and scene of the image.

VISUAL CHARACTERISTICS

[34]

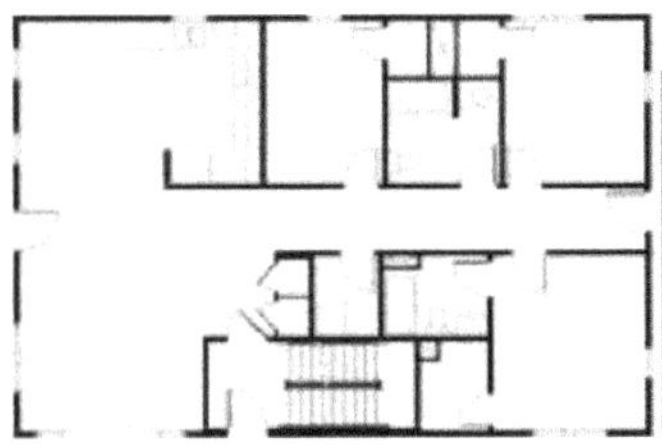

[35]

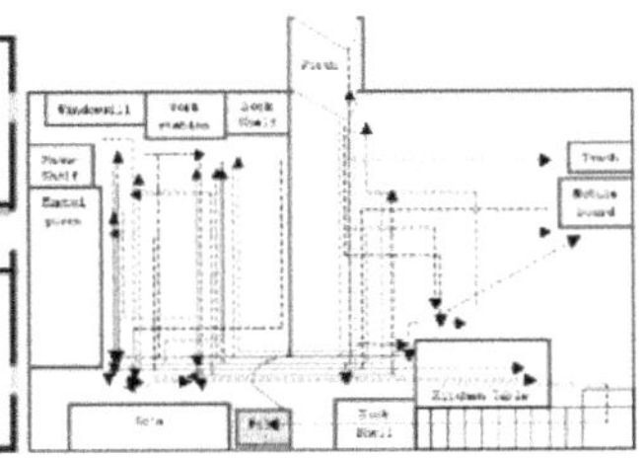

[9]

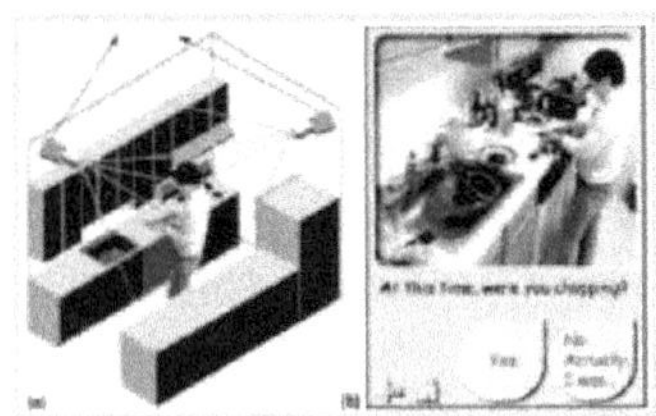

[31]

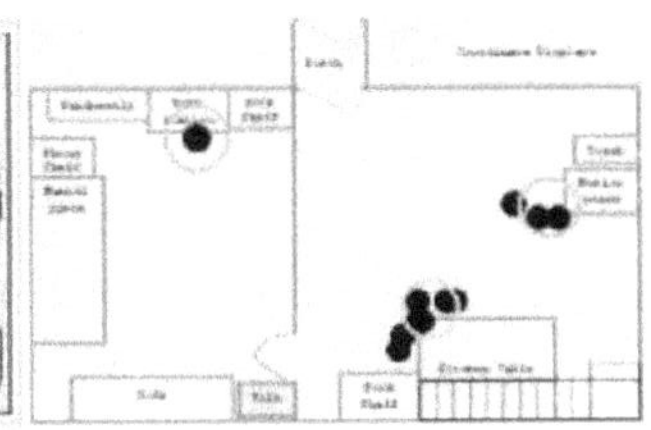

[10]

- Aerial line drawings and architectural drawings sometimes augmented with graphical representations of movement or routines in the home

[54]

[40]

[42]

- Photographs from a distance, like from across the street

The Object Oriented Observer

WHY THESE TYPES OF PICTURES?

The observer aims to show how an object is used and incorporated in the context and practices of everyday life in the home.

WHERE IS THE OBSERVER?

The observer is in the home with the participants and actively moves, looks into (e.g. drawers, books) and discusses with participants to understand how artifacts are used. He may also ask participants to perform actions or activities with artifacts as they normally would in order to document that as well.

VISUAL CHARACTERISTICS

[57] [15] [1] [57]

Tightly cropped artifacts in context, as they were found in the participants' houses

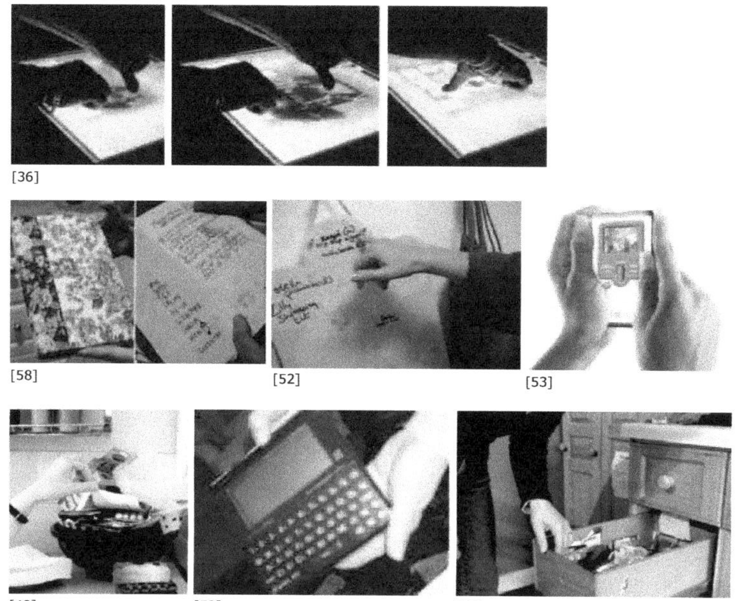

[36] [58] [52] [53] [49] [59] [49]

Photographs including at least one hand pointing or touching an artifact

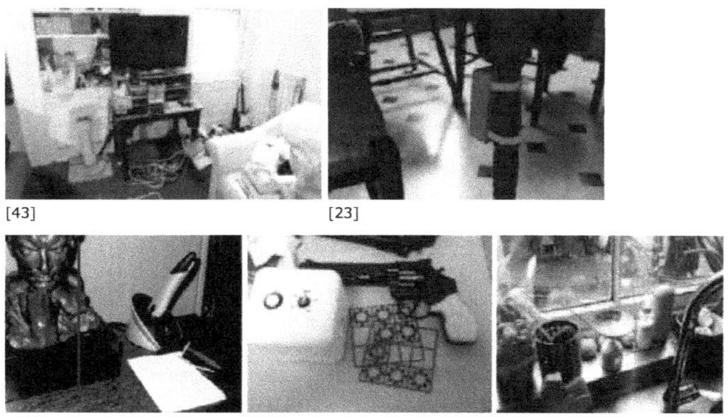

[43] [23] [45] [38] [24]

New technologies or interactive artifacts in the home

[14] [1] [51]

Collections of similar artifacts in context in the home

The People Oriented Observer

WHY THESE TYPES OF PICTURES?

The observer aims to foreground and emphasize how people use things and technologies in the home.

WHERE IS THE OBSERVER?

The observer is in the home with the participants as they demonstrate, use, or live with artifacts and technologies.

VISUAL CHARACTERISTICS

[57]

[26]

Photographs of people performing everyday actions in context

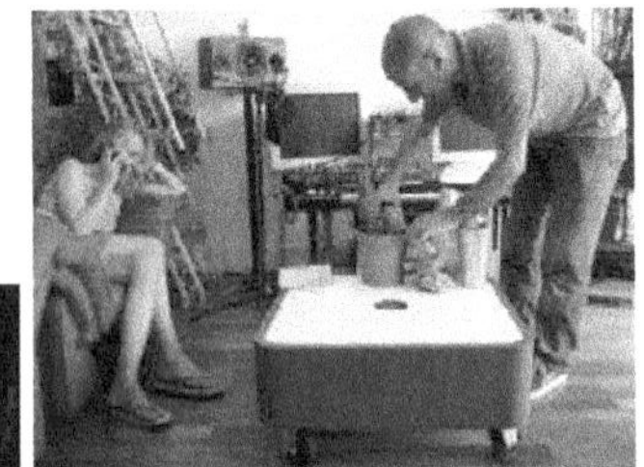

[20]

[22]

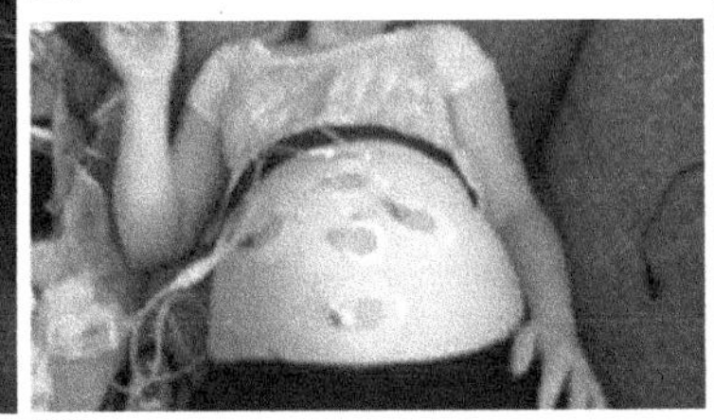

[27]

[30]

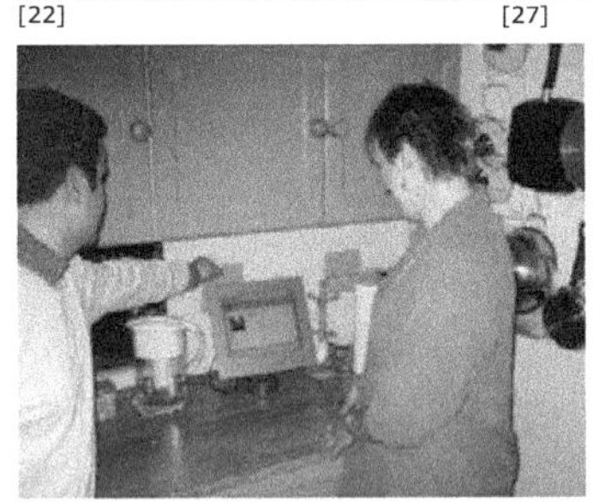

[47]

[45]

[30]

[3]

[46]

Photographs of people using a new technology in the home. The framing is concerned with the people and the technology first, the physical context second

The Evidence Collector

WHY THESE TYPES OF PICTURES?

The observer aims to gather and document the information that participants themselves have created (e.g., how they populated an app, or how they themselves photographed a thing).

WHERE IS THE OBSERVER?

The evidence collector is removed from the domestic experience entirely, but subsequently collects data that lets transpire participants' experience of the home.

VISUAL CHARACTERISTICS

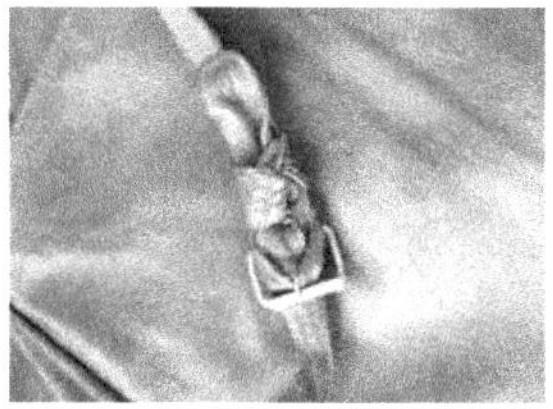
[39]

[56]

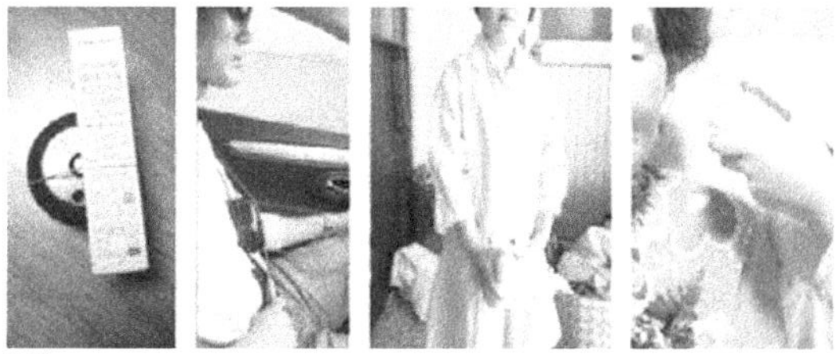
[38]

Relayed photos taken by participants (in self reporting practices)

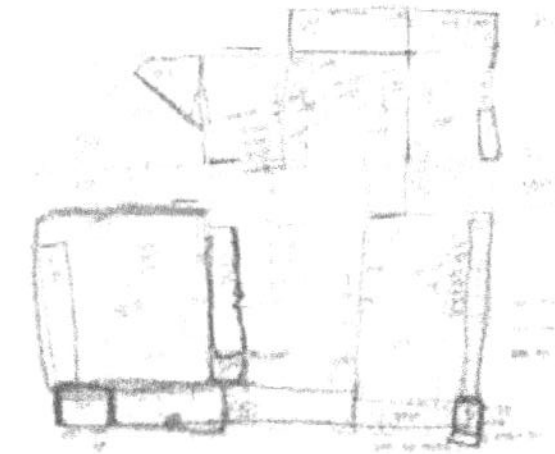
[37]

[45]

Photos of artifacts and notes created by participants

[3]

[19]

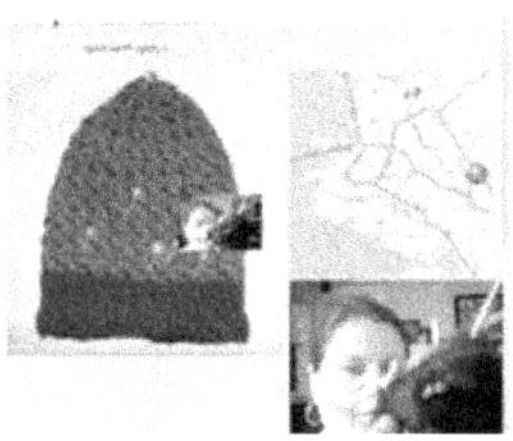
[46]

[32]

[47]

Photographs or screenshots of interfaces in use evidencing how participants used them

The Gaze Director Observer

WHY THESE TYPES OF PICTURES?

The observer aims to clearly identify and direct attention to a specific item in a photo or portion of the photo.

WHERE IS THE OBSERVER?

The observer is behind the lens when taking the photo, which is subsequently augmented using a computer to shape where the viewer does and does not look.

[48]

[55]

[9]

[10]

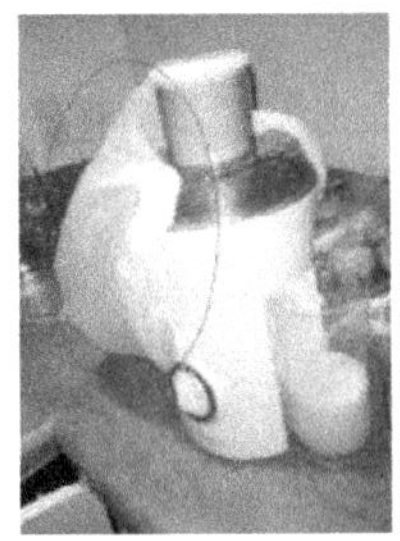

[39]

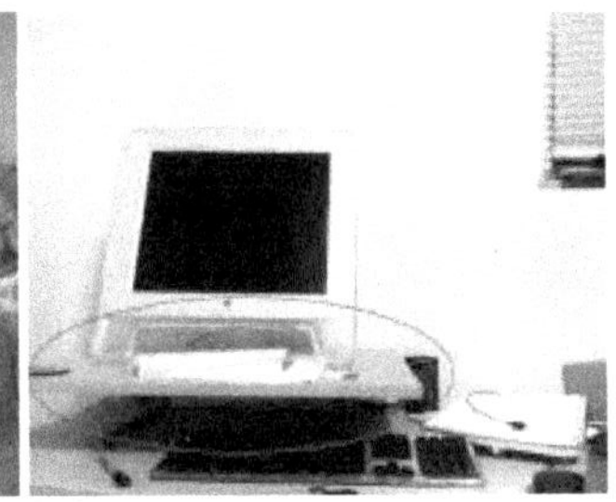

[39]

VISUAL CHARACTERISTICS

- Photos taken in a home, with an item within the room framed in red or in white
- Photos taken of an artifact, with a part of the artifact circled in red

The Composer Observer

WHY THESE TYPES OF PICTURES?

The observer aims to carefully construct an image to best show what an artifact or a system is.

WHERE IS THE OBSERVER?

The observer is behind the camera, but beforehand he sets up the scene to take the photo. The composer observer might also be behind his computer, crafting an interface on the screen which will then be used as a visual representation.

VISUAL CHARACTERISTICS

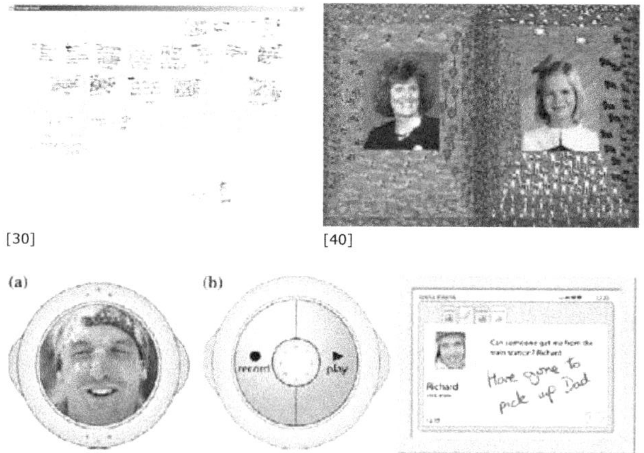

[30] [40] [51] [51]

- Screenshot or digitally created images that show an interface's state

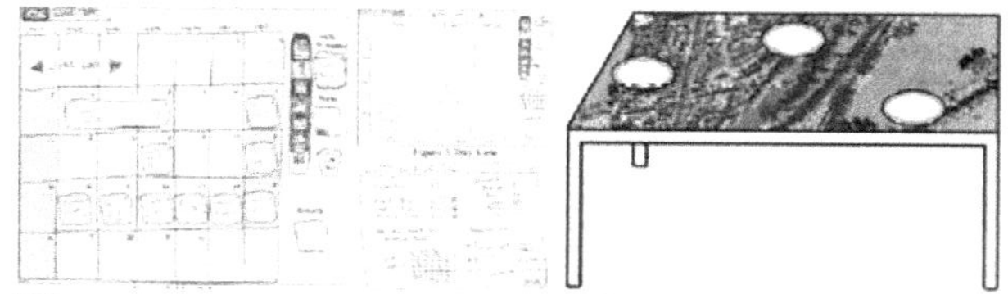
[41] [25]

- Digital or hand drawn sketches of a concept

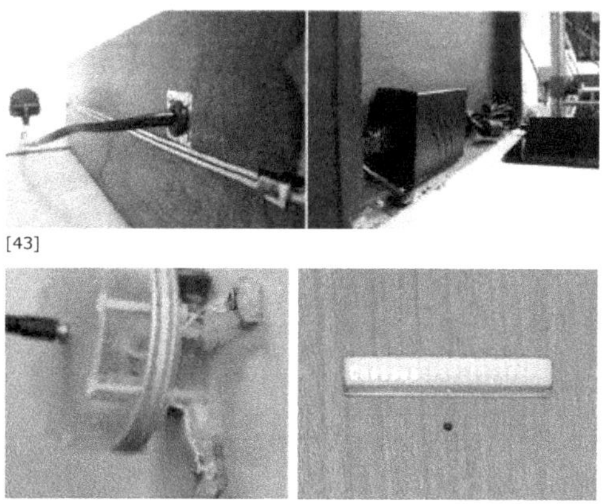
[43] [28] [25]

- Tightly cropped design details of a new technology or artifact, often where the digital and the computational meet

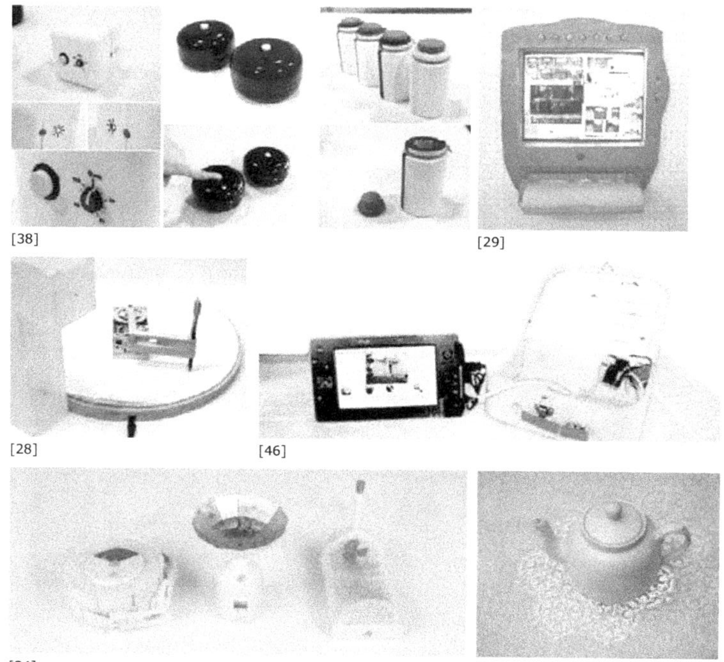
[38] [29] [28] [46] [24] [22]

- Artifacts photographed on a white or uniform background with controled lighting and framing

The Visionary Observer

WHY THESE TYPES OF PICTURES?

The observer aims to create a representation of a possible future of technology in or around the home.

WHERE IS THE OBSERVER?

The observer is active in constructing the images. He is both 'in front' and 'behind' the camera. And, through carefully crafting the image, he exercises an important authorial role.

VISUAL CHARACTERISTICS

[2]

[29]

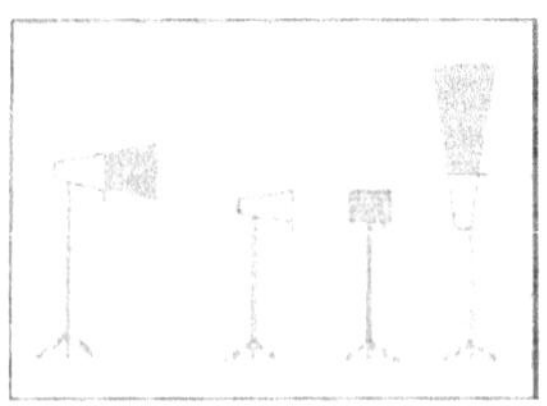

[18]

- Carefully crafted illustrations with an attention to the choice of colors, shades, and thickness of line

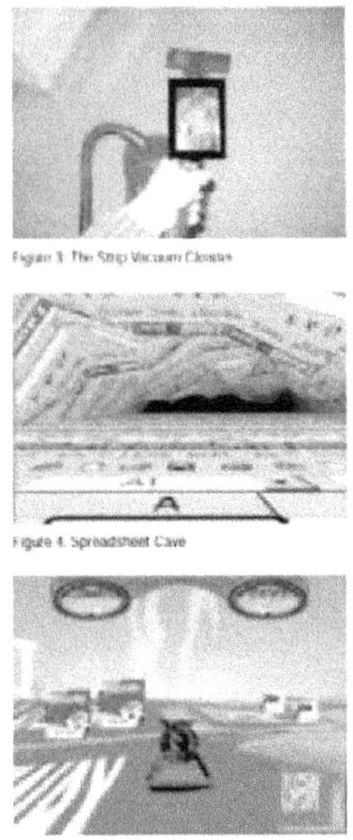

[7]

[54]

[60]

[17]

[20]

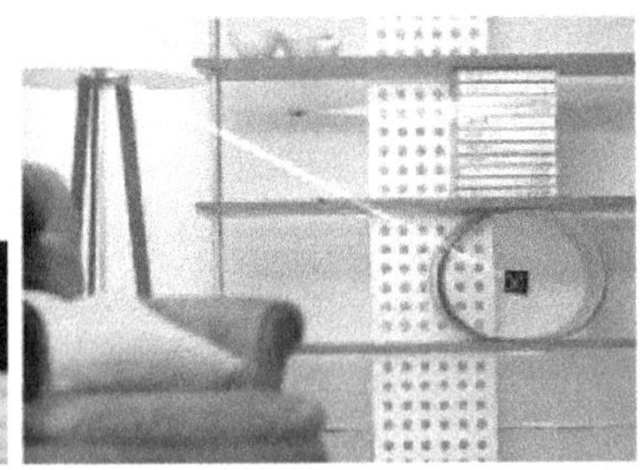

[22]

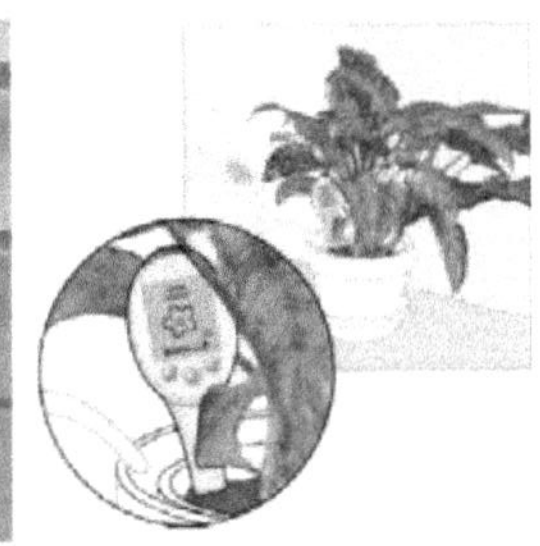

[53]

- Photomontages combining multiple photos, or addition of line drawing on top of photos. The images have an artistic and inspirational feel to them

Analysis

Matched and unmatched observers and epistemological commitments

Observers	Epistemological commitments
Detached observer	Objective observer
People oriented observer; Object oriented observer	Third person observer
Evidence collector	Relayed informant
Visionary observer; Composer observer	Experimenter
Gaze director observer	
	Author interpreter

In the previous pages, we have articulated the goals of the seven observers as well as their position when creating visual elements in their HCI research on the home. These insights can enable us to better understand the epistemological perspectives researchers take when conducting research in HCI on the home. In our critical literature review [13] based on the same corpus of literature, we identified five epistemological commitments grounded in our analysis. Looking at those five commitments in relation to the seven types of observers, we can see an interesting match between the two (see table). We highlight those relations in our analysis.

- Firstly, the detached observer takes photos from a distance or uses architectural and aerial views to understand ongoing practices in the home. The visual strategies used embody a rigor and a distance imposed between the observer and the situation and this refers back to ethnomethodology as a method and the epistemological commitment of the *objective observer*.
- Next, the object oriented observer and the people oriented observer both refer to the researcher being in the home with participants, doing a tour, asking about artifacts and potentially participating in everyday life. Photographs showing inconsistent lighting, blurriness, or unrefined framing are seen as a result of the rapidity and ad hoc manner in which they are taken and provide visual evidence that the researcher is physically present in the house emphasizing the epistemological commitment of the *third person observer*.
- Thirdly, the evidence collector relies on participants to create visual elements either by asking them to take pictures of their own domestic experience or by using a prototype that will record the participants' actions. The role of the researcher in this case is to collect, curate and relay this data as a way to answer research questions. This relates to the epistemological commitment of the *relayed informant*.
- Fourth, the composer observer and the visionary observer both carefully construct visual elements and use design to represent a current or future image of what technology in the home could be. This researcher plays an important authorial role and this relates to the epistemological commitment of the *experimenter*.
- Finally, we found that the gaze director observer embodied a strategy that cuts across the other observers and can be seen as an augmentation of other modes of observation through, for example, circling on top of field photographs. The epistemological commitment of the *author interpreter* also did not find a match in our visual analysis. This is unsurprising since this epistemological commitment was largely text based and argument structured.

On the following page we propose two complementary observers that can broaden the perspectives we take in HCI research on the home. First, the protagonist observer offers an alternative to the common 'interpreter' position taken in the detached observer, the object oriented observer, the people oriented observer and the evidence collector. A protagonist observer would be positioned in front of the camera within the domestic experience as a way to encourage first hand experience. Second, the absent observer proposes a complementary view to the generalized anthropocentric perspective to understanding the domestic experience. The absent observer leaves it to non-humans, such as things or pets, to share their own understanding of the domestic experience. This can allow researchers to consider a more egalitarian view in the home and highlight the relations that exist not only between humans and things or technologies in the home, but also the ones that exist between things.

The Protagonist Observer

WHY THESE TYPES OF PICTURES?

The observer aims to understand the experience of the home first hand.

WHERE IS THE OBSERVER?

The observer is positioned in front of the camera, or he points it towards his own experience of the home.

VISUAL CHARACTERISTICS

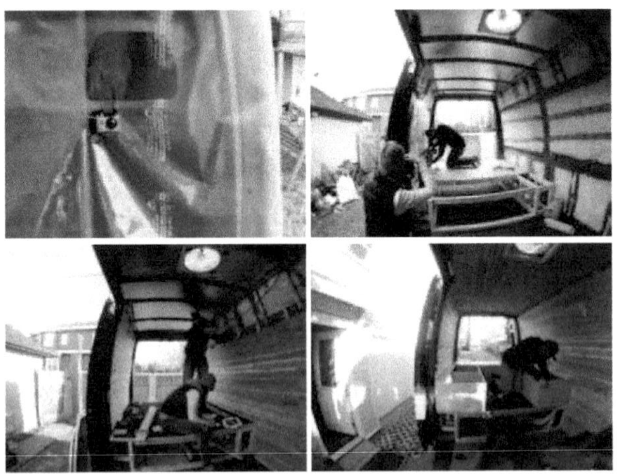

[12]

Still frames captured every minute to create timelapse videos

[19]

Photographs taken from the point of view of the researcher in his or her home

The Absent Observer

WHY THESE TYPES OF PICTURES?

The observer aims to capture the experience of the home from the perspective of non-humans (including objects or pets in the home).

WHERE IS THE OBSERVER?

The observer is completely removed from the situation and lets non-humans observe and report on the experience of the home. The researcher's role is in creating and installing those new methods enabling non-humans to gather data about the home.

VISUAL CHARACTERISTICS

[33]

[11]

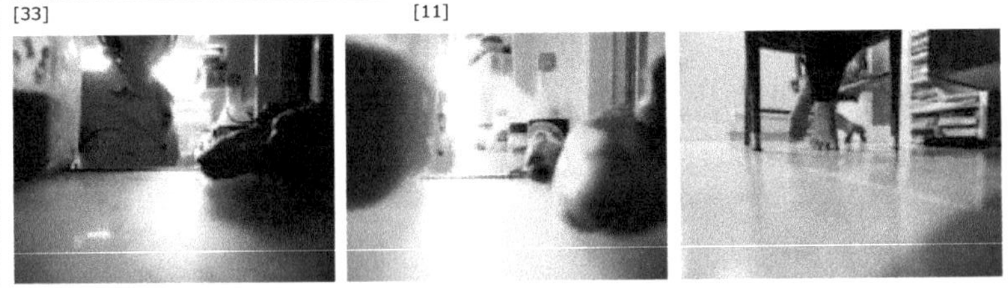

[13]

Photos of everyday scenes, from angles that are new to a human observer

Conclusion

© Lee Friedlander. New York City, 1966

© Lee Friedlander. New York City, 1968

"At first, my presence in my photos was fascinating and disturbing. But as time passed and I was more a part of other ideas in my photos, I was able to add a giggle to those feelings."

- Lee Friedlander [50]

In this pictorial, we have visually explored 121 works in HCI research for the home. Based on the visual elements of these works, we have proposed seven types of observers and two complementary observers for future research on domestic experience. In our future research, we aim to explore how the protagonist observer and the absent observer might operate in HCI research on the home.

The analytical method we used to reveal and communicate the seven types of observers is unique and novel in HCI. Next, we discuss the broader implications of this type of work in the context of the recent interest to visual literacy in HCI research [5,44].

Blevis [4] has articulated the value of visual thinking as a way to explore and make sense of the world through the making of digital imagery. In this pictorial, we illustrate how with visual thinking we were able to investigate and communicate the goals and the position a researcher might have when conducting research. Moreover, the images we used were published by researchers that may have not been fully aware of the power of their choice of images, the framing they applied, the treatment they gave, or the ways they collected the images. As visual literacy becomes more important in HCI, we hope our pictorial will help support researchers in being more self aware of the visual decisions they make. We take inspiration from the American photographer Lee Friedlander [50], who often acknowledges the presence of the photographer in his photos, where his own shadow or reflection becomes part of the composition of the image itself. With this comparison, we do not mean that the researcher should always become part of the scene he or she is observing, rather we are hoping to invite researchers to question the position they are taking when conducting HCI research on the home and beyond.

Acknowledgments

All images appearing in this paper were used with the permission of the authors themselves. We thank the Social Sciences and Humanities Research Council (SSHRC) of Canada for their support.

References

1. Rikke Aarhus and Stinne Aaløkke Ballegaard. 2010. Negotiating Boundaries: Managing Disease at Home. Proceedings of the SIGCHI Conference on Human Factors in Computing Systems, ACM, 1223–1232. http://doi.org/10.1145/1753326.1753509
2. Ryan Aipperspach, Ben Hooker, and Allison Woodruff. 2008. The Heterogeneous Home. Proceedings of the 10th International Conference on Ubiquitous Computing, ACM, 222–231. http://doi.org/10.1145/1409635.1409666
3. Morgan G. Ames, Janet Go, Joseph "Jofish" Kaye, and Mirjana Spasojevic. 2010. Making Love in the Network Closet: The Benefits and Work of Family Videochat. Proceedings of the 2010 ACM Conference on Computer Supported Cooperative Work, ACM, 145–154. http://doi.org/10.1145/1718918.1718946
4. Eli Blevis. 2011. Digital Imagery As Meaning and Form in HCI and Design: An Introduction to the Visual Thinking Backpage Gallery. interactions 18, 5: 60–65. http://doi.org/10.1145/2008176.2008190
5. Eli Blevis, Elizabeth Churchill, William Odom, James Pierce, David Roedl, and Ron Wakkary. 2012. Visual Thinking & Digital Imagery. ACM, 2715–2718. http://doi.org/10.1145/2212776.2212703
6. Eli Blevis, Sabrina Hauser, and William Odom. 2015. Sharing the Hidden Treasure in Pictorials. interactions 22, 3: 32–43. http://doi.org/10.1145/2755534
7. Mark Blythe and Andrew Monk. 2002. Notes Towards an Ethnography of Domestic Technology. Proceedings of the 4th Conference on Designing Interactive Systems: Processes, Practices, Methods, and Techniques, ACM, 277–281. http://doi.org/10.1145/778712.778750
8. John Bowers. 2012. The Logic of Annotated Portfolios: Communicating the Value of "Research Through Design." Proceedings of the Designing Interactive Systems Conference, ACM, 68–77. http://doi.org/10.1145/2317956.2317968
9. Andy Crabtree and Tom Rodden. 2004. Domestic Routines and Design for the Home. Computer Supported Cooperative Work (CSCW) 13, 2: 191–220. http://doi.org/10.1023/B:COSU.0000045712.26840.a4
10. Andy Crabtree, Tom Rodden, Terry Hemmings, and Steve Benford. 2003. Finding a Place for UbiComp in the Home. In UbiComp 2003: Ubiquitous Computing, Anind K. Dey, Albrecht Schmidt and Joseph F. McCarthy (eds.). Springer Berlin Heidelberg, 208–226. Retrieved February 14, 2014 from http://link.springer.com.proxy.lib.sfu.ca/chapter/10.1007/978-3-540-39653-6_17
11. Lorenzo Davoli and Johan Redström. 2014. Materializing Infrastructures for Participatory Hacking. Proceedings of the 2014 Conference on Designing Interactive Systems, ACM, 121–130. http://doi.org/10.1145/2598510.2602961
12. Audrey Desjardins and Ron Wakkary. 2016. Living in a Prototype: A Reconfigured Space. Proceedings of the SIGCHI Conference on Human Factors in Computing Systems, ACM Press, 12 pages.
13. Audrey Desjardins, Ron Wakkary, and William Odom. 2015. Investigating Genres and Perspectives in HCI Research on the Home. Proceedings of the 33rd Annual ACM Conference on Human Factors in Computing Systems, ACM, 3073–3082. http://doi.org/10.1145/2702123.2702540
14. Kathryn Elliot, Carman Neustaedter, and Saul Greenberg. 2005. Time, Ownership and Awareness: The Value of Contextual Locations in the Home. In UbiComp 2005: Ubiquitous Computing, Michael Beigl, Stephen Intille, Jun Rekimoto and Hideyuki Tokuda (eds.). Springer Berlin Heidelberg, 251–268. Retrieved

February 15, 2014 from http://link.springer.com.proxy.lib.sfu.ca/chapter/10.1007/11551201_15
15. Jodi Forlizzi, Carl DiSalvo, and Francine Gemperle. 2004. Assistive Robotics and an Ecology of Elders Living Independently in Their Homes. Hum.-Comput. Interact. 19, 1: 25–59. http://doi.org/10.1207/s15327051hci1901&2_3
16. Bill Gaver and John Bowers. 2012. Annotated Portfolios. interactions 19, 4: 40–49. http://doi.org/10.1145/2212877.2212889
17. Bill Gaver, Tony Dunne, and Elena Pacenti. 1999. Design: Cultural probes. interactions 6, 1: 21–29. http://doi.org/10.1145/291224.291235
18. Bill Gaver and Heather Martin. 2000. Alternatives: exploring information appliances through conceptual design proposals. Proceedings of the SIGCHI conference on Human Factors in Computing Systems, ACM, 209–216. http://doi.org/10.1145/332040.332433
19. W. Gaver. 2006. The Video Window: My Life with a Ludic System. Personal Ubiquitous Comput. 10, 2-3: 60–65. http://doi.org/10.1007/s00779-005-0002-2
20. William Gaver. 2009. Designing for Homo Ludens, Still. In (Re)Searching The Digital Bauhaus, Thomas Binder, Jonas Löwgren and Lone Malmborg (eds.). Springer London, 163–178. Retrieved October 22, 2013 from http://link.springer.com.proxy.lib.sfu.ca/chapter/10.1007/978-1-84800-350-7_9
21. William Gaver. 2011. Making spaces: how design workbooks work. Proceedings of the SIGCHI Conference on Human Factors in Computing Systems, ACM, 1551–1560. http://doi.org/10.1145/1978942.1979169
22. William Gaver, John Bowers, Andy Boucher, Andy Law, Sarah Pennington, and Nicholas Villar. 2006. The History Tablecloth: Illuminating Domestic Activity. Proceedings of the 6th Conference on Designing Interactive Systems, ACM, 199–208. http://doi.org/10.1145/1142405.1142437
23. William Gaver, Phoebe Sengers, Tobie Kerridge, Joseph Kaye, and John Bowers. 2007. Enhancing Ubiquitous Computing with User Interpretation: Field Testing the Home Health Horoscope. Proceedings of the SIGCHI Conference on Human Factors in Computing Systems, ACM, 537–546. http://doi.org/10.1145/1240624.1240711
24. William W. Gaver, John Bowers, Kirsten Boehner, et al. 2013. Indoor weather stations: investigating a ludic approach to environmental HCI through batch prototyping. Proceedings of the SIGCHI Conference on Human Factors in Computing Systems, ACM, 3451–3460. http://doi.org/10.1145/2470654.2466474
25. William W. Gaver, John Bowers, Andrew Boucher, et al. 2004. The Drift Table: Designing for Ludic Engagement. CHI '04 Extended Abstracts on Human Factors in Computing Systems, ACM, 885–900. http://doi.org/10.1145/985921.985947
26. Elizabeth Goodman and Daniela Rosner. 2011. From garments to gardens: negotiating material relationships online and "by hand." Proceedings of the SIGCHI Conference on Human Factors in Computing Systems, ACM, 2257–2266. http://doi.org/10.1145/1978942.1979273
27. Erik Grönvall and Nervo Verdezoto. 2013. Beyond Self-monitoring: Understanding Non-functional Aspects of Home-based Healthcare Technology. Proceedings of the 2013 ACM International Joint Conference on Pervasive and Ubiquitous Computing, ACM, 587–596. http://doi.org/10.1145/2493432.2493495
28. John Helmes, Alex S. Taylor, Xiang Cao, Kristina Höök, Peter Schmitt, and Nicolas Villar. 2011. Rudiments 1, 2 & 3: Design Speculations on Autonomy. Proceedings

of the Fifth International Conference on Tangible, Embedded, and Embodied Interaction, ACM, 145–152. http://doi.org/10.1145/1935701.1935730
29. Debby Hindus, Scott D. Mainwaring, Nicole Leduc, Anna Elizabeth Hagström, and Oliver Bayley. 2001. Casablanca: Designing Social Communication Devices for the Home. Proceedings of the SIGCHI Conference on Human Factors in Computing Systems, ACM, 325–332. http://doi.org/10.1145/365024.383749
30. Hilary Hutchinson, Wendy Mackay, Bo Westerlund, et al. 2003. Technology probes: inspiring design for and with families. Proceedings of the SIGCHI Conference on Human Factors in Computing Systems, ACM, 17–24. http://doi.org/10.1145/642611.642616
31. S.S. Intille. 2002. Designing a home of the future. IEEE Pervasive Computing 1, 2: 76–82. http://doi.org/10.1109/MPRV.2002.1012340
32. Tejinder K. Judge, Carman Neustaedter, and Andrew F. Kurtz. 2010. The Family Window: The Design and Evaluation of a Domestic Media Space. Proceedings of the SIGCHI Conference on Human Factors in Computing Systems, ACM, 2361–2370. http://doi.org/10.1145/1753326.1753682
33. Chris Keeney. 2014. Petcam: The World Through the Lens of Our Four-Legged Friends. Princeton Architectural Press, New York.
34. Cory D. Kidd, Robert Orr, Gregory D. Abowd, et al. 1999. The Aware Home: A Living Laboratory for Ubiquitous Computing Research. In Cooperative Buildings. Integrating Information, Organizations, and Architecture, Norbert A. Streitz, Jane Siegel, Volker Hartkopf and Shin'ichi Konomi (eds.). Springer Berlin Heidelberg, 191–198. Retrieved April 3, 2014 from http://link.springer.com.proxy.lib.sfu.ca/chapter/10.1007/10705432_17
35. Julie A. Kientz, Shwetak N. Patel, Brian Jones, Ed Price, Elizabeth D. Mynatt, and Gregory D. Abowd. 2008. The Georgia Tech Aware Home. CHI '08 Extended Abstracts on Human Factors in Computing Systems, ACM, 3675–3680. http://doi.org/10.1145/1358628.1358911
36. David Kirk, Shahram Izadi, Otmar Hilliges, Richard Banks, Stuart Taylor, and Abigail Sellen. 2012. At Home with Surface Computing? Proceedings of the SIGCHI Conference on Human Factors in Computing Systems, ACM, 159–168. http://doi.org/10.1145/2207676.2207699
37. Hee Rin Lee and Selma Šabanović. 2013. Weiser's Dream in the Korean Home: Collaborative Study of Domestic Roles, Relationships, and Ideal Technologies. Proceedings of the 2013 ACM International Joint Conference on Pervasive and Ubiquitous Computing, ACM, 637–646. http://doi.org/10.1145/2493432.2493499
38. Youn-kyung Lim, Daesung Kim, Jaesung Jo, and Jong-bum Woo. 2013. Discovery-Driven Prototyping for User-Driven Creativity. IEEE Pervasive Computing 12, 3: 74–80. http://doi.org/10.1109/MPRV.2012.57
39. Leah Maestri and Ron Wakkary. 2011. Understanding repair as a creative process of everyday design. Proceedings of the 8th ACM conference on Creativity and cognition, ACM, 81–90. http://doi.org/10.1145/2069618.2069633
40. Elizabeth D. Mynatt, Jim Rowan, Sarah Craighill, and Annie Jacobs. 2001. Digital Family Portraits: Supporting Peace of Mind for Extended Family Members. Proceedings of the SIGCHI Conference on Human Factors in Computing Systems, ACM, 333–340. http://doi.org/10.1145/365024.365126
41. Carman Neustaedter and A. J. Bernheim Brush. 2006. "LINC-ing" the Family: The Participatory

Design of an Inkable Family Calendar. Proceedings of the SIGCHI Conference on Human Factors in Computing Systems, ACM, 141–150. http://doi.org/10.1145/1124772.1124796
42. Jon O'Brien, Tom Rodden, Mark Rouncefield, and John Hughes. 1999. At Home with the Technology: An Ethnographic Study of a Set-top-box Trial. ACM Trans. Comput.-Hum. Interact. 6, 3: 282–308. http://doi.org/10.1145/329693.329698
43. William T. Odom, Abigail J. Sellen, Richard Banks, et al. 2014. Designing for Slowness, Anticipation and Re-visitation: A Long Term Field Study of the Photobox. Proceedings of the 32Nd Annual ACM Conference on Human Factors in Computing Systems, ACM, 1961–1970. http://doi.org/10.1145/2556288.2557178
44. Kyle Overton, Omar Sosa-Tzec, Nancy Smith, et al. 2016. Visual Literacy & HCI. ACM Press.
45. Catherine Plaisant, Aaron Clamage, Hilary Browne Hutchinson, Benjamin B. Bederson, and Allison Druin. 2006. Shared Family Calendars: Promoting Symmetry and Accessibility. ACM Trans. Comput.-Hum. Interact. 13, 3: 313–346. http://doi.org/10.1145/1183456.1183458
46. Daniela K. Rosner and Kimiko Ryokai. 2009. Reflections on Craft: Probing the Creative Process of Everyday Knitters. Proceedings of the Seventh ACM Conference on Creativity and Cognition, ACM, 195–204. http://doi.org/10.1145/1640233.1640264
47. Abigail Sellen, Richard Harper, Rachel Eardley, et al. 2006. HomeNote: Supporting Situated Messaging in the Home. Proceedings of the 2006 20th Anniversary Conference on Computer Supported Cooperative Work, ACM, 383–392. http://doi.org/10.1145/1180875.1180933
48. Yolande Strengers. 2011. Negotiating everyday life: The role of energy and water consumption feedback. Journal of Consumer Culture 11, 3: 319–338. http://doi.org/10.1177/1469540511417994
49. Laurel Swan, Alex S. Taylor, and Richard Harper. 2008. Making Place for Clutter and Other Ideas of Home. ACM Trans. Comput.-Hum. Interact. 15, 2: 9:1–9:24. http://doi.org/10.1145/1375761.1375764
50. John Szarkowski, Rineke Dijkstra, and Lee Friedlander. 2005. Lee Friedlander: Self Portrait. The Museum of Modern Art, New York, New York.
51. Alex S. Taylor, Richard Harper, Laurel Swan, Shahram Izadi, Abigail Sellen, and Mark Perry. 2007. Homes That Make Us Smart. Personal Ubiquitous Comput. 11, 5: 383–393. http://doi.org/10.1007/s00779-006-0076-5
52. Alex S. Taylor and Laurel Swan. 2005. Artful systems in the home. Proceedings of the SIGCHI Conference on Human Factors in Computing Systems, ACM, 641–650. http://doi.org/10.1145/1054972.1055060
53. Alex S. Taylor, Susan P. Wyche, and Joseph "Jofish" Kaye. 2008. Pottering by Design. Proceedings of the 5th Nordic Conference on Human-computer Interaction: Building Bridges, ACM, 363–372. http://doi.org/10.1145/1463160.1463200
54. Peter Tolmie, James Pycock, Tim Diggins, Allan MacLean, and Alain Karsenty. 2002. Unremarkable computing. Proceedings of the SIGCHI Conference on Human Factors in Computing Systems, ACM, 399–406. http://doi.org/10.1145/503376.503448
55. Quan T. Tran, Gina Calcaterra, and Elizabeth D. Mynatt. 2005. COOK'S COLLAGE. In Home-Oriented Informatics and Telematics, Andy Sloane (ed.). Springer US, 15–32. Retrieved April 3, 2014 from http://link.springer.com.proxy.lib.sfu.ca/chapter/10.1007/11402985_2
56. Ron Wakkary, Audrey Desjardins, and Sabrina Hauser. 2015. Unselfconscious Interaction: A Conceptual

Construct. Interacting with Computers: iwv018. http://doi.org/10.1093/iwc/iwv018

57. Ron Wakkary and Leah Maestri. 2007. The resourcefulness of everyday design. Proceedings of the 6th ACM SIGCHI conference on Creativity & Cognition, ACM, 163–172. http://doi.org/10.1145/1254960.1254984
58. Ron Wakkary and Karen Tanenbaum. 2009. A sustainable identity: the creativity of an everyday designer. Proceedings of the SIGCHI Conference on Human Factors in Computing Systems, ACM, 365–374. http://doi.org/10.1145/1518701.1518761
59. Susan P. Wyche and Rebecca E. Grinter. 2009. Extraordinary Computing: Religion As a Lens for Reconsidering the Home. Proceedings of the SIGCHI Conference on Human Factors in Computing Systems, ACM, 749–758. http://doi.org/10.1145/1518701.1518817
60. Susan P. Wyche, Alex Taylor, and Joseph Kaye. 2007. Pottering: A Design-oriented Investigation. CHI '07 Extended Abstracts on Human Factors in Computing Systems, ACM, 1893–1898. http://doi.org/10.1145/1240866.1240917

Thing Ethnography: Doing Design Research with Non-Humans

Elisa Giaccardi
Delft University of Technology
Landbergstraat 15
Delft 2628 CE, NL
e.giaccardi@tudelft.nl

Chris Speed
University of Edinburgh
78 Westport
Edinburgh, EH1 2LE UK
c.speed@ed.ac.uk

Nazli Cila
Amsterdam University of Applied Sciences
Wibautstraat 2-4
Amsterdam 1091 GM, NL
n.cila@hva.nl

Melissa Caldwell
University of California, Santa Cruz
353 Social Sciences 1
Santa Cruz, CA 95064 USA
lissa@ucsc.edu

DIS 2016, June 04-08, 2016, Brisbane, QLD, Australia
 ISBN 978-1-4503-4031-1/16/06...$15.00
DOI: http://dx.doi.org/10.1145/2901790.2901905

Abstract
Drawing from a study of everyday home practices from a material objects' perspective, this paper examines the potential that a thing ethnography holds for both design and anthropology. In doing so, the paper challenges anthropocentric assumptions about the world, and opens up ways of understanding relationships among people, objects and use practices that would be difficult to elicit through traditional observations and interviews alone.

Authors Keywords
Internet of Things; thing ethnography; data worlds; use practices; thing perspective; things as co-ethnographers; non-anthropocentrism.

ACM Classification Keywords
H.5.m. Information interfaces and presentation (e.g., HCI): Miscellaneous.

Introduction
As humans, we shape objects, and objects shape us in return. Acknowledging this ongoing interaction among people and objects calls for approaches in both design and anthropology that give both parties an equal role. However in current HCI and design research, humans take a central place [6, 8, 12]. This comes with the assumption that possibilities for framing and solving problems are bounded only to human imagination and capabilities.

In this paper instead, we argue that the perspective of a 'thing' that is actively situated within relations with other entities, and that has different trajectories than humans [7], can present new ways for humans and non-humans of collaboratively framing and solving problems.

Equipped with software and sensors, things can begin to provide access to fields and perspectives that would not be otherwise attainable from human ethnographers. We call the collection and interpretation of these perspectives *thing ethnography*. These accounts emerge at the intersection of the data and trajectories that things give access to, and the theoretically informed analysis that humans bring to it.

Motivation and Related Work

Within a user-centered design approach, the role of objects is usually to support people to imagine, discuss, and shape future practices at project time [2]. By extension, design becomes a kind of stabilizing process through which future practice(s) are imagined and realized [2, p. 122].

The perspective explored in our work by the notion of thing ethnography instead troubles distinctions between humans and non-humans, producers and produced, and in so doing supports ways of understanding and designing that take place *after*, *with* and *beyond* the design work at project time [3, 4, 5, 9, 11].

Ontological reworkings of the asymmetry between people and things are especially relevant for HCI work in the emerging field of the Internet of Things. These reworkings are necessary not just to interpret the data that objects collect, the stories they reveal, and the interventions they make in the lives of the people that use them [10]. They also offer design nuanced ways of thinking about and intervening into socio-material arrangements, most notably those between designers and users.

The objects in this study are mundane and everyday to humans, and as such, do not do the same work of ontological flattening that more autonomous or infrastructural things (such a washing machine or an electrical outlet) might produce. Yet, by harbouring different ideas about expertise and skills, and by redistributing design and control between project time and use practices, a thing perspective offers a 'design alternative' [1] based on a fundamentally different theoretical, methodological and even ethical relationship between humans and non-humans.

Pictorial's Visual Communication

The visual communication strategy adopted in this pictorial combines visual ethnographic narratives with abstract visualizations. Through this combination we intend to reinforce the reading and understanding of the insights generated at the intersection of the data and trajectories that things gave access to and our theoretically informed analysis.

Insights are distilled and offered at each page according to three overarching themes (*movement*, *temporality*, *agency*). These themes emerged from the analysis of the data collected by means of intelligent cameras from the 'perspective' of material objects (about methodology and analysis, see the following two sections).

In the lateral bars, emerging themes are explained and discussed (each theme is expressed by two insights), therefore visually bridging the concise presentation of individual insights to the consideration of broader matters of concern for both ethnographers and designers in HCI and interaction design.

Using Autographers to access a thing perspective

Focusing on everyday home practices, we selected three mundane objects: a kettle, a fridge, and a cup. Because these objects are often in proximity, it was thought that together they would reveal insights not just about themselves but also about their relationships with each other – that is, about *unexpected horizontal arrangements of various practices*. We refer to the data concerning these arrangements and thus the ecosystems in which things become thoroughly imbricated as *data worlds*.

We equipped these objects with small logging cameras called Autographers. Five households were given three Autographers for two days. Autographers provided detailed information about the use patterns of particular objects and their trajectories throughout space and time, as well as data on parallel activities and objects. What was especially important was that the Autographers were meant to capture both the intentional and unintentional use of objects – and thus the ecosystems in which they come to participate 'after design' – from the unique perspective of those objects.

As a form of intelligent technology, Autographers autonomously take pictures and capture data via five sensors (e.g., accelerometer to determine movement, color sensor, magnetometer, thermometer, and PIR proximity sensor). Autographers lack shutter buttons, and photographs are taken autonomously by the camera, rather than according to deliberate choices or intervention by the photographer. As such, these images captured events and vantage points that might have evaded the researcher. Autographer data revealed additional objects that were related to those activities, besides the key objects initially selected. Autographer data illuminated unexpected and otherwise invisible relationships among objects – a perspective that we could not elicit through observation and interviews alone [5].

Revealing things' data worlds

Autographers collected 3000+ photographs depicting interconnected practices around participants' cup, kettle and fridge. Time-lapse details of things' data worlds were aggregated into a visual narrative. These were analyzed in two ways: (1) *timelines*, which help us examine the sequence of events, temporal order and trajectories of objects, and (2) *movie clips* which showed the same scene from the perspective of our three objects, helping us explore what these objects 'experience' within the a specific time frame and context.

MOVEMENTS OF THINGS
[insight #1 and #2]

As the data showed, the things that inhabited our participants' kitchens and dining rooms demonstrated different degrees of **dynamism** and **emplacement**.

There are differences between things that move and things that stay in one place or remain within a narrowly defined area of space.

Paying attention to movement illuminates how things exist in relationships with one another: they inhabit communities of things and practices that are at times separate, and at times overlapping. This understanding invites questions about the ecosystems in which they are embedded.

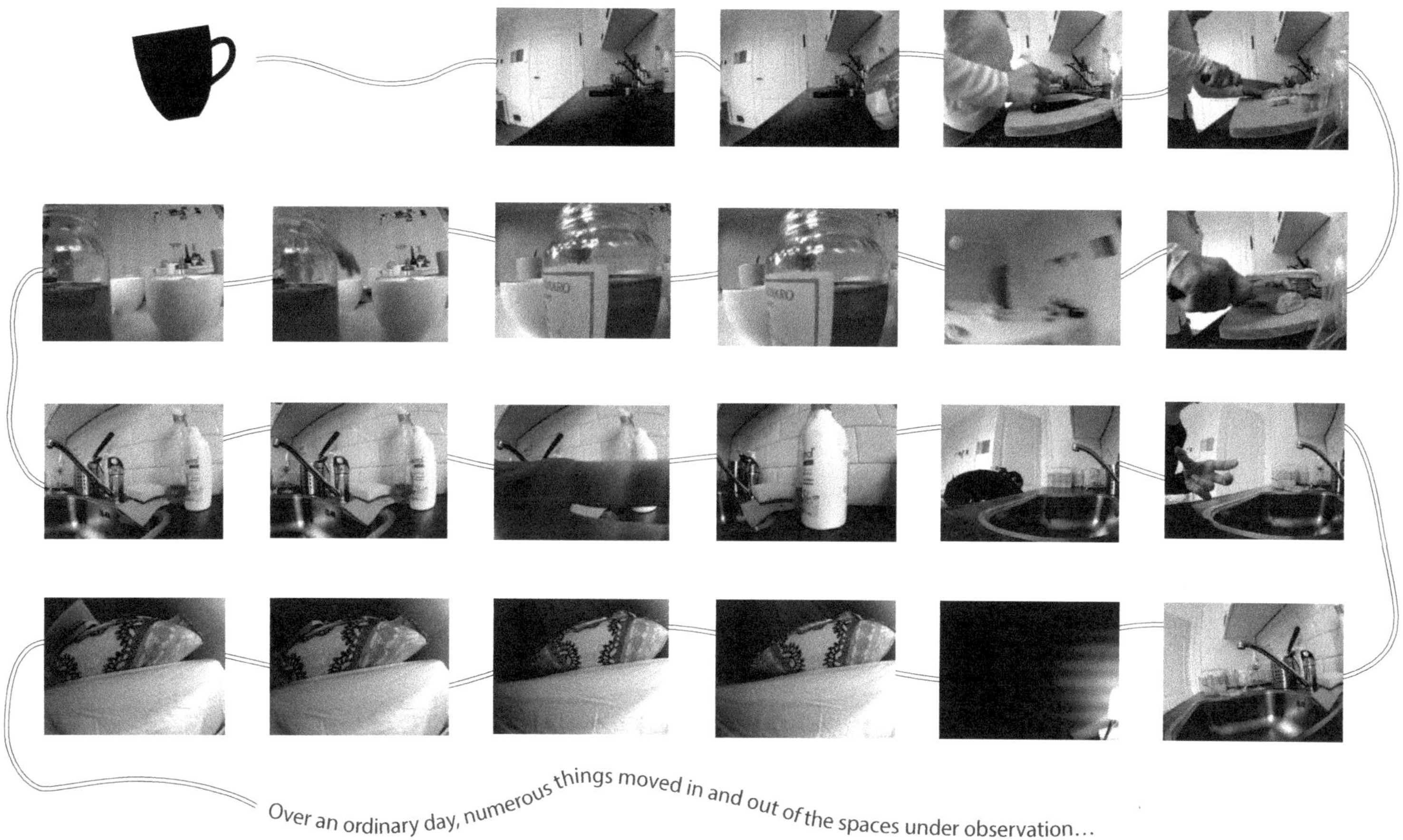

MOVEMENT

INSIGHT #1: Things that move

Things that move through space occupy multiple ecosystems and are also the connector among these ecosystems.

A simple table is simultaneously a thing that is actualized in a moment of praxis (i.e., when it is used as a flat top for eating) and a thing that has possibilities for other practices and futures beyond those for which it was intended, such as when it is turned into a convival tool for conversation.

MOVEMENT

INSIGHT #2: Things that do not move

Things that do not move through space can be subject to movement through time.

TEMPORALITY OF THINGS
[insight #3 and #4]

While the things under view in our study could be located in discrete temporal **moments**, these things also enjoyed their own, unique temporal **rhythms**.

Individual things do not have the same experience of time.

The different temporalities that unite and separate things from one another and from their human partners present opportunities to consider what is it about the nature of things (or their ecosystem) that enables them to create particular temporalities or make particular temporalities apparent or even visible.

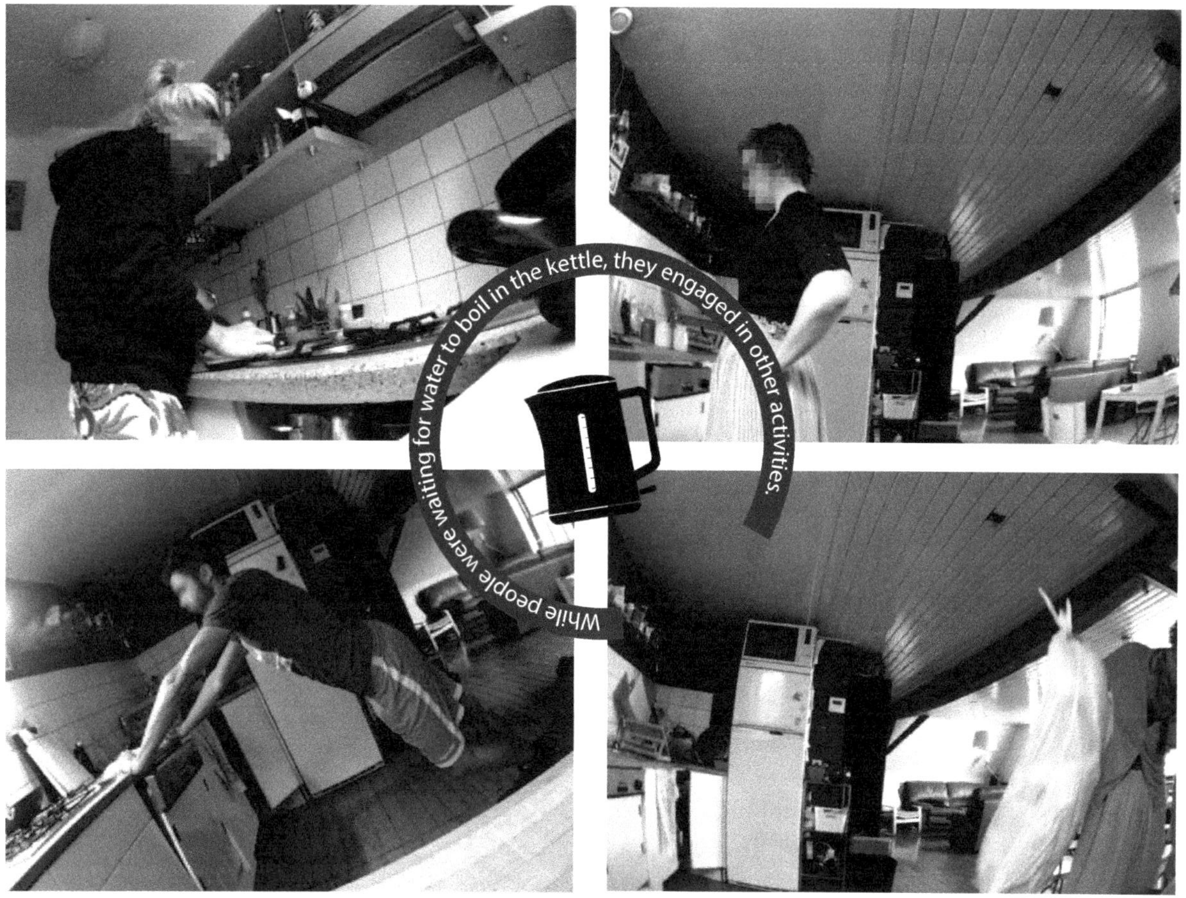

TEMPORALITY

INSIGHT #3: Things that make time

Some things create empty time that needs to be filled by other things.

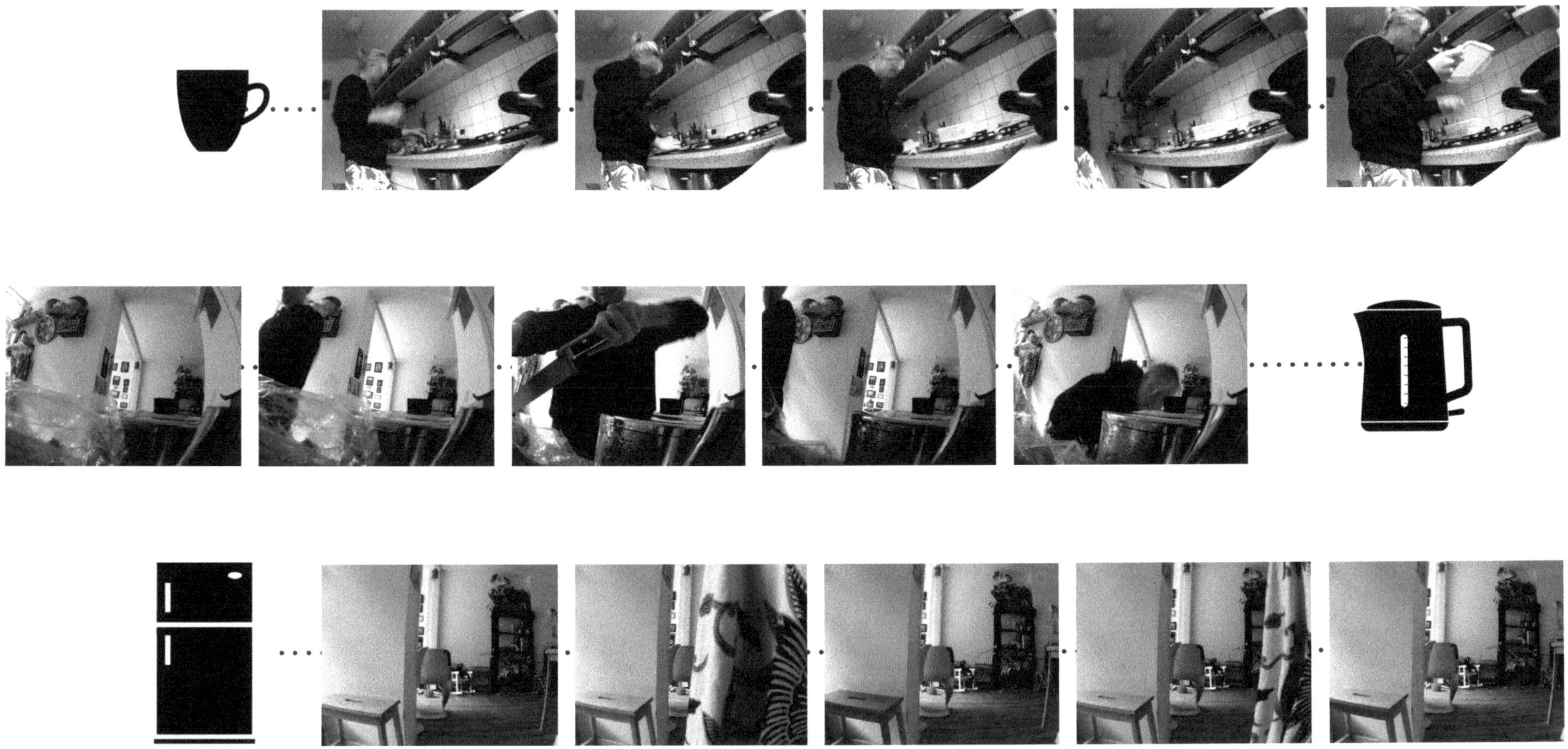

While cooking and waiting for the water to boil in the kettle, other activities filled the time: getting food out of the fridge, cutting, making a telephone call.

TEMPORALITY

INSIGHT #4: Things that fill time

Things occupy time and take up time.
In some cases, things fill time.

AGENCY OF THINGS
[insight #5 and #6]

The qualities of mobility and activity revealed by our data provoke intriguing questions about the nature of agency that inheres in things.

By changing the spaces and times of their own existence and of other entities with which they come into contact, things seem to exhibit an agency of their own.

Paying attention to the social relationships among things opens up spaces for rethinking not just how and where potentialities emerge, but whether there are dynamics of both **spontaneity** and **purposefulness** outside a subjective human experience, and where power is located.

When participants elect to make a call while they are waiting for their tea to steep, it seems as if it is the inanimate thing that is compelling the human to action.

AGENCY

INSIGHT #5: Things with power

At times, things seem as if they are compelling the human partner to respond; for example, when the human is confronted with empty time.

Participants were not aware of mundane practice such as storing their evening tea in a separate, sealed container.

AGENCY

INSIGHT #6: Things with politics

Things may capture what might seem unremarkable to the researcher orparticipant. Thus, as through a peephole, they are crucial for filling in the gaps and revealing to humans unexpected moments and unaware practices.

Conclusions

This paper contributes an initial exploration towards a non-anthropocentric methodology for using things as co-ethnographers. By expanding on the vocabulary proposed in [5], the terms *thing ethnography* and *data worlds* are introduced for the first time to the HCI and interaction design community, in the attempt to promote a more holistic way of understanding relationships among people, objects and practices.

The visual strategy experimented in this pictorial aims to reinforce such understanding. By visually combining findings and discussion, the pictorial intends to support the idea that in a thing ethnography insights are generated at the intersection of the data and trajectories that non-humans give access to, and the theoretically informed analysis that humans bring to it.

Finally, the paper usefully summarizes insights on the *movement*, *temporality* and *agency* of things that were revealed in [5], substantiating them with evidence from the original Autographers' data. We believe these insights contribute to illuminate future ontological and methodological reworkings of the asymmetry between people and things. These reworkings are especially relevant for design research in the emerging field of the Internet of Things, where data may be more diverse, complex or harder for humans to access and understand than images.

Acknowledgements

We would like to thank the reviewers for their insightful comments. This research was funded by the MIT Skoltech Initiative, Ideas Lab program (2014-2015).

References

1. Cross, N. (2007). *Designerly Ways of Knowing*, Basel: Birkhauser.
2. Donovan, J. and Gunn, W. (2012), 'Moving from Objects to Possibilities', in W. Gunn & J. Donovan (eds) *Design Anthropology*, Farnham, UK: Ashgate Publishing Company.
3. Binder, T., De Michelis, G., Ehn, P., Jacucci, G., Linde, P., Wagner, I. (2011), *Design Things*, Cambridge, MA: MIT Press.
4. Ehn, P. (2008), 'Participation in Design Things', in *Proc. PDC '08*, 92-101.
5. Giaccardi, E., Speed, C., Cila, N., Caldwell, M. (2016) 'Things as Co-ethnographers: Implications of a Thing Perspective for Design and Anthropology,' in R.C. Smith et al. (eds) *Design Anthropology Futures,* London: Bloomsbury (in press).
6. Greenbaum, J. and Kyng, M. (1991), *Design at Work: Cooperative Design of Computer Systems*, Hillsdale, NJ: L. Erlbaum Associates.
7. Grusin, R. (ed) (2015) *The Nonhuman Turn*, Minneapolis, MN: University of Minnesota Press.
8. ISO 9241-210 (2010), Human-centred design for interactive systems, http://www.iso.org/iso/catalogue_detail.htm?csnumber=52075
9. Kuijer, L. & Giaccardi, E. (2015), 'Considering Artifacts as Co-performers of Practice', in *Symposium on Animals, Automated Devices and Ecosystems: Dynamic Non-humans in Theories of Social Practice*, 9-10 October, Barcelona, Spain.
10. McVeigh-Schultz, J., Stein, J., Watson, J., Fisher, S. (2012), 'Extending the Lifelog to Non-human Subjects: Ambient Storytelling for Human-Object Relationships', in *Proc. MM'12*, 1205-08.
11. Redström, J. (2012), 'Introduction: Defining Moments', in W. Gunn and J. Donovan (eds), *Design Anthropology*, Farnham, UK: Ashgate Publishing Company.
12. Schuler, D. and Namioka, A. (1993), *Participatory Design: Principles and Practices*, Hillsdale, NJ: L. Erlbaum Associates.

Design Proposal for A Wireless Derouter: Speculatively Engaging Digitally Disconnected Space

James Pierce
University of California, Berkeley
Berkeley Center for New Media
and Jacobs Institute for Design
Innovation
pierjam@berkeley.edu

Abstract
This Pictorial uses design as a way to imaginatively and critically engage with digital disconnectivity as the obverse reaction to an increasingly hyperconnected, sped-up, and always-on digital world. Design is practiced here as a mode of inquiry and the outcomes presented as conceptual tools.

ACM Classification Keywords
Design; speculative design; wireless derouting

DIS 2016, June 04-08, 2016, Brisbane, QLD, Australia
© 2016 ACM. ISBN 978-1-4503-4031-1/16/06 $15.00
DOI: http://dx.doi.org/10.1145/2901790.2901908

This document uses design as a way to imaginatively and critically engage with digital disconnectivity as the obverse reaction to an increasingly hyperconnected, sped-up, and always-on digital world. Design is practiced here as a mode of inquiry, and the outcomes of this inquiry are presented as conceptual tools. With roughly equal parts criticism, cultural archiving, and speculative imagination, this work engages recent cultural countertrends of disconnecting, unplugging, and digital detoxing. Key issues articulated by researchers, artists, and designers include digital overload and distraction, anti-sociality and inauthenticity, and pervasive surveillance and privacy invasion.[1]

Critics have in turn reacted to nascent countertrends, raising concerns about the implicit politics of disconnecting. Some have observed that the strongest advocates for disconnecting are, ironically, among the privileged few most readily served by and invested in digital technology.[2]

This work brings together these issues, not to immediately resolve them, but to engage them as matters of concern and to imagine alternatives through design.[3] For this reason this work proceeds speculatively and tentatively, raising questions and concerns along the way and without (yet) arriving at firm conclusions or affirming specific design interventions.

What is offered instead is a catalog of concerns, a repository of ideas, and an interference device for clearing space to both populate and interrogate an emerging design field of digital disconnectivity. This field radiates outward from a design proposal for a wireless derouter, a device which disrupts wireless signals to create digitally disconnected spaces free from Wi-Fi, cellular, GPS, and other regulated radio frequencies. This proposal sketches the practical embodied and embedded operation of a wireless derouter along with models for conceptualizing disconnected space and ways of structuring and communicating its possible social and cultural functions.

As a proposal created for designers and researchers, the wireless derouter exhibits oscillatory conceptual functions. It functions as a simple antenna for amplifying and transmitting ideas. And it functions as an anti-antenna— an interference device—which clears space for new receptions: interrogations, critiques, and the generation of new speculative proposals for the future.

Design Proposals as Inquiry / The Proposal Document as Design Form

The rise of speculative, critical, and conceptual traditions of design has entailed experimentation with new design techniques and forms. Within these design practices, the conceptual design proposal stands out as a key tool and format for presenting design inquiry.[4] The purpose of the conceptual design proposal is not always to simply document finished work or to serve as an intermediary step within a cohesive ongoing design process. Instead the conceptual design proposal must be properly grasped as a finished unfinished form—one poised to inspire and aid in the generation of additional thoughts, forms, and interventions. Typically the goal of the speculative or critical design proposal is not to definitively affirm or advocate for the implementation of a design and its subsequent embedding within everyday contexts. Instead the function may be more vaguely and loosely articulated: speculation, critique, reflection, provocation, debate, dissensus (and always potentially more).[5] *Nonstandard academic publication formats, such as this DIS Pictorial, offer a much needed outlet for such work.*

Design Proposal for a Wireless Derouter: User's Guide

The genre and format of the design proposal accommodates diverse aesthetic and discursive styles, conceptual approaches, and methodological commitments. A few preliminary points will help the reader navigate the specifics of this design proposal.

Subtle and uncertain absurdity. This work employs visual and rhetorical language commonly found in design proposals from architecture, urban planning, and industrial and interaction design. Yet the content of the proposal is carefully poised between plausible and absurd, complicated by a number of continually shifting technical, legal, economic, social, and cultural factors.

Exaggerated commitment. Whereas many design proposals explore a diversity of possibilities, this proposal ostensibly commits to a single design direction: wireless derouting for the construction of disconnected personal, social, public, and civic spaces. But it must be understood that the conceptual point of the wireless derouter is to help clear space for imaginatively and critically engaging (and disengaging) digital disconnectivity.

Hybridizing designerly and scholarly forms. The first portion of this document is a design proposal for a wireless derouter composed of illustrations and text. The second portion—of equal importance — consists of notes, elaborations, and commentary. When faced with the question of whether the design proposal is design or scholarship, a suitable response is *why not both?*

Digital Connectivity

For many—but certainly not for all or equally—digital connectivity is no longer a luxury but a basic right.[6] Digital connectivity is rapidly becoming naturalized within industrialized contexts. Wi-Fi, cellular phones, and global positioning system (GPS) have joined television and AM/FM radio within the field of ubiquitous electromagnetic waves. Mobile devices allow virtually everything digital to be accessed anywhere, anytime, with the click of a button or swipe of a finger. Pockets of digitally disconnected space have become the exception—ones which we expect will soon be remedied.

Digital Disconnectivity

The countertrend is disconnecting. Sitting uncomfortably alongside digital connectivity are anxieties about an increasing pace of life, detachment from the physical world, social isolation, and inauthentic identity. This has given rise to buzzwords naming cultural countercurrents: digital detoxes, unplugging, disconnecting.[7]

On the surface disconnecting appears well-aligned with critiques of techno-utopian faith in technology and the neoliberal imperative to marketize every aspect of life.[8] Yet some argue that hyperconnectivity is nothing more than a first world problem of luxury, that the contemporary rhetoric around disconnecting is merely a means of recharging a productive capitalist workforce, and that the creation of alternative slow, disconnected spaces can only exist within the inequitable social relations of a speedy, hyperconnected world.[9]

Map of Digitally Connected Space

Alternatives to Ubiquitous Connectivity / Diversifications of Disconnectivity

There are clear signs of resistance alongside general acceptance of ubiquitous digital connectivity and enthusiasm for nascent and emerging technological paradigms, such as the Internet of Things (IoT) and "the cloud."[10] What alternatives exist to pervasive digital connectivity, always-on-ness, and one-click access to everything digital? How can we begin to map the landscape of resistances to hyperconnectivity, and the different values and interests at stake? Can we transcend the polarization of enthusiastic techno-utopians, on the one hand, and curmudgeonly luddites on the other? Or amplify this polarization to offer insight into desirable and undesirable futures?

The Interstitial Model

Occassional disruption to everyday routine is normal. Pervasive connectivity is in fact already punctuated by minor discontinuities and momentary interruptions. Interstices of disconnectivity are to be supported and embraced, rather than merely begrudgingly accepted as necessities.

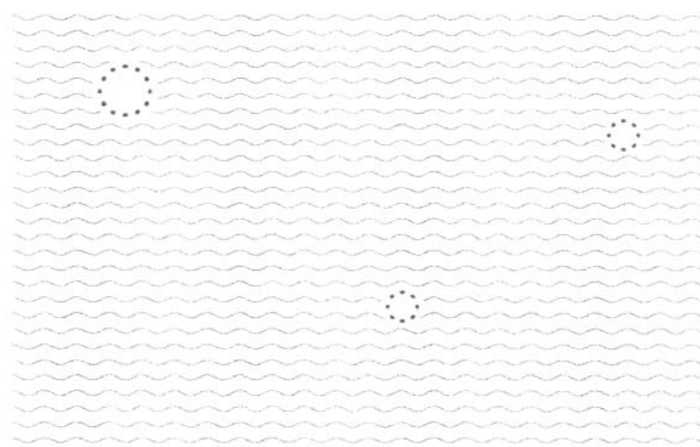

The Zoning Model

Disconnectivity is a legitimate personal, social, cultural, and economic need. As such, it must be zoned and regulated much like property, the built environment, and public infrastructure. However care must be taken to prevent discriminatory and detrimental disconnected zoning practices.

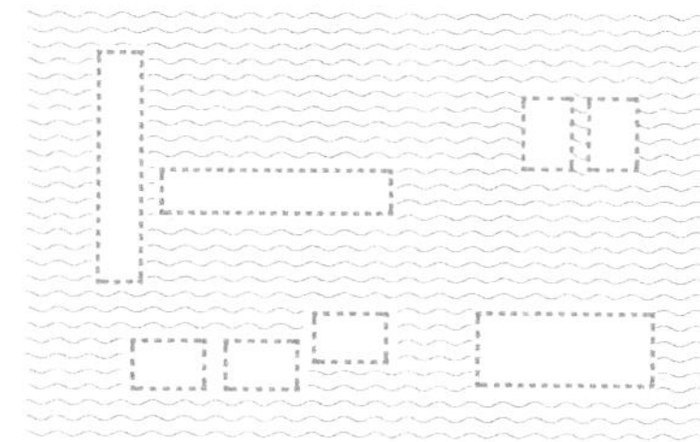

The Preservation/Restoration Model

Disconnected "dead zones" are rapidly disappearing.[11] The time has come to preserve and restore disconnected areas. Disconnected spaces of the future will serve social and ecological functions similar to the urban parks and natural preserves of today.[12]

The Inverse Model

The scales have tipped too far on the side of connectivity. It is time for an inversion. With certain exceptions such as emergency service connections, connectivity will be restricted to social and economic hubs. Connected space becomes the exception not the norm.

The Islands of Respite Model

Within the pervasive sea of connectivity, islands of disconnectivity are needed as alternative spaces for recuperation and refuge from our contemporary high-speed, hyperconnected, and always-on pace of life.

The Fuzzy Logic Model

The problematic polarization of connectivity/disconnectivity flows from the application of the binary logic of digital technology to the sociocultural level. A more integrative, pluralistic model is needed that recognizes spectrums and multiplicities of connectivity/disconnectivity.

Disrupting Digital Connectivity: Legal Matters

February 2012, Philadelphia, Pennsylvania, USA. A disconnectionist vigilante uses an illegal cell phone jammer to disrupt passengers on public buses who are engaged in obnoxiously loud phone conversations. News of the incident spreads through the media and "cell phone jammer" becomes a Google top 10 search over the weekend.[13] The U.S. Federal Communications Commission (FCC) issues a statement in response reminding consumers that it is illegal to use any device that "blocks, jams, or interferes with authorized communications." The FCC "has a zero tolerance policy in this area and will take aggressive action against its violators."[14]

Around the world, it is illegal to possess or operate devices that create digitally disconnected space by actively interfering with licensed radio waves. If digital connectivity is now a basic human right, a price that is paid is absolute disconnectivity is barred by law.[15]

Disconnective Counterproducts

There is more than a glimmer of consumer need and desire for disconnective technologies. A range of consumer products currently exist, from enhanced Do Not Disturb features on smartphones to productivity tools that block distracting websites and software applications. Artists, designers, and activists continue to create works that ambiguously function as practical disconnective tools.[16]

Wireless Derouting: Speculatively Engaging the Mundane

Many speculative designs are predicated on as-yet undeveloped technologies (science fiction), far-fetched social scenarios of use (social fiction), or both. The power of design speculation comes from its potential to imagine compelling yet unlikely or impossible scenarios becoming lived reality: actually materially and socially embedded within contexts of routine, ordinary, even mundane use.

Yet speculative design can also imaginatively engage the mundane through the design of technologies that are both technically feasible and socially plausible. Illegal technologies are one crucial area where speculative designs can be offered as a way to imaginatively and critically ask what-ifs and why-nots.

What if it were legal to use devices that actively block radio waves to create disconnected space? How would the construction of new interfaces, systems, and environments develop if such technologies were legalized? As speculative anti-infrastructure, how might wireless derouters function to create digitally disconnected spaces?

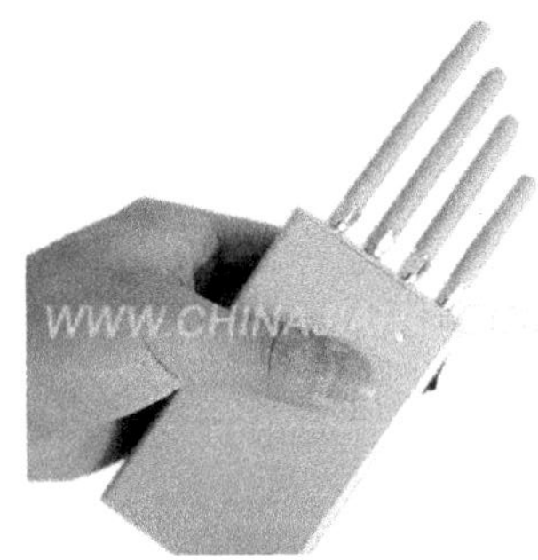

Portable GPS Jammer, 2G and 3G Mobile Phone Signal Jammer (US$ 115). Isolating Signal Bandwidths: GPS: 1500-1600Mhz , CDMA + GSM: 850-960Mhz, DCS (PHS) + CDMA + GSM: 1805-1990MHZ, 3G: 2110-2170MHz. Range of up to 15 meters. Chinajiaho.com.

A Wireless Derouter

Wireless derouters enable the construction of digitally disconnected spaces: spaces free from email, phone, SMS, Facebook, Twitter, Netflix, Instagram, Tinder, Wikipedia, Google search and myriad other applications. While such applications are useful and enabling, their unrestricted ubiquity means there is no longer the option to have strict disconnectivity. Wireless Derouters offer the possibility of something refreshingly different: wireless voids filled with digitally disconnected things.

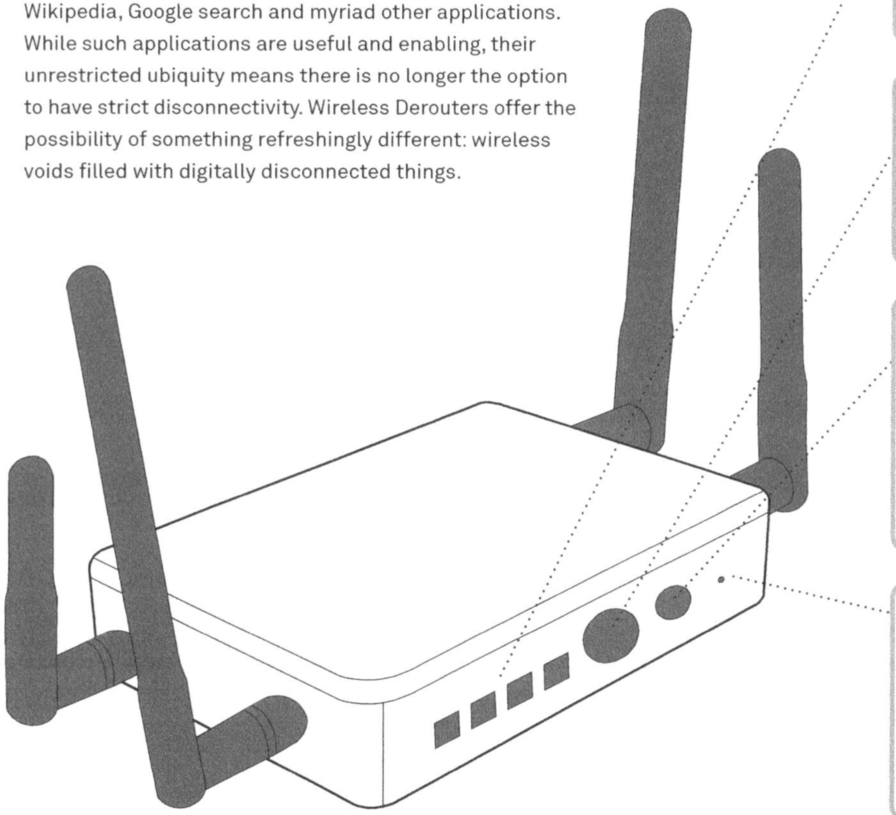

Signal Derouting Select

4 sets of wireless frequencies may be selected independently for derouting: WIFI/Bluetooth, 3G, 4G/LTE, and Cellular (CDMA/GSM/DCS/PCS).

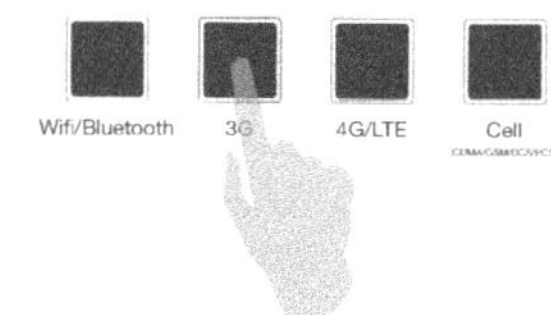

Distance (Radius of Disconnectivity)

The distance can be adjusted to create a sphere of disconnectivity with a radius ranging from 0.5 feet / 0.15 meters to 5 feet / 1.5 meters.

Readjustment Delay

The readjustment delay deters disabling the derouter by adjusting the distance to 0 or deselecting signals. The period of time required for a readjustment to take effect can be set from 15 seconds to 5 minutes.

Readjustment Delay Reset

The readjustment delay reset deters readjusting the signal select or readjustment delay.[17] Prior to making a readjustment you must press the reset using a small tool such as a paper clip.

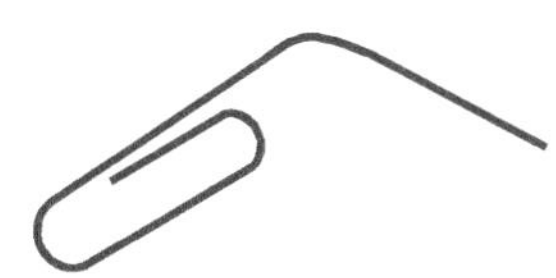

Wireless Nonspots[18] and Disconnected Nooks[19]
Wireless derouters can be used to construct permanent or temporary disconnected spaces for leisure, relaxation, work, socialization, and contemplation.

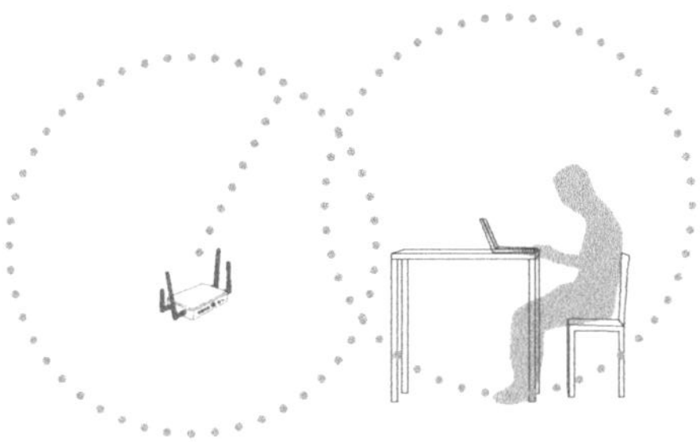

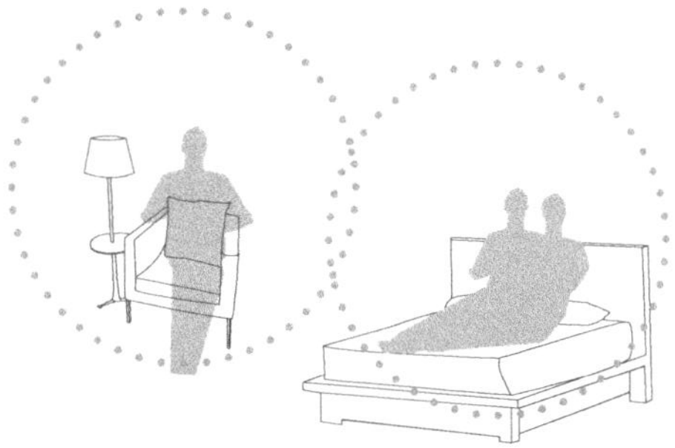

Disconected Public and Third Spaces
Disconnected spaces can be created for social and civic engagement, such as public squares, parks, libraries, bars, coffee shops, and places of worship.

Disconnected Events
Temporary disconnected spaces can also be created for events such as festivals, parties, conferences, work meetings, exhibitions, and performances.

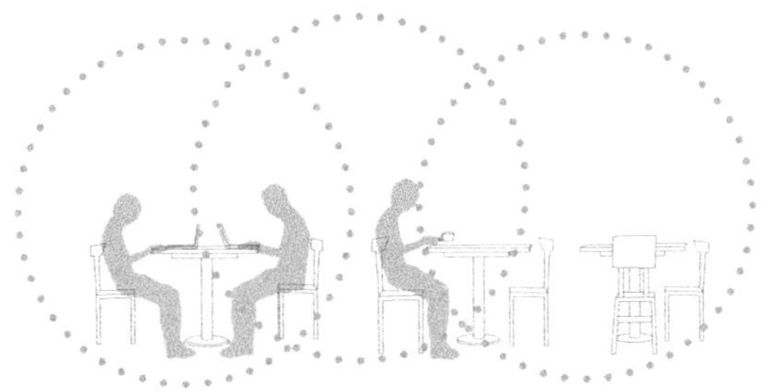

Communicating Disconnected Space
New systems will be needed to communicate digitally disconnected places and temporalities. Visual signage can be used to demarcate disconnected space and its social functions.

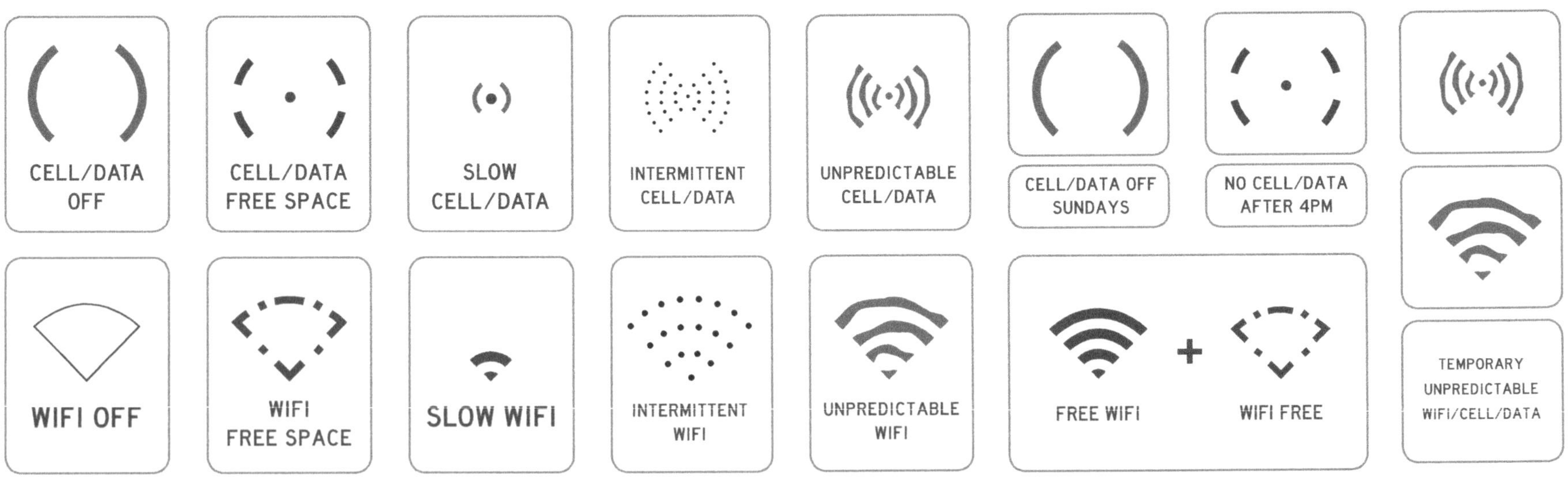

Off | Free (From) | Slow | Intermittent | Unpredictable | Temporal and Mixed Spaces

Concluding Transition

This work is unapologetically inconclusive and incomplete. The ideas that have been drawn here are tentative not definitive. The forms that have been presented appear preliminary and schematic. And a clear political position has not been explicitly advocated but rather suggested through skeptical and ambivalent proposals. But the conceptual and material lacunae formed by this design proposal are intentional. For they form potential: critical potential, speculative potential, even conventional, affirmative design potential.

Design is a tool for solving problems and improving our conditions. But design is also a tool for imagining, questioning, and reorienting. This proposal has been working as a conceptual anntena to detect and amplify clusters of concern, and as an interference device to clear space to create openings. Three clusters of concerns will draw this text to a close and transition into Notes, Elaboration, and Commentary, while hopefully continuing to extend beyond the page into other modes and forms of engagement.

1. The politics of disconnecting. Digital disconnectivity may momentarily feel freeing, but this does not mean this is the case always or for everyone equally. What are the implicit and explicit politics of disconnective technologies? Are they a politics to support, to critique, or both?

2. The potential for actual wireless derouters. Is a wireless derouter a good design concept? Would people actually want to use it? Maybe... or maybe not. One thing is for certain: it is difficult to practically and empirically investigate wireless derouting given the substantial legal barriers to operating devices that actively block radio waves.

3. Digital disconnectivity and the more and less distant futures. At this moment those of us living in a digitally hyper-connected world spend much of our time online. Increasingly our things are created, stored, and accessed in the cloud. All of this intensifies with predictions and promises of an internet of things, augmented realities, and artificial intelligences. What roles might disconnectivity play in the less and more distant futures? Amid growing concerns over intrusive and discriminatory surveillance, what opportunities lie in designing digitally disconnected spaces and things? If head, hand, and eye mounted displays and sensors continue to augment daily reality, will this intensify the need and desire for disconnected spaces and things? And if our future becomes filled with artificially intelligent domestic servants and companions, how will they feel about digitally disconnected space?

A wireless derouter is one specific direction to pursue towards both critical and affirmative ends. Yet perhaps the more powerful function of a wireless derouter is to serve as but one strong point within a broader space of possibilities. This proposals has worked to help plot a broader space with a set of models as alternatives to ubiquitous connectivity / diversifications of disconnectivity.

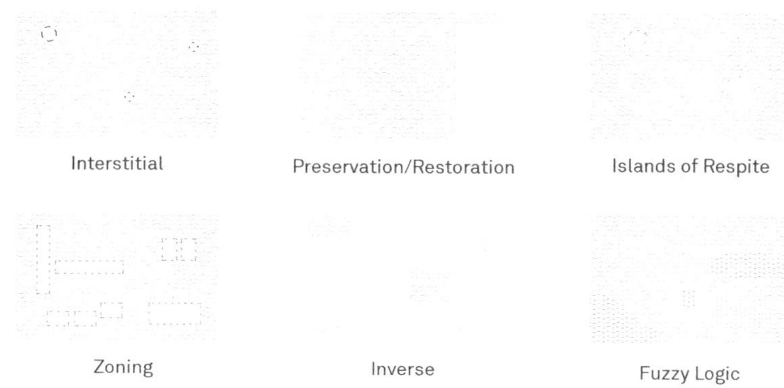

Continued engagement with these models promises to produce a richer and more diverse set of designs to stand alongside the wireless derouter and the use case scenarios proposed here.

Notes, Elaboration, and Commentary*

*

An intended function of the contents and format of these notes is to provoke and inspire by transitioning thought out of the main text and ultimately off of the page in multiple directions. Citations are typset in grey to help the reader distinguish between notes that are primarily references to related work and discursive notes which extend the main text by offering more substantive elaboration and commentary.

1

“Key issues articulated by researchers, artists, and designers include digital overload and distrac-

tion, anti-sociality and inauthenticity, and pervasive surveillance and privacy invasion." For example, researchers within HCI and adjacent fields have examined practices related to overwork and busyness (Leshed and Sengers, "'I Lie to Myself That I Have Freedom in My Own Schedule'"), smartphone anxiety (Harmon and Mazmanian, "Stories of the Smartphone in Everyday Discourse"), and social network account closures and hiatuses (Baumer et al., "Limiting, Leaving, and (Re)Lapsing"). Design researchers have organized programs around the design of technologies for slowness (Odom et al., "Designing for Slowness, Anticipation, and Re-visitation"), reflection and ambiguity (Sengers and Gaver, "Staying Open to Interpretation"), and limitations (Pierce and Paulos, "Counterfunctional things").

Adjacent to HCI, a number of scholars drawn attention to the negative impacts of digital connectivity. For example, in her book *Alone Together* Sherry Turkle has argued for how digital connectivity can create new forms of solitude and social alienation. Richard Harper discusses related issues with digital technology in his book *Texture*, arguing that simpler technologies that ostensibly offer less are often preferable to those digital technologies that offer increasingly more.

2

"Ironically, some of the strongest advocates for disconnecting are among the privileged minority most readily served by and invested in digital technology." See Morozov, "The Mindfulness Racket" and Sharma, *In the Meantime.* See also notes 8 and 9 below.

3

"This work brings together these issues, not to immediately resolve them, but to engage them as matters of concern and imagine alternatives through design." On design as a way of engaging matters of concern, see DiSalvo et al., ""Making public things."

4

"Visual and textual proposals are one format for presenting design inquiry." In the area of graphic design, branding, and architectures, see for example Metahaven and Schmidt, *Uncorporate Identity*. For examples within conceptual and critical architecture, see the work of Archigram and Superstudio. In product design, see for example Near Future Labs, "TBD Catalog" and Beaver, Pennington, and Kerridge, "Material Beliefs." For examples related to interactive design, see for example, Gaver and Martin, "Alternatives: Exploring Information Appliances Through Conceptual Design Proposals." For more recent examples in HCI and interaction design, see Aipperspach, Hooker, and Woodruff, "The Heterogeneous Home"; Pierce and Paulos, "Some Variations on a Counterfunctional Digital Camera"; Blythe et al, "Solutionism, the Game: Design Fictions for Positive Aging"; and Lawson et al., "Problematising upstream technology through speculative design: the case of quantified cats and dogs." On the use of proposals as a method and methodology, see Gaver, "How Design Workbooks Work."

5

"Speculation, critique, reflection, provocation, debate, dissensus (and always potentially more)." On dissensus and debate as functions of design, see for example, DiSalvo, *Adversarial Design*. On critique and speculation as functions of design, see for example, Dunne and Raby, *Speculative Everything*. On critical reflection as a function of design, see for example, Sengers et al., "Reflective Design." For a discussion of critically oriented design within HCI, see Pierce et al., "Expanding and refining design and criticality in HCI." For a broader discussion of alternative and oppositional functions of design, see Pierce, "Working by Not Quite Working."

6

"For many—but certainly not for all or equally—digital connectivity is no longer a luxury but a basic right." While space becomes increasingly digitally connected, access is not equally distributed and digital divides still exist both locally and globally. Internet access is limited for many even within developed countries. For example, a 2013 Pew Research study reported that one-third of Americans making less than $20,000 a year do not go online at all and another one-third go online but do not have home internet access. Of those making $30,000 or less, 45% of mobile internet users go online mostly with their cellphones. Zickuhr, Kathryn and Aaron Smith, "Home Broadband 2013."

In a recent initiative to bring the Internet to places of the world with low connectivity rates, Facebook has launched the highly controversial Internet.org partnership. From a net neutrality perspective, this initiative has been criticized for potentially creating a "second class internet." See, Newman, Lily Hay, "Mark Zuckerberg: 'It's Not Sustainable to Offer the Whole Internet for Free,'" Slate.

Are disconnected spaces elitist when voluntary and inequitable when imposed?

7

"This has given rise to buzzwords naming cultural countercurrents: digital detoxes, unplugging, disconnecting." A selection of examples that epitomize these cultural countercurrent are presented below:

(A) *Sketch by U.K. street artist Banksy.* See Hein, "Banksy's latest sketch is a terrifying reminder of your iPhone addiction."

(B) *Shutterstock.com image #235268062.* "Smart phone addiction concept. Human hand chained to a generic smart phone, high-quality 3D render. Green phone, chain, & nail polish. Metaphor for increasing reliance on technology and connectivity." Shutterstock, "Smartphone Addiction Concept."

(C) *Digital Detox Week, by Adbusters.* In 2009 Adbusters magazine, the promoters of social campaigns including Occupy Wall Street and Buy Nothing Day, rebranded TV Turnoff Week as Digital Detox week. The Oxford Online Dictionary defines digital detox as "a period of time during which a person refrains from using electronic devices such as smartphones or computers, regarded as an opportunity

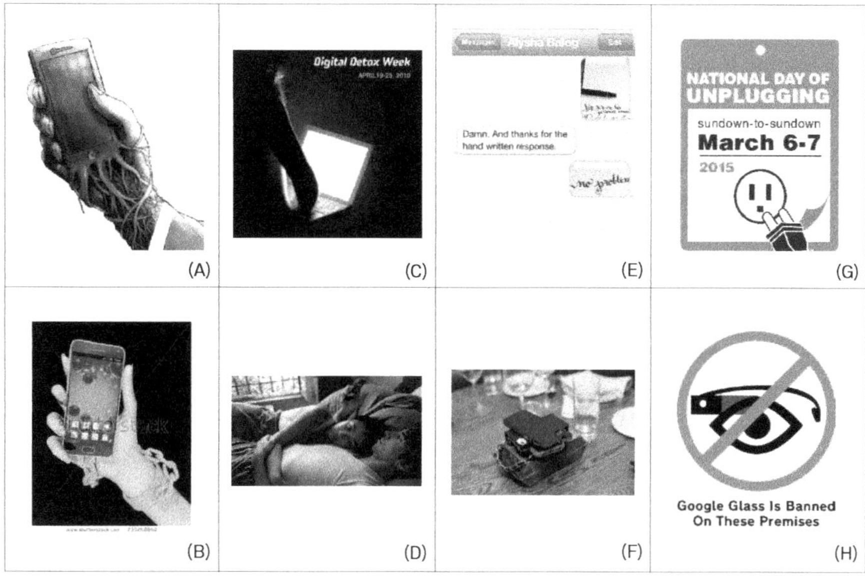

See note 7 for image credits.

to reduce stress or focus on social interaction in the physical world: break free of your devices and go on a digital detox." See, Stutner, "'Digital Detox' Becomes A Real-Life Word, Gets Added To Oxford Dictionary Online."

Digital detoxing is often framed as a matter of health, anxiety reduction, and increased mindfulness. There is no shortage of online articles extolling the benefits of digital detoxing with titles such as "7 Unexpected Benefits of a Digital Detox," "What Really Happens To Your Brain And Body During A Digital Detox," and "How To Prep For A Digital Detox In 6 Simple Steps."

(D) *"I forgot my phone" video still, by Miles Crawford and Charlene deGuzman.* The image of contemporary anxiety about pervasive digital connectivity and smartphone obsession is epitomized by the 2013 viral video "I forgot my phone" directed by Miles Crawford and written by Charlene deGuzman. The 2-minute film depicts a woman phone struggling to relate to everyone else around her tethered to their phones. The video currently has over 49 million views on YouTube. See, "I forgot my phone" published on Youtube.

(E) *Calligraphy text messages, by Cristina Vanko.* In August of 2013, artist Cristina Vanko handwrites all of her text messages by hand with a calligraphy pen. See Vanko, "I Sent All My Text Messages in Calligraphy for a Week."

(F) *Phone stacking game.* "Here's how it works: At the beginning of the meal, everyone puts their phone face down at the center of the table. As time goes on, you'll hear various calls, texts, and emails, but you can't pick up your phone. If you're the first one to give in to temptation, you're buying dinner for everyone else. If no one picks up, then everyone pays for themselves." Ha, "The Phone Stacking Game: Let's Make This A Thing."

(G) *National Day of Unplug, by Reboot.* "The National Day of Unplugging is a 24 hour period – running from sundown to sundown – and starts on the first Friday in March. The project is an outgrowth of The Sabbath Manifesto, an adaption of our ancestors' ritual of carving out one day per week to unwind, unplug, relax, reflect, get outdoors, and connect with loved ones." See, "National Day of Unplugging."

(H) *Google Glass ban signs, by Stop the Cyborgs.* These printable signs are offered by Stop The Cyborgs, a movement whose aim is "to stop a future in which privacy is impossible and where the iron cage of surveillance, calculation and control pervades every aspect of life." The purpose of the signage is to "encourage as many places as possible to become either 'Surveillance free zones' or 'Highly intrusive surveillance free zones.'" "Stop the Cyborgs." On January 15, 2015 Google announced it would cease production of its wearable Glass prototype but remained committed to the development of the product. In light of the news, the Stop The Cyborgs writes on their website that "resistance is not futile and that we can support technological progress without blindly accepting every creepy invasive technology that corporations want to foist upon us. It has also shown us that it is possible for public debate to help establish sensible norms around the use of technology in public places."

8

"On the surface disconnecting appears well-aligned with critiques of techno-utopian faith in technology and the neoliberal imperative to marketize every aspect of life." In *24/7:Late Capitalism and the Ends of Sleep*, Jonathan Crary offers a searing critique of digital connectivity enabled by new pervasive technologies. For Crary, sleep and other intervals of slow or vacant time are quickly being eroded as the last remaining refuges from capitalism. "Beginning with television, but especially in the last two decades," Crary writes, "one became familiar with the transitional moments when one shuts off an apparatus after having been immersed in any televisual or digital ambience for an extended period. ... One has a fleeting intuition of the disparity between one's sense of limitless electronic connectedness and the enduring constraints of embodiments and physical finitude. ... With increasingly prosthetic devices, these kinds of transitions occur everywhere, in every conceivable public or private milieu. ... Within 24/7 capitalism, a sociality outside of individual self-interest becomes inexorably depleted, and the interhuman basis of public space is made irrelevant to one's fantasmatic digital insularity." Crary, *24/7*, 88-89.

9

"Yet some argue that hyperconnectivity is nothing more than a first world problem of luxury..." Technology critic Evgeny Morozov interrogates the "disconnectionist movement" and asks us to consider why and by whom the virtues of disconnecting from technology are being preached: "In essence, we are being urged to unplug—for an hour, a day, a week—so that we can resume our usual activities with even more vigor upon returning to the land of distraction. ... why we disconnect matters: We can continue in today's mode of treating disconnection as a way to recharge and regain productivity, or we can view it as a way to sabotage the addiction tactics of the acceleration-distraction complex that is Silicon Valley." Morozov, "The Mindfulness Racket."

Morozov's words echo the concerns offered by Sarah Sharma writing about the politics of slowing down. Based on her ethnographic studies of temporality as it relates to practices such as corporate yoga, Sharma offers a counter-narrative to the emancipatory rhetoric around the design of slow spaces: "Slow spaces are spaces where anxieties about the pace of life are deliberately pacified in order to produce a different experience of time. As alternative temporal spaces they instead depend on the inequitable social relations of the fast and divisive world they rail against ... It is time to cast aside the individualistic and privileged weight of busyness, sacred space, and generalized precarity found in the laments over speed. If we want to grasp the complex intersections of social differences under global capital, we need to take the temporal seriously on its own terms." Sharma, *In the Meantime*, 19-21.

Sharma and Morozov both highlight interests in "disconnecting" and "slowing down" as largely upper and middle class conceits. Both Sharma and Morozov point out that the white-collar professionals and Silicon Valley technologists who are most loudly lamenting the excesses of technology are precisely the privileged few that already have more than enough. For Sharma and Morozov, among others, emerging digital countertrends in turn form the subject of counter-critique. While digital limitations hold the potential to be experienced as emancipatory, at the very same time they hold counter potentials to support overwork and speed under the guise of respite from the relentless productivity associated with modern technology and capitalism.

10

"'The Cloud.'" In *A Prehistory of the Cloud*, Tung-Hui Hu observers that "over the last twenty years, the Internet has been variously described as a "series of tubes," an "information superhighway", an "ecosystem," a "commons," a "rhizome," a "simulacra," a "cloud" ... Each terms brings with it an implicit politics of space." Hu, *A Prehistory of the Cloud*, xxiv.

What are the politics of space implicit in disconnectivity?

11

"Disconnected 'dead zones' are rapidly disappearing." A partial list of endangered disconnected spaces: subways, airplanes, basements, elevators, old construction with chicken wire wall supports, natural wilderness.

12

"Sanctioned areas of disconnected space serve social and ecological functions with similarities to urban parks and natural preserves." The emergence of digitally disconnected spaces could exhibit parallels with the cultural history of natural wilderness. Ancient explorers saw wilderness as dangerous, untamed space—the opposite of the profanely sacred spaces in need of preservation and restoration today. To early settlers of the United States, for example, wilderness was chaotic, terrifying territory. In contrast, cities were regarded as islands of security and order. In present day America the situation has flipped: wilderness is often regarded as exclusive space ideal for recreation and escape from chaotic, 24/7 urban life. Historian Robert Nash writes that "today's appreciation of wilderness represents one of the most remarkable intellectual revolutions in the history of human thought about land. ... Wilderness has evolved from an earthly hell to a peaceful sanctuary ... Such a perspective would have been absolutely incomprehensible to, for example, a Puritan in New England in the 1650s." Nash, Roderick, *Wilderness and the American Mind*, xii.

To current residents of so-called developed contexts, natural wilderness is a place to electrically "unplug" and digitally "disconnect" (though not necessarily to mechanically "unwind"). It is perhaps not so incomprehensible that urban dwellers of the near-term future will experience disconnected spaces not as frustrating and unsafe "dead zones" but rather as peaceful sanctuaries.

13

"A disconnectionist vigilante uses an illegal cell phone jammer to disrupt passengers on public buses who are engaged in obnoxiously loud phone conversations." See Gross, "Why the interest in illegal cell phone jammers?" See also FCC Enforcement Advisory responses, Federal Communications Commision, "DA-12-347A1," and Federal Communications Commision, "DA-11-249A1."

14

"It is illegal to use any device that 'blocks, jams, or interferes with authorized communications.' The FCC 'has a zero tolerance policy in this area and will take aggressive action against its violators.'" Federal Communications Commision, "DA-12-347A1."

15

"Around the world, it is illegal to possess or operate devices that actively create digitally disconnected space." There are thus some substantial legal challenges confronting wireless derouting research, design, and development. Countries that ban or restrict the ownership and operation of radio signal jammers include Australia, Brazil, Canada, EU, India, New Zealand, Pakistan, Singapore, South Africa, Sweden, Ukraine, United Kingdom, and United States. For example, in the United States, The Communications Act of 1934 "prohibits willful or malicious interference with the radio communications of any station licensed or authorized under the Act or operated by the U.S. Government (47 U.S.C. § 333)." Federal Communications Commision, "Jammer Enforcement."

Accordingly, it is illegal to block cellular telephone, GPS or Wi-Fi, even within the confines of one's private property. As a 2014 FCC advisory notice explains, "In order to prevent harmful interference to critical public safety communications and authorized radio services, federal law prohibits the marketing and sale of 'jammers,' i.e., equipment designed to intentionally block, jam, or interfere with licensed or authorized radio communications. This long-standing prohibition applies to any type of jamming equipment, including devices that interfere with cellular and Personal Communications Services (PCS), police radar, Global Positioning Systems (GPS), and wireless networking services (Wi-Fi). Jammers not only disrupt authorized radio services, but also jeopardize critical public safety communications, such as 9-1-1 calls, and could compromise law enforcement efforts. Ensuring the public's access to these vital services is critically important, and the Enforcement Bureau is committed to strict enforcement in this area." Federal Communications Commision, "FCC Enforcement Advisory No. 2011-03."

Passive, as opposed to active, jamming using fine-meshed Faraday cages or shields is often permitted by law. Electromagnetic field (EMF) shielding material is commercially available through retailers such as LessEMF.com, a site that caters to security and safety conscious users, such as those suffering from EHS (electromagnetic hypersensitivity). LessEMF offers an array of EMF shielding products including baseball caps, underwear, shirts, duvet covers, bed canopies, sleeping bags, and tents.

16

"Disconnective Counterproducts." A selection of disconnective counterproducts by various artists, designers, engineers, activists, entrepreneurs, and corporations:

(A) *I-Bomb, by Eric Paulos.* Creates an electro-magnetic pulse disabling and destroying electronics. See, "Experimental Interaction Unit."

(B) *Faraday Chair, by Dunne and Raby*. An unconventional chair offering refuge from everyday EMF radiation. See Dunne and Raby, "Hertzian Tales, 1994-1997." For a more sustained provocative engagement with electromagnetic space and radio blocking devices, see Dunne and Raby, Design Noir and Dunne, Hertzian Tales.

(C) *Web 2.0 Suicide Machine.* "Lets you delete all your energy sucking social-networking profiles." See the "Web 2.0 Suicide Machine" website.

(D) *Monotask phone covers, by Paolo Cardini.* 3D-printable covers covert your iPhone into a montasking device. 3D files available at the "Monotask covers" Thingiverse website.

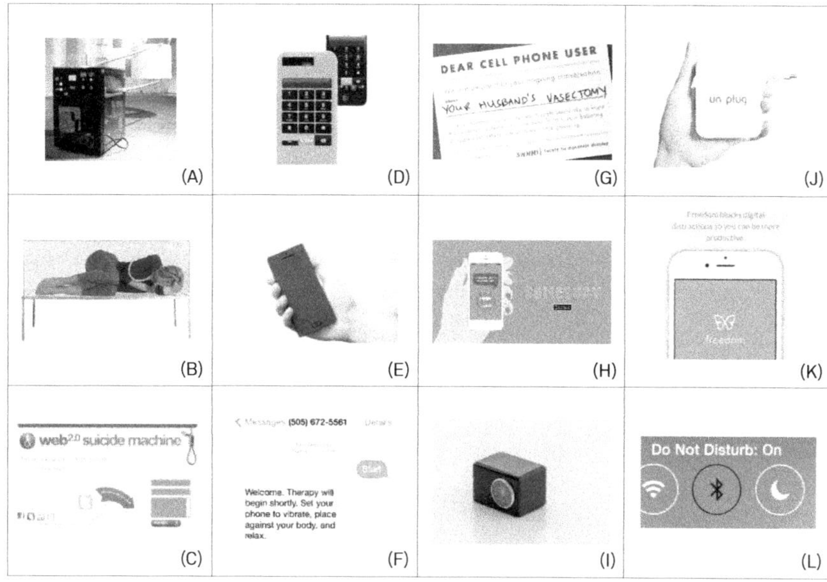

(A) (D) (G) (J) (B) (E) (H) (K) (C) (F) (I) (L)

See note 16 for image credits.

(E) *NoPhone.* "A fake phone for people who are addicted to real phones" Available from the Official NoPhone Store for US$ 10. The NoPhone Kickstarter crowdfunding campaign was successfully funding within 48 hours, raising US$ $18,316 from 916 backers. See, the "No Phone" website.

(F) *HERS: Treatment for Hyperactive Electronic Response Syndrome, by Luke Loeffler.* "Text 'start' to (505) 672-8718 and wait for a response." See Loeffler, "HERS" online project description. Work created for the Institute For New Feeling's Felt Book.

(G) *Dear Cell Phone User Cards, © 2004 Coudal Partners Inc. all rights reserved.* A method for combating obnoxious phone conversation SHHH! (Society for Handheld Hushing), cards available for download at the "Cloudal Partners SHHH" website.

(H) *Somebody iPhone app, by Miranda July.* An app for sending text messages that are delivered in person. "Conceived as an art work, created with Miu Miu, and launched with a companion film, the app that asked strangers to deliver messages between friends exploded in ways we couldn't have foreseen. Despite the ridiculous challenges, one in four messages were delivered, and an average of ten thousand people used the app every day. The next step could only be to form a real company — a start-up! — to expand and improve on our user's dedication. Or... to choose an end date and let Somebody go out as it came in: a wild experiment in public art, marking a particular moment in time." The iPhone app was removed from Apple's App Store on October 31, 2015. See the "Somebody" website.

(I) *MIc Jammer, by Allison Burtch, Eric Rosenthal, and Andy Sigler.* "Like taping over your webcam, but for audio." See, Burtch, "Mic Jammer" online project description.

(J) *Cyborg Unplug.* Pivacy appliance that detects and optionally disconnects devices known to pose a risk to personal privacy. Available from the "Cyborg Unplug" website.

(K) *Freedom app.* A productivity app that blocks distracting apps and websites. Available from the "Freedom" website. Other distraction-blocking apps include StayFocused, BrowseControl, FocusMe, Focus, Quiet, Anti-Social, SelfControl, StopProcrastinating, AppDetox, FocusNow, and Productivity Owl.

(L) *iPhone Do Not Disturb feature.* Silences calls, alerts, and push notifications. Allows scheduling and exceptions to be specified.

17

"Deters readjusting." The Readjustment Delay and Readjustment Delay Reset features can be read as examples of "undesigning interaction" through "self-inhibitive options." See Pierce, "Undesigning Technology," 961 and passim and Pierce, "Undesigning Interactions," 38 and passim.

18

"Wireless nonspots." Wireless nonspots offer non-options to connect. There is a subtle yet crucial distinction to be made between a non-option and an option-to-not. Within most digitally connected spaces there are numerous *options-to-not* connect: turning off Wi-Fi on your laptop, setting your phone to airplane mode, putting your digital devices away, etc. However *non-options* to connect, or the strict absence of connective options, are much more rare. Leaving your phone at home when you go out, for example, creates a non-option to connect via your phone. With the non-option to connect (i.e., without the option to connect, or disconnect), one is no longer tempted or enticed to do so. A non-option removes technological potential, effectively functioning as a *negative affordance*. In the case of a salient non-option it is a negative affordance of the perceived variety.

19

"Disconnected nooks." A simplified (and legal) do-it-yourself version of a wireless derouter can be constructed using a power strip, remote switch, or outlet connected to a wall switch. Simply connect your wireless router to a switch-controlled outlet. Turn the router off when you want to create disconnected space. Turn it on when you want to connect. The noticeable lag time upon startup while establishing a connection may help inhibit you in a way similar to the function of the derouter's Readjustment Delay feature. The setup will likely require negotiating socially shared connected and disconnected space.

Acknowledgments

Thanks to the anonymous reviewers and DIS Pictorials chairs (Eli Blevis, Sabrina Hauser, and Will Odom) for the instructive feedback on this submission. I also thank the creators of images and works I have referenced and reproduced within this proposal (in no particular order): Eric Paulos, Anthony Dunne and Fiona Raby (Dunne and Raby), moddr_ and Fresco Gamba and the Web 2.0 Suicide Machine team, Paolo Cardini, Chris Sheldon and Van Gould and the NoPhone team, Luke Loeffler, Institute for New Feeling (Scott Andrew, Agnes Bolt, and Nina Sarnelle), Coudal Partners, Miranda July, Allison Burtch, Eric Rosenthal, Andy Sigler, Fred Stutzman and the Freedom team, Reboot, Juilan Oliver and the Cyborg Unplug team, Banksy, Adbusters, Miles Crawford, Charlene deGuzman, Cristina Vanko, and Stop the Cyborgs campaign.

References

Aipperspach, Ryan, Ben Hooker, and Allison Woodruff. "The Heterogeneous Home." In *Proceedings of UbiComp 2008*, 222–231, 2008.

Baumer et al., "Limiting, Leaving, and (Re)Lapsing: An Exploration of Facebook Non-use Practices and Experiences," In *Proceedings of CHI 2013*, 3257–66, 2013.

Beaver, Jacob, Tobie Kerridge, and Sarah Pennington, eds. "Material Beliefs." London: Goldsmiths College, 2009.

Blythe, Mark, Jamie Steane, Jenny-Roe, and Caroline Oliver. "Solutionism, the Game: Design Fictions for Positive Aging." In *Proceedings of the CHI 2015*, 3849–58, 2015.

Burtch, Allison, "Mic Jammer," "Mic Jammer," http://www.allisonburtch.net/mic-jammer/, retrieved January 15, 2016.

"Cloudal Partners SHHH," http://www.coudal.com/shhhcards.pdf, retrieved January 15, 2016.

"Cyborg Unplug," https://plugunplug.net/, retrieved January 15, 2016.

Crary, Jonathan, *24/7: Late Capitalism and the Ends of Sleep*, Verso, 2013.

DiSalvo, Carl, *Adversarial Design*. The MIT Press, 2012.

DiSalvo, Carl, Jonathan Lukens, Thomas Lodato, Tom Jenkins, and Tanyoung Kim, "Making public things: how HCI design can express matters of concern." In *Proceedings of CHI 2014*, 2397–2406, 2014.

"Digital Detox," April 17, 2009, Internet Archive, https://web.archive.org/web/20090503022415/http://www.adbusters.org/campaigns/digitaldetox.

Dunne, Anthony and Fiona Raby, *Speculative Everything: Design, Fiction, and Social Dreaming*. Cambridge, Massachusetts; London: The MIT Press, 2013.

Dunne, Anthony, *Hertzian Tales: Electronic Products, Aesthetic Experience, and Critical Design*. Cambridge, Mass.; London: The MIT Press, 2008.

Dunne, Anthony and Fiona Raby, *Design Noir: The Secret Life of Electronic Objects.* Birkhauser, 2002.

Dunne and Raby, "Hertzian Tales, 1994-1997," http://www.dunneandraby.co.uk/content/projects/67/0, retrieved January 15, 2016.

"Experimental Interaction Unit," http://www.eiu.org/orig/experiments/i-bomb/info.html, retrieved January 15, 2016.

Federal Communications Commision, "DA-11-249A1" https://transition.fcc.gov/eb/Public_Notices/DA-11-249A1.html, retrieved January 15, 2016.

Federal Communications Commission, "DA-12-347A1," https://transition.fcc.gov/eb/Public_Notices/DA-12-347A1.html, retrieved January 15, 2016.

Federal Communications Commission, "Jammer Enforcement," https://www.fcc.gov/general/jammer-enforcement, retrieved January 15, 2016.

Gaver, "Making Spaces: How Design Workbooks Work," In *Proceedings of CHI 2011*, 1551–1560, 2001.

"Freedom," https://freedom.to/, retrieved January 15, 2016.

Gaver, Bill, and Heather Martin. "Alternatives: Exploring Information Appliances Through Conceptual Design Proposals." In *Proceedings of CHI 2000*, 209–16, 2000.

Gross, "Why the interest in illegal cell phone jammers?," CNN, 2012.

Ha, Anthony, "The Phone Stacking Game: Let's Make This A Thing," TechCrunch, 2012.

Harmon and Mazmanian, "Stories of the Smartphone in Everyday Discourse: Conflict, Tension and Instability." In *Proceedings of CHI 2013*, 1051–60, 2013.

Harper, Richard, *Texture: Human Expression in the Age of Communications Overload.* 2012, MIT Press.

Hein, Buster, "Banksy's latest sketch is a terrifying reminder of your iPhone addiction," http://www.cultofmac.com/293535/banksys-latest-sketch-terrifying-reminder-iphone-addiction/, retrieved January 15, 2016.

Hu, Tung-Hui, *A Prehistory of the Cloud*. 2015, MIT Press

"I Forgot My Phone," https://www.youtube.com/watch?v=OINa46HeWg8, retrieved January 15, 2016.

Institute For New Feeling's Felt Book, 2014-2015, http://www.institutefornewfeeling.com/feltbook, retrieved January, 15, 2016.

Lawson, Shaun, Ben Kirman, Conor Linehan, Tom Feltwell, Lisa Hopkins, and others. "Problematising Upstream Technology through Speculative Design: The Case of Quantified Cats and Dogs." In *Proceedings of CHI 2015*, 2663–2672, 2015.

Leshed and Sengers, ""I Lie to Myself That I Have Freedom in My Own Schedule": Productivity Tools and Experiences of Busyness," In *Proceedings of* CHI 2013, 905–14, 2013.

Metahaven (Daniel van der Velden and Vinca Kruk) and Marina Vishmidt eds., *Uncorporate Identity*. Lars Muller Publishers, 2010.

"MonoTask covers," http://www.thingiverse.com/thing:26578, retrieved January 15, 2016.

Morozov, "The Mindfulness Racket," New Republic, 2013.

Near Future Laboratory, "TBD Catalog." Excerpts available at https://www.dropbox.com/s/nejxlbin5fb6bse/TBD-Catalog-Excerpts.pdf

Newman, Lily Hay, "Mark Zuckerberg: 'It's Not Sustainable to Offer the Whole Internet for Free,'" Slate, May, 4, 2015.

"National Day of Unplug," http://nationaldayofunplugging.com/about-us/, retrieved January 15, 2016.

Nash, Roderick, *Wilderness and the American Mind*. Yale Univeristy Press, 1982, third edition.

"No Phone," https://www.kickstarter.com/projects/nophone-usa/the-new-and-unimproved-nophone, retrieved January 15, 2016.

Odom, William, Abigail Sellen, Richard Banks, David Kirk, Tim Regan, Mark Selby, Jodi Forlizzi, and John Zimmerman, "Designing for Slowness, Anticipation and Re-visitation: A Long Term Field Study of the Photobox," In *Proceedings of CHI 2013*, 1961–70, 2013.

Pierce, James, "Working by Not Quite Working: Resistance as a Technique for Alternative and Oppositional Design," PhD diss, Carnegie Mellon University, 2015. http://reports-archive.adm.cs.cmu.edu/anon/hcii/CMU-HCII-15-109.pdf

Pierce, James, Phoebe Sengers, Tad Hirsch, Tom Jenkins, William Gaver, and Carl DiSalvo, "Expanding and refining design and criticality in HCI." In *Proceedings of CHI 2015*, 2083–92, 2015.

Pierce, James and Eric Paulos, "Some Variations on a Counterfunctional Digital Camera," In *Proceedings of DIS 2014*, 131-40, 2014.

Pierce, James, and Eric Paulos, "Counterfunctional things: exploring possibilities in designing digital limitations," In *Proceedings of DIS 2014*, 375-84, 2014.

Pierce, James, "Undesigning Interaction." *interactions* 21 no 4(2014): 36-39.

Pierce, James, "Undesigning Technology: Considering the Negation of Design by Design," In *Proceedings of CHI 2012*, 957–66, 2012.

Sengers and Gaver, "Staying Open to Interpretation: Engaging Multiple Meanings in Design and Evaluation," In *Proceedings of DIS 2006*, 99-108, 2006.

Sengers, Phoebe, Kirsten Boehner, David Shay, and Joseph 'Jofish' Kaye, "Reflective design." In *Proceedings Critical Computing 2005*, 49-58, 2005.

Sharma, Sarah, *In the Meantime: Temporality and Cultural Politics*. Duke University Press, 2014.

Shutterstock, "Smartphone Addiction Concept," http://www.shutterstock.com/pic-235268062, retrieved January 15, 2016.

"Somebody," http://somebodyapp.com/, retrieved January 15, 2016.

"Stop the Cyborgs," http://stopthecyborgs.org/google-glass-ban-signs/, retrieved January 15, 2016.

Stutner, Suzie, "'Digital Detox' Becomes A Real-Life Word, Gets Added To Oxford Dictionary Online," Huffington Post, 2013.

Turkle, Sherry. *Alone together: Why we expect more from technology and less from each other.* Basic books, 2012.

Vanko, Cristina, "I Sent All My Text Messages in Calligraphy for a Week," Atlantic Online, 2013.

"Web 2.0 Suicide Machine." http://suicidemachine.org/, retrieved January 15, 2016.

Zickuhr, Kathryn and Aaron Smith, "Home Broadband 2013," Pew Research Center, 2013.

From Breakage to Icebreaker: Inspiration for Designing Technological Support for Human-Human Interaction

Xiaojuan Ma
Hong Kong University of Science and Technology, Hong Kong
mxj@cse.ust.hk

Ke Fang
Center for Research and Interdisciplinarity, France
ke.fang@cri-paris.org

Fengyuan Zhu
New York University, USA
zhufyaxel@gmail.com

ABSTRACT
This paper explores why and how accidental breakage of technologies can promote humans to interact and ultimately lead to positive behavioral, emotional, and relational change. Through a set of research activities, including meta-synthesis of daily anecdotes, design workshops, and a case study, we gain insights into what may hinder or trigger human-human communication, and propose the conceptual and actionable process of Breakage-to-Icebreaker (B2I) design. Instead of intentionally breaking a technology, B2I design embeds mechanisms into existing products and services, creating opportunities for users to interpersonally interact online and/or offline while enjoying the original features and functionalities. Finally, we envision a broader and extended use of B2I thinking in everyday design research and practices.

Author Keywords
Breakage; icebreaker; human-human interaction.

ACM Classification Keywords
H.5.m. Information interfaces and presentation (e.g., HCI): Miscellaneous.

INTRODUCTION
Pervasive use of information, communication, and mobile technologies enables people to build more connections and constantly stay connected [50]. However, the interpersonal relationship formed in the information age is typically shallower [36] with greater emotional distance [27]. In this paper, we draw insights from how accidental breakage of technologies improve interpersonal interaction, and propose a different thinking and tactics for designing support of human-human communication.

Despite the increased size and diversity of their social network [50], more and more people felt that they could not find anyone to discuss important matters with [25]. Prior research has shown that always remaining plugged erodes the quantity and quality of conventional offline human-human interactions [39]. A survey in 2013 suggested that 61% of people tended to keep checking emails, sending messages, and making calls after work – even when they are on vacation [10]. This not only cuts short their time with family and friends, but also makes them persistently stressed about other things during offline social interactions [1]. Although computer-supported cooperative work (CSCW) and computer-meditated communication (CMC) tools e.g., email, video / audio conferencing, and social media allow users to socialize beyond the constraints of space and time [22], they are a leaner means of communication compared to talking face-to-face [9]. The varying availabilities of social cues and degrees of responsiveness in CMC give rise to different depths in online relationships, some being more random, short-lived, impersonal, and superficial than the others [4, 48, 49].

Many researchers and practitioners have attempted to stimulate and foster online as well as offline interpersonal interactions by improving or inventing technologies, from social media (e.g., [41]), tangible interfaces (e.g., [19]), mobile applications (e.g., [45]), to public displays (e.g., [24]). These systems mainly emphasized on creating new channels or props for people to interact, such as providing richer media [19], prompting topics [24], and suggesting conversational partners [45]. Existing research has suggested that, without adequate motivation, people are reluctant to leave their comfort zone and take the desirable actions [14]. Therefore, the strength and endurance of the effects of these technological methods on supporting human-human interactions are yet to be studied.

On the contrary, some people have experimented with a different, "unplug" approach – physically or conceptually detaching heavy users of technology from all of their media devices to force them to socialize in person – in research [26] as well as in real life [44]. The "Phone Stack" game at dinner tables is one of such tactics [44]. In a broader sense, we might all have experienced in everyday life that some unintended breakage of technology leads to an unexpected breakthrough in social relationship. For example, control-swapped thermostats installed in two neighboring flats can increase the residents' chance of hanging out together, as they have to help adjust each other's room temperature. By breakage we mean accidental **functional, usability, or user experience breakdown**, e.g., no battery, unstable Internet collection, non-legible interface, or misleading appearance.

DIS '16, June 04-08, 2016, Brisbane, QLD, Australia
© 2016 ACM. ISBN 978-1-4503-4031-1/16/06…$15.00
DOI: http://dx.doi.org/10.1145/2901790.2901800

Note that we define breakage rather broadly. In some cases, the technology is intact, but users have a bad experience due to the context. Although breakage of technology may only be temporary, it may lead to enduring improvement on interpersonal relationship. This raises the question whether the underlying mechanisms that turn a broken technology into an icebreaker can be applied to design positive experiences with technology, which sounds like a paradox.

Extending James Pierce's framework of undesigning technology [35], we explore how to transfer insights from breakage of technology to thoughtful design of technology, particularly for **restoring, reinforcing, or promoting online and offline interpersonal communication** in the scope of this paper. We refer to this process as *Breakage-to-Icebreaker (B2I) design*, i.e., **embedding icebreaking mechanisms into existing products and services to create opportunities for users to interact and reflect while enjoying the original functionalities**. Note that although such mechanisms are inspired by abnormal, inconvenient, or uncomfortable experiences with a technology, our aim is not to reproduce such defects. Different from conventional affirmative designs that invent dedicated CMC systems, B2I design can use any technology as design materials. It encourages a novel way to view machines' role in mediating interpersonal interaction – a concern of the 3rd paradigm of Human-Computer Interaction (HCI) [18, 6].

Though breakage of technology in daily life is accidental and probably not repeatable, it is worth investigating the underlying factors in order to design positive experiences with technology. We conducted assorted activities to explore the conceptual and actionable process and techniques for the B2I design that gives people a "ticket to talk" [37, 42], including 49 anecdote interviews, material-oriented and goal-oriented design workshops with eight designers, and a case study. By analyzing the materials generated in these activities, we identified attributes of the potential user groups and scenarios, types of products and services that can serve as design materials, inhibitors and motivators of human interaction, effective icebreaking methods, and evaluation rubrics of design outcome. We further propose a set of design considerations and envision the use of B2I design in a broader context. The main contributions of this paper include:

1. We explore the design of technology to support online and offline human-human interaction based on insights drawn from examples of breakage of technology that accidentally serve the purpose in daily life.
2. We experiment with material-oriented (i.e., reshaping a given technology to reach a desirable state) and goal-oriented design (i.e., fulfilling a given goal by exploiting any existing technology) through two design workshops.
3. We evaluate, through a case study, a proposed conceptual and actionable process of B2I design of human-human interaction technologies derived from the meta-synthesis of anecdotes and the two design workshops.

RELATED WORK

In this section, we review existing use of technology to assist human-human interaction, and the movement of recycling, reusing, and repurposing a design.

Technological Support for Human-Human Interactions

Whether technologies benefit or impair interpersonal relationship remains controversial [25, 17]. Some early research indicated that lacking non-verbal cues in CMC may result in less social and emotional communication than face-to-face interactions [40]. In contrast, the hyperpersonal model proposed in [48] argues that CMC also evokes social and emotional exchange and is more socially desirable.

Leaving aside these debates, researchers and practitioners have affirmatively devised various technologies to foster interpersonal interactions. Examples of such intentionally introduced digital artifacts include intelligent interface for groups [19], gamified system to persuade personal contact [23], mobile applications to enhance sociality [45], and public displays to spur offline interaction [24]. However, there are occasions where "technological intervention results in more trouble or harm than the situation it's meant to address" [2], such as group dinner and family time [44].

Undesigning Technology

To address the above-mentioned situations, Pierce proposed the concept of undesigning technology, i.e., "intentional destruction, removal, or inhibition of an existing technology or the foreclosure of future technology" [35]. Undesigning technology is particularly feasible when the target activity does not necessary require the intervention of a digital or interactive technology, such as face-to-face meeting. However, when technology is a must-have component of the activity, whether it is to facilitate communication or for other purposes, could designers transfer the insights from breakage of technology to their design of positive utilization of technology? Our ultimate goal is to evoke reflection on and lasting improvement of interpersonal relationship rather than just faster, richer communication.

Recycle, Reuse, and Repurpose Everyday Design

The core concept of radically reshaping broken objects is somewhat different from the idea behind the research initiatives on designing repairable technologies, e.g., sustainable interface design [5, 30]. B2I design focuses more on transforming the essence of a technology according to the context in which it is used [31]. It attempts to leverage relationship-promoting properties uncovered in breakage that may be conventionally disfavored by the Human-Computer Interaction (HCI) community to evoke positive behaviors, experiences, and reflections. For example, Gaver et al. argued that ambiguity can facilitate designing for appropriation [15]. Dunne advocated for design with defamiliarization to bring in new perspectives [13]. Odom et al. showed that slowness can provoke reflection on relationship with domestic technology [31].

We seek to embed icebreaking mechanisms into existing products or services rather than intentionally re-creating technologies with flaws or troublesome situations (unlike [20]). Similar to the concept of everyday design introduced by Wakkary et al. [47], B2I design acquires the resourceful surroundings as design material for alternative use [30, 33, 20] – supporting interpersonal interaction. The mechanisms may be counterintuitive [36], but we try to maintain and leverage the ordinary functionality of the design materials.

In the rest of the paper, we present three activities that we conducted to extract insights of B2I design. First, we collect and analyze anecdotes in daily life about how unintentional breakage of technology triggers human-human interaction. Then, we describe two design workshops and a case study to evaluate the transfer of knowledge. We also derive a set of implications for future B2I design in a general setting.

LEARNING FROM EXPERIENCES: ANECDOTE STUDY

To gain an in-depth understanding of how a broken technology may turn into an icebreaker, we followed Wright and McCarthy's method [51] and engaged users and designers in dialogues centered on their experiences related to this phenomenon. More specifically, we collect and analyze 49 anecdotes from ordinary information technology users to gather concrete examples of participants, technologies, events, situations, thoughts, and feelings related to B2I incidents in daily life. These anecdotes contain rich information that might inspire and help communicate thinking behind the designs.

Method

In order to better guide the story-telling process, instead of having participants fill out questionnaires, we had conversations with them in person, either face-to-face or online. We first asked interviewees to recall their activities on a normal weekday especially with the use of a particular technology. This was a warm-up exercise for them to relax and get familiarized with recalling life stories. Later, we invited participants to share some personal memorable experience related to B2I. When participants finished eliciting their stories, we prompted them, through questions, to clarify and further elaborate on details concerning the context (e.g., time, place, original task), the broken technology, all parties involved, the actions and reactions, their emotional experiences during the process, the outcome and long-lasting effects (if any). We took notes and audio recorded the conversations which were transcribed into text.

Participants

We recruited participants through word-of-mouth and advertisement on various social media, e.g., Facebook, Weibo, and WeChat. We scheduled face-to-face, phone, or video interviews with 53 people who expressed interests in sharing past experiences with "some technical breakdown leading to the improvement of relationship with others."

Prior to the interview, we gathered basic demographic information from the 53 participants, among whom 31 were female, and 43% were in the age range of 18 and 25 (18% below 18, 28% in 26-35, 4% in 36-45, 5% in 46-55, and 2% above 55). These interviewees were regular information and communication technology users originally from 11 different countries and regions. Ten of them were high school students while the rest all had at least some college education in 15 different majors. The respondents' current occupation varied from student to faculty, engineer to designer, manager to official, and consultant to sport coach.

Data Processing

We extracted a total of 49 anecdotes. We excluded stories that were either with no technology directly involved or the final outcome of which had no strong association with human interaction. Below are some selected anecdotes.

A1. My phone has no GPS signal and I have to use a paper map. → More people come up to ask if I need any help.
A2. When I was pregnant, I could not see the readings on the weight scale. → My husband always helped me with it. We chatted more about my pregnancy.
A3. The printer in our office is really slow. → People waiting for printouts by the machine get to chat a lot.
A4. I accidentally put my digital watch to power saving mode and it goes to sleep after an hour. → People cannot help coming up and asking me if the battery is out.
A5. Our company's reimbursement system is extremely hard to use. → The HRs form an online support group.
A6. The text input of my WeChat was broken and I had to use voice chat with a co-worker discussing an urgent issue. → We felt closer and became friends later.
A7. The air condition in our classroom was super cold one day. → The boys were gentleman enough to lend us their jackets, though we seldom talk to each other before.

Here, A6 showcases functional breakage, and A2 is an example of user experience breakdown due to special context. We used a mix of qualitative and quantitative methods to analyze the anecdote transcripts. The three authors collaboratively applied the grounded theory method [8] to explore the data. Through iterative comparison and integration, we compiled a set of analytical, relational categories to summarize insights from the B2I anecdotes:

- Relation (who): relationship among the participants
- Location (where): context of B2I incidents
- Attribution (why): type of breakage of technology
- Function (what): medium of interpersonal interaction
- Rationale (how): inhibitors of interpersonal interaction
- Sequence (how): triggers of interpersonal interaction
- Means-end I (mechanism): verbal approach
- Means-end II (mechanism): physical approach
- Cause and Effect I (consequence): emotional outcome
- Cause and Effect II (consequence): Relational outcome

We are aware of the potential culture differences, and thus conducted a descriptive statistical analysis to investigate the frequency of the different analytical categories among the 49 anecdotes from diverse interviewees. Note that a story may involve multiple factors in the same category.

Insights into Breakage-to-Icebreaker Design Process

Table 1 summarizes the grounded theory results from anecdote study and interviews. We present example quotes and percentage count for each of the 10 analytical categories. In this subsection, we share some insights into some essential factors of B2I design.

Understanding Target and Context for Embodied Interaction

Based on the stories and feedback from the respondents (Table 1), we learned that B2I occurs more frequently and is more effective among weak ties (93.9% of the anecdotes). These are relationships that people often ignore or are less motivated to maintain, including strangers (30.6%), familiar strangers [34] such as people working (36.7%) or living (6.1%) in the same building, as well as acquaintances such as classmates (8.2%) and not-so-close friends (18.4%). Unlike strong ties such as immediate family (2.0%) and significant other (4.1%), people are less likely to actively initiate social interactions with weak ties in person or via CMC tools. As one person put in his story, "*I never thought that this uncle (a distant relative) would care about me, so I rarely contacted him. (A23)*" Another respondent also commented "*Who talk to their neighbors these days? If it were not for the broken WiFi, I may never knock on the neighbor's door. (A19)*" However, there are still occasions when B2I can make a difference in close relationships which is more critical than connecting with a weak tie. One designer provided an example, "*It (B2I) can serve as a good excuse to resolve a fight with my girlfriend (A6).*"

Furthermore, designers should take the target relationship into consideration when selecting design materials that can provide embodied interactions naturally occurring "in real time and real space" [11]. One interviewee gave her explanation, "*If my own computer is broken, I am more inclined to bother a good friend. I will not grab a random person in the building to help me fix it, as it is personal. But if a public computer goes wrong, anyone who might use it could help, right? (A33)*" More specifically, we analyzed the cases collected and found that 82.5% the relationship breakthrough between weak ties were initiated by some problem of certain information technologies for public or shared use, e.g., smart coffee machine, public WiFi hotspot, administrative software, and online store. In other words, a B2I design can utilize interactive systems that already locate in a common hang out area of the target users, to benefit from their innate tangibility and sociality [11].

Identifying the Inhibitors and Possible Motivators

There are many barriers that prevent people from having more interactions with others. Our analysis of the anecdotes highlights six key reasons why people do not talk to each other (Table 1): 1) physical isolation (12.2%); 2) social isolation (28.6%); 3) technological isolation (12.2%); 4) social awkwardness (20.5%); 5) social inappropriateness (16.3%); and 6) emotional indifference (10.2%). For instance, a female high school student commented that, "*A typical boy girl thing. We sit separately and mostly hang out with those of the same gender. What's worse, these boys are not cute enough and don't know how to speak to a girl in a good manner. Some are just too shy (A42).*"

The interviewees also shared some insights into what may force them to cross the interaction barrier. Urgency (22.4%) and inconvenience (20.4%) are both effective motivators for strong and weak ties, and the former is timelier. "*I was not so familiar with that guy, and normally we do not communicate via voice message. It's a little awkward. But I was very anxious to get the work done (A28).*" Emotional discomfort (20.4%) and physical pain (14.3%) are two other irresistible triggers. "*People just couldn't help warning me that my watch was dead, whether they knew me well or not (A4).*" "*The mosquitos really bother me, and I do not mind approaching someone who can keep these monsters away (A9).*" If interaction can bring in mutual benefits (16.3%), people seem to be more willing to talk to each other. "*I usually won't email someone not in my division this often. But in this case, we have to do so as both of us need to ensure that the emails get to the right person (A35).*" Some other possible factors include curiosity (12.5%) and financial concerns (8.2%), especially when they are substantial. "*It was until they saw a robot in the lobby talking by itself, did the students start asking me questions (A8).*" "*No one wanted to pay the cancelation fee, so we had to make sure that everyone was happy. We made calls and met for the first time just to go over the hotels (A31).*"

In a word, inhibitors to human-human interaction are diverse, and some are easier to overcome than the others. It is necessary to provide internal and/or external motivation to get people to step out of their comfort zone. The selection of motivating factors should relate to the intended scenarios and characteristics of the target relationships.

Choosing Mechanisms that Enhance Sensorial Presence

A person's sensorial experience with the other party's presence affects their understanding and relationship [46]. There are many ways to shorten the social and emotional distance. According to the Proxemics Theory [16], people use haptics, kinesics, vocalics, and chronemics to define territories during interpersonal communication [28]. It is particularly important to "*say the right thing, and do the right thing (A45),*" or it may lead to negative consequences.

Our respondents mostly mentioned the use of verbal and sensory channels (Table 1). Verbal communication can promote better understanding via instrumental dialogues (87.7% of the anecdotes, e.g., information exchange, demonstration / instruction, coordination, and warning) and

Category	Code	# Codes	% Anecdotes	Examples
Relation (Who)	Colleague / Officemate / Labmate	18	36.70%	Intern in the lab, HRs, co-workers, etc.
	Stranger	17	30.60%	Pedestrian, passengers, driver, people nearby, etc.
	Friend	9	18.40%	Female friends, a close friend, etc.
	Classmate / Schoolmate	4	8.20%	Boys in my class, etc.
	Roommate / Neighbor	3	6.10%	The guy next door, our neighbors, etc.
	Significant other / Date	3	6.10%	Boyfriend, my date, etc.
	Family / Relatives	2	4.10%	Uncle, my parents, etc.
Location (Where)	Office / Classroom	14	28.60%	In my department, in my class, in the lecture hall, etc.
	Transportation	7	14.30%	On the bus, in the subway station, etc.
	Online only	7	14.30%	Facebook, WeChat, online forum, etc.
	Restaurant	5	10.20%	Have a group dinner, café, etc.
	Public place (indoor)	5	10.20%	Museum, lobby, etc.
	Public place (outdoor)	5	10.20%	On the street, in a park, etc.
	Apartment / Dorm / Hotel	4	8.20%	In my flat, hotel in Greece, etc.
	Home	2	4.10%	At home, etc.
Attribution (Broken Type)	Failed operation	16	32.70%	Power off, no announcement, no GPS signal, etc.
	Difficult / Unfamiliar usage	12	24.50%	New coffee machine, hard-to-use interface, etc.
	Limited / Uneven resource	9	16.30%	Weak Wifi signal, only cools part of the room, etc.
	Missing function	7	14.30%	No speech output, no filter, no personalization, etc.
	Conflicted / Confused usage	6	10.20%	Swapped control, mistaken email address, etc.
	Uncomfortable usage	2	4.10%	Annoying sound, either too hot or too cold, etc.
	Unexpected outcome	2	4.10%	Random message, a pile of wasted paper, etc.
	Misguided appearance	2	4.10%	Looks smart, as if it were out of battery, etc.
Function (Medium)	Face to face conversation	38	73.40%	Discussion, shopping together, walk with me, etc.
	Messaging / Online chat	6	12.30%	Got a text, chatting online, etc.
	Social network	5	10.20%	Form a WeChat group, join a forum, etc.
	Phone call	3	6.10%	Called me up, etc.
	Email	1	2.00%	Emailed me
Rationale (Barrier)	Social isolation	15	28.60%	From another school, boys seldom talk to girls, etc.
	Social awkwardness / Shyness	10	20.30%	Geeky guys, too shy, etc.
	Social inappropriateness / Rudeness	8	16.30%	Cannot force him out of the cubicle, etc.
	Physical isolation	6	12.20%	Long distance relationship, in another city, etc.
	Emotional indifference	5	10.20%	Not interested in talking to him, etc.
	Technological isolation	5	8.20%	Everyone plays with their phones, etc.
Sequence (Trigger)	Urgency	12	22.40%	Need to get work done, cannot find my way, etc.
	Inconvenience	10	20.40%	Difficult to reach, have to go there each time, etc.
	Emotional discomfort	10	20.40%	Really frustrated, pretty nervous, stressed, etc.
	Mutual benefit	8	16.30%	Emails sent to the right person, both enjoyed it, etc.
	Physical discomfort	7	14.30%	My feet hurt, cannot bend down, etc.
	Curiosity / Fun	5	12.50%	Interested to see, give it a try, very curious, etc.
	Financial concern	4	8.20%	Get a discount, pay the bill, too expensive, etc.
Means-End I (Verbal)	Exchange information	17	34.70%	Exchange names and ideas, discuss possible ways, etc.
	Demonstration / Instruction	13	26.50%	Show me how to use the machines, give a demo, etc.
	Coordination	10	20.40%	Synchronize the control, take turns, arrange seats, etc.
	Compliment / Greeting / Blessing	4	6.10%	Compliment on the taste, say hello, etc.
	Warning	3	6.10%	Warned me the risk of wrist sprain, point out the hole, etc.
	Complaint	3	6.10%	Complain about the system, etc.
	Joke	3	6.10%	Tease myself, joke about it, etc.
Means-End II (Physical)	Shared object	15	30.60%	Shared Wifi hotspot, shared air condition, etc.
	Shared space	9	18.40%	Share the area with lights, etc.
	Body / Voice contact	8	14.30%	Holding hands, send me a voice message, etc.
	Gifting	3	6.10%	Get me a new headset, lend us their jackets, etc.
Cause and Effect I (Emotional)	Grateful	15	30.60%	Cannot get it done without him, really thankful, etc.
	Pleased / Satisfied	10	20.40%	Had a great trip, got to practice my English, etc.
	Fun / Interesting	10	20.40%	Never experienced this before, interesting to see, etc.
	Touched / Sweet	6	12.30%	It is so sweet, I am moved, etc.
	Surprised	6	12.20%	People did come up to me, she is not that hard to work with, etc.
	Sympathy / Empathy	3	6.10%	Sorry for the blind passenger, pity guy, etc.
Cause and Effect II (Relational)	Stronger emotional connection	27	53.10%	He really cares about me, we became close friends, etc.
	Better understanding	19	38.70%	Know my colleagues better, share our interests and tastes, etc.
	More interaction	16	32.70%	Interact more with the locals, participate in the conversationss, etc.

Table 1. Summary of codes of anecdotes, scenarios collected from focus group, and design examples.

stronger emotional connection via affective conversations (18.3%, e.g., greeting, compliment, complaint, and joke). In particular, voice brings people closer than written text. As one story noted, "*It was the first time I heard his voice. Voice message is definitely more personal than text (A28).*" We notice that all parties in the stories were taking a constructive attitude towards the breakdowns. It suggests that an effective icebreaking mechanism for B2I design should prevent destructive behaviors such as simply blaming the product or each other, and shift users' focus to reflecting on their interpersonal relationship.

Direct physical interactions (14.3%) create an even stronger sense of presence and intimacy [16]. It makes people feel that they are emotionally closer, which in turn reinforces interpersonal interactions. However, given the social norms, physical contact may be more suitable for stronger ties except in special occasions. "*I only hold on to the arm of my parents'. But if I sprained my ankle, I guess I would not mind borrowing the arm of someone nearby (A5).*"

In comparison, indirect contact in the physical world through shared object (30.6% of the anecdotes), shared space (18.4%), or gifting (6.1%) is of a wider use. Indirect physical contact may affect individuals' perception and behaviors in various ways. One respondent used being locked up together in a broken elevator as an example to elicit some of the mediating factors, such as a shared dedicated goal, an isolated non-distracted environment, common experiences and feelings, and common grounds of conversations. Several interviewees mentioned that some sensory stimuli which can easily invade a space, e.g., light, temperature, smell, and sound, and thus may stimulate shared emotional and social responses. "*We were hiding in our own cubicles, but the false fire alarm easily went through the dividers and dragged us all out. (A19)*"

Introducing Sustainable Outcome

All respondents agreed that a successful B2I design should lead to long-lasting emotional, behavioral, and relational change. People indicated in their personal stories that (Table 1), in the end they knew more about the person experienced B2I with them (38.7%), felt more emotionally connected (53.1%), and were more willing to interact with others in the future (32.7%). In some cases where the interaction only occurred once, particularly with strangers, the participants adopted a more positive, active attitude towards social interaction, as said in an anecdote, "*I love this city. People are so friendly. I interacted more with the locals during my visit which never happened before. (A38)*" In other words, a good B2I design should either reinforce the motivation and engage people in repeated, longer-term interaction, or leave a prolonged emotional impact.

LEARNING FROM PRACTICES: DESIGN WORKSHOPS

We have gained many useful insights from the daily experiences of target users, and would like to transfer the knowledge to actual designs practices. We consider B2I

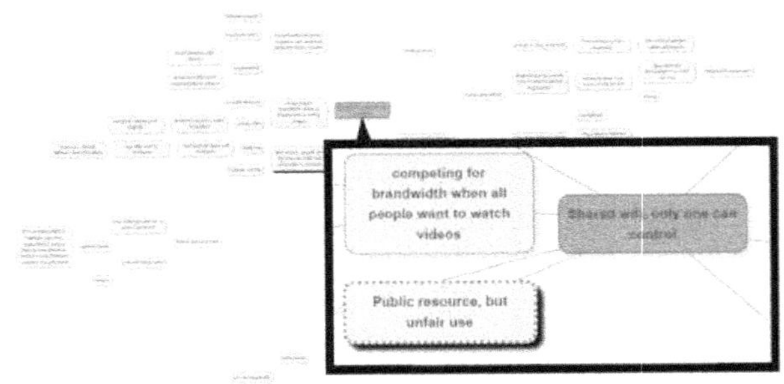

Figure 1. A mind map on shared WiFi hotspot from the material-oriented design workshop.

design to be a kind of everyday design [47]. For one thing, B2I design leverages the resourceful daily technologies as the design material. For another, B2I design does not necessarily need a professional designer, but can involve anyone who is willing to think critically and innovatively. We conducted two activities to transfer theories to practices: I) a material-oriented design workshops with three everyday designers and I) a goal-oriented design workshop with five everyday designers. The participants were recruited via word-of-mouth and advertisement on social media such as Facebook, Weibo, and Wechat.

Material-oriented Design Workshop

We conducted a material-oriented design workshop to explore the use of B2I thinking in actual design practice with three everyday designers (D1, D2 and D3) who liked to make things in their spare time. D1 (male, aged 26) was a master student in HCI, D2 (male, aged 22) was completely new to the field, and D3 (female, aged 30) was a professional designer with seven years of practices.

Session I: Warm-up Brainstorming

In the first part of the workshop, we organized a 40-minute warm-up brainstorming session to make sure that all the three designers correctly understood the basic concept of material-oriented B2I design. We presented them the design considerations derived from the anecdote study. We encouraged the designers to pick an ordinary product encountered in everyday life and creatively turn it into something useful for social interaction without worrying about feasibility or usability issues. The designers were able to generate many ideas with the help of mind maps [7]. The designers brought up seven examples of B2I design:

1. A set of water taps with swapped proximity sensors.
2. An emoticon-only chat tool.
3. An ice bucket that will block the WiFi signal around the table when having a bottle of beer in it.
4. A pair of stiletto that can detach the heel via a phone.
5. An automatic glass door that only opens when people on both side smile at it.
6. A TV that can only be viewed from a particular angle.
7. A children's game with random tasks for the parents.

We observed that their design materials were not restricted to interaction design; rather, the designers were better at

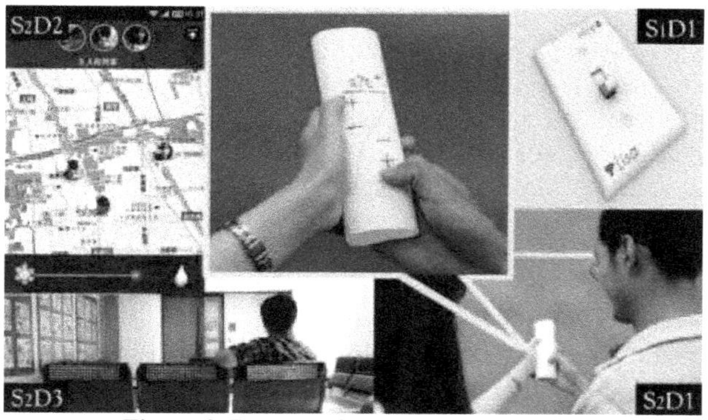

Figure 2. Results of parallel prototyping.

repurposing breakdown of everyday objects e.g., shoes and water tap. Additionally, many of the design outcomes were not only relational but also utilitarian or hedonic. In other words, the designers assigned B2I a broader definition.

Session II: Parallel Prototyping

We provided two products / services as the initial design materials, i.e., WiFi hotspot and air conditioner for a shared space. They both occurred several times in the anecdotes. In this session, the designers first collectively generated a mind map (Figure 1) for each case (45 min each), with emphasis on but not limited to our proposed B2I notions in Table 1. This process did not produce any specific design, but rather awareness of the issue and its linkage to other aspects relevant to social interactions. Mind mapping results served as design materials for parallel prototyping [12] (60 min each), during which the three designers independently proposed new B2I designs for each case.

Results of Parallel Prototyping

We share the six designs proposed by the designers for the cases of WiFi (S_1) and air conditioner (S_2) (Figure 2).

S_1D1: *WiFi Teeterboard* is a physical switch that mediates network speed between a team of two. Like a teeterboard, when flipped to one end, it gives one of the users high WiFi speed (e.g., 10MB/s) and a poorer speed (e.g., 1MB/s) to the other, and vice versa. Members have to communicate more about their current Internet usage and future plans.

S_1D2 : *Internet Exposer* grabs the URL that each member currently browses, and tries to expose it to all. However, users can sacrifice some of their bandwidth to cover up their URLs. In addition, employees are supervised by "social influence" rather than a compulsive URL screening, more beneficial for group dynamics and working culture.

S_1D3: *Share for More* is a network resource redistribution system that aims to increase sociality and sharedness. Limited network resources are not distributed evenly across a team. More are allocated to those who share information that they obtained from the Internet with others.

S_2D1: *Remotouch* is an air-conditioner remote design for rooms where family and friends get together. *Remotouch* only activates when two people hold it together. It reminds people to care for others' feeling, with their own hand, every time they want to change the temperature.

S_2D2: *Cool Map* is an application that indexes a map with users' perceived feelings of temperature rather than the actual temperature. Users can update their feelings with a slide bar and see others' feeling around them. It aims to encourage more icebreaking social interactions.

S_2D3: *Sense Me, Chat with Me* is a bench design in public space. The chair obtains users' physiologic and emotional status by sensors and the users' self-input, and visualize it at the back side of the bench, and can only be seen by others. The bench provokes icebreaking interactions among strangers when people care about others.

Designers' Reflection on Material-oriented Design

After the workshop, we interviewed the three designers and derived several implications from the interview.

Brainstorming a broad range of phenomena, mechanisms, experiences, values, and consequences related to design materials is essential to B2I design. Many ideas generated in this workshop were stimulated by more than one "spark". For example, D1's *Remotouch* incorporated the notions of "shared objects", "physical contact", and "mutual benefit". Various combinations may yield different design outcomes.

Interestingly, S_2D2 and S_2D3 exploited the concept of temperature rather than the initial product air-conditioner as the design material. The designers reported that their personal experiences inspire them to transplant the concept to another technology. D3 shared her thought process, "*Talking about air-conditioners' uneven cooling, it reminds me of another incident. My hands are cold when the room temperature is low. None of my friends knows about it until one day a thermal image camera accidently exposed my body temperature heatmap. The unexpected leak of my 'body index' turned out to be a good thing, because thereafter many of my caring friends offer to warm my hands from time to time. This is where the 'Sense Me, Chat with Me' idea comes from.*"

The three designers stressed several keys to the material-oriented design process: "*utilizing the power of habit and social norms (D1)*", "*repurposing everyday objects and devices (D2)*", and "*taking advantages of heuristics to naturally and seamlessly integrate the different elements together (D3)*". Take the automatic glass door proposed in the warm-up session as an example. The transparent glass allows users on both sides to see each other's smile, turning a mutual command for a mechanical operation into a social cue. Similarly, placing beer bottles into an ice bucket is a common practice, which is used to signal the start of a party both socially and technically (by blocking WiFi signals).

In the end, the panel of everyday designers made a remark that the material-oriented design process enabled them to "*think more out of the box*". "*Given a broken design, people's first instinct is to repair it. Sometimes we recycle*

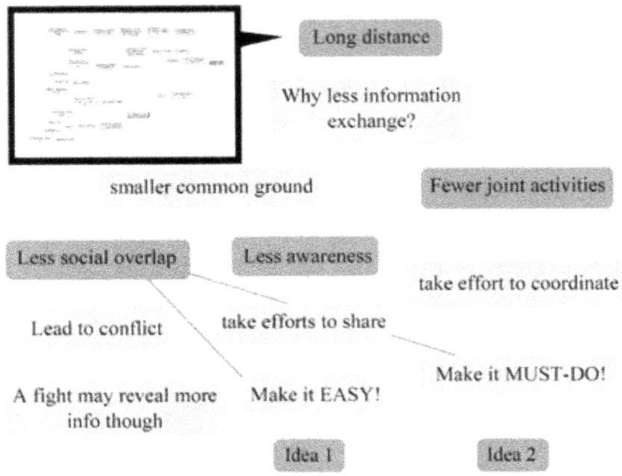

Figure 3. Simplified mind map in the goal-oriented design workshop (full mind map on the upper left).

some pieces to build a better system, but it is only near transfer. Finding a completely new use is unnatural, and the ideas generated could be somewhat arbitrary. But this is fun (D3)." This quote also indicates that B2I material-oriented design is a bottom-up process, which may not have clear patterns. On the contrary, the designers felt that a top-down, goal-oriented design may have a conceptual and actionable process to follow. Therefore, we conducted a second design workshop to explore the idea.

Goal-Oriented Design Workshop

We invited another five everyday designers (D4~D8, a least one year of everyday design experiences, Avg. age = 25.6, SD = 2.88 yrs., three females) to a goal-oriented design workshop. This workshop followed a traditional design process: specifying and solving a target problem. Designers were free to choose any design material.

Procedure

We asked designers to solve the problem of "*lovers going cold in a long-distance relationship (A34)*" in this workshop. The goal was to reinforce the ties and reactivate the interaction between lovers whose relationship is weakened by physical isolation (Table 1). Although close-ties were only mentioned in a small portion of the anecdotes, interviewees stressed that problems with a close-tie are more devastating than with a stranger. In addition, prior work showed that romantic partners were less satisfied with their relational quality than family or friends when communicating over various media [3]. The designers reviewed the categories in Table 1 and built a mind map (Figure 3) to explore the links among factors associated with a cooling-down long distance relationship. Designers could easily adapt mechanisms from the anecdotes that have fixed similar problems for their own design.

Goal-oriented Design Process and Outcomes

When sketching out the mind map, the designers found that although existing CMC tools can support low-cost, frequent communication between long-distance couples, physical isolation still causes inevitable damage to the relationship. For example, social overlap and common ground decrease as the distance enlarges, resulting in potential conflicts and misunderstanding. Also, remote couples are less motivated to coordinate and participant in joint events to pursue a shared goal, posing a challenge to their sense of belonging. "*We do not have much to talk about. He doesn't know the people or the context of some of the recent events. It will take me a long time to explain everything in order to avoid possible confusion, which I don't feel like doing. (D7)*" Such problems cannot be adequately addressed by scheduled conversations daily and meet-ups from time to time. The designers seek alternatives that could target these issues at a deeper level. Later, the designers got inspired by the notions and cases presented in Table 1 and came up with two designs, one for expanding social overlap and the other for promoting joint activities.

Idea1: *Random Messenger* takes random snapshots of all chat history throughout the day, and users can pick a few to send to the other party daily at their own will. It provides an opportunity for long-distance lovers to learn more about each other's social circle and recent activities. The design adopts notions such as "exchange information," "shared object," "curiosity," and "better understanding" in Table 1.

Idea2: *Solo-Media Player* is an online player that requires two people to synchronously watch the same video together, as one person only has the key to the video stream while the other can only unlock the audio. This design aims to encourage remote couples to watch video programs together online, and exchange thoughts and feelings. It can find references to notions e.g., "coordination," "shared object," "mutual benefits," "more interaction," etc.

Designers' Reflection on Goal-oriented Design

The designers proposed a five-phase tactics for B2I goal-oriented design: 1) specifying the target relationship and the desirable state; 2) locating the barriers; 3) identifying a suitable context or channel; 4) designing a mechanism that can provide sufficient motivation and provoke appropriate actions; and 5) reinforcing positive experiences.

The designers identified two ways to embed icebreaking features in an existing technology: as a *byproduct* (Idea1) of or as a *prerequisite* to the original functionality (Idea2). The former has less impact on the design material, but can be easily bypassed. In contrast, the latter better imposes the idea but can be viewed as counterfunctional [36] with "*the risk of arousing complaints against the product. (D5)*"

In addition, the designers highlighted some critical factors to be carefully managed, e.g., privacy and ethics. They did not want B2I design to trigger wars between lovers or with other parties that may be involved in the use of technology. However, they also indicated that a fight may sometimes heat up the relationship, as it "*reveals the 'true self' and communicates emotion and information intensely. (D8)*"

CASE STUDY

We conducted a case study on *Random Messenger* from the goal-oriented design workshop with three long-distance couples (Avg. age = 24.3, SD = 1.03 yrs., three females). The three couples (C1~C6) have been in a relationship for an average of 3.3 years and have not been co-located for 1.8 years on average. We held online interviews with each couple after they had tried Random Messenger for a week.

Case Study Process and Feedback

The three couples noted in a pre-study interview that distrust and lack of common topics are the two most urgent problems for long-distance relationships. Participants' feedback showed that Random Messenger could adequately remove these barriers, however, in an "abnormal" way.

Many reported that sharing chat history is an effective way to stimulate communication, especially for introducing new topics. "*I'm obsessed with analyzing the tone she talk to other people, someone I don't know, and guessing their relationship. We discussed a lot about this and I get to know more of her friends (C3).*" "*I saw his dialogue with a mutual friend. It caught my interest. We then continued with the topic raised in the conversation with this friend (C6).*"

Case Study Results and Implications

In the study we found that, due to the randomness, many of the chat snapshots were not "informative" enough for the other party. "*Before, we occasionally sent each other a snapshot that we thought was interesting. Random snapshot is different. It can be some information that the other party cannot follow at all (C1).*" However, all the three couples stated that it is exactly the non-informative feature that may better evoke interaction. "*Reading conversations out of my knowledge actually allows me to see a different side of her (C1).*" "*We both find the snapshots nonsense sometimes because of the lack of context; however, they successfully arouse our curiosity to know the story behind (C4).*" In other words, randomness is a useful ice breaker.

Random Messenger also intensified the issue of trust. Being unselective itself, Random Messenger put a test on both sides. C1 (male) shared an incident, "*Once, a snapshot of a female friend and me talking about having lunch together popped up. I hesitated for a while, but decided to send it to her. It was actually no big deal, though she might view it differently.*" And C1's girlfriend C2 added, "*Indeed. I think the girl likes him. I can take it because I can feel the trust between us.*" The couple recognized Random Messenger's active role in maintaining their mutual trust.

"Suspicious conversations" leaked by Random Messenger may stimulate jealousy, which was another common feeling besides curiosity as the participants noted. Fierce jealousy may be destructive, but a slight one is "*good in general, as it keeps us more passionate (C6).*" While curiosity incites interests in learning more about the other party, jealousy opens up an opportunity to regain a deeper understanding of self and feelings towards the relationship. "*In one snapshot, she told a boy that she would go to his place for the weekend. I was so jealous that I did not notice that the boy was a friend of mine and she was actually going to visit his girlfriend. Hilarious mistake. It made me realize how much I care about her, and I am not as mature as I thought (C3).*"

In summary, instead of trying to stabilize a relationship, Random Messenger gets users to experience the feeling of something "*being a bit out of control. (C5)*" Actually, Random Messenger incorporates the concepts of ambiguity [15] and defamiliarization [13] to reenergize social interactions, by critically adding excitement and challenges to a relationship that might be bland or is going cold.

The case study demonstrated the effectiveness of B2I design, and the feasibility of reshaping breakage of technologies. A near transfer with proper target- and context-based adaptation may quickly expand the use of existing B2I tactics. For example, some designs for long-distance relationship could also apply to other scenarios, e.g., left-behind children and their parents.

DISCUSSION

In general, B2I is a method to create antifragile systems that "benefit from shocks" and will "thrive and grow when exposed to volatility, randomness, disorder, and stressors and love adventure, risk, and uncertainty" [43]. Such systems have been found in molecular biology, finance, physics, etc. It suggests that B2I thinking can be applied to repurpose any object to foster target behaviors in a new domain, as long as designers can tolerate and carefully design counterfunctional mechanisms in a traditional sense.

Note that the antifragile mechanisms in B2I design, e.g., ambiguity and defamiliarization, might take the blame for interfering with the user experiences of the design material. Designers should ensure that the negative effect serves as the ticket to talk as shown in anecdote A5, which is only temporary and will ultimately lead to better outcomes.

Embedded B2I Feature should not Overrule the Product

Instead of developing technologies dedicated to promote interpersonal interaction from scratch, B2I design inserts features into exiting products and services shared among the target users, and repurposes part of the design materials. This approach has several benefits. First, B2I design can take advantage of the user base of the host product / service [11]. As designer D1 suggested in the material-oriented workshop, "*People need to use WiFi. In that sense, we don't have to persuade them to try out our feature.*" This is particularly true for the prerequisite type of B2I design. Second, the besides the intended improvement on interpersonal relationship, better experience with the design material can also serve as a motivator for the users. D1 gave an example, "*Eventually, our design (S_1D1: WiFi Teeterboard) allows users to avoid potential conflict over bandwidth and make better use of the WiFi service.*" More specifically, the designers proposed two approaches to leverage the original function of the design material as an incentive for active engagement in social interaction: 1) to secure resources and maintain service quality, e.g., S_1D2: *Internet Exposer*; and 2) to earn extra resources or higher priority, e.g., S_1D3: *Share for More*.

However, designers in both workshops stressed that the embedded icebreaking features should not detract the design material from its original purpose in any case. For example, D6 reflected on the design of Idea2: *Solo-Media Player* in the goal-oriented workshop, "*The (Solo-Media) player should work just like an ordinary video player, or with even better image and sound qualities when the remote couples are coordinated. Nobody wants to watch a crappy video after going through all these hassles. In addition, our design should be able to tolerate technical problems such as Internet delays or instability.*" As D4 remarked, "*We want the users to think our (B2I) designs as fun, perhaps helpful, add-ons to things that they have been so familiar with. Users are very picky. As soon as they find a decline in the service quality, they will turn to some other product. If that happens, we (as B2I designers) will be in trouble.*" In a word, B2I design might require some unconventional practices, but it should ultimately lead to positive experience with technologies and with humans.

Choice of Mechanism should Fit the Target and Context

The icebreaking features introduced by B2I design can be viewed as a trigger for desirable behaviors [14]. Whether the trigger serves as a facilitator, signal, or spark, is determined by users' motivations and abilities [14]. When users are willing to make changes such as in the long-distance relationship scenario, B2I design may take a more explicit, proactive approach. When users do not feel like socializing such as in a public place surrounded by strangers, B2I design can implicitly help establish common ground and mutual awareness, which can potentially turn into spark of human-human interaction. D3 explained her intent behind S_2D3: *Sense Me, Chat with Me*, "*My choice of public bench was inspired by the experience of a friend. Once he was sitting in a freezing cold waiting room. He wanted to get someone to adjust the temperature, but was not sure if other people in the room felt the same. He was afraid that asking around would make him seem demanding. My design would show that he was not the only one without having to ask. It creates a sense of togetherness and belonging, and people may be less reluctant to talk.*" All the designers agreed that B2I design should be noticeable but not intrusive. As D3 positioned her S_2D3 design, "*After all, it is a nice piece of interactive art.*"

Stronger Stimulus may be Needed for Significant Barriers

As shown in the anecdotes and reflected by the designers, sometimes the barrier that hinders interpersonal relationship is so thick that a gentle nudge will not break it, and thus it is necessary to apply a stronger stimulation. S_2D1: *Remotouch* is such an example. D1 justified his underlying design rational, "*When the two people fought over the control of air-conditioner (referring to one of the anecdotes), they insisted that the other person was being unreasonable and not considerate. By forcing them to touch each other's hand, Remotouch gives them a chance to really put themselves into the other person's shoes.*"

However, a strong stimulus should only be used when necessary. As D1 further added, "*Remotouch only requires users to hold the remote control together when it senses that there is a conflict, such as the temperature setting going back and forth. Once people achieved mutual understanding and reached consensus, it will returns to the normal mode. Otherwise, it will become annoying.*"

Violation of Ethics and Social Norm should be Reduced

There are usually multiple parties involved in the use of B2I designs. Designers should be conscious of any potential violation of ethics, and try to protect the rights and benefits of all the users. For example, the screenshots of chat history taken by *Random Messenger* not only concern the privacy of the remote couples, but also a third party that appears in the conversation. Therefore, *Random Messenger* does not send the screenshot automatically. Instead, the action needs to be screened and approved by the users.

In summary, B2I encourages designers to rethink the role of technology in humans' life. We need to critically take the view that a B2I design is a player in the ecologies between object, people, and environment [29], rather than merely a medium or tool for communication.

CONCLUSION AND FUTURE WORK

This paper presents the prosperity that insights from broken technology can be leverage to provoke humans to interact and ultimately lead to positive behavioral, emotional, and relational change. Via anecdote analysis, design workshops, and a case study, we gain insights into the conceptual and actionable process of Breakage-to-Icebreaker design. We derive a set of tactics to leverage antifragility without impairing users' relationship with technology. In particular, we identify two methods (byproduct and prerequisite) for embedding B2I mechanisms in existing technologies to exploit their innate tangibility and/or sociality. The goal is to evoke different embodied sensorial experiences of presence that affect perception of interpersonal relationship.

The insights presented in this paper were drawn from a limited number of examples. There should be an easier way to efficiently update and expand this collection, such as gathering data from social media to keep up with the latest innovation and locate better design materials. In addition, we will apply B2I design to other contexts such as persuading sustainable, healthy behaviors in the future.

ACKNOWLEDGMENTS

We thank the participants for their support.

REFERENCES

1. Stephen R. Barley, Debra E. Meyerson, and Stine Grodal. 2011. E-mail as a source and symbol of stress. *Organization Science* 22, 4: 887-906.
2. Eric PS. Baumer and M. Silberman. 2011. When the implication is not to design (technology). In *Proceedings of the SIGCHI Conference on Human Factors in Computing Systems*, 2271-2274.
3. Nancy K. Baym, Yan Bing Zhang, Adrianne Kunkel, Andrew Ledbetter, and Mei-Chen Lin. 2007. Relational quality and media use in interpersonal relationships. *New Media & Society* 9, 5: 735-752.
4. Aaron Ben-Ze'ev. 2004. *Love online: Emotions on the Internet*. Cambridge University Press.
5. Eli Blevis. 2007. Sustainable interaction design: invention & disposal, renewal & reuse. In *Proc. CHI '07*. 503-512.
6. Susanne Bødker. 2006. When second wave HCI meets third wave challenges. In *Proceedings of the 4th Nordic conference on Human-computer interaction: changing roles*, 1-8.
7. Tony Buzan. 2002. *How to Mind Map: The Ultimate Thinking Tool That Will Change Your Life*. Thorson, London.
8. Juliet Corbin and Anselm Strauss. 2014. *Basics of qualitative research: Techniques and procedures for developing grounded theory*. Sage publications.
9. Richard L. Daft and Robert H. Lengel. 1986. Organizational information requirements, media richness and structural design. *Management science* 32, 5: 554-571.
10. Jack Dickey. 2015. Save the American Vacation. Retrieved May 25 from http://time.com/3892050/american-summer-vacation/
11. Paul Dourish. 2004. *Where the action is: the foundations of embodied interaction*. MIT press.
12. Steven P. Dow, Alana Glassco, Jonathan Kass, Melissa Schwarz, Daniel L. Schwartz, and Scott R. Klemmer. 2010. Parallel prototyping leads to better design results, more divergence, and increased self-efficacy. *ACM TOCHI* 17, 4: 18.
13. Anthony Dunne. 1999. *Hertzian tales: Electronic products, aesthetic experience and critical design*. RCACRD Research Publications: London..
14. Brian J. Fogg. 2009. A behavior model for persuasive design. In *Proceedings of the 4th international Conference on Persuasive Technology*. 40.
15. William W. Gaver, Jacob Beaver, and Steve Benford. 2003. Ambiguity as a resource for design. In *Proc. CHI'03*. 233-240.
16. Edward Twitchell Hall. 1996. *The Hidden Dimension*. Anchor Books.
17. Keith N. Hampton, Lauren F. Sessions, Eun Ja Her, and Lee Rainie. 2009. Social Isolation and New Technology. *Pew Internet and American Life Project*, 4.
18. Steve Harrison, Deborah Tatar, and Phoebe Sengers. 2007. The three paradigms of HCI. In *Alt. Chi. Session at the CHI'07*, 1-18.
19. Eva Hornecker and Jacob Buur. 2006. Getting a Grip on Tangible Interaction: A Framework on Physical Space and Social Interaction. In *Proc. CHI'06*. 437-446.
20. Miwa Ikemiya and Daniela K. Rosner. 2014. Broken probes: toward the design of worn media. *Personal and ubiquitous computing*. 18, 3: 671-683.
21. Steven J. Jackson and Laewoo Kang. 2014. Breakdown, Obsolescence and Reuse: HCI and the Art of Repair. In *Proc. CHI'14*. 449-458.
22. Andrea Kavanaugh, John M. Carroll, Mary Beth Rosson, Than Than Zin, and Debbie Denise Reese. 2005. Community networks: Where offline communities meet online. *Journal of Computer-Mediated Communication* 10, 4: 00-00.
23. Regan L. Mandryk and Diego S. Maranan. 2002. False Prophets: Exploring Hybrid Board/Video Games. In *Proc. CHI EA'02*, 640-641.
24. Joseph F. McCarthy, Tony J. Costa, and Edy S. Liongosari. 2001. Unicast, outcast & groupcast: Three steps toward ubiquitous, peripheral displays. In *Ubicomp 2001: Ubiquitous Computing*. 332-345.
25. Miller McPherson, Lynn Smith-Lovin, and Matthew E. Brashears. 2006. Social isolation in America: Changes in core discussion networks over two decades. *American Sociological Review*, 71: 353–375.
26. Susan Moeller. 2010. *"24 hours unplugged." A day without media*. Retrieved July 11, 2014 from http://withoutmedia.wordpress.com/
27. Eric J. Moody. 2001. Internet use and its relationship to loneliness. *CyberPsychology & Behavior* 4, 3: 393-401.
28. Nina-Jo Moore, Mark Hickson, and Don W. Stacks. 2010. *Nonverbal Communication:Studies and Applications*. Oxford Univ. Press: New York.
29. Bonnie A. Nardi, and Vicki O'Day. 1999. *Information Ecologies: Using Technology with Heart*. MIT Press.
30. William Odom, James Pierce, Erik Stolterman, and Eli Blevis. 2009. Understanding why we preserve some things and discard others in the context of interaction design. In *Proc. CHI '09*. 1053-1062.
31. William T. Odom, Abigail J. Sellen, Richard Banks, David S. Kirk, Tim Regan, Mark Selby, Jodi L. Forlizzi, and John Zimmerman. 2014. Designing for slowness, anticipation and re-visitation: a long term field study of the photobox." In *Proc. CHI'14*. 1961-1970. ACM.

32. Nelly Oudshoorn and Trevor Pinch. 2003. *How Users Matter: The Co-Construction of Users and Technology (Inside Technology)*. The MIT Press.

33. Eric Paulos. 2009. The rise of the expert amateur: DIY culture and citizen science. In *Proc.UIST '09*. 181-182.

34. Eric Paulos and Elizabeth Goodman. 2004. The familiar stranger: anxiety, comfort, and play in public places. In *Proc. CHI'04*. 223–230.

35. James Pierce. 2012. Undesigning technology: considering the negation of design by design. In *Proc. CHI'12*. 957-966.

36. James Pierce and Eric Paulos. 2015. Making Multiple Uses of the Obscura 1C Digital Camera: Reflecting on the Design, Production, Packaging and Distribution of a Counterfunctional Device. In *Proc. CHI'15*. 2103-2112.

37. Harvey Sacks and Gail Jefferson. 1995. *Lectures on conversation*.

38. Dan Schawbel. 2012. Why Face-to-Face Networking Still Trumps Social Networking. Retrieved June 6, 2015 from http://business.time.com/2012/04/27/why-face-to-face-networking-trumps-social-networking/

39. Aric Sigman. 2009. Well connected? *Biologist* 56, 1: 14.

40. Lee Sproull and Sara Kiesler. 1986. Reducing social context cues. *Management Science*, 32, 11: 1492-1512.

41. Kaveri Subrahmanyam, Stephanie M. Reich, Natalia Waechter, and Guadalupe Espinoza. 2008. Online and offline social networks: Use of social networking sites by emerging adults. *Journal of Applied Developmental Psychology* 29, 6: 420-433.

42. Marcus Sanchez Svensson, and Tomas Sokoler. 2008. Ticket-to-talk-television: designing for the circumstantial nature of everyday social interaction. Proceedings of the 5th Nordic conference on Human-computer interaction: building bridges. ACM.

43. Nassim Nicholas Taleb. 2012. *Antifragile: Things that gain from disorder*. Vol. 3. Random House Incorporated.

44. Caroline Tell. 2013. Step away from the phone! Retrieved August 9, 2014 from http://www.nytimes.com/2013/09/22/fashion/step-away-from-the-phone.html

45. Eran Toch and Inbal Levi. 2012. What can 'people-nearby' applications teach us about meeting new people? In *Proc. UbiComp*'12. 802-803.

46. Seçil Uğur. 2013. *Wearing embodied emotions: A practice based design research on wearable technology*. Springer.

47. Ron Wakkary and Leah Maestri. 2007. The resourcefulness of everyday design. In *Proc. Creativity and Cognition'07*. 163–172.

48. Joseph B. Walther. 1996. Computer-mediated communication: Impersonal, interpersonal, and hyperpersonal interaction. *Communication Research*, 23, 1: 3–43.

49. Yi Wang and David Redmiles. 2015. Cheap talk, cooperation, and trust in global software engineering. Empirical Software Engineering. 1-35.

50. Hua Wang and Barry Wellman. 2010. Social connectivity in America: Changes in adult friendship network size from 2002 to 2007. *American Behavioral Scientist* 53, 8: 1148-1169.

51. Peter Wright and John McCarthy. 2010. Experience-Centered Design: Designers, Users, and Communities in Dialogue. *Syn. Lect. on HCI 3*, 1: 1–123.

CrowdUX: A Case for Using Widespread and Lightweight Tools in the Quest for UX

Hanna Schneider[a], Katharina Frison[b], Julie Wagner[a], Andras Butz[a]

LMU Munich, Germany
[a]firstname.lastname@ifi.lmu.de
[b]katharina.frison@googlemail.com

ABSTRACT
User studies and expert reviews are established methods for evaluating usability and user experience (UX) in user-centered design. However, practitioners often struggle to integrate these often time-consuming and costly methods in their design processes. As technological products and services are becoming increasingly mobile, their contexts of use are increasingly diverse and less predictable. While this changing context is hard to capture in lab studies, the same mobile technologies also provide possibilities for new study methods. In this paper we advocate lightweight mobile tools for crowdsourcing UX feedback. In cooperation with a design agency, we built two apps that allow users to express feedback with text, ratings and pictures whenever using a product. The second app assigns feedback to categories, while the first does not. In a case study we compared the quantity, relevance, and nature of the feedback collected with both UX evaluation apps to traditional evaluation methods. The feedback collected with the apps was considered highly useful by designers and provided more user stories and context than traditional evaluations.

ACM Classification Keywords
H.5.2. User Interfaces: Evaluation/methodology

Author Keywords
User Experience; Evaluation; Experience Sampling; User-centered Design; Crowdsourcing

THE DILEMMA OF MOBILE UX
The field of HCI has produced a large body of research on user-centered design strategies and methods and their use in developing interaction designs and concepts [38]. Many of these methods were originally developed for the design processes of desktop applications or web pages, but they are less suitable for interaction design or interface design beyond the desktop: For example, testing a headphone gesture interface in the lab might produce qualitative feedback or even quantitative measures about the usage itself and thereby document usability, but it will not provide any user stories or the type of feedback that will arise when users test the same headphone gestures in their everyday life, e.g., in a subway, and embarrass themselves in front of other passengers. What works well in the lab might be totally unacceptable in the wild.

In order to address this dilemma, we worked closely with designers at an international design agency[1]. Usability testing in the lab and expert reviews are part of their standard repertoire. However, running user studies on a regular basis during the short-cycled design process is made difficult by the necessary time for preparing the study, recruiting people, running the study, and then drawing proper conclusions from the results. In addition to laboratory studies, diary studies help them to understand how people use a product or a service in its real context of use. In diary studies participants regularly report events and experiences in their daily lives [6, 8]. However, diary studies are also time- and labour-intensive to prepare and analyse. Thus practitioners – especially smaller design agencies – generally often struggle with applying this method in their daily work [2, 17].

Together with the designers of our partner agency, we therefore developed two prototypes of a UX evaluation tool in the form of a mobile app, by which we were hoping to simultaneously address several of the problems above. If used consistently, we expected this approach to have the potential to decentralize the entire process of running UX evaluations and shift feedback generation to a much larger audience. Hence, we picked the term *CrowdUX* for our app as well as for the title of this paper.

Mobile Technology: A Double-Edged Sword
Pure usability is often regarded a commodity today [30]. As technologies are becoming increasingly mobile, predicting and understanding the context in which they will be used is increasingly difficult. Nevertheless, understanding this context and the overall user experience (UX) is essential for predicting the success of such a product.

DIS'16, June 04 - 08, 2016, Brisbane, QLD, Australia

ACM 978-1-4503-4031-1/16/06 $15.00
DOI: http://dx.doi.org/10.1145/2901790.2901814

[1] http://www.designaffairs.com

On the other hand, the same technological progress also created new opportunities: Today most people carry smartphones wherever they go. These devices are powerful tools for capturing the varying context of the user and for recording feedback with little overhead.

Collecting Feedback in the Wild?

In this situation, we were invited by a design agency to explore together with them the question "What will come after the Usability lab?". The agency develops designs and interaction concepts for a wide range of products and services from industrial designs (e.g., headphones and fridges) to purely virtual products (e.g., mobile and desktop software).

After analysing the work context, goals, and challenges the design agency faces, we formulated the following vision: What if we trusted a wider base of product users to give feedback autonomously (loosely speaking, by *crowdsourcing* the UX feedback)? Could this save money and at the same time capture both the context and the overall UX better? Can such a *Crowd-UX* become a new paradigm in UX engineering, just like *Crowdsourcing* and *Crowdfunding*?

To explore this vision we built a tool that is (1) technically lightweight for scalable roll-out and (2) facilitates a lightweight interaction, so that participants can easily integrate its use in their daily lives. The basic tool can be extended by gamification and motivational features to further encourage participation. With this prototype we then explored three research questions:

RQ1 Is the feedback collected with a UX evaluation app useful and relevant for designers?

RQ2 How does the interface design of the UX evaluation app (free-form vs. structured) influence feedback?

RQ3 What is the difference between expert and non-expert feedback when given through a UX evaluation app?

RELATED WORK

Before discussing *UX feedback* in the wild, we will first establish a common understanding of *UX* as opposed to pure *usability*. Starting from the literature, we will review shortcomings of existing UX evaluation methods and potential advantages of a lightweight UX evaluation app.

Usability vs. User Experience

The goal of the proposed UX evaluation application is to collect feedback on true *user experience* in addition to collecting feedback purely focused on *usability* (as usually done in lab studies) [43]. However, measuring and evaluating UX is a major challenge [25]. To test whether our proposed method is more or less suitable than traditional methods for collecting holistic UX feedback, we need to define how *UX* is different from *usability*. ISO 9241-210 offers a clear distinction between Usability and User Experience Evaluation. *UX* is defined as a "person's perceptions and responses resulting from the use and/or anticipated use of a product, system or service" [1]. However, a global understanding of *UX* has yet to emerge. One source of discrepancies is the gap between academia and industry [15].

In industry the term *UX* is often used as a collective term for efficiency, effectiveness, usability, user-centered design, or overall quality-of-use [3, 5, 15, 25]. In academia, various researchers have proposed frameworks to define and frame *UX*, e.g., Norman [32], McCarthy and Wright [27], Jordan [21], Hassenzahl [16], and Desmet and Hekkert [10].

In our work, we use a framework developed by Kort et al. [24, 42] (Figure 1) that merges ideas of the work from McCarthy and Wright [27], and Desmet and Hekkert [10]. This framework presents three aspects that are relevant for *UX*, namely *compositional aspects*, *aspects of meaning*, and *aesthetic aspects* and incorporates the temporal phases of an experience presented by McCarthy and Wright [27].

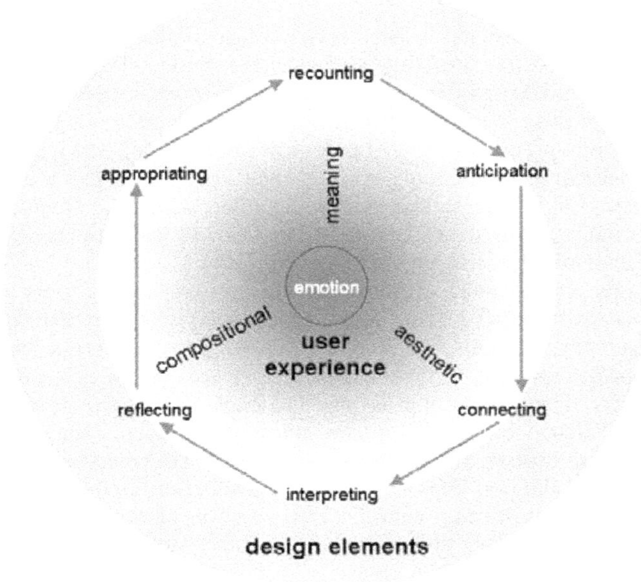

Figure 1. UX framework by Kort et al.[24] stressing *compositional*, *aesthetic*, and *meaning-related* aspects. Figure based on Kort et al.[24]

Compositional aspects address pragmatic properties of a product, e.g., usability and effectiveness. *Aesthetic aspects* address people's sensory perception, e.g., look and feel, sound or coloring of a product. This includes the user's understanding of how a product is working. *Aspects of meaning* address the hedonic properties of the product, which are cognitive processes concerning the users' higher goals, e.g., needs and desires. All these aspects are represented and can be influenced by properties of design elements of a product or service. To consider the user experience holistically, all three aspects need to be observed.

In their study, Vermeeren et al. [42] used these three aspects to categorize feedback. Their goal was to evaluate which method is most suitable to generate different kinds of feedback on a peer-to-peer television system. They found that lab studies and expert reviews were suitable to collect feedback on compositional aspects of a product while logging and sensing data was not. Both aesthetic aspects and aspects of meaning were found mainly in the laboratory study through spontaneous *think-aloud* utterances, as well as in retrospective interviews. We adopt a similar approach as Vermeeren et al. [42]. However, while they [42] compared traditional laboratory studies and expert reviews to logging and sensing data, we compare them to a UX evaluation app that trusts users to give feedback autonomously.

Why Crowdsourcing UX?

Formative feedback during the design process is important for understanding the cognitive and emotional impact of design decisions as well as for inspiring designers [4, 7, 37, 39]. A plethora of design research methods exists, as evidenced by the views of both Roto et al. [35] and Vermeeren et al. [43]. However, while many of these methods include receiving feedback from potential end-users, they do not meet practitioners' needs for *practicability*, understanding *context of use* and *scientific quality* [43]:

(1) *Practicability:* Many methods were developed in an academic context [22, 34, 41, 43]. However, in practice, designers require time-efficient, easy-to-use evaluation methods [41]. In their evaluation work, practitioners are often constrained by budgets and limited access to potential subjects (leading to low statistical reliability of their evaluation) [19, 23]. Hence, evaluation methods have to be adaptable to industry-specific settings and skills.

(2) *Lack of Context of Use:* Methods that collect momentary data (e.g., self-reports) are highly valuable in the design process [3, 43] . However, such methods are difficult to carry out in a valid and rigorous way and are therefore rarely used in practice [43]. Hence, designers often lack an understanding of the actual context of use of the products they are designing.

(3) *Lack of Long-Term Studies:* Evaluating the whole user experience from anticipation to recounting (as proposed by McCarthy and Wright [27]) is usually not practicable and too expensive [3, 18], even in bigger agencies.

In summary, existing research calls for *practicable* methods which allow to collect *long-term* data about the *context of use*. We investigate crowdsourcing UX feedback with a lightweight UX evaluation app as a method that aims to better meet these three challenges. We actually do not use the term *crowdsourcing* in its strict sense here, referring to micro task platforms such as Mechanical Turk. Instead, we use it as a somewhat catchy term for the opportunity to leverage the opinions and contribution of many potential users and to combine and evaluate them systematically. As participants have to be equipped with the product under evaluation, the appropriate number of participants for such a study is limited by the availability of the product (A software product may be installed remotely while a physical product has to be mailed).

How to Crowdsource UX

The opportunities of crowdsourcing have previously been discussed in the fields of design [44, 45] and product development [36]. Our goal was to find out whether this method is useful for a design agency concerned with the design of digital and physical products (RQ1). Moreover, practitioners who build and use a UX evaluation app have to make several decisions, e.g., whether and how feedback is structured or categorised (RQ2) and what expertise level their participants should bring (RQ3). To inform these decisions, we built on previous work on mobile diary studies [8, 9, 14], mobile ethnographies [28], and crowd-testing [26, 44, 45].

RQ1: Usefulness of a UX Evaluation App

The basic functionalities of our UX evaluation app are taking pictures, typing text (as recommended by [8, 20]) and evaluating the overall experience on a likert-scale (as successfully used by [28]). Even though others reported positive results with similar methods [8, 20, 28] a lack of participant engagement and a lack of guidance on how to give feedback present potential problems of the proposed method.

Fading participant commitment is a well-acknowledged limitation and challenge of diary studies [6, 14, 33]. Researchers typically address this by keeping diary entries short to complete [6], by using context-sensing to minimise the effort for the user [14], or by automatically reminding participants to stop, reflect on, and report the current experience [9, 14, 20, 33] (known as the experience sampling method, ESM).

Moreover, in the proposed method, the investigator is not present and can't give guidance when participants are unsure how to give feedback. For example, Muskat et al. [28] found that some participants would have needed guidance on *how* to give feedback and *what* to give feedback *on*. Even though their basic application (with the options to rate the overall experience, add a description, and media content) helped to capture critical events and opportunities of improvement of the museum experience under evaluation, participants were often uncertain what to capture and mentioned many different aspects in one feedback entry [28]. These problems might be reduced by providing guidance through structure in the UX evaluation - a design decision that we aim to evaluate in RQ2.

RQ2: Structured vs. Free-Form Feedback

While Muskat et al. [28] designed their mobile ethnography application to be open to all kinds of feedback, others developed and evaluated more structured feedback tools, e.g., allowing researchers to define per-capture questions that participants answer about each captured photo before uploading it [8]. Some feedback tools are structured according to a set of guidelines. Luther et al. [26], for example provided a feedback structure consisting of seven key design principles: Readability, Layout, Emphasis, Balance, Simplicity, Consistency, and Appropriateness. Similarly, Xu et al. [44, 45] structured feedback in five categories: elements, first notices, impressions, goals, and guidelines. They found that impressions feedback was perceived as most helpful by designers, followed by feedback on goals, with guidelines rated as the least helpful feedback [44]. Both the free-form feedback in Muskat et al.'s study [28] and the structured feedback in Luther et al.'s [26] and Xu et al.'s [44, 45] studies contained valuable information. In our study we aim to better understand the consequences of providing structure by comparing both versions in one case study.

RQ3: Experts vs. Non-experts
The proposed UX evaluation app can be used for tests with both UX and usability experts and non-experts. Expert feedback is often regarded as the gold standard [26, 44, 45]. However, the superiority of expert feedback is at least debatable. Existing research suggests that crowd critique (by a non-expert crowd) matches expert critique better than random critique [26] and in studies where large amounts of feedback were collected (e.g., large-scale prototype testing), non-expert crowd feedback was even more useful than feedback from a limited number of experts [23]. Furthermore, Luther et al. found that many assumed "false positives", issues identified by crowd workers but not by experts, pointed out legitimate issues [26]. Similarly, Nielsen and Molich [31]) revised their list of usability issues to include points only identified by novices but not by experts.

Taking a closer look at the nature of expert and non-expert feedback, it seems that expert feedback has essentially different qualities than non-expert feedback. For example, in Luther et al.'s [26] study a participant commented that novices provided "good emotional feedback" while experts offered "a higher-level technical critique". In our study we aim to gain a deeper understanding of the different nature of expert and non-expert feedback (RQ3).

In summary, similar approaches (e.g., mobile diaries, mobile ethnography, and crowd testing) have been successfully applied to gather user feedback in various contexts e.g., to evaluate the use of ubiquitous and mobile technology [8, 9, 14], the museum experience [28], or graphic design work [44, 45, 26]. In light of this promising previous work, we set out to get a better understanding of the applicability of this approach to the context of a design agency. Furthermore, we aim to investigate how the design of the UX evaluation app (free-form vs. structured) and the expertise (UX and usability expert vs. non-expert) influence the nature, the quantity and the quality of collected feedback.

DESIGN OF A LIGHT-WEIGHT UX EVALUATION TOOL
In a workshop with three designers of our partner agency, we defined requirements for our future UX evaluation tools:

(I) UX evaluation tools should collect 'lots of' and 'good' feedback with a high level of diversity.

(II) The time spent in study preparation and post-hoc analysis of the results should be minimized.

(III) Users should be contacted directly without the detour through expensive agencies; and users should spend less time in user studies leading to cheaper reimbursement.

In this paper, we primarily focus on the first requirement of the designers. We investigate how feedback quality, quantity and diversity compares between traditional user testing and our evaluation tools.

According to the designers we spoke to, UX evaluation tools of the future shall collect feedback of comparable (1) *quantity*, (2) *quality*, and (3) *diversity* to traditional user testing methods. Designers value (1) *feedback quantity*, i.e., the number of critical statements users provide: they are a source for qualitative quotes and provide a quantitative basis to argue for design decisions with managers and costumers. Designers value (2) *feedback quality* as an important inspiration for new design impulses and ideas which push the design process further. Designers value (3) *diverse* feedback, i.e., when the sum of feedback statements provides insight into various design aspects of the product such as usability, aesthetics or user experience stories [42] and thereby provides a holistic perspective on a product or service.

UI for Unmoderated Feedback Collection
Our partner design agency works on a heterogeneous set of products and services, ranging from traditional web pages, to services for renting bikes, to gestural interaction concepts for headphones. Traditional remote user studies applied in desktop environments are one way of unguided feedback collection. They are, however, not applicable for products where interaction takes place on other devices or in different places, e.g., outdoors. We decided to use mobile phones as a means for providing feedback as we can reasonably expect people to have them in reach in most situations. Users can provide text, video, images or audio to quickly describe the context, their feelings and thoughts.

Figure 2 shows the user interface of our prototype *CrowdUX*: users find a list of feedback items which can be edited or removed (see Fig. 2a) and a button to add new feedback (see Fig. 2b). New feedback is provided using a dialog wizard (see Fig. 2c) proposing – not enforcing – that users provide a title, a capture (photo, audio, or video), a description and a feedback rating. The rating is performed on a 7-point Likert scale from 1-very negative to 7-very positive.

Figure 3 shows a variation of *CrowdUX*, which we called *SortedCrowdUX*. It introduces two additional features: (A) a user-assessed categorization of feedback items (see Fig. 3a) and (B) an indication (on a color scale from red via white to green) of the amount of already provided feedback.

With the user-assessed feedback categorization, we expected users to provide more diverse feedback because the interface suggested a variety of potential feedback aspects. Users first decide on a category, e.g., branding or packaging (see Fig. 3 left) and then see a list of items provided for that category. Note that all actions from Figure 3 right are just as in *CrowdUX* (see Fig. 2). The 18 categories are derived from the HUX (Holistic User Experience) Framework [40] but we excluded some product-irrelevant categories (e.g., smell). As a promising side-effect, the categorized feedback reduces the post-processing time for designers because categories don't need to be assigned post-hoc. With the red-to-green visual feedback about users' *'performance'*, we expected to motivate users to provide more feedback in order to push the number up and the color from red to green.

Implementation of the Prototypes
For the implementation we used angularJS ESCMA Script 6 and HTML5. The feedback is stored locally with PouchDB[1]

[1] http://pouchdb.com/

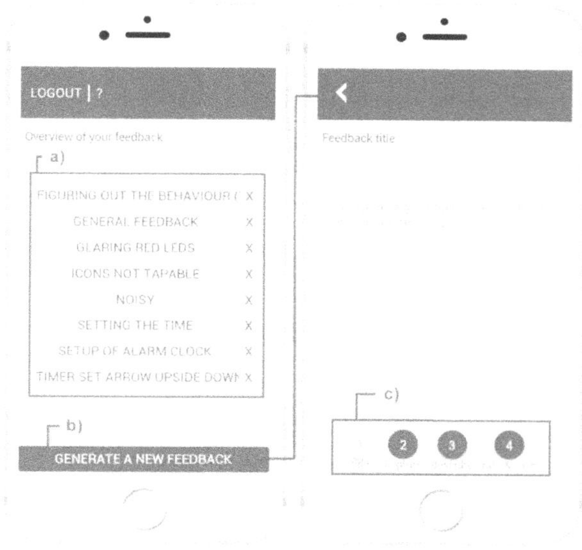

Figure 2. With *CrowdUX* users can provide feedback to products and services: left, (a) list of submitted feedback items, (b) button to create new feedback; right, dialog wizard guiding through feedback (c) title, capture (e.g., photo), description and rating.

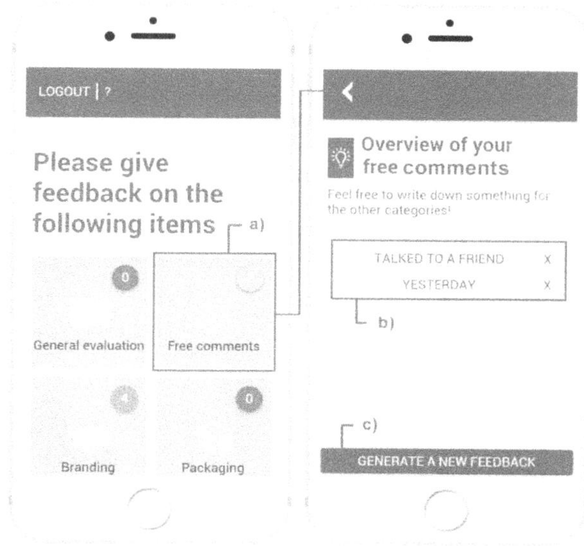

Figure 3. In addition to *CrowdUX*, with *SortedCrowdUX* users can categorize their feedback: left, (a) example tile representing the category "free comments"; right, (b) list of submitted feedback items in category "free comments", (c) button to create new feedback in category "free comments".

and remotely with CouchDB[2]. PouchDB is optimized to run in browsers and stores data if the user is offline. In case there is a connection, the data will be synchronized with CouchDB, a document-based database in which feedback is stored as single documents. Each user has her own personal database, to which she has to log in when starting the web-app. In this database feedback can be added, edited and deleted. Each entry has a time stamp. The administrator has access to the results of all participants on the CouchDB side. For the UI we used and adapted components of Angular Material[3].

CASE STUDY: APP-BASED VS. TRADITIONAL

The Designers in our partner agency traditionally involve two user groups, novices and experts, in their user testing: With novices they perform a laboratory study, while they ask experts to write an expert review. In our study, we compared collecting feedback through these traditional methods with collecting feedback through our prototypes. We were particularly interested in how feedback quantity, quality and diversity would differ between both types of evaluation and between both user groups.

Participants

We recruited 30 paid (5€) participants (14 female), and assigned 5 per condition, based on Nielsen's recommendation to test with 5 users for the best benefit-cost ratio [29]. We chose a lower compensation than most agencies would award their participants, (e.g., 50-100€), as a higher compensation is likely to reveal equally good or better results. 15 participants were UX-experts, defined as someone who has experience with both conducting and participating in user experience studies. Experts were employees of our partner agency, e.g., as UX designers or usability engineers and researchers in the area of UX and usability, assigned randomly to the three conditions. The other 15 participants were non-experts, defined as someone who has no experience with conducting and participating in user experience studies. Non-experts were, for example, students, teachers, or employees in Communication Management, PR, or Business Development. The average age of all participants was 30.

Method

We ran a between-subjects study with a 3 *StudyType* (*Traditional* vs. *CrowdUX* vs. *SortedCrowdUX*) × 2 *Expertise* (*non-experts* vs. *experts*) design. Each expert and non-expert in each *StudyType* received the travel alarm clock *KLOCKIS* from IKEA[4] for evaluation (see Fig. 4). In all conditions, we gave users 5 explicit tasks with the clock.

StudyType Traditional

The traditional procedure of our partner design agency includes user testing with non-experts and expert reviews by experts. In our study, non-experts were asked to participate in a 30 minute experiment. The experimenter asked them to perform 5 tasks (e.g., set the alarm) in a think-aloud fashion and collected feedback in subsequent interviews. We provided each expert with a clock and asked them to write a 1-page review of the product based on the same 5 tasks.

[2] http://couchdb.apache.org/
[3] https://material.angularjs.org/
[4] http://www.ikea.com

Table 1. Tasks and motivational messages sent to study participants via text messages though out the course of the 8-day study

SMS 1	SMS 2	SMS 3	SMS 4	SMS 5
Hi tester, welcome to the test week! Have you already set up the time of your new clock? How do you like your new clock? Cheers, testaffairs	Hey tester, have you already set the alarm for tomorrow? How do you like it? Use the app for your feedback! Good night and sleep well! Cheers, testaffairs	Hi tester, how are you? Are you still using testaffairs? Don't forget to give feedback. We need your opinion! Cheers, testaffairs	Hi tester, today is Sunday! I hope you don't need a clock! But how about eggs for breakfast? What do you think about the timer? Please use the app to give feedback! Thanks and cheers, testaffairs	Hi tester, the week is almost over, Thank you for your feedback! So, how do you generally evaluate the clock? Last chance to give feedback :D Everything matters! Cheers, testaffairs

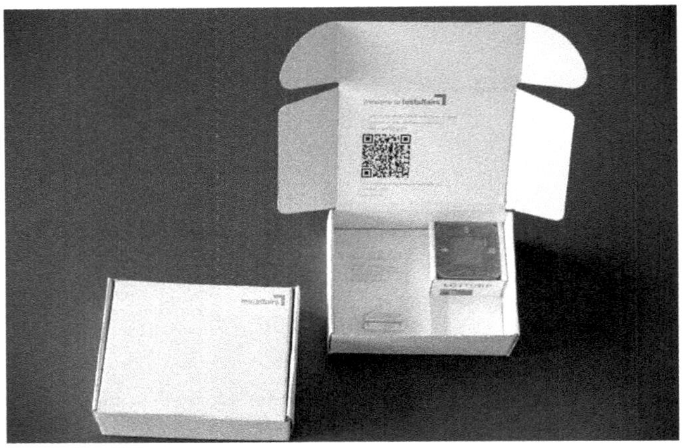

Figure 4. Each participant received a travel alarm clock *KLOCKIS* from Ikea for evaluation in a box with instructions.

StudyType CrowdUX and StudyType SortedCrowdUX
Both non-experts and experts were introduced to the feedback collection tools; they received an alarm clock and were asked to use the product at home during an 8-day period. All participants received another 5 tasks via text message on their phone and were reminded to keep posting feedback (see Tab. 1).

Data Collection
We stored all feedback in digital form: In *Traditional* we transcribed the interviews of non-experts and received digital reports from experts whereas in all other conditions we received the feedback they had posted digitally.

Data Cleaning and Postprocessing
We processed all textual feedback and separated it into *statements*. Semantically similar statements were consolidated into one *insight*.

Statements: we define statements as feedback that (1) contains one specific design aspect (2) of the alarm clock, and (3) is comprehensible. We split up feedback text, when it contained multiple statements: For example, a user might post one feedback: *"the alarm button is not visible, but the clock frame looks beautiful"*; in this case, we would have separated the feedback into two statements. We excluded 80 text statements of *Traditional*, 4 text statements of *CrowdUX* and 9 text statements of *SortedCrowdUX* because they were sarcastic, incomplete, incomprehensible, or did not contain feedback regarding *KLOCKIS*.

Insights: we define insights as semantically distinct information extracted from statements with relevance for the redesign of the product. Multiple statements often referred to the same issue or insight. For example, one user might have said *"the alarm button is not visible"* in *Traditional* and another user might have written *"I can not find the alarm button"* in *CrowdUX*. In this case both statements refer to the same insight.

Feedback Quality
Three designers from our partner agency, who did not participate in the study, assigned a priority ranging from 1 (low priority) to 5 (high priority) to each distinct insight. When designers assigned different priorities they discussed the insight together and agreed upon a priority together.

RESULTS

Highest Feedback Quantity with Traditional User Studies
Those conditions in which feedback was given orally yielded significantly more feedback than all other conditions. This is evidenced by an interaction effect between *Expertise* and *StudyType* $F_{2,24}=10.29$, $p < 0.0001$ on *feedback quantity* (see Fig. 5): Non-experts provided significantly more feedback in *Traditional* – on avg. 48.6 statements ($CI=[41.22, 55.98]$) – than in *CrowdUX* ($mean=14.2$, $CI=[6.82, 21.58]$) and *SortedCrowdUX* ($mean=16.2$, $CI=[8.82, 23.58]$). A Tukey post-hoc test reveals that experts show no significant difference between *StudyTypes*: on average, experts provided 13.2 statements in *Traditional* ($CI=[5.8, 20.6]$), 7.2 statements in *CrowdUX* ($CI=[-0.2, 14.6]$), and 8.6 statements in *SortedCrowdUX* ($CI=[1.2, 16.0]$).

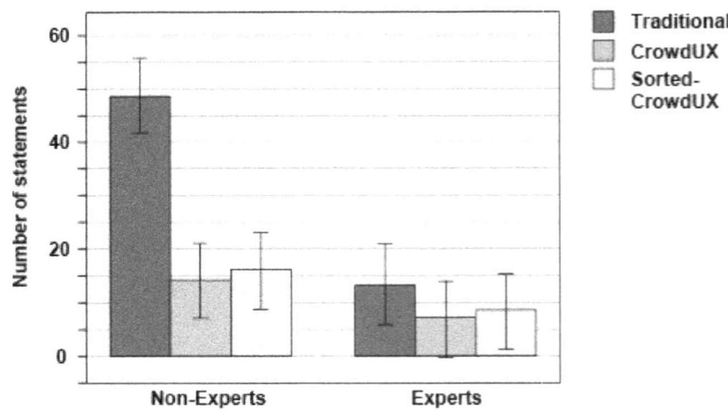

Figure 5. Number of feedback statements in each condition

This interaction effect can be explained by the fact that traditional user studies were the only evaluation method in our study in which feedback was given orally. In all other conditions participants had to express their feedback in writing, which takes more time and effort. Hence, participants wrote down only the most relevant feedback. This explanation is also consistent with the finding that written feedback on average was more relevant to designers than oral feedback.

Higher Relevance of App Feedback

Participants gave more feedback of priority 5 with *CrowdUX* and *SortedCrowdUX* than in the *Traditional* conditions. However, this difference is not statistically significant. On average 55.4% of the feedback in *SortedCrowdUX* (*CI*=[42.2, 68.6]), 48.3% in *CrowdUX* (*CI*=[35.1, 61.5]) and 39.6% in *Traditional* (*CI*=[26.4, 52.8]) had priority 5 (Fig. 6). Furthermore, expert feedback in *SortedCrowdUX* had a significantly higher percentage of priority 5 feedback (*mean*=70.3, *CI*=[57.1, 83.5]) than non-expert feedback (*mean*=42.6, *CI*=[28.9, 55.8]).

Receiving more dense feedback (less feedback with low priority and more feedback with high priority) saves design agencies the time and money needed to process and analyze feedback of low priority.

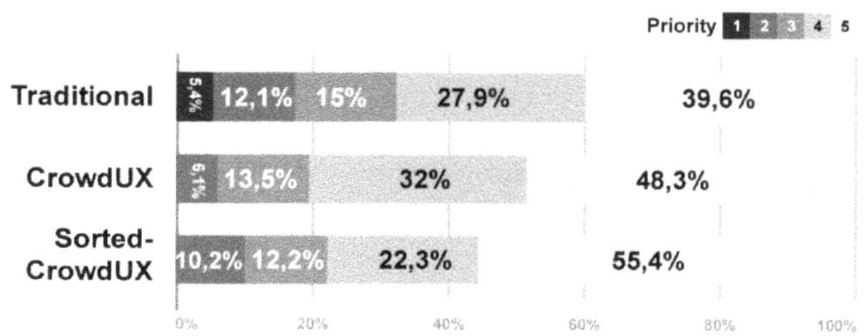

Figure 6. The average percentage of priority 5 feedback (out of all statements of a participant) was highest in *SortedCrowdUX*.

When looking closely, the higher density of feedback in *CrowdUX* and *SortedCrowdUX* was not only caused by the absence of low priority feedback, but also by additional high priority feedback that was not discovered in *Traditional*.

No Method Found All Important Insights

Out of 31 priority 5 insights in total, 23 were discovered in *Traditional* and 20 in both *CrowdUX* and *SortedCrowdUX*. Conversely, 8 priority 5 insights were missed in *Traditional*, and 11 each in *CrowdUX* and *SortedCrowdUX*. Hence, with 10 participants no single method found all important insights, indicating that combining methods might yield best results. Remarkably, even though *Traditional* yielded *3x* more feedback than *CrowdUX* and *SortedCrowdUX*, those statements contained only *1.15x* more priority 5 insights.

More Context with CrowdUX

Looking closer at the high priority insights missed in traditional user studies, it becomes evident that 62.5% of these insights are related to the context of use. One subject for example reported "I thought this clock has a radio clock and I do not have to set the time manually. Unfortunately I recognized - after waiting for five minutes - that this function does not exist". Other participants complained that the

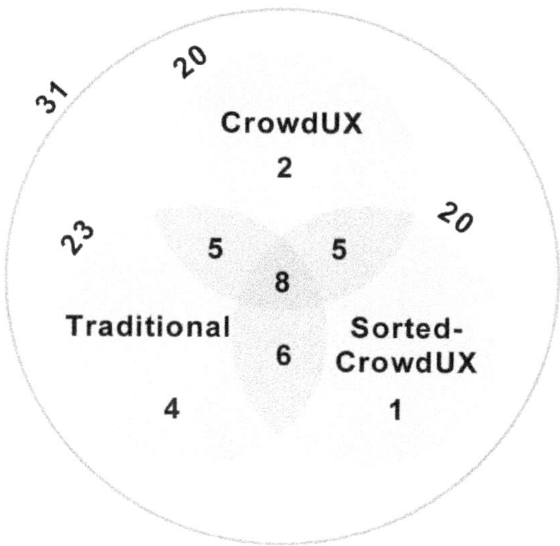

Figure 7. Of 31 insights with the highest priority, 23 were discovered in *Traditional* and 20 in each *CrowdUX* and *SortedCrowdUX* - no method discovered all important insights with 10 participants.

beeping of *KLOCKIS* (when being turned 90 degrees) is unpractical, when carrying it in a suitcase; they commented on the lack of time-zone adaption and automatic time setting; and they mentioned how much they enjoyed using the temperature function throughout the day. In contrast to usability issues, which are easily discovered in lab studies, this type of feedback entails scenarios of use, context of use and users' personal values and feelings when using the product.

To quantify what kind of feedback each method reveals, we distinguished between aesthetic, compositional and meaning feedback (according to the framework by Kort et al. [24]). Figure 8 shows the average amounts of each feedback aspect per condition. *CrowdUX* yielded the biggest proportion of *meaning* feedback (on average 37.3% of feedback given by a participant (*CI*=[26.4, 48.2]), which is significantly more than in *Traditional* ($F_{2,27}$=4.03, p = 0.026). In *Traditional* the average percentage of *meaning* feedback was 15.8% (*CI*=[4.9, 26.8]) and in *SortedCrowdUX* 25.6% (*CI*=[14.6, 36.5]).

This effect confirms that light-weight UX evaluation tools are in fact suitable for gathering context-rich user stories.

Traditional yielded the biggest proportion of *compositional* feedback (on average 63.3% of feedback given by a participant (*CI*=[49.4, 77.1]). In *CrowdUX* the average percentage of *compositional* feedback per participant was 38.7% (*CI*=[24.8, 52.5]) and in *SortedCrowdUX* 24.1% (*CI*=[10.2, 37.9]). This result is not surprising as studies in a usability lab are by nature focused on usability problems. *SortedCrowdUX* yielded the biggest proportion of *aesthetic* feedback per participant (on average 50.9% of feedback (*CI*=[36.7, 64.1]). In *Traditional* the average percentage of *aesthetic* feedback was 20.9% (*CI*=[7.2, 34.5]) and in *CrowdUX* 24.0% (*CI*=[10.4, 37.7]).

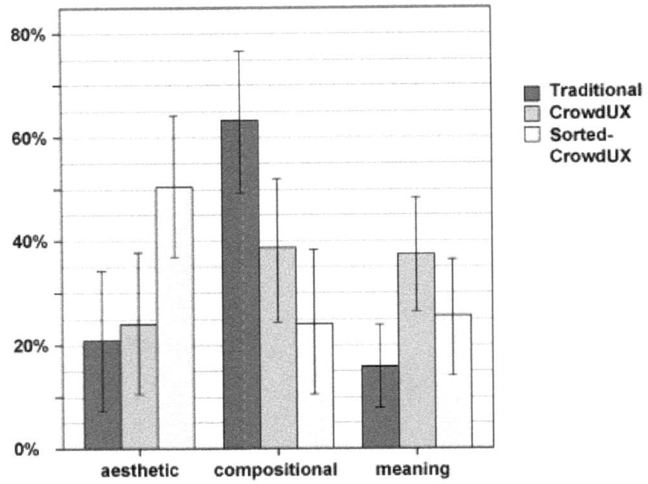

Figure 8. ***CrowdUX*** **revealed more user stories and context (concerning the** ***meaning*** **aspect) while** ***Traditional*** **revealed more feedback about usability issues (concerning** ***compositional*** **aspects) and** ***SortedCrowdUX*** **yielded feedback about** ***aesthetic*** **aspects.**

We suspect that this effect was partly caused by the feedback categories suggested by *SortedCrowdUX*. Hence, providing categories indeed seems to be a powerful tool to guide feedback. In particular, the feedback provided by experts was also found to be more useful when categories were provided.

Questions and Tasks Do Not Lead to More Feedback

The relatively smaller amount of feedback per participant with *CrowdUX* and *SortedCrowdUX* indicates that engaging users to give more feedback still is a major challenge of this type of mobile diary studies. In *CrowdUX* and *SortedCrowdUX* we sent participants text massages with questions, reminders, and tasks (in total five messages over the course of the 8-day study). Figure 9 shows the percentage of feedback items and observations triggered by each of these prompts: The percentage of self-initiated feedback per participant was significantly higher than the percentage of feedback triggered by other sources over all conditions $F_{1,29}$=67.33, $p < 0.0001$. In *Traditional* 13.0% of the feedback was triggered by a scripted question (CI=[7.7, 18.3]), 5.1% of the feedback was triggered by a task (CI=[−1.0, 11.2]), 11.5% of the feedback was triggered by a spontaneous question the instructor asked (CI=[9.0, 14.1]), and 64.1% of the feedback was self-initiated (CI=[56.1, 72.0]). In addition, the instructor made notes when she observed that the participant had difficulties. These instructor observations accounted for 6.3% of the discovered insights (CI=[4.7, 7.9]). In *CrowdUX* 15.6% of the feedback was triggered by a scripted question (CI=[10.3, 21.0]), 12.0% was triggered by a task (CI=[5.9, 18.1]), and 72.4% was self-initiated (CI=[64.4, 80.4]). In *SortedCrowdUX* 1.4% of the feedback was triggered by a scripted question (CI=[−3.9, 6.8]), 0.8% by a task (CI=[−5.3, 7.0]), and 97.3% was self-initiated (CI=[89.3, 105.3]). As there was no investigator present in *CrowdUX* and *SortedCrowdUX*, there were no observations or spontaneous questions in these conditions.

These results show that questions, tasks and reminders triggered only a small amount of feedback. Hence, these measures do not solve the problem of low participant engagement of mobile diary studies. Strategies that could help to tackle this problem include gamification [11], creative reimbursement strategies [33] or persuasive system design [13]. An alternative strategy for collecting sufficient feedback, of course, is to increase the number of participants.

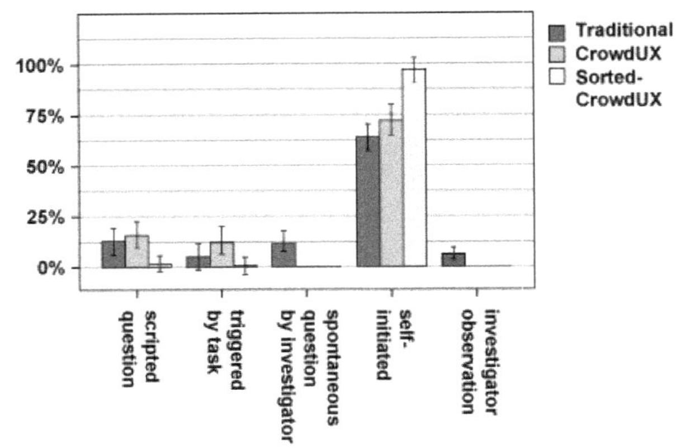

Figure 9. Most of the feedback in all three conditions was self-initiated by participants and not triggered by questions or tasks.

DISCUSSION AND CONCLUSION

In this paper, we have discussed methods for collecting user feedback through the use of light-weight tools in the form of mobile apps. In collaboration with a design agency, we conducted a case study comparing the feedback generated with a UX evaluation app by both experts and non-experts to feedback generated in traditional user tests and expert reviews. The goal of our case study was to better understand how the choice of method and participants influences the (quality and quantity of) feedback obtained from the perspective of a design agency.

RQ1: Lab Studies vs. UX Evaluation App

Our first research question was to evaluate whether feedback collected with a UX evaluation app is valuable for designers. Overall our results showed that this was the case: Feedback was understandable, rich, and relevant for designers. Moreover, evaluations with both *CrowdUX* and *SortedCrowdUX* yielded feedback that did not emerge in *Traditional* (Fig. 7). In particular, this feedback contained rich user stories and context of use while the *Traditional* method revealed more usability feedback.

RQ2: Structured vs. Free-Form Feedback

Our second goal was to understand the influence of design properties of the UX evaluation app. For this, we compared two versions of a UX evaluation app, one in which participants were asked to specify the category of feedback (*SortedCrowdUX*) and one in which they were not

(*CrowdUX*). We found that *SortedCrowdUX* yielded less user stories and context of use and more feedback regarding the aesthetics of the product. These results may reflect the fact that some of the proposed categories were related to aesthetics e.g., colour and haptics. While we used categories to guide feedback in certain directions, we were not aware that they could also prevent users from entering feedback that does not fit into any category, despite the existence of a category called *Other Comments*. Another drawback of providing categories was that users might have misunderstood some categories and therefore assigned feedback erroneously.

RQ3: Experts vs. Non-Experts

Our third research question was about the differences between expert and non-expert feedback. In *CrowdUX* we did not find significant differences in feedback quality between expert and non-expert feedback. However, *SortedCrowdUX* yielded especially useful feedback from experts.

Compared to non-experts, experts had a better understanding for the feedback categories defined by designers. Compared to expert reviews, evaluations with *SortedCrowdUX* allowed experts to spend time *living* with the product and they were more likely to discover issues related to the context of use, in comparison with evaluating the product in an artificial setting within 30 minutes. We hence argue that expert evaluations with *SortedCrowdUX* can leverage some of the same advantages as autoethnographies [12]. Simultaneously they can also provide the same benefits as heuristics in expert reviews [31]: Designers can choose the categories relevant for the design of a specific product before the evaluation.

Outlook: A Wide Spectrum of Usage Scenarios

We believe that lightweight UX evaluations as the ones in our case study can be a useful tool in many usage scenarios, including a variety of products and services in different phases of the development cycle, and including both local and global, as well as short- and long-term studies. The presented prototypes are extensible in various directions. First, in future work we plan to extend the prototype itself with the option to provide audio feedback and with gamification and creative reimbursement strategies and to investigate the effects. Second, in future work parameters such as the expertise of participants, length of study and categories could be integrated in the setup process of a study. In this way, designers could simultaneously leverage the benefits of three established methods: expert reviews, traditional user tests, and diary studies. As a third way to further explore the potential of the presented method, the prototypes could be used with remotely recruited crowdsourced participants, e.g. asking for feedback on a software product.

The Case for Widespread Lightweight Tools

In summary, our case study shows that lightweight UX tools have become technically feasible and present a valuable addition to traditional evaluation methods. Practicability and the possibility to collect information about the context of use are substantial advantages of the proposed method, making it especially suitable for projects with a tight budget and the need for rigorous evaluation.

ACKNOWLEDGMENTS

We thank Alexander Peters and Johannes Huber, designers at our partner agency, who contributed to our research project with insightful stories, experiences and opinions about the work context and the design processes in their design agency. Furthermore, we thank all participants for their time, feedback, and engagement throughout the study.

REFERENCES

1. ISO 9241:210:2010: Ergonomics of human-system interaction - Part 210: Human-centred design for interactive systems. Standard, International Organization for Standardization, Geneva, CH, March 2010.
2. Rui Alves, Pedro Valente, and Nuno J. Nunes. The state of user experience evaluation practice. In *Proceedings of the 8th Nordic Conference on Human-Computer Interaction: Fun, Fast, Foundational*, pages 93–102. ACM, 2014.
3. Javier A. Bargas-Avila and Kasper Hornbæk. Old wine in new bottles or novel challenges: a critical analysis of empirical studies of user experience. In *Proceedings of the SIGCHI Conference on Human Factors in Computing Systems*, pages 2689–2698. ACM, 2011.
4. Nigel Bevan. Classifying and selecting UX and usability measures. In *International Workshop on Meaningful Measures: Valid Useful User Experience Measurement*, pages 13–18, 2008.
5. Nigel Bevan. UX, usability and ISO standards. In *26th Annual Conference on Computer Human Interaction (CHI), ACM SIGCHI*, 2008.
6. Niall Bolger, Angelina Davis, and Eshkol Rafaeli. Diary methods: Capturing life as it is lived. *Annual review of psychology*, 54(1):579–616, 2003.
7. Michael Burmester, Kilian Jäger, Laura Festl, and Marcus Mast. Studien zur formativen evaluation der user experience mit der valenzmethode. *Reflexionen und Visionen der Mensch–Maschine-Interaktion–Aus der Vergangenheit lernen, Zukunft gestalten*, 9:567–572, 2011.
8. Scott Carter and Jennifer Mankoff. When participants do the capturing: the role of media in diary studies. In *Proceedings of the SIGCHI conference on Human factors in computing systems*, pages 899–908. ACM, 2005.
9. Sunny Consolvo and Miriam Walker. Using the experience sampling method to evaluate ubicomp applications. *IEEE Pervasive Computing*, (2):24–31, 2003.
10. Pieter Desmet and Paul Hekkert. Framework of product experience. *International journal of design, 1 (1) 2007*, 2007.
11. Sebastian Deterding, Dan Dixon, Rilla Khaled, and Lennart Nacke. From game design elements to gamefulness: defining gamification. In *Proceedings of*

the 15th International Academic MindTrek Conference: Envisioning Future Media Environments, pages 9–15. ACM, 2011.

12. Carolyn S. Ellis and Arthur Bochner. Autoethnography, personal narrative, reflexivity: Researcher as subject. 2000.
13. Brian J. Fogg. Persuasive technology: using computers to change what we think and do. *Ubiquity*, 2002(Dec.), 2002.
14. Jon Froehlich, Mike Y. Chen, Sunny Consolvo, Beverly Harrison, and James A. Landay. Myexperience: a system for in situ tracing and capturing of user feedback on mobile phones. In *Proceedings of the 5th international conference on Mobile systems, applications and services*, pages 57–70. ACM, 2007.
15. Marc Hassenzahl. User experience (UX): towards an experiential perspective on product quality. In *Proceedings of the 20th International Conference of the Association Francophone d'Interaction Homme-Machine*, pages 11–15. ACM, 2008.
16. Marc Hassenzahl and Noam Tractinsky. User experience – a research agenda. *Behaviour & information technology*, 25(2):91–97, 2006.
17. Mats Hellman and Kari Rönkkö. Is user experience supported effectively in existing software development processes? In *Proc. of COST294-MAUSE Workshop on Valid Useful User Experience Measurement (VUUM). Reykjavik, Island*, pages 32–37, 2008.
18. Kasper Hornbæk. Current practice in measuring usability: Challenges to usability studies and research. *International journal of human-computer studies*, 64(2):79–102, 2006.
19. Tobias Hoßfeld, Christian Keimel, Matthias Hirth, Bruno Gardlo, Julian Habigt, Klaus Diepold, and Phuoc Tran-Gia. Best practices for QoE crowdtesting: QoE assessment with crowdsourcing. *Multimedia, IEEE Transactions on*, 16(2):541–558, 2014.
20. Stephen Intille, Charles Kukla, and Xiaoyi Ma. Eliciting user preferences using image-based experience sampling and reflection. In *CHI'02 Extended Abstracts on Human Factors in Computing Systems*, pages 738–739. ACM, 2002.
21. Patrick W. Jordan. *Designing pleasurable products: An introduction to the new human factors*. CRC press, 2002.
22. Pekka Ketola and Virpi Roto. Exploring user experience measurement needs. In *Proc. of the 5th COST294-MAUSE Open Workshop on Valid Useful User Experience Measurement (VUUM). Reykjavik, Island*, pages 23–26, 2008.
23. Aniket Kittur, Ed H. Chi, and Bongwon Suh. Crowdsourcing user studies with mechanical turk. In *Proceedings of the SIGCHI conference on human factors in computing systems*, pages 453–456. ACM, 2008.
24. Joke Kort, Arnold P.O.S. Vermeeren, and Jenneke E. Fokker. Conceptualizing and measuring user experience. In *Proc. Towards a UX Manifesto, COST294-MAUSE affiliated workshop*, pages 57–64, 2007.
25. Effie L-C. Law, Virpi Roto, Marc Hassenzahl, Arnold P.O.S. Vermeeren, and Joke Kort. Understanding, scoping and defining user experience: a survey approach. In *Proceedings of the SIGCHI Conference on Human Factors in Computing Systems*, pages 719–728. ACM, 2009.
26. Kurt Luther, Jari-Lee Tolentino, Wei Wu, Amy Pavel, Brian P. Bailey, Maneesh Agrawala, Björn Hartmann, and Steven P. Dow. Structuring, aggregating, and evaluating crowdsourced design critique. In *Proceedings of the 18th ACM Conference on Computer Supported Cooperative Work & Social Computing*, CSCW '15, pages 473–485, New York, NY, USA, 2015. ACM.
27. John McCarthy and Peter Wright. Technology as experience. *interactions*, 11(5):42–43, September 2004.
28. Matthias Muskat, Birgit Muskat, Anita Zehrer, and Raechel Johns. Generation y: evaluating services experiences through mobile ethnography. *Tourism Review*, 68(3):55–71, 2013.
29. Jakob Nielsen. Guerrilla hci: Using discount usability engineering to penetrate the intimidation barrier. *Cost-justifying usability*, pages 245–272, 1994.
30. Jakob Nielsen. *Usability engineering*. Elsevier, 1994.
31. Jakob Nielsen and Rolf Molich. Heuristic evaluation of user interfaces. In *Proceedings of the SIGCHI conference on Human factors in computing systems*, pages 249–256. ACM, 1990.
32. Donald A. Norman. Introduction to this special section on beauty, goodness, and usability. *Hum.-Comput. Interact.*, 19(4):311–318, December 2008.
33. Leysia Palen and Marilyn Salzman. Voice-mail diary studies for naturalistic data capture under mobile conditions. In *Proceedings of the 2002 ACM conference on Computer supported cooperative work*, pages 87–95. ACM, 2002.
34. Virpi Roto, Marianna Obrist, and Kaisa Väänänen-Vainio-Mattila. User experience evaluation methods in academic and industrial contexts. In *Interact 2009 conference, User Experience Evaluation Methods in Product Development (UXEM'09), Uppsala, Sweden*. Citeseer, 2009.
35. Virpi Roto, Heli Väätäjä, Satu Jumisko-Pyykkö, and Kaisa Väänänen-Vainio-Mattila. Best practices for capturing context in user experience studies in the wild. In *Proceedings of the 15th International Academic MindTrek Conference: Envisioning Future Media Environments*, pages 91–98. ACM, 2011.

36. Jonathan Rubin. Can you crowdsource your user experience research? (online at http://www.digitalgov.gov/2014/12/09/can-you-crowdsource-your-user-experience-research/), December 2014.

37. D. Royce Sadler. Formative assessment and the design of instructional systems. *Instructional Science*, 18(2):119–144, 1989.

38. Liz Sanders. On modeling an evolving map of design practice and design research. *interactions*, 15(6):13–17, 2008.

39. Donald A. Schön. *The reflective practitioner: How professionals think in action*, volume 5126. Basic books, 1983.

40. Claude Toussaint, Marc Toussaint, and Stefan Ulrich. Hux–measuring holistic user experience. *Tagungsband UP12*, 2012.

41. Kaisa Väänänen-Vainio-Mattila, Virpi Roto, and Marc Hassenzahl. Towards practical user experience evaluation methods. *EL-C. Law, N. Bevan, G. Christou, M. Springett & M. Lárusdóttir (eds.) Meaningful Measures: Valid Useful User Experience Measurement (VUUM)*, pages 19–22, 2008.

42. Arnold P.O.S. Vermeeren, Joke Kort, Anita Cremers, and Jenneke Fokker. Comparing ux measurements, a case study. In *Proceedings of the International Workshop on Meaningful Measures: Valid Useful Experience Measurement, Reykjavik, Iceland, June*, volume 18, pages 72–78, 2008.

43. Arnold P.O.S. Vermeeren, Effie L-C. Law, Virpi Roto, Marianna Obrist, Jettie Hoonhout, and Kaisa Väänänen-Vainio-Mattila. User experience evaluation methods: current state and development needs. In *Proceedings of the 6th Nordic Conference on Human-Computer Interaction: Extending Boundaries*, pages 521–530. ACM, 2010.

44. Anbang Xu, Shih-Wen Huang, and Brian Bailey. Voyant: generating structured feedback on visual designs using a crowd of non-experts. In *Proceedings of the 17th ACM conference on Computer supported cooperative work & social computing*, pages 1433–1444. ACM, 2014.

45. Anbang Xu, Huaming Rao, Steven P. Dow, and Brian P. Bailey. A classroom study of using crowd feedback in the iterative design process. In *Proceedings of the 18th ACM Conference on Computer Supported Cooperative Work & Social Computing*, pages 1637–1648. ACM, 2015.

Trust Me: Doubts and Concerns Living with the Internet of Things

Peter Worthy, Ben Matthews, Stephen Viller
School of Information Technology & Electrical Engineering
University of Queensland
Brisbane, Queensland
p.worthy@uq.edu.au, matthews@uq.edu.au, viller@acm.org

ABSTRACT
An increasing number of everyday objects are now connected to the internet, collecting and sharing information about us: the "Internet of Things" (IoT). However, as the number of 'social' objects increases, human concerns arising from this connected world are starting to become apparent. This paper presents the results of a preliminary qualitative study in which five participants lived with an ambiguous IoT device that collected and shared data about their activities at home for a week. In analyzing this data, we identify the nature of human and socio-technical concerns that arise when living with IoT technologies. Trust is identified as a critical factor - as trust in the entity/ies that are able to use their collected information decreases, users are likely to demand greater control over information collection. Addressing these concerns may support greater engagement of users with IoT technology. The paper concludes with a discussion of how IoT systems might be designed to better foster trust with their owners.

Author Keywords
Internet of Things; Human Centered Design; Trust; Privacy; Data.

ACM Classification Keywords
H.5.2. User Interfaces: User-centered design.

INTRODUCTION
Internet of Things ("IoT") technology is becoming more pervasive. There are increasingly more connected devices in our environment, collecting and sharing data about us. The expected benefits extend beyond efficient and effective business process but also to societal benefits such as a 'more convenient way of life' [26]. To date, much of the research about IoT technology has focused on 'solving technical problems' with very little focus on 'issues related to potential adoption, usage and impact' [21]. People are expressing sociotechnical or 'human concerns' about issues such as privacy, security and trust [16]. These issues and concerns are based in the human values that have been implicated by the design, use, contexts of use, and interactions (both person-to-machine and person-to-person) of that technology [24].

Human values *"serve as guiding principles of what people consider important in life"* [9] going beyond monetary consideration [19]. In terms of technology, human values are what people consider to be important in terms of their relationship and interaction with that technology as well as any indirect effects from the use of that technology [9,12]. Values are the basis for our attitudes, choices and behaviours [12] and are influential in the creation, use and non-use of technology [27]. People's engagement with technologies such as IoT will be dependent upon how well that technology supports the human values that are implicated by that technology: its design; its use within the specific use context; and its social impact [17,23].

This paper presents five case studies that are part of an initial investigation into the human values that are implicated when living with IoT technology and how those values are enacted: expressed as concerns or doubts, or revealed in their behaviour. These case studies reveal important methodological considerations when investigating human values.

BACKGROUND AND MOTIVATION

Human Values and Concerns with Ubicomp and IoT
There is substantial overlap between Ubiquitous Computing and IoT technologies [2]. The sociotechnical or human concerns about Ubicomp centred around a general concept of privacy. However, the human value of privacy has a number of domains [8].

Information Privacy
As Ubicomp became more pervasive, the amount of data collected increased dramatically [21]. Smith et al (1996) explored the concern about information privacy using, amongst other methods, surveys and focus groups of consumers and expert judges. They concluded that human concerns about information privacy may be divided into 4 subscales: large amounts of identifiable data are being collected and stored; errors, both deliberate and accidental, may exist in that data; the data may be used for a purpose

DIS 2016, June 04 - 08, 2016, Brisbane, QLD, Australia

ACM 978-1-4503-4031-1/16/06…$15.00
DOI: http://dx.doi.org/10.1145/2901790.2901890

different than the stated purpose; and, the data may be used by people other than those who were initially authorized to use that data [25].

Being Tracked

Brown et al., [4] implemented a Ubicomp application that featured location tracking into a number of households. Based on interviews of household members, they found that people who were not members of a household but heard of the application, expressed concerns about being tracked. Based on a review of research available at that time, Abowd et al. [1] concluded that these manifest as concerns that people: do not know when and how they are being sensed; do not know what information is being collected; and, feel that something is being done "behind their backs" as they do not know what a computing system might actually be doing.

Big Data

Ubicomp has led to large amounts of data now being available [21]. From this comes a concern that data that was previously too difficult or laborious to collect is now being collected and used [1]. A consequent concern is that there is now large amounts of data containing information about a wide range of things that is open to the potential for abuse [4].

Smith et al., [25] found that people were concerned around "reduced judgment" where they feel as if they are being "treated as a number rather than an individual", and where incorrect decisions are made due to automated decision making and the reduction or absence of human moderation in the decision making process. They also found that people were concerned about, what they termed, the "mosaic effect" where data collected in separate database which, when used in isolation is innocuous, is aggregated with other data and used for a purpose not envisaged when the data was collected [19].

Investigating human values and concerns

Over recent years, the relationship between people and computers has been subject to significant transformations from factors such as: the *'end of interface stability'* where technology is embedded into objects in our environment and our own personal space; *'the growth of hyperconnectivity'* such that we, as people, are now more connected than ever; and *'the end of the ephemeral'* as we increase our digital footprint both in the amount of data that is captured but also the number of places that this data is stored [22]. These transformations mean that there are a wider range of issues, based in human values, that must be considered when designing new technology [13,20]. Unfortunately, human values are most often manifested through concerns such as 'counterproductivity, tension, or failure' [15] and these concerns may be a barrier to people's acceptance of technology [13,16].

IoT technology has the potential to deliver significant benefit to people and society in many different contexts [3,21]. However, to ensure people adopt and engage with IoT technology, that technology must support the human values implicated by it and its use. As designers, we need to identify and understand the human values implicated when living with the IoT and the concerns that may manifest when those values are neglected or impinged [6,21]. Whilst there is research examining people's experience of Ubicomp, at the present time, there is little research of the human values implicated from living with the IoT [8,21].

Beyond the people-computer relationship we are now realizing that digital data is a *"distinctive phenomenon worthy of treatment in its own right"*[5]. It is a sociotechnical system giving rise to interactional challenges that are based in human relationships [5] and is the subject of an emerging field called Human Data Interaction [5,11]. The field is concerned with data as it relates to people and data that is of a personal nature to people [5]. As a sociotechnical system, the issues that arise relate to both technological factors as well as social factors [5]. To support interaction between humans and data, humans must be central to any considerations regarding data collection, management and access [11]. One important challenge facing this field is the need to understand what must to be communicated and made explicit to people regarding the collection, management, use (including purpose for use) and ownership of personal data [5,11]. Another is addressing the complexities of dealing with human consent to pervasive and embedded systems, such as IoT and Ubicomp, to ensure that those technologies maintain genuine user agency in relation to the data that is collected [18].

METHOD

The values implicated by a system emerge from: the technology itself; the people involved the design and use of the technology; and, the social context in which that technology is used [10,27]. As values are 'enacted' through the use of the technology by many people, *'multiple interpretations of a single value arise, as well'* [27]. How these values "play out" will vary based on cultural factors at a specific point in time [9]. Further, a person's use of technology will change over time as that person as different situations arise [12]. Therefore it is important to explore and understand how different stakeholders enact values when interacting with a system in a specific real world use context and how these values evolve over time [13,27].

A device (see Figure 1) was developed to be installed in participant's domestic environment. The device was used as a technology probe [14] with the intention of supporting an initial investigation into the real world social setting where this type of technology would ultimately be deployed [7]. It used the Particle Photon™ microcontroller which was connected to Wi-Fi. It had a number of sensors connected to it. One sensor, either a Passive Infrared Sensor or a Sound Pressure senor, was used as a trigger for data to be sent to and recorded in an SQL database. The other sensors were either a temperature and humidity sensor or an air quality sensor. When triggered, the device would cause readings from the sensors to be recorded in the database. At the same time, neo-pixels inside the device would cause the device to glow.

Five participants were recruited to be involved in the study. These participants were recruited through the personal network of the researchers and, as such, there was an existing relationship with the main researcher as either family or acquaintances. Two of the participants, Terry and Elizabeth, are academics although neither work at the authors' university and both work in a field unrelated to Interaction Design or Human Computer Interaction.

The study involved the device being installed in their homes for between 10 to 14 days (depending on their individual circumstances). Prior the device being installed, participants were provided with an Information Sheet about the study and then provided written consent. Participants were then invited to ask any questions about either the study or the device. Participants were not told, as a matter of course, what kind of data would be collected by the device. The intention was to discern what sorts of enquiries people would make of the device. It was hoped that this would provide some insight into what factors were important given their initial perceptions of the device. However, all questions asked by a participant were answered truthfully and completely.

At the end of the study period, participants were interviewed. The interview was semi-structured. Three main topics were raised: 1. Participants were asked for their general reflections about living with the device. 2. An explanation of the nature of the data that was collected was provided. Then, participants were advised of possible inferences that could be drawn from this data (whether someone was active in the home or whether, potentially, no-one was present). Participants were then asked how they felt about this. 3. An explanation was provided to participants of the possibility for data, such as that collected in this study, to be more widely or openly available. Participants were also asked how they felt about this. Audio of the interview was recorded, transcribed and reviewed.

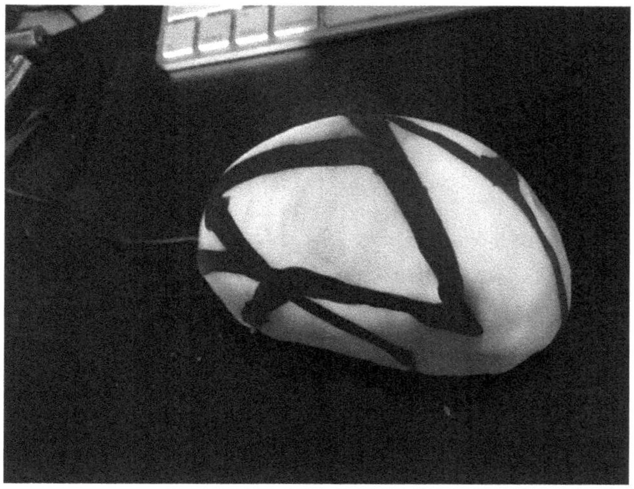

Figure 1. IoT device as deployed.

FINDINGS

Olga

Olga's first reflection on the device was that, after a very short period she mostly *"forgot"* about the device. However, on re-reading the few notes she had made in her diary, her main concern was about who would have access to the sort of information that was recorded. In particular, Olga did not want her family to be able to access the information *"because I live away from home, because I want to live away from my family"*. Olga indicated that whoever was going to have access to the information would need to be *"trustworthy"*.

Olga speculated on the sort of information that the device was recording about the environment and jokingly stated that "This place is a pigsty. I'm going to clean up." She wondered whether it was *"scanning"* the physical environment or if it was monitoring objects that were connected to either power or the internet. Prior to the device being installed, Olga had asked whether the device was capable of recording video and audio and was advised that it did not. The limitations of what the device was able to monitor were explained along with the ability to infer information from the data that was collected. Olga again mentioned the need for whoever had access to the data to be trustworthy *"because all humans have patterns then you'd be able to tell the pattern of the human."* Olga mentioned that, at times, she had worked on her hobby until around 2am. Had her family had access to this information they would have enquired into her activities. As a further example, Olga indicated that there were times that she chose not to accept telephone calls from her family for various reasons. If her family, through accessing data from the device, knew this it would simply lead to *"issues"*.

At another time, Olga had been relaxing and had not moved for a period of time. She expressed concern about the device 'knowing' about her inactivity: *"I've been sitting around for a while. I haven't actually gotten up and moved. That thing's gonna know!"* Olga expressed that she would not want others using information about her 'inappropriately'. At that point, Olga stated: *"I wouldn't want it in my place with me now without my permission"* indicating that both her knowledge and consent to such a device was important. Her main concern was a *"controlling factor"* and, in particular, *"sinister"* purposes. As an example, Olga mentioned targeted advertising speculating that data could gathered from a number of sources, such as reward cards and internet browsing history, to tailor the advertising to her own preferences.

Olga mentioned that she did feel that such information would have been useful to help monitor her elderly grandmother who had chosen to live at home. She felt that such a device would have been able to alert her or other family if her grandmother was not following 'normal' patterns of activity. She also felt that it would be useful if anyone ever broke into her house as there would, at least, be a record of the time that it occurred. On being asked to reflect on the amount and range of data that could be collected about her Olga felt that this was *"just the age that we are in"*. She felt that there was a need to *"protect"* herself however she felt that she was not *'computer savvy enough to actually protect all of the information that is going out'* about her even though she felt that she was more familiar with technology than many others. Currently, to manage this, Olga actively opted out of things such as store reward programs and chose not to use free Wi-Fi facilities at shopping centres and hotels.

After the interview had concluded, Olga made a comment that she elected to be part of the study and, in particular, was happy to have the device installed because she had known the researcher for a number of years and trusted the researcher. Because of this she felt confident that nothing was going to occur that would cause her any concern.

Terry

Similar to Olga, Terry's first reflection was that, at first, he was intrigued by the device and was actively watching for responses from the device. He actively showed the device to visitors to his house. However, after a few days, his attention to the device decreased. Terry felt that even when he did notice a response from the device he did not pay much attention to it because *"I guess we are used to things like phones lighting up and things doing things on their own"*. When asked to speculate on what he thought the device was monitoring, he thought that it was something simple such as temperature. He considered that it could have been monitoring downloads or browsing habits because it was connected to his Wi-Fi. Prior to the device being installed, Terry had asked if the device was recording video or audio and had been advised that it did not. The limitations of what the device was able to monitor was explained along with the ability to infer information from the data that was collected. When asked how he felt about this, Terry indicated that he had no concerns: *"I just think we or I have become used to, in the past couple of years, people being able to tell you stuff that is going on here."*

On being asked to reflect on the amount and range of data that could be collected about him, Terry indicated that he would accept that *"as long as I had control and prior knowledge of what people were doing"*. Terry indicated that he would like to have control similar to Facebook privacy settings where he would be able to indicate agreement to different aspects of sharing and the purpose for which the data was being used. He indicated: *"That's a bit like choosing whether you want your address to go to certain parties or not."* Terry indicated that if the data was being viewed as a large group, such as a postcode then he would be more comfortable. However, if the data was being used on an individual basis then he would specifically ask how the data was to be used and for what purpose. Terry indicated that, generally, he would agree for data about him to be collected and used. It was only when there was a negative consequence that he would then express concerns. He felt that he tended *"to be quite a naïve person when it comes to that sort of thing"*. If people were *"collecting data to make [his] life more difficult or to make profit, that was quite a different thing"*.

Also after the interview was completed, Terry indicated that as he had known the researcher for a period of time and understood that it was for research purposes he felt that he was more accepting of the device and did not feel the need to ask many questions or to be concerned about the collection of data. Importantly, Terry is an academic and is currently research active although not in this field.

Susan

Susan also first mentioned that she very quickly stopped thinking about the device, even if the device was glowing. Susan commented that she felt that the main reason for this was the familiarity with the researcher: *"And then well all just forgot about it which is, I think, I was writing about the fact that you had given it to us and I think that made a big difference to how we approached it."* A key factor was attitude – the willingness of people to explain new technology to a level appropriate to her needs. In her past experience, Susan had encountered people who, when providing her with technology, had not been willing to talk her through that technology: *"Whereas in the past, they used to be like 'I am a magician and this is a magic thing and it will do magic things to you, and you, bless your pretty little head, you do not need to concern yourself with these magic things'. And I would get grumpy and resentful… I think you were prepared to answer my questions, which is probably the other aspects of it."*

When reflecting on the type of data that was being recorded, Susan speculated that the device could not be recording video or audio. However, beyond that Susan was not concerned with the type of data that was being recorded. The limitations of what the device was able to monitor was explained along with the ability to infer information from the data that was collected. Susan indicated that this factor was significant: *"…that potentially really changes my feelings about who is collecting the data. Because if it is me collecting the data and I'm remotely away, then that's a very useful thing… But otherwise I, and in the kind of social media announcing that you're going away on holiday, that's a bit more disturbing."*

In relation to the concept of data being more widely available Susan felt that this would make her feel *"reasonably anxious"*. Susan felt that the context of the person that was the subject of the data was an important consideration, and provided an example of a relative who, due to the prominence of other family members, was often the subject of media attention. Susan felt that this person would not engage with this technology. Susan felt that in general terms most people would not be concerned about data collection and that she personally was *"not a very attractive target"* for anyone to want to use her data for any purpose that would be concerning to her.

However, Susan indicated that there were certain areas where she would feel more vulnerable and, if data was being collected about those areas she "*would want to know what's happening to the data"*. Susan's concern was that, in her experience, people had used data in *"very political ways to prove points"* and gave the example of an employer monitoring employees who were working remotely. Of particular concern to Susan was any data that may, in some way, represent mental health status, which she felt was also a political issue. Conversely, Susan felt that having this sort of information about her father might prompt her into contacting her father more frequently. However, she felt that this was somewhat unfair on her part. Susan reflected that *"Maybe I do think it's okay to share it with family. But again I'd want to be able to switch it off."* Further, in relation to this type of information, Susan felt that she would *"want to get some feedback that is what it is doing and sampling at that point in time, so that if I didn't want to share that data I could selectively remove that data"*. Overall Susan felt that she was not able to completely trust that collected data would not be used in a way to cause harm or concern.

Elizabeth and Troy

Elizabeth and Troy are married and live together. Elizabeth stated that initially, the device received a lot of attention. Further, Elizabeth indicated that she quite frequently noticed it glowing. This made her think about the possibilities for IoT technology in her home. However, this led her to thoughts of how vulnerable this sort of technology could be and how pervasive it could be in a domestic environment. When asked to elaborate on her concern about the vulnerability of the technology, Elizabeth first reinforced that knowing *"that you installed it for your study meant I didn't really have a concern"*. Her concern was how IoT technology could be used to manipulate people.

Elizabeth also raised a concern about security. She drew an analogy to spyware, where the IoT technology could be used to *"penetrate your use of technology"* to track passwords and access information such as banking details. This caused Elizabeth to consider the effort that would be required to maintain security if a household was filled with IoT devices: *"We have a fairly basic level of Internet of Things in this household. But imagine if we did? The level of security you'd have to go to, to ensure that it was secure, if you had things that were running the fridge, and your telephone and televisions and all that sort of stuff."*

Troy also reported that he noticed the device glowing. This caused him to speculate whether the device was monitoring when other technology devices were being used or being turned off. He indicated that initially he watched the device quite a bit in an attempt to determine what was causing the device to record data. When he felt that he was reasonably certain that it was monitoring the use of other technology he felt that his interest decreased and he became less aware of the device. Troy felt confident that it did not have the ability to track *"websites and website data"* however, initially, it did make him consider *"Could it be tracking my bank account details? Could it just be sitting in between all of the data that's coming in?"*

After the nature of the data that was being collected was explained to Elizabeth and Troy as well as how inferences could still be drawn from that data, Elizabeth commented that *"it's an interesting question, which is 'How do you feel about people collecting data just about you, your household, and making inferences about that?'"*. Elizabeth again commented that *"I'd have to be really really honest and say because it's you and your study and I'm a researcher I can feel good that it's going to contribute to something"*. However, she felt that if there had been some mandate for this sort of data to be collected where it was out of her control or beyond her choice, *"although it's the same thing [it] would maybe make us think differently about that [and] to someone making any kind of inferences or collect any kind of data about what's happening inside your own home"*. She felt that if the data was de-identified or if the data was going into a larger collection where inferences were generalized such that it had very little impact on her directly, she would have less concern.

Elizabeth felt that it was important to her to know what was being done with the data that was collected even if she had consciously provided consent to the collection of that data. Elizabeth gave an example of supermarket rewards programs, where data about shopping habits could be used to manipulate people to go back to the store more frequently. Elizabeth stated: *"Even though it may or may not impact on what I choose to do or how I experience it all, there's an aspect of I'd like to know and I'd like to have a choice about it"*.

At this point, Troy stated: *"But then again, you've got to worry about the argument about how much do you worry about stuff?"* Elizabeth agreed with this, acknowledging that there was most likely a large amount of data already being collected that's being used for different purposes, but she had not been concerned to date. However, she felt that it was about having an element of control: *"It's that element of agency that I think can still ... you'd never go down without a fight if you could"*. Elizabeth stated that she was concerned that inferences were being drawn about her from data where she did not have any opportunity to contribute to the inferences drawn. Further, her concern was about how data could be misinterpreted and used in a way to cause harm: *"How would somebody use that to twist and turn it on you?"*. However, she felt that she was *"not that interesting or important or dark enough for it to be known so therefore it doesn't really bother me"*. To some extent, Elizabeth felt the benefits of a smart home outweighed the risks that she personally faced.

DISCUSSION

Although this study and others of its kind face a number of significant limitations (about which we will have more to say shortly), there are also several interesting observations that can be made, and that present challenges for the design of IoT technologies.

Receding awareness

For the participants, the technology itself receded in their awareness quite quickly, in spite of the fact it consistently and visibly announced its activity and that its functionality (i.e. precisely what data was being collected) remained a mystery during the study. Although participants' own explanations for this varied (suggesting it should not be considered a phenomenon but perhaps manifestations of different phenomena), a version of it was reported in each of the households. The rapidity with which a new and ambiguous ambient technology can recede to become part of the furniture was surprising. This suggests users may only initially be cognizant of the data they are sharing and mindful of what that might reveal about them. Designers will need to build means of "resurfacing" ambient technologies into users' consciousness beyond intrusive or easy-to-dismiss notifications.

Social proximity and data control

Although intuitively it might be thought that participants would be happier, and feel safer, sharing potentially personal information about their activity with those closest to them (e.g. family and friends), that was certainly not universal. On one hand, Susan mused that *"maybe it's okay to share it with family"* (while reserving the right to switch it off), yet Olga expressed concern about the prospect of sharing data with family who were better placed to draw inferences from it, e.g. if she had chosen not to answer a phone call from them but they could, on account of the data being collected, see that someone was home. The "mosaic" effect [14] discussed earlier takes on a different aspect in such a case, as those close to us start with many more pieces to our puzzle, and therefore may be in some cases those from whom we wish to exert the greatest control over the data we share. Not all of our "mosaic" is digital data, and much of the most important, sensitive and/or revealing information about us is common knowledge to people who know us best. While differentiated control over what we share and to whom is a feature of many major social media platforms, these often assume that those personally closest to us are those with whom we want and need to share the most data.

Safety in numbers: de-identified, aggregate data

Relatedly, the prospect of sharing anonymous data, or data that would only be aggregated (e.g. as is the case in national census data) was explicitly identified by multiple participants as much less threatening. Systems that "clean" your data, e.g. de-identify and make less precise (e.g. by geographically and temporally blurring our data points) may be a valuable design strategy.

Hear no evil, see no evil

Elizabeth, Troy and Terry mentioned different aspects of the ways personal data can be used already, and the limited degree of active care or concern they had about how their data is used. Terry suggested that he would typically agree to the use of his data, and wait until something undesirable happened before mistrusting a service. Elizabeth and Troy wondered aloud how much data use should be something to proactively worry about. For many people living on the grid, there is limit to the amount of attention that the data we generate can be given. The challenge from this is to develop systems that recognize that people should be considered as central to any system that involves the collection of data about them, a core tenet for the emerging field of Human-Data Interaction [11].

Knowing why, or else trusting what for

For most of the participants, knowing the purposes the data would serve was identified as very important to them. On the surface this seems ironic, as they had all agreed to participate in a study in which the purpose of and the data collected by the IoT device was not disclosed. However, it makes sense in light of the fact that the participants were all known to the researcher. This emerged in their reflections—participants' concerns about this particular device were severely mitigated by their trust in the person who brought it to their house. Unsurprisingly, trust emerges as the key condition for participants' tolerance of the data they are generating and sharing with unknown others. Trust in the person or organisation who controls the functionality of the device, and who has access to the data, as well as how collected data is used are key considerations in people's acceptance of IoT technology in their domestic environments.

The usefulness of the probe

The probe, despite its minimal level of functionality and the pre-existing relationship with one of the researchers, was useful in providing some insight into the human values that are implicated when living with IoT technology. It supported the participants' developing of an understanding of the actual experience of living with IoT technology in a specific context and how that experience evolved over time. From this experience, it then supported the participants' exploration of different perspectives of living with this technology. This exploration provided rich information of: the values implicated by the technology; how those values were enacted by the participants; and, how values might be enacted in response to other IoT technology and in other contexts.

LIMITATIONS

This study was an initial exploration into human concerns that arose when people live with IoT technology. There are a number of easily identifiable limitations with this initial study, however. In designing our own IoT device and deploying it in people's homes, the situation created gave participants no choice or personal ownership over the device. This creates a very different set of circumstances in which people might ordinarily "live with" IoT devices, that have been selected, purchased and installed for personal benefit. Furthermore, this had the consequence that in deployment, participants did not experience a cost/benefit tradeoff—they were not "trading" their data as a commodity for some other value gained (as with, e.g. a system such as Strava), nor were they explicitly aware what data about their activities was being collected. In these respects, the experience of the participants in living with IoT was limited to living with a device that was itself an ambient reminder that data about them was being collected and shared with others.

Perhaps most of all, it is noteworthy that all participants made comment that the pre-existing relationship with one of the researchers was critical to their decision to allow the device to be placed in their homes and to record data.

Each of these is a significant limitation, but also highlights the complexity inherent to gaining access to the relevant phenomena encountered in living with IoT. Care must be taken designing and deploying bespoke technologies, recruiting people to live with them and report their experiences, since such a setup simulates but does not reproduce what has emerged as important considerations for these participants. The number of "I would have felt differently if…" reflections from the participants indicates that for the participants, the study did not reproduce the circumstances around IoT that they would find worrysome or disconcerting. And yet, by not reproducing these circumstances, we created a research setting in which participants identified and articulated the conditions under which they would be concerned with technologies such as this; that is the value of studies of this kind. But if we are to understand the doubts and concerns people actually encounter in IoT, we will need access to more distant participants, many of whom may be reluctant to participate in research conducted by people they do not know or trust.

This raises a methodological issue for design research. The means and manner of recruitment for embedded studies of this kind have vital consequences for what we can and cannot uncover. Field trials with volunteers (and particularly ones known to the researchers) who are aware of the purposes of the research, with all of the ethical safeguards that entails, create circumstances unlike those that the commercial Internet of Things instantiates. But while this represents a key limitation to the study, it remains that future studies may still require this or a similar pre-existing level of trust between researchers and participants, or perhaps substantial remuneration in order for participants to consent to participate in the first place. In each case, these researcher-participant dynamics have genuine consequences for the nature and quality of the data that is generated through the research.

ACKNOWLEDGMENTS

We would like to thank all of the participants for taking part in this study and for the information that they provided us.

The research on which this article is based was funded by an APA scholarship to PW.

REFERENCES

1. Gregory D. Abowd and Elizabeth D. Mynatt. 2000. Charting Past, Present, and Future Research in Ubiquitous Computing. *ACM Trans. Comput.-Hum. Interact.* 7, 1: 29–58. http://doi.org/10.1145/344949.344988
2. Luigi Atzori, Antonio Iera, and Giacomo Morabito. 2010. The Internet of Things: A survey. *Computer Networks* 54, 15: 2787–2805. http://doi.org/10.1016/j.comnet.2010.05.010
3. Luigi Atzori, Antonio Iera, and Giacomo Morabito. 2014. From "smart objects" to "social objects": The next evolutionary step of the internet of things. *IEEE Communications Magazine* 52, 1: 97–105. http://doi.org/10.1109/MCOM.2014.6710070
4. Barry Brown, Alex S. Taylor, Shahram Izadi, Abigail Sellen, Joseph Jofish' Kaye, and Rachel Eardley. 2007. Locating Family Values: A Field Trial of the Whereabouts Clock. In *UbiComp 2007: Ubiquitous Computing*, John Krumm, Gregory D. Abowd, Aruna Seneviratne and Thomas Strang (eds.). Springer Berlin Heidelberg, 354–371. Retrieved April 21, 2015 from http://link.springer.com/chapter/10.1007/978-3-540-74853-3_21
5. Andy Crabtree and Richard Mortier. 2015. Human data interaction: Historical lessons from social studies and CSCW. *ECSCW 2015: Proceedings of the 14th European Conference on Computer Supported Cooperative Work, 19-23 September 2015, Oslo, Norway*, Springer, 3–21. Retrieved March 28, 2016 from http://link.springer.com/chapter/10.1007/978-3-319-20499-4_1
6. John Curtin, Robert J. Kauffman, and Frederick J. Riggins. 2007. Making the "MOST" out of RFID technology: a research agenda for the study of the adoption, usage and impact of RFID. *Information Technology and Management* 8, 2: 87–110. http://doi.org/10.1007/s10799-007-0010-1
7. Paul Dourish. 2006. Implications for design. *Proceedings of the SIGCHI conference on Human Factors in computing systems*, ACM, 541–550. Retrieved July 12, 2015 from http://dl.acm.org/citation.cfm?id=1124855
8. Paul Dourish and Genevieve Bell. 2011. *Divining a Digital Future : Mess and Mythology in Ubiquitous Computing.* MIT Press, Cambridge, MA, USA. Retrieved May 2, 2015 from http://site.ebrary.com/lib/alltitles/docDetail.action?docID=10476094
9. Batya Friedman, Peter H. Kahn Jr, Alan Borning, and Alina Huldtgren. 2013. Value Sensitive Design and Information Systems. In *Early engagement and new technologies: Opening up the laboratory*, Neelke Doorn, Daan Schuurbiers, Ibo van de Poel and Michael

E. Gorman (eds.). Springer Netherlands, 55–95. Retrieved February 9, 2016 from http://link.springer.com/chapter/10.1007/978-94-007-7844-3_4

10. Batya Friedman and Helen Nissenbaum. 1996. Bias in computer systems. *ACM Transactions on Information Systems (TOIS)* 14, 3: 330–347.
11. Hamed Haddadi, Richard Mortier, Derek McAuley, and Jon Crowcroft. 2013. Human-data interaction. *Technical report, University of Cambridge, Computer Laboratory*. Retrieved March 28, 2016 from http://www-ipv4.cl.cam.ac.uk/techreports/UCAM-CL-TR-837.pdf
12. Richard HR Harper. 2008. *Being human: Human-computer interaction in the year 2020*. Microsoft Research Limited.
13. Richard Harper, Tom Rodden, Yvonne Rogers, and Abigail Sellen (eds.). 2008. *Being human: human-computer interaction in the year 2020*. Microsoft Research, Cambridge, England.
14. H. Hutchinson, W. Mackay, B. Westerlund, et al. 2003. Technology probes: inspiring design for and with families. *Proceedings of the SIGCHI conference on Human factors in computing systems*, 17–24. Retrieved January 31, 2013 from http://dl.acm.org/citation.cfm?id=642616
15. Cory Knobel and Geoffrey C. Bowker. 2011. Values in Design. *Commun. ACM* 54, 7: 26–28. http://doi.org/10.1145/1965724.1965735
16. Treffyn Lynch Koreshoff, Tuck Wah Leong, and Toni Robertson. 2013. Approaching a Human-centred Internet of Things. *Proceedings of the 25th Australian Computer-Human Interaction Conference: Augmentation, Application, Innovation, Collaboration*, ACM, 363–366. http://doi.org/10.1145/2541016.2541093
17. Christopher A. Le Dantec, Erika Shehan Poole, and Susan P. Wyche. 2009. Values as lived experience: evolving value sensitive design in support of value discovery. *Proceedings of the SIGCHI conference on human factors in computing systems*, ACM, 1141–1150. Retrieved March 24, 2016 from http://dl.acm.org/citation.cfm?id=1518875
18. Ewa Luger and Tom Rodden. 2013. Terms of agreement: Rethinking consent for pervasive computing. *Interacting with Computers* 25, 3: 199–203.
19. Jessica K. Miller, Batya Friedman, Gavin Jancke, and Brian Gill. 2007. Value tensions in design: the value sensitive design, development, and appropriation of a corporation's groupware system. *Proceedings of the 2007 international ACM conference on Supporting group work*, ACM, 281–290. Retrieved March 24, 2016 from http://dl.acm.org/citation.cfm?id=1316668
20. Roberto Pereira, M. Cecília C. Baranauskas, and L. D. Almeida. 2011. The value of value identification in web applications. *IADIS International Conference on WWW/Internet (ICWI)*, 37–44. Retrieved March 24, 2016 from https://www.researchgate.net/profile/Roberto_Pereira2/publication/216125524_The_Value_of_Value_Identification_in_Web_Applications/links/09e41504b7983e989b000000.pdf
21. F.J. Riggins and S.F. Wamba. 2015. Research Directions on the Adoption, Usage, and Impact of the Internet of Things through the Use of Big Data Analytics. *2015 48th Hawaii International Conference on System Sciences (HICSS)*, 1531–1540. http://doi.org/10.1109/HICSS.2015.186
22. Abigail Sellen, Yvonne Rogers, Richard Harper, and Tom Rodden. 2009. Reflecting Human Values in the Digital Age. *Commun. ACM* 52, 3: 58–66. http://doi.org/10.1145/1467247.1467265
23. Katie Shilton, Jes A. Koepfler, and Kenneth R. Fleischmann. 2013. Charting sociotechnical dimensions of values for design research. *The Information Society* 29, 5: 259–271.
24. Katie Shilton, Jes A. Koepfler, and Kenneth R. Fleischmann. 2014. How to See Values in Social Computing: Methods for Studying Values Dimensions. *Proceedings of the 17th ACM Conference on Computer Supported Cooperative Work & Social Computing*, ACM, 426–435. http://doi.org/10.1145/2531602.2531625
25. H. Jeff Smith, Sandra J. Milberg, and Sandra J. Burke. 1996. Information Privacy: Measuring Individuals' Concerns about Organizational Practices. *MIS Quarterly* 20, 2: 167–196. http://doi.org/10.2307/249477
26. Ovidiu Vermesan, Peter Friess, Patrick Guillemin, et al. 2011. Internet of things strategic research roadmap. *O. Vermesan, P. Friess, P. Guillemin, S. Gusmeroli, H. Sundmaeker, A. Bassi, et al., Internet of Things: Global Technological and Societal Trends* 1: 9–52.
27. Amy Voida, Lynn Dombrowski, Gillian R. Hayes, and Melissa Mazmanian. 2014. Shared Values/Conflicting Logics: Working Around e-Government Systems. *Proceedings of the 32Nd Annual ACM Conference on Human Factors in Computing Systems*, ACM, 3583–3592. http://doi.org/10.1145/2556288.2556971

DECO: a Design Space for Device Composition

Gary Perelman[1, 2], Marcos Serrano[1], Mathieu Raynal[1], Celia Picard[2], Mustapha Derras[2], Emmanuel Dubois[1]

[1]IRIT, University of Toulouse
Toulouse, France
{first_name.last_name}@irit.fr

[2]LRA, Berger-Levrault
Toulouse, France
{first_name.last_name}@berger-levrault.com

ABSTRACT
Numerous interaction devices are designed through device composition. However, there is no conceptual support for this process and designers are left out to explore the space of combinations in an ad-hoc manner. In this paper we propose a design space for device composition, DECO, which focuses on the physical aspects of the composition. This design space is built around two main axes, namely Physical arrangement, which describes how elements are physically combined, and Physical manipulation, which describes how users manipulate each element. We first classify existing devices using our design space and then compare four of them to illustrate their similarities and differences. Using DECO, we design a new compound device: RPM2. This device is based on the combination of a regular mouse with the Roly-Poly Mouse. We describe in detail the user-centered iterative design process that leads to the final prototype. Finally we propose a set of design guidelines to assist the use of DECO for device composition.

Author Keywords
Compound device; Design space; Device composition; Mouse.

ACM Classification Keywords
H.5.2. Information Interfaces and Presentation: User Interfaces: Theory and methods

INTRODUCTION
In recent years, numerous research projects have designed and implemented novel interaction devices resulting from the combination or aggregation of existing ones [12, 19, 22, 25, 29, 37, 41]. Among them, we can cite a touchscreen on a mouse as in LensMouse [41], an air balloon inside a mouse as in Inflatable Mouse [22], two keyboards fixed together as in FlipKeyboard [12], or two tablets glued to form a dual-sided device as in Codex [19]. These projects followed an empirical design approach resulting in the development of ad-hoc solutions combining existing devices, without relying on a systematic or structured process. While these combinations proved to be useful in several contexts, designers who want to produce such type of devices are left out to explore multiple design alternatives on their own.

DIS 2016, June 04-08, 2016, Brisbane, QLD, Australia
© 2016 ACM. ISBN 978-1-4503-4031-1/16/06...$15.00
DOI: http://dx.doi.org/10.1145/2901790.2901893

In this paper we investigate and refine the concept of **device composition** to promote the potential of combining existing devices to create new ones, and to leverage performing this combination in a more systematic manner. Device composition consists in **physically** putting together several existing devices to create a new one, hereafter referred to as a **compound device**. The concept of device composition can be related to the concepts of *multimodal interaction* and *composite device* [3, 16]. *Multimodal interaction* is based on the combination of several interaction modalities, each being defined as a couple of components: <device, language> [10]. In this paper we more specifically focus on the physical combination of two devices, instead of two modalities. The notion of *composite device*, as introduced by Bardram [3], defines the combination of interactive services and is thus far from the physical aspects considered in our approach.

In this work we develop the concept of device composition through the definition, illustration and evaluation of a design space for the physical combination of interaction devices. Our design space, **DECO**, is structured along two dimensions: 1) the physical arrangement, i.e. how the different devices are physically composed and 2) the physical manipulation, i.e. the way a user will manipulate each element of the compound device. Using DECO, we classify and compare existing devices to illustrate how our design space helps in describing and comparing different solutions.

In addition to the illustration of DECO on existing devices, we use this design space to elaborate a novel compound device supporting multi-dimensional interaction. This compound device aims at adding degrees of freedom to a traditional mouse. We describe in detail the user-centered iterative design process, using our design space, along four complete iterations involving user evaluations. These iterations prove that DECO contributes to the design of compound devices that are usable and perform well.

Our contributions are 1) the definition of the concept of device composition, 2) a design space, DECO, dedicated to device composition, 3) the classification and comparison of existing work using DECO, 4) the design and evaluation of a new compound device for multi-dimensional interaction and 5) an a set of design guidelines for applying DECO on device composition.

STATE OF THE ART

Our work is inspired by the large number of existing compound devices and by related work on composition toolkits and models for HCI. We synthesize these three sets of related works in this section and underline how DECO provides a novel perspective in terms of device composition.

Compound Devices

Device composition has largely been used in HCI. Such devices found in the literature can be classified into three main categories according to their interaction sense (input or output): 1) composition of two *input* devices to augment input interaction; 2) composition of two *output* devices to augment the output space; and 3) composition of *input* and *output* devices to provide an additional feedback on an input device (or vice versa). In this section we cite some examples without being exhaustive.

In the first category (*input-input*), a large body of work has been dedicated to the fusion of a mouse with another input device, most commonly with a tactile surface [2, 40]. A commercial example of this composition is the Apple's Magic Mouse. Some gamer's mice are based on a combination of a keyboard and a mouse [29]. Dedicated devices, such as the Lexip 3D [25] are based on the combination of a regular mouse with a joystick to offer additional degrees of freedom to support 3D manipulation tasks.

In the second category (*output-output*), most works are based on combining displays, such as Siftables, Codex, DualScreen or HoverPad [19, 23, 26, 32]. For instance, Siftables is based on the spatial combination of tiny screens [26]. Codex is a dual display mobile device [19]. Dualscreen combines two screens on a computer to share personal content to other users [23]. HoverPad is a compound device based on a self-actuated display on top of a tactile table [32].

Concerning the last category (input-output), one general approach is to add a display to an input device. For instance Yang et al. proposed LensMouse, based on adding a screen on the mouse [41] The opposite approach, i.e. adding input devices to a touchscreen, has been used in back-of-device prototypes [31, 36]. For instance, Sugimoto proposes to add a touchpad on the back of a PDA [36].

This general presentation of existing compound devices underlines their diversity and the multiplicity of composition alternatives. In the past, designers have explored this large composition space without any systematic or structured approach. In our work we propose a design space to support this exploration.

Composition toolkits in HCI

The idea of composition can be found in several HCI toolkits, from hardware platforms such as Arduino or Phidgets [35] to software IDEs such as OpenInterface or PureData [3, 9, 33].

Hardware toolkits help assembling and combining different sensors like pressure sensors, push buttons, light detectors, etc., resulting in a device based on sensor fusion. Phidgets [35] for example, propose multiple sensors that can be easily plugged together to create a device. Arduino [34] also proposes a set of actuators and sensors that can be combined to produce interactive devices. Hardware composition toolkits support the composition at a low level, i.e. at sensor granularity, but do not provide any help in guiding the design process or selecting design alternatives.

Other approaches developed the concept of composition at a software level. The OpenInterface platform [33] allows assembling abstract components and linking their input and output to develop a multimodal interaction. ContextToolkit [9] is another example using software components that encapsulate several types of sensors. It is then possible to combine those components to develop an interaction technique. Most of these software toolkits rely on analytical models to help identifying and structuring software components. However, they do not help determining how to design the physical combination of devices.

Rather than developing a concrete toolkit, the goal of the present work is to propose a theoretical framework. These existing software and hardware composition toolkits could actually be used to implement our theoretical approach.

Analytical approaches

In HCI, several works proposed to classify and describe input devices and their characteristics on the basis of the sensors used. Among them, Card's design space [8] defines three composition operators that can be used to combine sensors: Merger, Layout and Connection composition. Those three operators refer to the data composition (Merger), the spatial composition (Layout) and to the ability to plug the output of a sensor into the input of another sensor (Connection). Inspired by these three simple composition operators, our work is intended to propose a richer composition design space.

At a higher level of abstraction, multimodal properties were design to better describe the composition of interaction modalities. Allen [1] temporal properties define the temporal composition between two interaction modalities over time. The CARE [10] properties defines relationships between multiple modalities defined by a couple *<device, language>*. The fusion of modalities is performed at the language level. In our paper, we propose to refine these concepts by focusing on the composition of devices, not languages.

Closer to our approach, Hartmann et al. studied the combination of sensors with real devices [16] and enlightened the importance of the physical aspect. According to the authors, two devices or sensors that are designed to explicitly support their composition and that are aware of each other lead to a better resulting device. This type of composition is called "dovetail joint". Even if authors warn future designers against the risks of a bad composition, there is a lack of a design model that would better describe the properties of device composition.

To conclude, existing tools and properties describe the composition process at low level, using hardware or software toolkits, and at high level, using models to describe the composition of modalities. However we did not find any approaches focusing on the device composition process from a physical perspective. A design space to rationalize the composition process at a physical level would be a relevant complement to existing approaches, given the wide set of existing devices with different shapes, sizes or materials. To this end, we introduce DECO, a design space to inform the device composition process, using a set of relevant properties, in a similar way than other design methods such as annotated portfolio [7].

DEVICE COMPOSITION: DEFINITION

As seen in the previous section, existing work has paid little attention to identifying and analyzing the physical properties of device composition. Such consideration is crucial as it affects the interaction capabilities of the compound device. For instance, according to their relative position, two devices can be used simultaneously (e.g. a balloon and a mouse, as in Inflatable Mouse [22]) or only sequentially (a keyboard and a touchpad glued on its back, as in FlipKeyboard [12]). Altering the relative position of the components can also highly alter the resulting device: the LensMouse [41] would offer a completely different functionality if the touchscreen was placed on the side of the mouse instead of on its top.

Our concept of device composition takes this physical aspect into consideration. We define this concept as follows: a **device composition** is the physical assembly of several existing **elements**, according to a well-identified physical setting, and resulting in a **compound device**. The possible elements involved in a device composition include physical objects and devices.

This definition leads to two main design considerations:

- Physical arrangement: The integration of physical elements needs to consider their relative position and the alteration of their initial shape.
- Physical manipulation: Depending on the previous physical arrangement, different users' actions and body parts can be used to interact with the compound device. In addition, the device elements may be used sequentially or in a more interleaved manner, potentially allowing compound gestures.

These two design considerations are at the core of our design space, DECO.

DECO: A DESIGN SPACE FOR DEVICE COMPOSITION

The goal of DECO is to help designing new compound devices through **device composition** as previously defined. To achieve this goal, DECO is built around two axes: the *Physical arrangement* of elements (axis 1) and the *Physical manipulation* of the compound device (axis 2). We retain these two axes as they describe the two most important aspects of any device: its shape (**A1**) and its usage (**A2**).

Axis 1: Physical arrangement

The Physical arrangement axis (**A1**) depicts how the different elements are physically and/or spatially composed to create a compound device. These physical or spatial aspects have a direct impact on the device's final shape and on its physical manipulations, i.e. its usability and available DoFs. This axis describes the relative position of each element, how elements are physically linked together and how this arrangement varies over time. To address these considerations, we refine this axis into 3 properties: Topology, Fusion type and Dynamicity.

Topology. This property of DECO describes the spatial and physical organization of each element with respect to each other. We identified three possible categories for this axis: Enclosed, Glued and Separated (Figure 1).

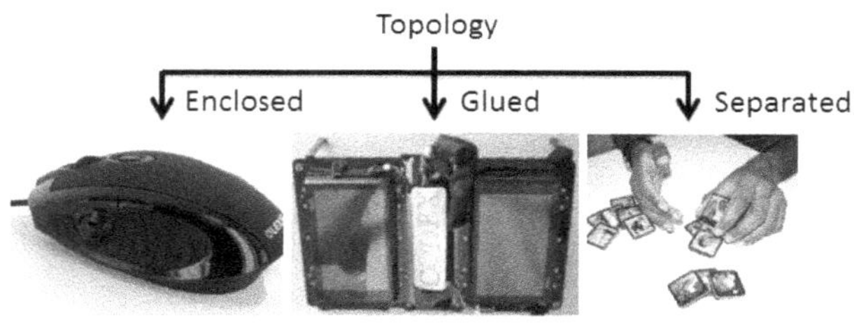

Figure 1: Illustration of the three *Topology* categories: *Enclosed* as in Lexip 3D [25], *Glued* as in Codex [19] and *Separated* as in Siftables [26].

Enclosed: The composition topology is *Enclosed* when one element is confined into another one. For instance, GlobeMouse [13] results from the insertion of a SpaceMouse into a 3DoF trackball. The Inflatable Mouse results from the insertion of a balloon into a mouse [22].

Glued: The composition topology is 'Glued' when elements are physically aggregated. This is the most common form of physical arrangement in compound devices. For instance, the LensMouse [41] is a compound device resulting from the assembly of a mouse and a touchscreen (elements are glued together, see Figure 2 - center). Codex [19] is a device created by fastening two tactile screens together (Figure 1 - center).

Separated: The composition topology is *separated* when multiple elements are spatially composed, i.e. their spatial relationship is detected. The pair of device (mouse, keyboard) for instance can not be considered as a compound device because they are not spatially composed. One example of *separated* compound device is Siftables [26]: these small displays are not *glued* together but can sense their relative position and orientation (Figure 1 - right). A particular instance of a *separated* topology is when the device is made of two separate elements not spatially related, but that can be *glued* if needed (see *dynamicity* later).

Fusion type. In the case of a *Glued* topology, a subsequent question is whether the physical shape of elements is altered to support the composition. Designers need to anticipate whether existing devices can be used or new ones must specifically be crafted. The Fusion type property describes which elements (if any) are altered during a composition. We identified three categories of *Fusion*:

(A-B) depicts the situation where elements are unchanged during composition: all elements are glued together without altering their original shape. For instance, a computer screen can simply be fixed to another one without further physical alteration as in the double-screen laptop Billboard [23] (Figure 2 - left). A similar approach is used in the FlipKeyboard [12], which is composed of a touchpad glued on the back of a keyboard.

(A←B) depicts the situation where the physical shape of element A has been modified (drilled, removed, reshaped, etc.) to accommodate or glue the element B. For instance in the case of the LensMouse [41] (Figure 2 - center), the mouse serves as a receptacle for a tactile screen: to place the touchscreen at an appropriate angle, the mouse cover has been altered and mouse buttons were also removed. In the Trackball Keyboard [37], a keyboard was carved to integrate a trackball on its top (Figure 4 - left).

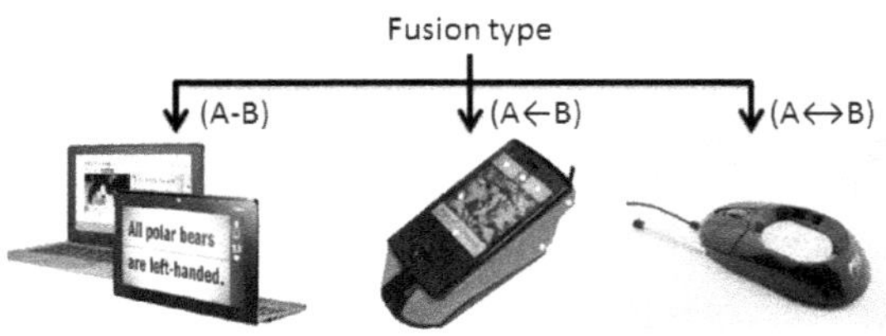

Figure 2: Illustration of the three *Fusion types*: *(A-B)* as in Billboard [23], *(A←B)* as in LensMouse [41] and *(A↔B)* as in Ink222 [20].

(A↔B) depicts the situation where the shape of both elements has been altered to support their composition. The Ink222 [20] mouse (Figure 2 - right) is a compound device based on a classical mouse and a touch tablet. In this case, the mouse was carved and the touch tablet was reshaped to fit a circular space. In the CapMouse [40] (Figure 6 - right), the mouse buttons have been removed and a touchpad has been adapted on top of the mouse.

Dynamicity. This property of DECO characterizes whether the Physical arrangement of a compound device changes over time. The physical arrangement is either *static*, i.e. defined once for all, or *dynamic*, i.e. it may change depending on the task, the user or the context (Figure 3). Usually, this property applies to the topology values *glued* and *separated*, when a device can shift from one to the other. For instance, Rooke M. [30] proposes multiple spatial arrangements between hexagonal bezel-less screens. Using *separated* screens, a user can perform selections and rotations whereas, using *glued* screens, a user can perform swipes or tilts (Figure 3).

Axis 2: Physical manipulation

The Physical manipulation axis of DECO describes how users manipulate the compound device's elements and aims to characterize its usage. From a physical perspective, focusing on the device usage means focusing on the device handling and on its expected manipulations. The Physical manipulation axis is thus described by 3 properties: Human effectors, Physical actions and Temporal usage.

Figure 3: Illustration of the *Dynamicity* property: *static* as in the Razer Naga [29] and *dynamic* as the Hexagonal bezel-less screens [30].

Human effectors. This property of DECO identifies the body parts acting on each element of the compound device. Anatomical dependencies between human effectors may largely influence their use in a compound device [24]. A human effector may be for example one finger, one hand, one foot, or the combination of several of them. This property is described by the body part(s) involved in the interaction with each element. For example, the Trackball Keyboard [37] is a compound device designed for a bimanual use, with one hand on each element: it can be described by the couple *<keyboard: non dom. hand; trackball: dom. hand>* (Figure 4 - left). The Inflatable Mouse [22] is designed to be used with the dominant hand: it can be described by the couple *<mouse: dom. hand; balloon: dom. hand>* (Figure 4 - right).

This axis allows identifying whether several elements of the compound device involve the same body part, as with the Inflatable Mouse. In this case, the physical actions applied to each element need to be compatible, which may imply to adapt or modify one of the elements.

Figure 4: Illustration of the *Human effectors* property. Trackball keyboard [37]: *<keyboard: non dom. hand; trackball: dom. hand> (left)*. The Inflatable Mouse [22]: *<mouse: dom. hand; balloon: dom. hand> (right)*.

Physical actions. This property of DECO describes the expected user's physical actions on each element. Examples of actions include translations, rotations, swipe, etc. Existing notation such as UAN [17] may also be used to describe more complex actions. The role of this property is therefore to help anticipate the ability of the user to produce the expected physical actions on each element, anticipate conflicts and consider different design alternatives.

This property is further refined by the **degrees of freedoms (DoF)** involved by each physical action. The CubicMouse [14], for example, is a compound device combining a cube and three rods (Figure 6). The cube has a 6DoF tracking sensor that allows logging the device's position and orientation. It can be described as follow: *<Cube: translations (3DoFs), rotations (3DoFs); StickX: translation (1DoF); StickY: translation (1DoF); StickZ: translation (1DoF)>*.

Temporal usage. This property of DECO describes how the physical actions are expected to be performed over time. The temporal usage of an interactive system has already been described in the literature. Allen properties [1] describe the temporal composition of modalities. Simplified later with two operators in the CASE model [27]: *Parallel* and *Sequential*.

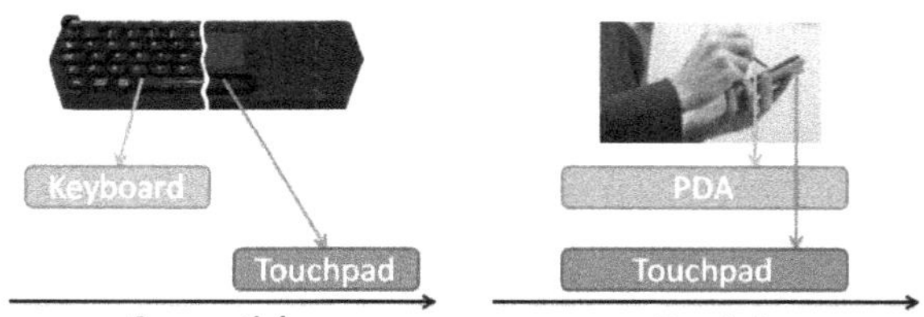

Figure 5: Illustration of the *temporal usage* property: sequential as in FlipKeyboard (left) and *parallel* as in HybridTouch (right).

In our design space we use these operators to define the temporal usage of elements in a compound device. Obviously, this property is influenced by the Physical arrangement and the Physical actions, which can prevent [20] or encourage [40] the concurrent usage of elements. For instance, the FlipKeyboard's [12] and HybridTouch [36] have the same Physical arrangement (*glued* on the back). However, in the FlipKeyboard, only one of its elements can be used at a time: the temporal usage is *sequential*. HybridTouch [36], based on the composition of a PDA and a touchpad, facilitates the concurrent usage of its two elements with a bi-manual interaction: the temporal usage is *parallel* (Figure 5).

CLASSIFICATION OF COMPOUND DEVICES

In this section we illustrate the use of DECO to describe a set of existing compound devices. We first give an overview of how these devices fit our space. Then we describe and compare in detail four existing devices to illustrate how our design space unveils their differences.

	Physical arrangement				
Topology	Enclosed	Glued			Separated
Fusion type		A-B	A<-B	A<->B	
Temporal usage: Sequential	GlobeMouse	Hexagonal bezel-less ☆, FlipKeyboard, Codex	Trackball Keyboard, LensMouse	Ink222	Hexagonal bezel-less ☆
Temporal usage: Parallel	Lexip 3D, Inflatable Mouse	Razer naga, Dualscreen, HybridTouch	PadMouse, CubicMouse, RPM2 ☆	Mouse 2.0	Siftable, HoverPad, RPM2 ☆

☆ = *Dynamic* compound device

Table 1. Compound devices from the literature in DECO.

Physical and temporal classification

Among the properties identified for the two axes of DECO, we adopted a graphical representation based on the physical topology, the fusion type, the dynamicity and the temporal usage. The two remaining properties (human effectors and physical actions) correspond to n-uplets that are less appropriate for a graphical representation. In the table above, compound devices from the literature are positioned with regard to these selected properties of DECO. A star is used to highlight *dynamic* compound devices (Table 1).

This graphical representation highlights the diversity of existing compound devices. It also reveals that the design space is relevant to classify existing work as each possible combination of properties (cell) is illustrated with an existing compound device.

Comparison of compound devices with DECO

To illustrate DECO more precisely, we selected four compound devices from the literature: the CubicMouse [14], the GlobeMouse [13], the PadMouse [2] and the CapMouse [40] (Figure 6). While these devices seem similar in certain aspects, DECO allows comparing them and exposing their similarities and differences (Table 2).

Figure 6: From left to right, the Cubic Mouse [14], the GlobeMouse [13], the PadMouse [2] and the CapMouse [40].

GlobeMouse. This compound device is based on the composition of a SpaceMouse and a trackball. The SpaceMouse is *enclosed* in the trackball shell. The physical arrangement of this compound device is *static*. Only one hand of the user is required to manipulate the compound device: *<SpaceMouse: dom. hand; trackball: dom. hand>*. The expected physical actions can be formalized as follow: *<SpaceMouse: translation (3DoFs); Trackball: rotation (3DoFs)>*. These actions can only be performed *sequentially*.

CubicMouse. This compound device is based on four main elements: a physical cube localized in 6D (position and orientation in a 3D space) and three rods passing through the cube center. The cube and the rods are *glued* together. The cube has been altered to allow the positioning of the rods (Fusion type: $A \leftarrow B$). The physical arrangement of the CubicMouse is *static*. The two hands of the user are required to manipulate the compound device: one for holding the cube and the other to adjust the rods <*cube: non dom. hand; rods: dom. hand*>. As discussed in the previous section, physical actions can be described as follow: <*Cube: translations (3DoFs), rotations (3DoFs); StickX: translation (1DoF); StickY: translation (1DoF); StickZ: translation (1DoF)*>. Physical actions on the rods and on the cube can be performed in *parallel*.

We use DECO to compare CubicMouse and GlobeMouse. The Physical arrangement of those devices differs, as their respective topology is *Enclosed* and *Glued*. The Physical manipulation differs too: the CubicMouse is a bimanual device, which offers a total of 9 DoFs, whereas the GlobeMouse can be used with one hand and offers 6 DoFs. Moreover, the CubicMouse provides a *parallel* usage and the GlobeMouse a *sequential* one. Our design space accurately highlights the differences between these two compound devices that differ both in terms of *physical arrangement* and *physical manipulation*.

PadMouse. This compound device is based on the composition of two elements: a regular mouse and a touchpad. The two elements are *glued* together. Only the mouse has been modified to produce the PadMouse: the mouse buttons have been removed to allow the composition with the touchpad (Fusion type: $A \leftarrow B$). A digital button on the touchpad replaces the mouse buttons. The physical arrangement of PadMouse is *static*. To be physically manipulated the compound device requires only one hand. It can be described as <*mouse: non dom. hand; touchpad: non dom. hand*>. Physical actions include 2D translations of the compound device and 2D touch on the touchpad, represented as follow: <*Mouse: translation (2DoFs); Touchpad: touch input (2DoFs)*>. Finally, it is possible to use the elements in *parallel*.

In light of DECO, the CubicMouse and the PadMouse are similar in terms of Physical arrangement (*glued*, fusion type $A \leftarrow B$, and *static*), but they strongly differ in terms of Physical manipulation. First, regarding the human effectors, the CubicMouse requires two hands whereas the PadMouse requires only one. In addition, the device composition has different effects in terms of DoF available: the buttons of the PadMouse were removed and their DoF replaced by the touchpad; in the CubicMouse, the DoF of each element were preserved. The comparison between these two devices highlights the ability of DECO to differentiate devices from the point of view of their physical manipulation, even if the physical arrangement is similar. This underlines the relevance of considering the physical manipulation as an axis of our design space.

CapMouse. This compound device is based on the composition of two elements: a regular mouse and a capacitive surface. These two elements are *glued* together but in this case, both elements have been modified to create the CapMouse (*Fusion Type* $A \leftrightarrow B$): the mouse buttons have been altered and the capacitive surface has been curved to fit the mouse shape. The physical arrangement of CapMouse is *static*. Under the capacitive surface, a single mouse button allows for mouse clicks. The *human effectors*, *physical actions* and *temporal usage* of this compound device are the same as in the PadMouse.

Although the CapMouse and PadMouse Physical manipulation are the same, their Physical arrangement highlights a fundamental difference. The CapMouse required physical modifications of both elements (fusion type $A \leftrightarrow B$), whereas the PadMouse only of one of its elements (fusion type $A \leftarrow B$). As a consequence, designers could easily prototype new versions of the PadMouse by replacing the touchpad with another rectangular tactile device, such as a smartphone or a smartwatch for example. In other words, in the $A \leftarrow B$ fusion, designers can simply consider device variations based on the replacement of B, while in the $A \leftrightarrow B$ fusion it would be more difficult as each element has been physically altered.

Summary: These four compound device descriptions and the most relevant comparisons using DECO enlighten the capabilities of our design space to accurately describe and distinguish existing solutions in terms of Physical arrangement and/or Physical manipulation (Table 2).

			GlobeMouse	CubicMouse	PadMouse	CapMouse
Physical arrangement	Topology	Enclosed	x			
		Glued		x	x	x
		Separated				
	Fusion type	A-B		x		
		A<-B			x	
		A<->B				x
	Dynamicity	Static	x	x	x	x
		Dynamic				
Physical manipulation	Human effectors	Dom. Hand	x	x	x	x
		Non Dom. Hand		x		
	Physical actions	Rotation	3 DoFs	3 DoFs		
		Translation	3 DoFs	6 DoFs	2 DoFs	2 DoFs
		Touch input			2 DoFs	2 DoFs
	Temporal usage	Sequential	x			
		Parallel		x	x	x

Table 2: Description of GlobeMouse, CubicMouse, PadMouse and CapMouse using DECO.

APPLICATION: RPM2

To assess the utility of DECO to generate new solutions, we report about the design and evaluation of a new compound device, RPM2, based on the combination of a regular mouse with a Roly-Poly Mouse (RPM) [28]. The RPM is a device, inspired by the roly-poly toy, with a circular basis that affords up to 5 DoF (2D translation and 3D roll and rotation).

Initial motivation

In this section, we detail the two main motivations that drove our design of a novel compound device combining the RPM and a mouse, namely the need to 1) overcome a technical challenge and 2) facilitate the adoption of RPM by making it compatible with the most widespread input device, the mouse.

The initial RPM prototype relies on an expensive infrared tracking system to log the position and orientation of the device. An embedded solution using a small 6 DoF sensor was proposed but lacks the precision of a laser mouse to track its 2D position. One solution to overcome this technical limitation is to combine the RPM with a mouse to benefit from its optical sensor. This solution has the additional advantage of drastically decreasing the cost of the resulting device.

To facilitate the adoption of RPM, we decided to envisage its usage as an extension of a classical mouse: RPM could then be used in conjunction with a mouse but also independently. From a DECO perspective, we wanted to propose a *dynamic* Physical arrangement: a device in which elements can be *glued* or *separated* depending on the usage context. For instance, when *glued,* the user can manipulate both elements with the dominant hand, while using the keyboard with his other hand. When the keyboard is no longer required, both devices could be *separated* and used in a bimanual mode, benefiting from higher precision with RPM.

Therefore, we decided to use DECO to guide our design process of a novel compound device combining the mouse and RPM. In the next section we illustrate the different versions of the new RPM (simply called RPM2) through an iterative user-centered design process using DECO. Participants involved in informal tests, pre-studies or evaluations (10 males and 2 females) were aged 24.8 on average (SD=3.6). All of them were right handed.

First iteration

We started by designing the *glued* version of the compound device: this version could potentially lead to physically altering one of the two devices (RPM or mouse) and therefore needed to be considered before exploring the *Separated* version. Our first step was to find the fusion type. We wanted to prototype a simple version of the device and improve it using DECO's second axis, the Physical manipulation. We built a cardboard prototype by using the fusion type *A-B* (no device is physically altered), since it is the simplest form of fusion.

The gluing mechanism relies on the use of an intermediate cardboard support. We made several prototypes by composing a USB mouse with a cardboard support on top of which RPM was placed, not altering any of the elements in the fusion process. We then varied the position of the mouse relative to the cardboard to test different physical compositions. This process led us to 5 different versions of the compound device according to the mouse position: on the left, on the right, on the front, on the back or under RPM (Figure 7). RPM was placed on the cardboard container but not attached to it to ensure free rotation of the device.

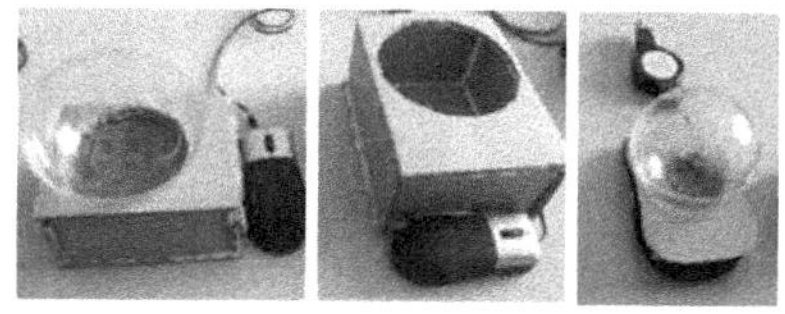

Figure 7: Cardboard prototypes of RPM2: the mouse is on the right side (left), on the back (center) or under (right) RPM.

We conducted a pre-study to evaluate the impact of the spatial *topology* of elements on usability and on the physical manipulations. We asked four users to manipulate all cardboard versions of RPM2. Users had to manipulate the compound device by performing translations, rotations, rolls and compound gestures (translation + roll). At the end of the experiment, users evaluated the device usability through an informal interview.

We found that the distance between the palm of the hand and the mouse, resulting from the cardboard support, had an impact on the usability of the device. This is due to the fact that, when RPM2 is translated, the cardboard slowly derives around RPM and the mouse is no longer aligned with the hand movement.

In addition, users declared that compound gestures were complex to perform on RPM2. This was also due to the distance between the two elements. As we wanted to keep the original RPM interaction properties, this was a main issue.

Second iteration: changing the fusion type

To solve the problems of the first prototype, we needed to allow the user to hold both the mouse and the RPM at the same time, i.e. reduce the physical distance between them. Using DECO, we searched for another fusion type that would get the two elements closer without altering the physical actions. In our context, a physical modification on RPM was impossible as it would impact the 3D rotation DoFs of the device. The fusion type *(A↔B)* was thus not appropriate. Therefore we decided to design a *(A←B)* fusion by considering how the mouse could be physically altered to incorporate RPM. One additional constraint was that both elements had to be *glued* without permanently fixing them to preserve the *dynamic* property of the device.

RPM2: Prototype v2

The second version of the compound device was overall smaller than the previous one as we removed the cardboard container. The cover of the mouse was replaced by a 3D printed version (Figure 8 - left). This cover was carved to hold RPM on it. A side effect was that we had to relocate the buttons on the side of the mouse. In parallel, we wanted to determine the optimal size of RPM as size could have an important impact on the physical manipulation of the device and on the user's comfort. To answer those design questions, we conducted a series of user tests.

In the first test, we varied the size of RPM to measure its impact on the *Physical actions*. Twelve users had to perform translations, rotations, rolls and compound gestures with the device. At the end of the experiment, participants were asked to evaluate the RPM size compared to the mouse size and they had to evaluate the device usability. The radiuses of the different RPM versions were 4, 5, 6, 8 and 10cm.

According to results, the optimal size for RPM was 5cm. With this size, both elements had almost the same width and allowed for a more comfortable hand posture. Moreover, users preferred to place the buttons on the left side of the mouse rather than on the right (Figure 8 - left) because pressing the buttons with the thumb (on the left) is less tiring than with the ring or little fingers (on the right). This confirms the importance of properly choosing the *human effectors* for each element.

To assess the device efficiency in a concrete task, we conducted a second test where we asked users to perform a 2D pointing task following the Fitts law [35] experiment protocol. Four users had to select among 25 circularly arranged targets using our device and a regular mouse. We evaluated six index of difficulty (defined as a ratio of the target size on the support circle size): 3.17, 3.70, 4.08, 5.93 and 6.33. Results showed that pointing with the mouse was faster than with RPM2. Pointing errors, i.e. missing the target, were significantly higher with our prototype. Participants' feedback revealed that the printed 3D support was hard to grasp: "The support is not steady, it's complicated to hold it correctly while I click." or "The support shape is not well suited. It was uncomfortable to grasp.".

RPM2: Prototype v3

Based on these results, we built a third version of the compound device. We removed the 3D printed support and directly carved the cover of a mouse to hold the 5cm RPM. With the best size for RPM defined, we explored the buttons location through another user test. The task was to perform translations, rotations, rolls and compound gestures with RPM2. Users had to manipulate two versions of the compound device: one on which the mouse was carved on the center and the buttons were placed on the left side (prototype v3a, Figure 8 – center); and one on which the mouse was carved on the right, leaving the original left mouse-button available (prototype v3b, Figure 8 –right). These two solutions required the use of different human effectors to press the button (thumb or index) but also to manipulate (rotate or roll) RPM.

The first result of this test is that users preferred the version with RPM on the center (prototype v3a). This is due to the fact that, when RPM is displaced on the right, the hand posture is particularly uncomfortable when performing rotations and rolls: the index finger lays on the left click while all the other fingers lay on RPM. Not only RPM manipulation is more complicated but also the posture is rather tiring. In addition, users found that compound gestures were easy to perform on the version carved on the center. In this version, the physical manipulation of RPM is performed using the three middle fingers.

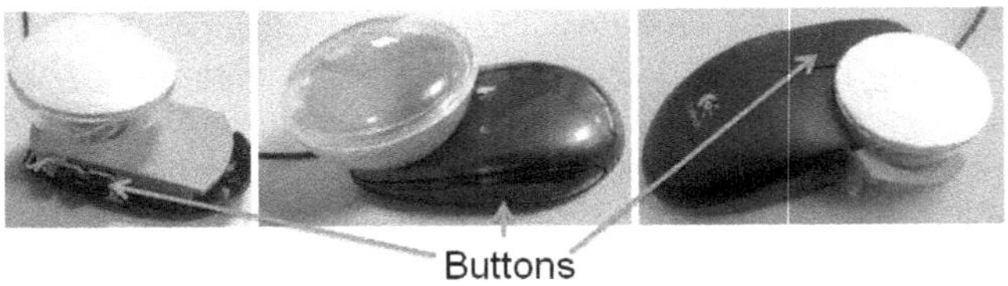

Figure 8: Different versions of the (A←B) compound device, from left to right: based on a 3D printed support (prototype v2), carved on the center of the mouse (prototype v3a) and carved on the right side of the mouse (prototype v3b)

Based on these results, we re-evaluated the compound device with four users in a 2D pointing task following the same protocol than before. Results showed a significant improvement in the compound device performance (10% better than the previous version). However, the prototype v3 still had a lower performance and a higher error rate than the regular mouse. Participants' feedback showed that this performance loss was due to a hard resistance of buttons, difficult and tiring to push with the thumb during a long period of time. Consequently, we improved the prototype by integrating softer buttons (Figure 9 – left).

Third iteration: Designing parallel temporal usage

After focusing on the Physical arrangement of the compound device, we focused on the temporal usage of its Physical manipulations. Our goal was to support compound gestures, i.e. *parallel* temporal usage of the device elements. While we included compound gestures in our previous iterations, we did not specifically focus on these gestures.

To evaluate the parallel usage of RPM2, we designed an experiment based on a multi-dimensional graphical task: rotate, scale and translate (RST, Figure 9 - center) [38]. Four users had to manipulate virtual rectangles in a 2D environment and dock them on a target rectangle. To move the rectangle, users first pressed the left click and then translated the device. To rotate and scale the rectangle, users could respectively rotate (left-right rotation) or roll (front-back rotations) the RPM. All three RST tasks could be performed in parallel with the RPM2 prototype v3a. At the end of the experiment users were asked to evaluate the device usability. We compared our device against the regular mouse, used as in PowerPoint (e.g. with anchors around the rectangle).

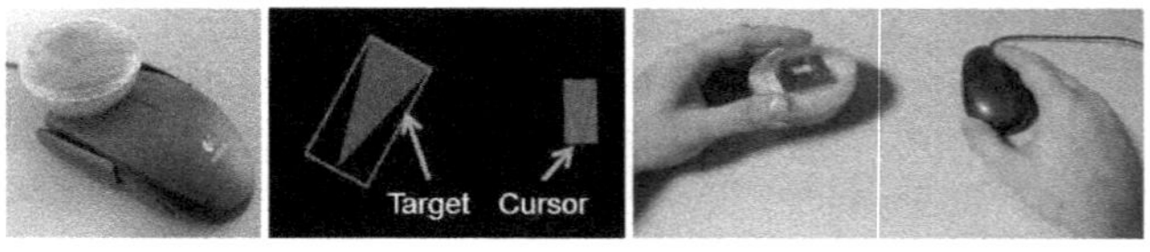

Figure 9: The *glued* RPM2 prototype v3 (left), a random trial from the RST experiment (center) and the *separated* RPM2 compound device (right).

The results reveal that our device is only 9% slower than the regular mouse, which means that our device is promising but the mapping between gestures and tasks needs to be improved. We observed that most users performed rotate, scale and translation in *parallel*. Actually, users found that RPM2 was "a good device because the manipulations are intuitive" and that "RPM2 is faster because I can scale and translate the rectangle at the same time".

These results clearly show that we succeeded in designing a novel compound device using our design space, DECO, as a designing tool. The prototype v3a is *glued* and the experiment results established the device usability and performance, close to a regular mouse. Our main goal being to propose a *dynamic* device, we carried a last iteration to validate its usage in a *separated* topology.

Fourth iteration: From a *Glued* to a *Separated* topology

In our compound device, RPM and the mouse are not physically fixed. Therefore to come up with the *separated* topology, we simply take each element with a different hand and uncouple them (Figure 9 - right). The mouse cover still has a hole that impedes using the device normally: a solution can be to use a mechanism to close the hole when RPM is removed. In this iteration, we did not build this solution and used a regular mouse without hole as we focused on the performance of the bimanual interaction.

The bimanual interaction technique is based on the use of a regular mouse with the dominant hand and the RPM with the other hand (*human effectors: <mouse: dom. hand; RPM: non dom. hand>*). This compound device still offers 5 DoFs and supports the following physical actions: *<mouse: translation (2DoFs), RPM: rotation (3DoFs)>*. The two elements can be used in *parallel* (temporal usage).

We evaluated the performance of this new version of RPM2 (RPM2-Separated) through a rotate, scale and translate (RST) experiment. We compared the bimanual technique with a regular mouse under the same conditions as in the previous iteration. Twelve subjects performed the experiment. Results revealed a significant difference between the two interaction techniques: the compound device performed faster than the mouse (22% faster). These results show that the *Separated* version of RPM2 performs better than its *glued* counterpart and illustrates the interest of developing a *dynamic* compound device: according to the task to perform, the user will be able to easily adopt the *glued* or the *separated* version of the compound device.

Summary

We proposed a novel *dynamic* compound device, the RPM2. It can be used as a *glued* compound device or as a bimanual *separated* compound device. A series of tests show that RPM2 is an efficient device in both Physical arrangements. To design these two versions of RPM2, we used DECO in a user-centered iterative design process: we guided our design process with the two axes of DECO and used its properties to iteratively propose several prototypes (Table 3).

	Physical arrangement				
Topology	Enclosed	Glued			Separated
Fusion type		A-B	A<-B	A<->B	
Temporal usage: Sequential		Iteration 1 →	Iteration 2 ↓		
Temporal usage: Parallel			Iteration 3 ☆ →		Iteration 4 ☆

☆ = *Dynamic* compound device

Table 3. RPM2 design iterations in DECO.

To sum up, this illustrative example shows that DECO is a useful tool for designing novel compound devices.

DISCUSSION

DECO to describe, compare and generate solutions

In this paper we presented DECO, a design space for device composition. As illustrated on the RPM2 case study, using DECO, designers can explore the implications of a given design by changing some parameters among DECO's axes. DECO's axes also constitute leverages for suggesting new design possibilities, based on properties observed in different situations of device composition. As such, DECO contributes to research through design [15].

To validate our design space, we used the approach proposed by Beaudoin-Lafon [4] to evaluate design models. This approach is based on three properties characterizing the ability of a model to describe existing solutions (descriptive power), compare existing solutions (evaluative power), and generate novel solutions (generative power). The relevance of such a validation has already been established in previous work seeking to evaluate interaction design approaches [11, 21]. Concretely, to validate the descriptive power of DECO, i.e. its ability to describe a wide range of different solutions, we described and classified existing compound devices using the *Physical arrangement* axis and the *Temporal usage* property of our design space. To validate the evaluative power of DECO, i.e. its ability to differentiate multiple solutions, we compared four of these devices and illustrated how DECO helps identifying their similarities and differences in terms of physical arrangement and manipulation. Finally, to validate the generative power of DECO, i.e. its ability to create new design solutions, we generated a novel compound device based on the combination of the regular mouse with the Roly-Poly mouse [28]: we used DECO to explore several design alternatives in a user-centered iterative design process.

Through this 3-part exploration, we demonstrated that DECO is a useful design space that can be used to describe, compare and generate novel compound devices.

Guidelines for generating compound devices

Generating and designing new devices often rely on an empirical approach that combines creativity and practical knowledge, as described in [39]. However, the lack of inspiration may affect the ideation phase of the design process. In the particular context of device composition, DECO is a structured analytical approach that seeks to offer designers a leverage to stimulate idea generation and to produce design alternatives. Combining such a formal approach with more informal design resources such as a brainstorming is possible and has already been proposed in HCI [6].

To help designers take advantage of DECO in a design process, we propose a set of lessons learnt during our experience in designing RPM2 with DECO.

Physical arrangement: One of the first steps, when designing an interactive device, is to analyze the users' requirements, tasks and context of use. These aspects may particularly impact the possibilities in terms of physical arrangement of the elements. At this design stage, using DECO should lead to choosing a specific topology. The two possible choices are an *Enclosed/Glued* topology, which leads to a single physical object, or a *Separated* topology, which leads to several objects.

In the case of a *Glued* topology, the advantage of starting with the *(A-B) fusion* is that it does not induce any modification on the initial devices. This allows evaluating early prototypes and getting feedback before considering physical alterations on any of the elements involved in the device composition.

Physical manipulation: The design of the Physical manipulation attributes needs to be reconsidered after each design iteration on the Physical arrangement. Even small physical changes in the prototype can induce large differences in terms of manipulation: for example, in our experience with RPM2, changing the size of the RPM considerably impacted its usability.

Finally, when the goal is to produce a *parallel* usage of the device, a good approach is to start designing and evaluating a *sequential* usage in the first iterations: the idea is to validate that each element can be properly manipulated and identify their potential in terms of manipulation (maximum range, stability, accuracy, etc.), before considering the combined manipulation.

Limitations and future work

In this paper we presented a first design space for device composition. We identified some limitations in terms of generalizability, granularity and property definition that we detail below.

In our work we mainly considered compound devices made of only two elements. While the related work on devices combining more than two elements is limited, we still need to generalize the use of our design space and assess its ability at describing, evaluating or helping generate compound devices based on more than 2 elements.

The definition of DECO has been largely driven by a critical analysis of compound devices presented in the literature. These solutions clearly focus on the combination of existing devices such as a mouse and a touchpad, i.e. the combination of two sets of sensors and physical objects. While we adopted the same approach to define the concept of device composition, DECO might also constitute a good support to analyze combinations at a finer grain of detail, i.e. at a sensor level. Future work will look into extending our design space to consider fusion composition.

In the future, we also plan to further analyze and refine the characteristics of the *Separated* topology. This case is particularly interesting for multi-surface systems, i.e. composing different interactive surfaces. We can for instance explore the geometric and spatial relationships between surfaces. Describing the Physical manipulations in this case will also require an extension of DECO to describe interactions such as mid-air or around-device gestures [5], which also have spatial properties.

CONCLUSION

In this paper we introduced DECO, a design space for device composition focusing on its physical dimensions. DECO is structured along two axes: Physical arrangement and Physical manipulation. The Physical arrangement axis describes the topology of the composition (Enclosed, Glued or Separated), the fusion type (which device is physically modified to produce the composition) and the dynamicity of the physical arrangement. The Physical manipulation axis describes the human effectors, i.e. the body parts, used to manipulate the device, the physical actions and the temporal usage of the elements. We used DECO to classify existing compound devices and compare alternative existing solutions. To illustrate the generative power of DECO, we designed a novel compound device by combining a mouse with the Roly-Poly Mouse in a user-centered design process. Finally, we proposed a set of guidelines to help designers apply our design space to create novel compound devices.

ACKNOWLEDGMENTS

This work was carried out as part of the research collaboration agreements IRIT-Berger Levrault (CNRS No.099856) and the ANR project AP2. The authors thank the members of the ELIPSE group for their useful suggestions.

REFERENCES

1. James F. Allen. Maintaining knowledge about temporal intervals. Commun. ACM, 26(11):832–843, 1983.
2. Ravin Balakrishnan and Pranay Patel. 1998. The PadMouse: facilitating selection and spatial positioning for the non-dominant hand. In *Procs of* CHI '98. ACM Press/Addison-Wesley Publishing Co., New York, NY, USA, 9-16.

3. Jakob E. Bardram, Christina Fuglsang, and Simon C. Pedersen. 2010. CompUTE: a runtime infrastructure for device composition. In *Procs of* AVI '10. ACM, New York, NY, USA, 111-118.
4. Michel Beaudouin-Lafon. 2004. Designing interaction, not interfaces. In *Procs of* AVI '04. ACM, New York, NY, USA, 15-22.
5. Louis-Pierre Bergé, Emmanuel Dubois, and Mathieu Raynal. 2015. Design and Evaluation of an "Around the SmartPhone" Technique for 3D Manipulations on Distant Display. In *Procs of* SUI '15. ACM, New York, NY, USA, 69-78.
6. Christophe Bortolaso, Emmanuel Dubois. 2013. Model Assisted Creativity Sessions for the Design of Mixed Interactive Systems: a Protocol Analysis. In INTERACT'13, Springer, LNCS 8119, p. 126-143, 2013.
7. John Bowers. 2012. The logic of annotated portfolios: communicating the value of 'research through design'. In *Procs* DIS '12. ACM, New York, NY, USA, 68-77.
8. Stuart K. Card, Jock D. Mackinlay, and George G. Robertson. A morphological analysis of the design space of input devices. ACM Transactions on Information Systems, 9(2):99–122, April 1991.
9. ContextToolkit http://contexttoolkit.sourceforge.net/
10. Joëlle Coutaz and Laurence Nigay. Les propriétés CARE dans les interfaces multimodales. In Actes de la conférence IHM'94, Lille, pages 7–14, 1994.
11. Coutrix, C., Nigay, L.: Mixed reality: a model of mixed interaction. In: Proc. of the Working Conf. on Advanced visual interfaces, AVI 2006, pp. 43–50. ACM Press (2006).
12. The FlipKeyboard. http://research.microsoft.com/en-us/um/people/bibuxton/buxtoncollection/detail.aspx?id=76
13. Froehlich, B., Hochstrate, J., Skuk, V., and Huckauf, A. The globefish and the globemouse: two new six degree of freedom input devices for graphics applications. CHI'06. ACM, 191-199.
14. Bernd Fröhlich and John Plate. 2000. The cubic mouse: a new device for three-dimensional input. In Procs of CHI '00. ACM, New York, NY, USA, 526-531.
15. William Gaver. 2012. What should we expect from research through design? In *Procs* CHI '12. ACM, New York, NY, USA, 937-946.
16. B. Hartmann , S. Doorley and S.R. Klemmer, Hacking, Mashing, Gluing: Understanding Opportunistic Design, IEEE Pervasive Computing, vol. 7, no. 3, pp.46-54, 2008
17. H. Rex Hartson, Antonio C. Siochi, and D. Hix. 1990. The UAN: a user-oriented representation for direct manipulation interface designs. *ACM Trans. Inf. Syst.* 8, 3 (July 1990), 181-203.
18. Michael Haupt, Michael Perscheid, Robert Hirschfeld, Lysann Kessler, Thomas Klingbeil, Stephanie Platz, Frank Schlegel, and Philipp Tessenow. 2010. PhidgetLab: crossing the border from virtual to real-world objects. In *Procs of* ITiCSE '10. ACM, New York, NY, USA, 73-77.
19. Ken Hinckley, Morgan Dixon, Raman Sarin, Francois Guimbretiere, and Ravin Balakrishnan. 2009. Codex: a dual screen tablet computer. In *Procs of* CHI '09. ACM, New York, NY, USA, 1933-1942.
20. Ink222 T&Mouse http://research.microsoft.com/en-us/um/people/bibuxton/buxtoncollection/detail.aspx?id=118
21. Jourde, F., Laurillau, Y., Morán, A.L., Nigay, L.: Towards specifying multimodal collaborative user interfaces: A comparison of collaboration notations. In: Interactive Systems. Design, Specification, and Verification, 15th Int. Workshop, DSV-IS, Kingston, Canada, pp. 281–286 (2008)
22. Seoktae Kim, Hyunjung Kim, Boram Lee, Tek-Jin Nam, and Woohun Lee. 2008. Inflatable mouse: volume-adjustable mouse with air-pressure-sensitive input and haptic feedback. In *Procs* CHI '08. ACM, New York, NY, USA, 211-224.
23. Lisa Kleinman, Tad Hirsch, and Matt Yurdana. 2015. Exploring Mobile Devices as Personal Public Displays. In *Procs* MobileHCI '15. ACM, New York, NY, USA, 233-243.
24. Lehman, S.L. and B.M. Calhoun, An identified model for human wrist movements. Experimental Brain Research, 1990. 81(1): p. 199-208.
25. Lexip 3D http://www.amazon.fr/Lexip-3DM-PRO-Souris-Filaire-Noir/dp/B00IZU1NE4
26. David Merrill, Jeevan Kalanithi, and Pattie Maes. 2007. Siftables: towards sensor network user interfaces. In *Procs of* TEI '07. ACM, New York, NY, USA, 75-78.
27. Laurence Nigay and Joëlle Coutaz. 1993. A design space for multimodal systems: concurrent processing and data fusion. In *Procs of* INTERACT'93 *and* CHI '93. ACM, New York, NY, USA, 172-178.
28. Gary Perelman, Marcos Serrano, Mathieu Raynal, Celia Picard, Mustapha Derras, and Emmanuel Dubois. 2015. The Roly-Poly Mouse: Designing a Rolling Input Device Unifying 2D and 3D Interaction. In *Procs of* CHI '15. ACM, New York, NY, USA, 327-336.
29. Razer naga mouse. http://www.razerzone.com/gaming-mice/razer-naga
30. Mike Rooke and Roel Vertegaal. 2010. Physics on display: tangible graphics on hexagonal bezel-less

screens. In Procs of TEI '10. ACM, New York, NY, USA, 233-236.

31. James Scott, Shahram Izadi, Leila Sadat Rezai, Dominika Ruszkowski, Xiaojun Bi, and Ravin Balakrishnan. 2010. RearType: text entry using keys on the back of a device. In *Procs of* MobileHCI '10. ACM, New York, NY, USA, 171-180.
32. Julian Seifert, Sebastian Boring, Christian Winkler, Florian Schaub, Fabian Schwab, Steffen Herrdum, Fabian Maier, Daniel Mayer, and Enrico Rukzio. 2014. Hover Pad: interacting with autonomous and self-actuated displays in space. In *Procs of* UIST '14. ACM, New York, NY, USA, 139-147.
33. Marcos Serrano, Laurence Nigay, Jean-Yves L. Lawson, Andrew Ramsay, Roderick Murray-Smith, and Sebastian Denef. 2008. The openinterface framework: a tool for multimodal interaction. In CHI EA '08. ACM, New York, NY, USA, 3501-3506.
34. David Sirkin and Wendy Ju. 2014. Make this!: introduction to electronics prototyping using arduino. In CHI EA '14.
35. Soukoreff, R. W., & MacKenzie, I. S. (2004). Towards a standard for pointing device evaluation: Perspectives on 27 years of Fitts' law research in HCI. International Journal of Human-Computer Studies, 61, 751-789.
36. Masanori Sugimoto and Keiichi Hiroki. 2006. HybridTouch: an intuitive manipulation technique for PDAs using their front and rear surfaces. In *Procs of* MobileHCI '06. ACM, New York, NY, USA, 137-140.
37. The trackball keyboard. http://www.ione-usa.com/ione-scorpius-35-trackball-keyboard.html
38. Jayson Turner, Jason Alexander, Andreas Bulling, and Hans Gellersen. 2015. Gaze+RST: Integrating Gaze and Multitouch for Remote Rotate-Scale-Translate Tasks. In *Procs of* CHI '15. ACM, New York, NY, USA, 4179-4188.
39. Anna Vallgårda and Ylva Fernaeus. 2015. Interaction Design as a Bricolage Practice. In Procs of TEI '15. ACM, New York, NY, USA, 173-180.
40. Nicolas Villar, Shahram Izadi, Dan Rosenfeld, Hrvoje Benko, John Helmes, Jonathan Westhues, Steve Hodges, Eyal Ofek, Alex Butler, Xiang Cao, and Billy Chen. 2009. Mouse 2.0: multi-touch meets the mouse. In *Procs of* UIST '09. ACM, New York, NY, USA, 33-42.
41. Xing-Dong Yang, Edward Mak, David McCallum, Pourang Irani, Xiang Cao, and Shahram Izadi. 2010. LensMouse: augmenting the mouse with an interactive touch display. In Procs CHI '10. ACM, New York, NY, USA, 2431-2440.

PeerPresents: A Web-Based System for In-Class Peer Feedback during Student Presentations

Amy Shannon
Carnegie Mellon University
Pittsburgh, USA
amyshann@cs.cmu.edu

Jessica Hammer
Carnegie Mellon University
Pittsburgh, USA
hammerj@cs.cmu.edu

Hassler Thurston
University of Rochester
Rochester, USA
jthurst3@u.rochester.edu

Natalie Diehl
University of Michigan
Ann Arbor, USA
diehlna@umich.edu

Steven Dow
University of California, San Diego
La Jolla, USA
spdow@ucsd.edu

ABSTRACT

Peer feedback systems enable students to get feedback without substantially burdening the instructor. However, current systems typically ask students to provide feedback after class; this introduces challenges for ensuring relevant, timely, diverse, and sufficient amounts of feedback, and reduces time available for student reflection. This paper explores the current landscape of peer feedback tools and introduces a novel system for in-class peer review called *PeerPresents* where students can quickly exchange feedback on projects without being burdened by additional work outside of class. Through an exploratory study with Google docs and a preliminary evaluation of PeerPresents, we find students can receive immediate, copious, and diverse peer feedback through a structured in-class activity. Students also described the feedback they received as helpful and reported that they gave more feedback than without using the system. These early results demonstrate the potential benefits of in-class peer feedback systems.

Author Keywords

Peer feedback; feedback systems; collaborative learning; classroom technology.

ACM Classification Keywords

K.3.1. Computer Uses in Education: Collaborative Learning; H.5.3 Group and Organization Interfaces: Computer-supported cooperative work.

INTRODUCTION

Giving and receiving feedback is a key activity for student learning, especially in open-ended domains like design and writing [3,7]. As demand for education in such domains increases, instructors increasingly turn to peer feedback systems to ensure students get personalized input on their work [7,17,27]. Peer feedback has been shown to improve learning by helping feedback receivers make connections between evaluation rubrics and their own work [29]; the activity also benefits the provider by helping them think critically about the evaluation criteria [9]. For mid-size to large classes, peer feedback can potentially increase the amount of feedback and shorten the amount of time to receive feedback, compared to receiving feedback from the instructor alone (e.g. [17]).

While peer feedback systems have helped address the increasing demand for feedback, the features and practices emerging around such systems can create new challenges for feedback providers. Many systems require peers to review a minimum number of other students' submissions, typically outside of class (e.g. [7].) In this arrangement, students often perceive peer reviews as an extra assignment [17], rather than as a learning opportunity. The PeerStudio project empirically demonstrated the value of rapid peer feedback [17], but students still need to schedule the feedback process around other commitments and may not be able to do the task quickly. To minimize workload, students typically only need to review the work of a few peers. Feedback receivers, therefore, only benefit from a small number of perspectives on their work, and those perspectives may vary widely in terms of quality and appropriateness [21]. The high variability and low diversity could be improved if a larger number of peers provided feedback. However, with current peer feedback systems, this would create an even larger burden on providers and limit the students' time to reflect on their own work.

Our work explores the possibility of moving peer feedback processes into the classroom. By pairing this process with student presentations, peers have a chance to comment on other students' work during class. This means students receive feedback by the end of class, potentially leaving more time to reflect. Also, by engaging the entire class, we hypothesize students will get more abundant and diverse feedback. Finally, past studies indicate that many students spend class time on non-learning activities, such as checking Facebook [16]. The intuition here is that in-class peer

DIS 2016, June 04 - 08, 2016, Brisbane, QLD, Australia

ACM 978-1-4503-4031-1/16/06···$15.00
DOI: http://dx.doi.org/10.1145/2901790.2901816

feedback can potentially supplant these off-task activities with ones that are beneficial for all students.

In this paper, we review prior work on peer feedback, as well as systems designed to facilitate peer feedback and audience interaction. We conducted an exploratory study where 53 students provided in-class peer feedback using shared Google Docs on student presentations in a project-based innovation course. This study demonstrated that in-class peer feedback could be successful, but that students need better support for reflecting on their feedback.

Based on these insights, we designed and developed a novel web-based, in-class peer feedback tool called *PeerPresents*. With this system, either students or faculty can design a rubric to guide the feedback process. Students can quickly access and participate on the system using any Web browser. Peers respond to rubric questions during and after the presentation, as well as vote on the responses from other students. Immediately after class, the students can see their feedback and use PeerPresents to organize and reflect on the help they have received.

As a preliminary evaluation of our novel tool, fifteen feedback providers used PeerPresents during practice research talks for six PhD students. The preliminary study demonstrated the value of structuring in-class peer feedback, and revealed further insights into how to elicit valuable peer feedback. In the discussion, we draw out implications for designing in-class peer feedback tools.

This paper presents the following contributions: 1) a taxonomy of existing peer feedback tools, 2) an exploratory study of an in-class peer feedback process using an off-the-shelf tool (Google docs), 3) a novel system called PeerPresents designed for in-class peer feedback, 4) a preliminary evaluation of the new feedback tool, and 5) reflections on lessons learned for in-class peer feedback exercises.

RELATED WORK

Numerous researchers have studied the benefits of peer feedback for all three parties involved: instructors, feedback receivers, and feedback providers. Peer feedback lowers the burden for instructors to generate feedback for the whole class. Students who receive feedback improve their self-regulated learning skills through the process of reflecting on feedback and revising their work [5]. Students who provide feedback learn to recognize what "good" work looks like and to correctly interpret standards or criteria [23]. Peer feedback also helps students improve their self-assessment abilities [19].

Qualities of Successful Feedback

Regardless of whether feedback comes from instructors, peers, or external reviewers, researchers have identified several key conditions that make feedback more successful for learning.

- *Relevant*: Feedback should focus on students' learning and performance, rather than on the students themselves or their personal characteristics [13]. Relevant feedback helps students understand the desired criteria (conceptual), compare their actual performance with these criteria (specific), and engage in action that closes this gap (actionable) [26].
- *Copious:* Researchers and educators value the peer feedback process because it allows students to get a higher quantity of feedback than if the instructor were the only feedback provider [28]. Generating sufficient feedback has most often been limited by the instructors' or peers' time constraints.
- *Timely:* Feedback should be timely, such that students receive it soon after they submit their work. A recent study on a peer feedback system for large online classes found that peer feedback helped students improve their grades, but only if the feedback was delivered within 24 hours [17].
- *Diverse:* Seeking diverse feedback helps in many domains, especially in design settings that need to account for multiple stakeholders [3]. Diverse feedback providers are more likely to offer novel perspectives and uncover unique issues [20].
- *Reflected On*: Reflecting on feedback helps students become better self-regulated learners [5,19,23]. Reflecting on feedback requires students to manage their own learning by interpreting standards and rubrics and revising their own work.

Certain structural features of current peer feedback systems create challenges to achieving all these goals. Peer feedback systems are typically designed for use outside of class, and often require students to provide feedback to a certain number of other students. This places a burden on students, reduces the likelihood that students will receive feedback in a timely manner, limits the number of perspectives represented in a student's feedback, and reduces the time available to work and reflect on their own assignment. Our research seeks to address these issues by introducing a system specifically designed for in-class feedback.

Design Considerations for In-Class Feedback

A number of additional factors come into play when considering in-class activities that could impact the design of peer feedback systems.

Time

There is limited time in any class session. Students and instructors may feel overwhelmed with adding another time-consuming activity to the class session [9], so implementing the in-class peer feedback system needs to be simple and time-efficient.

Management Logistics

Setting up and implementing a peer feedback process requires the instructor to manage numerous details, such as assigning peer reviewers or authoring rubrics. The instructor also might also need to evaluate both the original assignment and peer feedback itself in order to provide a grade [19]. (Numerous researchers also explore peer *as-*

sessment, where a student assigns another student a numerical grade on their assignment [e.g. [10]]; however, this paper focuses on qualitative peer feedback, not peer assessment.)

Risks for Students

Peer feedback requires students to make their work public, inviting potential risks such as loss of privacy, saving face, embarrassment, or even humiliation [19]. One indication that students are aware of these risks could be their reluctance to criticize peers when providing feedback [21].

Classroom Culture

Some researchers argue that peer feedback processes can only be carried out effectively when students understand the benefits of peer feedback, trust their peers, and benefit from an established collaborative learning climate [19]. Others point out the necessity for a non-threatening, collaborative atmosphere for peer feedback [24]. The instructor plays an important role in establishing a classroom culture that builds trust among peers and encourages learning without reducing learners' self-efficacy.

Attitudes Toward Technology Use

Most systems for peer feedback rely on digital technology to facilitate interaction, but instructors have a variety of attitudes towards using technology in class. While some instructors find technology beneficial to student learning [22], others decline to use technology in their class because of a lack of technical support or suitable software [4].

REVIEW OF EXISTING SYSTEMS

To understand the current state of peer feedback technology, we first investigated the successes and pitfalls of existing tools. We reviewed 31 different tools designed to capture qualitative feedback on student assignments, as well as tools designed to elicit responses from students during class or for general audience interactions (see Figure 1).

We discovered systems to review by following citation trails, searching academic and non-academic databases, and getting suggestions from experts. These systems supported activities such as peer feedback, student or instructor critique, facilitating discussion, answering questions during lecture, asking questions during lecture, and polling large groups. We compared the systems using a competitive analysis. Rather than presenting all 31 systems, we chose to summarize the systems most influential to the design of a system for in-class peer feedback.

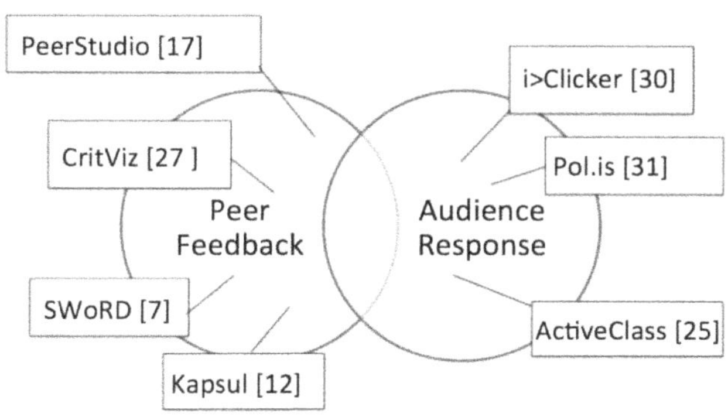

Figure 1. PeerPresents explores the intersection between peer feedback systems and audience interaction technology.

Feedback Systems

Most peer feedback systems are specifically designed for students to provide feedback outside of class [7,12,17,27]. We found one system designed for use during class [8], but this system—used to encourage novice group critique in a design course—also asked students to provide written feedback before the in-class critique session.

The peer review process is commonly characterized by a required number of reviews for each student [7,17], structured rubrics authored by the instructor to guide feedback [27], and a revision period before the final deadline [7]. In the case of PeerStudio, which facilitates rapid peer feedback to students in MOOCs, survey responses indicated that many students felt their schedule was too busy to revise. One student complained about the workload, saying that "(the instructors) expect us to read some forty page essays, then write the critiques and then review two other people, and then make changes on our work... twice a week" [17].

While some systems permit resubmission of assignments [7], reflecting on feedback was a task often ignored by peer feedback systems. Some provided only a way for students to view the feedback they received [12] without any additional support for sensemaking or reflection. One tool provided a leaderboard that allows students to see how their work ranked compared to classmates [27], but no support for understanding the reasons for their ranking. Even systems that allowed students to enter reflections on the feedback they received found that students rarely used this feature. For example, PeerStudio researchers found that only 100 out of 3600 students wrote reflections using the system [17].

Student/Audience Interaction Systems

To investigate the potential of in-class peer feedback, we reviewed tools designed for collecting input in real time during class. A number of systems support responses to pre-authored multiple-choice questions (e.g. [30]), and some require specific hardware [11].

In-class systems focused on being easy to use and often featured automatic real-time visualizations of student responses. For example, one system allowed students to ask questions during class and used voting as a way to highlight the most popular questions for the instructor [25].

We also reviewed systems designed to poll audiences who were not necessarily students in a classroom. Many systems were similar to in-class response systems in that they supported only multiple-choice responses and visualized responses in real time. Rather than relying on specific hardware like i>Clickers, these tools are often web-based and can be accessed via laptop or mobile devices. For example, Feedbackr, a tool designed to poll audiences

Peer Feedback Tools	In Class Use	Rubrics/ Scaffolding	Anonymous/ Pseudonymous	Voluntary Participation	Voting on Feedback	Reflection
Audience Response Systems	x			x	x	
CritViz [27]		x	x			
SWoRD [7]		x	x			
PeerStudio [17]		x	x			x
CSGC [8]	x	x			x	
PeerPresents	x	x	x	x	x	x

Figure 2. Features of existing peer feedback tools compared to PeerPresents.

during presentations, directs users to a short URL to view multiple choice questions, and the presenter can choose when each question is visible to audience members [14]. These tools commonly solicited anonymous responses from audience members.

Other systems designed to poll audiences went beyond multiple-choice questions. For example, Pol.is is a web-based polling system that uses machine learning and data visualizations to host large-scale discussions [31]. Once a topic has been created, Pol.is allows users to write a response or react (agree or disagree) to the responses of others. Then the system organizes users into groups who share similar opinions. These groups are visualized so that users can see whose thoughts align with their own and which reactions are most important to that group [31].

Lessons Learned from Other Systems

Our review of existing systems did not find any tools that focused both on peer feedback and real-time use during class. Existing peer feedback systems require extensive out-of-class time from students and may not promote or allow time for reflection, while existing in-class systems are typically limited to narrow types of interaction. However, both types of tools provide insights for the design of in-class peer feedback systems.

To encourage relevant feedback, we use scaffolding to guide the feedback process. To promote copious, timely, and diverse feedback, we bring the peer feedback process into the classroom. This allows students to receive feedback from potentially all peers by the end of class without requiring students to review a particular number of assignments or spend extra time outside class. We also implemented features to lower the risks for students to participate during class. Finally, we use student voting to highlight important comments to encourage presenters to reflect on their feedback. We developed additional constraints by examining how in-class systems were designed specifically for the classroom context.

Beyond the idea of facilitating peer feedback in-class, our system incorporates a number of novel features: question scaffolding, pseudonymous or anonymous participation, voluntary participation, voting, and reflection support. Figure 2 highlights the novelty of PeerPresents compared to existing peer feedback tools that influenced our system. We first discuss an exploratory study that proposes a process for in-class peer feedback using Google docs. We then discuss the novel design of PeerPresents and the preliminary evaluation of our system.

EXPLORATORY STUDY

As an exploratory study of the procedures and design issues for exchanging in-class feedback, we decided to create a "prototype" using off-the-shelf technology (Google Docs).

Method

We conducted an exploratory study with 53 students (35 female) in a project-based innovation course focused on the design of mobile service applications. The course, offered at a mid-western university, was comprised of undergraduate (37) and graduate (23) students; 95 percent of students regularly carried a laptop with them to class.

Students provided feedback to their peers during mid-term presentations on a group assignment. During two class sessions lasting two hours each, nine groups of students presented their business model ideas for a novel mobile app, such as Friendr, an app to help you find a friend to attend events with you, and SunnySideUp, an app for requesting breakfast delivery to your office or home.

To enable peer feedback, each presenting group prepared a business model document that they shared with the class through a Google doc. During and shortly after each presentation, the instructor asked students to provide feedback using Google's default commenting features, which students accessed using their laptops (see Figure 3).

To promote diversity of comments and to scaffold appropriate responses, students were encouraged to comment from one of four framing perspectives:

- Breakdowns: Think of problems that could cause this service to break down.
- Competitors: Think of existing and potential competitors to this service.
- Stakeholders: Think through the perspective of the people involved: users, providers, investors, marketers, and local businesses.

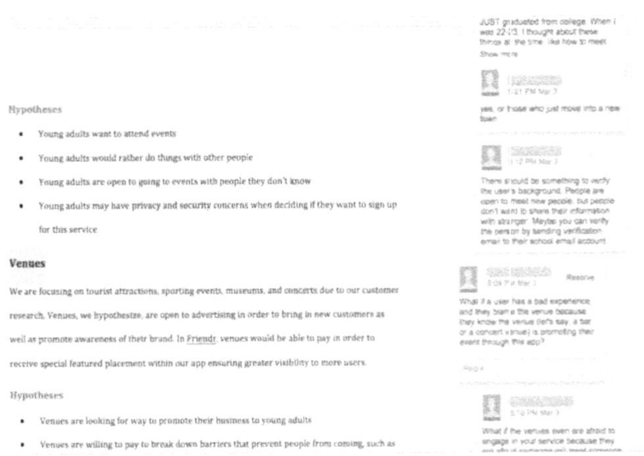

Figure 3. Business model for Friendr and the feedback they received as comments on a Google Doc.

- Scenarios: Think of additional scenarios where this idea could be applied.

These four framing perspectives were intended to stretch students to think about different factors that could affect the design of a mobile app. Students were assigned different perspectives for each presentation.

We collected and analyzed student and faculty comments on each presentation. After both sessions ended, students filled out an anonymous online survey about the experience; 84% participated. We collected data about class participation, students' technology use during class, and their attitudes about the perspectives they were assigned. Students were also asked to compare their participation in providing feedback during the presentations with how they provide feedback in other courses.

When surveyed about Facebook use during class, 40% of students reported using Facebook in class once a week and 27% reported using Facebook every class session. 24% reported once a month use, and only 9% said they never use Facebook in class.

Results

In presenting our results, we combine analysis of comment data with survey results to highlight five important criteria for student feedback that emerged from our literature review: relevant, copious, timely, diverse, and reflected-on.

Relevant: 80% of students who responded to the survey said that the comments they received were "helpful" or "very helpful." We find student beliefs about the helpfulness of comments a useful proxy for relevance; they are the ones who must interpret the comments and decide how to use feedback to revise their work.

Copious: Overall, 36 out of 53 students (68%) commented at least once during the two class sessions. Across the nine presentation documents, students made 242 comments, for an average of 26.7 comments per document and 7 comments per student. Of the 36 students who commented at least once, 33 (90%) reported that they felt they gave more feedback using written comments than they would have given verbally in class.

Timely: 88% of feedback was given during class, and was available to the presenting group immediately after their presentation. Of the feedback given after class, most was from the instructor giving grades on the assignment. Twelve student comments arrived after class had ended.

Diverse: 77% of comments used one of the four framing perspectives. However, only 14% used the perspective assigned to the student at that time; 63% of student comments came from a different perspective than the one assigned, and the remaining 23% of comments were not from any of the perspectives. In other words, students commented from a variety of perspectives even when asked to focus only on one. 38% of students reported their assigned perspective was "difficult" to adopt, and only 40%

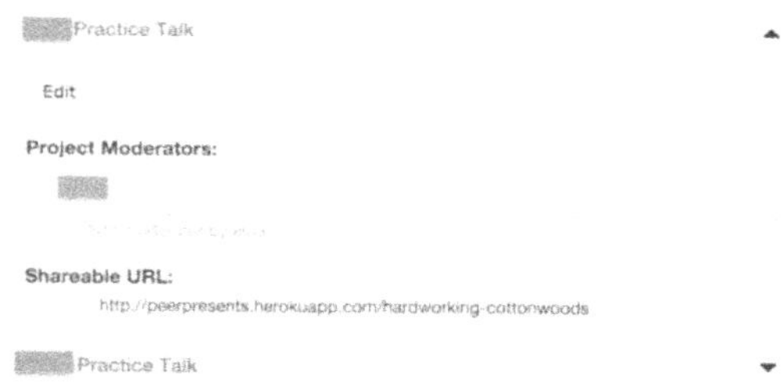

Figure 4. Presenting students can add team members, and distribute a short URL to feedback providers.

found the perspective "helpful" for inspiring new ideas while commenting. Given that 77% of comments came from one of the assigned perspectives – even when not assigned to that student – the data show that students found the scaffolding helpful, but felt restrained by having to comment from one perspective.

Reflected on: Out of 242 total comments, presenting students made only 5 comments in reply to the feedback their team had received. Based on the data we collected, we cannot draw conclusions about how students reflected on peer feedback.

Discussion

The exploratory study provides preliminary support that in-class feedback can be relevant, copious, timely, and diverse. This was achieved without implementing review requirements, mandating additional time outside of class, or requiring specific hardware. However, we see less evidence regarding how students engaged with the feedback received. Google Docs collapses longer comment threads, making it difficult for students to read all feedback on a document, or even know how much feedback is available. Google Docs also did not explicitly support reflection processes, and so future systems should address this need.

While in-class feedback did result in a diverse set of student comments, students did not seem to use the prescribed perspectives. Students were instructed to comment from a single perspective, but instead commented from many perspectives – creating even more diversity of feedback than we tried to scaffold. Students reported they did not use the framing perspectives as prescribed, partly because it felt limiting. We hypothesize that students are both willing and able to adopt multiple perspectives while commenting on a presentation. However, scaffolding may still be necessary to ensure that providing diverse feedback perspectives remains relevant to presenters' needs and the instructor's goals; we therefore reframe this as an issue of ensuring that peer feedback—which is naturally diverse in large classrooms—remains relevant. Future systems should focus on how to scaffold relevance, rather than diversity.

While we were initially concerned about placing a cognitive burden on students in the evaluation study, our preliminary observations tell us that students have a cognitive surplus during class, especially during peer presentations, which they often spend on non-academic activities like checking Facebook. A well-designed in-class peer feedback system could give students a pedagogically meaningful activity to potentially replace Facebook and other distractions with academic exercises.

Finally, the prototype did not support all students equally effectively. Most students felt comfortable giving and receiving comments on their work, but a minority of students (7 out of 45 survey respondents, or approximately 15%) felt that commenting during the presentation was distracting for the presenter. Additionally, some students reported feeling overly criticized and judged, or that commenting felt like a "hazing" process. This feeling of being judged may make peer feedback less effective and reduce learners' willingness to participate. Future systems could do more to address student risks and ensure peer feedback remains focused on the work, not on the personal characteristics of the student.

To address the findings from our exploratory study, we expanded our notion of in-class feedback to encompass the process before, during, and after class.

DESIGN OF A NOVEL IN-CLASS FEEDBACK TOOL

In our exploratory study, we validated the concept of exchanging peer feedback during class using web technology, and we gained insights on how to design a system that supports relevant, copious, timely, diverse, and reflected-on feedback. In creating PeerPresents, we focused on features that would build on the successes of the exploratory study while reducing the burden on the instructor, providing scaffolding to encourage relevant comments, mitigating risks for students, and encouraging reflection on feedback.

Before Class

Question scaffolding: To create effective scaffolds without placing an additional burden on the instructor, PeerPresents allows each team of presenting students to author rubric questions in preparation for their presentation (see Figure 6). These questions are presented to the class during the presentation, allowing presenting students to receive feedback better tailored to their goals. Not only do the questions provide a guide for students giving feedback, but the process of generating questions also encourages teams to reflect on what type of feedback would be most useful, and how to ask effective feedback questions. Presenting students can also decide when each question goes "live" for peers to answer.

Additionally, structuring feedback around questions rather than around, for example, slide numbers allows our system to accommodate presentations of many types – formal slide-based presentations, in-class role-play, video pitches, and more. Presenters can design questions that respond to the specific format of their presentation.

Permissions and Dissemination: In PeerPresents, students can add project group members to their presentation, so that the instructor does not have to input teams for the entire class. The system also automatically creates a short URL so presenters can easily direct classmates to their presentation (see Figure 4).

During Class

Pseudonyms: To help reduce the perceived risk around peer feedback, while still providing a degree of accountability, PeerPresents allows feedback providers to choose a pseudonym when accessing the system. This pseudonym appears on every comment they make, which is visible both to other students in class for voting and to the presenters for reflection. Because students can choose obscure or identifiable pseudonyms, students can decide in each class session how anonymous they would like to be.

Voluntary Feedback and Voting: During the presentation, peers can answer each question provided by the presenters as many or as few times as they choose (see Figure 6). They can also choose to provide comments in a "default" open-ended text box. PeerPresents did not support discussion

Figure 5. Presenting students see all the feedback they received, with the ability to tag, sort, and organize comments. (All names and pseudonyms removed for anonymous submission)

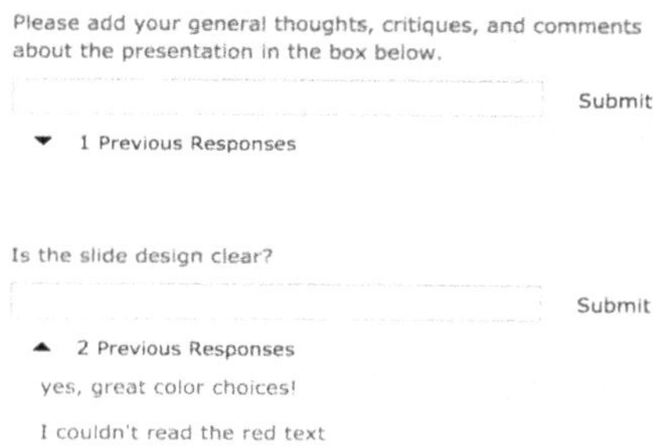

Figure 6. Peer feedback interface: Peers respond to specific questions as many times as they desire.

threads between students to minimize distractions during the presentation.

Peers can up-vote or down-vote comments from other students; this helps the presenters identify comments that are important, popular, or controversial. Comments are displayed in real time throughout the presentation on a separate voting page (see Figure 7).

After Class:

Reflection: Presenting students can immediately view all their feedback with the timestamp, author, up/down votes, and framing question (see Figure 5). Students can then tag and filter comments to organize their feedback in a meaningful way. The system provides default tags for students to mark Positive, Negative, and Important feedback. Any presenting team member can individually create additional tags, which are visible to all team members. The system also displays how many comments have been recorded under each author, question, or tag. Students can filter comments by author, question or tag, and sort comments by least or most recent, author, and number of votes. To increase familiarity, we designed the filtering and sorting process to resemble many consumer product websites.

Not only are these features novel within the design space of peer feedback systems (see Figure 2, above), they also work together to address the issues raised by our exploratory study and to improve the peer feedback process.

PRELIMINARY SYSTEM EVALUATION

To evaluate our system, we asked six PhD students to use PeerPresents while practicing for a PhD requirement talk—a twenty-minute research presentation followed by a ten-minute question period. This presentation is a requirement for the doctoral program in the authors' academic department. Faculty members judge each presentation on research content, communication style, and slide design.

Methods

Six students received comments on their presentations, and fifteen people (13 students and 2 faculty) provided feedback. We collected survey data asking participants to comment on their experience with the system with respect to the relevance, quality, timeliness, diversity, and reflec-

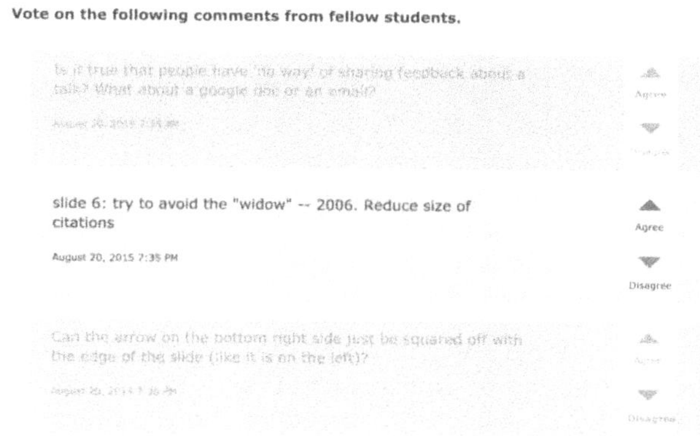

Figure 7. Students agree or disagree with the responses of other students providing feedback.

tiveness of feedback, and we analyzed the feedback provided by peers and faculty. The research team developed metrics to categorize comments into the following five types of feedback: *On Topic*: 1) research content, 2) communication style, 3) slide design, and *Off Topic*: 4) emotional support, and 5) other. We also tracked whether feedback made reference to a particular slide by number.

The practice session happened five days before the final presentations, so the talks were still in progress at this stage. This also meant that comments on communication style and slide design would be highly relevant, even if they might not be as important for practice talks in other contexts.

Given the constraints of the presentation context, we made some modifications to PeerPresents. First, the PhD program has a specific form for providing written feedback on these talks. Rather than have presenters develop their own questions to scaffold feedback, we used the same questions faculty would use to evaluate the real talk. For example, students would be evaluated on how the research was "situated in a larger theoretical context", if the research was "communicated in an understandable way", and whether "the slides followed good aesthetic design principles." All students would be evaluated by the same rubric.

After the practice session, we asked presenters to reflect on the feedback in a spreadsheet and to use the filtering features to mimic tagging and sorting their feedback. (This informed key features for the PeerPresents reflection page, which was under development at the time.)

Results

Relevant: Five out of six presenters responded that the feedback was relevant. In coding the comments across all presentations, we found that 89% of comments were on topic (45% content, 15% communication, 29% design) and only 21% were off topic. (Total percentages sum to over 100% because some comments included multiple types of feedback.) Despite concerns that off-topic feedback might be negative or judgmental, we found that the vast majority of off-topic feedback—90% of all off-topic comments—provided positive emotional support. Only 2% of comments were completely unrelated to the presentation or presenter (e.g. "hi" or "Lightning bolt! Lightning bolt!"), and none were negative.

We also found that 33% of the comments mentioned a specific slide number. Mentioning specific slides seemed particularly salient to presenters. Students commented that they "appreciated the feedback on specific slides" and "got specific details that I would not have gotten from discussion."

Finally, we found that instead of answering all questions on the feedback form, students put 44% of their feedback into first question visible at the top of the form, asking about the content of the talk in general. The second most frequently answered question (asking for feedback on communication skills) was the form's second question; it received 13% of all feedback.

Copious: Across all six presentations, there were 338 comments. Remarkably, feedback providers gave an average of 24 comments, something that would not have been possible during a 10-minute verbal feedback session. In the open-ended survey, participants responded that they "got a lot more feedback in this form, than traditional ways" and that it made it "easy to give lots of feedback."

Timely: All commenting happened either during the 20 minute talk or within the 10 minute Q&A period immediately following each talk. The total session for all six talks lasted three hours. According to our debrief discussions with presenters, all participants were eager to see their feedback immediately after their talk. When students knew that feedback could be available immediately after their presentation, they preferred not to delay even half an hour while another student spoke.

To minimize distraction, we asked students providing feedback to answer questions throughout the twenty-minute research presentation but wait to vote on others' comments until the ten-minute Q&A period. Participants expressed a desire to see others' responses to questions sooner, rather than waiting until after the presentation had ended.

Diverse: Participants were pleased with the diversity of their feedback. In addition to receiving comments regarding presentation skills, slide design, and research content, presenters also commented that they received a mix of detail-oriented and general feedback, and a balance of comments stating a problem and comments offering a solution. Presenters also recognized that the diversity in their feedback was in part due to the number of diverse perspectives represented in the audience.

Reflected On: We asked presenters to use the filtering features in a spreadsheet to mimic the feedback tagging and sorting features in PeerPresents. While not all presenters used the tagging feature, all mentioned frequently referring to their feedback during revision. One presenter told researchers her feedback contained a lot of "why" questions asking her to explain the validity or reasoning behind specific statements she made in the presentation, saying, "[the feedback] tells me I haven't found the right words or the right slides to tell the story yet."

Feedback providers voted on 120 of the 338 comments; 177 total up-votes and 7 total down-votes were given. The average feedback provider voted on 12 comments. Of the 113 comments receiving up-votes, 73 (65%) received only 1 vote and 30 (27%) received only 2 votes. No comment received more than one down-vote.

Most participants entered their real name as their pseudonym in the system. Twelve out of fifteen participants used their real name, or a variant on it, including five out of six presenters.

Discussion

Our preliminary evaluation of PeerPresents demonstrates that a custom in-class peer feedback system can yield relevant, copious, timely, and diverse feedback, as well as provide time and tools for reflection. In addition, we were able to address student concerns about negative personal judgments and minimize the burden on the instructor in setting up our system. We also identified a number of issues for future research and development.

Peer feedback as legitimate peripheral participation

As described above, we observed copious feedback being provided to presenters by their peers. However, we also observed that our system supports a variety of different levels of engagement and participation. Three feedback providers gave significantly more feedback than the average, with 80, 71, and 66 comments respectively. Others made only a few comments; four feedback providers made fewer than five comments apiece. The type of comments also varied: all fifteen gave feedback on slide design, nine spoke about communication skills, twelve about research content, and thirteen gave emotional support.

Building on theories of legitimate peripheral participation, we take this diversity of participation styles as a measure of the success of our system. Legitimate peripheral participation describes how novices become experts by participating in simple tasks that are well within their capabilities, but as part of a larger community in which they can receive feedback from more experienced members [18]. Similarly, PeerPresents does not require individual feedback providers to give a certain amount of feedback, but rather lets individuals choose the amount and type of feedback they are comfortable providing. This theoretical approach, however, suggests that it is important to make expert behavior visible to novices for modeling and learning purposes. For example, we can investigate the impact of design decisions such as highlighting faculty feedback with a different color.

Challenges of feedback questions

The PeerPresents system uses questions to inform peers about the feedback most relevant to presenters, and to remind them about presenter needs as they give feedback.

The system succeeded at focusing the feedback providers, as the vast majority of feedback was relevant. However, more than half of it was given in response to the first two questions on the feedback form (see Figure 6). These two questions received a variety of on- and off-topic feedback. The first question was a place for general open-ended feedback, and about 55% touched on the basic research content (as opposed to presentation style or slide design). The second question asked for input on communication skills, and here only about 59% of feedback touched on the presenter's communication skills and slide design. This suggests that feedback providers were able to use questions to scaffold relevant feedback, but that they sometimes provided feedback that did not match the question being asked (e.g. 36% of responses to the second question were about research content rather than communication skills). Providers also chose not to respond to questions later on the list.

We infer that feedback providers behaved this way because the feedback form contained nineteen questions. With so many questions, finding a particular question meant scrolling through multiple pages – time that feedback providers preferred to spend commenting. This is in line with prior work that suggests students often do not read rubrics in their entirety [1]. Additionally, the questions were intended to evaluate a finished presentation, not a work in progress. Students remarked that while there were too many questions, they also did not cover everything they wanted to comment on. Searching for a question that might not exist may have seemed like a fool's game when an open-ended comment box was convenient.

We found that the system worked, but that the question scaffolding may need further consideration. There may be a practical upper limit on how many questions commenters can effectively respond to. We did not test what makes an effective question for feedback, but we can learn from existing research on rubric formation (e.g. [2]) to provide guidance for helping students construct questions to guide feedback in future iterations of the tool.

Limitations on voting

On average, feedback providers made twice as many comments as votes, even though commenting required more time and effort. We noticed that general comments (like "you may want to talk slower"), or comments that were easy to agree with (like "you are a great speaker"), received the majority of the up-votes. We hypothesize that this happened because many of the feedback comments lacked context after the fact. For example, some feedback providers said they could not agree or disagree with someone else's comment because they did not remember the slide being referenced. Even when a comment did not mention a specific slide number, there was not always enough context after the fact for feedback providers to agree or disagree. While presenters were generally able to make sense of comments by referencing their own slide deck or recalling their presentation, the other feedback providers lacked the context they needed to be helpful up/down voters. While this difficulty may have been exacerbated by using the departmental feedback form instead of presenter-authored questions, we note the reconstruction of context as a future challenge for our work.

Very few of the votes were down-votes – only seven out of 184 votes. The lack of context may have made feedback providers even more hesitant to criticize than to applaud other people's comments, since they might be lacking context that would make the comment productive. Other research suggests that providing only upvoting, instead of upvoting and downvoting, can help minimize evaluation anxiety for students in a peer feedback context [15]. Removing the option to disagree with students in PeerPresents might benefit the classroom culture and help students feel more comfortable with the peer feedback process.

We also note that 35% of comments that pointed out problems also included a suggestion for how to address it; this could help mitigate the criticism. Taken together, this data makes us ask whether students are being sufficiently critical of one another's work, or whether additional scaffolding is needed to help feedback providers express appropriate criticism of the comments provided.

Pseudonymity and learning culture

While we provided the option for participants to use pseudonyms as identifiers in our system, the majority of participants chose to use their real names, or variants on their real names. While being identifiable may produce social risks for students in some contexts [6], in this study, being identifiable was seen as a positive. Because they personally knew each feedback provider, presenters found their knowledge of that person's background and expertise helped provide context for specific comments. Having the option to be identifiable also served as a partial way of allowing experts to model behavior. Because the faculty members attending the talk chose to be identifiable, students were able to give their comments higher priority.

This does not imply that identifiability is necessarily better that pseudonymity. What we observe is a particular learning culture, one in which all participants know each other well and had established trust before the study. This type of learning environment is conducive to productive peer feedback [19], and we hope to investigate how PeerPresents can foster such a classroom culture in a variety of learning environments, while still supporting learning environments that do not yet have these characteristics.

Class size

While we believe PeerPresents may be particularly helpful to instructors of large classes, our small-scale preliminary evaluation indicates that high-quality peer feedback can be useful for classes of all sizes. The 15 students in our preliminary tool evaluation were able to instantly give a detailed critique of their peers' work, allowing presenters to rapidly iterate and improve their presentations.

Distraction
One concern with using this tool in real-time is that the system could become a distraction during student presentations. For example, students might be reading and voting on peer's comments and stop listening to the presenter. Also, how will the presenter feel if everyone in the audience is looking at their laptops instead of at the slides or speaker?

In our preliminary study of the system, participants did not express distraction as a concern, neither when they were giving feedback nor when they were presenting. Perhaps this is because students in our study are accustomed to being on laptops during presentations. However, we recognize this would not be true for all classroom contexts. A fruitful avenue for future work will be to investigate how facilitate minimally disruptive in-class feedback.

Role of the instructor
PeerPresents does not specify what role the instructor plays while students are using the system. We envision that the instructor could use PeerPresents to help students develop good feedback skills, such as guiding students as they write feedback questions, providing comments through the system during presentations, and evaluating the quality of the feedback students provide. Further design work can explore the best ways to support how instructors might interact with PeerPresents.

Limitations
Our study recruited a limited sample to test PeerPresents, consisting of graduate students and faculty from a single department. We have implicitly compared our tool to a verbal Q&A session, rather than testing it in comparison to a similar system, or to other existing approaches such as email or paper-based feedback forms. Further, PeerPresents' reflection page was still under development during our initial evaluation; for example, participants may have organized their feedback differently in Excel than they would when using the PeerPresents reflection page. In addition, the exploratory study and preliminary system evaluation did not fully investigate the instructors' perspective towards implementing this type of system in their class. We expect to gain insights about what instructors need from this system when we deploy PeerPresents in classrooms.

FUTURE WORK
The issues discussed above suggest avenues for future research, as well as provide insights to help us iterate our tool. A more rigorous future evaluation of PeerPresents would compare this tool to analog methods as well as to other digital feedback systems. We also believe this system could be generalized to other contexts, such as conferences. In the longer term, we will be investigating the following three research areas related to in-class technology.

Scaffolding Question Formation and Reflection
Discerning what questions to ask when asking for feedback is a skill that many students may not have fully developed. We intend to explore ways PeerPresents can help students ask more helpful questions, and investigate how students reflect on the feedback they requested.

Studying Instructor Adoption
In-class tools only work when the instructor is willing and able to adopt them. While extensive literature on instructor adoption of education technology exists, there is no literature on adopting in-class peer feedback systems. We are well suited to contribute to this body of literature with future studies.

Investigating Classroom Culture
While most students responded positively to our tool, we recall the student from our exploratory study who compared the critique process to "hazing." On the other hand, many students in our exploratory and preliminary evaluation study used the tool to offer emotional support to their peers. We will investigate how PeerPresents can reduce the risk students feel when presenting and critiquing work in a classroom, both with and without an established culture of peer feedback.

CONCLUSION
In this paper, we have presented a successful prototype of an in-class peer feedback system for student presentations. PeerPresents is a browser-based system that enables presenting students to write feedback questions before class, which get prompted to peer feedback providers during class. On any device, peers can quickly provide feedback and vote on others' feedback. The system also provides tools for the presenting students to organize and reflect on feedback after class. Our preliminary evaluations demonstrate that in-class peer feedback systems can elicit relevant, copious, timely, and diverse feedback. By allowing students to generate scaffolding questions before class and enabling feedback provision during class time, we maximize the time for student reflection on feedback after class. We have also highlighted a new design space for classroom tools, and extracted generalizable design lessons for future work.

ACKNOWLEDGMENTS
We would like to acknowledge the support of the following grants: NSF #1122206, #1217096, and #1122320.

REFERENCES
1. Heidi Andrade and Ying Du. 2005. Student perspectives on rubric-referenced assessment. *Practical Assessment, Research & Evaluation*. Retrieved June 10, 2015 from http://www.pareonline.net/pdf/v10n3.pdf

2. Heidi Goodrich Andrade. 2005. Teaching with Rubrics: The Good, the Bad, and the Ugly. *College Teaching*. Retrieved June 10, 2015 from https://e-learn.sdu.dk/bbcswebdav/courses/E-learn_Support_Center/Andrade_2005_good_bad_ugly.pdf

3. Hugh Beyer and Karen Holtzblatt. 1997. *Contextual Design: Defining Customer-Centered Systems*. Elsevier. Retrieved September 24, 2015 from

https://books.google.com/books?hl=en&lr=&id=JxQaQgOONGIC&pgis=1

4. Charles Buabeng-Andoh. 2012. Factors influencing teachers' adoption and integration of information and communication technology into teaching: A review of the literature. *International Journal of Education and Development using Information and Communication Technology* 8, 1: 136–155. Retrieved September 24, 2015 from http://search.proquest.com/openview/938bbe87db68135bee298a6845a43dd9/1?pq-origsite=gscholar
5. Deborah L. Butler and Phillip H. Winne. 1995. Feedback and self-regulated learning: A theoretical synthesis. *Review of educational research*. Retrieved June 24, 2015 from http://rer.sagepub.com/content/65/3/245.short
6. Andrea Chester and Gillian Gwynne. 2006. Online Teaching: Encouraging Collaboration through Anonymity. *Journal of Computer-Mediated Communication* 4, 2. http://doi.org/10.1111/j.1083-6101.1998.tb00096.x
7. Kwangsu Cho and Christian D. Schunn. 2007. Scaffolded writing and rewriting in the discipline: A web-based reciprocal peer review system. *Computers & Education* 48, 3: 409–426. http://doi.org/10.1016/j.compedu.2005.02.004
8. Matthew W. Easterday, Daniel Rees Lewis, Colin Fitzpatrick, and Elizabeth M. Gerber. 2014. Computer supported novice group critique. *Proceedings of the 2014 conference on Designing interactive systems - DIS '14*, ACM Press, 405–414. http://doi.org/10.1145/2598510.2600889
9. Peggy A. Ertmer, Jennifer C. Richardson, Brian Belland, et al. 2007. Using Peer Feedback to Enhance the Quality of Student Online Postings: An Exploratory Study. *Journal of Computer-Mediated Communication* 12, 2: 412–433. http://doi.org/10.1111/j.1083-6101.2007.00331.x
10. Nancy Falchikov. 2001. *Learning Together: Peer Tutoring in Higher Education*. Psychology Press. Retrieved September 25, 2015 from https://books.google.com/books?hl=en&lr=&id=6liO0ynJM1oC&pgis=1
11. Carmen Fies and Jill Marshall. 2006. Classroom response systems: A review of the literature. *Journal of Science Education and Technology*. Retrieved May 20, 2015 from http://link.springer.com/article/10.1007/s10956-006-0360-1
12. Kadist Art Foundation. Kapsul. Retrieved September 10, 2015 from http://www.kapsul.org/about
13. Graham Gibbs and Claire Simpson. 2004. Conditions under which assessment supports students' learning. *Learning and teaching in higher education*. Retrieved June 24, 2015 from http://www2.glos.ac.uk/offload/tli/lets/lathe/issue1/issue1.pdf#page=5
14. Christian Haintz and Karen Pichler. Feedbackr. Retrieved September 10, 2015 from feedbackr.io
15. Iris Howley. 2015. Leveraging Educational Technology to Overcome Social Obstacles to Help Seeking.
16. R Junco. 2015. Student class standing, Facebook use, and academic performance. *Journal of Applied Developmental Psychology*. Retrieved January 17, 2016 from http://www.sciencedirect.com/science/article/pii/S0193397314001257
17. Chinmay Kulkarni, Michael S. Bernstein, and Scott Klemmer. 2015. PeerStudio: Rapid Peer Feedback Emphasizes Revision and Improves Performance. *Proceedings from The ...*. Retrieved June 10, 2015 from https://hci.stanford.edu/publications/2015/PeerStudio/Peerstudio.pdf
18. Jean Lave and Etienne Wenger. 1991. *Situated Learning: Legitimate Peripheral Participation*. Cambridge University Press. Retrieved October 28, 2014 from http://books.google.com/books?hl=en&lr=&id=CAVIOrW3vYAC&pgis=1
19. Ngar-Fun Liu and David Carless. 2006. Peer feedback: the learning element of peer assessment. *Teaching in Higher education*. Retrieved June 10, 2015 from http://www.tandfonline.com/doi/abs/10.1080/13562510600680582
20. Xiaojuan Ma, Li Yu, Jodi L. Forlizzi, and Steven P. Dow. 2015. Exiting the Design Studio. *Proceedings of the 18th ACM Conference on Computer Supported Cooperative Work & Social Computing - CSCW '15*, ACM Press, 676–685. http://doi.org/10.1145/2675133.2675174
21. Tim McMahon. 2010. Peer feedback in an undergraduate programme: using action research to overcome students' reluctance to criticise. *Educational Action Research* 18, 2: 273–287. http://doi.org/10.1080/09650791003741814
22. Shazia Mumtaz. 2000. Factors affecting teachers' use of information and communications technology: a review of the literature. *Journal of Information Techology for Teacher Education* 9, 3: 319–342. http://doi.org/10.1080/14759390000200096

23. David J. Nicol and Deborah Macfarlane-Dick. 2006. Formative assessment and self-regulated learning: A model and seven principles of good feedback practice. *Studies in Higher Education*. Retrieved June 24, 2015 from http://ewds.strath.ac.uk/REAP/public/Papers/DN_SHE_Final.pdf

24. Paul Orsmond, Stephen Merry, and Kevin Reiling. 2000. The Use of Student Derived Marking Criteria in Peer and Self-Assessment. *Assessment & Evaluation in Higher Education*. Retrieved June 24, 2015 from http://eric.ed.gov/?id=EJ608330

25. Matt Ratto, Benjamin Shapiro, Tan Minh Truong, and William Griswold. 2003. The ActiveClass Project: Experiments in Encouraging Classroom Participation. *Computer Support for Collaboartive Learning*. http://doi.org/10.1007/978-94-017-0195-2

26. D. Royce Sadler. 1989. Formative assessment and the design of instructional systems. *Instructional Science* 18, 2: 119–144. http://doi.org/10.1007/BF00117714

27. David Tinapple, Loren Olson, and John Sadauskas. 2013. CritViz: Web-based software supporting peer critique in large creative classrooms. *Bulletin of the IEEE Technical Committee on Learning Technology*. Retrieved June 10, 2015 from http://www.ieeetclt.org/issues/january2013/Tinapple.pdf

28. Kieth Topping. 1998. Peer assessment between students in colleges and universities. *Review of educational Research*. Retrieved September 24, 2015 from http://rer.sagepub.com/content/68/3/249.short

29. Haiyi Zhu, Steven P. Dow, Robert E. Kraut, and Aniket Kittur. 2014. Reviewing versus doing. *Proceedings of the 17th ACM conference on Computer supported cooperative work & social computing - CSCW '14*, ACM Press, 1445–1455. http://doi.org/10.1145/2531602.2531718

30. i>Clicker. Retrieved from https://www1.iclicker.com/for-education/

31. Pol.is. Retrieved September 10, 2015 from https://pol.is/2arcefpshi

Developing a Comprehensive Engagement Framework of Gamification for Reflective Learning

Chaklam Silpasuwanchai[*]
chaklam@kochi-tech.ac.jp

Xiaojuan Ma[†]
mxj@cse.ust.hk

Hiroaki Shigemasu[‡]
shigemasu.hiroaki@kochi-tech.ac.jp

Xiangshi Ren[*‡]
ren.xiangshi@kochi-tech.ac.jp

[*]Center for Human-Engaged Computing, Kochi University of Technology, Kochi, Japan

[‡]School of Information, Kochi University of Technology, Kochi, Japan

[†]Department of Computer Science and Engineering, Hong Kong University of Science and Technology, Hong Kong

ABSTRACT
Engagement is a key reason for introducing gamification to learning and thus serves as an important measurement of its effectiveness. Based on a literature review and meta-synthesis, this paper proposes a comprehensive framework of engagement in gamification for learning. The framework sketches out the connections among gamification strategies, dimensions of engagement, and the ultimate learning outcome. It also elicits other task - and user - related factors that may potentially impact the effect of gamification on learner engagement. To verify and further strengthen the framework, we conducted a user study to demonstrate that: 1) different gamification strategies can trigger different facets of engagement; 2) the three dimensions of engagement have varying effects on skill acquisition and transfer; and 3) task nature and learner characteristics that were overlooked in previous studies can influence the engagement process. Our framework provides an in-depth understanding of the mechanism of gamification for learning, and can serve as a theoretical foundation for future research and design.

Author Keywords
Gamification for Learning; Engagement; Framework.

ACM Classification Keywords
H.5.m. Information Interfaces and Presentation (e.g. HCI): Miscellaneous

General Terms
Theory; Design.

INTRODUCTION
Keeping learners engaged is a challenge in education. By contrast, games have the potential to stimulate the players interest and get them to commit time and effort. Therefore, many studies have applied game elements in the context of

DIS 2016, June 4–8, 2016, Brisbane, Australia.
Copyright © 2016 ACM ISBN ISBN 978-1-4503-4031-1/16/06 ...$15.00.
http://dx.doi.org/10.1145/2901790.2901836

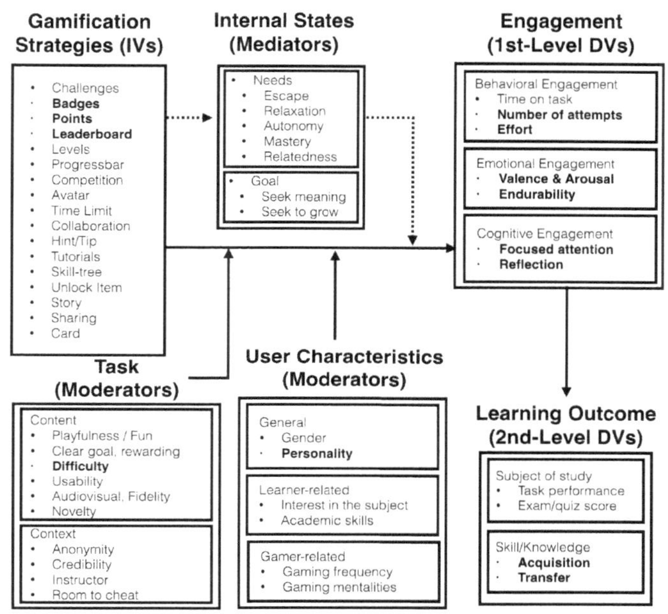

Figure 1. Our proposed engagement framework of gamification for learning. (Note: Bold components were investigated in the user study.)

education (a.k.a. gamification for learning [47]) to increase the learners desire to focus on the educational task at hand and consequently improve their learning performance, e.g., [19, 21].

Nevertheless, the effectiveness of gamification for learning remains controversial. For example, some studies found gamification effective [21, 54, 55], while others showed no significant or even negative effects [19, 24, 29]. This may be due to the novelty effect or other confounding factors such as the quality of the learning materials. Hence, previous research has explicitly called for a deeper understanding of the underlying mechanisms of gamification that facilitate or impede learning [19, 21, 32]. Since better engaging learners is one of the key reasons why gamification is introduced, the study of engagement can serve as a lens to investigate the efficacy.

Engagement is more than getting learners to perform and repeat desirable actions [49]. Truly engaged learners should also find themselves actively and persistently construct hypotheses, review learning outcomes, consolidate the knowledge gained, and adapt future strategies. In this sense, engagement in learning is a multi-faceted concept [4], and thus one should thoroughly consider all aspects when using engagement to measure the effectiveness of gamification. For example, time on task is a popular indicator of engagement [4,35]. However, only participating in the learning task for a short period of time does not mean that a learner is devoted. Focused attention [17] and perceived enjoyment [11,60,82] can also be sign of engagement. Therefore, it is necessary and helpful to define the different dimensions of engagement and their interplay, understand how they are evoked by various gamification strategies and produce assorted learning outcomes, and identify other factors that may impact this process.

This paper proposes and evaluates a comprehensive framework of engagement in gamified learning that covers all of these aspects (Figure 1). Existing gamification frameworks, e.g., *Octalysis* [85] and *Kaleidoscope* [48] focused primarily on motivational game elements. Little research has comprehensively looked into the different factors that may impact engagement as well as the relationships between these assorted factors. Our work is an initial attempt to explore this gap.

We develop the framework through a constructive meta-synthesis of existing literature. The framework defines three dimensions of engagement, i.e., behavioral, emotional, and cognitive engagement, as well as their connections with gamification strategies (main causes), learning outcomes (consequences), and other user- and task-related factors (moderators and mediators).

To explore the relations among the different components (or particular sub-dimensions within a component) of the framework, we conducted a controlled user study. More specifically, compared to non-gamified learning, we showed that points, badges, and leaderboards, the three most popular gamification strategies, can trigger divergent types of engagement and ultimately lead to different performance in skill acquisition and transfer. In addition, by employing basic cognitive tasks rather than a specific subject, we looked into the moderating effects of some aspects of the fundamental nature of a learning task. We also investigated how some learner characteristics may influence the efficacy of gamification on engagement. We conclude that engagement can be used to assess gamification for learning, but focusing merely on one facet of engagement may result in misjudgment. Our framework can help guide future design and research into gamification for learning.

RELATED WORK

In this section, we review related literature on engagement definitions, theories and models, even though they are not specifically for gamification in the learning context.

Definition and Dimensions of Engagement

There exist many definitions of engagement. Some are narrower, emphasizing on a single aspect such as attention [15, 16] or enjoyment [52]. Others are more comprehensive, considering engagement as an integrated user experience [4,23,58,63,67,75]. In the scope of this paper, we define engagement as *the behavioral, emotional and cognitive connection that exists between a user and the task at hand at any point in time and possibly over time* (adapted from [4, p. 2]).

This definition points out the three major dimensions of engagement evaluation. In particular, time on task, number of attempts, and effort are good indicators of behavioral engagement [4, 35]. Intense or enduring emotional responses, including but not limited to enjoyment, is another widely used cue of engagement [11,60,82]. In other words, emotional engagement can be measured by the valence, arousal, and endurance of the evoked affective state. Besides, cognitive engagement is related to the sense of involvement, focused attention, and deep reflection [15, 16].

User- and Task-related Factors on Engagement

Our definition of engagement suggests two other related factors: the user and the task. Since the idea of introducing game elements to the learning context is inspired by the ability of games to attract and retain players, we review existing theories on game engagement.

The *Immersion Theory* [13,43] proposes that game engagement is concerned with the merging of self and task. The *Player Typology Theory* [7,33] suggests that individual differences in user characteristics such as gender [44,57], gaming frequency [41], and mentalities [46] can influence player engagement. Furthermore, the *Self-Determination Theory* [20], the *Uses and Gratification Theory* [78], the *Eudaimonic Theory* [71] and the *Learning Theory* [27] postulate that individuals are more engaged when they have particular needs (e.g., escape, relaxation, autonomy, mastery, relatedness, etc.) or goals (e.g., seeking meaningfulness in life, learning to grow, etc.) to meet. These factors can be summarized as internal user states.

Second, the characteristics of a task can influence user engagement. For example, a task that can provide a strong sense of achievement [37, 84] or evoke playful (*Play Theory* [26,40,53,60]), tentatively positive emotions (*Pleasure Theory* [45]) is more engaging. In the context of gaming, other criteria for designing an engaging task include clear sets of goals and progress, clear and immediate feedback, a good balance between skills and challenges (*Flow Theory* [17]), effective error prevention and recovery mechanisms (*Usability Theory* [66]), and an aesthetically pleasing appearance (*Representation Theory* [52] and *Aesthetics Theory* [15]). The media [65,77] and fidelity (*Fidelity Theory* [36,59,79,83]) of task presentation can lead to different levels of engagement as well.

Comparison to Existing Engagement Frameworks

We have identified three key constructs for our framework of gamification for learning: multi-faceted engagement, user, and task. In this subsection, we compare our idea with the existing engagement framework in gaming to investigate possible room for improvement.

OBrien and Toms [68] depicted a dynamic loop between the point of engagement and disengagement. However, this model did not differentiate between mechanisms that may promote engagement such as challenge and metrics of engagement itself such as attention.

Bouvier et al. [9] modeled shifts of consciousness "from immersion and involvement to engagement, presence and flow". This model is related to the cognitive component of our framework.

Chen [16] described three dimensions of engagement – interest, attention and immersion. Chen's framework can be mapped to our framework in the cognitive dimension (attention, immersion) and to the internal user states component (interest).

Schoenau-Fog [38] proposes four components of player engagement: motivation (intrinsic, extrinsic), activities (gameplay), accomplishments (rewards), and affects (positive, negative). Motivation can be mapped to our user internal states component; activities are related to the task component; accomplishments are related to the gamification strategy component; and affects are related to the emotional dimension of engagement.

Brockmeyer et al. [12] developed *Game Engagement Questionnaire* which classifies engagement into absorption, flow, presence, and immersion. This model captures and describes the cognitive dimension of engagement.

Ijsselsteijn et al. [42] developed *Game Experience Questionnaire* which divides engagement into immersion, flow, competence, tension, challenge, positive affect, and negative affect. Immersion and flow can be mapped to cognitive engagement; positive and negative affect and tension can be mapped to emotional engagement; and competence and challenge are related to internal user states.

Sweetser and Wyeth [81] propose a player engagement model called "*GameFlow*" which is informed by Flow Theory. The model identifies eight elements: concentration, challenge, skills, control, clear goals, feedback, immersion and social interaction. Concentration and immersion are related to the cognitive component; feedback are gamification strategies, while control (autonomy), social (relatedness), challenge (competence), and goals are related to the internal user states component.

Nacke and Drachen [64] propose a PX (player experience) framework that identifies three layers of interaction: game system, players, and context. Game systems can be mapped to gamification strategies; players can be mapped to the user characteristics component, while context is linked to the task characteristics component.

Nabi and Krcmar [63] propose a tripartite model of media enjoyment composed of affective, cognitive and behavioral dimension that mutually exert influence on one another, which shares similar dimensions of engagement as our framework.

Iacovides et al. [41] proposes a *GIIL (Game Involvement and Informal Learning)* framework which indicates how different kinds of gameplay can lead to different kinds of learning experience. In addition, the more strongly a learner identifies him/herself as gamer, the more likely he/she is to become involved and learn from the gaming experience. Different gameplay may be related to gamification strategies as well as the task component. On the other hand, perception as a gamer is related to the user characteristics component.

This list of frameworks is not exhaustive, but we believe it is adequate to show that our framework integrates concepts that are scattered across assorted engagement frameworks. We better organize the different factors that are intertwined in previous frameworks into six constructs (gamification strategies, engagement, learning outcome, task, user characteristics, and user internal states) and clarify their relationships, making it easier to be applied in research and design.

META-SYNTHESIS

To construct a more specific engagement framework, we extract insights from existing research in gamification for learning. The literature review centered around four questions: Q1) What are the gamification strategies that researchers have explored to support learning? Q2) What are their effects on engagement? Q3) What are their effects on learning outcomes? And Q4) what are other related factors to engagement?

Source and Criteria

We searched databases that are commonly used for publications in gamification research including the ACM Digital Library (ACM), ScienceDirect (SD), and IEEE Xplore Digital Library (IEEE). We restricted our search from 2011 to 2015, given the surge of interest in gamification since 2011 [22]. The terms *gamification*, *learning* and *education* were used to search all publications. The search resulted in a total of 486 publications (DL = 278, SD = 152, IEEE = 56). For manageability, we narrowed down to 36 papers and articles (DL = 21, SD = 9, IEEE = 6) using the following criteria: 1) original full papers with empirical evidence, 2) papers published in peer-reviewed English forums, and 3) papers that were focused on gamification for learning rather than full-fledged educational games. The screening process was conducted by two researchers independently with high inter-rater reliability (Kappa = 0.889, $p < 0.05$).

Findings

Gamification for learning is a multi-disciplinary research area with increasing popularity in the recent three years (2013-2015), attracting the interest of the Education, Human-Computer Interaction (HCI), and Game Design communities (Figure 2). Gamification was applied most frequently in online learning environments (61.11%), classrooms (16.67%), desktop apps (13.89%), and mobile apps (8.34%), with computer science (58.33%) being the most commonly gamified subject.

A1: Gamification Strategies

We analyzed the frequency of the use of gamification strategies, and how often two strategies were used in conjunction (see co-occurrence matrix in Figure 3).

Challenges (16.91%) were one most commonly used strategies. Challenges were implemented in different forms including quizes [25], practical exercises [54], and quests [6]. Many strategies were used in conjunction with challenges. Levels (6.62%) [6], tutorials (2.21%) [3] and hints/tips [55] (2.94%) were used to provide comfortable pacing. Progress-bars (5.15%) [8] were used to indicate progress. Skill-trees

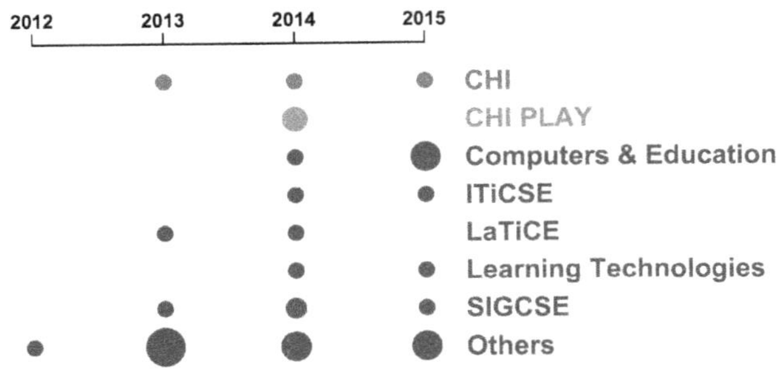

Figure 2. Number of publications by venues and years.

(2.21%) were used to provide a sense of autonomy. Time limits (3.68%) was used to provide extra pressure and excitement, and story (1.45%) was used to provide a fantasy context.

PBL (Points, Badges, and Leaderboards) was a collective strategy commonly used together. Points (11.76%) come in many forms, i.e., scores, XP [6], and bonus points [54]. Badges (18.38%) were awarded in two major ways: when players achieve certain steps of actions, or when players achieved certain ranks or scores. Leaderboards (11.03%) are used to rank users often providing competitive motivation.

Competition (5.15%) comes in two forms: (i) 1-on-1 competitions and (ii) team competitions. Collaboration (3.68%) comes in two forms: (i) collaboration to reach a goal and (ii) collaboration to compete with another team. Other strategies include the use of avatars (4.41%), sharing (1.47%), unlocking items (1.47%), and collectible cards (1.47%).

A2: Effects on Engagement

Our review shows that researchers deployed three measures of engagement, (i) behavioral, (ii) emotional, and (iii) cognitive (see Figure 4).

Behavioral engagement concerns participation and involvement, often measured by attendance, time spent and number of attempts. 14 out of 17 studies reported positive effects. Negative effects can be due to an over-emphasis on competition [19], novelty effect [29], and student attitudes towards the teacher [2].

Emotional engagement concerns affective reactions such as interest and boredom, commonly measured using questionnaires. 18 out of 22 studies reported positive effect on emotional engagement. Negative effects can be due to the application of gamification on already interesting tasks [34], or due to non-gamers tendency to pose negative attitude towards gamification [8].

Cognitive engagement focuses on the learners psychological investment in learning. Students may be behaviorally engaged but not cognitively engaged, such as attending class but not understanding or actively reflecting and thinking about the materials. Our analysis showed that, aside from self-reporting, very few studies actually measured cognitive engagement, with the exception of [55] where they analyzed whether the students had applied the techniques they learned as they completed the tasks.

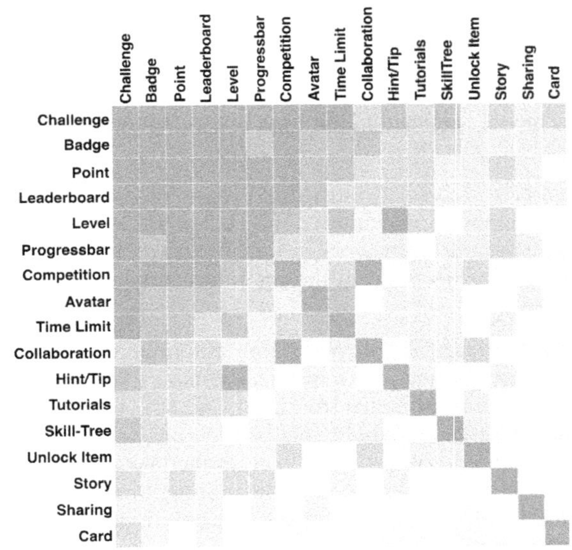

Figure 3. Co-occurrence matrix of gamification strategies.

Overall, behavioral and emotional engagement generally show that gamification is effective to make learners participate and enjoy more. However, cognitive engagement remains under-investigated, i.e., it remains inconclusive whether gamification can really make learners think deeply and reflect.

A3: Effects on Performance

We analyzed the effect of gamification on performance. Our analysis revealed mixed effects, i.e., 9 out of 18 studies showed positive effects, three showed negative effects and six showed no effects (see Figure 5). We further investigated the correlation between engagement and performance by dividing engagement and performance in each study into three categories: positive, neutral, and negative. Pearson's product moment correlation showed a significant correlation ($r = 0.895$, $p < 0.001$) between behavioral engagement and performance, but not between emotional engagement and performance, suggesting that fun may not always translate into better performance. We did not conduct the correlation analysis for the cognitive engagement due to its small sample size.

A4: Effects of External factors

It is well-documented that gamification is context-dependent [32, 76]. We classified past studies into user- and task-related factors.

User-related factors

Various external factors have been discussed. Studies on player types confirmed that different students perceived gamification differently [6, 8]. Goal orientations were found to have an effect where avoidance-oriented students tended to have lower motivation towards gamification [5,30]. Studies also suggested gender differences, i.e., females were observed to be less motivated by individual competition [51] and by the introduction of extra pressure [73]. Nevertheless, some studies did not find any significant effect of gender [50] suggesting further treatment is required. Gaming experience was suggested by [8] to

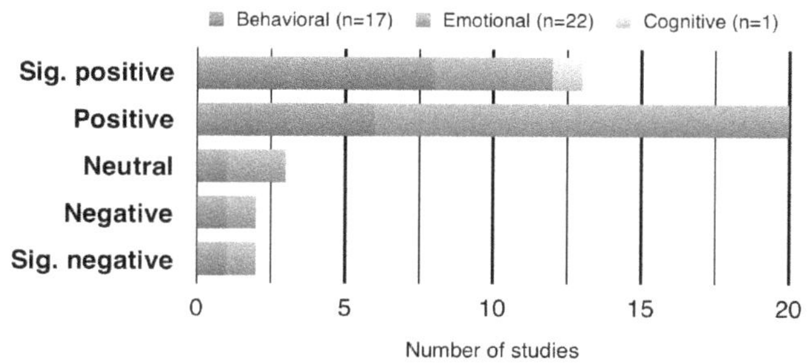

Figure 4. Engagement effects reported in studies. (Note: Positive and Negative are descriptive results.)

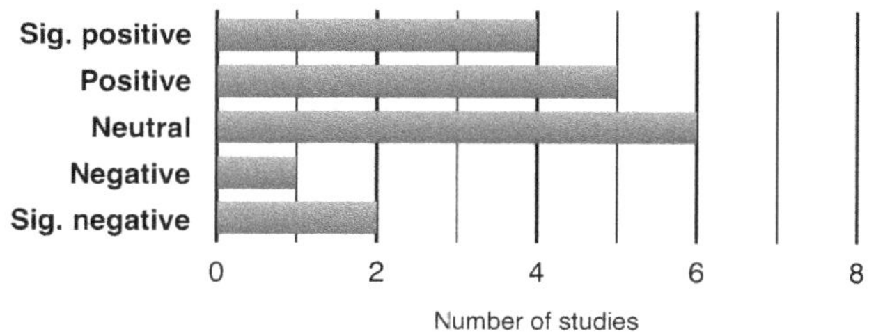

Figure 5. Performance effects reported in studies.

have an influence, i.e., non-gamers may have a tendency to be negative about gamification. There are though some factors such as personality [37] that have been explored in the video games domain but have been overlooked in gamification for learning. Such factors can also confound the results.

Task-related factors

Cheating in gamification can have a detrimental effect on user experience [69, 72, 73]. Such cheating allows users to advance levels by exhausting all possible directions or by tuning parameters rather than by mastering the scheme [49]. Anonymity of users was found to improve cooperative learning as it frees students from possible embarrassment [70]. Applying gamification to an already interesting task may have a negative effect, as gamification may seen to be manipulative [34]. Other negative factors include the novelty effect [29], lack of credibility of badges [18], and negative student attitudes toward the teacher [2]. There remains various factors to be tested in gamification for learning, such as difficulty, usability, and fun - all of which can possibly moderate the efficacy of gamification strategies.

ENGAGEMENT FRAMEWORK

Through our literature review and meta-synthesis, we are now ready to propose our initial framework on gamification for learning. The framework consists of six components (Figure 1): 1) gamification strategies as the independent variables, 2) users' internal states as the mediators, 3) user characteristics as the moderators, 4) the task as second moderator, 5) engagement as first-level dependent variables, and 6) learning outcomes as second-level dependent variables. All components are related factors of engagement.

We list all the gamification strategies studied in the literature. The effectiveness of gamification strategies is mediated by personal needs, motivations, and goals. The effectiveness of gamification strategies is also dependent on the task and user characteristics. The outcome of gamification strategies is engagement in three dimensions: behavioral (paying time and effort), emotional (showing positive affect), and cognitive (deep thinking). The second-order outcome of gamification strategies is learning performance, which is a consequential effect of engagement. Previous work mainly used exam scores to assess the quality of learning. We stress that the ultimate goal of learning is task-independent knowledge/skill acquisition and transfer (see [49]), and that these should be taken into consideration.

As mentioned earlier, the existing literature covers only part of the framework. Primarily, little study has investigated the dimensions of engagement and their relationships. In addition, most prior work focuses on exam scores but not on skill/knowledge acquisition and transfer which may be better indicators of active learning. Thus we conducted a user study to fill these gaps.

USER STUDY

This study explored how gamification strategies affect the three dimensions of engagement in the context of learning. We were also interested in exploring the relationship between the three dimensions of engagement and learning outcomes, as well as exploring some task and user-related factors. For designing the experiment, there are other factors that may confound the results, as shown in our framework, such as the quality of teaching materials, which should be eliminated or well-controlled. We thus designed a basic task experiment to control all possible subject-related confounding factors. Specifically, instead of teaching a particular subject of study, we tested how well participants could acquire some basic cognitive skills.

Experimental Tasks

We selected experimental tasks from cognitive psychology based on three criteria: 1) the basic tasks should target some fundamental cognitive skills required in various disciplines; 2) the basic tasks should be empirically validated with satisfactory psychometric properties; and 3) the number of basic tasks should be accomplished within a reasonable experimental time frame. Given these considerations, we selected *memory* and *problem-solving* skills since they are fundamental skills required in many disciplines from math and science, to art, language and literature (see [74] for memory, [61] for problem-solving). To represent each skill, we selected three memory tasks and three problem-solving tasks that were commonly used and validated [80] (see Table 1 for a full list of tasks).

Tools for Testing

We developed two interactive systems - non-gamified and gamified. The gamified version adopted three most common gamification strategies - Points, Badges, and Leaderboards (PBL). Points were provided as scores, corresponding to the measure of each task. Badges were awarded when certain thresholds were met (example in Figure 6). The thresholds of

	Learning Aspect	Sub-aspects	Measures
Yes-No Recognition (YNR)	Memory	Recognition	Total number of correct responses
Cued-Recall (CR)	Memory	Recall	Total number of correct responses
Free-Recall (FR)	Memory	Heavy Recall	Total number of recalled items
Wisconsin Card Sorting (WCST)	Problem-Solving	Flexibility	Total number of correct matches
Tower of London (TOL)	Problem-Solving	Planning	Average moves per problem, total time spent
Wason Selection (WS)	Problem-Solving	Deductive Reasoning	Number of failed attempts before getting right

Table 1. Overview of selected basic tasks.

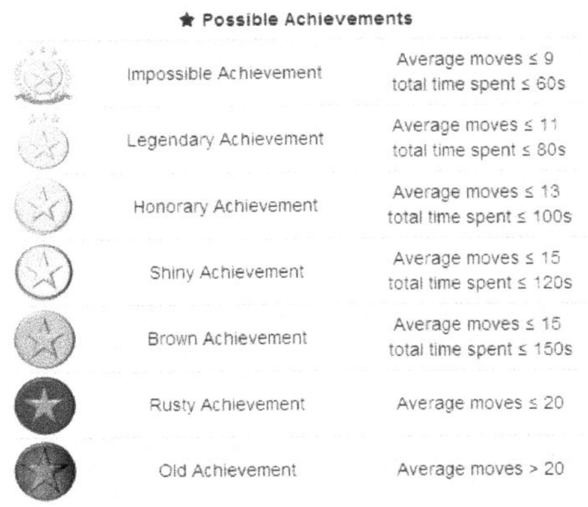

Figure 6. Sample screenshot of badges used in our study.

each badge level were determined through play-testing with nine users prior to the actual study. We designed a total of 42 badges, seven per task. Each badge contained a visual icon, a name, and unlocking conditions. Participants received notification when they successfully unlocked badges [31]. The Leaderboard ranked the accumulated performance scores of all participants. Participants could further filter and sort the scores according to each task. Since social presence and leaderboard positions can possibly impact the effectiveness of the leaderboard [10], we initially populate the leaderboard with data through the pilot study, where the data followed a normal distribution. Since we did not want to overburden participants with extra effort to jump to other pages, we embedded these gamification strategies in the task interface, as shown in Figure 7.

Experimental Design

This study used a two-factor mixed design. The first factor, *group*, was between-subjects, giving participants one of the two systems (gamified, non-gamified). The second factor, *task*, was within-subjects, providing repeated measures of two cognitive skills for each participant using six basic tasks.

Thirty participants were assigned to either gamified or non-gamified systems according to a balanced distribution of age, gender, gaming experience and pretest performance between

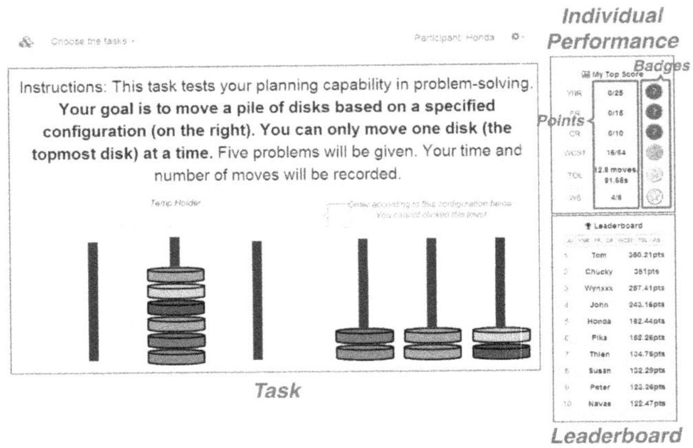

Figure 7. Sample screenshot of the gamification interface.

the two groups. It is important to note that the group assignment in the memory session was independent of the group assignment in the problem-solving session. A participant belonging to the gamified group in the memory session may belong to the non-gamified group in the problem-solving session. This is because memory and problem-solving ability can be very different, and thus it was difficult to take both skills into account at the same time when trying to balance pretest performances. Although this arrangement may yield possible carry-over effects from the first session to the second session, we tried to minimize this by counterbalancing the order of sessions across all participants.

The order of the skill session as well as the order of the tasks in each session was counterbalanced across participants. Each task was performed with three trials but participants were allowed to conduct more trials if they wanted to. Thus the minimum number of total trials was:

15 participants ×
2 groups (gamified, non-gamified) ×
6 basic tasks (for the two skill categories) ×
3 trials
= 540 trials.

Measurements

As proposed in our framework, this study measured three dimensions of engagement - *behavioral, emotional, cognitive* and two dimensions of learning outcome - *skill acquisition* and *skill transfer*.

Engagement

The number of extra trials in addition to the three compulsory trials was used to measure behavioral engagement. A subjective questionnaire on a 7-point Likert scale was used to measure the level of emotional engagement - *enjoyment, excitement, endurability*; behavioral engagement - *effort*; cognitive engagement - *attention, reflection*; and learning performance - *perceived competence*, and *perceived improvement*. To understand the efficacy of each gamification strategy, another subjective questionnaire was used to measure the preference of users toward points, badges, and leaderboard separately.

Gaze data were used to measure cognitive engagement (attention). Semi-structured interviews were conducted to provide qualitative reasons behind the collected data.

Learning Outcome

Skill acquisition was measured by skill improvements across the three trials (summarized in Table 1). *Skill transfer* was measured as the difference between pre- and post-test results. The tests consisted of the card-matching test [1] for assessing overall memory capability. For problem-solving, we employed three separate tests: the "Stroop test" for flexibility [14], the "5-discs Tower of Hanoi" for planning [28], and "4x4 Sudoku" for deductive reasoning [56].

Participants

Thirty participants (age 19 to 25, M = 22.1 years, 8 females) were recruited through the university portal. To prevent any possible predisposition towards gamification (see [8,41]), we excluded extreme gamers (those who play games every day for more than 8 hours a week). Instead, we selected participants who had no or only moderate gaming experience. All participants had experience with video games within a range of zero to five hours per week. None had experienced with any of the tasks. Each was paid $10.

Apparatus

The study was conducted on a high-performance desktop computer (Windows 7) connected to a Tobii X120 eye-tracker. The learning system was implemented using JavaScript and HTML5 and was run on a Chrome browser.

Procedure

Both memory and problem-solving sessions followed a similar procedure. We present the procedure of the memory session as an example: (1) Experimenters instructed participants on how each memory task worked. Then participants were allowed to familiarize themselves by trying each of the three memory tasks for around 5 minutes. (2) Experimenters demonstrated how the PBL worked. Participants were allowed to play and see how the PBL worked for another 5 minutes. Participants in the non-gamified group, instead, were shown only the non-gamified system. (3) Participants proceeded to do the three memory tasks, each task containing three trials. The order of the tasks was counterbalanced. After the three trials for each task, we instructed participants that they could continue playing for another 10 minutes. (4) Participants were asked to complete a post-test and two subjective questionnaires, followed by a semi-structured interview.

Results

The results are structured according to each metric as follows:

Extra Trials

We hypothesized that participants in the gamified group would commit more time and effort to the tasks. To confirm, we counted the number of occasions where users performed extra rounds of trials in each task, aside from the three mandatory trials (total possible number of occasions = 15 participants x 6 tasks; maximum average number of occasions = 6). We analyzed using Mann-Whitney U tests for extra trials (the

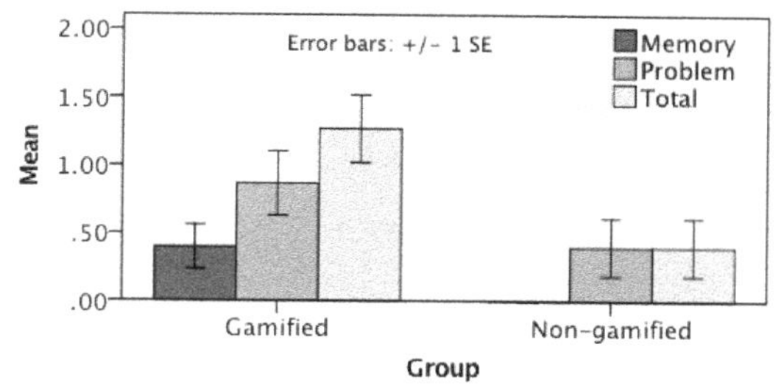

Figure 8. The average number of occasions where users performed extra trials between the two groups ($p < 0.01$).

Scales	Gamified	Non-gamified	Sig.
Enjoyment	5.21	4.64	-
Excitement	5.10	4.57	-
Endurability	4.05	3.03	-
Effort	5.73	5.11	$p < 0.05$
Attention	5.67	3.96	$p < 0.001$
Reflection	5.60	4.75	$p < 0.05$
Perceived Competence	4.85	4.55	-
Perceived Improvement	4.43	4.21	-

Table 2. Subjective measures in a seven-point Likert scale (7 as strongly agree).

Kolmogorov-Smirnov test and Levene's test indicated that the data was non-parametric).

A Mann-Whitney U test indicated a significant difference between the two groups ($U = 54.5$, $Z = -2.60$, $p < 0.01$) with the total number of occasions for the gamified group being 19 ($M = 1.26$, $SD = 0.96$) compared with 6 ($M = 0.40$, $SD = 0.83$) for the non-gamified group (See Figure 8). For those who did conduct more trials, there was no significant difference in the average number of additional trials between gamified (M = 2.88, SD = 0.48) and non-gamified group (M = 1.89, SD = 0.51).

We further analyzed whether the nature of the tasks (memory vs. problem-solving) affected the number of extra trials. A Mann-Whitney U test indicated a significant difference in memory tasks ($U = 75.01$, $Z = -2.40$, $p < 0.05$), with the total number of occasions for the gamified group being 6 ($M = 0.40$, $SD = 0.63$) compared with 0 (M = null) for the non-gamified group. The test though failed to find a significant difference in problem-solving tasks with the total number of occasions for the gamified group being 13 ($M = 0.87$, $SD = 0.92$) compared with 6 ($M = 0.40$, $SD = 0.83$) for the non-gamified group. To understand why there was a lack of significance in problem-solving tasks, we analyzed the post-study interviews. One common observation showed that players were already motivated to perform problem-solving tasks, regardless of the gamification strategies. On the other hand, memory tasks were perceived to be difficult and boring and adding gamification strategies helped boost user motivation.

Subjective Measures

We collected the participants' responses which were based on the level of emotional engagement - *enjoyment*, *excitement*, *endurability*; behavioral engagement - *effort*; cognitive engagement - *attention*, *reflection*; and learning performance - *perceived competence*, and *perceived improvement*. We used

	Enjoyment	Excitement	Endurability.	Effort	Attention	Reflection	Competence	Improvement
Enjoyment	-	**.658*****	**.740*****	**.578*****	**.446****	**.443****	**.604*****	**.365***
Excitement	**.658****	-	**.671*****	.170	**.398***	.288	.335	.210
Endurability	**.740*****	**.671*****	-	.274	**.547****	**.415***	**.492****	.278
Effort	**.578****	.170	.274	-	**.457***	**.606*****	**.563****	**.398***
Attention	**.446***	**.398***	**.547****	**.547****	-	**.548****	.301	.293
Reflection	**.443***	.288	**.415***	**.606*****	**548****	-	**.570****	**.371***
Competence	**.604****	.355	**.492****	**.563****	.301	**.570****	-	**.425***
Improvement	**.365***	.210	.278	**.398***	.293	**.371***	**.475***	-

Table 3. Correlation between subjective measures (R value of Kendall's tau test.) Note: * = $p < 0.05$, ** = $p < 0.01$, *** = $p < 0.001$.

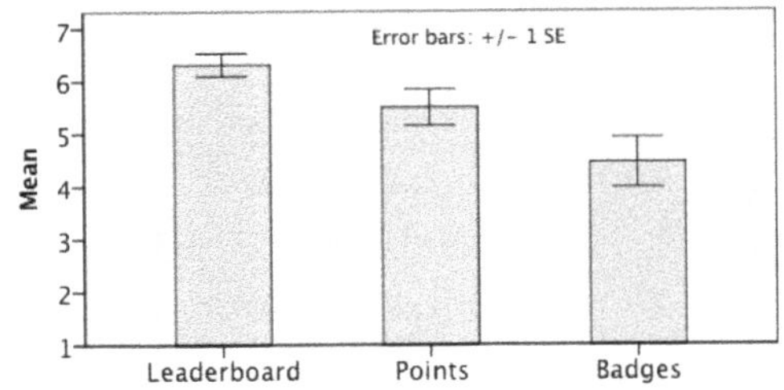

Figure 9. Preferences between points, badges, and leaderboard (7 = highly preferred). Pairwise comparisons confirmed differences between the Leaderboards and Badges ($p < 0.01$), and between Points and Badges ($p < 0.01$).

Mann-Whitney tests to analyze between-group questionnaire data. Results are illustrated in Table 2.

A Mann-Whitney U test indicated a significant difference between gamified and non-gamified groups in the level of *effort* ($U = 58.5$, $Z = -2.25$, $p < 0.05$), *attention* ($U = 20.0$, $Z = -3.89$, $p < 0.001$) and *reflection* ($U = 59.5$, $Z = -2.32$, $p < 0.05$).

We further analyzed whether the nature of the tasks made a difference. Regardless of the task, a Mann-Whitney Test indicated a significant difference between the gamified group and the non-gamified group in the level of *attention* (Memory, $U = 47.5$, $Z = -2.75$, $p < 0.01$; Problem-solving, $U = 30.0$, $Z = -3.51$, $p < 0.001$) and *reflection* (Memory, $U = 68.5$, $Z = -1.86$, $p < 0.1$; Problem-solving $U = 72.5$, $Z = -1.74$, $p < 0.1$). On the other hand, the data showed that only users in the problem-solving tasks have higher *endurability* ($U = 65.5$, $Z = -1.99$, $p < 0.05$) and higher *perceived improvement* ($U = 67.0$, $Z = -1.945$, $p < 0.05$). Post-study interviews indicated that users perceived memory tasks to be more difficult and thus commented that the addition of gamification helped motivate them. On the other hand, users commented that problem-solving tasks are already interesting, thus the addition of gamification has less effect. To crosscheck this consistency, using pairwise comparisons of Wilcoxon Signed Ranks test we analyzed the difference between memory and problem-solving tasks, regardless of the groups. Our results confirmed that users did perceive problem-solving tasks as more enjoyable and that users felt more self-competent - *enjoyment* ($Z = -2.87$, $p < 0.001$), *excitement* ($Z = -2.47$, $p < 0.01$), *endurability* ($Z = -2.72$, $p < 0.001$), *perceived competence* ($Z = -3.66$, $p < 0.001$), *perceived improvement* ($Z = -2.09$, $p < 0.05$), and *attention* ($Z = -2.22$, $p < 0.05$).

We further analyzed the correlations between each scale. Kendall's tau test was commonly used for analyzing correlations of non-parametric data. The result was illustrated in Table 3. We found a strong within-associations between dimensions of engagement. We also found an overall strong association between engagement and learning outcome, i.e., between enjoyment, endurability, effort, reflection with competence, and between enjoyment, effort, reflection on perceived improvement.

Our post-study interviews revealed both consistency and conflicts with the above results. For example, we observed an association between high behavioral engagement and high cognitive engagement. One participant commented that *"I really want to get better at this Tower of London Task, so I tried more and during each attempt, I reviewed my previous attempts and what did I do wrong, and aims to fix it in the next trial."*. Anyhow, we also observed some association between high behavioral and low cognitive engagement. One participant commented that *"I tried many attempts on the Wason task by randomly clicking, so I can get better scores eventually."*. We also observed a association between emotional engagement as cause, and behavioral and cognitive engagement as effect, e.g., one participant commented: *"I enjoyed a lot on Tower of London and Wisconsin Tasks, so I tried more and think more how I can improve."*. Nevertheless, we also observed that despite low emotional engagement, some participants still worked hard to improve themselves (high cognitive engagement): *"I really did not enjoy the memory tasks, but I wanted to do a good job so I concentrated hard on how to improve my memory and I tried many times"*.

Preference on PBL

We were also interested in exploring the impact of the three strategies (Points, Badges, Leaderboards) for the gamified group. A Friedman test was used to analyze within-subject questionnaires data. The test showed a significant difference ($\chi^2_2 = 12.038$, $p < 0.001$) in the preference of the three strategies, with Leaderboards scoring 6.31, Points scoring 5.49, and Badges scoring 4.44. A pairwise comparison of Wilcoxon Signed Ranks test confirmed the significant differences between Leaderboard and Badges ($Z = -2.77$, $p < 0.01$), and between Points and Badges ($Z = -2.60$, $p < 0.01$), but not between Leaderboards and Points (See Figure 9). Similar results were observed when split into memory and problem-solving tasks.

Gaze Data

Visual attention was typically measured in the form of fixations. Fixations were collected from gaze points with a minimum of 100ms on a specific target. We measured attention

		Non-gamified				Gamified			
Task	Measure	1st trial	2nd trial	3rd trial	Sig.	1st trial	2nd trial	3rd trial	Sig.
YNR	Correct responses	18.01	18.85	21	-	18.81	19.31	18.56	-
CR	Correct responses	3.23	3.54	3.62	-	3.56	3.5	3.75	-
FR	Correct responses	7.31	7.92	7.85	-	8.44	9.06	8.81	-
WCST	Correct matches	45.64	48.07	46.86	-	43.21	46.43	47.72	*
TOL	Time[1] ; # of moves[2]	151.47; 12.76	123.49; 12.69	126.59; 12.94	**[1]; -	152.87, 13.41	118.24, 12.48	119.525, 13.16	***[1];-
WS	# of failed attempts	3.60	3.20	2.44	*	3.67	2.34	1.47	***

Table 4. Users' mean performance on the three trials in the non-gamified and gamified groups. Note: * = $p < 0.05$, ** = $p < 0.01$, *** = $p < 0.001$.

span by calculating the average fixation duration on the Task area.

A Mann-Whitney U test indicated a significant difference between the two groups ($U = 56.5$, $Z = -2.33$, $p < 0.05$) with the average fixation duration for the gamified group being 500.2ms compared with 396.47ms for the non-gamified group. This data indicated that gamification can increase user attention span on the task. We did not find any significant difference between memory and problem-solving tasks.

To further understand user behaviors, we classified user patterns based on their gaze behaviors and their interviews. We classified two types of users: High-Achievers (56%) and Avoidance-Achievers (44%).

High-Achievers tend to be more motivated by the existence of PBL. In their typical gaze behaviors, before they started the task, they scanned the whole leaderboard; during the task, they were very focused on the Task area; after the task, they scanned the whole leaderboard again. They were less afraid of failure and enjoyed taking on more challenges. They were coded with common schemes such as "*It's challenging*", "*I do not want to lose to others*".

Avoidance-Achievers tend to be easily discouraged. In their typical gaze behaviors, before they started the task, they scanned the leaderboard; during the task, they were only partially focused on the Task area; after the task, their attention was scattered across the screen. Avoidance-achievers were easily demotivated when they looked at the top score in the leaderboard, or as soon as they completed certain tasks where they achieved relatively lower scores than others. They were commonly coded with schemes such as "*The top score is too high*", "*this game is so difficult*".

Skill Acquisition and Transfer

For user progress across the trials, the data conformed to the requirements for parametric evaluation: normal distribution using the Kolmogorov-Smirnov test and homogeneity of variance using Levene's test. Thus repeated measures ANOVA was used.

We hypothesized that the gamified group would achieve greater progress than the non-gamified group. Data showed that both the gamified and the non-gamified groups improved their skills over the course of multiple trials. ANOVA revealed significant differences in the performance of problem-solving tasks (see Table 4): non-gamified-TOL ($F_{2,40} = 4.99$, $p < 0.01$), non-gamified-WS ($F_{2,42} = 3.69$, $p < 0.05$), gamified-WCST ($F_{2,39} = 3.93$, $p < 0.05$), gamified-TOL ($F_{2,42} = 6.51$, $p < 0.001$), and gamified-WS ($F_{2,42} = 15.98$, $p < 0.001$); but not in memory tasks. The non-gamified group significantly improved their results between the first and third mandatory trials in TOL and WS, but not as much as in the gamified condition. Statistical tests confirmed the difference between the two conditions for WS ($F_{1,28} = 4.196$, $p < 0.05$) and a moderate main effect for TOL ($F_{1,28} = 2.55$, $p < 0.1$). Only the gamified group achieved significant improvement in WCST.

The pretest-posttest comparisons did not reveal any significant improvements in either the non-gamified group or the gamified group, thus skill transfer was not confirmed. This indicates that although the skills had significantly improved, skill-transfer may require more practice [62]. In summary, these results confirmed that PBL gamification can improve skill acquisition, while skill transfer would require more practice.

We analyzed the correlations between engagement (extra trials, subjective measures) and learning gain. In memory tasks, a Kendall's tau test found a significant correlation between *endurability* and the occurrences of extra trials ($r = 0.36$, $p < 0.05$), between the gain in the YNR task with *perceived improvement* ($r = 0.39$, $p < 0.05$), and between the gain in the FR task with *endurability* ($r = 0.28$, $p < 0.05$) and *reflection* ($r = 0.28$, $p < 0.05$). In problem-solving tasks, the test found a significant correlation between the occurrences of extra trials and *attention* ($r = 0.31$, $p < 0.05$) and *endurability* ($r = 0.26$, $p < 0.05$), between the gain in WCST task and *attention* ($r = 0.378$, $p < 0.05$), between the gain in TOL task and *enjoyment* ($r = 0.36$, $p < 0.05$) and *endurability* ($r = 0.29$, $p < 0.05$), and between the gain in WS task and *perceived competence* ($r = 0.36$, $p < 0.05$).

GENERAL DISCUSSION

We developed an engagement framework of gamification for learning. To further explore the framework, we conducted a user study investigating the three dimensions of engagement - behavioral, emotional, and cognitive, and learning outcome. The study confirmed the relationship within the three dimensions of engagement, between engagement and learning outcome, as well as the influence of user and task-related factors. The comparison also suggests that users paid more attention and put more efforts on gamified tasks, which are important indicators of engagement. In terms of learning outcome, users in the gamified condition only showed short-term improvement on problem-solving tasks over those in the baseline condition.

Within Different Dimensions of Engagement

We have confirmed strong associations within the three dimensions of engagement - behavior, emotion, and cognition. Anyhow, our study showed that it was not always the case (sometimes independent relationship). Thus we believe that judging the efficacy of gamification based on only one or two dimensions can be misleading. In addition, using multiple dimensions of engagement can allow designers to investigate which gamification strategies improve which dimensions of engagement, and thus different strategies can be tailored to different contexts of use.

Between Engagement and Learning Outcome

Our data also confirmed the association between different measures of engagement such as enjoyment, effort, attention, extra-trials and learning outcome. Investigating the link between engagement and learning outcome will be useful to better understand the task and the suitability of gamification strategies. For example, although we found a significant level of extra trials in memory tasks, we did not observe any significant learning gain in any memory tasks. This helps us understand that behavioral engagement does not lead to higher learning outcomes in the memory tasks, thus memory tasks may need other gamification strategies that emphasize other dimensions of engagement.

Task Factor

Although subject-related factors were controlled, we actually tested some task characteristics as moderators. We found that problem-solving itself is a strong motivator, even surpassing the effect of points and leaderboards. In contrast, memory tasks are less motivating, and thus PBL showed significantly positive effect in this case. This suggests that perhaps, for interesting tasks, simply providing gamification strategies in the form of indicators of progress or feedback is adequate. For boring tasks, extrinsic rewards may be necessary as an incentive to attract and retain users. In addition, applying non-typical gamification strategies (e.g., skill-tree) or totally changing the image of a task (e.g., package a memory task as a card-matching task) may enhance its inherent motivational value.

We also found the effect of the task on users' preference on PBL. What surprised us was the relatively low score for Badges. Post-study interviews ruled out usability or aesthetical problems with our Badges, but they highlighted one trend where participants were more focused on getting points and being on top of the leaderboard, rather than on badge collection. One possible explanation is that the performance-oriented nature of our tasks led to utilitarian involvement (e.g., getting better scores) rather than hedonic involvement (e.g., collecting badges).

User Factor

We also tested user characteristics as another moderator, specifically on high-achievers vs. avoidance-achievers. The design of PBL gamification should be given special consideration when targeting avoidance-achievers, which was also suggested by past study in the video games domain [37]. Our experiment showed a clear distinction between high-achievers and avoidance-achievers. Since the tasks were somewhat like an IQ test, participants may interpret their performance as a reflection of their intelligence level. Consequently, low-achievers were afraid to see their scores when they were around the average or lower levels, and this is likely to impair their self-confidence. An interesting future direction is to explore the design space of leaderboards, such as the different forms of leaderboards and the potential efficacy of personalization.

Basic Tasks

One of our contributions was to demonstrate how basic tasks can be used. Using standard tasks can simplify experimental design by eliminating possible confounding factors. It also allowed us to investigate the fundamental nature of the task factors. In any case, it was our intention to show the merits of basic tasks as a complementary method, rather than a replacement of existing "in-the-wild" testing methods. Such basic tasks can be employed first for preliminary controlled evaluation before a large-scale field test. Both will be needed to provide a solid replication of results [39].

Limitations and Space for Improvement

Some limitations may affect the results. First, this was a short-term study. As a result, we were not able to observe any improvement on knowledge transfer in the pretest-posttest comparison which may require a longer time to achieve significant results. However, as a result of this limitation, we used other metrics (e.g., progress) to complement our results. In addition, this user study did not cover some of the factors proposed in the framework, such as mediators where further future work will be conducted.

Second, there might be possible carry-over effects for some participants, since they can be in the non-gamified group for memory tasks, and in the gamified group for problem-solving based on their pretest performance. Foreknowledge of the existence of gamification may affect the validity of the results. To assess the impact of the carry-over effect, we excluded the data of participants who were in both the gamified and non-gamified groups and we re-ran the analysis. We received similar results; for example, we found significant differences in attitudes between the gamified and the non-gamified groups ($F_{1,25} = 6.42$, $p < 0.01$) and significance in persistence between the two conditions ($F_{1,105} = 5.02$, $p < 0.05$). This ensures that the carry-over effect did not have any significant impact.

CONCLUSION

We have proposed an engagement framework for gamification for learning. The distinguishing feature of the proposed framework is that it outlines the relationships between different factors around engagement. Understanding the relationships between different factors is essential for gamification for learning as past work and our study have consistently pointed out that gamification is highly context-dependent.

Our review shows that few studies have explored the dimensions of engagement in gamification for learning. We thus conducted a controlled user study. We have confirmed with past theories and models that engagement is multi-faceted, consisting of various dimensions and related factors. Thus, multiple measures of engagement should be used to provide accurate evaluation. We have also confirmed that engagement is influenced by contextual factors including task and user internal states, thus future work should adequately bring these contextual factors into consideration.

REFERENCES

1. Joshua M. Ackerman, Vaughn D. Becker, Chad R. Mortensen, Takao Sasaki, Steven L. Neuberg, and

Douglas T. Kenrick. 2009. A pox on the mind: Disjunction of attention and memory in the processing of physical disfigurement. *Journal of Experimental Social Psychology* 45, 3 (2009), 478–485. DOI: http://dx.doi.org/10.1016/j.jesp.2008.12.008

2. Afifa Amriani, Alham F. Aji, Andika Y. Utomo, and Kasiyah M. Junus. 2013. An empirical study of gamification impact on e-Learning environment. In *Proc. ICCSNT 2013*. 265–269. DOI: http://dx.doi.org/10.1109/ICCSNT.2013.6967110
3. Paul E. Anderson, Thomas Nash, and Renée McCauley. 2015. Facilitating Programming Success in Data Science Courses Through Gamified Scaffolding and Learn2Mine. In *Proc. ITiCSE 2015*. ACM, 99–104. DOI: http://dx.doi.org/10.1145/2729094.2742597
4. Simon Attfield, Gabriella Kazai, Mounia Lalmas, and Benjamin Piwowarski. 2011. Towards a science of user engagement. In *WSDM Workshop on User Modelling for Web Applications*. ACM.
5. Taipo Auvinen, Lasse Hakulinen, and Lauri Malmi. 2015. Increasing Students' Awareness of their Behavior in Online Learning Environments with Visualizations and Achievement Badges. *IEEE Transactions on Learning Technologies* PP, 99 (2015), 1–14. DOI: http://dx.doi.org/10.1109/TLT.2015.2441718
6. Gabriel Barata, Sandra Gama, Joaquim A.P. Jorge, and Daniel J.V. Gonçalves. 2014. Relating Gaming Habits with Student Performance in a Gamified Learning Experience. In *Proc. CHI PLAY 2014*. ACM, 17–25. DOI:http://dx.doi.org/10.1145/2658537.2658692
7. Richard Bartle. 1996. Hearts, Clubs, Diamonds, Spades: Players Who suit MUDs. *Journal of MUD Research 1* (1996), 1–27.
8. Kay Berkling and Christoph Thomas. 2013. Gamification of a Software Engineering course and a detailed analysis of the factors that lead to it's failure. In *Proc. ICL 2013*. 525–530. DOI: http://dx.doi.org/10.1109/ICL.2013.6644642
9. Patrice Bouvier, Elise Lavou, and Karim Sehaba. 2014. Defining Engagement and Characterizing Engaged-Behaviors in Digital Gaming. *Simulation & Gaming* (2014). DOI: http://dx.doi.org/10.1177/1046878114553571
10. Jason T. Bowey, Max V. Birk, and Regan L. Mandryk. 2015. Manipulating Leaderboards to Induce Player Experience. In *Proc. CHI Play 2015*. ACM, 115–120. DOI:http://dx.doi.org/10.1145/2793107.2793138
11. Elizabeth A. Boyle, Thomas M. Connolly, Thomas Hainey, and James M. Boyle. 2012. Engagement in Digital Entertainment Games: A Systematic Review. *Comput. Hum. Behav.* 28, 3 (2012), 771–780.
12. Jeanne H. Brockmyer, Christine M. Fox, Kathleen a. Curtiss, Evan McBroom, Kimberly M. Burkhart, and Jacquelyn N. Pidruzny. 2009. The development of the Game Engagement Questionnaire: A measure of engagement in video game-playing. *Journal of Experimental Social Psychology* 45, 4 (2009), 624–634.
13. Emily Brown and Paul Cairns. 2004. A grounded investigation of game immersion. In *Proc. CHI 2004*. ACM, 1297–1300.
14. Julie M. Bugg, Larry L. Jacoby, and Jeffrey P. Toth. 2008. Multiple levels of control in the Stroop task. *Memory & cognition* 36, 8 (2008), 1484–1494. DOI: http://dx.doi.org/10.3758/MC.36.8.1484
15. Peter Chapman. 1997. *Models of engagement: Intrinsically motivated interaction with multimedia learning software*. University of Waterloo.
16. Mark Chen, Beth E. Kolko, Elisabeth Cuddihy, and Eliana Medina. 2011. Modeling but NOT Measuring Engagement in Computer Games. In *Proc. GLS 2011*. 55–63.
17. Mihaly Csikszentmihalyi. 1990. *Flow : The Psychology of Optimal Experience*. Harper Perennial.
18. Katie Davis and Simrat Singh. 2015. Digital badges in afterschool learning: Documenting the perspectives and experiences of students and educators. *Computers & Education* 88 (2015), 72 – 83. DOI: http://dx.doi.org/10.1016/j.compedu.2015.04.011
19. Luis De-Marcos, Adrián Domínguez, Joseba Saenz-de Navarrete, and Carmen Pagés. 2014. An empirical study comparing gamification and social networking on e-learning. *Computers & Education* 75 (2014), 82–91. DOI: http://dx.doi.org/10.1016/j.compedu.2014.01.012
20. Edward L. Deci and Richard M. Ryan. 2000. The "What" and "Why" of Goal Pursuits: Human Needs and the Self-Determination of Behavior. 11, 4 (2000), 227–268. DOI: http://dx.doi.org/10.1207/S15327965PLI1104_01
21. Paul Denny. 2013. The effect of virtual achievements on student engagement. In *Proc. CHI 2013*. ACM, 763–772. DOI:http://dx.doi.org/10.1145/2470654.2470763
22. Sebastian Deterding, Dan Dixon, Rilla Khaled, and Lennart Nacke. 2011. From Game Design Elements to Gamefulness: Defining "Gamification". In *Proc. MindTrek 2011*. ACM, 9–15. DOI: http://dx.doi.org/10.1145/2181037.2181040
23. John Dewey. 1934. *Art as Experience*. Perigree.
24. Adrián Domínguez, Joseba Saenz-de Navarrete, Luis De-Marcos, Luis Fernández-Sanz, Carmen Pagés, and José-Javier Martínez-Herráiz. 2013. Gamifying learning experiences: Practical implications and outcomes. *Computers and Education* 63 (2013), 380–392. DOI: http://dx.doi.org/10.1016/j.compedu.2012.12.020

25. Usef Faghihi, Albert Brautigam, Kris Jorgenson, David Martin, Angela Brown, Elizabeth Measures, and Sioui Maldonado-Bouchard. 2014. How Gamification Applies for Educational Purpose Specially with College Algebra. *5th Annual International Conference on Biologically Inspired Cognitive Architectures* 41 (2014), 182 – 187. DOI: http://dx.doi.org/10.1016/j.procs.2014.11.102

26. Gregory P. Garvey. 2007. Drawing a line in the sand: border/boundary theories and games. In *Proc. Sandbox 2007*. ACM, 47–54. DOI: http://dx.doi.org/10.1145/1274940.1274952

27. James Paul Gee. 2003. *What video games have to teach us about learning and literacy*. Palgrave Macmillan Trade.

28. Vinod Goel and Jordan Grafman. 1995. Are the frontal lobes implicated in planning functions? Interpreting data from the Tower of Hanoi. *Neuropsychologia* 33, 5 (1995), 623–642. DOI: http://dx.doi.org/10.1016/0028-3932(95)90866-P

29. Lassi Haaranen, Petri Ihantola, Lasse Hakulinen, and Ari Korhonen. 2014. How (Not) to Introduce Badges to Online Exercises. In *Proc. SIGCSE 2014*. ACM, 33–38. DOI: http://dx.doi.org/10.1145/2538862.2538921

30. Lasse Hakulinen and Taipo Auvinen. 2014. The Effect of Gamification on Students with Different Achievement Goal Orientations. In *Proc. LaTiCE 2014*. 9–16. DOI: http://dx.doi.org/10.1109/LaTiCE.2014.10

31. Juho Hamari and Veikko Eranti. 2011. Framework for Designing and Evaluating Game Achievements. In *Proc. DIGRA 2011*.

32. Juho Hamari, Jonna Koivisto, and Harri Sarsa. 2014. Does Gamification Work? - A Literature Review of Empirical Studies on Gamification. In *Proc. HICSS 2014*. IEEE, 3025–3034.

33. Juho Hamari and Janne Tuunanen. 2014. Player Types: A Meta-synthesis. *Transactions of the Digital Games Research Association* 1, 2 (2014), 29–53.

34. Michael D. Hanus and Jesse Fox. 2015. Assessing the effects of gamification in the classroom: A longitudinal study on intrinsic motivation, social comparison, satisfaction, effort, and academic performance. *Computers & Education* 80 (2015), 152 – 161. DOI: http://dx.doi.org/doi: 10.1016/j.compedu.2014.08.019

35. Leland Harden and Bob Heyman. 2009. *Digital engagement: Internet marketing that captures customers and builds intense brand loyalty*. AMACOM.

36. Robert T. Hays and Michael J. Singer. 1988. *Simulation Fidelity in Training System Design: Bridging the Gap Between Reality and Training (Recent Research in Psychology)*. Springer.

37. Carrie Heeter, Yu-Hao Lee, Ben Medler, and Brian Magerko. 2011. Beyond player types: gaming achievement goal. In *Proc. Sandbox 2011*. ACM, 43–48.

38. Schoenau-Fog Henrik. 2011. The Player Engagement Process - An Exploration of Continuation Desire in Digital Games. In *Proc. DiGRA 2011*. 1–18.

39. Kasper Hornbæk, Søren S. Sander, Javier Andrés Bargas-Avila, and Jakob Grue Simonsen. 2014. Is Once Enough?: On the Extent and Content of Replications in Human-computer Interaction. In *Proc. CHI 2014*. ACM, 3523–3532. DOI: http://dx.doi.org/10.1145/2556288.2557004

40. Johan Huizinga. 1950. *Homo Ludens: A study of the play-element in culture*. The Beacon Press. DOI: http://dx.doi.org/10.2307/2087716

41. Ioanna Iacovides, Patrick Mcandrew, Eileen Scanlon, and James Aczel. 2014. The Gaming Involvement and Informal Learning Framework. *Simul. Gaming* 45, 4-5 (2014), 611–626. DOI: http://dx.doi.org/10.1177/1046878114554191

42. Wijnand Ijsselsteijn, W.M. van den Hoogen, Christoph Klimmt, Y.A.W. de Kort, Craig Lindley, Klaus Mathiak, Karolien Poels, Niklas Ravaja, Marko Turpeinen, and Peter Vorderer. 2008. Measuring the experience of digital game enjoyment. In *Proc. Measuring Behavior 2008*. 88–89.

43. Charlene Jennett, Anna L. Cox, Paul Cairns, Samira Dhoparee, Andrew Epps, Tim Tijs, and Alison Walton. 2008. Measuring and defining the experience of immersion in games. *International Journal of Human-Computer Studies* 66, 9 (2008), 641–661.

44. Jennifer Jenson, Suzanne de Castell, and Stephanie Fisher. 2007. Girls playing games: rethinking stereotypes. In *Proc. Future Play 2007*. ACM, 9–16.

45. Patrick W. Jordan. 2000. *Designing Pleasurable Products: An Introduction to the New Human Factors*. Taylor & Francis.

46. Kirsi P. Kallio, Frans Mayra, and Kirsikka Kaipainen. 2010. At Least Nine Ways to Play: Approaching Gamer Mentalities. *Games and Culture* 6, 4 (2010), 327–353.

47. Karl M. Kapp. 2012. *The gamification of learning and instruction: game-based methods and strategies for training and education*. Pfieffer.

48. Dennis L. Kappen and Lennart E. Nacke. 2013. The Kaleidoscope of Effective Gamification: Deconstructing Gamification in Business Applications. In *Proc. Gamification 2013*. ACM, 119–122. DOI: http://dx.doi.org/10.1145/2583008.2583029

49. Harri Ketamo and Kiili Kiili. 2010. Conceptual Change Takes Time: Game Based Learning Cannot be Only Supplementary Amusement. *Journal of Educational Multimedia and Hypermedia* 19, 4 (2010), 399–419.

50. Markus Krause, Marc Mogalle, Henning Pohl, and Joseph Jay Williams. 2015. A Playful Game Changer: Fostering Student Retention in Online Education with Social Gamification. In *Proc. L@S 2015*. ACM, 95–102. DOI: http://dx.doi.org/10.1145/2724660.2724665

51. Celine Latulipe, N. Bruce Long, and Carlos E. Seminario. 2015. Structuring Flipped Classes with Lightweight Teams and Gamification. In *Proc. SIGCSE 2015*. ACM, 392–397. DOI: http://dx.doi.org/10.1145/2676723.2677240

52. Brenda Laurel. 1993. *Computer as Theatre*. Addison-Wesley.

53. Nicole Lazzaro. 2004. Why we play games: Four keys to more emotion without story. In *Game Developer's Conference*. 1–8.

54. Wei Li, Tovi Grossman, and George Fitzmaurice. 2012. GamiCAD: A Gamified Tutorial System for First Time Autocad Users. In *Proc. UIST 2012*. 103–112. DOI: http://dx.doi.org/10.1145/2380116.2380131

55. Wei Li, Tovi Grossman, and George Fitzmaurice. 2014. CADament: A Gamified Multiplayer Software Tutorial System. In *Proc. CHI 2014*. ACM, 3369–3378. DOI: http://dx.doi.org/10.1145/2556288.2556954

56. NY Louis Lee, Geoffrey P. Goodwin, and P.N. Johnson-Laird. 2008. The psychological puzzle of Sudoku. *Thinking & Reasoning* 14, 4 (2008), 342–364. DOI: http://dx.doi.org/10.1080/13546780802236308

57. Kristen Lucas and John L. Sherry. 2004. Sex Differences in Video Game Play:: A Communication-Based Explanation. *Communication Research* 31, 5 (2004), 499–523.

58. John McCarthy and Peter Wright. 2004. *Technology as experience*. The MIT Press. DOI: http://dx.doi.org/10.1145/1015530.1015549

59. Alison Mcmahan. 2003. Immersion, Engagement, and Presence: A Method for Analyzing 3D Videogames. In *The Video Game Theory Reader*. Routledge, 67–86.

60. Elisa D. Mekler, Julia Ayumi Bopp, Alexandre N. Tuch, and Klaus Opwis. 2014. A Systematic Review of Quantitative Studies on the Enjoyment of Digital Entertainment Games. In *Proc. CHI 2014*. ACM, 927–936.

61. Lynn Meltzer. 2010. *Executive Function in Education: From Theory to Practice*. The Guilford Press.

62. Roxana Moreno and Mayer Richard. 2005. Role of guidance, reflection, and interactivity in an agent-based multimedia game. *Journal of Educational Psychology* 97, 1 (2005), 117–128.

63. Robin L. Nabi and Marina Krcmar. 2004. Conceptualizing media enjoyment as attitude: Implications for mass media effects research. *Communication Theory* 14, 4 (2004), 288–310.

64. Lennart E. Nacke and Anders Drachen. 2011. Towards a Framework of Player Experience Research. In *Proc. FDG 2011*.

65. Lennart E. Nacke, Mark N. Grimshaw, and Craig A. Lindley. 2010. More than a feeling: Measurement of sonic user experience and psychophysiology in a first-person shooter game. *Interacting with Computer* 22, 5 (2010), 336–343.

66. Jakob Nielsen and Rolf Molich. 1990. Heuristic Evaluation of User Interfaces. In *Proc. CHI 1990*. ACM, 249–256. DOI: http://dx.doi.org/10.1145/97243.97281

67. Donald A. Norman. 2003. *Emotional design: why we love (or hate) everyday things*. Basic Books.

68. Heather L O'Brien and Elaine G Toms. 2008. What is user engagement? A conceptual framework for defining user engagement with technology. *Journal of the American Society for Information Science* 59, 6 (2008), 938–955. DOI: http://dx.doi.org/10.1002/asi.v59:6

69. Siobhan O'Donovan, James Gain, and Patrick Marais. 2013. A Case Study in the Gamification of a University-level Games Development Course. In *Proc. SAICSIT 2013*. ACM, 242–251. DOI: http://dx.doi.org/10.1145/2513456.2513469

70. Asako Ohno, Takahiro Yamasaki, and Kin-ichiroh Tokiwa. 2013. A discussion on introducing half-anonymity and gamification to improve students' motivation and engagement in classroom lectures. In *Proc. IEEE HTC 2010*. 215–220. DOI: http://dx.doi.org/10.1109/R10-HTC.2013.6669044

71. Mary Beth Oliver and Arthur A Raney. 2011. Entertainment as Pleasurable and Meaningful: Identifying Hedonic and Eudaimonic Motivations for Entertainment Consumption. *Journal of Communication* 61, 5 (2011), 984–1004.

72. Manuel Palomo-Duarte, Anke Berns, Juan Manuel Dodero, and Alberto Cejas. 2014. Foreign Language Learning Using a Gamificated APP to Support Peer-assessment. In *Proc. TEEM 2014*. ACM, 381–386. DOI: http://dx.doi.org/10.1145/2669711.2669927

73. Lais Z. Pedro, Aparecida M. Z. Lopes, Bruno G. Prates, Julita Vassileva, and Seiji Isotani. 2015. Does Gamification Work for Boys and Girls?: An Exploratory Study with a Virtual Learning Environment. In *Proc. SAC 2015*. ACM, 214–219. DOI: http://dx.doi.org/10.1145/2695664.2695752

74. Susan J. Pickering and Gary D. Phye. 2006. *Working Memory and Education*. Academic Press.

75. Johnmarshall Reeve, Hyungshim Jang, Dan Carrell, Soohyun Jeon, and Jon Barch. 2004. Enhancing Students' Engagement by Increasing Teachers' Autonomy Support. *Motivation and Emotion* 28, 2 (2004), 147–169. DOI: http://dx.doi.org/10.1023/B:MOEM.0000032312.95499.6f

76. Chad Richards, Craig W. Thompson, and Nicholas Graham. 2014. Beyond Designing for Motivation: The Importance of Context in Gamification. In *Proc. CHI Play 2014*. ACM, 217–226. DOI: http://dx.doi.org/10.1145/2658537.2658683

77. Sam Rossoff, George Tzanetakis, and Bruce Gooch. 2010. Adapting personal music for synesthetic game play. In *Proc. FDG 2010*. ACM, 163–170.
78. Wilbur Schramm. 1961. *Television in the Lives of Our Children*. Stanford University Press.
79. Mel Slater, Martin Usoh, and Anthony Steed. 1994. Depth of presence in virtual environments. *Presence: Teleoperators and Virtual Environments* 3, 2 (1994), 130–140.
80. Esther Strauss, Elisabeth M. S. Sherman, and Otfried Spreen. 2006. *A Compendium of Neuropsychological Tests: Administration, Norms, and Commentary*. Oxford University Press.
81. Penelope Sweetser and Peta Wyeth. 2005. GameFlow: a model for evaluating player enjoyment in games. *Comput. Entertain.* 3, 3 (2005), 3.
82. Peter Vorderer, Christoph Klimmt, and Ute Ritterfield. 2004. Enjoyment: At the heart of media entertainment. *Communication Theory* 14 (2004), 388–408. DOI: http://dx.doi.org/10.1111/j.1468-2885.2004.tb00321.x
83. Bob G. Witmer and M.J. Singer. 1998. Measuring Presence in Virtual Environments : A Presence Questionnaire. *Presence: Teleoperators and Virtual Environments* 7, 3 (1998), 225–240.
84. Nick Yee. 2006. Motivations for Play in Online Games. *Cyberpsychology and Behavior* 9, 6 (2006), 772–775.
85. Chou Yu-Kai. 2012. Octalysis: Complete Gamification Framework. (2012). http://yukaichou.com/gamification-examples/octalysis-complete-gamification-framework

Linking Data to Action: Designing for Amateur Energy Management

Hanna Hasselqvist
KTH Royal Institute of Technology
Stockholm, Sweden
hannaha@kth.se

Cristian Bogdan
KTH Royal Institute of Technology
Stockholm, Sweden
cristi@kth.se

Filip Kis
KTH Royal Institute of Technology
Stockholm, Sweden
fkis@kth.se

ABSTRACT
Design of eco-feedback has primarily aimed at persuading individuals to change behaviours into more environmentally sustainable ones. However, it has been questioned how effective such feedback is in supporting long-term change. As an alternative focus for energy feedback, we present a case study of amateur energy management work in apartment buildings owned by housing cooperatives, and the design of an app that aims to stimulate and support cooperatives in taking energy actions that significantly reduce the cooperative's collective energy use. By linking energy data to energy actions, the users can see how actions taken in their own and other cooperatives affected the energy use, learn from each other's experiences and become motivated as energy amateurs. Based on our housing cooperative case, we reflect on design aspects to consider when designing for energy management in amateur settings.

Author Keywords
Sustainable HCI; Interaction Design; Energy; Housing Cooperatives; Amateur Community.

ACM Classification Keywords
H.5.m. Information interfaces and presentation (e.g., HCI): Miscellaneous.

INTRODUCTION
Designing interactive technologies to understand and reduce the use of energy and other resources is an ongoing challenge in HCI. Previous designs of persuasive technologies for sustainability, often termed "eco-feedback", have been criticised for having a narrow

DIS 2016, June 04-08, 2016, Brisbane, QLD, Australia
ACM 978-1-4503-4031-1/16/06.
http://dx.doi.org/10.1145/2901790.2901837

Figure 1. Housing cooperatives in Hammarby Sjöstad in Stockholm, Sweden. Image: CC-BY Hans Kylberg on Flickr.

approach, which may work to a certain extent in the short term but it is questionable whether they can support long-term sustainable change. One major criticism is directed to such technologies addressing the individual level but not acknowledging or addressing other levels (e.g. communities, corporations and governments) that greatly influence the way we use and consume resources [4, 10, 12]. Other points of criticism are that they do not discourage people from adopting new, more resource-intensive, practices [29] and that their potentially negative effects on for example privacy are not considered [5].

It has been suggested that the usefulness of feedback on energy use depends on the user's motivation [19, 25] and that it only is helpful for people who make rational decisions based on this feedback [30]. However, the practicalities of everyday life may get in the way of acting rationally [30, 7] and there can be also infrastructural barriers, such as opening hours of shared laundry rooms, to changing energy practices [23]. In apartment buildings, households are particularly limited in what they can influence since they may not be in control of heating, maintenance of the building or choice of appliances. Tensions between landlords and tenants can also prevent energy efficiency measures from being taken [8]. These issues further support the argument that actors and contexts beyond the individual need to be considered in energy reduction efforts.

While the focus of eco-feedback is mainly on changing behaviours, rather than taking one-time actions to increase energy efficiency [14], environmental research suggests that one-time actions aiming at long-term effects have higher potential in reducing energy use [15]. Advice may be needed for making investments in energy efficient technologies, and friends and neighbours can be important sources of information perceived as trustworthy [26].

One further shortcoming of many interactive technologies targeting energy reduction is that focus lies mostly on electricity use [14, 24]. This can be regarded as a consequence of the individual focus, since, for apartment buildings, electricity use is something that households are expected to be in control of. However, in many countries with temperate or cold climate, electricity is only a small part of the total energy use; for example, 25% of the energy is used for electricity in an average Swedish apartment household [13]. The other 75% are used for heating and hot water, typically provided through district heating. Heating, in terms of people's perception of thermal comfort and alternatives to traditional space heating, has been explored by for example [6] and [21]. However, since the energy use for heating and hot water is affected by many factors beyond the control of the individual households (e.g. insulation of the building and the pipes, temperature settings, and type of energy system), we see another interesting case in studying and designing for people in charge of the building-level energy work, rather than the "users" of energy.

We have chosen to focus our research on supporting energy reduction actions in housing cooperatives, which are common in Northern Europe. For example, 20% of the Swedish households live in apartments owned by housing cooperatives (37% in Stockholm, where our study is situated) [27]. Housing cooperatives are managed by boards of volunteers from among the dwellers. The boards can propose energy-related decisions such as maintenance or one-time investments, which may be implemented directly or voted upon by all the households in the cooperative. Some boards have designated *energy managers* who lead the energy work. The board members (including energy managers) do not necessarily have any experience of energy management, and they often need to rely on others in the housing cooperative community, or on energy professionals, for taking energy reduction actions.

With our focus on housing cooperative energy management, we aim to inform and perform design that promotes and facilitates collective energy reduction work in settings such as housing cooperative neighbourhoods. There are other examples in HCI [e.g. 16, 9] of designing for social interactions between neighbours to encourage energy reduction in communities. However, our case moves the design focus from energy use on a household level to building level energy use and energy reduction actions.

We regard both the apartment dwellers and the board volunteers as *energy amateurs*. Indeed, while few of them may pursue a profession related to the energy domain, the boards and the households see every year a major post in the cooperative budget allocated to energy. Without energy expertise, but with amateur knowledge of it, they strive to improve the cooperative's energy situation. Amateurs always act in social groups [28] and relate to others (amateurs or professionals) for learning and for assessing their "performance" in pursuing the respective field. Such social groups, in this case housing cooperatives and their energy-related federations, are termed *amateur communities* [3]. The amateur community framing is useful for us in design, as we have been involved, in other settings, in formulating design guidelines for such communities. We used and revised the guidelines in this case.

In this paper, we present a case study and initial design iterations aiming to reduce collective energy use in a district of Stockholm, where we have worked closely with six housing cooperatives and their energy managers. We detail on the amateur community framework and how it can help structure fieldwork and design, and comment on our field data in relation to this framework. The design of a housing cooperative energy app, which is used by the six cooperatives, is presented and reflected upon. Finally, we discuss how design can support amateur energy management, as a focus beyond the individual household, in settings other than housing cooperatives and we suggest additional design aspects to take into account for future support of collective energy management.

THEORETICAL FRAMEWORK: DESIGNING FOR AN AMATEUR COMMUNITY

We describe a view on voluntary amateur work that has inspired us in our fieldwork and design. The perspective was drawn from one of the authors' previous studies in amateur radio ([1] cf. [18]) and volunteer student association work [3], as well as on studies by Stebbins [28] on amateur sportsmen, archaeologists, and actors. Stebbins classifies the amateurs into *pre-professional* and *post-professional* and this is reflected by our energy managers; some are interested in energy but have never worked professionally with energy matters while others came into their energy manager role because of their former or present energy-related profession.

Amateurs were approached by HCI especially from the CSCW perspective, which is a sign of their collaborative nature, it is difficult to imagine an amateur who would not relate to a community. Grinter [17] presents work on amateur photography and the GROUP conference had a workshop on amateurs [31]. In the amateur community perspective, *amateur work* is fundamentally social and *challenge-driven* [3]. For example, one important amateur radio challenge is to realise radio connections with as little transmission power as possible, to places as remote as possible. Amateurs value contingencies related to their work and aim to negotiate them. Some leading amateurs *pioneer* new such spaces of contingency, that are a whole new family of challenges, for example a new type of radio transmission in the amateur radio domain. The way challenges are addressed is *reviewed by peers* and good performance in addressing them is regarded as a contribution to community and is subject to recognition.

An important concern in amateur contexts with volunteer work is whether there are enough members to address the community challenges. The amateur community perspective thus also looks at ways in which people can become members of the community and possibly evolve towards a core status and become leaders. Amateur learning is important in this case, and the *community of practice* learning perspective [22] is employed, with new amateurs being regarded as peripheral participants learning from their more experienced peers. To facilitate learning, a community should provide both easy (addressable) and very difficult challenges. Members are thus following a *gentle learning path.* A healthy amateur community is then a community that has a sufficient number of members at all stages of learning about the amateur practice. As more and more challenges are addressed by a member, their prestige among peers is growing [1, 3].

A designer who aims to help an amateur community needs to identify their challenges and spaces of contingency and support the amateur work within these spaces. The designer should also aim to create or support a gentle learning path for the community members. One such design process and design product aimed at amateur programmers in a student association is described by [2], where the design product is still in use over a decade after the researcher left the amateur setting.

It is important for any community to follow up on its progress and all the more so for an amateur community. A designer who works with an amateur community should aim to let them follow to what extent they have addressed their challenges and what are the new kinds of challenges recently pioneered.

From the amateur community perspective, our aim in the housing cooperative energy domain is thus to understand energy managers as energy amateurs, to understand their challenges and spaces of contingency, and to pinpoint the energy notions and practicalities that they need to learn about. We also aim, through design, to support peer learning and to create a gentle learning path so that housing cooperative members who find energy work interesting can in their turn become energy managers.

METHODS

The first step in our design process was to increase our knowledge of the current energy management work in Hammarby Sjöstad in Stockholm, Sweden. During 2014 and 2015 we joined three meetings with the local energy network (attended by energy managers from different cooperatives as well as energy providers, energy consultants and other local energy stakeholders) and we joined or arranged six meetings with representatives from the energy network management group. To better understand the technical challenges of the energy management work, we observed the energy system in one housing cooperative and we also had a meeting with an energy management company.

To discuss potential design interventions on a high level, we carried out two group interviews, early in the process, with two housing cooperative representative in each interview. During the interviews we presented, and received feedback on, four scenarios that described different ways of using ICT for community energy work in Hammarby Sjöstad.

We analysed our notes from the observations, meetings and interviews using the amateur community framework as reference, and we identified a number of design opportunities for ICT to support amateur energy management work. To include all opportunities in a first design was not feasible, so we decided to create a mockup with the features we found most promising and that were furthest away from the tools the energy managers already had access to. The semi-interactive mockup of a mobile app was discussed in a focus group with three energy managers and, based on the discussion, we later iterated our design and developed a first version of a functioning app. Invitations to try out the app were sent to 13 housing cooperatives who had already given the energy network management group access to their cooperatives' energy data. In the end of 2015 we carried out app signup meetings with five energy managers from different cooperatives and with the "energy management group" from a sixth cooperative. During the signup meetings, the energy managers created an account, we discussed their cooperative's energy data and energy actions taken, the energy managers added a couple of energy actions and gave us feedback on the app.

The focus group and app signup meetings were audio recorded and data was also collected through a survey that included: information about how experienced the energy managers were as housing cooperative board members and as energy managers, their rating of energy knowledge in their boards and among other members, and energy related information about the cooperative.

To increase the number of users we will in the future also offer the app to housing cooperatives outside of Hammarby Sjöstad. The recruitment will mainly target board members who make decisions or drive decision-making processes on issues affecting energy use, although they might not identify themselves as energy managers. To reach out to the cooperatives we will collaborate with building management companies or other organisations that regularly are in

Figure 2. Energy network meeting with energy managers and other energy stakeholders (from [32], used with permission).

contact with housing cooperatives on practical matters that may be related to energy use.

AMATEUR ENERGY MANAGEMENT IN HOUSING COOPERATIVES

Everyone who buys an apartment in Sweden must join the local housing cooperative, which owns and manages the buildings and is in charge of the energy needed for heating, cooling, hot water, and electricity in common areas (facilities electricity). The costs, including also loans on the buildings and maintenance costs, are then spread to the households in the form of a monthly fee. This process is managed by the housing cooperative board, which is elected among the cooperative members every year. In the city district we worked with, many boards had appointed an energy manager with the responsibility of attending to energy issues. The energy managers were invited to join meetings with a local "energy network" (see Figure 2), managed by an umbrella organisation including 40 housing cooperatives in the area. The housing cooperatives vary in size, the smallest cooperative in our study has 38 apartments and the largest has 137 apartments, and they have different energy issues and resources to address the issues.

The Board and the Energy Managers

No previous experience or knowledge is required to join a housing cooperative board and the work is usually unpaid or rewarded with a small pay. Nevertheless, the work of the board is fundamental for the existence of the housing cooperative. The role of the energy manager is not compulsory in the board but dealing with energy issues is an inevitable part of the work. Some of the energy managers volunteered for the position because they had previous energy related professional experiences (one energy manager was a building owner for many years and another worked for the Swedish Energy Agency), while others volunteered because they were equally inexperienced as everyone else in the board. The experience of board work in other housing cooperatives varied among our energy managers, from no previous experience up to 21 years of experience.

The energy managers' personal drivers and goals for engaging in energy management work were often related to sustainability or minimising energy waste, which in terms of amateur motivation can be framed as their challenge. However, cost was a crucial factor when it came to making energy related decisions in the cooperatives and cost reductions were many times drivers of the collective energy work, which one of the energy managers expressed as follows: *"Personally I actually only consider the environment [in the energy management work] but when I motivate it to the board it is money I talk about."* It was important that the board and housing cooperative members were convinced that any investment considered would pay off and for energy related investments a payoff time of ten years was perceived as reasonable. While sustainability might be considered, for example when investing in a new energy system, the energy managers did not think that environmental benefits would be enough to convince the board and the other members to make investments with uncertain payoff.

Being part of the board was a learning process for the energy managers, just as in other amateur work, and the local energy network further supported the learning. It was, however, difficult to sustain the learning process and keep the acquired knowledge in the housing cooperative due to the high turnover of community members. Of the nine contact persons in the cooperatives we initially collaborated with, five had changed a year later. It is not only knowledge about energy systems and previous work that is easily lost when people leave, but also the motivation to push for certain energy reduction actions.

Pioneering is an important aspect of amateur work, as it opens new types of challenges that other members of the respective community may appreciate and take in their turn. We have observed cases of for example a new type of contract with an energy management company being tested and an installation of a heat pump resulting in significant reductions of energy use. These cases were proudly presented at meetings with the energy network, which emphasises the importance of the peer audience in amateur work.

Other Housing Cooperative Members

In the amateur community perspective, ordinary housing cooperative members are peripheral participants who in the future may or may not take the amateur challenge and engage with energy matters. However, they are still affected by the cooperative's energy decisions, for example in terms of limitations of the indoor temperature, and they might be involved in making decisions on energy investments during the annual meeting. The energy managers experienced that the engagement from other members was highest when they were unhappy about something, for example if they thought it was too cold in the apartments, but people rarely offered help and many did not even attend the annual meetings. One energy manager described it as: "*some people have that hotel feeling, like... I want to have this fixed, you [the board] should fix this for me, preferably yesterday*".

Although ordinary housing cooperative members have little power to significantly reduce the collective energy use unless they become part of the board, their actions may in some cases affect the entire energy system negatively. One example is members renovating the kitchen and replacing the cooker hood. If the new hood does not match with the building's ventilation system, it can decrease the efficiency of the system in the whole building. The collective consequences are not visible and might not even be known to the individual member, and it is also difficult for the energy managers to detect such issues.

Energy Issues and Energy Actions

The buildings of the housing cooperatives in the study are relatively new; they were constructed between 2001 and 2007 as part of a renewal of the city district. The sustainability ambitions were high for the area, with energy efficient buildings being one goal. However, many buildings were not as efficient as expected and energy audits have shown a potential for housing cooperatives to reduce their energy use with 10-50 per cent [32].

There are many different types of possible energy reduction actions, from small (and inexpensive) optimisations of current energy systems, such as adjusting the ventilation frequency or reducing the temperature in entrances and garages, to costly investments such as installation of a heat pump for heat recovery. Consequently, the scope of the energy challenge for the amateurs is wide and the energy managers have different goals depending on the energy status of the housing cooperative.

We have also encountered examples of energy simply being wasted, such as high electricity use for ventilation because the ventilation filters had not been cleaned for a long time and outdoor lighting that always was on because vegetation had grown and covered the light sensors. The issues were in many cases pointed out by an energy auditor working in the area, while energy managers were unaware of the waste. One energy manager found out that his cooperative used electricity for heating the pavement (meant for melting ice in the winter) during the entire year: "*I was surprised, we were heating water in the autumn. There was a dry spot in the middle [of the wet pavement], you could see where the electricity was. It was ridiculous, I've still got pictures of it.*"

Energy, and energy waste, matters also in terms of money. In most housing cooperatives, energy is the second largest post among the expenses, after costs for loans on the apartment buildings. The measured district heating use (for heating and hot water) among the housing cooperatives in our study varied from 0.5 to 1.4 MWh during 2014, which equals costs of around €52,000 ($56,000) and €136,000 ($148,000) respectively. Since the costs are high, the savings can also be significant. One of the housing cooperatives in the study installed a system for heat recovery, which in the first year after installation cut the energy costs with €50,000 ($55,000), or about 40%, and they estimated the payoff time to eight years. However, a lot of work is required from the energy manager and the board for such investments to be realised and it is a long process that may take years of investigation, decision-making and implementation.

In addition, there was a need for involving energy professionals who could analyse the energy reduction potential, recommend solutions and carry out installations. While the amateur energy managers depended on the expertise of the professionals in such situations they also expressed concern regarding whom they could trust. Some housing cooperatives had bad experiences of being cheated by energy management companies and these companies were perceived as having vested interests. This is somewhat different from usual amateur-professional relations [28] where amateurs and professionals collaborate and learn from each other.

Energy Feedback and ICT Support

Through the main energy provider's website, the housing cooperatives can access detailed information about their use of district heating and facilities electricity. Energy data for the own cooperative can be viewed per hour or in different aggregations (see Figure 3) and there is some support for analysing historical data for the purpose of for example deciding on which type of energy contract to choose. This tool is only accessible for members of the board who have the necessary login information. Some of the energy managers we met had used the tool, for example to follow up on their energy work and see how they were progressing in their challenges, while others had never logged in to their accounts.

It is difficult for members outside of the board, who are

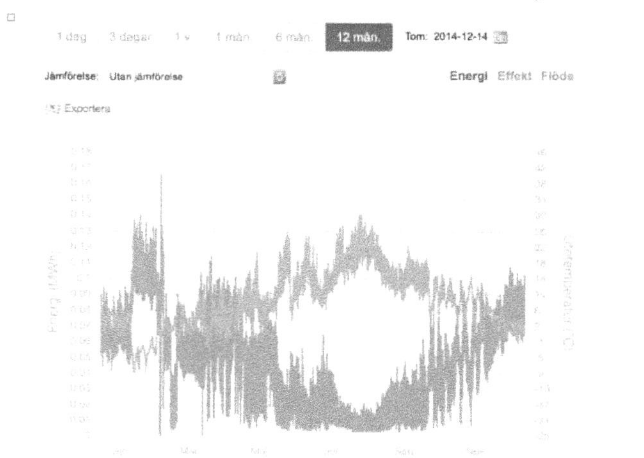

Figure 3. Example of energy data the housing cooperatives can access from the energy provider.

interested in the energy use of their own cooperative, to find information that is updated and easy to interpret. Indirect information in the form of yearly energy costs is provided in the cooperative's annual report, which sometimes also includes information about energy investments that have been made. However, this information can be hard to interpret for members not familiar with housing cooperative energy use. It is, for example, not obvious what is a "normal" annual energy cost, or what energy improvement work the cooperative should or could do. For comparison purposes, there is information about the cooperative's energy performance in the legally-required "energy declaration" of the buildings, which is a public document often available on the housing cooperative's website. While the energy declaration to some extent allows for comparisons, the data may not be particularly accurate since the declaration only has to be updated every ten years. Consequently, it might take a long time before the effect of energy reduction actions is visible in the energy declaration.

The energy network in Hammarby Sjöstad was interested in getting an overview of the energy performance of the buildings in the area, and a map-based visualisation (see Figure 4) was created with the energy performance data from the energy declarations. Although the overview was appreciated, and it emphasised that buildings that may seem similar from the outside can have very different energy performance, the visualisation was a static image and they would have liked a more dynamic overview with higher data accuracy.

From an amateur community perspective, none of the energy feedback the energy managers (and other housing cooperative members) had access to provided enough support for learning from peers, for assessing the work of their peers, for identification of suitable challenges or for community follow-up on the challenges. The tool from the energy provider facilitated the energy managers in analysing the energy use of their own cooperative and to follow up on their individual challenges, but it lacked a community perspective where challenges along with pioneering energy improvement work, are visible to the other energy managers.

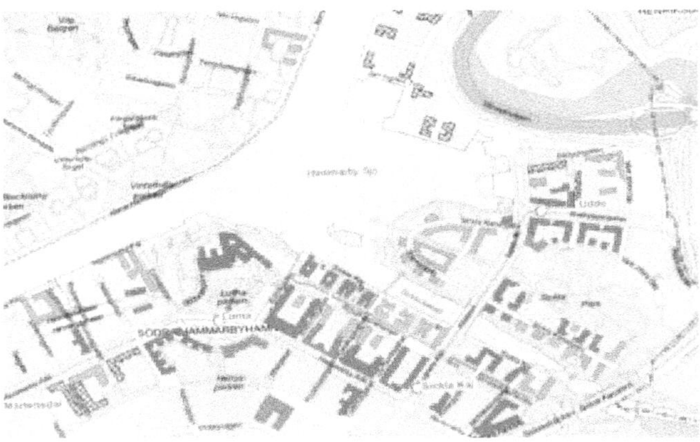

Figure 4. Overview of the housing cooperatives' energy use (from [32], used with permission).

THE HOUSING COOPERATIVE ENERGY APP

The aim of the app is to support peer learning between energy managers (both between different cooperatives and over time within a cooperative), to motivate them to find suitable challenges in terms of energy actions, to reward good work and pioneering by providing recognition, and to sensitise other members (peripheral participants) on the housing cooperatives to collective energy issues. We have developed a first version of the app that is currently used by energy managers in six housing cooperatives in Hammarby Sjöstad. For one cooperative also the household members have been invited to try the app and, in addition to the cooperative energy information, they can see their own household's monthly energy use (electricity and hot water). Below we describe the design rationale for the main features of the app as well as for the technical implementation and decisions related to privacy.

Energy Data Linked to Energy Actions

One of the key features in the app, which is not provided through any other energy feedback the energy managers have access to, is the mapping of energy actions to energy data as a way of supporting peer learning and providing follow-up on the energy reduction actions taken as part of their amateur challenge. Energy managers can add energy actions that their cooperative has taken along with information about the type of action, when it was carried out, the cost, and any additional information they think might be useful. After they are added, the energy actions appear as numbers in a bar chart displaying monthly or yearly energy use and the user can compare to the previous year's use to examine the effects of the actions (see Figure 5, left). The information about each action is found in an expandable list below the chart (see Figure 5, middle). All this information is visible to all app users in the district, which helps create a large peer audience, and helps make the energy reduction challenges apparent to prospective new energy amateurs, as well as to existing energy managers.

To make use of another cooperative's experience, more information may be needed than what is added to the action, for example if the energy manager from one cooperative is interested in details on how another housing cooperative optimised their energy system. Contact and communication ways are provided through a commenting function connected to each action (see Figure 5, right) and through an option for the energy managers to add an email address as contact point for energy related issues. Once the energy managers know which other cooperatives have taken energy reduction actions they are interested in, they can also start the discussion offline, during the energy network meetings. Our goal here was thus to spark interest

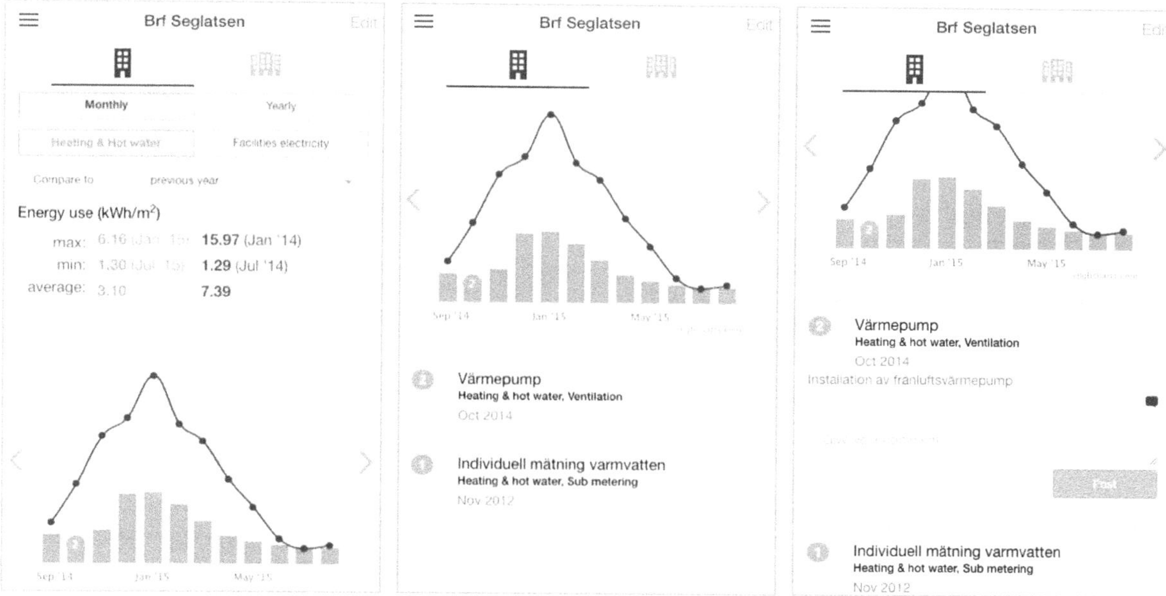

Figure 5. The housing cooperative energy app. Left: Visualisation of monthly energy use compared to previous year. Middle: The energy actions are listed below the graph. Action number 2 is an installation of a heat pump. Right: Each action can be commented on, for example to ask for more details on the action.

in peer learning and peer review of the energy actions and to promote pioneering of new kinds of actions.

The energy managers believed that the app would support them in learning from other housing cooperatives and they wanted to use the app to find cooperatives with similar challenges and see what actions they had taken. For example, one of the cooperatives was interested in changing the lighting in common areas to LED lights. He would like to connect with other cooperatives that had already gone through the process. The energy managers also thought the app would be helpful for deciding which companies can be trusted, based on the experience other housing cooperatives had with the respective company and what the effects were on the energy use. However, with only six cooperatives, and a few actions added, there is not yet enough data to browse between many different actions.

The purpose of linking energy data to actions is not only to support peer learning between energy managers in different cooperatives, but also to support learning within a cooperative when energy managers and other people in the board leave and are replaced by new members. This supports basic continuity in the amateur community. In some cooperatives there was no documentation (that the energy managers were aware of) related to the energy systems. In addition to documenting actions, the energy managers would like to have support for documenting calculations that are regularly made. As a first step, the app includes calculations of energy performance, which can be used to compare a cooperative's energy improvements over time or compare the energy use of different cooperatives.

Housing Cooperative Energy Comparisons

One way of motivating the energy managers, and allowing them to follow up on their energy amateur challenges, is to make it explicit how the own cooperative is doing in relation to similar cooperatives. In the app this is done by displaying an overview of the yearly energy performance of the housing cooperatives (see Figure 6). The comparison is based on the previous year's actual energy use and is calculated as the heating and hot water use divided by the heated area (kWh/m^2). To facilitate comparison, the energy performance is displayed both as a number and as a colour (from red for high energy use to green for low energy use). The calculation and the "energy classification" based on colour are designed to be similar to the energy performance calculations in the compulsory energy declarations. The essential difference is that in the app the information is

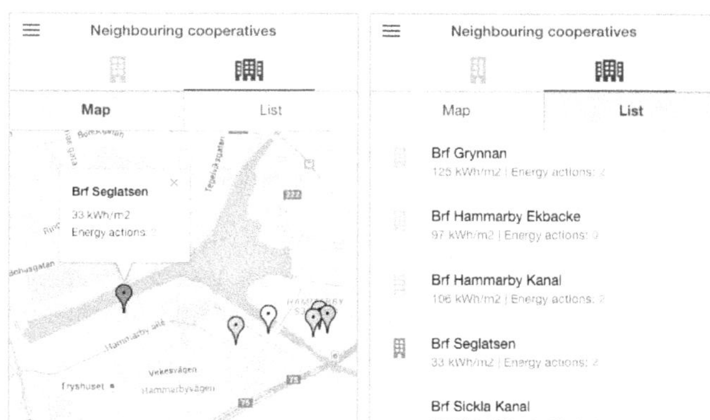

Figure 6. Overview of the housing cooperatives' energy performance and number of energy actions taken.

updated yearly instead of every ten years, which gives the housing cooperatives more direct feedback on, and recognition for, any improvements in energy performance. It is important that the energy performance is normalised for outdoor temperature, since it is otherwise impossible to compare energy performance between years.

Another type of comparison that is provided in the app is the possibility to compare a cooperative's monthly or yearly energy use, divided into "heating & hot water" and "facilities electricity", to the neighbourhood average (see Figure 7). Since the cooperatives in our study vary a lot in size (from around 5000 m^2 up to more than 15000 m^2), energy use is also presented as kWh/m^2 in the bar chart.

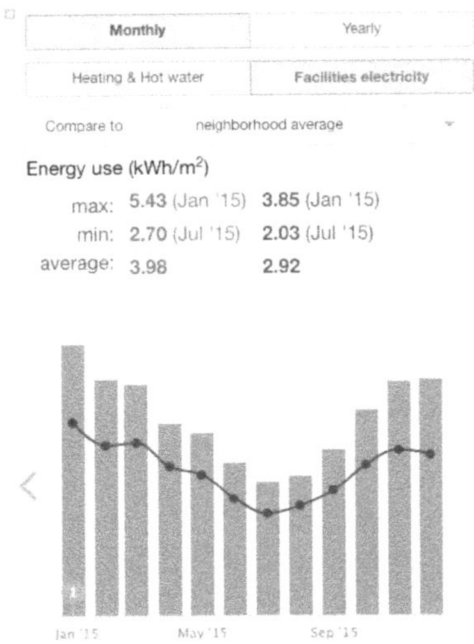

Figure 7. Energy use compared to neighbourhood average.

It is difficult to make fair comparisons of energy use since there are variations in what energy data is measured, how the size of the heated area is measured and how the building was constructed. If the comparisons are perceived as unfair, we see a risk of demotivating energy managers, and of making their challenges appear too difficult to address. However, a poor energy performance is not necessarily the same as the energy manager doing a poor job.

The energy managers stressed the importance of easily understanding the reasons for why the energy performance is at a certain level, for example: *"It would be really interesting to compare one self in a simple way: they have 70 apartments, 80 [kWh] per square metre and we have 135 [kWh/m²], 121 apartments, they have taken these actions. So you know what it is you are comparing to."* Therefore, after discussing these aspects with a few energy managers, the app presents housing cooperative information that affects the energy performance: the number of apartments in the cooperative, size in terms of heated area, the building's construction year, and type of ventilation system in the building (see Figure 8). This allows the energy managers to better decide what is an addressable challenge and what is non-addressable in the case of their

Figure 8. Information about the housing cooperative that is important for understanding the energy use.

own housing cooperative. In addition, to highlight good work and pioneering in all types of cooperatives, the map and list overviews do not only show energy performance but also number of energy actions taken. Thus, an energy manager in a housing cooperative that was poorly built from an energy perspective can still share experiences and get recognition for taking actions.

The aim of opening up the energy data is also to make differences between one's own and other cooperatives visible for housing cooperative members outside of the board and to sensitise them to the energy work of their cooperative. However, the energy managers doubted, based on the current level of engagement in the general housing cooperative work, that many members outside of the board would be interested in following their own cooperative's energy use. They rather saw potential in using the app for engaging members in specific questions, such as getting support for energy improvements and investments, by pointing out the energy progress that *other* cooperatives have achieved: *"It can be good if one makes an investment and then points out... now we are doing like this [in terms of energy performance], look at the one that did that... they are doing like this. Then one can... here we can earn money."*

Technical Implementation

The first version of the app, currently used by the housing cooperatives, is a web application primarily accessed through mobile devices, thus its design is optimised for mobile phone screens. We made this priority since the users saw the current features as useful for having a quick look at during board meetings or "on the go", rather than something they would sit down and work with. However, there are possible future features that may work better on a bigger screen, and by keeping it as a web application we can easily add those features later. In addition, one user did not own a smartphone and instead accessed the app on his computer.

Even though the app is used as a web app, it is built using the Ionic Framework[1] for building hybrid mobile applications. Hybrid apps are essentially web applications wrapped in special containers for each mobile platform that

[1] http://ionicframework.com/

makes them run on the phone as native, rather than web, apps. However, due to the fast design iterations at this stage, we decided to use it only as a web app in the first stages.

The energy data in the app is acquired through Metry[2], a web service that provides a unified API for accessing utility data from many utility providers in the country. Since different energy providers have different formats for the energy data, it would require a lot of work to access it directly from each provider.

Selected use data of the app is logged for the purpose of future study and analysis. The data includes a database access log as well as analytics data, gathered through the service Mixpanel[3], which captures the interaction in the app (e.g. logins, clicks, navigation).

Balancing Privacy and Openness

Since one of the core ideas of the app is to open up data that was previously only accessible to a few people in the housing cooperative, and share it with the members and other housing cooperatives, there were also privacy concerns to take into account for the design and implementation. In the app, all information that can be seen for the own housing cooperative is also visible to members of other cooperatives, but only the energy manager of a specific housing cooperative has the right to edit the cooperative information (e.g. type of ventilation system) and to add or edit actions.

We decided to present the energy data aggregated on a monthly and yearly basis, since that in most cases is enough for seeing what the effects are of actions taken. Daily or hourly data might also be sensitive, particularly for small housing cooperatives, since it could reveal when many people are not at home and assist burglars in identifying suitable times for breaking in. The energy managers did not see any problem with sharing monthly or yearly data, neither with sharing information about actions taken, basic information about the housing cooperative or their email address. However, some energy managers had concerns about making the information completely open, to people also outside of housing cooperatives, as they feared they might be contacted by a lot of companies offering their services. On the other hand, they thought it would be convenient if selected companies, such as energy consultants hired by the cooperative, could access their energy information through the app.

DISCUSSION

We have explored the potential of designing to support amateur energy managers in housing cooperatives as an alternative to the dominant, and by many questioned [e.g. 4, 5, 10, 12, 30], focus of eco-feedback aimed at individual behaviour change. While the setting of housing cooperatives is rather specific to Northern Europe, we believe there are other groups of energy amateurs where linking energy data to energy actions, and at the same time sharing this information, could be equally valuable. Other forms of small scale building ownership have similar issues of persons in charge lacking knowledge of energy management in buildings, or even awareness of that there are energy issues that can be addressed. Whether or not they identify themselves as amateur energy managers, we believe there are opportunities for design to support them in work that has a significant impact and long lasting effects. Although we are still in the early stages of a long learning and design process, and further design iterations and evaluation will follow, we already now have some initial reflections and recommendations on what we found are important considerations when designing for amateur energy management.

Supporting Energy Action

While eco-feedback has long focused on different ways of visualising energy data, we see an interesting, and less explored, potential in *linking energy data to energy action*. Our design presents some early attempts in this regard, by linking data to action with the aim of supporting documentation, reflection and learning in amateur energy work. Yet we believe that this is a rich ground for further exploration of other ways of designing and assessing the data-action linking.

For example, a different temporal perspective can be applied by linking past energy data with suitable future action, designing for a catalogue of possible actions and indicating their suitability for the situation as it emerges from past energy data. We also believe that designers should make use of and adapt simulations that exist in the "energy and the built environment" research area to link data to action in the future, not just in the past, and facilitate in assessing energy improvement impact and payoff times. Creative adaptation is required because existing simulations are not directed to energy amateurs, but more to professionals.

Designing at the energy community level also lifts a sensitivity, which we started to explore, for *awareness* within the community. Awareness of suitable energy actions, awareness of peers who may have the same issues or needs, awareness of good professional help one can get, are a few examples that illustrate opportunities for the designer. The CSCW field has long considered the awareness topic in workplaces, as a notion related to coordination [11], yet it has not been explored much in less formal (amateur) work settings such as energy communities. The awareness we would like to emphasise is closer to this collaborative awareness than to "energy awareness" that is prominent in eco-feedback.

Working with Long Time Perspectives

Energy work in housing cooperatives is a slow process that is further affected by the high turnover of board members.

[2] https://metry.io

[3] https://mixpanel.com

This is similar to energy work also in other settings, since energy investments take time to consider, plan for, decide on and carry out. In addition, the results of investments may not be immediately visible; in some cases a full year is needed to evaluate the effects. Thus it may take many years from an energy action is first initiated until the results show. For the design process, this means we must look for ways to assess our work and judge alternatives that are not directly dependent on actual energy reductions.

The combination of slow processes and the amateur (volunteer) context may lead to energy work being initiated by someone who leaves the community before the work is finished and without any handover. Another design goal should therefore be to bridge such gaps between energy managers. Our current design partly supports this by the option to document energy actions, but we also see a potential in involving actors on higher levels to ensure continuity. For example, energy management companies, which may work with a housing cooperative during a long time, could play a part in using the app for documentation of the work they are doing and introducing new energy managers.

Sparking Energy Interest

To find ways of sparking the interest of peripheral participants [22] is crucial for energy management to become a self-sustainable amateur practice. However, a consequence of the slow processes in energy management is that the content of our app does not change fast, and particularly to the less knowledgeable user the app will often "look the same". This is not what modern mobile users expect, and it is a challenge that must be considered when designing in an amateur energy management context. One possible way of addressing this is to combine energy data with local community information, which does not need to be energy-related. Another possible design approach is to highlight when there is new information that may be interesting for the user, such as actions taken by the own or a similar cooperative or data showing the effects of actions, and to make it easy for energy managers to share selected challenges or accomplishments in situations where they think peripheral participants would be interested.

A further challenge is that energy management work comprises, to a great extent, resource management decisions, which eco-feedback has been criticised for focusing too much on [30]. This is currently mirrored in the design of our app and while the resource management focus is appreciated by the energy managers, it may be less appealing to others in the community (including possible future energy managers). In fact, we found that the motivation for engaging in energy management work in the first place was often related to responsibility and environmental concern. We thus believe that design, to assist in sparking energy interest among others than the already engaged, should explore how such values can be designed for in relation to energy management work. Considering intrinsic values, such as caring about the environment, is also in line with suggestions [20] for how HCI can better utilise interactive technologies for sustainability purposes.

CONCLUSION

We have presented a case study of energy amateur management in housing cooperatives, which illustrates collective energy work that has a high impact on energy use in buildings. We have presented and reflected on the design of an energy app that aims to support peer learning among the amateur energy managers, identification of suitable amateur challenges and documentation of energy work. Linking energy data to energy actions was a key design feature in the energy management support and we believe there are further design opportunities in exploring combinations of data and actions. Additional aspects for design to consider are the slow processes and the long time perspective in energy work and the challenges in inspiring community members to become more involved in energy issues.

ACKNOWLEDGMENTS

This work has been supported by EU FP7 programme through the project CIVIS (no 608774) and the Swedish STandUP for Energy Initiative. We are also grateful to the housing cooperatives and energy network in Hammarby Sjöstad, and to our CIVIS project colleagues.

REFERENCES

1. Cristian Bogdan and John Bowers. 2007. Tuning In: Challenging Design for Communities through a Field Study of Radio Amateurs. In *Communities and Technologies 2007*, Charles Steinfield, Brian T. Pentland, Mark Ackerman and Noshir Contractor (eds.). Springer, London, pp 439–461. http://doi.org/10.1007/978-1-84628-905-7
2. Cristian Bogdan and Rudolf Mayer. 2009. Makumba: the Role of Technology or the Sustainability of Amateur Programming Practice and Community. *Communities and technologies - C&T 2009*, 205–214. http://doi.org/10.1145/1556460.1556490
3. Cristian Bogdan. 2003. IT Design for Amateur Communities.
4. Hrönn Brynjarsdottir, Maria Håkansson, James Pierce, Eric Baumer, Carl Disalvo, and Phoebe Sengers. 2012. Sustainably Unpersuaded: How Persuasion Narrows Our Vision of Sustainability. *CHI 2012*, ACM, 947–956.
5. Baki Cakici and Markus Bylund. 2014. Changing Behaviour to Save Energy: ICT-Based Surveillance for a Low-Carbon Economy in the Seventh Framework Programme. *ICT4S 2014*, 165–170.
6. Adrian Clear, Adrian Friday, Mike Hazas, and Carolynne Lord. 2014. Catch my drift? Achieving comfort more sustainably in conventionally heated

buildings. *DIS 2014*, 1015–1024. http://doi.org/10.1145/2598510.2598529

7. Enrico Costanza, Joel E Fischer, James A Colley, Tom Rodden, Sarvapali D Ramchurn, and Nicholas R Jennings. 2014. Doing the Laundry with Agents: a Field Trial of a Future Smart Energy System in the Home. *CHI 2014*, ACM.
8. Tawanna Dillahunt, Jennifer Mankoff, and Eric Paulos. 2010. Understanding conflict between landlords and tenants: implications for energy sensing and feedback. *Ubicomp 2010*, 149–158. http://doi.org/10.1145/1864349.1864376
9. Tawanna Dillahunt and Jennifer Mankoff. 2014. Understanding Factors of Successful Engagement around Energy Consumption Between and Among Households. *CSCW 2014*, 1246–1257.
10. Carl DiSalvo, Phoebe Sengers, and Hrönn Brynjarsdóttir. 2010. Mapping the landscape of sustainable HCI. *CHI 2010*, ACM, 1975–1984. http://doi.org/10.1145/1753326.1753625
11. Paul Dourish and Victoria Bellotti. 1992. Awareness and Coordination in Shared Workspaces. *CSCW 1992*, 107–114. http://doi.org/10.1145/143457.143468
12. Paul Dourish. 2010. HCI and environmental sustainability: the politics of design and the design of politics. *DIS 2010*, 1–10. http://doi.org/10.1145/1858171.1858173
13. Eon. Har du normal elförbrukning? Retrieved January 15, 2015 from http://www.eon.se/privatkund/Energieffektivisering/energiradgivning/normal-elforbrukning/
14. Jon Froehlich, Leah Findlater, and James Landay. 2010. The Design of Eco-Feedback Technology. *CHI 2010*, ACM.
15. Gerald T. Gardner and Paul C. Stern. 2008. The Short List: The Most Effective Actions U.S. Households Can Take to Curb Climate Change. *Environment: Science and Policy for Sustainable Development* 50, 5: 12–25. http://doi.org/10.3200/ENVT.50.5.12-25
16. Catherine Grevet, Jennifer Mankoff, and Scott D. Anderson. 2010. Design and evaluation of a social visualization aimed at encouraging sustainable behavior. *Proceedings of the Annual Hawaii International Conference on System Sciences*: 1–8. http://doi.org/10.1109/HICSS.2010.135
17. Rebecca Grinter. 2005. Words about images: Coordinating community in amateur photography. *Computer Supported Cooperative Work* 14, 2: 161–188. http://doi.org/10.1007/s10606-005-1053-7
18. Kristen Haring. 2007. *Ham Radio's Technical Culture*. MIT Press.
19. Helen Ai He, Saul Greenberg, and Elaine M Huang. 2010. One Size Does Not Fit All: Applying the Transtheoretical Model to Energy Feedback Technology Design. *CHI 2010*, ACM, 927–936.
20. Bran Knowles, Lynne Blair, Stuart Walker, Paul Coulton, Lisa Thomas, and Louise Mullagh. 2014. Patterns of persuasion for sustainability. *DIS 2014*, 1035–1044. http://doi.org/10.1145/2598510.2598536
21. Lenneke Kuijer and Annelise De Jong. 2012. Identifying design opportunities for reduced household resource consumption: exploring practices of thermal comfort. *Journal of Design Research* 10, 1-2: 67–85. http://doi.org/10.1504/JDR.2012.046140
22. Jean Lave and Etienne Wenger. 1991. *Situated Learning: Legitimate Peripheral Participation*. Cambridge University Press.
23. Johanne Mose Entwistle, Mia Kruse Rasmussen, Nervo Verdezoto, Robert S Brewer, and Mads Schaarup Andersen. 2015. Beyond the Individual: The Contextual Wheel of Practice as a Research Framework for Sustainable HCI. *CHI 2015*.
24. James Pierce and Eric Paulos. 2012. Beyond energy monitors: interaction, energy, and emerging energy systems. *CHI 2012*, ACM, 665–674.
25. Anneli Selvefors, I C Marianne Karlsson, and Ulrike Rahe. 2013. Use and Adoption of Interactive Energy Feedback Systems. *IASDR 2013*, 1771–1782.
26. Anneli Selvefors, I.C. MariAnne Karlsson, and Ulrike Rahe. 2015. Conflicts in Everyday Life: The Influence of Competing Goals on Domestic Energy Conservation. *Sustainability* 7, 5: 5963–5980. http://doi.org/10.3390/su7055963
27. Statistics Sweden. 2014. Statistikdatabasen. Retrieved May 11, 2015 from http://www.statistikdatabasen.scb.se/pxweb/sv/ssd/START__BO__BO0104/BO0104T04/?rxid=d4abd6aa-84eb-41db-b9d8-324c83482584
28. R.A. Stebbins. 1979. *Amateurs: on the margin between work and leisure*. Sage, Beverly Hills.
29. Yolande Strengers. 2011. Designing eco-feedback systems for everyday life. *CHI 2011*, ACM Press, 2135–2144. http://doi.org/10.1145/1978942.1979252
30. Yolande Strengers. 2014. Smart Energy in Everyday Life: Are You Designing for Resource Man? *Interactions* 21, 4: 24–31.
31. J. Thom-Santelli, E. Cook, K. Luther, J. Bardzell, A. Bruckman, and D. McDonald. 2009. Approaching Amateur, Workshop at GROUP 2009.
32. Helene Wintzell, Allan Larsson, and Willy Ociansson. 2013. *Under 100 - att lyckas med energi i Hammarby Sjöstad*.

SOLE Meets MOOC: Designing Infrastructure for Online Self-Organised Learning with a Social Mission

Hanna Celina, Ahmed Kharrufa, Anne Preston, Rob Comber, Patrick Olivier
Open Lab, Newcastle University
Newcastle upon Tyne, UK
{h.celina1,ahmed.kharrufa,anne.preston,robert.comber,patrick.olivier}@newcastle.ac.uk

ABSTRACT
We present the design, deployment and evaluation of three configurations of an online learning activity for would-be social innovators and activists, with the aim of understanding the factors that are critical to the design of an infrastructure to support such communities of learners. Our research was inspired and motivated by the example of SOLEs (self-organised learning environments) and builds upon the experiences of early connectivist MOOCs (massive open online courses). Our configurations were used to deliver three pilot courses on the topic of Sustainable Development, in partnership with United World Colleges (an organisation of international schools). Our work is distinctive in putting a focus on civic engagement and the autonomy of student learners throughout the course. Our primary design goals were to enable activist empowerment, self-organized learning, and the creation of social bonds to facilitate a lasting and self-sufficient international activist community. We base our analysis on a sample of 114 active learners and 33 mentors; including data from 223 applications, 705 Facebook posts, 48 participant survey responses and a variety of quantitative metrics.

Author Keywords
Online learning, civic engagement, civic education, activism, MOOC, e-learning, SOLE

ACM Classification Keywords
K.3.1 Computers and Education: Computer Uses in Education–*collaborative learning*

INTRODUCTION
Sugata Mitra's "hole in the wall" experiment explored whether children could learn effectively when exposed to technology and allowed to follow their natural curiosity [38]. Mitra's idea of self-organised learning environments (SOLEs) postulates that when learners are empowered to take responsibility for their learning and are given access to technology, they will learn at least as effectively as in formal school environments. One motivation of our research was to explore and apply this learner-agency based model where learners actively construct and even co-create knowledge during the learning process. Industrial-scale education, already foreseen by Fuller in 1962 [12], has become a reality with near-ubiquitous Internet access and as new models of MOOCs were developed and popularised in the first decade of the new millennium, primarily by universities: first with MOOCs inspired by connectivist theories of learning, then with behavioural cognitivist inspired MOOCs (that place a stronger emphasis on learning analytics and assessment).

Recently, non-governmental organisations have also been exploring the use of MOOCs; for example, Amnesty International conducted its first online course on edX in November 2015, recognizing the potential for raising awareness among learners and enabling their engagement as activists. To date, the generation of social impact through online learning has mostly been considered from the point of view of enabling access to citizens of developing world countries to high-quality, low-cost education (offered by the world's top providers).

The topic of activism itself, and the process of organising the work and efforts of volunteers online, has received significant attention in literature. Much work has focused on understanding the role of social media in creating political movements [16], on specific examples such as Occupy Wall Street [23] or the Arab Spring [22,24], and the potential of digital civic education to drive offline impact. Other familiar areas of concern include the coordination of crowdsourced work in online activist communities – with the creation of online encyclopaedias, including both successful [10] and unsuccessful implementations [33].

While both activism (including digital youth civic education) and online learning have been thoroughly researched, little attention has been paid to the transformational potential of online education design that combines the principles of developing and supporting communities of practice with the scale and diversity of MOOC-scale learning. The contribution of this work is twofold: (1) to show the potential of online courses as a way to facilitate creation of online learning communities for social innovation and activism; (2) to establish a set of best practices, based on our three design configurations, for

DIS 2016, June 04-08, 2016, Brisbane, QLD, Australia ACM 978-1-4503-4031-1/16/06. http://dx.doi.org/10.1145/2901790.2901848

infrastructures to support collaborative learning communities of would-be social innovators and activists. Our work is inspired by SOLE principles and builds upon best practices of connectivist MOOCs addressing many of their known challenges. We use the term 'infrastructure' here instead of the term 'platform', conventionally used in education technology research, in order to highlight the importance of the entire suite of internet tools and organizational processes that are normally used in preparing and running an online course, including the course website, any social media presence as well as the structure of communication between course organisers and learners.

RELATED WORK

A vast body of existing research has focused on understanding the learning process, motivations and outcomes of MOOCs. A further body of research also considers the topic of the development of online communities and coordinating online activism. However, the question of how using online education can support social change goals, through the development of communities of social innovators and activists, has not yet been widely explored.

Activism, communities of practice, online communities

Online activism encompasses a variety of online activities, including awareness/advocacy, organisation/mobilisation and action/reaction [34] and much of the existing research base addresses the role of social media in driving awareness about issues and the mobilisation of populations to act in response to these issues.

Role of social media

A primary focus of digital activism research is the role of technology and social media in creating political movements [16], particularly developing an understanding of how activist organisations can drive offline action in offline communities [17]. For example, a number of studies explored the dynamics of the role of social media in shaping political debates (reinforced by the absence of free media), affecting events on the ground and spreading democratic ideas across national borders during the Arab Spring [22,24]. Other work has shown the importance of social media for spreading political ideas as well as the importance of assuring the sustainability of movements such as Occupy Wall Street by decentralisation [23].

Analysis of youth online civic engagement revealed the changing nature of citizenship in the digital age – from *dutiful citizen* (who sees voting as a core responsibility of a citizen) to an *actualising citizen* (who typically distrusts government and does not view voting as core citizen responsibility, and instead focuses on the importance of loosely networked community actions). Several online communities exist which aim to empower young people to learn about volunteering opportunities and how to make an impact in their communities (DoSomething.org, PublicLab.org) or programs organised by leading global educational institutions (such as MIT's Center for Civic Media and Harvard's Berkman Center). Other approaches seek to promote young activist role models through their fellowship programmes, such as Global Youth Connect. Studies of activist website design [31] highlight that such sites do not focus on course-based education, but instead offer self-guided asynchronous access to educational and promotional materials.

Online communities

The literature on communities of practice has explored learning in a much wider sense as situated in the process of legitimate peripheral participation [30]. Wenger's later work on learning, meaning and identity creation further explored the dynamics of this interaction [53].

The most researched online community is Wikipedia, which has been analysed from several points of view as knowledge crowdsourcing experiment [11,51], as an example of an altruistic community [29] and as a social movement [28]. Significant effort has been devoted into understanding how successful online communities emerge and are sustained [42,43], including structural features [18]. A number of best practices have been broadly established, including: designing for sociability (in terms of community members' roles and responsibilities, codes of conduct, expectations) and usability (ease of use for novices and experienced users alike) [42]; building communities focused on design principles to achieve group identity and group cohesiveness; and reinforcing the "mission". In relation to online activists communities, the definition of a sense of 'we' and others has also been seen to be a key element of vibrancy and sustainability [42].

Ultimately, our research is motivated by the fact that while there is a robust framework for the design of online communities, and the nature of MOOC-based learning and communities is a topic of active exploration, the problem of designing online learning for social innovators and activists is largely underexplored.

MOOCs and SOLEs

The term MOOC was introduced in 2008 by David Comier to describe open access large-scale online courses, inspired at that time by the connectivist theory of learning introduced in 2004 by Siemens [47]. Today, the term MOOC is used to describe a vast variety of course offerings made by a plethora of organisers ranging from newly created EdTech start-ups to well-established universities.

Connectivism and cMOOCs

Connectivism was proposed by George Siemens as a new theory explaining learning which happens in a world where people are connected to each other and resources via technology [47,48,49]. Connectivism explains knowledge as a set of connections that are formed either in mind or in a society, and that form a network, which adapts as experiences are built [9]. Learning is described as a nonlinear process whereby learners tap into the knowledge network [47]. The key features of connectivist MOOCs (cMOOCs) are autonomy (learner's choice of learning pathways and materials to be studied), diversity (of learners in a course), openness (understood as open access) and connectedness/interactivity (the processes which enable learning) [32]. Engagement and learning motivation were the key questions considered in the scholarship about these first MOOCs [25,50]. Other research investigated designing the learning environment to allow for transformative learning to take place [27] and which of the several off-the shelf online applications were preferred by learners [26]. Several vocal critiques rejected connectivism as a learning theory [4] and then as a "naive and damaging blip in the educational media's long and carefully grounded history" [2].

Behavioural cognitivism and xMOOCs

cMOOCs inspired the second wave of courses (xMOOCs) which stood in contrast in both pedagogy and philosophical foundation. The scale of courses increased, with some reaching more than 100,000 registered students. This new generation of xMOOCs were inspired by behavioural cognitivism, and focused on the acquisition of information pre-defined in a linear curriculum, communicated to learners by means of online videos and articles, and assessed through online quizzes and automatically- or peer-reviewed assignments. Where in cMOOCs knowledge was generative, in xMOOCs it was declarative [45]. Furthermore, in xMOOCs the relationship between teacher and students is limited, and the knowledge is "transmitted" to students. Interaction in xMOOCs is mediated by (mostly) proprietary platforms, with course content typically protected by restrictive licenses that do not allow sharing [45].

Scholarly discourse on xMOOCs focuses on learning analytics (learners' unique learning paths through course content in a constrained and predefined platform environment), optimisation of user experience to minimise attrition, and assessment (in the context of MOOCs as substitute for brick-and-mortar based delivery) [46]. The lack of innovation in MOOC pedagogy is the predominant axis of critique, with MOOCs' unidirectional structure seen as failing to capture the transformational potential of education [44].

Supporting online collaborative learning

Since 2013 ('the year of the MOOC') the landscape of MOOCs has seen innovation in approaches to tackle the challenge of learner engagement, assessment and feedback. New takes on developing online interactions between learners and course organisers included DOCCs (distributed online collaborative courses), BOOCs (big open online courses), SMOCs (synchronous massive online courses), SPOCs (small private online courses) and corporate MOOCs [5]. In particular, recent experiments with SPOCs have shown promise. In March 2014 Harvard Business School launched HBX, a proprietary platform for executive business courses that demonstrated high engagement of learners in the course (by facilitating more interaction between students and organisers) [19]. Other edX courses have demonstrated a positive improvement on the quality of student assignment quality when a smaller group (132 students) is given assistance from a higher number (15) of teaching fellows [13]. Similar positive experiences in terms of student engagement and higher quality instruction were noted also in Harvard's CopyrightX course, where a pre-selected group of students engaged in group discussion, managed by a group of TFs, using videoconferencing [13].

Self-organisation in learning

SOLEs originated through Sugata Mitra's early research into unsupervised learning using computers [38]. Mitra points to self-organisation originating as a physics term, describing a system which exhibits an emerging behaviour via local interactions but without centralised control, which in its application to education Mitra calls "learning at the edge of chaos" [35]. The Internet allows for children to explore a variety of resources, many created with adults in mind, to decode meaning and answer big questions while working in small groups [35].

The earliest experiments of Mitra describe the learning that took place when young children, with no computer literacy are given access to computers – they learn to use the different functionalities, discover various programs and teach one another about their discoveries [36,37,38]. Later work included different configurations of these experiments [8,39]. The authors were inspired by this learner oriented, connectivity (to Internet and others) driven approach to learning and wanted to see what elements of the SOLE methods can be adapted to run a large scale online course that empowers a community of young activists.

DESIGN GOALS

Our goal was to establish the characteristics of an infrastructure to support online learning for would-be activists through the design, deployment and evaluation of actual courses. Our work in part returned to many of the ideas of cMOOCs (peer-to-peer interaction, diversity and high levels of learner autonomy), but also includes structural elements of successful online communities. This required us to address the inadequacies of existing platforms for building activist learning communities: both online learning platforms and targeted civic education social platforms.

However, although inspired by cMOOCs, which operated without a formal learning management system, we decided against this approach in its purest form (given some cMOOC learners' reports of chaotic experiences and feelings of being overwhelmed [26, 27, 32]) and instead included elements of structure that we believed would appeal to our younger, less experienced, learners. On the other hand, we did not want to use an LMS inspired by behaviourist approaches to education (such as Coursera) and while alternative LMSs, such as Moodle (see also Blackboard, Piazza, etc.), place some emphasis on user generated content and provide support for the creation of communities of practice (through its social features such as forums), we were concerned that student engagement and the creation of lasting social connections would be made difficult if we fully relied on custom infrastructure.

Given that our work is informed by connectivist and learner-agency and community-based theories, and the potential of integrating social media in education has been shown by several research studies [5,15], we instead utilised a custom designed website and a range of existing social media applications and utilities (Facebook, Google+, YouTube, Twitter, etc.). Task design included course materials such as syllabus, training materials for course organisers, mentors, learners, communication templates, etc. Additional design considerations concerned the methodology of learning and teaching, selection of interaction modes with expert lecturers, structure of weekly discussion sessions and type of assignments to be given out.

The online learning infrastructure had to respond to several design objectives: (1) to empower learners to begin their own social mission driven initiatives (with the support of the created learning community and through careful scaffolding); (2) to enable learners to get to know one another and share their unique experiences (through asynchronous communication via messaging and social media and synchronous discussion in small groups); and (3) to facilitate self-organisation of learners, who are both able to effectively follow unique learning paths and effectively follow course schedules and materials in an easy-to-use way both synchronously and asynchronously (videos, articles, content created and shared by others). Our approach was specifically tailored to the needs of people with high levels of self-efficacy and digital literacy.

ONLINE UWC: FROM IDEA TO IMPLEMENTATION

We ran three cycles of design, deployment and evaluation through three configurations of an extracurricular online course focused on the topic of sustainable development. The young learners (14-20 year-olds) were pre-selected based on their written applications. We gathered participant applications and participant and mentor feedback for each edition of the course, as well as a set of quantitative metrics such as group sessions participation or live and on-demand views of video lectures.

We changed and improved some elements of course design in each edition to compare results in the final stage. The goal of the first edition was to test the learning approach with a small pilot group of 10 learners before rolling out to a larger audience. The second edition focused specifically on learner engagement and mastering logistics by working with 86 learners in three different time zones (London, Hong Kong and New York). The third edition had 18 learners and focused on understanding the scaffolding process for projects and the role of mentors in the success of future courses. We conducted a detailed analysis at the end of each edition to provide grounds for design recommendations with the aim to establish which design elements help facilitate activism through collaborative learning while allowing the learners to have more control over their own learning.

The First Edition

The initial Online UWC infrastructure design was guided by theoretical best practices presented in online education literature [1,3,14,24,25]. We used Google Course Builder to build the website and present course schedule and materials given the simplicity of deployment as well as the ability to heavily customize the website in the future. We included social media communication channels to provide sociability tools for the participants required for the creation of social bonds [42], which were not part of Google Course Builder's design.

The course was designed to support user engagement, inspired by prior research findings [1,3,14,24,25]. Learners had to complete an application form prior to admission for the course as well as commit to paying a small fee, which served to promote commitment to the course [13,40]. Learners unable to pay the fee were asked to apply for financial aid, which was granted if candidates met (lenient) eligibility criteria. A key element of our design was the inclusion of mentors to help run the course whose presence has been shown to encourage higher level of engagement in online courses [40]. Our mentors were aged 15-30 and came from a variety of backgrounds (business, academia, NGOs) and were all alumni of United World Colleges. The main role of mentors was to be the point of contact for learners: troubleshoot technical difficulties, clarify any confusion about the course schedule, communicate via email, the website and on the Facebook group [7].

Additionally, the application process, which was open to candidates from all over the world, helped to assure that the admitted candidates shared a set of common values, a condition that helps create effective online communities [42] and had a basic working knowledge of English. What the learners, mentors and experts had in common was their passion for building a more peaceful and sustainable world.

The course design introduced enough structure to keep the learners oriented, while offering enough flexibility to help them negotiate their learning objectives, problem-solve and explore different areas of knowledge in real life conditions (as per SOLEs). The course schedule (including a communications calendar) followed a simple weekly structure (see Table 1) in order to help orient the learners, as recommended by previous research [14]. Learners were given their weekly assignments on Sunday, which typically consisted of links to assigned videos and readings (newspaper articles, TED talks). Each Wednesday, an expert lecturer would talk about the week's sustainability topic (via Hangout on Air, later shared on a YouTube channel). On Thursday, the learners took turns in chairing or facilitating a discussion on the week's topic. The weekly chairs received a short briefing over email to propose some ideas or structure that they should use in this learner-led discussion class. Learners were then given assignments to be completed by the following week (often in pairs or small groups).

Metric	When	Scale	SO*
Weekly email	Sun/Mon	All	No
Hangout on Air	Tue/Wed	All	Yes
Hangout	Thu	3-10	Yes
Assignment	Fri	All	Yes
Big FB group	Continuous	All	Yes
Small FB group	Continuous	3-10	Yes

Table 1. Approximate course schedule and interaction modes. *SO qualified whether or not task type included elements of self-organization.

We designed learning tasks to resemble the work of activists (e.g. working together in small groups to create written, rich media and video materials, discussions about means to solve environmental issues). Learners were challenged with real-world problems, which were relevant to their communities. We aimed to ensure that learners knew that they were not expected to hand in a traditional "paper" as a response to assignment prompts, but an output in a format of their own choosing, such as audio files, videos, animations, drawings, PowerPoint presentations, Prezis etc. Thus their imagination and technical skills were the only limit for how they chose to work together and present their results. Additionally, we emphasised the importance of experts having activist background, to serve as role models for the learners. The experts were sustainable development practitioners (activists, entrepreneurs, academics, etc.). They presented their career experiences as well as an overview of the topic grounded in their own experience during the weekly expert Hangouts.

Throughout the course learners were encouraged as much as possible to become course co-creators, to both increase their own sense of self-sufficiency, and to meet the design goal of self-organisation. Learners were encouraged to find more materials that were relevant to the topic of the week and share them with others. They interacted with lecturers and classmates live through Google Hangouts, and synchronously/asynchronously on Facebook, voted on the topics they most wanted to study, recommended and invited guest lecturers they found exciting, and were continuously challenged to co-create the curriculum through discussion with their classmates and the organisers.

Evaluation of the first course

Ahead of the second course, we conducted two rounds of feedback (one mid- and one post-first course) to enquire about learners' satisfaction with the model provided and to establish which design elements should be further explored in the second course configuration. Learners reported enjoying communicating with others in different countries and wished for even more opportunities to make personal connections. Out of 6 responses in the end-of-course survey, 1 learner said that the course did not give them the opportunity to meet others, and even of the 4 learners who answered "Yes, but…" hoped for more opportunities to get to know each other: *"I thought we could use more time getting to know each other. There are students I never got to know."* (C1R5)

Additionally, based on feedback questionnaires, several students were confused about the different modes of communication and were not clear about using the technology needed to participate in the course (6 out of 11 responses to question about improvement ideas mention learner confusion).

We also started accepting applications for the next course, which gave us more insight into student motivation. Based on a review of applications for the second course, we established that making a difference in communities was a primary driver for participation: 55 of the 189 approved explicitly mentioned themes relating to concern for their communities (local:27 and global:28), for example as participant C2S150[1] explained: *"I would like to learn more about sustainability because it is a way to make the world better, not just being worried about the social, climate and economic problems: learning about sustainability gives you instruments to use in your city, country and all over the world in order to take care of the planet and making it last for future generations."*

The Second Edition

Recognising the importance of community impact to applicants, we refocused the second edition around community projects – students were asked to consider ideas from the first week and were guided into implementation of their ideas throughout the course. Ahead of the October course, a new website was set up. In the first edition of the course we did not have a formal scaffolding process to create and discuss projects. Consequently, no community projects had been created in the course. The key feature of the new website was that it allowed users to create user profiles and set up projects. Students could share links to their projects, share them on Facebook, and like, follow and comment on their peers' projects.

We addressed the need to strengthen bonds between students by reinforcing the sense of community. For example, we implemented a suggestion offered by C1S4: *"I would suggest you to make people write a brief presentation including not just why do participate in course... But whatever they want to share and send the presentations to all participants before the course starts, it could help to know a bit more one other."* We used the first task as an opportunity to present oneself in the Facebook group and gave an example with custom creative videos we made. We also made sure that everyone had a chance to introduce themselves and felt comfortable in an online Hangout before diving into the class content (a message that was reinforced both through mentor training and

[1] For CxSy: "x" is the course edition, "Sy" a student; CxMy: "My" a mentor, and CxSMy: "SMy" is a student mentor.

student chair briefing notes). We also provided more structure to welcome newcomers in a prominent space on our new course website to ensure that learners, used to a traditional learning structure, would not be surprised by self-organised elements of the course.

Ahead of the course we also sought to create a community of mentors through repeated communications by emails and Hangouts, in which best practices were shared as well as help solicited in course material creation. We also gave the opportunity for one alumnus of the first course (familiar with its methods) to become the first student-mentor, and to investigate learner attachment to mentors we swapped mentors half way through the course. Finally, we strengthened the structure of the course by clearly defining a communication schedule for the courses, providing a schedule ahead of the courses and empowering mentors as intermediaries between students and course organisers. We had noticed that communication about course logistics took too much of the students' attention in the first course (54% of posts and comments related to discussing logistics).

Evaluation of the second course

Throughout the course 41 projects were set up (for 86 active students). Projects comprised an image, a short description, and next steps needed for implementation (see Figure 1). Students had to create a profile on the course website in order to create new projects, or follow or like other projects. Projects created on the website were generally well thought out and many included user created graphics. Ideas included education-related projects (creating a green contest or Model United Nations club at local school), environment related projects (reducing water usage, creating a recycling project), and social welfare projects (refugee inclusion project, homelessness).

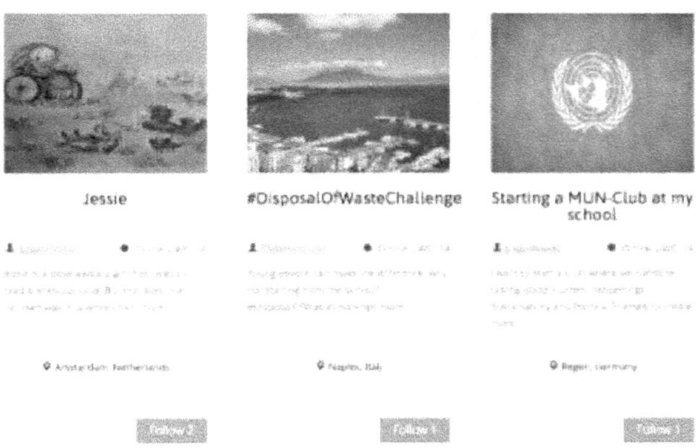

Figure 1. Example student projects set up on course website.

A refreshed, more attractive website paired with a social media marketing campaign resulted in a ten-fold increase in applicants. This larger scale deployment required us to consider design elements necessary to manage a larger user base. The course required significant time investment from course organisers (including administrative tasks such as splitting students and mentors into groups, coordinating scheduling and setting up calendar invitations for all groups, tracking attendance and assignment completion, answering questions from a much larger number of students etc.). Live lectures had to be organised in three different time zones. The 20 mentors who joined the learning community had to be induced into the community. As course organisers we noticed that the time commitment required to run the course per week almost doubled vs. the first edition.

Mentors helped prepare class materials ahead of the course and they also helped recruit a number of experts, which significantly helped the organising team. The student mentor (C2SM1) who participated in the course enjoyed the experience and did not report specific problems relating to their being an alumnus. Mentors also took on leadership roles as needed: "*In the second session it was the chair having difficulties with the tec[h]nical part. That is why I had to take over*" (C2M4). Swapping mentors half-way through the course did not have a positive impact on class. As student C2R3 observed: "*Switching mentors was more confusing than "rewarding".*" Mentor C2M5 confirmed this: "*I don't think changing the mentors was a good idea because we just started building a relationship of trust and fun together that was ended very abruptly.*"

Mentors provided feedback about interactions inside the small Hangouts. 13 out of 30 (43%) responses mentioned low attendance as a problem. Mentor C2M5 commented: "*What could be improved is to have a better "emergency plan" in case only a limited amount of students shows up and the planned discussion is not possible.*" Many students could not make it to class because of technical issues: "*We had 14 students assigned, out of which 5 made it. Some were having tech difficulties*" *(C2M1).* Other groups had the opposite problem: "*The hangouts are only designed for up to 10 people. As we have 14 in the group this meant some people couldn't join.*" (C2M4).

Mentor responses shed light on the different sources of technical issues faced by the students, including power shortages in their towns, slow internet connection, social media being blocked at school, and issues with unmuting microphone or unlocking the camera. 68% of mentor responses mentioned the presence of technical difficulties for one or more participant.

The Third Edition

The third edition aimed to explore a simpler interface to set up project ideas (without detailed user profiles or numerous description fields). We also further experimented with the role of the mentor. While in the first edition of the course we had assigned two mentors to each class, in this edition we assigned one mentor to half the groups. Additionally, we increased the number of student mentors: a third of mentors were alumni of previous courses.

Evaluation of the third course

We used a simple Google Slides template to limit friction at project set-up and encouraged students to update their entries throughout the course. While the overall number of projects per learner increased from 48% to 67%, the number of projects for which completion evidence emerged in the following 12 months decreased from 21% to 17%. The implications of not having mentor back-up became apparent when one of the mentors forgot about his session in the first week of the course, which resulted in several messages on the Facebook group from confused students. Similar events happened the following week (explaining an increase in logistics related posts and comments between the second and third). However, student mentors met expectations and were able to effectively run group sessions. Indeed, they were the only ones who provided feedback after the end of the course. Experiences of this edition highlighted the crucial role that mentors play for the effectiveness of an online community of young learners.

FINDINGS

By reflecting across the three editions of the course we are able to revisit our three primary objectives: (1) empowering students to begin their own social mission driven initiatives (2) enabling students to get to know one another and share their unique experiences; and (3) to facilitate self-organisation of students. Table 2 presents summary statistics for the three editions of the course.

Metric	2014-06	2014-10	2015-03
# Actives	10	86	18
% Graduated	70%	77%	67%
Students / Mentors	3.3	4.3	1.8
WT / Student	58	173	161
Posts / Participant	5.8	6.0	8.1
Projects Set Up	0	41	12
Impact Evidenced	3	18	3

Table 2. Summary statistics for the three editions of the course. Number of active students measured as students who attended at least one group discussion session. Watch Time (WT) denoted in minutes. Impact evidenced calculated as projects in which an individual took part (can be more than one per individual).

Promoting activist involvement

We can consider both the primary and secondary effects of creating this activist community through the three editions of the online course. The primary effect was that students learned about different ways in which they can get involved in their community and created 52 community projects throughout the three editions of the course. In participant surveys 76% of student respondents mentioned that the course helped them think about creating their own project, with the highest proportion (83% in the October 2014 course, and the lowest in the June 2014 course where projects were not emphasised or scaffolded throughout the course). In the feedback respondents clarified that project-focused lectures and feedback from peers in their class showed them the importance of iteration and community research before setting out to build a project (12 of 23 responses mentioned the importance of peers or expert lectures). Additionally, 2 of 23 students who responded positively mentioned they already had been involved in volunteering projects when they started the course.

Figure 2. Online UWC students present what they learned in the course at their school

Over a period of 12 months following the courses, evidence emerged of at least 24 instances of student involvement in activist endeavours. In the second course, United Youth Journalists projects emerged one month after the course. The initial post by C2S46 (we present its beginning below) shared details of a simple idea, which was discussed and iterated in 58 comments by other group members: *"I had this idea, I know in some ways it already exists but I was thinking about creating a website in English with who is interested in writing articles about his country."* This eventually led to the creation of a separate online community and consequently, an online magazine that has since published more than 110 articles [52]. What was striking about this example is that the project emerged not as a formal classroom assignment, but as an idea that was floated within the group after the course has ended and happened on the private discussion group. Students wanted to engage as equal partners – did not want help from course organisers – wanted to do their own project, which they would manage on their own. At the same time, this example evidenced the existence of a community that does not cease to exist after the class is over, and the benefit of using Facebook instead of custom software as a means of building and sustaining engagement in the learning community.

The secondary effect was that many of the projects were promoted outside of the direct online classroom and involved the creation of outside learning communities. The example above resulted in the creation of a Facebook page (which at the time of writing has over 3,500 followers) where members share their articles with their friends network, further expanding its reach. Other students provided evidence for conducting presentations about sustainable development issues in their schools (see Figure 2), further increasing the impact of their online participation to real-world communities.

Promoting community

As we adapted design elements to reinforce community building, we saw positive impact both on social aspects of the community and on activist outcomes. The second and third edition of the course, where we put a large emphasis on creating a community of learners (see Figure 3), saw a larger number of posts on the course's Facebook group per student. The second course, which had the highest number of participants, also saw the highest number of comments per participant (15 per student vs. 11 per student in the third edition and 2 in the first edition). As one student explained, getting to know others helped him share ideas: *"We weren't very comfortable around each other at first and it took us a while to actually be more comfortable and have good discussions"* (C2S6).

In the second course, we also observed that students wanted to go to a smaller subset of their group where they found interaction more manageable. When asked about their preferred mode of communication (multiple preferences were allowed), 100% of respondents in the first and third editions of the course (both had less than 20 participants) identified the overall course Facebook group, as compared to only 40% in the second course; 70% identified small discussion groups, 60% Hangouts and 50% email. By contrast, students in the third edition of the course (which was smaller than the second but where creating social connections was reinforced unlike in the first) were the most satisfied with the degree to which they got to know each other throughout the course (3.3 average score out of 4, with first course at 2.8 and second at 3.0).

Moreover, many students mentioned in their feedback that they enjoyed meeting others from different countries; for example: *"It was very interesting to find out new things about other countries. I also realized things about my country that I didn't know before." (C2R10)*. Other evidence of the strength of bonds formed was the fact that students were not only meeting in real life when they travelled to other countries, but they also shared these news in photo updates with the rest of the communities.

Figure 3. Example of playful community building during one group Hangout.

Promoting self-organisation

There were two ways in which evidence of self-organisation emerged throughout the courses: participants helping each other solve logistical and communication issues, and sharing external materials (articles, videos, or personal stories) to propose new discussion topics (see Table 3).

Type	2014-06	2014-10	2015-03
Assignments	12%	23%	40%
Relationships	4%	37%	16%
Logistics	54%	13%	27%
Content sharing	17%	12%	8%
Technical issues	7%	7%	8%
Self help	5%	4%	0%
Connection invites	0%	3%	0%
Other projects	1%	1%	1%

Table 3.. Percentage of topics of Facebook private group posts and comments per course edition.

Students self-organised to troubleshoot problems that related to both scheduling and technology. They also came up with ideas to better share course materials: one example from the first edition of the course included a suggestion to write up summary notes for group discussions so that those who were not able to participate can catch up. Taking live notes became a suggestion, which we shared with student chairs in future editions of the course.

Students also shared contact information to get in touch on external platforms (including WhatsApp, Instagram). Many individually connected as friends on Facebook to students, mentors and course organisers. Three posts on the topic elicited 52 responses from others wanting to share their contact details across other social media tools. Students contributed to co-creating course materials in several ways. They shared resources on Facebook and proposed discussion topics (~10% of posts and comments in all courses related to students sharing resources and discussion topics). In the first course one of the students proposed to get in touch with an expert they wanted to meet, approach them to arrange the Hangout (which was rated 4.3 out of 5 by course participants). 73% of the students who responded to the survey enjoyed the group discussion facilitated by the student chair.

Students contributed questions to drive discussion with lecturers (who only spoke for the first 15-20 minutes with the rest of the time devoted to answering student questions). A great example of interactivity in Hangout on Air lecture occurred during a Week 2 Video lecture on the topic of Inclusive Cities, which attracted a total of 40 comments [41]. Several provided feedback to the lecturer in case things were not clear or if Internet connection was intermittent. Students were making connections between the case studies presented by lecturers and their own contexts: *"What would you do for pass the ideas of Curitiba and Waterloo to a big city like Mexico City, for have a really impact considering the population size?" (C2S142)* or *"What do you suggest leaders like Stephen Harper (Canada's prime minister for those of you who don't know) do to act on climate change?" (C2S87)*. Students also provided live comments or question some of the materials presented by expert lecturers: *"We live in a Tropical country! And we don't have sidewalks. Use the bicycle as transportation to distant places is impossible because it's hot out there!" (C2S153)*.

Mentor survey results showed that 60% of responses about group discussions mentioned that the student chair performance was good: for example *"the student chair was very strong" (C2M15), "the student chairing went well"* (C2M5). At the same time, it should be noted that only 35% of discussion sessions were chaired by students, due to the small number of students (usually 3 or 4 per discussion session instead of 10 in a group). Mentors also referred to the under-preparation of some student chairs or technical difficulties that they faced, which led to mentors taking over.

As another element of self-organisation, we allowed students to find project partners from other countries and set-up working with them on joint projects. Students in all three courses reported enjoying the experience (81% of students who responded to this survey question), but while students valued the interactions, many voiced concerns and frustration about having to find other active students without the help of the platform (30% of the students who responded). The following response is representative of many students' frustrations: *"I don't understand how you expected us to work with students from other regions through the web. I did, but it was complicated to get together, there was a platform missing."* (C2S14)

As course organising processes improved (we launched a full weekly curriculum plan ahead of the March 2015 course) some elements of student organisation decreased but the content sharing element of self-organisation increased. This is evidenced by the fact that participants engaged in longer discussions, with content sharing posts made by students attracting 1 comment each on average in the first edition of the course, 2 in the second edition and 7 in the third. Students also posted longer comments (with some of them as long as 500+ word opinion papers).

DESIGN IMPLICATIONS

Our three editions of the course correspond to three configurations of infrastructure for supporting learning, and in summary demonstrated that it is possible to realise the characteristics we set as objectives using a loosely coupled set of media. However, this became increasingly difficult when the number of participants exceeded 100. In particular, while the social media channels used were clearly valuable for engaging students, they lacked several features necessary to foster community building and early stage project feedback processes. As a result we have identified several implications for the design of a learning infrastructure that will better meet our three objectives.

Logistics and mechanics of activist learning

Learning infrastructure should aim to minimize distractions that do not directly support our design objectives. An important way to enable this is to ensure the seamlessness of the logistics of the course and the mechanics of its operation for course organisers, mentors and students (especially as the scale of the course increases).

Organise the resources

Infrastructure must clearly lay out the rhythm, pacing and expectations of learning activities, as well as allow the students to interact with others, in a space that is dedicated to learning. It must allow the course organisers to drive dynamic communications and social media re-engagement. Infrastructure needs to provide an access point for students to course resources, schedules of key events, and assignments. Key features are likely to include access to the syllabus, recommended resources and links to live video lectures, and ways for students to find each other on social media and submit assignments and project ideas.

Enable creative expression in tasks

The creation of community projects (and any other assignments) should allow students to express themselves creatively, including allowing them to upload and embed pictures and video files. Students should not only have the capacity to like or comment a project, but also to search for projects that are of interest to them. Finally, task design should reinforce the importance of providing feedback.

Automate mundane tasks

From the course organiser's point of view, infrastructure must make it possible to recruit the students into the course, plan course interactions (such as weekly Hangout sessions and expert lectures, assignments and weekly emails), execute course interactions (e.g. send out the weekly reminder emails) and establish participation achievements after the course (e.g. participation and assignment completion data).

Supporting scale and sustainability

Several design components can support scale. Especially the complex task of setting up schedules and reschedules of group sessions needs to be devised for a large-scale deployment (i.e. more than 100 students). Students should be put into groups based on preferred time availability and maximum diversity within a group. Our three deployments, demonstrate the positive impact of mentors on learning, and mechanisms are required for recruiting mentors, both from previous course alumni and separately, ahead of the course. In particular, infrastructure must support the potential for students to transition from the role of student to mentor. Designing for scale also has implications across (as well as within) courses, as infrastructure must allow new organisers to create their own communities and courses, and include commissioning tools to help organisers sample interest before significant resources are devoted to curriculum development.

Focus on learning
The focus of the learning infrastructure should be the organisation of courses, and while it should allow for students to remain part of the community, as alumni and potential future student-mentors or experts, it should encourage members to only use the platform for brainstorming before moving to external platforms (such as custom built websites or Facebook communities) to continue building their projects and stay in touch with others as best suits their respective needs.

Community building and reinforcing community layers
Learning infrastructure should be structured around the community itself, rather than the content, and focus on the development of lasting collaborations between students and enablement of impact through activism.

Layer community engagement
All layers of community engagement are important for effective activist classes. Interaction in larger groups allows for students to get to know others from different countries and feel they are participating in a vibrant and lively community that allows for the spontaneous sharing of ideas and a diversity of perspectives in learner initiated online discussions. At the same time, smaller groups promote more in-depth conversations and give the opportunity to provide higher quality feedback as students become more familiar with each other, and more willing to share their thoughts. A key requirement is that students should be able to easily navigate between the different layers of the community, from big course groups to smaller discussion groups, as well as be able to find and communicate with individual students (e.g. pair up for group projects).

Surface student presence
Allowing students to know who is in their group and be able to connect with them easily is a fundamental requirement. When students can easily identify who else has been active in the course, they can connect with more ease to complete assignments together. When students and mentors know who is planning to attend a group Hangout discussion, they can adjust the schedule if needed ahead of time to ensure the required number of participants is met, and create a new event in the rare case that all 12 participants assigned to the discussion session would plan to attend. The students should also have the opportunity to negotiate the time of their attendance every week to suit their personal circumstances.

Reinforce community leaders
Strong community leaders (mentors, student-chairs) are key enablers of activist learning. Mentors help guide newcomers through the community, help facilitate engaging discussions and escalate more difficult questions to course organisers, but their recruitment and training takes time. The student-chair model works well with groups that have full participation showing potential for engaging learners in leadership roles. Larger scale learning environments will benefit from incorporating design elements that promote such learner leadership.

Self organisation: focus on central skills
Two types of self-organisation during the course were observed: one that was driven by frustration from the inefficiency of tools used, and one that involved students sharing their opinions and thoughts with others.

Tackle technology problems upfront
Technology issues have consistently been an issue for several participants – despite almost ubiquitous access to the Internet, both the connection strength and hardware used for connecting to class materials will likely cause challenges. Learning infrastructure must be capable of coordinating between tools that are familiar to the students (i.e. social media, video conferencing tools). It is also necessary to provide resources for learners to refer to, in the event of problems arising, and to encourage them to set up and test their technology ahead of key activities (e.g. the group Hangout).

Make negotiation of learning a habit
Course organisers should be able to provide a clear structure to a course but also allow students to negotiate the modes of their participation (e.g. by inviting additional expert speakers or submitting assignments on a personally selected topic). While many students and mentors may still choose the default, the platform should readily surface and reward innovation and customisation with a view to inspire others to experiment. Design elements which encourage students to negotiate their learning and actively co-create course content should be implemented.

CONCLUSIONS
Our study involved the design and deployment of three configurations of social media and communication technologies to deliver online learning, followed by the evaluation and analysis of, and reflection on, student and mentor behaviour and outcomes. Our design recommendations comprise several principles for creating infrastructure to support online learning targeted specifically at communities of would-be social innovators and activists. We see widespread application for such activist-oriented learning infrastructure, from NGOs (for many of which education activities are central to their mission) and companies (aiming to increase international knowledge sharing among employees), to traditional educational institutions seeking to re-engage their alumni communities.

ACKNOWLEDGMENTS
This work was funded by the Research Investment Fund at Newcastle University and EPSRC award EP/M023001/1 (DERC). Data supporting this publication is openly available under an 'Open Data Commons Open Database License'. Additional metadata are available at: 10.17634/154300-17. Please contact Newcastle Research Data Service at rdm@ncl.ac.uk for access instructions. Special thanks to Robin Tyne and Victoria Alleyne for their precious help and to all Online UWC students and mentors for their enthusiastic participation.

REFERENCES

1. Panagiotis Adamopoulos. 2013. What Makes a Great MOOC? An Interdisciplinary Analysis of Student Retention in Online Courses. *Thirty Fourth International Conference on Information Systems*: 1–21.
2. Jon Baggaley. 2014. MOOC postscript. *Distance Education* 35, 1: 126–132. http://doi.org/10.1080/01587919.2013.876142
3. Maha Bali. 2014. MOOC Pedagogy: Gleaning Good Practice from Existing MOOCs. *MERLOT Journal of Online Learning and Teaching* 10, 1: 44–56.
4. Frances Bell. 2011. Connectivism: Its place in Theory-informed research and innovation in technology-enabled learning. *International Review of Research in Open and Distance Learning* 12, 3: 98–118.
5. Marta Cuesta, Monica Eklund, Ingegerd Rydin, and Ann-katrin Witt. 2016. Using Facebook as a co-learning community in higher education. 9884, January. http://doi.org/10.1080/17439884.2015.1064952
6. Alex Cusack, 2014. *A Handy Cheat Sheet on MOOCs*. Retrieved on September 26, 2015 from https://www.edsurge.com/news/2014-01-10-a-handy-cheatsheet-on-moocs
7. Margarita V. Divall and Jennifer L. Kirwin. 2012. Using Facebook to facilitate course-related discussion between students and faculty members. American Journal of Pharmaceutical Education 76, 2: 1–5. http://doi.org/10.5688/ajpe76232
8. Paul Dolan, David Leat, Laura Mazzoli Smith, Sugata Mitra, Liz Todd, and Kate Wall. 2014. Self-Organised Learning Environments (SOLEs) in an English School: an example of transformative pedagogy? *The Online Educational Research Journal*.
9. Stephen Downes. 2012. Creating the Connectivist Course. *One Change a Day*. Retrieved on September 25, 2015 from http://moocblogcalendar.wordpress.com/2012/01/03/creating-the-connectivist-course/
10. Andrea Forte, Niki Kittur, Vanessa Larco, and H Zhu. 2012. Coordination and beyond: social functions of groups in open content production. p. 417–426. http://doi.org/10.1145/2145204.2145270
11. Andrea Forte and Amy Bruckman. 2008. Scaling consensus: Increasing decentralization in Wikipedia governance. *Proceedings of the Annual Hawaii International Conference on System Sciences*: 15–17. http://doi.org/10.1109/HICSS.2008.383
12. Buckminster Fuller, 1962. Education Automation: Freeing the Scholar to Go Back to His Studies. Southern Illinois University Press.
13. Stephanie Garloch, 2015. Is small beautiful? Online education looks beyond the MOOC. Harvard Magazine. Retrieved on August 17, 2015 from: http://harvardmagazine.com/2015/07/is-small-beautiful
14. Lourdes Guàrdia, Marcelo Maina, and Albert Sangrà. 2013. MOOC Design Principles. A Pedagogical Approach from the Learner's Perspective. *eLearning Papers* 33, May: 1–6.
15. Christine Greenhow and Cathy Lewin. 2015. Social media and education: reconceptualizing the boundaries of formal and informal learning. Learning, Media and Technology 9884, January: 1–25. http://doi.org/10.1080/17439884.2015.1064954
16. Noriko Hara and By Huang. 2011. Online social movements. Annual review of information science and Technology: 489–522. http://doi.org/10.1002/aris.2011.1440450117
17. Summer Harlow and Dustin Harp. 2012. Collective Action on the Web. Information, Communication & Society 15, 2: 196–216. http://doi.org/10.1080/1369118X.2011.591411
18. Lindsey Harness. 2011. Virtual Communities: Bowling Alone, Online Together. *Quarterly Journal of Speech* 97, 1: 117–120. http://doi.org/10.1080/00335630.2010.541279
19. Harvard Magazine. Harvard Business School Launches HBX. Retrieved on August 22, 2015 from http://harvardmagazine.com/2014/03/harvard-business-school-launches-online-hbx
20. Andrew Dean Ho, Isaac Chuang, Justin Reich, et al. 2015. HarvardX and MITx : Two Years of Open Online Courses Fall 2012-Summer 2014. *SSRN Electronic Journal*, 10: 1–37. http://doi.org/10.2139/ssrn.2586847
21. Andrew Dean Ho, Justin Reich, Sergiy O Nesterko, et al. 2014. HarvardX and MITx: The First Year of Open Online Courses, Fall 2012-Summer 2013. *SSRN Electronic Journal*, 1: 1–33. http://doi.org/10.2139/ssrn.2381263
22. Philip N Howard, Aiden Duffy, Deen Freelon, Muzammil Hussain, Will Mari, and Mrawa Mazaid. 2011. What was the role of social media during the Arab Spring ? Project on Information Technologu and Political Islam: 1–30. http://doi.org/10.1007/s13398-014-0173-7.2
23. Jeffrey S Juris. 2012. Reflections on #Occupy Everywhere: Social media, public space, and emerging logics of aggregation. American Ethnologist 39, 2: 259–279. http://doi.org/10.1111/j.1548-1425.2012.01362.x
24. Habibul Haque Khondker. 2011. Role of the New Media in the Arab Spring. Globalizations 8, 5: 675–679. http://doi.org/10.1080/14747731.2011.621287

25. Rita Kop. 2011. The challenges to connectivist learning on open online networks: Learning experiences during a massive open online course. *International Review of Research in Open and Distance Learning* 12, 3: 19–38.
26. Rita Kop and Fiona Carroll. 2011. Cloud Computing and Creativity: Learning on a Massive Open Online Course. *European Journal of Open, Distance and E-Learning*: 1–11. Retrieved from http://www.eurodl.org/?p=special&sp=articles&inum=2&article=457
27. Rita Kop, Helene Fournier, and John Sui Fai Mak. 2011. A Pedagogy of Abundance or a Pedagogy to Support Human Beings? Participant Support on Massive Open Online Courses. *International Review of Research in Open and Distance Learning* 12, 7: 74–93. Retrieved on September 26, 2015 from http://search.proquest.com/docview/1018483294?accountid=14624
28. Piotr Konieczny. 2009. Governance, Organization, and Democracy on the Internet: The Iron Law and the Evolution of Wikipedia. *Sociological Forum* 24, 1: 162–192. http://doi.org/10.1111/j.1573-7861.2008.01090.x
29. Stacey Kuznetsov. 2006. Motivations of contributors to Wikipedia. *ACM SIGCAS Computers and Society* 36, 2: 1–es. http://doi.org/10.1145/1215942.1215943
30. Jean Lave and Etienne Wenger. 1991. Situated learning: Legitimate peripheral participation. *Learning in doing* 95: 138. http://doi.org/10.2307/2804509
31. The John D, Catherine T Macarthur, and Foundation Series. 2008. Civic Life Online: Learning How Digital Media Can Engage Youth.
32. Jenny Mackness, S F J Mak, and Roy Williams. 2010. The Ideals and Reality of Participating in a MOOC. *Learning* 10, December 2011: 266–274. Retrieved from http://www.lancs.ac.uk/fss/organisations/netlc/past/nlc2010/abstracts/PDFs/Mackness.pdf
33. Benjamin Mako Hill. 2013. Almost Wikipedia : Eight Early Encyclopedia Projects and the Mechanisms of Collective Action. Massachusetts Institute of Technology: 1–38.
34. Martha Mccaughey (Editor), Michael Ayers (Editor). 2004. Cyberactivism: Online Activism in Theory and Practice. DOI:10.1080/01972240500253632
35. Sugata Mitra. 2014. The future of schooling: Children and learning at the edge of chaos. Prospects 44, 4: 547–558. http://doi.org/10.1007/s11125-014-9327-9
36. Mitra Sugata, Dangwa Ritu, Shiffon Chatterjee, Swati Jha, Ravinder S. Bisht, and Preeti Kapur. 2005. Acquisition of computing literacy on shared public computers: Children and the "hole in the wall." *Australasian Journal of Educational Technology* 21, 3: 407–426.
37. Sugata Mitra and Ritu Dangwal. 2010. Limits to self-organising systems of learning-the Kalikuppam experiment. *British Journal of Educational Technology* 41, 5: 672–688. http://doi.org/10.1111/j.1467-8535.2010.01077.x
38. Sugata Mitra and Vivek Rana. 2001. Minimally invasive education in India. *British Journal of Educational Technology* 32, 2: 221–232.
39. Newcastle University, 2014. *SOLE Central.* Retrieved on August 17, 2015 from: http://www.ncl.ac.uk/solecentral/
40. Daniel F. O. Onah, Jane Sinclair, and Russell Boyatt. 2014. Dropout rates of massive open online courses : behavioural patterns. *EDULEARN14 Proceedings*: 5825–5834. Retrieved on August 17, 2015 from http://wrap.warwick.ac.uk/65543/1/WRAP_9770711-cs-070115-edulearn2014.pdf
41. Online UWC. Empower Inclusive, Productive and Resilient Cities, Video lecture for Online UWC, broadcast on October 9, 2014, Retried on January 5, 2016: https://plus.google.com/events/c28gb6q0jclfhr8t29avmids3n0
42. Jenny Preece. 2000. *Online Communities: Designing Usability and Supporting Sociability.*
43. Yuqing Ren, Robert Kraut, Sara Kiesler, and Paul Resnick. 2011. Encouraging commitment in online communities. *Evidence-based social design: Mining the social sciences to build online communities*: 77–125.
44. Robert A. Rhoads, Jennifer Berdan, and Brit Toven-Lindsey. 2013. The Open Courseware Movement in Higher Education: Unmasking Power and Raising Questions about the Movement's Democratic Potential. *Educational Theory* 63, 1: 87–110. http://doi.org/10.1111/edth.12011
45. Osvaldo Rodriguez. 2013. The concept of openness behind c and x-MOOCs (Massive Open Online Courses). *Open Praxis* 5, 1: 67–73. http://doi.org/10.5944/openpraxis.5.1.42
46. Cathy Sandeen. 2013. Assessment's Place in the New MOOC World. *Research and Practice in Assessment* 8, Summer: 5–12.
47. George Siemens. 2004. Connectivism : A Learning Theory for the Digital Age. *elearnspace.org*. Retrieved on September 25, 2015 from http://www.elearnspace.org/Articles/connectivism.htm
48. George Siemens. 2005. Learning Development Cycle: Bridging Learning Design and Modern Knowledge Needs. *elearnspace.org*. Retrieved on September 25, 2015 from http://www.elearnspace.org/Articles/ldc.htm
49. George Siemens. 2006. Connectivism: Learning Theory or Pastime of the Self-Amused?

elearnspace.org. Retrieved on September 25, 2015 from http://www.elearnspace.org/Articles/connectivism_self-amused.htm

50. Carmen Tschofen and Jenny Mackness. 2012. Connectivism and dimensions of individual experience. *International Review of Research in Open and Distance Learning* 13, 1: 124–143.
51. Hang Ung and Jean-Michel Dalle. 2010. Project management in the Wikipedia community. *Proceedings of the 6th International Symposium on Wikis and Open Collaboration*: 13:1–13:4. http://doi.org/http://doi.acm.org/10.1145/1832772.1832790
52. United Youth Journalists. Retrived on January 15, 2016 from http://unitedyouthjournalists.com/.
53. Etienne Wenger. 1998. *Communities of practice: Learning, meaning and identitiy.*

The Prediction Machine: Performing Scientific and Artistic Process

Rachel Jacobs & Steve Benford
University of Nottingham
Nottingham, UK
rachel.jacobs@nottingham.ac.uk

Ewa Luger
Microsoft Research
Cambridge, UK
ewluge@microsoft.com

Candice Howarth
Anglia Ruskin University
Cambridge, UK
candice.howarth@anglia.ac.uk

ABSTRACT
This paper responds to an increasing interest in how data-driven interactive artworks can support a greater understanding of the relationship between humans and data. This paper extends this work by focusing on the *The Prediction Machine*, an interactive and data-driven artwork that arose from collaborations between an artist, climate scientists, HCI researchers and the wider public. A study of the practice-led process reveals: (a) how the artist 'performed' scientific data across multiple outputs; (b) how the artist walked a line between scientific and artistic process; (c) how the public experienced data across multiple components of the artwork; (d) how the artwork can be seen as process rather than a exhibition or artifact; and (e) how tensions between artistic strategies and scientific processes inherent in the creation of data-driven artworks might inform future work involving public engagement with scientific data.

Author Keywords
Interactive art; environmentally engaged art; environmental data; sensory; embodied; performance; participatory sensing; sustainable HCI; authenticity; scientific process; climate data; performing data; big data

ACM Classification Keywords
H.5 Information Interfaces and Presentation

INTRODUCTION
Previous work within HCI has shown that 'ecologically engaged art' has the potential to stimulate and frame public debate around sustainability [12]. Data-driven artworks can inform strategies for public engagement, allowing for sensory, performative and multiple interpretations of complex scientific data such as climate data [21], engage the public in emotional and dialogic experiences of this data on a human scale [7], and explore new ways to represent statistical and numerical scientific data [41]. The growth of interest in and inherent tension between 'big data' and 'personal data' has called into question the relationship between humans, data, its legibility and provenance, inspiring manifestos such as Human-Data Interaction (HDI) [24]. Within this context, we wish to explore how data-driven socially and environmentally engaged art practices can offer alternative strategies for placing the human at the center of data-driven innovations, raising questions around the human, social experience of data.

In response, the following study maps the development of a specific artwork – *The Prediction Machine* – that engages the public with issues of climate change through sensory, performative and physicalised representations of climate and weather data, designed to stimulate ongoing dialogues with the public [44]. *The Prediction Machine* is a complex artwork involving multiple public outputs including an exhibited artwork and a series of public workshops. The exhibited artwork (which we describe in detail later on) comprises two interactive machines (see **Figure 1**), reminiscent of Victorian era fortune telling machines. The first machine prints out predictions for our climate 30 years in the future. The second machine allows visitors to input their own promises and predictions for the future, and discover more about the scientific processes that support how the predictions were made.

Figure 1. Exhibition of both machines

By studying the process of developing and exhibiting this work we reveal the strategies and processes employed by the artist throughout multiple public engagements. Through an analysis of the key findings from the study we present a

DIS 2016, June 04-08, 2016, Brisbane, QLD, Australia
© 2016 ACM. ISBN 978-1-4503-4031-1/16/06...$15.00
DOI: http://dx.doi.org/10.1145/2901790.2901825

detailed 'behind the scenes view' of the artists' approach to creating the work in collaboration with an interdisciplinary team, and the public's responses to the workshop activities and exhibitions - that took place as part of it's public presentation. The subsequent discussion examines how these artistic strategies engaged the public with scientific processes; and how the artist walked a line between scientific and artistic approaches to interpreting and representing the scientific data embedded within the work.

RELATED WORK

Despite increasing access to scientific information, research shows there are still low levels of scientific comprehension amongst the public of complex scientific problems, particularly around often contentious issues such as anthropogenic climate change [22], leading to many challenges for the communication of scientific data to the public. Added to this, the difficulty of reporting and representing issues of uncertainty in relation to scientific data more generally [29, 37] is compounded by methods of representation of risk and uncertainty in the media [5]. In response to these challenges, there have been calls for new forms of communication – particularly in reference to future climate modelling – that enable the public to engage with these issues through localized, personal and emotional discourses [25,31], opportunities for storytelling [32] and new forms of data conceptualisations [14]. Giannachi [15] argues that these new approaches require narratives that engage us on an emotional level in order to bring into play our rational, cognitive and intuitive thinking, and that scientists are looking increasingly to art and citizen science to provide these alternative approaches.

Previous research has explored how interactive and information based artists, often working under the banner of 'Sci-Art', offer a unique contribution to engaging the public with complex scientific issues [2,29,33,42]. More traditional arts practices, particularly those that are environmentally engaged, often involve artists taking on the role of activists, positioning themselves counter to scientific and technological thinking and rejecting what they see as 'technocratic prescriptions' – where, through the empirical positions of these scientific processes, nature in particular is seen as separate to humans and culture [11]. One of the key questions raised from these contrasting practices is how artists can engage with science, yet without becoming 'instrumental' or 'illustrative' [9]. This is particularly relevant where scientific data is treated as a new material without interrogating the meaning or the 'scientific-ness' of the processes of data capture, management and interpretation [41].

Within this broad space, a collection of artists have emerged from the traditions of performance art [39], interactive art and mixed reality performance [4], who are increasingly engaging in collaborations across science and the arts as an opportunity for dialogue with ecologists, scientists, technologists and most significantly the public [12]. Artists within this domain have begun to develop strategies for engaging the public with complex representations of scientific data by interrogating these scientific processes and exploring ways to engage with scientific data through intimate, sensory, embodied, personal, human-scale narratives, metaphors and aesthetics [20,41]. The resulting works explore shared values and exchanges across interdisciplinary practices, often through process-led experiences [18] rather than relying solely on the performance or exhibition of a final artifact.

In parallel, HCI research has begun to explore the tools and systems that allow these types of interdisciplinary, artist-led collaborations to occur [8,16]. Since 2000, HCI has witnessed a broad turn to the artistic, looking towards the arts and interaction design to enhance the discipline through more provocative, cultural and social experiences. As this work has evolved, research is increasingly exploring what HCI can learn from these data driven environmentally and socially engaged arts practices around the capture and representation of real world data [1,23,27]. Similar questions are also being explored from an interaction design perspective, where Froehlich's [13] eco-feedback designs and Holmes' eco-visualisations are offering new *"ways to dynamically visualise invisible environmental data"*, [19]. Yet much of this work focuses on the impact of the final artifact as opposed to the processes and strategies that have been embedded within it.

Many of the challenges inherent in bringing the diverse approaches of the disciplines of science and art together towards a process of *'continuous dialogue'* [15] are mirrored within the scientific community where, despite acknowledgement of the need to communicate uncertainties and engage the public with science communication in ways that *'touch peoples emotions'* [10], scientists remain skeptical about the role of subjective experience, how the language and aesthetics of art and the role of the senses can aid understandings of science and data. This is particularly relevant for complex issues such as climate change [29].

In response, an emerging area of interdisciplinary research is converging around theories of 'performativity' [36] and notions of 'data-mixing' [41]. West et al. propose a *"recombination and reappropriation practice intended to trigger novel subjective experiences and associations"*, that can contribute to the current crisis of representation, where data and science is often seen as *"remote from experiential and aesthetic concerns"*. The notion of 'performing data' has emerged from a similar perspective, whereby artists are employing performative strategies that can enable subtle, temporal and emotional representations of data [27,36]. This work is beginning to question existing assumptions of the value of scientific knowledge, exploring who the data belongs to and how it should be interpreted, in turn raising important questions for how we design systems to support public engagement with scientific data.

APPROACH

We now present a study of *The Prediction Machine* that took place across three phases: (1) initial research and development; (2) public engagement through a series of workshops and; (3) public exhibitions. The development of the artwork took place alongside a broader research project that involved building a toolkit (*The Performing Data Toolkit*) designed to support a variety of artworks (including *The Prediction Machine*) to capture, mediate and represent different forms of scientific data - including weather, wave and bio data [43].

Our methodology is practice-led, drawing on two approaches that have recently been proposed in HCI. Specifically, the artwork has been created by a professional artist in response to a series of external commissions and exhibition opportunities. This approach was then studied using a combination of ethnography as practiced in the approach of *Performance-Led Research in the Wild* [3], augmented with self-reflection by the artist - who also took on the role of one of the researchers - as practiced in the approach of *Design from Within* [35]. The following account therefore draws on both external ethnographic observations and the artists' own view of their rationale and process to offer a holistic perspective on how the artwork was developed and experienced.

Participants

The participants in the study were focused on (a) the artist (b) workshop participants (c) visitors to the exhibition. The first phase of public engagement workshops took place whilst the main machine was being built, involving one monthly session over a period of six months. These workshops brought together 40 scientists, academics and members of the public over the duration of the six months, with a core group of 6 participants who attended regularly. The second phase of workshops took place alongside each exhibition with pre-established groups connected to the venues where the exhibitions took place. These included a women's craft group, a creative writing group and an older men's group. The visitors to the exhibition were also from a wide background, the first exhibition took place in a public town library during a school holiday, the majority of the audience involved families and library users not expecting to experience contemporary art or contemplate issues of climate change. The second exhibition took place in a contemporary art gallery as part of a themed exhibition about nature and the environment, where visitors tended to be prepared to view and interact with contemporary artworks. The final exhibition took place at a media centre where again the visitors expected to interact with often complex and challenging artworks.

Capturing and analysing data

The workshops and exhibitions were observed and recorded through manual field notes, which detailed participant and artist interactions. Data from the interviews and observations were analysed separately using a thematic framework. 18 workshop participants were interviewed and 20 visitors to the exhibitions. The interviews were first transcribed and then coded, the codes were then grouped within organising themes and photographs were also taken. The field notes were coded independently and themes arising from both the interviews and observations were contrasted. The following findings are grouped along common themes arising from both analyses.

Interviews with the artist occurred after each session and were semi-structured in the loosest sense. Across all interviews, the researcher raised four themes; (i) the intentions of the artist, (ii) the extent to which they felt these have been realized, (iii) areas of success/concern, and (iiii) their ongoing plans. Interviews ranged in duration from 20 minutes to 1 hour in length. Workshop participant and exhibition visitor interviews were much shorter in duration so as not to intrude upon the experience and so necessarily took a more classically semi-structured form including questions around (i) their background, (ii) rationale for involvement, (iii) things enjoyed/didn't enjoy (iiii) their feelings regarding the presentation of data within the workshops activities or exhibited artwork.

THE ARTWORK

The Prediction Machine consisted of multiple components including the exhibited data-driven artwork and broader participation through the series of public workshops. We now introduce the two machines that make up the exhibited artwork (Figure 2). We discuss the workshops later on.

Figure 2. Exhibition of both machines

The design of the two machines is based on the nostalgic and playful aesthetics of old fashioned (Victorian era) end-of-the-pier fortune telling devices. This aesthetic emerged from an ongoing dialogue between the artist, an engineer, furniture maker, creative programmers, and an accessibility advisor. The first machine that prints out the predictions is a wooden structure with a screen, a wooden wheel (functioning as a hand crank), a small dial, a slot, and a metal plate with instructions asking the user to *'Twist the dial to input your age, keep turning the crank to power the machine, collect your prediction from the slot.*

A screen and speakers built into the machine are powered by the hand crank that visitors are required to turn themselves, with some effort, in order to display information about the current temperature, rainfall and wind speed on the screen. This information is followed by a selection of videos showing participants from the workshops talking about their experiences of climate change and their predictions projected thirty years into the future. These videos are disrupted by the live weather data – with rain data causing rain to appear over the video image and temperature increases to brighten the image (Figure 3.).

Figure 3. Screen with the data visualisation and videos

Following this interaction, the machine prints out a prediction for the visitor's own future (Figure 4), generated for each individual based on the current weather data, location and their age entered using a dial on the front of the machine (seen just above the hand in Figure 5). The machine prints out a prediction about a world with increased temperatures, based on an increase of 3.7 degrees to the current temperature, captured by a weather station set up in the locality of the exhibition. This prediction is printed live whilst the user waits for the card to drop out of a slot at the front of the machine, for them to take away. The text of the predictions were devised and written by participants in the earlier workshops.

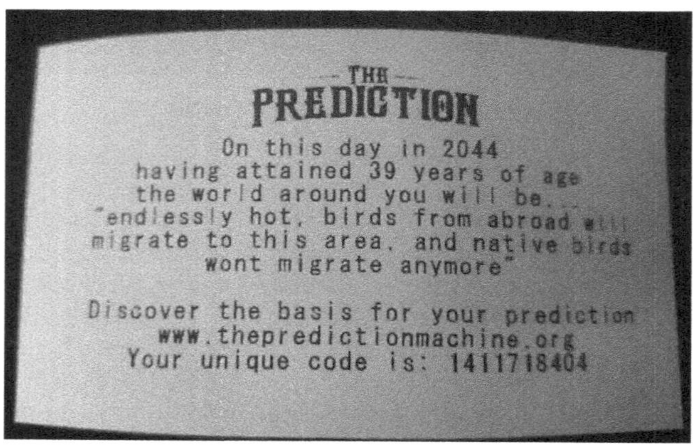

Figure 4. The prediction print out

The second machine (Figure 6) provides a touch screen through which users are invited to add their own promises or predictions for the future. It also explains the scientific processes that informed the artwork and presents a graph of 100 years of minimum and maximum temperature averages for the exhibition location.

Figure 5. Visitor turning the age dial and reading instructions

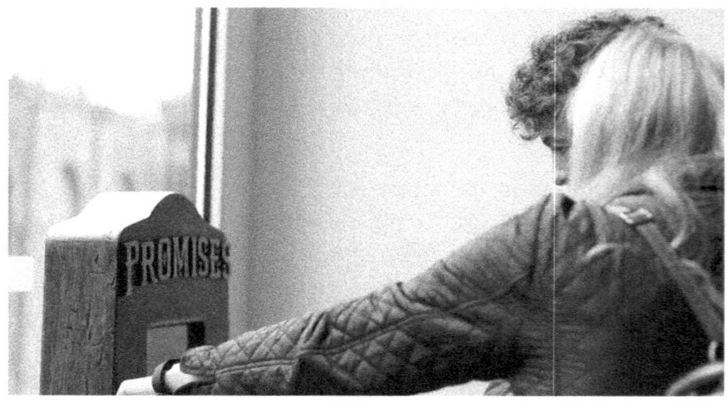

Figure 6. Visitors using the Promises machine

Both machines are connected to the weather station via the *Performing Data Timestreams Toolkit* [43] and designed to respond to temperature projections for 2030-2050 based on a climate modelling dataset provided by the Met Office UK's open data weather generator [45].

FINDINGS

The Prediction Machine is a complex artwork comprising of multiple components and outputs within a public context. The following description is a reflexive account offering three different perspectives of the artwork: the artist's rationale and the processes involved in developing the work; public engagement through a series of workshop activities; and how the audience experienced the artwork across a series of exhibitions of the interactive installation.

The following sections provide a thematic analysis of the findings of the study across each of these components. This analysis reveals the tensions and challenges experienced by the artist whilst walking the line between the artistic and scientific processes involved in 'choreographing' a data experience. The analysis then reveals how the public responded to the data across each component of the artwork. The resulting discussion considers the challenges and opportunities for future work, to inform both artists and HCI researchers working in this space.

The Artist's Rationale

The Prediction Machine is one of a series of artworks by the same artist that combines scientific and artistic processes to create *"playful and reflective"* experiences, responding to the capture and representation of climate and weather data. These works are informed by strategies from performance art, socially engaged arts, and interaction design, involving ongoing collaborations with climate scientists, HCI researchers and the public. This artwork also took place alongside academic research into the concept of 'performing data' – investigating how HCI can design systems to support performative strategies for engaging with scientific data.

In this case, *The Prediction Machine* was developed in collaboration with three climate scientists with expertise in hydroclimatic modelling, modelling the impacts and risks of climate change, and climate change communication. They advised on the presentation and interpretation of the climate and weather data across each component of the work. The artist also collaborated with HCI researchers who developed a system for the capture and mediation of this data. It was the artist's intention to create an interactive and performative experience as *"a process of dialogue"* through: (1) conversations between the artist, HCI researchers, climate scientists and the public; (2) the public engagement workshops; (3) a web presence; and (4) exhibitions of the two machines. The artist perceived each of these as being of equal importance – even if the audience didn't experience all of the components.

The artwork is designed to track 'moments of climate change' in our everyday lives and print out predictions for a future world impacted by these changes. The machines that make up the exhibition are alternately described by the artist as a warning system for possible extreme weather and climate change related events, and as an archive of local people's knowledge and memory of weather - providing alternative ways of imagining the future. Visitors to the exhibition were invited to take the predictions away with them as souvenirs of the moment in time when they interacted with the machines, inviting them to reflect for a moment on the weather outside and imagine a future climate scenario based on that moment. Both the artifacts in the exhibition and the workshop activities aimed to connect weather and climate data with personal and localised observations in this way. The artist outlined how she employed strategies for achieving these multiple outputs and experiences by *performing* a combination of *physical and digital interpretations* of the data and by *embedding* scientific data into the design of the machines.

Conversations took place between the artist, researchers and climate scientists around the complexity of the climate modelling used within the artwork and how this supports the audience's understanding of the scientific data embedded in the work. The artist suggests that by providing the public with the opportunity to 'enact' scientific processes of capturing and measuring data as part of their own subjective lines of enquiry they each attempted to move beyond merely instrumenting science – towards a position of interweaving scientific and artistic process.

Yet, some tensions arose from this process. A more complex model was suggested by some of the climate scientists who felt that the scientific process should be more clearly revealed to the public within the exhibited artwork. The final decision to use a very simple model (adding 3.7 C to the current temperature) was made in response to a variety of constraints: (a) the intricacies of understanding more complex climate models required a high level of support from the scientists; (b) it would require further bespoke developments to create these more complex algorithms; (c) it was felt by the artist that the public would not necessarily understand the more complex models, whereas the scientists assumed more information on the process would increase engagement. These tensions raised interesting questions about how non-experts are able to enact 'scientific processes' on their own within limited resources, and how effective authenticity is to public's engagement with these processes.

As a result of these dialogues, the artwork evolved to offer multiple interpretations that deliberately juxtapose past, present and future data to allow the often slow, temporal and complex nature of climate data to be narrated, represented and embodied. The neon sign on top of the first machine reacts to a combination of live temperature, rainfall and wind speed and then pulsates when an extreme reading appears. The central screen displays the live data as both numerical data and text, alongside videos that are visually disrupted by the data (see Figure 3). This screen also displays the numerical 'projected' weather data for 30 years in the future. The prediction cards then describe this future weather as a text description. On the second machine these processes are also revealed by contextualizing the data through the dynamic graphic visualisation of 100 years annual min/max temperatures in the location of the exhibition. The artist describes the challenges they experienced developing this process: *"when you are battling with data and looking at numbers or you're talking to people there's a point where you just have to shut down and go ok – how do I want this to sound, how is this going to engage people? I need to create the machines voice... what I could do, which would be the researchers way of doing it is just present direct quotes (for the predictions)... but the machine needs to have its own voice... I'm trying to think about the science and think about the participants... but that's the art bit in my mind"*

The artist also described how materials used in the construction of the machines, and the way the work is powered by a fusion of hand power (see Figure 7) and mains power embodied the broader themes of the work. For example, both machines are made from the same oak tree, felled by the furniture maker, who made them, in a local forest as it was being thinned. The oak casings of the machines are deliberately distressed to give a sense of timelessness and tactility to the objects themselves. The artist described why this contrast between the data-driven elements and the materiality and aesthetics were important to the public experience: *"the technology working the machine is complex and inherently of this technological age – but its' frame is designed to appear solid and timeless. I like the idea that although these machines respond to data in the here and now, they might visually tell another story – like they have bobbed up from the bottom of the ocean and survived a flood or a nuclear war".*

Figure 7. Powering the machine with the hand crank

The aesthetics of the disrupted videos, corrupted and decontextualised, the distressed woodenness of the machines, – the shakiness of the hand crank, the sounds of the printer and the design of the printed cards and the immediacy of the thermal printed cards were all designed by the artist were all designed to evoke a playful sense of nostalgia, intrigue and magic. This aesthetic was continued across the different elements of the exhibited work as a way to engage the public more playfully with the serious theme of climate change in contrast to the often difficult and 'depressing' nature of the predictions.

The public workshops

In addition to the two exhibited machines, the artist also engaged the public through workshops that, depending on when they took place, either provided participants with an opportunity to contribute to the design and content of the work or encouraged them to reflect on the final work as exhibited. The artist's rationale for the workshops was to engage participants in the process of meaning construction from sensed data. Participants were invited to engage in a series of activities that facilitated a process of observing, 'performing' and interpreting climate and weather data. Whilst each of these activities were distinct, it was clear that the ongoing framing carried out by the artist was instrumental in creating the conceptual thread that drew the work together. These activities then supported an ongoing dialogue and most significantly provided the predictions and video messages embedded in the work.

A schematic sketch drawn by the artist shows how each of these components should be seen as part of a whole process of 'performing data' (see Figure 8) including: (a) the capture of scientific data using sensors inputs; (b) creating multiple artistic outputs; (c) mediating data in interesting ways including scaling data, replaying old data when the sensors weren't live; (d) juxtaposing different types of data with historical, live, projected future data; and (e) juxtaposing scientific data with personal data and subjective narratives.

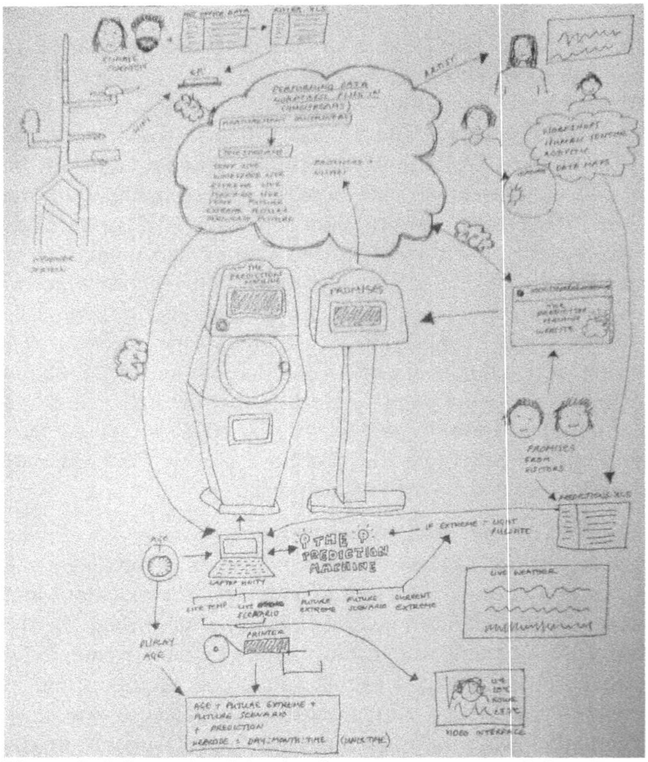

Figure 8. Schematic of the development process and data flow

From observations of the participants engagement with this process, specifically in the workshops, the most effective of these artist-curated activities were observed to be: drawing upon memory to consider physical features of weather, such as recollections from childhood; the use of poetry and fiction to illustrate experiential interpretations of future climate; asking participants to experience physically sensed components of weather and enact scientific processes by turning these experiences into data, plotting a point on a graduated scale; and finally, enacting the artistic process by representing the weather data and predictions visually, making felt collage 'maps' (see Figure 9).

During the first phase of workshops it was observed that as this process took place participants were increasingly able to discuss the data in terms of meaning construction. For example, in the first session participants tended to discuss their experiences of weather in highly narrative ways, whilst by the end of the workshops the participants were able to submit personalized narrative descriptions (for the predictions) that they could link back to the data. When asked at the end of this process, most of the participants reflected positively on the effect of these collective discussions within this process: *"I found that quite effective with pieces of paper... turning the human sensing into stories."*

"I think you might get what people already think rather than having it challenged and more well-rounded by a group discussion."

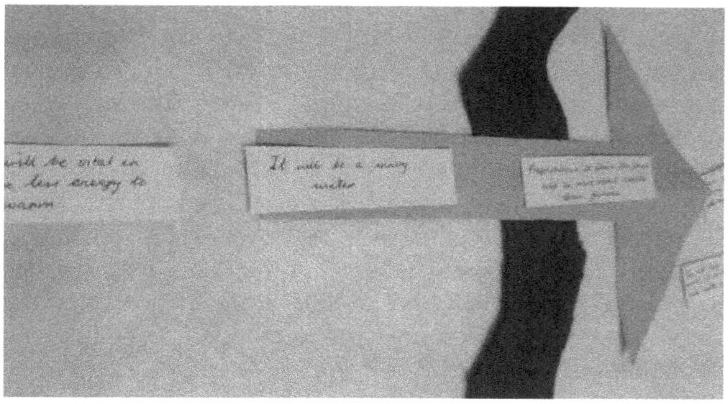

Figure 9. The felt collage data maps

One of the dominant themes that arose from the study was the artist's exploration of the line between the scientific-ness of the data and the artistic representations of data embedded in the artwork. Most significantly the workshops revealed that climate and weather data were seen by both the artist and many of the participants as the domain of 'experts', as the artist describes: *"I'm not the expert, although I've worked in this area for a long time, I'm still trying to work this out. It's actually us playing together and with the scientists and if there are experts in the room us all trying to muddle through it because I think we are all humans and we are all struggling with this even if we are experts or not... it's about having that kind of dialogue and playing around with different ways that we can interact with that."*

In contrast, during the first phase of workshops, where the participants were predominantly from academic or 'expert' backgrounds the creative strategies and approaches often appeared to challenge their assumptions of how scientific data should be interpreted and conceptualised. One participant suggested that, despite attending the workshop to learn about new ways to engage the public with issues of climate change, he struggled with understanding how the more sensory, creative activities could be an effective means to understanding the data: *"the human sensing thing I do struggle a bit with, so the questions there are can you sense air pressure, well no, we can't really to be honest, temperature, wind speed yeh, humidity, how fresh does the air feel, yeh but then there's the human... it's all very subjective, so that wasn't so valuable."*

Another participant also questioned how the 'subjective' interpretations proposed by the artist could be used to support understanding of numerical data and scientific processes: *"we've all kind of taken it in... you had to really get into it with your imagination, you couldn't just take it or leave it attitude, you had to really imagine what it would be like... if everybody did that on a large scale, gradually you'd find a shift in willingness to make the sacrifices... but the difficulty is getting it out of the subjective realm into actual numbers... how do you put those into numerical values instead of just saying it feels wetter, you need to say it feels like 90% humidity... so if there is some way of getting quantitative differences of course the way to do that is to look at... some of the data."*

One specific instance of this interplay between 'expert' and the more subjective 'lay' views in practice occurred during the third workshop. Participants began to describe their subjective experiences of higher than expected temperatures and there was some group discussion as to why this might be the case. Knowing that one of the participants was a retired meteorologist, the artist invited him, 'our resident expert', to comment and he contributed by standing in front of the group and describing slow moving weather systems whilst another 'expert' participant brought up a map of the current weather system on the projection screen. This interplay enabled the group to develop their more subjective dialogues in response to the quantitative data. This example was very much in contrast to some of the participants from the second phase of workshops, who didn't see themselves as experts or scientists. In this case the participants responses when asked about the meaning of the data were focused on their physical reactions and personalised thinking, rarely linking back to the numerical data: *"We got wet... that was the weather"*

"In the last 40 years we haven't had any real summer, unlike 1976, do you remember, it was very, very hot"

"The lads on the allotment often sit and have a cup of tea and quite a few of us agree, we seem to think that the seasons are moving, like you know you have spring from January to the end of March or whatever, we first noticed this once, it was about October we all sit out in brilliant sunshine"

The artist has previously talked about how strategies of combining scientific and artistic process might enable people to respond to the data in sensory, personalized, subjective and emotional ways, where the data functions as 'trigger data'. As opposed to more objective scientific processes and interpretations of numerical data, described as 'black box' data [28]. The artist expands on this idea within this context, suggesting the process: *"doesn't become about information sharing it becomes about allowing certain triggers to enable a dialogue."*

The artist described how these challenges were deliberately incorporated into the workshop activities and discussions: *"I'm going to ask (the participants) some questions around some of the problems I'm having with connecting data to a narrative and I'm going to bring up this whole issue that I've got, that I've got hopefully lovely predictions at one end and also empirical data on the other and there is a very difficult bit in the middle which connects the two together and how much we make it transparent or not, as part of the process and I want to work through that with them as well as myself, so they kind of inform that process."*

Figure 10. The Prediction Machine at the public library

The Exhibitions

The exhibitions took place at a public library, two contemporary art galleries, two Universities and at a science festival, over a period of one year. The exhibitions consisted of the two machines installed side by side, close to a window that had at least a partial view of the sky (and therefore the weather). Beside the machines stood an A4 sign with detailed instructions about how to interact, information about how the work was developed and how the live weather data was being captured.

The first exhibition (in a town library) consisted only of the main machine that prints out the predictions (Figure 10). This was extended in the later exhibitions to also include the second machine with an iPad touch screen – the 'Promises Machine'. This new machine was designed to respond to some of the tensions that arose from the discussions with the scientists and workshop participants around revealing and contextualizing the scientific processes that the predictions were based on, and to support more in depth reflections on the theme of climate change.

Tensions around the presentation of complex numerical scientific data outlined in the previous section were also reflected in the findings from the study of the exhibition. Visitors appeared to focus heavily upon their experience of the physical form of the machine and not the scientific data. The materiality of the machine was observed as a key factor to visitors' engagement with the work, with many visitors describing it as 'old fashioned' and 'beautiful'. This conflict between aesthetics, materiality, the artifacts and the embedded scientific processes was highlighted by one of the librarians: *"I think largely it's probably about the actual machine itself from what I've heard rather than about any views on climate change or anything like that. I mean there might be a few people that mentioned it but I think largely people just talked about the machine itself, how good... a beautiful Machine to use."*

When the second machine was added (in the later exhibitions) it was observed that many more people stayed close to the machine after using it, comparing and discussing their predictions, discussing how old they would be in 2045 and what that might mean to them.

The age dial on the main machine was designed to provide a personalised connection to the data and the fictionalised futures described in the predictions. This 'personalisation' appeared to work best for younger visitors, but was often problematic for the visitors over 60 who voiced concerns about whether they were going to still be alive and how relevant or frightening thinking generally about the future was at their age. Children were also observed as much less likely to attend to the data and information on the screens and were more interested in the artifacts generated by turning the wheel, describing to each other how you 'got something' if you 'turned the handle'.

The issue of temporality was a recurrent theme, in the occasional mismatch between visitor expectations, the time taken for a prediction to appear, and the time people were prepared to dedicate to follow up 'work' in order to complete or continue the experience and engage more fully with the data. Where the public appeared to relate most to the scientific data embedded in the machine was through their engagements with the narrative text descriptions of the data (the weather scenarios on the screen and the printed predictions). Visitors were found reading these aloud to each other whilst discussing them afterwards. In some cases the impact of these narrative descriptions were longer term – one audience member was observed talking about the predictions over half an hour after they interacted with the machine and another reported they had their prediction displayed on their desk at work six months later.

The librarian from the first exhibition also described how she and her colleagues continued to discuss their predictions over the two week period of the exhibition: *"The first one I did was not best... it will be quite warm and stuff like that, it was quite depressing - it will be global warming, it will be really hot... on the day I did it, it was quite mild for the time of year it sort of picks that up and gives you the worse prediction than if say it was colder... I think most of us have asked, 'what did you get?"*

One of the visitors to the later exhibitions described how they ignored the numerical datasets because of the strong aesthetics and interactive nature of the machines: *"I think my main attention was on, what is it, how does it work, what should I be doing, you know what I mean? It was quite task focused.... I was focused on the process of it rather than the theme of it'.*

Yet, this same visitor went on to describe how doing these tasks, and then being asked to submit his own prediction for the future on the second machine, triggered a process of thinking about climate change in relation to the data that he had been initially unaware of: *"actually just the words - in 2045 there will be bluebirds in the park - just came into my head so maybe at some level you can be thinking about something without consciously thinking about it ... its actually quite manipulative... it's like when you're doing something with your hands ... so maybe there's a bit of that 'cos you are focusing on something else, but you've been given a task and something pops up".*

DISCUSSION

Our study has charted how an artist set out to embed scientific data within an artwork with the goal of enabling people to make personalised connections to the complex themes of climate change and climate modelling. What stands out from our findings is the significance of *process*. First, the artwork is itself a process – more than merely two artifacts – that involved an artistic journey through a series of public workshops and exhibitions that both informed and responded to one another. Second, the underlying science is also a process – more than merely representations of scientific data – of capture, analysis and presentation. In the following sub-sections, we unpack and compare these two notions of process. Our discussion suggests that we might reconsider the ways in which these artists, who are increasingly working with real world data, often juxtapose live, historical and future projected data [6,7,20,26]. We might also reconsider how the emerging notion of 'performing data' within HCI [20,27] establishes a dialogue between two processes – artistic and scientific - raising new creative opportunities but also involving negotiating some key tensions.

Establishing dialogue

We begin with the notion of dialogue. Findings from the study of *The Prediction Machine* artwork shows us that the artist deliberately positioned the work to bring questions and dialogues about issues of climate change to the fore. The study reveals how the artist adopted various performative, socially engaged and dialogic strategies to support the interweaving of scientific and artistic processes:

- Engaging directly with numerical scientific representations, through both live and projected data
- Supporting participants and visitors to visibly transform this data into narrative text, through the data maps made in the workshops, weather scenarios, predictions and the submitted promises and predictions
- Juxtaposing this data with observations and more experiential/felt data, through videos, a lit-up sign, predictions, age data and the voltage on the hand crank

As a result of choosing this position the artist used the artifacts (the machines) and the narrative (the predictions) as triggers to address some of the tensions of combining scientific and artistic processes.

First and foremost, our study offers an example of how such artworks can establish an extended dialogue between artists, scientists and the public in order to surface some of the socio-political issues raised by the interweaving of artistic process and scientific data. We will now consider how this dialogue emerges through the juxtaposition of these processes.

Artworks as process

Hohl [18] suggests that through concrete visualisations, artifacts, objects and embodied experiences of data, artists can *"transform these conclusions into communicable formats that capture the public's imagination"*. Hohl then identifies three key components of this transformation: using 'actual data'; finding meaning within the process of making and not just in the resulting artifacts; and using open-ended dialogue. Our findings, as presented in the previous section, reveal how this occurred with *The Prediction Machine* as a performance of data - using data to 'trigger' personalized stories and emotional responses, that in turn connected people to the data in ways less likely to occur through more traditional science communication [31]. What is vital here is that as an artwork, *The Prediction Machine* is indeed, as Hohl suggests, a process not just an artifact. It is a series of workshops and exhibitions situated within a broader artistic journey. Moreover, the public is invited directly into this process and not just the experience of the resulting exhibited artifacts. Key to these findings is the catalytic role of the artist in using data to drive this process. Choreographing how the data is performed in the work was revealed as an often subtle and unseen process, 'curated' by the artist in order to provoke often unexpected, nuanced and longer-term engagements with the work.

Science as process

Of course, science can also be viewed in terms of process. For example, various scientific workflows involve capturing and analysing data from the natural world so as to generate hypotheses, or conducting experiments to test these hypotheses. While the participants in *The Prediction Machine* are not directly undertaking science or following these particular workflows, the artwork does serve to expose something of these scientific processes. Participants are invited to gather data, interpret it and make predictions at various stages of the workshops and also when engaging with the exhibited machines. Put another way, the artwork involves an artistic performance of scientific process.

Such practices are not unique to this work. Other artists such as Polli [26], Walker [30] and Jeremijenko [40],

Autogena and Portway [29] also focus on performative enactments of scientific processes as a part of their practice. As just one example, Walker's work on capturing data from the riders of amusement rides and displaying it to spectators is in a large part about the performance of selecting participants, visibly kitting them up with sensors and then interpreting their data on stage, all framed as the public performance of a 'thrill experiment' [30].

Yet, this sense of performing scientific process is not common to all data driven artworks. Many others tend to use found and pre-recorded data as a raw 'material' to inform their work, whilst separating the data from a scientific context and process. While being perfectly appropriate to the creation of artworks, we suggest that this may lead to not only a different approach to playing with the materiality of real world data, but perhaps also a less dialogic process of creating, interrogating and experiencing the data and its underlying provenance and meaning.

Juxtaposing artistic and scientific process

This artistic performance of science, in which scientific process is seen through the lens of an artistic process, is the basis for dialogue in *The Prediction Machine* and similar works. It is a juxtaposition of two epistemologies – science and art – that were for many decades seen as being separate or even fundamentally in opposition [38]. Our study suggests that this juxtaposition of processes can be a productive one, serving to inspire new art, but also to engage those involved – artists, scientists and the public – in extended dialogues. It is not, however, without its tensions. One core tension arises from the notion of data as a trigger to subjective experience, which appears to be particular to these forms of artistic processes [28,41]. Yet, connecting scientific processes with 'subjective' artistic strategies without very overt or transparent connections to the scientific process can still be seen as problematic and potentially ineffective by some of the scientific community, as shown by the responses of some of the 'expert' participants in the workshops and discussions with the climate scientists.

In response to these tensions the study revealed that through enacting and engaging with the capture and mediation of data the artist, visitors to the exhibition and participants in the workshops were able to discuss issues of data authenticity, certainty, and meaning. All of this data 'history' was then presented as part of the workshop process and through the interface on the second machine in the later exhibitions, allowing participants with a scientific background to experience an unusual (to them) subjective interpretation of the data while non-experts were offered a route into understanding and appreciating aspects of the scientific process.

More broadly then, our findings enable us to begin to frame the tensions and opportunities involved when artists walk a line between art, science and data. The artist actively positioned themselves in relation to scientific understandings of the data by collaborating with climate scientists and making conscious decisions about how the resulting discussions were embedded in the work. The artist also articulated the desire to abandon instrumentalist approaches to data representation, such as a reliance on direct visualization (e.g. graphs) and instead sought to play with notions of performativity, context and meaning, allowing participants to interleave their own subjectivities into the interpretive act of engaging with the data. In this way the artist chose to interrogate the 'positivist/scientific' approach of data representation without taking a more oppositional view - rejecting notions of scientific empiricism. Reflecting on the above discussion, we therefore suggest that there are many ways that artists work with complex scientific data including:

- Instrumenting science through the direct representation of scientific processes
- Re-enacting science through performative strategies
- Interweaving scientific and artistic processes by juxtaposing data alongside experiential, felt, sensory, aesthetic and personalised interpretations
- Using scientific data as a new material - without interrogating the scientific-ness of the data
- Creating critiques that might reject these scientific processes completely

We already know that, as with all human work, creating data is indivisible from value and subjectivity. In the case of this artwork we have begun to see how data can be curated to trigger subjective experiences in the viewer, suggesting that data does not have to be framed as objective to be meaningful. Interestingly, within this subjectivity there arises common themes informed by the findings of this study, that could influence future research within this space: the role of memory in the creation of recognised and meaningful contexts; the importance of constructing focused social 'spaces' and artifacts that trigger reflection and engagement; and the importance of everydayness in the construction of meaning around abstracted data.

CONCLUSION

We have explored how an interdisciplinary collaboration leading to an interactive data-driven artwork interweaved complex scientific processes with artistic strategies to engage the public with weather and climate data. What this study most significantly reveals is how such artworks can be understood as an artistic process in which aspects of scientific processes are interpreted and performed, leading to new dialogues between artists, scientists and the wider public. Complex artworks such as *The Prediction Machine* serve to offer these alternative views of data.

We suggest that these discussions have potentially far reaching implications for the design of systems to capture, mediate and represent real world and scientific data in the future, as well as implications for how we engage the public in complex and contentious scientific issues.

ACKNOWLEDGMENTS

We thank the partners, participants and visitors involved in The Prediction Machine, especially Dr Carlo Buontempo from the UK Met office, Dr Candice Howarth from the Global Sustainability Institute, Anglia Ruskin University and Prof Rob Wilby, Loughborough University. We also thank the 'Performing Data' team especially Jesse Blum, Paul Tennent, Pat Brundell, Brendan Walker, Joe Marshall, Holger Schnadelbach, Caroline Locke and Di Wiltshire. We gratefully acknowledge support from the RCUK Horizon Digital Economy Research Hub grant, EP/G065802/1, the EPSRC Impact Acceleration Account and Radar LU Arts. Supported using public funding by Arts Council England.

REFERENCES

1. Paul Aoki, R. J. Honicky, Alan Mainwaring, Chris Myers, Eric Paulos, Sushmita Subramanian, and Allison Woodruff. "A vehicle for research: using street sweepers to explore the landscape of environmental community action." In *Proceedings of the SIGCHI Conference on Human Factors in Computing Systems*, pp. 375-384. ACM
2. Bergit Arends, Davina Thackara, eds. 2003. *Experiment: Conversations in art and science.* Wellcome Trust
3. Steve Benford, Chris Greenhalgh, Andy Crabtree, Martin Flintham, Brendan Walker, Joe Marshall, Boriana Koleva. 2013. "Performance-led research in the wild." *ACM Transactions on Computer-Human Interaction (TOCHI)* 20, no. 3: 14.
4. Steve Benford, Gabriella Giannachi. 2011. *Performing mixed reality*. The MIT Press
5. Maxwell T Boykoff,. 2011. Who speaks for the climate?: Making sense of media reporting on climate change. Cambridge University Press, 2011.
6. Lisa E Bloom. 2011. Contemporary Art and Climate Change: The Aesthetics of Disappearance at the Poles. Available at: http://isea2011.sabanciuniv.edu/paper/aesthetics-disappearance-climate-change-antarctica-and-contemporary-sublime-work-anne-noble-co [Accessed August 6, 2013].
7. Annick Bureaud. 2011.Climate Change: Embodying the Data. Available at: http://www.leoalmanac.org/isea2011-panel-farfield2-the-data-landscapes-of-climate-change/ [Accessed July 26, 2013].
8. Jesse Blum, Martin Flintham, Derek McAuley, Rachel Jacobs, Matt Watkins, Rebecca Lee, Robin Shackford, Mark Selby, Silvia Leal and Gabriella Giannachi for their paper Timestreams: Supporting Community Engagement in the Climate Change Debate
9. Madeleine Bunting, Art and Climate An Essay: does the art stop when the persuasion starts?, 2008. *RSA Arts and Ecology Magazine*, RSA
10. David J Curtis, Nick Reid, and Guy Ballard. 2012. "Communicating ecology through art: what scientists think." *Ecology and Society* 17, no. 2: 3.
11. T. J. Demos. 2013. Contemporary Art and the Politics of Ecology: An Introduction. *Third Text*, *27*(1), 1-9.
12. Carl DiSalvo , Kirsten Boehner, Nicholas A. Knouf, and Phoebe Sengers. 2009. "Nourishing the ground for sustainable HCI: considerations from ecologically engaged art." In *Proceedings of the SIGCHI Conference on Human Factors in Computing Systems*, pp. 385-394. ACM.
13. Froehlich, J., Findlater, L., & Landay, J. 2010, The design of eco-feedback technology. In *Proceedings of the SIGCHI Conference on Human Factors in Computing Systems* (pp. 1999-2008). ACM.
14. Jennifer Gabrys, Kathryn Yusoff. 2012. "Arts, sciences and climate change: practices and politics at the threshold." *Science as culture* 21, no. 1: 1-24.
15. Gabriella Giannachi. 2012. Representing, Performing and Mitigating Climate Change in Contemporary Art Practice. *Leonardo*, *45*(2), 124-131
16. Jeffrey Goldman, Katie Shilton, Jeff Burke, Deborah Estrin, Mark Hansen, Nithya Ramanathan, Sasank Reddy, Vids Samanta, Mani Srivastava, Ruth West. 2009. "Participatory Sensing: A citizen-powered approach to illuminating the patterns that shape our world." *Foresight & Governance Project, White Paper*
17. Drew Hemment, Carlo Buontempo, and Alfie Dennon. 2013. Climate Bubbles: Artwork and Design Prototype. FutureEverything, Manchester
18. Michael Hohl. 2012. Making visible the invisible: art, design and science in data visualisation. University of Huddersfield
19. Holmes, T. G. 2007, Eco-visualization: combining art and technology to reduce energy consumption. In *Proceedings of the 6th ACM SIGCHI conference on Creativity & cognition* (pp. 153-162). ACM.
20. Rachel Jacobs, Steve Benford, Mark Selby, Michael Golembewski, Dominic Price, and Gabriella Giannachi. 2013. A conversation between trees: what data feels like in the forest. In *Proceedings of the SIGCHI Conference on Human Factors in Computing Systems* (pp. 129-138). ACM.
21. Rachel Jacobs, Steve Benford, and Ewa Luger. 2015. "Behind The Scenes at HCI's Turn to the Arts." In *Proceedings of the 33rd Annual ACM Conference Extended Abstracts on Human Factors in Computing Systems*, pp. 567-578. ACM

22. Dan M Kahan, Ellen Peters, Maggie Wittlin, Paul Slovic, Lisa Larrimore Ouellette, Donald Braman, and Gregory Mandel. 2012. "The polarizing impact of science literacy and numeracy on perceived climate change risks." *Nature Climate Change* 2, no. 10: 732

23. Stacey Kuznetsov, George Noel Davis, Eric Paulos, Mark D. Gross, and Jian Chiu Cheung. 2011. "Red balloon, green balloon, sensors in the sky." In *Proceedings of the 13th international conference on Ubiquitous computing*, pp. 237-246. ACM

24. Richard Mortier, Richard, Hamed Haddadi, Tristan Henderson, Derek McAuley, and Jon Crowcroft. 2013."Challenges & opportunities in human-data interaction." *University of Cambridge, Computer Laboratory*

25. Kari Marie Norgaard. Living in denial: Climate change, emotions, and everyday life. 2011. *MIT Press*

26. Andrea Polli. 2011. Communicating Air: Alternative Pathways to Environmental Knowing through Computational Ecomedia.

27. Paul Tennent, Stuart Reeves, Steve Benford, Brendan Walker, Joe Marshall, Pat Brundell, R. Meese, Paul Harter, 2012 "The Machine in the Ghost: Augmenting Broadcasts with Biodata," in Proceedings of the 2012 annual conference extended abstracts on Human factors in computing systems (CHI2012), Austin, TX, USA

28. Stephen Rimmer. Ed. 2009. Paralelo - Unfolding Narratives: in art, technology and Environment, Sao Paulo: MIS and Imprensaoficial.

29. Julian Ruddock, Mark Macklin, John Harvey, SciArt The confluence of art and science in conveying the uncertainties of climate change http://cargocollective.com/artscienceclimatechange/SciArt-the-confluence-of-art-and-science-in-conveying-the-uncertaintie (Accessed January, 14· 2016)

30. Holger Schnädelbach, Stefan Rennick Egglestone, Stuart Reeves, Steve Benford, Brendan Walker, and Michael Wright. 2008. "Performing thrill: designing telemetry systems and spectator interfaces for amusement rides." In *Proceedings of the SIGCHI Conference on Human Factors in Computing Systems*, pp. 1167-1176. ACM

31. Alexa Spence, Wouter Poortinga, Catherine Butler, and Nicholas Frank Pidgeon. 2011. "Perceptions of climate change and willingness to save energy related to flood experience." *Nature climate change* 1, no. 1: 46-49.

32. Daniel Stokols, Raul Perez Lejano, and John Hipp. 2013. "Enhancing the resilience of human-environment systems: a social ecological perspective." *Ecology and Society* 18, no. 1

33. http://www.symbiotica.uwa.edu.au uk (accessed January, 14· 2016)

34. Alex S. Taylor, Siân Lindley, Tim Regan, David Sweeney, Vasillis Vlachokyriakos, Lillie Grainger, and Jessica Lingel. 2015. Data-in-Place: Thinking through the Relations Between Data and Community. In Proceedings of the 33rd Annual ACM Conference on Human Factors in Computing Systems (CHI '15). ACM, New York, NY, USA, 2863-2872.

35. Robyn Taylor, Guy Schofield, John Shearer, Jayne Wallace, Peter Wright, Pierre Boulanger, Patrick Olivier. 2009. "Designing from within: humanaquarium." In *Proceedings of the SIGCHI Conference on Human Factors in Computing Systems*, pp. 1855-1864. ACM

36. Nicola Triscott. Art, Science, Technology & Society. http://nicolatriscott.org/2015/07/05/the-performance-and-performativity-of-science/ uk (Accessed January, 14· 2016)

37. Haydn Washington, H. 2013. Climate change denial: Heads in the sand. Routledge.

38. Snow, C. P., *The Two Cultures*. London: Cambridge University Press. 1959.

39. Kristine Stiles, Peter Selz. 1996, Theories and documents of contemporary art: a sourcebook of artists' writings (Vol. 35) University of California Press: 798-953

40. Weiner, J., 2013 The Artist Who Talks With the Fishes - NYTimes.com. *nytimes.com*. Available at: http://www.nytimes.com/2013/06/30/magazine/the-artist-who-talks-with-the-fishes.html?_r=0 [Accessed August 6, 2013]

41. Ruth West, Roger Malina, John Lewis, Scot Gresham-Lancaster, Alejandro Borsani, Brian Merlo, Lifan Wang, 2015, DataRemix: Designing the DataMade, "DataRemix: Designing The Datamade." Leonardo

42. Stephen Wilson, 2002 Information arts: intersections of art, science and technology, MIT press

43. http://www.performingdata.org.uk (Accessed January, 14· 2016)

44. http://www.thepredictionmachine.org (Accessed January, 14· 2016)

45. http://ukclimateprojections.metoffice.gov.uk/22540 uk (Accessed January, 14· 2016)

Live Participation: Augmenting Events with Audience–Performer Interaction Systems

Matti Nelimarkka [a,b,c] Kai Kuikkaniemi [a,b] Antti Salovaara [d] Giulio Jacucci [a,b,c]
[a] Helsinki Institute for Information Technology HIIT
[b] Department of Computer Science, Aalto University, Espoo, Finland
[c] Department of Computer Science, University of Helsinki, Helsinki, Finland
[d] School of Business, Aalto University, Helsinki, Finland
{matti.nelimarkka,kai.kuikkaniemi,giulio.jacucci}@hiit.fi, antti.salovaara@aalto.fi

ABSTRACT
Tools for supporting performer–audience interaction have been gaining increasing interest in HCI community recently. They encompass a wide range of systems from simple polls to live tweeting and backchannel chats. However, a lack of unifying conceptual framework hampers their efficient development and deployment in events. In this paper, we develop a notion of *live participation* and present a live participation system that aims to capture performer–audience interaction systems' salient design-relevant characteristics. With user studies, we identify central characteristics of live participation (RQ1) and explore the diversity of types of live participation situations (RQ2). The identified concepts—extended performance, integration work, and episodes—provide the groundwork for further design of live participation systems and more engaging audience interactions.

Author Keywords
live participation; co-located interaction; audience–performer interaction; events

ACM Classification Keywords
H.5.3 Information Interfaces and Presentation (e.g. HCI): Group and Organization Interfaces

General Terms
Human Factors; Design

INTRODUCTION
Many computer-augmented systems and tools have been developed and presented with a goal of supporting interaction between and among performers (e.g., presenters, teachers, event hosts, chairpersons etc.) and their audiences. These tools include, among others, question management systems [4, 18], audience response systems [21, 22], and backchannels [28, 45]. Also Twitter has been appropriated as a discussion board through live tweeting [9, 25, 29].

Together, these and other tools demonstrate a fertile application domain for human–computer interaction (HCI). However, to our knowledge, the possibilities of different performer–audience interactions in this application domain have remained unexplored comprehensively. We thus take the first steps to discuss the design opportunities and challenges in this domain that we call *live participation*. The term is a shorthand for computer-augmented performer–audience interactions where the emphasis is on audience members' concurrent involvement in the presentation or activity (i.e., "live") and their contributing role in it (i.e., "participation").

We are informed by research on *performance* as studied both in event studies (e.g., [14]) and in HCI (e.g. [19, 32, 44]). In a performance, one or many persons (i.e., performers) have a leading role in the orchestration of social interactions, and have something to show or offer to the rest of the people (i.e., audience) [35]. In particular, we focus on planned events where performers aim to disseminate information to an audience. Classes and presentations are prime examples of such contexts. Our work also focuses primarily on performers' needs (compared to, e.g., group support systems that aim for decision-making and problem solving purposes and where the performer's role is not as clear [31]).

For HCI and the design of interactive systems, live participation perspective opens new ways to explore computer-augmented social interactions. When audience–performer interaction in the real world is extended to a digital world, technology becomes the second venue for interaction—thus resulting in an *extended performance*. These two venues—mediated (extended performance) and non-mediated (on-stage performance)—are in interaction, leading to needs for performers to "bridge" the digital and physical performances, or *integrate* them.

We begin by outlining the existing research and by developing the concepts further. This provides a starting point for a conceptually informed empirical study on Presemo, a live participation system that contains a more comprehensive set of functions than other systems in the market or in academic

DIS 2016, June 4–8, 2016, Brisbane, Australia.

ACM ISBN ISBN 978-1-4503-4031-1/16/06 ...$15.00.
http://dx.doi.org/10.1145/2901790.2901862

research. In particular, we study, with a qualitative single-case study, *what characteristics are central in live participation* (RQ1). Endowed with this qualitative understanding, we continue by exploring the *diversity of types of live participation* (RQ2) with a multiple-case study of eight diverse contexts where the system has been used. The studies foregrounded new questions especially related to the social organization of live participation performances, and the range of opportunities for live participation.

PREVIOUS WORK

In this section, we review both the previous research on performance as well as the systems that fall under an umbrella of live participation.

Performances in Event Studies and HCI

Event studies—a sub-discipline of tourism research—have since early 1990s started to analyse the planning and execution of events (e.g., [13, 15, 16]). This research has covered a wide range of contexts from festivals to religious gatherings, and applies various perspectives to events. Among them is also the performance aspect that emphasizes that events are distinctly *socially framed and contextualised* [14]. For example, an academic conference has expected behaviour roles for presenters and the audience. These social roles define how they can engage in the event.

When technology is introduced to play a part in a performance, it has profound implications, as many HCI studies have already documented (e.g., [8, 32, 33, 37, 39]). Of interest have been the participants' different roles in performances, and what this implies to technological support for performance. 'Performers', 'audience', and 'bystanders' contribute to performances in different ways: Performers interact with the technology through publicly visible interactions. The audience members follow performers' interactions and are also themselves invited to interact with the technology. This makes them more performer-like [8, 32, 33, 37, 39]. Bystanders, in comparison, are those who do not focus on performers and do not engage in technology interaction either.

Based on systematic analyses on these situations, roles coincide with specific spatial locations in event performances. The centre-stage position, for example, is controlled by performers while the other staff can be found behind-the-scenes where they may manipulate technological equipment [32]. The performers' interactions may be visible (when they take place "centre-stage") or hidden (when they are in "backstage"). The interactions may be amplified with technology [33]. These works posit varying levels of importance for technology. Some researchers see technology in the core of the performance [37, 32] whereas others see it in a supplementary role [39].

Live Participation Systems

Live participation is an application domain where technology allows the audience to impact the direction of the event. Possible use contexts include teaching in classes [11, 17, 30] and conferences [18, 28]. Live participation can change the social set-up of an event [17, 30], transform users' roles [11], support the event flow by providing a non-interruptive channel for contributions [18, 28], lead to knowledge gains in peers' interaction [45], confuse participants due to cognitive challenges of following several information streams [28], and even lead to non-constructive commenting [6]. Therefore, researchers are familiar with these systems' audience-side implications, but less has been said about the implications on the performance and the performer, or the event as such.

To better understand these implications, we must further review the tools that have been developed and used in this application domain. We find it helpful to consider them along two categories: who *initiates* the interaction and who *controls* it. By initiation we refer to the actions that define when the first interactions take place and what their stimuli are for co-located participants' subsequent responses. Controlling, in turn, refers to the control and steering of the live participation process in the event context, and the unfolding of the computer-mediated interaction. We will organise our review of live participation technologies around three related categories.

Performer-Initiated & Performer-Controlled

Performer-initiated & performer-controlled technologies retain the control on audience engagement firmly in the performers' hands. For example, audience response systems ('clickers')—used most commonly in education—are tools with which teachers can present students with multiple-choice questions and quickly summarise the results. Based on the results, teachers may adapt their teaching and recap or elaborate concepts as needed—either for all the students or smaller groups [7, 12, 21, 22]. Work with these systems started in the 1960s, focusing on faster feedback loops between teachers and students. Later they came to serve also as discussion-starters [21]. The idea of a networked classroom in the 1990s also included audience response systems, as one of the means to improve the interactions (e.g., [24]). Even today, these systems's focus is on the interaction and its support through a mediated environment (e.g., [5, 24]).

The understanding of audience response systems and their impacts on learning and teaching is already mature, as has been shown in several reviews (e.g., [7, 12, 22]). Positive outcomes include increased engagement, interactivity, and enjoyment during the classes. These may lead to greater learning gains. Learning-enhancing practices include raising awareness and directing attention, improving cognitive processes, using the answers as part of (formative) evaluation, and pointing to questions to stimulate discussion [3].

Therefore, audience response systems emphasise the role of the performer who initiates and masters the interaction. They offer limited interaction methods; the current research, for instance, addresses predominantly multiple-choice responses. The audience has limited opportunities to express their views, usually from among a predefined set of options.

Audience-Controlled

In the other end of the spectrum are audience-controlled systems. Backchannels are an example of this category. Similarly to audience response systems, their purpose is to create a complementary communication channel for a specific environment, such as a conference or a classroom [28, 34, 45]. Most commonly, backchannels are message boards or chats, but live tweeting through a particular hashtag in Twitter has recently become increasingly popular [25, 27, 29].

When compared with audience response systems, backchannels are more general-purpose and free-form in the interaction they afford. As we have seen, audience response systems mainly support a teacher asking questions from an audience. Backchannels, in contrast, can be used by the audience to ask questions or seek clarifications from one's peers [10, 28, 45] or to share thoughts with them [11]. Especially panel moderators might follow and engage with backchannels [28] during panel discussions to elicit questions from the audience.

Backchannels offer many potential benefits, such as peer learning and co-construction of knowledge [28, 45], increased sense of flow [28], and audience engagement as active contributors rather than passive listeners [11].

The primary focus with backchannels is on improving the interaction among peers in the audience. This is achieved by providing a free-form space for sharing ideas and comments and allowing the audience to direct the discussion to topics of shared interest. However, if the performers cannot be part of this interaction loop (e.g., if the backchannel is hidden from them, or if they have to direct all of their attention to this interaction), their opportunities do not realise for the performers, and subsequently the opportunities of live participation cannot be fully capitalized.

Performer-Initiated & Audience-Controlled

Audience response systems (focused on performers and their needs) and backchannels (focused on the audience and their needs) can be complemented with a third category: the interaction between the audience and the presenter(s) using two-way tools—something that happens only in a limited sense in the two preceding categories.

Confusingly, many papers label also these systems as backchannels. Backchan.nl [18] lets the audience rate questions during a panel discussion and panellists to answer the highest-ranking questions. Similarly, Fragmented Social Mirror [4] lets participants ask the lecturer specific questions, to which either the lecturer or an assistant can reply.

We re-label these systems as *question management systems*, to reflect the audience-initiated interactions with performers. Interaction may also involve peer interaction, such as voting on various questions' relevance [18]. These systems engage audience in the creation of the performance through two-way interaction, and thus transform them to be more active. They are thus highly relevant to more engaging performances.

LIVE PARTICIPATION

The above-presented heterogeneous collection of empirical work has pushed us to consider the systems in a common framework. Informed by concept-driven research [41], we move forward to examine *live participation* and develop an interactive artifact to explore its implications. Our focus is on planned events and their information sharing.

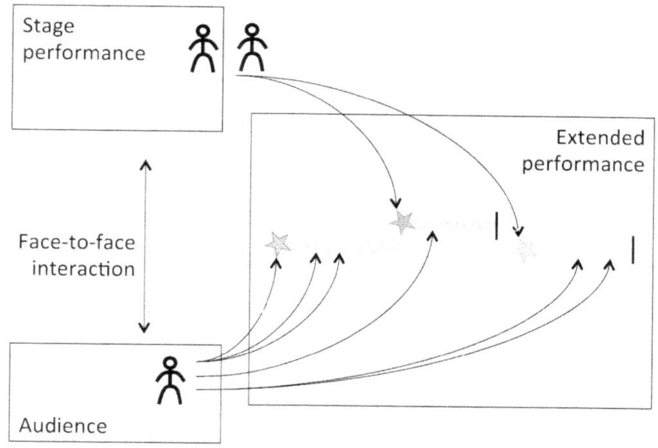

Figure 1: Live participation. The face-to-face stage performance is supported through a computer-mediated environment that allows audience-controlled, performer-initiated & performer-controlled, and [illegible] interaction episodes.

Live participation systems create a mediated space for interaction. Figure 1 presents live participation's three primary roles, building on performance literature[1] [8, 33, 32, 37, 39]: audience, on-stage performers and off-stage performers. We refer to the technology-augmented interactive elements of the performance as *extended performance*, to differentiate it from the physical performance ongoing on the stage.

Technology can amplify spectator experiences in artistic performances [33]. Similarly, in events, performers can use live participation systems to extend their performance to the mediated space as well. Therefore, the mediated space is not only another communication channel (as seen in group work, e.g., [26]), but in the best case becames also a part of the performance. Our choice to talk about "extended performance" rather than merely "extended communication channel", for example, reflects this ideal.

We observe that the extended performance requires *integration work* in order to become a natural part of the event and the performance. Integration work consists of any actions by performers that raise the audience's awareness of the mediated interaction space, encourage participation through it, and take the audience's contributions as part of the on-stage performance. Examples of integration work include framing and setting up the live participation activity, motivating the audience to use the live participation system, and reacting to audience contributions. The term's resemblance to articulation work—an important concept of computer-supported cooperative work—is not coincidental. Articulation work refers to efforts made to manage the distributed nature of cooperative work [36, 42]—in other words, the meta-work required to make the actual work possible. Similarly, integration work

[1] HCI community has had a liberal definition of "performance" (cf. [40]). We acknowledge that performances can take various forms. Our work may be generalizable to many situations, but we mostly consider presentations, classroom teaching, panels, and other contexts where the presenter-performers lead the interaction.

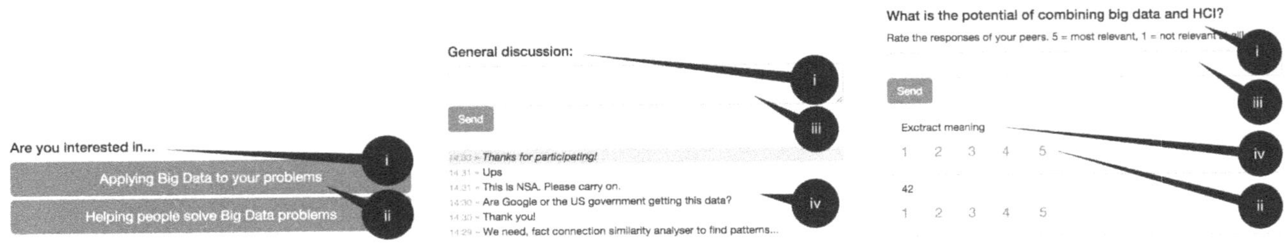

(a) Poll (b) Chat (c) Voting

Figure 2: Presemo's three interaction block types as they are seen in the audience members' devices. Blocks have a title (i) and can have performer-defined answer options (ii), an input field (iii) and user-generated content (iv).

addresses the efforts to establish a coherent performance both through the mediated and on-stage activities.

Accordingly, Figure 1 presents how audience follows two performances—on-stage and extended—and can contribute to the performance. In many live participation systems, this involves sending messages (e.g., [11, 28, 34]) or voting from predefined lists of possibilities (e.g., [3, 7]). Figure 1 visualizes the three different initiation–control interaction types with different colours. Those controlled by performers (red and green; e.g., polls and votes) have specific endings, while audience-controlled episodes (e.g., backchannel chats) have indefinite lengths.

If there are multiple on-stage performers, such as panellists (e.g. [18]), teachers (e.g. [3, 7, 11]) and presenters (e.g. [28]), they can share the responsibility of integration work. Events may also include off-stage staff who may support integration work by, for example, moderating audience members' messages [18, 4] and other contributions to the ongoing performance [28]. Figure 1 presents the on-stage and off-stage as separate actors that stand side by side.

Live participation relates to the previous frameworks in the following ways. Sheridan et al.'s [37] Performance Triad model posits the mediating technology in a central role in audience–performer interactions. Our model is more tuned to collocated settings where face-to-face interactions and mediated interactions may play equally important roles. Reeves et al.'s [33] spectator experience taxonomy orients to artistic performances where the technology is performer-controlled even when it is used in a shared manner with the audience. Finally, Spence et al. [39] presented systems where performers use media for storytelling. Also this approach gives precedence for performers who prepare the content beforehand and leave less control and agency for the audience. Live participation therefore differs also from this framework by being more oriented to the audience and its members' contributions of content.

These differences to existing frameworks arise from our attempt to focus on planned "live" events as an application domain for audience participation. For our use, "live" highlights the nature and the potential changes in the performance [2, 35]. For us, "participation", in turn, denotes the aspect of giving the audience a voice; either to influence the outcomes or to demonstrate their affect [23].

The desire to support performer–audience interaction has motivated use to develop Presemo—a system that supports live participation and integrates into a single system the various live participation functions that we reviewed above.

Presemo, an Integrated Live Participation System

Presemo's main design objective is to combine together the performer-initiated & performer-controlled, the audience-initiated & performer-controlled, and audience-controlled modes of live participation. In addition, Presemo also aims to support integration work and extension of the performance to the mediated environment. We have approached it through *episode-oriented* interaction design. Each usage of a live participation tool is part of a performer-defined episode. Such episodes can be, for instance, polling of answers for a question, a chat discussion, or a vote. We have aimed at making the initiation and closing of these episodes as flexible as possible for performers. One means for enabling this has been that the different episodes of an extended performance can be prepared in advance in Presemo. They are shown as "blocks" both in the composing mode as well as when they are active and interactable for the audience during a performance.

Each block offers the audience a single type of interaction opportunity. A plan for an event (i.e., the performance) may include multiple blocks, each one representing a different interaction session with the audience.

Presemo has the functionality for three types of interaction: polls (see Fig. 2a), chats wherein participants can send messages to everybody (see Fig. 2b), and voting, where the audience can first suggest options between which they then can vote (see Fig. 2c). These features map to the three modes of participation discussed above. The poll represents performer-initiated & performer-controlled audience interaction. The chat, depending on the performers' instruction, is audience-controlled and either audience-initiated or perfomer-initiated. The voting is performer-initiated & audience-controlled. We acknowledge that the design space for different blocks is not saturated with these three interactions. There remains room for considerable extension in future work.

New blocks can be both edited and created on the fly during a performance. In addition, performers can toggle the visibility and change the relative order of each block in real time both in a public screen and in the contents that audience members can

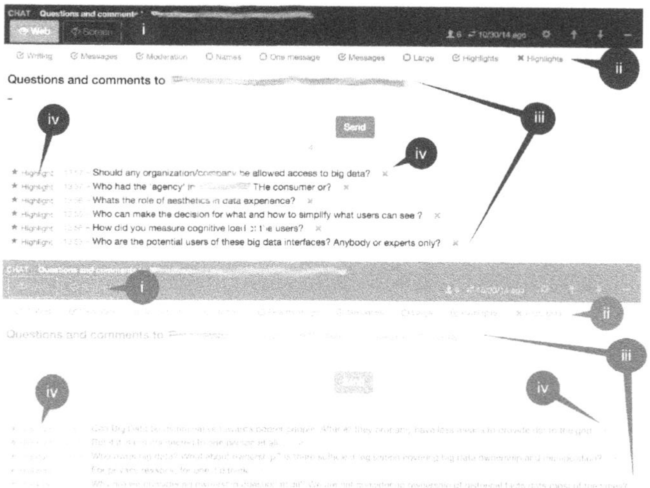

Figure 3: Presemo's full control interface for performers that allows for managing the blocks' visibility (i) and block-specific interaction mechanisms (ii). The interface shows the block's contents (iii) and allows content moderation (iv). In the figure, two voting blocks have been created.

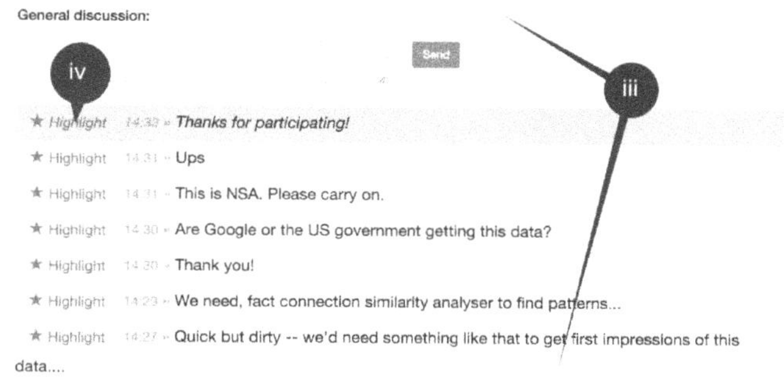

Figure 4: Presemo's simplified control interface. This interface shows the content (iii) and allows highlighting the content (iv).

see in their devices. This enables dynamically configurable presentations.

Audience members can use Presemo with any internet-equipped device. The system has been optimized for smartphone and tablet use, since these devices are usually most common in the audience. Using Presemo requires zero configuration: there are no logins or user accounts; instead, a simple URL is provided that the audience members can type in their web browsers.

To support performers' varying needs, we have developed two different control interfaces for managing Presemo. The full control interface (Fig. 3) allows for the performer to control the visibility of each block (i), configure block-specific options (ii), show user contributions (iii), and highlight or delete specific contributions (iv). The simplified control interface (Fig. 4) offers a narrowed-down set of functions, including only content showing (iii) and highlighting (iv). The need for two different control interfaces stems from our experience of actual Presemo use and facilitation that spans several years. We will discuss this further in the end of the work.

RQ1: CHARACTERISTICS OF LIVE PARTICIPATION

Having presented our instance of a live participation system—Presemo—we move to explore the characteristics (RQ1) and diversity (RQ2) of live participation. To study these aspects, we engaged in empirical case studies: a single-case study for the characteristics and a multiple-case study for the diversity (for more information about the cases, see Table 1 later in the paper). These cases demonstrate how live participation was taken into use in panels and discussion events (cases a, c, e, f), education (g, h) and conferences (b, d). They represent variety of audience sizes and organizers applying live participation and using Presemo. As Presemo has also been commercialized as an academic spinoff[2], these cases have been chosen from a series of in-the-wild studies.

We studied characteristics of live participation in an academic event, referred to as Case a in Table 1. It was a 1.5 hours panel where the panellists first presented their own work and then engaged in a discussion between themselves and their audience about the relationships of big data and HCI. The panellists sat next to public screens, facing the audience. The event also involved off-stage staff who sat in the front row in the audience (see Fig. 5) and managed Presemo's use via the full control interface.

We chose this case for a more detailed analysis because of several reasons. First, the large audience size made it comparable to the existing works in audience–performer interaction (e.g., [4, 11, 18, 28, 34]). Second, the case included two types of performances: the panellists' presentations and the discussion. Third, the audience consisted of mostly first-time users, which is the most common situation in live participation contexts. Finally, an academic panel allowed us to apply various data collection strategies, as the event was public and participants were supportive of research. We informed the audience about our study in the beginning of the panel, and no questions of our arrangements were raised.

We triangulated our analysis with video recordings, interviews, log data and a survey to analyse the interactions. We started the analysis from the video material and interviews where we applied the open-ended coding approach [38], first on the video material and later on the interview data. This way, the interview data analysis was informed by the video analysis and could be used to supplement the video-based observations [20]. In both of the datasets our coding focused on the performers' interactions with Presemo.

We carried out seven semi-structured interviews of 20 to 60 minutes each and rewarded interviewees with 25-euro (USD 30) gift cards. We inquired about event experiences and performer–spectator and spectator–spectator interactions. We continued with more detailed inquiries about the role of mediated and non-mediated communications in these interactions.

[2] See Screen.io, `http://www.screen.io`

Figure 5: Photograph from case study a, showing the public display (left), the panellists and of-stage staff (middle), and the audience (right).

Finally, we sent a questionnaire to all the conference participants, focusing on their experiences of the panel discussion. 24 participants—about one quarter of the panel audience—responded.[3] We probed for experiences about using Presemo, using a five-point Likert scale, to understand the experiences of the audience more broadly. The questionnaire items included both positive (e.g., 'Presemo was useful') and negative statements (e.g., 'Presemo was unnecessary'). We will consider the participants' responses descriptively in the analysis section.

We describe our findings on live participation through the following three characteristics.

Integration Work

The panel chair took the lead of integration work and used several methods to do this. He made verbal notes throughout the session regarding Presemo. He invited the audience to take part, framed the goal of participation during different stages of performance, and acknowledged audience's contributions and further presented them to the panellists. Also non-verbal actions, such as glancing at the public display, conveyed the notion of relevance of the content to those attending the panel discussion. Finally, he also highlighted audience's chat messages through Presemo and invited the panellists to discuss them. In an interview, one participant observed that

> I assume they [messages] kind of reflected the, again, the hive mind. So if the moderator [chairperson] selected those, it was because he was paying attention [Audience member, interview 3].

This indicates the perceived value this interviewee had towards the panel chair's attempt to use the content to lead the discussion. However, the panel chair was not the only on-stage actor conducting integration work. The panellists had monitors, which allowed them to see the content. We observed two cases wherein the panellists specially addressed a topic raised via Presemo in their on-stage discussion. One of the panellists engaging in this type of activity explained:

> [I] involved content from Presemo, to make it worthwhile for people to be interacting with it. So trying to address the comments that came through on it. So yeah, definitely a couple of times I explicitly referred to these comments. [Panellist, interview 5]

In this quote, we observe also the subtle ways of integrating the audience content without explicitly framing it as such.

Episodes

In this panel, a total of 11 blocks were used, seven of them ratings, three of voting and one of polling.

The panel started off with an introduction of Presemo and warm-up questions that aimed to familiarise the audience with its use. The chair presented the overall goal of the panel. During this time, the extended performance was mostly either performer-initiated & performer-controlled or audience-initiated & performer-controlled. This warm-up phase lasted roughly the first 25 minutes of the panel.

The second phase of the panel included customised chat blocks, each titled with "Questions and comments to N. N." Each block was shown during the respective panellist's opening statement. The panel chair used the content to ask questions after each presentation. Each block was then hidden from the audience. This represented a very typical pattern of audience-initiated & performer-controlled interaction. In total this took 35 minutes, and on average each extended performance episode lasted 8 minutes.

In the final phase, majority of blocks were freeform chats, and the chair involved its contents in summarizing statements about the panel. Here we saw audience-controlled interaction as well as audience-initiated & performer-controlled interaction. In total there were five blocks in this phase, shown and hidden in an alternating manner over a course of 35 minutes.

Extended Performance

The observed performer–audience interactions demonstrate Presemo's successful use in an extended performance. First, performers took content from Presemo and made it a part of performance (integration). Second, the blocks were shown and hidden based on the performance (episodes).

Also the off-stage staff's role in the creation of the extended performance was important. They commenced and closed episodes by hiding and showing respective interaction blocks as needed by the on-stage performers. To make sure that Presemo's use would be aligned with the event's different stages, planning had been necessary between the technical team, the panel chair and panellists before the performance.

However, as is typical in performances, the panel also involved improvisation. To facilitate further discussion, the technical staff opened an unplanned new block focused specifically on the privacy questions related to big data and HCI. This example demonstrates how the off-stage staff was involved in creating the extended performance beyond the original plans.

[3] We acknowledge that in our data-collection, response biases such as self-selection are clear; therefore, we use these statistical data to triangulate our other results and as an illustrative example.

Our survey indicated that live participation was overall successful, as more than 70% of the respondents agreed that 'Presemo influenced the overall flow of the sessions', and slightly more than 50% also agreed that Presemo allowed them to work with the panellists. These results mean that Presemo became an extended performance, instead of only a supplementary channel. Also, the audience considered its use meaningful instead and not an interruption. The performers enhanced the on-stage performance by making use of user-generated content. The system itself was changed based on the varying needs of the performance, also dynamically.

To sum up the answers to RQ1, we observed that integration work was distributed among several people, both on-stage and off-stage. We also observed how the panel chair, panellists and the off-stage staff were engaged in creation of the extended performance. Finally, we observed the episodic nature of the extended performance, where 11 different blocks provided a structure for the performance's different phases.

RQ2: THE DIVERSITY OF LIVE PARTICIPATION

To study the diversity of live participation, one needs to engage in studies in different cases and contexts. Thus we present a multiple-case study encompassing eight different contexts where Presemo was used, varying in terms of experience with Presemo (novel to experienced), audience size (20 to 400), audience members' familiarity with each other (from ad hoc groups to several years of collaboration), age of participants (from an elementary school class to working age), and use contexts (panels, education, conferences).

Although we have facilitated over a hundred Presemo sessions during the previous years, in the sampling of the cases for this paper we were limited to those ones where videotaping, logging and reporting of presentation contents was allowed. More details of the cases can be found from Table 1 where we describe the contexts, aims, and user roles from each case, as well as the number of blocks that were used in the events. We discovered diversity among several important dimensions, as presented in the following.

Aims and Means of Use

One of the most significant dimensions was the variance of goals why live participation was used (hereafter "aims") and the ways in which performers sought to reach the aims (hereafter "means"). Column "Aim" in Table 1 shows the purposes for which Presemo was used, as expressed by the performers. The aims can be categorized into four general categories: asking questions, activating audience, engaging the audience in knowledge co-creation and collecting information.

To analyse the means to reach these general aims, we analysed log data about blocks' titles (i.e., the textual prompts shown to the audience) across the eight cases. Our method followed the practices of qualitative thematic classification [43]. We asked two researchers *not* familiar with the cases, Presemo, or our own categorization, to group the block titles of each case (83 in total; the sum of blocks in Table 1) independently into categories. They then grouped the categories, discussed the results with us, and we developed the final grouping. We achieved reliable levels of inter-coder agreement of 87.8% and a Krippendorff's alpha of 0.855.

This process resulted in eight different means (see Table 2), some of which were used to serve several aims.[4] These eight means can be grouped into three conceptual categories following the distinctions between three types of initiation–control pairs that we already used to discuss existing live participation systems. We have highlighted the three categories with italicized sub-headings. Based on these analyses of aims and means, we find that Presemo afforded a wide variety of different ways of use, both ones giving agency to the performer and those giving it to the audience.

Audience Size

When we reviewed the literature on live participation systems, we found no previous papers that would have examined the scalability, in terms of number of participants, of different systems. Thus we do not know yet whether backchannels, Q&A systems and the like scale gracefully up or down from the typical range of 75–150 participants [11, 18].

Our eight case studies provide initial glimpses to the diversity of audience sizes to which the live participation concept can be generalized. Live participation seems usable at least with audience sizes ranging from 20 to 400. In most cases, the penetration rate among the participants who engaged in using Presemo varied between 40% to 100% (see column "Roles" in Table 1). In case e, we expect that the lower penetration was related to not having a public display to present the audience's contributions.

Although the benefits from using Presemo in these cases are difficult to measure, we received positive feedback from all the organizers. Therefore, we conclude that these cases may have not yet even reached the limits of scalability for live participation systems.

Performer Roles

We also observed various configurations of on-stage and off-stage performer roles (see column "Roles" in Table 1). Concerning the on-stage roles, we learned that not everyone on-stage is necessarily involved in live participation. Based on this, we have now developed a more detailed terminology for different live participation setups.

Chairpersons, for example, are on-stage performers who are actively using the system but mostly attend the other performers. However, they are often limited by their attentive capacity and therefore can at most show and hide blocks that are shown on screen. More demanding tasks such as reordering of the blocks or changing their contents may take too much attention from the face-to-face interactions.

Hosts are performers' "right hands" who especially in large events are in direct interaction both with the audience and the live participation, but interact less with the performers on stage. Unlike chairpersons or panel members, hosts do not

[4] The last means labelled as "event organization" is marked with "n/a", since it did not belong to the scope of live participation: performers only showed static content to the audience.

	Context	Aim	Roles	Blocks
(a)	An academic panel related to big data in HCI research. Panellists first presented their own work around the topic, after which audience and panellists discussed the opportunites and challenges together.	Ask questions from panellists and engage in knowledge co-construction.	Audience: 100 persons, of whom 40 used Presemo. On-stage: Five panellists seeing Presemo content and a panel chairperson with a simplified control interface. Off-stage: Two orchestrators who had full access to the control interface.	11
(b)	A marketing festival for sharing the latest news related to trends in information technology with corporations' representatives.	Activate the audience	Audience: 200 persons, of whom 100 used Presemo. On-stage: Five presenters and a host who had access to the simplified control interface. Off-stage: One assistant to the host, sitting next to the stage. Assistants providing technical support and managed the system via the control interface.	22
(c)	A strategy meeting discussing current and future trends in mobility with organisations' staff and external stakeholders, related to organization's strategy work	Ask questions and collect information for strategy work.	Audience: 400 persons, of whom 200 used Presemo. On-stage: Seven presenters and one host. Off-stage: An orchestrator, two moderators, and three technical support staff supporting the audience.	14
(d)	An state-of-the-art presentation and gathering of the industry where the latest information on industrial Internet development was shared and understand how various members of the relevant association apply industrial Internet thinking in their organisation. Presemo question was used much to collect factual information of participants, examined during the event and after it.	Collect information from participants and activate them.	Audience: 100 persons, most using Presemo. On-stage: Four presenters and one chairperson. The orchestrator was on-stage a few times to act as host of the event. Off-stage: An orchestrator and two moderators, both of whom pre-screened content.	20
(e)	An annual meeting of academic staff where the future of the research institute and university support services were presented. The first performer asked to be interrupred during his presentation, while the second and third presented preferred to go questions through in the end of his presentation.	Ask questions anonymously	Audience: 60 person, only few using Presemo. On-stage: three performers, none with direct access to Presemo content. Off-stage: two moderators, responsible of raising themes from Presemo to the stage.	3
(f)	A panel and discussion about the future of. Participants were a group of lead users. The performers asked questions and commented the results as their performance.	Collect information from the audience.	Audience: 150 persons, of whom 140 used Presemo. On-stage: Three panel members and two chairpersons, who had access to a simplified control interface. Off-stage: One orchestrator and two moderators.	9
(g)	A primary-school class for getting students engaged and to think about domestication of animals. The students answered two questions during 45 minutes class.	Activate the students	Audience: 20 students. On-stage: teacher, responsible both Presemo moderation and on-stage performance.	2
(h)	An university lecture focused on techniques for promoting good oral hygiene.	Activate the students	Audience: 50 students enrolled to lecture series. On-stage: teacher, responsible both Presemo moderation and on-stage activities	2

Table 1: Cases studied to examine diversity of live participation.

contribute to the main topic of the event, even if they are on stage.

Moderators and *orchestrators* work off-stage and help those on-stage to establish and maintain the extended performances. Moderators pre- and post-screen the content in the mediated interactions. Orchestrators, in turn, show and hide blocks in Presemo. Moderators were present in Cases a, c, d, and f, and orchestrators in Cases a–f. In cases g and h a single person was responsible for both the orchestration and content management, and was all the time on the stage.

The diversity of roles poses questions about live participation tools' interface design. If people in different roles have limitations in their attentive capacity, due to the contextual constraints, do they require different user interfaces? We will return to this question in the Discussion.

Episodes

Episodic extended performances were both our design goal in Presemo's development, and subsequently one of the characterising elements in the resulting live participation (see the section on RQ1). Episodicness makes it possible to be prepared for improvisation already before the event, through a pre-creation of interaction blocks.

To analyse the variation of episodes, we plotted, for each case, what means (as defined in Table 2) was used at any given time to advance the performance's aim. The results, shown in Figure 6, show how frequently the means was changed during each performance. These activity histograms allow us to discuss the episodes in these events.

First, in cases a, g, and h the performers switched the dominant interaction block during the course of the performance. These patterns are pointedly episodic as each moment is dominated by one type of means only.

In a more detailed analysis we confirmed that the episodic patterns were related to different stages of the event. For example, in the educational cases (g, h) the episodes coincided with first using Presemo for audience activation, and later for audience engagement. Even in cases where one means was dominant throughout the performance (such as in Cases c and

The means and its description	Example block titles	Supported aims*	Colour**
Performer-initiated & Performer-controlled			
Collection of precise information Collection of factual information from participants to assist with the presentation. The framing in terms of factual information indicates that each of the participants should know a single, correct answer.	"Your role in the company" (poll)	Collect	
Audience activation Closed-ended questions used during the performance and fully articulated and formulated by the performer team. These questions are often used as an input in the performance, thus as seeking various opinions and then discussing them.	"Evaluate the action (implementability)" (rating)	Collect	
Audience-initiated & Performer-controlled			
Audience engagement Open-ended questions used during the performance and contextualised as a part of the event. With audience engagement, there is a precisely defined, well-articulated aim for the interaction, presented in the framing of the activity.	"What are the problems in combining Big Data and HCI?" (rating)	Activate	
Interaction with performers Activities directed specifically to one particular performer on-stage, such as commenting on a presentation or asking questions of a certain performer.	"Questions and comments to [speaker name, organisation]" (chat)	Ask, Collect	
Audience-controlled			
General chat Allowing participants to discuss an open topic, without further elaboration on the purpose of the activity.	"General discussion" (chat)	Engage	
Specific chat Discussion of a topic that is related to the performance and has a special framing that contextualises the chat as part of the stage in question. However, this is open-ended and does not elaborate more precisely on the aim behind the interaction or the purpose of the chat activity.	"Talent on the Digital Frontier" (chat)	Activate	
Other			
Social lobby An 'anteroom' for the system, with activities familiarising the audience with live participation technology and examining how to use it before the event and performances start.	"How are you this morning?" (poll) "Welcome to [seminar name]" (chat)	Engage	
Event organisation Use of the live participation tool to support event set-up and organisation. This includes conveying information about event timetables, collecting feedback, and posting updates on the next stages of preparation for the event.	"11.20-12.05: Infoshots in Hall G, D and H" (chat) "Lunch Break 12.05-13.05" (chat)	n/a	

* The words refer to the aims presented in Table 1: Ask questions, Activate audience, Engage in knowledge co-construction, and Collect information.
** Used in Figure 6.

Table 2: The means by which blocks were used to support the aims of live participation.

e), different means had a lot of micro-level variation. While the graphs do not show it, Case c involved use of 14, and Case e use of 3 interaction blocks during the performance.

To summarize, while Presemo's design only included three different interaction block types, our analysis identified eight different ways (i.e., means) to use them to advance the performances' aims. Thus the same types of blocks, when considered as interactive episodes within a performance, were enacted by the performers in very different ways.

DISCUSSION

In this work, we have extended the previous research on performer–audience interaction by looking at various systems used for this target. Audience-response systems, question management systems and backchannels represent systems for a larger application domain that we have titled *live participation*. Furthermore, we presented Presemo, a tool whose design goes beyond those systems that have been designed with one prominent feature only. Our studies on Presemo explored live participation's crucial aspects (RQ1) and foregrounded a wide diversity of different uses (RQ2). With these studies and the conceptual work that we presented before the case studies we increased the understanding on performer–audience interaction on one hand, and tools with which it can be supported on the other.

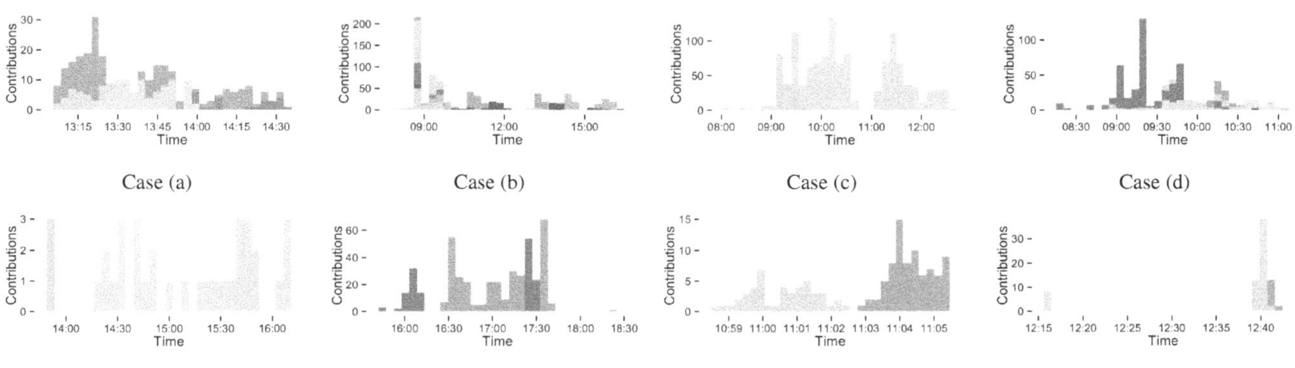

* Timeline only reflects time when Presemo was in use

Figure 6: Presemo use at events. For the colours' meanings, see Table 2.

We introduced a novel concept—*extended performance*—suggesting that the mediated space created through live participation system can be a venue that performers can use to engage the audience in their performances. Our work involved three approaches that had not been previously considered together: We applied performance research to events, we considered concurrently occurring face-to-face and mediated performances, and we included the audience as an active contributor to the performance. We described the challenges of managing these simultaneous interactions through a concept of integration work.

Our empirical focus was on performers and the ways in which they take advantage of live participation. Performers appropriated Presemo's three functionalities—polls, chat and voting—for four different aims through eight different means (see Tables 1 and 2). Based on eight case studies as well as other settings where we have facilitated Presemo's use, we consider the system design a success and find that it clearly supports performer–audience interaction. Performers have generally been happy with the experience of using Presemo.

Supporting Integration Work

Successful appropriation of a live participation system, as said, requires additional effort from the performer. We referred to this as *integration work*, meaning acts by which performers "bridge" the digital and the on-stage activities. Performers engage in integration work, for example, by including the audience-generated content into the on-stage performance and by articulating what they expect the audience to contribute. Some cases of integration work are straightforward: A performer may ask the audience a question that needs to be answered in the mediated space, and takes the result into account in the subsequent unfolding of the performance. Other cases of integration work may be more effortful, especially if performers cannot follow the interactions in the live participation system. For example, backchannel discussions may take place in forums not directly accessible to the performer. Integrating such hidden interactions in the ongoing on-stage performance is next to impossible.

A significant problem in sustaining the extended performance is that integration work is labourious. When the audience really engages in live participation, performers become easily overwhelmed by the amount of input. Indeed, we observed activity spikes where within a short amount of time tens or hundreds of contributions were entered.

Despite potential hardships, based on our experience, integration work is in the heart of successful performance augmentation with live participation. Because verbal integration work is effortful, we find more potential in non-verbal integration work. Non-verbal interactions' benefit lies in their lightweightness. Live participation systems shoud allow performers acknowledge audience members' contributions with simple positive signals. For example, performers could mark audience contributions as "read", or indicate if they "queue" a contribution for later discussion. Receiving such feedback from the performer could encourage participants to increase the quality and volume of further interactions.

As we reported, audience engagement may be "bursty". To avoid overwhelming the performers, automatic content management could be considered. Chat contents and open-ended answers could be summarized with real-time tag and keyword clouds. With speech-to-text analysis, content in the mediated space could be highlighted based on what the performer is talking at a given time (e.g., [1]). Also if several audience members submit similar content in a short time period, this could be brought up more strongly, for example, by grouping and highlighting these contributions. Finally, content could be rated or otherwise further processed by the audience, such as in Presemo and backchann.el [18].

Supporting the Extended Performance

Successful extended performance requires that the performer has an active presence also in the mediated space. If this is not possible, additional performers may be needed to ensure a sufficient mediated engagement with the audience.

With multiple performers, roles may be allocated for different people. To support *different roles* (see "performer roles"; RQ2), dedicated role-specific live participation interfaces may be needed. Presemo provides currently two such interfaces. The simplified interface (Figure 4) seemed best suitable for hosts while chairpersons benefit more from the full control of Presemo's functions, including block initiation and content moderation.

In single-performer situations in smaller (e.g., classroom) events, the support for an extended performance needs a different approach, as one performer needs to manage both the face-to-face and mediated interactions. Based on our experience, a clearly alternating pattern has been useful. When extended performances become clearly distinguishable sessions, they need well-designed initiations and wrap-ups that bring structure to the performance. Close-ended polls whose results are graphically presented to the audience meet these requirements, but should not be the only means for augmenting performances. New interaction formats are therefore an important topic for future research.

CONCLUSION

Live participation systems are a fertile application domain in HCI. They are actively developed and taken into use in various performances. Our paper has gathered these systems—ranging from close-ended audience response systems to open-ended live tweeting systems and backchannels—together, under a shared conceptual framework. We have also increased, through empirical case studies, conceptual understanding on these systems' salient characteristics of use.

Acknowledgements

We thank Petri Lievonen and Jukka Reitmaa in their contributions to Presemo's development. Presemo has been released under GNU-AGPL and is available at `https://github.com/presemo/`.

We thank TEKES for funding this work through LEAD and Re:Know projects. AS's work was funded by Academy of Finland through Creative Use project.

REFERENCES

1. Salvatore Andolina, Khalil Klouche, Diogo Cabral, Tuukka Ruotsalo, and Giulio Jacucci. 2015. InspirationWall: Supporting Idea Generation Through Automatic Information Exploration. In *Proceedings of the 2015 ACM SIGCHI Conference on Creativity and Cognition*. ACM Press, 103–106. DOI: http://dx.doi.org/10.1145/2757226.2757252

2. Philip Auslander. 2012. Digital Liveness: a Historico-Philosophical Perspective. *PAJ: A Journal of Performance and Art* 34, 3 (2012), 3–11.

3. Ian D. Beatty, William J. Gerace, and Robert J. Dufresne. 2006. Designing Effective Questions for Classroom Response System Teaching. *American Journal of Physics* 74, 1 (2006), 31–39. DOI: http://dx.doi.org/10.1119/1.2121753

4. Tony Bergstrom, Andrew Harris, and Karrie Karahalios. 2011. Encouraging Initiative in the Classroom with Anonymous Feedback. In *Proceedings of the 13th IFIP TC 13 International Conference on Human-Computer Interaction*. 627–642. DOI: http://dx.doi.org/10.1007/978-3-642-23774-4{_}49

5. Lorena Blasco-Arcas, Isabel Buil, Blanca Hernández-Ortega, and F. Javier Sese. 2013. Using Clickers in Class. The Role of Interactivity, Active Collaborative Learning and Engagement in Learning Performance. *Computers and Education* 62 (2013), 102–110. DOI: http://dx.doi.org/10.1016/j.compedu.2012.10.019

6. danah m. boyd. 2009. Spectacle at Web2.0 Expo... from my perspective. Available online at http://www.zephoria.org/thoughts/archives/2009/11/24/spectacle_at_we.html. (2009).

7. Jane E. Caldwell. 2007. Clickers in the Large Classroom: Current Research and Best-Practice Tips. *CBE Life Sciences Education* 6, 1 (2007), 9–20. DOI: http://dx.doi.org/10.1187/cbe.06-12-0205

8. Alan Dix, Jennifer G. Sheridan, Stuart Reeves, and Steve Benford. 2006. Formalising Performative Interaction. In *Interactive Systems. Design, Specification, and Verification*. 15–25.

9. Marian Dörk, Daniel Gruen, Carey Williamson, and Sheelagh Carpendale. 2010. A Visual Backchannel for Large-Scale Events. *IEEE Transactions on Visualization and Computer Graphics* 16, 6 (2010), 1129–1138. DOI: http://dx.doi.org/10.1109/TVCG.2010.129

10. Honglu Du, Mary Beth Rosson, and John M. Carroll. 2012. Communication Patterns for a Classroom Public Digital Backchannel. In *Proceedings of the 30th ACM international Conference on Design of Communication*. ACM Press, 127. DOI: http://dx.doi.org/10.1145/2379057.2379081

11. Honglu Du, Mary Beth Rosson, John M. Carroll, and Craig Ganoe. 2009. I felt like a contributing member of the class. In *Proceedings of the ACM 2009 International Conference on Supporting Group Work*. ACM Press, 233. DOI: http://dx.doi.org/10.1145/1531674.1531709

12. Carmen Fies and Jill Marshall. 2006. Classroom Response Systems: A Review of the Literature. *Journal of Science Education and Technology* 15, 1 (2006), 101–109. DOI: http://dx.doi.org/10.1007/s10956-006-0360-1

13. Donald Getz. 1991. *Festivals, special events, and tourism*. Van Nostrand Reinhold.

14. Donald Getz. 2012. *Event Studies: Theory, Research and Policy for Planned Events*. Routledge.

15. Joe J. Goldblatt. 1990. *Special Events: The Art and Science of Celebration*. Van Nostrand Reinhold.

16. Colin M. Hall. 1992. *Hallmark Tourist Events: Impacts, Management and Planning*. Belhaven Press.

17. Drew Harry, Eric Gordon, and Chris Schmandt. 2012. Setting the Stage for Interaction: A Tablet Application to Augment. In *Proceedings of the ACM 2012 Conference on Computer Supported Cooperative Work*. ACM Press, 1071–1081. DOI: http://dx.doi.org/10.1145/2145204.2145364

18. Drew Harry, Joshua Green, and Judith Donath. 2009. backchan.nl. In *Proceedings of the 27th International Conference on Human factors in computing systems*. ACM Press, 1361–1370. DOI: http://dx.doi.org/10.1145/1518701.1518907

19. Giulio Jacucci. 2015. Interaction as Performance: Performative Strategies in Designing Interactive Experiences. In *Ubiquitous Computing, Complexity, and Culture*, Ulrik Ekman, Jay David Bolter, Lily Diaz, Morten Sondergaard, and Maria Engberg (Eds.). Routledge, New York.

20. Brigitte Jordan and Austin Henderson. 1995. Interaction Analysis: Foundations and Practice. *Journal of the Learning Sciences* 4, 1 (1 1995), 39–103. DOI: http://dx.doi.org/10.1207/s15327809jls0401{_}2

21. Eugene Judson and Daiyo Sawada. 2002. Learning from Past and Present: Electronic Response Systems in College Lecture Halls. *Journal of Computers in Mathematics and Science Teaching* 21, 2 (2002), 167–181.

22. Robin H. Kay and Ann LeSage. 2009. Examining the Benefits and Challenges of Using Audience Response Systems: A Review of the Literature. *Computers & Education* 53, 3 (2009), 819–827. http://dx.doi.org/10.1016/j.compedu.2009.05.001

23. Christopher Kelty, Aaron Panofsky, Morgan Currie, Roderic Crooks, Seth Erickson, Patricia Garcia, Michael Wartenbe, and Stacy Wood. 2015. Seven Dimensions of Contemporary Participation Disentangled. *Journal of the Association for Information Science and Technology* 66, 3 (2015), 474–488. DOI: http://dx.doi.org/10.1002/asi.23202

24. David M. Lane and Rober S. Atlas. 1996. The Networked Classroom. In *The meeting of Computers and Psychology*. http://ctl.sri.com/publications/displayPublication.jsp?ID=321

25. Anders Olof Larsson. 2013. Tweeting the Viewer – Use of Twitter in a Talk Show Context. *Journal of Broadcasting & Electronic Media* 57, 2 (4 2013), 135–152. DOI: http://dx.doi.org/10.1080/08838151.2013.787081

26. Eun-Ju Lee. 2012. That's Not the Way It Is: How User-Generated Comments on the News Affect Perceived Media Bias. *Journal of Computer-Mediated Communication* 18, 1 (10 2012), 32–45. DOI: http://dx.doi.org/10.1111/j.1083-6101.2012.01597.x

27. Misa T. Maruyama, Scott P. Robertson, Sara K. Douglas, Bryan C. Semaan, and Heather A. Faucett. 2014. Hybrid Media Consumption. In *Proceedings of the 17th ACM Conference on Computer Supported Cooperative Work & Social Computing*. ACM Press, 1422–1432. DOI: http://dx.doi.org/10.1145/2531602.2531719

28. Joseph F. McCarthy and danah m. boyd. 2005. Digital Backchannels in Shared Physical Spaces. In *2005 Extended Abstracts on Human Factors in Computing Systems*. ACM Press, 1641. DOI: http://dx.doi.org/10.1145/1056808.1056986

29. Kimra McPherson, Kai Huotari, Yo-Shang F. Cheng, David Humphrey, Coye Chesire, and Andrew L. Brooks. 2012. Glitter: a Mixed-Methods Study of Twitter Use During Glee Broadcasts. In *Proceedings of the ACM 2012 conference on Computer Supported Cooperative Work Companion*. 167–170. http://dl.acm.org/citation.cfm?id=2141569

30. Matti Nelimarkka, Kai Kuikkaniemi, and Giulio Jacucci. 2014. A Field Trial of an Anonymous Backchannel Among Primary School Pupils. In *Proceedings of the 18th International Conference on Supporting Group Work*. ACM Press, 238–242. DOI: http://dx.doi.org/10.1145/2660398.2660399

31. Jay F. Nunamaker, Robert O. Briggs, Daniel D. Mittleman, Douglas R. Vogel, and Balthazard A. Pierre. 1996. Lessons from a Dozen Years of Group Support Systems Research: A Discussion of Lab and Field Findings. *Journal of Management Information Systems* 13, 3 (12 1996), 163–207. DOI: http://dx.doi.org/10.1080/07421222.1996.11518138

32. Stuart Reeves. 2011. *Designing Interfaces in Public Settings: Understanding the Role of the Spectator in Human-Computer Interaction*. Springer. DOI: http://dx.doi.org/10.1007/978-0-85729-265-0

33. Stuart Reeves, Steve Benford, Claire O'Malley, and Mike Fraser. 2005. Designing the spectator experience. In *Proceedings of the SIGCHI Conference on Human Factors in Computing Systems*. ACM Press, 741. DOI: http://dx.doi.org/10.1145/1054972.1055074

34. Jun Rekimoto, Yuji Ayatsuka, Hitoraka Uoi, and Toshifumi Arai. 1998. Adding Another Communication Channel to Reality. In *Conference summary on Human factors in Computing Systems 1998*. ACM Press, 271–272. DOI: http://dx.doi.org/10.1145/286498.286752

35. Richard Schechner. 2013. *Performance studies: An introduction*. Routledge.

36. Kjeld Schmidt and Liam Bannon. 1992. Taking CSCW seriously - Supporting Articulation Work. *Computer Supported Cooperative Work* 1, 1-2 (1992), 7–40. DOI: http://dx.doi.org/10.1007/BF00752449

37. Jennifer G. Sheridan, Alan Dix, Simon Lock, and Alice Bayliss. 2005. Understanding Interaction in Ubiquitous Guerrilla Performances in Playful Arenas. In *Proceedings of HCI 2004: People and Computers XVIII – Design for Life*. 3–17. DOI: http://dx.doi.org/10.1007/1-84628-062-1{_}1

38. David Silverman. 2000. *Doing Qualitative Research. A practical handbook*. SAGE Publications.

39. Jocelyn Spence, Stuart Andrews, and David M. Frohlich. 2012. Now, Where Was I? Negotiating Time in Digitally Augmented Autobiographical Performance. *Journal of Media Practice* 13, 3 (9 2012), 269–284. DOI: http://dx.doi.org/10.1386/jmpr.13.3.269{_}1

40. Jocelyn Spence, David Frohlich, and Stuart Andrews. 2013. Performative Experience Design: Where Autobiographical Performance and HumanComputer Interaction Meet. *Digital Creativity* 24, 2 (2013), 96–110. DOI: http://dx.doi.org/10.1080/14626268.2013.808964

41. Erik Stolterman and Mikael Wiberg. 2010. Concept-Driven Interaction Design Research. *Human-Computer Interaction* 25, 2 (2010), 95–118. DOI: http://dx.doi.org/10.1080/07370020903586696

42. Anselm Strauss. 1985. Work and the Division of Labor. *The Sociological Quarterly* 26, 1 (1985), 1–19.

43. Anselm Leonard Strauss and Juliet M. Corbin. 1990. *Basics of Qualitative Research*. Vol. 15. Sage Newbury Park, CA.

44. Julie R. Williamson, Lone Koefoed Hansen, Giulio Jacucci, Ann Light, and Stuart Reeves. 2014. Understanding Performative Interactions in Public Settings. *Personal and Ubiquitous Computing* 18, 7 (2014), 1545–1549.

45. Sarita Yardi. 2006. The Role of the Backchannel in Collaborative Learning Environments. In *Proceedings of the 7th International Conference on Learning Sciences*. 852–858. http://dl.acm.org/citation.cfm?id=1150034.1150158

Situated Encounters with Socially Engaged Art in Community-Based Design

Rachel Clarke[1]
Open Lab[1]
Newcastle University
{Rachel.Clarke} {P.C.Wright}
@newcastle.ac.uk

Jo Briggs[2]
Media & Communication Design
Northumbria University[2]
Newcastle-upon-Tyne
Jo.Briggs@northumbria.ac.uk

Ann Light[3]

Peter Wright[1]
School of Engineering & Informatics[3]
University of Sussex
Ann.Light@sussex.ac.uk

ABSTRACT
With the increased relevance of digital technologies in civil life comes the challenge of how to design research for citizen engagement. Drawing from three reflexive case studies presenting socially engaged arts (SEA) projects, we describe how, as artists, collaborators and researchers, we engaged in socially inclusive community-based projects. We argue that our roles required us to be both flexible and to adopt critical openness in practices of collaborative social facilitation. We conclude with insights to inform community-based research and enable nurturing and inclusive engagement in research design for the exploration of near-future digital technologies.

Author Keywords
Socially Engaged Art; community-based design; participation; civic engagement; social change

INTRODUCTION
Community-based design research is increasingly understood as complex, requiring commitments that that go beyond "formal methods" [10,16,18,45,46]. As researchers we adopt multiple approaches taking on flexible and responsive roles, sensitively adapting to situations as our understanding and relationships change during the process [22,31,36]. In community-based participatory and action research, involving artists is an increasingly common tactic used to open up alternative lines of inquiry, or build community confidence [20]. Artists develop approaches to envision alternative imaginaries, often overlooked in conventional research focused on linguistic forms of expression and representation [30]. The use of performance, photography and video for instance, can help elicit rich accounts of people's experience, and also make more explicit practitioners' implicated roles [4,24,27].

DIS 2016, June 04-08, 2016, Brisbane, QLD, Australia
ACM 978-1-4503-4031-1/16/06.
http://dx.doi.org/10.1145/2901790.2901882

In HCI and related research there is increased interest in design involving communities in sustained acts of civic engagement [45,46]. We argue that wider awareness of socially engaged arts (SEA) practitioner roles can be of benefit and part of our contribution is to help acknowledge this and open up further discussion. SEA has emerged within HCI over the past decade [13] facilitated by its orientation towards social change, social justice [12,34], sustainability [8,15], inclusion and participation [48]. And yet, while practices have been adopted in design research they still remain largely under-acknowledged.

We believe that we are in a privileged position to contribute by articulating the complexities and intricacies of community engagement from our own experiences. Our authorship consists of HCI researchers with backgrounds in SEA practice [6,12]; and well-established HCI academics who have worked extensively with SEA practitioners [33, 34,35,37] and drawn conceptual and theoretical insights from such work [38,51]. However, we also advocate for additional work to build and sustain more equitable and inclusive relationships between researchers and communities. This, we feel is particularly important where research is motivated by a desire to bring about "real-world" social change, but also requires caution and shared responsibility in accounting for the social and material consequences that may occur, when designing and using digital technologies.

In this paper we discuss how we position ourselves within community-based projects and how these positions both influence and are influenced by our process. As researchers we typically work with a multiplicity of narratives to engage with the perspectives of those with whom we work, while also articulating our own positions [3,22,31,43]. The inherently durational aspect of our work with and within communities is an important feature [10,45]; our positions are situated not just in place but also time, and subject to change. With a growing shift from designing for discrete interactive systems to designing for their extensive use across social, cultural and civil life [1,26] the insights we contribute have wide applicability to supporting community-based HCI design research practices.

Our contribution is centered on three reflexive accounts of discrete projects that we have developed since 2000. Our descriptions are detailed to foreground our roles and commitments to working as and working with SEA practitioners and researchers. By reflecting back we reveal how we performed multiple overlapping practitioner-researcher identities to ask: What were the motivations and expectations at the outset of what often became extended and sometimes-intense forms of engagement? What anticipated and unexpected roles did we adopt as the projects evolved? How did our identities evolve over time?

We sketch out the necessarily complex personas and entangled relations that were created through processes of working with communities. And we extend – and also trouble [9,21] – existing vocabulary for researcher identities and roles within community-based design. We present our case studies as sensitizing strategies [29] to provoke and open up discussion on some of the intricacies of designing and facilitating design research. We argue this way of working necessitates an ongoing commitment to critical openness, to work with uncertainty and a willingness to submerge ourselves and make sense of complexity [29].

SOCIALLY ENGAGED ART IN HCI

Arts-based practices within HCI research have made significant contributions to both the understanding of people's experiences with technology and to the design of aesthetics for digital interaction. As a subset of fine arts practice, SEA is a "process-based approach" [4] in that it is grounded on the 'facilitation of dialogue among diverse communities' [27 p.153] rather than on artifacts or exhibitions. Drawing from traditions of performance and activism [5,19,23], SEA within HCI has so far primarily been employed around issues of environmental sustainability [8,15].

Valuable theoretical insights from SEA and applied in HCI, have shown how researchers can support collaborative investigation of the very conditions in which problems are defined, technology is developed and/or used, and knowledge produced. We find these theoretical arguments compelling as they question what it means to "do good", or attempt to mobilize social change, or at least improve "real world" situations through research. Further, these insights attend to how we frame our research objectives by shifting the focus of design from tangible artifacts to the processes and practices of research, collaboration, facilitation and knowledge production. However, much of the existing work has focused on rhetorical reflections of brief episodes in time, and rarely accounts for more durational and relational aspects of engagement, or the shifting roles that researchers enact to address challenges and tensions encountered along the way.

Within the arts, practitioners are typically experienced in public engagement and its facilitation. We believe that there is value in critically reflecting upon what it is in particular that SEA practitioners *do*. Our aim is to exemplify and tease out some of these roles in relation to the durational complexities and social and political intricacies that community-based research often involves.

Between community and researcher identities

The community-based informatics and design literatures frequently outline the importance of researchers familiarizing themselves with particular community identities to enable meaningful participation [10,16]. This is considered important, so as not to conceptualize communities as homogenous and harmonious wholes and rather to understand the informal ways that relationships within communities are formed. However, researchers' roles and positions are rarely discussed and critically questioned in relation to how their values and assumptions inform the construction of research sites or framing of research questions. The two areas that have articulated this most fully are Action Research and Participatory Design.

Hayes describes how research is never 'value neutral' in that researchers bring personal values into the field [22]. She articulates these in terms of researchers becoming 'friendly outsider(s)' who work in close proximity to the community as '"coaches" skilled at opening up lines of communication and facilitating research activities with community partners' [p.8]. This is accompanied by recognition of particular expertise in and awareness of what digital technology is available and appropriate for a particular situation.

In Participatory Design, Light and Akama [36] highlight the emotional acuity required in facilitation roles, particularly those to support design research for community safety. Light and Akama highlight the importance of creating safe spaces for conflict and difference where people could feel comfortable sharing difficult experiences. Facilitating such spaces required additional time in working with participants' stories of loss and anger, before issues of safety could even be approached – an unanticipated but vital step in the design work.

In an eloquent exposition of researcher roles, Le Dantec and Fox [31] describe how these changed to help manage a complex research agenda over time. Their in-depth account from an under-reported community researcher perspective, advocates that the researcher step back from the work of designing digital interaction and instead focus on the design of the research goals and objectives with the community. Their description articulates complex work that necessarily *precedes* the design of any digital infrastructure or artifacts. This is not just about how researchers gain access to and/or become part of a community; but recognition of constant navigation of multiple and often conflicting identities. Le Dantec and Fox usefully highlight how these roles are not just positions that as researchers we define ourselves, but roles that are negotiated within and sometimes ascribed by the communities with whom we work. If we become a confidant this is because someone values us in this way.

We applaud the value of feminist scholarship to the design community in advocating for greater transparency in our reporting of values, positionality and reflexivity [3,21,43]. Indeed, hiding our positions and decision-making processes can disguise differences in power and influence. Yet, as Le Dantec and Fox [31] and Light and Akama [36] show, researchers' positions can change when their initial approaches do not fit with the aims or sensibilities of the community, or when different issues emerge. Positions, roles and identities are also open to others' interpretation and can mean different things to different people, requiring continual questioning and responsiveness [43].

It is therefore useful here to consider the limits of being able to *know*, and fully account for our positions with certainty. Feminist scholars have also argued that aiming for comprehensive transparency in reflexivity is bound to fail [43]. It is important to recognize the situated nature and partiality of knowledge production that does not claim complete transparency. Situatedness is never, in effect, completely knowable and reportable. In this sense researchers are always working with a shifting self, articulated through specific and ongoing social interactions, informed by the research inquiry and ongoing relationships with people. It is only through enacting and performing roles through with others that the complexity and uncertainty of identity becomes (partially) recognizable and understood [9].

Between art theory and practice

SEA literature offers further valuable perspectives on such negotiations to community-based design and associated research. The concept of *dialogical aesthetics* was adopted by art historian Grant Kester [27] as a way of characterizing SEA as emerging through direct community action or intervention. Kester argues that empathic listening within forms of communicative exchange is where value is created [27 p.90] – as opposed to it being manifest in a tangible artifact or other output. Communication here is described as particular and unique, in that these relational processes enable sharing of and reflection upon personal biographies in processes that are both specifically situated and yet open to change. A dialogical aesthetic then is an approach, a way of working in which practitioners and those involved can appreciate the process of engagement, from different centers of value. Kester describes this as 'performative' in that 'the identity of the artist and those involved is produced through situational encounters', rather than through forms of performativity associated with theatricality or spectacle [27 p.95].

In a similar vein, theorists such as Claire Bishop identify the value of SEA practices as working with and accounting for the complexity of social relations, the tangled knots of 'engagement, affect, inequality' [4 p.39]. Rather than highlighting empathic dialogue, Bishop underlines the 'undecidability' of aesthetic experience as an important characteristic [4 p.27]. She argues that this is not just achieved through rational verbal argumentation, but embedded through the affective experience of working with uncertainty and contradiction, collaboratively. Bishop's account includes a useful reflection on the multiplicity of people involved in artworks, how the projects are conceived, funded, align or contradict with the diverse values of those who participate or facilitate their production. Creating such events requires approaches to gathering people and resources together. The role of the artist in this sense is therefore decentralized as controlling the action by highlighting a meshwork of actors taking on roles ordinarily not associated with creative practice.

From a SEA practitioner perspective, Pablo Helguera [23] further highlights that artists' roles may be much more fluid within socially engaged work, balancing between project management, social work and protest. This can create feelings of vulnerability for all those involved, not least, in how artists' roles may be perceived by others. There is constant negotiation of roles and commitments within a community. Artists may indeed subscribe to values, such as 'the betterment of humanity … social justice, the defense of human dignity and worth, and the strengthening of human relationships' [23 p.35]. However, what distinguishes them in their role is a 'critical self reflexive dialogue' [p.35] that encourages reflection on these values and concerns, through practices of working with people. The emphasis here is placed less on extremes – of confrontation and harmony – and more on *practices of listening* to a community of narrators and translators. Those involved may 'willingly engage in a dialogue from which they extract enough critical and experiential wealth to walk away feeling enriched, perhaps even claiming some ownership of the experience or the ability to reproduce it with others' [p. 23]. Helguera highlights how SEA practitioners often have an overt agenda which emphasizes developing a 'platform or a network for the participation of others, so that the effects of the project may outlast its ephemeral presentation' [p.23]. So while SEA practitioners may not always stay closely involved in a project, they may contribute to mobilizing certain forms of action, awareness or resources that continue beyond their immediate involvement.

CASE STUDIES

We now sketch our roles in three case studies by presenting reflexive first person perspectives, gained from our experiences facilitating community-based projects. We do this as a sensitizing strategy [29] to illustrate the specificities of our positions as artist-practitioner-researchers. The case studies have been selected because they were all informed by SEA practices but show a spectrum of positions working across different contexts and timescales. Furthermore we chose them because we have intimate knowledge of how they began and felt we could contribute details of our changing positions across time.

The first project ***Weird View*** [6,40] was completed 15 years ago by second author, Jo Briggs, in collaboration with artist

Valentina Nisi and the residents of a terrace of houses in County Dublin. This work was not developed as HCI research but as a collaborative interactive social history artwork for exhibition, but nonetheless provides insights on relationships and concepts for digital media were developed. Our second project ***DemTech*** [33,34,35,37] began in 2007, led by third author Ann Light, and featured researchers with an interest in arts-based practice and SEA artists collaborating in a community-based project with older adults. It has since grown into a new community initiative for sustainable energy. More recent and continuing interdisciplinary HCI design research ***Photo-parshiya*** [11,12,14] began in 2011 initiated by first author, Rachel Clarke, working as an artist with a background in SEA and new to HCI research. This project enabled the continuation of a collaborative community-based research initiative with an international women's center. We report the cases in the first person, working from within, and using our combined reflections to critically frame and identify our changing roles.

As an organizational device, we move chronologically through the three projects and provide a brief overview of each, how we began them, how we developed working relationships and how we left these relationships or kept in touch. This allows us to reflect specifically on durational aspects of our positions and roles within the work, while recognizing the changes that time has brought in the way of new technical opportunities and challenges. For the purposes of this paper we focus on our roles and therefore do not detail our methods or include perspectives of those we worked with as these are more fully discussed in prior work detailed above.

Weird View

Weird View was a community digital art project produced as the "final exhibition" of a master's course at Trinity College Dublin, where, after 10 years as a visual artist, I was undertaking training in multimedia systems. The brief was to "collaboratively develop" an interactive artwork. I was keen to extend collaboration beyond the 30 multidisciplinary postgraduates and involve people as co-producers of the artwork drawing inspiration from similar community broadcast work of its time [47].

Getting Started (partner-friend-artist-computer postgrad)

Weird View was born tangentially to this institutional process and came about through existing close ties and circumstances relating to my partner. At a family funeral in Lucan, Co. Dublin, he was reunited with four siblings from across three continents. They all met, along with cousins and old friends, and at the reception – where the stories flowed along with the drink. It was here that the idea to capture childhood reminiscences emerged. The timing and open nature of the family project enabled and demanded its immediate development, to involve some of those who were only around for a few days [6].

I began unobtrusively, researching by word-of-mouth and collecting the names of all the residents of a terrace of 20 cottages over living memory. This helped to capture people's interest and paper lists were passed around the village and annotated. Meanwhile the project revealed its potential for the proposed exhibition and Trinity postgraduate and artist Valentina Nisi, came on board. Meanwhile my partner and his closest familial ties were key, in not only contributing further stories but also by enabling and fast-forwarding connections more widely, and engendering everyone's trust in me.

In her work on site-specific artwork and situated identities, Mwon Kwon says that the most meaningful participation builds on existing ties to a particular community or friendship group [28]. My partner had lived on the terrace all of his life and he was pivotal, making introductions, before wide use of email or mobile phones. So, while a relatively short, if intensive, 3-month project, *Weird View's* design capitalized on close relations going back decades.

Our collective aim then was to capture the "memories and myths" associated with the terrace. This approach enabled some artistic license, and divergence from more formal social history methods enabling interpretation of the "behind closed doors" stories, from different perspectives.

Collaborating (facilitator-partner-foreigner-student-multimedia designer)

A loosely ethnographic approach of "hanging out" including shooting video in the village generated interest, and sparked conversations in which we invited contributions of stories or memorabilia. Encouraging people to bring along and discuss family photos at informal get-togethers e.g. in the village pub, prompted shared reminiscences. For instance, Annie, a keen photographer, had recently moved to a residential home for the elderly and in her absence, her son participated on her behalf, bringing along Annie's three family photo albums that chronicled the terrace between the 40s and the 60s; both a useful talking point and rich visual material. Over around 6-weeks the project grew rapidly as stories were recounted and collected, reenacted and captured using digital media. A certain "tipping point" was reached as locals offered anecdotes or other help (e.g. props for the videos), and the project grew well beyond a friends and family story.

Collectively, a core of community storytellers (including my partner) and the wider community generated dozens of reflective accounts of village life, which we artists retold in audio-visual and interactive media [40]. Around 60 individual stories were selected for the final exhibition, in consultation with Marie, who'd grown up on the terrace and informally took the role of community investigator (i.e. she was consulted on what should and should not be reproduced for the final work in the absence of more formal consent processes). Marie had initially shown interest as she was keen to discuss her new email account, and, as someone working with digital technology, I was invited along to trouble-shoot her network connection, in the process establishing very good relations.

We purposefully took a light touch approach to selecting the stories to develop for the artwork in a tactic to avoid potential tension. We rejected darker stories e.g. on domestic abuse or alcoholism, since I felt an acute personal responsibility to my partner, his family, friends and wider community. As non-Irish nationals and as artists, Valentina and I both worked inside, and also outside of the community [7] with our difference, and our use of digital tools, facilitating relations by attracting interest. For most of our community storytellers, *Weird View* was a first experience of being involved in a project using digital technologies and they were fascinated. While our objective did not include digitally up-skilling the community, the informal exchange of technical know-how – from troubleshooting email to learning the basics of shooting video – proved a by-product of mutual value which helped to quickly strengthen new relationships.

By the end of the project we had collectively produced a networked tapestry of the stories, realized in current and emergent digital media (circa 2000), in an interactive narrative form that spoke to the multivocality of a community, including the sometimes-conflicting accounts of the same event. The final piece aimed to invite interaction with an intertwined narrative snapshot of village life at a juncture when Co. Dublin was undergoing rapid urbanization.

Moving on (memento maker-web master-former partner)

The exhibition took place in the Douglas Hyde Gallery and, a week later the Muintir Na Tíre (local village hall) (Fig. 1). Our storytellers were invited to both, and turned out in force at the village hall. This event proved a fitting finalé to the project and comprised an informal evaluative process that elicited feedback and many further stories. *Weird View* won the annual Trinity prize and the exhibition curator expressed some interest in further developing the work. However, in the relative chaos that follows intensive postgraduate courses, we failed to find a continuation. I produced a website and CD-ROM, simplifying the dual touch-monitor installation for single screen PC, as a memento for our storytellers. Developing the project as artists helped to open doors – as did working with the reputation of a renowned Irish university. Over its development, *Weird View* became an open exploration of community co-production in a project that was founded and reliant on both the newly available digital tools, and on the buy-in of the community for practices of community self-presentation through digital media. The input of our storytellers was fundamental beyond even project conceptualization and pre-planning – through familial and community connections and experiences going back decades.

As I took a job in the multimedia industries in Dublin, my collaborator Valentina went on to develop more spatially distributed interactive narratives at the newly formed Media Lab Europe [41,42]. I later accepted a lecturing job in England while my partner chose to remain in Lucan.

Fig 1. Top: Community storytellers watching Weird View in the Muintir Na Tíre and gallery installation. Bottom: Detailed view of one of the homes (photos: Jo Briggs and Tim Kovar).

Democratising Technology (DemTech)

Democratising Technology (www.demtech.qmul.ac.uk) was a research project that brought older people's community groups together with researchers to produce a generative, open-ended form of engagement with digital technology. We deliberately used arts methods to devise techniques that could be brought to bear on the design of our society and tools [32,34,35]. Informed by performance artist Lois Weaver's practice [49], she and I worked with participants' values and aspirations for the future, using performance development methods as a transformational tool to produce a workshop of techniques for engaging people to consider social values for future technologies. The project ran for 18 months from 2007-8 and included a series of events, in particular an exhibition, *The Not Quite Yet* (Fig 2.), at which several artworks based on the workshop research were shown, and also a public symposium '*On the Margins of Technology*' about participation and older people.

Getting Started (an obsessive about connected products)

DemTech was intended to link citizenship, technological futures, and people's sense of agency in participative ways, rather than tackle the design of specific artifacts. It grew from my obsession with what I called the *social implications of networking everything,* which I had been writing about for some time (e.g. [32]), and my background in drama. I wrote the bid when I worked as a design consultant and winning the grant helped propel me into an academic role. Lois and I used co-design methodology and arts theory on engagement [5,33,34,49] to create a new path to democratically influencing the shape of future technology. We wanted to start with structures that seed ideas rather than introduce scenarios that would dictate themes. We wanted to work with people not already using networked technology. We chose to work with older people as a widely diverse cluster with low take-up of digital tools, but rich and varied experience of life, earlier technologies and ways of living.

Collaborating (co-developer-observer-interviewer)
We sought experts on life experience, social relations and the ethics of technology. We recruited in the East End of London, around the university. Lois handled the outreach, explaining her approach to a range of community groups. The Geezers Club was one of the five groups that chose to be involved and about 10 of the Geezers (retired men) participated, allowing us to visit them during their usual meeting time and work with them. As part of *DemTech* exercises [35], they looked back to tools they had used in their lifetime and made up potential technologies. Inventions ranged from a teleporting device to magic money to a virtual holiday. But the striking development in this group was the will to reuse old skills and knowledge and to innovate in the field of renewable technology.

During the project, my role was to work closely with Lois to create activities that placed performance methods at the heart of imagining a networked future [34]. I observed workshops and analyzed our impact from each encounter. Lois' methods are devised to build confidence and silence self-criticism. It was evident that achieving these goals was essential to the collaboration and to fostering participants' sense of agency and articulacy.

As well as developing these methods with our community partners, we commissioned artists to work with the material generated in the workshops and to continue community liaison once the first phase finished. Each was briefed to create a piece of work for display as part of the *DemTech* exhibition *The Not Quite Yet* with one community group as partner. The goal was to learn more about aspects of artistic practice that support confident participation in digital design decisions. I was there to observe developments and analyze approaches, with a brief to see how arts work could support learning about and interacting with technology.

All three artists were known for creating work exploring power and participation, but how this comes out in their practice is different. We expected this to affect outcomes, noting one artist's practice was community-driven and collaborative, whereas another worked in live art, using her body, and the third used art in a conceptual way to critique digital culture. Conditions did not make exact comparison possible, but I could see the commitments of the artists made a difference [34]. Loraine Leeson, working with The Geezers, used approaches from conflict resolution, which include identifying what everyone involved wants and building on that. The project they co-devised concerned using lost skills to make a water turbine [34].

Keeping in touch (documenter-friend-believer)
Eight years after *DemTech* ended, The Geezers were still working on the legacy of their engagement with it. There was a redirection of effort in the community group towards inventing the turbine technology they had imagined in work for the show (Fig 2). When the project funding ran out, their initiative gained new adherents and new pots of money. They have continued to contribute to new turbine-related activities, in collaboration with an art gallery, a couple of charities, a secondary school, a barge-based restaurant and a social housing association, and drawn in professional engineers as well as further academics. They also worked with me again on a later project about participation. Although no design exercises towards specific ends were part of *DemTech*, what eventually emerged was a design for a fully-fledged water turbine from a community of ad hoc innovators, including and focused on The Geezers.

Fig 2. Socially engaged arts practitioner Loraine Leeson working with The Geezers in 2008 (photo: Jim Prevett).

I have continued to document this legacy, writing a history of the problems they encountered in getting the design tested [37]. But, in October 2014, a prototype water turbine was launched at a party on a barge in The Thames outside the British Houses of Parliament. I was there. It coped with the tides and worked for a short while. Then it broke.

The next iteration of turbine is being planned. I continue to be loosely involved, spotting funding opportunities and helping write applications, and will hope to see the Geezers I know at the next party, if they continue to keep well. Meanwhile, Loraine and I, who met through the project, will see each other for supper and I will catch up on the news, as she is still working closely with them.

Everyone agrees that the turbine – and its potential as a low-cost open-source energy generation tool – would not have come to pass were it not for *DemTech*. But equally the project cannot claim to have generated and sustained this secondary research activity and, despite the original focus, there was no special emphasis on the *digital* in the turbine work. Yet it seeded it. I have records of the men talking about their lost skills and their interest in being useful, in the housing situation along The Thames and what will power the new buildings. These conversations were held in the context of investigating values for future living and developing intervention methods. Lois elicited the sense of agency necessary to take action [35]. Loraine channeled the desire to act into a more structured form and has continued to steward them [37]. 10 years since getting the grant, I am enjoying the fulfillment of my vision that socially engaged art can have a meaningful, open-ended role in promoting participation in design and shaping future technology.

Photo-parshiya

The *Photo-parshiya* project took place between 2011 and 2014 and included a series of photography and design workshops, the creation of a bespoke digital artifact and pop-up exhibition involving staff and volunteers at an international women's center. Our focus was to bring people together to reflect on the role of technology for the presentation of excluded voices within institutional archives. The project was motivated by the desire to inform, over the long term, future digital tools and services that could benefit charitable organizations seeking to work with the cultural and heritage sectors.

Getting Started (artist-researcher-volunteer)

My involvement began when, as a new PhD researcher and new to HCI, I followed up on my interest in working with women who were born in South Asia, who had children and who had settled in the UK. The Center is an explicitly black feminist organization which values using the arts in the holistic support for immigration, employment advice, training, legal representation and therapeutic counseling for domestic violence. The Center's values and interests aligned with mine, which was informed in part by my previous experience of working as a SEA artist exploring online representation with women living in the UK who were born in South Asia and the Middle East. I introduced myself at the Center as an artist-researcher who was working with technology and showed staff and volunteers work I had produced before I started the PhD and also examples of digital prototypes from my research lab. I felt this was important to give them a sense of where I was coming from culturally, and to see how these artifacts were evaluated by people at the Center. Most importantly, this process helped to build trust, but also served to distinguish me from other researchers, who were seen by many staff and volunteers to extract from and not contribute to the values of the organization. I proposed to become a volunteer attending training and weekly meetings developing a series of informal drop-in arts workshops. This helped to discover people's interests and their existing use and experiences of digital technology and meanwhile to write a suitable ethics and confidentiality procedure that worked across institutions.

Collaborating (facilitator-confidant-analyst-broker-designer)

Focusing on creative making in the art sessions opened up a reflective space for women in which they felt able to more freely talk to one another. The women would often describe to each other and me, as facilitator, particular personal challenges that they were facing, and some of the tensions that they faced in building trusted networks within their neighborhoods and wider communities. In this sense the volunteering helped to re-define my initial focus from family connections, to how technology could support connections within and across the communities of women who came to the Center. At the same time, staff were also taking steps to develop a heritage project and we brought our interests together to develop a plan.

Given the diversity of experiences, cultures and ages of those who worked at the Center and accessed its services, I discussed with staff and volunteers a potential emphasis on photography. I had noticed particular tensions around visibility and how it was negotiated between people, in that there was a desire from some staff and volunteers to expose systems of injustice while also encouraging the women to take ownership for and crediting their contributions in making public the challenges they faced. However, there was also a growing nervousness about a collective online presence as the process of recording, archiving and reflecting on the work achieved raised issues around self-esteem and low confidence. Many women were learning English as an additional language while also, in some cases, accessing therapeutic support.

I then organized a series of structured workshops working with a small group, exploring how women were presenting themselves digitally, and where images were stored and shared, by the Center and across their trusted networks. I acted as a broker, moving between meetings with staff and volunteers and the workshops, which the women fitted in around their existing training and support. I tried to ensure everyone was kept informed, mapping out insights as they emerged and sharing these each week to further inform discussions and next steps.

Fig 3. *Photo-parshiya*; digital photo-album used as an alternative social and material archive for minority ethnic and refugee women's representation in heritage and photography workshops and pop-up exhibition (photo: Lalya Gaye)

During this time I informally discussed these insights, maintaining confidentiality, with my supervisors, and software developers in the lab to work towards a design that could respond to the sensitivities, desires and concerns of the women. There was a balance here; respecting the women's privacy and maintaining anonymity, while communicating but not overwhelming the developers with the complexity of the women's lives, nor focusing on a technological solution. From these conversations I created design sketches and discussed these with staff and volunteers. However, when the Center relocated to another building we re-evaluated the project, coming up with the digital photo-album idea in response to the new premises. Once developed (see Fig 3.), the artifact was installed for 4 months and used as part of a series of workshops run between me, staff and volunteers. Women created their own wireless necklaces that acted as a password key to give them control in adding or removing photographs to the album. In addition we held a pop-up exhibition and additional workshops with heritage professionals, to draw attention to the challenges of visibility, ownership and control in multi-cultural archives.

Keeping in touch (advocate-critical friend-neighbor)

While the use of the digital photo-album marked the official end of my PhD, I continued to contribute, feeding insights into a successful funding proposal developed by the Center to run a much larger project BAM Sistahood! I also presented to funders and negotiated, within my new role as a post-doctoral researcher, time to follow up project progress. As BAM Sistahood! is now concluding, my role has become more of a critical friend, available when specific advice is needed. I keep up to date with what's happening on the project through regular email bulletins, but also more informally I regularly see women who are still involved and have become neighborhood friends.

DISCUSSION

Community-based design presents an exciting challenge for HCI, yet there is a risk that a reliance on traditional human-centered methods may struggle to engage with the complexities of these contexts. Methods that employ finite and discrete engagements aimed at iterative refinement, and a homogenous view of people as "users" for technology interventions that solve problems may assume well-defined problems, goals and needs [50]. Yet this way of involving people risks framing particular identities, in turn limiting people's potential to inform the design process. In contrast, we have reflected on artist-researcher roles in SEA, to acknowledge the messiness, diversity and inequality of social relations within a variety of community contexts. This has helped to sketch out and problematize researcher responsibilities, project legacies, and researcher-community relationships, emphasizing how interactions around digital technology can be understood as more nuanced.

With a turn towards HCI research with a social agenda, it has become yet more necessary to gain a rich understanding of the longer term potential for technology and its role in making change. Meanwhile, we are being forced into an awareness of unintended consequences, through, among other things, a sudden attention to the crisis in resources. Reflecting on projects longitudinally means we can potentially see the social import of our actions. We could design for the short-term and make successful tools for the current moment, or we can vary our practices to respond to sites of investigation with genuine reciprocation and learning. Legacies are not always the successful use or adoption of the technologies themselves [45], but can include an understanding of the social processes that take place around the technology and connected to it This requires reflection on what is valued as part of our involvement and what persists when we move on.

We have detailed our particular approaches in how we have been open to understanding where a group or community is, where it wants to be and where it possibly could be in the future. In exploring futures together we did not achieve this through working with methods at a distance. We did so through sharing both our personal and professional values, and becoming involved as people, not in a narrowly and statically defined role such as "design researcher" or "ethnographer". Rather, we have mapped tentative steps, a willingness to accept a certain lack of control, and a sensitivity to existing structures and interests. In short we have taken a more humble position, that has moved us away from presuming that, through research alone, we may know how or indeed have the resources or ideas to make situations better, but rather, focused on questioning what better might mean with the communities with whom we have worked [39]. This has required us to adopt and encourage a *critical openness* to accept a multiplicity of roles and respond over time. We now sketch characteristics of critical openness that we have collectively found as useful orientations, in response to our case studies; responsibility and care, valuing relationships, and working openly with complexity.

Responsibility and care

While it may seem obvious to suggest that we take ethical and moral responsibility for our research when we have initiated and designed interventions, we mean something particular here. "Parachuting in" is the term used for work where researchers do not take the time to acquaint themselves with the lie of the land before seeking to offer alternatives. In the case studies, the flexible nature and indeterminate way that aspects evolved, meant that time became an important factor. We took time and built in practical ways to reflect and discuss emergent ideas and uncertainties and became flexible because we cared about how this work would be potentially meaningful for those involved. Flexibility, that is to go with the flow, was important in how we planned and designed our projects. But this also required commitments beyond what was initially planned, through shifts and expectations in our roles and responsibilities. In the case of *Weird View* artists were family friends and creative professionals and required responsible action for maintaining personal relationships. In *DemTech*, researchers were facilitators and then became documenters and friends, in the *Photo-parshiya* project the researcher moved from artist to volunteer to neighbor.

In the *DemTech* project, the artists who collaborated to create exhibitions did so in more socially oriented ways in order to listen to what was important for those involved. In doing so this seeded alternative opportunities for the group to explore their own concerns beyond the timeframe of the research project. What was sustained here went beyond the successful implementation of technology, and how it was adopted. What began to emerge, was how some of those involved were seeing themselves differently, and therefore taking on different roles in society. In the case of the Geezers, this was pronounced: they became the designers and researchers and even challenged dominant models of innovation. The project didn't focus on teaching skills to do this, but highlighted a process that encouraged confidence, so much so that 8 years after the project finished the group is continuing to iterate on their designs.

In this sense projects and researchers roles are of their time, situated in particular historical, cultural and research paradigms while being sensitive to subtle social changes as they take place over extended periods of time. Each project has needed this time for reflection, both during the projects themselves but also at a critical distance, in allowing time to pass and for further reflection to take place. This all points to ways of taking responsibility beyond the processes of intervention, and to investments in the processes of care in relationships. Staying in touch with people is key to understanding how effects of the project 'may outlast their presentation' [23 p.23] beyond the immediate use of artifacts.

Valuing relationships

With our backgrounds in SEA practice and working with practitioners, we have recognized how important social connections are considered meaningful and situated in the context of the particularities of the community. As others have argued [31], this is not of course, just one-way. There is also recognition of the potential impact of practitioner relationships within the community and the changes in self in taking on shifting roles and experiencing other perspectives. What is clear through a discussion of our case studies is that this requires committed involvement and significant amounts of reciprocity; give and take, building and maintaining friendships, spending informal time with people. These are elements that can often be considered not important for research, or at worst detrimental.

In *Weird View* this was most evident in the building of relationships with family members, followed by buy-in and involvement from the whole street. The informal exchange of sharing skills in email and digital media production, and the final distribution of the work within the community village hall, online and on CD-ROM, helped support the artists in achieving their goals. The artists were clear in this objective when introducing the ideas. This project spoke to the value of intensive working with a community, exploring stories in complex and sometimes contradictory ways, showing the value in bringing people together to explore a particular place at a particular moment in time. This includes emotional investment (good feelings, anxieties, willingness to oblige and commit to certain propositions as part of valuing those relationships as well as associated responsibilities) and the tangled knots of 'engagement, affect, inequality' [4 p39] that being involved necessitates. There is a genuine hope that people will get something out of it and an honesty that, as artists and researchers, we get something out of it too. This is not just the papers and the reports or even the final exhibitions – but also how we care and how responsible we might feel when things go well and when they do not. Our case studies show how researchers and practitioners adapt to roles within the communities, which requires a particular kind of openness. This resides in the process not in the outcome and is more of an attitude, a willingness to engage and commit to people. This is what marks the path of such approaches rather than a commitment to particular methods or technology.

Working openly with complexity

As technologies are increasingly pervasive and immersive, we need means to anticipate the reception that changes will have. In our case studies, our long-term and/or intensive engagement saw a willingness to travel with people in ways that were meaningful for the communities and gave insight into their values and hopes. In *DemTech* and the *Photo-Parshiya* project, we saw thematic moves, in prioritizing local responses that potentially jeopardized the original research goals. Inevitably, this can result in compromise and a need to justify reorientation in technologically intensive institutions focused on innovation of products and services. Nonetheless, insight and change came from not trying to tidy up contradiction and uncertainty but finding ways to work with it. If our goal is to understand the changing nature of human-computer relations, then we must be willing to be occasionally surprised.

In fact, we suggest that attention to complexity within community-based design requires a criticality that is an alternative to critical design or critical theory [2]. We prefer to frame criticality in terms of critical thinking as a practice that is not bound by rational or adversarial argumentation but is more closely connected to practical wisdom found in sharing stories of personal experience [25,38]. It exists in cultivating plurality in telling stories and collectively thinking of other endings. Our proposal is that criticality needs to be considered as a workable and mutable set of orientations guided, in part, by listening with communities.

In the case of *Weird View*, there was a critical commitment that aligned with the possibilities provided by experimentation with new digital forms of grass-roots broadcast and visual presentation. The artists created a multivocal form of work that spoke to the intimate topography and sociability of community they found, as a counter to formal media narratives bound by linear broadcast. The use of digital technology here helped to find a vocabulary that spoke to the sensitivities of this particular community as closely coupled with place, social identity and geography.

More than 10 years later, the *Photo-parshiya* project also embraced the polyvocal nature of digital representation, benefiting from the more recent developments in networked mobile technologies. This allowed for the co-creation of a digital mobile archive that enabled immigrant women often excluded from presentation and identification with official archives, to be included, so as to make sense of their individual and collective contributions. Criticality here meant paying attention to different concerns and sensitivities and asking what was at stake in sharing images and stories. It is interesting to ask too, whether the digital tools available at the time of the engagement impacted on the communities by enabling a different quality of relationship with the materials produced. We might hazard a guess that the social circumstances around the production of the materials and the style of intervention had more overall impact. Though the critical openness of SEA was present in both, the time scale alone dictates that relations would be different.

By contrast, *DemTech* embodied a questioning of human-technology relations at its core and sought to make this a feature of the project work. Light was working to reveal 'the "designed" therefore "designable" nature of tools and systems' as part of the method [35 p2242]. The project worked to enfranchise marginalized groups (in this case, older people) by finding their confidence and authority in a territory that, at best, often treats them as irrelevant. Critical practice is here very much a creative practice, seen particularly in this last example, where, beyond co-construction, communities set off to change the world on their own terms.

Being socially engaged within community

In taking on these cultural challenges and the complexity of social process that necessarily accompanies them, we do not create straightforward projects and hence we do not create straightforward narratives in describing the research process. Working with and honoring the complexity and the messiness of the processes involves a critical commitment not to produce clean accounts of data collection to be enacted or described as distinct methods away from the relationships in which they were developed. This eschewal may include attention to relational aspects of risk taking, negotiation, uncertainty and compromises, as emerging critical awareness and feelings of ownership change.

We propose that SEA can be appreciated as a set of meta-approaches that underline the interpersonal and relational at a scale that is much more human, for all its partiality. This is the core commitment. Criticality is therefore enacted, not as intellectual argumentation or slick design, but as a process of constant questioning, through improvisation, opportunism, and adaptation. Rather than relying on ways of doing that are already pre-formed, comfortable and which give neat results for research, SEA emphasizes responsiveness to immediate and enduring local concerns. As has been shown here, this has the potential to create lasting benefits for those involved and change in deep-seated relational aspects (across social, technical and economic systems), many of which show emancipatory effects. Yet this also requires commitments of time, not only within the formal timescales and roles written into project proposals, but into unknown futures of the communities we work within and our own.

CONCLUSION

As HCI increasingly seeks to design research in socially responsive ways, alternative approaches are valuable both to deliver new insights for development and to show the merit of different styles of engagement. While practices from SEA have been adopted across sustainability and the arts more generally to raise critical questions, the relational, empathic and community-based orientation of such work has sometimes been lost. The approach to engagement we have demonstrated here is not an add-on but fundamental to open-ended inquiry. In presenting case studies where SEA practitioners and researchers have worked with technology to raise questions about future design and use, taking time, responsibility and care, valuing relationships and working openly with complexity were key commitments. We do not suggest that such practices replace other forms of inquiry. Indeed there are many researchers working with similarly sensitive, engaging processes in relevant work in this area. What we have sought to show is that SEA approaches and their related understanding of human-computer relations can augment and inform community-based design as it is currently understood within HCI. They can support work in contexts where cultural issues and/or social structures are paramount, raise awareness of tolerances and capacities to complement work that is more quantifiable. Many of these insights are only to be discovered in building and exploring slower, invested and meaningful connections.

ACKNOWLEDGMENTS

We would like to thank all our collaborators including our community storytellers and Valentina Nisi (*Weird View*), Pat Healey, Gini Simpson, Lois Weaver, Lorraine Leeson and the Geezers (*DemTech*) plus volunteers and staff at the Angelou Center (*Photo-parshiya*). Publication of this paper was supported by RCUK EPSRC grant no: EP/K037366/1.

REFERENCES

1. Liam J. Bannon and Pelle Ehn. 2013. Design: Design Matters in Participatory Design in Jasper Simonsen and Toni Robertson (Eds.) *Routledge International Handbook of Participatory Design,* London and New York: Routledge. 37-63.
2. Jeffrey Bardzell, and Shaowen Bardzell. 2013. What is "critical" about critical design? In *Proceedings of the SIGCHI Conference on Human Factors in Computing Systems* (CHI '13), 3297-3306. DOI: http://doi.acm.org/10.1145/1978942.1978979
3. Shaowen Bardzell and Jeffrey Bardzell. 2011. Towards a feminist HCI methodology: social science, feminism and HCI. In *Proceedings of the SIGCHI Conference on Human Factors in Computing Systems* (CHI '11), 675-684. http://doi.acm.org/10.1145/1978942.1979041

4. Claire Bishop. 2012. *Artificial Hells: Participatory Art and the Politics of Spectatorship*. Verso Books, UK.
5. Augusto Boal. 1979. *Theatre of the Oppressed*. London: Pluto Press
6. Jo Briggs 2012. 'Weird (Re)View : Informing qualitative HCI methods? Reflections on a personal participatory arts project.' In: 'Perspectives on Participation' workshop in association with DIS'12. https://openlab.ncl.ac.uk/participation/activities/dis2012/
7. Jo Briggs, Celia Lury and Sarah Teasley. 2015. *Creative Temporal Costings: A collaborative study with Leeds Creative Timebank.* AHRC ProtoPublics Research Report. http://nrl.northumbria.ac.uk/24800/1/CTC_research_report_online.pdf
8. Hrönn Brynjarsdóttir Holmer, Carl DiSalvo, Phoebe Sengers and Thomas Lodato. 2015. Constructing and constraining participation in participatory arts and HCI. In *Int. J. Hum.-Comput. Stud.* 74: 107-123 (2015). doi:10.1016/j.ijhcs.2014.10.003
9. Judith Butler. 1990. *Gender Trouble*. London: Routledge.
10. John M. Caroll and Mary Beth Rosson. 2013. Wild at Home: The Neighborhood as a Living Laboratory for HCI. *ACM Trans. Comput.-Hum. Interact.*20, 3, Article 16 (Jul 2013). http://dx.doi.org/10.1145/2491500.2491504
11. Rachel Clarke, and Peter Wright. 2012. Evocative of experience: crafting cross-cultural digital narratives through stories and portraits. In *Proceedings of the 7th Nordic Conference on Human-Computer Interaction* (NordiCHI '12) 318-321. http://doi.acm.org/10.1145/2399016.2399066
12. Rachel Clarke, Peter Wright, Madeleine Balaam and John McCarthy. 2013. Digital portraits: photo-sharing after domestic violence. In *Proceedings of the SIGCHI Conference on Human Factors in Computing Systems* (CHI '13) 2517-2526. http://doi.acm.org/10.1145/2470654.2481348
13. Rachel Clarke, Jo Briggs, Ann Light, Sarah Heitlinger and Clara Crivellaro. 2014. Socially engaged arts practice in HCI. In *CHI '14 Extended Abstracts on Human Factors in Computing Systems* (CHI EA'14) 69-74. http://doi.acm.org/10.1145/2559206.2559227
14. Rachel Clarke, Paul Dunphy and Peter Wright. 2015. Photo-parshiya: Discursive Assemblages in an International Women's Center. In *Proc. Research through Design* (RtD '15) available at http://figshare.com/articles/RTD2015_08_Photo_parshiya_Discursive_Assemblages_in_an_International_Women_s_Center/1328007
15. Carl DiSalvo, Kirsten Boehner, Nicholas A. Knouf and Phoebe Sengers 2009. Nourishing the ground for sustainable HCI: considerations from ecologically engaged art. In *Proceedings of the SIGCHI Conference on Human Factors in Computing Systems* (CHI '09), 385-394. http://doi.acm.org/10.1145/1518701.1518763
16. Carl DiSalvo, Andrew Clement and Volkmar Pipek. 2013. Communities: Participatory Design for, with and by communities. In Jasper Simonsen and Toni Robertson (Eds.) *Routledge International Handbook of Participatory Design,* London and New York: Routledge. 182-209.
17. William H Dutton, and Grant Blank. 2011. *Next Generation Users: The Internet in Britain. Oxford Internet Survey 2011.* Oxford, UK: Oxford Internet Institute, University of Oxford.
18. Sarah Fox and Christopher Le Dantec. 2014. Community historians: scaffolding community engagement through culture and heritage. In *Proceedings of the 2014 conference on Designing interactive systems*, (DIS'14) 785-794. http://doi.acm.org/10.1145/2598510.2598563
19. Paulo Freire, 1970. *Pedagogy of the Oppressed*. New York, Continuum.
20. Alison Gilchrist. 2009. *The well-connected community: A networking approach to community development.* Bristol, Polity.
21. Donna Haraway. 1988. Situated Knowledges. The Science Question in Feminism and the Privilege of Partial Knowledge. *Feminist Studies*, Vol 14, No 3:575-599.
22. Gillian Hayes. 2011. The relationship of action research to human-computer interaction. *ACM Trans. Comput.-Hum. Interact.* 18, 3, Article 15 (Aug 2011). http://dx.doi.org/10.1145/1993060.1993065
23. Pablo Helguera. 2011. *Education for Socially Engaged Art: A materials and technique handbook*. Jorge Pinto Books, US.
24. Larissa Hjorth and Kristen Sharp. 2014. The art of ethnography: The aesthetics or ethics of participation? *Visual Studies* 29: 2, 128-135.
25. bell hooks. 2010. *Teaching critical thinking: Practical wisdom*. Routledge.
26. Helena Karasti, Karen S. Baker and Florence Miller. 2010. Infrastructure Time: Long-term Matters in Collaborative Development. *CSCW Vol 19, Issue 3*:377-417. doi:10.1007/s10606-010-9113-z
27. Grant Kester. 2004. *Conversation Pieces: Community and Communication in Modern Art*. University of California Press, US.
28. Miwon Kwon. 2002. *One Place After Another: site specific art and locational identity*. MIT Press.

29. John Law and Annemarie Mol (Eds.). 2002. *Complexities: Social Studies of Knowledge Practices.* Duke University Press.
30. John Law. 2004. *After Method: Mess in Social Science Research.* Routledge.
31. Chris Le Dantec and Sarah Fox. 2015. Strangers at the Gate: Gaining Access, Building Rapport, and Co-Constructing Community-Based Research. In *Proceedings of the 18th ACM Conference on Computer Supported Cooperative Work and Social Computing* (CSCW'15), 1348-1358. http://doi.acm.org/10.1145/2675133.2675147
32. Ann Light. 2002. Users as Designers- Challenge of the Network Age (08 May 2002), *Usability News.*
33. Ann Light, Lois Weaver, Pat Healey and Gini Simpson. 2008. Adventures in the Not Quite Yet: using performance techniques to raise design awareness about digital networks. In. *Undisciplined! Design Research Society Conference 2008* (DRS'08).
34. Ann Light, Gini Simpson Lois Weaver and Pat Healey. 2009. Geezers, Turbines, Fantasy Personas: Making the Everyday into the Future. In *Proceedings of Creativity and Cognition* 2009, 39-48. http://doi.acm.org/10.1145/1640233.1640243
35. Ann Light. 2011. Democratising Technology: Inspiring Transformation with Design, Performance and Props. *Proceedings of the SIGCHI Conference on Human Factors in Computing Systems* (CHI'11) 2239-2242. http://doi.acm.org/10.1145/1978942.1979269
36. Ann Light and Yoko Akama. 2012. The human touch: participatory practice and the role of facilitation in designing with communities. *Proceedings of the 12th Participatory Design Conference* (PDC'12). 61-70 http://doi.acm.org/10.1145/1978942.1979269
37. Ann Light. 2014. Citizen Innovation: ActiveEnergy and the Quest for Sustainable Design, in Boler, M. and Ratto, M. (Eds.) *DIY Citizenship: Critical Making and Social Media.* MIT Press
38. John McCarthy and Peter Wright, P. 2015. *Take [A]part: The Politics and Aesthetics of Participation in Experience-centerd Design*. MIT Press.
39. Annemarie Mol. 2008. *The logic of care: Health and the Problem of Patient Choice*. Routledge.
40. Valentina Nisi and Mads Haahr. 2004. Weird View: Interactive Multilinear Narratives and Real-Life Community Stories' in *Crossings: eJournal of Art and Technology* 4.1, Dec 2004.
41. Valentina Nisi, Ian Oakley and Mads Haahr, 2006 Inner City Locative Media: Design and Experience of a Location- Aware Mobile Narrative for the Dublin Liberties Neighborhood, *Intelligent Agent* 6 (2).
42. Valentina Nisi, Alison Wood, Glorianna Davenport and Ian Oakley, 2004. Hopstory: An interactive, location-based narrative distributed in space and time. *Technologies for Interactive Digital Storytelling and Entertainment* pp132-141.
43. Gillian Rose. 1997. Situating knowledges: positionality, reflexivities and other tactics. *Progress in Human Geography.* June 1997, Vol. 21 No.3: 305-320. doi: 10.1191/030913297673302122
44. Arnd Schneider and Christopher Wright (Eds.). 2010. *Between Art and Anthropology. Contemporary Ethnographic Practice.* Berg Press.
45. Nick Taylor, Keith Cheverst, Peter Wright and Patrick Olivier. 2013. Leaving the wild: lessons from community technology handovers. In *Proceedings of the SIGCHI Conference on Human Factors in Computing Systems* (CHI '13*)*, 1549-1558. http://doi.acm.org/10.1145/2470654.2466206
46. Alex Taylor, Siân Lindley, Tim Regan. David Sweeney, Vasillis Vlachokyriakos, Lillie Grainger and Jessica Lingel. 2015. Data-in-Place: Thinking through the Relations Between Data and Community. In *Proceedings of the SIGCHI Conference on Human Factors in Computing Systems* (CHI '15) 2863-2872. http://doi.acm.org/ 10.1145/2702123.2702558
47. *Tenantspin* http://superflex.net/activities/2002/05/01/superchannel_-_tenantspin
48. John Vines, Rachel Clarke, Peter Wright and Patrick Olivier. 2013. Configuring participation: on how we involve people in design. *Proceedings of the SIGCHI Conference on Human Factors in Computing Systems* (CHI '13) 429-438. http://doi.acm.org/10.1145/2470654.2470716
49. Lois Weaver. 2007. Make Something: a manifesto for making performance about making change. In Elaine Aston and Sue-Ellen Case (Eds). *Performing Global Feminisms*. Basingstoke, UK: Palgrave Macmillan.
50. Peter Wright. 2011. Reconsidering the H, the C and the I: Some Thoughts on Reading Lucy Suchman's Human-Machine Reconfigurations. *interactions* 18, 5 (September 2011), 28-31. DOI=http://dx.doi.org/10.1145/2008176.2008185
51. Peter Wright and John McCarthy. 2010. *Experience Centerd Design: Designers, Users and Communities in Dialogue.* Morgan & Claypool: USA.

Improv Remix: Mixed-Reality Video Manipulation Using Whole-Body Interaction to Extend Improvised Theatre

Dustin Freeman
dustin@cs.toronto.edu
Occipital
San Francisco, CA, USA

Ravin Balakrishnan
ravin@dgp.toronto.edu
Dynamic Graphics Project
University of Toronto
Toronto, Canada

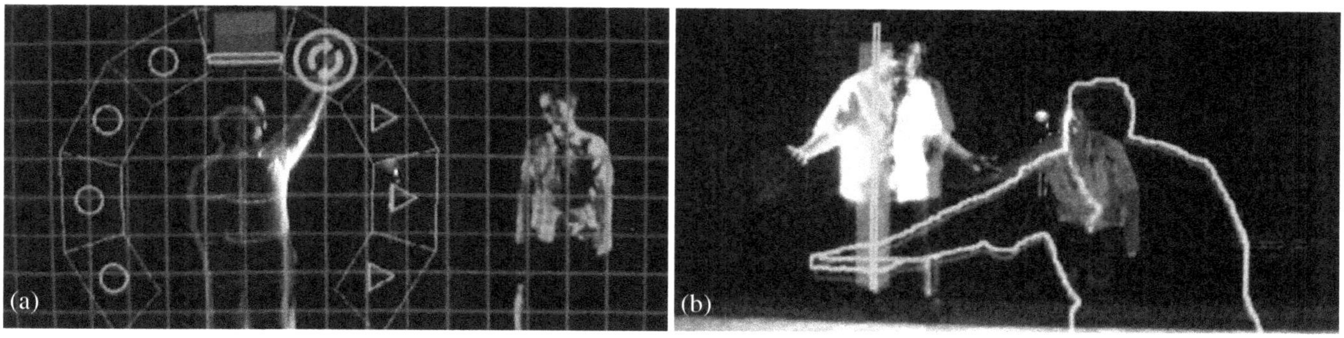

Figure 1. The view of Improv Remix from the audience. In the first frame, a live performer (left) accessing scenes using our novel Vitruvian Menu, and a video of a playback performer (right) is paused before playback. In the second frame, a live performer (right) scrubs his previous self (left).

ABSTRACT

Improv Remix is a mixed-reality system for live onstage video editing, using whole-body interaction, as an extension of improvised theatre. This work documents the process of analyzing an art form, then building technology that supports its extension. We tested the potential for video integration in improv in a exploratory workshop, then determined features and interaction techniques through iterative development with improvisors. We demonstrated the final iteration in a public showcase. Our contributions are (1) the documentation of the process, (2) a basic set of always-on interaction techniques tailored for performers standing adjacent to a large display, (3) methods to remix stage performance video, and, (4) a collection of creative use cases for the system, with an analysis of how the system extends improvisation.

Author Keywords

Whole-Body Interaction; Video; Improvised Theatre; Art; Mixed Reality;

ACM Classification Keywords

H.5.m. Information Interfaces and Presentation (e.g. HCI): Miscellaneous

DIS 2016, June 04 - 08, 2016, Brisbane, QLD, Australia.

ACM 978-1-4503-4031-1/16/06$15.00
DOI: **http://dx.doi.org/10.1145/2901790.2901894**

INTRODUCTION

The usage of advanced technology in theatrical improvisation is rare, and this observation prompted the authors' investigation. In this work we sought to extend, and thus be faithful to, modern theatrical improvisation, as observed through one of the authors' 14 years of personal experience.

It is not mandatory or even recommended that we use technology in the creation of art. However, many traditional art forms now have advanced digital tools developed for them (e.g. painting, sculpture, film). Even scripted (non-improvised) theatre now benefits from digital tools for complex lighting changes and projection mapping (e.g. Troikatronix's Isadora[1]) — why not modern theatrical improvisation?

With Improv Remix, we *extend* the features of improv, allowing performers to create content not possible before, while still feeling in the spirit of improv, and taking advantage of pre-existing skills of improv performers. Our approach is to enable recontextualization of previous scenes by providing techniques to record, re-project and manipulate video of the stage (Figure 1). Thus, the live, present performers appear with their video recordings on a synthesized *mixed reality* stage. The system allows improvisors to construct complex, multi-layered scenes. The interface is designed specifically to be used spontaneously from the stage itself, reducing iteration time between ideation and instantiation of new theatrical ideas. Often, the reuse of a scene's video out of its original context is unexpected, surprising, and enjoyable. While other stage performance contexts could benefit from a mixed-reality stage system, this work examines the specific case of modern improvised theatre.

[1] **http://troikatronix.com/isadora/about/**

To validate that use of mixed-reality video on stage was compelling, and to prototype the features for Improv Remix, we ran a set of workshops: informal drop-in session for performers to experiment, unstructured, with a prototype. The system as described in this paper was evaluated by presenting it at a set of showcases to an audience. Our showcases were in theatre spaces, with scheduled showtimes, where public audience members were invited to watch performers use Improv Remix, and then use it themselves.

FEATURES OF MODERN IMPROVISATION

Modern improvised theatre is popularly seen on the TV show *Whose Line Is It Anyway?* Improv scenes progress via unpredictable, exploratory content generation, to the joy of performers and audience members. Through this process, ideas are discovered that would have been difficult to do so otherwise. Sets under 5 minutes are called "shortform", and longer sets are called longform. Extending the genre of longform improvisation, which can explore a wide variety of themes, was the primary motivation for this work.

Here are some definitions for the purposes of this document: An *action* is anything a performer does, while an *interaction* is an action meant to be interpreted by a digital system. Actions that are *onstage* are intended to be part of the show, while actions that are *offstage* are not. A *live performer* is performing in the present, whereas a *playback performer* is a performance that was recorded previously, playing back now.

To extend an art form, we must deeply examine its fundamentals. We shall describe three inspiring features of improv, derived from the personal experience of one of the authors, who has spent 14 years as an improv performer, and 5 as a director.

Minimalism

Jerry Grotowski argued in *Towards a Poor Theatre* (1967) [9], that to compete with other medias such as film, theatre should strip away superfluous elements. Others have argued that theatre's liveness is what makes it unique, and the inclusion of technology can be problematic to keeping it so [5].

Improv intentionally minimizes influences on the spontaneous generation of content; most groups use neutral clothing and few props. Most special effects in theatre, such as sound effects, lighting or projections, are controlled by technicians from offstage, using a pre-arranged list of cues. This would inhibit improvisation's ability to customize for the present audience, or recent events, as occurred centuries past in *commedia dell'arte*. Thus, we argue that any system meant to be used during improvisation must have as few constraints and distractions as possible.

In the last century, when control of technology *onstage* has been increasingly experimented with, it is the opinion of the authors that the interactivity has not been fully realized. Either the technology intrudes so much on the show that it becomes cyborgized — that the show becomes *about* technology, or, the technology is merely responds to performers in an aesthetic way, as often appears in dance. In this paper, the goal of the technology is not be aesthetic, but rather support the pre-existing task at hand: improvised theatre, though admittedly a very novel version of it. A similar tool for dance would support dancers planning the steps in a performance or controlling lighting changes from the stage itself. The point of an Improv Remix performance is not the tool, in the sense that the point of a film is rarely to show off the video editor used in its creation.

Recontextualization

Recontextualization, or a callback, is taking previous events or themes in a performance and juxtaposing them against others in the present. The most prevalent longform (>5 minutes) improv structure is called the *The Harold* [10]. In a Harold performance, improvisors will do several short, and initially disconnected, scenes, and as the performance progresses, themes, locations and characters will be revisited, so that the performance has a high density of self-reference. Callbacks are frequent in stand-up and sketch comedy, where an innocuous joke or event at the beginning appears again at the end.

The term *Chekhov's Gun* originates from Russian playwright Anton Chekhov, who observed that "If you say in the first chapter that there is a rifle hanging on the wall, in the second or third chapter it absolutely must go off"[3]. In the beginning of a longform improvisational set, performers produce a series of initially disconnected ideas, but during the set they weave them together in amusing and unexpected ways. This feature of improvisation is amenable to additional techniques to call back previous ideas — in our approach, to enable playback and manipulation of video of performers themselves, in new contexts.

Coordinating Gestures

Improvisors use coordinating gestures to manage group content generation. This is performer-performer interaction as a layer external to in-character actions. Coordinating gestures are an existence proof that interaction and performance may co-exist. A secondary stakeholder in the design of coordinating gestures is the audience, who must be able to understand if an onstage action is part of a performer's acting, or the work of planning the scene. Here are three examples:

Sweep: A performer runs from one side of the stage to the other at the front. Similar to a film wipe, this indicates the group will transition to the next scene.

Tag-out: A performer from offstage taps an onstage performer. This indicates the offstage performer will replace the onstage performer as a new character.

"Cut to that!": A performer calls "cut to that!" to tell the group to transition to depicting an event just mentioned in the current scene.

Note that we cannot reuse any coordinating gestures already in common use in improvisation for our system, as performers will instinctively use them during performance. The nature of these gestures merely serve as inspiration for gestures we may use in Improv Remix, which must co-exist safely alongside currently-used gestures.

RELATED WORK

As a whole, this work explores a technological extension of an existing art form, via an iterative process, creating new interaction techniques to support an extended feature set. This approach is similar to similar to Kazi et al., who extended the art form of sand painting to a digital touch surface [16]. To contextualize the work in this paper, we will discuss the topics *Liveness*, *Mixed Reality*, *Interfaces for Live Video* and *Whole-Body Interaction*. While some work has explored theatrical improvisation as an interesting AI problem, this is out of scope for our current work [19].

One interesting prior work that covers a few of the topics is a scene in Blast Theory's *10 Backwards* where the actress uses a remote control to record and play back video of herself eating a bowl of cereal [28]. A camera on a tripod is facing her, and behind the camera is a large projection screen, where she and the audience can see the output from the camera. She records herself using the camera, and then plays herself back, trying to imitate her actions with slight exaggeration. She then records this exaggerated performance, and then repeats the same self-imitating procedure, eventually using the remote to go forwards and backwards frame-by-frame to imitate exact facial expressions.

Liveness

It is widely believed that liveness, the dramatic sensation that a performance is happening in the present, is important for compelling art, but it is unclear how to foster liveness with non-live (mediatized) components, such as pre-recorded video [1, 13, 22]. There has been much analysis of the relationship between live and projected images of performers [5]. *Gertie The Dinosaur* (1914) is an early example of combining live and pre-recorded interaction, where a physical prop transitioned from a live performer to an animated character [20]. In the Blast Theory example, the performer is not using a version of themselves that is exactly live, but is in the very recent past, similar to Improv Remix. *Sampling* content from another source is common in art, and an interesting examination of liveness in digital art [5, 21, 27]. Creative workers have observed that it appears to be human nature to ascribe meaning to chunks of content after it has been randomly assembled, as if a large part of the origin of the story is the observer themselves [18, 33].

Mixed Reality

For creating *Mixed Reality* in a theatre context, it is difficult technical problem to project images in-place on the stage without requiring any augmentation of audience members. Some works have had performers wear completely white clothing, so that the image of a human figure can be projected on top of them [5]. Tsuchida et al. created a system for rehearsing multi-person dances by placing a projection screen on top of a robot; the robot can move around the space arbitrarily and a calibrated projector can project human figures to that position [29]. The technique we use for Improv Remix is a variant on the extensively-used stage technique *Pepper's Ghost*, where a transparent projection screen is placed in front of a real, conventional scene, allowing virtual objects to appear (and disappear), apparently from the real scene [26].

Interfaces for Live Video

The interface used in the Blast Theory example is a basic TV remote, recording to or playing from a VHS tape. Even with this setup, a highly interesting performance can occur. However, there are many other instances of interfaces designed for live video output, particularly VJ software [8, 12]. Outside live network TV, we could find few cases that include live video input as well [7]. One feature in Improv Remix — polite playback — is automatic non-linear playback of video in response to live performers. There has been work on combining several mobile novice-recorded videos together — in one case, a human "director" is designated to manage all the input streams from various people [6]. There has also been much work on automatic editing of video [32, 31], and even semi-automatic editing with some user input [14]. For Improv Remix, we must parse a recorded performance into chunks based on audio; a similar technique appears in DemoCut to reduce content size for instructional video [4].

Whole-Body Interaction

In Improv Remix, interaction is possible with the limbs and the coarse position of the body. Early examples of work on unencumbered Whole-Body Interaction are CHARADE [2] and VIDEOPLACE [17]. Vogel explored the notion of *proxemics* with a large display, where different functionality could be present at different distances [30]. Shadow Reaching exploits perspective projection so the user can operate at different scales depending on their position [25].

Even outside theatre practice, there is concern on how interaction is perceived by observers. The interaction design values for a generic user (such as minimal effort, or avoiding awkwardness) [11, 24] are different from theatre performers' values [23]. Audience members are explicitly present to watch performers, and the nature of interaction can affect their perception of the performer. We argue that for theatre, we should choose interaction techniques so that they influence the semantics of the show as little as possible; by Reeves' analysis, this suggests that both manipulations and effects should be made clearly visible to the audience [23]. Juhlin and Önnevall's work on collaborative gestures in front of TV screens also shows support for gestural visibility between users as being important [15]. In the Blast Theory example, using an interface that is not novel to the audience (a TV remote) means that interactions with it are well understood, even though they may not see specifically which buttons the performer is pressing.

EXPLORATORY STUDY: WORKSHOPS

We ran informal exploratory workshops with a prototype enabling capture and playback of stage video. The purpose of the workshops was to (1) validate that using playback performers was compelling and (2) discover design issues and opportunities that Improv Remix would face. The backend is a bespoke colour and depth media storage container designed for simultaneous read and write of multiple video streams [2]. This container was later improved and used in the final system.

[2]Source `http://github.com/dustinfreeman/riffer`

Participants

We recruited participants by word-of-mouth (21 total, ages 20 to 60, all had at least 2 years experience with longform improvisation). No compensation was given.

Prototype

We used a Kinect to record colour and depth video, and projected it onto a wall at the rear of the stage area. Performers could play the last scene with a "clap" gesture, detected with the Kinect skeleton tracker. A new scene started recording when someone entered the stage area, and stopped once the stage was empty again. Scenes could be played back once or looped, controlled by the researcher from a laptop.

Procedure

Performers could drop in any time during the workshops' 6-hour duration. The researcher explained the prototype functionality if necessary. However, they preferred that experienced performers explain the prototype and its use cases to new arrivals. Occasionally the researcher would have to complete descriptions, or correct misunderstandings.

Results

Improvising with playback performers was found to be definitely compelling. Use cases were discovered during the workshop that we iteratively expanded on and explored in Improv Remix — these are described in a later section. Below we discuss issues identified during the workshops

Sightlines

When humans typically speak to each other, their torsos are directly facing. In a performance, performers will "cheat out", i.e. rotate their torsos unnaturally towards the audience so they are more visible. In the prototype, the playback performers were projected behind the live performers, while the audience was in front. This made it difficult for the live performers to present the front of their torso to the audience, while still being able to see the playback performers.

Distinguishing Interface Actions from Performance

Performers' interaction techniques were not robust. The clap gesture to play the last scene frequently caused false positives and often had to be disabled. The gesture to stop and start recording; walking on or off stage, appeared at the beginning and end of every recorded scene and was obtrusive.

The Importance of Spontaneity

To execute ideas, performers would have to describe them to the researcher operating the prototype. New ideas are vague and difficult to express, and if the performer was uncertain, they would abandon them. We feel that operation of the system from the stage itself, by performers, is very important.

Live and Playback Scene Responsiveness

A common use case was to record a *Template Scene*, consisting of a performer on one half of the stage, speaking to the empty half. Performers would play back this scene several times, responding creatively to the playback performer. However, the playback performer would tend to speak over the live performer, who would naturally react as if they were offended, constraining and derailing a scene.

IMPROV REMIX IMPLEMENTATION

Improv Remix represents the final iteration in a collaborative design process with experienced improv performers, intended to be well-suited to spontaneous interaction directly from the stage. Our resulting interaction techniques and feature set were selected to be simple, easy to teach indirectly, and frequently used. During the iteration process, we dropped (1) interaction techniques that were too finicky or difficult to teach and (2) features that did not create interesting performances. As such, the resulting system is not intended to represent a thorough, rich, expressive exploration of the interaction design space, but a polished, lightweight, pragmatically usable instance of a system that creates compelling performances.

During the process, we found a particularly important property — *exposure* — when a performer did an interaction, the degree to which an observer (audience members or other performers) could discern the intent and the effect of the interaction. To support coordinated improvised scene-making, it was beneficial to design interactions so that they were highly exposed. This is one reason why we kept all interactions whole-body, instead of pursuing other interaction techniques.

Example Usage

Here is an abstract description of an improv set using some features in Improv Remix. Interaction techniques will be described in later sections.

Alice starts behind the performance area, and Bob and Carlos start off to the side.

Alice steps forward, and records a performance of her monologuing about a topic (cats). When finished, she steps off the stage and the recording stops.

Bob walks into the performance area, and instantiates a playback performer of Alice's monologue on cats. Bob acts as a supportive listener, nodding in agreement with Alice's playback performer, and sometimes lightly clapping.

Before Alice's playback performer is finished, Carlos indicates to Bob to get off the stage. Bob leaves, and Carlos jumps on stage.

Carlos clears the stage of Alice's playback performer, and restarts it from the beginning, this time setting the interface to record his own performance as well.

While listening to Alice's playback performer, Carlos acts as an unsupportive audience member, loudly laughing, expressing disbelief, being offended and booing.

When Alice's playback performer finishes, Carlos steps off the stage. Improv Remix now has two performances in its library: Alice's cat speech, and Carlos being a rude listener.

Bob steps on stage and instantiates Carlos' playback performer. Bob begins a speech on another topic, acting as a mayor who is opening a new kids hospital. During the speech, Carlos' playback performer keeps interjecting rudely in apparent opposition to what Bob is proposing. Bob becomes increasingly comically frustrated.

Hilarity ensues.

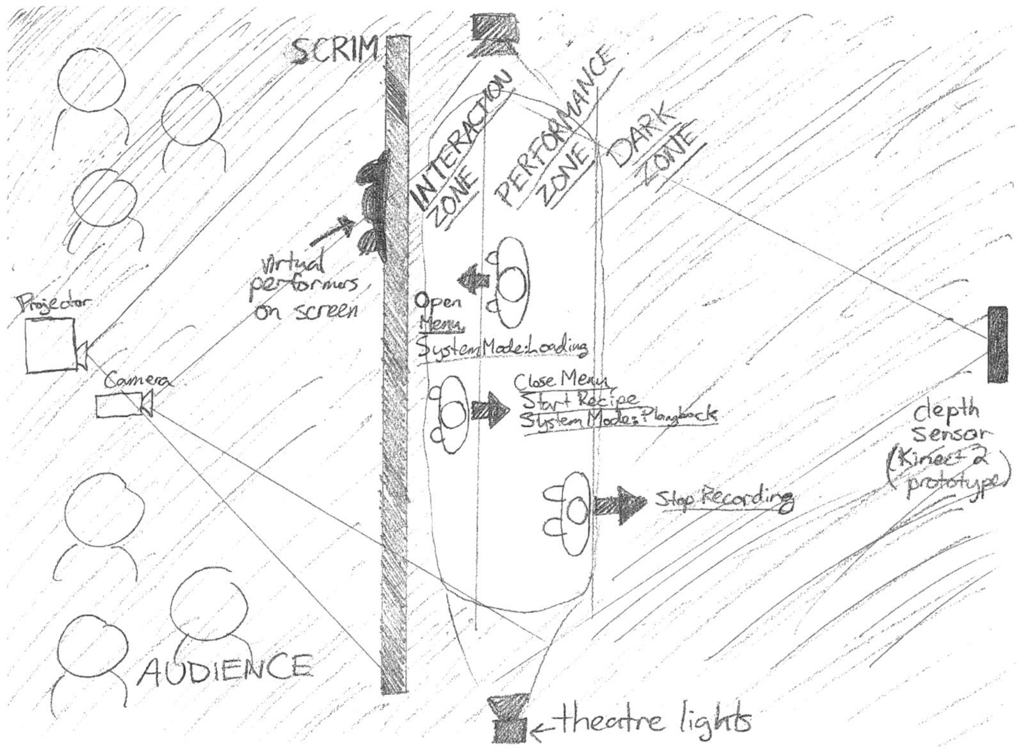

Figure 2. The final physical setup of Improv Remix. Middle: scrim. Left: projector, camera and audience. Right: lit performance space. Far Right: depth sensor (Kinect 2). Proxemic zones affect interface features: the Interaction Zone closest to the scrim, the Performance Zone in the lit area, and the Dark Zone past the light.

System Interface Overview

Improv Remix has three global modes: *Loading*, *Performance*, and *Library*. In Loading, performers instantiate playback performers using our novel *Vitruvian Menu* (Figure 3). In Performance, the interface is clean and any playback performers may be directly manipulated by live performers. In Library, a performer may browse all recorded performers, and slot them into the Vitruvian Menu for quick access.

We designed interactions to be robust in our inherently noisy and ambiguous environment. The scrim is invisible unless lit, so playback performers and UI elements appear to hover in mid-air. Having the scrim between live performers and the audience improves sightlines over our workshop prototype. We discovered the bright lighting inhibits visibility of UI elements that were farther away or used colour; thus, we used audio cues when possible.

Proxemic Zones

The stage has 3 proxemic zones (Figure 2): the *Interaction*, *Performance* and the *Dark*. A performer's zone is determined by distance from the rear depth camera, with hysteresis applied to prevent debouncing[3]. Audio feedback informs users of zone transitions. When a performer transitions zones, it affects system mode and recording: Stepping forward from the Performance Zone to the Interaction Zone sets the global mode to Loading, and the performer's Vitruvian Menu (described later) opens. The performer can choose to record a scene, or instantiate playback performers from previous scenes; we call this the *scene recipe*. The scene recipe does not execute until the performer steps back to the Performance Zone, which starts a 2.5 countdown until execution. To cancel a scene recipe, the performer steps back from the Performance Zone to the Dark Zone.

We use proxemic zones to enable performer access to the menu — this was found to be more robust than other approaches: (1) having the widgets always available, but in hard-to-reach places to prevent accidental activation, and (2) having the menu appear only if the user stood still for a period of time.

The Vitruvian Menu

Our novel *Vitruvian Menu* (Figure 3 a&b) is designed for a standing human; its name inspired by Leonardo Da Vinci's *Vitruvian Man*, as it is usable by arms and legs. We chose this user-relative design after finding that widgets with absolute position were difficult to acquire.

The Vitruvian Menu supports quick, spontaneous access of scenes, yet is also robust to the noisy nature of whole-body interaction. When the user's silhouette is overlapping with a button in the Vitruvian Menu, it gradually fills over 300 ms, and when untouched, it slowly un-fills; this mechanic, an extended form of dwell, ensures the button does not activate without a degree of certainty, but also makes it possible to

[3]Debouncing is an electronics term for strategies to prevent a switch rapidly alternating between states, by making a state "sticky", tending to preserve itself.

Figure 3. The Vitruvian Menu. (a) Closed, with only the Keystone visible. In the Keystone, we provide zone feedback. (b) Open, showing all scene slots, accessible by arms and legs. Icons in each slot indicate whether it has a scene, and its playback type in the Scene Recipe.

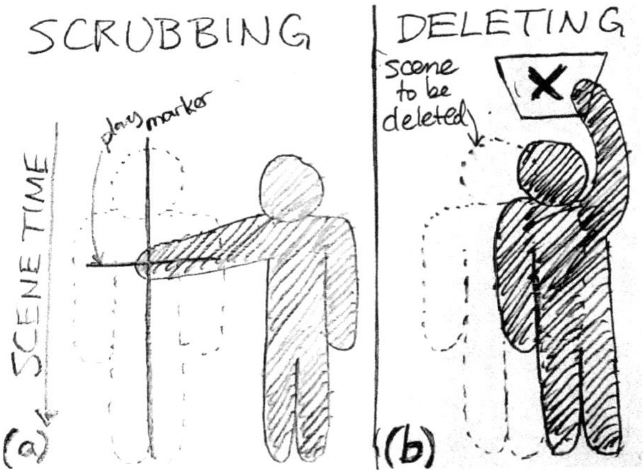

Figure 4. Interaction with Playback Performers: (a) Scrubbing a playback performer by reaching into its bounding box. The play marker is set to the centroid of the user's overlap with the timeline. (b) Deleting a playback performer by standing in its bounding box turning the Keystone into a delete button.

activate if the user has trouble maintaining overlap with the button. While activation by dwell is slow, other approaches were tried, such as (1) a specific gestural direction motion, and (2) instant activation if any part of the body touched a widget. However, these were found to not be robust enough for a performance setting.

When the performer is in the Performance Zone, their menu is closed, with just the Keystone visible; when the performer is in the Interaction Zone, the menu is open, with all buttons visible and Improv Remix in Loading mode. We use the Keystone to display feedback of the performer's current proxemic zone, while every other button is slot for a scene. Slots start empty, with Empty Circle icons resembling record buttons, whereas slots with scenes have Empty Triangle icons, resembling play buttons. When the user activates an icon it becomes solid, indicating that it is part of the scene recipe. An activated play icon means the system will instantiate a playback performer from that scene, and an activated record icon means that the system will record a new scene, and save it in that slot. When activated, a slot with a scene will cycle through possible playback behaviours: *none*, *play once*, *looping* and *polite* (described below).

Interaction with Playback Performers

Live performers may *scrub* or *delete* playback performers (Figure 4), by intersecting with a bounding box around the playback performer. We tuned this size of this so it was closer than natural acting speaking distance, to prevent accidental interaction.

Scrubbing

We define scrubbing as the ability to freely move a video backwards or forwards in time, where a release resumes normal play. Our scrubbing interface is composed of a vertical timeline, as well as a horizontal line representing the current play marker. To scrub the playback performer, the live performer touches the timeline, which sets the playback performer's play marker to that time. To avoid accidental scrubs when a live performer walks past a playback performer, we ignore silhouette overlaps with the bounding box above a threshold.

Scrubbing enables playful re-imagining of scenes, a powerful control which has not been possible before onstage. Scrubbing was found to be very intuitive by almost all who used it. In informal workshops, scrubbing was used innovatively by performers outside our primary target group. Dancers would finely control previous versions of themselves co-dancing with their arms, legs, elbows, knees, and even head. Vocal musicians set previous tracks to play at points that were easy to memorize, exploiting proprioception.

We found performers had fine control over the scrub position. Scrubbing is possible both from the Performance Zone and the Dark Zone. When performing with an audience, control from either zone takes on different characteristics; where hidden interaction from the Dark Zone feels like puppeteering. Due to perspective projection, scrubbing from the Performance Zone is best done with an ankle or a wrist, while from the Dark Zone, scrubbing may be done with the finger.

Deletion

Playback performers in *looping* or *polite* playback persist onstage until deleted manually. When a live performer and a playback performer overlap, a delete icon appears in the live performer's Keystone. Tapping the Keystone deletes all playback performers they overlap with. The stage can be quickly cleared by holding one's arm in the keystone while walking across, much like the *sweep* coordinating gesture in modern improv.

Playback with Manners: Polite Playback Performers

When a playback performer's mode is *polite*, its behaviour is to play random excepts from the original scene so as to create the appearance of the playback performer delivering new, often surprising, material. We accomplish this by using a naïve algorithm to parse the scene into suitable utterances and controlling their behaviour carefully so they appear to have manners with respect to the other stage occupants.

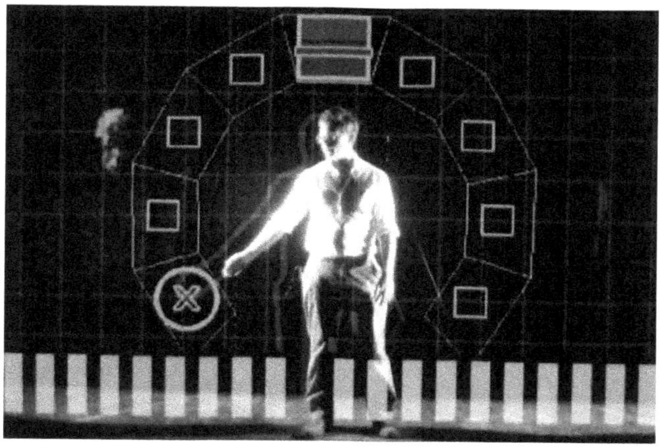

Figure 5. A performer using the Scene Library. To his left is the projected image of a puppet from his currently selected scene.

The default behaviour of a polite playback performer is to loop the longest non-utterance or "idle" section of the scene. This creates the appearance that the playback performer is listening, and avoids the jarring effect of freezing playback. Our system is careful when to trigger playback of utterances so that playback performers do not to talk over each other or live performers on stage. The *Manners Module* keeps a record of the last time the volume of the stage exceeded a threshold representing speech. If the onstage volume is silent for a given duration (we used 1.8 seconds) the manners module plays an utterance from a polite playback performer. If there are multiple onstage polite playback performers, the manners module maintains a circular queue, so that they take turns. After a playback performer finishes an utterance, it returns to looping the idle section.

The Scene Library

The Vitruvian Menu is meant for quick access, and thus only has 8 scene slots. Library mode is used to fetch scenes from the large quantity that may be generated over a typical 2-hour session (50+). To access the Library, the performer taps the Keystone when in the Interaction Zone (Figure 5). In Library Mode, a slot with a scene in it displays an X — if the performer activates this slot, they empty it. An empty slot has a square icon, indicating it can be filled with a scene. In the Library interface, scenes are represented by white rectangles on stage. The user selects a scene by walking left or right to stand over it, while the first frame of the selected scene is projected onstage. To fetch that scene into a specific empty slot, the user activates it.

SHOWCASE OBSERVATIONS AND USE CASES

We installed Improv Remix in a theatre space and ran three 2-hour public showcases. These were advertised over social media, and had approximately 50 attendees in total. We recruited 3 performers to create a demonstration of system features and known use cases. The structured demonstration of the system lasted an hour. In the second hour, audience members could come up and use Improv Remix, which including playback performers from earlier in the show.

The purpose of the showcases was to test the entertainment value of the system in front of a live audience. While a use case could be academically interesting in a workshop, we could not assume it would be in front of a live audience. The showcases also allowed us to observe if performers and audience members could invent use cases spontaneously

Physical Interaction

A performer created a chain of videos where he high-fived previous iterations of himself, with the audience clapping at each virtual impact. In a more complex example, a performer captured video of a pillar prop at three positions, and then instantiated them as looping, effectively static, objects. He made a puppet jump between the pillars (Figure 6a).

Collages

Performers layered several looping playback performers enacting a sound and/or physical action. In one example, performers recorded themselves individually dancing silently, intending to create a "dance party" when combined (Figure 6b). One of the performers played a song [4] on his smartphone next to his lapel mic. The resulting collage has him standing on the side of the stage, awkwardly swaying to the music, in contrast to the dancers. While the end result of a collage may be interesting, the audience can feel bored watching the build-up. It may be possible to make this payoff more exciting with performer practice, or it may be useful to bore the audience, lowering their expectations, before the payoff.

Music

One of our performers was an accomplished beatboxer and singer. He recorded himself beatboxing while dancing to create a layer, and then would begin to rap on top of that (Figure 6c). He constructed another example by singing the same song 3 times, and coordinated pointing to himself between the different video tracks (Figure 6d).

In many of these musical examples, the performer would construct the composition on the performer side of the scrim, then create a scene recipe of the prepared playback performers, and then excitedly run around to the audience side of the scrim to observe, with everyone else, the quality of their result. Musical samples from highly-skilled performers would often be brought back to accompany performers with less skill, and they would lip sync or react to the music. An interesting observation is that a short chunk of performance can become musical over the course of many (usually 10+) repetitions, regardless of orginial tone.

Constructed Scenes

The ability to record a scene while playing a previous one allows individual performers to construct complex scenes, exploiting timing and alignment. We have previously noted that the build-up of separate scenes intended to be combined is often not interesting. Here is one example where a performer recorded a series of scenes to that were interesting to watch under construction and satisfying in combination.

[4]with intentional irony, Robyn's *Dancing On My Own*

Figure 6. Example Use Cases: a) Physical interaction: A live puppet climbing static playback columns. The puppeteer hides his body in the Dark Zone; b) Collage: A dance party of several playback performers; c) Music: A beatboxer/dancer layering another instance of himself; d) Music, recontextualized: A performer replays two singing tracks so he may harmonize and gesture with himself; e) Constructed Scene: Part 1, an exuberant man beckons a duck; f) Constructed Scene: Part 2, a dishevelled (live) man responding to the beckons of a (playback) exuberant man; g) Responsive Scene via Scrubbing: a performer controls their own video from the Dark Zone; h) Polite Playback: A live performer records himself saying "true" or "false", then instantiates a polite playback performer and monologues, with his playback self informing him if he is lying; i) Failed Dissonance: The beatboxing playback performer re-appropriated alongside the dishevelled man. The dishevelled man's angry looks, originally intended for the exuberant man, appear to be directed at the beatboxer.

Scene 1: *Acting like a duck, the performer waddles from stage right to stage left, occasionally looking behind. Finally, it turns around and waddles back slightly faster, stands up and kisses an empty spot in the air.*

Scene 2: (Figure 6e) [With Scene 1 playing] *The performer stands on far stage right repeating exuberantly "Come here duck!" and beckoning as the duck, from Scene 1, waddles away. Finally, the performer loses his patience and loudly yells "Hey duck!", at which point the duck turns around and comes back. When it gets back to the performer, he picks it up and kisses it, saying "You're so cute!"*

Scene 3: (Figure 6f) [With Scene 2 playing] *A dishevelled man stands on stage left reading a newspaper. The exuberant man from Scene 2 repeats "Come here duck!", annoying and distracting the dishevelled man. Initially, the dishevelled man assumes that the exuberant man must be not be speaking to him. As the exuberant man continues, the dishevelled man becomes angry. Finally, the exuberant man from Scene 2 yells "Hey duck!" and the dishevelled man drops to the ground, ducking from possible danger. Seeing there is none, he charges the exuberant man, saying "Hey, buddy, what's the big idea!?". The exuberant man kisses him and the dishevelled man slaps him in response.*

Responsive Scenes

Both scrubbing and polite playback made for novel content which live performers had to respond to spontaneously.

Performer A asked the audience for 3 simple phrases, getting "It's raining", "These pretzels are making me thirsty." and "That's what she said". Performer A recorded himself saying these from stage right, facing (empty) stage left. Performer B, who had been sent out of the room, was called back and stood opposite playback performer A, while live performer A scrubbed his performer from the dark (Figure 6g).

One audience member created a polite playback performer saying "True" or "False" (Figure 6h). He then began a lecture and let his playback self choose whether the statement he just made was true. If a lie, he had to change his statement.

Failed Dissonance

Two seemingly unrelated scenes would often create an unexpected synthesis. A meaningless combination would be expected, but, in fact, often the dissonance *fails*. This effect is likely due to the unavoidable sense-making activities of human beings [18, 33]. We had two examples of failed dissonance: a) the dishevelled man from our Constructed Scene alongside our beatboxer, where his anger now appears directed at the beatboxer (Figure 6i) and b) An accidental recording of the beatboxer discussing and idea offstage, including the phrase "bastardized the equilibrium of harmonized core sounds". This was brought back amusingly against a multitude of other scenes, appearing to be overwrought and over-serious academic commentary on what is a bunch of silly messing around on a stage.

DISCUSSION: PERFORMERS AS SPECIAL USERS

Improv theatre performers are an unusual user group to design for, and here we will discuss observations of designing technology for them in a performance setting.

Instructing Interaction

We have made the specific choice in this project to not encumber the performers with hardware, and instead use coarse whole-body gestures, which are naturally noisy. Earlier in the project, we tried to search for gestures that would reliably not appear in theatrical performance, and could be reserved for system interaction. However, performance gestures are far too unpredictable, and if we banned certain, specific movements for performers, then performers became self-conscious. Fortunately, performers have a high degree of control over their bodies; when they are told they must pose or move in a certain way, they can consistently reproduce it. Performers are practiced at being cognizant of lighting on themselves and their visibility to the audience, and many theatre performers also have formal movement or dance training. The lesson is that "Do it exactly this way" works well, while "Don't do this" is received poorly.

Importance of Direct Control

A consistent observation during this work is that novel theatrical ideas are difficult, even tedious to explain in the middle of creative work. One goal of Improv Remix was to empower performers to have control of technical effects from the stage, thus, performers could execute half-formed ideas without having to articulate them, i.e. "brevity is the soul of wit". In the workshops, performers would occasionally abort ideas that were too difficult to articulate. It is not that performers are less persistent than the average user; just that they are used to generating a large amount of novel content quickly. If they are in a fast, creative mental state, as opposed to a seated formal discussion, then an impediment preventing them from prototyping an idea is in danger of making them abandon that idea for an "easier" one.

We noted that the coordinating gestures used in modern improvisation are fast and unambiguous to all performers on stage and the audience. The goal for our system was for its interaction to have the same degree of immediacy and clarity, which we termed *exposure*. We feel we achieved this, and performers were able to execute complex ideas without having to describe them. The visibility of interaction in our system also meant that there was no mystery as to how they achieved the result they intended, and others could replicate and build on their work.

Feature Elicitation

Improv is known for its "don't say no, say yes" rule. In truth, this is more nuanced — while rejecting an idea is often negative, improv teaching focuses on what to do with new information during a scene. Longform improv focuses on the "game of the scene" [10], a discovered pattern of behaviour that the performers may generatively explore and heighten or intensify. From a system developer perspective, this can run counter to the goal of finding a finite set of features to implement. Achieving a consistent and predictable map between user intention and result is not a good measure of success if our desire is to produce new tools for performers. Perhaps a better goal would be if a tool has properties that are initially surprising and novel.

Performers frequently asked questions of the form "Is it possible to...[X]" and the answer instinctively given back is whether X is possible with state-of-the-art equipment and algorithms, not whether it is possible to implement within the attention span of the asker. However, the system developer was cautious to say "no", as there was a worry that they will stop asking for interesting ideas. In practice, the best answer was "Yes, but not during this session".

Part of software development is finding and removing bugs. Performers' reactions to bugs was frustratingly positive — surprise and joy — as if the system was talking to them. Performers are trained to make every situation interesting — this means they are highly flexible in what others would consider a stressful situation (unexpected behaviour). It became difficult to work with this mindset during the early stages, when the goal of the developer was to end each workshop with a precisely-prioritized list of action-items.

CONCLUSION AND FUTURE WORK

We have presented *Improv Remix*: a design exercise in extending an art form through applied technology. Our primary contribution is our documentation of this process, from an analysis of the art form, to proposing an extension approach (performer control of video from earlier in the improv set), to designing a system, and observing use cases that would not have been possible before. This work has inspired the construction of novel interaction techniques, such as the *Vitruvian Menu*. We have also demonstrated a way to make verbal video content recombinable in a way that is satisfying to watch, with *polite playback*.

This work was inspired by existing practices; the goal was not to replicate them in digital form, but to extend and extrapolate from them. The extension work was specific to improvised theatre, though we feel there is general value in what we discovered to other theatre and art-making forms. We propose that extensions to other well-defined art forms and genres are possible using a process similar to that used in this work.

ACKNOWLEDGMENTS

This project would not be possible without Montgomery C. Martin, as the theatrical projection technical director. We also thank members of the DGP lab for putting up with a long-term physical setup, especially Haijun Xia, Jota, and John Hancock. We would also like to thank the members of the Toronto theatre community, especially Xander Williams, Alex James, Justine Cargo, Joe Law and Oliver Georgiou.

REFERENCES

1. Auslander, P. Live performance in a mediatized culture, 1999.
2. Baudel, T., and Beaudouin-Lafon, M. Charade: Remote control of objects using free-hand gestures. *Commun. ACM 36*, 7 (July 1993), 28–35.
3. Bill, V. T. *Chekhov–the Silent Voice of Freedom*. Philosophical Library, 1987.
4. Chi, P.-Y., Liu, J., Linder, J., Dontcheva, M., Li, W., and Hartmann, B. Democut: Generating concise instructional videos for physical demonstrations. In *Proc. of ACM UIST* (2013), 141–150.
5. Dixon, S. *Digital Performance: A History of New Media in Theatre, Dance, Performance Art, and Installation*. The MIT Press, 2007.
6. Engström, A., Esbjörnsson, M., and Juhlin, O. Mobile collaborative live video mixing. In *Proceedings of the 10th international conference on Human computer interaction with mobile devices and services*, MobileHCI '08, ACM (New York, NY, USA, 2008), 157–166.
7. Freeman, D. E., Santosa, S., Chevalier, F., Balakrishnan, R., and Singh, K. Laces: Live authoring through compositing and editing of streaming video. In *Proc. of ACM CHI* (New York, NY, USA, 2014), 1207–1216.
8. Graphics, L. D. M. Resolume VJ software.
9. Grotowski, J., Wiewiorowski, T., and Morris, K. Towards the poor theatre. *The Tulane Drama Review 11*, 3 (1967), 60–65.
10. Halpern, C., Close, and Johnson, K. H. *Truth in Comedy: The Manual for Improvisation*. Meriwether Publishing, 1994.
11. Hansen, L. K., Rico, J., Jacucci, G., Brewster, S., and Ashbrook, D. Performative interaction in public space. In *Proc. of ACM CHI EA* (2011), 49–52.
12. Hook, J., and Olivier, P. Waves: multi-touch vj interface. In *Proc. of ACM ITS* (2010), 305–305.
13. Hook, J., Schofield, G., Taylor, R., Bartindale, T., McCarthy, J., and Wright, P. Exploring hci's relationship with liveness. In *Proc. of ACM CHI* (2012), 2771–2774.
14. Hua, X.-S., Wang, Z., and Li, S. Lazycut: content-aware template-based video authoring. In *Proc. of ACM MULTIMEDIA* (2005), 792–793.
15. Juhlin, O., and Önnevall, E. On the relation of ordinary gestures to tv screens: General lessons for the design of collaborative interactive techniques. In *Proceedings of the SIGCHI Conference on Human Factors in Computing Systems*, CHI '13, ACM (New York, NY, USA, 2013), 919–930.
16. Kazi, R. H., Chua, K. C., Zhao, S., Davis, R., and Low, K.-L. Sandcanvas: A multi-touch art medium inspired by sand animation. In *Proc. of ACM CHI* (2011), 1283–1292.
17. Krueger, M. W., Gionfriddo, T., and Hinrichsen, K. Videoplace an artificial reality. In *Proc. of ACM CHI* (1985), 35–40.
18. Kulešov, L. V. *Kuleshov on film: writings by Lev Kuleshov*. Univ of California Press, 1974.
19. Magerko, B., Manzoul, W., Riedl, M., Baumer, A., Fuller, D., Luther, K., and Pearce, C. An empirical study of cognition and theatrical improvisation. In *Proceedings of the seventh ACM conference on Creativity and cognition*, ACM (2009), 117–126.
20. McCay, W. *Gertie the dinosaur*. Museum of Modern Art, 1909.
21. Murray, J. H. *Hamlet on the holodeck: The future of narrative in cyberspace*. Simon and Schuster, 1997.
22. Phelan, P. The politics of performance. *London and New York: Routledge 4* (1993).
23. Reeves, S., Benford, S., O'Malley, C., and Fraser, M. Designing the spectator experience. In *Proc. of ACM CHI* (New York, NY, USA, 2005), 741–750.
24. Rico, J. Evaluating the social acceptability of multimodal mobile interactions. In *Proc. of ACM CHI EA* (New York, NY, USA, 2010), 2887–2890.
25. Shoemaker, G., Tang, A., and Booth, K. S. Shadow reaching: a new perspective on interaction for large displays. In *Proc. of ACM UIST* (2007), 53–56.
26. Steinmeyer, J. The science behind the ghost: A brief history of pepper's ghost, 1999.
27. The Builders Association. Xtravaganza, 2002.
28. Theory, B. Ten backwards. DVD, 1999.
29. Tsuchida, S., Terada, T., and Tsukamoto, M. A system for practicing formations in dance performance supported by self-propelled screen. In *Proc. of ACM AH* (2013), 178–185.
30. Vogel, D., and Balakrishnan, R. Interactive public ambient displays: transitioning from implicit to explicit, public to personal, interaction with multiple users. In *Proc. of ACM UIST* (2004), 137–146.
31. Wang, J., Bhat, P., Colburn, R. A., Agrawala, M., and Cohen, M. F. Interactive video cutout. *ACM Trans. Graph. 24*, 3 (July 2005), 585–594.
32. Yip, S., Leu, E., and Howe, H. The automatic video editor. In *Proc. of ACM MULTIMEDIA* (New York, NY, USA, 2003), 596–597.
33. Zimmerman, E. Creating a meaning-machine: The deck of stories called life in the garden. *Second Person* (2007).

Sketchplore: Sketch and Explore with a Layout Optimiser

Kashyap Todi[1,2] kashyap.todi@uhasselt.be

Daryl Weir[1] daryl.weir@aalto.fi

Antti Oulasvirta[1] antti.oulasvirta@aalto.fi

[1]Aalto University Helsinki, Finland

[2]Hasselt University - tUL - iMinds Diepenbeek, Belgium

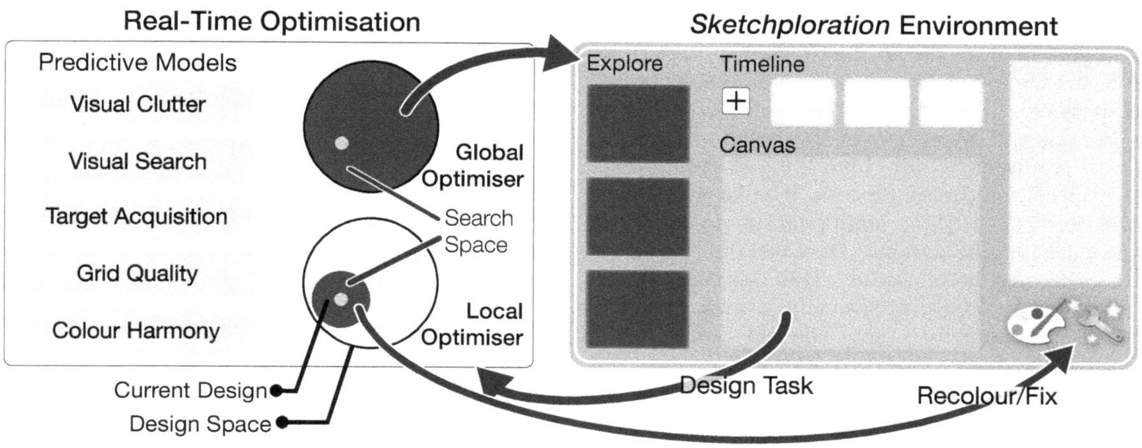

Figure 1: *Sketchplorer* is an interactive layout sketching tool supported by real-time model-based optimisation. The tool is designed to facilitate the creative and problem-solving aspects of sketching without requiring extensive input. While a designer is sketching, a design task is automatically inferred. The optimiser uses predictive models to make suggestions for local and global changes that improve usability and aesthetics. Suggestions appear on the side, and never override the designer's work.

ABSTRACT

This paper studies a novel concept for integrating real-time design optimisation to a sketching tool. Although optimisation methods can attack very complex design problems, their insistence on precise objectives and a point optimum is a poor fit with sketching practices. *Sketchplorer* is a multi-touch sketching tool that uses a real-time layout optimiser. It automatically infers the designer's task to search for both local improvements to the current design and global (radical) alternatives. Using predictive models of sensorimotor performance and perception, these suggestions steer the designer toward more usable and aesthetic layouts without overriding the designer or demanding extensive input.

Author Keywords

Sketching; Model-based optimisation; Visual Layouts

ACM Classification Keywords

H.5.2. Information Interfaces and Presentation: User Interfaces

DIS 2016, June 04–08, 2016, Brisbane, QLD, Australia.

DOI: http://dx.doi.org/10.1145/2901790.2901817

INTRODUCTION

This paper is motivated by the observation that optimisation methods have great untapped potential in design tools. We focus on the activity of *sketching layouts*, in which a designer places, colours, organises, and defines elements on a canvas. From a combinatorial perspective, the design of layouts is notoriously hard. For a canvas of 1024×768 pixels, divided into a 24×32 grid, as in the tool presented here, there are 158,400 one-element layouts and a whopping 10^{41} eight-element layouts. Although algorithms may not be able to find the optimal solution in such large search spaces, they can "parallelise" search, and find candidate solutions and suggest them to designers. This could help designers in exploration, who are known to be limited to a handful of designs per iteration [8]. Also, algorithms can complement designers by exploring design spaces neutrally without being constrained by past experiences, to produce designs that the designer might not otherwise conceive. Employing an optimiser might also improve the quality of designs for end-users (see [12, 33, 45]).

However, several hard research challenges emerge. First, layout design is a complex, multi-objective task addressing not only usability but also aesthetic qualities [15, 44]. Presently no algorithmic approach exists that can address both. Second, optimisation typically takes a long time, due to combinatorial complexity, and no solution has been shown for fast-paced, iterative design of layouts. Third, although optimisation methods can attack very complex design problems, their insistence on *precise* inputs contradicts sketching. To better fit with design practice, optimisers should radically reduce the effort for defining tasks (see e.g., [2]). Crucially, they should not attempt to override design thinking. Instead, final decisions should be left to designers, who possess knowledge that computers might not.

This paper investigates *'sketchploration'*, a novel concept to exploit interactive optimisation methods in design tools and in particular for layout sketching. We approach sketching as a *problem-solving* activity and a tool for *visual thinking* [6, 30]. The goal is to enable access to results of real-time optimisation, yet impose as few control requirements on the designer as possible, in order to support the natural flow of sketching. For this end, Sketchplorer, illustrated in Figure 1, relaxes typical requirements for controlling an optimiser in a way that respects the design process. Unlike with previous solutions (e.g., [2, 12]), no additional input is required from the designer. As the designer sketches, the system infers the designer's task automatically. The optimiser simultaneously searches for local improvements (small changes), and explores global alternatives (large changes). Importantly, it deploys several predictive models of user performance and perception adapted from literature. This allows it to make informed suggestions that "pull" the designer toward usable and aesthetic designs. Sketchplorer does not override the designers' sketch, but presents optimised designs as glanceable suggestions. Technically, sketchploration extends *model-based interface optimisation* [2, 12, 45] to real-time design exploration under ill-specified and changing design goals.

This paper presents the first investigation of the concept, focusing on *interactive layouts* familiar from GUIs, web pages, menus, and dialogs. It complements existing work by showing how an interactive optimiser can be integrated with fast-paced and unconstrained early-stage sketching. Our implementation presently supports 10 common types of elements and hierarchical (nested) placement. But concept could be implemented for any sketching tool that affords extending the workspace and communication with a server. The technical contributions include:

1. *Design principles* for integrating a model-based interface optimiser to a sketching tool.
2. *Extension of model-based interface optimisation* to interactive layouts by: 1) Formulation of (unconstrained) layout sketching as an optimisation problem, allowing for addressing the positions, sizes, and colours of elements. 2) A novel, theoretically informed objective function addressing five aspects important in layout use: perception of clutter, visual search performance, pointing performance, grid quality, and colour harmony.
3. *A dynamic optimisation approach* that 1) infers the designer's task from the current layout, 2) simultaneously explores and exploits in the design space and 3) reacts rapidly to changes in the current sketch.

We report results from two empirical evaluations—with end-users and with trained designers. We conclude that interactive model-based optimisation warrants more attention.

PRIOR ART: SKETCHING TOOLS AND UI OPTIMISATION

Our goal is to support sketching with computational methods. In this work, we investigate sketching as a tool for visual thinking and problem-solving, and do not delve into freehand drawing and rendering aspects of sketches. When understood as problem-solving, sketching is characterised by its quick, ambiguous, and uncertain nature [13, 42]. The goal of designers is not a point design, but rather exploration. Sketching unfolds as an iterative process of idea-generation, refinement (exploitation), and redefinition. Designers entertain multiple hypotheses and may backtrack to previous designs. Details to a sketch are added gradually, and they can be changed at any stage. Idea-generation in sketching has recognised limits and biases [8]. These properties make sketching both a challenge and an opportunity for computational support.

Sketching Tools and Interaction Techniques

Research on computational support for sketching originates from Sutherland's Sketchpad [37], which highlighted the benefits of a digital medium. We refer to a recent review [17] and here point out a few main trends in research.

First, improved recognition technologies have brought pen-and-paper like techniques to sketching [41]. Second, several interaction techniques have been proposed to enhance the drawing of shapes in sketching (e.g., [1]). Third, some approaches have looked at integration with other activities in design, and a better support for going back and forth between designs. SILK [23] and DENIM [25] explored several such techniques. Fourth, sketching has been extended from 2D spatial displays. For example, [19] enabled sketching for animations and dynamic authoring of illustrations. Fifth, design heuristics have been implemented in sketching tools. Examples include colour palettes [29], template-based sketching [18], and design guidelines. While these ensure that designs meet certain standards, they allow neither exploring designs nor refining them for some objectives.

Heuristic and Data-Driven Methods for Layout Generation

Heuristic approaches to layout generation have explored balance, consistency, or the golden cut (e.g. [11, 27]). Although heuristics can produce results that are visually appealing and resemble real designs, they do not predict effects on end-users. They lack means for conflict resolution. To our knowledge, there are no heuristic approaches that solve both spatial and visual aspects of layout.

Data-driven approaches such as Webzeitgeist [22] mine a large number of designs and can produce new ones for designer given inputs. Although colour, size, position, and grouping can be addressed, the approach results in basically "mimicry" of existing designs. It does not offer a principled way of setting objectives for goals like usability and aesthetics. They offer no guarantee that the outcomes are good beyond visual appeal.

Some work has been done on automatic generation and improvement of static graphical media such as posters, flyers, or slides. [31] used an energy-based model considering aesthetic heuristics, such as alignment, balance, and flow. DesignScape

[32] is a tool for assisting novice designers in creating graphical media. While our work, at first glance, resembles DesignScape, the assumptions and underlying mechanisms of the two systems are very different. DesignScape does not consider interactive layouts, which form the basis of GUIs. Additionally, the tool is meant to improve final-stage designs, based on realistic content. It is not designed for the uncertain and ambiguous nature of initial-stage sketching, where the actual content is still subject to change. With regard to underlying optimisation mechanisms, DesignScape uses a reduced design space which does not include element colour, and makes simplifying assumptions about aesthetics rather than using validated predicitive models from psychology.

Finally, there has been extensive work on automating layout generation based on constraint satisfaction. Interfaces are specified as a set of semantic and spatial constraints, and solver programs generate possible designs for given screen sizes. [26] reviews these techniques. However, the constraints still have to be constructed by a designer, and moreover the generated layouts have no guarantees about aesthetic quality or interaction performance.

Model-based Optimisation

Model-based user interface optimisation uses combinatorial optimisation to automate interface generation. The idea is to represent a design problem and design knowledge (e.g., user simulations, models, heuristics) as an objective function for a search algorithm that iteratively improves designs for the stated objectives. Unlike heuristic approaches, model-based optimisation relies on theories and predictive models of how users interact or perceive a layout and an algorithm that searches the design space systematically. The most well-known layout problem is the letter assignment problem. Fitts' law can be used together with bigram data on transition frequency to find keyboard layouts that minimise expected finger travel distance [24]. This idea has been extended to widget layouts in SUPPLE using branch-and-bound [12].

The first *interactive* design tool following model-based optimisation was MenuOptimizer [2]. It uses a model of menu search together with a consistency heuristic to optimise hierarchical menus for application. It integrated several types of support to the QtDesigner development environment. It introduced an interactive optimiser that proposed global and local changes like moving a menu item to improve user performance. However, it was designed for "point optimisation" and contained an overwhelming amount of controls and visualisations and insisted on problem specification for the optimiser. The authors concluded that designers mostly used global suggestions (suggestions for the whole menu system).

WALKTHROUGH AND DESIGN OVERVIEW

We had four objectives for integrating computational support to a design tool:

1. Support quick and ambiguous sketching, and leave room for uncertainty, by providing capabilities to defer the task of specifying details at any stage of the design process.
2. Allow fluent shifts between exploration and refinement.
3. Provide support for multiple hypotheses, and give an overview of progress, by providing a non-destructive, and editable, timeline of previous alternate designs.
4. Minimise user actions not related to the design activity itself by inferring details whenever possible.
5. Eliminate ambiguity, in designers' minds, while perceiving optimised results by communicating with the designer in a timely and predictable manner.

Walkthrough: Designing a Blog Page

This walkthrough illustrates the use of Sketchplorer from a designer's perspective.

Sketching the initial layout: Sketchplorer initially presents the designer with an empty canvas. The designer starts sketching by creating a structure for her design (Figure 2a). Drawn elements can be moved around, or resized, at any time. She ambiguously sketches out boxes, serving as proxies for the elements of her blog page. Sketchplorer dynamically infers hierarchy of elements, and does not require the designer to explicitly specify ordering or grouping. It starts computing both local and global suggestions in the background.

Refining and adding details: An *inspector* panel, similar to most commercial sketching tools, sits on the right-edge of the display, and can be pulled out at any time. This can be used to specify details, such as the element type, colour, and importance (usage probability) of objects on the canvas (Figure 2b). The designer now adds details to some of the elements. For instance, she indicates that her blog page has a heading and a paragraph element, and marks them as being of high importance for the optimiser. She also specifies that the image (site logo) is of low importance. Satisfied with the first version of the design, she taps the save ('+') button. This adds the current design to the designer's *timeline*, and provides a preview. The designs here can be retrieved, and edited, at any later time. This enables the designer to see the evolution in designs, borrow previous ideas, and select feasible alternatives.

Fine-tuning and local changes: While the designer sketches and refines, the system continuously streams the description of the current design to the optimiser. The local optimiser uses the current design as a starting point to suggest fixes and provide recolour options. Pulsating icons in the inspector panel appear when *fix* and *recolour* options are available (Figure 2c). The designer refers to these suggestions. She realises that by using the recolouring suggestion, she can make the paragraph of text stand out. She chooses one of the recoloured layouts, and continues working on her sketch.

Exploring new designs: By abstracting from the current design, the global optimiser retrieves unique designs, and returns them to the designer. An *explore* panel, residing on the left edge of the display (Figure 2d), is periodically updated with these designs. The designer browses through the list of alternatives, and finds two interesting alternatives. She adds the first to her list of saved designs, and drags the second onto the canvas, to continue working on it.

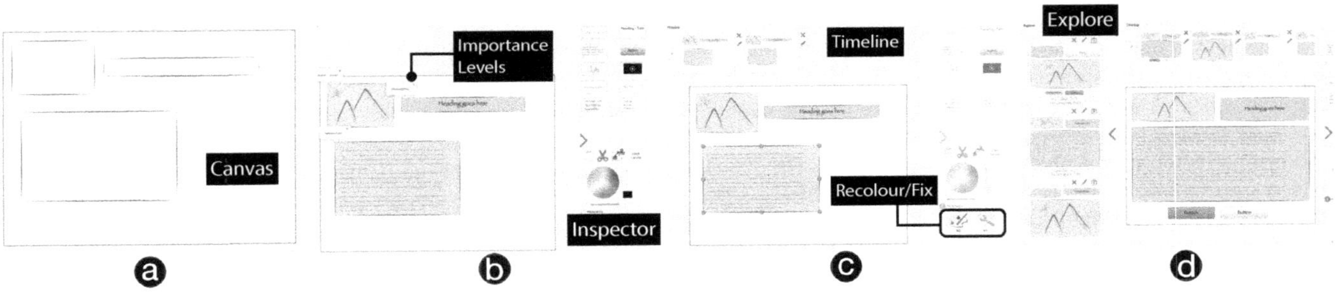

Figure 2: Overview of Sketchplorer. A large canvas is surrounded by the various features. Designers can (a) ambiguously sketch layout designs, and (b) refine and add details. They have immediate access to a timeline of saved designs. They can improve designs by (c) using *fix* and *recolour* suggestions, or (d) exploring globally optimised designs.

In a short duration, the designer's collection of *saved layouts* is populated with several feasible alternatives—some sketched by the designer, and the others with the aid of the optimiser. While the above phases appear to be linear, in practice, sketching and exploration phases are intertwined.

Overview of Interactions

Sketchplorer is designed for a multitouch environment using a large display, and uses touch gestures for all controls.

Sketching and refinement: Sketchplorer allows designers to either sketch ambiguous bounding boxes for layout elements, or pick out a specific element type and draw it on the canvas. It takes care to accurately order every element on the canvas, without requiring the user to explicitly *bring-to-front* or *send-to-back*. Each time an element is changed, so as to change the hierarchy, the ordering is dynamically adapted. Hierarchical groups of elements can be selected and manipulated at the same time. This inferred hierarchy is also essential for the internal representation of a layout in the optimiser. The colour picker allows designers to select the hue–saturation combination, and adjust the brightness. Double-tapping on an element reveals an in-place pop-over, and allows adding details without having to move to the inspector. Individual elements' importance can be adjusted in the inspector panel. Alternatively, an overlay can be enabled, that displays the importance of each element, and allows batch adjustments (Figure 2b).

Saved versions and timeline: Benefits of interactive timelines and alternate versions have been emphasised in HCI literature [38]. In Sketchplorer, the current design can be added to the timeline at any time. The timeline provides an overview of all saved designs, and any alternative design, or intermediate sketch, can be dragged back to canvas. This allows designers to compare designs, have an overview of the evolution of their designs, and iterate over sketches.

Integration with the optimiser: To the designer, the optimisation appears as a two-pronged approach, consisting of local and global optimisation. The local optimiser listens in on every change in the design, including changes in sizes and positions of elements. It creates fine-tuned designs, that maintain the overall composition of the original sketch, but improve certain aspects of it. Recolouring suggestions maintain the sizing and placement of elements, and offer harmonious recolouring suggestions, which also improve aesthetics and performance. In contrast, the global optimiser listens exclusively to changes in design tasks, and acts upon them. It abstracts away from exact details, allowing it to explore the entire design space, and generate unique designs. It performs exploration in real-time and periodically returns improved results that are immediately displayed to the designer in an expandable *explore* panel. The optimiser focuses on creating unique and improved solutions, not on refining or polishing a solution to make them perfect.

PREDICTIVE MODELS FOR INTERACTIVE LAYOUTS

Sketchplorer is the first user interface optimiser using models of human performance and perception to optimise both spatial and colour aspects of interactive layouts. We chose models that cover both aesthetic features, such as symmetry, and sensorimotor performance measures, such as target selection time. The models have also been validated in empirical studies and shown to align with user preferences and performance. In this way, we aim to produce layouts that are aesthetically pleasing and usable in a predictable way. However, note that the choice of models in the system is flexible. If there is evidence for another model being better than those we use currently, it is very simple to add this without changing the workflow of Sketchplorer.

Overview: The Colour Patches Task

In order to examine the effect of optimising for a model as an objective, and learn how the models affect optimisation, we created the *colour patches task*. Here, the optimiser's goal is to assign five rectangular elements to a 5×5 grid. Each element is a block or patch with a single colour. We assume that each patch is interactive, with a certain probability of being targeted. We sample these probabilities from a Zipf distribution. These probabilities are used to weight the average visual search and target acquisition times using a formula given later in the paper. To produce candidate designs, we traverse the elements in a random order and pick a random colour, size and position for each. The colours are chosen from Kelly's set of perceptually distinct colours [20], and the sizes are chosen randomly from three fixed sizes. For each objective, we evaluate many random designs to find the one with the lowest objective value, then perform small changes to search for local improvements in the design.

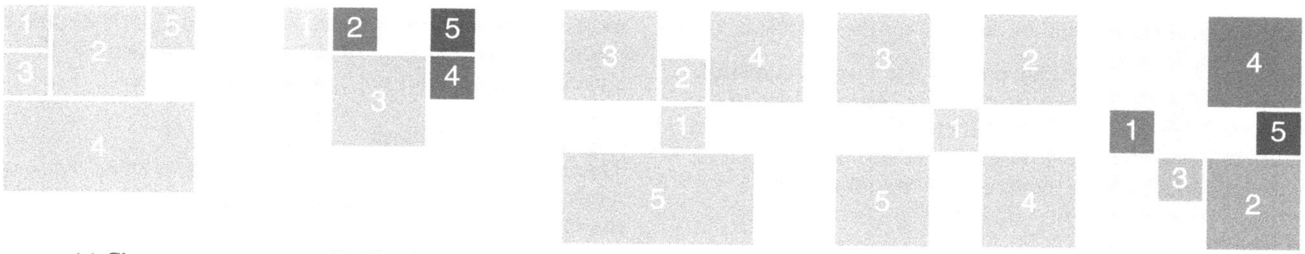

(a) Clutter (b) Visual search (c) Target acquisition (d) Grid quality (e) Colour harmony

Figure 3: Results for the colour patches task. These five layouts are outcomes when optimising for a *single objective at a time*. Sketchplorer combines these objectives into multi-objective search. Numbers refer to a ranking based on frequency of use.

Figure 3 shows the results. Elements are numbered by their usage probability, with 1 being the most common. The results show that each objective focuses on either spatial or colouring aspects, but may ignore or contradict the others. In the following sections, we will detail these results.

Visual Clutter

We use the Rosenholtz model [34] to minimise visual clutter. The idea is that as more objects are added to a display, it becomes more difficult to place a new object that it is perceptually unique and easy to identify. The layout elements have some distribution of visual features. As the number of elements grows, the feature distribution occupies more of the available space. This model has been shown to correlate with user perception of clutter, a correlate of aesthetic preference.

Given vectors of the features for each object on the display, we compute the mean and covariance $\boldsymbol{\Sigma}$ of these vectors. In our implementation, we consider only colour in our feature vector. The clutter of the display is then defined simply as the determinant of the covariance matrix, $|\boldsymbol{\Sigma}|$. This can be thought of as the volume of the 1 s.d. covariance ellipsoid. We take the inverse of the clutter score for the objective function.

Figure 3(a) shows the colour patch results for this model. Each item has the same colour, which makes sense as this choice minimises the volume of the colour covariance.

Visual Search

We implement the Kieras-Hornof model of visual attention [21] to maximise visual search performance by enhancing the perceptual uniqueness of commonly searched elements.

Prediction consists of two parts: (1) a set of availability functions determine whether the features of a target are perceivable from the user's current eye location; and (2) a simple GOMS-style algorithm estimates the time in milliseconds required to locate the target.The availability functions are based on the eccentricity from the current eye location e and angular size s of the target. Additive Gaussian random noise with variance $\sigma^2 = vs$ proportional to the size of the target is assumed. For each feature, a threshold t is computed as $t = ae^2 + be + c$ and the probability that the feature is perceivable is given by:

$$P(\text{available}) = 1 - \Phi\left(\frac{t - s}{\sigma^2}\right), \tag{1}$$

where $\Phi(x)$ is the c.d.f. of the standard normal. We further define $P(\text{available}) = 1$ when $e < 1°$, since targets in the fovea are always perceived.

We use parameter values from the original paper, which were shown to accurately predict visual search time for data from an older study [40]. Note that our implementation only uses colour as an availability feature, since the authors found size and shape could only reliably be perceived for targets close to the fixation location.

For memory effects we use a simple logarithmic model based on the number of previous acquisitions. We optimise assuming the user is an expert and has visually searched the interface 1000 times in total. However, this assumption can be easily changed for example to account for novices.

Figure 3(b) shows the visual search colour patches. Each item has a different colour to make it visually unique, and all items are clustered in the top left of the grid, where the simulated search begins. More important items are closer to the left corner. Note that this objective conflicts with the clutter metric, which rewards layouts where everything is the same colour. Thus, there is a tradeoff between aesthetics and visual search performance that can be controlled by adjusting the weights.

Target Acquisition

Following previous work on performance-optimisation of layouts [24, 45], we deploy a variant of Fitts' law [28] as our model of target acquisition. Fitts' law favours transitions between large elements at minimum distances, and estimates the upper bound of expert pointing performance. Including this model allows us to optimise for efficient selection of elements, rather than purely for aesthetics. T is the time it takes for an end-effector to reach a target from a given distance D. For target width W, T is given by:

$$T = \sum_{r \in R} t_r = \sum_{r \in R} \left[a + b \log_2\left(\frac{D}{W} + 1\right)\right] \tag{2}$$

where R is the set of responses when navigating to the target.

When optimising, we assume that users interact with the interface elements using touch. We use values of a and b from a recent study [10]. To compute D, we assume that the starting point of the finger is the centre of the display. We compute W according to the angle of approach. Fitts' law parameters for other input devices, such as the mouse, are readily available, and the optimiser can easily be adapted for these devices.

Figure 3(c) shows the colour patches for target acquistion. The most important element is centrally placed, close to the assumed starting position. The other elements are arranged around the center and have larger sizes so that they can be acquired without moving the finger far from the center.

Grid Quality

We use the Balinsky symmetry metric [3] as a measure of grid quality. It calculates the distance to the closest symmetrical layout. It was shown to correlate with aesthetic preferences.

We start with the layout vertex set $s = \{(x_1, y_1), \ldots, (x_n, y_n)\}$, rescaled such that the x-axis coincides with the axis of symmetry and the y-axis contains the centre of mass of the x_i. This is mapped to the complex plane to obtain a set $z_i = x_i + I y_i$. These points are horizontally symmetrical if they consist only of real values and complex conjugate pairs. A fundamental result in complex analysis states that this is equivalent to the stipulation that all coefficients a_j of the polynomial

$$P_n(z) = \prod_{j=1}^{n}(z - z_j) = \sum_{j=0}^{n} a_j z^j \tag{3}$$

are real. Thus, the asymmetry for a layout is obtained by constructing this polynomial and averaging the size of the imaginary parts of the coefficients. Vertical symmetry is scored in the same way, after a simple coordinate transformation. Our overall metric is an even weighting of these two scores.

Figure 3(d) shows the colour patches for this metric. As expected, the result is symmetric in both axes.

Colour Harmony

Harmonic colours are sets of colours that combine to provide a pleasant visual perception. Harmony is determined by relative position in colour space. There is no universal definition for a harmonic set. Here, we use the templates proposed in [7]. These consist of one or two sectors of the hue wheel, with given angular sizes. These templates can be arbitrarily rotated to create new sets.

The distance of a layout X from a template T is given by

$$D(X, T) = \sum_{e \in X} DH(e, T) S(e), \tag{4}$$

where $DH(e, T)$ is the arc-length distance between the hue of element e and the hue of the closest sector border in T, and $S(e)$ is the saturation channel of e. If a colour falls inside one of the sectors of T, $DH(e, T)$ is identically zero.

In order to rapidly evaluate many layouts, we precreate a set C of 78 harmonic sets by rotating the templates in fixed increments. We define the colour harmony H by:

$$H(X) = \min_{T \in C} D(X, T) \tag{5}$$

Figure 3(e) shows the colour patches with the best match to one of the harmonic sets. Patches 1–4 have similar hues but different saturations, and patch 5 has a hue on the opposite side of the colour wheel. Together these colours form a harmonic set with the Y-template defined in [7]. Note that the placement and ordering of the patches is somewhat chaotic, since this model does not consider those factors.

Scope and Limitations

These models allow us to deal with the positions, size, alignment and colour of layout elements. An optimiser is able to search for layouts that improve for user performance, but also for aesthetic qualities. If implemented alone, each objective drives a layouts to an unbalanced design favouring one aspect. A multi-objective optimiser allows finding good compromises. A limitation is that these models do not allow us to deal with semantic aspects of layouts, such as naming or grouping of elements. These decisions are currently left to the designer, but could be incorporated in future versions if models for these aspects are found.

DYNAMIC LAYOUT OPTIMISATION DURING SKETCHING

Layout design is a high-dimensional, NP-hard problem [9, 36]. Search is computationally expensive, as multiple objective values are calculated. Yet, when integrated with fast-paced sketching, only brief computation times are allowed. Further, the design problem is also under-specified, because the designer may not have time to specify point objectives and assumptions for each sketch.

Our approach builds on three ideas: First, we relax the requirement to specify a design task to an optimiser. Instead, we infer the “implicit” design task assumed in the sketch currently edited. The internal representation of the *design task*, in its simplest form, is comprised of the different layout elements placed on the canvas, and their ‘importance’ values, if specified. Using this, We can search alternatives without asking the designer anything. Second, we relax the assumption that the goal is to find the optimum design. Instead, we run several optimisers simultaneously that *explore* the design space with different assumptions. We pick a few diverse design ideas and pass them to the designer, and let his/her choices guide the search. Third, to accelerate search, we make use of the observation that there are far fewer (abstract) *design tasks* than there are (concrete) layouts. Using this observation, we pre-train an “associative memory” that has a good starting point for many design tasks that might occur. When Sketchplorer is running, it maps the present sketch to the closest seed in the associative memory to offer a good solution very quickly. By contrast, MenuOptimizer assumed a point-optimisation goal and enforced a complete reset of the optimiser's state when a single element was changed [2].

Definition: Layout Design Task

Layout design is similar to the letter assignment problem from keyboard optimisation [5] and to the *layout facility problem* (LFP), where the task is to place machines with fixed/varying size in a workshop [9, 36]. Layout design in HCI, as we address it here, is a special case, where the goal is to find a non-overlapping planar orthogonal arrangement of n coloured rectangular elements so as to minimise the cost function (see below). There are two differences to LFP: 1) elements can be coloured; and 2) the cost function is more complex. We make two further additions to the task. First, we define the task to involve *element types*, each with unique size constraints. Second, we allow groups. The elements can be nested as long as their bounding box edges do not overlap.

Internally, our optimiser represents a layout as a 2D array of pointers to information objects which store the colours, usage probabilities, etc. of the elements. We use an efficient maximal empty rectangles algorithm [39] to find places in this array where we can move or grow elements to modify the layout. Additionally, each element also has an internal array representing the positions of any child elements relative to itself. We treat the canvas in a recursive loop from the highest to the lowest level of this hierarchy.

Objective Function

We define a multi-objective task where we seek to minimise a weighted combination of the outputs of the five models:

$$U = \sum_{i=1}^{5} w_i S_i, \qquad (6)$$

where the weights w_i sum to 1 and the individual objectives S_i are normalised to the range [0, 1].

In addition, we introduce two optional canvas-level constraints. We compute *alignment* following an approach similar to [4], in which we count the number of 'alignment lines', or object edge positions, weighted by the average size of object edges lying on those lines. We compute *packing efficiency* as the proportion of the minimum bounding rectangle for the layout elements which is empty, averaged with the proportion of the overall canvas which is empty. These help the optimiser improve quicker in the grid quality dimension. They align elements horizontally and vertically and "pack" them. However, since they aggressively push search toward harmonic layouts, it may drive search to a local minima. We address this by introducing a filtering stage where we compare results for solution quality and diversity (see below).

Inferring the Design Task

We extract the *design task* by analysing the present layout being edited by the designer. We map a layout to a design task by 1) counting the number of occurrences for each element type, and 2) making a distinction between high and low importance items for each element type.

Dynamic Optimisation

During sketching, the optimiser system runs several optimisers simultaneously, each exploring the design space differently, and dedicated to a functionality in the Sketchplorer workspace. An overview is given in Table 1. The optimisers deploy two search heuristics.

Variable Neighbourhood Search (VNS) [14] is a strategy combining a neighbourhood-based meta-heuristic to a hill-climbing algorithm. This strategy was chosen to ensure good exploration of the design space, since it is able to increase the search radius if the search gets stuck. It allows larger and larger changes to be made in each iteration. In our case,

Sketchplorer Feature	Duration (s)	Search method	Neighbourhood size and type	Objective function
Recolour	1-10 s	VNS	Small; only colour changes	Colour only
Fix	1-10 s	VNS	Small; only spatial changes	All
Explore	1-10 s	AM	Large; only spatial changes	All
Explore	10-120 s	VNS	Medium; only spatial changes	All

VNS: Variable Neighbourhood Search, AM: Associative Memory

Table 1: Sketchplorer uses a multi-threaded optimisation strategy that both explores and exploits. To support dynamic changes in the task, two methods are used in parallel: Variable Neighbourhood Search and Associative Memory.

we run a steepest descent with different pre-set neighbourhood sizes. A neighbourhood is defined as a change to the colour, position, or size of an element. Small neighbourhood means that one iteration can only produce one change to a layout. Large neighbourhood means that multiple changes are allowed. The optimisers use VNS with small (e.g. 1, 2, 3) or medium radii (e.g. 4 to 10). Figure 4 shows good and failed designs produced in about 4 minutes on a laptop computer. Since Sketchplorer is targeted towards skilled designers, we take a mixed-initiative approach [16], and rely on the designer to identify good designs, and filter out unappealing or illogical ones.

Associative Memory (AM) [43] is executed in parallel. AM is a memory-based learning approach to dynamic optimisation problems. The idea is to populate the memory with good solutions offline, and map the current design task to its closest-matching task in AM, and use that as a starting point for search. We implemented *layout remapping* by searching AM for layouts with design tasks that were supersets of the current design, ordering the elements in each by usage probability, then searching for matched type pairs. We trained our AM for 6,600 randomly generated design tasks. The live optimiser loaded the AM in advance in order to respond quickly (within few seconds).

Filtering and Diversification of Results

Since the parallel searchers explore different parts of the design space, and we cannot show all results to the designer, we pool the results and filter them using a bi-objective pareto front criterion. We define this as the weighted (and normalised) sum of the objective score and *inter-layout distance*. Inter-layout distance is a score from 0 to 1 where 0 means identical layouts and 1 means that all elements have different locations. This diversifies search results and prevents identical designs from being shown to the designer.

SYSTEM IMPLEMENTATION

The tool is implemented in Objective-C. Multitouch input is detected using PQ Labs multitouch SDK, and interactions are recognised using customised gesture recognition. The optimisers are written in Python, and use parallelisation for speed-ups. When designers make changes to the current design, layout files (in JSON format) are sent from the design

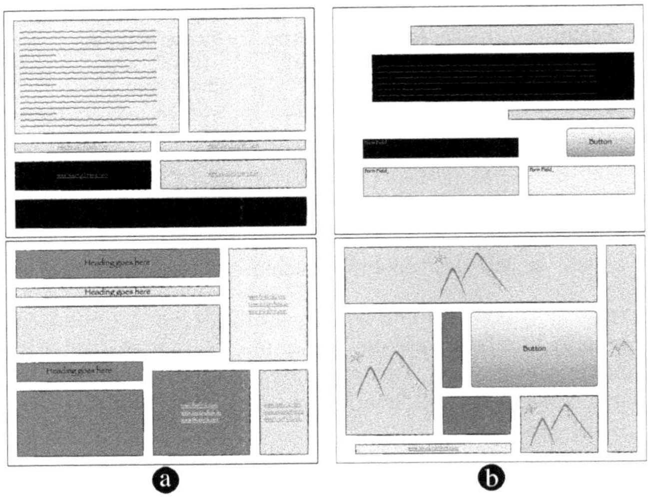

Figure 4: Examples of (a) successful and (b) unsuccessful global designs from the Associative Memory, *before* real-time optimisation. Designs were computed from randomised starting points, in 4 minutes each.

tool to the optimisers asynchronously. The optimisers run on dedicated laptops (we use Macbook Pros), and all devices communicate using ThoMoNetworking. Local vs. global design changes are identified using filename tags. To avoid outdated retrievals, the optimisers kill existing threads when a new file is received. Generated designs are immediately pushed back to the design tool.

STUDY 1: END-USER EVALUATION

Our first study addresses optimisation of the design of the Windows Phone home screen. This study involves no designer in the loop. The goal is evaluate our optimisation approach by testing its outputs with *end-users*. As the case we chose the Windows Phone home screen, a complex design task that could not have been addressed with previous approaches. The task allows multiple icon sizes, colours, and positions over three pages. We compare an optimised design against the baseline in a study where users are asked to select applications from the home screen. As dependent variables we look at selection time and measures of perceived aesthetics. As our baseline, we implemented the factory default of a Lumia 930 phone. Apps which were not preinstalled on the phone were added in a random order at the end of the default menu, as in an unpersonalised order-of-installation layout. Comparing against a real, commercial design provides a hard baseline for the layout optimiser.

Optimisation Task

The inputs to the optimiser are a list of 55 apps, together with usage probabilities from the LiveLab database [35]. We sampled the primary colours from the app icons manually. When generating layouts in the optimiser, we allowed as many 8×6 grid pages as necessary, and each icon was sized at 1×1, 2×2, or 2×4 grid cells. For some apps, the icon is a transparency, coloured according to system-wide accent colour. Others have icons with developer-chosen colours. For the system-coloured icons, the optimiser was free to choose from a set of 20 perceptually distinct colours [20].

Optimisation follows a different approach than in the live, dynamic optimisation task. We here performed multiple restarts of a random search procedure with different objective weights. For each weight set, we generated and evaluated 10,000 random layouts, then performed 3000 iterations of local search around each of the best three designs.

The menu with the best score over all weight sets was chosen as the design to evaluate with users. The models predicted that our optimised design would be better than the baseline in terms of visual search (score 0.106 vs. 0.117, a difference of ~270ms), selection (0.108 vs 0.104, ~90ms), and grid quality (0.005 vs. 0.013), similar in colour harmony (both 0.015), and worse in terms of clutter (0.028 vs 0.020).

Participants

We recruited 20 student participants (4 male), aged 20 to 36 (mean 26.7, s.d. 5.2). They had 2 to 8 years of experience with smartphones (mean 4.3, s.d. 1.8). Participants were required to not have prior experience with Windows Phone devices. Two participants were left handed. Participants were compensated with a cinema ticket.

Apparatus, Procedure, and Experimental Design

We implemented a logging application to display the menus and collect performance information on a Nexus 5 smartphone running Android 4.4.3.

Participants performed 275 trials with each menu. In each trial, they were shown a textual stimulus with the target name. After tapping to dismiss the stimulus, the first page of the current menu was shown. Participants had to navigate to and tap the appropriate icon. A hint button was available if they forgot the stimulus. The times of all taps and swipes were logged, along with any incorrect selections. The different apps were shown as stimuli between 1 and 25 times, depending on their usage probability. We used a smoothed version of the distribution used to train the optimiser, in order to increase the number of applications with more than 1 selection.

Participants performed the experiment while seated in a quiet room. They were asked to hold the phone in their non-dominant hand and tap with the index finger of their dominant hand. Order of conditions was counterbalanced.

After this, participants were shown images of the full layouts and asked to rate them from 1 to 5 in terms of overall aesthetic quality, use of colour, composition logic, and symmetry. They were also asked to indicate a preferred layout.

Results

As our principal performance metric, we use the average selection time over all trials, measured from the tap to dismiss the stimulus to the tap on the correct icon. We filtered out trials with selection errors or hint requests.

Figure 5 shows our results and the first page of each of the designs. Over all trials, there is no significant difference be-

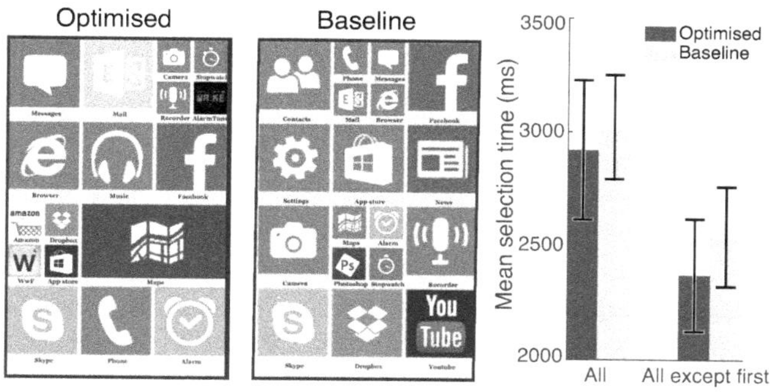

Figure 5: *End-User Study.* Left: Homescreens of the optimised and baseline designs. Right: Average selection times (95% CIs). The optimised design was significantly faster when the first selection for each app was excluded.

Figure 6: *Designer Study.* We evaluated Sketchplorer with 10 trained designers. Participants completed design tasks while using the different features supported by the design tool.

tween the average selection times between the two menus (paired t-test, $t(19) = -0.95, p > 0.05$).

However, when the first selection for each app in each condition is removed from consideration, the difference in selection time between the menus is significant (paired t-test, $t(19) = -2.67, p < 0.05$). This removal is justified given that users were mostly familiarising with the menus during the first selections. We also analysed only the latter half of trials for each app, to see if the learning benefit continued to grow. However, the results when doing this were very similar. This suggests that the majority of the learning takes place on the first selection. This result matches with our models that predict expert performance rather than that of novices.

For the aesthetic ratings, we found no significant differences between the overall ratings and logic of composition scores across the designs (Wilcoxon signed rank test, $Z = -1.80, -1.79, p > 0.05$). However, users rated the use of colour in the optimised design significantly higher than the baseline ($Z = 2.38, p < 0.05$), but the level of symmetry significantly lower ($Z = -2.65, p < 0.05$).

Half (10) of the 20 users expressed a preference for the optimised design over the baseline. Several participants noted that they disliked one or both designs because the menus did not prioritise the apps they themselves used. This reflects the app usage dataset, which is several years old.

Summary

To summarise, the optimiser was able to produce a significant performance benefit over a realistic baseline design. The observed differences were largely predicted by our models.

STUDY 2: DESIGN STUDY WITH A LIVE SYSTEM

To evaluate *Sketchplorer* as an integrated tool, we conducted a design study with trained designers. We aimed to evaluate whether Sketchplorer is effective in supporting creativity and problem-solving in sketching. We were interested in designers' insight and impressions, and not on validation of produced designs, as this had been investigated in the previous study. We did not direct them to use the optimiser's suggestions but were interested in seeing if this would happen spontaneously.

Study Design

We recruited a total of 10 participants (2 female), age ranging from 22 to 40 years (mean 29.4). All participants, except one, had an educational or professional background in design, and all of them had some experience using digital design tools. Participants were compensated with two cinema tickets.

All design tasks were performed on a 55-inch (140 cm) 4K display (3840 × 2160), with a PQ Labs G5S multitouch overlay. The display was tilted to a comfortable angle, and participants performed tasks in standing position (Figure 6). The design tool ran on a Macbook Pro (OS X 10.10). In addition, two Macbook Pros were used for the optimisers.

Procedure: After initial training, in which participants created simple designs and explored the tool, they were given a 'design brief' for the main study task. Similar to the example in the walkthrough, they were asked to create designs for a blog page. There were no strict requirements, and participants could freely decide on the exact elements, and their details. They were asked to create a few different designs, and could choose to make as many as they wished to, in a time frame of 30 minutes. Participants were free to save designs that were sketched with or without the aid of the optimiser. At the end of the task, they assigned ratings (1--5) to their saved designs, using a custom 'viewer' application. Importantly, the viewer did not reveal whether a given design had been entirely sketched by the participant, or if it was optimiser-assisted. Finally, we gathered further information through a questionnaire and a semi-structured interview.

Results

The study aimed at gauging whether Sketchplorer allowed designers to sketch freely, and their usage of different features the tool provided. On reviewing participants' list of saved designs, we found that 8 out of 10 participants had at least one optimiser-aided design in their saved list. Additionally, participant 10 stated to have borrowed an idea from the optimiser

ID	N(Saved)	N(Recolour)	N(Fix)	N(Global)
1	3	0	0	3
2	5	0	0	2
3	5	3	1	0
4	5	0	2	2
5	4	1	0	1
6	3	0	0	0
7	4	0	3	0
8	8	0	0	5
9	10	2	3	4
10	1	0	0	1

N(Saved) : Total number of saved layouts
N(Recolour) : Saved layouts with recolour-suggestions
N(Fix) : Saved layouts with fix-suggestions
N(Global) : Saved layouts with global-suggestions

Table 2: Summary of features used by each participant in Study 2. 9 out of 10 designers took advantage of suggestions offered by the optimiser, to achieve their final designs.

suggestions, but recreated it manually in his own sketch. On average, participants perceived optimiser-assisted designs to be equally good as designs they sketched alone. Table 2 summarises the optimiser-features used by the participants, in the saved versions.

Responses to the questionnaire and interview session were encouraging for Sketchplorer. Apart from minor technical glitches, participants commented that they could sketch out their ideas quickly and freely, and the multitouch interactions were easy and straightforward. The ability to have a large touch-friendly canvas was appreciated. All participants stated that they would certainly prefer a visual timeline in such design tools, over traditional save-dialogs, and such a feature would be useful in future tools.

With regards to the optimiser-related features, participants especially liked the *explore* option. They found the suggestions to be distinctly different, useful, and indicated that it would help them while designing. One commented, *"I kind of like how the suggestions turn my approach upside down, and I can get hints from there"*. There was a split between participants while rating the usefulness of *fix* and *recolour* during the given design task. A few participants found some of the *recolour* suggestions *"so 90s"* or *flashy*, and wished that the suggestions would be more subtle. One participant commented that they would rather explore new and different ideas, than 'fix' existing ones. However, participants also indicated that recolouring and fixing would help them in future design activities.

DISCUSSION

This paper has studied a new concept interactive design optimisation, backed by predictive models, and integrated to a sketching tool. By inferring design tasks implicitly, and by using a combination of exploration and exploitation, a layout optimiser can complement the sketching activities of a designer in real time, and enable her to explore larger design spaces without having to divert their attention to the optimisation process. During sketchploration, the designer–optimiser system is continuously both sketching (or, in optimiser terms, exploiting) and exploring. Crucially, the optimiser is not suggesting just anything for the designer. The predictive models of the optimiser try to "pull" the designer towards usable and aesthetic designs. A designer can reject designs that are unsatisfactory for some reasons that the optimiser may not include in its objective function. This way, the designer and the optimiser can iteratively approach a region of good designs without communicating an objective function. We are not aware of a similar approach in the past.

Results from two studies provide first evidence for the concept. Study 1 exposed end-users to a visual layout generated by the optimiser, comparing it against a commercial baseline design. The results were favourable, the optimised design was significantly better in average selection time, when measured after the first selection of an app. Colour harmony was rated higher, but the layout less harmonic. It is intriguing to note that the obtained data are mostly in alignment with the predictions made by the models.

Study 2 gauged Sketchplorer's ability to provide designers with a sketching environment conducive to sketchploration, and gathered insights about the different features. Most designers in our study added some of the optimisers' designs to their saved list of designs, used the features in their process, and rated the optimiser's outputs high. They in particular appreciated the explore feature. Given that the participants had educational and even professional background in design, we consider this a notable achievement.

Overall, we see sketchploration as a promising concept; one that can lead to not only empowering designers, but also to systematically improving usability and aesthetics, and raising the bar of design.

While our work lays the foundation for sketchploration, it also uncovers many challenges and opens up opportunities for future efforts. First, while this paper covers visual aspects of designs, it does not capture semantics or the dynamicity of interactions that interfaces afford. To further improve exploratory results, integrating these aspects is desirable. Second, our optimisation techniques are highly dependent on well-validated models; further development of accurate predictive models is a key factor to improvements in results. Third, although the optimiser's results were mostly good, we note that its performance was limited to designs with ten or fewer elements. Layout optimisation for HCI is a combinatorially challenging task that cannot be directly solved with standard methods. Finally, it can be beneficial to allow deeper exploration into design spaces, and provide designers with detailed insights of the entire space. In optimisation terms, the optimisation landscape could be visualised to allow more informed choices.

ACKNOWLEDGEMENTS

The project has received funding from the Academy of Finland project COMPUTED and the European Research Council (ERC) under the European Union's Horizon 2020 research and innovation programme (grant agreement 637991).
Among others, we would like to thank Andreas Karrenbauer and Gilles Bailly for their suggestions and comments, and Olli Savisaari and Perttu Lähteenlahti for their assistance.

REFERENCES

1. Seok-Hyung Bae, Ravin Balakrishnan, and Karan Singh. 2008. ILoveSketch: As-natural-as-possible Sketching System for Creating 3D Curve Models. In *Proceedings of the 21st Annual ACM Symposium on User Interface Software and Technology (UIST '08)*. ACM, New York, NY, USA, 151–160. DOI: http://dx.doi.org/10.1145/1449715.1449740
2. Gilles Bailly, Antti Oulasvirta, Timo Kötzing, and Sabrina Hoppe. 2013. MenuOptimizer: Interactive Optimization of Menu Systems. In *Proceedings of the 26th Annual ACM Symposium on User Interface Software and Technology (UIST '13)*. ACM, New York, NY, USA, 331–342. DOI: http://dx.doi.org/10.1145/2501988.2502024
3. Helen Y. Balinsky. 2006. Evaluating interface aesthetics: measure of symmetry. In *Electronic Imaging 2006*. International Society for Optics and Photonics, 607–608.
4. Helen Y. Balinsky, Anthony J. Wiley, and Matthew C. Roberts. 2009. Aesthetic Measure of Alignment and Regularity. In *Proceedings of the 9th ACM Symposium on Document Engineering (DocEng '09)*. ACM, New York, NY, USA, 56–65. DOI: http://dx.doi.org/10.1145/1600193.1600207
5. Rainer E. Burkhard and J. Offerman. 1977. Entwurf von schreibmaschinentastaturen mittels quadratischer zuordnungsprobleme. *Operations Res* 21 (1977), B121–B132.
6. Bill Buxton. 2007. *Sketching User Experiences: Getting the Design Right and the Right Design*. Morgan Kaufmann Publishers Inc., San Francisco, CA, USA.
7. Daniel Cohen-Or, Olga Sorkine, Ran Gal, Tommer Leyvand, and Ying-Qing Xu. 2006. Color Harmonization. In *ACM SIGGRAPH 2006 Papers (SIGGRAPH '06)*. ACM, New York, NY, USA, 624–630. DOI: http://dx.doi.org/10.1145/1179352.1141933
8. Nigel Cross. 2004. Expertise in design: an overview. *Design studies* 25, 5 (2004), 427–441.
9. Amine Drira, Henri Pierreval, and Sonia Hajri-Gabouj. 2007. Facility layout problems: A survey. *Annual Reviews in Control* 31, 2 (2007), 255–267.
10. Karim El Batran and Mark D. Dunlop. 2014. Enhancing KLM (Keystroke-level Model) to Fit Touch Screen Mobile Devices. In *Proceedings of the 16th International Conference on Human-computer Interaction with Mobile Devices & Services (MobileHCI '14)*. ACM, New York, NY, USA, 283–286. DOI: http://dx.doi.org/10.1145/2628363.2628385
11. Steven K. Feiner. 1988. A Grid-based Approach to Automating Display Layout. In *Proceedings on Graphics Interface '88*. Canadian Information Processing Society, Toronto, Ont., Canada, Canada, 192–197. http://dl.acm.org/citation.cfm?id=102313.102339
12. Krzysztof Gajos and Daniel S. Weld. 2004. SUPPLE: Automatically Generating User Interfaces. In *Proceedings of the 9th International Conference on Intelligent User Interfaces (IUI '04)*. ACM, New York, NY, USA, 93–100. DOI: http://dx.doi.org/10.1145/964442.964461
13. Mark D. Gross and Ellen Yi-Luen Do. 1996. Ambiguous Intentions: A Paper-like Interface for Creative Design. In *Proceedings of the 9th Annual ACM Symposium on User Interface Software and Technology (UIST '96)*. ACM, New York, NY, USA, 183–192. DOI: http://dx.doi.org/10.1145/237091.237119
14. Pierre Hansen and Nenad Mladenović. 2001. Variable neighborhood search: Principles and applications. *European journal of operational research* 130, 3 (2001), 449–467.
15. Marc Hassenzahl. 2008. The Interplay of Beauty, Goodness, and Usability in Interactive Products. *Hum.-Comput. Interact.* 19, 4 (Dec. 2008), 319–349. DOI: http://dx.doi.org/10.1207/s15327051hci1904_2
16. Eric Horvitz. 1999. Principles of Mixed-initiative User Interfaces. In *Proceedings of the SIGCHI Conference on Human Factors in Computing Systems (CHI '99)*. ACM, New York, NY, USA, 159–166. DOI: http://dx.doi.org/10.1145/302979.303030
17. Gabe Johnson, Mark D. Gross, Jason Hong, and Ellen Yi-Luen Do. 2009. Computational Support for Sketching in Design: A Review. *Found. Trends Hum.-Comput. Interact.* 2, 1 (Jan. 2009), 1–93. DOI: http://dx.doi.org/10.1561/1100000013
18. Levent Burak Kara, Chris M. D'Eramo, and Kenji Shimada. 2006. Pen-based Styling Design of 3D Geometry Using Concept Sketches and Template Models. In *Proceedings of the 2006 ACM Symposium on Solid and Physical Modeling (SPM '06)*. ACM, New York, NY, USA, 149–160. DOI: http://dx.doi.org/10.1145/1128888.1128909
19. Rubaiat Habib Kazi, Fanny Chevalier, Tovi Grossman, and George Fitzmaurice. 2014. Kitty: Sketching Dynamic and Interactive Illustrations. In *Proceedings of the 27th Annual ACM Symposium on User Interface Software and Technology (UIST '14)*. ACM, New York, NY, USA, 395–405. DOI: http://dx.doi.org/10.1145/2642918.2647375
20. Kenneth L. Kelly. 1965. Twenty-two colors of maximum contrast. *Color Engineering* 3, 26 (1965), 26–27.
21. David E. Kieras and Anthony J. Hornof. 2014. Towards Accurate and Practical Predictive Models of Active-vision-based Visual Search. In *Proceedings of the 32Nd Annual ACM Conference on Human Factors in Computing Systems (CHI '14)*. ACM, New York, NY, USA, 3875–3884. DOI: http://dx.doi.org/10.1145/2556288.2557324

22. Ranjitha Kumar, Arvind Satyanarayan, Cesar Torres, Maxine Lim, Salman Ahmad, Scott R. Klemmer, and Jerry O. Talton. 2013. Webzeitgeist: Design Mining the Web. In *Proceedings of the SIGCHI Conference on Human Factors in Computing Systems (CHI '13)*. ACM, New York, NY, USA, 3083–3092. DOI: http://dx.doi.org/10.1145/2470654.2466420

23. James A. Landay and Brad A. Myers. 1995. Interactive Sketching for the Early Stages of User Interface Design. In *Proceedings of the SIGCHI Conference on Human Factors in Computing Systems (CHI '95)*. ACM Press/Addison-Wesley Publishing Co., New York, NY, USA, 43–50. DOI: http://dx.doi.org/10.1145/223904.223910

24. Lissa Light and Peter Anderson. 1993. Designing better keyboards via simulated annealing. (1993).

25. James Lin, Mark W. Newman, Jason I. Hong, and James A. Landay. 2000. DENIM: Finding a Tighter Fit Between Tools and Practice for Web Site Design. In *Proceedings of the SIGCHI Conference on Human Factors in Computing Systems (CHI '00)*. ACM, New York, NY, USA, 510–517. DOI: http://dx.doi.org/10.1145/332040.332486

26. Simon Lok and Steven Feiner. 2001. A survey of automated layout techniques for information presentations. *Proceedings of SmartGraphics* 2001 (2001).

27. Simon Lok, Steven Feiner, and Gary Ngai. 2004. Evaluation of Visual Balance for Automated Layout. In *Proceedings of the 9th International Conference on Intelligent User Interfaces (IUI '04)*. ACM, New York, NY, USA, 101–108. DOI: http://dx.doi.org/10.1145/964442.964462

28. Scott I. MacKenzie. 1992. Fitts' law as a research and design tool in human-computer interaction. *Human–Computer Interaction* 7, 1 (1992), 91–139.

29. Barbara J. Meier, Anne Morgan Spalter, and David B. Karelitz. 2004. Interactive Color Palette Tools. *IEEE Comput. Graph. Appl.* 24, 3 (May 2004), 64–72. DOI: http://dx.doi.org/10.1109/MCG.2004.1297012

30. Mark W. Newman and James A. Landay. 2000. Sitemaps, Storyboards, and Specifications: A Sketch of Web Site Design Practice. In *Proceedings of the 3rd Conference on Designing Interactive Systems: Processes, Practices, Methods, and Techniques (DIS '00)*. ACM, New York, NY, USA, 263–274. DOI: http://dx.doi.org/10.1145/347642.347758

31. Peter O'Donovan, Aseem Agarwala, and Aaron Hertzmann. 2014. Learning Layouts for Single-PageGraphic Designs. *Visualization and Computer Graphics, IEEE Transactions on* 20, 8 (2014), 1200–1213.

32. Peter O'Donovan, Aseem Agarwala, and Aaron Hertzmann. 2015. DesignScape: Design with Interactive Layout Suggestions. In *Proceedings of the 33rd Annual ACM Conference on Human Factors in Computing Systems (CHI '15)*. ACM, New York, NY, USA, 1221–1224. DOI: http://dx.doi.org/10.1145/2702123.2702149

33. Antti Oulasvirta, Anna Reichel, Wenbin Li, Yan Zhang, Myroslav Bachynskyi, Keith Vertanen, and Per Ola Kristensson. 2013. Improving Two-thumb Text Entry on Touchscreen Devices. In *Proceedings of the SIGCHI Conference on Human Factors in Computing Systems (CHI '13)*. ACM, New York, NY, USA, 2765–2774. DOI: http://dx.doi.org/10.1145/2470654.2481383

34. Ruth Rosenholtz, Yuanzhen Li, and Lisa Nakano. 2007. Measuring visual clutter. *Journal of vision* 7, 2 (2007), 17.

35. Clayton Shepard, Ahmad Rahmati, Chad Tossell, Lin Zhong, and Phillip Kortum. 2011. LiveLab: Measuring Wireless Networks and Smartphone Users in the Field. *SIGMETRICS Perform. Eval. Rev.* 38, 3 (Jan. 2011), 15–20. DOI: http://dx.doi.org/10.1145/1925019.1925023

36. Surya P. Singh and Renduchintala RK Sharma. 2006. A review of different approaches to the facility layout problems. *The International Journal of Advanced Manufacturing Technology* 30, 5-6 (2006), 425–433.

37. Ivan E. Sutherland. 1963. Sketchpad: A Man-machine Graphical Communication System. In *Proceedings of the May 21-23, 1963, Spring Joint Computer Conference (AFIPS '63 (Spring))*. ACM, New York, NY, USA, 329–346. DOI: http://dx.doi.org/10.1145/1461551.1461591

38. Michael Terry, Elizabeth D. Mynatt, Kumiyo Nakakoji, and Yasuhiro Yamamoto. 2004. Variation in Element and Action: Supporting Simultaneous Development of Alternative Solutions. In *Proceedings of the SIGCHI Conference on Human Factors in Computing Systems (CHI '04)*. ACM, New York, NY, USA, 711–718. DOI: http://dx.doi.org/10.1145/985692.985782

39. Marc Van Droogenbroeck and Sébastien Piérard. 2011. Object Descriptors Based on a List of Rectangles: Method and Algorithm. In *Proceedings of the 10th International Conference on Mathematical Morphology and Its Applications to Image and Signal Processing (ISMM'11)*. Springer-Verlag, Berlin, Heidelberg, 155–165. http://dl.acm.org/citation.cfm?id=2023043.2023061

40. L.G. Williams. 1966. *A Study of Visual Search Using Eye Movement Recordings*. Technical Report. DTIC Document.

41. Jacob O. Wobbrock, Andrew D. Wilson, and Yang Li. 2007. Gestures Without Libraries, Toolkits or Training: A $1 Recognizer for User Interface Prototypes. In *Proceedings of the 20th Annual ACM Symposium on User Interface Software and Technology (UIST '07)*. ACM, New York, NY, USA, 159–168. DOI: http://dx.doi.org/10.1145/1294211.1294238

42. Yin Yin Wong. 1992. Rough and Ready Prototypes: Lessons from Graphic Design. In *Posters and Short Talks of the 1992 SIGCHI Conference on Human Factors in Computing Systems (CHI '92)*. ACM, New York, NY, USA, 83–84. DOI: http://dx.doi.org/10.1145/1125021.1125094

43. Shengxiang Yang and Xin Yao. 2008. Population-based incremental learning with associative memory for dynamic environments. *Evolutionary Computation, IEEE Transactions on* 12, 5 (2008), 542–561.

44. Yeonsoo Yang and Scott R. Klemmer. 2009. Aesthetics Matter: Leveraging Design Heuristics to Synthesize Visually Satisfying Handheld Interfaces. In *CHI '09 Extended Abstracts on Human Factors in Computing Systems (CHI EA '09)*. ACM, New York, NY, USA, 4183–4188. DOI: http://dx.doi.org/10.1145/1520340.1520637

45. Shumin Zhai, Michael Hunter, and Barton A. Smith. 2002. Performance Optimization of Virtual Keyboards. *Human–Computer Interaction* 17, 2-3 (2002), 229–269.

Impatience Induced by Waiting: An Effect Moderated by the Speed of Countdowns

Moojan Ghafurian
The Pennsylvania State University
moojan@psu.edu

David Reitter
The Pennsylvania State University
reitter@psu.edu

ABSTRACT

Countdowns and progress bars provide computer users with estimates of remaining wait times. These types of feedback are intended to manage their expectations and allow users to direct attention elsewhere. We suggest that they also moderate user's impatience, which affects decision-making in the subsequent task. In an experiment with 421 participants, impatience in a timing decision task was effectively and systematically manipulated through a countdown, as it affected timing and performance of the user's actions in the task. The effect persisted even after users gained task experience. More rapid countdowns reduced impatience. Post-hoc analysis also showed increased task satisfaction with rising countdown speed and suggested greater task satisfaction with a rapid countdown than with no waiting period at all.

Author Keywords

Impatience; Rationality; Countdown; Decision-making; Task satisfaction

ACM Classification Keywords

H.5.2; D.2.2; H.1.2 User Interfaces; Design Tools and Techniques; User/Machine Systems

INTRODUCTION

Despite dramatic improvements in speeds of computers and data transmission, computer users still face regular delays, e.g., to fetch data or finish computations. Further, there are situations where waiting is designed intentionally, e.g. to watch advertisements before a movie starts. Countdowns are useful tools in these situations to manage expectations, specifically where progress bars cannot be used (e.g., due to limited screen size or where continuous feedback is ineffective). Figure 1 shows a few of such examples.

Intuitively, waiting impacts user satisfaction, loyalty, and patience. However, the consequences of impatience for what a user does following the wait are largely unknown. In this study, we ask 1) whether impatience is persistent, extending beyond the waiting period, and 2) how it affects the task that

DIS 2016, June 04–08, 2016, Brisbane, QLD, Australia

ACM 978-1-4503-4031-1/16/06...$15.00
DOI: http://dx.doi.org/10.1145/2901790.2901830

Figure 1. People face countdowns daily, such as at a red traffic light (photo taken by Sasan Geranmehr), in a gym workout video, or smartphone application showing the remaining time of an exercise (from *Ab Workout* app), or watching a commercial while waiting for a video to play (from *YouTube*).

follows. If it negatively affects the following task, the next question is: what can a designer do about it? We study different ways to manipulate time perception in search for clear ways to decrease impatience and increase task satisfaction.

The situations we examine are those faced by regular computer users, although the implications go way beyond those interfaces. Delays are common when faced with technical systems (e.g., traffic lights and security checks), and people's decision-making may be severely affected [2, 8]. This is another good reason to make waiting more tolerable.

The hypothesis that countdowns can be manipulated to change time perception is backed by work on progress bars. Progress bars that speed up non-linearly were preferred by users [11]. Visually pulsating bars have been shown to decrease the perceived duration [12]. Studies in cognitive economics tell us that perception of duration is more influential when it comes to affective judgments than actual duration, and it is manipulated by presentation and other salient features of the task and wait period [6]. These studies seek to optimize human preferences, while we are also interested in actual decision-making: will computer users behave differently?

As a comparison to other types of feedback, countdowns are easy to manipulate. However, manipulating percentages is limited to changing their number from 1% to 100%, and deciding on a speed function for their progress. We face similar limitations for the design of progress bars. Given limited screen resolution and perceptual acuity, progress bars will either seem to move very slowly, or will be designed to move step-wise, pausing once or several times. If the delay is too long (in either percentages or prgoress bars), a pause will definitely occur at some point. Countdowns offer better flexibility. It is possible to start the countdown from a very large number and avoid having a pause, which can provide a better indication that the task is still in progress. That is why we believe it can be beneficial to use countdowns either along with progress bars or instead of percentages.

A previous study by the same authors suggested that impatience affects decision-making in the subsequent tasks. In this paper we manipulate countdowns and assess their effects on impatience, as well as on user satisfaction. We study the typical case of a program, where an exact estimate of the remaining time is unavailable or not necessary to convey.

BACKGROUND

People do not perceive time objectively [27], a bias that can mean over-estimating time intervals, especially in impulsive individuals [27]. As studies in cognitive psychology have shown, time perception depends on several factors. For instance, a user's level of attention influences time estimation and accuracy of the perceived time intervals [16, 4]: since information processing uses attentional resources, a high level of activity leaves people with fewer resources for time estimation, which leads to underestimating the time intervals. As a result, people pay less attention to the passing of time when they are processing a significant amount of information [1, 14]. So, people's perception of the speed of passing time changes with their level of activity. This is a reason why a person waiting in a line will find 10 minutes long compared to a person with only 10 minutes left to make an important deadline [3, 4, 19]. We expect that impatience can increase when a user perceives a delay to be longer than it is. However, when a delay sets the pace and provides a comparison interval for the actual task, that actual task might be perceived as shorter than it is. Conversely, the biases might also provide a mechanism to manipulate perceived waits and perceived task duration.

Perceived waiting time and the information provided in case of delay indirectly impact service satisfaction. This is because they affect the waiting time satisfaction of the users. Waiting time satisfaction is important as it moderates the effect of service satisfaction on costumer loyalty [2]. Furthermore, delays may have negative behavioral and emotional consequences. They can result in a significant deterioration of performance and negatively affect work productivity and work satisfaction [22]. Some user interfaces are also affected by impatience and associated dissatisfaction. Errors in speech recognition have been reported in telephony speech applications as a result of impatience caused by waiting. These errors were related to the duration of silence [7]. Ultimately, once impatience affects people's decision-making during critical tasks, it will have consequences for their health and security.

The presence of feedback extends users' tolerable waiting time [18]. In many tasks, the feedback shown during a delay is provided to users by showing a progress bar, countdown, or the percentage of the task being completed. Progress bars have been modified to reduce the perceived waiting time. Harrison et al. (2007) manipulated the speed of completion of the progress bars and reported significant effects on user perception of process duration. Users showed a strong aversion to pauses, especially towards the end [11]. In addition, the visual augmentation of progress bars are modified to reduce the perceived time. In another paper, Harrison et al. (2010) suggested that a backwards moving and decelerating progress bar has the best performance [12]. Further, Hurter et al. (2011) suggested the use of a temporary task while users are waiting. They propose an active progress bar design, where people can switch to a temporary activity (such as watching an animation or playing a game) while waiting [13].

To summarize, we know that people perceive time passing more slowly when their level of activity is low, such as while waiting for a task to start [4]. Further, we know waiting itself affects time judgments [4]. In the present experiment, we examine whether it is possible to influence people's impatience by manipulating countdowns. We hypothesize that waiting could affect people's experience negatively and affect the rationality of their future actions.

METHOD

In this section, we discuss in detail a task used to evaluate a user's impatience by eliciting timing decisions. We then describe how impatience was manipulated using a countdown that varied by experimental condition.

The timing task

The target task we give users requires deep cognitive processing and is designed to put them in situations where they have to make choices about *when* to act rather than how, as would be more common in many economic or behavioral decision-making tasks. As in many real-life situations encountered by, e.g., business or security professionals, decisions are made against the backdrop of a changing, stochastic environment. The task we selected allows us to compare the participants' timing choices in relation to a defined, non-obvious optimal strategy.

The task is a game, which we proceed to describe first in abstract terms, and then, in the next section, in its concrete scenario. It is inspired by the *FlipIt* game of "stealth takeover" [25]. *FlipIt* is a two player game, where players need to make one or more *moves* during a finite time span. These *moves* come at a constant cost, plus a variable payoff. The payoff depends on the actions of the players. One player's payoff is the lowest when preceding the other player, and highest when following it immediately. Thus, the players have to anticipate the other player's move (from previous experience) and trade the risk of wasting a move (by acting too early) against the benefits of acting early enough. This game has been used as a dynamic environment to study timing decisions under uncertainty [10, 20], even though it was conceived as a computer security simulation.

The generic FlipIt game is symmetric (both players attempt to move as soon as possible after the opponent, and the game runs for a fixed duration). Our game, which we call the *Cookie Monster Game* is asymmetric and has only one human player, who plays against a computer opponent. The computer opponent makes a move exactly once per 30-second round at an oblique time point sampled from a uniform distribution. We will outline the framing for the task in the next section for additional clarity. In two different variants of the *Cookie Monster Game*, Ghafurian and Reitter (2014) found impatience as a bias that affected decision-making in individuals and led to irrational decisions.

Scenario and Instructions

Participants play the *Cookie Monster Game*. Their opponent in the game, Cookie Monster, is a familiar figure from children's TV. Each round of the game starts with the player in the kitchen, cooking. Meanwhile, Cookie Monster is waiting for the player in the living room. In the living room, the player has 3000 cookies that s/he wants to protect from the Cookie Monster. The player knows that the Cookie Monster will definitely start eating them at some point and with a constant pace of 100 cookies per second. However, s/he does not know when. The player needs to develop a strategy to check on Cookie Monster. Anytime the player checks on him, s/he needs to give him 100 cookies to cover up for not trusting him and the game continues with the player going back to the kitchen. If s/he catches Cookie Monster while eating the cookies, the game ends. The number of the remaining cookies will be the points the player earns in the game. The subjects are paid according to their performance in the game, which corresponds to the overall points they earn in all the rounds.

Participants play six rounds of the game, with the first one (round 0) being a practice round. Each round of the game lasts 30 seconds, and players start out with $30 * 100$ points

Saving the checks ... 4

Figure 2. The countdown shown to participants, indicating that the delay is caused to save their selected checks.

(cookies). Participants decide on their strategy in advance by placing checks on the timeline before the round starts. The game ends after a successful check, and only the checks up to that point are associated with a cost for the player. Each second of latency in catching the opponent costs 100 points. So, e.g., for a 10-second game, with the opponent playing at $6.0s$, and the player checking twice at seconds 4.0 and 6.5, the payoff is $1000-0.5*100-200=750$ points. This setting creates an incentive to neither check too early, nor wait too long.[1]

Our game can be played as an online game where the player and the opponent make their moves as time progresses, or it can be played as a strategy game where the player predefines a strategy for each round. Both variants reflect different classes of real-life decision-making. To mirror realistic decision-making in tasks that general computer users would encounter, we have players define their strategy before watching it unfold. We expect that this motivates players to assess risks and timing more explicitly.

Countdown conditions

The experiment has a total of six between-participant conditions. Three of the conditions are the principal conditions of the experiment, one is the control condition, and the other two are the secondary conditions. In all except the control condition, we introduce a wait time of 15 seconds between defining the strategy (by setting checks) and actually watching the game. This delay is accompanied by a countdown, and a plausible explanation "Saving the Checks" (see figure 2). We define different speeds for countdowns to manipulate impatience and hypothesize that a faster countdown will moderate impatience.

In the three *principal* conditions, countdowns progress constantly, while the starting number of each countdown (and thus the pace of it) changes. The control and the principal conditions of the experiment are as follows:

- **NoWait (control)**: There is no delay (and thus no countdown) before the start of each round.
- **5CD**: There is a 15-second wait before start of each round, accompanied by an informational message "saving the checks" and a countdown from **5 to 1**. Therefore, each count lasts 3 seconds.
- **10CD**: A 15-second wait is accompanied by the same message and a countdown from **10 to 1**. Therefore, each count lasts 1.5 seconds.

[1] Risk-taking in discrete decisions is affected by the polarity of incentives [24].

- **15CD**: A 15-second wait is accompanied by the same message and a countdown from **15 to 1**. Therefore, each count lasts 1 second.

In addition, we explore two secondary conditions where the pace of the countdowns is not constant. We adopt a speed function proposed by Harrison et al. (2007), which gives the proportion of the number space completed as a function of the proportion of the delay completed (x): $f(x) = (x + (1-x)/2)^8$. Based on Harrison et al.'s findings, this speed function made waiting more tolerable for users, comparing to a constant pace and several other speed functions [11]. We utilize this speed function in the following, secondary conditions:

- **5CDM**: A 15-second wait is accompanied by a countdown from **5 to 1**. In this condition the speed of countdown changes based on the aforementioned speed function: starting with a slow pace and increasing with each count. Therefore, the first number (5) would last the longest and the last count (1) would last the shortest amount of time.

- **15CDM**: A 15-second wait is accompanied by the same message as before and a countdown from **15 to 1**. The speed of the counts increases as in the 5CDM condition.

The start values of 5 and 15 are chosen for the secondly conditions to be compared to one fast countdown (15CD, where each count lasts 1 second), and one slow countdown (5CD, where each count lasts 3 second) in the primary conditions.

Data Collection

442 North-America-based volunteers were recruited through Amazon Mechanical Turk (153 female, 288 male, and 1 unknown; age mean 33y, [18,77]). Each participant played 6 rounds of the game, where the first round (round 0) was labeled a practice round. A show-up fee of $0.40 and a bonus proportional to game performance were paid. Repeat participation was disallowed. 21 participants' data (6 female, 14 male, and 1 unknown) was discarded due to failure to fully attend to the game, according to the attention check (a performance criterion that was defined during the design phase). With participants typical work schedules and associated stress factors in mind, they were recruited and immediately run in several batches at approximately the same time of day, that is, in the afternoon in all North American time zones (4 p.m. Eastern time).

Study procedure

Participants first find and select the task (our experiment) on Mechanical Turk. At the beginning of the experiment, participants complete a survey with four demographic questions (e.g. age) , three basic integrity questions (e.g. "Please select the rightmost option"), and seven risk propensity assessing questions, which were developed and tested by Meertens & Lion (2008)[17]. The risk propensity questionnaire includes Likert-scale questions such as "I really dislike not knowing what is going to happen", or "I do not take risks with my health."

After submitting the survey, participants receive instructions with visual examples of how the game works. Figures 3 and 4 demonstrate similar visual feedback of the game that is shown to participants.

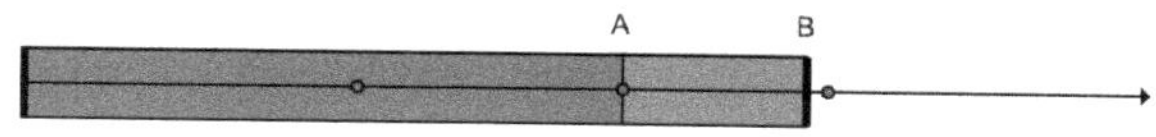

Figure 3. Visualization of a game in progress. The game has progressed to point B. The latest time the player has checked was at point A. No information about the situation after point A is known. The dots on the bar demonstrate the checks that were pre-set by the player.

Figure 4. Feedback shown after a round, when the opponent played at point A and the player made their last check at point B. At time B, the (small) extent of the opponent's dominance of the game was revealed. The player's payoff is proportional to the green area.

The game starts after reading the instructions. In each round, participants first define their strategy by setting the check times. What follows is the countdown (if any, depending on the condition), and then they watch the game. The countdown (if any) always takes 15 seconds; the screen is labeled "Saving the checks...N" where N is a number counting down (Figure 2). The game begins after this countdown. With this design, participants did not see a countdown until after deciding on the strategy during the practice round, which allows us to assess the early effects of countdowns in the following round (round 1).

Using a between-subjects design, the participants were assigned to the aforementioned experimental conditions. In the conditions as described above, the starting number of the countdowns changed, and as a result, so did the pace of counts.

Participants are prevented from switching to other windows on their screen, and their attention is monitored by requiring them to press a key immediately after the end of each round (which is random).

At the end of the experiment, participants had a chance to voluntarily leave comments about the game, technical issues, and their personal opinion.

ANALYSIS

The hypothetical rational player

A *rational* player would make optimal decisions, assuming exactly the same knowledge of a specific round of the game (and lack thereof) that a human player has. It perfectly understands the game's rules, and it makes no biased assumptions. Unlike humans, it is not limited in computational power (e.g., [9]). The rational player finds the actions that would maximize the expected utility, which will optimize the payoff assuming an infinite number of rounds [21].

The rational player in this game is proposed by the authors in [8]: We assume that the game is running, and the opponent's check is not caught yet. Considering one per time unit (1/100 or a hundredth of a second) to be the pay rate, and d to be the maximum duration of a round (30 seconds). The iterative solution to calculate the expected utility of a move at time t given the latest previous, unsuccessful move at time t_p is:

Table 1. Rational Strategies

Duration	Number and timing of Checks	Expected U.
3000	5: (800, 1401, 1802, 2203, 2604)	2432

All times in hundredths of seconds.

$$U(t,t_p) = -MoveCost + \sum_{k=t_p}^{t} \frac{1}{d-t_p}(k-t_p + d-t) + \max[0, \frac{d-t}{d-t_p} \max_{t<m<d} U(m,t)]$$

This function iterates over all the possible opponent move times k up to the proposed check time t, whose probability is the inverse of the remaining time $d-t_p$. The payoff for these consists of the initial period until the opponent moves, and the time period after our own move. Rational future moves are assumed and calculated iteratively if the opponent has not played so far.

The predefined rational strategy for our 30-second game is shown in Table 1.

We assume that a player's personal preferences [23] and current impatience status affect the timing of his or her future checks. The rational player model serves us in evaluating the person's strategy, one check at a time. Note that unlike in standard decision-making tasks designed to contrast risk-averse or risk-seeking behavior, there is only one optimal choice at any given time, and any risk-seeking or risk-averse behavior will reduce the participant's payoff. This means that participants were adequately incentivized to play rationally.

Strategy Analysis

To contrast the effects of different countdowns, we evaluate the game strategies by comparing the player's timing choices to what a rational player would do. We use the concept of the rational player as described above in a dynamic way: a model that optimizes the expected outcome at any point in time. The dynamic rational model finds the next best check given *the players's actions so far* and *the remaining time* of the game.

Assume that the participant has made the first check at time 300 (i.e., 3 seconds into the round). The time difference of participant's check to the rational model's check (Table 1) would be $\Delta t_1 = t_{rational} - t_{subject} = 800 - 300 = 500$. With 300 being the first check, the remaining time of the round would be 2700 and the dynamic rational model would check at times 1020, 1561, 2102, 2463, and 2644. Thus the next suggested rational check is at time 1020. If the participant's second check is earlier, at 700, then $\Delta t_2 = 1020 - 700 = 320$. The next remaining time is 2300, and the next rational suggestion would be to check at times 1312, 1925, 2385, and 2692. [2]

We report average Δt figures per round and condition. The measure is an indicator of how much people advance their timing in relation to a generally unknown, but anticipated time point. A high Δt implies earlier checks.

[2]time units are 1/100 (or hundredths) of a second

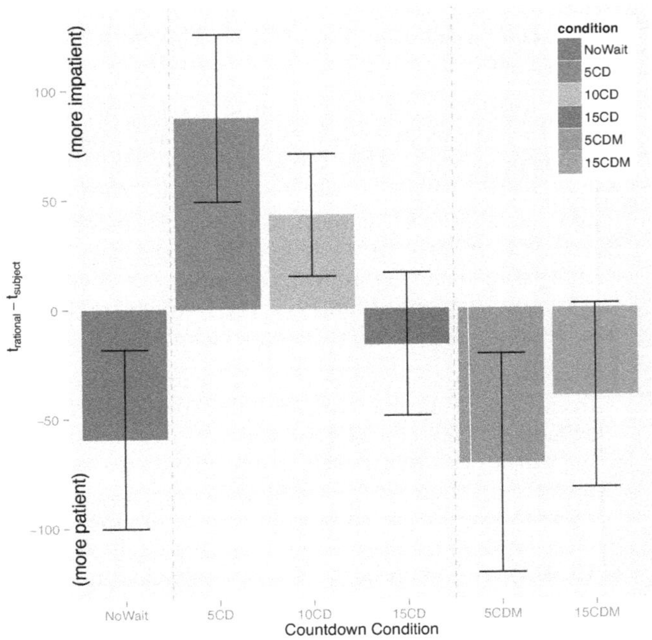

Figure 5. Δt, the deviation of check times from rational check times. Higher values indicate earlier checks. Participants who see the slower countdown chose earlier checks.

RESULTS

Δt for all participants and all conditions is shown in Figure 5. We first discuss the control and the principal conditions (NoWait, 5CD, 10CD, and 15CD) and then continue with discussing the secondary conditions (5CDM and 15CDM).

Results of the principal conditions

Δt for the principal conditions is shown in Figure 6. Slower counts increased participants' Δt , which implies reducing the waiting time between two checks.[3]

The first round, as the practice round, was removed from the analysis. However, participants first experienced waiting during this round.

Table 2. Regression model predicting the time difference between rational checks to the opponents' checks. Round number is centered.

Covariate	Estimate	SE	t	Pr (> |t|)
Intercept	-47.83	39.51	-1.210	0.227
CountDuration (s)	47.14	21.26	2.218	< .05
log (Round)	-27.39	11.40	-2.402	< .05

A regression model (Table 2) predicts Δt as a function of round number and the time that each count lasts in each condition

[3]We evaluated participants' risk preferences using a standardized survey evaluating Risk Propensity. No correlation is observed between risk propensity and Δt, which confirms that impatience is a personal preference and emotional status that is independent of general risk propensity. See also [8] (Fig.3).

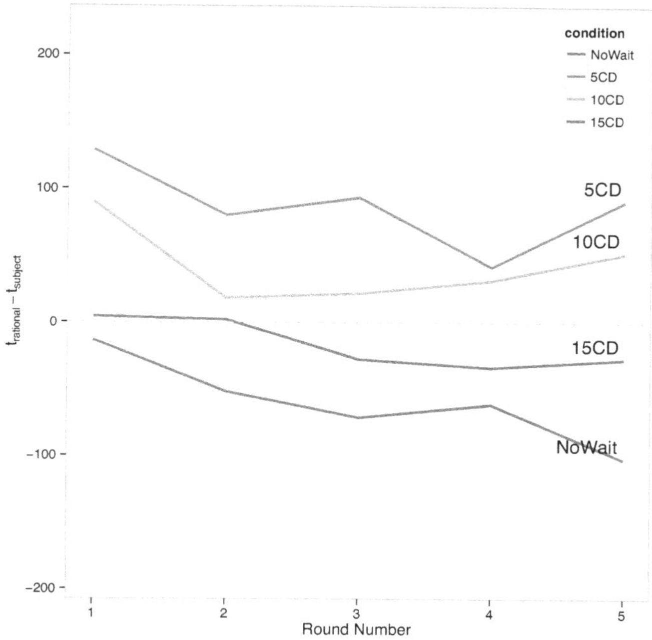

Figure 6. Δt for the principal conditions over all 5 scored rounds. See Table 2 for significance of differences.

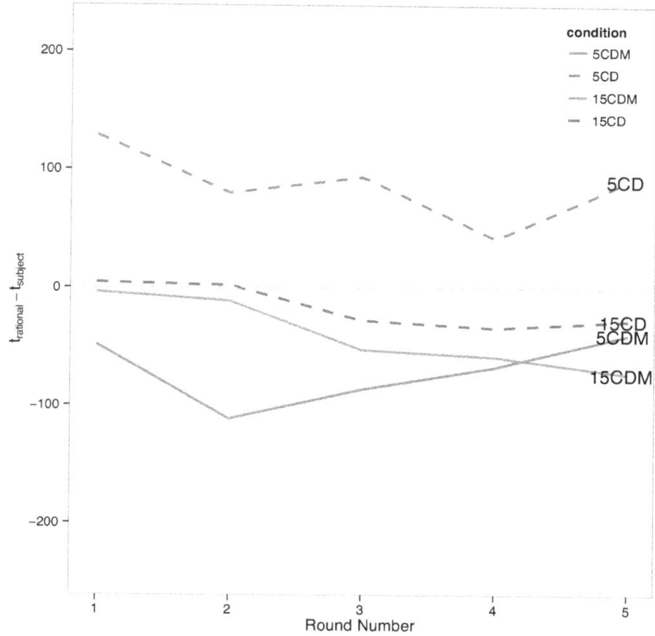

Figure 7. Participant's checks compared to the dynamic rational strategy for 5CDM, and 15CDM conditions. 5CD and 15CD from Fig.6 are shown for comparison. See Table 3 for significance of differences.

(CountDuration: 1 for 15CD, 1.5 for 10CD, and 3 for 5CD). All predictors are centered. Round number is log-transformed due to the nature of learning effect. Count Duration is positively correlated with Δt, which indicates that having slower counts results in checks that are earlier than what would be rational. A random intercept grouped by subject was fitted (as this is a repeated-measures study).

Further, the performance of participants in the 5CD condition is significantly different from the control (NoWait) condition ($se = 0.565, t = 2.513, p < 0.05$). However, as the speed of the countdown increases, this difference decreases. We do not see a significant difference between the performance of people in 15CD and the control (NoWait) condition ($se = 0.478, t = 0.857, p = 0.393$).

Results of the secondary conditions

We next evaluate the effect of a non-linear countdown speed. We use the secondary conditions to compare the effect of our proposed linear, fast countdowns to a nonlinear function that is proposed to be more tolerable for users when used in progress bars [11]. The secondary conditions 5CDM and 15CDM are compared to two of the principal conditions 5CD and 15CD. We consider 15CD as a fast countdown (each count takes 1 second), and 5CD as a slow countdown (each count takes 3 seconds). 5CDM and 15CDM use the same number of counts as 5CD and 15CD, but apply a dynamic countdown speed.

Δt values over rounds are shown in Figure 7.

People in the secondary conditions choose longer wait times between checks, meaning later check points compared to rational times (Δt). Participants in the 15CD condition make their moves closest to the rational player compared to the others (Fig. 5).

Table 3. Model of the effect of nonlinear speeds in the rapid and slow countdown conditions.

Covariate	Estimate	SE	t	Pr $(>|t|)$
15counts	-0.144	0.322	-0.449	0.654
5counts	0.864	0.40	2.167	$< .05$
log (Round)	-0.361	0.156	-2.318	$< .05$
15counts:nonlinear	-0.254	0.512	-0.495	0.621
5counts:nonlinear	-1.5786	0.587	-2.690	$< .01$

A mixed-effects regression model was fitted to the data matching two principal conditions (5CD, 15CD) and their two secondary counterparts (5CDM, 15CDM), coded as 5counts and 15counts, respectively (Table 3). Random intercept grouped by subject were fitted. The nonlinear speed significantly delayed people's check times in the slow countdown (5counts:nonlinear, $p < 0.05$), but this influence does not exist for the faster countdown (15counts:nonlinear, $p = 0.621$). These results also emphasize on the positive effects of fast countdowns.

Task satisfaction

We present a post-hoc study on participants' comments. Since leaving a comment was not required, many participants left without leaving one. A common type of comments was merely a copy of the ending message as is typical for studies on Mechanical Turk. We analyzed the remaining comments. Comments were pre-classified according to positive and negative sentiments using automated keyword spotting and manual verification. We found 82 positive comments. Some examples of these comments are: "very fun!", "Thanks. It was very fun & unique.", "interesting study"[4]. (Negative comments pertained to technical issues; they were rare.)

The proportion of positive comments of the participants in each condition is calculated. (The proportions are low as participants were not required to leave comments.) While we cannot assume anything about the silent participants, we can be sure that people who voluntarily spent time to leave even a simple, positive comment such as "thanks" actually did enjoy the task.

Figure 8 visualizes the proportion of positive comments for each condition. We see that in the principal conditions (5CD, 10CD, and 15CD), the rate of positive comments significantly decreases as the speed of countdown decreases ($se = 0.246, z = -1.984, p < 0.05$). Further, using the nonlinear function for the slow countdown (5CDM) significantly affected participant's decision-making and impatience during the game (compared to 5CD). However. it did not affect the rate of positive comments, or in other words, users' task satisfaction ($se = 0.615, z = 0.183, p = 0.855$).

To make sure that positive comments are not affected by the bonus participants received, and the difference is due to the manipulation of countdowns, we fit a regression model, predicting positive comments based on the amount of bonus received. We do not observe an effect of the payment on the positive comment ($se = 316, z = 0.232, p = 0.816$).

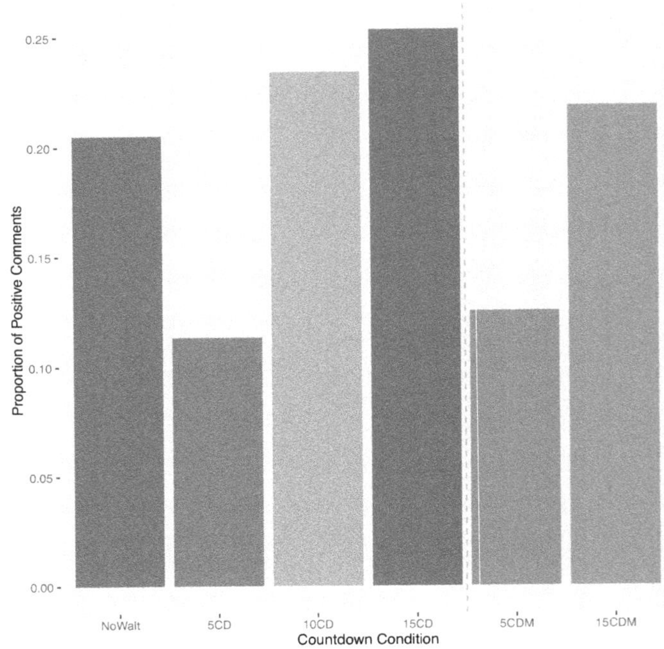

Figure 8. The proportion of the positive comments to all the comments for each condition. (Only one binary data point per participant.)

DISCUSSION

While waiting affects user's satisfaction and can result in negative behavioral and emotional consequences, the perceived waiting time plays an important role in moderating those consequences [2, 22]. In many situations people see countdowns during a delay or while waiting for a task to be started/completed. Examples of these countdowns are not limited purely to situations where the user is inactive, such as waiting at a traffic light. They are also used to show the remaining time of a task, such as a workout. While people's perception of the speed of time passing changes based on their level of activity [4, 3, 19], manipulating impatience and reducing it would be useful in all situations, regardless of activity.

In this study, we manipulated countdowns, which affected the computer users' impatience or their perception of delays. While the duration they actually waited was kept constant, the starting number of the countdown (and thus the speed of the counts), was different from condition to condition. Faster countdowns reduced impatience and resulted in a better decision afterwards, while people in the conditions with slower counts became more impatient and played more frequently.

In addition, we received a higher rate of positive comments from participants in the faster countdown conditions. This shows that this manipulation not only affected people's impatience and time perception, but also affected their task satisfaction.

Surprisingly, participants who experienced a 15-second delay and received rapid countdowns were more positive about the game compared to people who did not experience any delay (NoWait). Akin to a website with a faux progress bar, which gives the impression that a computer program is hard at work, participants may have been impressed by the system. The message saying "saving the checks" may have made the system seem more sophisticated. This suggests that experiencing a small delay accompanied by an appropriate UI design does not necessarily affect users negatively, and it can even impress users and affect their task satisfaction positively.

Finally, nonlinear countdowns used in the secondary conditions only improved decision-making in the slow countdown (5CDM), but it neither affected decision-making in the fast countdown (15CDM vs. 15CD), nor affected task satisfaction. This evidence suggests that making countdowns faster is more effective than making them non-linear, which we believe might also be true for progress bars.

More questions about the mechanisms behind the effect remain. Specifically, we cannot be sure about how time perception is affected by the countdowns, and whether a manipulation of duration perception or of expectations leads to altered judgments of the subsequent task duration. The alternative, simpler interpretation would be that persistent impatience is created that affects subsequent decision-making.

[4]Some other examples of the positive comments are: "Thanks. It was very fun & unique", "C is for cookie!! nom nom nom!", "Thanks, this was a really fun HIT!", and "I am struggling to contain my laughter from the first page of the study. The animated gif is NOT helping. Typos, 'bellow'(below)"

IMPLICATIONS FOR THE DESIGNER

The applications of these results are evident. An aforementioned example is adding fast countdowns while an advertisement is being played. As it makes waiting more tolerable for the users, this would be beneficial to both users and the advertising companies. We suggest using faster countdowns in situations where knowing an exact estimate of the remaining time is not beneficial (e.g. for a short advertisement, for downloading a file, or for specific softwares that are being installed).

As another example, we propose adding fast countdowns to red traffic lights. We know that Traffic safety is affected by impatience. Wissinger et al. (2000) investigated red light running and reported impatience as one of the most frequently mentioned reasons of red light running in focus groups [26]. Long et al. (2013) showed that lights with countdown assist drivers' decision-making and reduce hazardous maneuvers [15]. Chiou and Chang (2010) showed that red signal countdowns enhance intersection efficiency [5]. We suggest that using red lights with a faster speed of countdown can moderate impatience and affect the behavior of drivers and pedestrians.

The flexibility of a countdown is why we think they are beneficial, whether used alone or along with a progress bar. As it is discussed earlier, in situations where very long delays are expected, having a pause in progress bars and percentages is inevitable, due to their limitations. We believe that in those situations, using a fast countdown could have larger effects on time perception and impatience compared to a visual progress bar. We also suggest considering combining countdowns with progress bars (e.g. Figure 9). In addition, we point out that situations with long delays and a limited screen size exist where the speed of fast counts could have larger effects on time perception compared to a visual progress bar.

Finally, it is worth emphasizing that the context in which the countdowns are being manipulated is important. As an example, this would be a good manipulation for red lights (to decrease the level of both pedestrians' and drivers' impatience). We do not recommend this manipulation in situations where people need an accurate estimate of the remaining time (e.g., green light, where people need to estimate whether they have enough time to cross the street or not). If this manipulation is made in such contexts, it should be emphasized to people that the counts do not represent the remaining seconds.

CONCLUSION

Waiting for computers and technical systems to complete tasks is not only cause for annoyance, but also produces impatience that affects performance in subsequent tasks.

Manipulation of a common user interface device can mitigate this impatience: countdowns can be shown, and when they run more quickly or speed up towards the end, they can reduce impatience. This was visible, most importantly, in terms of task performance. User satisfaction was improved by greater speed of the countdown, but not by a nonlinear countdown.

The main contributions of this study are as follows. (1) We systematically induce impatience using a period of waiting and show that this impatience has knock-on effects on both

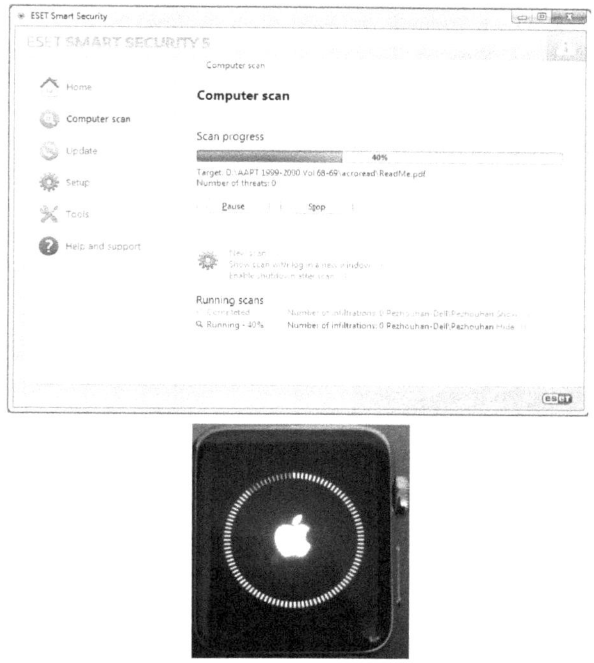

Figure 9. Progress bars used alone, or along with percentages. We recommend adding countdowns to them (e.g., above or below the progress bar in the first example, and in the middle of the screen in the second example). In the first example, impatience can result in stopping an important scan, which can endanger a users' security. The second example is an operating system being updated. For some of such firmware updates, stopping the process can cause harm to the system..

decision-making in subsequent tasks and user satisfaction. (2) We demonstrate that a faster countdown shown during an equally-long waiting period reliably decreases user's impatience, evidenced by later decisions. (3) We present evidence that user satisfaction is improved by waits accompanied by rapid countdowns compared to having no waiting period at all.

We believe this manipulation would be of interest in a wide range of situations, where people are waiting or face delays. Clearly perceiving a faster passage of time in these situations can result in a better user experience and improve the quality of work completed by the user in the context of such waits.

Acknowledgments

The authors thank Frank E. Ritter, Jens Grossklags, Jeremy Cole, and all anonymous referees for their comments on this study.

REFERENCES

1. Alessandro Angrilli, Paolo Cherubini, Antonella Pavese, and Sara Manfredini. 1997. The influence of affective factors on time perception. *Perception & Psychophysics* 59, 6 (1997), 972–982.

2. Frédéric Bielen and Nathalie Demoulin. 2007. Waiting time influence on the satisfaction-loyalty relationship in services. *Managing Service Quality: An International Journal* 17, 2 (2007), 174–193.

3. Richard A Block, Edward J George, and Marjorie A Reed. 1980. A watched pot sometimes boils: A study of duration experience. *Acta Psychologica* 46, 2 (1980), 81–94.
4. Paloma Botella, Francisco Bosch, Francisco J Romero, and Andrés Parra. 2001. Sex differences in estimation of time intervals and in reaction time are removed by moderate but not high doses of caffeine in coffee. *Human Psychopharmacology: Clinical and Experimental* 16, 7 (2001), 533–540.
5. Yu-Chiun Chiou and Chien-Hua Chang. 2010. Driver responses to green and red vehicular signal countdown displays: Safety and efficiency aspects. *Accident Analysis & Prevention* 42, 4 (2010), 1057–1065.
6. Barbara L Fredrickson and Daniel Kahneman. 1993. Duration neglect in retrospective evaluations of affective episodes. *Journal of Personality and Social Psychology* 65, 1 (1993), 45.
7. Peter Fröhlich. 2005. Dealing with system response times in interactive speech applications. In *CHI'05 Extended Abstracts on Human Factors in Computing Systems*. ACM, 1379–1382.
8. Moojan Ghafurian and David Reitter. 2014. Impatience, Risk Propensity and Rationality in Timing Games. In *Proceedings of the 36th Annual Meeting of the Cognitive Science Society (CogSci), Quebec City, Canada.*
9. Gerd Gigerenzer and Reinhard Selten. 2002. *Bounded rationality: The adaptive toolbox*. MIT Press.
10. Jens Grossklags and David Reitter. 2014. How task familiarity and cognitive predispositions impact behavior in a security game of timing. In *Computer Security Foundations Symposium (CSF), 2014 IEEE 27th*. IEEE, 111–122.
11. Chris Harrison, Brian Amento, Stacey Kuznetsov, and Robert Bell. 2007. Rethinking the progress bar. In *Proceedings of the 20th annual ACM symposium on User interface software and technology*. ACM, 115–118.
12. Chris Harrison, Zhiquan Yeo, and Scott E Hudson. 2010. Faster progress bars: manipulating perceived duration with visual augmentations. In *Proceedings of the SIGCHI Conference on Human Factors in Computing Systems*. ACM, 1545–1548.
13. Christophe Hurter, Audrey Girouard, Nathalie Riche, and Catherine Plaisant. 2011. Active progress bars: facilitating the switch to temporary activities. In *CHI'11 Extended Abstracts on Human Factors in Computing Systems*. ACM, 1963–1968.
14. Iris Levin and Dan Zakay. 1989. *Time and human cognition: A life-span perspective*. Elsevier.
15. Kejun Long, Yue Liu, and Lee D Han. 2013. Impact of countdown timer on driving maneuvers after the yellow onset at signalized intersections: An empirical study in Changsha, China. *Safety science* 54 (2013), 8–16.
16. Michele McClellan Stine, Richard J O'Connor, Bonnie R Yatko, Neil E Grunberg, and Laura Cousino Klein. 2002. Evidence for a relationship between daily caffeine consumption and accuracy of time estimation. *Human Psychopharmacology: Clinical and Experimental* 17, 7 (2002), 361–367.
17. Ree M Meertens and René Lion. 2008. Measuring an Individual's Tendency to Take Risks: The Risk Propensity Scale. *Journal of Applied Social Psychology* 38, 6 (2008), 1506–1520.
18. Fiona Fui-Hoon Nah. 2004. A study on tolerable waiting time: how long are Web users willing to wait? *Behaviour & Information Technology* 23, 3 (2004), 153–163.
19. María A Pastor and Julio Artieda. 1996. *Time, internal clocks and movement*. Vol. 115. Elsevier.
20. David Reitter, Jens Grossklags, and Alan Nochenson. 2013. Risk-seeking in a continuous game of timing. In *Proceedings of the 13th International Conference on Cognitive Modeling (ICCM)*. 397–403.
21. Herbert A Simon. 1986. Rationality in psychology and economics. *Journal of Business* (1986), S209–S224.
22. André J Szameitat, Jan Rummel, Diana P Szameitat, and Annette Sterr. 2009. Behavioral and emotional consequences of brief delays in human–computer interaction. *International Journal of Human-Computer Studies* 67, 7 (2009), 561–570.
23. Amos Tversky and Daniel Kahneman. 1974. Judgment under uncertainty: Heuristics and biases. *Science* 185, 4157 (1974), 1124–1131.
24. Amos Tversky and Daniel Kahneman. 1986. Rational choice and the framing of decisions. *Journal of Business* (1986), S251–S278.
25. Marten Van Dijk, Ari Juels, Alina Oprea, and Ronald L Rivest. 2012. FlipIt: The game of "stealthy takeover". *Journal of Cryptology* (2012), 1–59.
26. Leanne Wissinger, Joseph Hummer, and Joseph Milazzo. 2000. Using focus groups to investigate issues of red light running. *Transportation Research Record: Journal of the Transportation Research Board* 1734 (2000), 38–45.
27. Marc Wittmann and Martin P Paulus. 2008. Decision making, impulsivity and time perception. *Trends in Cognitive Sciences* 12, 1 (2008), 7–12.

Planning Adaptive Mobile Experiences When Wireframing

Qian Yang John Zimmerman Aaron Steinfeld Anthony Tomasic
School of Computer Science, Carnegie Mellon University, PA, USA
{qyang1, johnz, astein, tomasic}@cs.cmu.edu

ABSTRACT
Machine learning improves mobile user experience. Interestingly, envisioning apps with adaptive interfaces that reduce navigation and selection effort is not standard UX practice. When implementing an adaptive UI for our mobile transit app, we encountered a number of problems. Our original design did not log necessary information nor did it induce users to provide good labels. On reflection, we realized UX designers should identify and refine UI adaptions when sketching wireframes. To advance on this insight, we reviewed the interfaces of popular apps and extracted six design patterns where UI adaptation can improve in-app navigation. Next, we designed an exemplar set of wireframes, illustrating how UX designers might annotate their interaction flows to communicate planned adaptation and note the information (logs and labels) needed to make the desired inferences.

Author Keywords
Design patterns; interaction design; mobile interfaces.

ACM Classification Keywords
H.5.m. Information interfaces and presentation (e.g., HCI): Miscellaneous

INTRODUCTION
Machine learning (ML) has become an attractive and effective tool for improving mobile user experience (UX). Many of the most popular mobile apps regularly mine user behavior and context data in order to make personalized recommendations, filter out spam, predict travel time, and log behaviors like walking or sleeping. The increasing number of people who interact with these smart systems now expect more natural and intelligent interfaces [40].

The idea of improving UX with adaptive interfaces has been a topic of technical advancement. Mobile UI particularly benefits from adaptations that reduce navigation and selection efforts because (1) mobile tasks and contexts vary greatly, (2) small screens limit interaction and content space, and (3) the on-the-go usage often limits attention making every second count [4,8,10]. For example, the Starbucks app might learn a user pays with their phone and land the user on the payment screen when launched inside a Starbucks' store. Adaptive interfaces also benefit users with disabilities. These users pay a higher cost to navigate UIs in terms of cognitive and physical effort [28]. Recently, some interaction design experts have begun to claim that, "AI is the new UI"[6]. They view adaptation as the most important path forward for improving UX [6,20].

If AI really is the new UI, it seems planning interfaces and interaction flows that adapt should be a part of UX practice. Interestingly, this is extremely rare. Practice-focused design patterns as well as books and articles on wireframing do not discuss how to design for adaptation or how to collect the information needed for ML [7,15,33,39,42]. Most interaction design programs do not teach students to look for adaptation opportunities and build them into their designs. Finally, current mobile UI prototyping tools do not support the design of adaptive mobile UIs that change as they learn user preferences (see Cooper's great list of prototyping tools used by practitioners [38]).

We attempted to enhance our mobile transit app, Tiramisu, with an adaptive interface in order to reduce navigation and selection efforts. We encountered two problems that made this impossible. First, we had not logged the information needed to infer what users most likely wanted to do. Second, we had not properly motivated users to provide good labels that would support adaptation. In reflecting on these breakdowns, we realized that we should have planned for an adaptive UI when we first sketched our wireframes. By planning for an adaptive UI, we could have designed the logging systems and tailored the interactions to collect the required information.

Although challenging, recognizing learning opportunities when wireframing will be an important goal for future IxD practices. To advance on this challenge, we reviewed the interfaces of many popular mobile apps. We extracted six UI design patterns that define where and how adaptation might be applied. In addition, we generated an exemplar of a wireframed interaction flow. This flow shows both the pre-adapted and adapted interaction paths and documents the data needed to make an inference, a recovery method in the case of an inference error, and an inference quality needed to trigger adaptation. This flow functions as a boundary object, aiding designers in discussions with their development team.

DIS 2016, June 04-08, 2016, Brisbane, QLD, Australia
© 2016 ACM. ISBN 978-1-4503-4031-1/16/06…$15.00
DOI: http://dx.doi.org/10.1145/2901790.2901858

This paper makes three contributions. First, we discover and promote the lack of planning for adaptive UI in current UX practice. Second, we provide six mobile design patterns showing where and how adaptations might be added. Third, we provide an exemplar wireframed interaction flow that allows design teams to capture and communicate their plans for an adaptive mobile UI.

RELATED WORK

Adaptive User Interfaces

HCI refers to learning systems that reduce UI navigation and selection as adaptive UIs. Adaptive UIs automatically adjust content, layout, or visual presentation based on detected changes in device, context, task, or demands [2,21]. They typically employ a user profile and set of user models to personalize user experiences and to address heterogeneous user needs [23].

Online personalization benefits both users and service providers [24]. Successful personalization anticipates users' intentions and reduces their navigation (number of screens) and selection efforts (number of taps and inputs). For example, Netflix's movie recommendations reduce the effort needed to find a movie. Service provider benefits include improved customer satisfaction, persuasion, and loyalty. The service design and research community has recognized personalization as an important part of building and maintaining long-term customer relationships with a view toward creating *customer lifetime value* [37].

HCI researchers have investigated adaptive UIs both for personalization and for context-aware applications. Familiar examples include automating display of desktop interfaces on mobile devices (done prior to responsive design) (i.e. SUPPLE [12]) and reducing navigation by reconfiguring menu items and toolbars based on frequency of use (i.e., Microsoft's Smart Menu and the Windows XP Start Menu [13]). More recently, interfaces now also intelligently respond to use contexts [5]. They surface information or services users likely want by monitoring contextual clues such as the user's location (i.e., Cyberguide [1]), current behavior (i.e. Sensay [41]), or previous behavior to automate task completion (i.e. VIO [45]).

The ML community describes adaptive interfaces as a special class of ML systems [23]. To build such a system, developers collect examples, extract features and labels (the values they wish to predict), train a prediction model, and test the accuracy of the predictions [32]. Developers must reformulate the adaptation they want into a problem that ML methods can directly address, engineer an adequate set of the descriptors, and work with interaction designers to develop interfaces that accurately capture the required data to generate high quality output [22]. Some researchers address this challenge by developing the ML system and interface simultaneously, thereby allowing negotiation between the ML input requirements and the actions required for users to complete their tasks (e.g., [45]).

Adaptation and User experience

Past work notes that adding adaptation can be dangerous [28]. Adaptive UIs confuse users who perceive changes in system behavior as negatively inconsistent instead of positively personal, thus increasing cognitive workload [45] and decreasing their sense of control [16,44]. In response, researchers designed visual metaphors to make adaptations more predictable (vividly exemplified by eight adaptive interface strategies applied to pull-down menus [9]).

When to adapt comes down to a tradeoff between the quality of the inferring system and the risk/reward users associate with a successful or failed adaptive action. Working with developers, designers should engage in discussions about a systems inference performance because user satisfaction does not correlate directly with high accuracy [27]. The notion of "fail-soft" [25], inference errors that still move users closer to their goal, provides a great example of how to address the tradeoff between performance and user experience. For example, Internet search engines return a list of ranked links (moving the user closer) instead of taking them to a specific page.

High-performance ML requires carefully selected set of data descriptors that can accurately and directly characterize user intention [21,22,29]. ML often needs *ground truth* labels for good and/or bad examples that can be hard to lift from implicit user actions. ML developers also seek a minimal set of descriptors because use of less relevant and irrelevant features can confound learning [23]. Likewise, being careless with samples can lead to *overtraining* and biasing the results. Therefore, interfaces must often induce users to provide explicit labels in addition to implicitly inferring features [2,13]. UX teams planning for adaptation should carefully weigh the additional effort to log implicit behaviors and induce good explicit labels, the risk of inference errors, and the opportunity for improved user experience [17,30].

Rogers argues that context-aware technologies should NOT do things for people, but they should instead engage people more actively in their current activity [35]. More discussion on better positioning of automation in interfaces as a means of optimizing costs and benefits can be found in mixed-initiative interface research (e.g., [17]). Billsus et al. [2] generated a set of design recommendations for adaptive interfaces for news readers. Below we list the ones that are most likely to generalize to mobile UIs:

- Create an effective interface that works well before the personalization is running
- Adapt quickly to what the user does/wants and monitor for changes in taste/desire
- Support multiple modes of information access (such as providing both recommended set of items and an alpha-ordered set of items)
- Make recovery from a mistaken user-action easy to execute
- Respect the user's privacy

The idea of improving UX with ML is not new, and the HCI research community has done great work to demonstrate this functionality. The maturity of this area catalyzed the concept of *AI is the new UI* [6]. Our research attempts to bridge the prior technical advances on adaptive UIs with current UX design practices that largely ignore this opportunity and the challenges it brings.

A CASE STUDY: ADAPTIVE UI FOR TIRAMISU

We deployed a transit information app, *Tiramisu*, in 2011, and since its release, thousands of users have used this app [43]. We wanted to redesign the app to simplify interaction flows in response to issues users identified. Specifically, we wanted to collapse the navigation of several screens and eliminate the need for several selection actions by inferring what information users most likely wanted.

Tiramisu has an unusual interaction flow for a transit information app. It crowdsources real-time arrival information by encouraging users to share location traces from their phones as they commute. Upon launching, the app lands on a home screen that lets users choose to see *Nearby* stops and previously created *Favorite* stops (Figure 1a). When selecting *Nearby*, users transition to a map. They select a stop to reveal its name (Figure 1b) and tap the name flag to transition to a list of the bus routes that use the stop (Figure 1c). Here they see arrival times for upcoming buses. Selecting an arriving bus launches a popup (Figure 1d) where users indicate if they plan to board this bus (*Getting on*). This transitions them to a destination screen (Figure 1e) showing a list of downstream stops. Tiramisu collects the destination so it can stop sharing the location from the user's phone as they arrive at their destination. Selecting a

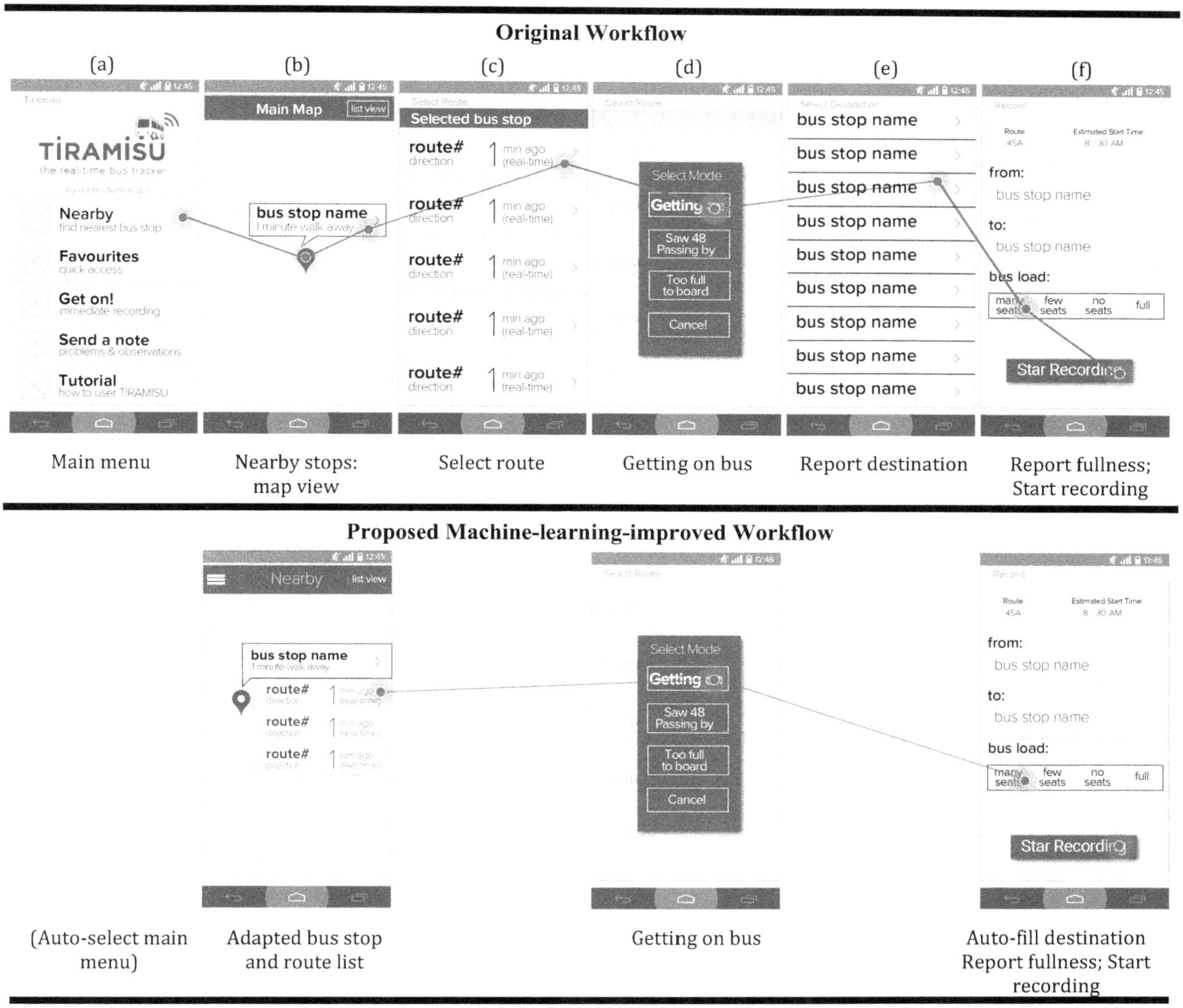

Figure 1. Tiramisu interface wireframes (Fonts resized for readability).

destination transitions the user to the tracing screen (Figure 1f). Here they must indicate vehicle fullness and then they can share a location trace by tapping *Start Recording*.

To see arrival times, users navigate three screens, make three selections by tapping, and scroll one list. To share a location trace needed to generate the real-time arrival information, users navigate six screens and a popup menu, make eight selections by tapping, and scroll two lists. Several users complained that it took too many screen and taps to share a trace. In addition, some complained about entering a destination. This level of effort was particularly onerous for blind users who used screen readers.

When planning the redesign, we wanted to collapse this flow to minimize navigation and selection effort. We selected three specific places to do this:

1. Infer the tab a user wanted, eliminating the home screen (Figure 1a);
2. If they wanted *Nearby*, then infer the stop, eliminating the map and stop selection and taking them right to the arrival times (Figure 1b);
3. When sharing a trace, infer the destination, skipping the destination screen (from 1e);

We assumed frequent users typically take the same trips at the same times, such as a daily commute to work. So based on time of day and location, we could infer origin and destination bus stops. Previous studies successfully predicted bus-riding patterns by mining time-location pairs from a history rides [26,31,34]. In an ideal case, the app would deliver the user to a list of desired arrival times when they launched the app. To share a trace, users would need to navigate two screens and a popup, while scrolling one list and making two tap selections. The adaptive UI would be significantly faster and require much less effort.

We encountered two problems that prevented the design improvements. First, our system did not log all the information we needed. For example, we could not tell which selection a user had made on the home screen. Our system logged calls to the database, not onscreen actions. Database calls to send arrival times could originate from (1) selecting a stop on the map, (2) looking up a stop from *Favorites*, or (3) refreshing a list of arrival times. Second, some logs contained poor quality data. Specifically, some of the destination selections users made contained the next stop on the route. We suspect that few took a bus to travel the distance of one stop. We inferred they might be simply selecting the first item on the destination screen in order to dismiss the screen and get to tracing. Both of these problems produced irreparable defects in the data.

Reflections

We reflected on the challenging state of our redesign efforts. We compared it to our previously successful pre-planned ML implementation to see if we could identify a breakdown in our process and improve future design efforts. After much discussion, we concluded that the breakdown happened when we wireframed the interaction flows.

We should have noted adaptation opportunities when sketching our initial wireframes. When wireframing interaction flows, a design team views the interface and task from the users' point of view. This perspective helps designers develop a sense of the users' intentions and identify the sets of actions users will likely repeat. Sketching should produce flow without the adaptation, to show the initial design and also adapted flows that document reduced navigation and selection. A set of flows might include one where the interface makes suggestions and others where better inference performance allows for more automation. After completing these sketches, we should have shared these with our development team so that tasks can be properly framed and plans can be made for logging the required information.

Most of the original design team members had several years of experience designing, developing, and evaluating intelligent products and services that used ML. *This was not our first rodeo*. We speculated on how much more difficult this might be for design teams with little to no experience working with ML systems. In looking at UX practice books that describe wireframing, interaction design classes that teach wireframing, and current practices of UX design teams, we observed that anticipating adaptation in order to reduce navigation and selection is not written about, taught, or a typical part of current UX practice. To help both ourselves and other UX designers with less experience, we decided to identify mobile interaction patterns that would likely benefit from adaptation.

ADAPTIVE UI PATTERNS

To help designers both recognize opportunities, we searched for mobile UI design patterns [3] that might benefit adaptation. We started by analyzing the 25 most popular mobile apps of 2015 [11]. We downloaded these and navigated their interfaces using our phones; collectively discussing and developing consensus for what constituted a pattern. As we used these apps, we also discussed other apps we regularly used as additional sources for patterns. We scoped our search to *in-app navigation* because (1) navigation is a common UI component shared among apps, (2) it is the focus of much of the wireframing stage of UX design, and (3) it does not require any changes to an operating system that most often falls well outside the purview of an apps UX team.

This process resulted in six mobile UI design patterns that signal where designers should consider adding adaption. For each pattern, we noted common UI elements along with approaches for executing the adaptation. Below we describe each pattern with its known uses and variations, the adaptation opportunities it offers, the forms it might take after learning, and any interaction challenges.

1. Landing

Use when: The landing page contains multiple subsections of function or content. Often each tab on a landing page represent a subsection; each tab links to a separate screen. Almost all applications we analyzed landed on a screen with tabs a tab panel in launching screen. Exceptions include apps with a single function, like *Boomerang*.

UI adaptation opportunity: Landing on the tab a user most likely wants based on collective and/or personal history. For *Tiramisu*, the home screen matches this pattern.

Most current content and media consumption apps, such as news, use a recommender to rank content, but they often employ a designer-selected default to land on a desired page. Adaptation would benefit users not served well by this default. Social network apps also personalize the listing of posts; however, they generally do not learn when users want to land on notifications or land on new posts.

Adapted presentations:
The wireframes below illustrate how this adaptation might unfold as predictions improve. Figure 2a shows the initial UI and Figure 2b and 2c show two stages of an adapted landing tab. The first stage reorders tabs, revealing hidden tabs based on prior usage (assuming the design has more tabs than can be displayed). The second stage automatically lands the user on the inferred tab. Automation should appear progressive and steady. The uniformity both in user experience and in the underlying data flow across the set of wireframes can reduce potential confusion.

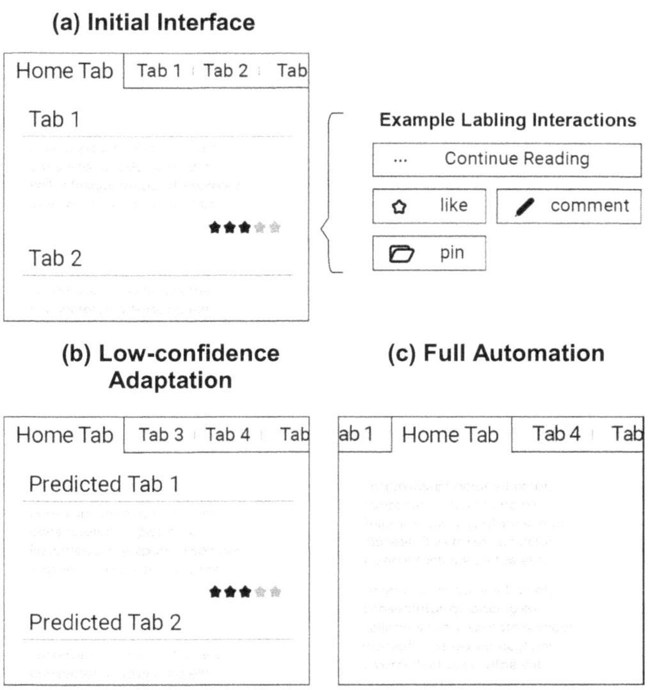

Figure 2. Wireframe patterns for automated tab landing.

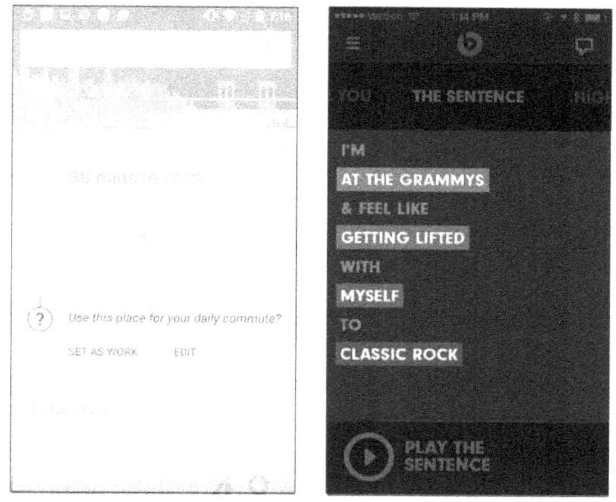

Figure 3. Interface examples that encourage explicit labeling. (a) Google Now Launcher (b) Beats music

Interaction Challenges
1). *Different triggers*: When adapting the landing, design teams should consider different scenarios. Behaviors might need to be different for a fresh launch, for bringing an app back into focus, or when transitioning in from another app.

2). *Quality labels:* On a tabbed interface, it can be difficult to infer if the app landed on the best tab simply by monitoring the time users take to navigate to a different tab. When the initial tab's visit time is short, it is difficult to infer if the user wanted a different tab or if they only needed a small amount of information from the default tab. Interfaces can explicitly ask users for labels. For example, *Google Now* (Figure 3a) prompts users with, "Is this card useful right now?" to validate a recommendation. Such direct labeling prompts should be used infrequently as they have great capacity to annoy users.

2. Single Selection

Use when: Interface contains single-selection lists, pickers (such as date and time), toggles, single checkboxes, list of radio buttons, etc.

UI adaptation opportunity: Reducing navigation or reducing selection effort situations where users must frequently make the same choice. For Tiramisu, the selection of a desired stop on the map screen and the selection of the destination when tracing both follow this pattern.

Adapted presentations: Figure 4 shows several options to reduce selection effort for a single-selection list based on the quality of a prediction. (4a) shows the initial control with a structured single-selection list. (4b) adapts the list by placing a highlight on the most-likely item. (4c) adapts the list by showing likely items at the top of the list followed by a structured list of all items. (4d) adapts the list by making a selection. Users can fix an error by tapping the control and selecting the correct item.

Interaction Challenge:

1) *Determining trigger quality:* Designers should work closely with the developers to select a performance threshold that triggers the adaptation. The design team understands the impact on user experience when the system performs correctly versus when it makes an error. The design and development teams should collectively determine thresholds.

2) *Selecting adaptation forms:* The design team needs to select a form or set of forms based on the type of choice being made. For very long lists, providing a ranked list at the top can speed interaction. When fully automating by making a selection, designers should consider how easily users can recognize an error and make a repair.

3. Form

Use when: Interface contains one or more text fields, a screen with form elements, tagging tasks, and others that have form like behaviors.

UI adaptation opportunity: Auto-completing repeated user inputs. Text input can be auto-completed by mining history. Multi-field forms, systems can monitor the first few inputs and then fill remaining items based on history of form filling. Familiar uses of this pattern include autocompleting multiple email recipients, filling in a user's contact information or address, and automatically tagging an uploaded photo as a specific person.

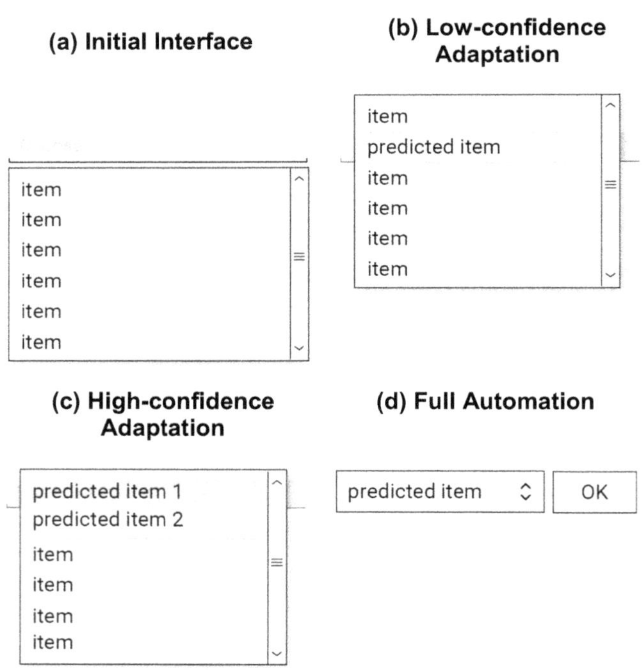

Figure 4. Wireframe patterns for automated list selection.

Interaction challenge:

1) *Recognizing errors:* HCI research shows that users sometimes struggle to recognize form-filling errors [45]. Visually distinguishing automated actions from explicit user actions can help. Also, teams can set very high quality thresholds for trigger adaptation for specific elements where an error might be catastrophic.

2) *Setting adaptation quality thresholds*: Auto-completing a longer form with no "undo" can penalize users who would need to make many individual deletions and corrections.

4. Multi-screen Transactions

Use when: A user task consists of many steps that span more than one screen.

UI adaptation opportunity: Automating the choices on one or more screens to reduce navigation and selection. Our Tiramisu redesign uses this adaption by automatically selecting the landing tab (eliminating the home screen) and automatically selecting the desired stop (eliminated the map and need to select a stop on the map).

Adapted presentations: Collapsing multi-screen transactions will be quite specific to an individual app. Amazon's "Buy-now with 1-click" feature provides a familiar example. The design uses a single selection to collapse payment selection and shipping screens, transitioning the user directly to the confirmation screen showing the item has been ordered. The Spotify music app offers another example. The app can detect the pace of a user's exercise (walk or run) and then automatically select songs that match the pace.

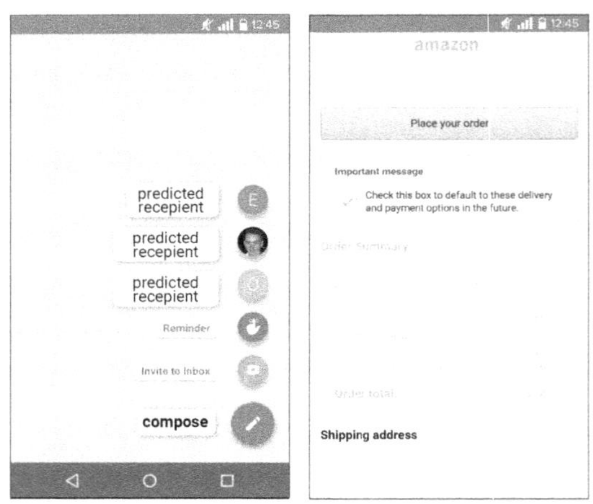

Figure 5. Shortcut screen transaction UI examples: (a) Gmail app provides a set of recipient shortcuts for composing new emails. (b) Amazon shopping app offers users options to automate ordering process to different extents.

Interaction challenges:

1). *Lack of Consistency:* When apps automate several simultaneous actions, it increases the likelihood of confusing users or of introducing errors that disrupt the user experience. Designers should carefully consider the value of the adaptation versus the potential for disruption.

2). *Recovery:* An adaptive UI that collapses a multi-screen transaction should provide an easy mechanism for users to recover in the event of an inference error. This recovery might be some sort of "undo" or other control that can rollback some or all of the actions taken. With highly accurate prediction models, such as spam detection, an even more complex recovery interaction may be required.

3). *Adaptation Threshold:* The inference quality threshold should be high for adaptation that makes several selections. Ways to increase confidence include single selection confirmations users make in order to trigger a multi-screen transaction and explicit user confirmation authorizing the app to automate this set of actions in future transactions.

5. User Generated and Incoming Contents

Use When: The app displays or handles sensor data; user created content such as text, audio, or photos; or content generated by people or machines that the app downloads or displays.

UI adaptation opportunity: Like multi-screen transactions, this pattern and its potential adapted layouts are often quite specific to the underlying task. Adaptation generally involves recognizing entities such as a face, a phone number or date string (as compared to other text), a voice, a user activity, etc. This pattern can be a means to automate selection, form filling, or collapsing multi-screen transactions.

Adapted presentations: Most will be specific to an individual task or recognized entity. Face detect has begun to emerge as a pattern that uses a box around a face next to a textbox showing the inferred name.

Interaction challenges: Determining the quality thresholds for triggering the adaptation. Communicating to users actions the app has taken on the users' behalf.

6. Attention-catcher

Use when: Interruptions or requests for the user's immediate attention, often in the form of pop-up windows and banners. Common examples include notifications; popups that encourage users to register, review, or login to the app using a social media account; and reminders to upgrade an app for an improved user experience.

UI adaptation opportunity: This adaptation attempts to determine either the best time to ask a user for this non-required information (when they are most-likely to provide it) or when it should no longer continue to ask the user for this information. The timing can be learned jointly as stepping-stones of a user-app relationship. Discovering the best timings for these requests opens up the design space to intelligently manage long-term user experiences.

Interaction challenges:

1). *Selecting default threshold:* Improperly set thresholds can be extremely annoying, so designers should be conservative, and consider if they should use this

Recognizing patterns in UI elements	Patterns	Entailed Interaction Challenges
• Landing page that contains multiple subsections of function or content, often presented by a panel of tabs;	**Landing**	• Differentiate actions for different landings; • Labeling correct/incorrect adaptations appropriately;
• Single-selection lists, including pickers, toggles and single checkbox radio buttons; • Extensive lists, including tab panel with overflow items, navigation menu used in combination with slide-out menu;	**Single Selection**	• Deliberate adaptation threshold
• Forms; Lists of checkboxes or toggles whose items are correlated; • One or more text fields or tags;	**Form**	• Differentiate actions of the agent and of the user; • Deliberate level of automation;
• A series of screens that constitute a user task;	**Multi-screen Transaction**	• Deliberate automation threshold; • Explain automation; • Ease correction;
• User inputs and uploads, including texts, audios, photos, videos and beyond;	**Incoming Content**	• Ease correction;
• Pop-up windows; • Banners;	**Attention-catcher**	• Deliberate threshold; • Allow dismiss;

Table 1: An overview of adaptive navigation UI patterns

adaptation.

2). *Allowing for easy dismissal:* Interaction flows should aid users pick up where they left off before the interruptions.

3). *Determining value proposition for nags:* Rewarding users with escalated experience with an eye on creating and managing long-term UX values.

IMPLEMENTING PATTERNS WHEN WIREFRAMING

We searched for and documented these six design patterns in order to help UX design teams recognize opportunities to add adaptation to their mobile interfaces. Once a team has identified an opportunity, they must construct interaction flows that communicate both the pre-adaptive and post-adaptive behaviors. These flows then need to be documented in a way that supports an effective exchange between the design team and the development team. To this end, we generated an annotated wireframe exemplar using our *Tiramisu* UI as an example.

We first went through several typical usage scenarios to envision a preliminary task flow. We identified adaptation opportunities: adaptive landing and three single selections (wanted bus stop, destination, and fullness). We then generated a preliminary set of features we felt would most likely be needed to make the inference. We selected these

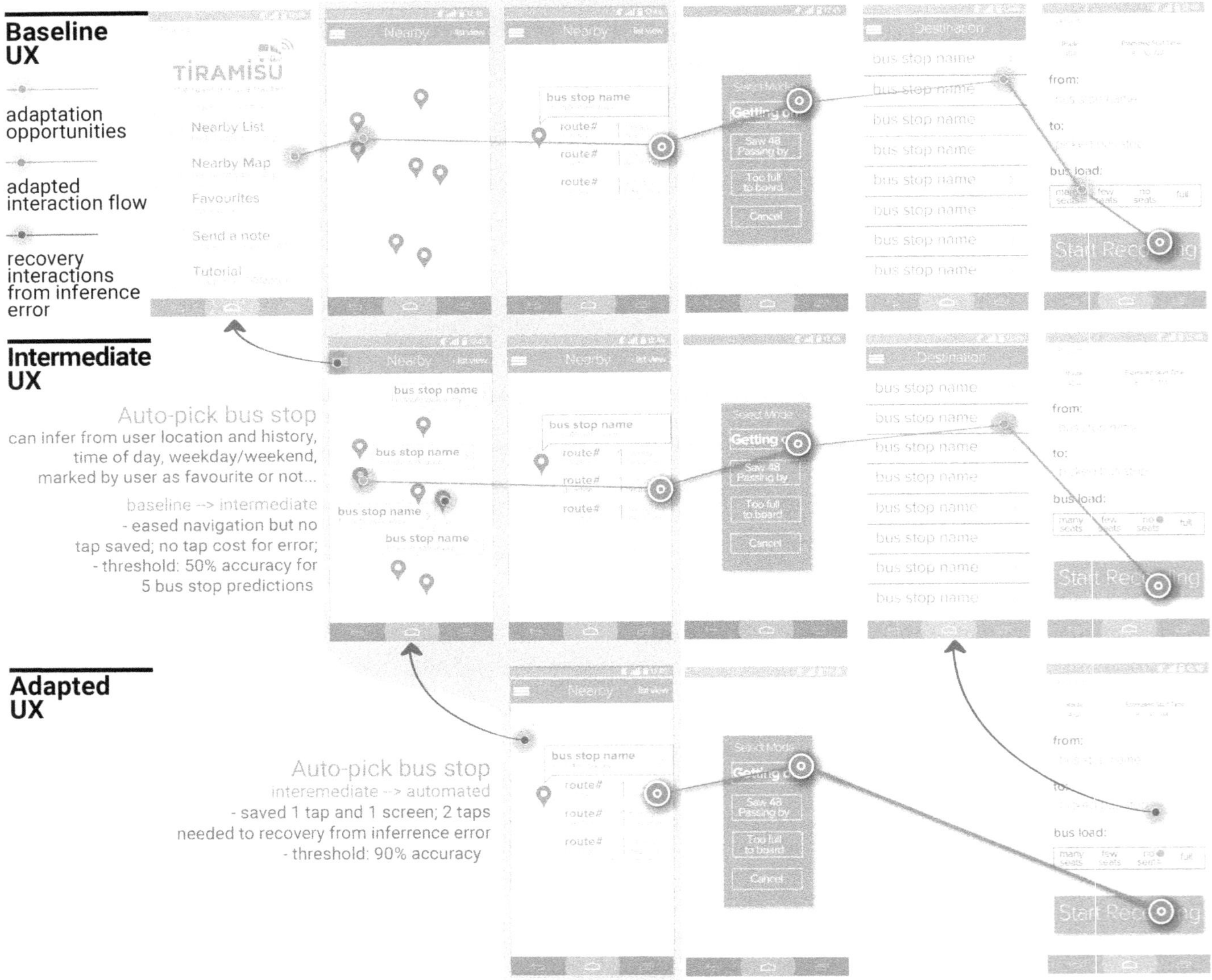

Figure 6: Proposed wireframe revision enabled by machine learning automations. Data collected over the early lifecycle of the app enabled great opportunities for machine learning to simplify in-app navigation. The blue dots represent user actions that we hope to automate; the green traces are the user actions needed when all adaptations are successful; red traces represents page transactions to recover from an inference error.

based on how we imagined most users would engage with the app the majority of the time. We wanted to capture the required features to aid in discussions with the development team on what should be logged. Next, we sketched the pre- and post adaptation interaction flows. When making the post-adaptation wireframes, we focused on users should recognize and recover from inference errors. We planned stages for the adaptation with an eye towards increasing automation as prediction quality increased. We annotated the flow across the wireframes to show the specific user actions (Figure 6 blue lines), and the steps needed to recover from an error (Figure 6 red lines). Finally, we note a rough estimation of the prediction threshold for each level of automation.

Figure 6 shows an annotated flow of wireframes generated through this process. The top shows the pre-adaption flow with highlights indicating the user selections. Below that are the adaptive flows. For each adaptation, we identified a preliminary set of features based on our understanding of user intentions and actions. The automatic selection of the most likely desired bus stop provides a good example; we suspected that the features time of day, day of week, and user location would have strong correlations. Transit rider mobility patterns often show a strong geo-temporal pattern, especially for weekdays. Whether the user has marked a nearby bus stop as a *Favorite* can also help an inference of the stop they most likely want information about. We listed these features on the wireframe.

Each stage of each adaptation, the wireframe notes the potential benefits and costs, and accordingly an estimated accuracy threshold required for triggering the adaptation (Figure 8 blue notes). For example, when accurately predicting the most likely stop a user might be interested performs poorly, the map highlights the five most likely stops (Figure6 – Intermediate UX – screen one). When none of these match the user's intention, they can continue to select the stop they want from the map with no interaction penalty. When successful, the prediction saves navigation efforts and the number of selection actions needed remain the same as the interaction with no adaptation. Considering both the benefit and cost of automation are minimal, we expect the accuracy threshold should be relatively low (i.e. 50%).

Design teams should use these annotated interaction flows as a boundary object to discuss adaptation with their development team. Both teams can use the flow as a common structure for either simulating user experiences or modeling underlying data. They can also find issues in their common interests (such as the user actions to mine for inferences and the accuracy thresholds for interface changes) annotated on the wireframe, offering starting places for both teams to build upon collaboratively.

DISCUSSION

Adaptive UIs

Everyday people use more and more mobile apps that employ ML to enhance user experience. Like others in the HCI and IxD communities, we promote the idea that *ML is the new UI*. Adaptive UIs that proactively improve user experience represent one aspect of this trend, and HCI researchers have produced a strong technical foundation through their development of dynamically adaptive UIs.

The idea of adaptive UIs has not yet become a standard part of UX design and development. One traditional challenge researchers noted with their acceptance comes from users who expect consistency in software behavior [13]. We suggest this might be less of a problem today than in the past. Today, almost all of the mainstream online tools and mobile apps continuously update their interfaces, exposing users to a frequent pace of UI change never seen with traditional desktop applications and operating systems. We suspect today's users have become more robust to interface changes and will thus more easily accept and appreciate adaptive UIs. In addition, with the increasing exposure to ML-enhanced systems, users are becoming more familiar with the possibility that systems make inference errors. Now seems the perfect time to push on the idea to make adaptive UIs a standard part of UX practice.

The software development community has learned over many years that HCI and user experience should be considered early in the development process and not added as an afterthought at the end. These considerations range from usability [18], to usable privacy [14], to accessibility [36] and even sustainability [19]. Similarly, this paper promotes the idea that an adaptive UI that learns from a user's interaction history how to reduce navigation and selection effort should also be considered at the early stages of the design process; specifically, when sketching wireframes and interaction flows. Our attempt to enhance our own app with an adaptive UI revealed an unanticipated barrier. Because we had not planned for adaptation, our initial design did not collect good labels and our system did not log the information needed to make high quality inferences. The lack of planning for adaptive UIs in current UX practice stands as a barrier to operationalizing UI adaptation technology in current products and services.

Creating effective interaction designs that both collect data from users and seed valuable adaptation remains a design challenge. Promises of adapted interactions often come at the expense of usability. In order to make confident predictions, machine-learning systems need to induce more explicit inputs from users. This tradeoff is best demonstrated by comparing a new user's experiences with *Tiramisu* and with *Transit,* a mobile app with similar functionality but no personalization (Figure 7). How can designers induce and regulate interactions in order to collect data and labels? How can interactions externalize users' intentions and capture their behaviors? How can UX teams find harmony between adaptations and user engagement? We have seen many creative solutions employed in other services that intend to produce a ready source of training data. For example, web music player *Beats* invites users to complete a narrative of "I'm (at a party), feeling like (chilling out) with (my friends) to (old school hip-hop)" and the player *plays the sentence* with recommended sound tracks. This example employs an entertaining dialog that motivates users to contribute information; information that can be used as labels for personalization.

UX designers should consider the risk of inference errors. Many open research questions remain around how to calculate the benefit of successful adaptation against the harm caused by inference errors. Much more research is needed on interfaces that make it easier for users to recognize and make repair to these errors.

We see significant opportunities in the design of new tools that support UX designers in utilizing machine learning; tools that help them step beyond the static flows they produce today. Our work provides a set of staged adaptive UIs (pre-adaptation UX, partial adaptation UX, and fully adapted UX). These will not fit into current prototyping tools that assume a single interaction flow. We encourage more design researchers to work on the challenge of integrating adaptation into current wireframing and interface prototyping tools. The prototyping tools should support designers in detailing staged adaptive interaction flows and with collecting rationales for the information that should be logged.,

ML Is the New UX

Our work narrowly investigates generating adaptive UIs, and it promotes the idea of building this into the early stages of the design process. However, adaptive UIs represent only one small way that ML can enhance UX. If interaction designers and HCI practitioners really believe that *ML is the new UX*, more work needs to be done to advance current UX education and practices.

Most of the ML enhancements to user experience, from spam filters to activity and context recognition systems, start as ideas within ML development teams. These ideas then get passed to HCI and UX teams to integrate into an interaction design. UX teams play little to no role in generating the ideas around what could or should be done. In our experience, most UX designers are not prepared to effectively envision new ML-enhanced products and services. They lack a tacit knowledge of ML as a design material. Today UX teams either never consider adding ML to enhance their designs or they think of them too much like magic and generate ideas that cannot be effectively implemented. They need more education on what ML can do, and they need practice tools that support them in investigating and communicating their design ideas.

To deliver of the idea that ML is the new UX, IxD and HCI researchers must develop new means that help UX teams develop a tacit understanding of ML as a design material. They must invent new prototyping tools that allow design teams to effectively communicate their concepts to development teams and to investigate all of the implications these concepts generate, such as the risk of errors or the need to induce users to provide explicit labels for training.

The idea that ML is the new UX opens up a large space for more and more IxD and HCI research that builds off the latest trends in industry and that offers new ideas for how the emerging power of ML can be operationalized in interaction designs. Parallel to these research efforts should be work to integrate ML as a design material into IxD and HCI education. Students coming from these programs should have an understanding of what this technology can do and of how to assess the costs and benefits of adding it into a new design.

LIMITATIONS AND FUTURE WORK

Through this paper we hope to formulate some changes to HCI and interaction design research, practice, and education that will shape how designers envision interactions. We also hope to start a serious discussion around the larger issues related to the idea that ML is the new UX. The presented work is intended to provide another start point for this emerging conversation.

One limitation of the presented work, including both the design patterns and the example of how to capture an adaptive UI in an interaction flow of wireframes, is a lack of evaluation. We generated the patterns and documentation approach to address a specific design challenge we faced with the intention that they might generalize to design teams who wish to make mobile UIs adaptive. We do not know if these patterns will aid design teams in identifying places to add adaptation or with their search for an effective interaction form. We do not know if the annotated interaction flows will generate effective conversations between ML developers and UX design teams. We will continue this work and evaluate and refine our patterns and wireframe exemplar, working with practitioners and researchers. We encourage the IxD and HCI research community to join us, and build new prototyping tools that support and shape adaptive interactions.

ACKNOWLEDGEMENT

The contents of this paper were developed under a grant from the National Institute on Disability, Independent Living, and Rehabilitation Research (NIDILRR grant number 90RE5011-01-00). NIDILRR is a Center within the Administration for Community Living (ACL), Department of Health and Human Services (HHS).

REFERENCES

1. Gregory D. Abowd, Christopher G. Atkeson, Jason Hong, Sue Long, Rob Kooper, and Mike Pinkerton. 1997. Cyberguide: a mobile context-aware tour guide. *Wireless Networks* 3, 5: 421–433. http://doi.org/10.1023/A:1019194325861

2. Daniel Billsus, Clifford a Brunk, Craig Evans, Brian Gladish, and Michael Pazzani. 2002. Adaptive Interfaces for Ubiquitous Web Access. *Communications of the ACM* 45, 5: 34–38.
3. Jan O. Borchers. 2001. A pattern approach to interaction design. *AI & Society* 15, 4: 359–376. http://doi.org/10.1007/BF01206115
4. Robert Bridle and Eric McCreath. 2006. Inducing shortcuts on a mobile phone interface. *Proceedings of the international conference on Intelligent user interfaces (IUI '06)*, 327. http://doi.org/10.1145/1111449.1111526
5. Dermot Browne. 2014. *Adaptive User Interfaces*. Elsevier.
6. John Brownlee. 2015. Apple Finally Learns AI Is The New UI. Retrieved December 25, 2015 from http://www.fastcodesign.com/3047199/apple-finally-learns-ai-is-the-new-ui
7. Christian Crumlish and Erin Malone. 2009. *Designing Social Interfaces: Principles, Patterns, and Practices for Improving the User Experience*. "O'Reilly Media, Inc."
8. Razak Eun Lee, Young and Benbasat. 2003. Interface Design for Mobile Commerce. *Communications of the ACM* 46, 12: 48–52.
9. Leah Findlater and Krzysztof Z. Gajos. 2009. Design Space and Evaluation Graphical User Interfaces. *AI Magazine*, Höök 2000: 68–73. http://doi.org/10.1609/aimag.v30i4.2268
10. Leah Findlater and Joanna McGrenere. 2008. Impact of screen size on performance, awareness, and user satisfaction with adaptive graphical user interfaces. *Proceedings of the 26th SIGCHI Conference on Human Factors in Computing Systems*: 1247–1256. http://doi.org/10.1145/1357054.1357249
11. Dan Frommer. 2015. These are the 25 most popular mobile apps in America. Retrieved January 17, 2016 from http://qz.com/481245/these-are-the-25-most-popular-2015-mobile-apps-in-america/
12. Krzysztof Z. Gajos, Daniel S. Weld, and Jacob O. Wobbrock. 2010. Automatically generating personalized user interfaces with Supple. *Artificial Intelligence* 174, 12-13: 910–950. http://doi.org/10.1016/j.artint.2010.05.005
13. Kz Gajos, Mary Czerwinski, Ds Tan, and Ds Weld. 2006. Exploring the design space for adaptive graphical user interfaces. *Proceedings of Advanced visual interfaces*: 201–208. http://doi.org/10.1145/1133265.1133306
14. Jason Hong. 2009. Usable Privacy and Security : A Grand Challenge for HCI Usable Privacy and Security : A Grand Challenge for HCI.
15. Steven Hoober and Eric Berkman. 2011. *Designing Mobile Interfaces*. "O'Reilly Media, Inc."
16. K. Höök. 2000. Steps to take before intelligent user interfaces become real. *Interacting with Computers* 12, 4: 409–426. http://doi.org/10.1016/S0953-5438(99)00006-5
17. Eric Horvitz. 1999. Principles of Mixed-Initiative User Interfaces. *Proceedings of the SIGCHI Conference on Human Factors in Computing Systems (CHI '99)*. http://doi.org/10.1145/302979.303030
18. Natalia Juristo and Ana Moreno. 2008. Moving usability forward to the beginning of the software development process. *Human Computer Interaction*, Bass 1999.
19. Azam Khan, Lyn Bartram, Eli Blevis, Carl DiSalvo, Jon Froehlich, and Gordon Kurtenbach. 2011. CHI 2011 sustainability community invited panel. *Proceedings of the 2011 annual conference extended abstracts on Human factors in computing systems - CHI EA '11*, ACM Press, 73. http://doi.org/10.1145/1979742.1979484
20. Cliff Kuang. 2013. Why a New Golden Age for UI Design Is Around the Corner. *Wired Magazine 21.09*. Retrieved December 28, 2015 from http://www.wired.com/2013/08/design-and-the-digital-world/
21. Miroslav Kubat, Robert C. Holte, and Stan Matwin. Machine Learning for the Detection of Oil Spills in Satellite Radar Images. *Machine Learning* 30, 2-3: 195–215. http://doi.org/10.1023/A:1007452223027
22. Pat Langley. 1997. Machine Learning for Adaptive User Interfaces. In *KI-97: Advances in Artificial Intelligence*, Gerhard Brewka, Christopher Habel and Bernhard Nebel (eds.). Springer Berlin Heidelberg, Berlin, Heidelberg, 53–62. http://doi.org/10.1007/3-540-63493-2
23. Pat Langley. 1999. User Modeling in Adaptive Interfaces. *UM '99 Proceedings of the seventh international conference on User modeling*, Springer-Verlag New York, Inc., 357–370. Retrieved from http://citeseer.ist.psu.edu/viewdoc/summary?doi=10.1.1.29.8715\nhttp://citeseerx.ist.psu.edu/viewdoc/download?doi=10.1.1.29.8715&rep=rep1&type=pdf
24. Min Kyung Lee. 2013. Designing personalization in technology-based services. Retrieved January 9, 2016 from http://dl.acm.org/citation.cfm?id=2575012
25. Henry Lieberman, Hugo Liu, Push Singh, and Barbara Barry. 2004. Beating Commons Sense into Interactive Applications. *AI Magazine* 25: 63–76.

26. Xiaolei Ma, Yao-Jan Wu, Yinhai Wang, Feng Chen, and Jianfeng Liu. 2013. Mining smart card data for transit riders' travel patterns. *Transportation Research Part C: Emerging Technologies* 36, January 2016: 1–12. http://doi.org/10.1016/j.trc.2013.07.010

27. Sean M. McNee, John Riedl, and Joseph A. Konstan. 2006. Being accurate is not enough: How Accuracy Metrics have hurt Recommender Systems. *CHI '06 extended abstracts on Human factors in computing systems - CHI EA '06*, ACM Press, 1097. http://doi.org/10.1145/1125451.1125659

28. Kyle Montague, Vicki L Hanson, and Andy Cobley. 2011. Adaptive Interfaces : A Little Learning is a Dangerous Thing. In *Universal Access in Human-Computer Interaction. Design for All and eInclusion*. 391–399. http://doi.org/10.1007/978-3-642-21672-5_43

29. Issam El Naqa and Martin J. Murphy. 2015. What Is Machine Learning? In *Machine Learning in Radiation Oncology*, Issam El Naqa, Ruijiang Li and Martin J. Murphy (eds.). Springer International Publishing, Cham, 3–11. http://doi.org/10.1007/978-3-319-18305-3

30. D. Narayanan, J. Flinn, and M. Satyanarayanan. 2000. Using history to improve mobile application adaptation. *Proceedings Third IEEE Workshop on Mobile Computing Systems and Applications*, December: 31–40. http://doi.org/10.1109/MCSA.2000.895379

31. Le T Nguyen, Heng-tze Cheng, Pang Wu, Senaka Buthpitiya, and Ying Zhang. 2012. *PnLUM : System for Prediction of Next Location for Users with Mobility*.

32. Kayur Patel. 2010. Lowering the Barrier to Applying Machine Learning. *Adjunct Proceedings of the 23Nd Annual ACM Symposium on User Interface Software and Technology*: 355–358. http://doi.org/10.1145/1866218.1866222

33. Jenny Preece, Helen Sharp, and Yvonne Rogers. 2015. *Interaction Design: Beyond Human-Computer Interaction*. John Wiley & Sons.

34. Rudy Raymond, Takamitsu Sugiura, and Kota Tsubouchi. 2011. Location recommendation based on location history and spatio-temporal correlations for an on-demand bus system. *Proceedings of the 19th ACM SIGSPATIAL International Conference on Advances in Geographic Information Systems - GIS '11*, ACM Press, 377. http://doi.org/10.1145/2093973.2094027

35. Yvonne Rogers. 2006. Moving on from Weiser's Vision of Calm Computing: engaging UbiComp experiences. *Ubicomp '06*: 404–421. http://doi.org/10.1007/11853565_24

36. Brian J. Rosmaita. 2006. Accessibility first!: a new approach to web design. *Proceedings of the 37th SIGCSE technical symposium on Computer science education - SIGCSE '06*, ACM Press, 270. http://doi.org/10.1145/1121341.1121426

37. Roland T. Rust and Tuck Siong Chung. 2006. Marketing Models of Service and Relationships. *Marketing Science* 25, 6: 560–580. http://doi.org/10.1287/mksc.1050.0139

38. Emily Schwartzman. Designer's Toolkit: Prototyping Tools, Reviews and rankings to help you find the best prototyping tool for the job. Retrieved January 7, 2016 from http://www.cooper.com/prototyping-tools

39. Ahmed Seffah and Homa Javahery. 2005. *Multiple User Interfaces: Cross-Platform Applications and Context-Aware Interfaces*. John Wiley & Sons.

40. Ling Shao, Caifeng Shan, Jiebo Luo, and Minoru Etoh. 2010. Multimedia Interaction and Intelligent User Interfaces: Principles, Methods and Applications. Retrieved January 13, 2016 from http://dl.acm.org/citation.cfm?id=1869926

41. Daniel Siewiorek, Asim Smailagic, Junichi Furukawa, et al. 2003. SenSay: A Context-Aware Mobile Phone. 248. Retrieved January 15, 2016 from http://dl.acm.org/citation.cfm?id=946249.946884

42. Jenifer Tidwell. 2010. *Designing Interfaces*. "O'Reilly Media, Inc."

43. Anthony Tomasic, John Zimmerman, Aaron Steinfeld, and Yun Huang. 2014. Motivating Contribution in a Participatory Sensing System via Quid-pro-quo. *Proceedings of the 17th ACM conference on Computer supported cooperative work & social computing.*: 979–988. http://doi.org/10.1145/2531602.2531705

44. Daniel S. Weld, Corin Anderson, Pedro Domingos, et al. 2003. Automatically personalizing user interfaces. *IJCAI'03 Proceedings of the 18th international joint conference on Artificial intelligence*, Morgan Kaufmann Publishers Inc., 1613–1619. Retrieved December 26, 2015 from http://dl.acm.org/citation.cfm?id=1630659.1630944

45. John Zimmerman, Anthony Tomasic, Isaac Simmons, et al. 2007. Vio: a mixed-initiative approach to learning and automating procedural update tasks. *Proceedings of the SIGCHI conference on Human factors in computing systems - CHI '07*, ACM Press, 1445. http://doi.org/10.1145/1240624.1240843

Surveying Expert-Level Gesture Use and Adoption on Multi-Touch Tablets

Jeff Avery
University of Waterloo
Waterloo, Canada
j2avery@uwaterloo.ca

Edward Lank
University of Waterloo
Waterloo, Canada
lank@uwaterloo.ca

ABSTRACT
Multi-touch interaction on mobile devices typically consists of taps and swipes - simple gestures that don't exploit the full range of technical and human capabilities. Some devices offer more sophisticated, expert-level gestures, but these haven't yet been widely adopted. To determine what factors might be preventing widespread adoption of expert-level gestures, we examine the use of multi-tasking features on the iPad as representative of widely available, but optional, expert-level gestures. We survey a group of 106 iPad users about their device habits, awareness of expert-level gestures, and how they are used in everyday tasks. We determine that users have a fairly high awareness of expert-level gestures, and willingness to perform them, but often find them difficult to discover and challenging to learn. We conclude with design implications for future research.

Author Keywords
multi-touch; tablet; expert-level gestures; online survey.

ACM Classification Keywords
H.5.2. User interfaces; interaction styles.

INTRODUCTION
Users of modern multi-touch devices such as smartphones and tablets have a relatively high level of skill in using multi-touch gestures to interact with them [14], but the multi-touch gesture sets used are typically restricted to a small subset of one and two-finger gestures, e.g. tap, double tap, drag/flick and pinch/spread (Figure 1). However, modern multi-touch smartphones and tablets are capable of accepting at least ten simultaneous points of contact [17,18], and human kinesthetic models suggest that humans are capable of richer and more expressive forms of interaction that utilize multiple fingers [4]. This suggests a gap between the technical capabilities of multi-touch devices, the kinesthetic abilities of end-users, and the gesture sets that have been implemented for these devices.

DIS 2016, June 04 - 08, 2016, Brisbane, QLD, Australia

ACM 978-1-4503-4031-1/16/06...$15.00
DOI: http://dx.doi.org/10.1145/2901790.2901895

There have been attempts to introduce more sophisticated interactions through the use of expert-level gestures: Apple provides trackpad-swipe gestures on their MacBook Pro [17,18], Microsoft has implemented bezel-swipes on the Surface Pro [19], and numerous research projects have attempted to improve multi-touch functionality by adding targeted expert-level gestures [3,7,12]. These include systems such as BiTouch [15], Cyclostar [7] and ZoomPointing [1,11]. The Apple iPad is an example of a commercially successful multi-touch input device with an limited set of extended multitasking gestures [20]. We call these expert-level gestures *enhanced gesture sets*, and define them as gestures not included in common gesture sets (such as Figure 1).

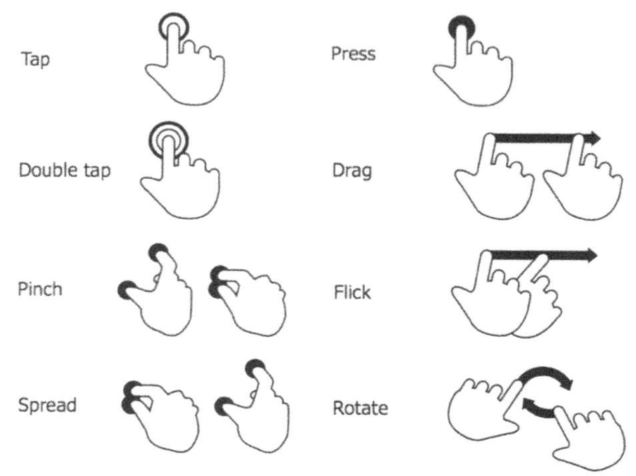

Figure 1: Typical Gesture Set

While expert-level gestures may be initially challenging to recall and perform, with appropriate time and training, user performance improves significantly [6]. Despite the benefits and the availability of enhanced gesture sets, in observations of user interaction on multi-touch platforms [8,14] it appears that these gestures are used infrequently.

In this paper, we examine the use of three enhanced, direct multi-touch gestures on an iPad, which we consider a realization of an enhanced gesture set. To examine real-world usage, we designed and ran an anonymous survey on SurveyMonkey, where we recruited experienced iPad users and asked them questions about their device usage. First, we attempted to determine if end-users were already aware of the existence of these gesture sets. Second, we explored how frequently they used these advanced gestures. Finally, we explored user perceptions of the enhanced gesture set, and willingness to adopt them post-survey.

Overall, our goal is to validate the perception of slow adoption (to verify whether users really are slow to adopt such gestures) and, if so, to determine some of the causes for this slow adoption rate. For example, are new awareness mechanisms needed? Are gestures too complicated to learn or use? Do users perceive the current set of gestures as adequate and see no need for enhanced gesture sets? This paper summarizes the survey results and the design implications for multi-touch gesture sets.

SURVEY DESIGN

A number of authors have attempted to describe the population of iPad users, but have typically focused more narrowly on characterizing application use [2,16]. We are not aware of any attempts to determine how users interact with their iPads; this lack of data motivated our survey.

We chose an online survey as a data collection method for the same reasons proposed by Kjeldskov et al. [5]: external validity. Our goal is to collect responses related to software features used "in-the-wild" during day-to-day interactions, which is difficult to accomplish in a controlled lab environment. A similar approach was taken by Snowdon et al. [13] when assessing a mobile map navigation technique.

In our survey, we focus on three specific expert-level direct-touch gestures on the iPad: Multitasking, App-Switching and Pinch-to-Home. Multitasking on the iPad allows a user to display a list of all running applications, and either switch to that application or close it. It can be activated by either double-pressing the home button on the iPad, or via an expert-level gesture, swiping-up with four fingers. Pinch-to-Home exits the currently running application and returns the user to their home screen. This can be accomplished by single-pressing the home button, or performing a four-finger clutch gesture. Finally, App-switching allows a user to switch to the next or previous running application. This is activated by swiping left or right with four fingers, for the previous or next running applications. This feature can only be activated with these gestures.

The advantage of focusing on iPad gestures is consistency in the implementation: Apple has made these gestures available in the same form, across a large number of devices. These gestures also provide *optional* functionality; users that have adopted these gestures had to deliberately seek out and learn how to use them.

Apparatus and Participants

Our survey was created and hosted on SurveyMonkey [21]. Data was collected in two sessions: Dec 1 2015, 3:13 to 4:45 PM EST, and Jan 13, 2016, 11:00 PM to Jan 14, 2016 10:31 AM. Data collection was spaced across two different time periods, to get a broad spectrum of respondents who may be using the devices in different contexts. A target number of participants was specified in each case, and SurveyMonkey automatically closed the survey once the target was reached for a given period. SurveyMonkey advertised the study ("task"), handled recruiting and managing participants, and supplied anonymized results after data collection was complete. We recruited 123 participants; 17 participants stated that they "did not own an iPad" and their responses were discarded. Our remaining 106 participants (55F, 35M, 16 unreported), had a mean age of 43.1 years (SD 15.4).

Survey Design

Our survey design was guided by Muller et al. [9,10]. Our survey contained 35 questions across 5 sections (Figure 2). After answering the first question about device usage, participants were allowed to skip any of the remaining questions that they did not wish to answer.

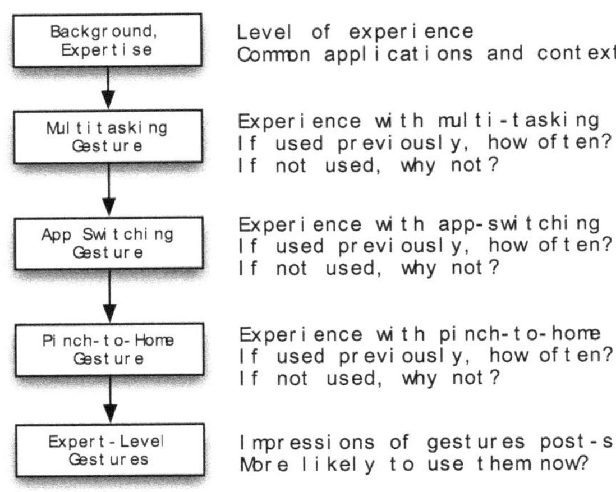

Figure 2: Survey Design

Section one asked demographic questions and general questions about iPad usage. The second through fourth sections of the survey asked questions about the three specific expert-level gestures of interest noted earlier: Multitasking, App-Switching and Pinch-to-Home. For each expert-level gesture, we asked about a participant's familiarity with that gesture, and branched based on their response: if they had used a gesture previously, we asked about frequency of use, preference compared to non-gestural activation method, and general satisfaction; if they were unfamiliar with a gesture, we explained how to use it, asked them to attempt it on their iPad, and then polled them on ease-of-use and and impressions. This branching is a technique suggested by Muller [9,10]; it is well-suited to online surveys, and allows us to vary questions based on level of expertise. Finally, the last section of the survey asked about revised opinions of expert-level gestures.

In our analysis, we report both raw scores (e.g. mean Likert scores), and significant results from Pearson's Chi-squared "goodness of fit" tests performed against various measures. Unanswered questions are excluded from the results.

RESULTS

Introduction

From the first section of the survey, we were able build a profile of an average iPad user. 72.6% of respondents use full-size iPads with a 9.7" display (77/106), 22.6%, use an iPad Mini with a 7.9" display (24/106), and 4.7%, use an iPad Pro with a 12.9" screen (5/106). 59.4% of participants reported devices from 2013 or later (63/106). All of the iPads reported support the expert-level gestures of interest to us in our survey.

Our users are relatively experienced: 60.8% have owned an iPad for at least 2-3 years (62/102), while 15.7% have owned it for a "longer period" (16/102). Daily usage was high: 72.6% use it for at least 30 minutes (77/106), and 41.5% use it for more than 60 minutes each day (44/106). As expected, most users use their iPads for media consumption and social media (Figure 3). Although there was no correlation between age and experience-level (X^2=17.1, NS), there were differences in usage patterns: for instance, younger participants watched more videos (X^2=15.9, p<0.01), while participants age 30-44 used social media features the least (X^2=15.8, p<0.01).

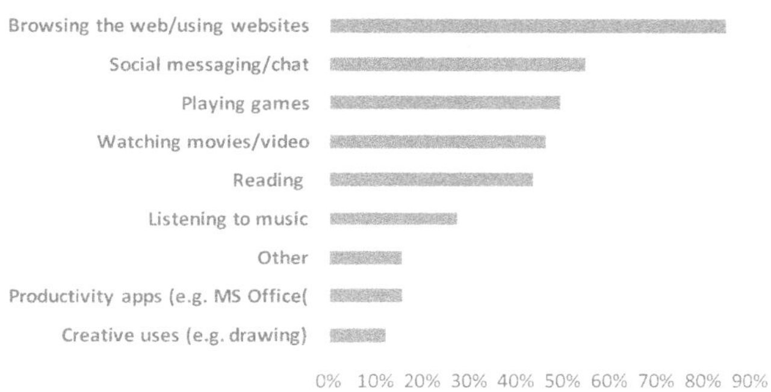

Figure 3: Common applications reported

We asked users about their satisfaction levels with the device on a 5-point Likert scale: 61.3% "strongly liked" their device (65/106), 29.2% "liked" it (31/106), and 9.4% were neutral (10/106). When asked what Apple could change to "make it a better device", common answers were to make the device cheaper (11/83), more durable (7/83) or improve connectivity (6/83). A number of respondents suggested minor software changes (11/83). The largest category were satisfied with current features (19/83). There was no correlation between age and satisfaction (X^2=8.1, NS) or gender and satisfaction (X^2=2.9, NS).

Prior Knowledge

Multitasking is the ability to bring up a list of running applications, either by double-pressing the home button or swiping-up with four fingers. Participants were asked about their prior experience with the multi-tasking gesture: 6.7% had used only swipe-up (7/104), 32.7% had used the home button (34/104) and 34.6% had used both activation mechanisms (36/104). 10.6% were aware of the swipe-up gesture but hadn't used it previously (11/104), and 15.4% had never heard of the feature (16/104). There was a positive correlation between iPad and multitasking experience (X^2=51.8, p<0.01), suggesting that experienced users are more likely to use this gesture.

App switching is the ability to quickly switch between running applications, without needing to activate multitasking or return to the home screen. This feature can only be activated as an expert gesture, by performing a three-finger swipe left or right from within a running application. 52.0% of participants had used this feature previously (51/98). 24.5% had heard of the feature but never used it (24/98), and 23.5% had never heard of it (23/98). There was no correlation between overall iPad and app-switching experience (X^2=17.4, NS).

Pinch-to-Home is the ability to exit and application and return to the home screen of the iPad. This can be accomplished by single-pressing the home button, or performing a four-finger clutching motion while an application is running. 43.0% of participants had used this feature (40/93), 25.8% had heard of it but never used it (24/93), and 31.2% were previously unaware of the gesture (29/93). There was no correlation between overall iPad and app-switching experience (X^2=17.1, NS).

Usage

Respondents who had used swipe-up to multitask performed the gesture infrequently: 49.4% rarely used it (38/77), 29.9% occasionally used it (23/77), and only 15.1% used it frequently (16/106). When given the choice, 76.6% preferred to use the home button to activate multitasking (59/77), 11.7% used the swipe-up gesture (9/77), and 11.7% used both mechanisms (9/77). Open-ended comments suggested that the swipe-up was sometimes "difficult to activate" compared to the home button (16/41). The physical button, for many participants, was easier to activate (14/41) and more familiar (12/41). Participants who did not use multitasking appear to have been mostly unaware of the feature: 65.4% didn't know it existed (17/26) and only 23.1% claimed that they don't need this functionality (6/26).

Participants who reported using app-switching, tended to use it infrequently: 39.2% used it rarely (20/51), 41.2% used it occasionally (21/51), and only 19.6% used it frequently (10/51). Participants who didn't use it appear to have been unaware of the gesture: 62.2% reported that they didn't know that it existed (28/45), 15.6% claim that they don't need this functionality (7/45), and 5.9% found it difficult to use (3/51).

Participants who used pinch-to-home also used it infrequently: 35.0% used it rarely (14/40), 45.0% used it occasionally (18/40) and 20.0% used it frequently (8/40). However, most respondents prefer the home button: 70.0% used the home button exclusively (28/40), 20.0% used both methods (8/40), and only 10.0% (4/40) used the pinch-gesture exclusively. Reasons for this preference included familiarity (9/20), ease-of-use and convenience (8/20).

Impressions

Multitasking was viewed favorably, with 82.5% neutral or higher (31/97 "neutral", 39/97 "like", 10/97 "strong-like"). It was generally considered easy to use, with 84.5% neutral or higher (31/97 "neutral", 39/97 "easy", 12/97 "very easy"). App-switching was also viewed favorably, with 82.0% rating it neutral or higher (26/89 "neutral", 35/89 "like", 12/89 "strong like"). It was generally reported as easy to use, with 85.4% rating it neutral or higher (26/89 "neutral", 34/89 "easy", 16/89 "very easy"). Pinch-to-Home was viewed very favorably: 92.0% of participants rated it neutral or higher (39/88 "neutral", 35/88 "like", 7/88 "strong like"), and 87.5% found it easy to use (27/88 "neutral", 38/88 "easy" and 12/88 "very easy"). Across each of these gestures, there was a positive correlation between experience and user satisfaction with that specific gesture (multitasking X^2=41.1, $p<0.05$; app-switching X^2=64.2, $p<0.01$; pinch-to-home X^2=102.0, $p<0.01$).

Post-survey impressions of expert-level gestures were very favorable: 94.5% were neutral or higher (29/91 "neutral", 42/91 "like", 15/91 "strong like). This is higher than any single gesture score, suggesting that overall impressions improved as the survey progressed. Open-ended feedback was generally favorable, with many respondents indicating that the gestures required no further changes (14/36 for multitasking, 15/28 for app-switching and 13/31 for pinch-to-home). Complaints were that the gestures were complex and difficult to learn for some (8/41 overall), or difficult to discover (2/36 for multitasking, 6/28 for app-switching). As one respondent stated, "how do you find out about any of these? you have to accidentally run into them or spend hours googling ipad shortcuts" (sic).

Adoption

With multitasking gestures, 15.2% claimed that they are more likely to use them in the future (15/99), with 31.3% (31/99) suggesting that they would be interested to "try it and see". There was a significant positive correlation between prior multitasking experience and satisfaction (X^2=41.1, $p<0.05$), and between satisfaction with the gesture and a willingness to continue using the gesture post-survey (X^2=96.4, $p<0.01$).

With app-switching gestures, 12.1% (11/91) claimed that they were more likely to use swipe-left and right to app-switch following this survey; 36.3% (33/91) claimed that they would be interested to "try it". There was a significant positive correlation between prior app-switching experience and satisfaction (X^2=64.2, $p<0.01$), and between satisfaction and a willingness to continue using them post-survey (X^2=102.4, $p<0.01$).

With pinch-to-home gestures, 19.3% (17/88) of participants suggested that they were more likely to use pinch-to-home after being made aware of it. 34.1% (30/88) suggested that they might "try it and see". There was also a significant positive correlation between pinch-to-home experience and satisfaction (X^2=102.0, $p<0.01$), and between satisfaction and a willingness to continue using this gesture post-survey (X^2=120.4, $p<0.01$). When asked afterwards if the survey would impact use of these gestures in the future, 18.6% (17/91) of participants reported that they expected to use them more, and 35.1% (32/91) thought that the survey "might" have some impact.

DISCUSSION

Our respondents are experienced iPad users, using their devices frequently for media consumption, playing games and interacting on social media. This aligns with previous studies of consumer behavior [16]. However, despite this casual-use profile, our participants reported occasional-to-frequent use of expert-level gestures: 45.0% used swipe-up for multitasking, 60.8% used swipe-left/right for application switching and 65.0% used the pinch-to-home gesture. Familiarity with gestures was high, with awareness of 51.9% for swipe-up, 76.5% for swipe left/right and 68.8% for pinch-to-home. This is surprising, given that these features are not well-advertised.

After exposure during the survey, user impressions of these gestures were relatively high, and actually improved to 94.5% by the end of the survey (novice participants were asked to attempt them, which may have influenced this result). User satisfaction was directly correlated with experience level, suggesting that these gestures may require effort to master, and that users need time to effectively learn to use these gestures. Open feedback suggests that participants initially found these gestures difficult to discover, but that they worked well after some practice.

Significantly, 53.7% of respondents thought that increased awareness provided through this survey might increase their likelihood of using these gestures, suggesting that lack of awareness was an obstacle preventing adoption. These results suggest we need clear awareness mechanisms to make novices aware of these gestures, understand how they work and what options they might provide. Over time, these awareness mechanisms become less valuable, and may be hidden or curtailed as users gain proficiency.

CONCLUSIONS

Expert-level gestures afford an opportunity to expand the capabilities of multi-touch devices towards more complex tasks, but their adoption is hampered by discoverability issues, particularly for novice users. Future work should consider the effectiveness of different awareness mechanisms in helping novice users to learn to effectively utilize advanced gestures.

ACKNOWLEDGEMENTS

This paper is based on work supported by the Natural Science and Engineering Research Council of Canada (NSERC) and through a Google Faculty Fellowship.

REFERENCES

1. Pär-Anders Albinsson and Shumin Zhai. 2003. High precision touch screen interaction. CHI '03: Proceedings of the SIGCHI Conference on Human Factors in Computer Systems, 105-112.
2. Elaine B Coleman, Randy Hellman, Desiree Davis, Kari Cafouros, and Aric Ackerman. 2010. The iPad Effect. *Alert!*
3. Emilien Ghomi, Stephane Huot, Olivier Bau, Michel Beaudouin-Lafon, and Wendy E Mackay. 2013. Arpège: learning multitouch chord gestures vocabularies. CHI '13: Proceedings of the SIGCHI Conference on Human Factors in Computer Systems, 209-218.
4. Ralph Hill, Peter Rowley, William Buxton, Ralph Hill, and Peter Rowley. 1985. Issues and techniques in touch-sensitive tablet input. ACM SIGGRAPH Computer Graphics 19, 3: 215–224.
5. Jesper Kjeldskov and Jeni Paay. 2012. A longitudinal review of Mobile HCI research methods. MobileHCI '12: Proceedings of the ACM Conference on Human-Computer Interaction with Mobile Devices and Services, 69-78.
6. G Julian Lepinski, Tovi Grossman, and George Fitzmaurice. 2010. The design and evaluation of multitouch marking menus. CHI '10: Proceedings of the SIGCHI Conference on Human Factors in Computer Systems, 2233-2242.
7. Sylvain Malacria, Eric Lecolinet, and Yves Guiard. 2010. Clutch-free panning and integrated pan-zoom control on touch-sensitive surfaces: the cyclostar approach. CHI '10: Proceedings of the SIGCHI Conference on Human Factors in Computer Systems, 2615-2624.
8. M.R. Morris, J.O. Wobbrock, and A.D. Wilson. 2010. Understanding users' preferences for surface gestures. *Proceedings of Graphics Interface 2010*: 261–268.
9. Hendrik Muller, Aaron Sedley, and Elizabeth Ferrall-Nunge. 2014. Survey Research in HCI. In Ways of Knowing in HCI, Judith S Olson and W A Kellogg (eds.). Springer, New York, 575-666.
10. Hendrik Müller and Aaron Sedley. 2015. Designing Surveys for HCI Research. CHI '15 Extended Abstracts, 2485–2486.
11. M. Negulescu, J Ruiz, and E Lank. 2011. ZoomPointing revisited: supporting mixed-resolution gesturing on interactive surfaces. ITS '11: Proceedings of the ACM International Conference on Interactive Tabletops and Surfaces: 150–153.
12. Alex Olwal, Steven Feiner, and Susanna Heyman. 2008. Rubbing and tapping for precise and rapid selection on touch-screen displays. CHI '08: Proceedings of the SIGCHI Conference on Human Factors in Computer Systems, 295-304.
13. Caroline Snowdon and Christian Kray. 2009. *Exploring the use of landmarks for mobile navigation support in natural environments*. ACM, New York, New York, USA. http://doi.org/10.1145/1613858.1613875
14. Z Tuncer, M Selim, M Liwicki, G Kormann, and S Allee. Evaluation of Multi-Touch Gestures. *gil-net.de*.
15. J. Wagner, S. Huot, and W.E. Mackay. 2012. BiTouch and BiPad: Designing Bimanual Interaction for Hand-held Tablets. CHI '12: Proceedings of the SIGCHI Conference on Human Factors in Computer Systems, 2317-2326.
16. J Yarow. 2012. *How people actually use the iPad: Results from our exclusive survey*. Business Insider. Retrieved Dec 12, 2015 from http://www.businessinsider.com/ipad-usage-survey-results-2012-7
17. iOS Developer Library. *developer.apple.com*. Retrieved December 12, 2015 from https://developer.apple.com/library/ios/navigation/
18. Android Developer Library. *developer.android.com*. Retrieved December 12, 2015 from http://developer.android.com/guide/index.html
19. Use touchscreen gestures on Microsoft Surface | Zoom, scroll, tap, copy, paste. *microsoft.com*. Retrieved December 14, 2015 from https://www.microsoft.com/surface/en-ca/support/touch-mouse-and-search/using-touch-gestures-tap-swipe-and-beyond?os=windows-8.1-update-1
20. Adopting Multitasking Enhancements on iPad: Getting Oriented. *developer.apple.com*. Retrieved December 12, 2015 from https://developer.apple.com/library/ios/documentation/WindowsViews/Conceptual/AdoptingMultitaskingOniPad/
21. SurveyMonkey: Free online survey software & questionnaire tool. *surveymonkey.com*. Retrieved December 12, 2015 from https://www.surveymonkey.com/

Design Interactions in ʔeləw̓kʷ — Belongings

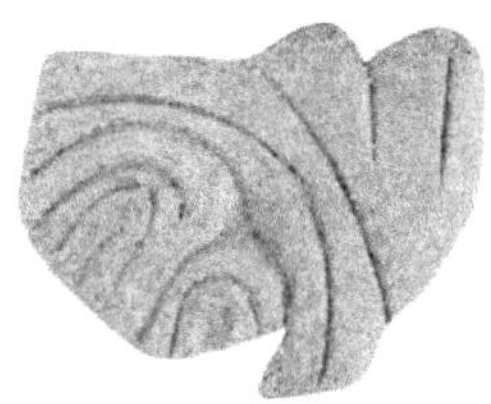

ʔəy̓ə́y̓mət — beautiful belongings

Reese Muntean
Simon Fraser University
250-13450 102nd Avenue
Surrey, BC V3T 0A3 Canada
rmuntean@sfu.ca

Kate Hennessy
Simon Fraser University
250-13450 102nd Avenue
Surrey, BC V3T 0A3 Canada
hennessy_kate@sfu.ca

Alissa Antle
Simon Fraser University
250-13450 102nd Avenue
Surrey, BC V3T 0A3 Canada
aantle@sfu.ca

Brendan Matkin
Simon Fraser University
250-13450 102nd Avenue
Surrey, BC V3T 0A3 Canada
bmatkin@sfu.ca

Susan Rowley
University of British Columbia
6393 NW Marine Drive
Vancouver, BC, V6T 1Z2 Canada
sdmrowley@gmail.com

Jordan Wilson
University of British Columbia
6393 NW Marine Drive
Vancouver, BC, V6T 1Z2 Canada
jordanphwilson@gmail.com

DIS 2016, June 04 - 08, 2016, Brisbane, QLD, Australia

ACM 978-1-4503-4031-1/16/06 $15.00
DOI: http://dx.doi.org/10.1145/2901790.2901912

Abstract

Our pictorial visually describes ʔeləw̓kʷ — Belongings, an interactive tangible tabletop installed in the Museum of Anthropology at the University of British Columbia. The tabletop was designed to communicate the continuity of Musqueam culture, convey the complexity of belongings that were excavated from Musqueam's ancient village site, and reconnect those belongings to traditional practices and oral histories through tangible interactions with the table—all while highlighting that cultural knowledge should be treated with respect. In this pictorial, we will show how the design process was shared among researchers, curators, and the exhibit Advisory Committee and highlight some of the key design decisions that came out of this collaboration.

Authors Keywords

Tangible interaction; intangible cultural heritage; digital heritage; Museum of Anthropology; Musqueam Indian Band; c̓əsnaʔəm.

ACM Classification Keywords

H.5.2. Information interfaces and presentation (e.g., HCI): User Interfaces, Evaluation/Methodology.

Introduction

ʔeləw̓k̓ʷ — Belongings is an interactive tangible table at the Museum of Anthropology (MOA) at the University of British Columbia in Vancouver, Canada and was developed for the *c̓əsnaʔəm, the city before the city* exhibition. The exhibition is a partnership among the Musqueam Indian Band, the Museum of Vancouver, and MOA along with the University of Waterloo. In three unique but related exhibitions, the institutions introduce visitors to c̓əsnaʔəm, an ancient Musqueam village and cemetery near the Fraser River on which part of modern day Vancouver was built.

Using replicas of ancient belongings excavated from c̓əsnaʔəm and everyday objects in contemporary Musqueam lives, the table shares stories of the Musqueam community's past and how their culture and traditional knowledge continue today. In this pictorial, we will show how the design process was shared among researchers, curators, and the exhibit Advisory Committee and highlight some of the key design decisions that came out of this collaboration.

The Fraser River, as seen from the Musqueam Cultural Education and Resource Centre

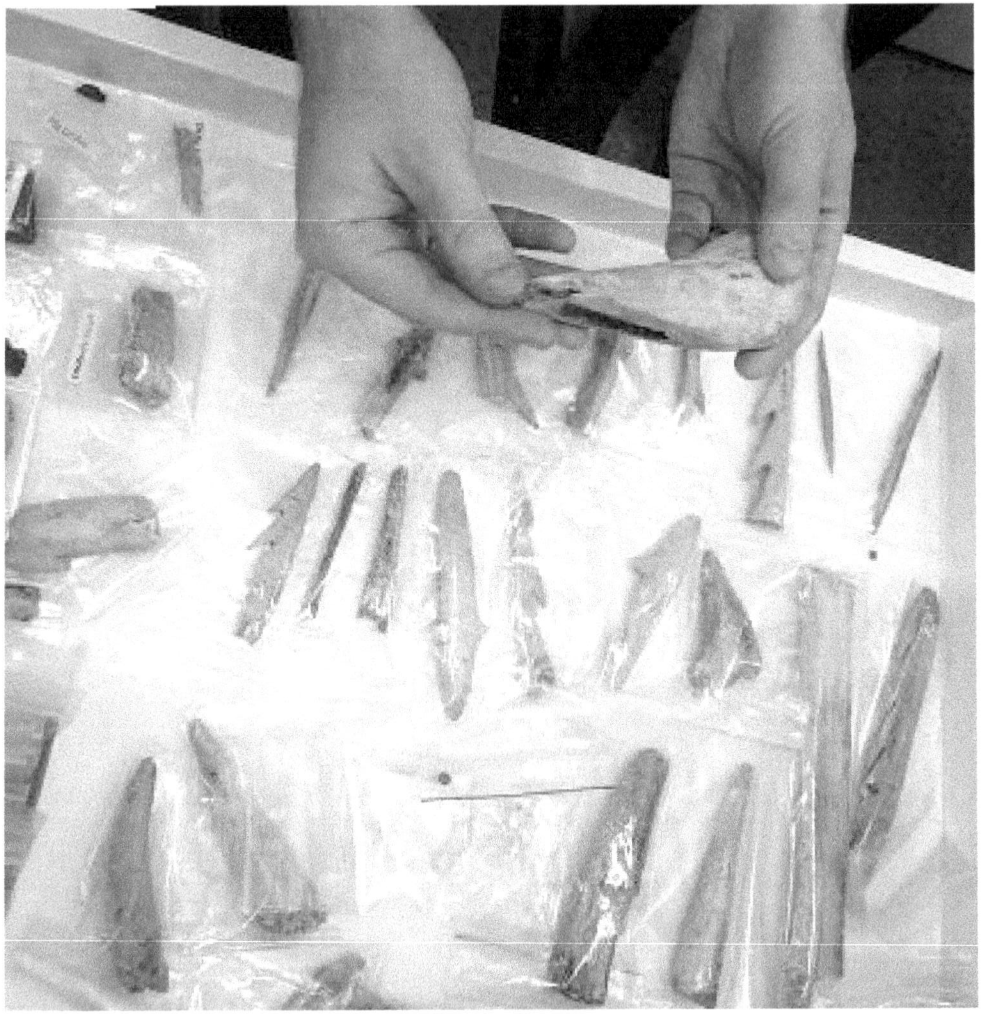

Speaking of Belongings

Archaeologists generally refer to the material culture they excavate as "artifacts". Our Musqueam collaborators understand these items to have been created by, and to continue to belong to, their ancestors. For this reason we refer to them as ʔeləw̓k̓ʷ, a hən̓q̓əmin̓əm̓ term meaning belongings. By reframing Musqueam's material culture using this term, we emphasize the continuity of intangible forms of knowledge that are intrinsically connected to belongings.

Relationships and Networking

Today, museums are building new relationships with contemporary Indigenous peoples, This includes repatriating belongings and ancestral remains that were dispersed in collections around the world during a period following the implementation of the Indian Act (1884) in which the Indigenous populations were at their lowest ebb [7]. Museums are also struggling to find ways to represent intangible cultural heritage in the museum space [4]. The development of the ʔeləw̓k̓ʷ — Belongings tabletop exhibit has roots in a paradigm shift in North American museology focused on building new relationships with First Peoples [1] and addressing these challenges of showcasing and safeguarding intangible cultural heritage [11].

One of the reasons we were even able to produce this work is the continuing relationship between the Musqueam Indian Band and MOA. Particularly successful in laying the groundwork for ʔeləw̓k̓ʷ — Belongings was the collaborative effort among Musqueam, the Stó:lō Nation, the U'mista Cultural Society, and MOA to create the online portal known as the Reciprocal Research Network (RRN), which makes dispersed collections of ancient belongings accessible digitally to communities and researchers [8, 9]. The thumbnail photos below show some of the belongings excavated from c̓əsnaʔəm that are in the Laboratory of Archaeology, housed at MOA, accessed through the RRN during the ʔeləw̓k̓ʷ — Belongings design process, and incorporated into the final tabletop installation.

The ʔeləw̓kʷ — Belongings team looks through ancient belongings that are part of the Laboratory of Archaeology at MOA.

Development Process and Goals

Susan Rowley, Jordan Wilson, and Lisa Uyeda at MOA worked with Kate Hennessy, Alissa Antle, Rachael Eckersley, Perry Tan, Brendan Matkin, and Reese Muntean at Simon Fraser University's School of Interactive Arts and Technology (SIAT) to develop the tabletop application. With a tight deadline and only five months to complete the project, we immediately scheduled weekly two-hour in person meetings. The meetings were initially used for brainstorming, activity design, and presenting ideas and work. Outside of these meetings Rowley and Wilson would gather and organize the content for the table (e.g. historical images, quotes from Musqueam community, information about fishing) and check in with the elders on the Advisory Committee regarding our progress. SIAT students would hold additional meetings during the week to design the visuals, graphics, and interactions, as well as write the code. During the first meeting, we outlined a number of goals for the tabletop. In this pictorial we will touch on some of the decisions we made to achieve our goals of helping visitors understand the complex stories connected to belongings and communicating Musqueam values and cultural knowledge.

Inspiration

Once we had the basic idea for a tangible tabletop and knowing that we had certain goals in mind to showcase the stories of belongings and also highlight the continuity of Musqueam culture, we needed an activity and focus to bring this all together. We landed upon salmon fishing. Many of the ancient belongings from c̓əsnaʔəm were related to fishing, an activity that is still an important part of life today. We were inspired by the fish cutting table of Sonny Williams of the Scowlitz First Nation – shown here – which was photographed as part of a project that Hennessy and Muntean were working on up the Fraser River with the Stó:lō Nation.

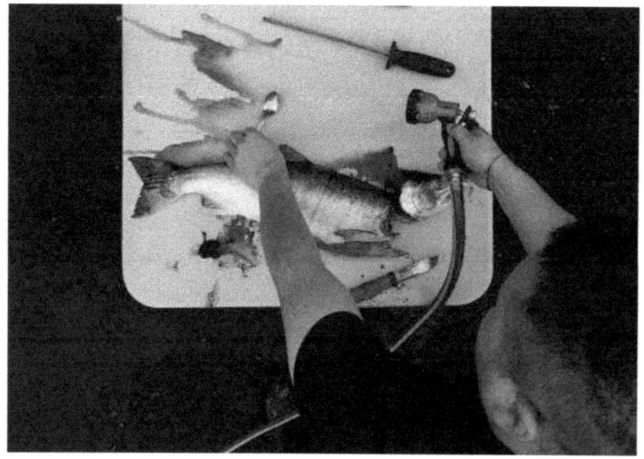

Processing Fish

We saw a wonderful opportunity to show the continuity of Musqueam's own fishing culture and values and how these traditions continue today. Wilson and Muntean teamed up with the Musqueam Fisheries Commission to photograph the process of cutting and cleaning salmon outside of the community smokehouse for the main image on the digital table.

* Photo ©Jordan Wilson

Final Fish-Cutting Image

Here is the image that appears on the ʔeləw̓k̓ʷ — Belongings table. Using a top-down view, visitors are able to place themselves in the scene cutting fish, surrounded by related tools and items, making the image one of the present day.

Replicating Belongings

As we came up with the concept of the interactive salmon cutting table, we also needed to select physical belongings that would interact with the table, incorporating ideas from tangible computing as well as museological discourse around objects themselves embodying knowledge. Indeed, we agreed that "a necessary condition for the generation of knowledge is engagement with objects" [10].

Rowley and Wilson selected the six ancient belongings that best tell the stories of Musqueam practices and continuity of culture. The Musqueam Indian Band gave permission for molds to be made of the original belongings. Replicas of belongings provided the opportunity for museum visitors to spend time with Musqueam belongings from c̓əsnaʔəm and to interact with them and handle them in a way that the exhibition of real belongings would not allow.

One of our key design decisions was to include both ancient and modern belongings as a way to show how common the ancient belongings were in day to day life and to get visitors thinking about their importance. Six modern belongings were also selected. The juxtaposition of the ancient and contemporary belongings were effective in that people would explore unfamiliar belongings while the modern belongings would encourage them to question how how they are all relevant to Musqueam culture [5, 6].

Our process of recreating belongings: exploring our options, selecting ancient belongings, making molds, and sealing and painting the final replicas.

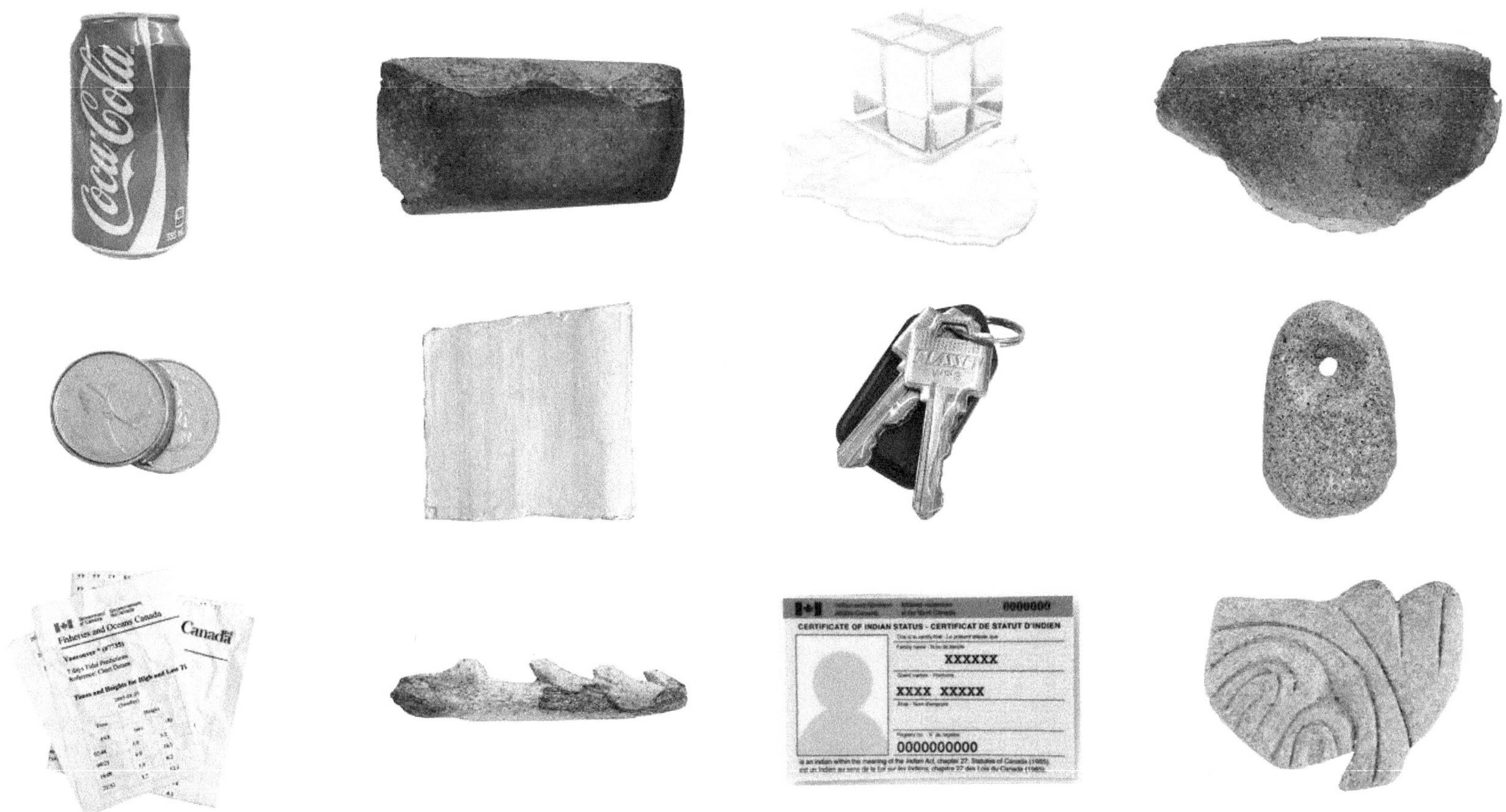

Interactions with Belongings

The final set of belongings includes six ancient (adz, slate blade, cedar bark, net weight, decorated piece, and harpoon) and six contemporary belongings (Coke can, ice cube, quarters, keys, status card, and tide chart). The physical interactions with these belongings and the digital tabletop helped visitors connect the histories of the belongings to one another as well as to present-day issues, showing just how complex these stories can be. The belongings serve as entry points and inputs for interacting with the tangible table. These belongings, along with activator rings, enable different sets of interactions to reveal layers of multi-modal information [2], evoking cultural forms [3] and revealing complex stories about each belonging's place in Musqueam life and how the related practices have shifted and were sustained over time.

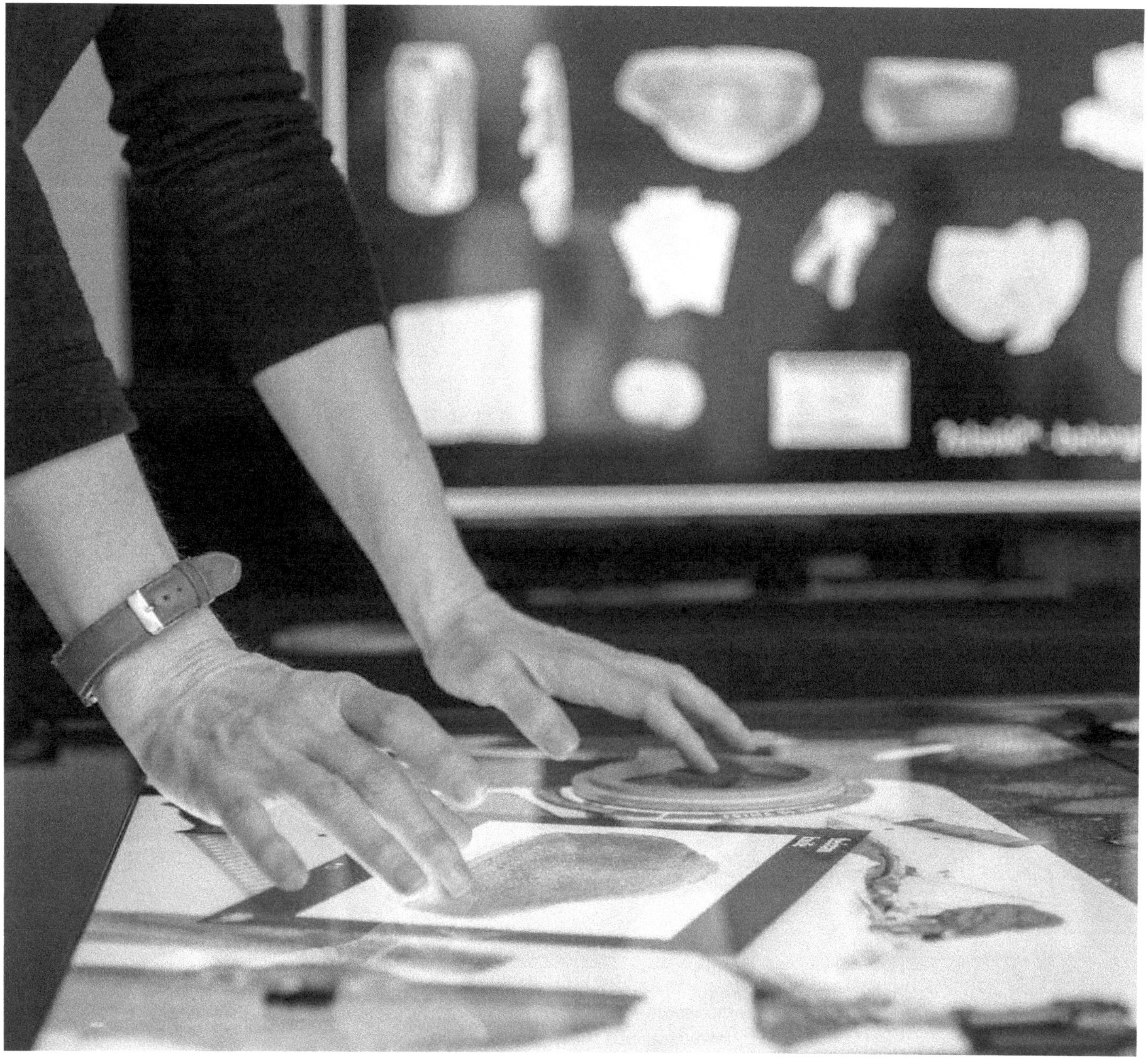

The ʔeləw̓kʷ — Belongings system comprises a Samsung SUR40 table, three monitors, twelve replicas, and two activator rings. One monitor plays a series of photographs detailing the process of cutting and cleaning a fish, and the remaining monitors are connected to each of the ring tools.

The System of Belongings

To reconnect the day-to-day cultural practices to belongings both ancient and modern, we focused on stem tə ʔi ? (What is this?), tatəl̓ət (Understanding it), snəw̓eyəɬ (Teachings since childhood), and cyəθəs (Having stories). These are the four categories etched into the activator rings and that appear in the digital ring interface. Using these concepts, we led visitors through a series of interactions to learn about belongings' form and function (What is this?), connect belongings to the fish-cutting table image (Understanding it), match ancient belongings with modern personal items (Teachings), and ultimately unlock stories from Musqueam community members about the process of learning and their traditional culture (Having stories). An example of two of these belongings and their connections are detailed in a flowchart on the following page.

What Is This

When you first place a belonging in one of the rings on the table, basic information appears on the table. Here, text and images appear explaining that the belonging is a Coke can or that it is a jadeite adz used for carving.

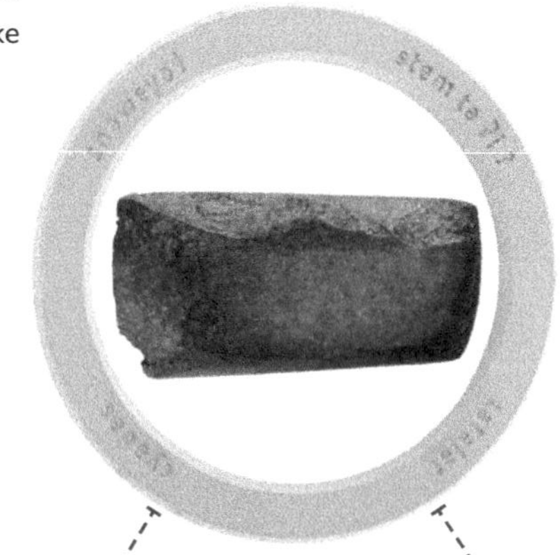

Teachings

Each ancient belonging pairs to a modern belonging, and when visitors enter the teachings category they will be prompted to make that connection. The Coke can and adz pair in this way to tell the story of historic and contemporary trade routes.

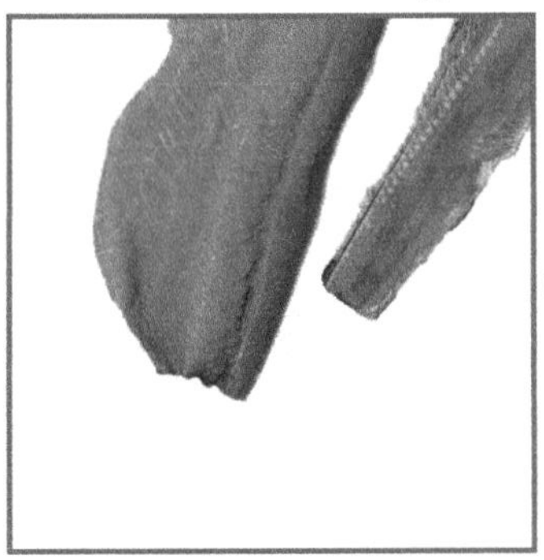

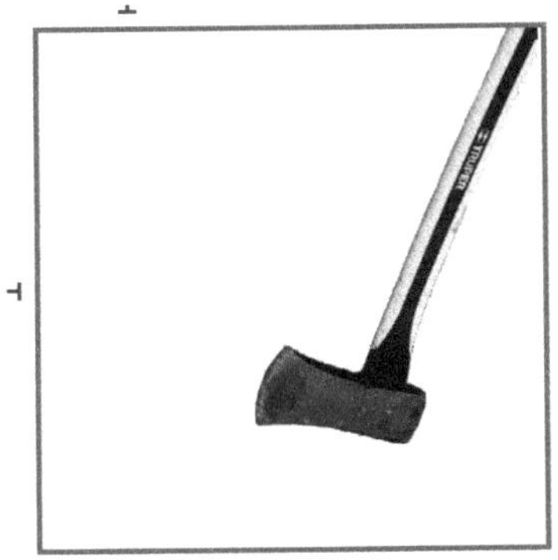

Understanding It

In the Understanding It category, visitors match a belonging to its corresponding area on the fish cutting table. The Coke can matches to the salmon fillets to access information about the changes in traditional diet brought about by issues including access, overfishing, and pollution.

Understanding It

When visitors connect the adz to the axe, its modern counterpart, they learn about how the adz was used, the long history of carving, and the importance in the community. Community members share their grandparents' stories of building boats, and images and text show the structure of the long houses.

Having Stories

Once a visitor explores the first three categories of information, the monitor associated with the ring plays a video of a community member sharing stories about learning cultural practices and their own lived experiences.

Conclusion

The flowchart on the previous page aims to clarify how belongings connect to one another, to the underlying fish cutting image, and to the community voices that reveal the intangible heritage associated with them. These connections and interactions are made with each of the twelve belongings. It is a complex web of relationships, but this was also what we wanted to convey to visitors. In taking the time to interact with the tabletop and navigate these complexities, we are sharing with visitors the ideas of earning knowledge and that cultural knowledge should be treated with respect.

These belongings – the tangible interface – respond to the challenge of representing the significance of both archeological and everyday belongings in a museum space. The choice of ancient and modern belongings for the tangible interface further highlights cultural continuity and how ancient belongings connect to contemporary Musqueam life. While engaging with the belongings, visitors are engaging with Musqueam cultural knowledge, but also issues of access, preservation, and continuity of culture that are central to discussions of digital heritage.

* Photo ©Jordan Wilson

References

1. Council of Canadian Academies. (2015). Leading in the Digital World: Opportunities for Canada's Memory Institutions (Assessment). Ottawa, Canada: Council of Canadian Academies.

2. Giaccardi, E., & Palen, L. 2008. The Social Production of Heritage through Cross-media Interaction: Making Place for Place-making. International Journal of Heritage Studies, 14(3), 281–297. http://doi.org/10.1080/13527250801953827

3. Horn, M. S. 2013. The Role of Cultural Forms in Tangible Interaction Design. In Proceedings of the 7th International Conference on Tangible, Embedded and Embodied Interaction (pp. 117–124). New York, NY, USA: ACM. http://doi.org/10.1145/2460625.2460643

4. Kurin, R. (2004). Museums and intangible heritage: Culture dead or alive? ICOM News, 57(4), 7–9.

5. Muntean, R., Hennessy, K., Antle, A., Rowley, S., Wilson, J., & Matkin, B. 2015. ʔeləw̓kw – Belongings: Tangible Interactions with Intangible Heritage. Journal of Science and Technology of the Arts, 7(2), 59. http://doi.org/10.7559/citarj.v7i2.159

6. Muntean, R., Hennessy, K., Antle, A., Rowley, S., Wilson, J., Matkin, B., ... Wakkary, R. 2015. ʔeləw̓kw – Belongings: A Tangible Interface for Intangible Cultural Heritage. In EVA 2015. London. http://doi.org/10.14236/ewic/eva2015.41

7. Phillips, R. B., & Johnson, E. (2003). Negotiating new relationships: Canadian museums, First Nations, and cultural property. In Politics and the Past: On Repairing Historical Injustices (pp. 149–67).

8. Rowley, S. (2013). The Reciprocal Research Network: The Development Process. Museum Anthropology Review, 7(1-2), 22–43.

9. Rowley, S., Schaepe, D., Sparrow, L., Sanborn, A., Tadermacher, U., Wallace, R., ... Goffman, T. (2010). Building an on-line research community: The Reciprocal Research Network. Museums and the Web 2010: Proceedings. Retrieved from http://www.archimuse.com/mw2010/papers/rowley/rowley.html

10. Srinivasan, R., Boast, R., Furner, J., & Becvar, K. M. (2009). Digital museums and diverse cultural knowledges: Moving past the traditional catalog. The Information Society, 25(4), 265–278.

11. UNESCO Culture Sector - Intangible Heritage - 2003 Convention : (n.d.). Retrieved September 25, 2015, from http://www.unesco.org/culture/ich/en/convention

Photography

All photography ©Reese Muntean unless otherwise noted.

Acknowledgments

Special thanks to the Musqueam Indian Band, Museum of Anthropology at the University of British Columbia, Maia Jensen at the SIAT Solid Space Fabrication Lab, and Grand NCE.

The Form Design of the Datacatcher: A Research Prototype

Andy Boucher
Interaction Research Studio
Goldsmiths, University of London
London, UK
a.boucher@gold.ac.uk

Abstract
This pictorial exposes aspects of the decision-making process during the form design of a research prototype called the Datacatcher: a mobile electronic device that receives a continuous stream of location-based sociopolitical messages. Manifesting a physical device generated a myriad of demands on top of our research agenda that included issues with both technology and manufacturing. This pictorial will demonstrate how research through design has to tackle issues beyond core research questions in creating research devices, and suggest that because such seemingly irrelevant concerns are crucial for how research questions are embodied, those concerns themselves become integral to the research.

Authors Keywords
Design; research through design; form; prototype; batch production; mobile device.

ACM Classification Keywords
H.5.m. Information interfaces and presentation (e.g., HCI): Miscellaneous.

DIS 2016, June 04 - 08, 2016, Brisbane, QLD, Australia

ACM 978-1-4503-4031-1/16/06...$15.00
DOI: http://dx.doi.org/10.1145/2901790.2901907

Introduction
The Datacatcher is an always-on mobile device designed to display data about its location from a number of online sources, intended to highlight sociopolitical differences across the UK. Topics include average house prices, typical income, the number of pubs or GP surgeries. Turning the device's dial one way scrolls through all the messages that have appeared on the device; turning it the other way accesses a set of poll questions that

Figure 1. A batch produced version of the Datacatcher, a research device that displays a continuous stream of location aware sociopolitical messages.

can be answered using the dial to select among alternatives. Questions cover a range of topics from pollution to politics, including some that are more playful (e.g. 'What are the dogs like here? handbag / working / attack'). 130 of these devices were batch produced during a research project run by the Interaction Research Studio to investigate Third Wave HCI [5].

This pictorial reflects burgeoning interest in visual documentation, using images to provide insight into the design process that brought the Datacatcher into being. This responds in part to observations that the complex processes involved in designing devices should be better represented in the HCI literature [2,6,8,10]. The photographs used in this pictorial are themselves an output of a reflexive process to document the design thinking and making involved in the multiplicity of practices that constitute research through design [7]. They are curated in order to illustrate key stages in the design process, however they should not be viewed as indicative of a linear model of design [4] but rather as particular moments, or way points, in the complex biography of the Datacatcher that are indexical to its making. Moreover, I end my account prior to the completed devices being given to participants, as their experiences with the devices are described elsewhere [3].

The research agenda of the Datacatcher project was to design a device that would support multiple orientations to data that gave a sense of the sociopolitical texture of the neighbourhoods where it is used. The messages are derived from public and private datasets, such as the census and credit agency data. The message feed on the device was aimed at making data more transparent and empowering — indeed, during a test of an early version of the Datacatcher, one participant said that it presented 'Big Data for little people'. To understand the various engagements the Datacatcher would afford, we planned to distribute all of the prototypes to people in the Greater London area to use for several months. We planned to hire two documentary filmmaking teams to capture these experiences and it would be through the participants voices that we would create a kind of polyphonic, fragmentary story of living with the devices (see figure 11).

Background

In terms of how artefacts are typically manifested, used and evaluated the Datacatcher is an unusual example as it is a

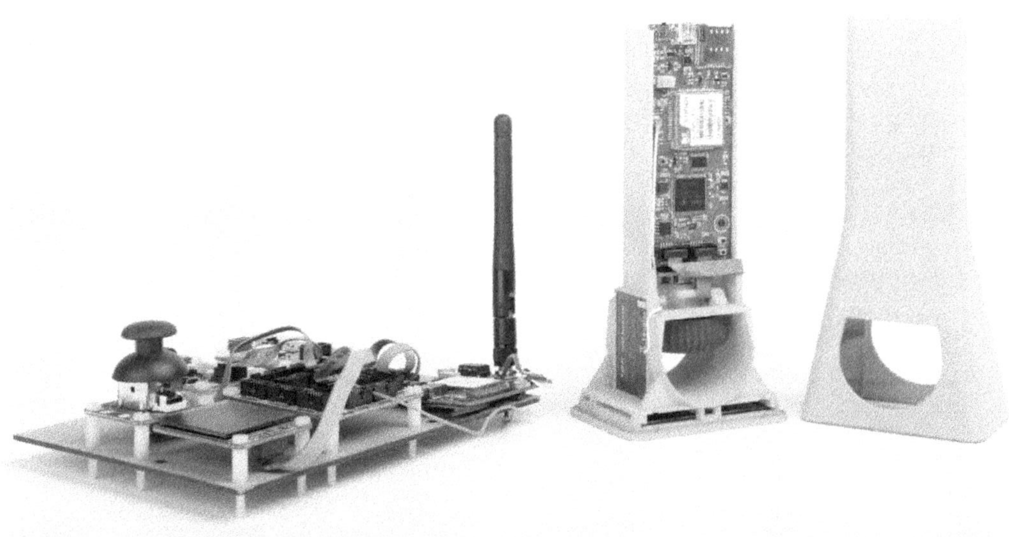

Figure 2. Left, a proof of concept prototype built from NET Gadgeteer [9] modules. Right, the batch production version of the Datacatcher featuring a single, bespoke, printed circuit board.

device that is a product of research through design. Its design brief has a lineage that reaches back into a funding proposal and into the previous work of the design team that created it [1]. It is a technological device, but is not a tool for performing tasks, nor does it facilitate gaming or entertainment, nor does it connect to anything that might generate a revenue stream and despite its name, it doesn't harvest data for anyone other than the participant using it. It is a product designed and built for exploration and does not sit within the consumer landscape often used to locate electronic artefacts. However, it does share qualities with devices that belong to categories that the Datacatcher does not. It has a screen, a control and a battery that needs to be charged. It connects to the Internet through the cell phone network. It is robust and safe to use, and if a problem arises then there is a telephone support line.

Form Design

This pictorial will use visual material to help describe some of the more detailed considerations driving the design of the Datacatcher's form. Although this may seem of little relevance to the project's key research questions, the form design itself is key to the identity of the Datacatcher, how it will be used, and crucially how people's expectations of the device are shaped by how it looks and feels. As with other research through design projects, the research questions are supported by and to a certain degree presented through the form design [1].

The Datacatcher is designed as a handheld object that has a screen on one end and a large control dial set in a recess underneath. On the end opposite of the screen is a small on/off switch and a charging socket. At the time of writing the devices are about a year old and have been used by hundreds of people both in a long-term field trial and subsequent public engagement events. A common initial question from people who have used it (other than why it isn't an app [3]) is why is it shaped like a torch/flashlight? Although the Datacatcher shares affordances with this familiar form, it was not our intention to imitate such an object (even though some users have described the device as illuminating). Instead, our design decisions were shaped by a constellation of criteria and demands that resulted in the device being handheld, powered by a large battery and with an output that appears from the end plane of the form.

Proof of Concept

The Datacatcher's design team is experienced in making technical research prototypes [1], yet producing 130

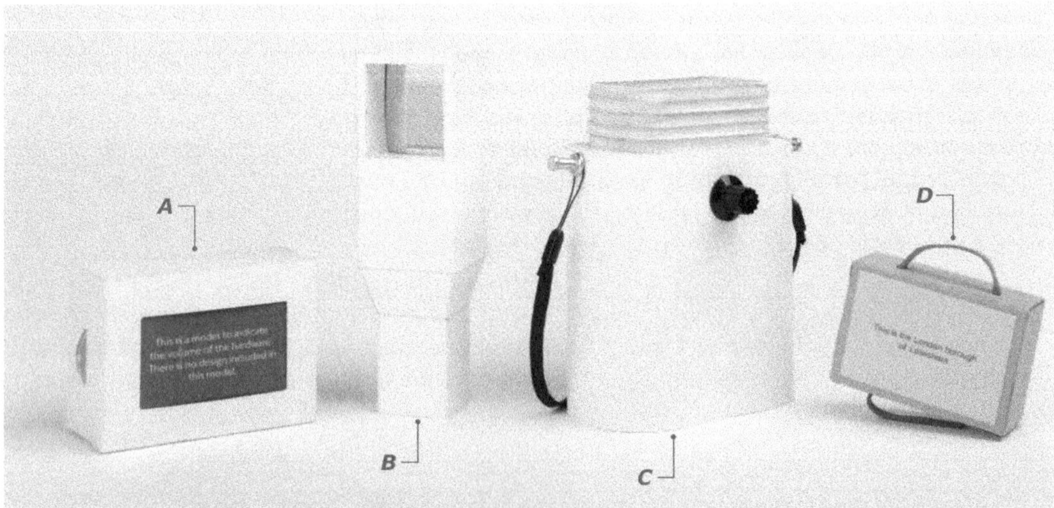

Figure 3. Sketch models. (A) This simple form echoes a 'pager' and encloses the expected volume of electronics and battery at an early stage in the design process (B) A handheld case similar to an 'otoscope' featuring a translucent screen that would overlay text on the view through the display. (C) A model of a device that would hang around the neck like a pair of binoculars featuring a screen that can be viewed by glancing through the top aperture. (D) A device that loops or hangs onto other objects to become a small personal or public display.

highly finished and robust devices raised new and unexpected challenges. The sheer scale of the production introduced issues with materials, processes and manufacturing, and the technical complexity of building what was essentially a GPRS cell phone from scratch was a few steps beyond our comfort zone. Early in the design process we created a working prototype using modules based on the .NET Gadgeteer platform [9] that could receive a continuous feed of location-specific messages compiled on a remote server (see Figure 2). This version was built around a cell phone module (GPS was too power-hungry for a device intended for continuous use), which would report cell tower identifications back to our server that could be used as a rough proxy for the device's location. Although this method was coarse, it was more than adequate for the granularity of most datasets. The prototype also featured a small e-ink type of monochrome display that would be used in the final version of the prototype, even though we would evaluate many others during the design process.

The Design Brief

We added lessons from the working prototype to refine our brief prior to the beginning the form design:

- A mobile device which streams sociopolitical information in response to the device's location
- that would connect to a remote server compiling data scraped from data sources such as government sites, credit agencies, the UK census, Twitter™ and Wikipedia™ and
- allow participants to contribute their own, location relevant opinions
- using GPRS cell phone technology to approximate location and
- be capable of being switched on continuously for days between battery charges

Mission Creep

The brief focuses on our core research agenda for this project, but it also introduces demands that are outside this. Resolving issues with manufacturing, radio interference and power management became a sizeable part of our research activity and these are embodied in the final form of the Datacatcher as much as the core research interests were. Dealing with concerns beyond our key research questions is common to many of our research through design projects, though often unreported. The rest of the pictorial aims to demonstrate

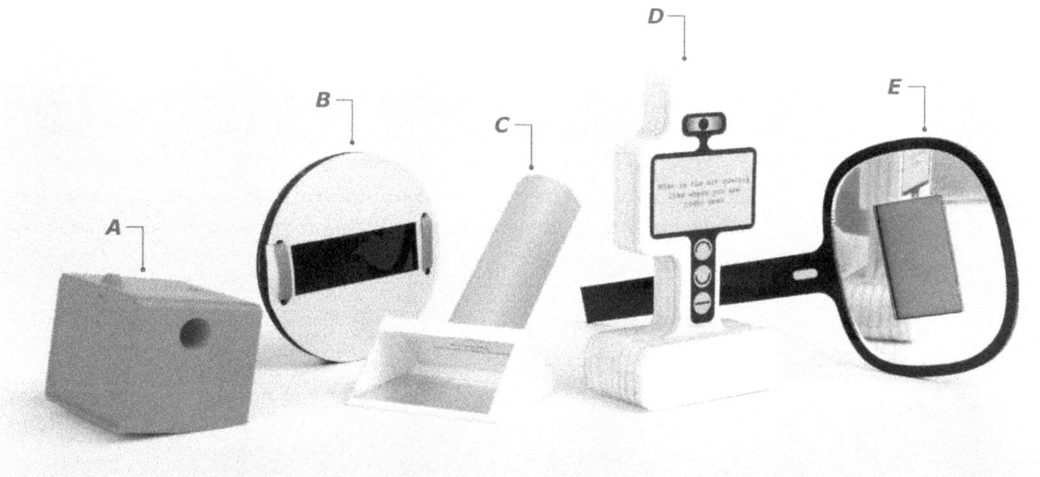

Figure 4. Sketch models. (A) An iteration of the previous pager style model with detailing to tilt the screen on flat surfaces and a cut-through hole allowing a cycle lock to pass through. (B) Exploring flexible materials such as rubber and foam around a hard screen. (C) A periscope model, where the screen is viewed via a mirror and a handle that acts as a dial. (D) This concept includes user-poll buttons which allow positive, neutral or negative responses to questions and has a large volume in the base to house batteries as we began to realise the need for a substantial power source. (E) This maquette incorporates the screen within a convex handheld mirror, in response to a proposal suggesting that the Datacatcher should focus users on their surroundings rather transporting them away, as is the case with most mobile technology.

some of the decision making and development made during the form design process of the Datacatcher that shows how fundamental issues seemingly outside our key research agenda became influential during our research activity.

Initial Ideas

Figures 3 & 4 show a small selection of the numerous sketch models that were made to explore early questions of how the Datacatcher might be used (At home? Carried by hand? Mounted on a car dashboard? Perhaps left in a public space as a form of electronic graffiti?). During this period of study we investigated some very specific usage scenarios, and one idea that was quite obsessively explored was the notion of providing various methods to attach the device to other objects. Two maquettes shown in figure 3 (D) & 4 (B) both feature built-in elasticated bands for strapping to articles such as bags, buggies, handlebars or clothing, while the prototype on the far left of figure 4 (A) features a hole cut through the body designed to allow be used with a bicycle D-lock for securing the device in public locations. The idea of a cut–through became a feature of the final form, provide a space for the dial and thumb, while retaining the ability to be used as an attachment point.

The idea introduced with the simple pager-style sketch (A, figure 3) was the notion that the screen should be the main point of visual contact when holding the device, and that all of the physical bulk of the batteries and electronics should disappear behind the screen. We returned to this concept repeatedly in sketches. Over time it combined with the upright form of the otoscope style model (B, figure 3, and popular among our team), and modified further to take into account the apparent need for a large battery (see below). The result was a convergence on the form factors shown in Figure 5, all of which place the display on the end plane of a cylindrical form.

The Battery

As we progressed with the electronic hardware development, it became clear that we would need a high-capacity power source. So we abandoned ideas of using user-replaceable AA batteries and began exploring options with rechargeable lithium-ion battery packs (as seen in the device on the far right of figure 5). We eventually had to use a relatively large 4600mAh battery pack that added considerable volume to the handle in the Datacatcher's final form. This was softened by significantly filleting

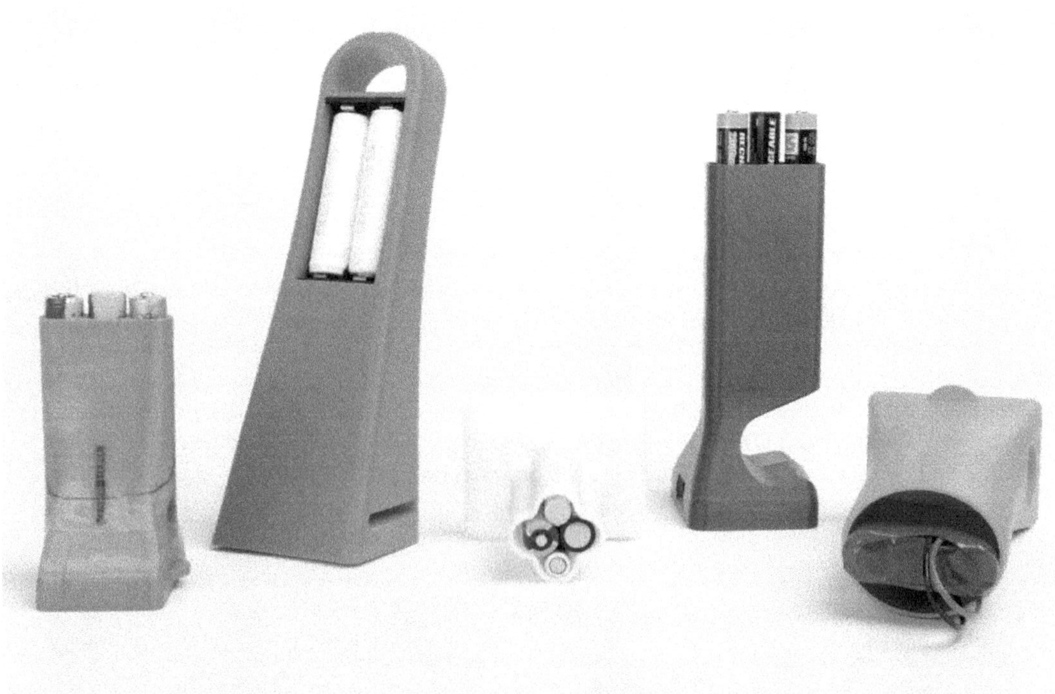

Figure 5. We began incorporating batteries in proposals for the Datacatcher form. All the models on this image incorporate different specifications of high-performance batteries housed within the device's handle. Most use combinations of rechargeable AA and AAA batteries that that we hoped would meet the power requirements of the device as well as having the advantage of being user replaceable. However, we were developing hardware in parallel to the form design and it became clear at this stage that the device would demand a larger power source if we were going to achieve several days usage with a single charge.

(rounding) the edges of the device to wrap around the battery, but it did add an appreciable weight to the device, which some participants commented on as being a slight drawback [3]. However we imagined that the usability of the Datacatcher would be impaired if users were expected to have to charge the device more often than a smart phone and so we decided that compromising the form with the added bulk would be worthwhile. None of our participants subsequently complained about battery life during the field trial.

Getting Real

We had been 3D printing 'sketches' in house on a machine which uses an additive process called fused deposition modelling (FDM). This builds objects by laying down molten plastic in layers. While this process is very useful for development, it doesn't produce parts particularly quickly and the end results can be fragile, so this process would be unsuitable for production in large numbers. We initially investigated low-volume injection moulding solutions for the final production, however we were keen on the appeal of the seamless cases that we could make on our FDM machine because they felt so comfortable in the hand. Injection moulding the parts would have added a split-line or seam lengthways through the case, which would both lose the appeal of the 3D printed cases and add a kind of ordinariness which we believed would be detrimental to the field study. The only way to produce the form we had been converging on would be through using additive manufacture.

After some investigation, we elected to develop the final form for a technique called selective laser sintering (SLS) which is a process that can produce incredibly strong parts by fusing nylon powder, we could also subcontract the production of all the cases to a bureau specialising in additive manufacturing. An additional advantage with this

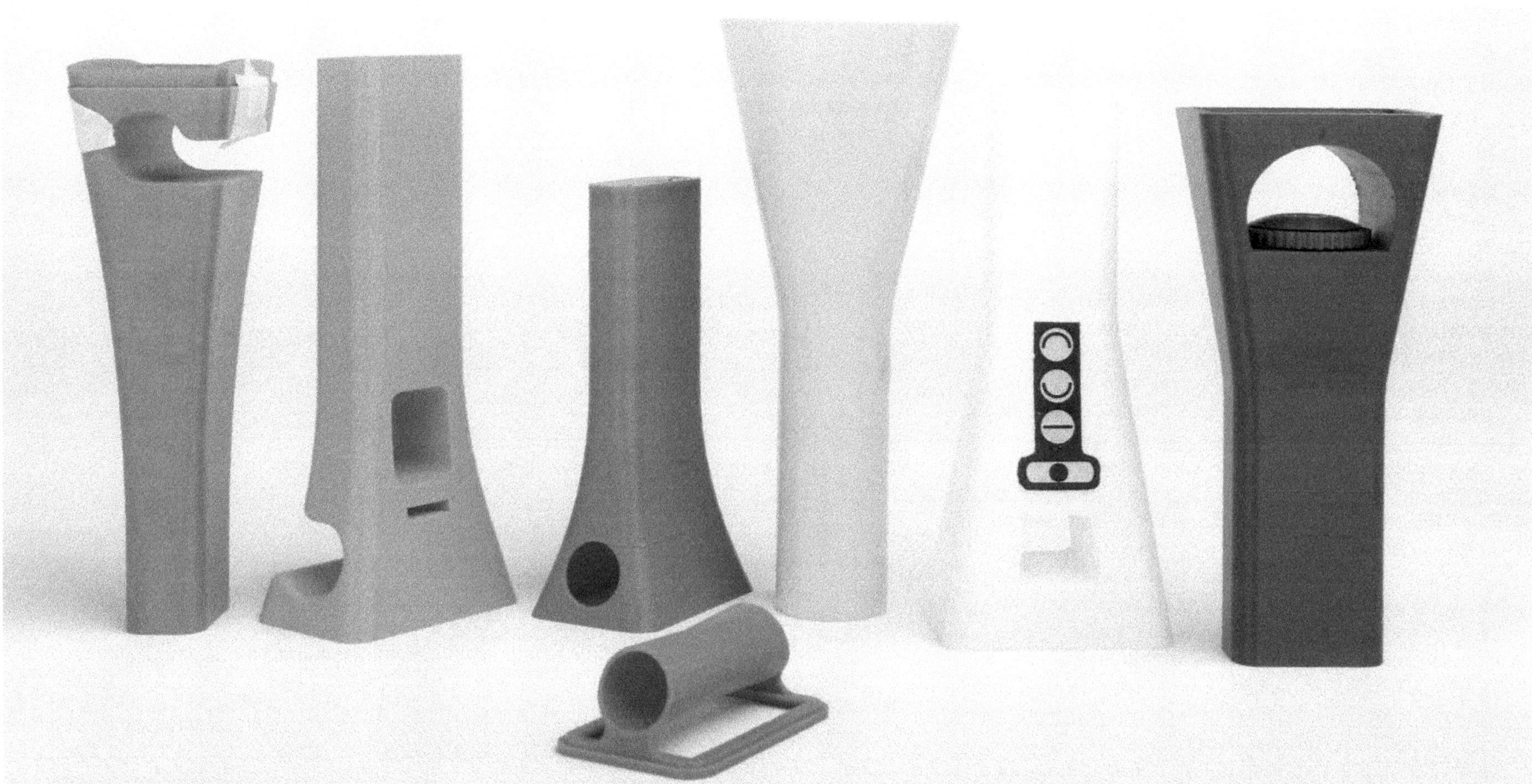

Figure 6. Maquettes produced with a 3D printer, that begin to address batch production opportunities and issues.

process was that we could develop the form using our in-house 3D printer before handing the final design over to be manufactured, as the build technique is so similar. So we set about developing the Datacatcher with as few parts as possible, while taking full advantage of the fact that using the additive process we could make parts that are impossible to produce using traditional moulding techniques. The manufacturing process would enable us to maintain the cut-through hole that we were developing. The blue model, center of figure 6, was our first attempt at building the hole into an inner core or chassis of the Datacatcher.

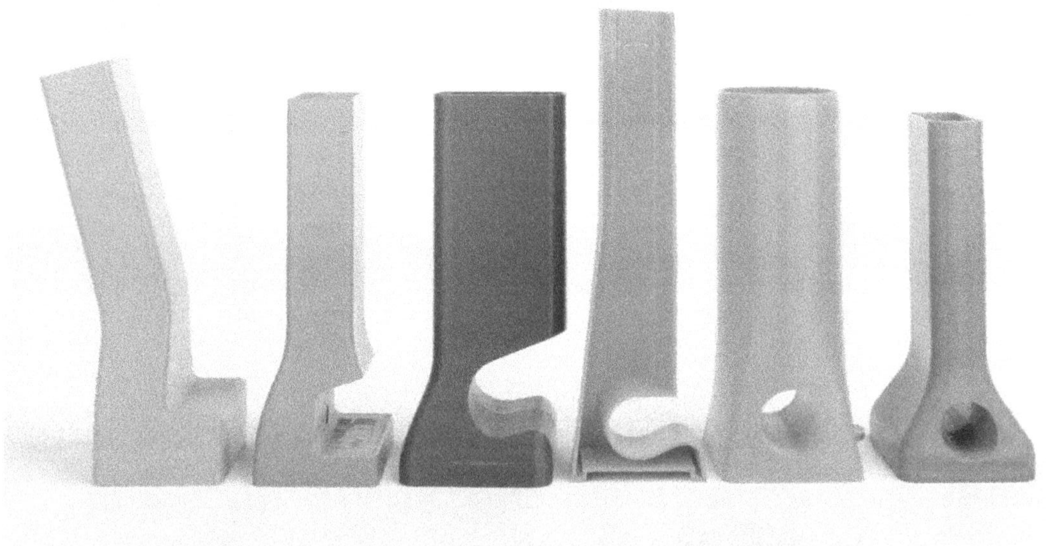

Figure 7. The development of the cut-through from hook to hole. The blue model on the far right is the first to have the tunnel of the hole printed within the inner core section, which matches up with the two holes in the outer sleeve.

The Hole

The final cut-through hole evolved from both the earlier concept of adding accessories such as a cycle locks and a later idea having a built-in hook that could be used to hang the device. Eventually, the hole became the place to locate the thumb operated dial-interface of the Datacatcher, but can also be used to hold the device from the thumb when being carried around. This design feature also creates a space for the internal antenna away from the planes of the PCB and the display, significantly improving radio reception. As an object, this detail also helps place the device in a category outside the landscape of commercial electronics. The casing would be irrational to mass-produce, and so the Datacatcher would become unusual object to encounter: it looks different and feels different to other computational devices.

The Inner Core

As we developed the form for production on a 3D printer, we narrowed the number of parts down to three. The cut-through hole proved challenging when rationalising these components, but was the perfect feature for showcasing the possibilities of additive manufacturing over conventional plastic moulding. Figure 8 is the near-final form of the outer sleeve, and various iterations of LCD screen holder and inner core. The inner core was the part that required the greatest development as this had to incorporate the structure of the cut-through hole, the battery, electronics, encoder (dial), antenna and power switch. As we developed the inner core, we were able to reduce the number of parts from three to two (figure 9), as we worked out a way to incorporate the LCD screen holder by developing a slot for it to slide into. The inherent strength of SLS and the possibilities of additive manufacturing allowed us to develop components that would be impossible to produce by any other method. The simplicity of the outer core belies the complexity of the inner core, which features several printed fasteners allowing the two parts of the case to be held together with just one screw.

3D Printer Variance

We had designed, developed and optimised the design of the housing on our own FDM printer before outsourcing the production of 130 units using SLS. In theory, the resulting parts should have been identical, however were very different. Using the same 3D data, a part printed on an FDM machine is not identical to a part printed on a SLS machine. There are different tolerances with each method and most importantly, there are different characteristics to way each very slightly shrink and warp after building.

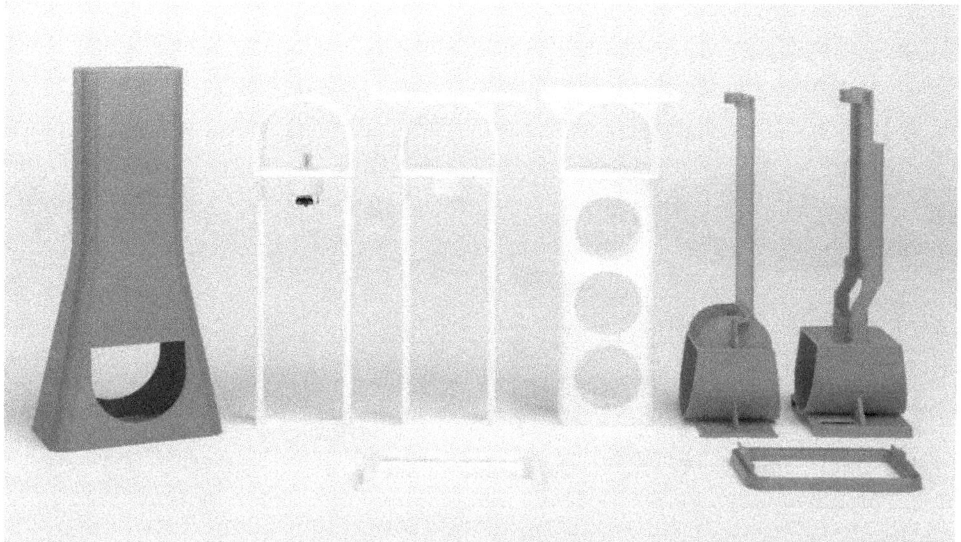

Figure 8. Developing an inner core separate from the outer sleeve. The inner core is designed to hold all the internal electronics and parts and for quick assembly. Despite sub-contracting as much of the manufacture as possible, all assembly was carried out in-house.

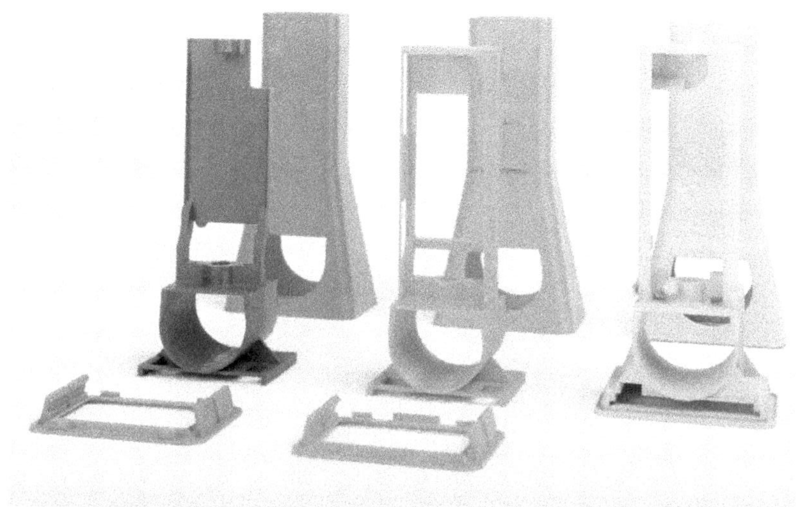

Figure 9. As we developed the inner core, we were able to reduce the number of parts from three to two as we worked out a way to incorporate the LCD screen holder by developing a slot for it to slide into. The simplicity of the outer sleeve belies the complexity of the inner core.

The Datacatcher housing consisted of two parts, designed to clip together with a fine seam where they join around the screen edge. We had optimised the design using our FDM machine and the versions we had made were perfect, but the first samples returned to us that were built on an SLS machine were terrible: the clips did not work and the display and PCB would not slide into the channels built to hold them. Worst of all, the joint between the display bezel and sleeve was inconstant and crooked.

After much back and forth with three different bureaus, we modified the design to achieve the same quality of fit as the ABS printed versions, adding and removing microns from clips and shut lines of 3D drawings. However key to the quality assurance was specifying exact orientation and position of each multiple in the SLS machine's build chamber: A major difference between the SLS and FDM process is that each SLS build takes roughly the same time as the material chamber has to be progressively filled with nylon powder whether it is being fused by the laser or not. This means that bureaus tessellate as many parts as possible into each build and we found that different angles that our components were being built in greatly affected the consistency of the final part, creating rounded edges and steps on flat surfaces. Our final specification to the bureau was not just a refined 3D drawing but also the exact position of each multiple in the build chamber. This level

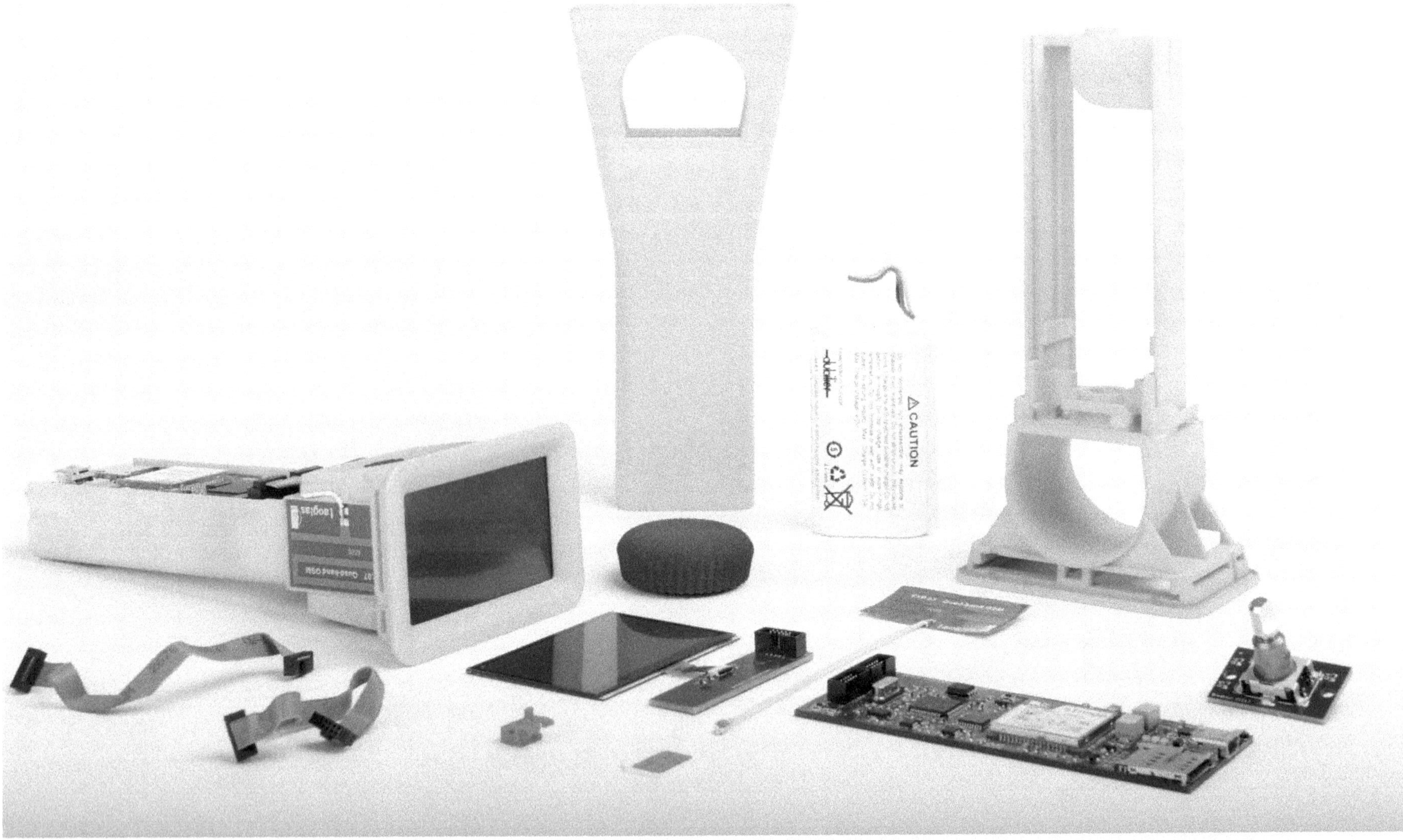

Figure 10. An assembled inner core of a Datacatcher next to a disassembled one. Parts that attach to the inner core are right to left: rotary encoder, mainboard PCB, cell phone antenna, battery, LCD screen and breakout board, dial, SIM card, switch cover, ribbon leads.

Figure 11. A selection of stills from documentaries of participants describing their experiences of living with their Datactcher. All 54 films can be accessed at vimeo.com/channels/datacatcher

of engagement with a production process may at first seem irrelevant to our research interests, but controlling the quality of the physical form is crucial if the form is embodying the research agenda.

Discussion

In the Interaction Research Studio, we practice research through design and much of our day-to-day activity involves dealing with issues that are not directly related to core research questions. Tackling these issues though is fundamental in being able to manifest research prototypes that can adequately serve our research agenda, to the extent that these non-core issues become part of the research itself. The Datacatcher project was a large and ambitious endeavour. The key research questions were addressed via the manipulation and the redistribution of big data by a remote server, exploiting cell phone infrastructure to deliver sociopolitical location-aware short messages to a device.

The device though has to embody the whole experience and capture the essence of the research agenda. The form design is crucial for this and the Datacatchers had to be detailed so as to resolve issues we had manipulating so much technology to deliver the messages. Had the device been uncomfortable to hold, difficult to read, tricky to charge, demanding to operate, or just fragile, none of our participates would have engaged with our research questions as they would have been too preoccupied with its problems. Design is crucial for research through design, and it needs to be acknowledged as being part of the research itself.

Acknowledgments

This research was supported by the European Research Council's advanced investigator award no. 226528, 'Third Wave HCI'. The Datacatcher team were: Robin Beitra, Dave Cameron, William Gaver, Mark Hauenstein, Nadine Jarvis, Liliana Ovalle, Sarah Pennington and James Pike. With thanks to: Paul Basford, Matias Bjorndahl, Kirsten Boehner, John Bowers, Alan Boyles, Richard Cook, Chaka Films, Michael Guggenheim, Marine Guichard, Ben Hooker, Nia Hughes, Robin Hunter, Tobie Kerridge, Doh Lee, Ros Lerner, Jamahl Lindsay, Eleanor Margolies, Kitty McMahon, Mary Mead, Sebastian Melo, Lee Murray, Liliana Ovalle, Belen Palacios, Veronika Papadopoulou, Cristina Picchi, Matthew Plummer-Fernandez, Jonathan Rowley, Jared Schiller, Kate Sclater, Charles Staples, Alex Taylor, UsCreates, Nicolas Villar, Alex Wilkie, Justin Wilson.

References

1. Bowers, J. (2012). The Logic of Annotated Portfolios: Communicating the Value of 'Research Through Design.' *In Proc. of DIS 2012. ACM, New York, 2012. 68–77*
2. Dalsgaard, P. and Halskov, K. (2012). Reflective Design Documentation. *In Proc of the DIS 2012. ACM, New York, 2012. 428–37.*
3. Gaver, W., Boucher, A., Jarvis, N., Cameron, D., Hauenstein, M., Pennington, S., Ovalle, L., Bowers, J., Pike, J., Beitra, R. (2016). The Datacatcher: Batch Deployment and Documentation of 130 Location-Aware, Mobile Devices That Put Sociopolitically-Relevant Big Data in People's Hands: Polyphonic Interpretation at Scale. *In Proc. of CHI 2016. ACM, New York, 2016.*
4. Godin, B. (2006). The Linear Model of Innovation: The Historical Construction of an Analytical Framework. *Science, Technology & Human Values 31: 639–667*
5. Harrison, S., Sengers, P., Tatar, D. (2011). Making epistemological trouble: Third-paradigm HCI as a successor science. *Interacting with Computers, 23 (5), 385-392.*
6. Koskinen, I., Binder, T. and Redström, J. (2009). Lab, Field, Gallery, and Beyond. *Artifact, 2, 1 (2009), 46--57.*
7. Jarvis, N., Cameron, D,. and Boucher, A. (2012) Attention to detail: annotations of a design process. I*n Proc. NordiCHI '12. ACM, New York. 11-20.*
8. Pierce, J. (2014). On the Presentation and Production of Design Research Artifacts in HCI. *In Proc. of DIS 2014. ACM, New York, 2014. 735–744*
9. Villar, N., Scott, J. and Hodges, S. (2011). Prototyping with Microsoft .net gadgeteer. *In Proc. TEI 2011. ACM, New York, 2011. 377-380*
10. Zimmerman J., Stolterman, E. and Forlizzi. J. (2010). An analysis and critique of Research through Design: towards a formalization of a research approach. *In Proc. of DIS 2010, ACM Press, 310-319.*

Virtual Trainer: A Low Cost AR Simulation of a Sudden Cardiac Arrest Emergency

Tom Djajadiningrat
High Tech Campus, Building 33
5656AE Eindhoven
The Netherlands
tom.djajadiningrat@philips.com

Pei-Yin Chao
pei-yin.chao@philips.com

Christian Richard
christian.richard@philips.com

Patray Lui
patray.lui@philips.com

DIS 2016, June 04-08, 2016, Brisbane, QLD, Australia
ACM 978-1-4503-4031-1/16/06.
http://dx.doi.org/10.1145/2901790.2901914

Abstract
Sudden cardiac arrest is a leading cause of death. Because treatment must be delivered within minutes and emergency services take time to arrive, survival is strongly influenced by bystander intervention. However, bystanders are often hesitant to help. Training is a major factor in increasing the chances of bystander help. Current training uses 3D manikins which are costly and require instruction by a professional coach. We propose to make training more accessible through a low-cost approach. Our design allows trainees to practise on an interactive cloth printed with a life-sized manikin and defibrillator whilst receiving augmented reality guidance on a TV.

Authors Keywords
augmented reality; manuals; emergency care

ACM Classification Keywords
H.5.2. User Interfaces: training, help and documentation H.5.1. Multimedia Information Systems: Artificial, augmented, and virtual realities

Introduction
Time matters most in sudden cardiac arrest (SCA). As a rule of thumb, the victim's chance of survival decreases with 10% for every minute without cardio-pulmonary rescitation (CPR). Most people want to help, yet are unsure what to do. Some may even not do anything at

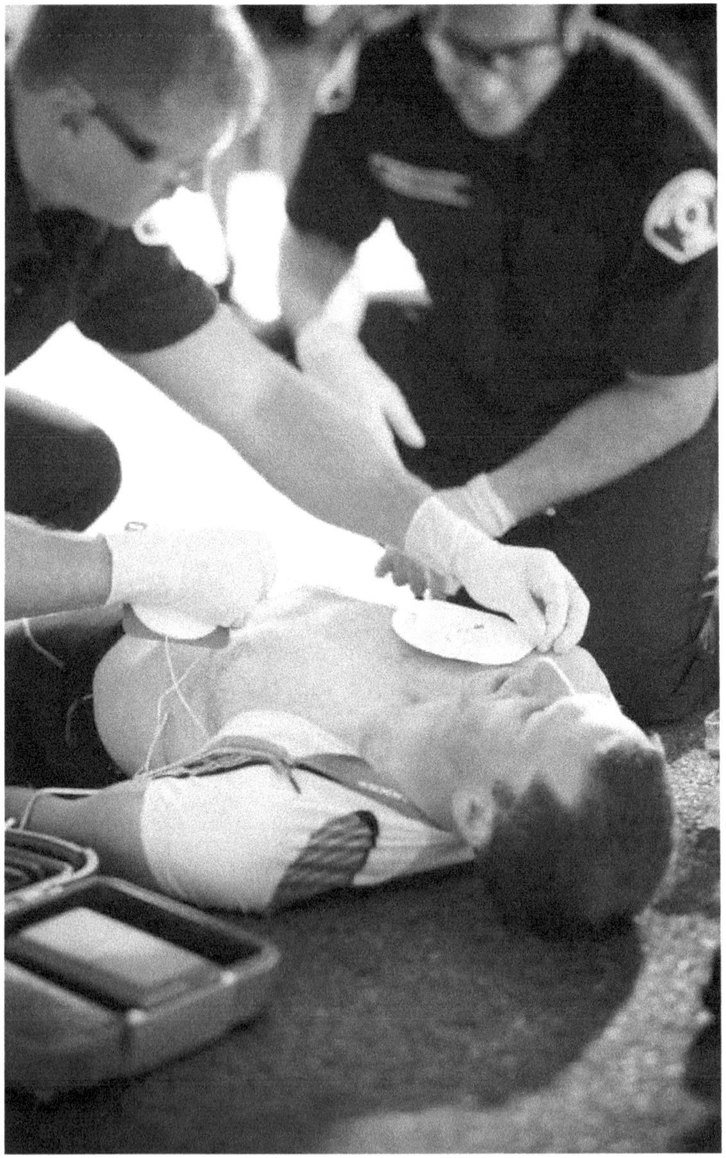

An emergency response team applying electrode pads to a sudden cardiac arrest victim. Because every second counts in SCA, bystanders should already start at least resuscitation and preferably defibrillation before EMS arrives.

all. Only one-third (32%) of SCA victims receive bystander CPR and only 2% are treated with automatic external defibrillators (AEDs) by bystanders (Roger et al. 2012). If bystanders provide CPR and use an AED to treat the victim before EMS arrives, survival rates increase from 10% to 38% (Weisfeldt et al., 2010).

Why are bystanders so hesitant? From usability experts in our company we hear the following. Lay responders:

- are insecure and face uncertainties that make them slow to act. They have questions such as "Can I use this on a child, a woman? Will it shock me?"
- have trouble interpreting instructions, regardless of how easy they are.
- place hands and pads in the wrong place, all the time.
- get 'flustered' or may even panic when confronted with the chaos and noise of an emergency scene.
- find it hard to press the shock button, even if it is the life of their partner at stake.

According to Swor et al. (2006), a bystander trained in CPR is the strongest predictor of a victim actually receiving CPR, stronger than a public location of the cardiac arrest, a bystander-witnessed event, and the bystander's educational level. Regular training is significantly associated with willingness to provide CPR (Sipsma et al., 2011). Strikingly, SCA survival rates vary widely and are higher where CPR is part of the school curriculum or community training programs are in place. The most common way to learn resuscitation and defibrillation is with a CPR mannequin, a dummy AED and instruction by a emergency care professional. Professional CPR manikins are expensive (i.e. 250-1500 USD) as is professional coaching. Our ambition was to create a low-cost training solution for resuscitation and defibrillation which could make training more accessible.

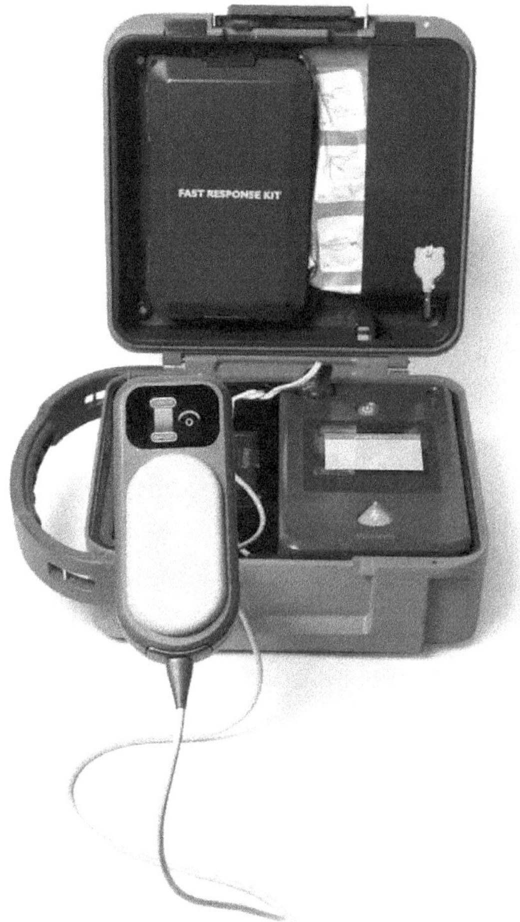

An automatic external defibrillator (AED)
An AED case with foil-packed electrode pads in the lid, an LCD-bsed interface and a triangular shock button. The device in front is an resuscitation metronome which helps the first responder achieve the right speed and depth of compression. It is put on top of the victim's chest and held underneath the hands.

What is resuscitation and defibrillation?

In case of sudden cardiac arrest, the heart contracts erratically and is no longer capable of transporting oxygenated blood around the body. The basic principle behind resuscitation is simple: rhythmically pressing down on the victim's chest causes the heart to get trapped between sternum and spine and this squeezing action takes over the function of the heart. Important are the speed (110 compressions/min.) and depth (5cm) of resuscitation. Proper resuscitation is highly intensive and tiring.

Defibrillation, requiring an automatic external defibrillator (AED), involves delivering a electric shock to the patient to bring heart muscle contractions back in sync. The shock is delivered through two electrode pads which need to be stuck to the victim's body.

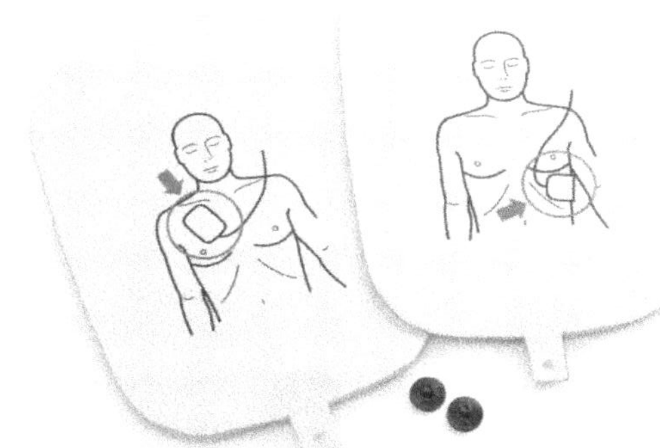

Despite the graphics, untrained lay responders still find it difficult to place the pads correctly on the victim's body.

Ideation workshop: exploring an AR-based coach

We were interested in using augmented reality to guide trainees through an SCA emergency. Augmented reality can be seen as having two components: a computer vision component which can track objects and a display component which can show a co-located virtual overlay on top of the physical world. Both aspects are useful in virtual training. By tracking objects in the real world we can see whether users are doing the right thing and suggest corrections if needed. Through a virtual overlay we can show animated and adaptive guidance.

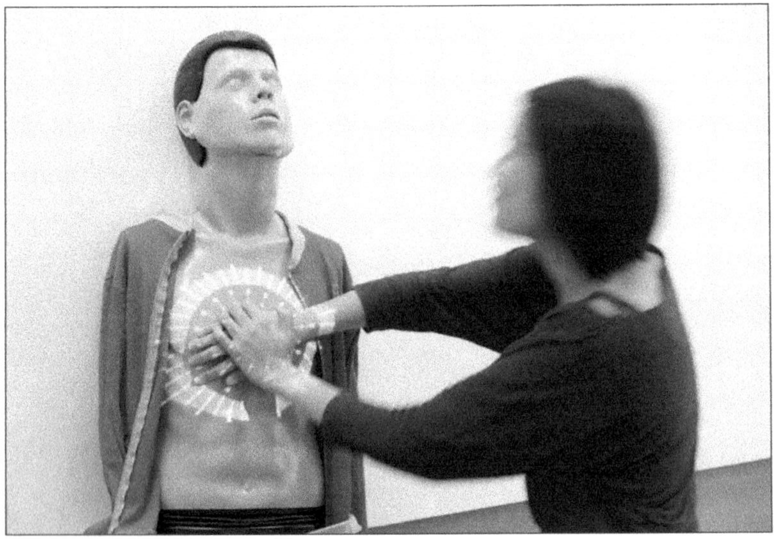

Using projection to simulate a resuscitation metronome

Here we use projection of a Flash movie as a quick way of investigating what a resuscitation metronome could look like in AR. In particular we were interested in how to visually communicate both speed and depth through animation. The figure that is projected on is a professional resuscitation manikin.

Low-fi, embodied ideation

An SCA emergency is highly physical and contextual. It involves the victim's body, the first responder's body and various tangible objects, most notably the AED and pads. Because CPR and defibrilliation need to be done in a high stress situation, the trained response should ideally be almost automatic, relying more on muscle memory than cognition (Farnell, 1999; Ingold, 2001). Considering the importance of embodiment, we acted out the scene using low-fi, physical prototyping, sometimes even for the augmentation (Burns 1994; Ylirisku & Buur, 2007).

Using low-fi physical prototyping to explore augmentation

This still from one of our acting out movies shows a trainee performing resuscitation on a drawn manikin in front of a TV. A mirror took the place of the TV, scouring pads with string served as electrode pads. Using a wizard of oz approach, another actor (out of view) moved the pink cardboard hands with the correct hand posture up and down to indicate the optimal speed of resuscitation.

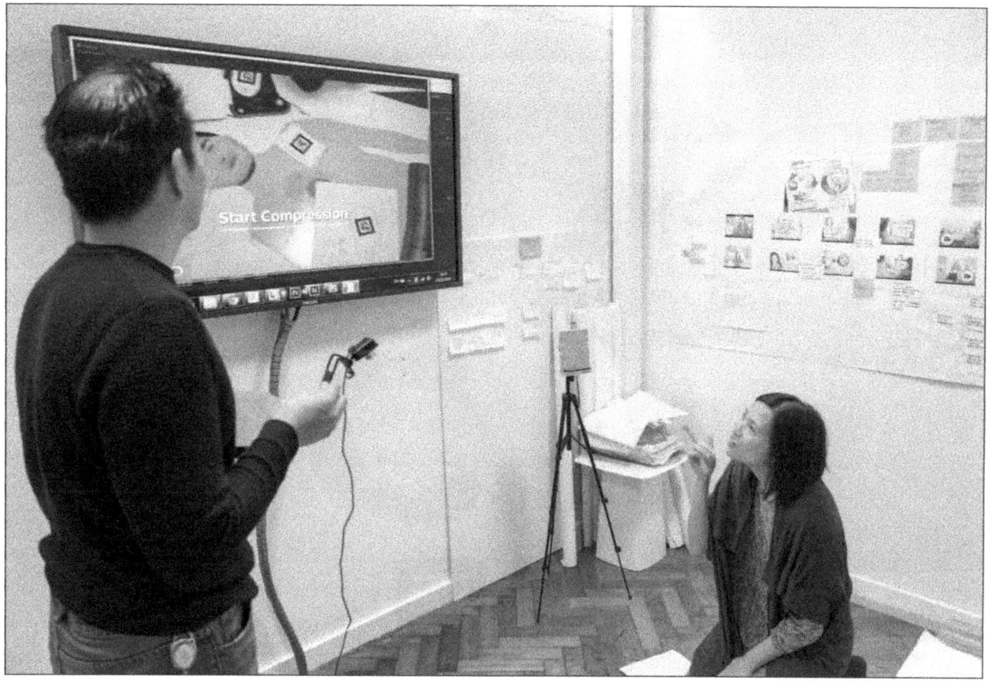

Acting in mirror image

Though the mirror in the ideation session helped us get started, once we tried with a mirrored camera image we found it made interaction difficult. In particular following guidance on placing the pads turned out to be highly confusing. Through experimentation with a webcam we found that the camera need not look over the shoulder of trainee as long as 'north' for the camera coincides 'north' for the trainee.

Placing and sizing AR markers

A seemingly trivial yet tricky aspect of AR is to make sure the markers are well visible to the camera. We used a wide angle webcam to capture as wide a scene as possible. Because AR depends upon computer vision, the visibility of the markers is crucial. The size of the markers, lighting and reflectivity of the material on which the markers are printed all have a strong influence on the robustness of the augmentation and the stability of virtual objects.

Cloth instead of paper

Whilst originally we thought of using a paper poster printed with a victim and an AED, we switched to a screen-printed textile mat. This makes the mat both easier to fold and transport and more robust. It also got rid of some of the reflection problems we had with paper.

The conscious decision for a female victim

It is known that while males and females are equally at risk of sudden cardiac arrest (SCA), females are less likely to be resuscitated. Kramer et al. (2014) point out how CPR on females may be inhibited by socio-cultural norms about exposing female victims' chests and call for more realistic female patient simulators. This inspired us to switch from a male to a female victim and add fold-away clothing which exposes a bra.

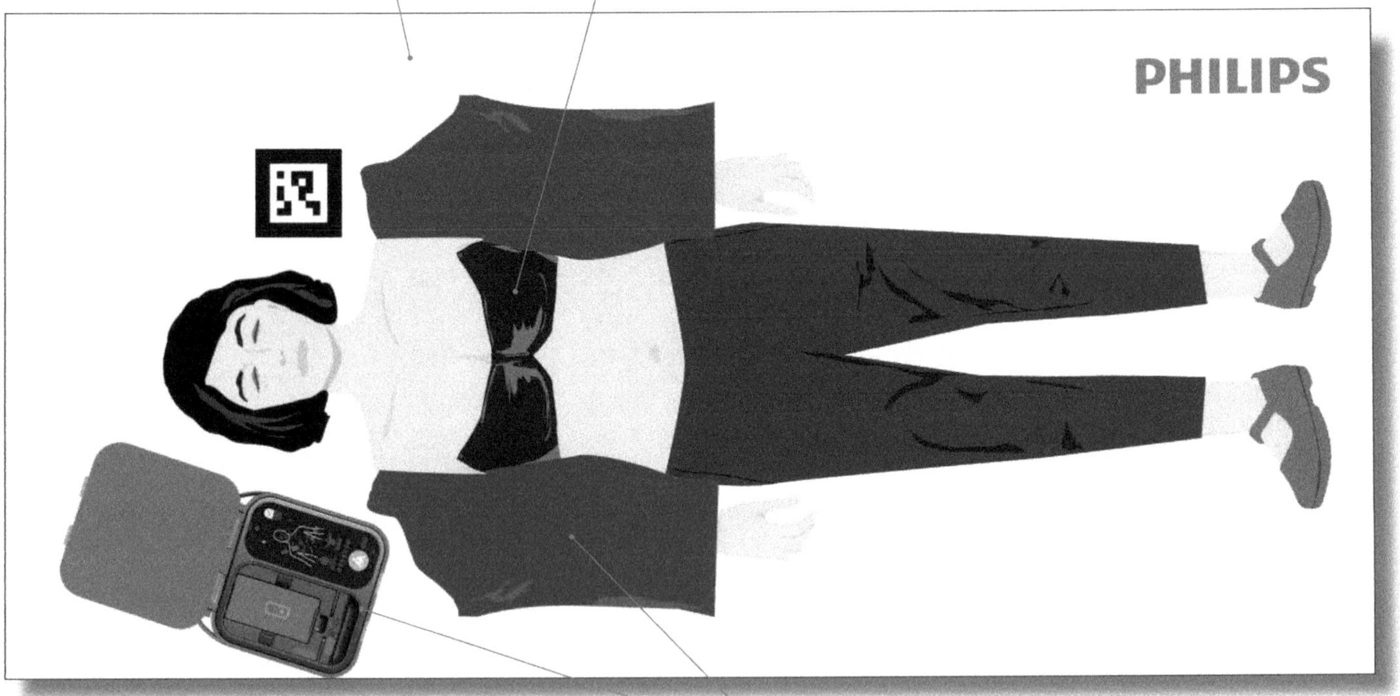

Training muscle memory for 'the motions that matter'

Even though VirtualTrainer could never be a high fidelity simulator because of its low cost approach, we still wanted to make trainees go through 'the motions that matter' in order to train muscle memory. We therefore added AR markers to the foldable clothing so that the system could detect whether the trainee had actually gone through the act of removing it. Similarly, we added a cloth 'lid' to the AED to train the opening action.

Storyboarding

To get a grip on the full interaction flow, we made extensive use of storyboarding. The storyboard fulfilled several roles. It helped us to get feedback from stakeholders and manage their expectations before finalizing the design. It also helped us in discussions on how far we were with interaction programming, physical design, and 2D and 3D assets. Finally, it helped us communicate with photographer and videographer on how best to document the final demonstrator once it would be finished.

John practises SCA emergency response using the Virtual Trainer. This low-cost simulator consists of an app, a smartphone arm mount and an interactive cloth printed with a life-size victim and AED.

The display of the VirtualTrainer app is routed to the TV. The app augments the image captured by smartphone's camera with guidance. An arrow shows John to first open the AED.

John selects the beginner checkbox. At this most basic level the system takes him by the hand and provides maximum amount of guidance and explanation. The higher the level, the less guidance the trainee receives. Regardless of level, John's actions are always monitored.

Animated arrows instruct John to remove the clothing, a crucial step that is sometimes overlooked. The shirt can be opened so that John actually needs to go through the physical actions. This also confronts John with the embarassment hurdle he may feel when the victim is a female stranger.

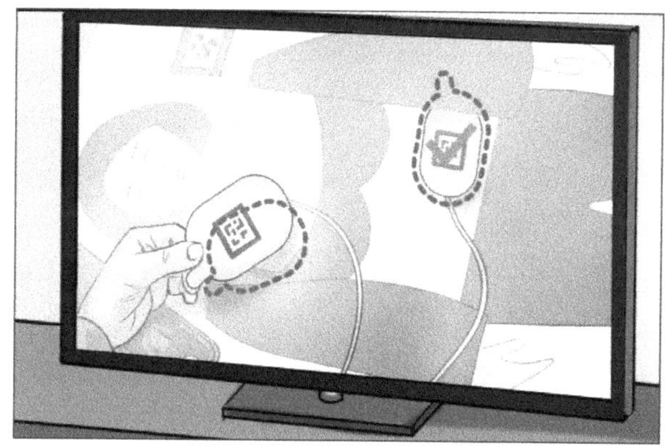

The system comes with a pair of tangible practice pads. By means of dotted outlines John is shown where to put these pads on the body. The system monitors the position and orientation of the pads to check whether John accurately places the pads and places a checkmark once they are placed correctly.

Using an animation, the Virtual Trainer shows John how to adopt the interlocking hands grip, the most effective hand posture for chest compressions.

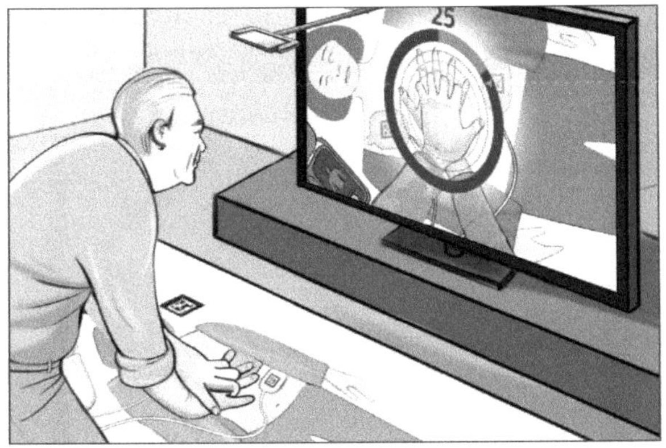

An auditory beat and visual feedforward indicate 110 compressions/min. with optimal depth and release. A timer shows how much longer he needs to continue. Trying to keep pace, John realises how physically demanding resuscitation is.

The system has decided to deliver a shock. It indicates that John should stay clear from the body and shows a count down bar.

When the countdown has finished, a shock is visualized.

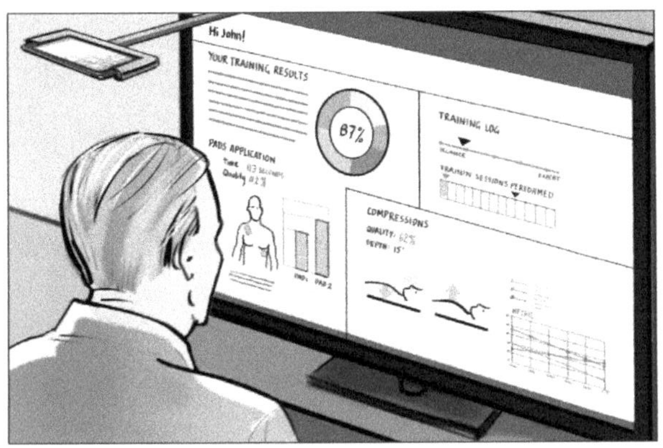

At the end of the session, John is shown a report summarizing his performance. This includes the time taken, the number of errors, the correctness of the pad placement and the effectiveness of his resuscitation.

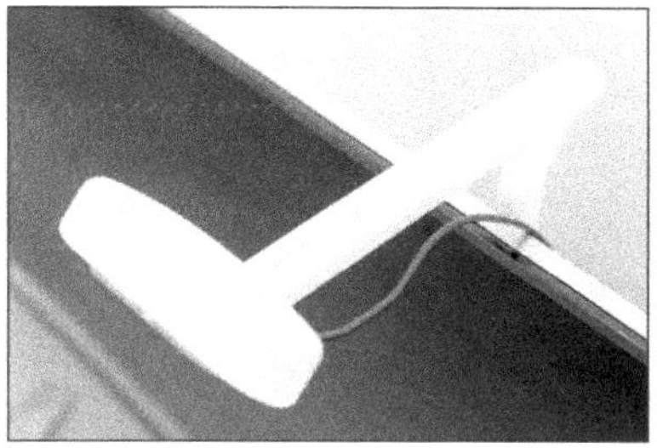

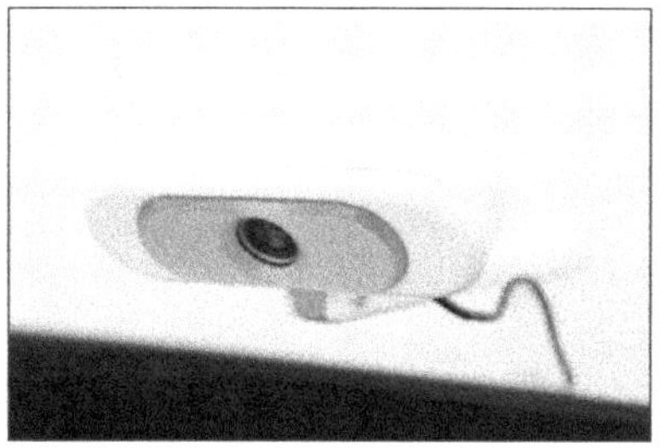

Webcam instead of smartphone
For our demonstrator, we chose to use a webcam connected to a laptop instead of an AR app on a smartphone. This allowed for faster development with less time-consuming compilation as well as a more robust set-up since the laptop could be connected straight to the TV. Modern TVs could in fact work directly with a webcam as they have the necessary computational power on-board. For actual product development, compilation for iOS or Android should pose no problems.

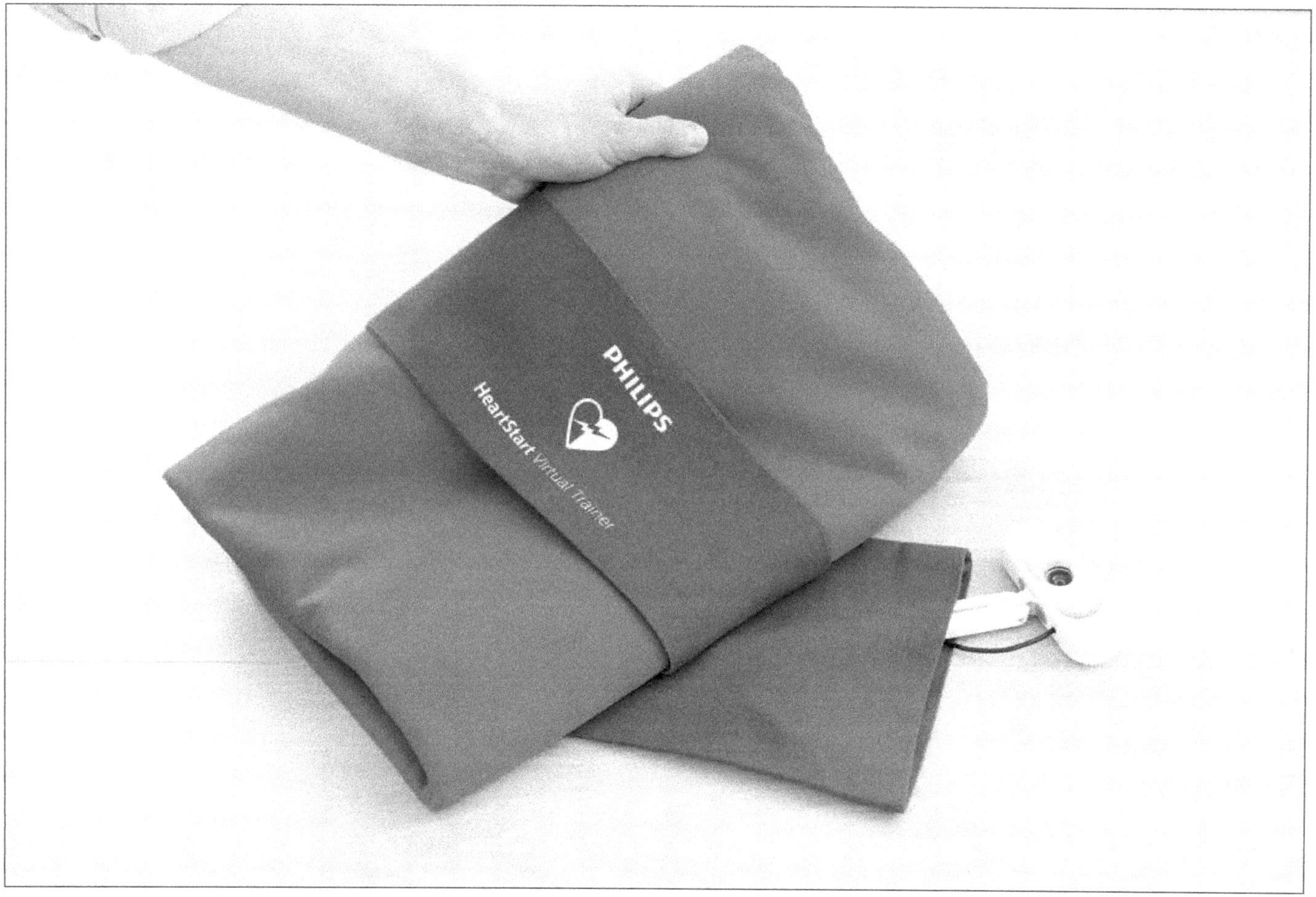

The low cost package
Virtual Trainer comes as an interactive cloth and a webcam which are to be used in combination with a TV.

Final demonstrator

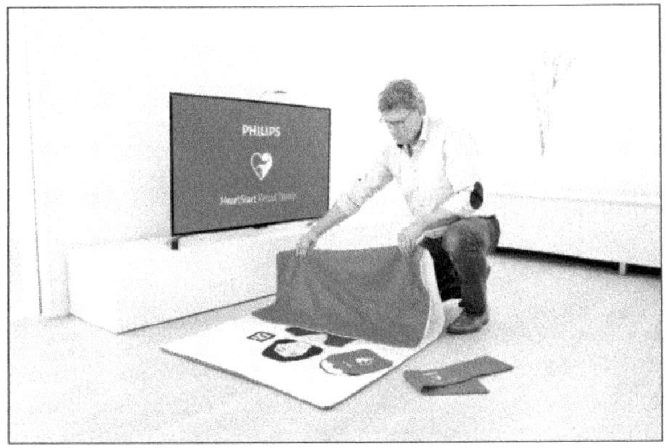

The interactive cloth is laid down in front of a TV. It is printed with a life-sized mannequin and a defibrillator (AED). A camera is attached to the TV and tracks the trainee's actions, allowing augmented reality guidance to be shown on the TV.

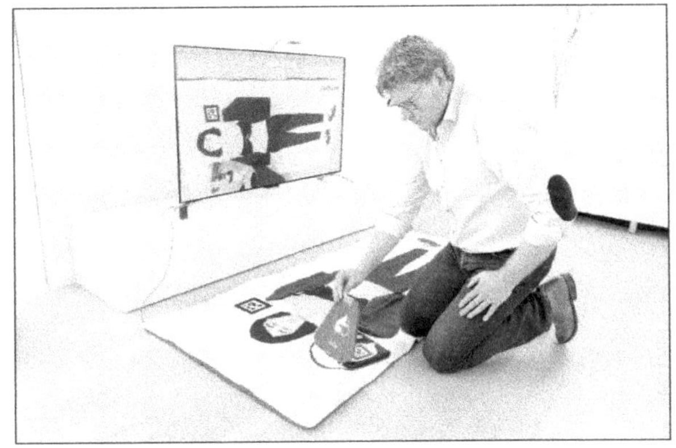

Though the mannequin and AED are flat, they have tangible qualities where it matters, allowing the trainee to practise the most important actions. Here the trainee needs to go through the motions of opening the lid of the AED.

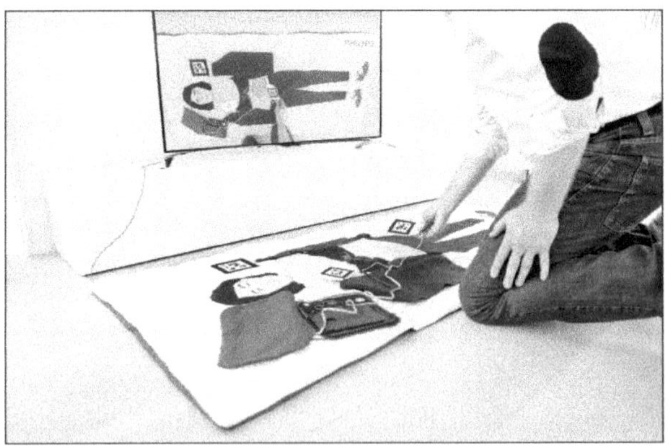

AR guidance shows the user what to do and a coach tells him what to do. Here dotted outlines indicate where to put the pads which are tracked by the camera. Once they are in the right place this is confirmed through tick marks on the pads.

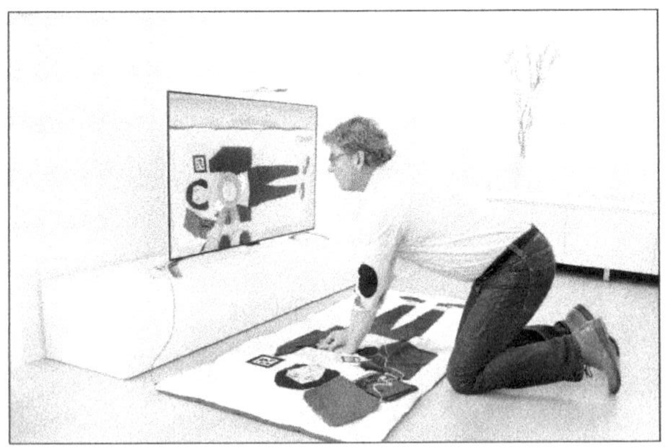

Inside the mat there is a pressure sensor. An animated metronome provides guidance on the required speed and pressure during resuscitation. When speed or pressure are off the coach gives additional instructions by voice (e.g. "Press harder").

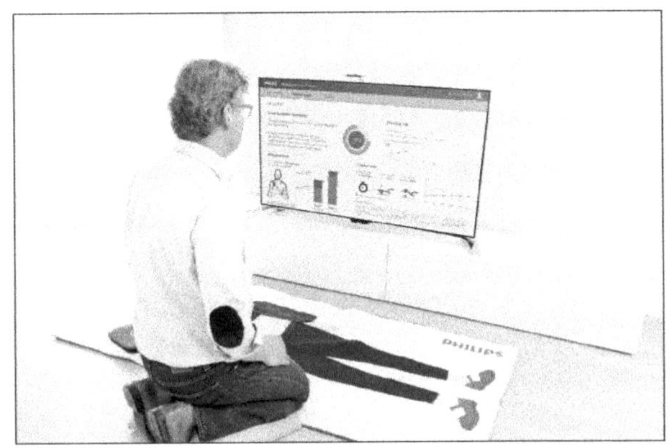

At the end of the session, the user is shown analytics, e.g. if any mistakes where made and how much time the user spent on time-critical actions.

We shot a three minute contextual video explaining the purpose and use of VirtualTrainer. This allowed us to circulate the concept more widely than by means of the demonstrator alone. We gathered feedback from various people within the company including business stakeholders, usability experts and designers from our emergency care unit.

Discussion

We share some of the feedback we received and add our own reflections.

1. AR offers both guidance and monitoring
Though AR is typically associated with virtual overlays, we found that the computer vision functionality of AR can be very useful by itself to monitor the user's actions. This is most obvious in VirtualTrainer's expert mode in which users receive no AR guidance but do benefit from an analysis of their actions.

2. Acting out is a natural ideation companion for AR
In AR, embodiment can play a very strong role as it opens up possibilities for rich user actions and spatial, situated feedback. We found that that acting out with physical props was a powerful way of exploring embodied AR scenarios. This is particularly the case for co-location, the notion that virtual objects can be accurately placed within the user's real-world environment.

3. There are two loci of attention: mat and TV
Trainees need to split their attention between their actions on the cloth and the guidance shown on the TV. Suggestions to overcome this were to use projection or head-mounted displays. Both add cost and complexity and do not gel with our vision of a low-cost solution. For now, our recommendation is to put the TV as low as possible to minimize ergonomic discomfort, i.e. neck strain.

4. Training could have value for diverse target groups
In addition to community training or training at schools, VirtualTrainer could be provided to individuals who buy an AED for peace of mind at home. This would offer family of people at an increased risk of cardiac arrest the possibility to be better prepared. Another target group could be policemen and firemen who do not have the same level of medical training as an EMS team yet are often among the first on the ground at an emergency scene.

5. Virtual Trainer as part of our emergency care offering
Virtual Trainer could be offered as part of an end-to-end emergency care offering to help improve the effectiveness of our AEDs. It could also form the basis of a product-service combination which offers training and certification for users. Virtual Trainer could also have a PR role, showing to the outside world that our company sells more than 'just the product' and works on training solutions to optimize the life-saving capabilities of our AEDs.

Acknowledgements

We gratefully acknowledge David Bentham, Jeroen Raijmakers, Geert Christiaansen, Sean Carney, SeYoung Kim, Marleen van Leengoed, Ozgur Tasar, Kurt Fischer, Anja Janssen, Vincent Jeanne, Helle Ullerup and Hans van der Pluijm for their feedback and contributions to Virtual Trainer.

References

1. Burns, C., Dishman, E., Verplank, W., and Lassiter, B. (1994). Actors, hairdos & videotape—informance design. In Conference Companion on Human Factors in Computing Systems (CHI '94), Catherine Plaisant (Ed.). ACM, New York, NY, USA, 119-120.
2. Farnell, B. (1999) Moving bodies, acting selves. Annu Rev Anthropol 28:341–373.
3. Ingold, T. (2001) Beyond art and technology: the Anthropology of Skill. In: Schiffer HB (ed) anthropological perspectives on technology. University of New Mexico Press, Albuquerque, pp 17–33.
4. Ylirisku, S and Buur, J. (2007). Designing with Video. Focusing the user-centred design process. Including DVD with 34 video samples. Springer 2007.
5. Kramer, C.E., Wilkins, M.S., Davis, J.M., Caird, J.K., & Hallihan, G.M. (2015). Does the sex of a simulated patient affect CPR? Resuscitation, The Official Journal of the European Resuscitation Council, Volume 86, 82–87.
6. Roger, V.L., et al. (2012). Heart disease and stroke statistics-2012 update: A report from the AHA. Circulation. Vol. 125(1), 188-197.
7. Sipsma, K., Stubbs, B.A., & Plorde, M. (2011). Training rates and willingness to perform CPR in King County, Washington: a community survey. Resuscitation. 2011 May;82(5):564-7.
8. Swor, R., Khan, I., Domeier, R., Honeycutt, L., Chu, K., and Compton, S. (2006). CPR training and CPR performance: do CPR-trained bystanders perform CPR?. Acad Emerg Med., 13: 596–601
9. Weisfeldt, M.L., Sitlani, C.M., Ornato, J.P., et al. (2010). Survival after application of automated external defibrillators before arrival of the emergency medical system: Evaluation in the Resuscitation outcomes consortium population of 21 million. J Am Coll Cardiol. Vol. 55(16): 1,713-1,720.

The Tuning of Materials: A Designer's Journey

Elvin Karana
Delft University of Technology
Landbergstraat 15
2628 CE Delft NL
E.Karana@tudelft.nl

Elisa Giaccardi
Delft University of Technology
Landbergstraat 15
2628 CE Delft NL
E.Giaccardi@tudelft.nl

Niels Stamhuis
Delft University of Technology
Landbergstraat 15
2628 CE Delft NL
nielstamhuis@gmail.com

Jasper Goossensen
Delft University of Technology
Landbergstraat 15
2628 CE Delft NL
jasper.goossensen@gmail.com

DIS 2016, June 04-08, 2016, Brisbane, QLD, Australia
© 2016 ACM. ISBN 978-1-4503-4031-1/16/06...$15.00
DOI: http://dx.doi.org/10.1145/2901790.2901909

Abstract
A growing number of scholars have started to look at materials as part of the unfolding of social and cultural practices. Yet, to date, relatively little is known about how to purposefully design for a particular practice in which materials, with their unique qualities, act as co-performers. This paper presents the journey of a designer who includes the explorations on the performative qualities of materials in design ideation. This journey aimed to explore how the material and the performance can 'lead the way' in the potential unfolding of a social practice such as 'tuning a radio'.

Authors Keywords
Materials experience; design; performative qualities of materials; connected everyday.

ACM Classification Keywords
H.5.m. Information interfaces and presentation (e.g., HCI): Miscellaneous.

Introduction
Reversing the emphasis from researching people and their individual relationships with material artifacts to materials experience, which takes the properties and experiential qualities of materials as conditions for ongoing encounters and performances and ultimately the development of practice, is a paradigmatic shift for designers [1]. It requires designers to envision and create a situation in which a desired practice is likely to unfold; and even

Original concept: At the Technical University of Delft the lives and practices of expats were researched by the Faculty of Industrial Design Engineering to uncover opportunities for new interactions with everyday products. We have translated the research findings into a series of conceptual products where the ghost of the land of origin seeps through in day-to-day use. The Geist radio is one of these connected product concpets that helps expat families develop and maintain a sense of connectedness and belonging. By adjusting the knob of the Radio, a family can navigate a bespoke spectrum of radio channels ranging from their native country to the place where they currently reside. If a family adjusts the knob on a frequency of their hometown, for example, the Radio will transmit local radio streams. The mundane performance of turning the dial to transverse the space in between 'homes' physically manifests and bridges the chasm that defines the social and cultural experience of being an expat.

Design brief: We commissioned to a trained interaction designer external to the original design team to re-design the Geist radio by focusing on the performative qualities of the materials that will embody the design. What if this radio is made of rubber? How would we interact with it? How can such material carry the design intention? We asked the designer to select a material(s) which evoked a way of tuning between channels that was unique to an expat's everyday routines. Next to the design brief, we provided the designer with the [anonymized] framework, which we introduced in [1]. The designer kept a design diary to document his design journey, thoroughly showing his action steps and decisions making process.

more importantly, a situation in which people are equipped and empowered to assimilate the design into their ongoing performances. In other words, it requires considering materials as 'co-performers' of practice together with people [2].

'Materials experience' is a phrase that acknowledges the experience people have with and through materials [3]. It acknowledges the aesthetic aspects of experience as much as its performative character. Accordingly, the notion of materials experience suggests that designers should qualify the material not only for what it is, but also for what it does [4], what it expresses to us, what it elicits from us, what it makes us do. To facilitate this understanding, in an earlier publication [1], we introduced the four levels of materials experience in which materials are experienced: sensorial, interpretive, affective and performative. While the first three levels have been explored to a great extent [3, 4, 5, 6, 7], relatively too little has been done in understanding the role of materials in shaping our ways of doing.

HCI researchers have started to investigate how to capitalize on the social life of material artifacts and the role of material properties [e.g., 8, 9, 10] in the context of a variety of practices, from coordinative practices to home practices and creative processes of making. This corpus of HCI research is primarily informed by ethnographic work, and increasingly grounded in material studies and studies in material cultures. But as pointed out in [11], the situated engagement with materials and forms of interaction that are not necessarily familiar has been a largely unexplored topic in the HCI research field.

This paper visualizes step by step and briefly discusses our first attempt of understanding how a trained interaction designer might go about re-conceptualizing the social practice of 'tuning a radio,' and his material explorations.

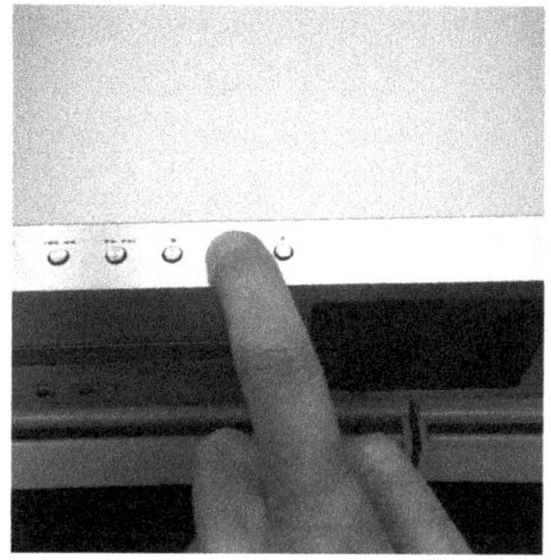

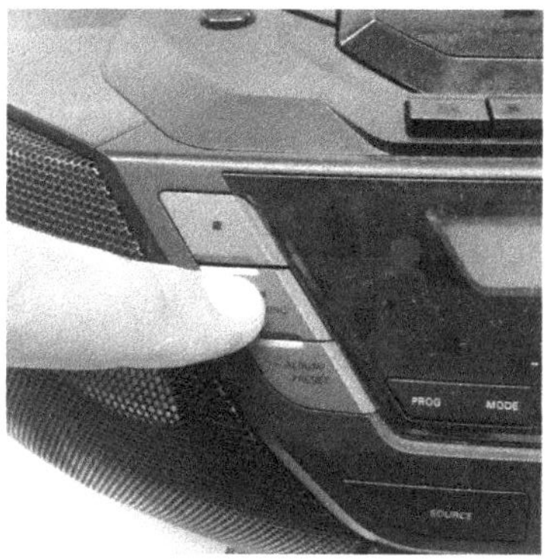

Understanding
tuning a radio

The designer started with a product benchmarking by collecting radios that differ in their ways of tuning. In order to experience different ways of tuning, the designer prefered to visit shops rather than searching radio designs in the Internet. The process of tuning a radio in search of a right channel has an iterative character involving searching, finding, listening, again searching, etc.

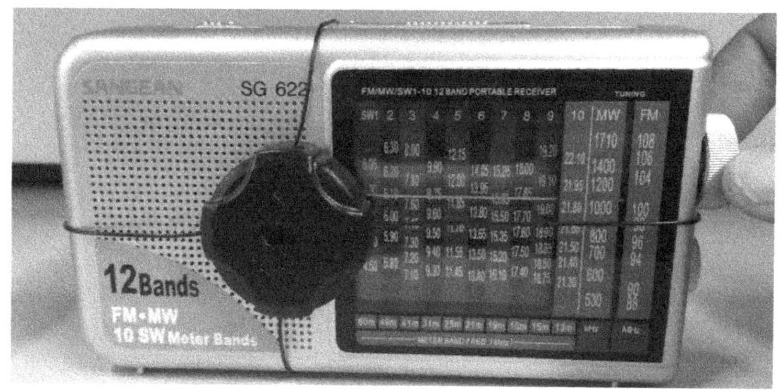

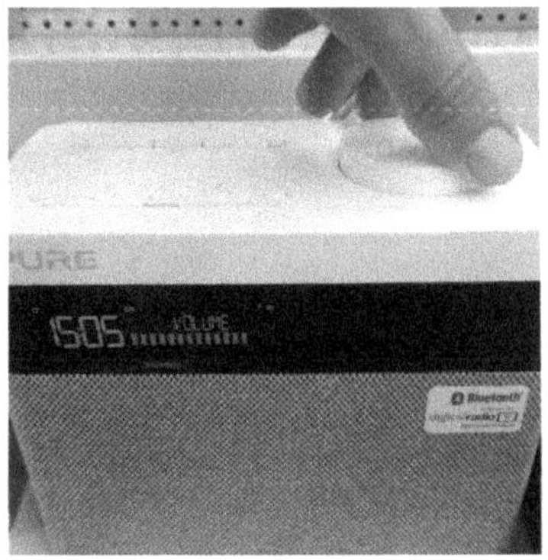

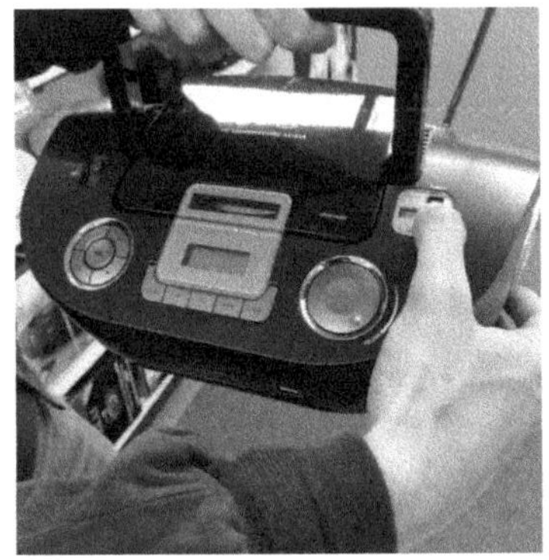

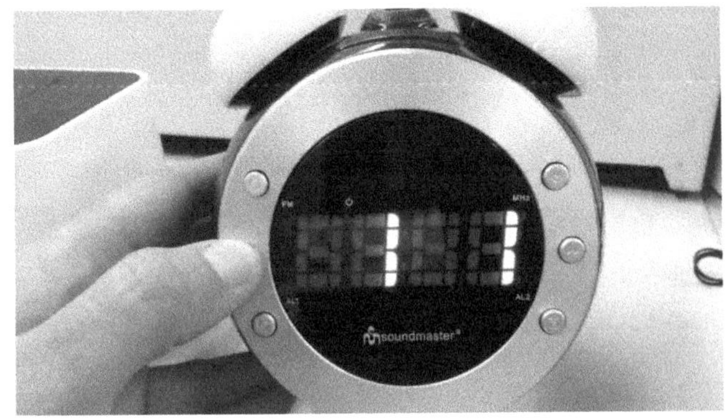

According to the designer, for expats, missing home is a mix of melancholic longing for something far away and pleasant sense of connectedness. He interprets the tuning of the Geist Radio accordingly: "*The tuning will implicate hope (in search of a channel) and disappointment (when the desired channel is missed/ cannot be caught). These iterations of acts and affects will happen each time one searches for the next radio station, till a pleasant sense of conncetedness is elicted when a satisfying channel is caught*". The designer defined this overall tuning experience of the Geist Radio as 'sad-isfaction'.

sad-isfaction
The quality of being content with melancholia

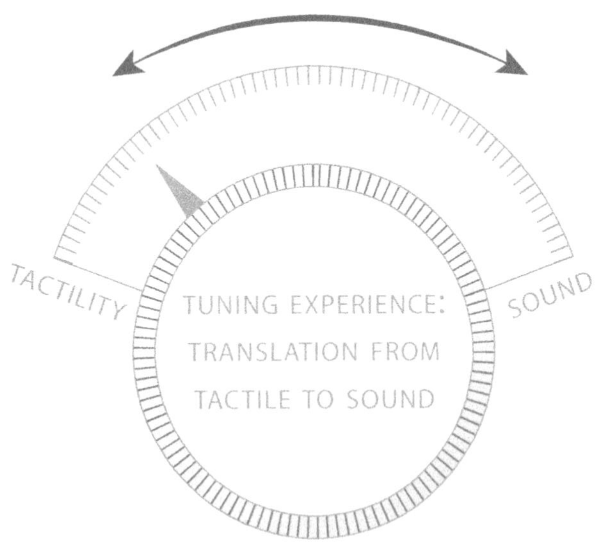

Material explorations

Then, the designer asked himself: What kind of material qualities would facilitate this way of tuning in and out of a sense of melancholia? Or the other way around; if different types of materials would facilitate the tuning for 'sad-isfaction', how would the quality of the performance change? The designer explored the performative qualities of some everyday materials to answer these two questions.

Plastic shattered ball

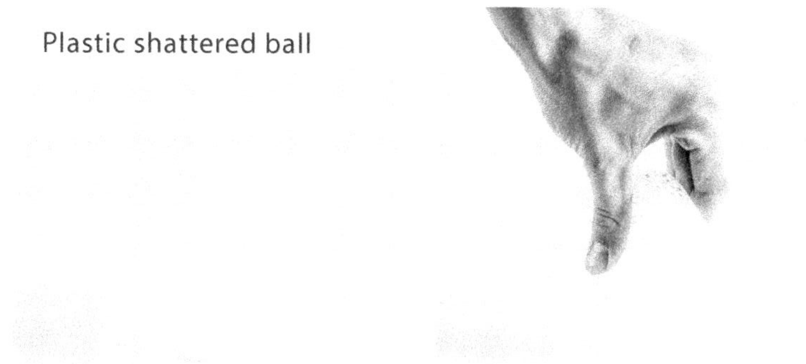

Plastic hair donut

Hard plastic bowl

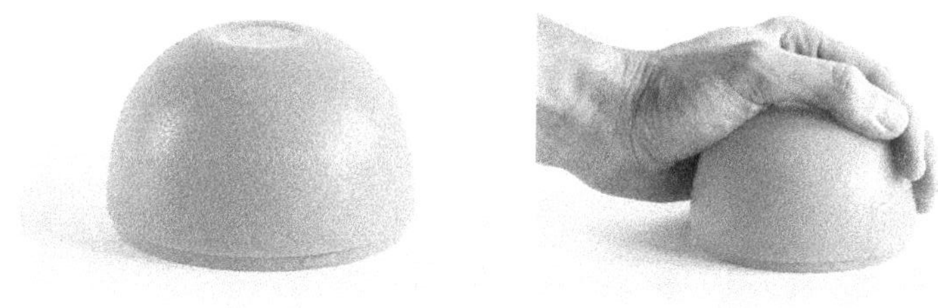

Cloth sponge

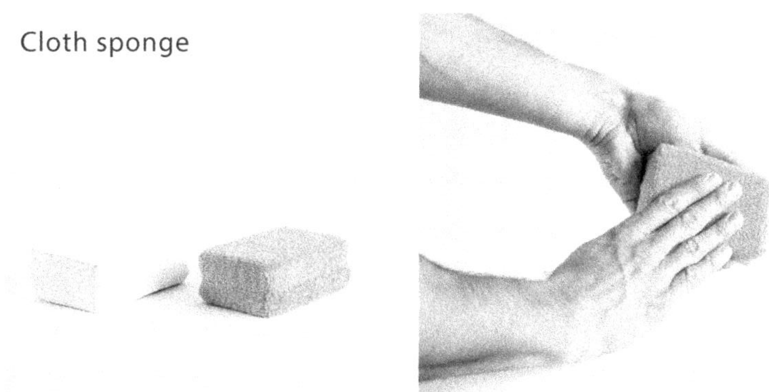

Silicon hair balloon

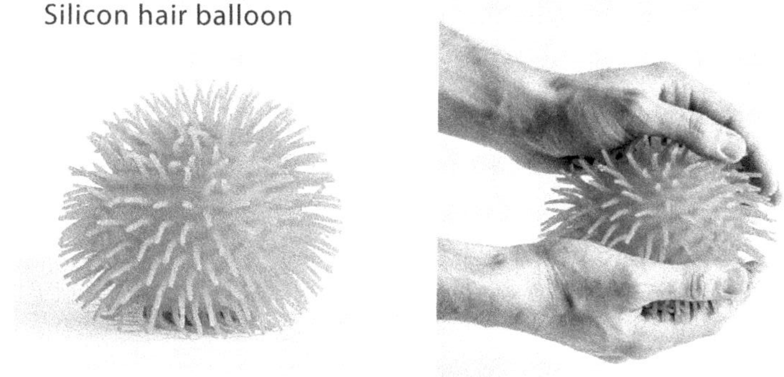

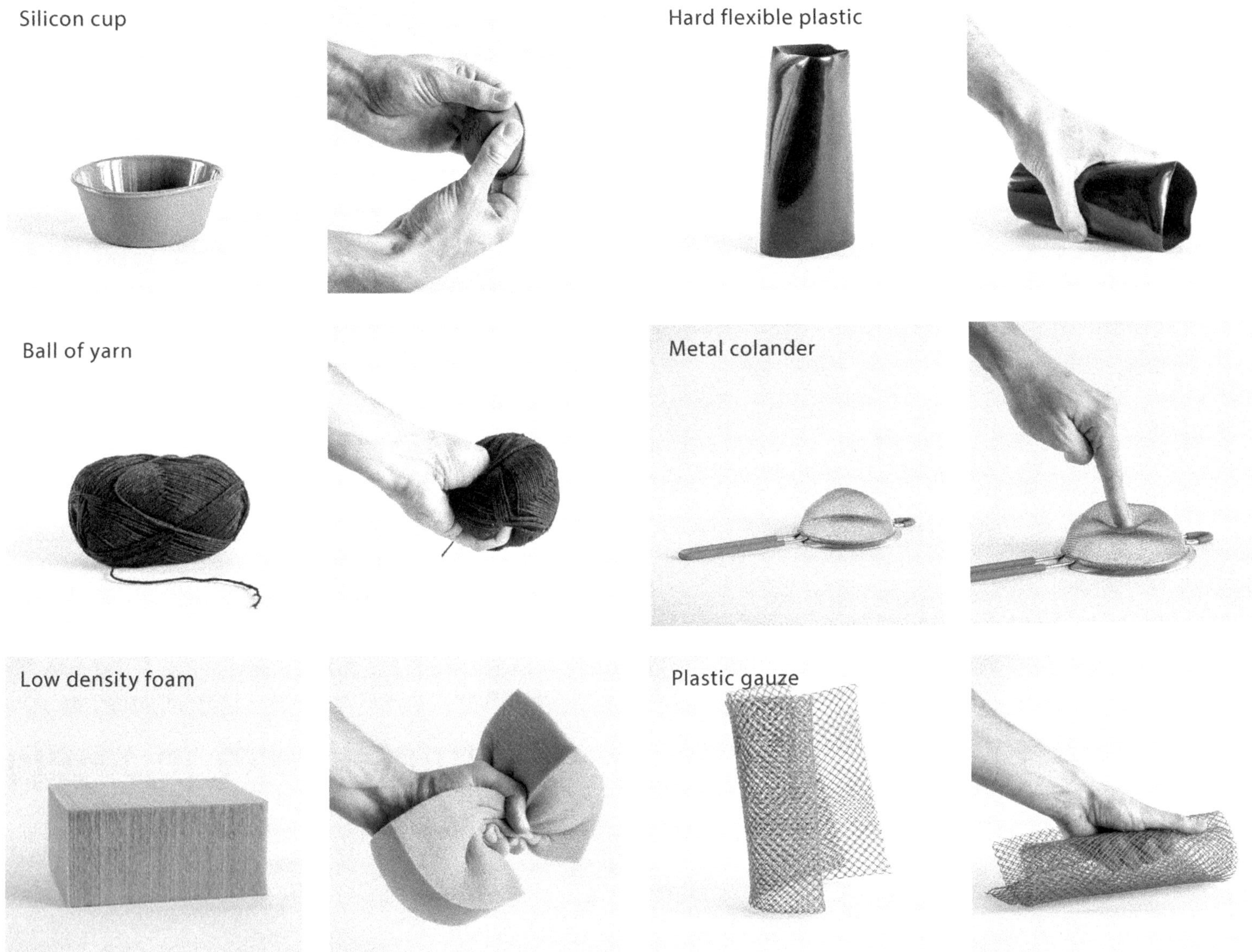
Silicon cup
Hard flexible plastic
Ball of yarn
Metal colander
Low density foam
Plastic gauze

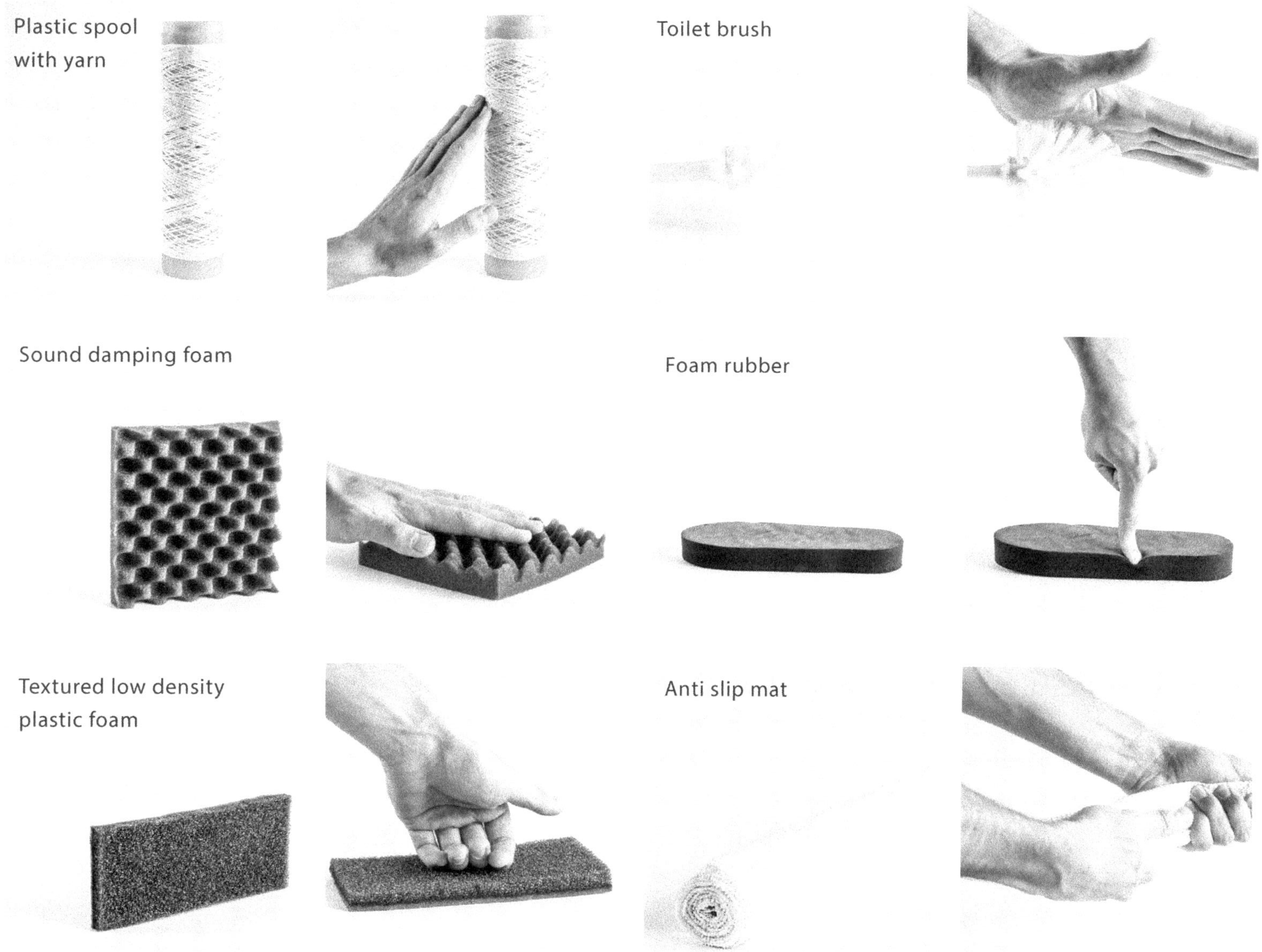
Plastic spool with yarn
Toilet brush
Sound damping foam
Foam rubber
Textured low density plastic foam
Anti slip mat

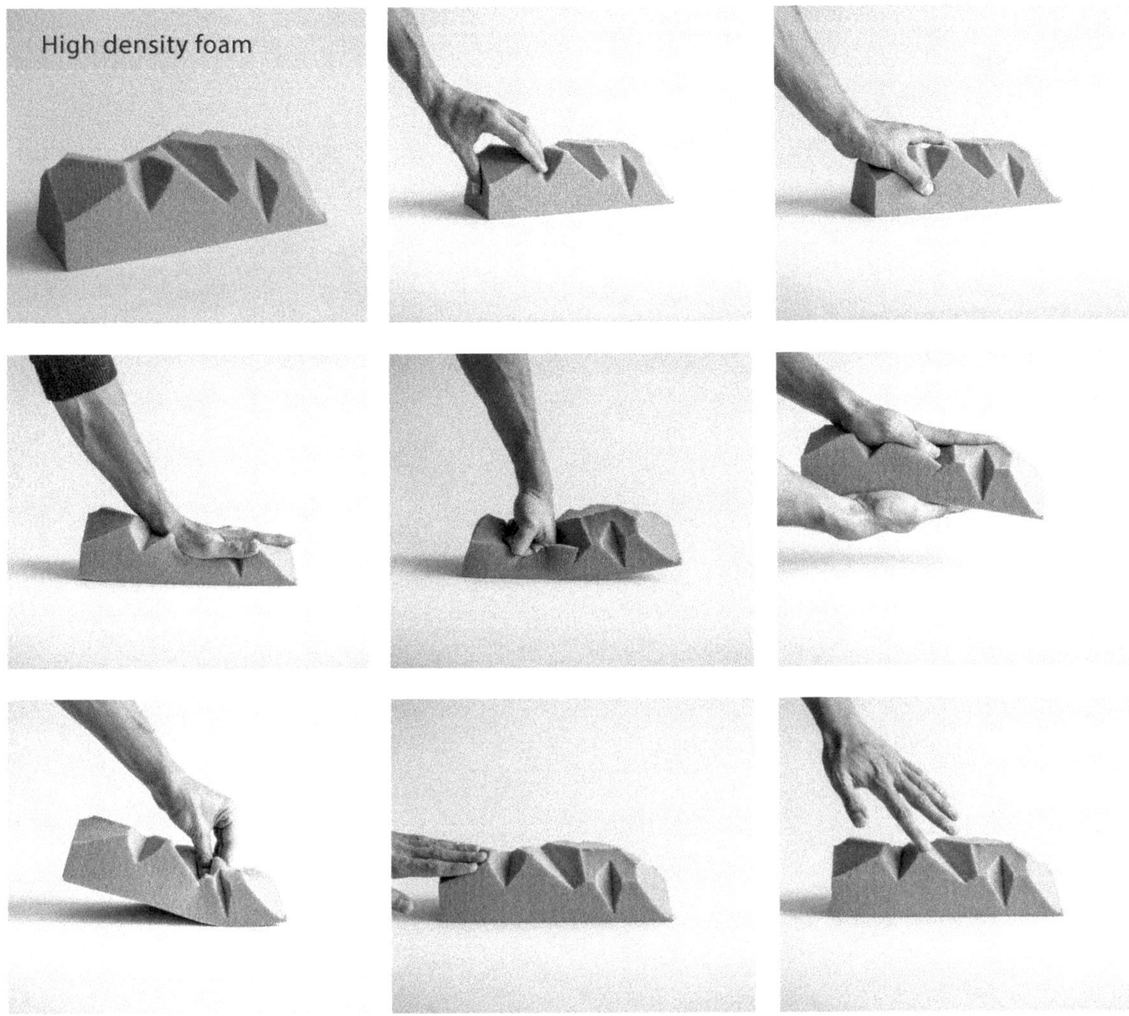

All samples have different sensorial qualities (e.g. soft, flexible), associations and meanings; as well as different forms. As emphasized in [1], in a situational whole the four experiential levels, sensorial, interpretive, affective and performative, affect each other in a non-sequential manner.

Materials experience vision

The designer summarised various findings under a cohesive whole as 'Materials Experience Vision' to guide his decisions through the process of design. The Materials Experience Vision expresses how a designer envisions a material's role in creating/contributing to functional superiority and a unique user experience when embodied in a product [12]. It may accommodate various statements that could be interpretative (e.g., the material will express naturalness), affective (e.g., the material will surprise people), or performative (e.g., the material will require delicate use), in relation to the aimed ultimate experience (i.e. sad-isfaction).

sensorial: soft, rounded, textured, coarse, matte, warm

interpretive: personal, dynamic, natural, safe, warm, elegant, sober, calm

sad-isfaction

performative: kneading, exploring, stroking, caressing

affective: melancholia, nostalgia, empathy, desire, longing, lingering

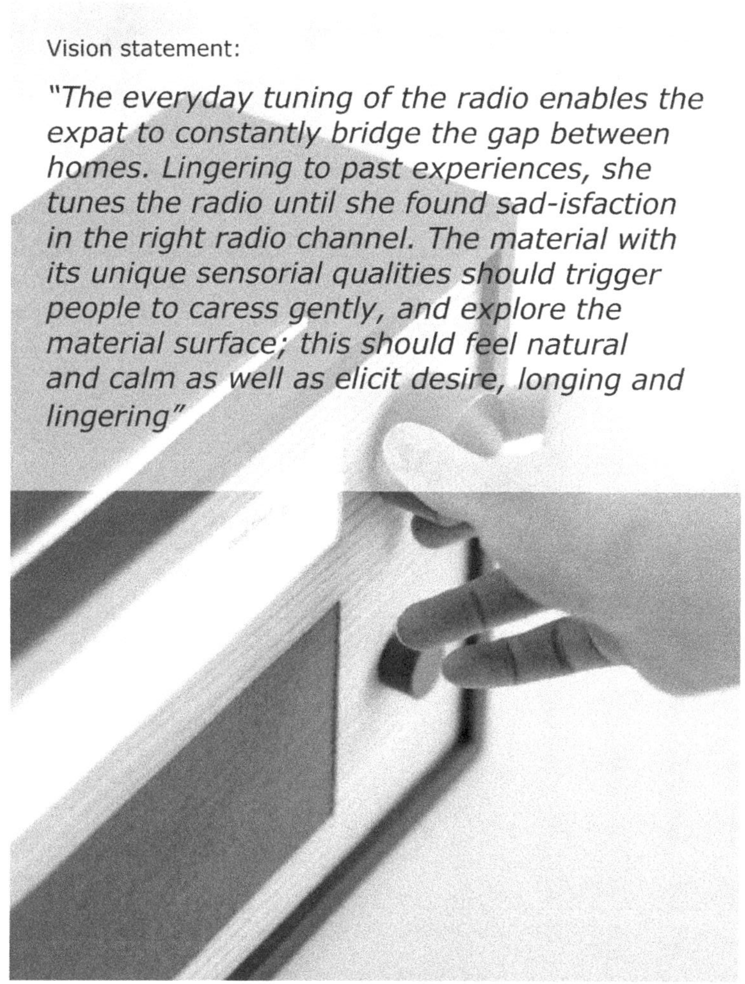

Vision statement:

"The everyday tuning of the radio enables the expat to constantly bridge the gap between homes. Lingering to past experiences, she tunes the radio until she found sad-isfaction in the right radio channel. The material with its unique sensorial qualities should trigger people to caress gently, and explore the material surface; this should feel natural and calm as well as elicit desire, longing and lingering"

Product concepts

Three product concepts focusing on three different ways of tuning were created.

In the first concept, pressing and kneading the 'foam'-like material manifest the tuning. In this configuration there is not a very clear distinction between what is home and what is abroad, the channels are mixed and the foam is the window into the radio landscape from which the right channel has to be found through interacting with the material. The focus of this concept is to explore the relationships between the soft quality of foam and the lingering and searching character of melancholy by kneading and pressing.

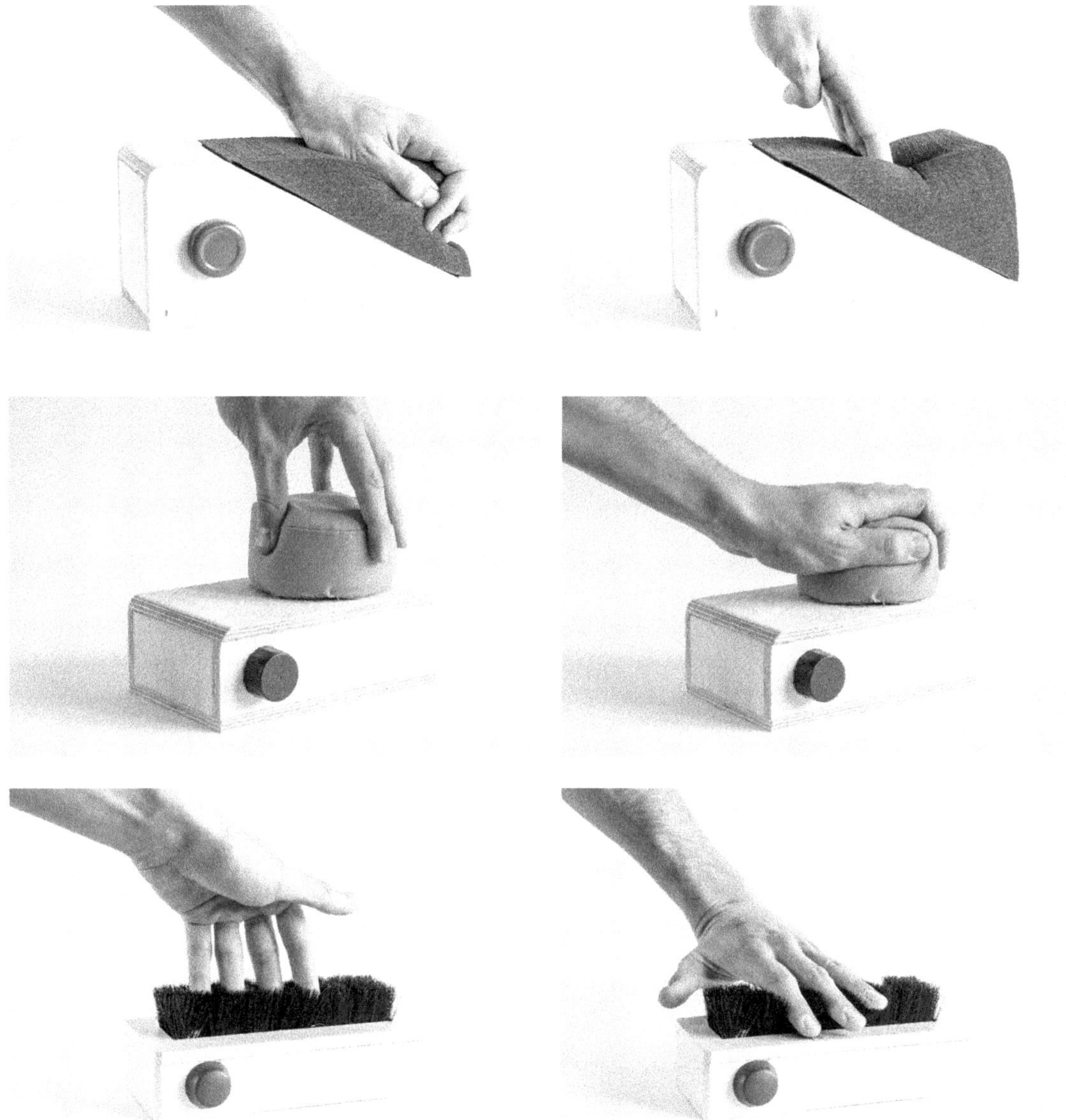

The act of kneading is explored in the second concept too, yet this time guided by a specific direction (through its knob like shape). The knob could even be taken off and carried along through the house, so tuning can be done on different places depending on various activities that take place through the house.

The focus of the last concept is to explore the quality of hairs, and the tuning in between two places by letting the position of the hand determine the place in between homes. The character of the practice is searching, exploring, dreaming from melancholia.

The last concept was selected because of its ability to tune from one place into the other (left to right). Wandering in between the hairs or tapping and caressing them provides different ways of tuning for a clear reception. Also, the hairs resemble on the one hand the experience of hearing the noise of the radio, and on the other hand support melancholic interactions with a lingering, explorative character.

Conclusions

This paper describes a designer's journey in search of the performative qualities of materials for tuning, within the given context of a radio for expats. In doing so, the paper discusses the design process of taking into consideration 'the performative' in material selection and embodiment. Yet, it does not discuss the quality of the final designs.

In the attempt to anchor the performative qualities of tuning in an experience he could empathize with, the designer begins his journey by positing the practice of tuning in relation to expats. What may 'tuning' mean for an expat? The designer's actions steps can be summarized as below:

- Understanding the performance/practice (i.e. tuning): The designer understands and empathizes with what 'tuning' means for expats.
- Material explorations: The designer explores what material qualities would facilitate different ways of tuning.
- Materials experience vision: The designer articulates what the design intention for the ultimate materials experience is; and envisions how the quality of the performance in relation to the material properties/qualities would be.
- Concept creation and prototyping: The designer makes the transition from design intention to material/ product design.

Informal discussions with the designer showed that while each step has its own specific challenges, the most challenging action was to identify and bridge the performative qualities to the given practice. It appeared evident that when users and practice (expats and tuning, in this case) are fixed in the design brief and the choice of material is subordinate, performative qualities can be explored and identified only after traversing first the interpretive level (tuning as 'sad-isfaction'). While results show the given practice has 'opened up' by adding performative considerations of material qualities (i.e. pressing, caressing, lingering etc. not just functionally turning a dial), we are left with an itching question. What if the initial design brief had unconventionally bracketed the user? Or what if we provided the designer with a particular material to design a new way of tuning? How would process and outcomes have been different? Elaborating on the effects of such different beginnings (i.e. performance only, material + performance, etc.) on the design process and outcomes, and facilitating the design process by tools and methods, for instance Material Driven Design [12], is our endeavor for future work.

References

1. Giaccardi, E. and Karana, E. 2015. Foundations of Materials Experience: An Approach for HCI. In Proceedings of the ACM Conference on Human Factors in Computing Systems (CHI '15), 2447-2456.
2. Kuijer, L., Giaccardi, E. 2015. Considering Artifacts as Co-performers, in Animals, automated devices and ecosystems: A symposium on the agencies of dynamic non-humans in theories of practice, 9-10 October, Barcelona.
3. Karana,E., Pedgley, O., Rognoli, V. (Eds.). 2014. Materials experience: Fundamentals of materials and design. Oxford, UK: Butterworth-Heinemann.
4. Manzini, E. 1986. The material of invention. Milan, Italy: Arcadia Edizioni.
5. Rognoli, V. 2010. A broad survey on expressive-sensorial characterization of materials for design education. METU Journal of The Faculty of Architecture, 27(2), 287-300.
6. Zuo, H., Hope, T., Jones, M. 2014. Tactile Aesthetics of Materials and Design. In E. Karana, O. Pedgley, & V. Rognoli (Eds.), Materials experience: Fundamentals of materials and design (pp. 277-286). Oxford, UK: Butterworth-Heinemann.

7. Karana, E. 2009. Meanings of Materials. Dissertation Delft University of Technology.
8. Kirk, D.S., Sellen, A. 2010. On human remains: values and practice in the home archiving of cherished objects. TOCHI, 17(3), Article No. 10.
9. Odom, W. et al. 2009. Understanding why we preserve some things and discard others in the context of interaction design. CHI'09, 1053-1062.
10. Rosner, D. 2012. The material practices of collaboration. In CSCW'12, 1155-1164.
11. Fernaeus, Y ., Vallgårda, A. 2014. Ajna: negotiating forms in the making of a musical cabinet. DIS'14, 915-924.
12. Karana E., Barati, B., Rognoli V., Zeeuw Van Der Laan, A. 2015. Material Driven Design (MDD): A Method To Design For Material Experiences. International Journal of Design, 9(2), 35-54.

Live Prototyping

Willem Horst
dknl design
Møllebaken 1, 1 DK-6400
Sønderborg, Denmark
willem@dknldesign.com

Ben Matthews
Information Technology & Electrical Engineering
The University of Queensland
Brisbane, Australia
matthews@uq.edu.au

ABSTRACT
The technical skills required to effect functional and material changes to high fidelity prototypes can create barriers to the participation of other stakeholders in prototyping activities. In this paper we present an industrial case in which a 'live' prototyping approach was trialled during the development of a new programmable radiator thermostat. A live prototype is an interactive prototype that permits real-time modifications to its interactivity within a collaborative session. We analyse collaborative events that were staged around a live prototype in order to demonstrate the ways in which the prototype worked as a platform for various stakeholders to participate in design, Practical benefits for development included the rapidity with which separate design iterations could be implemented in plenum and the ease with which changes to the interface could be rolled back when unforeseen difficulties were encountered. The live prototype also exposed latent issues in the complex organisation of an industrial design undertaking, including misalignments between stakeholders, institutional design constraints, and implicit design rationale. Additionally, by being modifiable and easily shareable, it also served as a physical form of documentation of the current state of the interface to other stakeholders. As an approach, live prototyping opened up the possibilities, constraints and organisational contexts of prototyping to stakeholders.

Author Keywords
prototyping; live prototyping; participation; interactive prototype; co-design; design methods.

ACM Classification Keywords
H.5.2. User Interfaces: Prototyping; User-centered design.

INTRODUCTION
Prototyping in interaction design is a staple of the design process. For several decades, prototypes have been seen not only as a means of anticipating downstream design or use problems, but as an essential tool to engage stakeholders in collaborative design. Prototyping features centrally in the early and influential participatory design accounts [3,10,31], used as e.g. invitations for participation [8] and tools for inquiring into contexts of use [24].

In this study, we share this principal concern with the use of prototyping for participation, and in particular its consequences for design in an industrial setting. On one hand, prototyping is an important collaborative practice, a means of involving others in design. On the other hand, the activity of prototyping is itself a designerly one, where the actors who shape prototypes are engaged in a process of design inquiry through which they explore and better understand the design space within which they work [18,20]. Within design research, there exist a number of important discussions of the general properties and applications of prototypes for design, based on an understanding of central design texts and carefully documented studies [11,20] or grounded in decades of experience at companies such as IBM [28] or Apple [17]. Design research is already in possession of a number of definitions and analytic distinctions with which to understand the use and usefulness of prototypes in design. It is our intention neither to add to these, nor to criticise them, but to present an analysis of a single prototyping case that addresses a central challenge of participation with respect to technical design work, in a way that constructively complicates some of the pictures of prototyping in design found in these discussions.

The particular tension that we wish to explore in this case relates to the possibility for the prototype to facilitate the participatory inclusion (and exclusion) of others in the design process. There is clearly a degree of technical skill required to work with any design medium (whether it be pencil and paper, clay, styrofoam, a CAD package, a programming language). This specialist knowledge creates challenges for the inclusion of non-designers in collaborative prototyping activities. Over the past decades, the field of interaction design has developed multiple strategies and formats that can work to alleviate this difficulty, among them 'informance' [5], scenarios [7], generative tools [29], paper prototypes [27] and design 'games' [4] as means of enabling non-designers to engage in design-relevant activities. These kinds of activities are frequently undertaken in the earlier stages of design, where there is still considerable scope for changes to the concept

DIS 2016, June 04 - 08, 2016, Brisbane, QLD, Australia

ACM 978-1-4503-4031-1/16/06…$15.00
DOI: http://dx.doi.org/10.1145/2901790.2901807

under development, including its form, construction and interactivity [28].

In later stages of the design process, where more sophisticated prototypes have been developed, different kinds of formats for participation are typically used. Once there is a 'working prototype', for instance, formal evaluations such as usability tests are frequently employed. At this stage, feedback on the prototype is obtained, and specifications for changes to it might be suggested.[1] The participation of others at this point in the process is often limited to 'input', in contrast to the greater degrees of influence characteristic of the kinds of less technical formats (paper etc.) discussed above. As prototypes become more intricate, and as the work required to effect changes to them become more time consuming, a disjunction between participation and prototyping activities emerges. We notice, then, that the activity of prototyp*ing* functional or 'polished' versions of a concept are often of necessity the exclusive province of designers and engineers.

In this paper, we present an industrial case in which a series of interactive prototypes were deployed during the development process as a means of engaging other stakeholders in prototyp*ing*, i.e. in being able to shape, in near real-time, the functionality and interactivity of the prototype itself. We refer to this approach as 'live prototyping'. Live prototyping is an activity that brings the act of prototyping to the foreground, by 'performing' prototyping in an event with stakeholders who are actively engaged and guide the prototyper with suggestions and input. Doing live prototyping requires (a) an interactive prototype, (b) in which real-time modifications to its interactivity can be made, (c) and one that travels, i.e. is re-deployable within a collaborative session involving non-technical/design stakeholders. One obvious benefit of such a prototype is that it allows for quick iterations in plenum. However, in this paper we are not simply promoting a rapid prototyping approach, but rather wish to bring to attention some of the consequences for design of using such a prototype to involve (non-technical and other) stakeholders in prototyping activities.

In the following sections we first introduce the industrial case, with a brief overview of the challenges in the project, the stakeholders involved, and the functionality of the product. We analyse the live prototyping events to demonstrate how the prototype was staged and how it worked. Our discussion focuses on the ways the prototype worked as a tool for design, as a platform for participation, as well as a means of inquiring into the collaborative and organisational environments in which the product was under development.

DATA

This paper is based on the first author's involvement as an externally hired interaction design consultant in the development of the living eco® radiator thermostat (eco®) at Danfoss Heating Solutions. We focus on the first 7 months of the development of the interface, up to the 'display freeze' when all the elements of the interface were locked. In this time the first author spent approximately 200 working hours on this project, organizing 6 workshops with different stakeholders of which 3 are described here. During this period a series of 3 usability tests were conducted by an external company, and 1 internal usability test was done at Danfoss. In the remainder of this paper, the first author will be referred to as the *interaction design consultant* (IDC) when describing the case, and it was he who developed and introduced the live prototype for the project. The live prototype was deployed in several workshops in the course of the development of the thermostat user interface. In describing this case, we draw on the first author's experience of having actively participated in the events we describe, in addition to other documentary sources: project communications (emails, attachments, prototype versions), video recordings of the workshops where the live prototype was deployed, and subsequent interviews with several of the participants about the prototype and its usefulness to the project and the company.

PROJECT BACKGROUND

The eco® is a programmable radiator thermostat containing electronics and a user interface, which can be mounted onto any radiator and has a similar form factor as a conventional radiator thermostat. Based on the schedule set by the user and the temperature measured by the temperature sensor, a small motor controls the radiator valve to regulate the temperature. The product offers users the possibility to customise their heating use, for example by automatically lowering the set temperature at night or during working hours[2].

The Danfoss Heating Solutions department responsible for its development usually develops mechanical products, such as conventional radiator thermostats. The eco®, as a *programmable* radiator thermostat *with a user interface*, was a new kind of product for this department, which had consequences for the execution of this particular project. Firstly, their milestone plan for new product development – a modified version of the StageGate model – did not describe deliverables for interaction design. Therefore, the Design Line Specialist with a background in design engineering took responsibility for the interface, alongside

[1] We would not term this 'collaborative prototyping', since in many cases, changes to the design medium (whether programming language, CAD model or material forming process etc.) can only be made by those with particular expertise.

[2] For more information about the product, including a simulation of the interface, see http://homeowners.danfoss.com/products/radiatorthermostats/living-eco/.

his responsibility for the construction of the product. Another consequence was that the development team had to collaborate with different internal and external partners, since they did not have all the necessary in-house expertise (e.g. software, electronics and interaction design). Finally, the design of the interface called for a different kind of prototype than they were accustomed to work with. Normally, they only work with mechanical prototypes, but in this project they also needed an interactive (software) prototype, which could be deployed in formal usability tests.

Before the prototyping of the interface began, the development team had already made several important design decisions that were 'locked'. The product would have 3 buttons, a circular segment display 25mm in diameter and would be powered by batteries. The team had also made an initial specification for the interface through 4 workshops, resulting in 13 walk-through use scenarios and a proposal for the segment display (see figure 1a). At this point the project team was working towards what they called the 'display freeze'. This was the final determination of precisely which LCD segments needed to be on the display, including the icon design, position, and size (see figure 1b). Danfoss had planned to conduct usability tests with the interactive prototype as a means of ensuring that the interface would be usable and could support the range of programming functions of which the radiator was capable, such as the ability to fully customise a week-long heating schedule.

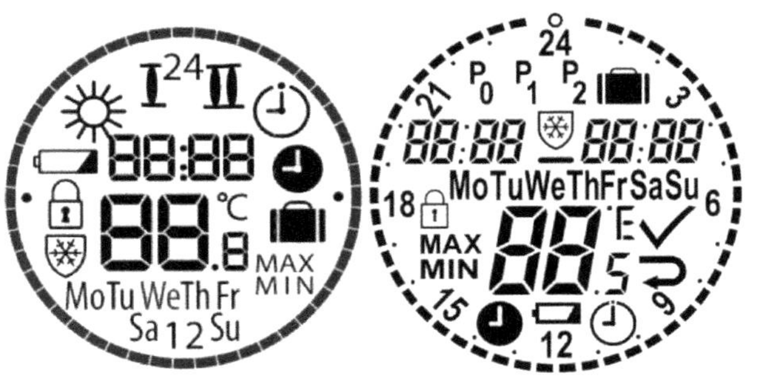

Figure 1. (a) initial segment proposal and (b) segments after display freeze (six months later)

THE LIVE PROTOTYPE

The first author was brought in as an interaction design consultant to develop an interactive prototype, and negotiated to this consulting project as a case in his PhD research concerning collaborative prototyping processes. The prototype was created to be deployable in usability tests, but additional time was spent to make the prototype easily configurable without the need for re-coding the software, so that a number of iterations of the interface could be generated within a project meeting. In the initial email to the other developers the first author outlined the two-fold purpose of the prototype: "The prototype has 2 purposes: (1) it is a demo that has to be used in a user test, and (2) it is a development tool [to be used] across departments" (email, 2 June 2009). Making the prototype with this degree of flexibility and deploying it in an industrial case was a means of doing action research, where the consequences of the interventions could be analysed for evidence of their utility. Historically, the organisation has a tradition of conducting experiments with design practice in active development projects[3]; in general, there was an organisational and management culture that was receptive to exploring an experimental prototyping approach.

The interactive prototype was software that could run on any computer and shared with other developers and external partners. For testing and evaluation a touch-screen computer was used, simulating the three buttons and with the vector graphics at the right scale to mimic the 25 mm diameter segment display, in order to accurately assess the readability of the icons (see figure 2).

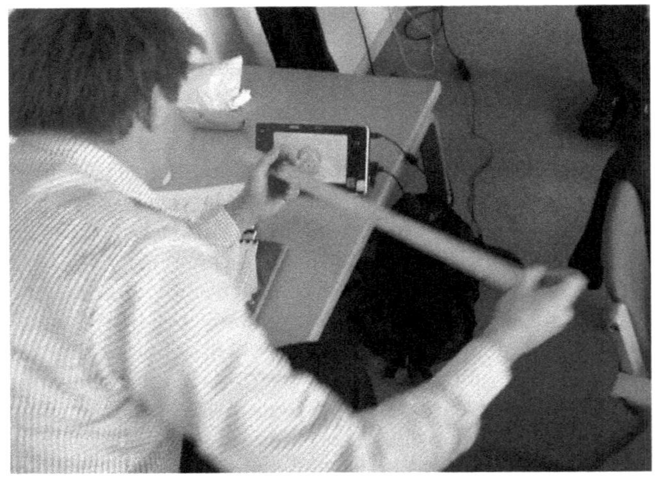

Figure 2. Internal participant measuring the display size on the touch screen to check its dimensions in the stakeholder workshop

The prototype was developed using Adobe Director and it was structured around external files. For example, each screen was described in a separate text file, similar in structure to an xml file, specifying which graphics to use, which variables to manipulate, and which actions to take. Other text files described the various time-outs, blinking frequencies and variables; a readme described the default and valid values for these parameters. Since these could be changed with standard text editors, such as Notepad or TextEdit, it became possible to make rapid changes to the interface outside the development environment. The first author also developed additional supportive tools specifically for this prototype – an editor for the segment display and a screen exporter – that required no additional software to run. This made changes to these aspects of the

[3] This is evidenced by the running history of exploratory work conducted at Danfoss in the past fifteen years by Jacob Buur and colleagues. Select examples include [2,22,25].

interface easier and much faster, to the point where these changes could be implemented 'live' during meetings and workshops.

LIVE PROTOTYPING WORKSHOPS

The live prototype was employed in two workshops at Danfoss among internal and external stakeholders. It was later used in two individual workshops with single users. The first author participated in each of these sessions. In the first workshop described here, the prototype was introduced to a large group of stakeholders, where the focus was on developing a shared understanding and allowing the participants to come with suggestions for improvements before going into the first usability test. The second workshop with three participants focused on solving specific usability problems encountered in the first test and working out the details of a new proposal to be tested again. The individual user workshops were done as complementary usability tests where emerging usability problems introduced by the new design changes could be detected and addressed. Each workshop was recorded on video.

The general setup in these workshops was similar. A static version of the prototype ran on a touch screen PC, and served as a reference point of the state of the prototype before the workshop. A live version of the prototype ran on the first author's computer, and was changed during the workshop based on suggestions from the participants. If more than two people participated a projector was used to enable everyone in the room to follow along (see figure 3).

Figure 3. The live prototype being used in the stakeholder workshop

Stakeholder workshop

The first workshop was a meeting of ten internal and two external stakeholders, and was the first time the live prototype had been tried as a tool in this process. Participants included the Design Line Specialist (DLS), the Product Portfolio Director (PPD), a Design Engineer (DE), a Marketing Engineer (ME), the R&D Director and the R&D Senior Director. In addition, two usability consultants (UC1 and UC2) from an external company who were to carry out the first usability tests on the interface a week later also participated in this session. A goal of this meeting was to specify a version of the interface that could be implemented in the upcoming usability tests. After a brief presentation of the interface, participants were invited to give feedback and suggest design changes. As suggestions were being made, the Interaction Design Consultant implemented some of these changes in a live version of the prototype. These changes were evaluated in the meeting, and recommendations were made for further changes to the interface before the first usability test. The transcribed discussion below exhibits a number of the issues that were at stake in this particular development project:

DE: Now we have the possibility to have several different periods, but we aren't able to have different temperatures in those periods?

DLS: No, that is something we chose not to do.

DE: Can our competitors do that?

PPD: Yes. Yes, that is something we have to include.

DLS: So we have to be able to, on [a display the size of] a 10 kroner coin, choose a flexible temperature change for every single period?

... (several lines of transcript omitted for brevity)

DLS: Of course it is possible, and we have also played with it, but there is a significant difference in the user interface, if we include the temperature parameter in programming the schedule.

... (several lines of transcript omitted for brevity)

ME: I can't see a reason to be able to in the advanced menu set the temperature on Tuesday to be 23 degrees, on Wednesday to be 24 degrees and on Thursday 26 degrees. It can't see a reason for that. I see much more value in that you can define the periods.

DE: So when they are setting the schedule they think: "Why can't I do this?" Our competitors can.

DLS: Yes, but does it add value?

DE: Yeah, yeah

UC1: In any case there is the problem with this trade-off on the user-friendliness. It means that if you have to 'go on compromise' with the user-friendliness, you could say, that you can't even reach that functionality. You can say it has a price.

In this segment[4], a number of constraints and rationale emerge in discussion regarding the interface of the thermostat that has been demonstrated. The interface allows the possibility to set both 'comfort' (high) and 'saving' (low) temperature periods in a 24-hour period. The discussion, initiated by DE, relates to whether the product permits the user to set different comfort temperatures in a day's heating program. The DLS explains it was a *deliberate choice* to not have this feature. The issue is not a technical one—the thermostat is technically capable to support this function—but as DLS implies, it is a matter of restricting the complexity of the configurable functions to access on an LCD interface that is only 25mm in diameter

[4] Transcript excerpts have been translated to English.

(the size of "a 10 kroner coin"). DE and PPD introduce an alternative consideration: whether that is functionality that competitors' products offer. This begins an extended discussion about the merits (or otherwise) of this decision.

The balance between the feature set of the product, its competitive comparability to existing products, and the burden that the inclusion of any additional functions might bear on the simplicity and usability of the interface were live issues throughout the development. As we will shortly show, these were also issues that were explored in and through the proposal and implementation of changes to the interface by various participants.

Usability workshop

Shortly after the stakeholder workshop the first usability tests were held, in which a number of usability problems were identified and presented in a usability report. More than 40 usability problems of varying degrees of severity were identified, and a number of subsequent changes were made to the prototype to address these problems. Following these tests and changes, a second collaborative live prototyping workshop was then held with the Design Line Specialist (DLS), a consultant from the external usability consultancy (UC1) and the Interaction Design Consultant (IDC, also the first author). The aim of this event was to discuss the changes already made, and to make further changes in preparation for the next round of usability tests.

Much of this workshop was spent discussing when to show a 'preview' of a program, which is the visualisation of the comfort and savings periods around a 24-hour clock. Since these periods are different in each program by default, and can be modified by users, the preview is intended to give users an idea what will happen when they choose to run a particular program (see figure 4).

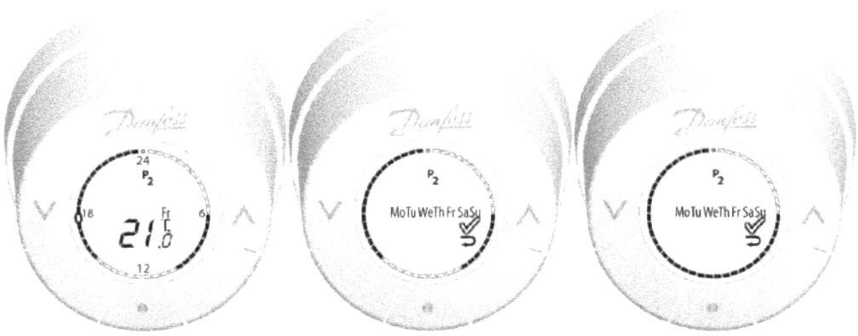

Figure 4. From left to right: the home screen visualising the comfort and saving periods of the running program; the 'approve schedule' showing a preview when it is Friday; and the same screen showing a preview when it is Saturday

The discussion is focused on two screens: the 'confirm program' screen, where users can confirm to run the program they selected, and the 'approve schedule' screen, where users can approve (or modify) the schedule for a program; when a schedule is approved the selected program will run. In the version of the prototype prepared before this workshop, a preview of the periods on Monday is shown on both occasions. The following transcript starts when discussing the 'approve schedule' scenario, where the preview of Monday is confusing:

DLS: Maybe we should remove it [the preview] altogether? Then it is very visual that now you are not on the days anymore, now you can choose okay or back.

... (several lines of transcript omitted; prototyping while discussion continues)

IDC: Is this how it should be?

DLS: Perfect. That just gives the feedback that now you are choosing something.

IDC: Here ['confirm program' screen] we also have [the preview of] Monday that we show, that is why I also had it there.

... (several lines of transcript omitted; prototyping while discussion continues)

UC1: The question is if it would be better to show the preview of the current day. In case you have changed it. To see what will actually happen when I choose this program.

... (several lines of transcript omitted; prototyping while discussion continues)

IDC: So if I go here ['approve schedule' screen] I don't get any preview, and if I go here ['confirm program' screen] I see the preview of today.

DLS: Super.

UC1: Yes, that's really good.

... (several lines of transcript omitted; prototyping while discussion continues)

IDC: Doesn't this ['approve schedule' screen] look a bit strange? Because I don't have a clue what I'm approving right now. I understand we can't just give a preview of Monday, but shouldn't we have a preview of today also here, maybe? Because this 'run' [in the 'approve schedule' screen] actually means the same as that 'run' [in the 'confirm program' screen]

UC1: Yes.

DLS: Yes.

Various options were suggested and implemented within this session. When several of these were tried out, however, there remained question marks over which of them, if any, were likely to make the most sense to users. At the end of the session, this exchange reveals the team's experience of having worked through many of these options:

DLS: I'm looking forward to see the next round [of usability tests].

UC1: Me too, definitely. It is hard to anticipate how much will be needed. We can sit here and change this and that, but the things we have changed now, I'm thinking, we are of course working towards eliminating problems, but it is hard to exclude that what we are changing now will introduce new problems. That would be unfortunate, but that is how it will be, and in the end it will help to prioritise some things, so they become more clear. Those are the trade-offs, right.

IDC: Then we also know what the focus should be in the user manual, what they can do without and what they need the manual for and show it clearly and step-by-step how to....

User workshops

Closer to the 'display freeze' deadline (see figure 1), two user workshops were done with individual users and a live prototype as an alternative kind of usability evaluation. Each user focused on a particular task, performing it while thinking out loud, and reflecting on the problems he or she encountered. In a dialogue different proposals to tackle problems were implemented, and immediately evaluated to detect and address any emerging, unforeseen usability problems the changes might introduce. Instead of a usability report at the end of each workshop, there was an updated prototype, which was then shared with the development team.

ANALYSIS

Obviously, there were a number of advantages in running such internal meetings and user involvement sessions with a live prototype. Some of these were anticipated consequences, relating to the original intention of creating a prototype that could be modified 'live'. Others became apparent through our analysis of the material from the live prototyping sessions and subsequent interviews with project participants. As fitting for an industrial case study such as this, we attach no special claim as to the (future) generalisability of these findings [c.f. 32]; rather, we advance them as empirically-grounded observations from this particular case.

Allowing for rapid iteration in plenum

First, working with a live prototype permitted the rapid iteration, in plenum, of different design proposals. This is evidenced by the fact that 13 distinct iterations of the interface were prototyped *within* these collaborative sessions. Many of these changes were implemented in session as a result of suggestions made by the participants themselves. Different screen layouts, modes of function selection or accessibility were not just identified or proposed, but were implemented, stepped through, and evaluated. In this case of the preview function, this is what happened (from the usability workshop):

UC1: What do you think? If you see a preview should you then see an indication of what day you are seeing the preview of?
IDC: I can quickly try that.
UC1: What do you think?
DLS: Let's see how it looks. Then you would get an idea of what kind of program it is.
UC1: I can't say right away whether this will interfere with something. It actually makes sense to have an indication all the time: where am I, what is it I'm choosing…
DLS: Yes, that's right.

The default configuration that previewed the schedule was unconvincing and alternatives were proposed and prototyped. This leads us to three related observations.

Exposing tradeoffs of different design alternatives

Similarly, the configurable prototype permitted discussion of the tradeoffs of different design alternatives. What, and whether, certain settings should be made available to change frequently exposed the tradeoff between the simplicity and navigability of the small 3-button LCD interface versus the range of technical functions of the product. This is precisely the way UC1 expresses the 'tradeoff' at the end of the transcript from the stakeholder workshop in section 5 above; a little later in that same session it was expressed in a different way by the Communication Technology Manager (CTM): "We have really many functions, and I seriously doubt to what extent these advanced functions will be used in really many installations. Because it's simply too difficult to figure out. We can of course write that we can do these fine things on the box, which our competitors can also do, so we have a product that matches that… it is only in our marketing that it gives something". In this project, the balance between maximizing the number of features needed to claim a competitive advantage, while minimizing the added complexity to the user interface was a balance explored through collaboratively specifying changes to the interface.

Permitting 'rollback' changes

Additionally, since the prototype was easily modifiable it also permitted that any implemented changes could be rolled back when as were discovered within these sessions to introduce unanticipated complications or confusions in interaction. One clear example of this emerged in a live prototyping session with a user (conducted in English). At this point, a suggested change to the interface has just been implemented, and the user is stepping through it (silences are marked in tenths of seconds).

US1: This is already nicer than (0.6) uuhh (0.3) oh no wait. See, if I for example make a mistake here, then I have to go back to this [screen]. Yeah.
IDC: So would it be easier-
US1: But actually it is not so much easier.

This realisation ("oh no, wait"),[5] initiates a discussion between the user and the interaction designer about other possible implementation options that might obviate the *new* difficulty that the proposed changes had introduced. An essential advantage of making the prototype live becomes simply the volume of design options that can be proposed, implemented, stepped through, evaluated and then *rolled back again if necessary* in a short session such as this user trial, which lasted less than an hour.

In our analysis of these sessions, however, we became interested in aspects other than simply how the prototype worked as a (conventional) prototype, i.e. as a communication tool between team members, as a concept generation device, or as a means of anticipating downstream implementation or usability issues [6,16]. We were also struck by how the live prototyping sessions worked as platforms for the involvement of others in prototyping itself, and while doing so, facilitated a set of conversations between stakeholders that made it as much a tool of organisational inquiry as an instrument to advance the design of the interface towards production. A set of our related observations in this regard follows.

[5] The particle 'oh' has been shown in English conversation to signal a (cognitive) 'change of state' of the speaker. See Heritage [13] for a recent exposition.

Repurposing beyond design and development

The prototype was repurposed within the Danfoss organisation beyond a testing vehicle and development tool. The prototype itself was shown at a roadshow exhibition for potential customers in Poland. It was used for technical training of installers before the physical prototype was finalised. Moreover, it served internally as the specification for the software developers as well as the development of a 'try me' feature on the website, supported with a document using exported screenshots from the prototype. The screen export function was also used to make pictures for internal presentations and to make illustrations for the user manual.

Being used without the main prototype developer

Live prototyping was mainly done in workshops facilitated by the interaction design consultant who built the prototype, but the interviews revealed that other developers had also engaged in live prototyping themselves, making use of the 'supportive tools' that enabled changing the prototype without coding [14]. For example, the Design Line Specialist had used a live prototyping approach to fine-tune the details of the interface, either in informal internal tests or in formal usability tests with end-users. In the following interview transcript, he compares the live prototype to a static software prototype that had been used on a different ("living connect") project.

IDC: I have seen there was also a MMI prototype of the living connect [a different product in the same product line], that you had in the same phase. How were these two prototypes different or similar would you assess?
DLS: You could say that the connect prototype is not flexible; we cannot change anything. I cannot change anything in it myself. I can use it as a communication tool, or some status update: "Well, now it is like this." But I have no possibility to modify it, or develop with it, you could say.
IDC: You are saying you made changes to it. How did you do that? There is a graphic editor, and there are text files.
DLS: Yes exactly, [I changed the text files]. Things we have played around with a lot are the default values in it: blinking frequencies, time-outs and such things. You call it participation workshops, where you test directly with a user and correct immediately, until you reach a satisfying result.
IDC: And you have done that?
DLS: Yes, we have indeed. As a developer you lose the feeling for those parameters, time-outs and frequencies and things like that. So there it was very easy to go in and find the values, by being able to adjust them until the end-user says: "Now it is good."

The time-outs of the backlight have an impact on both the user experience and the battery life of the product. The Design Line Specialist was able to find an appropriate balance by changing these values himself, and evaluating them immediately with an end-user, without the need for an external consultant to reprogram the prototype.

Exposing misalignments between stakeholders

In negotiating various changes that were possible to be made to the prototype, the participants' discussions revealed various misalignments between them regarding the priorities that the product should ideally be fulfilling. These included its competitive range of features, its sale cost, its usability, its size and its marketability. Seeing and experiencing the prototype, finding difficulties or limitations with the interface, and proposing solutions to those within the meeting allowed these various misalignments in values to surface in discussion. Because of the detail of the prototype, however, these competing concerns did not arise as general or abstract issues, but in response to specific UI decisions, such as precisely what settings to offer on the Advanced Menu, or how the user might recover from having made a mistake in a program setting. The resolution (even if only temporary) of these issues were able to be determined *through the interface*, as changes to it were proposed, tried, and evaluated in session, rather than e.g. as the formulation of changes to design specifications that would be implemented sometime later by developers.

Revealing the specific reach of institutional constraints

Several institutional (or corporate) design constraints also became visible through this active negotiation of the changes to be implemented in new versions of the interface during these sessions. Consider the following exchange from the stakeholder workshop:

DE: So what's the difference? [between the black and white clock icons on the LCD display]
INTERN: The one is time and date, that's the black clock. The white one that is schedule. And those are standard icons.
DLS: They are standard icons for all of Danfoss.
... (several lines of transcript omitted for brevity)
UC1: How can it be that both are standard icons?
INTERN: I know they are taken from one standard, but I don't know if that's the design line.
DLS: Can't we just change that one?
(ALL): (laughing/growling)
DE: Back to that black clock. Is there no other way to do that?

The design line exists in order to ensure a semblance of corporate consistency across a wide range of products. The Danfoss design line consists of a set of standards that include specific icons for different functions. While probing the interface, one of the new participants encounters the two different clock icons (the white schedule and the black time/date) and asks about their difference. The several turns at conversation here culminate in the Design Line Specialist joking that they might suggest changing the design line. This results in group laughter and growls, simultaneously demonstrating that the obstinacy of the design line as something with which each product must conform is a well-known (and sometimes unpopular) constraint in the organisation. The questioning of other icons also met with the 'design line' explanation. The restrictions imposed by the Company-wide design line are therefore notorious at Danfoss. As such, the existence of the constraint itself was not news to the participants. What is noteworthy is that such constraints were encountered in and through the prototype, not as generic requirements for the interface, but as specific restrictions on design options that are currently on the table and in the process of being negotiated.

Similar institutional constraints emerged elsewhere in our material, such as the impending 'display freeze' (mentioned earlier) and the limitation of the number of segments that the LCD display needed to support. Like the design line, these constraints were encountered as constituents of the suggestion and consideration of specific changes to the display/interface. The specific *reach* of those institutional constraints, their relevance to the current issue being discussed, is something that is only exposed through interaction concerning the various options made available through these live prototyping sessions.

Embodying implicit design rationale

Relatedly, the rationale for certain decisions was also topicalised in discussion as perceived difficulties were anticipated and encountered. The examples we have already considered show how decisions had been justified as a means of satisfying a design line constraint, or in order to conserve LCD elements on the display, or in order to simplify the interface. The ability to propose alterations, implement them and discuss their merits provided opportunity for the design team to share their reasoning for the existence of certain features with other stakeholders, and to expose that reasoning to scrutiny.

Becoming a novel form of design documentation

An unexpected subsequent use of the live prototype was that it became a new form of design documentation for the distributed stakeholders in this project. At the end of each of these prototyping sessions, the prototype itself had undergone a series of revisions, and various features of the interface had changed. These changes had been discussed, and evaluated, and ultimately a new version of the interface stabilised within each meeting, becoming ready for subsequent organisational use, as in e.g. a usability test. These decisions were documented by the resultant state of the live prototype itself, rather than as, e.g., a list of specifications for changes to be made. Moreover, they had already been tested (to a degree) by the participants in the room. Because the prototype could be exported as an executable file, it could also be shared with absent stakeholders, who could step through the new version and see the changes that had been made for themselves. An external agency developing a software simulation for the product website is an example of such a stakeholder, as the Global Webmaster discussed in a subsequent interview. "Knowing that I could always say to them [the website simulation developers]: 'just look at the prototype'. So for me that is the greatest benefit, of knowing that they have something in-house, in Warsaw, they can look at and see. [...] I think they received a second version not long after the first one. But that was easy just to mail it to them and say: 'look, this is the latest'."

COSTS, LIMITATIONS & IMPACTS

In sum, from the examples we have presented in this single case, a core value of working with a 'live' prototype is that design rationale, tradeoffs, departmental agendas, institutional constraints and the like can become publicly and collectively *discoverable* through exploring the interface itself, rather than needing to be discursively *reportable* by the responsible designers or consultants, or worse, remaining implicit during the process.

While there are clear benefits in constructing a prototype that can be quickly and easily configured in collaborative settings, and although this can significantly increase the quantity of design iterations that can be done together with other (especially non-technical) participants, the initial effort to create a configurable prototype that works in this way obviously adds to the development time. Clearly, the volume of additional work required to build a live prototype depends on many things. These include the particular technology in view, the complexity of the interface, the stage of the project (i.e. the number of interface decisions that are still negotiable), the skill of the prototyping team and the particular prototyping media, each of which may have costly implications for development time. Although this approach to prototyping appears ideally suited to environments where there are many distributed stakeholders, where establishing collective ownership and influence over the shape of the outcome is especially important for the project's intra-organisational success, the costs versus the benefits of prototyping in this way will vary greatly depending on the organisations and projects in view. Furthermore, live interactive prototypes are inherently constrained, as interactivity, workflows and feedback must already be specified. Unlike other, much less expensive methods for collaboratively prototyping and evaluating interactive interfaces, live prototyping does not provide a medium for design anywhere nearly as malleable as less technological approaches such as "wizard of oz" techniques. And indeed, the choice of which elements and parameters of the interface are modifiable is stipulated outside of collaborative sessions by (again) the designers and technologists who (still) control the construction of the flexible prototype. As our data shows, these decisions (e.g. which parameters can be tweaked) are incredibly consequential for the content and direction of the stakeholder discussions that take place around the interface. These are important limitations of this approach.

However, these workshops clearly had a traceable impact on the ultimate design of the interface. Although pinpointing which design decisions were made in these workshops is not straightforward, a strong indication is given by the timestamp on the text files describing the screens. Because these describe the interaction flow, refer to the icons used, and describe only a single screen each, each screen has a precise date and time at which they were last modified, enabling us to recover which decisions were finalised during a live prototyping workshop. Figure 5 shows an overview of the eighteen screen definitions of the prototype at the time of the 'display freeze' in reverse chronological order. The screens that were finalised during the workshops describe here are highlighted. Of the eighteen screen definitions, eight were finalised during these workshops, whereas ten were implemented according to specifications formally determined outside these sessions. In this way we can say that these workshops have enabled (non-prototyping) participants to have a direct impact on the final design.

Name	Size	Type	Date Modified
confirm_p2.txt	1 KB	Text Document	2009-11-23 20:06
confirm_p1.txt	1 KB	Text Document	2009-11-23 20:06
setdayschedule.txt	1 KB	Text Document	2009-11-23 20:04
Home.txt	1 KB	Text Document	2009-11-23 19:06
HomeTR.txt	1 KB	Text Document	2009-11-23 18:53
Quick.txt	1 KB	Text Document	2009-10-12 12:03
Locked.txt	1 KB	Text Document	2009-09-23 19:47
set_date_firsttime.txt	1 KB	Text Document	2009-08-25 13:46
firsttime_set_time.txt	1 KB	Text Document	2009-08-25 13:45
set_travel_date.txt	2 KB	Text Document	2009-08-25 13:04
confirm_p4.txt	2 KB	Text Document	2009-08-25 13:04
Advanced.txt	1 KB	Text Document	2009-08-04 14:18
date_confirm.txt	1 KB	Text Document	2009-08-04 13:07
set_date.txt	1 KB	Text Document	2009-08-04 12:58
confirm_p0.txt	1 KB	Text Document	2009-07-30 15:17
set_time.txt	1 KB	Text Document	2009-07-29 16:49
set_min.txt	1 KB	Text Document	2009-06-16 12:48
set_maxmin.txt	1 KB	Text Document	2009-06-15 13:53

Figure 6. Screen definition text files; screens finalised in live prototyping workshops are highlighted

DISCUSSION

Naturally, the set of observations we have collected above about the uses and consequences of live prototyping are, we suspect, shared with some other kinds of collaborative prototyping activities. Given our observations, however, it is particularly the *organisational* aspects of our analysis that distinguish the kinds of things we say about prototyping from many of the general discussions of prototypes that appear in design research. For example, Lim et al. [20] introduce a nuanced set of distinctions with respect to the 'nature' of prototypes: that prototypes can be understood in terms of their *filtering dimensions* (e.g. the selective aspects of the intended product that the prototype foregrounds in its constitution, such as size, functionality or interactivity) and *manifestation dimensions* (e.g. how it is materially constructed, or to what level of detail) which aptly define the prototype in design-centric terms—i.e. in terms of what, how and how many aspects of the product are represented in the prototype. Similarly, Houde and Hill [17] distinguish prototypes in terms of whether they model an artefact's *role, look and feel,* or *implementation.* When prototypes are conceived as design tools, representations [6], or even communication devices [9], the emphasis is naturally placed upon what is represented, and/or how it supports the continuing development of the concept. What may disappear from view are many of the organisational corollaries of prototypes and prototyping activities. Part of the value of an analysis such as we present here is the extent to which it draws attention to the organisational contexts of prototyping. As we have tried to show, opening up the prototyping process to other stakeholders actually opened up the organisation itself, such that the locally relevant logics of decisions, constraints and rationales became explicitly topicalised, yet specific to the participants' own perspectives, and relative to particular design options for the interface.

We would therefore struggle to locate many of our observations about the consequences of live prototyping within any of the prototyping frameworks or taxonomies of which we are aware, including those that have been constructed from different uses of prototyping within industrial cases [19]. What the prototype 'is', including precisely the aspects of the product that a prototype prototypes (e.g. its 'filtering dimensions'), is not merely a matter of its specific materialisation, the prototyper's intentions, nor of its relation to the final product, but is also constituent of the setting in which it is introduced, the participants who engage with it, the tasks they are presented and the discussions it occasions. It is on this basis that we are able to constructively complicate a design-centric view of what prototypes are. Our contextual and organisational observations are of a kind that are generally neglected in design prototyping literature, yet they bear directly upon what prototypes are conceived to be, and how they can be (alternatively) effective in the swampy lowlands of industrial design practice. This conceptual point stands in close relation to some recent developments in design studies that are formulating notions of design that are not inherently tied to design intent [1,23,26].

Naturally, we are not the first to draw attention to organisational and contextual issues in prototyping. Other scholars have identified related roles of prototypes in industrial design and development projects. Schrage [30] draws attention to the importance of the prototype as a tool for dialogue within an organisation, a vehicle for persuading managers and "a weapon in interdepartmental power struggles" (p.201). The breadth and diversity of the roles of prototypes that Schrage identifies are, to our knowledge, unmatched in studies of industrial prototyping. But it is also a breadth that comes at the expense of detailed empirical examples. His observations (such as those quoted above) ring true, but they are made in passing, supported only by anecdotes. More convincing examples are found in ethnographies. In one longitudinal study of a software research and development laboratory, Matthews [21] described the way in which an itinerant prototype of an 'internet fridge' circulated (physically and discursively) through the organisation, becoming a token of the technological competence of its developer, and in this way affording new opportunities for intra-organisational collaboration. Henderson's [12] ethnographic study of the development of a medical lens insertion device stands as a detailed document of the organisational *politics* of prototyping, and the kinds of power struggles into which prototypes can be drawn. Henderson analyses her case in order to demonstrate how engineering representations, including prototypes, are susceptible to different (and politically interested) readings, are mobilised as devices to conscript intra-organisational support, and become a site of disciplinary squabbles and a locus of organisational influence. In this paper, we have extended this family understandings of the ways prototypes can work within organisations, analysing them in terms of the ways in which they function as devices for revealing institutional values and constraints, exposing latent characteristics of the organisational context, participants' interests, and local particulars of the project. Yet we have also shown how they can be deliberately crafted to be open, inclusive and collaborative, altering the kinds of institutional politics of prototyping identified by Henderson and Schrage.

The implications of this view of prototyping highlight a set of issues than have not commonly been raised. Rather than holding our focus on which aspects of a product are captured in a prototype, to what level of detail, and how those are materially, temporally and visually expressed in service of what purposes (although these remain vital issues for design prototyping), we are led to ask who can be involved in prototyping, how their participation in a session can be invited and structured, and when (or how early) they can be involved. For example, the involvement of external usability consultants together with the product portfolio director and product marketers in the same prototyping session was instrumental in exposing some of the tradeoffs between usability issues and the feature set of the product. Furthermore, the role of the designer/prototyper in this case also shifts towards one of facilitation of this involvement. This does not mean that less designerly work is involved. In this instance, the prototype itself becomes a carefully designed artefact with its own set of stakeholders; it must be deliberately crafted so that the designer can actually cede some control over the functional, interactive and material qualities of design to these other stakeholders [15]; and in this way it also contributes (methodologically) to the ways in which prototypes can feature as in constructive design research [33].

CONCLUSION

Live prototypes serve as platforms for active involvement and participation in the development process with different stakeholders. This paper has described a case in which this prototyping approach was used at Danfoss Heating Solutions during the development of a product for market production. We have described examples of the ways in which a live prototype worked as a development tool, yet also exposed latent issues in the complex organisation of an industrial design undertaking, including misalignments between stakeholders, institutional design constraints, implicit design rationale and unforeseen consequences of design decisions. Additionally, by being collaboratively modifiable and easily shareable, it also served as a form of documentation in lieu of written specifications, and was subsequently repurposed within the organisation.

In particular, the approach of live prototyping is intended to serve as a means of bringing other non-technical stakeholders into the technical arena in which concrete determinations of the constitution of a designed product are set—i.e. into the act of prototyping itself. This opposes the otherwise 'natural' separation between evaluation activities with stakeholders (e.g. users) and "making" activities of designers and engineers. In this case, iterative loops involving problem identification, re-design proposals, implementation and evaluation were condensed such that multiple iterations could be performed in a single workshop session with multiple stakeholders.

ACKNOWLEDGEMENTS

We gratefully acknowledge the participation and support of Danfoss Heating Solutions, in addition to the interaction design research environments at Syddansk Universitet (SDU-Design) and The University of Queensland.

REFERENCES

1. Thomas Binder. 2002. Intent, form and materiality in the design of interaction technology. In *Social thinking - software practice*. MIT Press, Cambridge, 451–468.

2. Susanne Bødker and Jacob Buur. 2002. The design collaboratorium—a place for usability design. *ACM Transactions on Computer-Human Interaction* 9, 2: 152–169.

3. Susanne Bødker and K. Grönbæk. 1991. Cooperative prototyping: users and designers in mutual activity. *International Journal of Man-Machine Studies* 34, 3: 453–478.

4. Eva Brandt and J. Messeter. 2004. Facilitating collaboration through design games. *Proceedings of the eighth conference on Participatory design: Artful integration: interweaving media, materials and practices-Volume 1*, 121–131.

5. C. Burns, E. Dishman, W. Verplank, and B. Lassiter. 1994. Actors, hairdos & videotape - informance design. *CHI '94 Conference Companion*, ACM Press.

6. Jacob Buur and M. M. Andreason. 1989. Design models in mechatronic product development. *Design Studies* 10, 3.

7. John M. Carroll. 1995. *Scenario-Based Design: Envisioning Work and Technology in System Development*. John Wiley & Sons.

8. Pelle Ehn and Morten Kyng. 1991. Cardboard computers: mocking-it-up or hands-on the future. In *Design at work: cooperative design of computer systems*. Lawrence Erlbaum Associates, Inc, Mahwah, NJ.

9. Thomas Erickson. 1995. Notes on design practice: stories and prototypes as catalysts for communication. . John Wiley & Sons, Inc., New York, NY, USA, 37–58. Retrieved April 18, 2011 from http://portal.acm.org/citation.cfm?id=209227.209231
10. J. Greenbaum and Morten Kyng. 1991. *Design at work: cooperative design of computer systems.* Lawrence Erlbaum, Hillsdale, NJ.
11. B. Hartmann. 2009. Gaining design insight through interaction prototyping tools.
12. Kathryn Henderson. 1995. The political career of a prototype: visual representation in design engineering. *Social Problems* 42, 2: 274–299.
13. J. Heritage. 2005. Cognition in discourse. In *Conversation and cognition*, Hedwig te Molder and Jonathan Potter (eds.). Cambridge University Press, Cambridge, 184–202.
14. Willem Horst. 2011. Supportive tools for collaborative prototyping. *Making Design Matter: Proceedings of the 4th Nordic Design Research Conference*, 318–323.
15. Willem Horst. 2011. Prototypes as platforms for participation.
16. Glen I. Horton and David F. Radcliffe. 1995. Nature of Rapid Proof-of-concept Prototyping. *Journal of Engineering Design* 6: 3–16. http://doi.org/10.1080/09544829508907898
17. S. Houde and C. Hill. 1997. What do prototypes prototype. *Handbook of human-computer interaction* 2: 367–381.
18. S. R Klemmer, B. Hartmann, and L. Takayama. 2006. How bodies matter: five themes for interaction design. *Proceedings of the 6th conference on Designing Interactive systems*, 140–149.
19. H. Lichter, M. Schneider-Hufschmidt, and H. Zullighoven. 1994. Prototyping in industrial software projects-bridging the gap between theory and practice. *Software Engineering, IEEE Transactions on* 20, 11: 825–832.
20. Y. K Lim, E. Stolterman, and J. Tenenberg. 2008. The anatomy of prototypes: Prototypes as filters, prototypes as manifestations of design ideas. *ACM Transactions on Computer-Human Interaction (TOCHI)* 15, 2: 1–27.
21. Ben Matthews. 2004. Studying design: an interpretive and empirical investigation of design activity.
22. Ben Matthews, Jacob Buur, and Margot F. Brereton. 2001. Brick games in boardrooms: making use context tangible. In *Designing in context*, P. A. Lloyd and Henri Christiaans (eds.). Delft University Press, Delft University, 187–198.
23. Ben Matthews, Marcelle Stienstra, and Tom Djajadiningrat. 2008. Emergent interaction: creating spaces for play. *Design Issues* 24, 3: 58–71.
24. P. Mogensen. 1992. Towards a provotyping approach in systems development. *Scandinavian Journal of Information Systems* 4, 1: 5.
25. Jesper Pedersen and Jacob Buur. 2000. Games and movies: towards innovative co-design with users. In *Collaborative design*. Springer, London, 93–100.
26. Johan Redström. 2008. RE: Definitions of use. *Design Studies* 29, 4: 410–423.
27. M. Rettig. 1994. Prototyping for tiny fingers. *Communications of the ACM* 37, 4: 21–27.
28. J. Rudd, K. Stern, and S. Isensee. 1996. Low vs. high-fidelity prototyping debate. *interactions* 3, 1: 76–85.
29. Elizabeth Sanders and P. J Stappers. 2008. Co-creation and the new landscapes of design. *CoDesign* 4, 1: 5–18.
30. M. Schrage. 1996. Cultures of prototyping. In *Bringing design to software*, Terry Winograd (ed.). ACM Press, New York.
31. Douglas Schuler and Aki Namioka. 1993. *Participatory design: principles and practices.* Lawrence Erlbaum Associates, Hillsdale, NJ.
32. Robert E. Stake. 1994. Case studies. In *Handbook of qualitative research.* Sage Publications, Thousand Oaks, Calif., 236–247.
33. Stephan Wensveen and Ben Matthews. 2015. Prototypes and prototyping in design research. In *The Routledge Companion to Design Research.* Routledge, London, 262–276.

A Design Approach for Authenticity and Technology

Norman Makoto Su
School of Informatics and Computing
Indiana University Bloomington
normsu@indiana.edu

Erik Stolterman
School of Informatics and Computing
Indiana University Bloomington
estolter@indiana.edu

ABSTRACT
Today's sensor-rich and socially-networked world forces us to ask whether technology is moving us away from an authentic life. We all have different views on what constitutes an authentic life with technology and, through our actions, try to stay true to those views. We describe a design approach called "Designing for Authenticity" that draws from the existentialist philosophy of Søren Kierkegaard. It allows researchers engaged in immersive fieldwork to articulate the possible patterns of authentic living with technology. It also outlines a strategy to design artifacts that indirectly communicate to users the experiences of those living in different modes of authenticity. Yet, our approach gives the designer's own informed convictions weight in advocating that one should commit to a spiritual life-view with technology. To illustrate our approach, we subject previously published research on Irish traditional musicians to our designing for authenticity approach.

Author Keywords
Authenticity; design approach; philosophy; existentialism; spirituality; techno-spirituality; Kierkegaard

ACM Classification Keywords
H.5.m. Information Interfaces and Presentation (e.g. HCI): Miscellaneous

INTRODUCTION
There is a consensus amongst scholars [1, 8] that one part of ubiquitous computing's vision [58]—technology of different forms will permeate all facets of our lives—has come to fruition. We can use technology anywhere and anytime. Indeed, it is now difficult to imagine any activity not somehow mediated with technology. Today's sensor-rich and socially-networked world comes with a familiar refrain: technology moves us away from an *authentic* life, a life that lives up to the full potential of humankind. For example, research has described how technology is blamed for eroding conversational skills [53], supplanting traditional practices [52], and removing our connection to nature [3] or society [14].

ACM 978-1-4503-4031-1/16/06...$15.00.
DOI: http://dx.doi.org/10.1145/2901790.2901869

This rhetoric reflects a central challenge of modernity: balancing the purported benefits of technology adoption with the corrosive effects it may have on one's goals and values. In particular, technology's inescapable nature impels subcultures [30] to now confront the potential conflicts between technology and their mores. Among religious groups, members leverage technology for convenience and financial reasons while technically not violating their faith (e.g., Amish "workarounds" [19] and home automation for Orthodox Jews [59]). The specialized skills passed down from generation to generation in isolated subcultures are in danger of being displaced by technology (e.g., the deterioration of wayfinding skills amongst younger Inuit due to the proliferation of GPS devices [4]).

Research in HCI and its related fields often employ the term "authenticity" in a loosely colloquial manner to explain why users limit, disparage, discontinue, delay, or refuse the use [7, 46] of digital artifacts in their lives. In asking why we choose to use technology in the ways we do, such work has on occasion brought to light an individual's personal beliefs on what constitutes "the good life" [5].

This paper outlines a new design approach that focuses on authenticity—treating it as a fundamental concept that humans deeply think about, have feelings about, and act upon. We begin with a definition of authenticity [6] that encapsulates this relation between one's actions and personal philosophy:

> A *mode of existence* arising from self-awareness, critical reflection on one's goals and values, and responsibility for one's own actions; the condition of being true to oneself. [emphasis added]

This existential-slant toward authenticity emphasizes that human agency is the pathway towards achieving a way of living that embraces human potentiality (being true to oneself).

Our interest is in the intersection of authenticity with technology. We make two observations here. First, it is a matter of active public debate as to what constitutes an authentic life with technology. For instance, some believe cameras disengage us from the real world (e.g., from truly appreciating the art in a museum [44] or the performance in a live concert [17]). Others believe humanity has always been intact despite such technological advances [15, 42]. In sum, individuals hold different beliefs on authenticity, each of which prescribe a particular integration of technology that avoids violating one's life-view. Second, while striving to follow a chosen model of authentic living, people are aware of the hypocrisy of their own technological practices. Simply put, we veer away from authenticity for practical reasons. One might, for example, compromise personal views on privacy and surveillance by joining online social networking services for social and professional capital [39, 18, 50]. For some this is acceptable; for others, it is a choice racked with guilt or unease.

We propose a design approach—"Designing for Authenticity"—as a first step toward addressing these concerns, specifically the multifarious nature of authenticity and our difficulty in choosing an authentic mode of living. The genesis of this approach comes from the efforts of Su and Duggan [52] to puzzle out the varied beliefs and reactions to a system called TuneTracker that was designed, developed, and deployed for Irish traditional musicians—a subculture whose members for centuries have scarcely relied on digital technology. Despite being informed by an immersive two-year ethnography of folk musicians in Dublin [51], some of the study's informants felt TuneTracker's design represented the actions of an immoral and inauthentic musician at odds with tradition. Other informants, however, did believe TuneTracker respected tradition and, in fact, embodied the ways of an authentic folk musician. The approach in this paper is one possible way to understand and act on these mixed findings.

Our design approach draws from the work of Søren Kierkegaard, arguably the first existentialist philosopher. Kierkegaard recognized that authenticity—the "condition of being true to oneself"—differed across people. Yet, he also believed and wished to communicate that one particular mode of existence best exemplified authenticity. Designing for authenticity turns to two of Kierkegaard's major concepts: *spheres of existence* and *indirect communication*. With spheres of existence, Kierkegaard attempted to map out our possible modes of existence. Each sphere has its own view on what one must do to have a fulfilling and meaningful life. Indirect communication describes Kierkegaard's peculiar method of disavowing authorship of his own writing in order to more persuasively present the positive and negative aspects of each sphere of existence. This encourages the reader to make their own commitment, without the author's reputation or authority being a factor, on what sphere of existence to adopt.

Designing for authenticity marries interaction design with Kierkegaard's philosophical concepts. Spheres of existence provides a broad foundation for the designer who has achieved both (a) a thick description of the domain of interest (e.g., through ethnography [26]) and (b) a heartfelt *conviction* regarding the varied lifestyles of that domain to begin to articulate, in a penetrating manner, the benefits and pitfalls of adopting a certain approach to authenticity with technology. In this sense, designing for authenticity takes to heart Le Dantec et al.'s [38] point that "what gets lost when we talk about values in the abstract...is the visceral relationship to values as lived experience." Through our approach, designers can begin a dialogue on how their designs may cohere or intervene with users' lifestyles. Indirect communication outlines a strategy for designers to brainstorm or create technological tools for users to critically understand the role of technology in different notions of living authentically.

Most radically, designing for authenticity is prescriptive. It asks users to simultaneously consider different modes of existence and to deeply commit to their chosen sphere of existence. Furthermore, it challenges the user to strive towards what Kierkegaard called the *religious* sphere of existence—a life-view which he believed epitomized authenticity. In our design approach, we broadly interpret the religious sphere as a spiritual, transcendental mode of existence that cannot be explained in rational terms.

Because Kierkegaard is regarded as a Christian philosopher (whose influence unequivocally extends to the secular world), we wish to make abundantly clear that we are *not* arguing for or against a life that follows Christianity or any other religious denomination. Yet, we believe Kierkegaard was right in asserting that if we are to talk about the authentic, we cannot escape the metaphysical. Buie similarly argues that since spirituality is part of most people's lives, HCI needs more studies that understand and design technology that support these modes of existence [11]. Further, Kierkegaard is advocating for a more personal, spiritual inwardness for ourselves, a self not encumbered by the politics and shallow traditions of institutions (in his time, the Church of Denmark).

This paper presents a nascent step in making authenticity a first-class object of inquiry in design. Through the example of Su and Duggan's research on Irish traditional musicians, we demonstrate the use of our design approach. Their research is an apt exemplar because it describes efforts to design for a subculture where concerns of authenticity with technology are particularly visible. However, our primary goal is not to present the sociotechnical practices of musicians (for that, see their work [51, 52]), but to help readers understand, use, and build upon our design approach. First, we demonstrate how spheres of existence provide a useful framework for conceptualizing disparate views on authenticity and technology amongst Irish traditional musicians. Second, we present a hypothetical transformation of TuneTracker's design into a new design—Indirect TuneTracker—that adopts Kierkegaard's strategy of indirect communication. Lastly, we contrast our design approach with past, analogous work, followed by suggestions for future work on designing for authenticity.

ILLUSTRATING OUR APPROACH: IRISH TRAD MUSIC

We illustrate designing for authenticity through a previous three-year study on the intersection of technology and Irish traditional (trad) musicians by Su and Duggan [51, 52]. Participatory observation and interviews with 27 trad musicians were conducted in Dublin, Ireland. To set the stage, we describe what trad musicians do and then summarize their published work.

Irish trad musicians gather together in *sessions* to play Irish music together in a public space (e.g., a pub). Most trad musicians do not use nor can read sheet music. Sets of tunes are played in a session. A set is two or three tunes played in succession without a pause. Tunes in a set usually have the same meter/rhythm (e.g., jig, barndance, hornpipe, polka, slide, or reel). Each tune in a set is repeated three times in a row. The musician who starts a tune is usually expected to lead by choosing what tunes follow one after another (thus forming a set). Unlike jam sessions in genres like jazz where improvisation is valued, trad music is essentially monophonic music in which the melody is played in unison. However, unobtrusive harmonic or percussive backing by guitar/bouzouki or bodhrán (an Irish drum) is now common. Each session has its own particular yet ever-changing repertoire of tunes. Session tunes are also influenced by their regional styles (e.g., Sligo fiddle playing or Roscommon flute playing). Each session can be said to have its own particular repertoire of tunes.

Ethnographic investigations found that professional Irish trad musicians draw from a multitude of analog and digital sources (e.g., CDs, YouTube clips, and transcriptions) to reach an "authentic" representation of a tune [51]. Amateur musicians, however, vacillate between different representations of tunes, finding it difficult to reach an acceptable, authentic form for a tune. "Tradition," for those steeped in Irish traditional music, means embracing aural learning, respecting old masters, knowing the provenance of tunes, upholding the social aspect of playing, believing in etiquette in sessions, and possessing a flexible and ambiguous notion of what a tune is. This notion of a tune includes playing with ornaments and variations that respect the melody, having incomplete, hazy knowledge of tunes that are filled in by other musicians during collaborative playing, and a reliance on memory (professionals know thousands of tunes by heart) rather than sheet music.

In response to these findings, the TuneTracker system was created by Su and Duggan [52] to address the gap between amateur and professional musicians. TuneTracker was a continuously running system installed in The Cobblestone (a pub in Dublin famous for its Irish traditional music sessions). TuneTracker dynamically tracks the tunes played by musicians in a session and publishes the names of those tunes on a public website. It statistically analyzes tune playing trends to give musicians a sense of what tunes are popular. Such information can be used, for example, to suggest what tunes need to be learned to be able to play along in a session. TuneTracker's reception revealed divergent viewpoints [52] on the interplay between TuneTracker and authenticity in trad music. We now turn to understanding these viewpoints by describing and applying Kierkegaard's *spheres of existence*. In our writings below, the Irish musicians, TuneTracker, and Indirect TuneTracker serve as rhetorical and pedagogical tools (founded upon empirical data) to illustrate our design approach in action.

UNPACKING AUTHENTICITY: SPHERES OF EXISTENCE

Kierkegaard outlines three spheres of existence: the aesthetic, the ethical, and the religious. Each sphere dictates a particular life style—a guide on how one should live, what one's goal in life should be, and what kind of commitment is required to have a fulfilling life. The spheres also elucidate the inherent tensions and dread exhibited in such life styles. Spheres are less about categorizing behaviors or activities and more about representing the possibilities of living that are available to all of us. In addition to translations and the prefaces of Kierkegaard's *Fear and Trembling* [37], *Either/Or* [36, 35], and *Two Ages: The Age of Revolution and the Present Age* [34], our exposition of Kierkegaard owes much to Garff's [25] prodigious biography of Kierkegaard, Mullen's [41] work on Kierkegaard's significance in modern society, Evans's [21] primer on Kierkegaard, Walsh's [56] aesthetic perspective into Kierkegaard's existentialism, and an introductory chapter on Kierkegaard by Guignon and Pereboom [27]. In accordance with previous scholarship on Kierkegaard, we will use the terms *spheres of existence*, *stages of existence*, *modes of existence*, *life styles*, and *life-views* interchangeably.

We now present three life-views of the authentic Irish trad musician. We first describe each sphere of existence's virtues and faults according to Kierkegaard's writings. We then reimagine or frame Su and Duggan's data and findings on traditional musicians into these spheres. We emphasize that these re-imaginings are our own translations. By following Kierkegaard's philosophy and our convictions, our translations advocate, albeit indirectly, the religious sphere as the most "authentic" life-view.

I. THE AESTHETIC SPHERE: MASTERING PLEASURE

In the aesthetic sphere, enjoyment and pleasure is the goal of the individual. The aesthete lives for the immediate. Happiness is gained through the satisfaction of immediate desire. As a result, the aesthete experiences time in fleeting moments. The aesthete is a poet who investigates human nature through *irony*. As a critic of human nature, irony allows the aesthete to detach themselves and passively observe—without commitment—the world. This ironic posture [41, p.19] allows the aesthete to play with and imagine the possibilities available to their life. The poet embraces an emotional and critical viewpoint of social laws and mores.

There are a spectrum of individuals described in *Either/Or* who adopt an aesthetic lifestyle. The Countess is a person obsessed with health and beauty. The genius seeks enjoyment through the development of a particular talent or skill. The hedonist seeks pleasure in a multitude of forms (wealth, beauty, and status). The seducer conquers one woman, only to seek another one.

These individuals represent the most shallow adopters of this sphere, the *immediate aesthete*. However, the immediate aesthete risks boredom; when one continually seeks momentary, immediate pleasures, life becomes a series of fragmented projects. Their lives become governed by chance and fortune.

The *reflective aesthete* represents the pinnacle of the aesthetic sphere. Borrowing an agricultural metaphor—"a rotation of crops"—the reflective aesthete proposes two methods to combat boredom. The first is to simply exhaust the soil and move onto another field. Yet, this method is doomed to fail since the search for something new will itself become boring. The second is to carry out "genuine crop rotation...changing the method of cultivation and the kinds of crops." In this method, one chooses to "live with intensity rather than seeking extensive experiences" [20, p.78].

This requires one to adopt the discipline of *remembering and forgetting*. Essentially, the reflective aesthete tries to experience things intensively so that they can remember it at any moment. They sacrifice permanent commitments such as marriage or friendship and moderate enjoyment (since it is not "intense" enjoyment). The aesthete can thus guard against, to some extent, the ephemeral nature of their moments: "We must learn to keep our enjoyment under control, so as not to indulge in an experience too long or allow it to acquire too strong a hold on us" [56, p.90]. One makes their own life a project through detachment and happily observes themselves enjoying life. This ensures total freedom and self-control of our lives.

Problems: Chasing the Dragon. Two key problems plague the aesthete [21, p.85–89]: the loss of immediacy and the inescapability of the ethical. First, the reflective aesthete will never escape dependence on the external world. There is a constant worry of not being able to secure what is desired as well as diminishing returns for continued effort to create "interesting" experiences for themselves. The life of the aesthete is one of alienation. By always living in the immediate, random events of joy may give satisfaction, but random events of illness may destroy the immediate aesthete. There is no chance for a stable identity. Second, the aesthete seems to lack any moral compass. The Seducer, for example, is willing to go to extreme deception to, with cold calculation, seduce a woman while claiming no violation of the ethical because no commitment has been made to begin with.

Perhaps the most significant criticism comes from Kierkegaard's commentary on our *present age* [34]. Stepping back from the individual to the societal level, the present age is "the social instantiation of the aesthetic sphere" [13]. The present age is a "sensible, reflecting age, devoid of passion, flaring up in superficial, short-lived enthusiasm and prudentially relaxing in indolence" [34, p.68]. The present age is where everyone knows everything, and nothing is done with fervor. Information overload drains the meaning from our life. Our life becomes one of endless sampling, like trying on different suits.

One of the present age's most stifling phenomenon is *leveling* [34]: everyone is put on the same level, individualism is stifled by *the public*, and a mass of unsubstantial "anonymous" gather without repercussion. Privacy is no longer valued; instead individuals crave gossip generated by the press. Unlike the past when individual bravery was admired, such acts are deemed foolish or regarded with cynicism (as an acrobatic stunt). In the present age, we can have our cake and eat it too—neither sacrifice, nor commitment is necessary.

I. The Aesthetic Musician: Music for My Own Pleasure

Newcomers to Irish traditional music seek ways to immediately join a session. The aesthetic trad musician revels in the thrill of playing together. The worst musicians read off sheet music during a session (a social taboo) or use the TunePal smartphone app to *in situ* identify tunes being played in a session and show the music notes for tunes. Regular session musicians are likely to glare at the aesthete who is actively reading the written notes instead of sitting, listening, and recording the tune for later learning. For the aesthete, the only goal is to play along. This will avoid the consequence of being bored, sitting with an unused instrument. She insists on getting the chance to play her own sets of tunes, rather than playing other people's tunes. She wants to learn difficult, virtuosic tunes that will impress, yet few will want to play together.

The immediate aesthete is never concerned with the history of tune playing in a session. Sessions often have regular participants, tunes, rhythms, etc., that only become apparent through continued participation. She quickly becomes bored of a session, jumping from one pub to another in an attempt to find the "right" session for her, like many suits.

Ultimately, the aesthetic musician reveals herself to be an automaton with a limited repertoire. She learns tunes from sheet music, fails to socialize with others, and ignores the context of the tunes themselves. She remains steadfastly fixated on her own tunes, and does not seek to adapt her playing to the styles/variations of the local session. Technology, both old (sheet music) and new (apps), facilitates her goal of immediate tune playing.

To avoid boredom, she may elevate herself into a reflective aesthete, coveting tunes to ensure that their performance gives her desires maximum intensity. Although she believes strongly in living in the moment, through continuous experimentation with tunes and sessions, she is never bored and constantly challenged in her pursuits. She avoids being tied down to social conventions in Irish traditional music. She becomes quite adept at appreciating the beauty of music, the aesthetic pleasure of listening and playing. That is her only concern.

TuneTracker encourages the aesthete to alienate herself from the community of trad musicians. She knows everything about the session instantly—she knows what tunes are played, what the statistical trends are (e.g., what are the top 10 tunes played last week), and can quickly prepare herself to perform with the other musicians. She devours the practice of making local (potentially private) tunes a global phenomenon. She has little respect for old timers or established players—the heroes of Irish music. The ethical is inescapable. She feels shunned by the other musicians, and her connection with others is on a shallow level. She has no control over whether her tunes will be played, nor whether she can play with others. She has all the information but they are just probabilities, and she finds that the tunes played are very much dependent on who is there.

TuneTracker is a great leveler. It compresses the session into a nameless list of tunes compiled by an emotionless system. We don't know who played which tunes—individualism is lost. Instead of faces in the crowd of a pub, we have the public, anonymous spectators of the Internet. What was once locally public but globally private is now public across the board.

II. THE ETHICAL: COMMITTING TO COHERENCE

To live an ethical life requires a monumental commitment to construct a coherent life project. Rather than being free to create oneself, as one in the aesthetic sphere does, our freedom allows us to find one's place, task, and calling in the world. One must find a civic-self in service to others.

Here, existence is orderly and predictable. For the ethicist, courage is to have the self-discipline to commit oneself to his chosen goal in society. In Kierkegaard's terms, the ethical life is not devoid of an awareness and relation to God [20, p.116]. God is a being embodying humanity (someone we can relate to) who has given you a pathway to follow in life.

Perhaps the best exemplar of the ethicist's actions is his willingness to commit to marriage. Whereas the aesthete makes love a thing of passion and spontaneity, the ethical makes marriage one's duty. Rather than regarding marriage as the immediate, the ethical gives love a rich, deep history. Marriage gives love endurance and coherence. Marriage does not make love a burdensome duty, but allows us to structure love with depth via commitment so that two people can create a history.

The aesthetic sphere is ultimately unsatisfying to those in the ethical sphere [20, p.97]: "Humans have, as they mature, a fundamental need to live spiritually meaningful lives, and this requires them to possess ideals to which they are committed and which define them as selves."

Problems: Equating Duty with Faith. Kierkegaard saw Hegelianism (succinctly put, fulfilling one's responsibility in the institutions of society) as "an intellectual expression of the kind of society he saw around him in Europe, the society that he called 'Christendom'" [21, p.xxii]. In Christendom, becoming Christian merely entails possessing the values society deems as good. In our present age, Kierkegaard scoffs at the notion that one can become a true Christian by, for example, performing good deeds, attending the Christian Church, or becoming a monk. Instead, Kierkegaard believed becoming Christian required a life changing, costly commitment that few people are willing to make. Such a commitment is not captured in the ethical sphere.

The problems with the ethical are illustrated in Kierkegaard's most famous work, *Fear and Trembling* [37]. The book does a close reading of the famous Biblical story, *The Binding of Isaac* [Genesis 22:1–15 English Standard Version]. God commands Abraham to sacrifice his son, Isaac. Without question, Abraham willingly takes his son to Mount Moriah to be sacrificed but, at the last minute, an angel stops him, and a ram appears to take the place of his son. Why is it then that we consider Abraham as the ultimate embodiment of faith, yet, when judged through an ethical perspective, his actions (filicide) are reprehensible? The ethical sphere does not understand faith nor religion.

II. The Ethical Musician: Embracing Tradition

The ethical trad musician seeks to find one's place in trad music and in the local session itself. He is willing to decisively sacrifice the immediate (the desire to play many tunes in sessions) to find his place and duty in a session. Here, the social rules that govern sessions gives our musician the guidance to become part of the traditional music community. The session is a rational, orderly entity with implied etiquette. Tradition dictates "toughing" it out. He sits in many sessions for hours on end without being able to play a single tune. Yet, he is willing to listen, record, and converse about the history of tunes in the session thereby gaining a deeper representation of what tunes are about. Rather than desire to simply play, he desires to play harmoniously with his session mates. Rather than acting as a tourist, he is willing to stick with a session and become part of its history. Thus, the ethical musician takes responsibility for his actions. Although the aesthetic musician may regard the ethicist as removed from joy, the ethicist would counter that his life-view allows him to give music its proper profundity as a socially situated practice with a rich local history.

Within the ethical sphere, the schools of thought are pluralistic. There is one camp of ethical trad musicians that, as their moral code, embrace more progressive developments in trad music. These musicians define "tradition" to include jazz techniques, electronic instruments, and unorthodox, modern tunes. Instead of viewing tradition as old tunes played by old masters in old places, they seek out recordings by up and coming trad musicians who push the envelope of traditional music.

The ethical musician is quick to admonish those in the session who use technology as an immediate aesthete would. TuneTracker does not prescribe music, nor does it have agency. Rather, it is a *tool* for the ethical musician to use. TuneTracker ensures that ongoing traditions are preserved for future generations. TuneTracker welcomes newcomers into the session, thereby upholding the ethic that sessions are egalitarian affairs open to people from all walks of life. Sessions are locally and globally open to listening and participating.

For some ethicists, however, TuneTracker represents an active agent who has no role in traditional music—it does not maintain nor spread music in traditional means (e.g., aurally). As such, it is subject to abuse by the aesthetic musician. The aesthetic musician may use TuneTracker to bypass the duties to tradition that the ethicist holds dear. Some ethicists believe the session is a public space locally but a private space globally. TuneTracker violates this ethic, forcing the session's gates open to the Internet world.

Although the ethicist makes a concrete choice in becoming part of the tradition, he still can never escape a kind of despair over sacrificing the aesthetic. For one, he is not sure his choice is the *right* choice. Is he choosing his task in life correctly? Can he derive pleasure in his playing? Second, he may be embracing "Christendom" in the form of sanctioned, government-sponsored ways of traditional playing (e.g., Ireland has Comhaltas, an organization dedicated to promoting and preserving Irish traditional music). Is this ethical duty *enough* to be a traditional musician?

III. THE RELIGIOUS: THE UNATTAINABLE INFINITE

The religious sphere is defined by its difficulty to be conceptualized. It requires a sort of commitment that few can live up to or understand. Abraham is willing to sacrifice his son; he is willing to, as Kierkegaard writes, make the movement of resignation. He is resigned to sacrificing the finite (things of the material world, in this case, Isaac), for the infinite (spiritual). Clearly, making such a movement of detaching oneself from finite things is difficult and full of *suffering*. As we live in the religious sphere, we suffer guilt, "a constant awareness that one's own powers are insufficient to express infinitude" [27, p.13]. This is called a double movement. First, Abraham wishes to have a son (at a very old age) and loves him. Second, he uses all his courage to sacrifice this granted wish. This movement is conducted by what Kierkegaard calls a *knight of resignation* (the first variant of the religious).

However, Kierkegaard provides an alternative, less gloomy scenario to the above. Rather than always living in guilt and relying on our own will to become religious, Kierkegaard says we must passionately commit to the *paradox* that God is both a temporal and eternal being. In other words, we have faith in things beyond our understanding—this is a movement that *cannot be done rationally*. This is in contrast to the ethicist who sees God as nearly human—someone relatable.

To accomplish the above, the *knight of faith* similarly does a double movement, but "*at the very same time that he resigns the finite he receives and accepts it back 'by virtue of the absurd'* " [27, p.14]. Abraham was prepared to sacrifice Isaac, but he agrees to have him back when a ram is offered by God instead. Even as Abraham "accepts Isaac back, he does not relinquish the movements involved in infinite resignation...he maintains his intense love, his resignation, and his acceptance, all at the same time" [27, p.15]. What we end up with is this strange, miraculous, and contradictory situation of truly giving something up but being able to take it back.

This absurdity brings home the point of the monumental task needed to become a knight of faith. It is an ill-conceived notion to try and logically explain what faith is. In fact, most of us cannot be knights of faith because we cannot readily identify such people in everyday life. They are like aliens to us. Although those in an ethical life have self-confidence in their relation to God (something within grasp), the "religious individual...has made discoveries about the difficulties of becoming an integral self [and is] someone who is no longer confident of the God-relation as a goal to be achieved through action" [20, p.117].

III. The Religious Musician: Music at Another Level

We preface this section by noting that we will adopt Kierkegaard's style of writing. In his writings, Kierkegaard was speaking of the Christian God (although a conception of God removed from institutions that differed from many of his contemporaries), but, here, we take the analogy of God as the spirituality or infiniteness of music. We use words like God, faith, and salvation in a more rhetorical manner to convey that music is both something larger than oneself and an inward experience. Based on the lived experience through ethnographic work and our own convictions/translations, like Kierkegaard, we advocate this as the authentic life-view.

We cannot know nor identify the religious musician. As what Kierkegaard calls "a knight of faith," she is completely foreign to us. Yet, we know she is someone who has made a monumental commitment to the "spirit" of music. An ethicist may follow the teachings and writings of traditional musicians, but simply doing one's civic duty does not make one a traditional musician. Faith itself is a gift from God that is not human.

A traditional musician who exists in a religious life has renounced attachments to finite things and has given up satisfaction on Earth for the promise of eternal happiness with God. She is one who painfully experiences a recognition of the impossibility that it is to become a truly authentic musician and to ever really "know" a tune. You will always fall short. It is an acknowledgment of the contradictions inherent in society's moral compass and what is demanded from you as a musician. It is nonsensical to claim to be a religious musician. Striving to be a Christian musician is not a "gradual achievement of perfection but inversely...a deepening recognition of the imperfection of our striving" [56, p.239]. The religious musician constantly repeats the practice, listening, playing, learning, etc., of tunes, their history, and their social meaning not for the sake of achieving perfection, but to repeatedly relive the earnestness with which the musician believes in God (the spirit of music).

Professional musicians—and especially those who have been steeped in the culture (i.e., have a long familial history of Irish traditional musicians)—have a certain humor about traditional music. The painfulness of the situation of earnestly striving but never reaching infinitude can be mitigated by seeing the situation in a comic, rather than tragic sense. The religious musician humbly accepts that one cannot simply create oneself—at some point she needs cooperation from the divine to live authentically. A religious musician is not a product of self-creation but self-development.

We can perhaps glean some hints on what it takes to be a religious musician from this Facebook post by Harry Bradley, a professional Irish flute player (winner of the 2014 Gradam Ceoil TG4 award, the "Grammy awards" for Irish trad musicians):

> Here's what's on my mind: People sometimes ask me advice on how to play music (first mistake!). Here's what I SHOULD say to them, but am usually too shy or distracted to: Don't aspire to play shi* just because it is the flavour of the month. Lavish your attention on the music, learn to hear it: Learning to hear it is the key to learning to do it...It's not for everyone, Brian. I quite accept that people just play music for enjoyment, as a hobby etc...
>
> Sessions are fine sometimes, often they are a pain in the hole if I want to play well. I see thier [sic] social function and all that, but I can't always say they are good for my or other people's playing...
>
> I don't give a sh*t what other people think really, never did (well, maybe a few certain people at times). That's part of going for it: Keep your head down and your eye on the ball. If I did give a sh*t then I probably wouldn't be playing in the way that I do which, if not particularly accomplished, is at least a bit distinctive.

First, Harry calls the question of "how to play" a mistake. Second, he tells musicians to not go for the immediate, the flavor of the month. Third, he wants you to sacrifice yourself to the music, to hear it for itself. He acknowledges that people play "for enjoyment, as a hobby." But to really become a musician, something that you may never be, requires monumental commitment. Lastly, Harry criticizes sessions as sites for musicianship, which conflicts with mainstream ethics that sessions are part of the tradition in Irish trad music. In this sense, the religious musician is prepared to embrace activities that seem at odds with the ethical, or tradition. Ultimately, it is a solitary pursuit where a musician embraces both the infinite and finite to achieve the grace of God.

The religious musician embraces and loves music with all her heart, but then is willing to sacrifice it to paradoxically receive it back. The religious musician has full faith that she will receive God's salvation. She embraces the contradiction in renouncing "her worldly concerns, but she also continues [in absurdity] to hope for happiness within her life" [12, p.81].

TuneTracker does not capture the tradition of the religious musician. It can be used in an ethical or aesthetic manner, but it does not convey the absurdity of the situation and our inevitable, irrational step towards faith. TuneTracker rationally reduces God into tune names and statistics that we can process and then delude ourselves into thinking we can become authentic musicians. The religious musician may find TuneTracker amusing but ultimately lacking in communicating the infinitude of that which is traditional music. We cannot recognize in TuneTracker what it takes to be an authentic trad musician.

DESIGNING WITH INDIRECT COMMUNICATION

Having described our re-imagining and framing of the varied viewpoints on authentic living by traditional Irish musicians, we now turn to explaining Kierkegaard's writing strategy and its utility to design. Kierkegaard is daunting for the new reader because he purposefully distances himself from his own writings. Most of his major writings are authored by fictional writers (sometimes multiple). First-person prefaces sometimes have mysterious stories of how the main text's manuscript was accidentally found and thus published. With obviously made-up names such as Johannes de Silento, Johannes Climacus, A, and Judge William, Kierkegaard was not trying to hide his authorship. Instead, through *indirect communication*, Kierkegaard asks his readers to do a *double reflection*. This subjective understanding requires that "a person first grasp the relevant concepts (first reflection), but then go and think through what it would mean to apply those concepts to the person's own life (second reflection)" [20, p.30]. Indirect communication also allows Kierkegaard to remove himself as an authoritative figure—the reader must, on their own, reach their own conclusions on writings from a possibly unreliable narrator regarding how to live. Lastly, Kierkegaard believed it is simply impossible to explain directly and in written text spiritual matters on how to live rightly. Evans [20, p.35] notes that "I can help another person learn to love what I love, but my love cannot simply be transferred to the other person...what I communicate to the other is necessarily indirect."

We suggest that designing for authenticity not only means describing spheres of existence but designing artifacts to *indirectly* represent these spheres of existence. Kierkegaard needed to somehow communicate, albeit indirectly, via his own writings on what an authentic mode of living is. Inspired by his writings, we believe designers can similarly communicate, as Kierkegaard did, ways of living.

Ultimately, Kierkegaard's writings were to help reintroduce Christianity into Christendom. That is, save us from the deception that Christendom *is* Christianity. He argued that this cannot be done directly: "An illusion can never be destroyed directly...This is what is achieved by the indirect method, which, loving and serving the truth, arranges everything dialectically for the prospective captive, and then shyly withdraws (for love is always shy), so as not to witness the admission which he makes to himself alone before God—that he has lived hitherto in an illusion" [33, p.332]. It is through the indirect method that Kierkegaard seeks to draw out our commitment to his notion of the (reformed) religious sphere.

INDIRECT TUNETRACKER

In mid-19th century Copenhagen, Kierkegaard could only use paper books and articles to indirectly communicate to his readers. Now, we can imagine a variety of digital forms—tangible devices, wearable interfaces, mobile apps—to create an interactive artifact of indirect communication. We can thus consider the possibility of designing a hypothetical version of the TuneTracker system that indirectly communicates the different life-views of traditional musicians we have discussed earlier. Namely, can we take advantage of the persuasive power of indirect communication to convey different views on authenticity? What would this "Indirect TuneTracker" look like?

Kierkegaard himself describes several requirements in carrying out indirect communication. First, Kierkegaard suggests that rather than directly stating that a particular life-view is *the* way to be authentic, the system would describe such a way of life as both *concrete* and a *possibility*. An Indirect TuneTracker needs to describe, not exaggerate [56, p.208] (i.e., concoct an imaginary fairy tale) to be concrete:

> The subjective [existential] thinker is not free, therefore, to present an imaginary, illusory self-portrait, using the variety of enhancing scenes and settings ordinarily employed in poetic construction.

Second, Climacus (pseudonymous author of *Concluding Unscientific Postscript*) asks that the existential human communicate to others in the form of the possible. Instead of directly telling others of one's actions to be admired, the existential human should present that which is admirable universally to humans and present that as an "ethical requirement, as challenge to the recipient to exist in it" [56, p.208]. Rather than simply depicting neutral "data" on tune playing with TuneTracker, Indirect TuneTracker could explicitly challenge the user to become a more authentic being. For example, Indirect TuneTracker may turn off or hide features that support an aesthetic life-view to force the user to consider the possibility of an ethical life.

Third, Climacus warns that we must consider what we describe based on whom we are describing to. For example, a religious person who depicts eternal happiness to an aesthetic person would be missing the point. It does not adequately describe what it means to be a religious person: "It would be more appropriate...to describe instead what that person has suffered for the sake of eternal happiness" [56, p.208]. The constant suffering of musicians to achieve their *movement into* the religious sphere would need to be conveyed in Indirect TuneTracker. For example, one might imagine tunes accompanied by some depiction of the same tune played by various musicians whom continue to master the tune. Aside from simply depicting tune practices, an Indirect TuneTracker could convey information about the participants in the session. A sense of how often they participate and how they continually learn as if beginning from scratch would communicate this suffering.

Our exposition of Kierkegaard's indirect communication suggests that a hypothetical Indirect TuneTracker could have several *modes*, each of which depict a different sphere of existence depending on the user, and which also challenge people to consider other spheres of existence:

Aesthetic mode. Indirect TuneTracker could allow users to quickly print off sequences of tunes being played at sessions, suggest what tunes the user should learn based on statistics collected, and report deviations from standard sets, etc. Videos could be provided of intense moments in the session (perhaps detected by quicker tempos and louder playing) to allow the reflective aesthete to relieve past session moments.

Ethical mode. An Indirect TuneTracker that would resonate with the ethical musician could emphasize commitment, the moral order of sessions [9], respect for old masters, etc. Tune names could be published on a website with additional information such as the players' names, what old masters played the tune, the regional variants, and links to audio recordings. The system could indicate what place the player has in the session (e.g., whether the session is too "advanced" for a player). An ethical system could also require the player to get a password from a local player in order to access the system's records to expose the collaborative and locally public but globally private nature of sessions.

Religious mode. The illusion of Christendom that Kierkegaard was attempting to rail against is the illusion that blindly following laws and rules grants one religious faith. In the context of Irish traditional musicians, merely reading up on session etiquette and fulfilling one's duty in playing, teaching, or preserving Irish traditional music is not enough to be a knight of faith nor resignation. In addition, Christendom conveys an unrealistically rosy picture of religion. Resignation and suffering are part of the religious sphere. TuneTracker is implicitly a positive system, conveying lists of tunes that anyone can conceivably play and thus become part of tradition. Instead, however, an Indirect TuneTracker could convey the hopelessness of becoming an authentic musician. For example, Indirect TuneTracker could list the innumerable tunes that are out there yet to be learned. Here Indirect TuneTracker serves to "wound" the players from behind by portraying the infiniteness that a player must strive for. It could convey the lengthy continued period that the same tunes are continually played. This may convince the player to give up on a commitment to learn many tunes for an absolute commitment to mastery of a few tunes. Then one must suffer—not necessarily physical pain but suffer by recognizing one's dependence on God as a knight of resignation.

By supporting such modes, this hypothetical Indirect TuneTracker is able to indirectly communicate to people from different spheres of existence.

Lastly, an Indirect TuneTracker could point to ways to move from one existential sphere to another. Climacus describes *boundary zones* between spheres of existence. Humor is described as a boundary zone between the ethical and religious spheres. For those teetering on the edge of the ethical into the religious, humor offers a way to tolerate the suffering involved in the religious sphere. The humorist knows the contradiction between the finite and infinite, or the fact that in the real world it seems one has the power to do many things yet is powerless to do "anything by oneself to transform one's existence into conformity with the ideal" [56, p.216]. An Indirect TuneTracker could ease the possibility of suffering proffered by the religious sphere by introducing elements of humor—showing the possibility of a knight of faith. Authenticity in traditional music is more than the music itself, and the camaraderie felt when musicians of all different walks of life play together shows an awareness that many of us strive for the impossible and perhaps can laugh at it all as well. We do not know how Indirect TuneTracker could convey humor, but the interviews with professional Irish traditional musicians by Su [51] revealed a particular lighthearted and cavalier attitude towards learning Irish music. This contrast between the high standards and respect demanded by seasoned musicians with the lax attitude towards the skill involved in music might somehow be captured and represented in an ironic, contradictory manner on Indirect TuneTracker.

TOUCHING UPON AUTHENTICITY IN HCI

Authenticity and similar concepts have been mentioned in HCI, CSCW, and media studies literature. Authenticity as a concept is often understood as something "natural" taken away by technology and a reason for limiting technology use, and it stands in contrast to deceptive practices afforded by online identity. Authenticity has also been taken to mean something inherent in "traditional" materials that modern, material objects lack. Although the scope of this paper limits a comprehensive survey of the domains that mention authenticity, we will discuss authenticity as related to its pervasiveness in everyday activities, disclosure and honesty in social media, and materiality.

The way in which new technologies seem to force us to mediate our everyday practices everywhere has been labeled by some a challenge to authenticity. Harmon and Mazmanian [29] describe an ongoing discourse between the benefits and detriments in choosing to increase technological integration or "dis-integrate" the smart phone from daily life. Similar to how Harmon and Mazmanian place smartphone tropes within idealized *subject position* trajectories (e.g., from Luddite to multitasker), our use of Kierkegaard's spheres of existence can be seen as an attempt to reconcile various behaviors into modes of living authentically. Ames [2] observed that college students had to reconcile their own definition of what an authentic, natural relationship to others was with the authenticity forced upon them by the technological behaviors afforded by the mobile phone (e.g., constant connectivity and non face-to-face interactions). Each mobile user has his or her own conception of an "authentic" conversation (which may change depending on the context). Su and Wang [53] describe the role of mobile phones in the conversation of pubs. In some cases smartphones serve to enhance authenticity by creating richer conversations, but in other cases they ruin the spontaneity of debates by presenting hard facts (e.g., via Wikipedia searches). In studies to visually depict data in digital artwork in the house and in galleries, designers and artists faced challenges in maintaining and conveying the authenticity—the validity—of their data when mediated through technology [31, 57].

Social media has been the subject of studies that examine the intersection between online media and authenticity. Authenticity is oppositionally situated against activities of deception and lying [32] in domains such as online dating [28] and social media profiles [49]. In this regard, authenticity is a colloquial term for profile photos that truthfully and honestly depict their subject. Research has also investigated the online practices of celebrities and how they convey their "real-ness" to their fans and the public [16, 40]. Marwick and boyd's [40] work is one of the few that draws from a philosophical work on authenticity. They use a definition of authenticity rooted in "passion and interiority" that Kierkegaard would likely sympathize with. However, they see authenticity as a social construct—for example, some social media such as Twitter demand more practices (e.g., tweets that are emotionally candid) that are (or seem) authentic. Here, the focus is on the ability of technologies to support both authentic and inauthentic practices of identity.

Lastly, there is work concerned with new forms of materiality and their authenticity. In a study of virtual possessions, Odom et al. [43] found their formlessness led to a perception of inauthenticity; they were less "real" than material possessions and were not unique objects. In a study of book restoration [45], authenticity was tied to respecting a book's original condition (e.g., by allowing restorations to be reversible). The authors suggest future design may seek to create digital artifacts that similarly demand such respect from restorers.

These studies present an insightful—albeit, a kaleidoscopic—view of what people do to achieve authenticity (whether for themselves or some object) and what researchers understand as authenticity. However, authenticity itself—what it means for different people and how our actions are shaped by such meanings—is remarkably under-studied in HCI. Most of the research mentioned above engages with authenticity without any elaborate or substantial examinations of the meaning of authenticity in relation to previous work in philosophy or other disciplines. In this article, we have proposed one alternative approach, designing for authenticity, that makes authenticity the key concern when analyzing technology's role in our humanity as well as in the design process.

OPEN INTERPRETATION VS. PRESCRIPTION

Designing for authenticity adopts some of the tenets of reflective design [47]. In particular, we find inspiration from Sengers et al.'s call to design systems that show the choices one makes in everyday activities and offer new, unexpected choices.

Yet, designing for authenticity is a prescriptive framework. The power of Kierkegaard's writings lies from his conviction that the religious sphere is the life we ought to strive towards while acknowledging that few of us will achieve a place in it. The belief in our ultimate dependence on God guides his views on the positive and negative elements of each sphere of existence. Designing for authenticity adopts Kierkegaard's method and belief, which are inseparable. Our analysis of Irish traditional musicians and the hypothetical design of Indirect TuneTracker is reflective, but it utilizes reflection as a strategy to guide and persuade our users to adopt a particular view of technology that complements the religious sphere of existence.

It is instructive to consider alternatives to our own approach. Sengers and Gaver [48] outlined an innovative approach to purposefully explore designs that are open to multiple interpretations. Designs that downplay the system's authority and thwart any consistent interpretation, for example, are ways to give the user's own interpretations equal footing to the designer. Many of these designs are exploratory and anarchic in character, embracing any number of possibly conflicting uses. *Value-sensitive design* (VSD) [24] emphasizes a tripartite methodology of conceptual, empirical, and technological investigations on values of moral import [55], such as human well-being. Borning and Muller's thoughtful critique of VSD [10] states, "There are huge problems with both the position that there are some values that are or should be universally held...We suggest that VSD should take a more pluralistic position on this question of universal values, and simply say that this is a contested issue." Approaches like these advocate open pluralistic interpretations not predetermined by any designer.

In contrast, designing for authenticity is a very rational approach to embracing a form of irrationality (the irrationality of the religious sphere) or openness but with a very clear goal and purpose. To employ this prescriptive framework requires a deep understanding of the design space. The ethnography of Irish traditional musicians and TuneTracker's subsequent design and deployment gave the authors of that study a deep conviction on what an authentic life-view was and should be for these musicians. Our framing and re-imagining of Indirect TuneTracker seeks to convey this conviction. Designing for authenticity presents "a pluralistic position" on life-views and their contested nature (e.g., ethical vs. aesthetic life styles), but ultimately says that there are universal values we should seek. It also presents, even if indirect, how to go about achieving such values. To put it another way, a system embracing indirect communication presents several designs with an authoritative interpretation for the user to choose, although only one of those designs is the desired, authentic choice.

This does not mean that the only measure of success for the Indirect TuneTracker is when users reach the highest level of existence (the religious sphere). Existentialism posits our life is open-ended and subject to our choices; yet, "reflection by itself cannot determine choice" [21, p.20]. We must make existence a struggle by actively *committing* to unify our life [27]. Such a commitment requires one not to make decisions from a detached, scientific perspective, but emotionally and deeply—Kierkegaard called this seeing *truth subjectively*. Pursuing something passionately, even if false, is better than pursuing something apathetically. And, designing with indirect communication—leaving it up to the user to reach their own conclusions—has the potential to make a user passionately seek an authentic self. For example, though our Indirect TuneTracker may fail to guide our users to the religious sphere, we may claim some measure of success if its users passionately commit to a particular sphere (e.g., the aesthetic sphere).

We are not claiming that designing for authenticity is *the* framework for authenticity, nor are we discounting the merits of reflective design strategies. It is certainly useful, for example, when creating designs in new spaces and new forms or when trying to escape subtle biases in design thinking to ensure that multiple interpretations from users are neutrally explored. However, if one has gained a deep, lengthy, and passionate understanding of a domain, designing for authenticity may provide a means to analyze and design with prescription as a goal. Kierkegaard's philosophy and his notion of the aesthetic, ethical, and religious sphere, we believe, has universal relevance to any domain where technology intersects.

CONCLUSION: DESIGNING FOR AUTHENTICITY

Presumably, Kierkegaard did not intend his philosophy to be applied to different domains of everyday life (e.g., particular hobbies). The application of Kierkegaard to a specific ethnographic fieldsite necessitates changes in the interpretation of his philosophy, for example, when it comes to the notion of the "religious sphere." Although there is no doubt that some famous composers (e.g., Haydn and Bach) have been inspired by the Christian God, this was not the notion that has been used in this study, nor does this study advocate a specific religious orientation (if at all). It is, however, not difficult to see how, just as with any religiously motivated work, one can learn a great deal from Kierkegaard. Noted Kierkegaard scholar Carlisle (a Buddhist herself) [12, p.156-157] suggests that if we were to remove the Christian element from Kierkegaard, we might "pay less attention to themes such as love and suffering which come so naturally to a Christian thinker." If, as we believe, authenticity is about these themes of humanity, and moreover, its relationship with modern technology poses new challenges, we would do well to heed the guidance philosophy can provide in melding authenticity with interaction design [22].

What we have proposed in this paper is a means by which, colored by our own experiences, fieldwork, and readings of Kierkegaard, we can conceptualize and organize different patterns of living "authentically" with technology. Moreover, this conceptualization can help us to outline how technologies can be designed to indirectly communicate these modes of living for self-reflection. Through indirect communication, the user can passionately choose the best sphere of existence to adopt. Technologies that adopt designing for authenticity will reveal other spheres of existence, possibly prompting one to move from one sphere to another. Ultimately, designing for authenticity seeks to guide users into the religious sphere of existence. Thus, we believe designing for authenticity provides a powerful approach for not only puzzling out different philosophies of technology's role in authenticity, but for designing technologies that present these philosophies in non-neutral ways.

Our approach brings to question the authority of designers. Studies have acknowledged that the designer's views play a large (sometimes unconscious) role in shaping their creations, even if they embraced a user-centered approach [60, 23]. Moreover, the disciplines from which HCI practitioners draw their design methods naturally lead to systems with particular goals (e.g., constraining organizations [54]). Later iterations of VSD argue for better transparency regarding the designer's own values [10]. So, in some sense, giving designers authority when it comes to values is not anything new. Although newer approaches to design may acknowledge the researchers' or designers' power, they typically impose a certain modesty in their authority. In contrast, designing for authenticity, the way we have developed it here, may be controversial because it not only seems to give the designer the right to impose their belief of authenticity on "hapless" users, it also gives the designer a method by which they can indirectly point to a specific lifestyle. The latter may be perceived as a disingenuous tactic because users are ostensibly presented with several spheres of existence from which they are free to strive for one—yet, the designer's intent, if following the Kierkegaardian thinking we have laid out, is to steer the user to the religious sphere.

The concerns around the authority of the designer in relation to authenticity are valid, important, and complicated. Therefore we do not see our presented approach to be the final word; instead, we see future opportunities to elaborate or extend designing for authenticity from a broad and more philosophical approach into concrete methods (as was done with VSD) or well-defined theory. However, we wish to note that designing for authenticity ultimately rests on the designer or researcher responsibly employing methods that give them a deep understanding of the domains they are creating for—i.e., embedding, critiquing, and reflecting longitudinally enough such that they can articulate an authentic life while acknowledging their inability to live up to the ideas and ideals their designs attempt to convey to their users. Part of this rigor involves, just as user-centered design does, "living" with and respecting users' varied lifestyles with technology. Any approach that purports to address authenticity, we believe, needs to make transparent that living authentically with technology means to understand its complex, emotional, and sometimes irrational nature, and that communicating this difficult choice cannot be done simply (i.e., through direct communication). Lastly, our approach's goal is not simply to push people into the "right" sphere. Instead it is important to see truth subjectively (cf. previous section) by attending to authenticity with verve—how you believe rather than what you believe is vital. This is a form of modesty, albeit different from past approaches.

Lastly, Kierkegaard's philosophy provides one answer to, "What justifies designer action in authenticity?" Movements such as sustainability and ICT4D have successfully mobilized designer action through compelling, *global* arguments that humanity can rally around. Yet, authenticity is a deeply individualistic, variegated concept. To simply say that everyone has a different notion of authenticity is not enough—designers should responsibly (and rigorously) judge and act on what they think is the right way to live without judging the individuals themselves. These are precisely the actions that existential philosophers like Kierkegaard exemplify.

In sum, this paper was an effort to make sense of the varied opinions of authenticity found through both intensive fieldwork and a subsequent system developed with the intent to respect authenticity. Designing for authenticity allowed us to understand the ways in which we try our best to live fulfilling and worthwhile lives with technology. Designing with indirect communication is a concrete reification of not only our rigorous, respectful sympathy for people's joys and struggles, but a particular belief of what an authentic life should be.

REFERENCES

1. Gregory D. Abowd. 2012. What Next, Ubicomp?: Celebrating an Intellectual Disappearing Act. In *Proceedings of the 2012 ACM Conference on Ubiquitous Computing (UbiComp '12)*. ACM, New York, NY, USA, 31–40. DOI: http://dx.doi.org/10.1145/2370216.2370222
2. Morgan G. Ames. 2013. Managing Mobile Multitasking: The Culture of iPhones on Stanford Campus. In *Proceedings of the 2013 Conference on Computer Supported Cooperative Work (CSCW '13)*. ACM, New York, NY, USA, 1487–1498. DOI: http://dx.doi.org/10.1145/2441776.2441945
3. Morgan G. Ames, Janet Go, Joseph 'Jofish' Kaye, and Mirjana Spasojevic. 2011. Understanding Technology Choices and Values Through Social Class. In *Proceedings of the ACM 2011 Conference on Computer Supported Cooperative Work (CSCW '11)*. ACM, New York, NY, USA, 55–64. DOI: http://dx.doi.org/10.1145/1958824.1958834
4. Claudio Aporta and Eric Higgs. 2005. Satellite Culture: Global Positioning Systems, Inuit Wayfinding, and the Need for a New Account of Technology. *Current Anthropology* 46, 5 (Dec. 2005), 729–753. DOI: http://dx.doi.org/10.1086/432651
5. Aristotle and Terence Irwin (Trans.). 1999. *Nicomachean Ethics* (2nd ed.). Hackett Publishing Company, Inc., Indianapolis, IN, USA.
6. authenticity, n. September 2015. *OED Online*. Oxford University Press. http://www.oed.com/view/Entry/13325 accessed September 13, 2015.
7. Eric P.S. Baumer, Morgan G. Ames, Jed R. Brubaker, Jenna Burrell, and Paul Dourish. 2014. Refusing, Limiting, Departing: Why We Should Study Technology Non-use. In *CHI '14 Extended Abstracts on Human Factors in Computing Systems (CHI EA '14)*. ACM, New York, NY, USA, 65–68. DOI: http://dx.doi.org/10.1145/2559206.2559224
8. Genevieve Bell and Paul Dourish. 2007. Yesterday's tomorrows: notes on ubiquitous computing's dominant vision. *Personal and Ubiquitous Computing* 11, 2 (Feb. 2007), 133–143. DOI: http://dx.doi.org/10.1007/s00779-006-0071-x
9. Steve Benford, Peter Tolmie, Ahmed Y. Ahmed, Andy Crabtree, and Tom Rodden. 2012. Supporting traditional music-making: designing for situated discretion. In *Proceedings of the ACM 2012 Conference on Computer Supported Cooperative Work (CSCW '12)*. ACM, New York, NY, USA, 127–136. DOI: http://dx.doi.org/10.1145/2145204.2145227
10. Alan Borning and Michael Muller. 2012. Next Steps for Value Sensitive Design. In *Proceedings of the SIGCHI Conference on Human Factors in Computing Systems (CHI '12)*. ACM, New York, NY, USA, 1125–1134. DOI: http://dx.doi.org/10.1145/2207676.2208560
11. Elizabeth A. Buie. 2014. User Experience and the Human Spirit. In *CHI '14 Extended Abstracts on Human Factors in Computing Systems (CHI EA '14)*. ACM, New York, NY, USA, 335–338. DOI: http://dx.doi.org/10.1145/2559206.2559962
12. Clare Carlisle. 2006. *Kierkegaard: A Guide for the Perplexed.* Contiuum International Publishing Group, London, UK.
13. Clare Carlisle. 2011. Kierkegaard's Despair in An Age of Reflection. *Graduate Faculty Philosophy Journal* 32, 2 (2011), 251–279. DOI: http://dx.doi.org/10.5840/gfpj20113223
14. Nicholas Carr. 2014. *The Glass Cage: Automation and Us* (1st ed.). W. W. Norton & Company, New York, NY, USA.
15. Héctor L. Carral. 2015. Stop saying technology is causing social isolation. (18 Oct. 2015). https://medium.com/digital-culturist/stop-saying-technology-is-causing-social-isolation-1e004de63a5e
16. Melissa A. Click, Hyunji Lee, and Holly Willson Holladay. 2013. Making Monsters: Lady Gaga, Fan Identification, and Social Media. *Popular Music and Society* 36, 3 (July 2013), 360–379. DOI: http://dx.doi.org/10.1080/03007766.2013.798546
17. Graham Dugoni. 2015. Your Smartphone Is Ruining Precious Experiences. (10 June 2015). http://www.popsugar.com/node/37636606
18. Nicole B. Ellison, Charles Steinfield, and Cliff Lampe. 2007. The Benefits of Facebook "Friends:" Social Capital and College Students' Use of Online Social Network Sites. *Journal of Computer-Mediated Communication* 12, 4 (July 2007), 1143–1168. DOI: http://dx.doi.org/10.1111/j.1083-6101.2007.00367.x
19. Lindsay Ems. 2014. Amish Workarounds: Toward a Dynamic, Contextualized View of Technology Use. *Journal of Amish and Plain Anabaptist Studies* 2, 1 (April 2014), 42–58. http://hdl.handle.net/1811/59690
20. C. Stephen Evans. 2006. Introduction. In *Kierkegaard: Fear and Trembling*, C. Stephen Evans and Sylvia Walsh (Eds.). Cambridge University Press, New York, NY, USA, vi–xxx.
21. C. Stephen Evans. 2009. *Kierkegaard: An Introduction.* Cambridge University Press, New York, NY, USA.
22. Daniel Fallman. 2011. The New Good: Exploring the Potential of Philosophy of Technology to Contribute to Human-computer Interaction. In *Proceedings of the SIGCHI Conference on Human Factors in Computing Systems (CHI '11)*. ACM, New York, NY, USA, 1051–1060. DOI: http://dx.doi.org/10.1145/1978942.1979099
23. Diana E. Forsythe. 1996. New Bottles, Old Wine: Hidden Cultural Assumptions in a Computerized Explanation System for Migraine Sufferers. *Medical Anthropology Quarterly* 10, 4 (Dec. 1996), 551–574. DOI: http://dx.doi.org/10.1525/maq.1996.10.4.02a00100

24. Batya Friedman, Peter H. Kahn Jr, Alan Borning, and Alina Huldtgren. 2013. Value Sensitive Design and Information Systems. In *Early Engagement and New Technologies: Opening Up the Laboratory*, Neelke Doorn, Daan Schuurbiers, Ibo van de Poel, and Michael E. Gorman (Eds.). Number 16 in Philosophy of Engineering and Technology. Springer Netherlands, 55–95. http://link.springer.com/chapter/10.1007/978-94-007-7844-3_4

25. Joakim Garff. 2005. *Søren Kierkegaard: A Biography*. Princeton University Press, Princeton, NJ, USA.

26. Clifford Geertz. 1973. Thick Description: Towards an Interpretive Theory of Culture. In *The Interpretation of Cultures*. Basic Books, New York, NY, USA, 3–30.

27. Charles B. Guignon and Derk Pereboom. 2001. Kierkegaard. In *Existentialism: Basic Writings*, Charles B. Guignon and Derk Pereboom (Eds.). Hackett Publishing, Indianapolis, IN, USA, 1–17.

28. Jeffrey T. Hancock and Catalina L. Toma. 2009. Putting Your Best Face Forward: The Accuracy of Online Dating Photographs. *Journal of Communication* 59, 2 (June 2009), 367–386. DOI: http://dx.doi.org/10.1111/j.1460-2466.2009.01420.x

29. Ellie Harmon and Melissa Mazmanian. 2013. Stories of the Smartphone in Everyday Discourse: Conflict, Tension & Instability. In *Proceedings of the SIGCHI Conference on Human Factors in Computing Systems (CHI '13)*. ACM, New York, NY, USA, 1051–1060. DOI: http://dx.doi.org/10.1145/2470654.2466134

30. Dick Hebdige. 1979. *Subculture: The Meaning of Style*. Routledge, London, UK.

31. Rachel Jacobs, Steve Benford, Mark Selby, Michael Golembewski, Dominic Price, and Gabriella Giannachi. 2013. A Conversation Between Trees: What Data Feels Like in the Forest. In *Proceedings of the SIGCHI Conference on Human Factors in Computing Systems (CHI '13)*. ACM, New York, NY, USA, 129–138. DOI: http://dx.doi.org/10.1145/2470654.2470673

32. Adam N. Joinson, Jeffrey Hancock, and Pam Briggs. 2008. Secrets and Lies in Computer-Mediated Interaction: Theory, Methods and Design. In *CHI '08 Extended Abstracts on Human Factors in Computing Systems (CHI EA '08)*. ACM, New York, NY, USA, 3993–3996. DOI: http://dx.doi.org/10.1145/1358628.1358975

33. Søren Kierkegaard and Robert Bretall (Ed.). 1973. *A Kierkegaard Anthology* (1st Princeton Paperback ed.). Princeton University Press, Princeton, NJ, USA.

34. Søren Kierkegaard, Howard V. Hong (Trans.), and Edna H. Hong (Trans.). 1978. *Two Ages: The Age of Revolution and the Present Age, a Literary Review*. Princeton University Press, Princeton, NJ, USA.

35. Søren Kierkegaard and Walter Lowrie (Trans.). 1959. *Either/Or, Volume II*. Princeton University Press, Princeton, NJ, USA.

36. Søren Kierkegaard, David F. Swenson (Trans.), and Lillian Marvin Swenson (Trans.). 1959. *Either/Or, Volume I*. Princeton University Press, Princeton, NJ, USA.

37. Søren Kierkegaard and Sylvia Walsh (Trans.). 2006. *Kierkegaard: Fear and Trembling*. Cambridge University Press, New York, NY, USA.

38. Christopher A. Le Dantec, Erika Shehan Poole, and Susan P. Wyche. 2009. Values As Lived Experience: Evolving Value Sensitive Design in Support of Value Discovery. In *Proceedings of the SIGCHI Conference on Human Factors in Computing Systems (CHI '09)*. ACM, New York, NY, USA, 1141–1150. DOI: http://dx.doi.org/10.1145/1518701.1518875

39. Clare Madge, Julia Meek, Jane Wellens, and Tristram Hooley. 2009. Facebook, social integration and informal learning at university: 'It is more for socialising and talking to friends about work than for actually doing work'. *Learning, Media and Technology* 34, 2 (June 2009), 141–155. DOI: http://dx.doi.org/10.1080/17439880902923606

40. Alice Marwick and danah boyd. 2011. To See and Be Seen: Celebrity Practice on Twitter. *Convergence: The International Journal of Research into New Media Technologies* 17, 2 (May 2011), 139–158. DOI: http://dx.doi.org/10.1177/1354856510394539

41. John Mullen. 1981. *Kierkegaard's Philosophy: Self Deception and Cowardice in the Present Age*. The New American Library, Inc., New York, NY, USA.

42. Randall Munroe. 2015. xkcd: The Pace of Modern Life. (2015). http://xkcd.com/1227/

43. William Odom, John Zimmerman, and Jodi Forlizzi. 2014. Placelessness, Spacelessness, and Formlessness: Experiential Qualities of Virtual Possessions. In *Proceedings of the 2014 Conference on Designing Interactive Systems (DIS '14)*. ACM, New York, NY, USA, 985–994. DOI: http://dx.doi.org/10.1145/2598510.2598577

44. Gediminas Rapolavicius. 2015. Museum 'Bans' Cameras, Asks People To Sketch Artwork To Truly Appreciate It. (2015). http://www.boredpanda.com/museum-bans-cameras-start-drawing-rijksmuseum/

45. Daniela K. Rosner and Alex S. Taylor. 2011. Antiquarian Answers: Book Restoration As a Resource for Design. In *Proceedings of the SIGCHI Conference on Human Factors in Computing Systems (CHI '11)*. ACM, New York, NY, USA, 2665–2668. DOI: http://dx.doi.org/10.1145/1978942.1979332

46. Christine Satchell and Paul Dourish. 2009. Beyond the User: Use and Non-use in HCI. In *Proceedings of the 21st Annual Conference of the Australian Computer-Human Interaction Special Interest Group: Design: Open 24/7 (OZCHI '09)*. ACM, New York, NY, USA, 9–16. DOI: http://dx.doi.org/10.1145/1738826.1738829

47. Phoebe Sengers, Kirsten Boehner, Shay David, and Joseph 'Jofish' Kaye. 2005. Reflective Design. In *Proceedings of the 4th Decennial Conference on Critical Computing: Between Sense and Sensibility (CC '05)*. ACM, New York, NY, USA, 49–58. DOI: http://dx.doi.org/10.1145/1094562.1094569

48. Phoebe Sengers and Bill Gaver. 2006. Staying Open to Interpretation: Engaging Multiple Meanings in Design and Evaluation. In *Proceedings of the 6th Conference on Designing Interactive Systems (DIS '06)*. ACM, New York, NY, USA, 99–108. DOI: http://dx.doi.org/10.1145/1142405.1142422

49. Lauren F. Sessions. 2009. "You Looked Better on MySpace": Deception and authenticity on the Web 2.0. *First Monday* 14, 7 (July 2009). DOI: http://dx.doi.org/10.5210/fm.v14i7.2539

50. Meredith M. Skeels and Jonathan Grudin. 2009. When Social Networks Cross Boundaries: A Case Study of Workplace Use of Facebook and Linkedin. In *Proceedings of the ACM 2009 International Conference on Supporting Group Work (GROUP '09)*. ACM, New York, NY, USA, 95–104. DOI: http://dx.doi.org/10.1145/1531674.1531689

51. Norman Makoto Su. 2013. The Social Life of Tunes: Representing the Aesthetics of Reception. In *ECSCW 2013: Proceedings of the 13th European Conference on Computer Supported Cooperative Work, 21-25 September 2013, Paphos, Cyprus*, Olav W. Bertelsen, Luigina Ciolfi, Maria Antonietta Grasso, and George Angelos Papadopoulos (Eds.). Springer London, 207–228. http://link.springer.com/chapter/10.1007/978-1-4471-5346-7_11 DOI: 10.1007/978-1-4471-5346-7_11.

52. Norman Makoto Su and Bryan Duggan. 2014. TuneTracker: Tensions in the Surveillance of Traditional Music. In *Proceedings of the 2014 Conference on Designing Interactive Systems (DIS '14)*. ACM, New York, NY, USA, 845–854. DOI: http://dx.doi.org/10.1145/2598510.2598559

53. Norman Makoto Su and Lulu Wang. 2015. From Third to Surveilled Place: The Mobile in Irish Pubs. In *Proceedings of the 33rd Annual ACM Conference on Human Factors in Computing Systems (CHI '15)*. ACM, New York, NY, USA, 1659–1668. DOI: http://dx.doi.org/10.1145/2702123.2702574

54. Lucy Suchman. 1993. Do categories have politics? The language action perspective reconsidered. *Computer Supported Cooperative Work (CSCW)* 2, 3 (1993), 177–190. DOI: http://dx.doi.org/10.1007/BF00749015

55. Jeroen van der Hoven and Noemi Manders-Huits. 2009. Value-Sensitive Design. In *A Companion to the Philosophy of Technology*, Jan Kyrre Berg Olsen, Stig Andur Pedersen, and Vincent F. Hendricks (Eds.). Wiley-Blackwell, 477–480. http://onlinelibrary.wiley.com/doi/10.1002/9781444310795.ch86/summary

56. Sylvia Walsh. 2010. *Living Poetically: Kierkegaard's Existential Aesthetics*. Penn State Press, University Park, PA, USA.

57. Jinyi Wang, Mudassar Ahmad Mughal, and Oskar Juhlin. 2015. Experiencing Liveness of a Cherished Place in the Home. In *Proceedings of the ACM International Conference on Interactive Experiences for TV and Online Video (TVX '15)*. ACM, New York, NY, USA, 3–12. DOI: http://dx.doi.org/10.1145/2745197.2745198

58. Mark Weiser. 1991. The Computer for the 21st Century. *Scientific American* 265, 3 (1991), 94–110.

59. Allison Woodruff, Sally Augustin, and Brooke Foucault. 2007. Sabbath Day Home Automation: "It's like Mixing Technology and Religion". In *Proceedings of the SIGCHI Conference on Human Factors in Computing Systems (CHI '07)*. ACM, New York, NY, USA, 527–536. DOI: http://dx.doi.org/10.1145/1240624.1240710

60. Steve Woolgar. 1990. Configuring the user: the case of usability trials. *The Sociological Review* 38, S1 (May 1990), 58–99. DOI: http://dx.doi.org/10.1111/j.1467-954X.1990.tb03349.x

Social Justice-Oriented Interaction Design: Outlining Key Design Strategies and Commitments

Lynn Dombrowski
Human-Centered Computing
Indiana University, IUPUI
lsdombro@iupui.edu

Ellie Harmon
Information Science
University of Colorado Boulder
ellie@ellieharmon.com

Sarah Fox
Human Centered Design & Engineering
University of Washington
sefox@uw.edu

ABSTRACT
In recent years, many HCI designers have begun pursuing research agendas that address large scale social issues. These systemic or "wicked" problems present challenges for design practice due to their scope, scale, complexity, and political nature. In this paper, we develop a *social justice orientation* to designing for such challenges. We highlight a breadth of design strategies that target the goals of social justice along six dimensions – *transformation, recognition, reciprocity, enablement, distribution,* and *accountability* – and elaborate three commitments necessary to developing a social justice oriented design practice – *a commitment to conflict, a commitment to reflexivity, and a commitment to personal ethics and politics.* Although there are no easy solutions to systemic social issues, a social justice orientation provides one way to foster an engagement with the thorny political issues that are increasingly acknowledged as crucial to a field that is not just about technological possibility, but also about political responsibility.

Author Keywords
Social justice, social change, design, interaction design, politics of design, social issues

ACM Classification Keywords
H.5.m. Information interfaces and presentation (*e.g.*, HCI): Miscellaneous

INTRODUCTION
In recent years, members of the design and HCI communities have shown increased interest in addressing large-scale social challenges through their design and research practices. These research and design agendas include projects focused on economic and social development [64, 116], sustainability [33], food insecurity [35], homelessness and housing [7, 78, 122], street harassment [28], and domestic abuse [22, 29]. Such systemic or "wicked" problems [75] present new challenges for our theoretical and design practices, in part due to their scale, scope, and complexity [see also 12]. Moreover, as noted by design and urban planning scholars Rittel and Webber, wicked problems are also characterized by their lack of a clear objective answer or solution. Rather, interventions in these kinds of complex social issues always raise questions of privileging some values and stakeholders over others [104]. Research and design projects that examine or intervene in large scale social issues thus require scholars to engage directly in (or against) both state (*e.g.* laws, the national-social politics of welfare programs) and personal level politics (*e.g.* the implicit and explicit ethical and moral stances of designers, research participants, and funding agencies). Grappling with these politics is particularly challenging given the field's historical inclinations towards treating technological development as unquestionably progressive, or approaching research and design in an apolitical and ahistorical manner [see critiques by 9, 83, 123]. The recent growing interest in research related to large scale social issues underscores the imperative to heed more general calls for HCI researchers and designers to ask not only what is technologically possible, but also how to design ethically, responsibly, and with accountability – and to thoughtfully consider whether design is even an appropriate intervention in a given situation [8, 9, 12, 14, 32, 33, 43, 60, 83, 111, 114]. In this paper, we develop *social justice-oriented interaction design* as one response to these concerns and provocations.

Design is inherently about change – not just in the creation of new material artifacts, but in the ways that new technological objects afford new practices, social habits, and ways of living and interacting. As design scholars Dunne and Raby write, design is always engaged in a process of "changing reality rather than simply describing it or maintaining it" [39]. However, progressive change does not happen naturally. As Bardzell and Light argue, a focus on designing for the status quo – *e.g.*, for what a majority of research participants already want or need – often leads to the re-entrenchment of problematic inequalities and power relations, privileging elite social groups and marginalizing others [9, 83]. In this paper, we argue that an explicit engagement with social justice can help guard against this tendency, and facilitate more equitable social change by providing a set of strategies and commitments to guide

DIS 2016, June 04 - 08, 2016, Brisbane, QLD, Australia

ACM 978-1-4503-4031-1/16/06...$15.00
DOI: http://dx.doi.org/10.1145/2901790.2901861

design practice in favor of polyvocal participation in mechanisms for social change.

Broadly speaking, taking a social justice approach means attending to the ways that individuals experience oppression, including how benefits, burdens, obligations, power, opportunity, and privilege have been (in)equitably distributed within society. As an *orientation* to design – rather than a specific technique or method – the approach described in this paper differs from prior methods such as value-sensitive design and participatory design. Often these methods are compatible with social justice and might be used as part of a social justice oriented design practice. However, rather than a new method, a social justice *orientation* might be thought of as a constellation of modes and sensitivities, including a mode of knowing and relating, and sensitivities to inequality and marginalized voices. In the literature review, we draw on a multi-faceted definition of social justice [85] because it helps attune the researcher or designer to the various ways that social issues can manifest throughout a design practice. When intervening in complex social situations, we acknowledge that there is rarely a clear 'right' answer. Thus, we also understand social justice as a horizon to work towards; an always ongoing process and practice rather than a clearly defined utopia that offers itself up for idealized achievement. Rather than centering on a particular set of values, a social justice orientation centers on a commitment to a design practice rooted in conflict, participation, and politics. It is an approach, orientation, sensitivity, and mode of work that must be carried through the entirety of a design practice, across and between multiple projects, and throughout the process of any one project – from problem framing to participant engagement.

In the rest of this paper, we first give a brief introduction to social justice as a concept rooted in political philosophy, outline some of its multiple histories, and articulate a working definition of social justice that emphasizes its multi-faceted nature by drawing on the work of political philosopher H.P.P. Lötter [85]. We then review a subset of recent HCI work that engages with large scale social issues. Drawing on cases from sustainability, ICTD, and community informatics, we show how a social justice orientation offers a response to existing open questions, and also raises important new challenges for research. In the latter half of the paper, we highlight concrete strategies for practicing social justice-orientated interaction design. These strategies target the goals of social justice along six dimensions: *transformation*, *recognition*, *reciprocity*, *enablement*, *distribution*, and *accountability*. Although there are no easy solutions to systemic social issues, we draw on our own and others' design research to show how a social justice orientation provides one way to directly and responsibly engage the ethical and moral issues that are increasingly acknowledged as central to the future of HCI. In the closing discussion, we reflect back on these practical strategies through the articulation of three personal commitments vital to the ongoing work of practicing design from a social justice orientation: *a commitment to conflict*, *a commitment to reflexivity*, and *a commitment to personal ethics and politics*.

BACKGROUND

The term 'social justice' is often attributed to Luigi Taparelli D'Azeglio, an Italian Jesuit philosopher of the mid-1800s whose work was based on the teachings of St. Thomas Aquinas [125]. Though, as others note, it is far more likely that the concept(s) predated the term [*e.g.*, 115]. Since the end of the second world war, western political philosophers, most notably John Rawls, have adopted the term to refer to formulations of justice that center on the ongoing – and always incomplete – attempt to balance the benefits and burdens of a social system such that they are fair or equitably shared [103; See also, 48, 69, 87, 94, 96, 110, 120]. While prior conceptions of justice often centered on abstract assessments of a system's morality with respect to some ideological grounding, Rawls' concept of social justice centered on the assessment of a system based on *the perspectives of those subject to its control* [103]. Though widely referenced, subsequent critique of Rawls has highlighted his persistent silence on race, which is all the more problematic given that he was writing within the United States, a society built on 'white privilege' and the racial subordination of non-white peoples [88]. Thus, we can begin to see that social justice might best be understood not as a single concept, but as a constantly evolving mechanism for thinking through how power, privilege, and access affect social structures.

While we focus on social justice, it is beyond the scope of this paper to discuss social justice in all of its complexity. There are many different types of social justice, no single, agreed-upon definition, and no clear consensus on how to work towards it or to verify its achievement. For the purposes of understanding what social justice means for design practice, we pragmatically adopt a concept of social justice developed by contemporary South African political theorist H.P.P. Lötter. In doing so, we are not holding his conception above any other, but find this framework useful in the exercise of thinking through social justice and its relationship to design by attending to multiple facets of this complex and unstable concept.

Lötter argues that social justice in the context of modern constitutional democracies is a "cluster concept" [85], a framework that is multi-dimensional by nature. His conceptualization thus accounts for multiple, contiguous aspects of justice. In grappling with the philosophical adage "justice is to give everyone their due" (and its inherent normativity), he formulates six dimensions of justice: *recognition*, *reciprocity*, *enablement*, *distribution*, *accountability*, and *transformation*. The multi-dimensional aspect of Lötter's definition is particularly useful for our purposes because it allows us to highlight concerns of social justice as they intersect with multiple moments and encounters within design practice. We will elaborate on specific sensitivities of each dimension later in the paper when we outline corresponding strategies for practicing social justice oriented interaction design. At its core, Lötter's conception of social justice centers on the social concerns, obligations, and ethical commitments created through social interactions. Drawing from this work, we note that social justice explicitly takes into account how historicity, identity, and social and political context (*e.g.*, class, race, gender, ability, health and wellness, and so on) impact people's lived experiences. This definition is compatible with work such as [21, 23, 25, 86], and – especially important for our purposes – is inclusive of concerns about how technology is designed and developed, how policy impacts information and communication practices and experiences, and how marginalization and oppression impact people's experiences of and practices with technology.

Design stands to play an important role within social change as ephemeral ideas about social justice are operationalized in processes of design, implementation, and use. As a philosophical concept, social justice provides one foundation for responding to open questions about how to conduct HCI design and research in ethically and politically responsible ways, and for developing specific strategies for engaging with the politics of design.

CASES: HOW A SOCIAL JUSTICE ORIENTATION CAN BENEFIT HCI DESIGN AND RESEARCH

HCI engages with large-scale social issues in a variety of domains, from education to health disparity. We believe that many of these domains could benefit from an engagement with social justice. In service of space and clarity, we examine only three such domains in this section. We take work in sustainability, ICTD, and community informatics as cases for showing how an engagement with social justice responds to open questions in socially-engaged design, and generates new concerns for future research.

Sustainability: From Individual to Systemic

Although emergent as a prominent research area only within the last decade, HCI research related to ecological concerns has exploded in recent years, and "sustainability" now owns a place in calls for participation as a targeted application domain (including at DIS 2016). In an extensive 2010 review of sustainable HCI, DiSalvo *et al.* showed that a vast majority of early research (70% of the works they examined) focused on designing tools or systems targeted at *individual consumers* with an additional (unreported) number of works targeted at individuals in some other capacity – *e.g.,* "as citizens rather than as consumers" [33]. This focus on the individual was well-aligned with another common theme found in their survey – an approach rooted in *persuasive design*. The intersection of persuasive design with a focus on individual actions characterizes a set of canonical projects in sustainable HCI: technologies designed to help users reflect on and alter their own behaviors in order to consume less energy or water, produce less waste, or otherwise minimize their personal ecological impact [*e.g.*, 92, 76, 68; see also 20]. Scholars have since argued that a focus on individual choice neglects the complex social dynamics, economics, and politics that produce situations of (un)sustainability in the first place, thus limiting the broader impacts of design projects framed from this perspective [54, 20, 12]. Instead of identifying isolated problems that might be solved at the individual level, these scholars call for designers to grapple with sustainability "holistically" or "systemically." Partially in response to such calls, some recent projects have focused on designing for sustainability at the infrastructural level. For example, Pierce and Paulos [100] describe a "local energy indicator" focused not just on the individual, but instead on making visible the variable availability of distributed and renewable energy sources – such as solar and wind – within a larger energy grid.

Calls within HCI to address sustainability systemically echo the calls of researcher-practitioners in urban studies and regional planning who have faced similar challenges in the design of "green" cities. Researchers in these domains have shown that a de-politicized approach to designing for sustainability – even if 'at scale' and rooted in community-centric, and community-led models – does not "result in 'win-win-win' [119] outcomes for economic development, environmental improvement, and social equity" as once believed [51]. Instead, these scholars note that sustainability is "inextricably linked to human equality. Wherever in the world environmental despoliation and degradation is happening, it is almost always linked to questions of social justice, equity, rights, and people's quality of life in its widest sense" [2]. Thus, without a direct engagement with the concerns of social justice – explicit work to surface the "undercurrents of class, gender and race/ethnicity-based conflict around socio-ecological relations" – sustainability projects "often *reproduce* social inequalities" [51] and undermine their own transformative potentials.

These scholars propose the notion of "just" sustainabilities to describe sustainabilities that go beyond "green," and aim to "ensure a better quality of life for all, now and into the future, in a just and equitable manner, whilst living within the limits of supporting ecosystems" [2; see also 109]. This work suggests that addressing sustainability as a systemic rather than individual issue is not just a matter of "scaling up" in a quantitative way. It is not just about involving more people, or scaling up the site of design, *e.g.,* from individual behavior to infrastructural technologies. Rather, *just* sustainabilities demand new ways of accounting for difference and inequity at the societal scale as cornerstones of truly sustainable design.

Beyond critique, these researchers also provide models for mitigating and resisting the re-entrenchment of inequity. Goodling and Harrington [51] describe the case of a justice-oriented transformation of a "complete streets" initiative in the city of Portland. When first introduced, the city-wide grant program offered technical and financial support to community groups seeking to make ecological and community-oriented improvements to local streets. Initially, however, applicants almost exclusively came from a small set of affluent neighborhoods. Recognizing that this disparity in grants was rooted in already-existing inequities – *e.g.*, having the time to navigate the grant program's bureaucracy or being a member of the social networks necessary to learn about the program in the first place – the city proactively changed program administration. In collaboration with graduate students at Portland State University, they began identifying and explicitly reaching out to underserved neighborhoods. Only with this explicit attention to equity within the administrative process was the city able to achieve the goals of the program – to enhance the ecological sustainability of the city as a whole.

Within HCI, Håkansonn & Sengers [54] have called for new attention to the relationships between sustainability and other social challenges such as the temporal, technical, and labor politics of contemporary capitalism. As they conclude, "HCI researchers concerned about sustainability can, and should, go beyond being 'about' being green" [54]. For example, "issues around busyness and having time to reflect on one's values [81] may be as important for a sustainable HCI to address as issues directly around consumption" [54]. Bringing a social justice orientation to sustainable interaction design is one way to push research further in this kind of holistic direction because it explicitly directs attention to the ways that sustainability is inextricably tied up in, rather than isolated from, the politics of class, race, labor, economy, and geography. In working towards *just* sustainabilities [2], our attention is drawn to the systemic and relational rather than to the individual; we are asked to explicitly grapple with the ways that a project of sustainable design might lead to the entrenchment or creation of socioeconomic disparities; we are provoked to take a political and ethical stance that centers not just on being "green," but on being more broadly equitable.

In responding to calls for more systemic research, a social justice orientation also helps to foreground new concerns about how to account for, and address, entrenched differences and inequities as part of a sustainable HCI agenda. In particular, it reminds us to ask who is (and is not) served by design, and suggests that sustainable HCI should be targeted not just at those who might afford (monetarily or temporally) to spend a weekend installing personal solar panels, to reflect on (and alter) consumptive practices, or to optimize energy usage patterns in alignment with a distributed solar or wind-powered electric grid. From a social justice orientation, sustainability is never about one person's resource consumption, but is always rooted in a multiplicity of stakeholders, power relations, and the already-existing unevenness of social life. The strategies for social justice oriented interaction design described in the latter half of this paper provide concrete tools for recognizing and responding to the linkages between the social challenge of sustainability and the persistence of inequities across social strata.

ICTD: From Technical to Political

Researchers in ICTD – information and communication technologies and development – study, design, and build computing technologies to bolster socioeconomic and international development efforts [116]. For example, past projects have focused on designing and deploying novel technology configurations in order to improve Internet access in rural and unconnected spaces [117, 98, 107, 97]. ICTD projects are often framed as explicit attempts to leverage the capacity of technology for social change in the service of addressing what have been identified as underlying social challenges such as widespread poverty or a lack of access to education. This area of work thus takes on deeply entrenched social issues, including educational, economic, developmental, and health disparities.

However, as researchers have found, projects focused on predominately *technical* approaches to social change often fail because they lack social and political sustainability [see 117, 62, 57, 5, 121, 67]. An inattention to the specificities of local politics and the power relations among the multiple stakeholders involved in a development project often contributes to the increased marginalization of oppressed groups while further entrenching existing power structures [see 45, 82, 89]. Recent critiques have argued for the need to re-politicize design and engineering practices, especially in the ways that designers and researchers identify and frame problems [82], to rethink assumptions about what makes 'poverty' a thing to fix [66, 45], and to be wary of perpetuating already-uneven economic relations by transforming individuals into consumers [66, 41]. Moreover, as Escobar [40] has argued, including more people and stakeholders alone is not enough. Thus, open questions in ICTD center not only on participant inclusivity, but also on how to reconfigure the constellations of power in which an outsider, a designer or developer, is often in the primary position of control.

Such critiques underscore a need for ICTD designers to engage more explicitly with precisely the key concerns of social justice – the multiplicity of stakeholders, power relations, and the unevenness of social and political systems. In this direction, some recent ICTD projects have embodied an explicit focus on social change through resisting forms of oppression, such as sexism, classism, racism, and ableism (*e.g.*, [102, 112, 70]). Irani *et al.* affirm that "all design research and practice is culturally located and power laden" and argue for a more explicitly political engagement with social issues like poverty because apolitical stances often occlude "the sometimes highly political causes of poverty" [66]. In their analysis, they draw from Ferguson, an anthropologist, to highlight how these development projects, by aligning with commercial interests, frequently ignore the political and historical trajectories that produce and perpetuate the conditions of poverty [45; see also 82, 89]. Likewise, Warschauer & Ames call for a more integrative approach among policymakers, practitioners, scholars, and designers to develop "an understanding of how to organize large-scale social improvement efforts involving technology" [121]. Similarly, Burrell and Toyama also call for interdisciplinary approaches and highlight the value and importance of reflexivity in the research and design process [18].

Taking a social justice orientation to design practice is one way to respond to these calls. The practical strategies and personal commitments which we outline in the final two sections can help designers to explicitly foreground the politics surrounding oppression and draw attention to the ways that some interventions may reproduce inequalities. Even if imperfect in execution, working towards the horizon of a more socially just society, means making the effortful attempt to reconfigure power structures within the design process. Although some recent work has focused on oppression, a more holistic engagement with social justice – including issues concerning the multiplicity of stakeholders, designer's engagement, and the economic, historical, and political framings of social issues – would help us better attend to and engage with the multiple politics of design. A shift from the technical to political highlights the ways that designers may unknowingly reduce or ignore the complex social situations for smaller, more tractable problems. Bringing a social justice orientation to ICTD work preferences attention to the complex economic, historical, and political trajectories of social issues and can help to raise related concerns that might otherwise remain invisible as well as to guide analysis through the development of more holistic framings of sociotechnical situations.

Community Informatics: From Charity to Social Change

A third cluster of work that aims to intervene in social challenges is design and research within the space of community informatics. In seeking to find practical ways to address a variety of complex social issues – such as homelessness, health disparity, street harassment, and domestic abuse – HCI researchers have often partnered with local nonprofit organizations [*e.g.*, 122, 78, 79, 28, 35]. Although non-profit and "charitable" organizations exist along a broad spectrum, many of these organizations aim to address social issues predominately through a charity model [53, 101]. Charity, as an orientation toward people and social challenges, focuses on providing aid to individuals identified as disadvantaged and can be problematic and limiting for the following reasons: it provides insufficient or inappropriate resources to address issues [53, 77, 101]; it defunds public sector services [101]; it is undemocratic in how to address issues [50]; and finally, such approaches tend to ignore the structural inequalities that produce the need for charity [50, 73]. Although there are many complex interrelations among non-profits, organizations commonly referred to as "charities," and other institutions in histories of social change, it is important to recognize the ways in which taking up charity as an orientation towards change can be problematic. Amplifying the current practices of charity-based nonprofits' may not be the most effective way to address all social issues.

Recently, there have been calls for rethinking traditional approaches to community informatics. Working in the area of civic engagement, Korn and Voida call for design strategies that create friction and generate contestation in order to "provoke people not only to take up more active roles in their communities but to question conventional norms and values about what it means to be a citizen as well" [71]. Studying housing justice activists, Asad & Le Dantec examine "how different kinds of civic engagement exist on digital platforms in spaces outside formal political and institutional channels" and as a means to resist institutional authority [7]. DiSalvo calls more generally for politically–oriented "adversarial design" to provoke discussion, debate, and contestation [30]. Such scholarship raises questions about how designers' participation and engagement with social issues are situated within larger cultural, political, social, and economic systems.

When forming partnerships – with "charities" or otherwise – designers and researchers must take care with respect to the types of practices and services they wish to amplify and how they engage and participate with the multiple stakeholders. Designers must attend to and reflect on how the practices they seek to augment are situated within a cultural, historical, and political milieu when working towards equity. Any work between vulnerable, marginalized populations and organizations seeking to help these populations raises questions about the politics of engagement and participation given the often-dramatic differences in social standing, power, and circumstance of these multiple participants.

A social justice orientation highlights how charity alone as a method to address large systemic social issues will likely not bring out the desired social change. Social justice draws to the fore concerns of equity, participation, engagement, and the larger consequences of practices, partnerships, and politics within design practices. It places these concerns at the heart, rather than the periphery, of design inquiry. It can help us more fully attend to and reflexively engage with the politics of collectively envisioning different futures and the pragmatic social changes necessary to achieve them.

DESIGN STRATEGIES FOR SOCIAL JUSTICE

In this section, we show how a social justice orientation can be enacted within a design practice. As we have seen thus far, social justice is a multi-faceted, complicated concept. There are many concerns associated with achieving social justice, and multiple paths along which one might work towards achieving its goals. In this section, we return to the work of Lötter [85], as inspiration for a set of concrete design strategies which respond to six different dimensions of social justice. These exemplar strategies, among many possible, help ground a social justice orientation within design practice. These strategies include designing for *transformation, recognition, reciprocity, enablement, distribution, and accountability*. For each of these, we draw on our own and others' work to identify concrete examples of how to practice design with a social justice orientation.

Designing for Transformation

In our first design strategy, we highlight the fluidity and malleability of social justice as a concept. Social justice is not (and should not be) a stable concept – it is always evolving with more robust and inclusive understandings of the issues, problematics, concerns, causes, and catalysts of social justice. Per Lötter, "conceptions of justice change over time [to reflect new social norms] and therefore just ways and means must be found to comply with a new, improved conception of [social] justice" [85]. Thus, a social justice oriented understanding of *transformation* suggests the usefulness of a long-term approach to designing for the evolving, emergent social, economic, and political relations that produce inequalities. Designing for such transformation draws our temporal orientation from immediate innovation towards a focus on the role that structural inequalities (*e.g.*, government institutions, the cultural milieu, access to education) may play in perpetuating social injustices.

Large social issues, such as food insecurity, sustainability, racism, sexism, and ableism develop from multifaceted interactions among individuals, communities, governments, organizations, and so on. Recent work within HCI, notably sustainable HCI, recognizes individual actions have a limited effect on large-scale social challenges, and has called for further understanding of problems beyond the individual [20, 36, 37, 72]. Such work asks designers to consider the "political and cultural context" [37] so they might develop effective solutions to large-scale societal problems. This broadening of the design space promotes designers to move beyond individual action and toward designing for collective action, by focusing on regional and national contexts [47, 52]; activist groups [52, 6, 33, 99], and/or nonprofit organizations [78, 122].

Designing for Recognition

The second design strategy for social justice that we explore here is rooted in the notion of *recognition*. From a social justice orientation, recognition focuses on identifying unjust practices, policies, laws, and other phenomena, as well as identifying those people who are most negatively impacted by such phenomenon [85].

Within design practice, recognition can happen when designers articulate and frame a problem and its collection of key issues [31, 108]. Problems do *not* exist *a priori*. Designers formulate "problems" when they define and articulate the collection of issues on which to focus their attention. The act of defining a problem simultaneously creates the acceptable parameters by which they can be addressed (*i.e.*, solutions that contend with the problem) by narrowing the focus of the potential design solutions. Therefore, problems are always developed understandings of situations that focus and delimit the design space [74, 31, 108].

One example of recognition can be found in the work of Dimond *et al.* in analyzing the impact of storytelling via Hollaback's web and mobile platforms. Hollaback, a social movement organization whose mission is to end street harassment, created these platforms to enable people to share stories and reflect on experiences of street harassment, an under-recognized problem which they define as "harassment in public spaces directed towards traditionally marginalized groups such as women, nonwhites, and LGBTQ (Lesbian, Gay, Bi, Transgender, and Queer) people" [28]. Hollaback helps individuals share stories and identify this phenomenon as harassment. Per the authors, street harassment is "not necessarily problematized or even recognized as a phenomenon" and, thus, a central goal of their design project involved "diagnosing street harassment as a problem" [28]. In this case, designing for recognition occurs at two levels. First, in framing a design or problem space, the creators of Hollaback explicitly aimed to address a social challenge that had previously been under-recognized, but that was a manifestation of unjust social relations and affected specific marginalized groups. Second, in creating a storytelling platform, the Hollaback team designed a system that did not attempt to simplistically or single-handedly 'solve' or eliminate street harassment, but rather to facilitate individuals' sharing of personal stories in such a way as to encourage others' identification of harassment, oppression, and marginalization as a legitimate social problem to be addressed via multiple avenues.

As a mode of reworking "participation" in the design process, recognition also encourages us to create open, transparent, and inclusive decision-making processes about which issues are deemed important when understanding a problem [42]. In practice, this encourages not only partnering with collaborators for extended periods to understand their challenges, resources, and goals, but also incorporating participatory methods within design practice.

In sum, designing for recognition means focusing on identifying unjust practices, laws, and policies and other phenomena. This identification can happen in a variety of ways including shedding light on the severity of an experience, situating historical injustices, legitimizing issues and concerns, translating experiences to enroll allies, and so on. Recognizing a phenomenon as a problem is the first step necessary to work towards social change.

Designing for Reciprocity

Building on recognition, after an injustice has been identified, *reciprocity* describes the relationship between those who are owed justice and what needs to occur for the obligations of justice to be fulfilled [85]. Often this requires an implicit or explicit agreement of what is considered to be the fair expectations or obligations between those who are owed justice and interpersonal, social, and institutional relations [85]. Thus, reciprocity as a design strategy focuses on engendering more fully equitable relationships.

Developing equitable relationships can be difficult given that people often do not agree on whether restitution is owed or how to address past injustices. Reciprocity encourages a focus on how to engender different forms of participation that could lead to more equitable engagements. There are many different types of relationships and stakeholders that could be envisioned in the design process from allies to oppressors. Reciprocity can be framed as mutually beneficial social arrangements and therefore, it encourages developing opportunities for change within uneven relations. One strategy for designing for reciprocity is to design platforms with the potential to change those inequitable relations. For example, in Dombrowski's design research on food justice, she worked alongside urban farmers who wanted to develop an alternative online marketplace with the goal of changing their uneven economic and social relations with their more affluent local businesses [34]. The urban farmers expressed concerns about feeling marginalized within the local food scene and desires to be seen as a resource to their affluent counterparts in more mutually beneficial ways. To develop new avenues for selling food to upscale restaurants ideologically invested in the local food movement, they proposed designs that would enable them to market and sell their produce to high-end consumers for a fair price, foster their reputation, and communicate with consumers. For these urban farmers, more equitable social and economic relations were the goal, not the starting point, of the envisioned design intervention. Here, reciprocity focused on developing relationships and devising methods to engender more equitable arrangements between farmers and their more prosperous counterparts, opening the possibility for more equitable reciprocity.

In sum, designing for reciprocity focuses on relationships and the ways in which those relationships maybe need to change to become more equitable for all stakeholders. While the presented design example highlighted a mutually beneficial system, fostering more equitable relationships may not always be seen as mutually beneficial, but can also encourage spaces for open contestation and conflict.

Designing for Enablement

The fourth design strategy for social justice focuses on *enablement*, facilitating and developing opportunities for people to fulfill their potential and to develop their own capacity. Oppression occurs when people are unduly constrained by "institutions, laws, policies, and human behavior" [85] or unable to engage in their own development [124]. Thus, enablement has a multi-level focus on developing opportunities for change, including scaffolding individual behavior change as well as the practices and polices related to fostering structural change. Enablement as an ideal focuses on creating possibilities for change and for decisions about what to change.

For design, enablement might be understood in terms of fostering human capacity or helping people take advantage of opportunities by creating platforms for participation and self-determination. For example, work by Parker *et al.*, focused on building community capacity around healthy eating by developing "community mosaic," a public infrastructure for sharing ideas among community members, promoting reflection, and encouraging behavior change [99]. This work exemplifies enablement because it focuses on creating a platform to help "lay people encourage others in their neighborhood to eat healthfully by sharing how they have been able to make healthy eating decisions themselves—information that is, hopefully, locally and culturally relevant to other community members" [99]. Individuals' stories were shared on a large public display in a local community center. Importantly, rather than standardizing behavior, the system fostered individuals' own reflection and decision making by prompting sharing aimed at inspiring others to eat healthy. Enablement centers not just on facilitating action, but also on deciding *which* actions to enable. In this example, decision-making occurred through formative focus groups in which the local community decided to emphasize, "how the community is succeeding at eating healthfully (instead of focusing on challenges)" [99]. Beyond nutrition and health, enablement is applicable within other domains in which individuals develop their own capacity such as education, healthcare, sustainability, and employment.

Designing for Distribution

Another design strategy for social justice is the equitable *distribution* of the benefits and burdens of social systems [85]. Benefits include wealth, goods, opportunities, and access to resources; burdens, on the other hand, include undesirable work, taxes, lack of adequate income, and environmental pollution.

With respect to designing interaction and sociotechnical systems, there are several strategies for fostering just distributions. First, one can examine areas focusing on a type of inequality. For example, Dombrowski *et al*'s work [35], focused on food insecurity, a lack of equitable access to healthy food [118]. In their work, they co-designed a collaborative location based information system with local nonprofit organizations seeking to better distribute food resources to their local community [35]. In this example, the design of the information system attempts to reimagine how a physical good – food, in this case – and information can be reconfigured across a network of nonprofit organizations and stakeholders to promote additional access and resource use. Their design envisions more equitable arrangements of resources by expanding the possibility of who can access and make use of those resources. Equitable distribution refers not only to physical goods, but to informational resources, access, and opportunities. Beyond this example, design has examined more equitable redistributions of resources, such as clean water [16], educational opportunities [106], economic opportunities

[27], and issues pertaining to information access and use [95, 17, 93]. Even further, equitable distribution can also entail how to use information and the ability to recognize what kinds of information are need to address a problem or need [90, 13]. Thus, distribution as a concept does not only refer to physical goods, but also immaterial resources such as power, knowledge, privilege.

There are limits to understanding material redistribution as a mechanism of social justice; better distributions of resources will not produce justice if they are neither sustainable nor made through equitable decision making processes. Therefore, beyond more equitable resource allocation, a more holistic definition of distributive justice encapsulates not only material resources, but also redistribution of the production mechanisms for technology and information. Within HCI, we see this type of distributional justice ethic reified through methods that broaden the scope of participation in the design process (*e.g.*, participatory design; action research; cooperative design) by aligning with typically marginalized populations (*e.g.*, [78]). By incorporating people who are typically excluded from the design process, designers may render visible alternative design spaces consistent with collaborators' particular cultural practices and preferences [44] and also engender designs that fight oppression and persistent marginalization and promote social change.

Designing for Accountability

Our final design strategy for social justice focuses on *accountability*, which includes holding responsible those who foster or unduly benefit from the oppression of others and identifying and assigning appropriate sanctions, penalties, or even punishments [85]. While determining causes and responsibility for injustice is an important step for social change, assigning sanctions when a sense of social justice has been violated can be difficult – if not impossible – for those in relatively low-positions of social standing and power. Therefore, one strategy for designing for accountability is developing coalitions and "alliances built on common cause … as a way to sustain political and ethical action" [64].

For example, Amazon Mechanical Turk (AMT) workers, or online crowd workers, "felt their work was regularly rejected unfairly or arbitrarily" and desired more fair compensation [64]. To address these concerns, Irani and Silberman designed and developed Turkopticon, which enables crowd workers to share and aggregate reviews of their employers, where previously only the employers could review employees. Doing so develops the potential for new forms of accountability by rendering interactions between workers and employers visible to other workers. In the case of Turkopticon, designing for accountability is not about requiring people to act in a specific way, but rather providing mechanisms for sharing and aggregating previously unseen knowledge among a previously marginalized group to help them make more informed decisions about which jobs to accept and destabilize the employer-dominated power structure.

Lastly, we would like to highlight Suchman's work on located accountability, where she advocates for a perspective on design and design practice to engender how "our vision of the world is a vision from somewhere … which makes us personally responsible for it" [113; see also 55]. Such a view of design and accountability helps designers understand how accountability can play a role in the relations of design, production, and use of technological systems. This could help designers to hold themselves accountable to other stakeholders who may be impacted by their design decisions, ranging from the inclusion criteria for direct stakeholders, to contemplating the types of materials used to produce the final design.

DISCUSSION

In this paper, we have outlined a social justice orientation to interaction design. The six pragmatic design strategies just presented create tractable ways to engage with social issues; however, as we stated earlier, in developing a social justice *orientation*, we have refrained from prescribing specific actions or stepwise methods. Thus, the presented design strategies should be understood as a preliminary and necessarily incomplete set of pragmatic approaches rooted in a theoretical and multi-dimensional analysis of social justice. We view social justice as a horizon to work towards. No developed solution will be perfect given the tradeoffs and conflicts among stakeholders that necessarily occur in design. Rather, designers should find ways to ground themselves within these imperfectly resolvable social, political, and economic situations and to focus on a process with a set of guiding goals that allow one to improvise as new situations and specific challenges arise. In this final section, we reflexively consider the ways that the six pragmatic strategies connect with a more pervasive and fundamental set of guiding personal commitments within a design practice. These three key commitments include *a commitment to conflict, a commitment to reflexivity, and a commitment to personal ethics and politics*.

Three Key Commitments in the Design Process

A Commitment to Conflict

Taken for granted ways of doing design often suppress, smooth over, or simply fail to surface conflicts. In many cases, conflict can seem to be a hindrance to design. For example, as Irani found in her study of hackathons, potential participants who were perceived by other designer-attendees as too "political" were often excluded from project and social groups – either explicitly or implicitly. The need to keep the project moving forward on a short timeline meant that anything other than depoliticized "feedback" was seen as disruptive and problematic for the success of the design project [63]. By contrast, a social justice orientation to design aligns with HCI scholarship that calls for favoring "polyvocality, diversity, and multiple perspectives" within the design process [38]. Prior work on polyvocality within HCI states that "decision-making [in the design process] involves more than having a voice; it means having a say" [15]. However, when embracing a diversity of perspectives, experiences, opinions, and goals conflict is likely to occur. There are multiple points where vigorous disagreement can occur within the design process, including attending who is allowed to speak, who controls the agenda and scope of the design process, problem framing, and determining how to address an issue.

In the design process, partnering with those who have experiences with and/or work to end oppression (*e.g.,* based on class, race, gender, ability, sexual or gender orientation) is a good starting point for understanding their particular experiences. Such work involves different types of stakeholders with different values, agendas, politics, ideals, and experiences that are productive in identifying "important information for analyzing our shared world" [42]. However, this means that problems do not have clear answers, because understanding a situation and coming to consensus becomes quite complicated given all of the experiences and external factors that influence a person's subjectivity during decision-making processes, including which problems are even worth addressing.

Earlier we discussed, in *designing for recognition,* that designers have to make explicit effort to legitimatize and render visible people's detrimental experiences with social issues. To complicate matters further, power (*i.e.*, social standing, influence, etc.) also impacts how articulations of social and technical problems are received. As Harding, a feminist science studies scholar, points out, "Marginalized groups have interests in asking questions [about power, oppression, and inequality], and dominant groups have interests in not hearing them" [56]. Marginalized voices can be silenced through deliberate coercive actions or by a distinct lack of opportunity to speak or to be heard. Therefore, conflict in discussions – either anticipated or direct – should be understood not as a problem, but as a healthy sign that the project is tackling questions worth discussing. By anticipated conflict, we refer to the ways in which others may anticipate or imagine other's reactions to discussions and decisions. By direct conflict, we refer to the open contestation that can occur during discussions of problems or proposed interventions. Arguments about healthy conflict align well with prior scholarship on conflict, politics, and deliberation within HCI and beyond [30, 83, 91]. Conflict is likely to occur when *designing for accountability* given that this dimension demands an acknowledgement of past injustices – something that is difficult for many people to do and is not often a part of everyday social interactions. Making a commitment to conflict means that the designer must take on the effortful task of helping to facilitate what may sometimes be uncomfortable conversations. Aligning with those who are oppressed and marginalized is one way to work against a cycle of oppression and representational inequity, as is recognizing our own privilege, constraints, and limits of our embodied knowledge within the design process and decision making.

A Commitment to Reflexivity

Attending to polyvocality in the design process includes acknowledging the designer's positionality, values, and politics. A long-standing debate amongst the HCI Values in Design community has focused on examining whose values should drive the design process and how those multiple, and sometimes contradicting and competing, opinions should influence the design process and how we understand technology [3, 79, 4, 46, 49]. While it would be problematic not to focus on users and acknowledge their values, experiences, and practices in the design process (which is the very definition of user-centered design), it is equally problematic to presume that designers' merely serve as amplifiers of their users' values. The relationship between the design process and different stakeholders' (*e.g.,* designers, researchers, community partners) positionality, values, and politics is far more complicated. Much of the existing work within Values in Design and HCI tends to downplay the role of the designer's values and their own subjective experience, which likely stems from designer's desires to be seen as more objective and neutral, and therefore more scientific [114]. It may also stem from wanting to "give voice" to the marginalized. However, taking a social justice approach involves active reflection on how designers' own beliefs and values influence design processes and outcomes, and how their "vision of the world is a vision from somewhere" [114; see also 55].

Works within HCI that raise concerns about subjectivity and reflexivity (*e.g.,* reflective HCI [111, 84, 1], critical HCI [11, 10], activist HCI [61, 19, 65], third-paradigm HCI [58]) have identified similar issues and often advocate that that designers and researchers should turn an analytical gaze to their own practices. Such works suggest that scholars should critically reflect on the practices that their work seeks to amplify, and the ways in which those practices are situated within a larger cultural and political milieu. Similarly, when *designing for enablement* and *distribution*, we must attend to not only *what* is enabled or distributed, but also *how* the design process unfolds and the designer's position and role within those processes. To engage issues of researcher and designer politics and their visions 'from somewhere,' Light calls for designers to "engage in researcher reflexivity; challenge the hegemonic dominance, legitimacy and appropriateness of positivist epistemologies; theorize from the margins; and problematize gender" [83]. Harrison *et al.*, likewise suggest that the "phenomenological situatedness of users, designers, and researchers" is central to design research, and argue that researchers, "should articulate to the extent possible the intellectual and political commitments that the authors bring to a particular project" [58]. There are limits to reflexivity [105] and prior work has called for recognizing the flexibility and relationally in our ability to know [79], particularly in moments when others, including our partners, question our positions, assumptions, and difference. However, this does not obviate a responsibility to attempt to integrate within the design process an acknowledgement of, and critical reflection on, one's own positionality. A social justice orientation is rooted in similar concerns, and provides a complementary set of strategies for researchers to bring political issues of class, race, gender, status, and sexual orientation to their projects' fore.

A Commitment to Ethics and Politics

A social justice perspective acknowledges the oppression a marginalized person has undergone, and that the oppression likely originates from or is influenced by external factors beyond the individual's control. It suggests asking, "why is this person experiencing this need in the first place?" Within *designing for transformation*, we discussed how social justice as a term is not stable and continually evolves more robust and inclusive understandings of concerns related to social justice. In doing so, a social justice-orientation widens the arena in terms of how context and situations are understood in relation to how oppression is experienced. Therefore, calls to action include contending with the individual's immediate needs, and attempts to address the larger context and imbalanced power relations that produce the potential for and actual oppression.

Importantly, we want to acknowledge the different political philosophies a social justice orientation can include. While the term social justice is often associated with inclinations that are considered liberal or "left leaning", social justice as a philosophy can include other political stances, values, and starting points. For example, in her work on science and technology policy, Cozzens demonstrates how different political philosophies (*e.g.,* libertarianism; utilitarianism; contractarianism; and communitarianism) all engage with the concept of justice differently; resulting in varied understandings of state obligations [24]. Therefore, social justice does not necessarily equate to "left leaning" politics and can be inclusive of a wider political spectrum.

However, what is crucial for embodying a social justice orientation is an explicit engagement with and commitment to *a* personal political and ethical stance. Attending to our own situated politics as designers and researchers provokes us to ask tough moral questions about our involvement in design and research projects. This attention is raised explicitly within strategies for *designing for reciprocity* as it focuses on fostering equitable relationships, including those between designers and their partners. By examining how personal politics inform our projects, we can produce more robust theoretical contributions focused on the capacity and constraints of interventions addressing social inequality.

Open Questions and Challenges

Before concluding, we want to acknowledge that significant pragmatic challenges confront a social justice-oriented design practice as researchers must contend with bureaucratic realities: securing funding, caring for students, obtaining ethics approval, working within institutional commitments, maintaining multiple community partnerships, and so on. These pragmatic challenges are a nontrivial component of conducting engaged work, and require attention within the realm of the mundane details of our disciplinary reward structures and institutional norms.

Another important open question centers on the politics of being an ally for an issue one does not directly experience. Political ecology research examining philanthropic nonprofit and non-governmental organizations states that "new configurations of networked relationship [can] obfuscate the workings of neoliberal imperialism; thus reinforcing global power hierarchies in which hegemonic powers are depicted as humanitarian 'saviours' whilst enforcing 'accumulation by dispossession' in the periphery" [26 citing 59]. That is, some efforts may appear philanthropic in nature, but upon further examination may actually reinforce oppression or the status quo, as many of these activities may be in "opposition to [local] agency and progressive social movements" [26]. Further explorations of the ethics and possibility of being a "good" ally for social justice causes within HCI are needed.

CONCLUSION

In summary, we understand social justice to be a fluid, multi-dimensional concept that evolves as we develop more robust and inclusive understandings of the concerns, causes, and catalysts of social change. We have aimed to honor this fluidity by outlining an *orientation* to design rooted in social justice – rather than presenting a specific technique or singular stepwise method. We understand this social justice orientation as comprising a constellation of modes and sensitivities, including a mode of knowing and relating, and sensitivities to inequality and marginalized voices. In outlining a social justice orientation to design, this paper provides several contributions: we described a multi-faceted concept of social justice relevant to interaction design and useful as a means to directly engage with the ethical and moral issues in design practice; we described concrete, pragmatic design strategies that create tractable ways to practice social justice oriented design along six dimensions; and finally, we outlined three key commitments necessary for carrying a social justice orientation through a design and research practice given that social justice as a horizon to work towards; an always ongoing process and practice rather than a clearly defined utopia that offers itself up for idealized achievement.

ACKNOWLEDGEMENTS

We thank our generous colleagues who gave us feedback on this work, including Lilly Irani, Carl DiSalvo, Amy Voida, Chris Wolf, Jed Brubaker, Melissa Mazmanian, Gillian R. Hayes, Geoffrey Bowker, and our anonymous reviewers. This work was supported in part by the Intel Science & Technology Center for Social Computing and The Newkirk Center For Science and Society.

REFERENCES

1. Philip E. Agre. 1997. *Computation and Human Experience*. Cambridge University Press, New York, NY, USA.
2. Julian Agyeman, Robert D. Bullard, and Bob Evans. 2003. *Just sustainabilities: development in an unequal world*. MIT Press, 2003.
3. Tamara Alsheikh, Jennifer A. Rode, and Siân E. Lindley. 2011. (Whose) value-sensitive design: a study of long- distance relationships in an Arabic cultural context. In *Proceedings of the ACM 2011 conference on Computer supported cooperative work* (CSCW '11), 75-84. http://dx.doi.org/10.1145/1958824.1958836
4. Morgan G. Ames, Janet Go, Joseph 'Jofish' Kaye, and Mirjana Spasojevic. 2011. Understanding technology choices and values through social class. In *Proceedings of the ACM 2011 conference on Computer supported cooperative work* (CSCW '11), 55-64. http://dx.doi.org/10.1145/1958824.1958834
5. Mike Ananny and Niall Winters. 2007. Designing development: Understanding One Laptop Per Child in its historical context. In *Proceedings of the 2nd IEEE/ACM International Conference on Information and Communication Technologies and Development (ICTD '07)*, 107–118. http://dx.doi.org/10.1109/ICTD.2007.4937397
6. Paul M. Aoki, R. J. Honicky, Alan Mainwaring, Chris Myers, Eric Paulos, Sushmita Subramanian, and Allison Woodruff. 2009. A vehicle for research: using street sweepers to explore the landscape of environmental community action. In *Proceedings of the SIGCHI Conference on Human Factors in Computing Systems* (CHI '09), 375-384. http://dx.doi.org/10.1145/1518701.1518762
7. Mariam Asad and Christopher A. Le Dantec. 2015. Illegitimate Civic Participation: Supporting Community Activists on the Ground. In *Proceedings of the 18th ACM Conference on Computer Supported Cooperative Work & Social Computing* (CSCW '15), 1694-1703. http://dx.doi.org/10.1145/2675133.2675156
8. Liam Bannon. 2011. Reimagining HCI: toward a more human-centered perspective. *interactions*18, 4 (July 2011), 50-57. http://dx.doi.org/10.1145/1978822.1978833
9. Shaowen Bardzell. 2010. Feminist HCI: taking stock and outlining an agenda for design. In *Proceedings of the SIGCHI Conference on Human Factors in Computing Systems* (CHI '10), 1301-1310. http://dx.doi.org/10.1145/1753326.1753521
10. Jeffrey Bardzell and Shaowen Bardzell. 2013. What is "critical" about critical design?. In *Proceedings of the SIGCHI Conference on Human Factors in Computing Systems* (CHI '13), 3297-3306. http://dx.doi.org/10.1145/2470654.2466451
11. Shaowen Bardzell, Jeffrey Bardzell, Jodi Forlizzi, John Zimmerman, and John Antanitis. 2012. Critical design and critical theory: the challenge of designing for provocation. In *Proceedings of the Designing Interactive Systems Conference* (DIS '12), 288-297. http://doi.acm.org/10.1145/2317956.2318001
12. Eric P.S. Baumer and M. Six Silberman. 2011. When the implication is not to design (technology). In *Proceedings of the SIGCHI Conference on Human Factors in Computing Systems* (CHI '11), 2271-2274. http://dx.doi.org/10.1145/1978942.1979275
13. France Belanger and Lemuria Carter. 2006. The Effects of the Digital Divide on E-Government: An Emperical Evaluation. In *Proceedings of the 39th Annual Hawaii International Conference on System Sciences - Volume 04* (HICSS '06), Vol. 4, 81-88. http://dx.doi.org/10.1109/HICSS.2006.464
14. Susanne Bødker, 2015. Using IT to "do good" in communities? *The Journal of Community Informatics.* Vol 11. No 2.
15. Tone Bratteteig, Keld Bødker, Yvonne Dittrich, Preben Holst Mogensen, and Jesper Simonsen. 2013. Methods in Participatory Design. In Jesper Simonsen and Toni Robertson (eds.). *Routledge International Handbook of Participatory Design*. Routledge.
16. Deana Brown, Gary Marsden, and Ulrike Rivett. 2012. *WATER alert!*: using mobile phones to improve community perspective on drinking water quality in South Africa. In *Proceedings of the Fifth International Conference on Information and Communication Technologies and Development* (ICTD '12), 230-240. http://dx.doi.org/10.1145/2160673.2160703
17. Giuseppe Bruno, Emilio Esposito, Andrea Genovese, and Kholekile L. Gwebu. 2011. A Critical Analysis of Current Indexes for Digital Divide Measurement. *The Information Society* 27, 1 (January 2011), 16-28. http://dx.doi.org/10.1080/01972243.2010.534364
18. Jenna Burrell and Kentaro Toyama. 2009. What Constitutes Good ICTD Research? *Information Technologies and International Development.* Volume 5, Number 3, 82–94.
19. Daniela K. Busse, Alan Borning, Samuel Mann, Tad Hirsch, Lisa P. Nathan, Andrea Grimes Parker, Ben Shneiderman, and Bryan Nunez. 2013. CHI at the barricades: an activist agenda?. In *CHI '13 Extended Abstracts on Human Factors in Computing Systems* (CHI EA '13), 2407-2412. http://dx.doi.org/10.1145/2468356.2468787
20. Hronn Brynjarsdottir, Maria Håkansson, James Pierce, Eric Baumer, Carl DiSalvo, and Phoebe Sengers. 2012. Sustainably unpersuaded: how persuasion narrows our

vision of sustainability. In *Proceedings of the SIGCHI Conference on Human Factors in Computing Systems* (CHI '12), 947-956. http://dx.doi.org/10.1145/2207676.2208539

21. Sumi Cho, Kimberle Williams Crenshaw, and Leslie McCall. 2014. Toward a field of intersectionality studies: Theory, applications, and praxis. *Signs* 38.4 (2013): 785-810
22. Rachel Clarke, Peter Wright, Madeline Balaam, and John McCarthy. 2013. Digital portraits: photo-sharing after domestic violence. In *Proceedings of the SIGCHI Conference on Human Factors in Computing Systems* (CHI '13), 2517-2526. http://dx.doi.org/10.1145/2470654.2481348
23. Patricia Hill Collins. 2002. Black Feminist Thought: Knowledge, Consciousness, and the Politics of Empowerment. Routledge.
24. Susan E. Cozzen. 2007. Distributive justice in science and technology policy. *Science and Public Policy*, 34 (2).
25. Kimberle Crenshaw. 1991. Mapping the Margins: Intersectionality, Identity Politics, and Violence against Women of Color. *Stanford Law Review* 43, 6: 1241–1299. http://doi.org/10.2307/1229039
26. Patricia Daley. 2013. "Rescuing African bodies: celebrities, consumerism and neoliberal humanitarianism." *Review of African Political Economy* 40.137, 375-393.
27. Tawanna R. Dillahunt. 2014. Fostering social capital in economically distressed communities. In *Proceedings of the SIGCHI Conference on Human Factors in Computing Systems* (CHI '14), 531-540. http://dx.doi.org/10.1145/2556288.2557123
28. Jill P. Dimond, Michaelanne Dye, Daphne Larose, and Amy S. Bruckman. 2013. Hollaback!: the role of storytelling online in a social movement organization. In *Proceedings of the 2013 conference on Computer supported cooperative work* (CSCW '13), 477-490. http://dx.doi.org/10.1145/2441776.2441831
29. Jill P. Dimond, Casey Fiesler, and Amy S. Bruckman. 2011. Domestic violence and information communication technologies. *Interacting with Computers* 23, 5 (September 2011), 413-421. http://dx.doi.org/10.1016/j.intcom.2011.04.006
30. Carl DiSalvo. 2012. *Adversarial Design*. The MIT Press.
31. Carl DiSalvo, Thomas Lodato, Laura Fries, Beth Schechter, and Thomas Barnwell. 2011. The collective articulation of issues as design practice. CoDesign: International Journal of CoCreation in Design and the Arts. Vol 7, Issue 3-4.
32. Carl DiSalvo, Jonathan Lukens, Thomas Lodato, Tom Jenkins, and Tanyoung Kim. 2014. Making public things: how HCI design can express matters of concern. In *Proceedings of the SIGCHI Conference on Human Factors in Computing Systems* (CHI '14), 2397-2406. http://dx.doi.org/10.1145/2556288.2557359
33. Carl DiSalvo, Phoebe Sengers, and Hrönn Brynjarsdóttir. 2010. Mapping the landscape of sustainable HCI. In *Proceedings of the SIGCHI Conference on Human Factors in Computing Systems* (CHI '10), 1975-1984. http://dx.doi.org/10.1145/1753326.1753625
34. Lynn Dombrowski. 2015. Sociotechnical Food Justice: Examining and Designing Public Interventions for Systemic Social Issues. Ph.D. University of California, Irvine. In Print.
35. Lynn Dombrowski, Jed R. Brubaker, Sen H. Hirano, Melissa Mazmanian, and Gillian R. Hayes. 2013. It takes a network to get dinner: designing location-based systems to address local food needs. In *Proceedings of the 2013 ACM international joint conference on Pervasive and ubiquitous computing* (UbiComp '13), 519-528. http://dx.doi.org/10.1145/2493432.2493493
36. Paul Dourish. 2007. Seeing like an interface. In *Proceedings of the 19th Australasian conference on Computer-Human Interaction: Entertaining User Interfaces* (OZCHI '07), 1-8. http://dx.doi.org/10.1145/1324892.1324894
37. Paul Dourish. 2010. HCI and environmental sustainability: the politics of design and the design of politics. In *Proceedings of the 8th ACM Conference on Designing Interactive Systems* (DIS '10), 1-10. http://dx.doi.org/10.1145/1858171.1858173
38. Paul Dourish and Scott D. Mainwaring. 2012. Ubicomp's colonial impulse. In *Proceedings of the 2012 ACM Conference on Ubiquitous Computing* (UbiComp '12), 133-142. http://dx.doi.org/10.1145/2370216.2370238
39. Anthony Dunne and Fiona Raby. 2013. Speculative everything: design, fiction, and social dreaming. MIT Press.
40. Arturo Escobar. 1991. Anthropology and the development encounter: the making and marketing of development anthropology. *American Ethnologist*, 18(4), 658-682.
41. Arturo Escobar. 1995. Encountering Development: the making and unmaking of the Third World. Princeton University Press Princeton.
42. Virginia Eubanks. 2011. Digital dead end: Fighting for social justice in the information age. MIT Press.
43. Daniel Fallman. 2011. The New Good: Exploring the Potential of Philosophy of Technology to Contribute to Human-Computer Interaction. In *Proceedings of the SIGCHI Conference on Human Factors in Computing*

Systems (CHI '11), 1051-1060. http://dx.doi.org/10.1145/1978942.1979099

44. Andrew Feenberg. 1995. Alternative Modernity: The technical turn in philosophy and social theory. University of California Press, Berkley and Los Angles, CA.
45. James Ferguson. 1990. The anti-politics machine: the development, depoliticization, and bureaucratic power in Lesotho. Cambridge University Press.
46. Mary Flanagan, Daniel C. Howe, and Helen Nissenbaum. 2008. Embodying values in technology: Theory and practice. *Information technology and moral philosophy*: 322-353.
47. Marcus Foth, Eric Paulos, Christine Satchell, and Paul Dourish. 2009. Pervasive Computing and Environmental Sustainability: Two Conference Workshops. *IEEE Pervasive Computing* 8, 1 (January 2009), 78-81. http://dx.doi.org/10.1109/MPRV.2009.13
48. Paulo Freire. 2000. *Pedagogy of the oppressed.* Bloomsbury Publishing.
49. Batya Friedman. 1997. *Human values and the design of computer technology*. No. 72. Cambridge University Press.
50. Paul Gomberg. 2002. The fallacy of philanthropy. *Canadian Journal of Philosophy* 32.1: 29-65.
51. Erin Goodling and Cameron Harrington. 2015. "Reversing Complete Streets Disparities: Portland's Community Watershed Program." Chapter 10 in Steven Zavetoski and Julian Agyeman (ed.), *Incomplete Streets: Processes, practices, and possibilities.* Routledge.
52. Elizabeth Goodman. 2009. Three environmental discourses in human-computer interaction. In *CHI '09 Extended Abstracts on Human Factors in Computing Systems* (CHI EA '09), 2535-2544. dx.doi.org/10.1145/1520340.1520358
53. Julie Guthman. 2008. Thinking inside the neoliberal box: The micro-politics of agro-food philanthropy. Geoforum, 39(3), 1241–1253.
54. Maria Håkansson and Phoebe Sengers. 2013. Beyond being green: simple living families and ICT. In *Proceedings of the SIGCHI Conference on Human Factors in Computing Systems* (CHI '13), 2725-2734. http://dx.doi.org/10.1145/2470654.2481378
55. Donna Haraway. 1998. Situated knowledges: The science question in feminism and the privilege of partial perspective. *Feminist studies*: 575-599.
56. Sandra Harding. 1998. Is Science Multicultural? Postcolonialisms, Feminisms, and Epistemologies. Bloomington: Indiana University Press.
57. Roger W. Harris. 2015. How ICT4D Research Fails the Poor. *Information Technology for Development.* 1-16.
58. Steve Harrison. Phoebe Sengers, and Deborah Tatar. 2011. Making epistemological trouble: Third-paradigm HCI as successor science. *Interacting with Computers,* 23(5), 385–392.
59. David Harvey. 2003. *The New Imperialism.* Oxford: OUP
60. John Harvey, David Golightly, and Andrew Smith. 2014. HCI as a means to prosociality in the economy. In *Proceedings of the SIGCHI Conference on Human Factors in Computing Systems* (CHI '14), 2955-2964. http://dx.doi.org/10.1145/2556288.2557367
61. Gillian R. Hayes. 2011. The relationship of action research to human-computer interaction. *ACM Trans. Comput.-Hum. Interact.* 18, 3, Article 15 (August 2011), 20 pages. http://dx.doi.org/10.1145/1993060.1993065
62. Richard Heeks. 1999. Information and communication technologies, poverty and development. *Institute for Development Policy and Management.*
63. Lilly Irani. 2015. Hackathons and the Making of Entrepreneurial Citizenship. *Science, Technology, and Human Values.* 40(5), 799-824.
64. Lilly C. Irani and M. Six Silberman. 2013. Turkopticon: interrupting worker invisibility in amazon mechanical turk. In *Proceedings of the SIGCHI Conference on Human Factors in Computing Systems* (CHI '13), 611-620. http://dx.doi.org/10.1145/2470654.2470742
65. Lilly Irani and M. Six Silberman, 2016. Stories We Tell About Labor: Turkopticon and the Trouble with "Design". In *Proceedings of the SIGCHI Conference on Human Factors in Computing Systems* (CHI '16). ACM, New York, NY, USA.
66. Lilly Irani, Janet Vertesi, Paul Dourish, Kavita Philip, and Rebecca E. Grinter. 2010. Postcolonial computing: a lens on design and development. In *Proceedings of the SIGCHI Conference on Human Factors in Computing Systems* (CHI '10), 1311-1320. http://dx.doi.org/10.1145/1753326.1753522
67. Steven J. Jackson, Alex Pompe, and Gabriel Krieshok. 2011. Things fall apart: maintenance, repair, and technology for education initiatives in rural Namibia. In *Proceedings of the 2011 iConference* (iConference '11), 83-90. http://dx.doi.org/10.1145/1940761.1940773
68. Li Jönsson, Loove Broms, and Cecilia Katzeff. 2010. Watt-Lite: energy statistics made tangible. In*Proceedings of the 8th ACM Conference on Designing Interactive Systems* (DIS '10), 240-243. http://dx.doi.org/10.1145/1858171.1858214

69. John T. Jost and Aaron C. Kay. 2010. Social justice: History, theory, and research. *Handbook of social psychology*. dx.doi.org/10.1002/9780470561119.socpsy002030
70. Gereon Koch Kapuire, Heike Winschiers-Theophilus, and Edwin Blake. 2015. An insider perspective on community gains: A subjective account of a Namibian rural communities' perception of a long-term participatory design project. *International Journal of Human-Computer Studies* 74: 124-143. http://dx.doi.org/10.1016/j.ijhcs.2014.10.004
71. Matthias Korn and Amy Voida. 2015. Creating Friction: Infrastructuring Civic Engagement in Everyday Life. *Aarhus Series on Human Centered Computing* 1.1 (2015): 12.
72. Bran Knowles, Lynne Blair, Mike Hazas, and Stuart Walker. 2013. Exploring sustainability research in computing: where we are and where we go next. In *Proceedings of the 2013 ACM international joint conference on Pervasive and ubiquitous computing* (UbiComp '13), 305-314. http://dx.doi.org/10.1145/2493432.2493474
73. Erica Kohl-Arenas. 2015. The Self-Help Myth: How Philanthropy Fails to Alleviate Poverty. *University of California Press*.
74. John Kolko. 2010. Sensemaking and Framing: A theoretical reflection on perspective in design synthesis. In *proceedings of the 2010 Design Research Society conference*.
75. John Kolko. 2012. *Wicked Problems: Problems Worth Solving: A Handbook & A Call to Action*. Austin Center for Design.
76. Stacey Kuznetsov and Eric Paulos. 2010. UpStream: motivating water conservation with low-cost water flow sensing and persuasive displays. In *Proceedings of the SIGCHI Conference on Human Factors in Computing Systems* (CHI '10), 1851-1860. http://dx.doi.org/10.1145/1753326.1753604
77. Robert W. Lake, and Kathe Newman. 2002. Differential citizenship in the shadow state. *Geo Journal* 58: 109-120.
78. Christopher A. Le Dantec, Jim E. Christensen, Mark Bailey, Robert G. Farrell, Jason B. Ellis, Catalina M. Danis, Wendy A. Kellogg, and W. Keith Edwards. 2010. A tale of two publics: democratizing design at the margins. In *Proceedings of the 8th ACM Conference on Designing Interactive Systems* (DIS '10), 11-20. http://dx.doi.org/10.1145/1858171.1858174
79. Christopher A. Le Dantec and Sarah Fox. 2015. Strangers at the Gate: Gaining Access, Building Rapport, and Co-Constructing Community-Based Research. In *Proceedings of the 18th ACM Conference on Computer Supported Cooperative Work & Social Computing* (CSCW '15). ACM, New York, NY, USA, 1348-1358. DOI=http://dx.doi.org/10.1145/2675133.2675147
80. Christopher A. Le Dantec, Erika Shehan Poole, and Susan P. Wyche. 2009. Values as lived experience: evolving value sensitive design in support of value discovery. In *Proceedings of the SIGCHI Conference on Human Factors in Computing Systems* (CHI '09), 1141-1150. http://dx.doi.org/10.1145/1518701.1518875
81. Gilly Leshed and Phoebe Sengers. 2011. "I lie to myself that i have freedom in my own schedule": productivity tools and experiences of busyness. In *Proceedings of the SIGCHI Conference on Human Factors in Computing Systems* (CHI '11), 905-914. http://dx.doi.org/10.1145/1978942.1979077
82. Tania Murray Li. 2007. The will to improve: governmentality, development, and the practice of politics. Duke University Press.
83. Ann Light. 2011. HCI as heterodoxy: Technologies of identity and the queering of interaction with computers. *Interact. Comput.* 23, 5 (September 2011), 430-438.
84. Jonas Löwgren and Erik Stolterman. 2004. Thoughtful Interaction Design: A Design Perspective on Information Technology. The MIT Press.
85. H.P.P. (Hennie) Lötter. 2011. Poverty, Ethics and Justice. University of Wales Press.
86. Leslie McCall. 2014. The complexity of intersectionality. *Signs* 40.1.
87. David Miller. 1999. Principles of social justice. Harvard University Press.
88. Charles Mills. 2009. Rawls on Race/Race in Rawls. *The Southern Journal of Philosophy*. Vol 47.
89. Timothy Mitchell. 2002. Rule of experts: Egypt, techno-politics, modernity. University of California Press.
90. Karen Mossenburg, Caroline J. Tolbert, and Mary Stansbury. 2003. Virtual Inequality: Beyond the Digital Divide. George Washington University Press, Washington, D.C.
91. Chantal Mouffe. 1999. Deliberative democracy or agonistic pluralism?. *Social research* 745-758.
92. Tatsuo Nakajima, Vili Lehdonvirta, Eiji Tokunaga, and Hiroaki Kimura. 2008. Reflecting human behavior to motivate desirable lifestyle. In *Proceedings of the 7th ACM conference on Designing interactive systems* (DIS '08), 405-414. http://dx.doi.org/10.1145/1394445.1394489
93. Taewoo Nam and Djoko Sigit Sayogo. 2011. Who uses e-government?: examining the digital divide in e-

government use. In *Proceedings of the 5th International Conference on Theory and Practice of Electronic Governance* (ICEGOV '11), 27-36. http://dx.doi.org/10.1145/2072069.2072075

94. Kai Nielsen. 2003. Globalization and justice. Prometheus Books.
95. Pippa Norris. 2001. Digital divide: Civic engagement, information poverty, and the Internet worldwide. Cambridge University Press, New York, NY.
96. Martha C. Nussbaum. 2004. Beyond the social contract: capabilities and global justice. An Olaf Palme lecture, delivered in Oxford on 19 June 2003. *Oxford Development Studies* 32.1 (2004): 3-18. 166.
97. Elisa Oreglia, Ying Liu, and Wei Zhao. 2011. Designing for emerging rural users: experiences from China. In *Proceedings of the SIGCHI Conference on Human Factors in Computing Systems* (CHI '11), 1433-1436. http://dx.doi.org/10.1145/1978942.1979152
98. Tapan S. Parikh and Kaushik Ghosh. 2006. Understanding and designing for intermediated information tasks in India. *IEEE Pervasive Computing* 5, 2., 32–39.
99. Andrea Parker, Vasudhara Kantroo, Hee Rin Lee, Miguel Osornio, Mansi Sharma, and Rebecca Grinter. 2012. Health promotion as activism: building community capacity to effect social change. In *Proceedings of the SIGCHI Conference on Human Factors in Computing Systems* (CHI '12), 99-108. http://dx.doi.org/10.1145/2207676.2207692
100. James Pierce and Eric Paulos. 2012. The local energy indicator: designing for wind and solar energy systems in the home. In *Proceedings of the Designing Interactive Systems Conference* (DIS '12), 631-634. http://dx.doi.org/10.1145/2317956.2318050
101. Janet Poppendieck. 1999. Sweet charity?: Emergency food and the end of entitlement. Viking Penguin.
102. Gary W. Pritchard and John Vines. 2013. Digital apartheid: an ethnographic account of racialised hci in Cape Town hip-hop. In *Proceedings of the SIGCHI Conference on Human Factors in Computing Systems* (CHI '13), 2537-2546. http://dx.doi.org/10.1145/2470654.2481350
103. John Rawls. 1971. A Theory of Justice. Cambridge, MA: Harvard University Press.
104. Horst W. J. Rittel and Melvin M. Webber. 1973. Dilemmas in a General Theory of Planning. *Policy Sciences*. 4. 155-169.
105. Gillian Rose. 1997. Situating knowledges: positionality, reflexivities and other tactics. *Progress in human geography* 21.3: 305-320.
106. Parisa Khanipour Roshan, Maia Jacobs, Michaelanne Dye, and Betsy DiSalvo. 2014. Exploring How Parents in Economically Depressed Communities Access Learning Resources. In *Proceedings of the 18th International Conference on Supporting Group Work* (GROUP '14), 131-141. DOI=http://dx.doi.org/10.1145/2660398.2660415
107. Nithya Sambasivan, Ed Cutrell, Kentaro Toyama, and Bonnie Nardi. 2010. Intermediated technology use in developing communities. In *Proceedings of the SIGCHI Conference on Human Factors in Computing Systems* (CHI '10), 2583-2592. http://dx.doi.org/10.1145/1753326.1753718
108. Donald Schön. 1983. The reflective practitioner. Basic Books.
109. Kristin Scrader-Frechette. 2002. Environmental Justice: Creating Equality, Reclaiming Democracy. New York: Oxford University Press.
110. Amartya Sen. 2011. The idea of justice. Harvard University Press.
111. Phoebe Sengers, Kirsten Boehner, Shay David, and Joseph 'Jofish' Kaye. 2005. Reflective design. In *Proceedings of the 4th decennial conference on Critical computing: between sense and sensibility* (CC '05), Olav W. Bertelsen, Niels Olof Bouvin, Peter G. Krogh, and Morten Kyng (Eds.), 49-58. http://dx.doi.org/10.1145/1094562.1094569
112. Larry Stillman. 2013. Participatory action research & inclusive information and knowledge management for empowerment. In *Proceedings of the Sixth International Conference on Information and Communications Technologies and Development:* Notes - Volume 2 (ICTD '13), Vol. 2, 163-166. http://dx.doi.org/10.1145/2517899.2517903
113. Lucy Suchman. 2002. Located accountabilities in technology production. *Scandinavian journal of information systems.* Vol 14 Issue 2.
114. Lucy Suchman. 2011. Anthropological Relocations and the Limits of Design. *Annual Review of Anthropology.* 40. 1–18. doi:10.1146/annurev.anthro.041608.105640
115. Elizabeth F. Thompson. 2014. Social Justice in the Middle East. In The Routledge International Handbook of Social Justice, Michael Reisch, ed. London: Routledge, 61-73.
116. Kentaro Toyama. 2010. Human–Computer Interaction and Global Development. *Foundations and Trends in Human-Computer Interaction.* 4, 1 (January 2010), 1-79. DOI=http://dx.doi.org/10.1561/1100000021 225.
117. William David Tucker and Edwin H. Blake. 2008. The role of Outcome Mapping in developing a rural telemedicine system. In *Proc. IST-Africa.*
118. United States Department of Agriculture. 2013. Household Food Security in the United States in 2012.

Retrieved From: http://www.ers.usda.gov/publications/err-economic-research-report/err155.aspx#.UipsnGRt4qk

119. Robert O. Vos. 2007. Defining sustainability: A conceptual orientation. *Journal of Chemical Technology and Biotechnology*, 82 (4), 334–339.

120. Michael Walzer. 2008. *Spheres of justice: A defense of pluralism and equality*. Basic Books.

121. Mark Warschauer and Morgan Ames. 2010. Can One Laptop per Child save the world's poor?. *Journal of International Affairs* 64.1.33.

122. Jill Palzkill Woelfer and David G. Hendry. 2011. Designing ubiquitous information systems for a community of homeless young people: precaution and a way forward. *Personal Ubiquitous Comput.* 15, 6, 565-573.

123. Sally Wyatt. 2003. Non-users also matter: The construction of users and non-users of the Internet. In Oudshoorn and Pinch (Ed.), *How Users Matter: The Co-construction of Users and Technology*. MIT Press.

124. Iris Marion Young. 1990. *Justice and the Politics of Difference*. Princeton, NJ: Princeton University Press.

125. Joseph Zajda, Suzanne Majhanovich, and Val Rust. 2006 eds. *Education and Social Justice*. Dordrecht: Springer Netherlands. link.springer.com/10.1007/1-4020-4722-3.

Privacy & Social Media in the Context of the Arab Gulf

Norah Abokhodair*
University of Washington
Seattle, USA
noraha@uw.edu

Sarah Vieweg
Qatar Computing Research Institute
Doha, Qatar
svieweg@qf.org.qa

ABSTRACT
Theories of privacy and how it relates to the use of Information Communication Technology (ICT) have been a topic of research for decades. However, little attention has been paid to the perception of privacy from the perspective of technology users in the Middle East. In this paper, we delve into interpretations of privacy from the approach of Arab Gulf citizens. We consider how privacy is practiced and understood in technology-mediated environments among this population, paying particular attention to the role of Islam and cultural traditions in constructing norms around privacy. We then offer culturally sensitive design principles and suggestions for future research that incorporates previously unexplored characteristics of privacy, which play a role in how users navigate social media.

Author Keywords
Privacy; Saudi Arabia; Qatar; Social Media; Arab Studies; Middle East; Islam; Social Computing.

ACM Classification Keywords
H.5.m. Information interfaces and presentation (e.g., HCI): Miscellaneous.

INTRODUCTION
Layla is a 23-year-old Saudi girl. After finishing her undergraduate degree at King Saud University in Riyadh, she started working at a multinational consulting firm in her hometown. This particular firm is one of the few workplaces in the country in which gender segregation laws are relaxed and Layla can attend meetings with men. After a few months, Layla started receiving friend requests on Facebook from male colleagues. While she does not mind being friends with males on Facebook, she is aware that it would disturb her family. In the given situation, Layla was faced with a conundrum: should she placate her family and follow their wishes, or participate in social networking that may prove useful in her professional life?

DIS 2016, June 04-08, 2016, Brisbane, QLD, Australia
© 2016 ACM. ISBN 978-1-4503-4031-1/16/06 $15.00
DOI: http://dx.doi.org/10.1145/2901790.2901873

Previously, Layla used her Facebook account to keep in touch with female friends and family. Maintaining a small group of friends on Facebook was culturally acceptable and safe. However, if she is to immerse herself in the culture of her new workplace, make friends, and advance her career, she may have to take on the task of managing her social media sites in ways that satisfy both the traditional expectations placed on her by her family, and the professional expectations placed on her by her colleagues.

Motivation
Social Media Sites are playing an increasingly important—yet frequently problematic—role in the everyday lives of users in the GCC[1]. They bring about challenges in terms of the ways this population experiences privacy and manages identity. We are aware of various conceptions of privacy that exist across cultures, but when it comes to commonly used tools such as social media sites and microblogging services, the assumptions around privacy that are embedded in technology design do not necessarily make it easy for those who adhere to Islamic interpretations of privacy to use them. In other words, we can say that a particular interpretation of privacy is foisted upon the users of these technologies, and if those users regard and practice privacy differently, then re-use and appropriation must take place. In this paper, we focus on how social media users in the Arab Gulf manage their interactions, and their identities, while maintaining traditional expectations and practicing privacy in culturally acceptable ways.

Privacy, Religion and HCI
Researchers have long discussed, researched, and debated definitions of privacy and how it should be considered and incorporated into technology design. Recently, scholars have questioned the notion of a universal definition of privacy, suggesting instead that it is a socially constructed and culturally bound concept [10,29,31]. While various outcomes and applications have arisen from the studies to date, limited research approaches privacy from a point of view that does not focus on interpersonal boundaries [9], but allows for alternative interpretations of "privacy."

* This research was conducted while an intern at Qatar Computing Research Institute (QCRI)

[1]The GCC stands for the Gulf Cooperation Council—six Muslim majority countries near or on the Arabian Gulf that share cultural and historical ties.

For technology users from the Arab Gulf, the Arabic language, religious affiliation, and cultural expectations are factors that play a critical role in technology adoption and use. In particular, understandings of privacy are tied to expectations and norms that have foundations in Muslim religious practice. The importance of privacy is borne of the responsibility to maintain the sanctity of one's body and one's home, in addition to upholding the honor and good name of one's extended family.

Researchers have noted ways in which Muslim social media users enact norms that dictate modesty and consider the importance of reputation, self-image and family honor, [1,7,34,44], but a focus on privacy vis-à-vis social media use has yet to be theorized. Looking at privacy through the lens of digital technology in an Arab Gulf setting raises provocative questions about the ways in which cultural norms and expectations that are rooted in tradition come to pass when they are interpreted via modern media.

Our aim is to contribute to the literature on privacy in two ways. First, introduce and explain privacy vis-à-vis social media use, with an eye toward Arab Gulf understandings and enactments of privacy. Second, we provide evidence regarding how privacy is enacted in digital environments through analysis of face-to-face interviews. Combined, these serve as a foundation for design opportunities that take a more encompassing view of privacy.

RELATED WORK

Previous research contributes to understandings of privacy as it is understood in the Arab Gulf, but questions—and the need for additional theorization regarding privacy—remain. Privacy is often viewed as a concept of the self as an individual, apart from a group [9]. While this is true in many previously studied user groups, we note that in the Arab Gulf the basic idea of *the self* and *the group* is conceptualized such that asserting one's individuality is viewed in a negative light. Membership in a family and tribe are of the utmost importance; there is no individual separate from a family [12,20]. This perception of the self extends elsewhere, as explained by Bidwell regarding her research on Facebook use in rural Africa: "In the everyday acts, linguistics, and philosophy of precolonial African society, personhood was constituted by others—both living and dead—and identity was perceived as undifferentiated and fixed to a social position" [12]. This idea of formulating the self through others is a process that applies also to Arab Gulf culture, and as this relates to privacy, the notion of "personal privacy" takes on a different tenor.

Privacy in Design

Scholars have also noted how conceptions of privacy become inscribed in technology design [7, 17, 22, 23, 43]. As the design and HCI communities strive to establish a broader understanding of values imbued in technology design, there is risk in continuing to omit alternative perspectives toward privacy. We strongly support the idea that "A first step toward designing for privacy entails understanding what privacy means to those who will use and be affected by the use of the technology" [23].

This is not to say that researchers and scholars have not carefully considered the highly contextual, culturally-bound nature of privacy within the realm of technology use. Palen and Dourish [31] delve into the ways in which technology is viewed and implemented vis-à-vis cultural norms. The authors consider privacy through the lens of Altman, which leaves room for us to interpret what is meant by "privacy," and not be beholden to a particular perspective. Altman present privacy as a dynamic, dialectic process "conditioned by our own expectations and experiences, and by those of others with whom we interact" [9 in 31]. Building on their work, Barkhuus emphasizes that "privacy is not an easily measurable unit…we as HCI researchers and practitioners need to approach the notion through more contextually grounded measures" [11].

However, while many have thoughtfully analyzed and theorized privacy and technology use, there has been little research that brings Gulf Arab notions of privacy into the conversation. One study that does focus specifically on privacy and social networking in the GCC is by Faisal et al. [20]. They evaluate privacy behaviors, trust concerns, and attitudes of social media users in Kuwait. The study included 222 surveys, with results showing that a high level of privacy awareness and trust are major factors that affect how Kuwaiti youth participate on social media. In addition, they note that Kuwaitis "tend to be conservative and favor collective over individual interests." Overall, they stress that privacy is a high-stakes value in collectivist and honor-based societies, and a violation of privacy "leads to shame and loss of face" [20].

Contributing to the body of research on privacy enactment via digital technology among GCC users, and answering the call made by [11] for "a more nuanced treatment of the notion of privacy" we add to the conversation around Gulf Arab interpretations of privacy. We provide a description of privacy from the perspective of citizens of the region, and go on to elucidate how the enactment of privacy affects their behavior in digital environments.

UNDERSTANDING PRIVACY IN THE GCC

In GCC countries, knowledge and practices around morality and ethics are primarily derived from Qur'anic text, and the example (*Sunnah*) of the prophet Muhammad. Together, these constitute the principle sources of *sharia law*, which is the foundation for both the judicial system, and societal norms and expectations regarding behavior. The need for, and expectation of, privacy plays a prominent role in daily life. To adequately grasp how privacy is viewed in the GCC, it is important to first explain what privacy is from an Islamic perspective. We do so by providing background on how privacy is viewed in the Arab Gulf. We then focus on the Islamic roots, and discuss why the consistent enactment of privacy is tantamount to following sharia law.

While prevalent conceptions of privacy focus on the individual, and their relationship to "a group," (namely, notions of seclusion and control) [9] Gulf Arab notions of privacy are bound up in the importance of modesty. [37] explains that "the notion of privacy in the Arab-Islamic paradigm is largely related to the requirement of modest self-presentation for Muslims in public, particularly women…the underlying meaning of privacy in the Arab-Islamic culture is respect and not seclusion." Presenting oneself as modest, in both dress and behavior, is of great importance to being a respectable member of Gulf society, and privacy plays an important role in how modesty and respect are maintained.

Research that focuses on Arab notions of privacy comes from fields including healthcare, marketing, and architecture. Drawing on experiences with the psychiatric care of Arab patients in the United States, [27] note that privacy is vigorously guarded, and medical personnel are often viewed as intrusive when asking questions that Western patients consider routine. It is not uncommon for Arab patients to answer questions in a way that pleases the medical professional, but not necessarily be honest about a condition or symptom, so as to maintain privacy [27].

From an architectural perspective, Sobh and Belk provide detail about traditional home design in the Gulf Arab countries, where houses are typically designed with an inward-facing center to protect the family from the public eye [37]. The idea is to maintain the sanctity of the home, which is considered sacred and pure, and which must be guarded from the gaze or intrusion of non-family members.

When it comes to marketing, particularly of Western products/ideals in the Arab Gulf, Sobh and Belk again point to slippage in current approaches that fail to understand the importance of privacy. For example, some advertisements show gatherings of mixed-gender, non-family members in a home, which is forbidden in Gulf Arab culture. The privacy of females in particular is of the upmost importance, and the idea of a mixed-gender gathering is nonsensical [37].

The Islamic vision of privacy

To elaborate on these approaches toward privacy, we must delve into the significance privacy has in the GCC. The way in which privacy translates so as to be understood by a non-Gulf Arab audience involves several concepts.

"Hurma" (حرمة) is an Arabic word that symbolizes the concept closest to the notion of privacy in the English vocabulary. Depending on the context, hurma has two meanings: 1) anything that is unlawful to obtain or look at without permission or 2) a woman, a sacred space (mosque or home) or a sacred time (holy month). These are all considered pure, and should remain guarded; any intrusion on their sanctity is considered sinful [18].

In the Quran, privacy is first mentioned in the context of instructing people to seek permission before entering another's home. The purpose is to protect the sanctity—or hurma—of the house and the body. One is required to knock on a door three times before accessing another's space. This rule is in place to avoid walking in on another while in a state of undress, or while with one's spouse/family. Entering without permission risks exposing one's "awrah"(عورة) . In Islam, awrah literally means the intimate parts of one's body. In the GCC, everyone is instructed to cover certain body parts; what is covered and when depends on the specific situation and the level of conservativeness. For women in the GCC, awrah can extend beyond the hair to include the arms, the legs, and in some cases the face. Awrah and hurma can be used together to indicate the unlawfulness of obtaining or seeking access to others' sacred body parts and spaces.

In addition, Saudi Arabia upholds the right to privacy in its Basic Law of Government: "Dwellings are inviolate. Access is prohibited without their owners' permission. No search may be made except in cases specified by the Law." [39]. In the GCC, the rule associated with privacy is "haq al-khososyah"(حق الخصوصية), which is an "individual's right to protect some aspects of their private life and maintain confidentiality to safeguard his/her reputation and aspects of his/her life that are kept away from the interference of people" [5]. When GCC citizens protect their hurma and/or awrah, they are enacting their right to haq al-khososyah.

We suggest that privacy as practiced in traditional Islamic cultures, especially in the Gulf, involves three aspects; awrah, hurma, and haq al-khososyah. We can think of awrah as an object, something tangible that must be protected. Hurma is the value, borne of Islamic teachings that asserts the sacredness of awrah. Haq al-khososyah is the law that guards and protects one's right to invoke hurma in the interest of protecting awrah. In Figure 1, we depict awrah at the center, as it is of the most value; it is the object to be shielded. We show hurma encompassing awrah; it is the space that surrounds the awrah, protecting it. Haq al-khososyah encircles both hurma and awrah; it empowers people to legitimately protect their awrah.

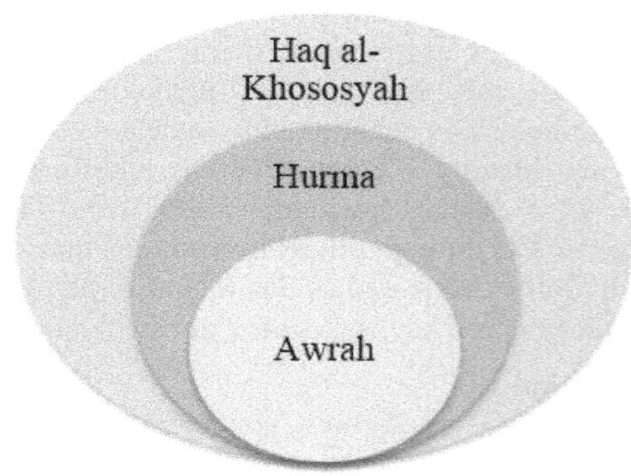

Figure 1: Islamic Interpretation of 3 aspects of "privacy"

Privacy is again mentioned in the Quran in relation to a law that promotes the respect of others by warning Muslims to refrain from bad manners that can lead to an invasion of others' privacy. This is based on the prohibition of spying, gossiping, and mistrust. When a rule is introduced in a holy text, Muslims are obligated to follow it. Failure to follow these rules is considered a sin. Therefore, respecting others' privacy, and maintaining one's own privacy, is a decree from God. GCC citizens' practice of and adherence to privacy as part of their daily lives stems from the pursuit of the blessings of God, or "barakah" (بركة). This endeavor leads to the creation and maintenance of a respectful image.

THE STUDY

The population we focus on are citizens of two of the six Gulf Cooperation Council (GCC) countries—Saudi Arabia, and Qatar. The GCC is a political and economic union that implements similar regulations in trade, finance, and religion (among other matters), and whose governments and leadership maintain close ties with each other. Islamic principles and tribal traditions are thoroughly intertwined and provide the foundation for GCC customs, laws and practices. Virtually all citizens of the GCC are practicing Muslims; the majority adheres to conservative interpretations of Islamic texts which dictate their daily lives. Arabic is the official language of the GCC, and the language of the Quran; it is the primary language taught at public schools and used in official government processes. However, English is commonly spoken; it is the second most common language among citizens of the GCC and is used in many day-to-day interactions. In addition, English classes are compulsory in schools.

GCC society is collectivistic in nature. Patriarchal norms direct behavior; the reputation of one's family and tribe are of the utmost importance and take precedence over individual status, needs and/or self-image. In collectivistic cultures, individuals identify as part of strong and cohesive long-term commitments to a whole [42] that can be seen in the relationship people have with their immediate and extended family, and their tribe. In the Quran, the practice of maintaining a relationship with kin is referred to as 'silatur-rahim' (maintaining the bonds of kinship) meaning one must "deal properly with relatives, supporting them with whatever possible and warding off bad things. "[It involves] visiting the relatives, asking about them, checking on them, giving them gifts when possible, helping their poor members, visiting their sick members, accepting their invitations, having them as guests, feeling proud of them and elevating them" [35 in 2]. In Qatar and Saudi Arabia, it is a regular practice to allocate some time during the weekend and the holidays for visits between relatives. This practice is highly encouraged in Islam and there are verses in the Quran that warns people from severing or abandoning these ties.

Additionally, citizens of these countries follow strict social conventions akin to unspoken rules. For example, gender segregation is an important aspect of life in the GCC. This practice concerns the interaction between women and men who are not close blood relatives (non-mahram[2]). Gender segregation is actively enforced in Saudi Arabia and commonly practiced in Qatar (though it is not legally required). This segregation is in place "to regulate women [and to] prevent other men from encroaching on the male honor of the family" [3]. When in public, women must wear loose robes over their clothing called *abaya*, cover their hair and sometimes their faces with a *shayla* and *niqab* respectively, all to avoid the "unwanted gaze" of unrelated men. These are everyday practices borne of an adherence to modesty and respect. However, women are not expected to wear the shayla and abaya when in the company of other women, nor around mahrams.

Citizens of the GCC are also avid users of social media. Recently, Saudi Arabia was ranked second globally and first among Arab countries for using Snapchat [8]. Additionally, in 2014, the kingdom also recorded a rate of over 7.8M active Facebook users, as well as the fastest-growing population on Twitter with more than 5M active users and 150M tweets per month [38]. Numbers are similarly high in Qatar: 65% of Qataris are on Instagram, 44% are on Facebook, and 46% are on Twitter [32]. Fast adoption, high rates and regular use of social media will continue to grow in the region. However, despite the popularity of social media, users find it necessary to employ workarounds that allow them to use these technologies in culturally appropriate ways.

Privacy is a "multifaceted" notion [15]; it is interwoven with notions of trust, identity, seclusion and autonomy. In the Arab World, and in the GCC in particular, honor, shame, and modesty are also factors that influence how privacy is approached and carried out. We are interested in how "privacy" as practiced in the Gulf is enacted through the use of technologies that were not developed with this user group in mind. We asked participants about their uses and habits regarding social media, and talked about their opinions and preferences. In analyzing interview data, it became clear that privacy was a concern.

Method

The authors have both been actively conducting research in The GCC The first author is a Saudi Arabian female, the second author is an American female who has lived and worked in Qatar for several years. Each of us has previously interviewed citizens of the region about their views and habits regarding social media use. Through this ongoing research, we came to realize that when discussing social media use, privacy was a topic that was frequently discussed among all participants.

In embarking upon joint research that considers privacy in a Gulf Arab context, we found ourselves constrained by definitions and conceptions of privacy that are based in a perspective that is largely theorized and defined in

[2] A *mahram* is a male relative that a Muslim woman cannot marry, or to whom she is already married, e.g. father, husband, brother, son.

American and Western European perspectives. These perspectives do not translate in a way that allows for "privacy" in a Gulf Arab sense to be fully acknowledged or understood. This challenge is not unique to this research, and we have observed that other researchers who approached the topic of privacy in the Arab Gulf often juxtapose their explanations of privacy with "Western" definitions [1, 2, 20, 37].

Participants

The first author focuses on Saudi Arabia, and the second on Qatar. Each recruited participants through personal and professional connections, who then recommended additional participants. We used a "snowball" sampling approach due to the difficulty of recruiting research participants in the GCC. It is challenging to find people to participate in qualitative research due to the perception that discussing one's personal life with a relative stranger is an invasion of privacy. For many Arab people, discussing personal matters is uncomfortable and typically avoided, especially outside of the family. In fact, Al-Munajjed [3] states, "a researcher is not readily accepted in a traditional milieu that frowns upon those enquiring into other peoples' lives." In addition, in Saudi Arabia, gender segregation is widely practiced, and recruiting willing participants requires using personal connections to find people who will sit down with someone not of their own gender.

Interviews

Our sample for this research is comprised of thirty-three face-to-face interviews with eleven men and twenty-two women that lasted from 21 minutes to 2 hours. We conducted interviews in English and Arabic between August 2014 and November 2015. Participants are citizens of either Saudi Arabia or Qatar, at least 18 years old, and all have at least some college education. Participants are native speakers of Arabic, and are fluent or bilingual in English.

The first author is bilingual in Arabic and English, and asked participants for their preferred language. At the outset, most preferred English, though code-switching and borrowing occurred. When discussing sensitive topics, the first author found that participants tended toward English when they spoke about experiences grounded in the time they spent in the US and Western Europe. In addition, based on our observations and personal experience, there is a sense that speaking English is "cool," and young people like to speak English when given the opportunity. The second author conducted all interviews in English. Before we met participants, we told them we would speak about general social media use. We started the interviews with semi-structured questions such as "What social networking sites do you use? What do you like/dislike about them? Do you wish anything were different about a particular site? What challenges do you face in using social media?" These general questions led to free-flowing conversations that were often confessional in nature. Participants spoke about social media use, but also shared secrets about culturally unaccepted activities such as dating and attending mixed-gender gatherings.

Overall, we do not claim that our sample is representative of either country, nor the region. In general, in conducting this interpretive/descriptive research, our aim is to settle upon "a specification of the characteristics of the sample, so that one can make judgment about the applicability of the findings" [19]. I.e. our goal was to tap into this population, identify themes in the data, and use those themes as the foundation for culturally aware design principles.

Data Analysis

Authors transcribed their own interviews, paying close attention to paralinguistic cues such as tone, pauses and laughter. In addition, when Arabic was spoken, the first author took context into consideration, i.e. she was careful to preserve the meaning, not simply the syntax of the interview. We then performed open coding on the transcripts to generate high-level themes. This step involved an iterative process that generated specific themes from more general themes [40]. Additionally, we conducted action-implicative discourse analysis [40]—focusing on mentions of privacy—to gain insight into how privacy was interpreted, enacted, and framed vis-à-vis social media use.

Analyzing Interview Data

We draw from a range of analytic methods to understand and interpret our data. First, we draw from action-implicative discourse analysis (AIDA) [40,41]. Performing AIDA first involves transcribing the text, and capturing words, vocal sounds (e.g., um, hmm), and repetitions. Next, analysts use theoretically informed induction, in which "tapes and transcripts are repeatedly studied to identify interesting practices, where notions of what is interesting are shaped by knowing what observed practices would challenge or extend theorizing" [40]. In our study, we focus not only on the interview transcripts, but also on observations, and background knowledge of the context and culture. This type of analysis focuses on language use as part of the participant's lived experience, i.e. we look at what the interviewees are saying within the context of the Arab Gulf culture. This allows us to understand participants' discourse as an information source regarding their beliefs and views.

Being "cultural insiders" is an advantage in this situation as it allows us to better explicate and explain the values as commonly practiced in Gulf societies. We generated themes based on our readings of the whole group and triangulated results with each other throughout our analysis.

FINDINGS

On the meaning of "Privacy"

Readers will note that throughout this paper, we have not provided a definition for "privacy." This is due to our commitment to understand privacy based on the views and enactments of our population [22], and to consider it as an ever-evolving, locally-constructed phenomenon. Our approach to framing privacy stems from referring to Nissenbaum's framework of 'contextual integrity,' which is concerned with the norms that regulate the flow of certain types of information [29]. We rely upon contextual integrity as the benchmark for how we understand privacy in the context of our user group. Based on an analysis of our interviews, we see how privacy is about more than managing personal boundaries. When asked about their views of privacy, participants often referred to societal expectations rather than personal limits or beliefs. They spoke of an ongoing boundary negotiation that encompassed their entire families, and how they act as representatives to meet societal expectations. This is illustrated in a male Saudi's (M3) response to a question regarding privacy:

"It [privacy] is not about me and my beliefs; it is about the audience and what they believe in and their objective."

M3 is very clear in his assertion that in the case of a Saudi audience, the maintenance of privacy is not related to what he believes is permissible or ethical, but is instead driven by societal expectations.

A Saudi view of privacy is expanded upon by (F5), a female who spent a year living in London studying for her master's degree, and who has since returned to Saudi Arabia. When asked about her sense of privacy in Saudi compared to London, she said:

"Privacy is a lot more of a right over here [in Saudi] than anywhere else. People actually respect your privacy here, where in the West you will be asked too many details. Generally speaking, the idea of privacy in the West is hard to achieve...sometimes it is something you have to stand up for. Like if you want to buy something at the pharmacy there [London] they ask you for a photo ID. They don't ask for one over here unless it is something super serious."

To F5, the benign request for ID at a pharmacy—which is not a common practice in Saudi—to purchase over-the-counter medication, is seen as a violation of her privacy. She explains that in Saudi Arabia privacy is not something that must be actively pursued, because it is a given, communal, expected value that is enacted through lifestyle, local norms, expectations, and laws.

This idea of privacy as a communal effort is elucidated by (F7), a Saudi female:

"Privacy is important but it is not in my hand...I wouldn't say it is a need."

The phrase "it is not in my hand" refers to the understanding among citizens of the GCC that privacy is achieved by a group; individuals do not approach privacy with the goal of protecting only themselves. In effect, F7 is saying that privacy is a collective practice that she alone would not be able to achieve.

Private accounts

In our sample most participants (especially females) maintain private social media accounts. In the below excerpt, a Saudi male, (M8), explains the tension between wanting to be online—which entails conforming with the rules of the platform—and the need to adhere to social expectations, which dictate that private accounts are the default choice. The key challenge for GCC users is negotiating modernity while maintaining their authenticity and tradition. In other words, the challenge is *managing transcendence* and coherence in the age of social media [1].

In explaining the reason she had to make her Facebook account private, (F4), a female Saudi, says: *"[B]ecause of the community and because of the environment. Personally I don't find something wrong about being a public person [on social media] but if you don't comply necessarily with all the rules around you in your environment, then sometimes it is not a good idea."*

Overall, the option to have a private social media account is not something that is always necessarily chosen because a user wants to maintain a private account, but because if they do *not* have a private account, the societal and familial backlash they would likely encounter is too great a risk. Privacy is not personal; it is the foundation for how entire families and tribes uphold their reputations.

Information Disclosure and Boundary Regulation

In his writing on privacy regulation theory, Altman argues against a definition of privacy that relies upon the idea of the withdrawal of an individual from the group. Instead, he advocates for an understanding of privacy as a process of optimization [9]. This interpretation provides a nuanced way in which to understand the privacy behavior of social media users in the Gulf. The ways users find the right balance between withdrawal and disclosure is very much tied to the idea of optimization; figuring out how, within the expectations of their culture, can they successfully use social media to share, communicate and have fun, while at the same time, maintain family honor?

Other social media researchers have studied the relationship between privacy concerns and the level of information disclosure and boundary regulation as a protective measure. Marwick and boyd [26] discuss tactics Twitter users adopt to navigate multiple audiences while avoiding "context collapse," or the divulging of information to the wrong audience. In addition, Farnham and Churchill [21] provide an in-depth discussion around issues of "the singularity of identity" on social media. The authors assert that there are many consequences for the user from the assumption that technology users have a unique, all-encompassing, solitary identity. They assert that "in reality, people's lives are 'faceted'; that is, people maintain social boundaries and show different facets" depending on the situation.

Our interviews support the claims of [26] and [21]. We heard about the acquisition and management of multiple accounts that reflect different personas on Facebook or other sites, the maintenance of accounts on different social media for different audiences and purposes (e.g. maintaining an account on Twitter for work-related posts, and Facebook for socializing with friends); the use of pseudonyms, and the management of boundaries between friends' circles and the information they could see online.

Participants also talk about different degrees of information disclosure on social media, which depend on both audience and platform. For example, a user may want non-Saudi friends to see a particular post or photo, but not Saudi friends nor family. Or, a female may want to show a photo of herself without her shayla to only female friends and mahrams. In addition, it is important to note that images carry far more weight, and risk, than text. If a photo or video is spread outside a user's intended audience, it can bring great shame and embarrassment to the user and their family. In some cases, the inappropriate sharing of an image can severely threaten reputation, which has far-reaching consequences on livelihood, including marriage prospects, career opportunity, and general well-being.

To illustrate the significance of photos, below is an excerpt from (F6), Saudi female, in which she shares her concern regarding her father gaining access to her account:

"I have my dad blocked on Facebook (laughing). The moment I learned he opened an account I blocked him because at the time he opened it I was getting tagged on a lot of pictures that I didn't want my family to see. Pictures of traveling photos or wearing shorts, etc.) I didn't even want to risk (loud voice) something accidently being set on the wrong privacy setting. Even though I always had my privacy setting on pretty high. The only things I allow to be shown are the things I allow. I have ten different friends groups. I have 'limited', 'more limited' 'most limited'...I have six to seven different levels of privacy."

F6 goes through great lengths to make sure that her Facebook account is finely tuned to ensure particular information is shared only with the chosen audience(s). If her father or other family members were to see that she has photos in circulation that show her wearing shorts for example, her reputation would be severely damaged, and her family's honor would be brought into question.

Regarding the preservation of family honor, a male Saudi, M3 describes his privacy settings on Facebook:

"It is four layers. I am an old school Facebook (illustrates his layers on paper). To me, basically, you have a big circle here which have the pictures and the tags, the tags, the tags (he is repeating them to stress their importance)...the tags are full of details on college life and many things, so I don't want to have anyone seeing them."

M3 stresses that while he is an avid user of Facebook, and had already configured his privacy settings to be quite strict, there are still things he cannot control, such as tagging by other users. Features on social media sites—such as the "like" and "tagging" features on Facebook—can have unintended consequences for users who are in a position to have their image put at risk by the accidental sharing of photos or information. Females in particular are in danger of exposure, as they bear great responsibility in upholding their family's reputation [36].

(M1), a male Saudi, describes some of these concerns:

"Four years ago when Facebook changed the privacy settings, one of my friends liked a picture of my family, the picture had my sister in it, and I got really upset and embarrassed that he could see that picture of my sister in it, so I deactivated my account for about six months, I think."

The participant has a responsibility to protect his hurma, in this case, his sister's reputation. A non-mahram was able to view a photo of his sister, which was in effect an exposure of his sister's awrah (in this case, her face). This is a shameful act, and one which brought embarrassment to the participant and his family.

In another interview a Saudi female (F2), who studied at a foreign university, explains that she needed to "*minimize her participation on Facebook*" to maintain an acceptable image back home. This came as a result of a scenario that not only affected her, but her family as well. She was chosen to appear in a promotional video for her university—she explains:

"*I was filmed* [unveiled]*...in a video...and I was tagged and some people from my hometown Googled me and saw it and didn't like it, and told my mom and she was pissed...All I remember is my sister calling and asking me to untag my name...But that just made me go back and check each picture on Facebook and check* [if it was] *private to make sure something like that will not happen again.*"

The function of tagging led to others from the student's community to become aware of the video. While she was proud of her participation, her family and those in her hometown saw her actions as unacceptable; she failed to adhere to khososyah. However, it is important to note that if a male were in the same situation, it would be a source of pride for his family, because the male face is not considered awrah; showing his face is acceptable, if not brag-worthy.

Similarly, (F3), Saudi female, explains that her participation on social media is affected by societal constraints:

"I don't like that people could see pictures I am tagged in. Maybe it is fear of judgment or I didn't mature enough to justify it. Like if someone confronted me [about my photo] I wouldn't know what to say."

F3 is expressing a fear of social stigma, which is a common theme in our data. Stigma and the maintenance of reputation have more serious consequences for women and their families in the GCC than they do on men. Therefore, users of social media are very aware of the consequences associated with any privacy violation. E.g., women often do not use photos of themselves in profile pictures because they are afraid that if a photo falls in the wrong hands someone could blackmail them with it. In the GCC, the acquisition and distribution of female photos is prohibited, as it is considered an attack on the family hurma [2,6,44].

Physical proximity is another factor that plays into what users post to their social media. (M4), a Saudi male participant who studied abroad, discusses his information disclosure practice on Facebook once he returned to Saudi:

"When I was there [in the US] it was different (long pause)…I would post anything I want if it was proper and if it is on me only I wouldn't be ashamed of it, I would keep it public even. But here [in Saudi] I would not."

When he was abroad, M4 had a different sense of privacy, one that made it personal, and in which only he faced consequences of information disclosure. Upon returning home, and being in close proximity to his family, he felt the need to modify his behavior regarding social media, and to conform to expectations.

These examples exemplify how users navigate social networking sites in a way to make them culturally appropriate, to make them "their own." Actions and behaviors that may seem innocent and/or innocuous to some can be viewed as intrusive by a citizen of the GCC. At the same time, the ways in which privacy is understood and built into systems does not meet their needs. The interpretations of privacy that tend to prevail in technology design can have significant consequences on users who do not subscribe to this same view. To illustrate, the first author asked M4 to imagine the following scenario:

You wake up and your account is public—everything you worked on in terms of privacy settings is gone.

*"I don't want to imagine that (nervous laughter)…I am actually going in and removing all these tags…sh*t, may Allah forgive me, yeah that would hurt…hurt reputation, my relationship, relationships with people"*

Upon hearing this completely hypothetical situation, M4 became so nervous and fearful of the remote possibility that his privacy settings would be reset that he decided to remove all tags of himself in any photo. While this is an extreme example of a participant making a hasty decision about his Facebook account, it highlights an outlook that pervades throughout the GCC: the importance of *honor*.

Honor

Honor—*'ird*—is the single most important value that drives cultural norms and expectations in the GCC [16]. The ways in which honor manifest are subtle and nuanced, though it touches upon all aspects of daily life. It is the responsibility of each individual to uphold 'ird. By doing so, they protect their family and maintain good societal standing. As explained by [16]: "much of the organization of the Arab family can be understood in terms of *'ird* as a controlling value, legitimating the family structure and the 'modesty code' required of both men and women."

'ird is connected to the chastity of women, and has a sacred characteristic in GCC society [16]. The connection of 'ird to chastity is additionally highlighted by [28]: "[C]hastity and sexual modesty [are] also very highly valued. Applied primarily to women, these values [are] not only tied to family honor but [are] held to be a religious obligation as well." In this sense, chastity refers to more than a women's sexuality; it implies the need for them to display chaste behavior in all situations. In face-to-face settings, chaste behavior is implied by wearing appropriate garments, not interacting with non-mahrams, and not calling attention to oneself. In digital environments, women invoke chastity by using privacy settings, in addition to other tactics, to protect hurma, awrah, and above all, family 'ird.

'ird is the foundational attribute that motivates the beliefs and actions of our participants as they navigate various social media. Through our analysis, discussions of privacy can all be traced to participants' concerns regarding the maintenance of 'ird. So, while privacy is the word that is often used, the overarching theme or incentive bound up in protecting privacy in digital environments is directly related to the protection of 'ird.

The significance of 'ird is evident in this excerpt by (F8), a female Saudi. She explains: "*…here in Saudi privacy is forced on you. You have to be private….it is not a choice to be secluded…it is society telling you as a women to be private…because of religion, culture, society…and it is just expected of you to be private…if you post something that is a bit too public people will call you and be like 'why are you posting this? You are sharing too much information.'*"

F8 is referring to her responsibility to protect her family's reputation through the control of information sharing. In speaking about posting something "a bit too public," she is referring to her position as someone under surveillance by her family [44]. In effect, F8 has very little choice in what she can post; she can test limits, but this will likely result in admonishment, and her family will remind her that she must maintain privacy (i.e. protect their 'ird), at all times.

The earlier excerpt from M1—the man who deactivated his Facebook account as a result of photos of his sister being posted—is another example that highlights 'ird. If M1's sister shared pictures of herself in a hijab, it would not be an issue. However, a photo of her in an uncovered state was circulated, and a friend of M1's "liked" it, which brought shame to M1, and possibly damaged his 'ird.

In the following example, (M5) discusses his return to Saudi Arabia after being in the US. Though his friends are the same, there is now a greater risk associated with being closer to family and friends who will judge him for sharing:

"As Saudis we know how to keep our private life private and what is suppose to be public, we still keep private."

First author: *"Like what?"* M5: *"Your name, your work, your mother's name...the worst example we have here...a lot of guys are ashamed of their mothers' name."*

In his reference to "mothers' names," M5 is referring to the significance of honor and shame as they manifest in everyday situations. In the GCC, men experience shame if their male friends know their mother's name; this custom is borne of tribal practices that persist today. A man's mahram women (mother, wife) are usually referred to by nicknames or in the abstract (e.g., "the family," "the mother of my children"). In this regard, men "consider the names of their female relatives a private part of their lives that they do not want to share with others" [4], i.e. female relatives' names are awrah, and must be protected. If names are known to other men, then 'ird is damaged. As this relates to digital behavior; the onus is on men to ensure that female relatives' names are not released nor spread.

Gender

Gender is a theme that is referenced, either blatantly or subtly, in every interview. Participants discussed privacy in terms of protecting awrah and maintaining hurma, and gender plays a significant role in these discussions.

The Maintenance of Hurma

When "privacy" is used by our participants to describe values, they are invoking the concepts hurma, awrah, and khososyah. For example, in this excerpt from an interview with a female Qatari (F1) who is speaking about Instagram, we learn why she has a private account:

"...for us as Muslims...you have to be respectful...I had some incidents on my Instagram, like I had to actually block some people and I unfollowed a lot of people... because some of them are very rude...or inappropriate. That's why I made it private... like, my photos are private, and I don't trust [others] and I block, block, blocked them."

F1 discusses how she manages her Instagram account to make it an acceptable, respectable place for her to interact with others while maintaining her values. She carefully guards her account, and does not allow outsiders to intrude upon it. The participant references Islam as the reason for her behavior, i.e. she seeks barakah while eliminating society's judgment. In effect, she is protecting her hurma, which in this case, is her social media account.

Societal expectations regarding gender roles also trump personal views. In this example, (M2), a Saudi male, explains his views on his sisters covering their hair when they travel outside Saudi Arabia. He is not strict about whether his sisters cover; they often remove their hijabs when they are with him. However, he finds it troubling if they were to publically post a photo of themselves on Facebook without a hijab. When asked if he would permit his sisters to post a photo of themselves uncovered, he says:

"In general I will say no because of the culture; even though I don't mind it, but everyone else will mind it...it is culture backed by religion, it is both not one without the other. For example, when my sisters open their snaps [videos from Snapchat] and I am near them, they hide their phones so I don't see their friends without the veil."

This quote illustrates the gravitas placed on conforming to expectations regarding what is permissible for females, as well as the obligation to protect others' hurma. M2's sisters are careful to protect their friends' awrah, in this case, images of themselves uncovered.

A gendered focus on protecting hurma is also discussed by F5 when she explains her process in moving from an all-female Instagram account to a mixed gendered account, and the actions associated with such a merger:

"When I first started using Instagram I didn't have guys because I wanted to put pictures of me and my friends because some of them are wearing the hijab. Then I started having guys on my Instagram, so I removed [them]."

In discussing photos, (F9), a Qatari female said that most will add pictures of flowers, or objects, but not their faces. If a female's photos are misused, it will bring disrespect to her family. The participant describes her fear:

"...somebody will steal my pictures, and he will do some modification, and create a problem...and the boys, in the family will be very much embarrassed, and they will create a big issue for the girl."

F9 is alluding to the enactment of khososyah by females in order to guard social media accounts, which they consider hurma, as they are places in which awrah may be exposed. Overall, we can think of the gender roles that manifest as an aspect of teamwork; men and women understand expectations—and test limits—as they use social media within the boundaries of their culture.

CULTURALLY SENSITIVE DESIGN FOR PRIVACY

Our discussions highlight the ways in which particular values are enacted through the use of digital technologies. Notably, these values are not necessarily understood—much less taken into consideration—when designers and developers create and/or augment technologies. Working within this vein of inquiry, we assert that a way to reduce cultural bias is to consider cross-cultural studies of privacy. By looking to research that examines various cultures and the value tensions associated with technology use, we give designers and developers the necessary tools to produce technologies that are appropriate for a broad audience.

That said, challenges persist in finding a systematic way to translate theoretical insights into technical design principles. Addressing such an endeavor is the goal of *value sensitive design (VSD)*, an approach that incorporates values into the process of designing artifacts [22]. VSD is a "theoretically grounded approach to the design of technology that accounts for human values in a principled and comprehensive manner throughout the design process." VSD also takes into account *indirect stakeholders,* i.e. those who do not interact with technology but who are affected by it [22]. Indirect stakeholders were prominent in our discussions, as in how they influence users' decisions about what information to share, and through which medium. Similar to VSD is the approach of Privacy by Design (PbD). PbD focuses solely on privacy, with the goal of "protecting privacy by embedding it into the design specifications of technologies, business practices, and physical infrastructures" [14]. Our data show how participants appropriate privacy settings to accommodate their needs. These findings, together with our knowledge of VSD and PbD, provide a foundation for principles regarding culturally sensitive technology development.

Burgeoning Design Opportunities

Designing around a notion of privacy bound up in honor, modesty and reputation is unchartered territory. Before we attempt to translate these complex and nuanced perceptions of privacy into design principles, we sought participants' opinions. In follow-up questions, we asked: "what would you do to improve <X>?" and "how do you imagine <X> changing to meet your needs?" Participants' responses resulted in several suggestions:

"Private" as default setting. Participants expressed lack of trust in some platforms because of incidents in which privacy were settings were reverted to 'default,' which was *public*. One way to avoid this is to make the default setting 'private.' This is in line with the PbD principle: "If an individual does nothing, their privacy still remains intact. No action is required on the part of the individual to protect their privacy—it is built into the system, by *default*." [14].

"Real name" and "one account" policies. Some participants confessed to managing more than one account on Facebook in particular—one for family and "judgmental" friends, and one for "open minded" friends. Some also said they use nicknames as profile names. We learned that although many refer to this practice as the use of "fake names," the names are in fact representations of themselves that they like to present to particular audiences; the digital platform is the space where they experience self-expression that cannot be had elsewhere. Policies that require users to maintain only one profile in their "real" names stymy this freedom that is highly valued by those who seek more autonomy than what their cultures permit.

We join others in calling for such policies to be more lenient and flexible [13,25]. In addition, we recommend the development of an interface that allows for management of multiple accounts. Due to the fear of context collapse, and the all too real possibility of harming one's family through information sharing, the ability to easily maintain more than one account would be a welcome feature by many.

Gender sensitive recommendation system. The example of Layla we highlight in the introduction demonstrates a situation where non-mahram were friend suggestions. However, the practice of gender segregation often extends to digital environments. So, we follow [7] in recommending a modification to *friend suggestion* algorithms to support same gender-and/or "kin relationship" suggestions. As a result, we anticipate a reduction in uncomfortable incidents for women in particular.

LIMITATIONS AND FUTURE WORK

While our research has uncovered many and varied findings, we do not claim that they hold for the entire GCC, nor for either country in particular. We interviewed thirty-three participants, all of whom are educated, English-speaking, and most of whom spent time abroad. We acknowledge that this group is likely more open-minded than many of their compatriots. However, this initial study provides the foundation for future work that will involve a larger, more diverse set of respondents, and ask more probing questions about privacy, social media use, and how to best design with values in mind. Overall, our preliminary findings support the need for further theorization that provides an enriched understanding of "privacy."

DISCUSSION AND CONCLUDING REMARKS

With the goal of supporting the HCI community in our mission towards more inclusive and culturally-sensitive design [22], we introduce the Islamic perspective of "privacy," and explain why it is critical to understand. *Hurma, awrah,* and the protection of them—*khososyah*—all come under the umbrella of maintaining honor. Our data point to how social media users in Saudi Arabia and Qatar interpret these concepts. While conventional interpretations of these actions indicate that our participants are discussing the enactment of "privacy," what is taking place involves more than what is typically viewed as "privacy management." The ways in which "privacy" is enacted among our participants goes beyond concerns for safety, security, and the ability to separate oneself from a larger group in a controlled manner. We are in fact observing adherence to Islamic teachings, maintenance of reputation, and the careful navigation of social media activity so as to preserve respect and modesty.

Contextually-grounded understandings of the ideologies and norms that guide social media use by a diverse population helps designers and researchers to not only create more inclusive, culturally-sensitive tools, but to understand how their own biases and values—while not knowingly harmful or problematic—create limitations that require considerable effort on behalf of some users to be able to safely and effectively use them.

This is the first contextually grounded study that explores how privacy is understood and enacted via social media by Gulf Arab Muslims. Our aim is to recognize the consequences of designing technologies with a limited view of "privacy." This research looks at what "privacy" is from a wider spectrum of users and investigates various foundations of the concept. We anticipate this will lead to design principles that will better guide developers and researchers going forward.

REFERENCES

1. Norah Abokhodair. 2015. Transmigrant Saudi Arabian Youth and Social Media: Privacy, Intimacy and Freedom of Expression. In *Proceedings of the 33rd Annual ACM Conference Extended Abstracts on Human Factors in Computing Systems (CHI EA '15)*, 187-190.
2. Hashem A. Al-Makrami. 2015. Online self-disclosure across cultures: A study of Facebook use in Saudi Arabia and Australia. PhD thesis, Queensland University of Technology.
3. Mona Al-Munajjed. 1997. *Women in Saudi Arabia today*. New York: St. Martin's Press.
4. Maha Al-Nowaisser. 2005. Who Is to Blame for the Name Shame-Game?. Accessed January 14, 2016. http://www.arabnews.com/node/267149.
5. Zamel Al- Rakad. 2005. The right to privacy. *Alriyadh*. Retrieved from http://www.alriyadh.com/110341
6. Yeslam Al-Saggaf. 2004. The Effect of Online Community on Offline Community in Saudi Arabia. *The Electronic Journal of Information Systems in Developing Countries 16*.
7. Tamara Al-Sheikh, Jennifer A. Rode, and Siân E. Lindley. 2011. (Whose) value-sensitive design: a study of long-distance relationships in an Arabic cultural context. In *Proceedings of the ACM 2011 conference on Computer supported cooperative work* (CSCW '11), 75-84.
8. Sultan Al-Sughair. 2015. Snapchat use: KSA tops Arab countries.Arab News. Retrieved January/2016, from:http://www.arabnews.com/saudi-arabia/news/779826
9. Irwin Altman. 1976. Privacy: A Conceptual Analysis. *Environment and behavior, 8*(1), 7-29.
10. Irwin Altman. 1977. Privacy regulation: Culturally universal or culturally specific?. *Journal of Social Issues*, *33*(3), 66-84.
11. Louise Barkhuus. 2012. The mismeasurement of privacy: using contextual integrity to reconsider privacy in HCI. In *Proceedings of the SIGCHI Conference on Human Factors in Computing Systems*(CHI '12). 367-376.
12. Nic Bidwell. 2010. Ubuntu in the network: humanness in social capital in rural Africa. *interactions, 17*(2), 68-71.
13. Danah Boyd. 2011. "Real Names" Policies Are an Abuse of Power." *Zephoria*. Personal Blog.Retrevied Jan/2016. http://www.zephoria.org/thoughts/archives/2011/08/04/real-names.html.
14. Ann Cavoukian. 2009. Privacy by design: The 7 foundational principles. *Information and Privacy Commissioner of Ontario*, Canada.
15. Judith Wagner DeCew. 1997. *In pursuit of privacy: Law, ethics, and the rise of technology*. Cornell University Press.
16. Peter C. Dodd. 1973. Family honor and the forces of change in Arab society. *International Journal of Middle East Studies, 4*(01), 40-54.
17. Paul Dourish, Ken Anderson. 2006. Collective information practice: emploring privacy and security as social and cultural phenomena. *Human-computer interaction, 21(3), 319-342.*
18. Fadwa El Guindi. 1999. *Veil : modesty, privacy and resistance*. Oxford, UK
19. Robert Elliott, Ladislav Timulak. 2005. Descriptive and interpretive approaches to qualitative research. *A handbook of research methods for clinical and health psychology*, 147-159.
20. Maha Faisal, Asmaa Alsumait. 2011. *Social network privacy and trust concerns.* Paper presented at the Proceedings of the 13th International Conference on Information Integration and Web-based Applications and Services.
21. Shelly D. Farnham, Elizabeth F. Churchill. 2011. Faceted identity, faceted lives: social and technical issues with being yourself online. In the *Proceedings of the ACM 2011 conference on Computer supported cooperative work* .
22. Batya Friedman, Peter H. Kahn Jr., Alan Borning, and Alina Huldtgren. 2006. Value sensitive design and information systems. *Human-computer interaction in management information systems: Foundations*, 5, 348-372.
23. Batya Friedman, Kristina Hook, Brian Gill, Lina Eidmar, Catherine Sallmander Prien, and Rachel Severson. 2008. Personlig integritet: a comparative study of perceptions of privacy in public places in Sweden and the United States. In *Proceedings of the 5th Nordic conference on Human-computer interaction: building bridges* (NordiCHI '08) , 142-151.
24. Silvia Lindtner, , Ken Anderson, and Paul Dourish. (2012)Cultural appropriation: information technologies as sites of transnational imagination. In *Proceedings of the ACM 2012 conference on Computer Supported Cooperative Work* (CSCW '12), 77-86.
25. Jessica Lingel, Tarleton Gillespie. 2014. One Name to Rule Them All: Facebook's Identity Problem. The Atlantic. Atlantic Media Company, Web. Retrevied: Jan/2016.http://www.theatlantic.com/technology/archive/2014/10/one-name-to-rule-them-all-facebook-still-insists-on-a-single-identity/381039/.

26. Alice E. Marwick, Danah Boyd. 2011. I tweet honestly, I tweet passionately: Twitter users, context collapse, and the imagined audience. *New media & society*. 13.1: 114-133.
27. Afaf Ibrahim Meleis.1984. The Arab American And Psychiatric Care. *Perspectives in Psychiatric Care, 22*(2), 72-76.
28. Helen Chapin Metz. 1993. *Saudi Arabia: A Country Study*. Washington: GPO for the Library of Congress, Federal Research Division.
29. Helen Nissenbaum. 2009. *Privacy in context: Technology, policy, and the integrity of social life.* Stanford University Press.
30. Justin Osofsky, Todd Gage. 2015. Community Support FYI: Improving the Names Process on Facebook. *Facebook Newsroom*. Retrevied 16 Jan. 2016.
31. Leysia Palen, Paul Dourish. 2003. Unpacking privacy for a networked world. In *Proceedings of the SIGCHI Conference on Human Factors in Computing Systems* (CHI '03), 129-136.
32. Damian Radcliffe,. 2015. Social Media in the Middle East: The Story of 2014. Retrieved August 2015 from https://damianradcliffe.files.wordpress.com/2015/01/damian-radcliffe-social-media-in-the-middle-east-the-story-of-2014.pdf
33. Edward W. Said. 1979. *Orientalism.* New York: Vintage.
34. Bryan Semaan, Gloria Mark. 2012. 'Facebooking' Towards Crisis Recovery And Beyond: Disruption As An Opportunity. In *Proceedings of the ACM 2012 conference on Computer Supported Cooperative Work* (CSCW '12), 27-36.
35. Sergany. 2010. The importance of ethics and values in Islamic civilization. Retrieved January, 16, 2016 from http://rasoulallah.net/index.php/en/articles/article/11939
36. Asifa Siraj. 2011. Meanings of modesty and the hijab amongst Muslim women in Glasgow, Scotland. *Gender, Place & Culture, 18*(6), 716-731.
37. Rana Sobh, Russell W. Belk. 2011. Privacy and gendered spaces in Arab Gulf homes. *Home Cultures, 8*(3), 317-340.
38. SocialClinic. 2014. The State Of Social Media In Saudi Arabia.Vol 3. Retrieved from http://www.thesocialclinic.com/the-state-of-social-media-in-saudi-arabia-vol-3/
39. The_Shura_Council. 1991. The Basic Law Of Government, article 37. Retrieved from http://www.shura.gov.sa/wps/wcm/connect/ShuraEn/internet/Laws+and+Regulations/The+Basic+Law+Of+Government/Chapter+Five/
40. Karen Tracy. 1995. Action-implicative discourse analysis. *Journal of Language and Social Psychology* 14.1-2: 195-215.
41. Karen Tracy. 2007. The discourse of crisis in public meetings: Case study of a school district's multimillion dollar error. *Journal of Applied Communication Research* 35.4: 418-441.
42. Harry C. Triandis 1995. *Individualism & collectivism.* Boulder: Westview Press.
43. Balse Ur, Yang Wang. 2013. A cross-cultural framework for protecting user privacy in online social media. In *Proceedings of the 22nd International Conference On World Wide Web Companion.*755-762.
44. Sarah Vieweg, Adam Hodges. 2016. Surveillance & Modesty on Social Media: How Qataris Navigate Modernity and Maintain Tradition. In *Proceedings of the ACM Conference on Computer-Supported Cooperative Work and Social Computing (CSCW 2016).*

www.ingramcontent.com/pod-product-compliance
Ingram Content Group UK Ltd.
Pitfield, Milton Keynes, MK11 3LW, UK
UKHW051419290926
15471UKWH00009B/1684

9 781450 345972